T0184926

Lecture Notes in Computer Science 9114

More information about this series at http://www.springer.com/series/7409

Philipp Cimiano · Flavius Frasincar
Geert-Jan Houben · Daniel Schwabe (Eds.)

Engineering the Web in the Big Data Era

15th International Conference, ICWE 2015
Rotterdam, The Netherlands, June 23–26, 2015
Proceedings

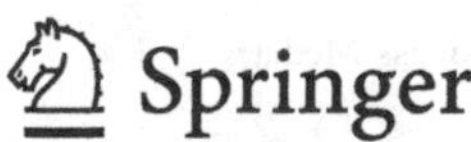

Editors
Philipp Cimiano
Bielefeld University
Bielefeld
Germany

Flavius Frasincar
Eramus University Rotterdam
Rotterdam
The Netherlands

Geert-Jan Houben
Delft University of Technology
Delft
The Netherlands

Daniel Schwabe
Pontifical Catholic University
of Rio de Janeiro
Rio de Janeiro
Brazil

ISSN 0302-9743 ISSN 1611-3349 (electronic)
Lecture Notes in Computer Science
ISBN 978-3-319-19889-7 ISBN 978-3-319-19890-3 (eBook)
DOI 10.1007/978-3-319-19890-3

Library of Congress Control Number: 2015942219

LNCS Sublibrary: SL3 – Information Systems and Application, incl. Internet/Web, and HCI

Springer Cham Heidelberg New York Dordrecht London

Printed on acid-free paper

Springer International Publishing AG Switzerland is part of Springer Science+Business Media
(www.springer.com)

Preface

The Web has become such an important tool in our daily lives that it is difficult to imagine living in a world without it. In addition to the original goal of satisfying an information need, the Web has grown to become a popular platform for doing business, education, entertainment, communication, etc. Developing software for the Web needs to meet an increasing number of challenges that have not been previously faced by any software platform, in good part spurred by its functional versatility, as well as its ubiquity fostered by the ever-growing presence of Web-enabled electronic devices. Web engineering aims to address these challenges by adapting software engineering to the Web context, as well as providing new methodologies, techniques, and tools to address Web application design, development, and maintenance.

This volume contains the full research papers, short papers, industry papers, the descriptions of posters, demonstrations, and tutorials, and extended abstracts for the keynotes of the 15th International Conference on Web Engineering (ICWE 2015), held during June 23–25, 2015, in Rotterdam, The Netherlands.

ICWE is the flagship conference for the Web engineering community. Previous editions of ICWE took place at Toulouse, France (2014), Aalborg, Denmark (2013), Berlin, Germany (2012), Paphos, Cyprus (2011), Vienna, Austria (2010), San Sebastian, Spain (2009), Yorktown Heights, NY, USA (2008), Como, Italy (2007), Palo Alto, CA, USA (2006), Sydney, Australia (2005), Munich, Germany (2004), Oviedo, Spain (2003), Santa Fe, Argentina (2002), and Cáceres, Spain (2001). The 2015 edition of ICWE was centered on the theme of "Engineering the Web in the Big Data Era," hereby highlighting the impact big data has on Web engineering research today. Big data promises new data usages contributing to a change in our daily practices. As the Web is a valuable producer and consumer of big data, it is imperative to analyze the consequences and impact of the big data paradigm in the Web engineering field.

ICWE 2015 presented eight research tracks, namely, Web Application Modeling and Engineering, Mobile Web Applications, Social Web Applications, Semantic Web Applications, Quality and Accessibility Aspects of Web Applications, Web Applications Composition and Mashups, Web User Interfaces, and Security and Privacy in Web Applications, and an industry track aimed at concentrating expertise and contributing to the identity of the Web engineering community.

The ICWE 2015 edition received 110 submissions distributed over nine tracks (eight research tracks plus one industry track), out of which the Program Committee selected 26 full research papers (24% acceptance rate), 11 short papers (34% acceptance rate), and seven industry papers. Additionally, the Program Committee accepted 11 demonstrations, six posters, and four contributions to the PhD symposium, where PhD students received personalized advice and guidance on their work from senior researchers in the Web engineering field. Also accepted were two tutorials lecturing on the advanced topics of (1) "Enabling the Web of (Linked Open) Data," and (2) "The Web of Data for E-Commerce: Schema.org and GoodRelations for Researchers and

Practitioners," three workshops entitled (1) First International Workshop on Natural Language Processing for Informal Text (NLPIT 2015), (2) First Workshop on Pervasive Web Technologies, Trends and Challenges (PEWET 2015), and (3) First International Workshop in Mining the Social Web (SoWeMine 2015), and one challenge on Rapid Mashup.

The excellent program would not have been possible without the support of the many people who helped with the organization of this event. We would like to thank all the track, tutorial, demonstrations/poster, workshop, PhD symposium, sponsorship, publicity, metadata, and registration chairs for their hard work. Our thanks also goes to Enrique Alfonseca (Google Research), Peter Mika (Yahoo Research), and Mike Thelwall (University of Wolverhampton), who accepted to be our keynote speakers. Special thanks are extended to Oscar Diaz and Peter Dolog for their advice and encouragement in setting up ICWE 2015 in Rotterdam. We would like to also thank Michael Krug and Martin Gaedke for hosting the conference website, and Kim Schouten and Damir Vandic for building and maintaining the website. We are grateful to our local organizers Ursula David and Marianne Kroek-Buijs for their logistical support, and Springer for publishing this volume. In addition, we thank the reviewers for their meticulous work that allowed us to select the best papers to be presented at ICWE 2015. Last, but not least, we would like to thank the authors who submitted their work to this conference and all the participants who contributed to the success of this event.

June 2015

Philipp Cimiano
Flavius Frasincar
Geert-Jan Houben
Daniel Schwabe

Organization

Technical Committee

General Chair

Flavius Frasincar — Erasmus University Rotterdam, The Netherlands

Vice General Chair

Geert-Jan Houben — Delft University of Technology, The Netherlands

Program Committee Chairs

Philipp Cimiano — Bielefeld University, Germany
Daniel Schwabe — Pontifical Catholic University of Rio de Janiero, Brazil

Track Chairs

Web Application Modeling and Engineering

Oscar Pastor — Universitat Politècnica de València, Spain
Marco Winckler — University Paul Sabatier, France

Mobile Web Applications

In-Young Ko — Korea Advanced Institute of Science and Technology, South Korea
Volker Gruhn — University of Duisburg-Essen, Germany

Social Web Applications

Alessandro Bozzon — Delft University of Technology, The Netherlands
Sven Casteleyn — University Jaume I of Castellon, Spain

Semantic Web Applications

Sören Auer — University of Bonn, Germany
Heiko Paulheim — University of Mannheim, Germany

Quality and Accessibility Aspects of Web Applications

Luis Olsina — National University of La Pampa, Argentina
Markel Vigo — The University of Manchester, UK

Web Applications Composition and Mashups

Cinzia Cappiello	Politecnico di Milano, Italy
Cesare Pautasso	University of Lugano, Switzerland

Web User Interfaces

Ali Mesbah	University of British Columbia, Canada
Fabio Paterno	University of Pisa, Italy

Security and Privacy in Web Applications

Martin Gaedke	Chemnitz University of Technology, Germany
Christian Hammer	Saarland University, Germany

Industry

Marco Brambilla	Politecnico di Milano, Italy
Maja Vukovic	IBM T.J. Watson Research Center, USA

Tutorials Chairs

Franciska de Jong	Erasmus University Rotterdam, The Netherlands
Moira Norrie	ETH Zurich, Switzerland

Workshops Chairs

Florian Daniel	University of Trento, Italy
Oscar Diaz	University of the Basque Country, Spain

Demonstrations and Posters Chairs

Roberto De Virgilio	Roma Tre University, Italy
Gustavo Rossi	National University of La Plata, Argentina

PhD Symposium Chairs

Irene Garrigos	University of Alicante, Spain
Manuel Wimmer	Vienna University of Technology, Austria

Program Committee

Web Application Modeling and Engineering

Luciano Baresi	Politecnico di Milano, Italy
Hubert Baumeister	Technical University of Denmark, Denmark
Devis Bianchini	University of Brescia, Italy
Alessandro Bozzon	Delft University of Technology, The Netherlands
Marco Brambilla	Politecnico di Milano, Italy

Jordi Cabot	Inria-École des Mines de Nantes, France
Richard Chbeir	LIUPPA Laboratory, France
Florian Daniel	University of Trento, Italy
Oscar Diaz	University of the Basque Country, Spain
Schahram Dustdar	Vienna University of Technology, Austria
Marina Egea	Indra, Spain
Sergio Firmenich	UNLP and CONICET, Argentina
Flavius Frasincar	Erasmus University Rotterdam, The Netherlands
Piero Fraternali	Politecnico di Milano, Italy
Jose Luis Garrido	University of Granada, Spain
Irene Garrigos	University of Alicante, Spain
Sujoy Gupta	AppDirect, USA
Guy-Vincent Jourdan	University of Ottawa, Canada
Gerti Kappel	Vienna University of Technology, Austria
Alexander Knapp	Universität Augsburg, Germany
Maristella Matera	Politecnico di Milano, Italy
Santiago Melia	Universidad de Alicante, Spain
Jose Ignacio Panach Navarrete	Universitat de València, Spain
Vicente Pelechano	Universitat Politècnica de València, Spain
Alfonso Pierantonio	University of L'Aquila, Italy
Werner Retschitzegger	Johannes Kepler University Linz, Austria
Gustavo Rossi	UNLP, Argentina
Fernando Sánchez	Universidad de Extremadura, Spain
Daniel Schwabe	Pontifical Catholic University of Rio de Janiero, Brazil
Francisco Valverde	Universitat Politècnica de València, Spain
Manuel Wimmer	Vienna University of Technology, Austria
Gefei Zhang	Celonis GmbH, Germany
Jürgen Ziegler	University of Duisburg-Essen, Germany

Mobile Web Applications

Marcos Baez	University of Trento, Italy
Matthias Book	University of Iceland, Iceland
Dickson K.W. Chiu	The University of Hong Kong, SAR China
Olga De Troyer	Vrije Universiteit Brussel, Belgium
Federico Michele Facca	CREATE-NET, Italy
Angel Jimenez-Molina	University of Chile, Chile
Philipp Leitner	University of Zurich, Switzerland
Vicente Pelechano	Universitat Politècnica de València, Spain
Thomas Richter	Rhein-Waal University of Applied Sciences, Germany
Gustavo Rossi	UNLP, Argentina
Quan Z. Sheng	The University of Adelaide, Australia
Beat Signer	Vrije Universiteit Brussel, Belgium
Giovanni Toffetti Carughi	IBM Research Haifa, Israel

Social Web Applications

Ioannis Anagnostopoulos	University of Central Greece, Greece
Maria Bielikova	Slovak University of Technology in Bratislava, Slovakia
Marco Brambilla	Politecnico di Milano, Italy
Richard Chbeir	LIUPPA Laboratory, France
Alexandra Cristea	University of Warwick, UK
Gianluca Demartini	University of Sheffield, UK
Tommaso di Noia	Polytechnic University of Bari, Italy
Vania Dimitrova	University of Leeds, UK
Peter Dolog	Aalborg University, Denmark
Jutta Eckstein	IT communication, Germany
Filomena Ferruci	Università di Salerno, Italy
Geert-Jan Houben	Delft University of Technology, The Netherlands
Roman Klinger	Universität Stuttgart, Germany
Zakaria Maamar	Zayed University, UAE
Lourdes Moreno Lopez	Universidad Carlos III de Madrid, Spain
George Pallis	University of Cyprus, Cyprus
Jan Paralic	Technical University Kosice, Slovakia
Iv Ramakrishnan	Stony Brook, USA
Filippo Rica	University of Genoa, Italy
Thomas Richter	Rhein-Waal University of Applied Sciences, Germany
Elena Simperl	University of Southampton, UK
Philipp Singer	Knowledge Management Institute, Austria
William Van Woensel	University of Dalhousie, Canada
Vincent Wade	Dublin University, Ireland
Erik Wilde	EMC Corporation, USA
Guandong Xu	University of Technology Sydney, Australia
Gefei Zhang	Ludwig Maximilians University of Munich, Germany

Semantic Web Applications

Christian Bizer	University of Mannheim, Germany
Sarven Capadisli	University of Bonn, Germany
Pieter Colpaert	Ghent University, Belgium
Oscar Corcho	Universidad Politècnica de Madrid, Spain
Jose Manuel Gomez-Perez	Intelligent Software Components S.A., Spain
Thomas Gottron	University of Koblenz-Landau, Germany
Paul Groth	VU University, Amsterdam
Peter Haase	Fluid Operations, Germany
Eero Hyvönen	Aalto University and University of Helsinki, Finland
Tomi Kauppinen	Aalto University School of Science, Finland
Christoph Lange	University of Bonn, Germany
Robert Meusel	University of Mannheim, Germany
Daniel Oberle	SAP, Germany

Harald Sack	University of Potsdam, Germany
Axel Schulz	TU Darmstadt, Germany
Raphaël Troncy	EURECOM, France
Ruben Verborgh	Ghent University, Belgium
Maria Esther Vidal	Universidad Simon Bolivar, Venezuela
Evelyne Viegas	Microsoft Research, USA

Quality and Accessibility Aspects of Web Applications

Silvia Abrahao	Universitat Politècnica de València, Spain
Amaia Aizpurua	University of the Basque Country, Spain
Myriam Arrue	University of the Basque Country, Spain
Domenico Bianculli	University of Luxembourg, Luxembourg
Giorgio Brajnik	University of Udine, Italy
Andrew Brown	BBC, UK
Cinzia Cappiello	Politecnico di Milano, Italy
Luis Carrio	University of Lisbon, Portugal
Alex Chen	Nanyang Technological University, China
Nádia Fernandes	University of Lisbon, Portugal
Simon Harper	The University of Manchester, UK
Caroline Jay	The University of Manchester, UK
Maristella Matera	Politecnico di Milano, Italy
Emilia Mendes	The University of Auckland, New Zealand
Cu Duy Nguyen	University of Luxembourg, Luxembourg
Hironobu Takagi	IBM Research, Japan
Arie van Deursen	Delft University of Technology, The Netherlands
Marco Winckler	Université Paul Sabatier, France
Yeliz Yesilada	The University of Manchester, UK

Web Applications Composition and Mashups

Saeed Aghaee	University of Lugano, Switzerland
Boualem Benatallah	University of New South Wales, Australia
Christoph Bussler	Oracle Corporation, USA
Sven Casteleyn	University Jaume I of Castellon, Spain
Florian Daniel	University of Trento, Italy
Oscar Diaz	University of the Basque Country, Spain
Hao Han	Kanagawa University, Japan
Geert-Jan Houben	Delft University of Technology, The Netherlands
Agnes Koschmider	Karlsruhe Institute of Technology, Germany
Peep Küngas	University of Tartu, Estonia
Maristella Matera	Politecnico di Milano, Italy
Nikolay Mehandjiev	The University of Manchester, UK
Michael Weiss	Carleton University, Canada
Eric Wohlstadter	University of British Columbia, Canada

Web User Interfaces

Carlos Duarte	University of Lisbon, Portugal
Cristina Gena	University of Turin, Italy
William G.J. Halfond	University of Southern California, USA
Guy-Vincent Jourdan	University of Ottawa, Canada
Josip Maras	University of Split, Croatia
Maristella Matera	Politecnico di Milano, Italy
Carmen Santoro	ISTI-CNR, Italy
Nikolaos Tsantalis	Concordia University, Canada
Marco Winckler	Université Paul Sabatier, France

Security and Privacy in Web Applications

Adam Doupe	Arizona State University, USA
Schahram Dustdar	Vienna University of Technology, Austria
Martin Johns	SAP Research, Germany
Aniket Kate	Saarland University, Germany
Sergio Maffeis	Imperial College London, UK
Maristella Matera	Politecnico di Milano, Italy
Mohammadreza Mousavi	Halmstad University, Sweden
Phu H. Phung	University of Illinois at Chicago, USA
Raphael M. Reischuk	Saarland University, Germany
Nicola Zannone	Eindhoven University of Technology, The Netherlands

Industry

Marco Brambilla	Politecnico di Milano, Italy
Marina Egea	Indra, Spain
Maja Vukovic	IBM T.J. Watson Research Center, USA

Additional Reviewers

Panos Alexopoulos
Ritwik Banerjee
Seyed-Mehdi-Reza Beheshti
Juergen Cito
Ronald Denaux
Hariton Efstathiades
Birhanu Eshete
Bin Fu
Magnus Knuth
Christoph Pinkel
Dinesh Reddy
Petar Ristoski
Dominique Ritze
Roberto Rodriguez-Echeverria
Jessica Rosati
Paolo Tomeo
Joerg Waitelonis
Youquan Wang
Jie Yang

Local Organizing Committee

Local Arrangements Chairs

Ursula David	Erasmus University Rotterdam, The Netherlands
Marianne Kroek-Buijs	Erasmus University Rotterdam, The Netherlands

Registrations and Finance Chair

Susan Dijkstra	Congress Bureau, The Netherlands
Irene van der Wel	Congress Bureau, The Netherlands

Sponshorship Chairs

Viorel Milea	Erasmus University Rotterdam, The Netherlands
Damir Vandic	Erasmus University Rotterdam, The Netherlands

Publicity Chair

Guandong Xu	University of Technology Sydney, Australia

Proceedings Chair

Katja Temnow	Bielefeld University, Germany

Metadata Chair

Cord Wiljes	Bielefeld University, Germany

Website Chairs

Kim Schouten	Erasmus University Rotterdam, The Netherlands
Damir Vandic	Erasmus University Rotterdam, The Netherlands

ICWE Steering Committee Liaisons

Oscar Diaz	University of the Basque Country, Spain
Peter Dolog	Aalborg University, Denmark

Sponsoring Institutions

The conference chairs and conference organizers would like to thank our sponsors:

ERIM Erasmus Research Institute of Management

ERASMUS UNIVERSITEIT ROTTERDAM

Google™

ISWE International Society for Web Engineering e.V.

rotterdam partners

Keynotes

News Understanding for Knowledge Graph Freshness

Enrique Alfonseca

Google Inc.
ealfonseca@google.com

Abstract. This talk will describe ongoing work at Google Zurich towards event understanding and headline generation from news collections. From a web-scale corpus of English news, we mine and cluster syntactic patterns using sentence compression techniques, each cluster constituting an event description. At inference time, we can query the model with the patterns observed in an unseen news collection, identify the event that better captures the gist of the collection and automatically produce updates for the knowledge graph, and retrieve the most appropriate pattern to generate a headline.

Keywords: Information extraction · Event understanding · Sentence compression

Most Open Information Extraction (Open-IE) systems [2] extract textual relational patterns between entities automatically [3, 8] and optionally organize them into paraphrase clusters. These pattern clusters have been found to be useful for different applications, including Question Answering [4, 7] and relation extraction [5, 9].

A related Open-IE problem is that of automatically extracting and paraphrasing **event patterns:** those that describe changes in the state or attribute values of one or several entities. Applications include news understanding for e.g. generating news alerts, keeping structured knowledge bases up-to-date, or automatically generating headlines for news or news collections.

An existing approach lo learn paraphrases of event patterns is to build on the following weak supervision signal: news articles that were published on the same day and mention the same entities should contain good paraphrase candidates. A core component of these models is the automatic extraction of extraction patterns from the original sentences. Most previous works generate these patterns using heuristics, i.e., hand-written rules or lexico-syntactic regular expressions [1, 3, 8]. In our work we have explored the use of *Sentence compression* and *memory-based* extractors as viable alternatives, allowing us to trade-off coverage and accuracy for the extracted patterns.

Two state-of-the-art event paraphrasing systems that are based on this assumption are NewsSpike [11] and Heady/Idest [1, 6, 10]. This talk will focus on the latter, which has evolved from a Bayesian model (a Noisy-OR neural network) into a deep neural network model, where patterns are represented with a distributed representation in an embedding space, with the assumption that closeness in that space correlates with semantic closeness, with significant improvements in model accuracy.

References

1. Alfonseca, E., Pighin, D., Garrido, G.: HEADY: News headline abstraction through event pattern clustering. In: Proceedings of the 51st Annual Meeting of the Association for Computational Linguistics, Sofia, Bulgaria, pp. 1243–1253, 4–9 August 2013
2. Banko, M., Cafarella, M.J., Soderland, S., Broadhead, M., Etzioni, O.: Open information extraction from the Web. In: Proceedings of the 20th International Joint Conference on Artificial Intelligence, Hyderabad, India, pp. 2670–2676, 6–12 January 2007
3. Fader, A., Soderland, S., Etzioni, O.: Identifying relations for open information extraction. In: Proceedings of the 2011 Conference on Empirical Methods in Natural Language Processing, Edinburgh, UK, pp. 1535–1545, 27–29 July 2011 (2011)
4. Fader, A., Zettlemoyer, L.S., Etzioni, O.: Paraphrase-driven learning for open question answering. In: Proceedings of the 51st Annual Meeting of the Association for Computational Linguistics, Sofia, Bulgaria, pp. 1608–1618, 4–9 August 2013 (2013)
5. Grycner, A., Weikum, G.: Harpy: hypernyms and alignment of relational paraphrases. In: Proceedings of the 25rd International Conference on Computational Linguistics, Dublin, Ireland, pp. 2195–2204, 23–29 August 2014 (2014)
6. Krause, S., Alfonseca, E., Filippova, K., Pighin, D.: Idest: learning a distributed representation for event patterns. In: Proceedings of the 2015 Conference of the North American Chapter of the Association for Computational Linguistics Human Language Technologies (2015)
7. Lin, D., Pantel, P.: Discovery of inference rules for question-answering. Nat. Lang. Eng. **7**(4), 343–360 (2001)
8. Mausam, Schmitz, M., Bart, R., Soderland, S., Etzioni, O.: Open language learning for information extraction. In: Proceedings of the 2012 Conference on Empirical Methods in Natural Language Processing, Jeju Island, Korea, pp. 523–534, 12–14 July 2012 (2012)
9. Moro, A., Navigli, R.: Wisenet: building a wikipedia-based semantic network with ontologized relations. In: Proceedings of the 21st ACM International Conference on Information and knowledge management (CIKM 2012), Maui, USA, pp. 1672–1676. ACM, 29 October–02 November 2012
10. Pighin, D., Colnolti, M., Alfonseca, E., Filippova, K.: Modelling events through memory-based, Open-IE patterns for abstractive summarization. In: Proceedings of the 52nd Annual Meeting of the Association for Computational Linguistics, Baltimore, USA, pp. 892–901, 22–27 June 2014
11. Zhang, C., Weld, D.S.: Harvesting parallel news streams to generate paraphrases of event relations. In: Proceedings of the 2013 Conference on Empirical Methods in Natural Language Processing, Seattle, WA, USA, pp. 1776–1786, 18–21 October 2013

Making the Web Searchable

Peter Mika

Yahoo Labs
125 Shaftesbury Avenue
London, UK
pmika@yahoo-inc.com

Abstract. The key idea of the Semantic Web is to make information on the Web easily consumable by machines. As machines start to understand web pages as sources of data, search on the Web will move well beyond the current paradigm of retrieving pages by keywords. Instead, search engines will start to answer complex queries based on the cumulative knowledge of the Web. In this presentation, we will review the brief history of Semantic Search in academic research and in developments across the search industry. We also look ahead to highlight the research challenges that have surfaced and remain unsolved.

Improving access to the vast amount of human knowledge on the Web can be achieved in two principally different ways. Information Retrieval is traditionally concerned with improving the process of retrieval, given the content of the Web, as well as information on the structure of the Web and usage patterns of Web users [2]. Largely complementary to these efforts, the Semantic Web [1] has emerged as an effort to re-engineer the Web in a way that its contents become easier for machines to process. In this presentation, we will discuss the convergence of these approaches in what is known as Semantic Search, i.e. improving retrieval by exploiting the explicit semantics of information on the Web.

We begin by summarizing the relatively brief history of the scientific and engineering efforts towards realizing the Semantic Web, focusing in particular on the standards and tools for describing the content of web pages using additional metadata embedded in HTML. We will highlight the significant extent to which embedded metadata is already adopted on the Web, driven by an increasing number of applications but also facilitated by increasing collaboration around initiatives such as `schema.org`.

We then turn to discussing what these developments mean for search engine providers and other consumers of web content, starting from the very first application of embedded metadata, i.e. displaying more visual and interactive summaries of web pages [6]. We will explain in more detail the workings of entity retrieval and recommendation systems that power the "Knowledge Graph" experiences in large scale search engines such as Yahoo Search, and some of the research challenges associated, including the focused crawling of structured data [8], information integration [5, 7], ranking [3, 9] and query interpretation [4].

We will close by discussing some of the future directions in Semantic Search, in particular the challenge of going beyond entity-based, informational experiences to solving more complex tasks that require interaction with the user. We will also point out the increasing shift in web search from desktop to mobile, and some of the opportunities and challenges of the mobile context.

References

1. Antoniou, G., Groth, P., van Harmelen, F., Hoekstra, R.: A Semantic Web Primer, 3rd edn. MIT Press (2012)
2. Baeza-Yates, R.A., Ribeiro-Neto, B.A.: Modern Information Retrieval, 2nd edn. ACM Press / Addison-Wesley (2011)
3. Blanco, R., Mika, P., Vigna, S.: Effective and efficient entity search in RDF data. In: Proceedings of 10th International Semantic Web Conference, Bonn, Germany, pp. 83–97 (2011)
4. Blanco, R., Ottaviano, G., Meij, E.: Fast and space-efficient entity linking for queries. In: Proceedings of the Eighth ACM WSDM Conference, Shanghai, China, pp. 179–188 (2015)
5. Dalton, J., Blanco, R., Mika, P.: Coreference aware web object retrieval. In: Proceedings of the 20th ACM CIKM Conference, Glasgow, United Kingdom, pp. 211–220 (2011)
6. Haas, K., Mika, P., Tarjan, P., Blanco, R.: Enhanced results for web search. In: Proceeding of the 34th International ACM SIGIR Conference, Beijing, China, pp. 725–734 (2011)
7. Herzig, D.M., Mika, P., Blanco, R., Tran, T.: Federated entity search using on-the-fly consolidation. In: Proceedings of the 12th International Semantic Web Conference, Sydney, NSW, Australia, pp. 167–183 (2013)
8. Meusel, R., Mika, P., Blanco, R.: Focused crawling for structured data. In: Proceedings of the 23rd ACM CIKM Conference, Shanghai, China, pp. 1039–1048 (2014)
9. Pound, J., Mika, P., Zaragoza, H.: Ad-hoc object retrieval in the web of data. In: Proceedings of the 19th WWW Conference, Raleigh, North Carolina, USA, pp. 771–780 (2010)

Sentiment Strength Detection for Social Media Text: Artificial Agents, Answer Ranking and Art Installations

Mike Thelwall

Statistical Cybermetrics Research Group,
University of Wolverhampton,
Wolverhampton, UK
M.Thelwall@wlv.ac.uk

Abstract. This talk will describe a simple, fast, intuitive and flexible lexical method to detect sentiment strength in short informal text and will illustrate it with a range of research and commercial applications. Implemented in the software SentiStrength and optimised for social web text, the method can process 14,000 tweets per second with human level accuracy in many cases. The talk will demonstrate the program and its evaluations and show how it has been translated from the original English version to many other languages. It is free for researchers to use and its current applications include art installations, answer ranking, opinion mining, stock market prediction, customer feedback analysis, and sentiment-aware artificial agents.

Keywords: Sentiment analysis · Opinion mining · Social web · Twitter

The sentiment strength detection program SentiStrength [4] was developed in response to a need for the sentiment analysis of the huge number of informal texts written every day in social network sites, Twitter and elsewhere on the social web. Emotion psychology suggests that the most fundamental affective distinction is between positive and negative sentiment, with finer grained expressions of emotion being more culturally dependant. Moreover, humans process positive and negative sentiment in parallel to some extent. SentiStrength was therefore designed to detect the strength of positive and negative sentiment separately in social web texts.

SentiStrength uses a primarily lexical approach to detect sentiment. It has a list of about 2700 word stems, each with a pre-defined positive or negative sentiment strength score. For example, if a text contains the word *excellent* then the list suggests the presence of strong (4 out of 5) positive sentiment. There are 18 additional rules for special cases, such as negation, questions, booster words (e.g., *very*), emoticons and sentiment spelling (e.g., *niiiice*). This approach is fast (14,000 tweets/sec on a basic PC) and gives human-level accuracy on most of the social web texts that it has been tested on [6]. Its scores also tend to reflect the stated judgments and bodily responses (e.g., sweating, heartrate) of the people reading or writing it [1]. Because all sentiment resources, such as the sentiment term list, are stored in plain text files separately from the code, SentiStrength can be customised for specialised versions and other languages without the need for new code, except for agglutinative languages [8] and languages without word boundaries (e.g., Chinese).

In addition to being used in social science research to detect patterns of sentiment in the social web, SentiStrength has been used in a wide variety of other applications. The most prominent use is for detecting sentiment in the feedback given to question answerers in Yahoo Answers. The results boost the ranking of the answers given by people who receive more positive feedback [2]. SentiStrength also supports the logic of autonomous agents responding to human text. For example, users in one virtual world reported deeper engagement with a virtual bartender when his facial expression and body posture reacted to the sentiment in their conversation [3]. SentiStrength's ease of customisation has also allowed it to be used in applications when sentiment is commonly expressed in unusual ways. For example, it was used to drive lightshows on the London Eye during the London 2012 Olympics and on the Empire State Building during the Super Bowl 2014 by detecting sentiment in relevant tweets and translating the results into patterns of light. In both cases, simple changes were needed to detect context-specific expressions, such as *Go Hawks!*. SentiStrength has also been used to analyse tweets about prominent political and news events. It incorporates automatic methods to optimise its term list and term weightings for such topic specific applications [5] but struggles with sarcasm in online political arguments [6], and with using context from ongoing discussions to improve sentiment scores [7].

References

1. Kappas, A. Tsankova, E. Theunis, M., Kuester, D.: Cyberemotions: subjective and physiological responses elicited by contributing to online discussion forums. In: 51th Annual Meeting of the Society for Psychophysiological Research (2010)
2. Kucuktunc, O., Cambazoglu, B.B., Weber, I., Ferhatosmanoglu, H.: A large-scale sentiment analysis for Yahoo! Answers. In: Proceedings of the 5th ACM International Conference on Web Search and Data Mining (2012)
3. Skowron, M., Pirker, H., Rank, S., Paltoglou, G., Ahn, J., Gobron S.: No peanuts! Affective cues for the virtual bartender. In: Proceedings of the Florida Artificial Intelligence Research Society Conference. AAAI Press (2011)
4. Thelwall, M., Buckley, K., Paltoglou, G. Cai, D., Kappas, A.: Sentiment strength detection in short informal text. J. Am. Soc. Inf. Sci. Technol. **61**(12), 2544–2558 (2010)
5. Thelwall, M., et al.: Damping sentiment analysis in online communication: Discussions, monologs and dialogs. In: Gelbukh, A. (ed.) CICLing 2013, Part II. LNCS, vol. 7817, pp. 1–12. Springer, Heidelberg (2013)
6. Thelwall, M., Buckley, K., Paltoglou, G.: Sentiment strength detection for the social web. J. Am. Soci. Inf. Sci. Technol. **63**(1), 163–173 (2012)
7. Thelwall, M., Buckley, K.: Topic-based sentiment analysis for the Social Web: the role of mood and issue-related words. J. Am. Soc. Inf. Sci. Technol. **64**(8), 1608–1617 (2013)
8. Vural, G., Cambazoglu, B.B., Senkul, P., Tokgoz O.: A framework for sentiment analysis in Turkish: application to polarity detection of movie reviews in Turkish. Comput. Inf. Sci. III, 437–445 (2013)

Contents

Web Application Modelling and Engineering

Mobile Web Applications

Social Web Applications

Semantic Web Applications

PhD Symposium

Demonstrations

Posters

Tutorials

Web Application Modelling and Engineering

Beyond Graph Search: Exploring and Exploiting Rich Connected Data Sets

Omar Alonso[1] and Jaap Kamps[2](✉)

[1] Microsoft Corp, Mountain View, CA, USA
omalonso@microsoft.com
[2] University of Amsterdam, Amsterdam, The Netherlands
kamps@uva.nl

Abstract. Modern Web data is highly structured in terms of entities and relations from large knowledge resources, geo-temporal references and social network structures, resulting in a massive multidimensional graph. This graph essentially unifies both the searcher and the information resources that played a fundamentally different role in traditional information retrieval. Graph search-based systems offer major new ways to access relevant information. Graph search affects both query formulation (complex queries about entities and relations building on the searcher's context) as well as result exploration and discovery (slicing and dicing the information using the graph structure) in a completely novel way. This new graph based approach introduces great opportunities, but also great challenges, in terms of data quality and data integration, user interface design, and privacy.

1 Introduction

With the explosion of social networks, the term *graph* has become more ubiquitous than ever. When people talk about the Facebook graph or the Twitter followers graph, to name a couple of examples, the focus is on the relationships and their semantic meaning (e.g., friend, like, re-tweet, etc.) instead of just web objects like a page or an image. On the more traditional search engine arena, there has a been a lot of work on extracting more useful information from web pages so they can reflect these relationships. These efforts have produced new experiences for users.

Bing and Google have now graphs (named Satori and Knowledge Graph respectively) that can contribute more information to the search engine results page (SERP) than just ten blue links. Figures 1 and 2 show different strategies to present more information that is not usually displayed by the typical blue links. In the case of Bing, the input box autocomplete incorporates bits of the web page (image and snippet) as the user enters the query. For Google, a similar effect takes place but instead of showing the content on the pull-down, the extra information is rendered next to the search results. The benefit for the user is very clear: instead of issuing a query, examining the results, modifying the query

P. Cimiano et al. (Eds.): ICWE 2015, LNCS 9114, pp. 3–12, 2015.
DOI: 10.1007/978-3-319-19890-3_1

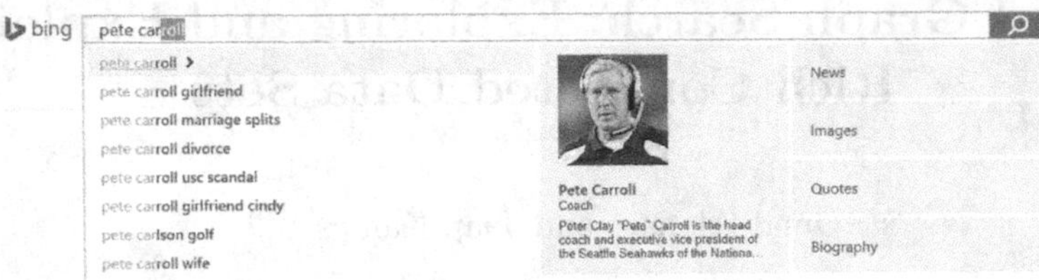

Fig. 1. Interactive autocomplete showing person name and basic information in Bing

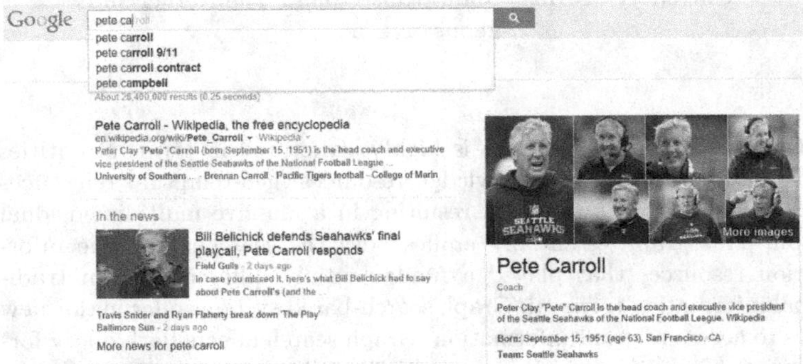

Fig. 2. Interactive autocomplete showing more information next to the SERP in Google

and examining again, this new model allows a more interactive *exploration* of what is possible before *exploiting* the relevant content that is being presented.

In 2013 Facebook introduced Graph Search, a search feature that allowed users to express more semantic queries for searching social content. The first version of Graph Search focused on four main areas (people, photos, places, and interests) and it was rolled out in English only. While still premature, it was possible to perform new types of queries and get results that were very different from what was the norm in a traditional SERP. Figure 3 shows examples of entity-based structured queries within Facebook graph search. At the time of writing, Facebook is replacing the novel graph search with a more traditional search over postings at the searcher's personal timeline[1].

Clearly, this approach is not limited to web, and can be applied to other highly structured data. Just to give an example, the hansards or parliamentary proceedings are fully public data with a good graph structure linking every speech to the respective speaker, their role in parliament and their political party. Graph search allows us to explore politics from the viewpoint of individual members of parliament or government.

In this position paper we outline challenges, opportunities and possible research avenues for designing and building search services that can take full advantage of the potential of graphs and semantic information that can go beyond recommending friends or web links. Instead, we are interested in solutions that

[1] http://search.fb.com/

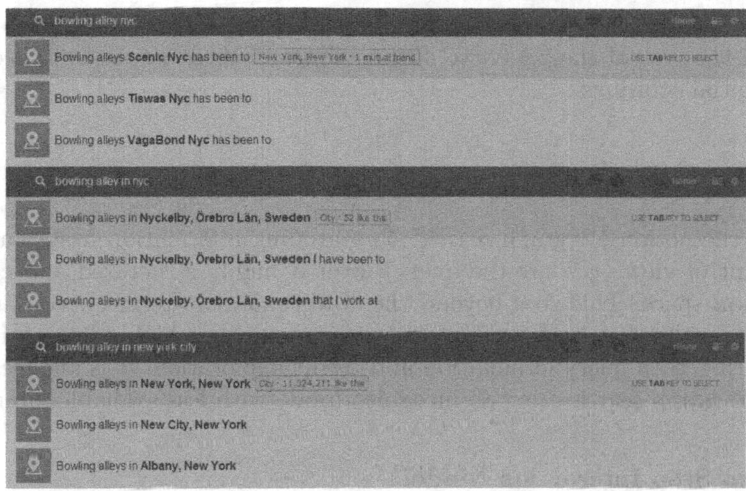

Fig. 3. Interactive autocomplete options within Facebook Graph Search

help users express information and navigate results better through the entire search space.

All the past and current efforts on using graph search have an exploratory information need in common. Information on the Web is becoming increasingly structured in terms of entities, types and relations from large knowledge resources, geo-temporal references and social network structures, resulting in a massive multidimensional graph that is very rich in content and connections. This graph essentially unifies both the searcher and the information resources that played a fundamentally different role in traditional information retrieval, and offers major new ways to access relevant information. In other words, the user is the default query. Or, *you* are the continuously running query on the system. Any user user input is added to this context.

Graph search affects both query formulation as well as result exploration and discovery. On the one hand, it allows for incrementally expressing complex information needs that triangulate information about multiple entities or entity types, relations between those entities, with various filters on location, temporal constraints or the sources of information used (or ignored), and taking into account the rich profile and context information of the searcher (and his/her peers at various degrees of separation). On the other hand, it is an enabling mechanism for more powerful ways to explore the results from various aspects and viewpoints, by slicing and dicing the information using the graph structure, and also using the same structure for explaining why results are retrieved or recommended, and by whom.

This new graph based approach introduces great opportunities, but also great challenges, both technical ranging from data quality and data integration to user interface design, as well as ethical challenges in terms of privacy; transparency, bias and control; and avoiding the so-called filter bubbles [16], that is, a personal universe of information created just for a user using an array of personalizing filters. In the rest of the paper we outline some of these issues and shed light into potential solutions.

2 Open Questions

We view the notion of "graph search" as searching information from your personal point of view (*you* are the query), over a highly structured and curated information space. This goes beyond the traditional two-term queries and ten blue links results that users are familiar with, requiring a highly interactive session covering both query formulation and result exploration. It is also desirable to support graph search using an incognito mode with less available filters.

2.1 Two Step Interaction Model

Interaction plays a central role on this new model. The user starts by writing a query and the engine is expected to assist by providing potential query completions. At certain keystrokes, the engine will show results that will change as the user explores more the query formulations. The goal for the user is to maximize the knowledge gain while minimizing the cost of interaction. This is even more prominent in mobile scenarios where any assistance is welcome given the real estate limitations and potential input errors.

Incremental Structured Query Input. Creating a *graph query* requires incremental construction of a complex query using a variety of building blocks. Current search engines treat this as a form of query suggestion or query completion, which offers tailored suggestions trying to promote longer queries that cover multiple entity types and relations and various filters. Suggestions and entity types may be based on the user's own activity. This goes beyond prevailing autocompletion techniques, with previews and surrogates from traditional result pages or SERPs moving to a more dynamic query suggestion.

Dynamic Structured Result Set Exploration. Results are highly personalized: they are unique for the searcher at a given point in time. The result set is highly structured: rather than just showing the top-10 results from an almost infinite list, a faceted exploration based on user's interests or augmentation of the SERP is needed. The structure is dynamically derived from the graph structure and the user's point of view, rather than a rigid facet and facet value hierarchy.

2.2 Data Quality and Data Integration

Building a knowledge graph requires significant effort on data acquisition, cleaning, and integration at many levels: are there trade offs in simplicity and level of detail (such as the classic knowledge representation trade-off)? What levels of granularity and comprehensiveness are needed for effective deployment? What type of quality is needed and adequate? Is any noise level acceptable? How to deal with near duplicate detection, conflation, mappings, or entity disambiguation at scale?

2.3 Query Classification

Graph search also requires a new query classification scheme, beyond the traditional division into navigational, informational, and transactional queries. Is there a new way to characterize queries in this new model? Does the notion of information need change? It is the ultimate form of personalization, with the searcher not only responsible for the query but also determining the (slice of) the data being considered? What shifts in control and transparency are needed to accomplish this?

2.4 Graph Search Evaluation

This also presents a range of new evaluation problems. How to evaluate the overall process, given its personalized and interactive nature? How to evaluate the first stage as essentially a form of query autocomplete? And how to evaluate the second stage as to explore and exploit the result set? Can we evaluate user satisfaction and engagement differently?

2.5 Ethics and Privacy

Access to personal data is fraught with ethical and privacy concerns, is there similarly structured public data for scientific research? As an extreme form of personalization, how to avoid the uncanny cave, filter bubbles and echo chambers? How ethical is it to privilege a particular query refinement suggestion over the many other possible candidates?

2.6 When (not) to Use Graph Search?

Rather than a universal solution, the graph search is particularly useful for specific types of information needs and queries. This is also depending on the character of the data available. For example, the Facebook Graph Search emphasized the social network structure, friends and other persons, locations and location-tagged objects. Social network data is abundantly available (although getting access presents a major barrier) but also notoriously skewed. Rather the searcher's personal point of view, it can also be used to show results from the viewpoint of any person in the network. There are many interesting sets of data – both historically or modern – that capture both the persons and related information: think of parliamentary data in public government, or intranet data in enterprises and organizations. For example, the *hansards* or parliamentary proceedings are fully public data with a clear graph structure linking every speech to the respective speaker, their role in parliament and their political party.

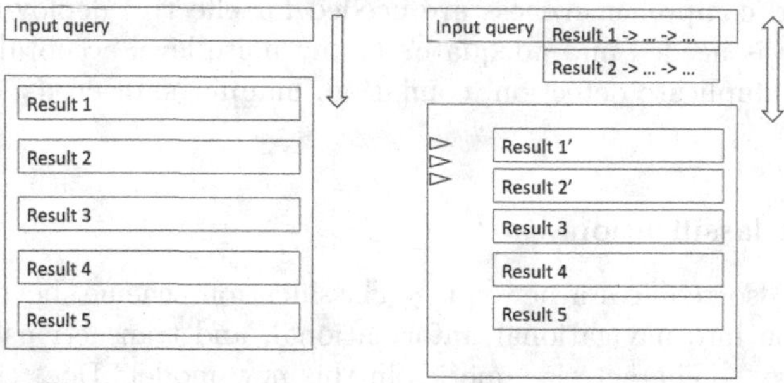

Fig. 4. Incremental Query Exploration Page (IQEP)

3 Potential Solutions

Graph search requires a highly interactive session covering both query formulation and result exploration. There is a seamless integration of what is shown as results depending of how far the user is expressing the query.

3.1 Query Exploration

There is a shift towards the control of the searcher, necessitating new tools that help the user construct the appropriate graph search query, and actively suggest refinements or filters to better articulate their needs, or explore further aspects [9]. This leads to a far more dynamic interaction than with traditional result lists, or modern hit lists showing summaries of a static set of results.

This suggests a new form of "query autocomplete" that invites and allows users to issue longer queries constructed based on entities, relationships, and templates. In contrast to SERP, we define IQEP as the *Incremental Query Exploration Page*. IQEP allows the user to explore more the result set as part of the input query. We can think of IQEP as an interactive mechanism that *promotes* relevant results selected by the user from the traditional SERP to the input box. In that sense, there is no static separation between query and search results. The more the user focuses or exploit a query term or entity, the more relevant content is moved upstream. Figure 4 shows IQEP as a bi-directional channel that moves results from the search list to the input box or vice versa (upstream/downstream). This mechanism enables the user to not only see what is possible but also to backtrack in case the content is not relevant or interesting enough anymore.

There are a range of suitable evaluation methods that we can use. The most obvious way is by direct evaluation of query suggestion and SERP. There is also a range of criteria useful for behavioral observation in the wild testing: users should issue longer queries, multiple filters, dwell-time, active engagement, structured-query templates. There are query segments where this type of querying is expected to be most useful: torso and tail queries (medium and rare occurrences based on query log distributions); exploratory scenarios. Traditional head or navigational queries, that is highly popular ones, seem less interesting, although these could be part of a more complex underlying information need.

This goes beyond Broder's taxonomy [4]: queries are all navigational, informational, and transactional *but* they are entity-focused. Queries may aim to return a single or a small set (not unlike traditional Boolean querying over structured data), or there is a need for data analytics on the whole set of results.

3.2 Result Exploration

This proposed shift towards the control of the searcher—small changes in the query can lead to radically different result sets—necessitating active exploration of slices of the data to explore further aspects.

This suggest a new form of search results unique for every user. Similarly to the query exploration mechanism, this interaction encourages users to explore over entities, relationships, and filters. Unlike traditional faceted search options, the result space is highly dynamic, and requires adaptive exploration options tailored to the context and searcher, at every stage of the process.

This is a radical departure from the traditional ten blue links available in any search engine. The IQEP moves from links to answers, and from answers to suggesting (expressions of) needs. This is an complete shift from the traditional dichotomy between query (the searcher's responsibility) and results (the system's responsibility). Traditional search results have moved to a hit list of result summaries (still a fix set of results, but the shown summaries are tailored to the searcher and her query). These summaries in terms of entities are now answers rather than links to answers. Now these results, or previews of them, are moving into the search box, in the form of structured query suggestions with some sort of preview indicating of the consequences on the result set (often in terms of numbers of results, or entity previews).

There are many options for the evaluation of components: (adaptive) captioning, (adaptive) filters, graph query templates. E.g., captioning should describe (relative to the entity), explain (relative to the user), and be contrastive (relative to the IQEP). There are standard experimental evaluation methods from Human-Computer Interaction and User Interface design [8]. With a running service, evaluation in the wild is very suitable. There are various implicit and explicit criteria: users should explore the result set, usage of multiple filters, dwell-time, active engagement, structured-query templates. Torso and tail queries, and exploratory scenarios are the most suitable query segments.

3.3 Barriers to Success

In order to work on graph search as a research community, we need to understand the problem better, and need to have sharable resources to do applied research and build common benchmarks.

The consequences of graph search are quite fundamental. Graph search has the potential to give users more power by unleashing semantically annotated information with many entities and relations between them. It brings the control back to the searcher, rather than leave it in the hands of the algorithm. Graph-based search systems also have the potential to solve part of the old information retrieval problem of conceptual search.

In terms of IR research and required evaluation methods, as discussed in the sections above, there are various open problems. What we need is to work on sharable research data, that exemplifies most of the characteristics we want to study. There is no need to be on Facebook or Twitter, or hand over your personal data. Similar small data sets and systems are available (e.g., so.cl, NYT, Parliamentary data, etc.) It will be hard to share a realistic subset of social network data but it should be possible to construct a simulated set.

What would be a concrete task to study on this data? Instead of implementing all features, it is would be useful to select a few components like query suggestion box, filters as facets, and captions to show the potential.

Search engine user interfaces has been very stable in the last 15 years. The input box and the ten blue links are the still the most optimal way to show search results. Can we do better in terms of user experience? This would give users a lot of flexibility and options. However, remains to be seen if users would adopt such dynamic interface.

At a high level, graph search seems limited to familiar entity types (e.g., Facebook entities) and templates. How far can this scale? Will this work on truly open domains? Finally, there are a number of ethical issues such as privacy, transparency, bias and control, and filter bubbles.

4 Related Work

There has been published research on models for seeking information that are related to our approach, in particular information foraging [17] and information encountering [5].

There is considerable industrial activity around social graphs. The most famous example is Facebook Graph Search, a feature that allows users to perform more sophisticated searches on their social network. Bing has been integrating Facebook into their web search results for the last couple of years. Similarly, Google has been annotating search results with Google+ profiles. In terms of published literature, both Google and Microsoft have reported studies on different aspects of social annotations, e.g. [7,14,15].

Hearst [8] covers extensively issues with search user interfaces design and evaluation. In particular she addressed the user interface and user experience challenges of search results moving from the found links, to the HIT page as snippets, and now to the query auto-suggest box as previews of possible query extensions.

Graph search, or personalized search over a highly structured and curated information space, is closely related work on exploratory search and sense making

[13,18]. The graph structure provides natural facets for exploring the data, from a local point of view, allowing for a more dynamic structure than traditional faceted search using rigid, global, hierarchical structure.

There are crucial links with work on searching structured data [6,10], and work on the appropriate query languages [11,12]. These branches of research in particular focus on complex querying of structured text or data, whereas the graph search addresses also, and perhaps primarily, the process of constructing series of complex queries interactively.

5 Conclusions

This position paper introduced the notion of "graph search" as searching information from your personal point of view (*you* are the query), over a highly structured and curated information space. Graph Search has fundamental consequences for web engineering and offers tremendous opportunities for building new systems and tools that allow users to explore information from many different angles. At the same time, using a graph to go beyond recommending friends or links requires solid knowledge of many components that need to work together. We presented the open questions and outlined a number of challenges and research directions that present some of the greatest challenges to work on in the coming years.

Acknowledgments. This research was supported in part by the Netherlands Organization for Scientific Research (ExPoSe project, NWO CI # 314.99.108; DiLiPaD project, NWO Digging into Data # 600.006.014).

We gratefully acknowledge discussion on this topic at the Exploiting Semantic Annotations in IR workshops (CIKM 2013 and CIKM 2014) [2,3], and at the Dagstuhl Seminar on Evaluation Methodologies in Information Retrieval [1]. A workshop devoted to this topic is planned at the SIGIR 2015 conference.

References

1. Alonso, O., Kamps, J.: Graph search and beyond. In: Agosti, M., Fuhr, N., Toms, E., Vakkari, P. (eds.) Evaluation Methodologies in Information Retrieval, Dagstuhl Reports, vol. 3 (10), chap. 4.3, pp. 108–111. Dagstuhl (2014)
2. Alonso, O., Kamps, J., Karlgren, J. (eds.): Proc. ESAIR 2014. ACM Press (2014). http://dl.acm.org/citation.cfm?id=2663712
3. Bennett, P.N., Gabrilovich, E., Kamps, J., Karlgren, J. (eds.): Proc. ESAIR 2013. ACM Press (2013). http://dl.acm.org/citation.cfm?id=2513204
4. Broder, A.: A taxonomy of web search. SIGIR Forum **36**(2), 3–10 (2002)
5. Erdelez, S.: Information encountering: a conceptual framework for accidental information discovery. In: Proc. of ISIC. Taylor Graham Publishing, London (1997)
6. Exploiting semantic annotations in information retrieval. Workshop (2009–2014)
7. Fernquist, J., Chi, E.: Perception and understanding of social annotations in web search. In: Proc. of WWW. International World Wide Web Conferences Steering Committee (2013)

8. Hearst, M.: Search User Interfaces. Cambridge University Press (2009)
9. Hearst, M.: How can search interfaces enhance the value of semantic annotations (and vice versa)? In: Proc. of ESAIR (2013)
10. Initiative for the evaluation of XML retrieval. Evaluation Forum (2002–2014)
11. Kamps, J., Marx, M., de Rijke, M., Sigurbjörnsson, B.: Articulating information needs in XML query languages. ACM TOIS **24**(4) (2006)
12. Libkin, L., Martens, W., Vrgoč, D.: Querying graph databases with XPath. In: Proc. of ICDT. ACM Press (2013)
13. Marchionini, G.: Exploratory search: from finding to understanding. Communications of the ACM **49**(4), 41–46 (2006)
14. Muralidharan, A., Gyongyi, Z., Chi, E.: Social annotations in web search. In: Proc. of CHI. ACM Press (2012)
15. Pantel, P., Gamon, M., Alonso, O., Haas, K.: Social annotations: utility and predictive modeling. In: Proc. of SIGIR. ACM Press (2012)
16. Pariser, E.: The Filter Bubble. Penguin (2011)
17. Pirolli, P.: Information Foraging Theory: Adaptive Interaction with Information. Oxford University Press (2009)
18. Pirolli, P., Russell, D.M.: Introduction to this special issue on sensemaking. Human-Computer Interaction **26**(1–2), 1–8 (2011)

Leveraging Social Patterns in Web Application Design

Devis Bianchini(✉), Valeria De Antonellis, and Michele Melchiori

Department of Information Engineering, University of Brescia,
Via Branze, 38, 25123 Brescia, Italy
{devis.bianchini,valeria.deantonellis,michele.melchiori}@unibs.it

Abstract. In this paper we propose a multi-layered model meant for the selection of data services for web application design. Our aim is at complementing existing data service selection criteria, e.g., matching based on (semantic) data coming from the services, by also considering the experience of other developers, who used the services in the past for designing their own web applications. In this sense, it becomes crucial the importance that a developer gives to past experiences of other developers in selecting a data service, that might depend on the social relationships that relate the developers each other as well. The model proposed in this paper takes into account these challenging issues by considering available data services, web applications where services have been aggregated, and social relationships between web application developers, which identify different kinds of *social patterns*.

1 Introduction

Modern web applications should be created also exploiting information made available in the form of data services, that enable to access data from different web sources. Data services need to be selected, before being properly integrated to become meaningful and valuable. Let's consider a web application developer, working for the marketing department of an enterprise, who has to build an application that integrates information about potential markets, sales and demographic data. This application requires to merge data coming from sources internal to the enterprise (e.g., information about the target clients) and external data sources (e.g., providing information about demographic data), made available as data services. On the one hand, data services may be selected according to their pertinence with respect to the application that is being designed, e.g., entailed by the (semantic) type of data coming from the sources [1–3]. On the other hand, there are many functional and non functional aspects, such as the ones related to quality of service [4,5] or service trustworthiness and reputation [6], that are not always available within data service descriptions, although they could improve service selection strategies [7]. Nevertheless, in an enterprise context, such as the one depicted in our running example, it is frequent that a developer, who learns by examples, searches for advices based on design experiences of other developers (of the same enterprise or different ones), rather than relying on votes/ratings

P. Cimiano et al. (Eds.): ICWE 2015, LNCS 9114, pp. 13–23, 2015.
DOI: 10.1007/978-3-319-19890-3_2

assigned to data services by developers over the Web. Moreover, even if developers' votes would be available to rate data services, approaches for data service selection that rely on such votes [7,8] do not consider another important aspect: the relevance of a data service may depend on the web application design project that is being carried on; such relevance might be high since the service has been already used in similar applications. Finally, in the enterprise context we are considering credibility of developers, who know each others, can be assumed as high, compared to a development scenario where services are ranked and used by developers over the Web. Therefore, for the moment, we do not use advanced developers' credibility assessment techniques such as the ones described in [7–9]. It is reasonable to assume that developer's preference is for experts who can be contacted/engaged, because some mutual social or organizational relationships exist among them. Such relationships constitute particular structures that in [10] are called *social patterns*, that can be fruitfully exploited for data service selection.

The main contribution in this paper is a *multi-layered model*, meant for supporting the selection of data services for web application design purposes, and of metrics specifically based on the model elements. The model is organized on three levels. At the lowest level (*data service layer*), the available data services and corresponding metadata are taken into account to enable service search. At a second level (*web application layer*), the model includes past experiences of collection and aggregation of data services to design web applications; these experiences act as a bridge between the data service layer and the *social layer*, that includes the developers, who experienced the collection of data services, organized according to different social patterns, that reflect different ways developers learn from each other experience in web application design.

The paper is organized as follows. In Section 2 we describe the multi-layered model. In Section 3 we propose the criteria for data service selection based on past experiences and social patterns, with some hints on preliminary experiments that are being carried on. Finally, future work are discussed in Section 4.

2 The Three-Layer Model

Data Service Layer. The multi-layered model we propose in this paper is shown in Figure 1. We define a (web) data service s as a single operation, method or query to access data from a web data source Σ. We model a data service s as a set of service inputs s^{IN} and a set of service outputs s^{OUT}. Service outputs represent data that are accessed through the service s, service inputs are parameters that are needed to invoke the service and access data. We denote with $\mathcal{S}$ the overall set of available data services and with $\Sigma[\mathcal{S}]\subseteq\mathcal{S}$ the set of data services made available by the source Σ. Examples of data services are the methods of a Web API (for instance, the method of GeoData Demographics API[1] that provides demographic data for a given zone), queries formulated by using search-specific languages (such as Yahoo! Query Language,

[1] http://geodataservice.net.

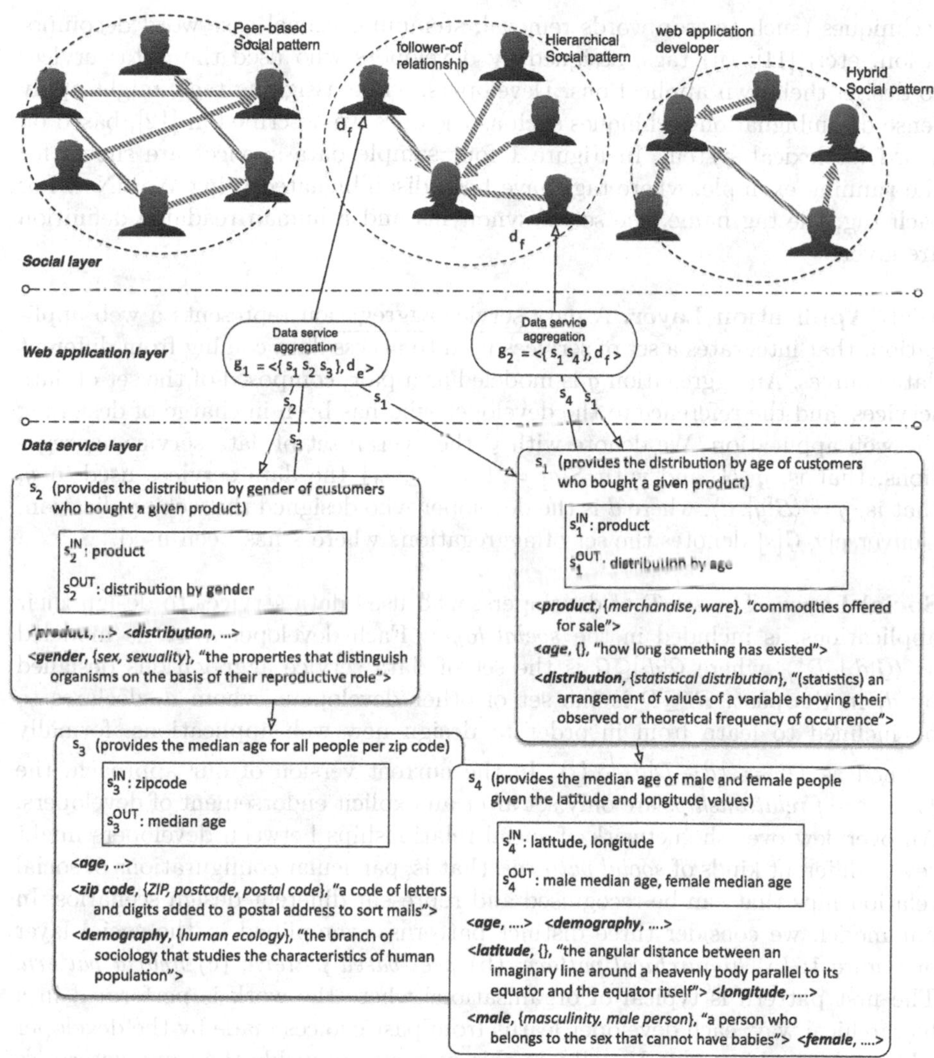

Fig. 1. The multi-layered model for data service selection

`https://developer.yahoo.com/yql/`), services delivering data in tabular format (e.g., Google Fusion Tables, `tables.googlelabs.com/`) or in row format (such as Factual, `http://www.factual.com`). Data services are usually wrapped as web services, that can be implemented according to different styles (e.g., using REST or WSDL).

A data service s is also associated with some *metadata*, that in the current version of the model contains (semantic) tags, used to enable coarse-grained search of the data services. In our model, we admit different ways of assigning (semantic) tags to data services: (i) keywords extracted from the data service name, I/O names and textual description through the application of text mining techniques (such as stop words removal, stemming, camel case word decomposition, etc.) [11]; (ii) tags, assigned by developers who used the data services to design their own applications. Developers, while assigning tags, might apply sense disambiguation techniques such as the ones we described in [12], based on WordNet lexical system. In Figure 1 four sample data services are shown for the running example, where tags have been disambiguated using WordNet. For each tag, the tag name, the set of synonyms and a human readable definition are given.

Web Application Layer. A data service aggregation represents a web application, that integrates a set of services used to access data coming from different data sources. An aggregation g is modeled as a pair, composed of the set of data services, and the reference to the developer who has been in charge of designing the web application. We denote with $\mathcal{G}$ the overall set of data service aggregations, that is, $g \in \mathcal{G}$, and with $\mathcal{S}[g] = \{s_1, \ldots, s_n\}$ the data services used in g, that is, $g = \langle \mathcal{S}[g], d \rangle$, where d is the developer who designed the web application. Conversely, $\mathcal{G}[s]$ denotes the set of aggregations where s has been used.

Social Layer. The set $\mathcal{D}$ of developers, who used data services to design their applications, is included in the *social layer.* Each developer $d_i \in \mathcal{D}$ is modeled as $\langle \mathcal{G}[d_i], \mathcal{D}^* \rangle$, where $\mathcal{G}[d_i] \subseteq \mathcal{G}$ is the set of data service aggregations designed by d_i in the past, $\mathcal{D}^* \subseteq \mathcal{D}$ is the set of other developers, whom d_i declares to be inclined to learn from in order to design new web applications, formally defined as $\mathcal{D}^* = \{d_j \in \mathcal{D} | d_i \xrightarrow{f} d_j\}$. In the current version of our approach, the *follower-of relationships* are only set after an explicit endorsement of developers. An overview over the network of social relationships between developers might reveal different kinds of *social patterns*, that is, particular configurations of social relationships that can be recognised and represent different design scenarios. In our model, we consider three distinct patterns, exemplified in the social layer of Figure 1: (a) *hierarchical pattern*; (b) *peer-based pattern*; (c) *hybrid pattern.* The first pattern is typical of organisations where the work is performed in a hierarchical way: each developer learns from past choices made by the developer who leads the hierarchy. Usually, in this case we are inside the same enterprise or across different departments of the same enterprise. The second pattern is typical of a totally collaborative environment, both within the same enterprise and across different ones, where a leadership in the selection of data services can not be identified. The third scenario represents an hybrid situation, where a developer is or has been involved in different web application design projects and, maybe depending on the particular application domain, has different other developers whose past choices could be considered to learn from. Automatic detection of social patterns, based on social network properties such as degree centrality, betweness centrality and closeness centrality [13], will be addressed in future work.

3 Data Service Selection Driven by Social Patterns

3.1 Problem Statement

Given a developer $d^r \in \mathcal{D}$, hereafter denoted as the *requester*, who is designing a new web application starting from a set of available data services $\mathcal{S}$, given the set $\mathcal{G}[d_k]$ of data service aggregations designed in the past by developer $d_k \in \mathcal{D}$, our aim is at supporting d^r in performing data service selection, by proposing an ordered set of candidate data services $\mathcal{S}^* \subseteq \mathcal{S}$ taking into account the past experiences in $\mathcal{G}[d_k]$ for each developer d_k such that $d^r \xrightarrow{f} d_k$, that is, for each developer from whom d^r explicitly declared to learn from. The request s^r is formulated as a set of desired (semantic) tags and a set of data services, that have been already included in the application, namely $s^r = \langle \{t^r\}, g^r \rangle$, where $\{t^r\}$ is a list of tags and $g^r = \{s_1, s_2, \ldots s_n\}$ is the list of already selected data service descriptions. Tags in the set $\{t^r\}$ can be disambiguated using WordNet as well. For example, the following request s^r is formulated to find a `demography` data service, annotated with a `postal code`, to produce a distribution of people by `sex`. The service must be used in a web application, that is being designed and already contains data services s_1 and s_2 (see Figure 1):

$s^r = \langle\ t_1^r = \{\langle$**postal code, {zip code, ZIP, postcode}, "a code of letters and digits added to a postal address to sort mails"**$\rangle\}$;

$t_2^r = \{\langle$**sex, {gender, sexuality}, "the properties that distinguish organisms on the basis of their reproductive roles"**$\rangle\}$;

$t_3^r = \{\langle$**demography, {human ecology}, "the branch of sociology that studies the characteristics of human populations"**$\rangle\}$;

$g^r = \{s_1, s_2\}\rangle$

3.2 Data Service Selection

The overall similarity between s^r and each available data service $s \in \mathcal{S}$, denoted with $Sim(s^r, s) \in [0, 1]$, is used to filter out not relevant data services and is computed as linear combination of two matching techniques:

$$Sim(s^r, s) = \omega_s \cdot Sim_{tag}(s^r, s) + (1 - \omega_s) \cdot Sim_{agg}(s^r, s) \in [0, 1] \quad (1)$$

$Sim_{tag}(s^r, s)$ is based on WordNet and has been widely described in [12],:

$$Sim_{tag}(s^r, s) = \frac{2 \cdot \sum_{t^r, t} TagAff(t^r, t)}{|\{t^r\}| + |\{t\}|} \in [0, 1] \quad (2)$$

where $TagAff(t^r, t) = 0.8^L$, if there is a path of L hyponymy/hypernymy relations between t^r and t. In the running example, $Sim_{tag}(s^r, s_3) = 0.667$ and $Sim_{tag}(s^r, s_4) = 0.862$, since $TagAff(\texttt{zipcode}, \texttt{postalcode}) = 1.0$, $TagAff(\texttt{sex}, \texttt{male}) = 0.8$, $TagAff(\texttt{sex}, \texttt{female}) = 0.8$, $TagAff(\texttt{postalcode}, \texttt{latitude}) = 0.64$, $TagAff(\texttt{postalcode}, \texttt{longitude}) = 0.64$. $Sim_{agg}(s^r, s)$ quantifies the average similarity between g^r and the aggregations where s has been used in the past. Such similarity relies on the Dice formula and is computed as:

$$AggSim(g^r, \mathcal{S}[g]) = \frac{2 \cdot \sum_{i,j} Sim_{tag}(s_i, s_j)}{|g^r| + |\mathcal{S}[g]|} \in [0,1] \tag{3}$$

The rationale here is that the more similar are data services used in the two compared aggregations according to their tag similarity, the more similar are the two aggregations as well. For example, since g^r already contains s_1 and s_2, we have

$$Sim_{agg}(s^r, s_3) = \frac{2 * (1.0 + 1.0 + 0.667)}{3+3} = 0.889 \quad Sim_{agg}(s^r, s_4) = \frac{2 * (1.0 + 0.862)}{3+2} = 0.745 \tag{4}$$

The weight $\omega_s \in [0,1]$ is used to balance the impact of similarity based on (semantic) tags and similarity based on data service aggregations. If $g^r = \emptyset$, that is, the developer is looking for the first data service to be included in the new web application that is being designed, then $\omega_s = 1$. In the running example, $Sim(s^r, s_3) = 0.8224$ and $Sim(s^r, s_4) = 0.7801$, where $\omega_s = 0.3$. Data services included in the search results (that we denote with $\mathcal{S}' \subseteq \mathcal{S}$) are those whose overall similarity $Sim(s^r, s) \geq \tau$, where τ is set by the requester.

3.3 Data Service Ranking

Each data service $s \in \mathcal{S}'$ is ranked taking into account both its overall similarity compared to the request, $Sim(s^r, s)$, and the value assigned to s through a ranking function $\rho : \mathcal{S}' \mapsto [0,1]$, that is based on the ranking of developers in terms of number of their followers at the Social layer. In particular, the better the ranking of developers who used the data service s, the closer the value $\rho(s)$ to 1.0 (maximum value). The $Sim(s^r, s)$ and $\rho(s)$ elements are combined in the following harmonic mean:

$$rank(s) = \frac{2 \cdot \rho(s) \cdot Sim(s^r, s)}{\rho(s) + Sim(s^r, s)} \in [0,1] \tag{5}$$

In the following, we further discuss how we estimate the ranking of developers for evaluating $\rho(s)$. For simplicity, let's denote the ranking of a developer $d \in \mathcal{D}$ as $DR[d] \in [0,1]$. The value $\rho(s)$ is computed as follows:

$$\rho(s) = \frac{\sum_{k=1}^{n} DR[d_k]}{N} \in [0,1] \tag{6}$$

where $\{d_k\} \subseteq \mathcal{D}$ are the developers who used the data service s in their own web application design projects, $DR[d_k]$ is the ranking of developer d_k, N is the number of times s has been selected (under the hypothesis that a developer might use a data service s in $m > 1$ projects, then $DR[d_k]$ is considered m times). The computation of $DR[d]$, based on the number of followers of d, depends on the type of social pattern, among the ones shown in Figure 1, as discussed in the following.

Hierarchical Social Pattern. This pattern can be represented through a tree structure, where children nodes *follow* their own parent node and only one parent is allowed for each child. Now, let's consider the structure shown in Figure 2(a), where we partially expanded the social layer of Figure 1. The developer d_c is the requester and has to choose among data services that have been used in the past by developers d_a, d_b, d_d, d_e and d_f, whose social relationships are depicted in figure. In particular, note that d_e and d_f designed the two aggregations g_1 and g_2, that contain data services s_3 and s_4, respectively.

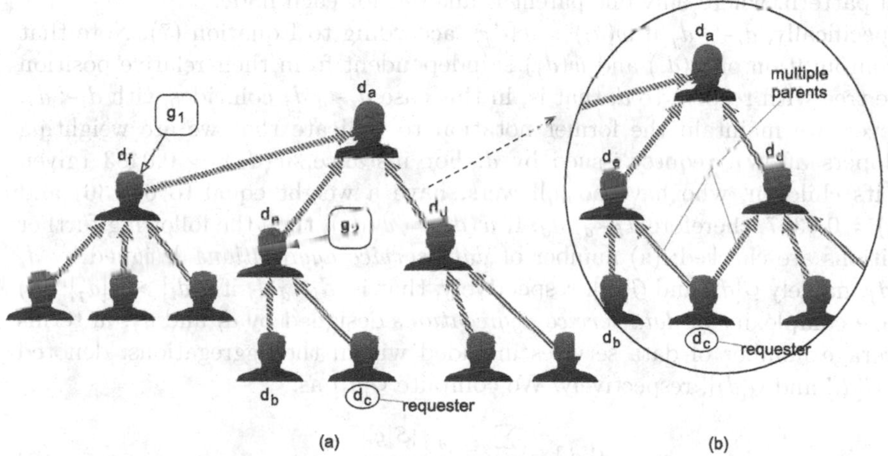

Fig. 2. An example of hierarchical social pattern (a) and a variant of the example, that represents a hybrid social pattern (b)

In this scenario, a developer d_i is ranked better than another developer d_j, under the viewpoint of a requester d, denoted with $d_i \prec_d d_j$, if one of the following conditions holds:

1. **condition (C1)** - d_i is one of the ancestors of d in the tree, while d_j is not; the rationale is that d always prefers to learn from developers, for whom d explicitly declared a *follower-of relationship*; for instance, considering the example in Figure 2(a), $d_e \prec_{d_c} d_d$;
2. **condition (C2)** - both d_i and d_j are ancestors of d in the tree, and $\ell(d, d_i) < \ell(d, d_j)$, where $\ell(d, d_i)$ denotes the distance (in terms of number of *follower-of relationships*) between d and d_i; for instance, in Figure 2(a), $d_e \prec_{d_c} d_a$, since $\ell(d_c, d_e) = 1 < \ell(d_c, d_a) = 2$, ; the rationale here is that developer d_c prefers to follow the examples of closer developers, for whom d_c explicitly declared a *follower-of relationship*.

In all the other cases, there is not a direct *follower-of relationship* or a chain of such relationships from the requester d to d_i or d_j, therefore the precedence

$d_i \prec_d d_j$ or $d_j \prec_d d_i$ is chosen, according to the number of d_i and d_j followers and in turn of the followers themselves, in a recursive way. The following formula is used, inspired by the PageRank metric:

$$w(d) = \frac{1-\alpha}{|\mathcal{D}|} + \alpha \cdot \sum_{k=1}^{n} w(d_k) \tag{7}$$

where: $w(d)$ is the weight of developer d; $|\mathcal{D}|$ is the number of developers; n is the number of developers d_k who follow d; $w(d_k)$ is the weight of developer d_k; α is the *dumping factor*, that, following the studies of the PageRank metric, has been set to 0.85, to weight the most those developers who have more followers. This metric has been adapted to the proper tree structure of the hierarchical social pattern, where only one parent is allowed for each node.

Specifically, $d_i \prec_d d_j$ if $w(d_i) > w(d_j)$, according to Equation (7). Note that the computation of $w(d_i)$ and $w(d_j)$ is independent from their relative position in the tree with respect to d, that is, in this case $d_i \prec_d d_j$ coincides with $d_i \prec d_j$. However, we maintain the former notation to indicate that we are weighting developers after a request issued by d. For instance, $w(d_f) = 0.0483$ (given that its children, who have no followers, have a weight equal to 0.0136) and $w(d_d) = 0.0367$, therefore $d_f \prec_{d_c} d_d$. If $w(d_i) = w(d_j)$, then the following further conditions are checked: (a) number of *data service aggregations* designed by d_i and d_j, namely $\mathcal{G}[d_i]$ and $\mathcal{G}[d_j]$, respectively, that is, $d_i \prec_d d_j$ if $\mathcal{G}[d_i] > \mathcal{G}[d_j]$; (b) average complexity of *data service aggregations* designed by d_i and d_j, in terms of average number of data services included within the aggregations, denoted with $\hat{\mathcal{G}}[d_i]$ and $\hat{\mathcal{G}}[d_j]$, respectively. We compute $\hat{\mathcal{G}}[d_i]$ as:

$$\hat{\mathcal{G}}[d_i] = \frac{\sum_{g \in \mathcal{G}[d_i]} |\mathcal{S}[g]|}{|\mathcal{G}[d_i]|} \tag{8}$$

where $|\mathcal{S}[g]|$ denotes the number of data services in g and $|\mathcal{G}[d_i]|$ denotes the number of aggregations in $\mathcal{G}[d_i]$. Therefore $d_i \prec_d d_j$ if $\hat{\mathcal{G}}[d_i] > \hat{\mathcal{G}}[d_j]$. For the example shown in Figure 2(a), the final ranking is: $d_e \prec_{d_c} d_a \prec_{d_c} d_f \prec_{d_c} d_d \prec_{d_c} d_b$. Note that, $d_e \prec_{d_c} d_f$ even if $w(d_e) < w(d_f)$, since in our approach our aim is at giving more importance to the developers among which *follower-of relationships* have been explicitly declared. The final developer's ranking $DR[d]$ used in Equation (6), is computed as:

$$DR[d] = \frac{N - (pos(d) - 1)}{N} \in [0, 1] \tag{9}$$

where $pos(d)$ represents the position of d in the ranking and N is the total number of ranked developers. For example, $DR[d_e] = (5-0)/5 = 1$, $DR[d_f] = (5-2)/5 = 0.6$. Therefore, according to Equation (6), $\rho(s_3) = 1$ and $\rho(s_4) = 0.6$, that is, $rank(s_3) = 1.556/1.778 = 0.875$ and $rank(s_4) = 0.9688/1.404 = 0.687$, according to Equation (5).

Peer-Based Social Pattern. This pattern can be represented through a graph, where there is not a hierarchical structure to be recognized. Therefore, conditions **C1** and **C2** meant for the hierarchical social pattern are not applicable, due to the possible presence of cycles. In this case, we use the following equation to weight developers:

$$w(d) = \frac{1-\alpha}{|\mathcal{D}|} + \alpha \cdot \sum_{k=1}^{n} \frac{w(d_k)}{C(d_k)} \tag{10}$$

The equation is a slight variation compared to Equation (7): $w(d)$ is the weight of developers d; $|\mathcal{D}|$ is the number of developers; n is the number of developers d_k who follow d; $w(d_k)$ is the weight of developer d_k; α is the *dumping factor* (set to 0.85); $C(d_k)$ is the number of developers followed by d_k, where, in this case, $C(d_k)$ can be greater that 1, while in the case of hierarchical pattern $C(d_k)$ can be at most equal to 1, due to the constraint on the single parent node. If $w(d_i) = w(d_j)$, then the following further conditions are checked: (a) number of *data service aggregations* designed by d_i and d_j; (b) average complexity of *data service aggregations* designed by d_i and d_j, in terms of average number of data services included within the aggregations. The final developer's ranking $DR[d]$ is computed according to Equation (9).

Hybrid Social Pattern. This pattern can be represented through a tree structure, where children nodes *follow* their own parent node and also multiple parents are allowed. Therefore, conditions **(C1)** and **(C2)** still hold. Now, let's consider the structure shown in Figure 2(b), where a new *follower-of relationship* from d_c to d_d has been added. In the scenario depicted in Figure 2(b), conditions **(C1)** and **(C2)** are not satisfied, because, for the developer d_c, both d_e and d_d are ancestors, but $\ell(d_c, d_e) = \ell(d_c, d_d)$. Therefore, we add the following additional condition:

3 **condition (C3)** - both d_i and d_j are ancestors of d in the tree, $\ell(d, d_i) = \ell(d, d_j)$, where $\ell(d, d_i)$ denotes the distance (in terms of number of *follower-of relationships*) between d and d_i, and $w(d_i) > w(d_j)$, where $w(d)$ is computed as shown in Equation (10); for instance, in Figure 2(b), $d_d \prec_{d_c} d_e$, since $\ell(d_c, d_e) = 1 = \ell(d_c, d_a)$, but $w(d_e) = 0.0309$ and $w(d_d) = 0.0425$.

In all the other cases, there is not a direct *follower-of relationship* or a chain of such relationships from the requester d to d_i or d_j, therefore the final developer's ranking $DR[d]$ is computed as for the peer-based social pattern. Preliminary laboratory experiments are being performed to test the effectiveness of our approach, on a proper dataset that is compliant with the model depicted in Figure 1. First experiments show how our system presents better results in the first positions of the search outcome. As expected, considering only $Sim_{tag}()$ values for selecting relevant data services is not effective, since the use of a specific data service for a particular web application cannot be inferred by only inspecting tags used to classify the service; instead, also Sim_{agg} values and ranking based on social patterns should be exploited to this purpose. This has been investigated by varying the ω_s parameter. In the first experiments, we are obtaining satisfying results for $\omega_s = 0.3$ (see Equation (1)): this means that in the dataset considered in the experiments, the importance of past developers' experiences in using candidate data services is even greater than the information coming from data service (semantic) tagging.

4 Conclusions

In this paper, we proposed a multi-layered model and proper metrics relying on it, meant for supporting the selection of data services for web application design purposes, taking into account also past experiences of other developers in collecting and aggregating data services in similar contexts, i.e., to build similar applications. Moreover, we modeled the network of social relationships between developers as third layer of the model, in order to exploit it for estimating the importance that a developer assigns to past experience of other developers. Further information might be integrated within the model, such as quality features among metadata and automatic annotation of service interfaces at the data service and web application layers, to refine the selection step. Extension of the approach to different contexts, where high credibility of developers cannot be assumed, will require the introduction of additional social patterns and the integration of credibility estimation techniques, such as the ones described in [7–9]. Finally, extensive experimentation (also considering real cases of web application design) has to be completed.

References

1. Li, Y., Wang, Y., Du, J.: E-FFC: an enhanced form-focused crawler for domain-specific Deep Web databases. J. of Intelligent Information Systems **40**(1), 159–184 (2013)
2. Quarteroni, S., Brambilla, M., Ceri, S.: A Bottom-up, Knowledge-Aware Approach to Integrating and Querying Web Data Services. ACM Trans. on the Web **7**(4), 44–76 (2013)
3. Bozzon, A., Brambilla, M., Ceri, S., Mazza, D.: Exploratory Search Framework for Web Data Services. VLDB Journal **22**, 641–663 (2013)
4. Bianchini, D., De Antonellis, V., Melchiori, M.: QoS in ontology-based service classification and discovery. In: 15th International Workshop on Database and Expert Systems Applications, pp. 145–150. IEEE Computer Society, Los Alamitos (2004)
5. Dillon, S., Stahl, F., Vossen, G.: Towards the web in your pocket: Curated data as a service. In: Nguyen, N.T., Trawinski, B., Katarzyniak, R., Jo, G.S. (eds.) Advanced Methods for Computing Collective Intelligence, pp. 25–34. Springer, Berlin Heidelberg (2013)
6. Balakrishnan, R., Kambhampati, S., Manishkumar, J.: Assessing Relevance and Trust of the Deep Web Sources and Results Based on Inter-Source Agreement. ACM Trans. on the Web **7**(2), 32 (2013)
7. Al-Sharawneh, J., Williams, M., Wang, X., Goldbaum, D.: Mitigating risk in web-based social network service selection: follow the leader. In: 6th Int. Conference on Internet and Web Applications and Services, pp. 156–164. IARIA XPS Press (2011)

8. Malik, Z., Bouguettaya, A.: RATEWeb: Reputation Assessment for Trust Establishment among Web Services. VLBD Journal **18**, 885–911 (2009)
9. Bianchini, D., De Antonellis, V., Melchiori, M.: Capitalizing the designers' experience for improving web API selection. In: Meersman, R., Panetto, H., Dillon, T., Missikoff, M., Liu, L., Pastor, O., Cuzzocrea, A., Sellis, T. (eds.) OTM 2014. LNCS, vol. 8841, pp. 364–381. Springer, Heidelberg (2014)
10. Fuxman, A., Giorgini, P., Kolp, M., Mylopoulos, J.: Information systems as social structures. In: 2nd Int. Conf. on Formal Ontologies for Information Systems, pp. 12–21. ACM, New York (2001)
11. Gupta, V., Lehal, G.: A Survey of Text Mining Techniques and Applications. J. of Emerging Technologies in Web Intelligence **1**(1), 60–76 (2009)
12. Bianchini, D., De Antonellis, V., Melchiori, M.: Semantic collaborative tagging for web APIs sharing and reuse. In: Brambilla, M., Tokuda, T., Tolksdorf, R. (eds.) ICWE 2012. LNCS, vol. 7387, pp. 76–90. Springer, Heidelberg (2012)
13. dos Santos, T., de Araujo, R., Magdaleno, A.: Identifying Collaboration Patterns in Software Development Social Networks. J. of Computer Science, 51–60 (2010)

Liquid Stream Processing Across Web Browsers and Web Servers

Masiar Babazadeh[(✉)], Andrea Gallidabino, and Cesare Pautasso

Faculty of Informatics, University of Lugano (USI), Lugano, Switzerland
{masiar.babazadeh,andrea.gallidabino,cesare.pautasso}@usi.ch

Abstract. The recently proposed API definition WebRTC introduced peer-to-peer real time communication between Web browsers, allowing streaming systems to be deployed on browsers in addition to traditional server-side execution environments. While streaming applications can be adapted to run on Web browsers, it remains difficult to deal with temporary disconnections, energy consumption on mobile devices and a potentially very large number of heterogeneous peers that join and leave the execution environment affecting the quality of the stream. In this paper we present the decentralized control approach followed by the Web Liquid Streams (WLS) framework, a novel framework for streaming applications running on Web browsers, Web servers and smart devices. Given the heterogeneity of the deployment environment and the volatility of Web browsers, we implemented a control infrastructure which is able to take operator migration decisions keeping into account the deployment constraints and the unpredictable workload.

1 Introduction

Real-time Web applications which display live updates resulting from complex stream processing topologies have recently started to impact the Web architecture. Web browsers are no longer limited to synchronous request-response HTTP interactions but can now establish full-duplex connections both with the server (WebSockets) and even directly with other browsers (WebRTC). This opens up the opportunity to shift to the Web browser more than a simple view to be rendered over the results of the stream, but also the processing of the data stream operators. Similar to ongoing Rich Internet Application trends [1], the idea is to offload part of the computation to clients that are becoming more and more powerful. This however requires the flexibility to adapt operators to run on a highly heterogeneous execution environment, determine which is the most suitable location for their execution, and deal with frequent outages, limited battery capacity and device failures.

More in detail, while building data streaming applications across Web browsers with WebRTC and WebSockets can be a relatively simple task, managing the deployment of arbitrary topologies, disconnections, and errors without a central entity may become increasingly difficult. The volatile nature of Web browsers (whose tabs may be closed at any time) implies that the system should

P. Cimiano et al. (Eds.): ICWE 2015, LNCS 9114, pp. 24–33, 2015.
DOI: 10.1007/978-3-319-19890-3_3

be able to restart leaving operators on other available machines. At the same time, CPU and memory consumption as well as data flow rate should be managed and regulated when operators become too taxing on the hosting browser. Whenever a host used up all its resources and causes bottlenecks, the hosted streaming operators should be relocated to other available machines. Special care should be taken in presence of portable devices such as smartphones or tablets, whose battery should be saved whenever possible.

In this paper we show how we deal with these problems in the Web Liquid Streams (WLS) framework. WLS allows developers to implement distributed stream processing topologies composed of JavaScript operators deployed across Web browsers and Web servers. Thanks to the widespread adoption of JavaScript, the lingua franca of the Web, it is possible to deploy and run streaming applications on any Web-enabled device: from small microprocessors, passing through smartphones, all the way to large virtualised Cloud computing clusters running the Node.JS [2] framework. The focus of this paper concerns the WLS distributed control infrastructure which is able to deal with faults and disconnections of the computing operators as well as bottlenecks in the streaming topology. Moreover it is in charge of optimizing the physical deployment of the topology by migrating and cloning operators across Web browsers and Web servers to reduce energy consumption and increase parallelism.

The RESTful API of the first version of WLS, which supported distributed stream processing only over Web server clusters has been previously described in [3]. In this paper we build upon the previous results to present the second version of WLS, which makes the following novel contributions:

- A decentralized infrastructure to deploy both on Web servers and Web browsers a graph of data stream operators in order to reduce the end to end latency of the stream while enforcing given deployment constraints.
- A control infrastructure able to deal with bottlenecks in the stream topology.
- A technique for cloning and relocating operators to dynamically parallelize computationally intensive operators, which can make use of volunteer resources and react to unpredictable workload changes.

The rest of this paper is organized as follows: Section 2 discusses related work, Section 3 introduces the Web Liquid Streams framework while Section 4 describes its control infrastructure. Section 5 shows a preliminary evaluation of the control infrastructure and Section 6 concludes the paper.

2 Related Work

Many stream processing frameworks have been proposed over the years [4,5]. Here we discuss the ones which inspired our work on WLS. Storm [6] is a distributed real-time computational environment originally developed by Twitter. Stream operators are defined by custom created "spouts" and "bolts", used to allow distributed processing of streaming data. Storm presents a two-fold controller infrastructure to deal with worker failure and node failure. Storm only features a server-side deployment, while we extend this concept in WLS by including Web browsers as part of the target deployment infrastructure and use standard Web protocols to send and receive data.

D-Streams [7] is a framework that provides a set of stream-transformations which treat the stream as a series of deterministic batch computations on very small time intervals. In this way, it reuses the fault tolerance mechanism for batch processing, leveraging MapReduce style recovery. D-Stream features a reconfiguration-style recovery for faults, which was inspirational for our controller; nonetheless, the D-Streams topology cannot be changed and adapted to the workload at runtime. Another related framework is MillWheel [8] by Google. MillWheel helps user build low-latency data-processing applications at large-scale without the need to think about how to deploy it in a distributed execution environment. Our runtime works at the same level of abstraction, but targets a more diverse, volunteer computing-style set of provided resources.

With the rapid growth of mobile smart phones, many efforts targeted improving their energy efficiency and explored how to deal with energy-intensive applications by means of Cloud offloading [9]. With approaches like MAUI [10] or ThinkAir [11], programmers annotate part of the code to be offloaded, and the runtime is able to tell if the offloading of the annotated parts could save energy on the client that would remotely invoke the corresponding methods.

Some research effort has been dedicated towards self-adaptation of streaming applications. A self-adapting optimizer has been presented in [12] where the authors introduced an online and offline scheduler for Storm. Another optimization for Storm has been proposed in [13], where the authors present an optimization algorithm that finds the optimal values for the batch sizes and the degree of parallelism for each Storm node in the dataflow. The algorithm automatically finds the best configuration for a topology, avoiding manual tuning. Our work is very similar, yet the premises of having fully transparent Peers are not met, as WLS is unable to access the complete hardware specifications of a machine from the existing Web browser HTML5 APIs. A more general approach in describing streaming optimizations has been taken in [4], where authors suggest a list of stream processing optimizations, some of which have been applied in our framework (i.e., Operator Fission, Fusion or Load balancing).

The concept of liquid software has been introduced in the Liquid Software Manifesto [14], where the authors use it to represent a seamless multi-device user experience where software can effortlessly flow from one device to another [15]. Likewise, in [16] we described an architectural style for liquid Web services, which can elastically scale taking advantage of heterogeneous computing resources. In the presented cases, the liquid quality is applied to the deployment of software components. In this paper we focus our efforts on the stream software connector and how to characterize its liquid behavior.

3 The Web Liquid Streams Framework

The Web Liquid Streams (WLS) framework helps developers create stream processing topologies and run them across Web servers, Web browsers, and smart devices. This Section introduces the main abstractions provided by WLS and how they can be used to build Topologies of streaming Operators written in JavaScript. To build streaming applications, developers make use of the following building blocks: **Peers** are physical machines that host the computation. Any Web-enabled device, including Web servers, Web browsers or microprocessors is eligible to become a Peer. In a streaming application, **Operators** receive the data, process it and forward the results downstream. Each Operator is associated to a JavaScript file, which describes the processing logic. The **Topology** defines a graph of Operators, effectively describing the data flow from producer Operators to consumers. The structure of the Topology can dynamically change while the stream is running. Peers can host more than one Operator at a time, and Operators on the same Peer can be part of different streaming Topologies. The way Operators and Peers are organized is dynamic as the number of Operators and their resource usage can change at runtime. Operators can be redundantly deployed on multiple Peers for increased scalability and reliability.

When implementing an Operator, developers do not need to worry about communication protocols as it is the WLS runtime's task to deploy the Operators on the physical hosts based on the Topology description and deployment constraints, and thus taking care of abstracting away the actual stream communication channels. To do so, the runtime includes a control infrastructure able to deal with disconnections and load fluctuations by means of Operator migration.

3.1 Liquid Stream Processing

We use the Liquid Software metaphor [14–16] to visualize the properties of the flow of data elements through the Operators that are deployed over a large and variable number of networked Peers owned by the users of the platform. The nature of the Peers can be heterogeneous: big Web servers with a lot of storage and RAM, Web browsers running on smart phones or personal computers, but also Web-enabled microcontrollers and smart devices such as Raspberry PI or Tessel.IO. Users of the system can share their own resources in a cooperative way by either connecting to the system through a Web browser or a Web server. WLS is able to handle the churn of connecting and leaving Peers through a gossip algorithm [17] , which propagates across all Peers the information about connected Peers where Operators can be deployed.

As a liquid adapts its shape to the one of its container, the WLS framework adapts the operators and the stream data rate to fit within the available resources. When the resource demand increases (i.e., because of an increase in the stream rate, or the processing power required to process some stream elements), new resources are allocated by the controller. Likewise, these will be elastically de-allocated once the stream resource demand decreases.

3.2 Operator Cloning and Migration

We implemented two basic mechanisms on the Operators: cloning and migration [18]. Operator cloning is the process of creating an exact copy of the

Operator on another Peer to solve bottlenecks by increasing the parallelism. The process can be reversed once the bottlenecks are solved and there is no need to keep more than one Peer busy.

Migration is the process of moving one Operator from one Peer to another at runtime. Migration in WLS can be triggered when a Peer expresses its willingness to leave the system, or when the battery level of a device reaches a predefined threshold. In that case, the Operators are migrated on other Peers to prevent disconnection errors when the battery is completely drained out. During the migration, the controller creates copies of these Operators on the designated machines and performs the bindings to and from other Operators, given the Topology structure. Considering [18], WLS performs a re-initialization of the relocated code on the new execution environment.

4 Decentralized Control Infrastructure

By uploading a file containing the Topology description through the WLS API [3], users of the system can deploy and execute their Topologies on a subset of the available Peers, which will be autonomously and transparently managed by WLS. Topologies can also be created manually through the command-line interface of the system or through a graphical monitoring tool. Upon receiving a Topology description or manual configuration commands, the system checks if the request can be satisfied with the currently available resources. If that is the case, WLS allocates and deploys Operators on designated Peers and starts the data stream between them. In this section we present the autonomic control infrastructure that automatically deploys Topologies and sends reconfiguration commands through the same WLS API. Each Web server Peer features its own local controller which deals with the connections and disconnections of the Web browser Peers attached to it as well as the parallelisation of Operators running on it (by forking Node.js processes). A similar controller is deployed on each Web browser Peer, where it parallelises the Operator execution spawning additional Web Workers. Likewises it monitors the local environment conditions to detect bottlenecks, battery shortages or disconnections and to signal them to the corresponding controller on the Web server. This establishes a hierarchical control infrastructure whereby each Operator is managed by a separate entity, coordinated by the controller responsible for managing the lifecycle and regulating the performance of the whole Topology.

4.1 Deployment Constraints

The control infrastructure deals with disconnections of Peers, load fluctuations and Operator migrations. In this paper we target the ability of the controller to deploy, migrate, and clone Operators across Peers seamlessly in order to face disconnections, but also to improve the overall performance of the Topology in terms of latency and energy consumption. To do so, the controller takes into account a list of constraints that are specified in the Topology description. The constraints are presented here in descending order of importance: i) **Hardware Dependencies**, for example the presence on the Peer device of specific hardware sensors or actuators must be taken into consideration by the controller as first-priority deployment constraint. An Operator that makes use of a gyroscope sensor cannot be migrated from a smart phone built with such sensor to a Web server. ii) **Whitelists or Blacklists**. Operators can be optionally associated with a list of known Peers that must (or must not) be used to run them. The list can be specified using IP address ranges and should be large enough so that if one Peer fails another can still be found to replace it. iii) **Battery**, whenever a Peer has battery shortage, the controller should be able to migrate the Operator(s) running on such Peer in order not to completely drain out the Peer battery. At the same time, a migration operation should not be performed targeting a Peer with a low battery level. iv) **CPU**. The current CPU utilization of the Peer must leave room to deploy another operator. Since JavaScript is a single-threaded language, we use the number of CPU cores as an upper bound on the level of parallelism that a Peer can deliver.

These constraints are used to select a set of candidate Peers, which are then ranked according to additional criteria, whose purpose is to ensure that the end-to-end latency of the stream is reduced, while minimizing the overall resource utilization. This is important to reduce the cost of the resources allocated to each Topology, while maintaining a good level of performance.

4.2 Ranking Function

The following metrics are taken into account by the controller for selecting the most suitable Peer for each Operator: i) **Energy** consumption can be optimized, for example when the computation of an Operator is too taxing on a battery-dependent Peer. In this case a migration may occur, moving the heavy computation from a mobile device to a desktop or Web server machine. Thus, the priority is given to fully charged mobile Peers or to fixed Peers without battery. ii) **Parallelism** can be achieved by cloning a bottleneck Operator. For example, a migration or a cloning operation may be expected if the computation is very CPU-intensive and the Peer hosting the Operator not only has its CPU full but it is also the Topology bottleneck. Thus, higher priority is given to Peers with larger CPUs and higher CPU availability. iii) **Deployment Cost Minimization** by prioritizing Web browsers instead of making use of Web servers, WLS tries to avoid incurring in additional variable costs given by the utilization of pay-per-use Cloud resources.

These metrics can be accessed on a Web server through the Node.js APIs, while on the Web browser we can again use the HTML5 APIs to gather the battery levels and a rough estimate of the processing power. The ranking function is evaluated by the controller at Topology initialization to find the best deployment configuration of the Operators, and while the Topology is running to improve its performance and deal with variations in the set of known/available Peers. For each Peer, the function uses the previously described constraints and metrics to

Algorithm 1. Peer Ranking for Topology Initialization

```
Data: Known Peers, Topology
Result: Peers Ranking
P ← Known Peers ;
foreach Operator o in Topology do
    foreach Peer p in P do
        if !compatible(o, p) then
            P ← P \ p ;
        end
    end
end
if P = ∅ then
    return cannot deploy Topology
else
    foreach Peer p in P do
        Poll p for its current metrics M_i(p);
        Compute ranking function r(p) according to Eq. (1);
    end
    return Sorted list of available Peers P according to their rank r(p)
end
```

compute a value that describes how much a Peer is suited to host an Operator. The function is defined as follows:

$$r(p) = \sum_{i=1}^{n} \alpha_i M_i(p) \tag{1}$$

where α_i is the weight representing the importance of the $i-th$ metric. M_i is the current value of the metric obtained from the Peer p. The result gives an estimate of the utility of the Peer p to run one or more Operators on it. In case the utility turns out to be negative, the semantics implies that the Peer p should no longer be used to run any operator. Whenever a Topology has to start, the controller polls the known Peers and executes the procedure shown in Algorithm 1.

The controller first determines which of the known Peers are compatible with the Operators of the topology. Then it polls each Peer for its metrics. Once received, the Ranking is computed and stored for further use. The Peers are then ordered from the most suited to the least suited, then for each Operator to be deployed the controller iterates the list top to bottom it decides which Peer will host it. This deploys the whole Topology and when all Peers confirm that the Operators have been deployed the flow of the data stream begins. As the Topology is up and running, the ranking function is periodically re-evaluated by the controller to check the status of the execution and adapt the topology to changes in workload (reflected by changed CPU utilization of the Peers) and changes in the available Peers (and thus deal with disconnections), as well as changes to the Topology structure itself (e.g., when new operators are removed from or added to it).

4.3 Disconnection Recovery

Whenever a Peer abruptly disconnects (i.e., a Web browser crashes), the controller notices the channel closing (through the JavaScript error event handling) and starts executing a recovery procedure in order to restore the Topology by restarting the lost Operators on other available Peers. The recovery is similar to the migration decision algorithm: the controller restarts the lost Operators on Peers satisfying the deployment constraints and with the highest ranking possible. It may be possible that the channel closing was caused by temporary network failures. In this case, if the Peer assumed lost comes back up, the controller brings it back to a clean state by stopping all Operators still running on it. The Peer may be later assigned other Operators if needed.

5 Preliminary Evaluation

The goal of the evaluation is to observe the differences between a deployment strategy to address bottlenecks using a random ranking function (random controller) as a baseline with respect to a more accurate deployment decision making approach, based on the devised ranking function defined in Eq. (1) (ranking controller). As additional control, we also performed experiments with a reverse ranking controller (Ranking^{-1}), which makes the worst possible decisions.

The Topology we use to evaluate the ranking controller consists of three Operators: the first takes as input a stream of tweets, the second encrypts them using triple DES and the third stores the encrypted result on a server. Given the unpredictable dynamics of the Twitter Firehose API we decided to sample 100000 tweets and use them as benchmark workload. The size of the messages exchanged along the stream is thus less than 1Kb.

For this experiment we used a Samsung Galaxy S4, one Mac Book Pro i7 with 16GB RAM running OSX, a Windows 7 machine 2.9GHz quadcore and three iPads 3 WiFi for the encryption Operator, while two servers for the producer and the consumer Operators (the producer with twenty-four Intel Xeon 2GHz cores and the consumer with four Intel Core 2 Quad 3GHz cores, both running Ubuntu 12.04 with Node.JS version 0.10.15.). All the resources using a Web browser are running Google Chrome version 40.

Figure 1 shows the resource usage of the experiments, comparing the number of processes and Peers used in the experiment. We see that in the first random approach, the deployment of the CPU-intensive Operator is on an iPad (single process), which then gets cloned on the MacBook, the best machine, resulting in a very low median latency. The other runs show a mix of deployment scenarios resulting in a not-so-optimal median throughput and with higher resource usage (two or more Peers). The ranking controller is able to detect the best machine where to run the CPU-intensive Operator and thus not only keeps the latency

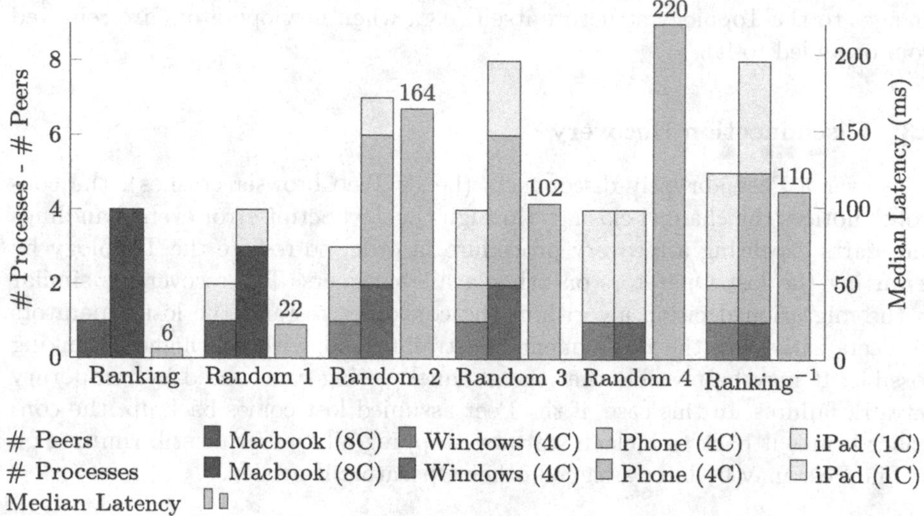

Fig. 1. Liquid Deployment and Bottleneck Handling: Comparison of Random vs. Ranked resource allocations and their median end-to-end latency

very low, but also uses a smaller amount of resources. The reverse ranking controller instead uses the iPads, the Phone and the Windows machine (in this order) to clone the Operator, resulting in a very high resource usage.

6 Conclusion and Future Work

In this paper we presented a control infrastructure for distributed stream processing across Web-enabled devices. The controller extends the Web Liquid Streams (WLS) framework for running stream processing topologies composed of JavaScript operators across Web servers and Web browsers. The control infrastructure is able to choose a suitable initial deployment on the available resources connected to WLS. While the streaming topology is running, it monitors the performance and is able to migrate or clone Operators across machines to increase parallelism as well as to prevent and react to faults given by battery shortages and disconnections. The controller is able to do so by using a ranking function which orders the Peers that are compatible with each Operator for choosing the most appropriate Peer for a deployment or migration. The initial evaluation presented in the paper shows how the controller reflects the best possible deployment given a set of resources, resulting in a balanced message throughput along the topology graph, and reduced end-to-end stream latency.

We are currently performing an extensive performance evaluation covering additional features of the WLS framework (e.g., more fine-grained CPU performance characterization, support of stateful operators, operator consolidation). Moreover, we would like to improve the current allocation approach, which is extremely simple and greedy. It does not consider characteristics of the Operators and of the data, which may affect computation time and Peer load.

Acknowledgments. We are grateful to Monica Landoni for her help. The work is supported by the Hasler Foundation with the Liquid Software Architecture (LiSA) project and by the Swiss National Science Foundation with the Fundamentals of Parallel Programming for Platform-as-a-Service Clouds project (Grant Nr. 153560).

References

1. Casteleyn, S., et al.: Ten years of rich internet applications: A systematic mapping study, and beyond. ACM Trans. Web **8**(3), 18:1–18:46 (2014)
2. Tilkov, S., et al.: Node.js: Using javascript to build high-performance network programs. IEEE Internet Computing **14**(6), 80–83 (2010)
3. Babazadeh, M., Pautasso, C.: A RESTful API for controlling dynamic streaming topologies. In: Proc. of WWW Companion, Seoul, Korea, April 2014
4. Hirzel, M., et al.: A catalog of stream processing optimizations. ACM Comput. Surv. **46**(4), 46:1–46:34 (2014)
5. Babazadeh, M., et al.: The stream software connector design space: frameworks and languages for distributed stream processing. In: Software Architecture (WICSA). IEEE/IFIP (2014)
6. Apache: Storm, distributed and fault-tolerant realtime computation (2011)
7. Zaharia, M., et al.: Discretized streams: an efficient and fault-tolerant model for stream processing on large clusters. In: Proc. of USENIX HotCloud, pp. 10–16 (2012)
8. Akidau, T., et al.: Millwheel: Fault-tolerant stream processing at internet scale. In: Proc. VLDB Endow., pp. 734–746 (2013)
9. Kumar, K., Lu, Y.H.: Cloud computing for mobile users: Can offloading computation save energy? Computer **43**(4), 51–56 (2010)
10. Cuervo, E., et al.: MAUI: making smartphones last longer with code offload. In: Proc. of MobiSys, pp. 49–62. ACM (2010)
11. Kosta, S., et al.: Thinkair: dynamic resource allocation and parallel execution in the cloud for mobile code offloading. In: INFOCOM, 2012 Proceedings IEEE, pp. 945–953 (2012)
12. Aniello, L., Baldoni, R., Querzoni, L.: Adaptive online scheduling in storm. In: Proc. of DEBS, pp. 207–218. ACM (2013)
13. Sax, M.J., et al.: Performance optimization for distributed intra-node-parallel streaming systems. In: ICDE Workshops, pp. 62–69. IEEE Computer Society (2013)
14. Taivalsaari, A., et al.: Liquid software manifesto: the era of multiple device ownership and its implications for software architecture. In: Proc. of COMPSAC 2014, pp. 338–343. IEEE Computer Society (2014)
15. Mikkonen, T., Systa, K., Pautasso, C.: Towards liquid web applications. In: Proc. ICWE 2015. Springer, Rotterdam (2015)
16. Bonetta, D., Pautasso, C.: An architectural style for liquid web services. In: 9th Working IEEE/IFIP Conference on Software Architecture (WICSA 2011) (2011)
17. Jelasity, M., et al.: Gossip-based aggregation in large dynamic networks. ACM Trans. Comput. Syst. **23**(3), 219–252 (2005)
18. Fuggetta, A., et al.: Understanding code mobility. IEEE Trans. Softw. Eng. **24**(5), 342–361 (1998)

Mixing and Mashing Website Themes

Linda Di Geronimo, Alfonso Murolo(✉), Michael Nebeling, and Moira C. Norrie

Department of Computer Science, ETH Zurich, CH-8092 Zurich, Switzerland
{lindad,amurolo,nebeling,norrie}@inf.ethz.ch

Abstract. WordPress offers users a wide choice of themes defining the structure, functionality, layout and presentation of a website together with its content types. These themes are shared by the WordPress community, enabling users to benefit from the skills of others. However, it is not possible to mix themes, so users often have to choose from a set of themes that only partially meet their requirements. We have developed a theme editor that allows users to combine both static and dynamic elements of existing themes using simple drag-and-drop operations. These elements are adapted to reflect the content and structure of the website under construction so that there is no distinction between design-time and run-time. We discuss in detail technical challenges along with our solutions for developing such an editor and integrating it into the WordPress platform. Further, we describe how the solutions could be generalised to other modern content management systems.

Keywords: Website theme · Theme generator · Web development tool · Content management system

1 Introduction

WordPress[1] has gone well beyond its origins as an open source blogging platform to become the most widely used content management system (CMS) with over 60% of the market share and estimates that it is used in nearly a quarter of the top 10 million websites[2]. Many of these sites manage large amounts of data and offer rich functionality including the integration of third party services.

Each WordPress site is an instance of a theme which defines the structure, functionality, layout and presentation of the website as well as the types of content to be managed and published. One of the main reasons for the initial popularity and widespread adoption of the platform was its support for end-user development of websites. Users could set up their website in a matter of minutes by selecting a theme, specifying a few customisation options through an administrative dashboard and adding content. In this way, they could not only create a website without any coding or deployment effort but also benefit from the design skills of other users who shared their themes.

[1] http://www.wordpress.org

[2] http://www.w3techs.com, 23.7% on 8 April 2015.

P. Cimiano et al. (Eds.): ICWE 2015, LNCS 9114, pp. 34–51, 2015.
DOI: 10.1007/978-3-319-19890-3_4

Over time, not only has the platform been extended to provide richer functionality and improved support for both end-users and developers, but the WordPress community has itself developed and shared vast numbers of themes. Furthermore, the WordPress platform provides a simple means for developers to extend the functionality of a theme through its plugin mechanism and the community has also developed and shared thousands of plugins. While some themes and plugins have been developed by professional agencies, many of them are freely shared within the community. For example, over 37'114 plugins are available at `wordpress.org`[3]. WordPress can therefore be considered as one of the most successful and influential examples of the power of crowdsourcing.

However, one limitation of the theme concept is that it only supports all-or-nothing reuse since it is not possible to mix elements of different themes. Consequently, users are forced to choose from a set of candidate themes each of which may only partially meet their requirements. To address this issue, we have developed a visual theme editor that allows users to compose their websites by mixing and mashing elements of existing sites. Both static and dynamic elements can be selected and reused via simple drag-and-drop operations. Developers can choose whether to retain the styling of the copied elements, apply the styling associated with the theme under creation or modify the styling via normal editing operations. When a dynamic element is reused, it is immediately adapted to reflect the content and structure of the website under construction. This means that developers can already see their website in operation at design-time. In this way, there is no distinction between design-time and run-time and, from the user point of view, no distinction between a website and a theme. To achieve this, it was necessary to integrate the theme editor into the WordPress platform and structure themes in terms of reusable components.

An overview of our approach of providing an editor that generates themes constructed from reusable components was presented previously in a short paper at ICWE2014 [1]. In this paper, we take the work further and present the main technical challenges and solutions of being able to dynamically mix and mash themes within the WordPress platform. Further, we discuss how the approach could be generalised to other popular modern CMS such as Drupal[4] and Joomla[5] which do not have the same theme concept as WordPress.

We start in Sect. 2 by reviewing existing WordPress theme generators as well as previous work addressing the technical challenges of reusing elements of websites. An overview of our approach is then presented in Sect. 3 before going on to provide details of how themes are structured in terms of reusable components in Sect. 4. Details of the steps involved in generating a theme and its components as well as dynamically reusing them in different content contexts are given in Sect. 5, with a review of the technical challenges and solutions in Sect. 6. We follow this in Sect. 7 with a discussion of how the approach could be generalised to other CMS. Concluding remarks are given in Sect. 8.

---

3 http://www.wordpress.org, 8 April 2015.
4 http://www.drupal.org
5 http://www.joomla.org

2 Background

WordPress has evolved into a flexible and powerful platform capable of supporting a wide variety of websites. If a developer can find a theme that fully meets their requirements, the process of developing a website can be done through the dashboard where customisation parameters can be set, pages created, navigation menus defined and sidebars configured. The functionality of the theme can also be extended through the dashboard by selecting and adding plugins. However, as soon as a developer is faced with the task of adapting or extending a theme, they have to start working at the level of the HTML, CSS, JavaScript and PHP files as well as learning about the core WordPress model and system operation.

Developers often work on a need-to-know basis, learning only enough to solve the particular task at hand. Since WordPress offers developers a very loose framework in which to work, many different approaches are used to achieve the same look and functionality. Consequently, the documentation and tutorials vary a lot in terms of guidelines and solutions offered and it is clear from reading tutorial-style books on theme development, e.g. [2,3] as well as online forums[6], that many developers simply copy and paste bits of code with the hope that it will achieve the desired effects. However, often these attempts to reuse code fail because they are inconsistent with how other parts of the site have been developed.

A number of WordPress theme generators are available to support end-user development of themes. These focus on creating new themes from scratch but many of them have serious limitations. For example, Templatr[7] only allows users to select from a fixed set of layouts, while Lubith[8] enables users to customise layout via drag-and-drop operations, but does not support the customisation of functionality. Further, many generators are not integrated into the WordPress platform, so it is not possible to perform content-related tasks at design-time and it can lead to compatibility problems across versions. It was therefore our goal to develop our theme editor on top of, and fully integrated into, WordPress.

Other tools and frameworks, for example Themify[9], have been developed to facilitate the customisation of themes. The budget limitations of a customer usually determine the amount of customisation that can take place and hence tools that make it easier for developers as well as end-users to create or customise themes can have a major impact on the quality of websites produced. However, often the required customisations could be achieved by simply mixing elements of different themes but this is currently not supported. In a recent survey of 110 WordPress developers [4], 75% indicated that they would like to be able to mix the functionality of different themes, while 56% answered that they would like to be able to mix layout elements.

Approaches that allow end-users to design their websites by selecting and combining parts of existing websites have been explored by researchers in the

[6] for example, http://www.wpbeginner.com

[7] http://templatr.cc

[8] http://www.lubith.com

[9] http://themify.me

HCI community [5,6]. Their studies demonstrated the benefits of the design-by-example paradigm, but their solutions only addressed the reuse of elements of website design in terms of layout and presentation and not the dynamic aspects dealing with functionality and content. Modern websites tend to make heavy use of JavaScript and jQuery[10] and, rather than being static, pages are often dynamically generated. This is particularly true in the case of CMS in general, and WordPress in particular, where "the Loop" is used to define the content to be displayed in an element of a web page in terms of a database query and templates to extract data from the query result.

Extracting components from an existing web page involves identifying and extracting all the necessary HTML, CSS, JavaScript and resources. Various techniques for this have been proposed in the mashup research community. For example, Ghiani et al. [7] allow users to select mashup components from arbitrary websites through direct manipulation of the GUI. Note that to extract and reuse elements of WordPress themes, it is necessary to not only extract components of a web page, but also the PHP functionality of the theme defining the dynamic parts of the page, i.e. the code that generates these elements. This raises many new challenges that have not been addressed previously.

To support reuse, component models for web development have been proposed to ensure that pages are constructed from reusable components. WebComposition [8] was an early effort in this direction where they proposed an object-oriented support system for building web applications through hierarchical compositions of reusable application components. MashArt [9] is a system developed in the mashup community that enables advanced users to create their own applications through the composition of user interface, application and data components. More recently, an extension to WordPress was proposed that allows websites to be developed from a component model that supports composition at the data, application and interface levels [10]. The approach requires developers to model the different aspects of a website and specify the composition logic. In contrast, our goal is to support end-user development by allowing themes to be created using a visual editor where users can simply drag and drop elements of existing themes that encapsulate presentation, content and functionality.

As detailed in the next sections, our approach combines many features of the related work described above. To support reuse, we first defined a metamodel for themes that can be used to structure them in terms of reusable components. Second, we developed a theme editor that enables users to mix and mash elements of web pages at the GUI level, thereby hiding the details of the component model but ensuring that the created themes conform to the model. In an earlier paper [1], we described how this approach could be used to support the design-by-example paradigm advocated by the HCI community in contrast to the model-driven approaches proposed by the web engineering community [11–13]. Here we take this work further by detailing the technical challenges underlying the approach and the solutions that we developed. Specifically, we describe the implementation of our theme editor and how it was integrated into the WordPress platform.

---

[10] http://jquery.com

3 Approach

Our overall goal is to allow end-users and developers to create themes by reusing elements of existing themes that can be searched and browsed in an online gallery. We illustrate this in Fig. 1 by showing elements of two web pages that have been selected and copied into a web page under construction.

Fig. 1. Components from left and right web pages mixed at GUI level in middle page

At first sight, this appears very similar to the previous research within the HCI community where users can design a website by selecting elements from galleries of examples. However, there are important and far-reaching differences. First, as mentioned before, they only handle static web pages and have no support for the reuse of client-side functionality. Second, they only deal with web pages rather than with themes defining how web pages are generated from database content. We illustrate the different layers involved in extracting and reusing a component of a theme in Fig. 2.

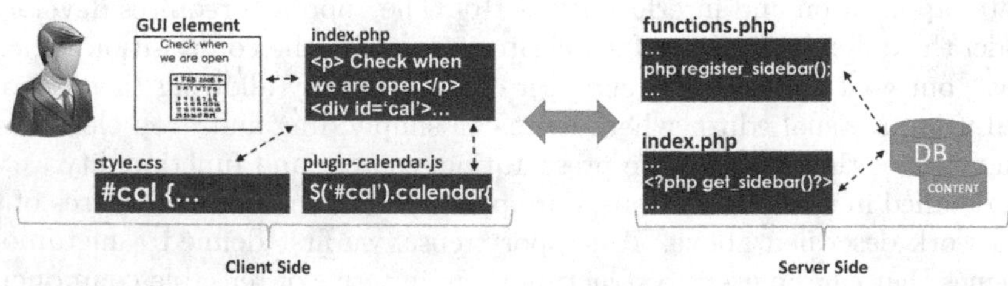

Fig. 2. Layers involved in extracting and reusing a theme component

On the left of Fig. 2, we show a rendered component of a web page and how it is defined in the underlying theme. A user should be able to extract and reuse this component by simply selecting the corresponding element within the rendered web page and copying it into their new page via drag-and-drop. They should also be able to choose whether to keep the source styling or adopt the target styling and be able to use basic editing operations to change its size, position or style. For more advanced users, there should be an option to switch to a mode where they can edit CSS code directly.

To achieve this, the corresponding DOM elements need to be identified and the required CSS and JavaScript code extracted along with the HTML. The first step of identifying the DOM elements is common to all projects dealing with the extraction and reuse of components of a web page. However, to import a selected element into a new theme, we also need to identify and extract the parts of the underlying theme that were responsible for generating them. This means that we need to extract code from the source theme's PHP templates stored on the server-side. We achieve this by exposing parts of the server-side code shown on the right of Fig. 2. Access is read-only and limited to the particular theme rather than the entire WordPress installation so that other software and users do not gain access to credentials and therefore control over the database and private data. It is further important to note that when the selected element is imported into the theme under construction, there is an immediate switch from executing queries against the WordPress database for the source theme to the database associated with the target theme.

In addition, as shown on the right of Fig. 2, some properties of a WordPress site such as content shown in a sidebar or a header are defined on the server-side and customised through the WordPress administrative interface and so we also need to handle these correctly when extracting and reusing elements.

To support our requirements, we have developed a visual theme editor with both design and reuse capabilities. This means that it can be used to design new themes from scratch or to compose new themes by mixing and mashing components of existing themes accessed in a gallery. This is important not only because it offers users full flexibility in how users create and customise their themes, but it also provides the initial motivation for users to participate that is essential to any crowdsourcing model [14]. By providing a visual editor with full capabilities for creating, positioning and styling both static and dynamic elements of a theme, including creating nested structures of arbitrary complexity, the functionality of the editor is comparable to that of the most powerful theme generators. The tool therefore has value to users and developers even without the ability to reuse components of existing themes. The themes generated by the tool are referred to as X-Themes since they are structured according to our metamodel and represented as a set of reusable components. As soon as an X-Theme is generated, it is added to the interactive gallery of existing themes accessible to the X-Themes editor and its components are immediately available for reuse. In this way, we can avoid the cold start problem and motivate users to participate.

The X-Themes editor is realised as a WordPress plugin and, once installed and activated, can be accessed via the main menu of the administrative interface. An advantage of making the editor available as a plugin is that it provides an easy means of deploying the tool to the vast developer community, while achieving our goal of integrating it into the WordPress platform.

4 Metamodel

A theme can be considered as a skeleton for a website that defines the essential form and function of the site with the dynamic content missing. It therefore defines the types of content, the structure and navigation of the site, the functionality, the presentation styles and any static content including images.

In the case of WordPress, a theme mainly consists of a set of PHP templates, CSS stylesheets and images. The templates are structured in a hierarchy to represent not only the home page and structural elements of pages such as header, footer and sidebar, but also templates for displaying different kinds of content. Since the WordPress platform was originally developed for blogging sites, the basic content types are posts and pages. While a default template should be provided for pages that display posts, it is possible through a naming scheme to construct a whole hierarchy of page templates ranging from customised pages for specific posts and categories of posts to a generic post page. Details of the WordPress model including the full template hierarchy are given in [15].

The model underlying the WordPress system is not as well-defined or documented as research systems with clearly defined concepts and a metamodel. Also, there is a lot of flexibility in terms of how and where different aspects of a theme are defined. Most parts of themes are tightly coupled and often not kept separate, making it difficult to identify, extract and reuse them. Until now, separation was up to the developer who, if following good principles of design, could manually separate code components to support future reuse. But it is important to remember that many WordPress developers are part-designer/part-developer with limited training in principles of software engineering [4].

We therefore defined a metamodel for themes consistent with the WordPress model, but introducing a notion of Components. Fig. 3a shows the core elements of the metamodel that define the structure of a theme and references to each component's resources so that they can be further accessed and reused. Specifically, we have defined Component as the reusable super-type of the model. A component can be an *LComponent* or an *FComponent*. An LComponent specifies the layout structure of a part of the page, and it is defined by CSS and HTML markup. An FComponent embeds functionality which can be defined through PHP or JavaScript logic, the former on the server-side and the latter on the client-side.

In order to give complete freedom in design, LComponents can contain other LComponents, allowing an arbitrarily nested structure, as shown in Fig. 3a. However, although LComponents can be placed with freedom within the page, FComponents instead need to be linked to an LComponent, in which they are loaded and displayed.

The code defined in the FComponents can either be integrated directly into pages via inclusion, or through widgets which provide easy access to plugins. Plugins are a means of extending the functionality of a theme and may either be integrated into a theme or added later by a user.

Elements such as headers, footers and sidebars are part of the core WordPress model, and custom content types can be added to support application-specific

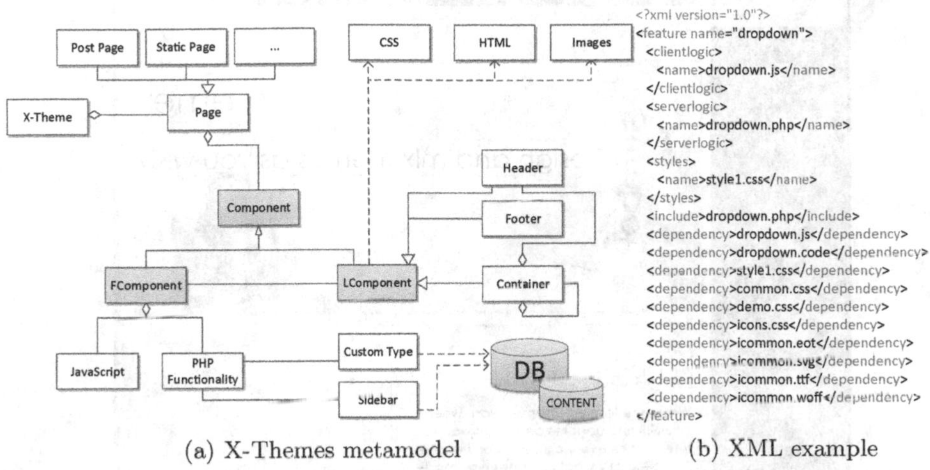

(a) X-Themes metamodel (b) XML example

Fig. 3. Metamodel and XML representation

data. For example, custom types could be defined in an e-commerce system to manage product data. The actual database and content are defined by an instance of a website and not the theme and therefore are not targeted by our reuse mechanism.

The generated X-Themes are structured so that all the resources and code required for each component are stored in a separate directory. The model distinguishes between server-side resources such as PHP templates, resources which enhance the client-side experience such as JavaScript and other required files such as images. For each component, we store a representation of this information in XML which is then used during theme generation to include all the required resources. The XML representation of a component is also used when a user drags-and-drops that component into a theme to identify which resources need to be loaded into the editor and displayed.

An example of the XML representation of a component is shown in Fig. 3b. The elements *serverlogic*, *clientlogic* and *styles* are used to identify the primary resources needed for a component to work. Moreover, a general *dependency* element is used to specify additional resources required, such as images and non-standard fonts. An *include* element specifies the file responsible for starting the execution of component.

All elements of the metamodel also have a DOM-based implementation which annotates the design created within the editor by exploiting the HTML5 *dataset* API. These annotations are then used in the generation and the reuse steps detailed in Section. 5. For example, during theme design, the root element of the component for the navigation menu represented in Fig.3b will be annotated with the *data-clientlogic* attribute specifying a DOM reference to enable fast access from the JavaScript modules of our editor.

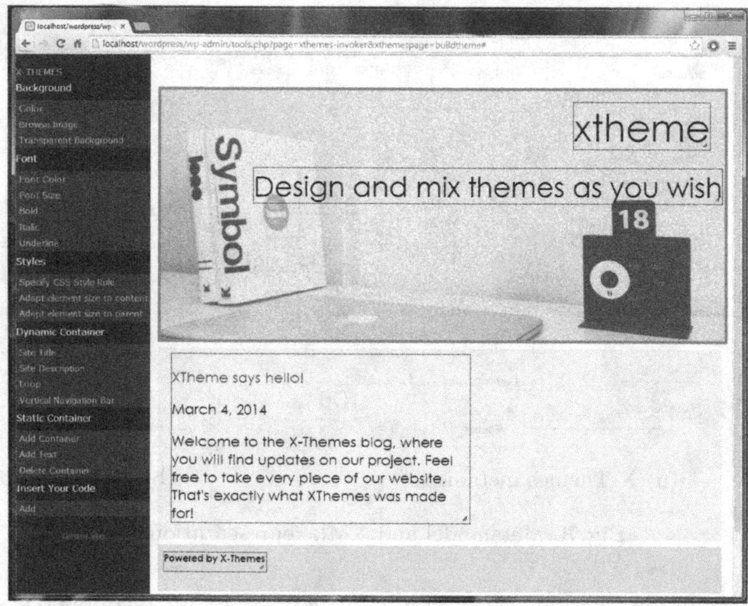

Fig. 4. X-Themes editor

We note that while the metamodel was designed around the original WordPress model, we were careful to design it in a such a way that it could be generalised to other CMS as described later in Sect. 7.

5 Implementation

The X-Themes editor is accessible through the dashboard of WordPress, and its interface is shown in Fig. 4. There is a menu on the left and the main three elements of a web page—header, body and footer—in the main editing area. Users can create an arbitrary nesting of containers within the main elements. The user can perform basic style customisations such as changing the font and background through menu options, while more expert users can also add and edit CSS rules directly.

Containers can be associated with functionality by creating or copying components into containers. To create a new FComponent, the user can import the necessary HTML, PHP, CSS and JavaScript files. When this is done, the editor performs two operations. First, it executes the FComponent directly and shows it running in the design being edited. Second, it creates a package, which is a zip archive, containing not only the source files specified by the user, but also the metamodel information as specified in Section 4. In this way, the tool creates a new FComponent which can be reused either via a drag-and-drop from the generated X-Theme accessed in an online gallery or through the zip archive. When the user is finished editing, they click on the *generate* button and their

X-Theme will be generated and immediately available for use via the WordPress dashboard, and for reuse via the X-Themes gallery.

We will now describe the generation process in detail referring to Fig. 5. We will first present the steps of the generation process shown on the left and then the reuse process on the right.

1. Design. When the editing of a theme is complete, the editor generates a set of templates for that theme together with the files defining its components and associated metadata based on the X-Themes metamodel. We will assume a simple example of a design with only two LComponents in the header and one in the body as shown in Fig. 6 to explain the steps.

1.a) **Design theme** Since our editor is a web-based tool, the design will be a subtree of the DOM structure of the page. It is important to know that the theme header, body and footer are handled as LComponents individually since this is how they are handled in WordPress. The DOM structure will contain the elements of the example together with the contents of the user's WordPress installation in the markup. As mentioned in Section 4, the root elements of the component subtrees have annotations based on the HTML5 *dataset* API to represent metadata for our model.

1.b) **Metamodel Generation**. A browser node recursively builds metamodel strings for each of the components present in the design. This involves recreating the XML structure, shown in Fig. 3b, by reading the HTML5 dataset *attributes*, reversing the mapping between the XML-based implementation of our metamodel and the DOM-based one, as explained in Section 4. In the case of Fig. 6, it builds an XML string for LC1, LC2 and FC as well as for the three default LComponents. Within the same recursive traversal, it also builds strings with

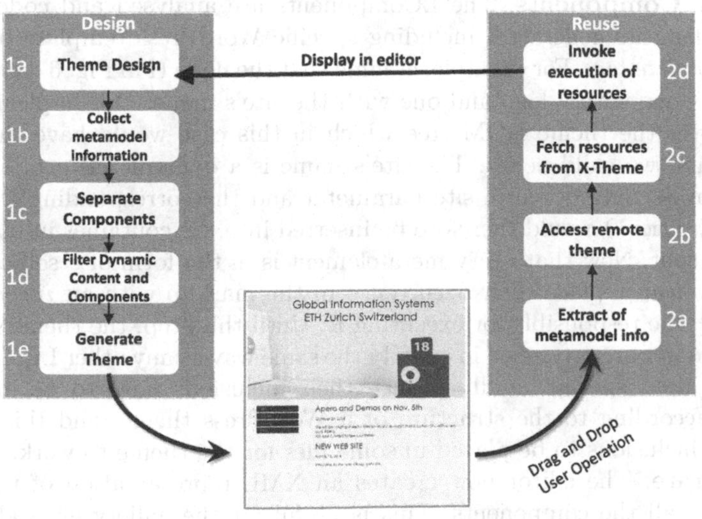

Fig. 5. X-Themes' process of generation and reuse

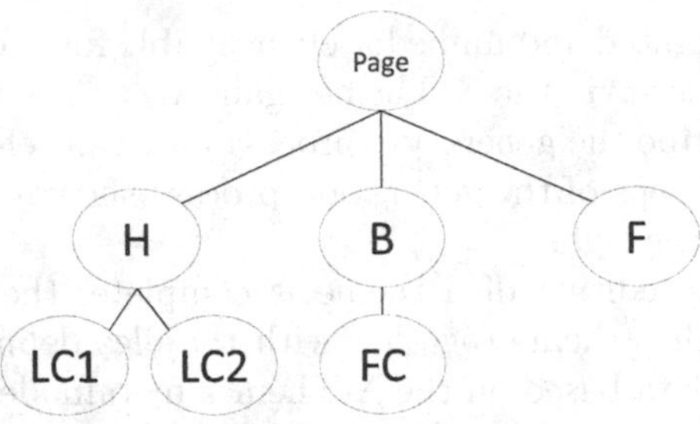

Fig. 6. Simple example design structure of an X-Theme

CSS style rules for each component so that they can be bound to the corresponding metamodel element, which from now on are referred to as *meta-elements*.
1.c) **Separate Components**. The first use we make of our XML specification is to distinguish the individual meta-elements and allocate a directory for each of them. For each meta-element, all files which have to be executed or loaded with it are saved in its directory, along with a copy of the PHP code (in a different format) that will allow future reuse. Also during this step, the CSS style information, which up until this point is represented as a string in inline rules, is separated out into CSS files. The theme's header, footer and body get processed in the same way. For the example in Fig. 6, this means it would create a separate self-contained structure for LC1, LC2 and FC nodes in the tree as well as for H, B and F. It is important to note that up to this point, the content originally shown to the user for each LComponent is still part of the markup saved to the PHP files.
1.d) **Filter Components**. The LComponents are analysed and code for any dynamic elements generated, including specific WordPress template functions, namely *template tags*. For example, assume that the node H in Fig. 6 contains two containers—one with a logo and one with the site's name. Our implementation operates over the theme DOM tree which in this case would have the parent node and its two child nodes. The site's name is a dynamic element since this information is contained in a site parameter and the corresponding PHP code `bloginfo('name')` would therefore be inserted into the container in place of its original output. Now that every meta-element is in the form of a self-contained package, we can replace their occurrence in the markup with an *include()* call to the PHP file responsible for executing it. Until this step, the theme's header, body and footer are processed in exactly the same way as any other LComponent. They now need special handling since their inclusions have to be in specific locations according to the structure of a WordPress theme, and this requires additional inclusions to be placed in some files for the theme to work.
1.e) **Generate**. The editor now creates an XML representation of the theme that defines all the components. This is useful for the gallery as it allows the complete theme structure to be analysed from a single source.

2. Reuse. On the right of Fig. 5, we show the main processing steps to extract an FComponent of an existing X-Theme for inclusion in the theme being edited. We name this approach **Clone-and-execute** since it performs local clones of the FComponent and executes it through an AJAX call accessing the WordPress API. It is important to note that we chose to develop a special approach for the reuse of simple LComponents and will explain this in our review of the implementation given in Section 6.

2.a) **Metamodel extraction**. When the user selects and drags an FComponent, such as a navigation menu implemented in PHP/JavaScript and CSS, the editor accesses the metamodel information of that FComponent and acquires references to the theme's location in the source web server. Moreover, for each file of a meta-element, each metamodel description contains references which are local to the source theme. These sub-references are also retrieved and act as an input for the next step.

2.b) **Theme Access**. The theme HTTP location and the local sub-references are now chained together to obtain an absolute HTTP-based location for each individual dependency of the meta-element itself. In this way, the editor propagates the selection and is ready to get the FComponent. Note that resources stored in remote WordPress installations first have to be cloned in order that the FComponent can be executed in the editor.

2.c) **Fetch resources**. The selected resources (JavaScript, CSS, PHP, images, etc.) are then fetched in order to clone them in the user's WordPress installation. The access is done via the HTTP protocol directly on the source theme server and the necessary connections made to download the required files. Note that only the resources in the component's directory get copied during this process. Remote resources that are referenced but not part of the WordPress installation do not get copied, for example a picture from a different website linked via a remote URL. Moreover, as remote access to PHP is not possible for security reasons, our implementation instead uses a copy of the FComponent's PHP code created when the X-Theme was generated.

2.d) **Execution**. After every resource has been selected, accessed and copied locally, the FComponent can be executed in the context of the X-Themes editor running on the user's own WordPress installation and accessing their database transparently. We perform this through an AJAX request to an endpoint meant to evaluate meta-elements coming from reused components and requiring access to the WordPress API. This endpoint is registered through some WordPress specific functions, namely *hooks*, which allow us to execute our code taking advantage of the WordPress API. Unfortunately, this approach comes with some disadvantages which will be explained in more detail in Section 6. Since our meta-element is sent to this AJAX endpoint within WordPress, all PHP and the WordPress-related queries can be executed and the result is used as output to the user. Once the AJAX response has been received, the editor will dynamically load any other CSS or JavaScript code that is required. As a result, the FComponent can directly display the actual contents of the target database rather than the source one. For example, any imported navigation menus, would immediately reflect the structure and labels defined by the user in the administrative dashboard for the theme under creation rather than those that appear in the source theme.

Allowing users to design their own themes by letting them reuse any PHP or JavaScript code raises potential security issues. For example, it would be possible to have a malicious FComponent containing JavaScript code which accesses other components through the DOM and somehow modifies them. While out of scope at this stage, the topic of detecting and preventing such side-effects is one direction for possible future work.

6 Review of Technical Challenges and Solutions

As is often the case when a system is extended to support goals for which it was not originally designed, realising the theme editor as a WordPress plugin brought many challenges. Specifically, there were many issues that had to be addressed to enable run-time components to be dragged-and-dropped from a web page running in a browser and deal with coherence of the components, the performance/efficiency of reuse and the re-execution of such components in a totally new environment. Moreover, while realising the editor as part of the WordPress dashboard offered potential advantages in terms of deployment and acceptance in the community, it meant that some compromises were necessary to display the editor within the WordPress administration pages. We will first discuss the main choices and compromises that we had to make to coexist with the WordPress dashboard, and then detail the trade-offs related to efficiency and performance.

As shown in Section 5, our tool makes heavy use of AJAX requests. Our X-Themes editor is reachable from a page registered to the WordPress dashboard through hooks and we also had to declare AJAX endpoints for our plugin in the same way, namely as a page in the WordPress dashboard. This is how many CMS achieve extensibility in contrast to the plugins developed for desktop applications such as MS Office and integrated development environments. The overall advantage of this approach is that the entire definition of the WordPress API is already complete before the flow of execution reaches the hooking point where the developer's plugin is executed, and therefore all of the required dependencies have been correctly prepared for the plugin to work. WordPress offers many hooks, some of them before an HTML component is generated and some of them after. Unfortunately, this means that the dashboard is prepended or appended, depending on the position in the flow of our target hook, to every AJAX request started by the editor, introducing noise that has to be filtered within the HTTP responses.

There were also challenges faced while developing the reuse process detailed in Section 5. When the user performs a drag-and-drop reuse operation, we could choose between two reuse techniques planned for our editor which act as a trade-off between reliability of the reused component and performance:

- *Clone-and-execute*: This is the approach presented in the reuse process in Section 5. It creates separate HTTP connections to retrieve each of the files. With slow source web servers, this can perform quite poorly.
- *Copy-and-filter*: CSS rules are identified and inlined to the markup. Then, we filter the output of WordPress template tags (which are PHP functions) from markup and replace it with the resulting output of the same functions in the target installation. This approach can be performed almost instantly, but it is not applicable when using components which have JavaScript or other PHP dependencies. Moreover, this approach can also cause issues when trying to infer which CSS rules are applied to the selected components.

During our implementation, we tested the tool on both fast and slow source servers and decided to opt for an approach that makes the choice of technique applied dependent on the type of component to be migrated. If the component is an LComponent, the editor filters out WordPress template tags and replaces their output from the resulting markup with a Copy-and-filter approach in the target installation. When it comes to bigger and more complex FComponents involving JavaScript and PHP dependencies, the editor applies a Clone-and-execute approach and triggers the correct execution of all the required resources for each component. The reason is that the Copy-and-filter approach heavily relies on the capabilities of matching calls to WordPress functions and replacing them with the correct output from the target installation. Unfortunately, this cannot always be guaranteed and, generally, it may be an unsafe approach: Some elements might be missed and therefore the data of the target website might not be incorporated into the new design. This makes the Clone-and-execute approach more reliable than the Copy-and-filter, but it can be much slower.

Another potential issue of the Copy-and-filter approach also has performance implications. Dragging an LComponent to the X-Themes editor requires knowledge of which CSS rules must be applied so they can be inlined. This could be implemented in two ways. The first method is to ask the browser about the computed style of each element, which is, however, not cross-browser compatible and may have serious performance issues for complex LComponents. Therefore, we chose the option of implementing our own algorithm which visits every CSS rule specified in the loaded stylesheets and only includes it if it influences the display of the corresponding elements. While this works well for most CSS rules that explicitly target DOM elements by ID or class, it can still raise performance issues in the case of many page-wide or deeply cascaded CSS rules.

7 Generalisation of Approach for Other CMS

The approach implemented for X-Themes was conceived with the goal of being general enough to be applied to other CMS. The metamodel itself avoids platform-specific concepts. This could be thought of as implying that the metamodel provides limited support for specific platforms, however we argue that our metamodel can support platform-specific concepts through taxonomy-like

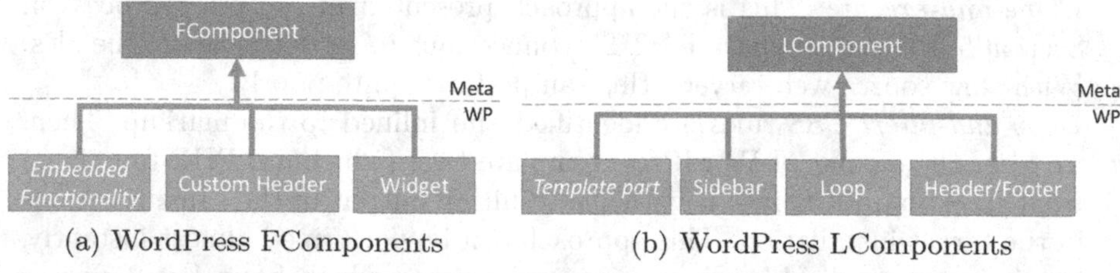

(a) WordPress FComponents (b) WordPress LComponents

Fig. 7. WordPress theme concepts implemented as elements of our metamodel

extensions of LComponents and FComponents which in turn can be powered by platform-specific implementations of theme generators.

We will begin by presenting which concepts of WordPress we have been able to represent in our metamodel and then map these to similar ones in other widely used CMS, providing details of how these concepts work in each target CMS and how they can be implemented as an instance of our metamodel. According to W3Techs[11], WordPress is the most widely used CMS with over 60% of the market share. The main competitors sharing the podium are Drupal and Joomla, with 7.3% and 5.1% of the market share, respectively. We will therefore use these to explain how the approach can be generalised by analysing what the equivalent concept of a theme is in each of these CMS, and providing an insight into the differences and similarities between each of the platforms and WordPress. We will then assess how well the concepts of each platform can be handled in our proposed approach.

In all three platforms, themes consist of template files used to generate output for different parts of the theme. The level of granularity of the template hierarchy is specific to each CMS and varies a lot. However, all of these platforms provide the opportunity to code specific layout details or functionality within the templates.

WordPress provides a lot of freedom in terms of the way in which a theme can be developed. Some developers choose to embed functionality within the theme templates, while others try to create a more decoupled structure making use of more advanced concepts such as *sidebars* and *widgets*. The former are areas of the template which can be configured through the administrative dashboard to show specific *widgets* providing functionality such as showing some dynamic content or overviews of other content areas of the website. Widgets can also be registered from plugins providing functionality that will be accessed through widgets. Additionally, developers often exploit functionality provided by the WordPress platform itself such as *Customisable headers*.

As shown in Fig. 7, sidebars have been implemented in X-Themes as an LComponent, since they shape where and how widgets can be displayed in the page. Widgets, on the other hand, often introduce functionality, for example a search box, and therefore are implemented as FComponents. Moreover, we have an interest in reproducing the functionality that the widgets provide and not

[11] http://www.w3techs.com/on8April2015

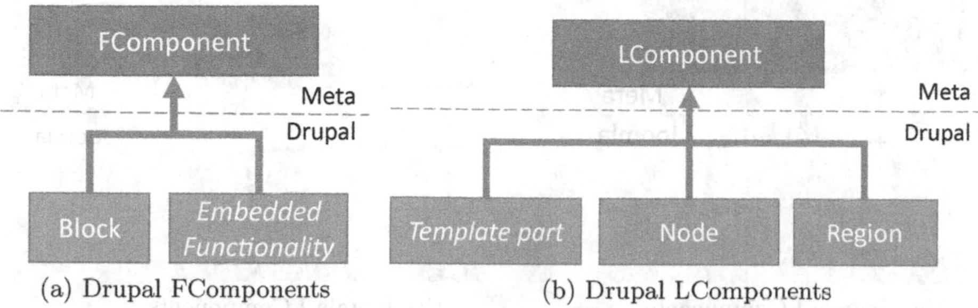

(a) Drupal FComponents (b) Drupal LComponents

Fig. 8. Drupal theme concepts implemented as elements of our metamodel

only the way the content is shown, therefore a *clone-and-execute* approach is more suitable for widgets. *Customisable headers* allow users to specify either a single or set of header images to be shown randomly and so have also been implemented as FComponents through the re-execution of content.

Drupal provides theme developers with similar tools for dynamically configuring a theme but uses the concepts of *regions* and *blocks*. *Regions* are areas of the layout designed to host atomic *blocks* of content, which have been defined by users or through so-called *modules* which act as plugins. Differently from WordPress, regions and blocks have default templates and specific templates. However, similarly to WordPress, we can distinguish components that specify layout from those that may involve functionality. Consequently, individual regions can be implemented as LComponents and blocks as FComponents as shown in Fig. 8. Further, the sidebars of WordPress can be mapped to Drupal's regions, and widgets to blocks. Drupal uses the concept of nodes to represent individual units of data, which are generally shown iteratively, and therefore is equivalent to the Loop in WordPress. Therefore, we are able to implement Node through an LComponent.

Joomla also distinguishes between components that define layout and those that define functionality as shown in Fig. 9. In the case of Joomla, positions are declared which have special placeholder code in the theme template, and these are detected and processed by the Joomla template engine, which replaces them with the template generated for the so-called *modules*. Positions and modules can be realised as LComponents and FComponents, respectively. It is clear that Joomla's positions can be mapped to Drupal's regions. We can do the same with Joomla's modules, which can be mapped to Drupal's blocks. The automatic query of the current content being viewed, handled by the Loop in WordPress and the execution of Nodes in Drupal, is handled by a specific Joomla module, internally called *component*.

Although the three CMS use different terminology and the details of the concepts and features offered vary, they all distinguish between components that deal only with layout and those that offer functionality. In addition, they all provide some means of querying and displaying the content that is equivalent to the Loop in WordPress and also support extensibility through some kind

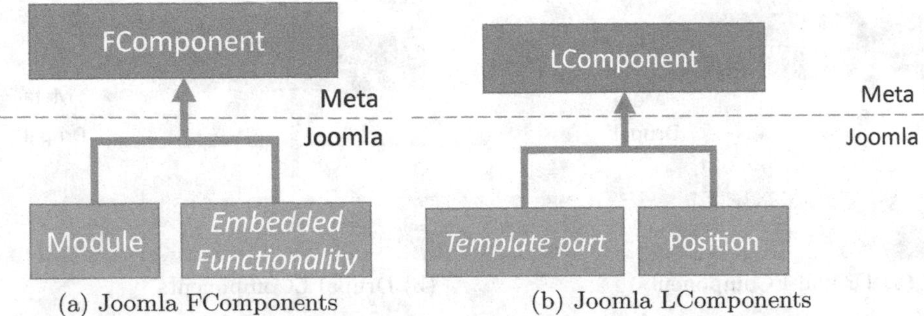

(a) Joomla FComponents (b) Joomla LComponents

Fig. 9. Joomla theme concepts implemented as elements of our metamodel

of plugin mechanism. As discussed, it is therefore possible to map the main concepts of all of these CMS to our metamodel, extending the LComponent and FComponent hierarchies where necessary to deal with specialisations.

8 Conclusion

We have shown how the arbitrary reuse and mixing of both layout and functionality of WordPress themes can be supported. Compared to previous work, users are able to select, reuse and combine parts of existing themes, transparently propagating the reuse to dynamic resources that define functionality on both the client and server sides. Since a theme must be based on the metamodel in order for it to be an X-Theme and accessible to the visual editor, we have defined a manual procedure for converting existing themes to an X-Theme, and are currently investigating semi-automated approaches.

There are also other research questions that we plan to address in the future. The first of these concerns data-intensive web sites which require the integration of custom post types to manage data. In previous work within our group, a tool was developed that generates a WordPress plugin with custom post types based on an entity-relationship data model defined by a developer [16]. We have now started to investigate an alternative approach that lets the user annotate sample data content from mockups or other similar websites and then automatically generates a data schema which is implemented as custom post types in the WordPress platform [17].

Acknowledgments. We acknowledge the support of the Swiss National Science Foundation who financially supported part of this research under project FZFSP0_147257.

References

1. Norrie, M.C., Nebeling, M., Di Geronimo, L., Murolo, A.: X-Themes: supporting design-by-example. In: Casteleyn, S., Rossi, G., Winckler, M. (eds.) ICWE 2014. LNCS, vol. 8541, pp. 480–489. Springer, Heidelberg (2014)
2. McCollin, R., Blakeley-Silver, T.: WordPress Theme Development. Packt Publishing (2013)

3. Casabona, J.: Building WordPress Themes from Scratch. Rockable Press (2012)
4. Norrie, M.C., Di Geronimo, L., Murolo, A., Nebeling, M.: The forgotten many? A survey of modern web development practices. In: Casteleyn, S., Rossi, G., Winckler, M. (eds.) ICWE 2014. LNCS, vol. 8541, pp. 290–307. Springer, Heidelberg (2014)
5. Hartmann, B., Wu, L., Collins, K., Klemmer, S.R.: Programming by a sample: rapidly creating web applications with d.mix. In: Proc. of the 20th ACM Symp. on User Interface Software and Technology (UIST). ACM (2007)
6. Lee, B., Srivastava, S., Kumar, R., Brafman, R., Klemmer, S.: Designing with interactive example galleries. In: Proc. of the 28th Conf. on Human Factors in Computings Systems (CHI). ACM (2010)
7. Ghiani, G., Paternò, F., Spano, L.D.: Creating mashups by direct manipulation of existing web applications. In: Piccinno, A. (ed.) IS-EUD 2011. LNCS, vol. 6654, pp. 42–52. Springer, Heidelberg (2011)
8. Gellersen, H., Wicke, R., Gaedke, M.: WebComposition: An Object-Oriented Support System for the Web Engineering Lifecycle. Computer Networks **29**(8) (1997)
9. Yu, J., Benatallah, B., Saint-Paul, R., Casati, F., Florian, D., Matera, M.: A Framework for rapid integration of presentation components. In: Proc. of the 16th Intl. Conf. on the World Wide Web (WWW). ACM (2007)
10. Leone, S., de Spindler, A., Norrie, M.C., McLeod, D.: Integrating component-based web engineering into content management systems. In: Daniel, F., Dolog, P., Li, Q. (eds.) ICWE 2013. LNCS, vol. 7977, pp. 37–51. Springer, Heidelberg (2013)
11. Ceri, S., Fraternali, P., Bongio, A., Brambilla, M., Comai, S., Matera, M.: Designing Data-Intensive Web Applications. Morgan Kaufmann (2002)
12. Houben, G., Barna, P., Frasincar, F., Vdovjak, R.: Hera: development of semantic web information systems. In: Cueva Lovelle, J.M., Rodríguez, B.M.G., Gayo, J.E.L., Ruiz, M.P.P., Aguilar, L.J. (eds.) ICWE 2003. LNCS, vol. 2722, pp. 529–538. Springer, Heidelberg (2003)
13. Knapp, A., Koch, N., Zhang, G.: Modeling the structure of web applications with ArgoUWE. In: Koch, N., Fraternali, P., Wirsing, M. (eds.) ICWE 2004. LNCS, vol. 3140, pp. 615–616. Springer, Heidelberg (2004)
14. Quinn, A.J., Bederson, B.B.: Human computation: a survey and taxonomy of a growing field. In: Proc. of the 29th Intl. Conf. on Human-Computer Interaction (CHI). ACM (2011)
15. Williams, B., Damstra, D., Stern, H.: Professional WordPress Design and Development. Wiley (2013)
16. Leone, S., de Spindler, A., Norrie, M.C.: A meta-plugin for bespoke data management in wordpress. In: Wang, X.S., Cruz, I., Delis, A., Huang, G. (eds.) WISE 2012. LNCS, vol. 7651, pp. 580–593. Springer, Heidelberg (2012)
17. Murolo, A., Norrie, M.: Deriving custom post types from digital mockups. In: Proc. of the 15th Intl. Conf. on Web Engineering (ICWE). Springer (2015)

Identifying Inter-Component Control Flow in Web Applications

William G.J. Halfond(✉)

University of Southern California, Los Angeles, USA
halfond@usc.edu

Abstract. As web applications become more complex, automated techniques for their testing and verification have become essential. Many of these techniques, such as ones for identifying security vulnerabilities, require information about a web application's control flow. Currently, this information is manually specified or automatically generated using techniques that cannot give strong guarantees of completeness. This paper presents a new static analysis based approach for identifying control flow in web applications that is both automated and provides stronger guarantees of completeness. The empirical evaluation of the approach shows that it is able to identify more complete control flow information than other approaches with comparable analysis run time.

1 Introduction

Modern web applications have become increasingly sophisticated, interweaving complex interactions and combining data from multiple sources. As web applications become more complex, automated testing and verification techniques specifically tailored for web applications have risen in importance. Many of these techniques require detailed information about the control flow of a web application. For example, to identify multi-module vulnerabilities [2], access control vulnerabilities [22], or eliminate navigation errors [10]. For early web applications, identifying this control flow was as simple as following the links embedded in each of the application's web pages. However, control flow in modern web applications is more complex and limitations of techniques for identifying control flow have meant that testing and verification techniques have to rely on less accurate methods. Unsurprisingly, two control flow related vulnerabilities, "Failure to Restrict URL Access" and "Unvalidated Redirects and Forwards" have made the infamous OWASP Top 10 Web Application Security Risks list.

The architecture of modern web applications makes their control flow more complex than that of traditional (e.g., desktop) software. On the server-side of a web application, modules of code, called *components*, can expose methods that allow them to be directly executed over the web. Examples of components include Java Servlets and PHP pages. In turn, a component may generate data or *object programs*, code that is intended to be interpreted and executed in another context. Object programs can be written in "web" languages, such as JavaScript

P. Cimiano et al. (Eds.): ICWE 2015, LNCS 9114, pp. 52–70, 2015.
DOI: 10.1007/978-3-319-19890-3_5

and HTML, or with protocols, such as HTTP, which allow developers to control the behavior of an end user's browser (e.g., using a redirect or authentication request). In web applications, not only is there control flow within each component, such as jumps, loops, branching, and method calls, written in the application's general purpose programming language, there is also inter-component control flow. This additional control flow is defined by the combination of the semantics of the object programs, which themselves can interact with other components and users. Control flow models that fail to account for all of these additional types of control flow may be incomplete and represent only a subset of the potential runtime behaviors of a web application.

Researchers and web application developers have recognized the importance of checking web application control flow. In early web applications, errors in control flow typically manifested themselves as dead links. Researchers found that web crawlers [3,14,23], were very effective at detecting these types of errors. However, as web applications became more dynamic, the effectiveness of these approaches was reduced. Subsequent work did not directly address this problem, but did provide a diverse set of techniques that could be used to verify and enforce correctness and security properties of web applications [1,10,12,15,20]. Unfortunately, their primary assumption is that there exist techniques for accurately specifying control flow. In practice, the approaches rely on either the developer to manually specify the control flow, which is time-consuming and error-prone, or on web crawlers, which cannot provide strong guarantees of completeness. Several automated static analysis techniques (e.g., [2,5,19,22,25]) have attempted to derive more complete control flow models, but do not account for all possible types of control flow.

This paper presents a new approach for statically identifying control flow in web applications that addresses the limitations of previous approaches. The approach is based on static analysis of the code of a web application. The static analysis identifies control flow related constructs defined by the generated HTML and JavaScript of the web application and by server-side commands generated by the general purpose language of the web application. This information is combined with traditional control flow information to provide a more complete model of a web application's control flow. As shown in the evaluation, the approach is more complete than other approaches and its running time is fast enough to allow it to be used to generate control flow information for a range of testing and verification tasks [10–12,21,22,24,26].

2 Web Applications Control Flow

Web application control flow includes both traditional control flow constructs, such as jumps, branches, and loops, as well as the following new types of control flow that are specific to web applications:

Dynamically Generated HTML. Web pages are displayed in a user's browser and provide the user with the ability to interact with the web application. Certain types of HTML tags can also affect the control flow, either automatically or when they are clicked on by the end user. These tags include: <a>, <form>, <img>, <meta>, <frame>, and <script>.

JavaScript. is a scripting language widely used to write programs that are embedded in HTML pages and that can interact with the web page's document object model (DOM) and the end-user. The embedded programs can perform a range of functions that can affect the inter-component control flow of a web application. These can be done by referencing the location property of the DOM and accessing the navigation functionality of the browser. Note that inter-component control flow related to *JavaScript* does not include control flow within the *JavaScript* programs, only the actions that cause a user to navigate from one component to another.

HTTP Commands. Components communicate among themselves and with the end user's browser by sending messages using the Hyper-Text Transport Protocol (HTTP). A component issues HTTP commands by calling a special API-based command and passing it an HTTP response code and a message parameter. Certain HTTP response codes cause the browser to redirect to the location specified in the HTTP message. These codes are 300, 301, 302, 303, and 307. For all of these, the message is specified in a special HTTP header field that is defined by a message of the form "Location: *target*" where *target* is a URL that indicates where the user should be redirected. A lesser known HTTP refresh header can also be used in much the same way as the HTML <meta> tag.

Component Inclusion. In many web application frameworks, it is possible to issue a command that imports the contents of another component. For example, both PHP and JSP have a variant of the `include` command. These commands import the contents of the target component at the point of the command. This can be done either statically via precompilation or dynamically at runtime. These commands affect control flow since the imported components are themselves executable code.

Direct Entry. Users are able to enter the URL of a web component directly in a web browser's location bar. This action causes the root method of the target component to execute. *Direct Entry* can occur even if a link to the target component has not been exposed and the developer did not intend for the component to be an entry point into the application. In the security literature, *Direct Entry* control flow is also known as "forced browsing" and can lead to workflow vulnerabilities [2]. *Direct Entry* control flow can be further refined by the type of encoding used by the HTTP requests, such as GET or POST.

3 Motivating Example

Figure 1 shows a partial listing of a web application component, `Login.jsp`, that manages a user logging in to a web application. The component is implemented as a servlet in the Java Enterprise Edition (JEE) web application framework.

The input to `Login.jsp` is a `Request` object for accessing the HTTP message sent to the component and a `Response` object for sending content to the end

```
void service(Request req, Response resp)
 1. JspWriter out = resp.getOutputStream();
 2. String session = req.getParam("session");
 3. if (isValidSession(session)) {
 4.  sendHttpCmd(resp, 302, "Default.jsp");
 5. } elsif (session.equals("login")) {
 6.  String login = req.getParam("uname");
 7.  String password = req.getParam("pword");
 8.  if (isClean(login) && isClean(pword)) {
 9.   if (loginOK(uname, pword)) {
10.    sendHttpCmd(resp, 302, "Default.jsp");
11.  }
12.  } else {
13.   sendHttpCmd(resp, 303, "Error.jsp");
14. }
15. } else {
16.  out.print("<html><body>");
17.  out.print("<script language='JavaScript'>");
18.  out.print("function goBack() {");
19.  out.print("window.location.href="Index.jsp";
20.  out.print("}");
21.  out.print("</script>");
22.  out.print("<h1>Login Page</h1>");
23.  out.print("<form method=POST" + " action='Login.jsp'>");
24.  out.print("<input type=hidden value=" +  "'login' name=session>");
25.  out.print("User:<input type=text name=uname>");
26.  out.print("Password:<input type=" + "password name=pword>");
27.  out.print("<input type=submit value='Login'>");
28.  out.print("<input type=submit value='Back'" + " onClick='goBack()'>");
29.  out.print("</form>");
30.  out.print("<a href='Reset.jsp'>" + " Reset password</a>");
31.  out.print("</body></html>");

void sendHttpCmd(Response resp, int code, String msg)
33. String location = "Location: ";
34. location += urlEncode(msg);
35. location += "\n\n";
36. resp.sendHttpMessage(code, location);
```

Fig. 1. Implementation of servlet, `Login.jsp`

user. At line 2, `Login.jsp` accesses a name-value pair, `session`, that is used by the application to track the logged-in status of the end user. If the session corresponds to a valid session, an HTTP command is issued at line 4 that causes the end user to redirect to the default servlet. This is done by calling `sendHttpCmd` and passing in three parameters, the first is the `Response` object, the second is the intended HTTP response code, and the third is the URL of the component to which the end user will be redirected. If the user does not have a valid session, but the session variable is equal to "login," then the servlet accesses the supplied username and password (lines 6 and 7) and checks the credentials at lines 8 and 9. If the login is successful, then at line 10 a redirect command is executed that allows the end user to proceed to the default servlet; otherwise, the user is redirected to an error page at line 13. Finally, if neither condition at line 3 or 5 applies, then the servlet prints a web form that allows the user to submit a username and password (lines 15–31). This web form, when submitted, sends the username and password back to the `Login.jsp` servlet. Alternatively, the user can click on the link generated at line 30 if they have forgotten their password or go back to the previous page that triggered the login request by clicking on the button generated at line 28. Clicking this button triggers the execution of the JavaScript function generated at lines 18–20.

`Login.jsp` illustrates several types of inter-component control flow. These include *HTTP Commands* at lines 4, 10, and 13; *Dynamically Generated HTML* via the HTML page produced at lines 16–31; and *JavaScript* via the script tag at lines 17–21 and called at line 28. The control flow links the `Login.jsp` servlet to `Index.jsp`, `Default.jsp`, `Error.jsp`, and `ResetPassword.jsp`. A web crawler could miss several of the control flow links during a crawl of the example application. For example, it is likely a web crawler could not accurately guess the constraints on the user input imposed at line 8. Therefore, the crawler would find the error page referenced at line 13, but not the default page referenced at line 10.

4 Approach

The goal of the proposed approach is to identify inter-component control flow in web applications. The proposed approach has four steps that together account for the different types of control flow. The first step targets control flow defined by the components' generated object programs, *Dynamically Generated HTML* and *JavaScript*, and is explained in Section 4.1. The second step, explained in Section 4.2, identifies server-side API-based control flow, which includes *HTTP Commands* and *Component Inclusion*. Section 4.3 details the third step, which identifies *Direct Entry* related control flow. The fourth step, in Section 4.4, combines the identified control flow into an Inter-Component Control Flow Graph (ICCFG).

4.1 Control Flow in Generated HTML Pages

Control flow due to *Dynamically Generated HTML* and *JavaScript* is defined in the HTML output of the components of a web application. To identify this control flow, the approach builds on prior work in web page string analysis [8,9] to compute the set of HTML pages that each component can generate at runtime. To do this, the approach analyzes each method of the component and computes a parameterized summary of the HTML that could be generated by the method. The methods are analyzed in reverse topological order with respect to the component's call graph to ensure that a method's summary is computed before those of calling methods. All methods that are part of a recursive call are analyzed together as one "super method." When the analysis of the component terminates, the summary of the root

$$\texttt{Gen}[n] = \begin{cases} \{\{\}\} & \text{if } n \text{ is method entry} \\ \{n\} & \text{if } n \text{ generates output} \\ \{n\} & \text{if } n \text{ is a callsite} \\ & \text{and target}(n) \text{ has a summary} \\ \{\} & \text{otherwise} \end{cases}$$

$$\texttt{In}[n] = \bigcup_{p \in pred(n)} \texttt{Out}[p]$$

$$\texttt{Out}[n] = \{p | \forall i \in \texttt{In}[n], p \leftarrow \textbf{append}(i, \texttt{Gen}[n])\}$$

$$\textbf{summary}(m) = \left\{ p | \forall s \in \texttt{Out}[exit(m)] \prod_{n \in s} \texttt{resolve}(n) \right\}$$

Fig. 2. Data-flow equations for identifying generated HTML [8]

method represents all of the possible HTML pages that could be generated by the component.

Within each method, the approach uses iterative data-flow analysis to compute the set of HTML pages. This analysis computes the fixed point solution to the equations shown in Figure 2. As shown in the figure, each node n in the method is assigned a `Gen` set based on whether it directly generates HTML data, calls a function that then generates HTML data, or does not contribute at all to the generated HTML. A node can be identified as generating HTML content based on the signature of its target invocation method. The `In` and `Out` sets propagate this information. The general intuition behind the equations is that nodes that can directly or indirectly generate HTML content are appended together, so the `Out` set of the exit of a method is a set of ordered sets (representing paths) of nodes that can generate HTML.

Once the `Out` set of the method's exit node reaches a fixed point, the approach uses the `resolve` function to convert each node to a set of strings that represents its generated HTML. The `resolve` function handles two general cases. (1) If the node directly generates output, `resolve` computes a finite state automata (FSA) representation of its strings. For nodes that print a constant string or variable defined without string operations (e.g., no concat or insert), the approach identifies the reaching definitions of the string values. For variables defined using a string expression, the approach uses the Java String Analysis (JSA) to compute an approximation of the possible string values [4]. If `resolve` encounters the use of a string that is defined as one of the formal parameters to the enclosing method or external to the method, then the `resolve` function leaves a placeholder in the returned results. (2) If the node represents a call site to a method with a summary, `resolve` replaces any placeholders in the target's summary with the call site's corresponding arguments. The result of calling `resolve` on each node in each ordered set is appended together to create an FSA based representation of the HTML content that could be generated along each path in the application.

When the analysis terminates, each component is associated with a set of FSA based representations of its potentially generated HTML. The approach traverses the generated representation using standard parsing techniques, and identifies strings that define control flow related tags and JavaScript. The approach analyzes the contents of these tags to identify their control flow information.

The relevant tags include: <`a`> allows for the creation of hyperlinks that can be clicked on by the user to move from the current page to the target of the hyperlink; <`form`> allows the user to submit data in a web form, which causes control flow to transfer from the current page to the target component specified by the tag; <`img`> contains a URL-based attribute that defines its source. In some cases the source points to a component that dynamically generates an image and causes execution of the target component. To prevent inclusion of uninteresting control flow that would be identified in this case, the approach uses the heuristic of not including control flow generated by the <`img`> tag if its source URL has a suffix that corresponds to a static image type; <`meta`> can define a "refresh" attribute, which redirects the end user to another URL after a certain amount of time has elapsed; <`frame`> and <`iframe`> include a URL attribute that indicates a target component is to be executed and then displayed in a portion of the HTML page.

To identify *JavaScript* related inter-component control flow, the approach first identifies JavaScript contained by <`script`> tags, embedded as event handlers, and included from external files. Next, the approach parses the JavaScript to identify statements that implement *Component Inclusion*, *Dynamically Generated HTML*, or *HTTP Commands* control flow. For example, statements that reference the `location` property, use the Document Object Model's (DOM) navigation model to send the user to another URL, generate HTML, or load additional JavaScript. Since each of these statements requires an argument specifying the target of the operation, the approach attempts to identify the values that could be referenced at each statement. This is done using an algorithm almost identical to Algorithm 1, where the identified statements are the analyzed command points. The difference between this analysis and the one explained in Section 4.2 is that these `resolve` functions return string values based on reaching definitions and only model the effect of concatenation used at the identified statements to join reaching string values. This more limited `resolve` function is used because there is not yet a JSA equivalent for JavaScript. Once the potential values at each of the identified statements have been calculated, the approach parses the arguments to identify the HTML tags used to define *Dynamically Generated HTML* control flow, the targets of *HTTP Commands* related control flow, or the code included by *Component Inclusion* constructs.

Example. In `Login.jsp`, only one of the four paths generates HTML content, the path that follows the false branch at line 5. The HTML page generated along this path is comprised of the string data generated at lines 16–31. The output of these nodes is appended together to form one string that contains the HTML output generated by the corresponding nodes. This string is then analyzed by an HTML and JavaScript parser to identify control flow information. This analysis identifies three control flow edges: a form that directs control flow back to `Login.jsp`, a hyperlink that directs control flow to `ResetPassword.jsp`, and a call to a JavaScript function that redirects the user to `Index.jsp`.

Algorithm 1. Identify API-based control flow

```
Input: C: web application component
Output: set of edges identified in C
methods ← methods of C in RTO
for all m ∈ methods do
   for all stmt ∈ m do
      if stmt is a CP then
         codes ← {FP, CI, 301, 302...} ∩ resolveCodes(stmt)
         if codes ≠ ∅ then
            targets ← resolveTarget(stmt)
            linenumber ← getLineNumber(stmt)
            summary(m) ← summary(m) ∪ createEdges(C, targets, codes)
         end if
      else if isInvoke(stmt) ∧ summary(getInvkTarget(stmt)) ≠ ∅ then
         target ← getInvkTarget(stmt)
         mappedEdges ← map(summary(target), stmt)
         for all e ∈ mappedEdges do
            targets ← resolveTarget(e)
            codes ← resolveCodes(e)
            linenumber ← getLineNumber(e)
            summary(m) ← summary(m) ∪ createEdges(C, targets, codes)
         end for
      end if
   end for
end for
return summary(root method of C)
```

4.2 Server-side API-Based Control Flow

The approach identifies server-side API-based control flow using a static analysis based technique. The general intuition behind this approach is to first identify the application's command points (CP) – points in an application where commands are issued to perform either *HTTP Commands* or *Component Inclusion* based control flow. The approach analyzes the CP to identify the possible values of their arguments. This is done by analyzing the chain of definitions and uses of the arguments. The identified values are parsed to extract control flow information. For CPs related to *HTTP Commands*, parsing the arguments identifies the HTTP response codes and the value of the `Location` header. For CPs related to *Component Inclusion*, the parsing identifies the component to be included at that point.

Algorithm 2. CreateEdges: helper function for creating edges

Input: C: web application component; *targets*: set of edge targets; *codes*: set of codes for the edges
Output: *edges*: set of edges created

for all $target \in targets$ **do**
    for all $code \in codes$ **do**
        edges $\leftarrow$ edges $\cup$ (nameOf(C), target, code, linenumber)
        if $code = CI$ **then**
            edges $\leftarrow$ edges $\cup$=(target, nameOf(C), code, linenumber)
        end if
    end for
end for
return edges

The algorithm for identifying server-side API-based control flow is shown in Algorithm 1. The input to the algorithm is a web component C, and the output is a set of edges, which contains the control flow defined in C. Each edge in *edges* is a tuple of the form $\langle source, destination, code, linenumber \rangle$. The first element of the tuple, *source*, is the name of the component from which the edge is originating. In most cases, this is the canonical name of C. The second element of the tuple, *destination*, represents the target component to which control flow is redirected. The third element, *code*, is the HTTP response code that is part of the message or the value "CI" for edges related to *Component Inclusion*. The last element, *linenumber*, is the line number in the component where the command is issued. This is used in the fourth step (Section 4.4) when the inter-component control flow information is combined with the CFGs of the individual components of the web application.

The analysis begins by creating a list of the methods of C. As in Section 4.1, the methods are analyzed in reverse topological order with respect to the component's call graph to ensure that a method's summary is computed before those of calling methods (line 1). All methods that are part of a recursive call are analyzed together as one "super method." Then for each method, m, each statement, *stmt*, is processed (lines 2–22).

If the statement is a CP (line 4), then `resolveCodes` is called on the statement to identify the possible HTTP codes that could be used at that point (line 5). The function `resolveCodes` is a simplified version of the `resolve` function introduced in Section 4.1, but is for resolving integer instead of string values. The set of values returned by calling `resolveCodes` is intersected with a set that contains HTTP control flow related codes, the symbol that is used to denote a placeholder for formal method parameters "FP," and the symbol for *Component Inclusion*, "CI" (line 5). If the intersection is non-empty (line 6), then `resolveTarget` is called to determine the value of the message used at the CP (line 7). The `resolveTarget` function is similar to the `resolve` method, but is customized to extract information related to *Component Inclusion* and the "Location" header. Then the line number that corresponds to *stmt* is identified (line 8). A helper function, `CreateEdges`, shown in Algorithm 2 is called to generate the inter-component control flow edges. In `CreateEdges`, the algorithm creates a new edge for each code and target. If the code relates to *Component Inclusion*, then an additional control-edge is added that shows control flow returning from the target back to the source. This reflects that *Component Inclusion* includes the target component's control flow and then continues execution within the original component.

If the statement is not a CP, then it is checked to see if it invokes a method that has a summary associated with it (line 11). If this is the case, the target of the invocation is identified (line 12). Next, function `map` takes the statement and summary of the target method and replaces any placeholders in the method summary with the corresponding argument provided at the invocation call site (line 12). For each mapped edge, the corresponding resolve calls are performed to identify the possible locations and codes that could be executed at that point (lines 15 and 16). This is done since the substituted argument for either the location or code could be resolvable in the current method context or may itself be defined by a parameter to the current enclosing method. With the potential codes and locations discovered by the calls to the resolve functions, new edges are created by calling `createEdges` (line 18).

Once each of the methods have been processed, the summary of the root method of the component contains all of the *Component Inclusion* and *HTTP Commands* control flow edges that can be generated by the component at runtime. If there are any placeholders remaining in the summary, these edges are noted as being defined by external input to the component. The root method's summary is returned as the output of the algorithm.

Example. To illustrate the second step of the approach, consider the example servlet, whose implementation is shown in Figure 1. Analysis of `Login.jsp` begins by analyzing method `sendHttpCmd`, since it is the first method in reverse topological order. The algorithm examines each statement of the method and identifies the CP at line 36 of `Login.jsp`. Next it attempts to resolve the value of the `code` variable that specifies the HTTP response code that will be issued at that point. The definition-use chain (DU) leads back to the second formal parameter of the method, so a placeholder (FP_2) that specifies this relationship is generated and returned by the call to `resolveCode` at line 6 of the algorithm. The formal placeholder is in the set of valid control flow related codes at line 7 of the algorithm, so the algorithm next tries to resolve the message sent at line 36 of `Login.jsp`. The DU chain leads back to the third formal parameter, so here again a placeholder is generated and returned (FP_3). No other statements in `sendHttpCmd` match either of the conditions at lines 5 or 20 of the algorithm, so a single edge of the form ⟨`Login.jsp`, FP_3, FP_2, 36⟩ is added to `sendHttpCmd`'s summary.

The algorithm then analyzes method `service`. The condition at line 20 of the algorithm is true for nodes 4, 10, and 13, since all call method `sendHttpCmd` and this method has a summary. The algorithm maps the statement's argument to the method's summary. For node 4, this creates ⟨`Login.jsp`, `Default.jsp`,

302, 4⟩; for node 10 this creates the edge ⟨`Login.jsp`, `Default.jsp`, 302, 10⟩; and for node 13 the edge ⟨`Login.jsp`, `Error.jsp`, 303, 13⟩ is created. The edges generated for each of the statements are added to the summary of `service`. No other statements in `service` match either of the conditions at line 5 or line 20 of the algorithm, so processing of `service` is finished and its summary is returned as the output of the algorithm.

4.3 Control Flow Based on Direct Entry

The third part of the approach identifies control flow related to *Direct Entry*. There are two steps in this identification. The first identifies if a component is able to receive requests directly from an end user. This is done by analyzing the component to determine if it meets the necessary conditions specified by the web application framework to receive requests. For example, in the Java Enterprise Edition (JEE), a component must implement one of a set of specific interfaces. These conditions can be checked via static analysis. If the component satisfies the conditions, an inter-component control flow edge that originates from the user and connects to the component entry points is identified. Once an edge is identified, the approach attempts to refine the information by determining the type of HTTP request method encoding (e.g., GET or POST) required to access the component. In certain frameworks, such as JEE, the HTTP request method indicates which procedure will be treated as the root method. For example, the presence of a `doPost` method implies that the component can handle POST requests. In PHP, the name of the global variable used to access input parameters indicates the expected request method. If it is possible to identify the request method, then the added edges are updated to include an annotation specifying the request method.

Example. The example presented in Figure 1 has several edges related to *Direct Entry* control flow. The first of these is an edge annotated with the "POST" request method that runs from the user to the entry node of `Login.jsp`. This is created because `Login.jsp` implements the JEE servlet interface method "doPost." This edge is of the form ⟨User, `Login.jsp`, "Direct", 0⟩, where the linenumber is not defined. Additionally, there are four other components identified as targets in in Sections 4.1 and 4.2: `Default.jsp`, `Error.jsp`, `Index.jsp`, and `ResetPassword.jsp`. For the purpose of illustration, we assume that these are analyzable by the approach and also implement the necessary entry points, which leads to edges being added from the user to each of their entry points.

4.4 Combining Control Flow Information

The Inter-Component Control-Flow Graph (ICCFG) includes inter-component and intra-component control flow. Intra-component control flow can be identified by standard techniques for building control flow graphs. Inter-component control flow edges that have a non-zero line number associated with them are added by

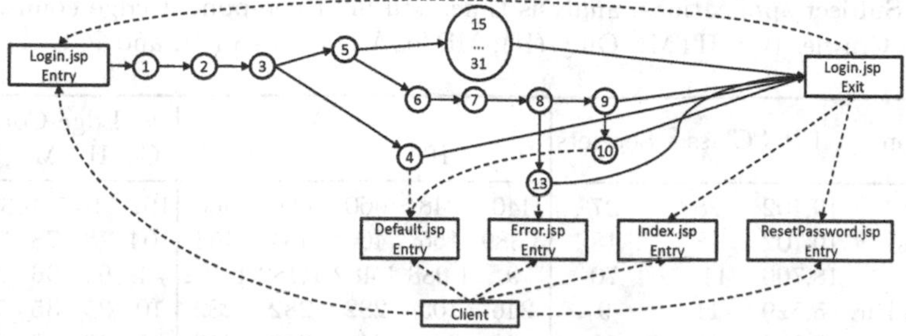

Fig. 3. Inter-component control flow graph for servlet `Login.jsp` shown in Figure 1

specifying that the source of the edge is the node that corresponds to the line number in the source component and connecting it to the edge's destination. Destination edges are connected to the entry node of the target component. In the case of inter-component control flow edges for which there is a zero or undefined line number, their source is the exit point of the source component and the destination is determined the same as edges with defined line numbers. For any edge with the user as the source, a "Client" node is created in the graph and all such edges' source runs from this node to the target component. Control flow edges that are derived from *Component Inclusion* are handled slightly differently in terms of their connection to specific nodes in the traditional control flow graph. The reason for this is that the naive approach to connecting these edges leads to the generation of a cycle at the node that performs the *Component Inclusion*. This would happen because both the outgoing edge and returning edge would be connected to the same node in the source component. To address this, the source node n is split into two corresponding nodes n_{call} and n_{return}. The outgoing edge to the included component is connected at its source to n_{call} and its destination to the entry node of the included component. The corresponding return edge is connected at its source to the exit of the included component and its destination to n_{return}.

The ICCFG for servlet `Login.jsp` is shown in Figure 3. This graph includes the traditional intra-component control flow of the component as solid lines and the inter-component control flow edges as dotted lines. Due to space constraints the control flow edges that go from nodes 4, 10, and 13 to method `sendHttpCmd` are omitted. Additionally, the control flow graphs for `Default.jsp`, `Error.jsp`, `Index.jsp`, and `ResetPassword.jsp` are not included in this example.

5 Evaluation

This section presents the results of an empirical evaluation of the approach. For the evaluation, the author implemented the analysis in a prototype tool, ICE (Inter-component Control-flow Extractor). The accuracy and runtime cost of ICE was compared against web crawling and three static analysis based approaches. The research questions are: **RQ1:** How long does it take to analyze the subject applications using each of the evaluated approaches? **RQ2:** What is the precision of each approach? **RQ3:** What is the recall of each approach?

Table 1. Subject applications, analysis time, and inter-component edge count. Techniques are Crawler (C), HTML Only (H), MiMoSA (M), SXS (S), and ICE (I)

Application	LOC	Classes	Servlets	Time (s)					Edge Count				
				C	H	M	S	I	C	H	M	S	I
Bookstore	19,402	28	27	440	248	660	660	660	192	118	118	368	415
Classifieds	10,702	18	18	3,389	156	464	464	464	104	78	78	174	198
Daffodil	18,706	119	70	9	1,088	1,482	1,482	1,482	31	92	96	96	101
Employee Dir.	5,529	11	9	246	105	282	282	282	10	35	35	51	65
Events	7,164	13	12	288	248	346	346	346	51	46	46	79	91
Filelister	8,671	41	10	6	90	191	191	191	7	19	19	19	160
Portal	16,089	28	27	2,486	262	755	755	755	294	116	116	491	517
Webmail	17,078	81	24	2,822	1,373	1,900	1,900	1,900	56	59	59	59	76

5.1 Experiment Setup

Subject Applications. For the evaluation, a set of eight subjects were analyzed. Details of the applications are shown in Table 1. All of the applications are available as open source. They were chosen because their implementations are a mix of static HTML, JavaScript, Java servlets, and regular Java code.

Implementation of Analyses. ICE was compared against web crawling and three static analysis based techniques. The static analysis based techniques were reimplemented for the evaluation since their original implementations were for PHP based web applications or were still at a prototype stage. Although none of the considered approaches were originally intended for control flow identification, they extract similar types of information and represent the most closely related approaches known to the author.

ICE: The implementation of ICE is in Java and leverages several previously developed program analyses: Soot, for generating control flow graphs; Indus, for data flow information; and JSA for evaluating string expressions. HTMLParser was used to parse the string representing the web pages and JavaScript was analyzed using Rhino.

Crawler: Approaches based on web crawling are well-known and widely-used for analyzing web applications. For this evaluation, two crawling based approaches were combined, CrawlJax [18], a state of the art crawler for AJAX based web applications, and a generic Spider based on VeriWeb [3]. Both approaches are used because preliminary results indicated that they were highly complementary; CrawlJax was better at finding control flow information related to JavaScript commands and Spider was better at finding control flow information that was not represented as a "clickable" unit in the web page. For both approaches, input specifications that allowed them to navigate login screens was provided. For CrawlJax a custom list of "clickable" elements was also provided for each subject application.

HTML Only: This technique is representative of several static analysis based approaches that analyze a web application and identify HTML output [5,19,25]. The computed HTML output is then parsed for control flow constructs. Although it is clear that these techniques will not be able to identify other forms of control flow, it is included since it represents a widely used approach.

SXS: Sun and colleagues propose a static analysis based technique for identifying access control vulnerabilities in PHP based web applications [22]. As part of this technique, they construct a sitemap that models several types of elements that are also relevant for constructing the ICCFG. Their approach handles some *HTTP Commands* related constructs, *Dynamically Generated HTML*, *Component Inclusion*, and *Direct Entry*, but not *JavaScript*.

MiMoSA: Balzarotti and colleagues propose a static analysis based technique for identifying multi-module vulnerabilities in PHP based web applications [2]. As with SXS, the authors must identify certain types of control flow in the web applications in order to discover these vulnerabilities. This control flow modeling includes limited support for *HTTP Commands*, heuristics for links generated by *JavaScript*, *Dynamically Generated HTML*, and *Direct Entry*. There is no support for *Component Inclusion*.

5.2 Experiments

To collect the experiment data, each of the five approaches was run on the eight subject applications. The machine used to run the results was an Intel Core i7@2.8Ghz with 8GB DDR3 RAM running Ubuntu 10.10 with 2GB RAM dedicated to the JVM heap. For each run, Table 1 shows the time for the analysis to execute ("Time") and the size of the edge set ("Edge Count"). Each approach is abbreviated by the first letter of its name.

5.3 Discussion of Results

The timing results in Table 1 show that analysis time varied significantly by application and analysis. Several of the worst run times were generated by Crawler. Even though web crawling is generally a fast technique, Crawljax loads and renders every crawled page, which incurs a high overhead, but is necessary to accurately model the effect of JavaScript. Full static analysis of daffodil and webmail was also very expensive. Investigation of the two applications showed that several large servlets represented pathological worst cases for the analysis, with almost every other line either a

Table 2. Recall (%) of the considered techniques: Crawler (C), HTML Only (H), MiMoSA (M), SXS (S), and ICE (I)

Application	Recall				
	C	H	M	S	I
Bookstore	40	27	27	88	100
Classifieds	50	37	37	87	100
Daffodil	5	91	95	95	100
Empl. Dir.	14	52	52	77	100
Events	56	48	48	86	100
Filelister	1	10	10	10	100
Portal	54	21	21	95	100
Webmail	32	78	78	78	100
Average	32	46	46	77	100

nested branch or output generating statement. Overall though, the results are positive for ICE. For 6/8 applications the runtime was under fifteen minutes and for 2/8 it was under thirty-two minutes. Note that SXS, MiMoSA, and ICE have the same runtime because they use the same implementations of the algorithms in Section 4.1 and 4.2.

The edge count results in Table 1 show that ICE, followed by SXS, consistently had the highest discovered edge count. The Crawler and the two other static analysis approaches each had higher edge counts for half of the subjects. The primary contributing factor to this was whether the application made extensive use of *Component Inclusion*. For Crawler it was trivial to discover these edges because they were present in the crawled page. However, HTML and MiMoSA did not consider the semantics of *Component Inclusion* in their analysis. Bookstore, Classifieds, Events, Employee Directory, and Portal used *Component Inclusion*, which led to Crawler having a higher edge count for four of them. Employee Directory made very limited use of *Component Inclusion* and many of these edges were actually redundant with edges already in the including page.

Table 2 shows recall results for the approaches. ICE had perfect recall; of the remaining approaches, SXS had the highest recall followed by a tie between HTML and MiMoSA, and Crawler last. To explain these results, the distribution of the edges over the different control flow types was analyzed. The primary differentiators between ICE and SXS was that ICE could handle all types of HTTP requests, whereas SXS could only handle HTTP requests related to the 302 response code. The differentiator between SXS and HTML/MiMoSA was primarily SXS' ability to handle *Component Inclusion*. Although MiMoSA is able to handle limited forms of *JavaScript* and *HTTP Commands* control flow, neither of the specific constructs it could handle were prevalent in the applications' code, which explains why there was very little difference between the two approaches. Lastly, there were several reasons for Crawler's low recall. The primary reasons was that many pages required the Crawler to interact with it in specific ways in order to reveal additional response behaviors. Since the Crawler could not randomly guess this, it was generally unable to access these pages. Filelister was particularly low for all approaches, except ICE, because almost 88% of its inter-component control flow was done via *HTTP Commands*. For all applications, all approaches were able to achieve 100% precision.

Overall, the results were very positive for ICE. It was able to discover a more complete set (i.e., higher recall) of control flow than all other approaches, and the runtime of ICE was comparable to the other approaches.

5.4 Threats to Validity

External validity is concerned with whether the results of this evaluation could generalize to other web applications. The primary threat to this validity is that the subject applications do not use as much JavaScript as AJAX based web applications. This threat is mitigated by the fact that most of the JavaScript complexity in AJAX applications is *intra* and not *inter* component control flow.

Regardless, most of this control flow would still be discovered by the technique outlined in Section 4.1 for *JavaScript*. The presence of this type of control flow would not change the results of ICE versus the other static analysis approaches, but could increase the relative number of edges found by Crawler. Also, even though the subject applications are all written in Java, the approach would be generally applicable to other web application frameworks and languages, such as PHP, Perl, or .NET, since all of these provide analogous APIs for sending HTTP commands and generating HTML content.

Internal validity addresses whether the conclusions about ICE's performance can be made based on the experiment design. The primary threat is that the techniques compared against were reimplemented for the study. To reduce this threat, the author made optimistic assumptions about the capability of the other techniques. Case in point, it was assumed that HTML, SXS, and MiMoSA could compute HTML pages as well as ICE and could be extended to handle the broader range of HTML constructs identified in this paper. This means that the performance of SXS and MiMoSA is higher than would be expected in practice because neither technique could properly handle object oriented code in PHP, and MiMoSA, as defined in the original paper, cannot safely handle dynamically generated HTML or HTTP messages.

6 Related Work

Early approaches for identifying control flow were based on the use of web crawlers that traversed the links of a web page, discovering web pages as they went [3,14,23]. More recent approaches add support for the interpretation of client-side JavaScript [17]. However, since they only interact with the web application via its generated HTML pages, they cannot offer any guarantees of completeness with regard to server-side control flow, such as *HTTP Commands* or *Component Inclusion*. Furthermore, it is common for web applications to only display certain pages after interactions that meet specific constraints. Therefore, it is likely the approaches could be incomplete with respect to *Dynamically Generated HTML* and *JavaScript* as well. Other approaches have proposed the use of captured user session data to build models of the target web application [7,13]. However, they can only model portions of the code that have been exercised by users, and would be incomplete with respect to the complete behavior of the web application.

Another large group of approaches uses specifications provided by the developer [1,10,12,15,20]. These specifications are typically provided using a formal language, such as UML or state-based models. These approaches allow developers to capture the *intended* control flow semantics of web applications. The drawback of manual specification is that the intended and actual control flow can differ. Furthermore, the development of complete and precise manual specifications for large web applications can be very time-consuming. Other approaches have proposed the development of new languages and frameworks that make much of the implicit control flow of web applications explicit in the structure and semantics of the language [6,16], but require developers to learn a new language and web application framework.

Other researchers have also proposed the use of static analysis to identify elements of web applications related to control flow. Deng, Frankl, and Wang proposed an early technique that used static analysis to identify link targets and paths through a web application [5]. As compared to the proposed approach, their technique could only be used to discover control flow related to a subset of *Dynamically Generated HTML*. Tonella and Ricca proposed an approach that could identify dynamically generated object programs [25]. This information was used to build web application system dependence graphs that accounted for certain types of control and data flow. As compared to their approach, the proposed approach takes into account a larger set of control flow related constructs on the client and server-side, such as JavaScript and HTTP redirects, and has a more precise method of determining string values based on method summarization and string analysis.

There is also an extensive amount of research that uses control flow related information to verify and test web applications. The proposed approach complements this body of work by providing a more complete mechanism for identifying control flow. For example, several approaches use control flow models to verify or enforce web application behaviors [10–12,26]. Security related approaches could also benefit from the automated control flow generation to more completely check properties related to session handling [6]. Lastly, other approaches use a web crawling based approach to build control flow models of web applications for testing and slicing [21,24] and the use of the proposed approach could increase the effectiveness of these techniques.

7 Conclusion

This paper presents a new technique for automatically identifying control flow in web applications. The technique is based on static analysis and analyzes each component of a web application to identify a wide range of of control flow types. The identified control flow is combined into a new representation, the Inter-Component Control-Flow Graph, which shows both traditional and inter-component control flow. The proposed approach was evaluated in terms of its runtime cost and accuracy of the identified control flow and compared against those achieved using a web crawling based approach and other static analysis based approaches. The results were positive; the proposed approach had a higher level of recall, and precision and runtime costs comparable to the other approaches. Overall, the results indicate that the approach is useful for accurately identifying web application control flow and, as such, could be used to help to improve testing and verification techniques for web applications that require control flow information.

References

1. Andrews, A.A., Offutt, J., Alexander, R.T.: Testing Web Applications by Modeling with FSMs. Software Systems and Modeling **4**(3), 326–345 (2005)
2. Balzarotti, D., Cova, M., Felmetsger, V.V., Vigna, G.: Multi-module vulnerability analysis of web-based applications. In: Proceedings of the 14th ACM Conference on Computer and Communications Security, CCS 2007, pp. 25–35. ACM, New York (2007)
3. Benedikt, M., Freire, J., Godefroid, P.: VeriWeb: automatically testing dynamic web sites. In: Proceedings the International World Wide Web Conference. ACM Press, New York, May 2002
4. Christensen, A.S., Møller, A., Schwartzbach, M.I.: Precise analysis of string expressions. In: Cousot, R. (ed.) SAS 2003. LNCS, vol. 2694, pp. 1–18. Springer, Heidelberg (2003)
5. Deng, Y., Frankl, P., Wang, J.: Testing Web Database Applications. SIGSOFT Software Engineering Notes **29**(5), 1–10 (2004)
6. Desmet, L., Verbaeten, P., Joosen, W., Piessens, F.: Provable protection against web application vulnerabilities related to session data dependencies. IEEE Transactions on Software Engineering **34**(1), 50–64 (2008)
7. Elbaum, S., Rothermel, G., Karre II, S.: Leveraging User-Session Data to Support Web Application Testing. Transactions On. Software Engineering **31**(3), 187–202 (2005)
8. Halfond, W.G.J.: Automated checking of web application invocations. In: Proceedings of the 23rd IEEE International Symposium on Software Reliability Engineering (ISSRE), pp. 111–120. IEEE, New York (2012)
9. Halfond, W.G., Orso, A.: Automated identification of parameter mismatches in web applications. In: Proceedings of the Symposium on the Foundations of Software Engineering, pp. 181–191. ACM, New York (2008)
10. Hallé, S., Ettema, T., Bunch, C., Bultan, T.: Eliminating navigation errors in web applications via model checking and runtime enforcement of navigation state machines. In: Proceedings of the IEEE/ACM International Conference on Automated Software Engineering, ASE 2010, pp. 235–244. ACM, New York (2010)
11. Han, M., Hofmeister, C.: Modeling and verification of adaptive navigation in web applications. In: Proceedings of the 6th International Conference on Web Engineering, ICWE 2006, pp. 329–336. ACM, New York (2006)
12. Han, M., Hofmeister, C.: Relating navigation and request routing models in web applications. In: Engels, G., Opdyke, B., Schmidt, D.C., Weil, F. (eds.) MODELS 2007. LNCS, vol. 4735, pp. 346–359. Springer, Heidelberg (2007)
13. Haydar, M.: Formal framework for automated analysis and verification of web-based applications. In: Proceedings of the 19th IEEE International Conference on Automated Software Engineering, pp. 410–413. IEEE Computer Society, Washington, DC (2004)
14. Huang, Y., Huang, S., Lin, T., Tsai, C.: Web application security assessment by fault injection and behavior monitoring. In: Proceedings of the International World Wide Web Conference, pp. 148–159. ACM, New York (2003)
15. Jia, X., Liu, H.: Rigorous and automatic testing of web applications. In: Proceedings of the International Conference on Software Engineering and Applications, pp. 280–285. ACTA Press, Cambridge, MA (2002)
16. Licata, D., Krishnamurthi, S.: Verifying interactive web programs. In: Proceedings of the International Conference on Automated Software Engineering, pp. 164–173. IEEE Computer Society, Washington, DC (2004)

17. Mesbah, A., Bozdag, E., van Deursen, A.: Crawling ajax by inferring user interface state changes. In: Schwabe, D., Curbera, F., Dantzig, P. (eds.) Proceedings of the International Conference on Web Engineering, pp. 122–134. IEEE Computer Society, Washington, DC (2008)
18. Mesbah, A., van Deursen, A.: Invariant-based automatic testing of ajax user interfaces. In: Proceedings of the 31st International Conference on Software Engineering (ICSE 2009). Research Papers, pp. 210–220. IEEE Computer Society, Washington, DC (2009)
19. Minamide, Y.: Static approximation of dynamically generated web pages. In: Proceedings of the International World Wide Web Conference, pp. 432–441. ACM Press, New York (2005)
20. Ricca, F., Tonella, P.: Analysis and testing of web applications. In: Proceedings of the International Conference on Software Engineering, pp. 25–34. IEEE, Washington, DC (2001)
21. Ricca, F., Tonella, P.: Web application slicing. In: Proceedings of the International Conference on Software Maintenance, pp. 148–157. IEEE Computer Society, Los Alamitos (2001)
22. Sun, F., Xu, L., Su, Z.: Static detection of access control vulnerabilities in web applications. In: Proceedings of the USENIX Security Symposium, p. 1. USENIX Association, Berkeley (2011)
23. Tonella, P., Ricca, F.: Dynamic model extraction and statistical analysis of web applications. In: Proceedings of the Fourth International Workshop on Web Site Evolution, pp. 43–52. IEEE, Washington, DC (2002)
24. Tonella, P., Ricca, F.: A 2-Layer model for the white-box testing of web applications. In: Proceedings of the International Workshop Web Site Evolution, pp. 11–19. IEEE Computer Society, Washington, DC (2004)
25. Tonella, P., Ricca, F.: Web Application Slicing in Presence of Dynamic Code Generation. Automated Software Engineering **12**(2), 259–288 (2005)
26. Yang, J., Huang, J., Wang, F., Chu, W.: Constructing control-flow-based testing tools for web application. In: Proc. of the 11th Software Enginnering and Knowledge Enginnering Conference (SEKE), p. 1. World Scientific Publishing, Singapore (1999)

Deriving Custom Post Types from Digital Mockups

Alfonso Murolo(✉) and Moira C. Norrie

Department of Computer Science, ETH Zurich, 8092 Zurich, Switzerland
{alfonso.murolo,norrie}@inf.ethz.ch

Abstract. Interface-driven approaches to web development often migrate digital mockups defining the presentation, structure and client-side functionality of a website to platforms such as WordPress that manage the content of the website and implement server-side functionality. In the case of data-intensive websites, generation of data types that manage the application-specific content is usually performed manually during the migration process. We propose an approach that allows WordPress custom post types to be derived based on an analysis of sample content used in digital mockups.

Keywords: Digital mockups · Data schemas · Custom post types

1 Introduction

It is common practice to develop websites using an interface-driven approach which starts with mockups of a website and, through a series of steps, adds first client-side and then server-side functionality. In the case of data-intensive websites, at some stage, data types need to be defined and data content added. Mockups provide a basis for communicating with the client to establish agreement not only on the visual appearance of their website, but also the required content and functionality. They frequently start as sketches on paper which are evolved into digital mockups implemented using HTML, CSS and JavaScript.

While filler text such as *lorem ipsum* is often used in mockups to represent content, some developers stress the importance of using real examples of content. Reasons for this include avoiding possible breaks in the design when real content is loaded as well as enhancing discussions with clients about the content to be managed and how it should be displayed. Moreover, it is reported in [1] that clients sometimes appear to feel more in control of the design process when they are presented with real samples of content and more likely to give feedback on the way that content is shown rather than purely the look and feel of the design.

Given estimates that nearly a quarter of the top ten million websites are running on WordPress[1], adding server-side functionality often involves transforming a digital mockup into a WordPress theme. As with other content management

[1] 23.7% according to w3techs.com on 8 Apr 2015.

P. Cimiano et al. (Eds.): ICWE 2015, LNCS 9114, pp. 71–80, 2015.
DOI: 10.1007/978-3-319-19890-3_6

systems (CMS), WordPress provides a generic schema for managing content which, in the case of WordPress, is based on posts and pages. This data schema can be extended with custom post types to manage application-specific data. A number of plugins are available to help users define their custom post types and integrate support into the administrative dashboard for creating and managing the associated data and, in some cases, data dependencies. Researchers have shown how developers could be further assisted by providing a meta-plugin that allows them to define their data schema in terms of an entity-relationship (ER) model and using this to automatically generate bespoke plugins for managing their data [2]. However, as reported in a survey of modern web development practices carried out in 2014 [3], many WordPress developers have no formal education in computer science and are unfamiliar with ER models.

We propose an approach where data types can be generated from sample content used in mockups to further simplify the process of developing data-intensive sites. The process consists of two steps: first generating a conceptual model of data entities based on an analysis of sample content and, second, creating an implementation for that model as WordPress custom post types. The first part is semi-automatic in that users annotate parts of the content and then guide the generation process which is based on automatic matching and clustering techniques. The generation of WordPress custom post types also requires code to be generated for every layer, including the server-side code capable of storing data in the database as well as the GUI to input and edit data. The user can also choose to populate the database with the extracted sample data.

We start with a review of related work in Sect. 2. We then present an overview of the approach in Sect. 3 before outlining our content matching algorithm and process for generating custom post types in Sect. 4. Concluding remarks are given in Sect. 5.

2 Background

Although mockups are widely used in practice, relatively little research has investigated how paper or digital mockups of websites could be used to automate parts of the development process. Within the HCI community, DENIM was an early project that generated simple versions of a website from sketches of pages and storyboards [4]. More recently, some researchers within the web engineering community have proposed tools to automatically generate APIs (MockAPI) [5] and application prototypes (MockDD) [6] from digital mockups in the form of wireframes. In both cases, users annotate the mockups to specify data entities and operations. In the case of MockDD, either a WebML [7] or UWE model [8] is generated and the existing tools associated with these models can then be used to generate the code for the website. In this way, they combine interface-driven and model-driven approaches within the overall development process.

An approach commonly aimed for in practice is the use of a visual editor to create a high-fidelity mockup of a website from which the code can be generated automatically. For example, in the case of WordPress, a number of theme generators are available that allow a user to design their website using a graphical tool and then generate the HTML, CSS, JavaScript and PHP files that define the WordPress site. However, existing theme generators are often restricted in terms of the flexibility and functionality that they offer to users. For example, Templatr[2] offers a fixed set of layouts while Lubith[3] allows users to customise layout but not functionality. Further, they do not provide specific support for data-intensive websites where application-specific data has to be managed.

Our approach is based on high-fidelity mockups that detail not only visual features and functionality of a website but also content. By analysing the samples of real content provided in the mockup, we aim to generate the data schemas and code necessary to create and manage the associated data with a minimum amount of interaction from the user.

The problem of generating data schemas from sample content is closely related to previous work on tools to extract data from web pages - the so-called *deep web*. In this research area, the goal of numerous projects is to generate wrappers that enable data published on dynamically-generated web pages to be extracted and/or queried. Generally, a wrapper uses a set of extraction rules to perform pattern matching over a page. Various approaches exist for generating wrappers—a problem known as *wrapper induction*—and these can be classified according to three main characteristics: the difficulty of the task, the techniques used and the degree of automation [9].

Works such as *NoDoSE* [10], *IEPAD* [11], *DeLa* [12] and *RoadRunner* [13] aim at generating wrappers based on a semi- or fully-automatic analysis of DOM structures and models derived from them, taking one or more pages as input and trying to discover repeating patterns in these pages through regular expressions and clustering. However, these approaches have various drawbacks such as requiring large amounts of data as input, sometimes consisting of groups of pages from the same website, or extensive amounts of user interaction.

The work by Lu et al. [14,15] distinguishes itself from the ones previously mentioned because it proposes a system for aligning and annotating similarly structured data through clustering given a set of data records obtained from queries to website. The main difference here is that they use forms to perform queries on websites for which they want to generate a wrapper, and therefore detect similarities between the query results. This is one of the closest works to ours, however, the main difference is that their goal is to create an annotation wrapper to be used on similar pages of the same website through form inputs, while ours is purely to locate and extract data records within single web pages for use in the development process.

Other works such as ViWER [16] and ViDE [17] propose the use of visual cues to detect data records. An example of visual cues can be the size of bounding boxes of the data records or block trees which segment regions of a page to isolate data records. While these works demonstrate the significance of visual cues, their techniques do not scale well if data records can have an increasng amount of small differences in lower levels of the subtree local to each record, or with the

---

2 http://templatr.cc

3 http://www.lubith.com

increasing amount of data-rich visual block trees. However, we acknowledge the importance of visual cues in the detection process and also use them in our approach.

In summary, while we could build on many ideas from previous research on wrapper induction, none of these methods fully meets our requirements. Further, while their primary goal is to perform content matching to be able to query data published in web pages, our target is to derive custom post types for managing such data and its implementation in WordPress. In the next section, we introduce the approach that we have developed before explaining the techniques we use.

3 Approach

Our tool implements a semi-automated process which requires users to annotate parts of the sample data content in a digital mockup. For example, assume a user is developing a website for a research group where one of the pages will list publications. In the digital mockup, a real sample of content would be provided, as shown in Fig. 1. A user can then annotate parts of that data by selecting an element with the mouse and labelling it. For example, for the first publication in the list, they might label the first author, the title and the conference as denoted by labels with a solid border.

After labelling, the user invokes the matching process and the tool searches for similar examples, propagating the labelling to all similar data items found. The system generated labels are shown in Fig. 1 with a dashed border. Note that, as part of this matching process, fields which have more than one occurrence (e.g. *author* in a publication) are also detected and labelled.

The overall process involves performing incremental matching from different parts of the digital mockup until all sample content of application-specific data has been labelled. Once this has been done, conceptual data types for the

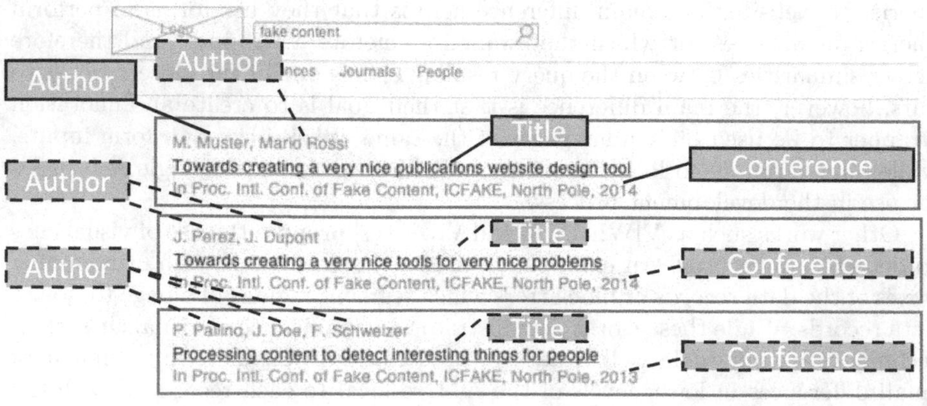

Fig. 1. Matching sample data in an HTML mockup

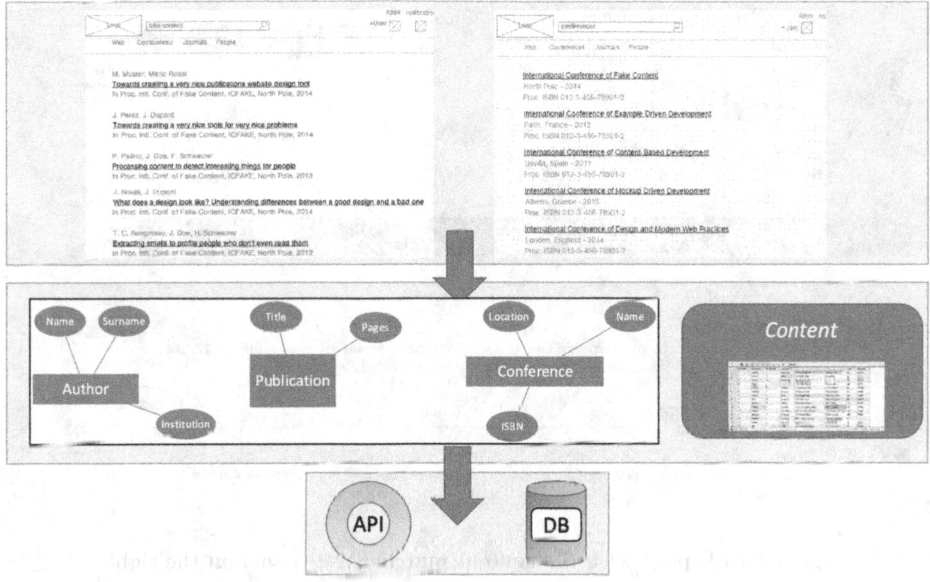

Fig. 2. Derivation of WordPress custom post types from sample data content

website are generated as indicated in Fig. 2. In a second step, the tool generates an implementation of these data types as WordPress custom post types. This involves the generation of an API, which allows basic CRUD operations, together with the required elements of the user interface required to allow users to perform data management. We note that WordPress custom post types are simpler than relational data schemas, since there is no support for relationships. However, we are currently investigating techniques for detecting relationships between entities and implementing them in WordPress in order to be able to handle more general database schemas in the future.

The results of the matching process may not always work as well as the example shown in Fig. 1 on the first attempt. For this reason, the user is offered a control panel as shown in Fig. 3 where they can experiment with various settings until they get the desired result (e.g. adjustable tolerance levels to potentially enlarge the set of matched records at the cost of increasing false positives). We explain this using a second example where the sample content comes from an existing website rather than a mockup. Since there is no real distinction technically between a digital mockup of a website and an actual website, the same process can be applied to examples of existing websites that meet the criteria of parts of the website under development, thereby supporting a design-by-example paradigm. For instance, the DBLP website[4] could be used to provide an example of a site with a list of publications and it would even be possible to extract the data to populate the database of the website under development.

[4] http://dblp.uni-trier.de/

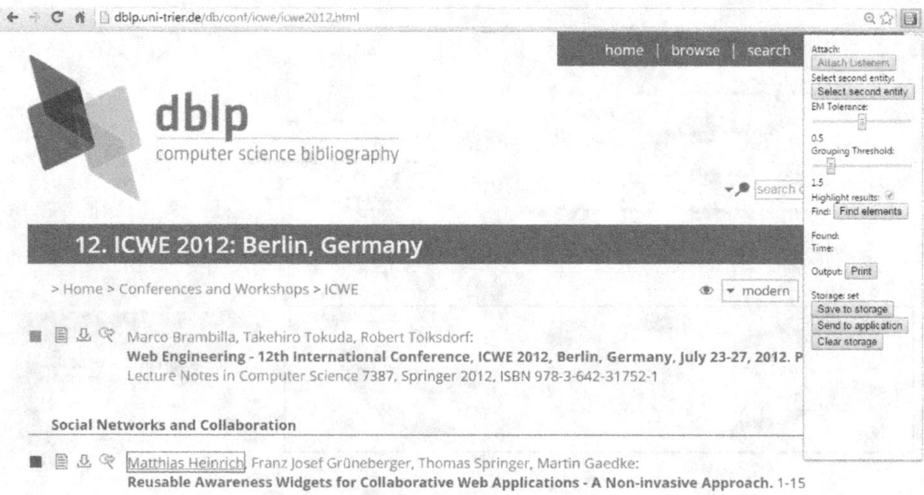

Fig. 3. DBLP page with the content matcher user panel on the right

In such a use case, the user would load the page and start annotating elements as shown in Fig. 3. The elements that can be annotated are highlighted as the user moves the cursor over them. The users might select and label a single author as indicated in Fig. 3. Assume they then also label a single title and a page reference in proceedings.

The user can then start the matching process. In this example, although the user annotated only the first author, all the authors are correctly matched as similar and labelled by the system. Fig. 4 shows a screenshot after the matching process. Each publication is recognised as a data unit as indicated by the shading

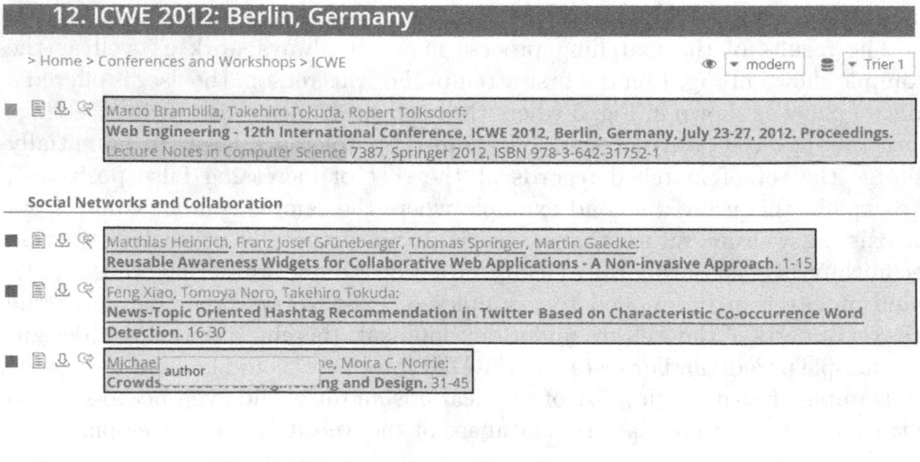

Fig. 4. Content matching results

and the elements underlined are the ones that have been labelled either by the user or the system. We can see therefore that all authors have been individually labelled. The user can inspect the labels by moving the cursor over the elements.

However, there are parts of the data that are not underlined which means that the system has successfully distinguished these as different from the labelled elements. For example, it recognises that *Lecture Notes in Computer Science* is neither an author nor a title based on various factors such as the form, the position and the presentation of the element, but has no way of determining what kind of entity it is. When the user detects errors in the identification of elements and their labelling, as well as incomplete coverage, they can then refine the process through a combination of annotating additional elements and experimenting with settings in the control panel that will be explained in the next section when we describe the matching algorithm.

All of the matched content, together with its detected structure, is sent to a WordPress plug-in that we have developed. This plug-in creates the custom post types along with the corresponding UI and server-side PHP code to manage the default CRUD operations. Once the generation has been completed, the generated PHP files can be embedded directly into a WordPress theme enabling the corresponding data to be created and managed through the administrative dashboard.

4 Algorithm

As described in the previous section, the matching process requires the user to first label individual fields of a data record. To minimise the demand on users, our goal was that they should only have to label parts of a sample data record such as the first occurrence of a repeated field, for example the first author in the list of authors of a publication, before starting the matching process.

The matching process is divided into various steps and it makes use of both structural and visual cues in several of the steps. We will now explain each step in turn.

1. **Record boundaries detection.** The preliminary phase starts by detecting the boundaries of the annotated data record. Once the labelled fields are stored, the matcher starts to look for a least common ancestor (LCA) for these fields. A least common ancestor is the closest node in the hierarchy that is an ancestor for all of the elements labelled by the user. Our algorithm performs best when each data record has a different LCA. However, this cannot be guaranteed in every possible case. There can be template-generated pages that will not necessarily have a unique LCA for every data record. We will provide details on how our algorithm behaves in such cases later in this section.
2. **Finding similar records.** Once the boundaries of the first record have been found, the algorithm has identified a DOM subtree similar to that of similar data records in the page, modulo some differences that will be record-specific. This phase starts retrieving all the elements in the page which have the same

HTML tag as the LCA, and compares their subtrees with the subtree with the LCA as root. To obtain a measure of the difference between two subtrees, we use an approximation algorithm called pq-gram distance [18], which calculates the tree edit distance problem efficiently. For each subtree, we calculate the pq-gram distance and compare it against a threshold called the *tolerance factor*. If the distance is less than this factor, we consider this subtree a possible match. At this stage, completely different elements which have a structure similar enough to be matched by the approximation algorithm would be part of the set of matched subtrees as false positives, so we next need to try and exclude them.

3. **Cross-record propagation.** We now propagate the labels specified by the user across all the matched records. We have to make sure we can replicate the user's selection in each subtree through XPath-based relative paths. If we are unable to replicate the selection, we remove the current subtree from the matched collection. On the contrary, if we can manage to replicate all of the user's selections in the current subtree, we keep it as a true positive.
4. **Local label propagation.** At this stage, each of the subtrees which has been recognised as similar contains the labelling made by the user and can be considered as a data record. We now aim at replicating the labels to all the elements which have a similar meaning, for example all authors of a publication within an identified publication data record. To do so, we use agglomerative hierarchical clustering. For each data record, we group siblings of the labelled elements according to a *distance function*, and use a complete linkage criterion between the clusters. As a stopping criterion for the hierarchical clustering, we check the distance between the clusters against a threshold, called the *grouping factor*. The distance function $dist(x, y)$ takes into consideration various factors which can be both visual and structural cues, namely:
   - The tag equality ϕ. Let t_1 and t_2 be the tags of the elements x and y, respectively. The tag equality is 1 if $t_1 == t_2$; otherwise, it is 0.
   - The structural tag discontinuity score Δ_t, which increases as the elements are further away, separated by elements of a different tag.
   - The field discontinuity score Δ_f, which increases as the elements between those being compared have been labelled as different fields.
   - The *style distance ratio* Δ_s as a measure of the distance between x and y in terms of their visual cues. It is defined as the following ratio:

     $$\Delta_s = \frac{\Delta_{css}}{max(\Delta_{css} + S, 1)}$$

     where Δ_{css} is the number of CSS rules which differ between the two elements being considered, and S is the number of CSS rules which are similar.

   Then, the distance function is calculated as follows:

   $$dist(x, y) := \Delta_s + \phi(t_1, t_2) + max(\Delta_t, \Delta_f)$$

   Since this distance function is used in hierarchical clustering, the elements which are considered to be very similar in structural and visual terms, and which happen to be presented in a contiguous fashion (e.g. all the links to the authors may be presented one after the other) will be put into the same cluster. If the elements are instead discontiguous, or are elements of a different type (e.g. ANCHOR or SPAN), the distance will be increased. We now need to decide which label should be applied to a cluster and this is done by majority voting. Each element in the cluster will have the chance to be counted as a vote for the corresponding label, if it has one. However, if it does not have one, the element will not be considered in the vote.

It could happen that the elements in the page appear to be visually separated in the browser, but have an LCA in common with all of the data records. The above algorithm would fail to identify a unique LCA for a data record, and the whole procedure might fail to correctly identify the other data records. In such a case, we need the user to specify a second example data record. This would allow the system to detect that the LCA for the two data records is the same element, and therefore they belong to the same subtree. However, the matching algorithm does more than just fault detection. We have developed a pattern matcher which behaves as a regular expression matcher for DOM elements. We can create a regular expression which, based on the user's selection, tries to detect the boundaries of a data record within the siblings. For example, we can create a regular expression which can detect a sequence of "one or more A elements followed by one or more SPAN elements". Once the boundaries of each data record in the page have been detected, we can artificially modify the DOM and create an element which will act as an LCA for each of them.

5 Conclusion

We have presented a method for deriving custom post types from digital mockups of websites with real samples of content. Although our primary aim was to support interface-driven development, the method also supports a design-by-example paradigm where users can base their design on parts of existing web sitse with similar data content.

We are currently investigating generalisations of the approach to support more powerful schema paradigms, such as relational schemas based on entity-relationship models. This involves the detection of more complex schema structures that involve relationships or aggregations, together with a collection mechanism which can incrementally match multiple data types and can be exploited to infer relationships. Additionally, we want to consider even more hybrid approaches in terms of structural and visual cues that can be considered while performing element clustering. We also plan to extend support for HTML text nodes which can be a challenge when detecting data records in HTML mockups or websites. Alongside these extensions and enhancements of the current method, we want to generalise the architecture of our tool to support the generation of data schemas and server-side APIs for target platforms other than WordPress so that it could be applied more generally to web application development.

References

1. Blakeley-Silver, T.: WordPress 2.8 Theme Design: Create Flexible, Powerful, and Professional Themes for Your WordPress Blogs and Websites. Packt Publishing Ltd. (2009)
2. Leone, S., de Spindler, A., Norrie, M.C.: A meta-plugin for bespoke data management in wordpress. In: Wang, X.S., Cruz, I., Delis, A., Huang, G. (eds.) WISE 2012. LNCS, vol. 7651, pp. 580–593. Springer, Heidelberg (2012)
3. Norrie, M.C., Di Geronimo, L., Murolo, A., Nebeling, M.: The forgotten many? a survey of modern web development practices. In: Casteleyn, S., Rossi, G., Winckler, M. (eds.) ICWE 2014. LNCS, vol. 8541, pp. 290–307. Springer, Heidelberg (2014)
4. Newman, M.W., Lin, J., Hong, J.I., Landay, J.A.: DENIM: An Informal Web Site Design Tool inspired by Observations of Practice. Human-Computer Interaction **18**(3) (2003)
5. Rivero, J.M., Heil, S., Grigera, J., Gaedke, M., Rossi, G.: MockAPI: an agile approach supporting API-first web application development. In: Daniel, F., Dolog, P., Li, Q. (eds.) ICWE 2013. LNCS, vol. 7977, pp. 7–21. Springer, Heidelberg (2013)
6. Rivero, J.M., Grigera, J., Rossi, G., Luna, E.R., Montero, F., Gaedke, M.: Mockup-Driven Development: Providing Agile Support for Model-Driven Web Engineering. Information and Software Technology **56**(6) (2014)
7. Ceri, S., Fraternali, P., Bongio, A., Brambilla, M., Comai, S., Matera, M.: Designing Data-Intensive Web Applications. Morgan Kaufmann (2002)
8. Hennicker, R., Koch, N.: A UML-Based methodology for hypermedia design. In: Evans, A., Caskurlu, B., Selic, B. (eds.) UML 2000. LNCS, vol. 1939, pp. 410–424. Springer, Heidelberg (2000)
9. Chang, C., Kayed, M., Girgis, M.R., Shaalan, K.F.: A Survey of Web Information Extraction Systems. IEEE Transactions on Knowledge and Data Engineering **18**(10) (2006)
10. Adelberg, B.: NoDoSE a tool for semi-automatically extracting structured and semistructured data from text documents. In: Proc. 9th ACM SIGMOD Intl. Conf. on Management of Data (SIGMOD). ACM (1998)
11. Chang, C., Lui, S.: IEPAD: information extraction based on pattern discovery. In: Proc. 10th Intl. Conf. on World Wide Web (WWW). ACM (2001)
12. Wang, J., Lochovsky, F.H.: Data extraction and label assignment for web databases. In: Proc. 12th Intl. Conf. on World Wide Web (WWW). ACM (2003)
13. Crescenzi, V., Mecca, G., Merialdo, P.: Roadrunner: towards automatic data extraction from large web sites. In: Proc. 27th Intl. Conf. on Very Large Data Bases (VLDB). Morgan Kaufmann (2001)
14. Lu, Y., He, H., Zhao, H., Meng, W., Yu, C.: Annotating structured data of the deep web. In: Proc. 23rd Intl. Conf. on Data Engineering (ICDE). IEEE (2007)
15. Lu, Y., He, H., Zhao, H., Meng, W., Yu, C.: Annotating Search Results from Web Databases. IEEE Transactions on Knowledge and Data Engineering **25**(3) (2013)
16. Hong, J.L., Siew, E., Egerton, S.: ViWER-Data extraction for search engine results pages using visual cue and dom tree. In: Proc. 1st Intl. Conf. on Information Retrieval & Knowledge Management (CAMP). IEEE (2010)
17. Liu, W., Meng, X., Meng, W.: Vide: A Vision-Based Approach for Deep Web Data Extraction. IEEE Transactions on Knowledge and Data Engineering **22**(3) (2010)
18. Augsten, N., Böhlen, M., Gamper, J.: Approximate matching of hierarchical data using Pq-Grams. In: Proc. 31st Intl. Conf. on Very Large Data Bases (VLDB), VLDB Endowment (2005)

Asqium: A JavaScript Plugin Framework for Extensible Client and Server-Side Components

Vasileios Triglianos(✉) and Cesare Pautasso

Faculty of Informatics, University of Lugano (USI), Lugano, Switzerland
{vasileios.triglianos,cesare.pautasso}@usi.ch
http://asq.inf.usi.ch/

Abstract. JavaScript has become a language for programming complex Web applications, whose logic is deployed across both Web browsers and Web servers. Current software packaging mechanisms for JavaScript enable a basic level of modularity and reuse. However, they have not yet reached full maturity in terms of enabling system extensions with features contributed as third-party plugins, while encapsulating them adequately. In this paper we present a novel plugin system for JavaScript applications, which integrate Node.js modules with HTML5 Web Components. It provides abstractions for: real time and loosely coupled communication between front-end and back-end components, persistent state storage, and isomorphic usage of JavaScript. Plugins can use hooks and events to contribute functionality and embed it into the main application flow, while respecting the common asynchronous non-blocking programming paradigm of JavaScript. We demonstrate the expressiveness of the framework as it is used to build ASQ: an open, extensible educational Web platform.

1 Introduction

Engineering extensible Web applications that span across the server and the client tiers is a challenging task, which can be alleviated by introducing a suitable plugin system. Reusable plugins [1] can thus be properly packaged to be deployed to extend both tiers of the Web application, despite limitations of the current Web technology platform. One limitation is the mismatch between the front and back-end programming languages for implementing the business logic. With the advent of Node.js, a JavaScript runtime environment for server-side applications, the full stack of the application logic can be written in one language. However, using one language for both the client- and server-side components of a plugin is not adequate on its own to efficiently develop, deploy, version and publish the plugin components so that they can be executed on their corresponding hosts. Another issue related to the double scope of such a plugin system is the asynchronous, event-based communication between the client- and server-side components of the plugin.

On the front-end, the main objective is to create encapsulated components, also known as widgets, that may feature User Interface and/or some

P. Cimiano et al. (Eds.): ICWE 2015, LNCS 9114, pp. 81–98, 2015.
DOI: 10.1007/978-3-319-19890-3_7

business logic implemented using HTML5, CSS, and respectively JavaScript. Until recently, Web front-end technologies (e.g., AngularJS, jQuery) dealt poorly with CSS styles and Javascript encapsulation: CSS styles and JavaScript global variables often bled, unintentionally affecting markup and code that was not in the original scope of the author.

On the server-side, the existing Node package manager (`npm`) mechanism for modularizing, packaging and distributing Node.js modules only ensures their dependencies are satisfied. A complete plugin system would provide additional Application Programming Interfaces (API) to interact with the core of the application featuring decoupled interfaces, event-based communication, performance isolation and failure containment, ease of deployment, avoidance of code repetition, all in compliance with the hosting system's conventions and data flow.

While some of the problems mentioned in this section have individual solutions, in this paper we present the first approach that, to our knowledge, implements a JavaScript based plugin system for the client and the server that offers a unified and integrated solution to all of these problems.

The work is motivated by the needs of the ASQ platform [2]. ASQ is a research platform offering a Web-based lecture delivery system that aims to provide presenters with awareness of the audience's comprehension of the presented material. The flow of an ASQ presentation involves presenting slides, asking questions, gathering real time feedback and discussing the results in class; we call this the 'present-ask-answer-assess-feedback' cycle. Questions are an integral part of ASQ, and one of the early design decisions was to allow content authors to create custom question types that can fit into the existing flow and extend it with new functionality, hence the need for a powerful plugin system to make the platform versatile and extensible.

The rest of this paper is structured as follows. In Section 2 we present the main requirements for extensible Web applications. Section 3 discusses the architecture and implementation details of the proposed plugin system, while the motivation for this work and a case study follow in section 4. Finally, we present the state of the art in Section 5 and we conclude this paper with an overview of future research directions for this work in Section 6.

2 Design Goals

From our experience with the design of ASQ and after analyzing the architecture of several modern Web applications featuring real-time updates, we have collected the following required characteristics that should be satisfied by a plugin system to enhance the extensibility of the Web application.

Application Domain Compliance. The domain of each application dictates the respective entities and their privileges, the flow of information between them and the security constraints that govern them. Plugins should adhere to these constraints rules. As an example, in the case of ASQ, the presenter is in control of information flow which follows variations of the *present-ask-answer-assess-feedback* cycle. A plugin that would automatically show assessment results without the presenter's consent would violate the domain rules.

Open Event Model. Since plugins extend the application with new functionality, it is likely that they may introduce new events which may not be part of the existing 'information flow' events of the application. While the latter are expected to be gracefully handled by a plugin, it is also very important to be able to extend the possible events exchanged within an application with custom ones, as long as they do not violate the main application flow.

Persistence Flexibility. Web applications often use more than one storage technology to tailor the way different parts of their data model are managed. For example, some aggregation operation is performed on some data and the extracted result gets propagated to the clients in real-time; similarly we may also store the raw data for deferred processing. These could result in using a simple fast in-memory key-value storage and slower document-based disk storage respectively. Plugins should be able to take advantage of both strategies.

Encapsulation and Theming. While encapsulation seems like an obvious desirable characteristic which is readily available by most modern programming languages and Web frameworks, until recently it was very hard to create encapsulated front-end components due to limitations of the HTML/CSS platform. Even if the component authors are careful enough to use high specificity CSS selectors there is no guarantee that the rest of the third-party style rules present in a page will not target the widget markup. To avoid bleeding JavaScript global variables [3], developers may choose to use closures. But this approach will make it harder to expose functionality of their widget to third-party code. Some of these problems have workarounds that fail to conceal the fact that JavaScript was not designed for large scale applications. For example the CommonJS and AMD[1] standards allow better encapsulation of JavaScript code at the cost of precompilation which negates the role of JavaScript as an interpreted language. Theming could make matters worse, since rules should either be very specific, which leads to hard-to-maintain codebases; or generic which could result in unintentional style rule leaks towards non-target elements.

Isomorphism. Developing isomorphic [4] Web applications has the benefits of using the same code both on the front-end and the back-end, a milder learning curve for new developers, better communication between front-end and back-end teams and smaller technology stack. JavaScript is the de-facto browser language and demonstrates good asynchronous performance server-side which renders it an ideal candidate for isomorphic applications.

Easy Deployment and Publication. As any piece of software, plugins may go through many iterations and releases, undergoing common steps such as: testing the code in isolation, followed by functional testing within the host system. If everything is complete in terms of target features and successful testing, the plugin gets released so that its users can update to the latest version. This process

[1] Asynchronous Module Definition.

can be tiresome and error prone since there are many file transfers involved and a lot points of failure: moving code between the plugin's source code directory, which in most cases is under some kind of revision control, and the target host system; deploying to remote servers; separating the client-side from the server-side components; and ensuring the compatibility of different versions in plugin-to-plugin dependencies. Streamlining these processes can help both plugin developers and consumers.

3 Plugin Architecture

In this section we present the architecture of our plugin system, asqium, and how it fulfills the design goals of the previous section (Table 1). The proposed design tries to strike a balance between expressiveness and compliance. An increasingly popular approach to achieve expressive freedom without sacrificing compliance to domain constraints is the curation (or screening) of plugins by a dedicated curator team or directly by the community that consumes the plugins [5]. This shifts the weight from the architectural design to the publishing process thus, resulting in less restrictive APIs where most of the restrictions' focus is on creating plugins that are safe (for example to prevent them, where possible, from accidentally deleting data or unintentionally slowing down the User Interface) rather than secure.

The server-side architectural units of our design are: the core and its exposed APIs, the proxy objects and the plugins. The core implements APIs to be consumed by plugins and a very minimal set of business logic. The majority of business logic that is fundamental to the operation of the system is implemented as bundled plugins, as opposed to optional extensions that are implemented as third-party plugins. The exposed APIs are hooks, events, database and settings. The hooks end events APIs undertake the duty of communication and message passing. The database API gives access to the models and the persistence stores of the application. The settings API allows plugins to store and access settings information for a wide range of system and plugin related tasks. Proxy objects act as the interface to the core APIs. The back-end components of a plugin are Node.js modules. On the client-side we distinguish the Event middleware, the core application and the plugins. The core application implements the information flow of the application. It is in control of the WebSocket layer and is also responsible for establishing the initial communication with the front-end components of plugins. The front-end components of plugins are based on the Web Components technology. For the rest of the paper, in the context of plugin components, 'modules' refers to back-end components and 'Web Components' to front-end components (Fig. 1).

3.1 Server-Side Plugins

Server plugins are implemented as npm modules. The only mandatory dependency from the plugin system is extending a base class which offers some conveniences for the developers like declarative mapping of hook names to callbacks

Table 1. Architectural Decisions and Design Goals

Design Goal	Architectural Decisions for Plugins
Application Domain Compliance	Curation of plugins by the community. Hooks to support the information flow of the application.
Open Event Model	Front-end and back-end code of plugins can exchange custom event types.
Persistence Flexibility	Implementation-agnostic persistence API.
Encapsulation and Theming	Web components mitigate the problem of CSS and Javascript bleeding. Custom elements like `core-style` can be shared across plugins to support theming.
Isomorphism	Business logic in both client and server implemented in Javascript
Easy Deployment and Publication	Single repository for both the front- and back-end. Front-end component installed with bower. Back-end component installed with npm.

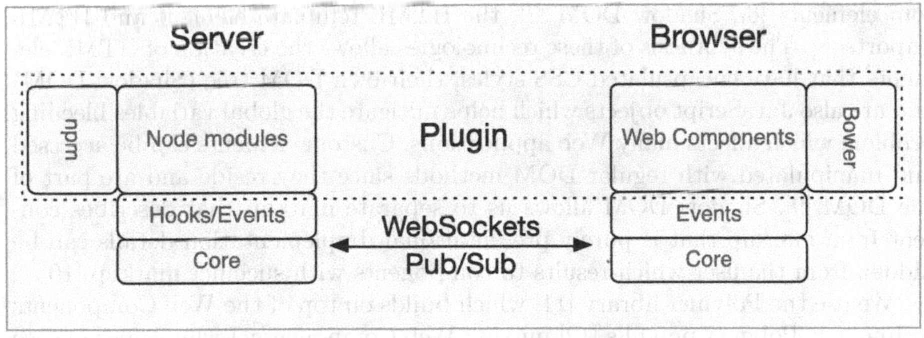

Fig. 1. Plugin structure: Back-end modules and Front-end Web components

and lifecycle methods. There are four lifecycle methods: `install`, `uninstall`, `activate` and `deactivate`, which are called from core when a system user tries to perform one of the corresponding actions. This allows plugins to perform tasks like creating settings, populating the persistent store or performing cleanup.

Proxy Object. Proxy objects are used as a single façade interface between plugin modules and the host system. A proxy object (Fig. 2) exposes all the available APIs that a plugin may use to interface with the core, like hooks, events, settings and database APIs. The implementation of a proxy object is provided by the core. Each time the core instantiates a plugin, it passes the plugin constructor a new instance of a proxy object. Conversely, the core does not directly call methods on plugins: instead it executes hooks or publishes events to which the plugin can subscribe. This ensures that the core remains decoupled from the plugins.

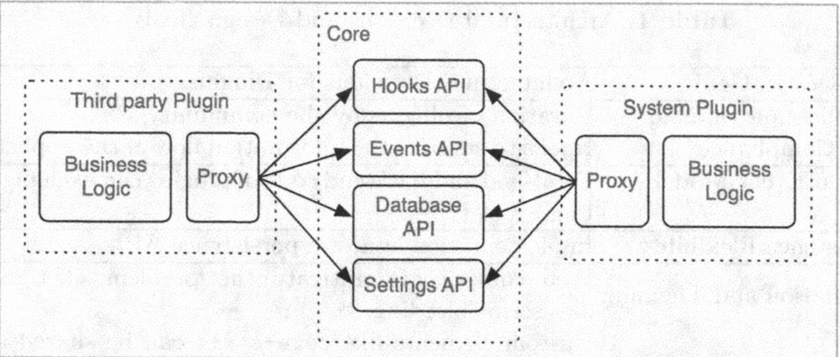

Fig. 2. Proxy object used as the entry point façade for the plugin contributed business logic to access the core APIs

3.2 Front-End Components

Web Components is an umbrella term covering four Web Technologies: Custom elements [6], Shadow DOM [7], the HTML template element and HTML imports [8]. The synthesis of these technologies allows the creation of HTML elements that have encapsulated CSS styles, their own DOM tree (Shadow DOM) and are also JavaScript objects which helps mitigate the global variables bleeding problem which affects many Web applications. Custom elements can be accessed and manipulated with regular DOM methods since they reside and are part of the DOM [9]. Shadow DOM allows us to separate markup that describes content from markup that is purely presentational. Implementation details can be hidden from the user which results to components with succinct markup [10].

We use the Polymer library [11] which builds on top of the Web Components technology. Polymer polyfills [12] missing Web Components Technologies in case they are not available in a browser and adds some functionalities like databinding and declarative element registration. A typical Web Component defines one or more Custom Elements that encapsulate the User Interface and front-end business logic of the plugin. The plugin subscribes and publishes events to communicate with the rest of the application. Thus, the only dependency between front-end components and the front-end core of the application is the pub/sub implementation which is already present in the form of the EventTarget interface that most DOM Elements implement.

3.3 Communication and Message Passing

Server-Side. We distinguish two modes of server-side task execution and discuss the corresponding communication patterns between participating plugins to accomplish them:

1. **Input Transformation Tasks with Completion Acknowledgement.** These are tasks where each participating plugin applies a transformation to some input. The result is passed to the next participating plugin until there is no plugin

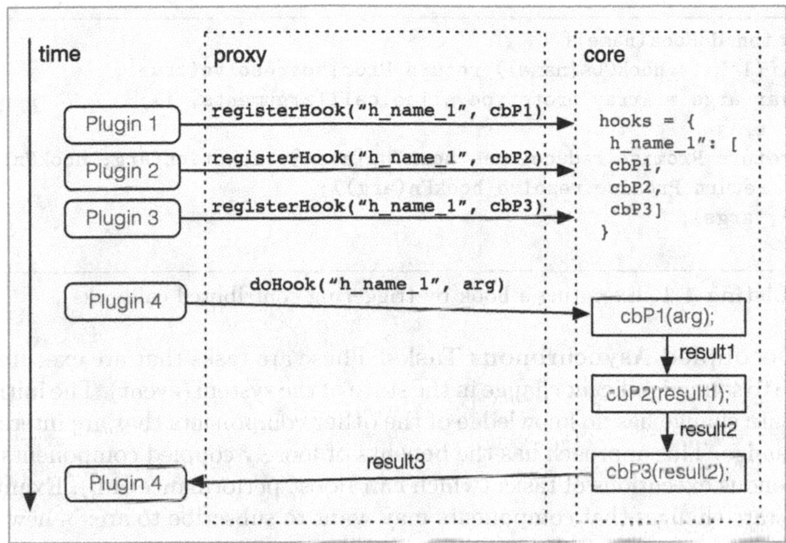

Fig. 3. Hook lifecycle: registration and chained invocation

left in which case the final output is returned to the initiator of the task. Here we only consider the case where order is not important. Participating components can process these tasks in parallel or asynchronously. This is because all participating components are operating on the same data which can lead to unexpected results. Nevertheless, a plugin may execute asynchronous code, which is encouraged for I/O operations, as long as it returns control to the callee when it has finished execution in order to proceed with the next plugin. This can be implemented with callbacks and/or Promises [13]. Examples of such tasks are: knowing when an answer from a student has been processed and persisted to the database in order to update progress information; composing a piece of information that needs to be sent as part of a single HTTP response to the client, like the head of an HTML document.

To target this type of execution, we implemented a hook system. The hook system allows plugins to register for a hook providing the name of the hook and the function (callback) to be invoked when this hook is executed. Hooks identify specific tasks of the Application that require sequential execution and result passing between chained invocations of logic that is contributed by one or more plugins. Hook callbacks have an arity of one, with the only argument being the result of the previous callback execution for the same hook. The initial value for the argument is provided from the initiator of the hook execution similar to a reduce function. Any plugin can initiate a hook execution and any plugin can register. The `doHook` function in Listing 1.1 executes all callbacks for a specific hook. Notice the use of `Promise.reduce` that waits for each task to return either a Promise or a value and then continues with the next callback.

```
function doHook(name){
    if(! this.hookCbs[name]) return Promise.resolve(true);
    var args = Array.prototype.slice.call(arguments, 1);
    //execute callbacks sequentially
    return Promise.reduce(this.hookCbs[name], function(arg, hookFn){
      return Promise.resolve(hookFn(arg));
    }, args);
}
```

Listing 1.1. Executing a hook by triggering contributed callbacks

2. **Decoupled Asynchronous Tasks.** These are tasks that are executed as response to some significant change in the state of the system (event). The initiator of the state change has no knowledge of the other components that are interested in the change. This approach has the benefits of loosely coupled components and asynchronous executions of tasks (which can boost performance [14]). Examples of such state changes that components may want to subscribe to are: 'a new user has come online' or 'a checkbox was ticked'. Event notifications are produced and propagated with message passing according to the pub/sub pattern. A plugin subscribes for an event which may be triggered from the core or other plugins. The dispatcher of the event has no expectations for a completion acknowledgement or some result to be returned. Event-based communication is encouraged in JavaScript development since there's native support in both the server (Node.js - EventEmitter) and the client (DOM - EventTarget).

Client-Side. Our approach is to use pub/sub style communication for plugins and the core using an EventEmitter-like library, and within the plugins a combination of DOM events communication and method invocation. The reason we do not use EventTarget DOM elements as event producers and consumers for non-DOM-related events is to maintain a uniform (isomorphic) interface for event creation and handling across both modules and Web Components. More in detail, the host application awaits for all plugins to be instantiated by listening for a `polymer-ready` event (Listing 1.2). Then it dispatches through the `document` an `app-ready` event for which plugins should have a listener for. As a payload to the event message is the EventEmitter instance that is going to be used as the event bus of the whole application. Plugins can subsequently publish/subscribe to events on the EventEmitter instance (Listing 1.3). The `app-ready` event is the only document dispatched event between a plugin and the application. The rest of the communication is carried out through the EventEmitter.

```
var eventBus = new EventEmitter2();
document.addEventListener("polymer-ready", function(){
  var event = new CustomEvent('app-ready', { 'detail': {appEventBus : eventBus} });
  document.dispatchEvent(event);
});
```

Listing 1.2. Seeding the EventEmitter instance to front-end plugins

```
document.addEventListener('app-ready', function(evt){
    evt.detail.appEventBus.on('asq:question_type',
        this.onQuestionType.bind(this));
}.bind(this));
```

Listing 1.3. A front-end plugin receiving the EventEmitter instance and using it to subscribe for events

Server-Client Plugin Communication. Real-time Web applications establish low-latency, low-overhead bidirectional communication streams between client and server through WebSockets. Plugins from both sides register for events on an intermediate layer that receives events from the WebSockets layer. The intermediate layer is tasked with filtering events and only re-emitting those that can be consumed by plugins. An EventEmitter-like instance is used to publish or subscribe to events. To send custom messages to the server, Web components use dedicated events, specifying their unique plugin name in the ‘type‘ field of the event. This ensures that modules will process this event since they can subscribe to receive it.

Server generated events targeted to client counterparts of a plugin use the same event structure but an extended identification mechanism. The rationale behind this is that there can be many connected clients that have an instance of the target Web Component and that may be in the scope of a specific event. For example a user may have opened two instances of our application in two separate browser windows; or we may want to target all users that have a specific role in our application, e.g. all the administrators. Our system uses the Socket.IO library to provide WebSocket functionality which allows grouping socket connections in rooms and namespaces [15]. This allows a server plugin to easily target logically grouped clients. Listing 1.9 demonstrates a simple use case of this pattern where a server-side plugin emits an event which targets its client-side counterpart running on clients that belong to the `ctrl` event namespace.

3.4 Persistence

The persistence APIs and behaviour is designed under the assumption that the persistence layer comprises schema-less document or key-value stores like MongoDB and Redis. Enforcing the schema of the data is possible, and recommended, at the business logic layer.

API Interface. Proxy objects provide plugins with an interface to the data stores used by the core. The interface is intended to help to accelerate common development tasks for plugins and mitigate common pitfalls. In our experience, a plugin usually needs two types of persistent data. The first concerns general settings for controlling the plugins' behaviour, for example: activated vs deactivated states, options of the control panel of the plugin, or general configuration options. RDBMS-based applications offer one or more tables dedicated to this cause. RDBMS require data stored in tables to conform to strict schemas.

A common strategy to enable storage of arbitrary data in a single table, is to serialize all data types, including hashmaps and arrays, into strings. Such a concession is not required in document based databases, therefore all types of setting data from all plugins and the core can be stored in one collection (the equivalent of a table)[2].

The second type is data for the plugin business logic. In this case plugin data may either share the same structure as the core generated data or introduce new structures. Again, small mismatches in similar data can be mitigated, as we will demonstrate in the evaluation section, by the schema-less nature of document stores; allowing the plugins to share the same collections as the core. There are cases however, where plugins need to store data that are unrelated with the existing data. In such cases plugins can create their own collections.

Schema and Data Migration. Plugins for traditional Relational Database Management Systems (RDBMS) usually have some logic that migrates the schema and stored data of related database tables from one version of the plugin to another. A lot of modern document based or key-value stores are schemaless and as such there is no need for schema migration. However, for simplicity, data should be kept consistent in structure, so a data migration plan remains necessary. Migration operations can be performed during the `install` lifecycle method of a plugin.

3.5 Plugin Isolation

At runtime, a plugin's code should run in isolation from the code of other plugins and in case of failure, if possible, it should not cause the rest of the application to fail as well. To minimize dependencies and thus the possibility for failures the only way a plugin can interface with the core is through the proxy object instance. The event and hooks systems are agnostic of the presence of plugins. All lifecycle methods of plugin modules that are called from the core are contained in try-catch blocks. This holds true for hooks as well: when a hook is executed the code that initiates the hook execution should catch and handle any errors that may occur from invoking a registered callback contributed by a potentially faulty plugin.

3.6 Deployment and Release Engineering

Npm is the package manager for Node.js modules. It is configured via a `package.json` file. Bower is a package manager for front-end assets like JavaScript libraries and CSS frameworks. It is configured by a `bower.json` file. Our plugin framework uses both to specify the modules and Web components contributed by the plugin respectively (see Fig. 1). The host system can specify the plugin as a dependency using the respective package managers. This design has a number of benefits:

[2] In some cases performance may be affected if some conditions are not met. For example collections with documents that vary greatly in size may induce write penalties.

1. reuses established package managers.
2. allows for a single code repository for the entire plugin.
3. enables to ignore files that are not required by a specific counterpart of the plugin. Npm uses either the `files` field in the `package.json` file for an inclusive list of files or a `.npmignore` file in the project's root directory that lists files to be excluded. Bower supports an `ignore` field in the `bower.json` file to specify which files to exclude.
4. makes it convenient to use the latest version of the plugin code while testing. This can be achieved either by using the tip of a specific code branch or by symlinking the package (be it an npm or a bower package) using built-in package manager commands.

The npm module part of the plugin can be deployed by the command `npm install <package-name>` which will install it in the `node_modules` directory of the server side code. Given correct implementation of the server-side plugin lifecycle methods, plugins can be installed, uninstalled, activated and deactivated while the application is executing, allowing us to hot-swap implementations while testing. The Web Component part of the plugin can be installed by specifying it as a dependency in the `bower.json` file or the front-end components of the host system. Additional building steps can be implemented to allow code transformation, minification and other release engineering tasks.

4 Evaluation

In this section we present a concrete use case to show that the plugin system delivers the extensibility we need as part of the ASQ [2] project.

4.1 ASQ Application Flow

ASQ is principally aimed at computer science lectures but can be used in any context where presenters require real-time fine grained audience feedback. Presenters add questions to the slides of their presentation, which are implemented in HTML5 and JavaScript, and broadcast the presentation. The audience members connect, follow the slides and answer questions. Continuous feedback is provided to the presenter who may choose to share parts or all of it with the audience. Examples of feedback include incoming answer events, automatic assessment results and more. There might be additional steps involved in the cycle, e.g., peer or self assessment of answers.

Overall, ASQ is designed to take advantage of the plugin system described in this paper to address the following extensibility requirements:

– Content authors should be able to create custom question types or extend existing ones. Types can range from simple multiple choice questions to advanced code editing questions with automatic unit-test assessment.

– Content authors should be able to create custom feedback logic and visualizations to target different presentational needs and accommodate for heterogeneous data coming from different question types. To better illustrate this, let us assume two different question types: multiple choice questions, where the answer is the combination of the checked options; and a highlight question, where the answer is the highlighted parts of a given text. Whereas it makes sense to render audience responses as a barchart or a pie chart in the former case it may not provide a meaningful visual representation for a heatmap question. A better choice may be to create a heatmap which maps each character position of the text with a color intensity that is proportional to the number of times the specific character position was highlighted by the audience.

– Presenters should be able to enable lecture flow and interaction patterns that match the usage context, their teaching style, the applied pedagogy and the nature of the question types. Examples include: the ability to have synchronized slides between presenter and audience within the classroom and free navigation for viewers during studying (presentation context); the ability to display assessment results in real time versus a specific point in time, or individual versus aggregated results (teaching style); the ability to allow students to work individually or in groups (applied pedagogy); the ability to have automatic, self or peer assessment strategies (applied pedagogy and question type complexity).

– Easily swap data-mining and analytics plugins to compare different techniques and algorithms to increase teacher awareness.

– Easy integration of complex external services and data sources without polluting the system architecture.

4.2 ASQ Architectural Overview

ASQ is a client/server application that uses both HTTP and WebSocket protocols for communication. An overview of the architecture is depicted in figure 4. In the back-end, an HTTP server coupled with the business logic of the application serves static assets, bootstrap data (such as WebSocket connection configuration) and initial HTML which is first rendered server-side using a dynamic template framework. Subsequent client-server communication is WebSocket based for reduced latency and higher throughput. Different roles connect to different 'namespaces', which are pools of connection ids implemented by a software layer on top of WebSockets, albeit in the same host and port.

The business layer persists model data like users, presentations and questions in MongoDB, a document based storage. The application also utilizes a Redis server tasked with two functions: storing simple key-value data like session identifiers and providing a pub/sub implementation that helps scale the WebSocket component of the application.

In the front-end, after an initial page load through HTTP, the application uses mostly WebSocket for communication. The core of the business logic is role-based, so presenters get a different main script than the viewers; and also view-based. For example presenters currently have two discrete views: the 'beamer' view which displays the presenter's version of the presentation and the 'control panel' which displays feedback information like number of connected users, incoming answers, statistics, next and previous slides and more.

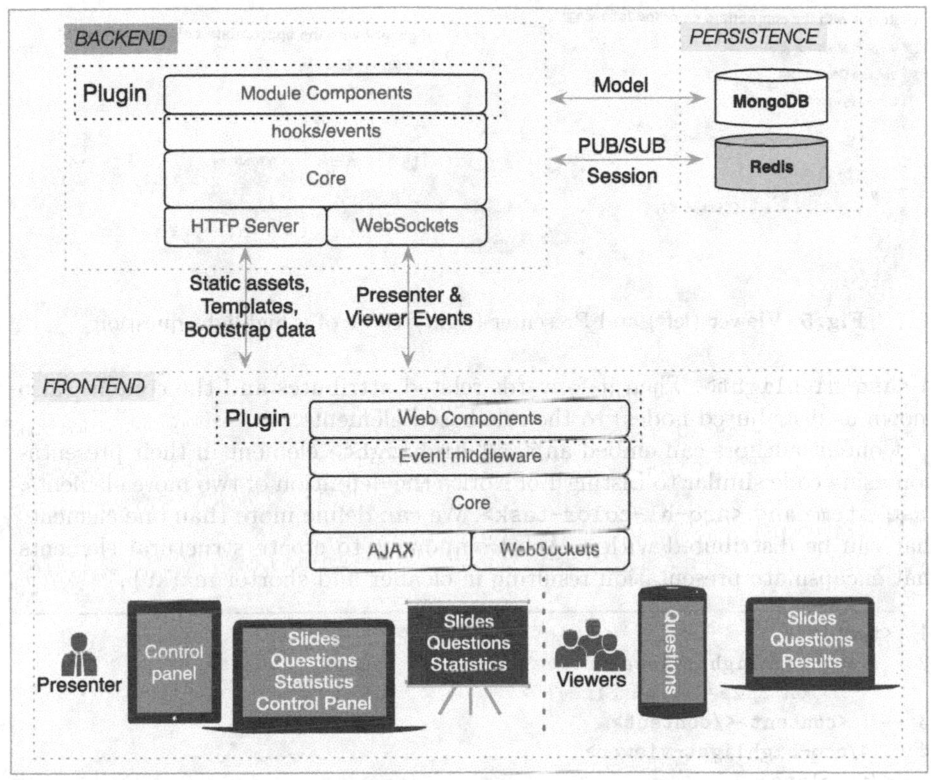

Fig. 4. ASQ architecture with the plugin system

4.3 Crafting a Plugin for ASQ

In this section we demonstrate how we can use the presented plugin system to craft a question type plugin for a highlight question. We will name the plugin 'asq-highlight'.

Creating the User Interface. A custom question type has different appearance and functionality based on the role and view of the user. In our case, an audience viewer faces a text editor with highlight capabilities showing the text to be highlighted (left of Fig. 5). On the beamer view (right of Fig. 5) the presenter can toggle between two modes: a heatmap over all audience answers or the correct solution. On the control panel, the presenter can display the highlight solution for any of the audience members or compare two or more answers with a heatmap.

To implement the User Interface we create a Custom Element, `<asq-highlight>`, that will be the façade for two role-based elements `<asq-highlight-viewer>` and `<asq-highlight-presenter>`; Listing 1.4 shows this in effect. The template of `<asq-highlight>` uses a conditional template (a Polymer feature) to render the appropriate element based on the role attribute

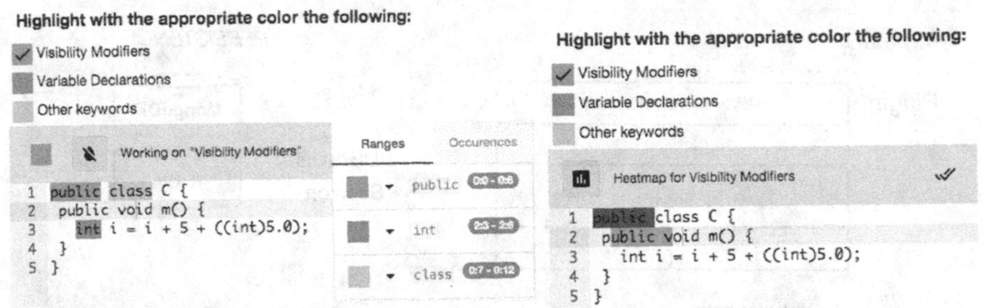

Fig. 5. Viewer (left) and Presenter (right) views of a highlight question

of <asq-highlight>. Then it forwards related attributes and the content (also known as distributed nodes) to the role-based elements.

Content authors can embed an <asq-highlight> element in their presentation using code similar to Listing 1.5. Notice the definition of two more elements, <asq-stem> and <asq-hl-color-task>. We can define more than one elements that can be distributed with a Web Component to create structural elements that encapsulate presentation resulting in cleaner and shorter markup.

```
<template if="{{role == roles.VIEWER}}">
  <asq-highlight-viewer mode="{{mode}}" theme="{{theme}}"
      fontSize="{{fontSize}}">
    <content></content>
  </asq-highlight-viewer>
</template>
<template if="{{role == roles.PRESENTER}}">
  <asq-highlight-presenter mode="{{mode}}" theme="{{theme}}"
      fontSize="{{fontSize}}">
    <content></content>
  </asq-highlight-presenter>
</template>
```

Listing 1.4. Template of the <asq-highghlight> element.

```
<asq-highlight theme="textmate" mode="java" fontSize="1em">
    <asq-stem><h3>Highlight with the appropriate color the
        following:</h3></asq-stem>
    <asq-hl-color-task color="d9534f">Visibility
        Modifiers</asq-hl-color-task>
    <asq-hl-color-task color="428bca">Variable
        Declarations</asq-hl-color-task>
    <asq-hl-color-task color="f0ad4e">Other keywords</asq-hl-color-task>
    <code>public class C {
  public void m() {
    int i = i + 5 + ((int)5.0) + ((int)5f);
  }
}</code></asq-highlight>
```

Listing 1.5. Markup to create the showcased highlight question

Implementing Server-Side Business Logic. The server-side module of asq-highlight will respond to two hooks: `parse_html` which is triggered when a user uploads an HTML presentation file; and `answer_submission`, triggered when an audience member submits an answer to a question.

For `parse_html` we are interested in extracting the representation of all `<asq-highlight>` elements present in an HTML string and persisting them in the 'questions' collection of our models persistence store (MongoDB). Listing 1.6 shows the implementation of the callback for `parse_html`. `this.asq` refers to the proxy instance used to persist the extracted question metadata.

```
function parseHtml(html){
  //cheerio is a Node.js library for HTML manipulation
  var   = cheerio.load(html, {decodeEntities: false});
  var hlQuestions = [];
  // extract question metadata from custom elements
   (this.tagName).each(function(idx, el){
    hlQuestions.push(this.processEl( , el));
  }.bind(this));
  //store metadata via persistance API
  return this.asq.db.model("Question").create(hlQuestions)
  .then(function(){
    return Promise.resolve( .root().html());
  });
}
```

Listing 1.6. `parse-html` hook callback for asq-highlight

When a viewer submits an answer to a set of questions, a core plugin fires the `exercise_submission` hook and for each individual question an `answer_submission` hook (Listing 1.7). Asq-highlight provides a callback for `answer_submission` in order to persist the Answer to the database as in Listing 1.8.

Notice the invocation of `this.calculateProgress` which calculates how many of the audience members have answered the question identified by `questionUid` and brodcasts the result to all connected clients. This method executes asynchronously and is a good example of event notification. The abbreviated version in Listing 1.9 shows how the event published from the server can target multiple clients.

```
function handleSubmitEvent(submission){
  //execute 'exercise_submission' hook
  yield hooks.doHook("exercise_submission", submission)
  //execute 'answer_submission' hook for each answer
  yield Promise.map(submission.answers, function(answer){
    return hooks.doHook("answer_submission", answer);
  });
}
```

Listing 1.7. triggering submission hooks in plugins, server-side

```
answerSubmission: coroutine(function *answerSubmissionGen (answer){
  var questionUid = answer.questionUid
  this.validateAnswer(answer);
  yield this.asq.db.model("Answer").create({
    question   : questionUid,
    answeree   : answer.answeree,
    session    : answer.session,
    submitDate : Date.now(),
    submission : answer.submission,
  });
  this.calculateProgress(answer.session, ObjectId(questionUid));
  //this will be the argument to the next hook
  return answer;
}
```

Listing 1.8. submission hook execution

```
var event = {
  questionType: 'asq-highlight',
  type: 'progress',
  questionUid: question_id.toString(),
  heatmapData: JSON.stringify(heatmapData),
}
this.asq.sendSocketEventToNamespaces('asq:question_type', event,
    session_id.toString(), 'ctrl')
```

Listing 1.9. sending an event to all presenter clients

5 Related Work

Architect [16], Intravenous [17], Seneca [18] and Wire [19] are all Node.js architectural frameworks that handle well dependency injection and offer ways to declare modules and their dependencies. They are positioned in the application composition layer on top of the npm modules layer. Front-end components are not in the scope of these frameworks.

This work is heavily influenced by the plugin systems of popular Web-based content management systems. More specifically the hooks construct can be found in similar contexts in Wordpress [20], Ghost [21] and Moodle [22] which are two blogging platforms and an open-source learning platform respectively. Moodle has also the notion of event-driven communication between back-end plugins and the core [23]. In these systems client-server communication between plugin components is performed mainly through HTTP/AJAX. By default, the back-end components cannot push any data to the front-end without the latter having issued an AJAX request first to pull the data [24].

Hoodie [25] is a Node.js framework with CouchDB store technology, whose main goal is to abstract away the back-end to facilitate the job of front-end developers. To accomplish this, the front-end application communicates with the back-end only through the Hoodie Javascript API. Using CouchDB's changes feed Hoodie is always aware of things that happen to the user's data and makes them available via events which allows keeping multiple devices syncronized. It support plugins which have a: *a*) frontend component; *b*) backend component; and *c*) an admin view. Frontend components communicate with back-end components through tasks similar to the client-server event mechanism described in Section 3.3. A task is a special object that can be saved into the database from the Hoodie front-end. Front-end plugin components deal only with the Hoodie API and do not have visual entities. Any related markup or CSS styles live in the static assets of the main application outside of the plugin directory. Hoodie thus lacks a way to encapsulate markup and styles for front-end plugins. Hoodie also does not have the concept of hooks.

6 Conclusion

In this paper we present the design of asqium: a plugin system for JavaScript/HTML5 Web applications that need to be extended with components running both as back-end modules and as front-end Web components. In addition to achieving the extensibility of the resulting Web application, the plugin system takes care also of basic infrastructural chores, such as event-based communication, persistent storage, and composition of synchronous and asynchronous functions contributed by multiple plugins. The plugin system has been implemented as the foundation of the ASQ educational Web platform, which has provided the motivation for the work and has been used as a case study to evaluate the plugin API expressiveness. We are looking forward to involve the Web Engineering community in further developments. The code for the plugin system implementation is available at https://github.com/ASQ-USI/ASQ/tree/master/lib/plugin. The back-end plugin base is an npm package which can be found at https://github.com/ASQ-USI/asq-plugin.

As a future research direction, we want to explore ways to enable seamless plugin data and state synchronization between different devices and the ability to cache plugin data that are produced when the client is offline and synchronize them upon re-establishing internet connectivity. This will provide a solid foundation on which liquid Web applications [26] can be engineered.

We are also working on ways for plugin authors to prioritize the callback execution associated with hooks and in general specify temporal dependencies between events of different plugins. Finally, we also want to shift our focus towards security and access control. We aim to introduce execution contexts for plugins, that correspond to user-granted privileges, by introducing Role-based Access Control (RBAC) at the plugin level.

Acknowledgments. The work is partially supported by the Swiss Commission for Technology and Innovation with the Spottedmap project (Grant Nr. 16328.1).

References

1. Mayer, J., Melzer, I., Schweiggert, F.: Lightweight plug-in-based application development. In: Aksit, M., Mezini, M., Unland, R. (eds.) NODe 2002. LNCS, vol. 2591, pp. 87–102. Springer, Heidelberg (2003)
2. Triglianos, V., Pautasso, C.: Interactive scalable lectures with ASQ. In: Casteleyn, S., Rossi, G., Winckler, M. (eds.) ICWE 2014. LNCS, vol. 8541, pp. 515–518. Springer, Heidelberg (2014)
3. kangax: Detecting global variable leaks (2009). http://perfectionkills.com/detecting-global-variable-leaks//
4. Bédard, J.: Isomorphic javascript (2015). http://isomorphic.net/
5. Onishi, A.: Plugins: When the time is right. In: Pro WordPress Theme Development, pp. 273–295. Apress (2013)
6. Dimitri, G.: Custom elements. W3c working draft, W3C (December 2014). http://www.w3.org/TR/2014/WD-custom-elements-20141216/
7. Dimitri, G., Ito, H.: Shadow dom. W3c working draft, W3C (June 2014). http://www.w3.org/TR/2014/WD-shadow-dom-20140617/
8. Dimitri, G., Hajime, M.: Html imports. W3c working draft, W3C (March 2014). http://www.w3.org/TR/2014/WD-html-imports-20140311/
9. Penades, S.: An Introduction to Web Components. In: Web Components London, webcomponents.org (January 2015)
10. Walton, P.: Web components and the future of CS. In: Proc. of SFHTML5 (November 2014). http://webcomponents.org/presentations/web-components-and-the-future-of-css/
11. Polymer, P.: Polymer Homepage (2015). https://www.polymer-project.org/
12. Sharp, R.: Detecting global variable leaks (October 2010). https://remysharp.com/2010/10/08/what-is-a-polyfill
13. ECMA: Draft specification for es.next (ecma-262 edition 6). Ecmascript working draft, ECMA (February 2015)
14. Bonetta, D., Binder, W., Pautasso, C.: TigerQuoll: parallel event-based JavaScript. In: Proc. of PPoPP, pp. 251–260 (2013)
15. Rauch, G.: Rooms and Namespaces (2014). http://socket.io/docs/rooms-and-namespaces/ (accessed: February 25, 2015)
16. c9: architect (2015). https://github.com/c9/architect
17. Jacobs, R.: intravenous (2015). https://github.com/RoyJacobs/intravenous
18. Rodger, R.: seneca (2015). https://github.com/rjrodger/seneca
19. cujoJS: wire (2015). https://github.com/cujojs/wire
20. Mullenweg, M., Boren, R., Jaquith, M., Ozz, A., Westwood, P.: Wordpress (2011). https://wordpress.org/
21. Wolfe, H., O'Nolan, J., Davis, P., Williams, J.: Ghost (2015). https://ghost.org/
22. Dougiamas, M.: Moodle: A virtual learning environment for the rest of us. TESL-EJ **8**(2), 1–8 (2004)
23. Moodle developer documentation, M.: Event 2 (2015). https://docs.moodle.org/dev/Event_2 (accessed: February 25, 2015)
24. Mesbah, A., Van Deursen, A.: A component-and push-based architectural style for ajax applications. Journal of Systems and Software **81**(12), 2194–2209 (2008)
25. Hoodie, H.: Hoodie Homepage (2015). http://hood.ie/ (accessed: February 25, 2015)
26. Mikkonnen, T., Systa, K., Pautasso, C.: Towards liquid web applications. In: Proc. of the 15th International Conference on Web Engineering (ICWE). Springer, Rotterdam (2015)

Mobile Web Applications

Mobile-IDM: A Design Method for Modeling the New Interaction Style of Mobile Applications

Giovanni Coppola, Alessandro Fiore(✉), Luca Mainetti, and Andrea Pandurino

Department of Innovation Engineering, University of Salento,
Via Monteroni 73100, Lecce, Italy
{giovanni.coppola,alessandro.fiore,luca.mainetti,
andrea.pandurino}@unisalento.it

Abstract. Mobile applications (apps) offer designers the opportunity to experiment with novel interaction grammars (e.g., gestures, context-aware events), whose implications for conceptual modeling still need to be fully understood. The research panorama only proposes a few design methods for apps, which are mainly released as extensions of existing ones. This, in addition to the short lifecycle that characterizes apps, leads to the risk of inappropriate modeling techniques being adopted. To bridge this gap, we propose a new design method, named Mobile-IDM, to model the interaction between the user and the app from a logical point of view. As it is based upon IDM and Rich-IDM, from which it inherits its design semantics, Mobile-IDM exploits the dialog metaphor to facilitate the establishment of a common ground between designers and web engineers to obtain good usability of the interaction. We demonstrate through a case study the simplicity and other advantages of our approach.

Keywords: User experience design · Mobile application · Design methodologies · IDM · Rich-IDM

1 Introduction

The statistics related to the uptake and the use of mobile devices, such as tablets and smartphones, are staggering. Just consider the fact that in the world 1,75 billion people use a smartphone in 2014 [1] and, in many European countries, it is not unusual to find people who have more than one device.

Technological development has also led manufacturers to produce devices with more powerful processors, more capacious memories, and more sophisticated hardware innovations (such as GPS, touchscreens, accelerometers, NFC, and other types of sensors). By combining these developments with the increasing diffusion of high-speed wireless Internet connections, it is possible to use mobile devices to perform a series of daily life tasks.

To satisfy the needs of the users, the number of applications present in online stores has exploded. At the end of 2014, the Google Play Store and Apple App Store contained about 1.43 million and 1.21 million applications, respectively. Actually, many of these have very similar features, allowing the user to perform the same

P. Cimiano et al. (Eds.): ICWE 2015, LNCS 9114, pp. 101–115, 2015.
DOI: 10.1007/978-3-319-19890-3_8

activities in a different way. Of course, the user will choose a specific application instead of another one according to their satisfaction in interacting with it.

For these reasons, it is necessary to rethink the user interface (UI) design methods for mobile applications in order to improve the quality of user interaction and, in general, the user experience. An important aspect that needs to be considered is the type of device on which the application will be used, as there are devices with different screen sizes and with different operating systems (Android, iOS, Windows Phone). These systems have different user interface elements and they already provide their own guidelines for interface modeling (for example, Apple does not permit the application's distribution on the App Store if these guidelines are not followed).

In this paper, in order to cater for some new distinctive characteristics enabled by mobile applications, we propose a design method for mobile applications called Mobile-IDM. Mobile-IDM is an innovative extension of Rich-IDM (Rich Interactive Dialogue Model) [2][3], which is traditionally used for modeling Rich Internet Applications (RIAs). Mobile-IDM integrates the theoretical constructs of dialogue theory (defined in IDM [4]), enabling the fundamental user interaction requirements, with the interaction and navigation grammar of the mobile device, to be captured. As a result, our approach aims to serve as a simple conceptual common ground between advanced design features and user interaction concerns. The features of Mobile-IDM, which are based on a few, simple conceptual primitives, allow us to hypothesize some key advantages: they are expressive enough to efficiently model the interaction between the user and the mobile application and they are structured enough to be directly connected to the user experience requirements as captured in IDM. In the last part of this work, we apply Mobile-IDM to a real case study in order to better describe its characteristics and to demonstrate the advantages of our approach.

The paper is organized as follows. The related work on web and mobile application design is summarized in Section 2. Section 3 presents the open issues that exist in the area of mobile application modeling approaches. A brief introduction on the IDM framework is reported in Section 4. Section 5 presents the Mobile-IDM approach, explaining its notation and semantics. Section 6 illustrates an application of Mobile-IDM (through a real case study) in order to address the issues highlighted in Section 3. Finally, in Section 7 the conclusions summarize our key messages and outline future research directions.

2 Related Work

In this section, we provide a general survey of the related work about web or mobile application design. In the literature, we can find several approaches for designing browser-based applications.

Hera [5] is a design methodology composed of several steps that define the many aspects of a system using models with graphical notations. This approach is supported by the Hera Presentation Generator, a tool capable of generating webpages from Hera models.

In [6], the authors propose a development framework for web applications on heterogeneous devices. The framework is based on a semiautomatic process capable of customizing the application for specific target devices and transforming HTML pages into generic application artifacts.

The Web Modeling Language (WebML) [7] is a notation for modeling web applications at the conceptual level. It enables the high-level description of a website under distinct orthogonal dimensions: its data content (structural model), the pages that compose it (composition model), the topology of links between pages (navigation model), the layout and graphic requirements for page rendering (presentation model), and the customization features for one-to-one content delivery (personalization model).

The Interaction Flow Modeling Language (IFML) [8], an extension of WebML, is a modeling language dedicated to the definition of "User Interaction" dynamics. The IFML language is abstract and independent from the implementation technology. As a result, IFML supports the platform-independent description of graphical user interfaces for applications accessed or deployed on such systems as desktop computers, laptop computers, PDAs, mobile phones, and tablets. The focus of the description is on the structure and behavior of the application as perceived by the end user.

TERESA [9] is a tool that allows the development and UI generation for multi-device interfaces starting from tasks defined by CTT (Concur Task Tree) notation. TERESA is able to support UI generation for a wide set of implementation languages: XHTML MP, VoiceXML, X+V, SVG, Xlet, and the gesture library for MS. This means that designers and developers have a consistent environment that allows them to build applications for a variety of platforms, which support various modalities.

RUX [10] designs the UI of RIA applications through four levels of definitions. The concepts and tasks level contains the data and business logic and can be modeled using a web design methodology, such as in WebML. The RUX-model strategy is fully compliant with many web design methodologies such as WebML or UWE (UML-based Web Engineering [11]).

UWE uses a specific UML profile and allows the model-driven development of web applications. The UWE design process has a requirement model, a content model, a navigation model, and a presentation model, which provides an abstract view of the Web UI.

OOHDM [12] proposes a design process where the interface and its behavior are explicitly analyzed and examined. The implementation step of the OOHDM design process is platform-dependent and maps the conceptual design on the specific RIA technology. In this step, the static aspect of the interface is modeled using Abstract Data Views (ADV) [13] while ADV-charts [14] are used to define the status and the behavior of each interface element. The OOHDM approach describes the application pages by defining their views and their charts to model the changes. The ADV approach has also been used within the process of Web Model Refactoring [15] towards RIA. This approach aims at transforming standard web interface elements into others, adding new interaction facilities that capture RIA features.

These methods, even if not properly designed for mobile applications, may be used in this field thanks to their platform independence. Furthermore, they offer useful guidelines about user interaction modeling. Nevertheless, a few methods explicitly intended for mobile applications can be found in the literature.

In [16], the authors propose a maieutic process for modeling mobile applications by taking into account the user's point of view. This approach starts by detecting the needs of the users and ends by transferring them into a system of functions and applications without limiting the satisfaction of superficial requirements.

In [17], the use of market elements is recognized as a leading factor in the success of a mobile software product. Thus, the authors recommend the use of the market-based New Product Development (NPD) for improving current mobile development.

In [18] an agile approach to mobile application development called Mobile-D is reported. Mobile-D is based on development practices borrowed from XP (eXtreme Programming), enjoys the scalability of methods inspired by the Crystal family of methodologies, and provides life-cycle coverage as defined by the RUP (Rational Unified Process).

Finally, MobileIFML [19] proposes an extension of IFML that is tailored to mobile applications. MobileIFML comprises the development of automatic code generators for cross-platform mobile applications based on HTML5, CSS, and JavaScript.

3 Open Issues

Considering the approaches discussed above, it is important to notice that many of the examined methodologies do not cover all of the specific aspects of mobile applications. For example, RUX does not consider the semantic and communicative value of the elements that compose the UI. Thus, it does not model the information flow that leads the user during navigation. In Hera the flow is modeled from a more conceptual perspective. None of the analyzed methods directly refers to mobile UIs, although we can find a number of important points for consideration. For instance, Hera and WebML provide a way to represent contextual information and how to use it. Furthermore, WebML suggests using several views for modeling the UI, one for each platform target.

In addition, the considered research on mobile applications does not focus on the user experience but rather on the design process in general. In particular, MobileIFML faces the problem from a technological and implementation perspective, providing a tool for automatic code generation. Our approach, instead, allows user experience to be designed for mobile applications starting from a conceptual level, which supports requirements analysis.

Most of the time clients require mobile applications to be developed as swiftly as possible and for multiple platforms and devices. From the technological perspective, the increasingly frequent use of cross-platform frameworks (e.g., PhoneGap, Titanium, Xamarin) testifies to this trend. Therefore, conceptual design becomes essential in the development of mobile applications in order to avoid errors in modeling functionalities and user interaction, even at the expense of technological aspects. Having a methodology that allows designers to model these aspects is a key factor in the success of a mobile application.

4 Introducing the IDM Methodology Framework

The IDM framework (Fig. 1) uses the theory of dialogue as the basis for describing human–computer interaction, considering every element of the interface as a dialogue fragment. The interface's elements are built using several dialogue types and techniques (such as form filling, menu selection, icons, etc.). Thus, suitable modeling is based on the collaboration between domain and communication experts, and user experience experts and engineers.

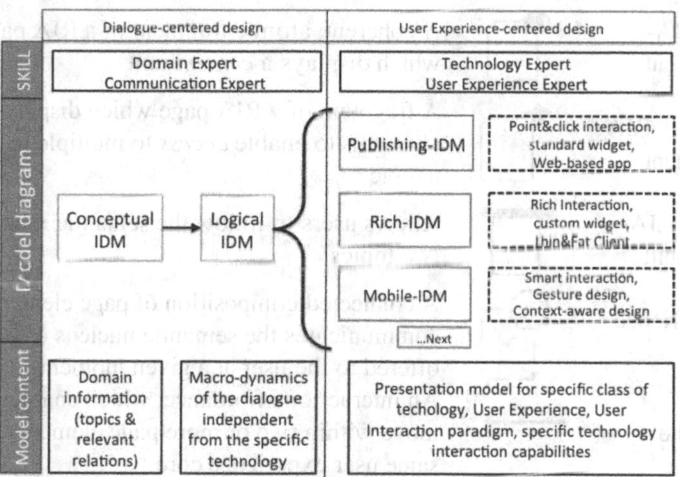

Fig. 1. IDM Methodology Framework

The first phase of the design is to describe the application at the conceptual level, focusing on the dynamics of the dialogue: the IDM primitives [4] can be used to catch the essential interactive and navigation features of information-intensive applications. These primitives are organized in two main design layers: Conceptual IDM (C-IDM) and Logical IDM (L-IDM). C-IDM is used to describe the "conceptual schema" of the application, defining the topics of the dialogue and the relations between its elements. In other words, it is used to shape the deep dialogic structure of the interaction [20]. Starting from the C-IDM design, the L-IDM schema models the decisions that are typically dependent on a specific fruition channel through which the application may be conveyed.

The second phase of the framework, instead, focuses on the user experience design, which is based on the specific class of technology. In particular, Publishing-IDM (P-IDM) considers several design aspects of the webpages, such as the layout or the frame position inside the page, while Rich-IDM is used for modeling RIAs.

4.1 Adapting Rich-IDM to Mobile Applications

Rich-IDM [2] [3] is a methodology for modeling the user experience of RIAs. It is currently being used in several research and industrial projects as it provides a description of the complex interaction offered to users in RIAs, including non-trivial relationships, behaviors, and views. Rich-IDM provides several primitives in order to model all the specific aspects of RIAs. In particular, the UX Core Element and the Context View Element allow the user's attention to be focused on the main elements of the dialogue, a fundamental requirement given the large amount of information contained in rich Internet pages. Table 1 describes the notation and the semantics of Rich-IDM primitives.

Table 1. The Rich-IDM design primitives

Name	*Notation*	*Design semantics*
Content RIA-Page Element		A coherent, atomic fragment of a RIA page, which displays a *content* unit
Introductory RIA-Page Element		A fragment of a RIA page which displays mechanisms to enable *access* to multiple instances of a topic
Transition RIA-Page Element		Allows users to follow the semantic relation of two topics
User Experience Core	X	A connected composition of page elements, which communicates the semantic nucleus of what is offered to the user at a given moment
RIA-Handle		An interaction affordance, which enables users to move within two or more page elements of the same user experience core
Context View		A set of user experience cores which maintain navigational context, orientation, and fluid transition between the cores
Default Element		Indicates the default RIA-Page Elements

The main Rich-IDM features are: i) expressiveness to capture interactive features at a high level of abstraction; ii) semi-formality to facilitate the establishment of a common ground between designers and software engineers; and iii) traceability of the design to important usability requirements. For these reasons, this method is well suited to modeling the user experience in the case of mobile applications, although it is necessary to use in a different way some primitives adapting them to the new contexts. Unlike RIAs, the screen size that is available in mobile devices is usually very limited for the purpose to show information to the user. Thus, in order to define and to organize the informational content, it is fundamental to redefine the User Experience Core usage. In fact in RIA, the UX Core element is used to indicate the objects containing the dialogue focus. It contains the dialogue elements that are the reasons for which the page has been created. Instead, in a mobile application, the UX Core designs the fundamental elements for satisfying the requirements of the page. Furthermore, the RIA-Handle primitive assumes an even more important role. In RIAs, users have the possibility of interacting with the page elements in different ways (e.g. drag & drop) using only the mouse in order to perform the actions. In this case, the RIA-Handles describe how the user can activate the transition to the target using standard input methods (e.g. mouse, touchpad). Instead in a mobile app the user can use many gestures (see fig. 5) to interact with the content but he/she can perform only a limited numbers of actions due to the screen sizes (e.g. drag & drop does not exist). Thus, the role of the RIA-Handle is limited in the mobile application but we have to consider the important function of gestures to optimizing the ergonomics of content navigation. In detail, it is important not only the use of the gestures but also how the gestures are used; e.g. it is our opinion that many swipes to see all the page content does not help the user experience.

Finally, also the Context View primitive is useful to model user interfaces of mobile application. In RIAs, it allows gathering related UX Cores with a same "look&feel" defining a specific navigational context; thus, it provides to the user the concept of section of RIA site. The mobile application characteristics suggest the use of a single Context View because the mobile apps are vertical application focused on specific aspect and, thus, the change of context is not needed. Moreover, the change of "look&feel" may confuse the user. Consequently, in the case of reverse engineering, the presence of more Context View could indicate an incorrect modeling of the application.

However, mobile applications have specific features that the Rich-IDM method is not able to model correctly.

5 Mobile-IDM

In this section, we provide readers with an introduction to Mobile-IDM, presenting its notation and primitives in order to overcome the lacks of Rich-IDM in the context of mobile application design. Starting from a common L-IDM information design, several M-IDM models of the same application, one for each combination device/orientation, can be obtained with Mobile-IDM. This can lead to a large number of models, although they are more readable than a single model in which all possible combinations are specified as variants. Table 2 illustrates the Mobile-IDM notation and its design semantics. Then, it follows a brief description of the distinctive aspects of mobile applications and how they can be modeled using Mobile-IDM.

5.1 Context-Aware Identifier

Modern mobile devices are able to discover and take advantage of contextual information such as user location, time, user activity, and preferences. These types of information (often obtained by the sensors on the device) are used by mobile applications to automatically adapt their behavior according to the context. Thus, it is possible to improve the user experience by providing users with what they probably need in a specific place, at a specific time, and for a specific task. However, in case of mobile applications, the question is: "How can the designer model the elements in the mobile application that are related to the context?"

In order to resolve this need, Mobile-IDM introduces the *Context-aware Identifier*. It models the dialogue elements that contain context-aware information. It may be associated with a single RIA Page Element or to a User Experience Core. Additional specifications can be attached to Context-Aware Element through textual annotations. For example, the designer can describe how the marked element adapts its content or its appearance (see Fig. 2). Thus, the Context-aware Identifier makes explicit the context-aware behavior of information elements in accordance to the goal of providing an easy to use tool.

5.2 Notification Identifier

A push notification allows an application to notify the user about updated contents or events, thus creating a new interaction flow with the user. The notifications become a point of access to the application, directly showing the updated content and making the interaction suddenly change.

It is needed to provide designers a solution for indicating the elements that are communicated to the users through a notification. How could we do this?

Table 2. The Mobile-IDM notation and design semantics

Name	*Notation*	*Design semantics*
Context-aware Identifier	C	Model the elements of the mobile application that contain context-aware information
Notification Identifier	!	Model the element that, after a notification, can become the first cue of the dialogue
Interaction Core Container		Model the user interaction with multiple RIA-Page Elements, describing navigation and presentation according to a specific strategy
Landmark Identifier	L	Indicate the RIA-Page elements that should be accessible from anywhere

Mobile-IDM offers the *Notification Identifier* to specify the above elements. Formally, this primitive says that the RIA-Page Element gets displayed when the user opens a notification. Again, the designer can add a textual annotation in order to better describe the interaction (Fig. 3). Considering the IDM dialogue metaphor, we can imagine the notification as the beginning of a dialogue made by the application itself rather than by the user.

5.3 Landmark Identifier

The limited screen size of mobile devices forces the user to navigate through several screens before reaching the desired information. Thus, in order to improve the user experience, is essential that a mobile design method offers a primitive able to model a direct access to specific application elements.

In web applications, the landmarks are often used allowing a quick access to single information elements (instances) such as the homepage, contacts, credits etc. Mobile-IDM extends the semantics of landmarks, providing designers with the *Landmark Identifier*, which models a dynamic link to a specific information class – an entity, or a topic according to the dialogic metaphor – or an application feature such as highlights, point-of-interest etc. Thus, the linked information could be not simple static elements (such as an individual topic or a RIA Element) but dynamic ones, typically related to the current context of application such as its spatial position and time.

Using the Landmark Identifier, the designer can specify the linked contents by putting them into a container marked with the label "L" (see Fig. 4). Formally, the landmarks are modeled with the Introductory RIA-Page Elements that should be accessible from anywhere. The Landmark Identifier primitive could be combined with the Context-aware Identifier and the Notification Identifier to model the context-aware and dynamic behavior of the information flow.

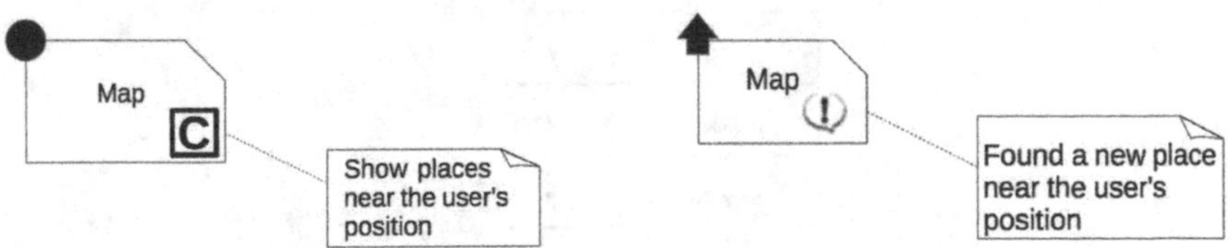

Fig. 2. Example of Context-Aware Identifier **Fig. 3.** Example of Notification Identifier

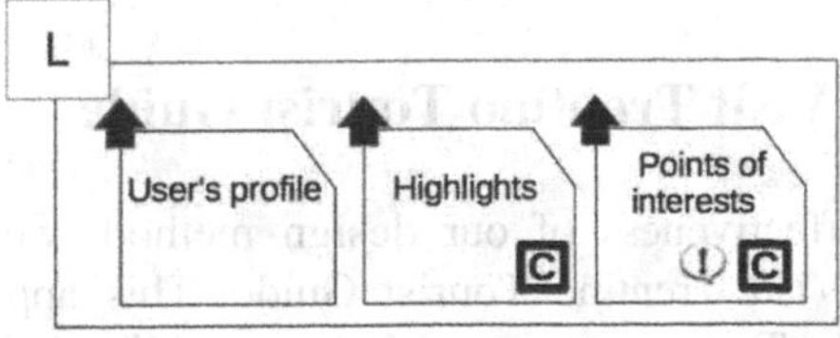

Fig. 4. Example of a Landmark Identifier

5.4 Interaction Core Container

In a mobile application it is needed to establish the best navigation strategies – according to the type and the quantity of contents – to ensure a good user experience. For example, in some cases it is useful to display the contents along a predefined order (Guided Tour strategy), in others it is convenient to navigate in a free manner (All-to-all strategy), and in some circumstances it is better to adopt a mixed strategy or to show all contents at the same time, without any transition between them (Simultaneous Presentation). How can the designer be encouraged to explicitly model these aspects?

Mobile-IDM meets this need providing designers with the *Interaction Core Container*. It is a container of RIA-Page Elements that belong to the same User Experience Core. In the Interaction Core Container the designer can specify one of the four Navigation Strategies defined in IDM (Guided Tour, All-to-all, Mixed, Simultaneous presentation) and an interaction mode from a list of basic gestures (see Fig. 5). This list can be extended with other elements to fulfill the designer's needs. In order to make the modeling more stringent, it can be added a number to define how many actions are needed to navigate all elements within the Interaction Core. For example, a "Swipe/Flick icon" associated with a number "2" defines that the swipe gesture is limited to a length equal two times the width of the screen. The absence of this number models an interaction without a predefined number of gestures.

Considering the IDM semantics, the Interaction Core Container allows designers to describe how the dialogue takes place, according to a specific strategy.

Interaction mode	Notation
Vertical Scroll	
Swipe/Flick	
Tap	
Double Tap	
Long Press	
Pan	

Fig. 5. Interaction modes

6 Case Study: Visit Trentino Tourist Guide

To demonstrate the effectiveness of our design method, we modeled an existing mobile application – Visit Trentino Tourist Guide. This app aims to help tourists organize a holiday in the Trentino region of Italy, providing information about places, sport centers, reception facilities, and other points of interest or services.

On the basis of our consideration about the context view primitives (explained in the 4.1 paragraph), we assume that there is only one context view; thus, the following diagrams do not report the context view in order to improve its readability.

For a lack of space, here we only analyze the topic "Discover point of interest," which allows the exploration and discovery of attractions thanks to the Introductory Acts shown in Fig. 6. These elements provide access to various categories of points of interest, giving a strong semantic value to the dialogue.

The first part of this case study is based on a reverse engineering of the application, which is actually only available for smartphones in portrait mode. In this way we demonstrate the descriptive capabilities of Mobile-IDM. The second part of the case study focuses on the outcome of a forward engineering process and allows the effectiveness of Mobile-IDM to be demonstrated.

Fig. 7 shows the Mobile-IDM model related to the smartphone with portrait orientation scenario. It is mapped with several screenshots of the application in order to demonstrate how the UIs are graphed with Mobile-IDM. For example, let us suppose that the user wants to search for the most interesting tourist places in the Trentino region.

The interaction starts from the main screen of the application by selecting the Introductory RIA-Page Element. Next, the user browses through a series of other pages that filter the results ("Tourist Sector" and "Types of touristic places") until the application shows a list of possible points of interest. The user can select (with a tap gesture) a particular point of interest to view its detail page. This page is modeled with four RIA-Page Content Elements grouped into an Interaction Core, which also defines the navigation strategy and the interaction mode. In particular, the number "2", which is associated with the notation, defines that the scroll is limited to a length equal to two times the length of the screen.

Thus, we have demonstrated that every aspect related to user interaction can be correctly represented with Mobile-IDM. Moreover, the resulting model is easy to read for designers that do not have specific skills in web engineering.

During the forward engineering phase, we supposed a landscape version of the application. A possible modeling is shown in Fig. 8. Thanks to the greater width of the screen, the designer can specify more Introductory RIA-Page Elements, which are grouped into Interaction Core labels. Obviously the height of the screen is smaller compared with portrait mode, so the designer must specify a larger number of vertical scrolls to display all the contents. To model this aspect we added the number "3" near to the icon of the scroll gesture.

Furthermore, we added a Notification Element and a Context-Aware Element to design the application behavior in the presence of context information. When the user displays the map in the information page of a point of interest, the application shows both the point's position and the user's. Moreover, the system notifies the user of the presence of other points of interest in the neighborhood of the user. A single tap on the corresponding notification allows the user to directly open the information page of that point. Finally, Fig. 9 shows a possible model for tablet devices. In this case, the larger size of the screen allows more contents to be displayed simultaneously. When the user selects a desired point of interest, the information pages of other points of interest in the same category can be displayed and browsed with a swipe gesture.

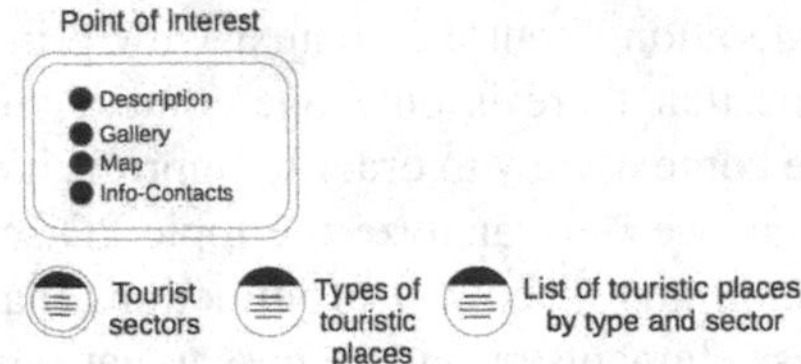

Fig. 6. "Discover Point of Interest" topic: L-IDM model

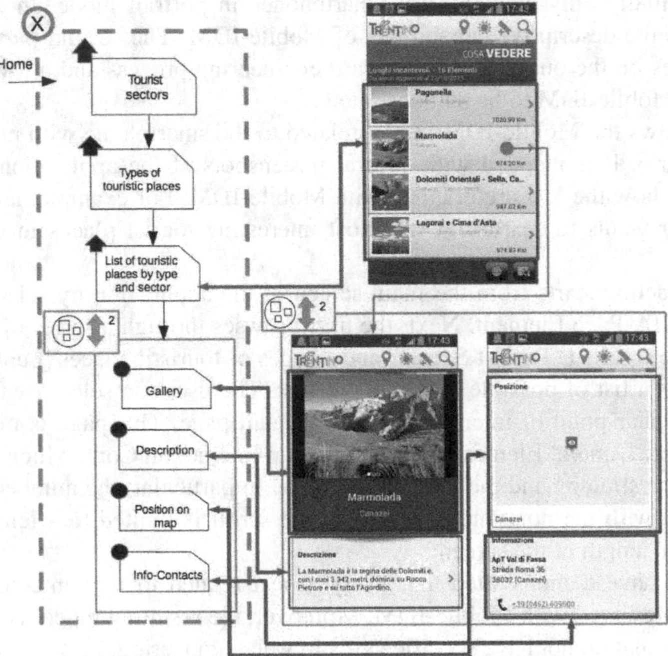

Fig. 7. Mobile-IDM model of Visit Trentino for smartphone (portrait orientation)

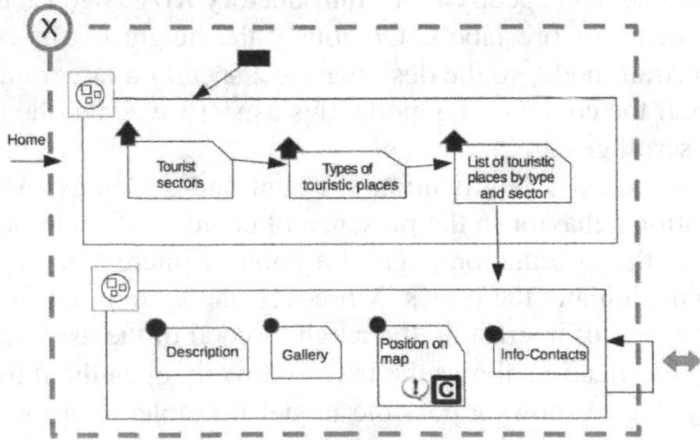

Fig. 8. Mobile-IDM model of Visit Trentino for smartphone (landscape orientation)

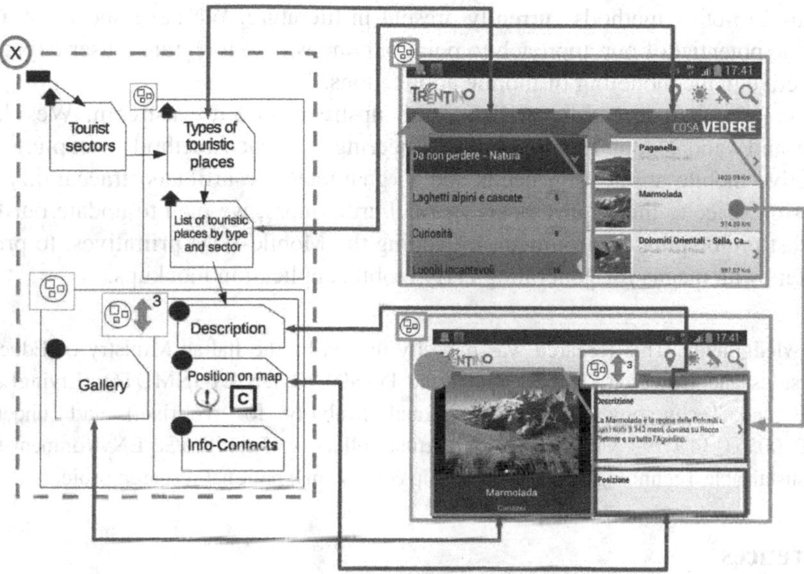

Fig. 9. Mobile-IDM model of Visit Trentino for tablet devices

Mobile-IDM is able to model this interaction simply using a RIA-Handle that comes out and falls into the Interaction Core and the swipe interaction mode. Thus, thanks to Mobile-IDM, we can design the user interaction taking into account screen sizes and device orientation.

7 Conclusions and Future Work

Mobile applications are a real revolution in the field of software engineering, as they have totally changed the interaction paradigm. To balance the trade-off between small screen sizes of mobile devices and the need to ensure good usability, cognitive workload, and efficiency, we have codified a new set of high-level modeling constructs based on the IDM/Rich-IDM approaches. Mobile-IDM primitives provide a common vocabulary between interaction designers (focusing on user requirements) and software engineers (focusing on translating those requirements into feasible and successful solutions).

Furthermore, we have defined some steps toward developing the same application for multiple types of devices, adapting at design time the information architecture and the interaction to the context of the device, with the aim of improving the user experience. Thanks to Mobile-IDM, the interaction between user and application is represented from a logical rather than a technological point of view. This simplifies the communication among designers and engineers as well as aiding the comprehension of stakeholders who do not have computer skills in the development process. Focusing on the design of the user experience and on the semantic modeling of the interface, Mobile-IDM offers a different perspective to mobile application design if compared to other methods currently present in literature. We have shown in a case study the potential of our approach to point out one way to integrate a user experience perspective in the modeling of mobile applications.

Future research directions will be both upstream and downstream. We plan to evolve and validate our requirement engineering reference method to capture other distinctive mobile application needs and to guarantee the artifacts' traceability from the design space to the requirements space. Furthermore, we plan to update our Rich-IDM fast prototyping environment, by adding the Mobile-IDM primitives, to provide designers with means for generating early mobile application mockups.

Acknowledgments. This research was partially funded by the Italian Ministry of Education, Universities and Research (MIUR) under the PON04_a2 DICET-INMOTO (LivingLab on Culture and Technology - Information and Mobility for Tourism) and under the PON02_00563_3470993 VINCENTE (A Virtual collective INtelligenCe ENvironment to develop sustainable Technology Entrepreneurship ecosystems) national research projects.

References

1. Smartphone Users Worldwide Will Total 1.75 Billion in 2014 (n.d.) retrieved April 1, 2015. http://www.emarketer.com/Article/Smartphone-Users-Worldwide-Will-Total-175-Billion-2014/1010536#sthash.cIJSOYbN.dpuf
2. Pandurino, A., Bolchini, D., Mainetti, L., Paiano, R.: Dialogue-based Modeling of Rich Internet Applications: The Rich-IDM Approach. Int. Journal of Web Information Systems **8**(2), 157–180 (2012)
3. Paiano, R., Pandurino, A., Mainetti, L.: Rich-IDM: transforming the user experience of legacy applications. In: 2011 13th IEEE International Symposium on Web Systems Evolution (WSE), pp. 81–85. IEEE Press, New York (2011)
4. Bolchini, D., Paolini, P.: Interactive Dialogue Model: A Design Technique for Multi-Channel Applications. IEEE Trans. Multimedia **8**(3), 529–541 (2006)
5. Frasincar, F., Houben, G.-J., Barna, P.: Hypermedia Presentation Generation in Hera. Inform. Syst. **35**(1), 23–55 (2010)
6. Banavar, G., Bergman, L., Cardone, R., Chevalier, V., Gaeremynck, Y., Giraud, F., Halverson, C., Hirose, S., Hori, M., Kitayama, F., Kondoh, G., Kundu, A., Ono, K., Schade, A., Soroker, D., Winz, K.: An Authoring Technology for Multidevice Web Applications. IEEE Pervasive Comput. **3**(3), 83–93 (2004)
7. Ceri, S., Fraternali, P., Bongio, A.: Web Modeling Language (WebML): A Modeling Language for Designing Web Sites. Comput. Netw. **33**(1–6), 137–157 (2000)
8. Interaction Flow Modeling Language (IFML) Beta1. Object Management Group, Inc., Needham (2013)
9. Paterno, F., Santoro, C., Mantyjarvi, J., Mori, G., Sansone, S.: Authoring Pervasive Multimodal User Interfaces. Int. J. Web. Eng. Tech. **4**(2), 235–261 (2008)
10. Linaje, M., Preciado, J.C., Sánchez-Figueroa, F.: A method for model based design of rich internet application interactive user interfaces. In: Baresi, L., Fraternali, P., Houben, G.-J. (eds.) ICWE 2007. LNCS, vol. 4607, pp. 226–241. Springer, Heidelberg (2007)
11. Preciado, J.C., Linaje, M., Morales-Chaparro, R., Sánchez-Figueroa, F., Zhang, G., Kroiβ, C., Koch, N.: Designing rich internet applications combining UWE and RUX-method. In: Eighth International Conference on Web Engineering, 2008. ICWE 2008, pp. 148–154. IEEE Press, New York (2008)

12. Urbieta, M., Rossi, G., Ginzburg, J., Schwabe, D.: Designing the interface of rich internet applications. In: Latin American Web Conference, 2007. LA-WEB 2007, pp. 144–153. IEEE Press, New York (2007)
13. Cowan, D.D., Lucena, C.J.P.: Abstract Data Views: An Interface Specification Concept to Enhance Design for Reuse. IEEE Trans. Softw. Eng. **21**(3), 229–243 (1995)
14. Carneiro, L.M.F., Cowan, D.D., Lucena, C.J.P.: ADVcharts: A Visual Formalism for Interactive Systems. ACM SIGCHI Bull. **26**(2), 74–77 (1994)
15. Rossi, G., Urbieta, M., Ginzburg, J., Distante, D., Garrido, A.: Refactoring to rich internet applications. A model-driven approach. In: Eighth International Conference on Web Engineering, 2008. ICWE 2008, pp. 1–12. IEEE Press, New York (2008)
16. Gerstheimer, O., Lupp, C.: Needs Versus Technology—The Challenge to Design Third-generation Mobile Applications. J. Bus. Res. **57**(12), 1409–1415 (2004)
17. Vainio, A.M., Tuunanen, T., Abrahamsson, P.: Developing software products for mobile markets: need for rethinking development models and practice. In: Proceedings of the 38th Annual Hawaii International Conference on System Sciences, 2005. HICSS 2005, p. 189b. IEEE Press, New York (2005)
18. Abrahamsson, P., Hanhineva, A., Hulkko, H., Ihme, T., Jäälinoja, J., Korkala, M., Koskela, J., Kyllönen, P., Salo, O.: Mobile-D: an agile approach for mobile application development. In: OOPSLA 2004 Companion to the 19th Annual ACM SIGPLAN Conference on Object-Oriented Programming Systems, Languages, and Applications, pp. 174–175. ACM, New York (2004)
19. Brambilla, M., Mauri, A., Umuhoza, E.: Extending the interaction flow modeling language (IFML) for model driven development of mobile applications front end. In: Awan, I., Younas, M., Franch, X., Quer, C. (eds.) MobiWIS 2014. LNCS, vol. 8640, pp. 176–191. Springer, Heidelberg (2014)
20. Pandurino, A., Bolchini, D., Mainetti, L., Paiano, R.: Streamlining complexity: conceptual page re-modeling for rich internet applications. In: Harth, A., Koch, N. (eds.) ICWE 2011. LNCS, vol. 7059, pp. 289–301. Springer, Heidelberg (2012)

Profiling User Activities with Minimal Traffic Traces

Tiep Mai, Deepak Ajwani(✉), and Alessandra Sala

Bell Laboratories, Dublin, Republic of Ireland
{tiep.mai,deepak.ajwani,alessandra.sala}@alcatel-lucent.com

Abstract. There is a need to strike a balance between the pursuit of personalized services based on a fine-grained behavioral analysis and the user privacy concerns. In this paper, we consider the use of web traces with truncated URLs, where each URL is trimmed to only contain the web domain, to remove sensitive user information. In order to offset the accuracy loss in user activity profiling due to URL truncation, we propose a statistical methodology that leverages specialized features extracted from a burst of consecutive URLs representing a micro user action. These bursts, in turn, are detected by a novel algorithm which is based on our observed characteristics of the inter-arrival time of HTTP records. On a real dataset of mobile web traces, consisting of more than 130 million records and 10,000 users, we show that our methodology achieves around 90% accuracy in segregating URLs representing user activities from non-representative URLs.

1 Introduction

Behavioral analysis of mobile users based on their web activities has the potential to transform their online experience. It enables service providers to personalize their deliverable, specialize their content, customize recommendations and target advertisements based on user context. For the network operators, it opens up the possibility of provisioning their resources and dynamically managing their network infrastructure (particularly, with the realization of network function virtualization) to effectively serve the varying user and content demand in order to deliver advanced quality-of-service experience.

However, behavioral analysis also raises serious concerns about user privacy. Users are uncomfortable if personalization is taken too far. In the wider philosophical debate between personalized services based on user behavior analysis and preserving the user privacy, there is a need to find a middle ground that will allow for potential benefits of personalized services and still safeguard the fine-grained sensitive user information.[1]

Ideally, the data set for such analyses should be stripped of all sensitive user information, while still allowing for inference of medium-grained user activity.

[1] Specific search queries, personal entertainment preferences, purchased products, location etc. are generally considered highly sensitive user information.

P. Cimiano et al. (Eds.): ICWE 2015, LNCS 9114, pp. 116–133, 2015.
DOI: 10.1007/978-3-319-19890-3_9

This is becoming even more important with the tightening privacy legislations in various countries [1,4,7,18], increasing regulation (e.g., [8]) and heavy penalties for data breaches which has made network operators as well as service providers (e.g., [26]) more careful about the data sets they collect, store and share. The operators would like to store the minimal amount of data to still be able to perform complex analytics, raising the important question of determining the *thin boundary* between the required data for necessary analytics and the data that can enable mining of highly sensitive fine-grained user traits. In this context, we consider the usage of truncated URLs, wherein each URL is trimmed to only contain the web domain. For instance, the HTTP URL *finance.yahoo.com/q?s=BAC* is truncated to *finance.yahoo.com* (to hide the fact that the user had queried for Bank of America Corp. stock price), the URL *https://www.google.com/#q=postnatal+depression* is truncated to *www.google.com* (to avoid leaking the sensitive health query of the user) and the URL *www.amazon.com/Dell-Inspiron-i15R-15-6-inch-Laptop/dp/B009US2BKA* is truncated to *www.amazon.com* (to avoid leaking the searched or purchased product). Already, many network operators only share the truncated URL data-sets with third-party analysts, owing to privacy considerations. For the non-HTTP traces (e.g., HTTPS encapsulated in IP packets), even the network operators, themselves, have limited information available. While a reverseDNS service can be used to extract the URL from the IP address, it does not recovers the content type or the query parameters. Thus, it is important to explore whether high accuracy can still be obtained in profiling user activities if an analyst is restricted to only using truncated-URL web trace. In this paper, we investigate this issue.

Specifically, we focus on the task of identifying URLs that are representative of user activities, which is often an important step in profiling user activities. We note that the remaining task of mapping the representative URLs to activity categories (and creating user profiles) can be done using either manual labeling of interesting categories or in an automated way by using external databases or web analytics services (e.g., Alexa [2]).

The key challenge in filtering out the representative URLs from noisy truncated traffic trace is that a truncated trace lacks many crucial features for such a filtering. These include the file name suffix (e.g., .jpg, .mp3, .mpg etc.) that is usually a good indicator of the content type as well as number, type and values of parameters in the URL strings. Nonetheless, we show that even with the truncated URLs, we can achieve a highly accurate automated classification of web-domains into those that represent the user activity and those that don't. The key insight that we bring in this paper is that a user's traffic trace is composed of many data bursts. A burst usually corresponds to a *micro user action* like a web click, chat reply, etc. and is typically associated with a unique activity. We show that novel features related to burst measurements, such as positioning of a URL in a burst, the number of URLs in the burst containing the web-domain etc., can improve the accuracy of filtering the noise (unintentional traffic such as spam, analytics, advertisements as well as other non-representative traffic such as images, multimedia, scripts) out of the traffic trace, by around 20%, offsetting the loss due to URL truncation.

To achieve this result, we need to decompose a traffic trace of a user into its constituent data bursts. The problem here is that there is a significant variation in the traffic pattern across different users, at different timestamps and different activities. Even the distribution shape of the inter-arrival time of HTTP records differs significantly from one user to another. We resolve this problem by proposing a novel burst decomposition algorithm that adapts itself to any distribution shape, rather than relying on specific distributions.

We provide an extensive experimental evaluation over more than 130 million HTTP records generated from 10,000 users over a period of 30 days. The experimental analysis demonstrates that our methodology provides high accuracy (around 90%), in segregating representative URLs from non-representative URLs.

Our approach, thus, enables the network operators to personalize services without risking the leakage of more sensitive user data (as the sensitive information need not be stored or shared). Specifically, it enables many medium-grained personalization applications, including, but not restricted to, product recommendation and targeted advertisement. For instance, knowing when their users read, shop, browse and play games, enables telecom operators to create better pricing schemes that are personalized and targetted for different users and demographics. Such profiling of user activity also opens up many avenues for network optimization to service providers. For instance, system resources can be better allocated to match the data access rate and desired delay time for gaming activities at specific time in the day and better caching strategies can be designed.

Outline. In Section 2, we show that there is a considerable variation in the user activity, that necessitates the data-dependent feature extraction and complex statistical models to deal with this problem. Section 3 presents an overview of our methodology. In Section 4, we argue that there is a considerable variation in the distribution shapes of the inter-arrival time of HTTP records and thus, the burst decomposition techniques that rely on specific distribution shapes do not work well across the entire user spectrum. In Section 5, we show how we can remedy the situation by using a threshold on the inter-arrival time of HTTP records, that adapts to the distribution profile of each user. Section 6 presents the results of domain classification using the features extracted from burst measurements. Section 7 presents an overview of some related work.

2 Variation in User Activity

The main goal of our investigation is to develop an automated procedure to filter out representative URLs from the noisy trace of truncated HTTP records. In this section, we describe our dataset. We show that in this dataset, there is a significant variation between different users in terms of non-representative traffic, user activities, number of HTTP records etc. In the next section, we propose a

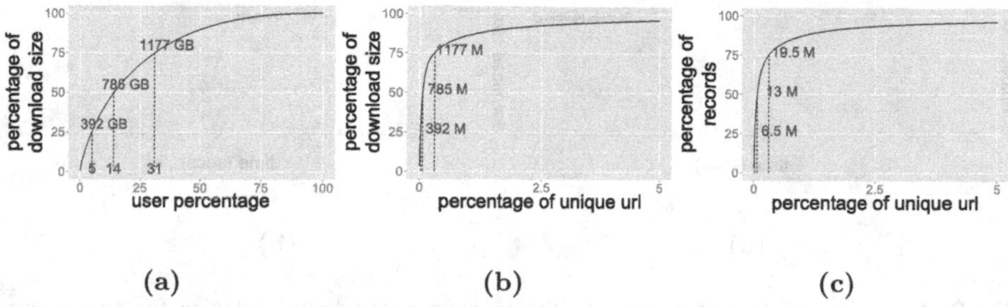

Fig. 1. Summary statistics for the traffic trace of a randomly chosen batch of 2000 users

novel methodology that employs robust algorithms for extracting user-dependent features to overcome this high variation in user activity.

Dataset. Our dataset consists of more than 130 million web-logs generated from randomly selected 10,000 users over a period of 30 days from an anonymous network operator. In our traces, each record contains information fields such as user hashed ID, truncated-URL, download size, upload size and timestamp. Note that our dataset is not restricted to any particular domain or limited to a small set of volunteer users. Being a network-side dataset, it is fairly large and diverse in terms of the domains and the users covered. The flip side of this is that it is also very noisy – it contains not just the URLs that a user types in his browser, but also all the redirects, secondary URLs (pictures, embedded videos etc.) and unintentional data (scripts, analytics, advertisement, spam etc.).

Variation in Total Traffic. We first observe that there is a significant variation in the HTTP traffic generated by different users. For instance, the number of HTTP records ranges from low tens for some users to tens of thousands for other users, over the 30 day period of study. In fact, a majority of HTTP download traffic (75%) is generated by just 31% of user (Figure 1a). We observe even more skewed distribution for the traffic in terms of the generating activity domain. Less than 0.5% of domains generate 75% of traffic in terms of download size (figure 1b) and HTTP record counts (Figure 1c). Note that even though a large majority (99.5%) of URLs together constitute only a small portion (25%) of the traffic, these less popular URLs are more likely to characterize the unique features of different users and therefore, they play a critical role in differentiating user specific behavior. Thus, it is vitally important to correctly classify these URLs into those that represent the user activities and those that don't.

Variation in Type of Traffic. Even among the users with similar total traffic, the kind of web activities and the fraction of non-representative URLs in the traffic trace varies considerably between the users. For instance, Figure 2 shows the web trace snapshot of two users, illustrating two different activity patterns. Different colored segments in this figure represent traffic from different domains, which can be either representative or non-representative. The trace of the first

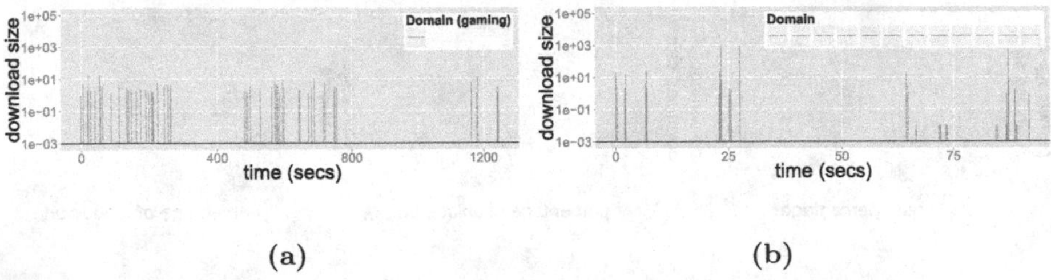

(a) (b)

Fig. 2. Snapshot of timestamped HTTP records with download size for two users, showing a significant variation in amount of non-representative traffic

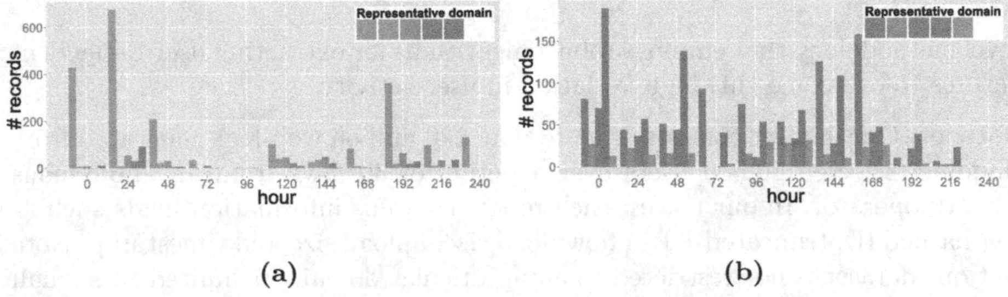

(a) (b)

Fig. 3. Daily record count of top 5 user activities for two users; different colored bars represent different user activities such as reading, searching, gaming

user (Figure 2a) has only one domain, i.e. gaming, and in fact, repeated records from a single URL for more than 1300 seconds. For this user, there is no non-representative traffic to filter out. However, the web browsing activity of another user shown in Figure 2b alternates between a large number of domains (scripts, multimedia, HTML CSS, advertisements, analytics etc.) in less than 100 seconds, even though he/she is browsing a single web-page during this time. This variation in activity patterns is reflected in download size, inter-arrival time as well as number of HTTP records. In addition, the timestamp patterns of HTTP records also varies significantly from one user to another (see Figure 2).

Variation in User Behaviors. We also observe that there is a significant variation between different users in terms of the activities themselves. To summarize the aggregated variation of the top-k domains of both representative and non-representative traffic, we use the following global entropy-based metric to measure this variation:

$$S_a = \frac{-\sum_i \frac{n_i}{nk} \log(\frac{n_i}{nk}) - \log(k)}{\log(nk) - \log(k)}, \quad (1)$$

where n_i is the number of times that URL i appears in the top k domains, satisfying $\sum_i n_i = nk$. By Equation (1), the variation metric S_a is maximized at 1 when all users have different non-overlapping top k domain set and is minimized at 0 when all users have the same non-ordered top k domain set. For the web trace data, S_a is 0.484 with 1455 distinct domains from among the top $k = 5$ domains for the 2000 users. The discovered S_a value suggests that there is a significant variation in the top activities among the different users. We show this intuition graphically in Figures 3a and 3b, where we depict the activity variation of two users over time. For this figure, we filtered out the non-representative domains manually, selected top 5 representative domains for each user according to the number of HTTP records. Figure 3 presents the daily record counts for each representative domain and demonstrates both the temporal and activity variations in terms of activity types and the magnitude across two randomly selected users.

Summary. These above variational statistics imply that the methods to extract features for separating noise from the representative URLs have to adapt to changing user patterns. In particular, the variation in the total traffic and the timestamp patterns necessitates user-adaptive solutions that we explore in the next sections.

3 Our Methodology

In this section, we present an overview of our methodology to automatically classify the web-domains into those that represent the user activities and those that don't. The key feature of this methodology is the usage of novel features derived from the burst decomposition of a user's web-trace that improves the accuracy of the classification, offsetting the loss due to URL truncation.

The main intuition behind our methodology is that a user's browsing activity consists of several data bursts. These data bursts correspond to micro user actions, such as a web click or a chat reply. In each burst, there are some URLs representing the user activity intermixed with other unintentional web-traffic such as advertisements, web-analytics etc and secondary URLs corresponding to multimedia associated with the representative URL. Our statistical methodology decomposes the web-trace back into its constituent data bursts. It then leverages specialized features from data bursts (e.g., the position of a URL in a data burst, the number of unique URLs in a data burst, burst duration, burst download size etc.) to segregate the representative web-domains from the remaining web-domains. In Section 6, we show that the usage of features derived from data burst help in significantly improving the accuracy of the segregation task.

A key challenge in our methodology is the decomposition of the web-trace into data bursts. As highlighted already in Section 2, there is a considerable variation in the traffic patterns of different users. We found that even the distribution of inter-arrival time of HTTP records is very different for different users. This makes it particularly difficult to model these data bursts and to find good thresholds to decompose the web-trace into data bursts. We solve this problem by having different thresholds for different users and ensuring that the threshold computing function is robust with respect to the distribution shape. This is achieved using a novel technique to generate thresholds for each user that adapts to any distribution of inter-arrival time.

4 Inter-arrival Time Distribution Models

In this section, we study the inter-arrival time of HTTP records with a view to finding good thresholds that will decompose a user's traffic-trace into burst of records that represent micro user actions.

As described in Section 3, the key concept behind burst is that when a user performs a micro action like web click, chat reply etc., it not only generates many HTTP records related to the representative activity, but also a large number of secondary records such as advertisements, web analytics, webscripts etc. These records are all intermixed. When the user completes the current micro-action, e.g. reading the current web page, and starts a new one, e.g. opening the next page, a new burst is generated with its associated records. So, the observed inter-arrival time records are the combined results of within-burst and out-of-burst records. However, we expect that the within-burst HTTP records are closer together and the out-of-burst records are far apart in time. By computing an appropriate *separation threshold* on the inter-arrival time, we aim to decompose the traffic into its constituent bursts.

Since traffic patterns and the inter-arrival time distributions for different users are very different, we can't expect a global threshold to work well for all users. Instead, we compute a different threshold for each user specific to his/her traffic patterns. If the difference between the time-stamp of a record and its predecessor is greater than the computed *separation threshold* for that user, the record marks the beginning of a new burst. Otherwise, the record belongs to the burst of its predecessor.

To learn the *separation threshold* for each user, our first approach is to learn the probability density function of inter-arrival time for the users. By computing the best-fitting parameters for this density function for each user and defining the separation threshold as a function of those parameters, we can decompose the traffic trace for each user into its constituent bursts.

We modeled personalized inter-arrival time distributions by exploring different density functions, such as exponential distribution, pareto distribution and mixtures and concatenations of these distributions (details provided in [14]). From the analysis, we found that even these general density functions are not flexible enough to accommodate highly varied and personalized inter-arrival time of different users. Thus, we concluded that even though this formalism is principled, there is a need for a more robust technique to separate within-burst and out-of-burst records, that is *independent* of the personalized distribution shape of a user.

5 Burst Decomposition Using Adaptive Thresholds

In this section, we propose a robust burst decomposition algorithm that is independent of the distribution shape. Our technique only relies on the general

Algorithm 1. Burst Decomposition

1. Divide inter-arrival times into bins b_i of length l with counts c_i
2. Calculate $k_i = \frac{c_i}{\sum_{j=1}^{i} c_j}$
3. Find the smallest index $i^\star$ that $k_{i^\star+j} < p \; \forall j = 1..J$
4. Define the inter-arrival threshold $\tau^\star = l \times i^\star$
5. Group consecutive URLs with inter-arrival times $\tau < \tau^\star$ into bursts.

characteristics of the inter-arrival time distribution (cf. [14]), but not on any specific model. The only characteristic of the inter-arrival time distribution that we use is that there is a within-burst component with high arrival-rate of records (and small inter-arrival time), an out-of-burst component with low arrival-rate (high inter-arrival time) forming a long tail and that these two components are separable with a threshold. Our aim in this section is to have a threshold that adapts itself to any inter-arrival time distribution, subject to this general property.

We first observe that an optimal threshold $\tau^\star$ is expected to lay in a low probability range and should satisfy the following conditions:

- $\forall\, x < \tau^\star$, $p(x)$ should, generally, be high and show the presence of bursts
- $\forall\, x >= \tau^\star$, $p(x)$ should, typically, have low values and imply user inactivity periods

In order to satisfy the above conditions, $\tau^\star$ has to intercept the minimum x point where the probability density function of inter-arrival time distribution decays to fairly close to zero and the density of $p(x)$ values beyond $\tau^\star$ is minimal.

However, to quantitatively measure the significance of each $p(x)$ value, we need a *scalar indicator* that would determine when a $p(x)$ value is minimal. This approach would suffer from the selection of a global scalar indicator that would fail in detecting the intrinsic variations of the density proportion between the within bursts and out-of bursts components for different users.

Therefore, instead of using this approach of quantifying $p(x)$, we leverage the conditional density, i.e. $\frac{p(x)dx}{\int_0^x p(y)dy}$, to determine $\tau^\star$. Note that, $\frac{p(x)dx}{\int_0^x p(y)dy} \approx \frac{c_i}{\sum_{j=1}^{i} c_j}$ which is the probability that a time sample belongs to bin i, conditioning on the fact that it belongs to a bin less than or equal to i: $k_i = \Pr(x \in b_i | x \in b_{1:i})$. In other words, k_i measures the contribution of the current bin to the accumulated probability.

Our Algorithm 1 searches for $\tau^\star$ by starting from the smallest value of the inter-arrival time density such that the extended probability by increasing decaying point is insignificant, compared to the accumulated probability at that point (as captured by k_i). Specifically, the threshold $\tau^\star$ is found when the contributions of J consecutive bins are less than a predefined probability, for a pre-specified parameter J.

The burst decomposition algorithm will group all the records with inter-arrival time less than the obtained $\tau^\star$ into actual bursts.

In the next section, we provide evidence that this algorithm detects meaningful bursts that significantly improve the classification accuracy in identifying the domains that represent user activities.

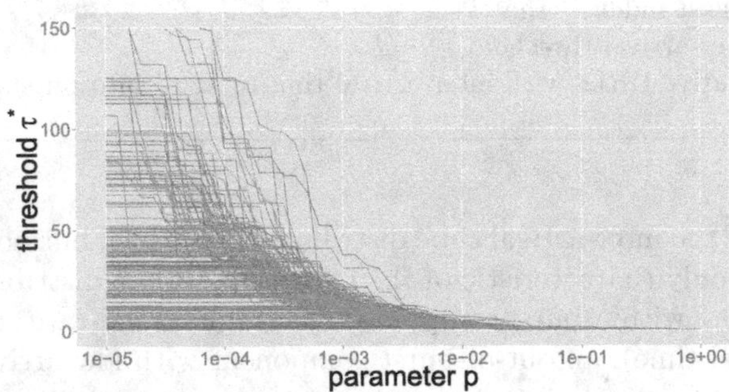

Fig. 4. Calibrating parameter p by examining the variation of user behaviors through the threshold $\tau^{\star}$

We estimate the values of the scalar indicator, p, used in the Algorithm 1 based on an analysis of the corresponding $\tau^{\star}$ values across all users. In Figure 4 we only report the $\tau^{\star}$ behaviors of 200 users as representative of entire $\tau^{\star}$ values computed across all users. It is easy to notice that for $p = 0.01$ the $\tau^{\star}$ would range from 1 to 10 seconds, which is a reasonable range to separate inter-arrival time values between within burst and out-of bursts for activities such as web browsing, reading, shopping, etc. Hence, this value of p was used in our experimental analysis.

Next, we examine the results of our algorithm with respect to users with substantially different behaviors. Even though the distribution shapes and the number of records characterizing these three users are very different, the algorithm successfully finds a user specific $\tau^{\star}$ as shown in Figure 5.

6 Domain Classification

In this section, we describe our classification model for identifying the representative URLs and show that it is possible to achieve very high accuracy for this task even with truncated URLs. Features extracted from the burst decomposition presented in Section 5 play a crucial role in significantly improving the accuracy of our classification model.

Classification Model Formalization. We use a logistic regression model for the domain classification problem. Our model for logistic regression is as follows:

$$y_i \sim \text{Bernoulli}(q_i), \tag{2}$$

$$\ln(\frac{q_i}{1-q_i}) = \mu_i = \beta_0 + \sum_l \beta_l x_{i,l}, \tag{3}$$

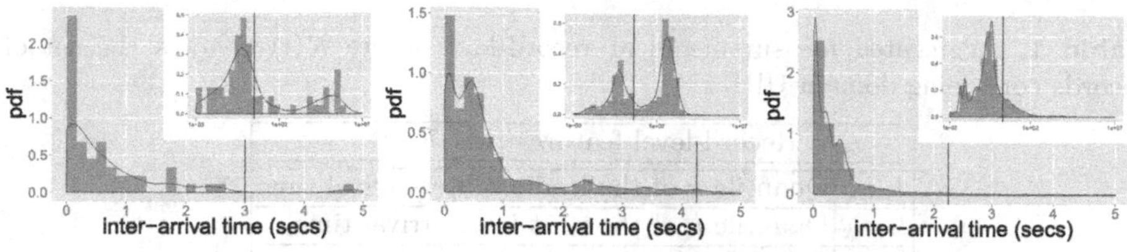

(a) Low activity user: 71 records. (b) Medium activity user: 6764 records. (c) High activity user: 35116 records.

Fig. 5. User dependent τ^* obtained from burst decomposition algorithm

where y_i is the binary label ($y_i = 1$ if URL i is representative and $y_i = 0$ otherwise) and $x_{i,l}$ is the specific classification feature that we derive from record-level and burst-level analysis in Section 6.1 and 6.2. The representative probability q_i is computed by the *logistic function* on a linear predictor μ_i and all the parameters are estimated by the Iteratively Re-Weighted Least Squares (IRWLS) method [20].

The domain classification follows three steps. First, we manually label 400 URLs into two classes: representative and non-representative domains. Second, we extract five sets of web traces generated out of $2K$ random users each, perform the burst decomposition and obtain aggregated measurements independently for each set. Finally, half of the labelled URLs of the first set are used in training the classifier, which is validated by the other half of the first set and the remaining four. We use five different sets to validate the robustness of our approach.

We demonstrate the accuracy of our classification approach in two steps. We first study the accuracy obtained by only using the record-level features and ignoring the burst-level features. Then, we show the improvements we gain by adding the burst-level features which are derived upon the detected bursts from our burst decomposition algorithm.

Record-level Features. The key part of our modeling is feature engineering, or identifying the right set of features to achieve a high accuracy. For the record-level features, shown in Table 1, we use the aggregated measurements across all users and compute the quantile values k by ranging k from 5 to 95 with an increment step equal to 5. These features were carefully selected to achieve a high accuracy with record-level features. Specifically, for each record we collect the leading and following inter-arrival time and the upload and download size. These features are examined as covariates in our domain classification model.

6.1 Accuracy with Record-level Features

Accuracy. As shown in Table 2, the resultant accuracy with the record-level features is quite poor. For the five sets of web traces, the accuracy varies between 69.7% and 72.9%, implying that around 30% of the URLs are misclassified.

Table 1. Aggregated measurements at record-level where $\mathcal{R}(i)$ denotes the set of records containing domain URL i

Record-level features (wrt $\mathcal{R}(i)$)	
$t_{r,l,k}$	Quantile k of the leading inter-arrival time
$t_{r,n,k}$	Quantile k of the next inter-arrival time
$s_{r,u,k}$	Quantile k of the upload size
$s_{r,d,k}$	Quantile k of the download size

Table 2. AIC and classification accuracy with record-level features

	AIC	BIC	Classification accuracy on 5 sets of 2K users each.				
$\mathcal{C}_{\mathcal{R}}$	242.82	252.72	69.7	72.9	71.0	70.8	71.4

Table 3. Estimated values (β_l), standard deviation (σ_β), p-values and significance (SIG) for logistic regression model with record-level features

Feature	β_l	σ_β	p-value	SIG
Intercept	−1.41	0.38	$1.8e-4$	***
$s_{r,d,75\%} - s_{r,d,25\%}$	−0.03	0.01	$4.7e-4$	***
$s_{r,u,50\%}$	0.86	0.26	$1.0e-3$	***

Among the analyzed features we have discovered two particularly important: $x_{\cdot,1} = (s_{r,d,75\%} - s_{r,d,25\%})$ and $x_{\cdot,2} = s_{r,u,50\%}$ by the stepwise model selection procedure. The first is the difference between the 75 and 25 quantile statistics of the download size per domain and the second is the 50 quantile statistic of the upload size. The estimated coefficients for this model is shown in Table 3, implying that domains with small variation of download size and high value of upload size have higher chance of being representative domains. However they are the most relevant features at record-level, their discriminatory capacity still remains limited.

6.2 Accuracy with Burst-level Features

In this section, we show how the accuracy improves with features measured at burst-level.

Burst-level Features. By leveraging the burst decomposition algorithm, we segment our web traces in a series of consecutive bursts and we measure burst-specific characteristics. Specifically, for each URL i, we choose a list of aggregated measurements, shown in Table 4, where $\mathcal{B}(i)$ denotes the set of bursts containing URL i. We observe that two burst features, i.e. $o_{b,j}$ and $u_{b,j}$ ($j = 1:2$), in Figure 6 are particularly important in improving the domain classification results. The first measure, i.e. $o_{b,j}$, describes the probability that a URL is ranked j in its burst and the second, i.e. $u_{b,j}$, quantifies the probability that there are j unique domains in the burst containing the URL ($j = 1:2$). Similar to record-level features, these aggregated measurements are examined as covariates in our domain classification model.

Table 4. Aggregated measurements at burst-level where $\mathcal{B}(i)$ denotes the set of bursts containing URL i

Burst-level features (wrt $\mathcal{B}(i)$)	
$o_{b,j}$	The probability that URL i is ranked j-th ($j = 1:9$)
$u_{b,j}$	The probability that a burst containing URL i has j unique URLs ($j = 1:9$) in the burst
$d_{b,k}$	Quantile k of burst duration
$t_{b,l,k}$	Quantile k of the leading inter-arrival time of a burst
$t_{b,n,k}$	Quantile k of the next inter-arrival time of a burst
$s_{b,u,k}$	Quantile k of the burst upload size
$s_{b,d,k}$	Quantile k of the burst download size

Table 5. Estimated values (β_l), standard deviation (σ_β), p-values and significance (SIG) for logistic regression model with all features

Feature	β_l	σ_β	p-value	SIG
Intercept	-3.30	0.52	$2.2e-11$	***
$\overline{o}_{b,j=1}$	22.87	3.32	$5.5e-12$	***
$u_{b,j=2}$	-9.51	3.45	0.01	**

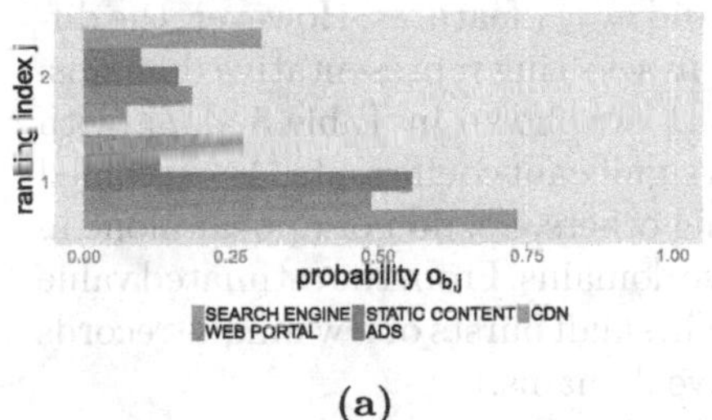

(a)

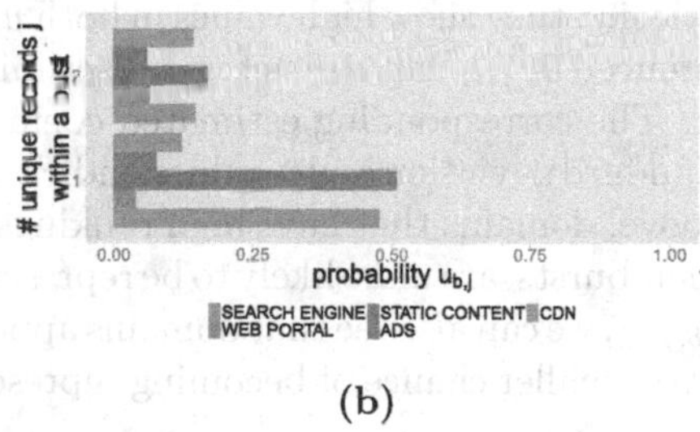

(b)

Fig. 6. The probability $o_{b,j}$ that a URL is ranked j in its burst and the probability $u_{b,j}$ that there are j records in the burst containing the URL ($j = 1:2$) for different domains

Discriminating Features. We perform a model selection procedure, based on AIC, to select the most discriminating features for our classification model and starting from those listed in Table 4. We observe that the feature $\overline{o}_{b,j=1} = o_{b,j=1} - u_{b,j=1}$ is selected with high significance. The intuition behind this is that the URLs which usually come first in bursts are more likely belonging to the representative class. Thus, $o_{b,j=1}$ is a good distinguishing feature between representative domains *(SEARCH ENGINE, WEB PORTAL)* and non-representative domains *(ADS, CDN)* (as shown in Figure 6). Solely using this feature will misclassify domains from *STATIC CONTENT* class as representative (as these are also likely to come first in burst). This class includes many CSS HTML pages and static images on web-pages. However, the exceptions such as those from *STATIC CONTENT* class have a high probability of being alone in their bursts, as shown by $u_{b,j=1}$ in Figure 6. Thus, the feature $\overline{o}_{b,j=1}$ is able to distinguish between most representative and non-representative domains.

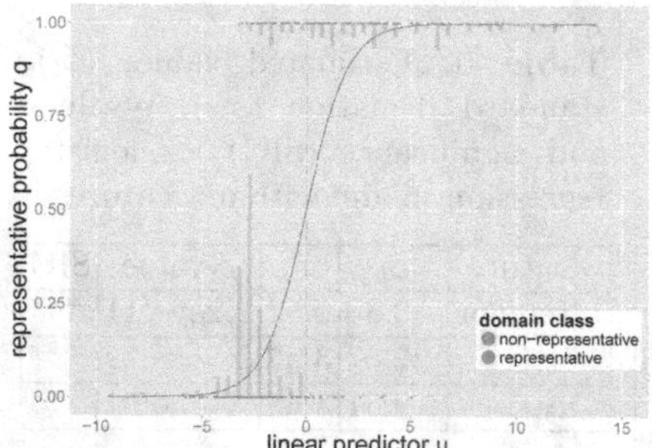

Fig. 7. Logistic curve of the predictor and the histograms of labelled observations

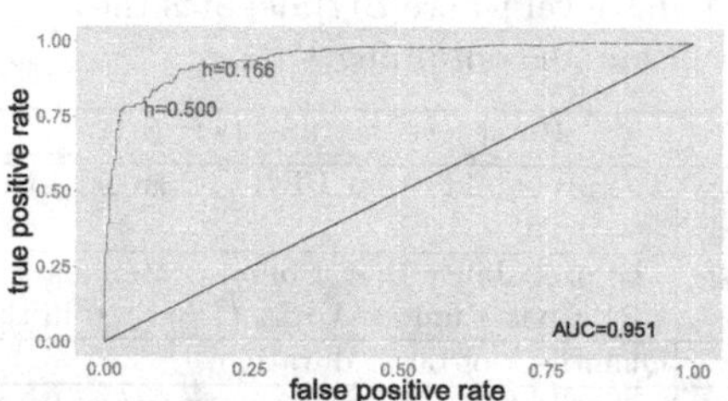

Fig. 8. Receiver operating characteristic curve

Note that the domains in the *SEARCH ENGINE* class have a unique characteristic, i.e. they show high values in both $u_{b,j=1}$ and $o_{b,j=1}$ features. However, the differenced $\overline{o}_{b,j=1}$ can still act as a discriminator in selecting representative domains.

The corresponding estimated coefficients β_l are shown in Table 5 along with standard deviation and p-values, indicating all significant coefficients. As explained above, domains that have high rankings among others, i.e. do not appear alone in their bursts, are more likely to be representative domains. From the estimated value $u_{b,j=2}$, we can also see that domains appearing in small bursts of few unique records have smaller chance of becoming representative domains.

6.3 Trade-off Between Classification Metrics

The relation between the linear predictor μ_i and representative probability q_i is plotted in Figure 7, together with the binary labelled observations and histogram of each domain class. The red vertical line represents the decision boundary such that all URL with $q_i \geq h = 0.5$ are put into representative class and the other are in the non-representative class. Hence, the ratio between the points on the left and right of the red line at row $q = 0$ corresponds to the ratio between true negative-ness and false positive-ness. Similarly, the ratio between true positive-ness and false negative-ness is at row $q = 1$.

In Figure 7, we use the boundary value $h = 0.5$, corresponding to the case of minimizing the number of misclassification cases to separate between representative and non-representative records. However, from a decision theory point-of-view, as the false-positive and false-negative penalties are usually different, we may want to optimize the boundary value by customizing these penalties based on application specific requirements. For instance, let's consider an application that generates users's profiles. These kind of applications may want to put a higher penalty for false negatives (representative URLs incorrectly classified as non-representatives) than for false positives (non-representative URLs correctly classified as representative). This is because when determining the activity of a burst, there is an opportunity to prune out the noise (non-representative URLs)

Table 6. Trade-off between accuracy, sensitivity, precision and specificity

h	0.500	0.166
Precision	0.93	0.77
Negative Predictive Value	0.90	0.95
Sensitivity	0.78	0.91
Specificity	0.97	0.87
Accuracy	0.91	0.88

Table 7. AIC and classification accuracy

	AIC	BIC	Classification accuracy				
$\mathcal{C}_{\mathcal{B}}$	112.80	122.69	90.0	88.3	90.2	89.2	90.5
$\mathcal{C}_{\mathcal{R}}$	242.82	252.72	69.7	72.9	71.0	70.8	71.4

further, while the representative URLs lost in the process are unlikely to be re-inserted later on. Thus, these applications should be calibrated to improve sensitivity, i.e. the ratio of correctly classified representative URLs to the total number of representative URLs.

Because the penalties are problem-specific and not obvious in many contexts, we show the trade-off between true positive rate (complement of false negative rate) and false positive rate with the receiver operating characteristic curve (ROC) in Figure 8. The figure also illustrates another optimal boundary point in purple for the case of minimizing the sum of false positive and false negative rates. The high value of area under the curve (AUC), [9], again confirms the good performance of our classifier.

Table 6 provides further statistics on the trade-off between false positives and true negatives for two different values of the boundary, that were shown in Figure 8. These trade-offs are characterized in terms of precision, negative predictive value, sensitivity, specificity and accuracy. We note that while the value of $h = 0.5$ results in higher precision and accuracy, the $h = 0.166$ results in better sensitivity. Thus, for applications with more emphasis on accuracy, we may choose $h = 0.5$, while for applications where sensitivity is crucial, we may select $h = 0.166$.

Accuracy. The usage of burst-level features, and in particular $\overline{o}_{b,j=1}$, results in significant improvement in the accuracy of the classification model. As shown in Table 7, the accuracy improves from around 70% to around 90%; AIC value drops from 242.82 without burst-level features to just 112.8 with these features; and finally, the BIC drops from 252.72 to 122.69.

Altogether, these results show that it is possible to achieve a 90% accuracy in segregating representative URLs from non-representative URLs by using burst-level features on truncated URL web-traces. In other words, the burst decomposition and the extraction of specific features from the bursts overcome the information lost due to URL truncation. Note that this accuracy is in terms of the number of URLs correctly classified as being representative or non-representative. Popular URLs are more likely to be correctly classified by our methodology and thus, the accuracy in terms of number of records, download size (e.g., to answer questions like how much download is generated corresponding to each activity type) or number of bursts (identifying the activity for each burst) is likely to be significantly higher.

7 Related Work

The past research related to identifying URLs representing user activities falls into the following categories:

1. Filter out the unintentional traffic by relying on URL suffixes (e.g., .mp3, .js etc.), URL header patterns, HTTP referrers and HTTP blacklists. This category critically relies on full HTTP web-traces. For some papers (e.g., [24]) in this category, the setting even allows to take a peek into a user's full network traffic (including a deep packet inspection of the content). The full HTTP URLs can reveal highly sensitive user information and their usage raises serious privacy concerns. For instance, Song et al. [16] highlighted a practical privacy attack that exploits seemingly-anonymous recorded information of shortened URL service such as HTTP referrer URLs, countries, browsers, platform, etc to infer the clicking pattern of a specific user. In contrast, our focus is on inferring medium-grained user behavior analysis from minimal traffic traces (truncated-URLs) and on techniques that will allow us to offset the accuracy loss due to URL truncation.
2. Providing an activity description at a very coarse level (e.g., peer-to-peer networking, HTTP browsing, chatting etc.) by filtering out URLs based on connection port number, packet payload, statistical traffic patterns etc. [15,25], primarily for the purpose of network traffic analysis and traffic classification (e.g. for CDN). This is clearly different from our HTTP domain-level segregation.
3. Manual blacklisting of URLs to filter out spam, adult content or advertisements. This has obvious scalability limitations and it is very expensive to manually maintain the blacklists. Furthermore, the existing blacklists (see [23] for a list of many manual blacklists) are for specific purposes (such as spam, adult content, advertisements) and do not contain all non-representative URLs (such as multimedia associated with the main content).

Our work deals with a large, diverse, but noisy traffic trace from a network-side. This allows us to perform a detailed study that is not limited to a few domains or restricted to a few volunteer users. This is in contrast with many publications on behavior analysis that deal with data from users or service-providers.

Privacy Preserving User Profiling. There has been considerable work in recent years on privacy preserving personalization. Herein, we list a few approaches:

Bilenko and Richardson [5] also consider the problem of user profiling while mitigating the privacy concerns. However, their approach is based on storing the sensitive information on the client side, in the form of cookies or browser local storage. The storage of this sensitive information still leaves a user vulnerable to privacy violations. On the other hand, our user profiling does not require the sensitive information to be stored at all. Similar client-side approaches in the context of personalized search (e.g., [21]) and online advertisements (e.g., [19]) have also been studied.

Nandi et al. [3] take an alternative approach to privacy preserving personalization. They replace the user traces by traces of group of similar users. However, this requires user segmentation, which in turn, requires significant historical data. Also, this results in an aggregate level personalization and not an individual level personalization.

Also, there are some theoretical solutions based on k-anonymity [17] and l-diversity [13] for preserving privacy. However, it is not clear if they can be useful for profiling personalized time-series data. There are also some approaches (e.g. [12]) that add random or correlated noise to the data to preserve the privacy. However, such approaches also introduce more noise in the user profiles.

Burst Detection. Kleinberg [11] proposed a discrete state space model as a burst detection algorithm, with applications in email streams. However, the focus of this solution is the varying exponential distribution's rate, modelled by the hidden state. The rate characterizes the email arrival of a temporal local period but does not provide a clear distinction between within-burst and out-of-burst records. For example, even when the rate goes down to the smallest value, the positive skewness of exponential distribution still favours small inter-arrival time samples. Such an approach is unlikely to work for our problem of segregating two inter-arrival time classes.

Karagiannis et al. [10] showed that the accuracy of exponential distribution varies with different backbone packet traces. In general, exponential distribution has nice mathematical features such as memoryless-ness and closed-form solutions of sum-concat-minimum operators. However, its light tailed property may not be a good match to some datasets.

8 Discussion

We have proposed a novel methodology to identify URLs representing user activities from a truncated URL web-trace. Our statistical methodology offsets the loss in accuracy due to URL truncation by considering additional features derived from the burst measurements. To enable the computation of burst-level features, we propose a novel technique for burst decomposition.

Once the set of representative URLs is identified, one can compare the (live) streaming web-traces of users to infer medium grained activities in real-time and offer personalized services. Burst decomposition can play a critical role in this part as well. Once the user-adaptive thresholds are identified, our burst decomposition algorithm can be used to decompose the streaming trace into bursts and a unique URL representing the activity in that burst can be identified using the identified set of representative URLs.

We consider that our methodology can be very useful for providing personalized services, while being considerate about more sensitive user privacy data. For instance, state-of-the-art techniques to predict click-through-rate (CTR) rely on behavioral targeting of fine-grained user data [6], such as advertisement clicks, web-page clicks, page views and search query data. A medium-grained user profiling, such as the one created by our technique, can be used to provide good

CTR predictions while preserving privacy considerations. Similarly, user segmentation based on behavioral targeted advertisement (e.g., [22]) can also benefit from our medium-grained profiling. Our profiling can also be employed to re-rank the search results for a more personalized experience (similar to the approach in [21]). More generally, we hope that our work will lead to deeper studies on the usage of truncated URL traces, as a means to striking the fine balance between personalized services and user privacy.

References

1. European Communities (Electronic Communications Networks and Services) (Privacy and Electronic Communications) Regulations (2011). http://dataprotection.ie/documents/guidance/Electronic_Communications_Guidance.pdf
2. Alexa: Actionable Analytics for the Web (2015). http://www.alexa.com
3. Nandi, A., Aghasaryan, A., Bouzid, M.: P3: a privacy preserving personalization middleware for recommendation-based services. In: Proceedings of 4th Hot Topics in Privacy Enhancing Technologies Symposium (HotPETS 2011) (2011)
4. BBC (2014). http://www.bbc.com/news/technology-25825690 (accessed November 2014)
5. Bilenko, M., Richardson, M.: Predictive client-side profiles for personalized advertising. In: Proceedings of the 17th ACM SIGKDD International Conference on Knowledge Discovery and Data Mining, pp. 413–421. ACM (2011)
6. Chen, Y., Pavlov, D., Canny, J.F.: Large-scale behavioral targeting. In: Proceedings of the 15th ACM SIGKDD International Conference on Knowledge Discovery and Data Mining, pp. 209–218. ACM (2009)
7. European Data Protection Supervisor (2011). https://secure.edps.europa.eu/EDPSWEB/webdav/site/mySite/shared/Documents/Consultation/Opinions/2011/11-05-30_Evaluation_Report_DRD_EN.pdf (accessed November 2014)
8. Facebook: Facebook and the Irish Data Protection Commission (2011). https://www.facebook.com/notes/facebook-public-policy-europe/facebook-and-the-irish-data-protection-commission/288934714486394 (accessed November 2014)
9. Fawcett, T.: An introduction to ROC analysis. Pattern Recognition Letters **27**(8), 861–874 (2006)
10. Karagiannis, T., Molle, M., Faloutsos, M., Broido, A.: A nonstationary poisson view of internet traffic. In: INFOCOM (2004)
11. Kleinberg, J.M.: Bursty and hierarchical structure in streams. In: KDD, pp. 91–101 (2002)
12. Li, F., Sun, J., Papadimitriou, S., Mihaila, G.A., Stanoi, I.: Hiding in the crowd: privacy preservation on evolving streams through correlation tracking. In: Proceedings of the 23rd International Conference on Data Engineering, ICDE, pp. 686–695. IEEE (2007)
13. Machanavajjhala, A., Kifer, D., Gehrke, J., Venkitasubramaniam, M.: L-diversity: privacy beyond k-anonymity. TKDD **1**(1) (2007)
14. Mai, T., Ajwani, D., Sala, A.: Profiling user activities with minimal traffic traces (2015). ArXiv e-prints
15. Nguyen, T.T.T., Armitage, G.J.: A survey of techniques for internet traffic classification using machine learning. IEEE Communications Surveys and Tutorials **10**(1–4), 56–76 (2008)

16. Song, J., Lee, S., Kim, J.: I know the shortened urls you clicked on twitter: inference attack using public click analytics and twitter metadata. In: Proceedings of the 22Nd International Conference on World Wide Web, pp. 1191–1200. WWW 2013, International World Wide Web Conferences Steering Committee, Republic and Canton of Geneva, Switzerland (2013). http://dl.acm.org/citation.cfm?id=2488388.2488492
17. Sweeney, L.: k-anonymity: A model for protecting privacy. International Journal of Uncertainty, Fuzziness and Knowledge-Based Systems **10**(5), 557–570 (2002)
18. TechCrunch (2015). http://techcrunch.com/2014/10/01/hamburg-google/ (accessed March 2015)
19. Toubiana, V., Narayanan, A., Boneh, D., Nissenbaum, H., Barocas, S.: Adnostic: privacy preserving targeted advertising. In: Proceedings of the Network and Distributed System Security Symposium, NDSS 2010. The Internet Society (2010)
20. Wood, S.N.: Generalized additive models: an introduction with R. Chapman and Hall/CRC Texts in Statistical Science Series. Chapman and Hall/CRC Press (2006)
21. Xu, Y., Wang, K., Zhang, B., Chen, Z.: Privacy-enhancing personalized web search. In: Proceedings of the 16th International Conference on World Wide Web, WWW, pp. 591–600. ACM (2007)
22. Yan, J., Liu, N., Wang, G., Zhang, W., Jiang, Y., Chen, Z.: How much can behavioral targeting help online advertising? In: Proceedings of the 18th International Conference on World Wide Web, WWW, pp. 261–270. ACM (2009)
23. Zeltser, L. (2014). http://zeltser.com/combating-malicious-software/malicious-ip-blocklists.html
24. Zhang, F., He, W., Liu, X., Bridges, P.G.: Inferring users' online activities through traffic analysis. In: Proceedings of the Fourth ACM Conference on Wireless Network Security, pp. 59–70. WiSec 2011. ACM (2011)
25. Zhang, J., Xiang, Y., Wang, Y., Zhou, W., Xiang, Y., Guan, Y.: Network traffic classification using correlation information. IEEE Trans. Parallel Distrib. Syst. **24**(1), 104–117 (2013)
26. Zuckerberg, M.: Our commitment to the facebook community (2011). https://www.facebook.com/notes/facebook/our-commitment-to-the-facebook-community/10150378701937131 (accessed November 2014)

Towards Liquid Web Applications

Tommi Mikkonen[1], Kari Systä[1], and Cesare Pautasso[2(✉)]

[1] Department of Pervasive Computing, Tampere University of Technology, Tampere, Finland
{tommi.mikkonen,kari.systa}@tut.fi

[2] Faculty of Informatics, University of Lugano (USI), Lugano, Switzerland
c.pautasso@ieee.org

Abstract. As the complexity of rich Web applications grows together with the power and number of Web browsers, the next Web engineering challenge to be addressed is to design and deploy Web applications to make coherent use of all devices. As users nowadays operate multiple personal computers, smart phones, tablets, and computing devices embedded into home appliances or cars, the architecture of current Web applications needs to be redesigned to enable what we call Liquid Software. Liquid Web applications not only can take full advantage of the computing, storage and communication resources available on all devices owned by the end user, but also can seamlessly and dynamically migrate from one device to another continuously following the user attention and usage context. In this paper we address the Liquid Software concept in the context of Web applications and survey to which extent and how current Web technologies can support its novel requirements.

1 Introduction

Today, the average consumer in the U.S. or Europe has two primary computing devices – a personal computer, usually a laptop, and a smartphone, with more new mobile devices and tablets activated every day. We are on the move from a world in which each person has two or three devices to a world in which people will use dozens of computing devices – laptops, phones, tablets, game consoles, TVs, car displays, digital photo frames, home appliances, wearable computers, and so on. All these devices are connected to the Web, and their users are provided with computation that is constantly available, capable of delivering meaningful value even in few moments, without requiring active attention from the users part [1].

The architecture of current Web applications is not living up to these expectations. Content is increasily made available on the Web and users have many ways to access the content published on the Web, but they are exposed to extra complexity caused by the large number of Web-enabled devices at their disposal. Additional complexity comes from the fact that user content is spread to several devices and Internet services. Managing all these as separate entities is currently a tedious task, while at the same time users expect casual experiences. Since all these devices are already connected to the Web, orchestrating their actions to simplify users' lives would be a natural extension of the Web platform.

P. Cimiano et al. (Eds.): ICWE 2015, LNCS 9114, pp. 134–143, 2015.
DOI: 10.1007/978-3-319-19890-3_10

To create software that fits with the multi-device paradigm, the architecture of current Web applications needs to be redesigned to enable what we call *Liquid Software* [2]. Such Liquid Web applications not only can take full advantage of the computing, storage and communication resources available on all devices owned by the end user, but also can seamlessly and dynamically migrate from one device to another continuously following the user attention and usage context.

In this position paper we apply the Liquid Software concept to the design of Web applications and survey to which extent and how current Web technologies can support its novel requirements. The rest of this paper is structured as follows. In Section 2, we provide background for the concept of Liquid Software. In Section 3, we discuss engineering Liquid Applications in the light of present Web technologies. In Section 4, we provide an extended discussions regarding our findings pointing out future research directions, summarized in Section 5.

2 Liquid Software: Background and Related Work

The notion of Liquid Software was originally proposed in [3]. In our interpretation, the essential feature of Liquid Software is support for hassle-free multi-device experiences, falling to the following categories [4]:

1. **Sequential Screening**. A single user runs an application on different devices at different times. The application adapts to the different devices capabilities while respecting the actual user needs in different usage contexts.
2. **Simultaneous Screening**. A single user uses the services from several devices at the same time, i.e., the session is open and running on multiple devices at same time. Different devices may show an adapted view of the same user interface or the system may have a distributed user interface where different devices play their own roles.
3. **Collaboration scenario.** Several users run the same application on their devices. This collaboration can be either sequential or simultaneous.

All the above scenarios share similar challenges in adapting the user interface to different devices and in synchronizing the data and state between devices. Synchronization of the data and state are important because the devices and users need to be aware of the results of their actions previously or simultaneously done in other devices. This is essential both for immediately transferring the work from one device to another, but also to enable seamless, real-time collaboration.

2.1 Liquid User Experience Scenarios

Today, browsers are used to access many Cloud services and Web applications, and users can already use several devices to access those services. In some cases, it is sufficient for users to share a hyperlink (URL with optional parameters) to exactly reproduce and restore the state of the user interface of the application from one browser to another. For example, the hyperlink may be used to identify the video to be played and also the position within the video the playback should start from. In this case, the client navigation state can be reliably identified and reconstructed elsewhere, assuming that the result of de-referencing the hyperlink is the same everywhere.

With more complex Web applications, so called Rich Internet Applications [5], it may not be possible to use a simple hyperlink to describe the large amounts of local state accumulated on the client during a user work session, and thus it may not be so simple to migrate the application across browsers. For example, Google Docs can be seen as a Liquid Application since one or multiple users can use it from multiple client devices either simultaneously or sequentially. While the state of the edited document (i.e., the data) gets synchronized in real-time, the state of the editor user interface is not. This means that when switching from one browser to another, even if the document remains the same, the editor configuration (e.g., the position of the caret within the document, or the configuration of the tool bar) will not be transferred across sessions.

Our ambition is not limited to centralized cloud services like Google Docs, or even to Rich Internet Applications. Many applications run locally in users devices and only sporadically contact to a server or cloud. At the moment mobile devices have many native mobile applications. Some of them are standard utilities like addressbook, some are mobile interfaces to common Internet services. We foresee that many of them will be implemented as Web applications, but still include a lot of local computation in the device. Local behavior, data and state are needed for better user experience and to cope with less than ideal network characteristics, and to access to local resources, like sensors and the file system. The fact that part of the application and its data resides in the client leads to different kinds of liquidity: liquidity between device and Cloud and liquidity between devices. If the applications or their components can move flexibly between devices and servers, the system may optimize factors like response times, networking costs or battery-life [6]. For instance, if the network latencies slow down the response times, the system may move the communicating components to the same host. Also, if we assume that a substantial part of the application logic and state is stored in the client device, liquid user experiences require liquidity of applications between devices using proximity-based communication.

So far, perhaps the most vivid example of a liquid behavior is the new Handoff capability in Apple iOS 8 [7]. One example scenario of Handoff is one where composing of an email may have started in a phone but finished with a PC that has bigger screen and a real keyboard. The participating devices need to be registered in iCloud with the same identity, and the devices mush be able to communicate over Bluetooth. Handoff can be seen as a mechanism to implement a liquid user experience, since it enables sequential screening for a single user. The applications need to be rewritten to take advantage of the Handoff API and pre-installed across all devices; most of the common Apple applications are already compatible with Handoff. Each device runs a specific version of the application, hence the user interface is implicitly adapted to take advantage of the device capabilities (e.g., multi-touch, screen size, and resolution).

In comparison to Handoff, Liquid Software should support heterogeneous devices across software ecosystem boundaries. This way, developers would need to implement only one application, which then can adapt itself to run everywhere. In our vision Liquid experiences are built using the Web – where applications already now are deployed on demand and through Responsive Web Design [8] are also adapted to fit on the local device display on the fly. Moreover, properties such as openness and freeness from predatory control make the Web a natural choice over native applications that are bound to a particular operating system, manufacturer, or ecosystem [9].

2.2 Liquid vs. Solid Software

In the multi-device world, the user experience of the applications may span across multiple devices [10]. Controlling the behavior of the applications as they migrate from one device to the next forms a new field of research, where proximity, gestures, and previous actions define the flow of user interaction. This has been well demonstrated by a video by the glass company Corning (https://www.youtube.com/watch?v=6Cf7IL_eZ38), where applications are used seamlessly with personal devices, shared screens, and embedded devices in a fashion that best fits the context as well as the particular use case at hand.

Based on the above, Liquid Software is by no means a single technology, but rather a mindset for developing applications to be executed on multiple, heterogeneous computing devices [2]. Liquid Applications then satisfy the SAFE qualities [11] – they are Scalable, Adaptive with respect to their environment, Flexible thus supporting heterogeneity, and Elastic with respect to their workload. The essential elements that make such software different from traditional, "solid", single-device applications are the following:

– **Code mobility**: dynamic relocation of executable code. One categorization of code mobility has been given by Fuggetta et al. in [12]. In that work *strong mobility* means that the code can move together with its state while in *weak mobility* the execution is re-initialized in the new location.

– **State synchronization**: ensuring that the state of the software (and in particular, its user interface) is preserved after the relocation. Fugetta et al. differentiate *migration* from *cloning* [12]. Liquid Applications take advantage of both of these mechanisms. The use case where the user wants to move the ongoing work from a smart phone to a PC (sequential screening), requires strong mobility with migration since the applications move with their states. In use cases where several users collaborate simultaneusly, cloning of the runtime state of the software is needed.

– **Adaptation** The applications as a whole and their components need to adapt to different contexts, runtime environments and hardware capabilities.

Conversely, solid software is characterized by the inability to change its execution environment, without going through a complex and expensive redeployment, reconfiguration, and re-initialization process – or, in general, by associating software with a single computer.

Data and State. In this work we distinguish the application data from the application state. With data we refer to the content that users store persistently across usage session, while state is the information that the application needs in order to continue its own execution after being relocated. This division is similar to the division given in [12] where the data was called *Data Space Management.* In the current Internet some of the resources are local to the device, while some data is available through the network. The user expectation of Liquid Applications is that all relevant data is available regardless of the device, and that modifications done in one location need be synchronized and made visible to all hosts. Companies like Apple, Google or Microsoft are solving this issue by providing data synchronization to the cloud. However, these solutions remain isolated from each other and are difficult to integrate with Web applications due to their file-based abstraction.

3 Engineering Liquid Web Applications

Creating Liquid Applications requires revising the role of traditional layers used to design Web applications as well as using new implementation mechanisms.

3.1 Layers Revisited

As explained earlier, Liquid Applications and their architecture vary in three different dimensions 1) simultaneous vs. sequential multi-device usage, 2) single vs. multiple users collaboration, and 3) thin vs. thick client. These dimensions are not necessary binary choices, and there may be a spectrum of intermediate solutions. For example, the "thickness" of Liquid Web applications may vary depending on the available resources and needs at hand. Fig. 1 shows a possible architecture where the application logic is split between server and client and data is persisted by the server-side. The client part of the logic with related state and user interface (UI) are about to migrate to another device. Below we discuss how the liquid quality impacts each architectural layer: User Interface, Logic, Data and State in the light of these scenarios.

User Interface. The first challenge is to support the adaptability to different device characteristics and usage contexts, but new challenges emerge when interaction includes collaboration between different devices or users. Simultaneous usage will require that the data model shown through the user interfaces

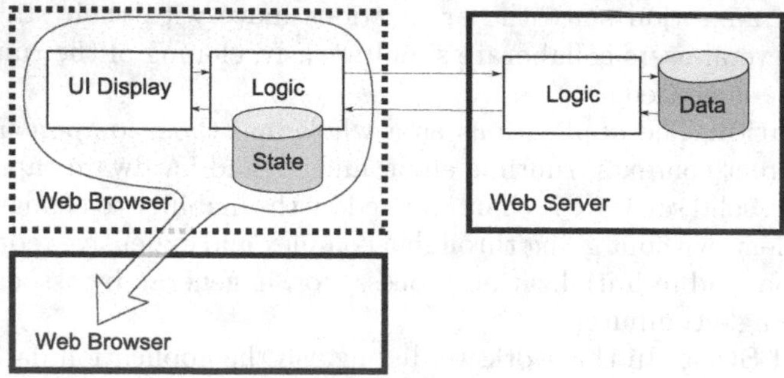

Fig. 1. Liquid Web Application Architecture

of different devices is kept synchronized. Furthermore, the user interface should support interactions that are based on coordinated input and output involving multiple devices. For example, the touch screen of a mobile device could act as an input device for driving the larger display of a laptop. These scenarios could also be combined so that different users look at the same shared display but use their own devices for input. The thicker the client is, the more there are possibilities to implement adaptation in the device, but on the other hand synchronization and coordination between devices become easier in centralized and server-based approaches.

Logic. Similarly to the user interface, also the logic that implements Liquid Applications needs be runnable in different client devices and also adaptable different devices and device combinations. If multiple screens or multiple users work on the same application simultaneously, the desired behaviour may be the same for all devices, or different users and devices may play different roles in the overall logic. In the dimension of thin and thick client, the logic may be split between server-side (e.g., in the Cloud) and client-side (e.g., on the mobile device) in various ways depending, e.g., on the available computational power, quality of the network connection, and the battery charge level of the device. The logic may also change its location dynamically. To support these scenarios, components need to be designed to be portable, for example across devices and between device and server, which is already supported by existing Web technologies (e.g., JavaScript, HTML5, Web components).

Data. In the case of Liquid Software we assume that the data managed by a Web application is available and accessible from all devices and contexts. Furthermore simultaneous screening requires that changes on data become visible on all screens immediately. If multiple users work with the same data, the system needs to handle ownership and access control of the data as well as conflict detection and resolution. Solving of these problems has a direct dependency on the design decision concerning the thin vs. thick dimension. The desired functionality can be achieved through centralization of the data layer, or by replicating and synchronizing a copy of the shared data across all devices.

State. The state of the application encapsulates enough information for migrating or cloning an application to a new location and to continue the execution there. The easiest way to move the state is to serialize the entire process or its whole virtual machine. From the user's point of view it is only important that the user can smoothly move the application to an another device and continue working with minimal disruption. This does not mean that all details on the state need to be preserved, but only the parts that are relevent for the user and for running the application in the new context. It should also be noted, that many applications are client-server systems and part of the state remains on the server. In these cases, the server-part and client-part can move independently from each other. If the client part – usually the user interface – moves, the server part does not need to move. In some systems, all relevant state may be on the server, and changing from one client to another does not require the transfer of any state beyond a URL identifying the server-side state.

3.2 Mechanisms

In the context of the Web, liquidity builds on numerous already existing techniques and mechanisms that are already commonly applied, or at very least, they have been experimented with in research projects. Next, we address the building blocks for achieving liquidity in existing Web browsers.

Responsive Web design. The primary weapon for tackling user interface issues in different devices used for accessing Web services is Responsive Web Design [8]. In its purest form, a key issue in responsive design is how to design the layout and the elements so that they can easily be customised for different screen sizes and device types, with focus usually only on eventual visual appearance on the screen. In general, due to the differences in browsers used in desktops and mobile devices, the development of Responsive Web Designs calls for architecture where some of the functionalities are always executed on the server side. While this simplifies the development, as these functionalities need not be tested with every possible client device, there are also complicating factors, since the state of the user interface must still be transferred from one device to another. Concrete technologies for composing Responsive Web Designs include using proportion-based grids and flexible images, where element sizing takes place using relative units instead of absolute ones, and CSS3 media queries, where different styles can be used for different devices. For the developer, the above facilities are usually visible through a library that supports Responsive Web Design, such as Bootstrap (http://getbootstrap.com) or Foundation (http://foundation.zurb.com).

Liquid Middleware. A key component in designing Liquid Applications is a middleware system that provides support for code and data mobility. Several such systems have been proposed in the field of agent systems [13–15]. In connection with Web applications, there are three different levels to perform a migration from one device to another:

- **Web application**. In our own work, we have shown how to serialize, migrate and deserialize Web applications in two contexts: 1) *Agent framework* enables HTML5 mobile agents that demonstrate that both application code and runtime state can be moved together with the application code [15], and 2) *Lively Kernel extensions* allow Web applications written using the Lively Kernel Web framework to migrate from one computer to another [16]. Both approaches require that the developer follows certain conventions to record state variables to be transferred as well as to define initialization and termination procedures.
- **JavaScript virtual machine**. In the context of browsers, migration can be realized through the underlying JavaScript virtual machine. Unlike the Web application level migration, migrating the JavaScript VM and the corresponding DOM tree state implies that any Web application can be moved automatically, without requiring developers to explicitly depend on a specific mobility framework, apart from what is necessary for adapting the user interface to different contexts with Responsive Web Design techniques.
- **Operating system level migration**. The most extensive approach to code migration is to transfer the whole virtual machine or operating system image

from one host to another. Obviously, such operation requires extensive virtualization, details of which fall beyond Web technologies. Moreover, with such migration, also considerations regarding the time it takes to transfer the image arise.

Data Synchronization. As discussed earlier, there is a need to synchronize updates on data shared by several devices. This can be done in the following ways: 1) keep all data in a centralized server and access data always from that server; 2) on the other extreme, keep all data replicated across all user devices and employ a decentralized, peer-to-peer synchronization tool (such as BitTorrent Sync, AeroFS, and the like); 3) build a system of several primary providers that all other devices use through a unified interface - for example VisualREST [17]. The preferred option depends on the need for simultaneous, concurrent access from multiple devices and thus the need for conflict avoidance/resolution. If a thin client approach is taken, all data is stored in server and addressed from the client. Possible caching would then be implemented with appropriate protocols – like in HTTP. Various Backend as a Service (BaaS) systems allow linking Web applications to hosted backend cloud storage systems and associated services such as push notifications, user management and social network integration. BaaS systems offer well-documented APIs that can be used from Web applications simply by adding a few lines of boilerplate code. For instance, there are systems such as Firebase that focus on making cloud side data storage as simple and effortless as possible. In our designs, this dimension is best considered in the context of Cloudberry [18].

4 Discussion

We claim that Web is a suitable platform for Liquid Software. This claim is backed by several technical experiments and prototypes we have been working on [6,15,16,18]. In the following we propose the next step - design and implementation of a general software framework for Liquid Web applications. The framework is still based on Web technologies and standards, but we propose some changes to existing designs.

The users should be provided with an interface that allows smooth control of liquidity. This means that the top-level user interfaces of devices should complemented with new user interface gestures. One example of such gesture is *hypedragging* [19] that users can use for pushing applications away from the device their are currently running on. Alternatively, a pull approach is also possible, where users indicate the target device on which the application should be moved on. Another requirement for user interface is adaptability of the user interface. Design and implementation of adaptive user interfaces usually takes extra effort, and we should develop frameworks and tools that make implementation of adaptive user interfaces easy.

A further important component of the software framework is the middleware that supports mobility of the code and execution state. The mechanisms should be as automated as possible and extra effort for the developer should be as small as possible. For example, serialization and de-serialization of the state should be automated but the developer may need to declare what is the relevant part of the state. Likewise, it should be possible to develop applications that can observe and react to specific events happening during the migration. The ideas presented in HTML5 Mobile Agents [15] can act as a starting point, but the primary use case should be achieving a liquid user experience of Web applications. In addition, the middleware should support application architectures where same component can run both on server and client. The ability to make optimal use of all available resources of the execution environment has been investigated as part of the Liquid Web Services architectural style [11].

Finally, the architecture should include a *Liquid Storage* abstraction that makes relevant data available and synchronized to users and applications who need it. This can be achieved using different centralized or decentralized replication mechanisms that are abstracted away by the storage abstraction, which should work in a way similar to HTML5 local storage. The data API of Cloudberry and EDB [20] include several ideas our design could reuse.

Ultimately, our research goal is is to develop a new *liquid.js* framework that utilizes the above framework components and make creation of Liquid Applications easy. The liquid.js toolkit will simplify the migration of stateful components and their adaptation to heterogeneous execution environments.

5 Conclusions

From the end-user perspective, liquid software essentially means that the software has a built-in ability to perform adaptive, live migration. The role of the Web is then to act as a platform-independent execution environment, which provides suitable abstractions for relocation, serialization, migration, and adaptation that are needed to develop such applications. All the facilities already exist today, but require use of special frameworks or even application specific code. All these should be either standardized by bodies like W3C, or be simply included to mainstream Web frameworks that today largely define solid application models in the first place.

There are plenty of future research to be carried out in the field of liquid applications. First and foremost, security challenges associated with using multiple devices, with some of them being used by multiple people, are many, and we have largely overlooked them in this phase. Secondly, Internet-of-Things (IoT), as well as its Web-oriented counterpart, Web-of-Things (WoT), introduce challenges that resemble liquid software – managing a large number of computing units, storage and sensors/actuators that are not pre-allocated or pre-configured simply falls beyond what existing application models can deliver. We believe that liquid software provides a suitable metaphor to envison the behavior of software systems as they are deployed in such complex and heterogeneous environments.

Acknowledgments. The work is partially supported by the Hasler Foundation (Switzerland) with the Liquid Software Architecture (LiSA) project.

References

1. Weiser, M.: The computer for the 21st century. Scientific American **265**(3), 94–104 (1991)
2. Taivalsaari, A., Mikkonen, T., Systä, K.: Liquid software manifesto: the era of multiple device ownership and its implications for software architecture. In: Proc. of the 38th IEEE Computer Software and Applications Conference (COMPSAC), pp. 338–343 (2014)
3. Hartman, J.H., Bigot, P.A., Bridges, P.G., Montz, A.B., Piltz, R., Spatscheck, O., Proebsting, T.A., Peterson, L.L., Bavier, A.C.: Joust: A platform for liquid software. IEEE Computer **32**(4), 50–56 (1999)"
4. Google: The new multi-screen world: Understanding cross-platform consumer behavior (2012). http://services.google.com/fh/files/misc/multiscreenworld_final.pdf
5. Casteleyn, S., Garrigós, I., Mazón, J.N.: Ten years of Rich Internet Applications: A systematic mapping study, and beyond. ACM Trans. Web **8**(3), 18:1–18:46 (2014)
6. Babazadeh, M., Gallidabino, A., Pautasso, C.: Liquid stream processing across web browsers and web servers. In: Proc. of the 15th International Conference on Web Engineering (ICWE 2015). Springer, Rotterdam, NL, June 2015
7. Gruman, G.: Apple's Handoff: What works, and what doesn't. InfoWorld, October 7, 2014
8. Marcotte, E.: Responsive Web Design. Editions Eyrolles (2011)
9. Mikkonen, T., Taivalsaari, A.: Cloud computing and its impact on mobile software development: Two roads diverged. Journal of Systems and Software **86**(9), 2318–2320 (2013)
10. Levin, M.: Designing Multi-device Experiences: An Ecosystem Approach to User Experiences Across Devices. O'Reilly (2014)
11. Bonetta, D., Pautasso, C.: An architectural style for liquid web services. In: Proc. of the 9th Working IEEE/IFIP Conference on Software Architecture (WICSA), pp. 232–241 (2011)
12. Fuggetta, A., Picco, G.P., Vigna, G.: Understanding code mobility. IEEE Trans. Softw. Eng. **24**(5), 342–361 (1998)
13. Dömel, P.: Mobile telescript agents and the web. In: Proc. of the 41st IEEE International Computer Conference. COMPCON 1996, p. 52 (1996)
14. Feldmann, M.: An approach for using the web as a mobile agent infrastructure. In: Proc. of the International Multiconference on Computer Science and Information Technology, vol. 2, pp. 39–45. PTI (2007)
15. Systä, K., Mikkonen, T., Järvenpää, L.: HTML5 agents: mobile agents for the web. In: Krempels, K.-H., Stocker, A. (eds.) WEBIST 2013. LNBIP, vol. 189, pp. 53–67. Springer, Heidelberg (2014)
16. Kuuskeri, J., Lautamäki, J., Mikkonen, T.: Peer-to-peer collaboration in the lively kernel. In: Proc. ACM Symposium on Applied Computing, pp. 812–817 (2010)
17. Mäkitalo, N., Peltola, H., Salo, J., Turto, T.: VisualREST: a content management system for cloud computing environment. In: Euromicoro Conference on Software Engineering and Advanced Applications, pp. 183–187. IEEE (2011)
18. Taivalsaari, A., Systä, K.: Cloudberry: An HTML5 cloud phone platform for mobile devices. IEEE Software **29**(4), 40–45 (2012)
19. Rekimoto, J., Saitoh, M.: Augmented surfaces: a spatially continuous work space for hybrid computing environments. In: Proc. CHI, pp. 378–385. ACM (1999)
20. Koskimies, O., Mikola, T., Taivalsaari, A., Wikman, J.: EDB: a multi-master database for liquid multi-device software. In: Proc. MobileSoft. ACM (2015)

Social Web Applications

User Interface Adaptation Using Web Augmentation Techniques: Towards a Negotiated Approach

Diego Firmenich[1,2] (✉), Sergio Firmenich[1], Gustavo Rossi[1], Marco Winckler[3], and Damiano Distante[4]

[1] LIFIA, Facultad de Informática, Universidad Nacional de La Plata and CONICET, La Plata, Argentina
dfirmenich@tw.unp.edu.ar,
{sergio.firmenich,gustavo}@lifia.info.unlp.edu.ar

[2] DIT, Fac. de Ingeniería, Universidad Nacional de la Patagonia San Juan Bosco, Comodoro Rivadavia, Argentina

[3] ICS-IRIT, University of Toulouse 3, Toulouse, France
winckler@irit.fr

[4] Unitelma Sapienza University, Rome, Italy
Damiano.distante@unitelma.it

Abstract. The use of Web augmentation techniques has an impact on tasks of owners of Web sites, developers of scripts and end-users. Because the Web sites can be modified by external scripts, their owners might lose control about how Web site contents are delivered. To prevent this, they might be tempted to modify the structure of Web pages thus making harder to execute external scripts. However, communities of Web augmentation scripters are increasing since end-users still have needs not yet covered by Web sites. In this paper we analyze the trade-offs of the introduction of Web augmentation scripts. In order to mitigate some negative effects, such as the loss of control, we propose an approach based on negotiation and coordination between actors involved in the process. We present a set of tools to facilitate the integration of scripts and to foster their dissemination for the benefit of all actors involved.

Keywords: Web augmentation · Client-side adaptation · Script developers

1 Introduction

Web augmentation techniques have been proposed as a way for extending Web sites features without affecting the server-side code [2]. Most of the popular Web augmentation tools extend the Web browser functionalities via plugins that can run client-side scripts to manipulate the structure of Web pages. The potential of these techniques for adapting existing Web sites is huge and this can be easily illustrated by some advanced applications [10][11]. Web augmentation techniques are used to adapt sites according to users' needs that have not been originally taken into account during the design of the Web site. The flexibility provided by Web augmentation techniques motivates individual and communities of coders to develop scripts. For example,

P. Cimiano et al. (Eds.): ICWE 2015, LNCS 9114, pp. 147–164, 2015.
DOI: 10.1007/978-3-319-19890-3_11

YouTube center[1], which adds several new functionalities (e.g. download and repeat videos) for improving the user experience, has been proved very popular with more than 15K downloads. The very existence of communities might also allow end-users to provide direct feedback to developers via requests for new augmenters instead of asking the Web site's owners to change the original site [8]. Moreover, some existing tools such as WebMakeUp [7] claim to support end-user development of Web augmenters. Thus, Web augmentation might compete with other existing techniques for adapting Web sites. When compared with closed adaptation techniques broadly-used by large Web applications for supporting personalization [3], Web augmenters allow users to go beyond of the adaptation features predefined by the Web site's owner. Some Web sites provide APIs that can be used to build extension-based adaptation of contents. For developers, APIs extensibility usually implies to follow specific guidelines and constraints. Moreover, there is no guarantee that the API will provide all the sought adaptation mechanisms. Besides, without prior commitment of the participants involved in the process, the development of Web augmenters can also be frustrating since Web augmenters might stop working when owners decide to change the Web site design [5]. As for the Web site owners, neglecting users' need for adaptation and the creative potential of community of coders, might make them less competitive.

In this paper we analyze the trades-off of Web augmentation approaches and we claim that benefits can be shared among actors involved in the process. An analysis of different strategies for Web site adaptations and the actors involved in the process is presented in section 2. In section 3 we propose a negotiated approach for Web augmentation adaptation. The aim is to delegate to the crowd of users the specification of the changes they are looking for, delegate to coders (users with programming skills) the implementation of the augmenters and finally let the Web site's owner integrate augmenters into their Web sites. Such an approach is duly supported by a platform which is described in section 4. In section 5 we propose an assessment based on cost estimation. In section 6 we discuss the contribution at the light of existing work and lastly in section 7 we present conclusions and future work.

2 Actors, Strategies and Trade-offs for Adapting Web Interfaces

The adaptation of user interfaces (UI) requires the definition of what are the goals of the adaption, what is adapted, what events trigger the adaptation, and which programming techniques are used to perform the adaptation [3]. In the context of this work, the goal of adaptation is to modify any aspect of the UI at client-side (either rendering and/or behavior). For that purpose adaptations might change the way users perform tasks (e.g. replacing scroll navigation between the top/bottom parts of a Web page by adding navigation buttons), the contents in display (e.g. enriching the page with information obtained from other sources), and/or the page's structure and layout.

[1] YouTubeCenter. Available at: *https://greasyfork.org/es/scripts/943-youtube-center*, last access: 12/2/2015.

These adaptations should be triggered by DOM events in the client-side. As for the techniques, the main focus of this study is on Web augmentation.

The development, deployment and use of Web adaptation techniques affect many actors, including the *Web site owner*, the *coders of scripts* and the *end-users*. The term *Web site owner* designates here the development team that has full control of the original Web site. In opposition, *coders of scripts* refer to developers who implement augmenters to support adaptations on the client-side. *End-users* refer to the user populations that consume Web site contents (being adapted or not to their profile). We identified four strategies for adapting Web applications involving these actors:

- *Closed adaptation* refers to adaptation techniques that are embedded as part of the original Web site and totally under the control of *Web site owner*. This kind of adaptation might encompass adaptations processed on the server-side and/or on the client-side. In any case, developers don't have any constraint for accessing to the code source of the Web site. Adaptations can be built upon users' characteristics that have been obtained by explicitly collecting users' profile (via Web forms) or implicitly (by tracking the behavior of ordinary visitors) [13]. In closed adaptation, the Web site is modified as the result of a direct relationship between the *Web site owners* and the *end users*. End-users contribute with information that can be used to personalize the adaptation and they only have access to adaptations that have been predefined by the Web site owners. Typically, recommendation systems, collaborative filtering systems, or hybrid systems [15] belong to this category.
- *Extension-based customization* is obtained with the help of dedicated APIs which allow external developers to adapt the Web site. This kind of adaptation strategy is well known in applications such as Google Drive[2] or Facebook[3]. By using APIs, *external coders* can create new forms of adaptations that have not been considered yet by *Web site owners*. Overall, adaptations require a triangulation between what *Web site owners* make adaptable via an API, what *coders* can do with such API and the *end-users'* expectations. Advanced programming skills, deep knowledge about the original Web site and the functions provided by the API are required to create adaptations. Thus, *coders* are somewhat dependent of the availability of API delivered by the original Web site. Besides that, end-users need to be supported with some tool for browsing and installing the available extensions.
- *Web augmentation* is a term used to address techniques that allow the adaptation of existing third-party Web applications in the client-site in such a way that no prior authorization from *Web site owners* is required [3]. Web augmentation techniques can be fine-tuned to work on a specific Web site but they can also be generic enough to work in any kind of Web site. The most common solutions for implementing *Web augmentation* techniques is Web browser extensions (i.e. plugins) that once installed modify the Web sites visited by the users. End-users may take advantage of a large set of scripts uploaded by their creators to public repositories[4]. Most of the popular augmenters are implemented using JavaScript, which means that coders need to have advance skills in imperative programming. The relation-

[2] The Drive Platform. Available at: *https://developers.google.com/drive/* Last access: last access: 12/2/2015.
[3] The Facebook API. Available at: *https://developers.facebook.com/* Last access: last access: 12/2/2015.
[4] Repositories list: *http://wiki.greasespot.net/User_Script_Hosting*. Last accessed: 2/4/2015.

ship between actors is simplified by excluding *Web site owners* from the adaptation process.
- *End-User Web augmentation* is a concept built upon *Web augmentation techniques* for empowering end-users with tools allowing them to program their own scripts [4][7]. The underlying idea is that users with little programming skill can be guided through a set of visual tools that hide the complexity of the code used to perform the adaptations on a Web site. This kind of techniques assume that end-users can work by their own, so that they do not longer depend on *coders* and/or *Web site owners* for having their Web sites personalized. For example, in [8] authors propose an environment where users can modify on the fly Web pages as a means to express requirements and/or to personalize the interaction with the site.

Adaptation strategies define different types of relationship between actors. Table 1 shows how *Web site owners'* and *end-users* are involved in a *closed adaptation* strategy. This is the most traditional approach for Web adaptation. Users often have to provide personal information (explicitly via a user account, or implicitly by user footprints whilst navigating the Web site). Closed adaptation, by definition, excludes the possibility of collaboration with external coders so all the costs of adaptation are supported by Web site owners. But site owners have at least full control on the adaptations provided to end-users.

Table 1. Trade-offs on Closed Adaptation

Web site Owner	Coder	End-user
- Implementation of adaptations models is expensive + User can provide personal information for portraying a user profile to tune adaptations + Full control of adaptation mechanisms proposed to users - Adaptation mechanism are dependent of a Web site	-	+ Users do not need to install anything on the browser - Costs limit the daptation to large and specialized Web sites + Can support personalization via recommendation and collaborative filtering systems - Users must have create an account and a profile to get the benefits of adaptations - Requiring user profile/feedback raise privacy issues + Adaptations can be tune to the usual tasks with the site - Might not be enough to support users requirements - Users have to learn how adaptation works in every site

Table 2. Trade-offs on Extension-based Adaptation

Web site Owner	External Coder	End-user
- Implementation of APIs has direct costs, including for training and advertisement + Control of functions that are made available through the API + Code provided by external coders might contribute to the popularity of the owners' Web site - Still requires programming on the top of APIs to implement the required adaptations - The owner don't have control of API-based adaptations	+ Often free of costs for coders + Support and documentation might be free of charges + Coders can build they applications on the top of existing Web sites, which is often cheaper than starting from scratch - Coders creativity can be limited to functions available in the API - Might not be enough to support adaptations envisaged by coders + Coders can contribute to create new adaptations	+ Users do not need to install anything on the browser +/- There is no guarantee that applications using APIs are free of charges for the end-users - Might not be enough to support the adaptations required by users + Let users to customize the application by installing extensions

By exposing an API to the community *Web site owners* allows the collaboration with an external community of *coders*, see Table 2. Deploying an API implies significant costs for the Web site owners but might also contribute to the popularity of the Web site, for the benefits of *external codes* and the *Web site owners* alike. To ensure protection on the backend, adaptability through APIs is often limited to a few functions which do not necessary grant access to information about the user profile. If one hand such strategy allows some level of control, it might also limit creativity of *external coders*. For the users, *extended adaptation* will only work in a few Web sites and do not necessary cover all users' needs for personalization.

In the case of *Web augmentation* strategies, it is the *Web site owner* who is excluded from the process, such as Table 3 and 4 show. The relationship occurs only between *end-users* who become the clients of *coders* who develop augmenters that operate on client-side without the supervision and control of the *owners'* of the Web. In such cases, *Web site owners* are excluded from the adaptation process and have no control in how the contents are delivered to end-users. *Web site owners* might be tempted to regularly modify the DOM structure of Web pages thus making harder to execute external scripts, which is a hard blow for *external coders* and *end-users*. Adaptations are often volatile and should be reapplied every time users return to the Web site.

Table 3. Trade-offs on Web Augmentation Adaptation

Web site Owner	External Coder	End-user
-	+ Coders creativity is not limited by APIs - Adaptations might stop working if the DOM of Web page is updated + By tracking downloads of extensions proposed to the users coders can assess popularity and infer user needs + The independence of APIs allows the development of augmenters focused on specific tasks that might be generic and thus be applied in many Web sites + There is no limitation about what aspects of the client-side application the coder may adapt on the Web site - Different augmenters developed by different coders might spoil the alterations between them	+ Users have diverse alternatives for adapting Web sites - Might not be enough to support all the adaptations required by users - Require users to install extensions + Users can reuse adaptation tools in a seamlessly way whilst navigating the Web - It is hard to take into account the user profile in generic augmenters, so that users might lose the benefits of recommendation systems or collaborative filtering systems - Adaptation mechanism provided natively may be spoiled - Since augmenters are not verified, some of them may be malicious

Table 4. Trade-offs on User-Driven Web Augmentation

Web site Owner	External Coder	End-user
-	-	+ Users are empowered with tools to perform the adaptations they want
		- End-users must develop programming skills for using EUP tools
		- Adaptations can be limited by users knowledge and skills, as well as the functions delivered in EUP environments

3 Towards a Negotiated Web Adaptation Approach

All existing adaptation strategies remarkably fail to provide seamless collaboration between actors involved. For that, we present a negotiated approach to Web adaptation which relies on three basic principles: first, all actors must find advantages in the collaboration; secondly, actors must collaborate; last but not least, tooling is essential to incentivise actors collaboration. We next present a view at glance of the approach and a detailed description of the distribution of tasks among the actors and how the execution of individual tasks can contribute to advantages for all.

3.1 The Approach in a Nutshell

Fig 1. illustrates some advantages actors can find in this kind of relationship. For example, *Web site* owners can stablish a trustful relationship with *coders* that guarantee that augmenters are not malicious. The negotiation between *Web site owners* and *coders* also benefit *end-users* who, by extension, can trust that third-party augmenters have been checked by owners of the Web site they trust. By keeping *end-users* in the loop benefits both the *Web site owners* who can continue to collect information about users and even share such as information with *coders* for improving their augmenters according with user needs. The negotiated approach also implies that a kind of commitment can be reached and for that actors must collaborate. Close collaboration and commitment often demand the implementation of coordination and communication tasks [14], which require additional resources (in terms of time and cognitive effort to maintain relationships running). To prevent that additional coordination and communication tasks come to plunge the advantages of such collaboration, the negotiated approach proposes that actors can work independently (as much as possible) and only perform the tasks for which they might foresee a direct advantage. To support such as a light-tight collaboration, we rely on a distribution of tasks among the participants and the existence of appropriate tool support as presented in Fig 2.

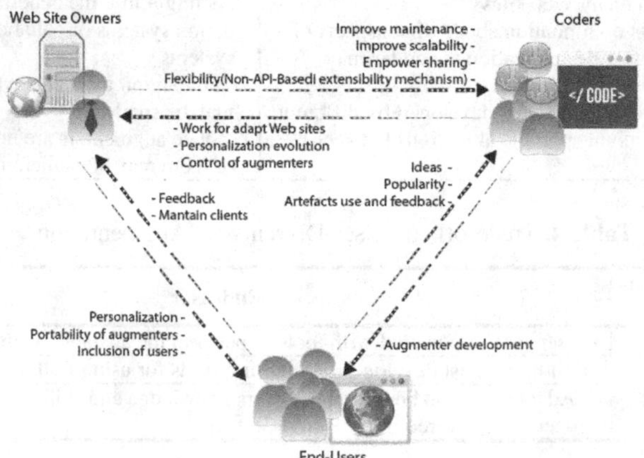

Fig. 1. Relationships between actors in a negotiated adaptation approach

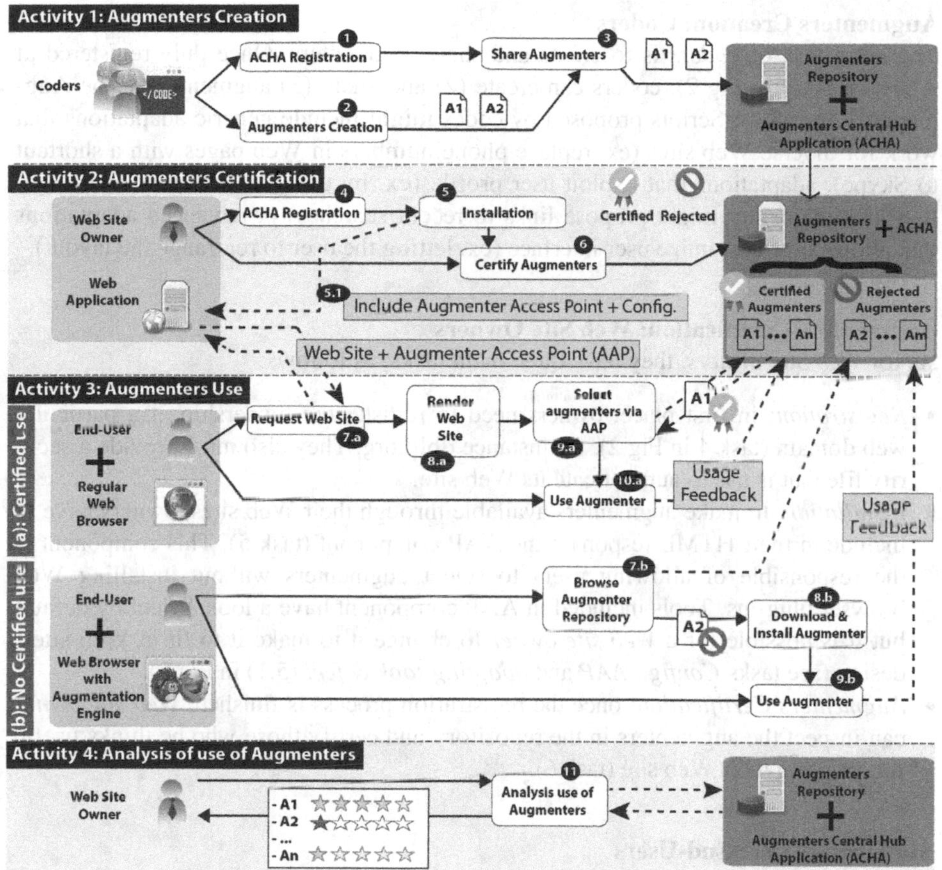

Fig. 2. Tasks allocation in a negotiated adaptation based on a Web augmentation approach

3.2 Analysis of Actors' Tasks

Hereafter we analyze implications for individuals of tasks imposed by the approaches shown in Fig 2. Notice that these tasks cannot be performed without appropriate tool support. For that a set of tool have been developed, including:

- *Augmenter repository:* is a Web site that contains the augmenters;
- *Augmenters Central Hub Application (ACHA):* is the front-end application that allows the management (search, inclusion, etc.) of augmenters into the repository.
- *Augmenters Access Point (AAP):* is a client-side component embedded on the Web sites registered in ACHA thus providing direct access to certified augmenters.

A full description of these tools is provided in section 4. Nonetheless, we make explicit reference to these tools whilst describing the tasks the different actors have to perform in a negotiated approach.

Augmenters Creation: Coders

The main task of *coders* is to create and share augmenters. Once duly registered at ACHA (task 1 in Fig 2), coders can create (2) and share (3) augmenters at the Augmenter Repository. Scripts proposed by codes might include generic adaptations that work for diverse Web sites (ex. replace phone numbers in Web pages with a shortcut to Skype), adaptations that exploit user profile (ex. by using user history of navigation, the augmenter might propose links to recent searches) or advanced adaptations that allows user customize user interface (ex. letting the user to rearrange the layout).

Augmenters Certification: Web Site Owners

As for *Web Site owners*, they have three main tasks, as follows:

- *Registration*: in first place, owners need to register the ownership of a particular web domain (task 4 in Fig 2), for instance dblp.org. They also must provide a security file that is use to authenticate its Web site.
- *Installation*: to make augmenters available through their Web sites, owners have to include in their HTML responses the AAP component (task 5). This component is the responsible of allowing users to select augmenters without installing Web browser plug-ins. Tools included in AAP component have a look & feel by default but it is possible for a *Web site owner* to change it to make it to fit in Web site's design (see tasks *Config AAP* and *adapting look & feel* (5.1) in Fig 2).
- *Augmenters Certification*: once the registration process is finished, *Web site owner* can inspect the augmenters in the repository and certify those who he thinks useful for adapting their Web site (task 6).

Augmenters Use: End-Users

The negotiated approach gives to end-users a major role as they ultimately have full control of adaptations that are going to be performed on the Web site. As we shall see in Fig 2, users have many duties with respect to the selection of certified (activity A1) and/or non-certified augmenters (activity A2):

- *Use of certified augmenters (a)*: when users visit a Web site (task 7.a) for which there are certified augmenters, the Web is rendered in the client (task 8.a) embedding the AAP tool. By using the AAP tool (task 9.a) *end-users* can select the desired augmenters which are then downloaded and executed transparently in the client-side (task 10.a). At the same pace, the ACHA record in the repository the information that a user has downloaded and used a given augmenter.
- *Use of non-certified augmenters (b)*: *end-users* use augmenters that do not have been certified by *Web site owners*. Non-certified augmenters do not automatically appear through the AAP when visiting a Web site. However, by using ACHA, users may browse non-certified augmenters (task 7.b). If the augmenter is relevant, the user may download it (task 8.b), and use with some external Web Augmentation engine such as GreaseMonkey (task 9.b). Note that this activity is not necessarily carried out by all the Web application users, but by those that are aware of the existence of the mechanisms for adapting third-party existing applications.

Analysis of Use of Augmenters: Web Site Owners
As show by task 11 in Fig 2, Web Site Owners can obtain feedback of use of the existing augmenters. Information about users using non-certified augmenter (task 9.b) of a Web site becomes part of the knowledge base of ACHA. This information is available for Web site owners who, thereupon, can decide to investigate (or not) why users are using such augmenters and what are they need for adapting the Web site.

4 An Platform for Web Augmentation Dissemination

In this section we present further details about the tool support that we have developed to demonstrate the feasibility of our negotiated approach. Section 4.1 presents a few underlying requirements that we have identified as essential for automating (as much as possible) user tasks. This follows with the presentation of the set of tools that have been developed to support the approach and concrete example of tool usage.

4.1 Underlying Requirements

These components were defined to address several aspects we believe to be really important for a negotiated adaptation approach:

- *Easy to install*: tools installation should be as simple as possible for the *Web application owners*. With this in mind the only actions required to the owner are the registration of the corresponding Web application in ACHA and also to add a JavaScript library on the Web pages (which contains the AAP among others). In the development of current applications supported by Web frameworks, it usually would mean to add a line of code in the main template of the application.
- *Customizability* of the look & feel for augmenters: besides to be easy to install, we allow Web application developers to define specific styles and behavior to the end-user tool (Augmenter Access Point tool) in order to make it compatible with the look & feel of the application.
- *Plug & Play*: it is essential for *end-users* to be able to select, activate and deactivate augmenters. Users must feel in control of the usage of adaptation but should guide them in the process.
- *Compatible and extensible*: the negotiated approach and the corresponding tool set should be compatible with existing augmenters in the community. In this way, our current implementation is compatible with existing user scripts, which are probably the most popular kind of artefacts. For that, our tool set must also provide an *Augmenter Engine Emulators* to make possible to execute any kind of scripts featuring augmenters.
- *Independence of Augmenter Repository*: the external repository shown in Fig 2 is proposed as a public standalone Web application. However, if *Web site owners* don't want to consume augmenters from the public repository, they instantiate a version of both the Augmenter Repository and ACHA in a private Web server accessible to a small community of *coders*.

4.2 Set of Tools Supporting the Approach

We have developed a bipartite system composed by a client-side library and a server-side Web application. On a dedicate Web server-side, the tools include:

- *Augmenters Repository and Augmenter Central Hub Application*: Augmenter Repository centralizes all the augmenters created by coders. The Augmenter Central Hub Application (ACHA) allows to manage the repository according to each role, i.e., that ACHA exposes different views and functionality for repository accordingly with the responsibilities of coders, owners and end-users.

At the client-side, there is the Augmenter Access Point component (AAP), a JavaScript library that encompasses three subcomponents cooperating with each other:

- *End-User Augmenter Selection Tool*: this tool aims at helping the selection of augmenters by end-users. This tool takes into account the current context, i.e. which Web page of the application is loaded; this is because an augmenter not necessary works for the whole application but just one or a set of nodes.
- *Augmenter Injector*: this tool is used for downloading and executing certified augmenters. The tool also record the user selection, so that the next time a user visits the same Web page, the corresponding augmenter is automatically executed.
- *Augmenter Engine Emulator*: this component allows the emulation of diverse APIs such as GreaseMonkey. It was implemented to make our approach compatible with any possible Web augmentation artefacts.

4.3 Illustration of Tools in a Case Study

The case study presented in this section is based on the Web site dblp.org. For the sake of illustration, in these examples we adopt the perspective of actors whilst presenting tools and the corresponding tasks. Moreover, all the examples below make reference to adaptions of the original page shown in Fig 3.

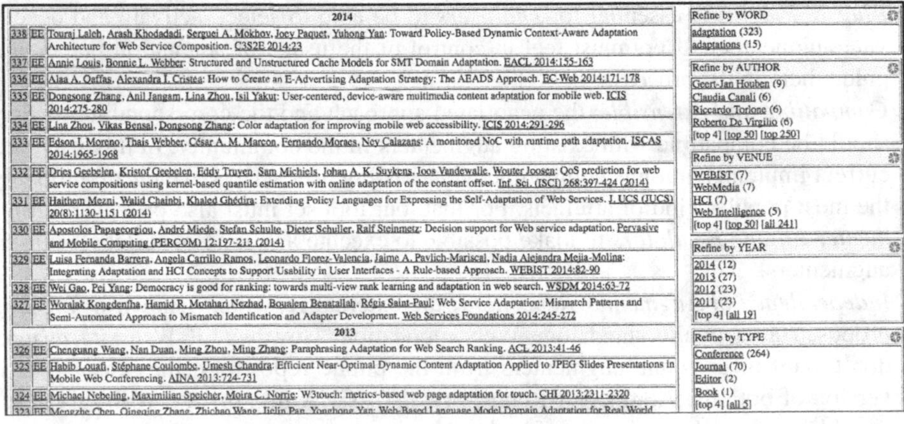

Fig. 3. Original search page of the DBLP web site

Coders

We assume that a coder has developed two augmenters that are aimed at improving the user experience of DBLP's users by implementing adapting features that are not yet available there such shown by Fig 4.

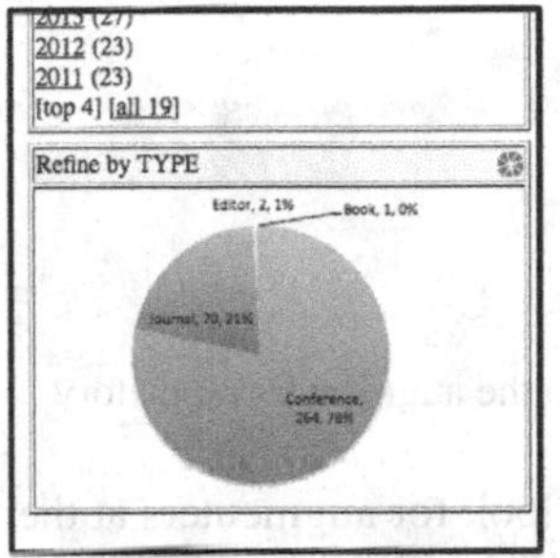

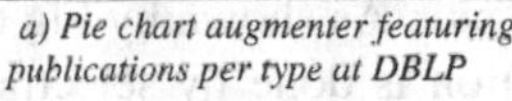
a) Pie chart augmenter featuring publications per type at DBLP

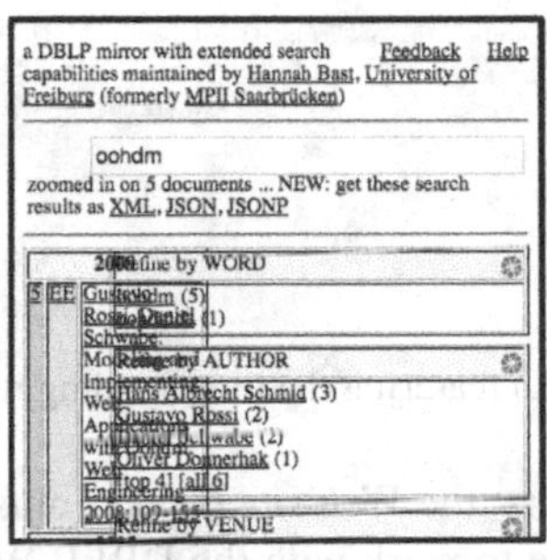

b) original DBLP page

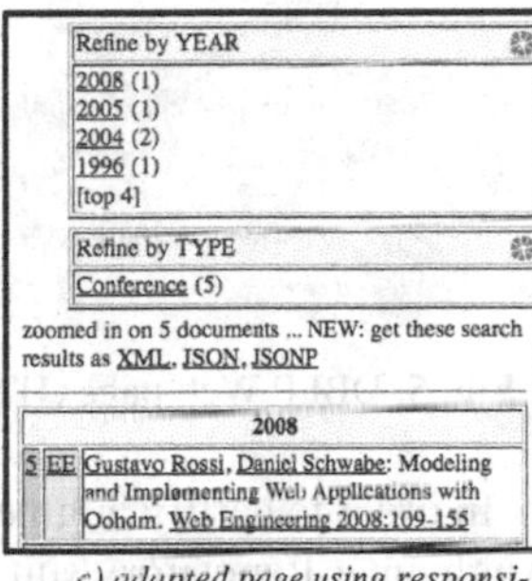

c) adapted page using responsiveDBLP augmenter

Fig. 4. Example of augmenters created by coders and waiting to be shared with the community

The first is an augmenter that is able to parse a DBLP Web page, extract information about publications and create a pie chart graph that can be injected into the Web site for depicting publication as shown in Fig 4.a. The second augmenter is aimed at modify the layout of Web page responsive to screen size. Fig 4.b shows the original Web page when visualized in a small screen and how visualization problems are fixed by the augmenter called *responsiveDBLP* Fig 4.c.

The augmenters illustrated by Fig 4 are ready to be used but the owners of the DBLP Web site did not have certified them yet. In order to get a certification and improve the visibility of these augmenters, we assume that the coder decides to share them via a public instantiation of both the Augmenter Repository and the ACHA, hosted at *UserRequirements*.org. For that, *coders* must create a user account on ACHA, define a user story describing the adaptations provided by each augmenter and finally upload it using the Web form.

Web Site Owners

Let's assume that the owners are particularly interested by the augmenter *responsibleDBLP* shown Fig 4 mainly because such augmenters might save lots of work for making the DBLP responsive. For including the *responsiveDBLP* into the DBLP Web site, the owners have at first to register at *UserRequirements.org* which can be accomplished by following these steps:

- Create a user account in ACHA, hosted in *UserRequirements.org*
- Register themselves as owners of the domain *dblp.org*
  - Certificate ownership: in order to demonstrate that they are actually the owners of dblp.org, they must download from ACHA a file containing a security token for *dblp.org* and upload the security token file to the web application root
  - Log in in *UserRequirement* and validate domain. ACHA will check that the security token file is already in the owners' Web server.

With these steps, ACHA accepts the association between that user account and the specified domain *dblp.org*. Once affiliated, owners need to add the Augmenter Access Point component into their main HTML. This only implies to add one line of code for adding a JavaScript file, line 5 in the code shown in Fig 5.

```
1  <!DOCTYPE html>
2  <link rel=stylesheet type="text/css" href="http://www.dblp.org/autocomplete-php/autocomplete/logging.css">
3    <script type="text/javascript" src="http://www.dblp.org/autocomplete-php/autocomplete/autocomplete.js"></script>
4    ......
5    <script src="http://www.dblp.org/../AugmenterAccessPoint.js" onload="URM_init('augs.userrequirements.org');"></script>
6    ......
7  <html>
8  <head>
9    ......
10   <title>CompleteSearch DBLP</title>
11   ......
12 </head>
13   ......
```

Fig. 5. DBLP Web page (HTML) featuring the links binding it to the augmenters repository

In order to certify augmenters, the *Web site owners* must look for augmenters at the Augmenter Repository suitable to work with the DBLP Web site. As shown by Fig 6, once the augmenter *responsiveDBLP* is found, the certification is done by selecting actions enable/disable options. It is also possible to download the augmenter for inspecting the code source and run it to see how it works. These tests are addressed mainly to check if augmenters are compatible with the current Web site DOM, however, owners may add further tests about the augmenter execution in order to prove if the adaptation is not spoiling relevant original content or functionality. Also from the ACHA, Web site owners can monitor user's feedback on this augmenter.

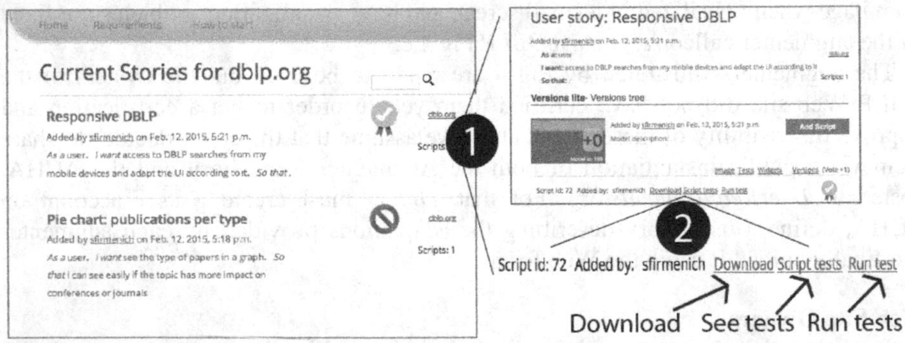

Fig. 6. Management of augmenters at the Web site repository: *UserRequirements.org*

End-users

When DBLP end-users visit the Web site they will be notified that certified augmenters exist by a green binding point at the up corner of the screen, as shown at the left side of Fig 7. The interaction between the end-user, the Web browser and our components is shown in Fig 8. When the user clicks on it, a menu is deployed showing augmenters available (this is the Augmenter Selection Tool). To active/deactivate an augmenter, end-users only need to click on the corresponding name in the list. Via this menu, end-users can also see the description of the augmenter left by the coders and further details about its popularity. Note that, as Fig 7 shows, the only augmenters available are those certified by the Web site owners in this case Responsive DBLP.

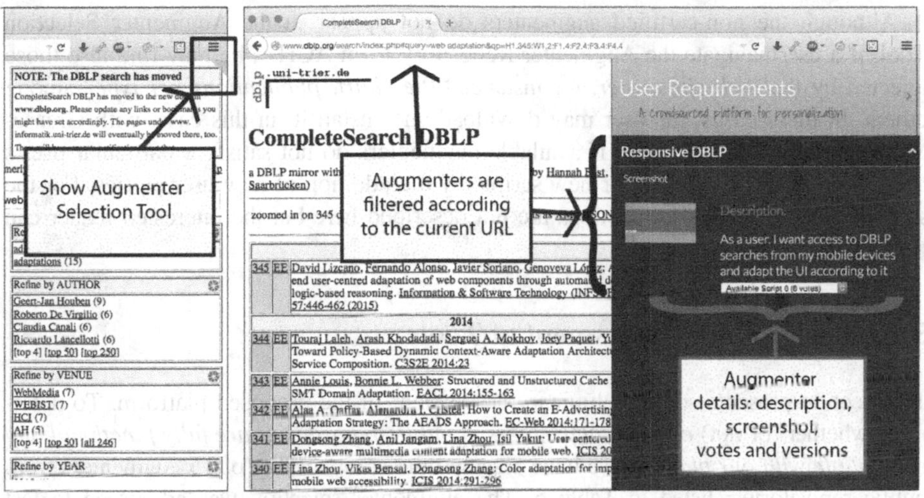

Fig. 7. Using augmenters at the DBLP web site

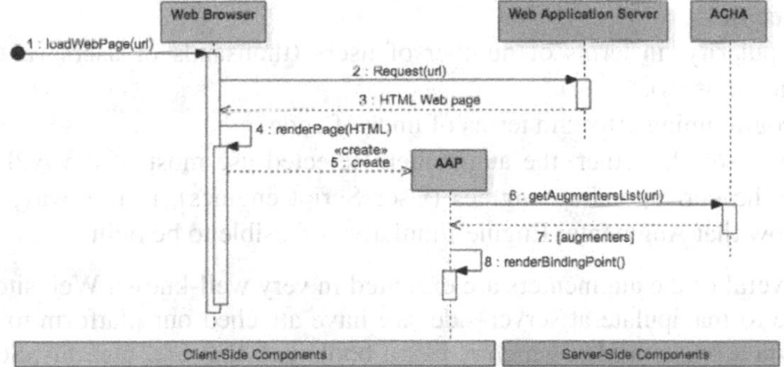

Fig. 8. Interaction when a Web site embedding AAP is rendered

Fig 9 shows the selection of an augmenter from the AAP and how it connects with the Augmenter Repository to delegates the execution to the Augmenter Injector.

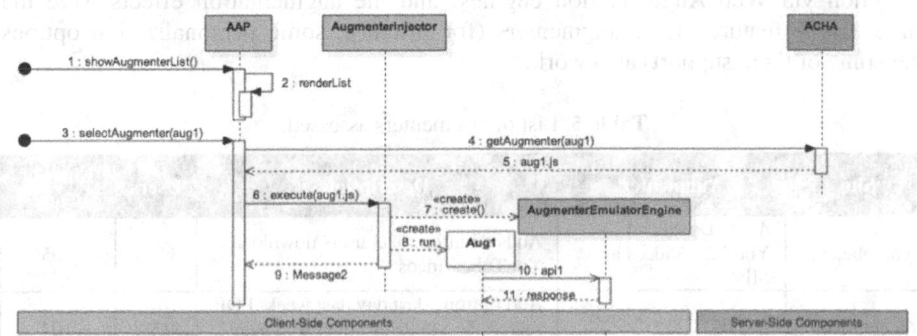

Fig. 9. Interaction when the end-user wants to enable an augmenter

Although the non-certified augmenters do not appear in the Augmenter Selection Tool, if a user navigate the Augmenter Repository from ACHA, he may find also those rejected by the *Web site owner*, for instance "*Pie chart: publications per type*" among others. In these cases, the user may download and install it, in this case, with Grease-Monkey engine. Besides that, if available augmenters do not satisfy a particular user's need, he may ask to *coders* for new scripts by the addition of new user stories. For the sake of conciseness these functions are not described here but the interested reader can find further information at [8].

5 Preliminary Assessment of Tools

This section presents some preliminary assessment of the proposed platform. To determine whether (or not) *existing augmenters in public repositories are fully functional and compatible with our platform* we have assessed the compatibility of 15 augmenters from public repositories, listed in Table 5. The augmenter selection was addressed to test different features:

- Generality: report if the augmenter works for any Web site or it is Web site-specific.
- Popularity: in terms of number of users (thousands of users *versus* a few known users).
- Programming effort: in terms of lines of code.
- API use: altogether, the augmenters selected use most of the API provided by the corresponding engines (User Script engines), in this way, we could show that Augmenter Engine Emulator is feasible to be built.

Since several of the augmenters are executed in very well-known Web sites that we are not able to manipulate at server-side, we have attached our platform to these applications via a bookmarklet, which is just a bookmark that executes JavaScript code when the user clicks on it. This JavaScript code is executed with the same privileges that native JavaScript code, then it is a sufficient prove of that augmenters may work from inside the application if the platform is also loaded. This also explains the case study presented in Section 3.1. The result was that the 100% of augmenters listed in Table 5 ran successfully with our platform. We have compared the result with the execution via Web Augmentation engines, and the augmentation effects were the same. Every feature of the augmenters (for instance, some personalization options that some of them support) also worked.

Table 5. List of augmenters assessed

Site	Augmenter	Description	Users	Lines of Code
Youtube.com	*Aug1*: Download YouTube Videos as MP4	Adds a button to let users download YouTube videos.	3.711	765
Google.com	*Aug2*: Google Search Extra Buttons	Add buttons (last day, last week, PDF search etc.) to results of search page of Google	150	104

Table 5. (*Continued*)

Imdb.com	*Aug3*: IMDB+	Add external links to IMDb. Every feature can be enabled/disabled in settings.	353	156
* (any Web site)	*Aug4*: Mouseover Popup Image Viewer	Shows larger version of thumbnails. Also supports HTML5 video.	8.580	1.207
* (any Web site)	*Aug5*: Google Translator Tooltip Expanded	Translates the selected text into a tooltip automatically.	493	1.227
Imdb.com	*Aug6*: Search IMDb Item on Netflix	Places a "Search for this on Netflix" button on the main page of any TV show/movie page on IMDb	141	34
Trello.com	*Aug7*: Trello-minimize lists	Minimize width of lists with toggle button	10	159
* (any Web site)	*Aug8*: Fixed Scroller Anywhere	Scroll by fixed pages	38	630
Wikipedia.org	*Aug9*: Wikipedia Inline Article Viewer	Adds a hover event to internal article links on wikipedia pages, which open the article inline in a dhtml frame.	3	512
Geocaching.com	*Aug10*: Geocaching Map Enhancements	Adds Ordenance Survey maps and grid reference search to Geocaching.com, plus other enhancements.	47.648	2.726
Twitter.com	*Aug11*: Twitter Instagram Cards - Photo Viewer	Now that Instagram have pulled their twitter support, this script adds back inline instagram photos.	361	46
* (all Web site)	*Aug12*: Universal Syntax Highlighter	It highlights plain text source code URLs in several languages. Based on the SpiralX auto highlighter	42	114
Google.com	*Aug13*: Endless google	Load more results automatically and endlessly.	4.732	142
Google.com	*Aug14*: Google Cache comeback	Brings back links to cached pages in the Google search results	15.208	248
Youtube.com	*Aug15*: Youtube to mp3	Convert youtube video to MP3	1.724	77

6 Related Work

The present work has interconnections with many relevant research areas such as personalization and adaptation techniques of Web applications, development of frameworks for supporting client-side adaptation and transcoding, end-user programming and communities of developers. Since 1996, most of the papers related to adaptive hypermedia systems were focused on Web applications [3][16]. Most of the well-known methods for the design of Web applications have incorporated the design of adaptation mechanisms. User profile modeling [13] has become also an important concern in adaptive Web applications, as well as the design of recommendation systems. However, the use of the Web not only is still increasing, which was the main factor mentioned by Brusilovsky [3], but also the way in which the Web is used has been mutating. There are several Web Augmentation communities around of existing repositories. Most important communities (in terms of size) are related to two kinds of artifacts, userscripts and userstyles. The formers are JavaScript-based augmenters such as those described in this paper. Currently, there are several userscripts repositories, altogether hosting more than 180 thousands of augmentation artifacts and several of these artifacts have been installed more than a million times. With all these existing repositories, it is clear that Web Augmentation is a current trend among the crowd of users. However, all these communities actually work without the intervention of Web site owners.

From the academy, in more recent years many works have investigated the potential of using End-User Programming techniques for allowing users to customize their applications [4][9]. Participation of the crowd of end-users is often presented as a suitable alternative for personalization, which often requires appropriate tool support and methodological approach for personalization [6]. Indeed, many works such as [7] focus on tool support for allowing end-users to tune Web sites. The results are promising but the impact in terms of number of users that can be reached by such as an approach is limited, given the skill level required to build such applications [12].

Some studies [17] have highlighted the importance of the involvement of communities of developers involved in the creation of scripts for adapting Web applications. Moreover, some authors [12] try to explain the role played by developers in the process. Other approaches tackle frequent design and implementation issues that appear when developing Web augmentation artefacts. For instance, some authors have studied how augmenter may be more resilient to DOM changes or even to improve the augmenters' reusability (i.e., usable in several Web sites) [5]. The same authors have proposed a security model in order to control what augmenters could do in a Web site [1], which is clearly utilizable in our approach. Nonetheless, very few works have investigated the relationship and possible interactions between other actors involved in the process, namely the owners of Web sites being adapted by external scripts.

7 Conclusions and Future Works

In this paper we have presented a negotiated approach that involves end-users, owners of Web sites and external communities of coders specialized in the development of Web augmentation scripts to perform client-side adaptation of Web sites. The underlying idea is to share the tasks required for Web-side adaptation among the actors involved in the process and that, for the benefits of all. By exposing the advantages that all actors might found in process, our negotiated approach presents a new perspective for the research in the areas of Web scripts development and Web site adaptation. Indeed, we claim in this paper that a deep analysis of tradeoffs for all actors is essential for deciding design options for implementing Web applications. In this respect, the comparative analysis of advantages and drawbacks of adaptations approaches for each role is a contribution of this paper at its own right.

The negotiated approach is not a panacea and probably don't solve all adaptation problems. Indeed, it is not aimed at replacing adaptation mechanisms that work pretty well and already fulfill a purpose. Nonetheless, we do claim that a negotiated approach opens up a new perspective for the research in the area in particular with respect to the way we involve actors in the adaptation process, in terms of tools required to support a distributed architecture for client-side adaptation and about mechanisms for observing the evolution of end-user needs for adaptation of Web site contents.

Indeed, this work allows starting to investigate many interesting research questions that for Web engineering, for example: In which extension end-users are able to comprise and collaborate with Web site owners and communities of coders? How user's needs that require adaptation of Web sites evolve overtime? How communities of coders can make a bigger impact on existing Web sites? How to prevent those communities of coders can damage the presentation of Web site contents? How to improve trustful relationship between users that have different interests in the adaptation of Web applications? How to ensure long term compatibility between Web sites and external scripts?

It is evident that for supporting the approach, and ultimately the underlying research questions, appropriate tool support is necessary. For that we have developed a set of full-fledge tools that are publicly available and we invite the interested readers to take a look at the Web site http://UserRequirements.org for further information. The tools are fully functional and can be used either by end-users, community of coders and Web site owners as it was dully illustrated in the present paper. Since the availability of such tools is very recent, we still don't have collected enough material to make any assertion about the usability and/or user experience of people using these tools. Due to the inner nature of the negotiated approach, studies in a long run are required to make the necessary observation of all users and confirm if our hypothesis (dressed here merely as an estimation effort) hold on.

As part of our future work, we have already started to advertise the platform around the community so that we can have a substantial number of users (in different roles) for supporting further analysis. We are also planning to pursue the study about compatibility between scripts and Web sites.

References

1. Arellano, C., Díaz, O., Iturrioz, J.: Crowdsourced web augmentation: a security model. In: Chen, L., Triantafillou, P., Suel, T. (eds.) WISE 2010. LNCS, vol. 6488, pp. 294–307. Springer, Heidelberg (2010)
2. Bouvin, N.O.: Unifying strategies for web augmentation. In: Proc. of the 10th ACM Conference on Hypertext and Hypermedia (1999)
3. Brusilovsky, P.: Adaptive Hypermedia. User Modeling and User-Adapted Interaction (UMUAI) **11**(1–2), 87–110 (2001). Springer
4. Díaz, O., Arellano, C., Aldalur, I., Medina, H., Firmenich, S.: End-user browser-side modification of web pages. In: Benatallah, B., Bestavros, A., Manolopoulos, Y., Vakali, A., Zhang, Y. (eds.) WISE 2014, Part I. LNCS, vol. 8786, pp. 293–307. Springer, Heidelberg (2014)
5. Díaz, O., Arellano, C., Iturrioz, J.: Interfaces for scripting: making greasemonkey scripts resilient to website upgrades. In: Benatallah, B., Casati, F., Kappel, G., Rossi, G. (eds.) ICWE 2010. LNCS, vol. 6189, pp. 233–247. Springer, Heidelberg (2010)
6. Arellano, C., Díaz, O., Iturrioz, J.: Opening personalization to partners: an architecture of participation for websites. In: Brambilla, M., Tokuda, T., Tolksdorf, R. (eds.) ICWE 2012. LNCS, vol. 7387, pp. 91–105. Springer, Heidelberg (2012)

7. Firmenich, S., Rossi, G., Winckler, M., Palanque, P.: An approach for supporting distributed user interface orchestration over the Web. Int. J. Hum.-Comput. Stud. **72**(1), 53–76 (2014)
8. Firmenich, D., Firmenich, S., Rivero, J.M., Antonelli, L.: A platform for web augmentation requirements specification. In: Casteleyn, S., Rossi, G., Winckler, M. (eds.) ICWE 2014. LNCS, vol. 8541, pp. 1–20. Springer, Heidelberg (2014)
9. Firmenich, S., Rossi, G., Winckler, M.: A domain specific language for orchestrating user tasks whilst navigation web sites. In: Daniel, F., Dolog, P., Li, Q. (eds.) ICWE 2013. LNCS, vol. 7977, pp. 224–232. Springer, Heidelberg (2013)
10. Garrido, A., Firmenich, S., Rossi, G., Grigera, J., Medina-Medina, N., Harari, I.: Personalized Web Accessibility using Client-Side Refactoring. IEEE Internet Computing **17**(4), 58–66 (2013)
11. Han, H., Tokuda, T.: Towards flexible and lightweight integration of web applications by end-user programming. IJWIS **6**(4), 359–373 (2010)
12. Jones, M.C., Churchill, E.F.: Conversations in developer communities: a preliminary analysis of the yahoo! pipes community. In: Proceedings of the Fourth International Conference on Communities and Technologies (C&T 2009), pp. 195–204. ACM, New York (2009)
13. Kobsa, A.: Generic user modeling systems. In: Brusilovsky, P., Kobsa, A., Nejdl, W. (eds.) Adaptive Web 2007. LNCS, vol. 4321, pp. 136–154. Springer, Heidelberg (2007)
14. Malone, T.W., Crowston, K.: The interdisciplinary study of coordination. ACM Comput. Surv. **26**(1), 87–119 (1994)
15. Adomavicius, G., Tuzhilin, A. Toward the Next Generation of Recommender Systems: Survey of the State-of-the-Art and Possible Extensions. IEEE Trans. Knowl. Data Eng., 734–749 (2005)
16. Rossi, G., Schwabe, D., Guimarães, R.: Designing personalized web applications. In: Proceedings of the 10th International Conference on World Wide Web (WWW 2001), pp. 275–284. ACM, New York
17. Stolee, K.T., Elbaum, S., Sarma, A.: Discovering How End-User Programmers and Their Communities Use Public Repositories: A Study on Yahoo! Pipes. Information and Software Technology **55**(7), 1289–1303 (2013). retrieved October 9, 2014. http://linkinghub.elsevier.com/retrieve/pii/S095058491200211X

Using Query-Log Based Collective Intelligence to Generate Query Suggestions for Tagged Content Search

Dirk Guijt[1] and Claudia Hauff[2](✉)

[1] Sanoma, Hoofddorp, The Netherlands
dirk.guijt@sanoma.com
[2] Web Information Systems, TU Delft, Delft, The Netherlands
c.hauff@tudelft.nl

Abstract. One of the standard features of today's major Web search engines are query suggestions, which aid the user in the formulation of their search queries. Over the years, a number of different approaches have been proposed which have commonly been evaluated in the standard Web search setting. In this work, we build a query suggestion pipeline based on the collective intelligence stored in log data collected from a more constrained search engine which uses tags to index the content. This constrained environment, though large-scale, differs considerably from standard Web search with respect to its users, indexing process and Web coverage. We implement a number of suggestion approaches based on query-flow and term-query graph models and investigate to what extent they are applicable in this more constrained environment.

Keywords: Query suggestions · Query-flow graphs · Search sessions · Collective intelligence · Tags · Tagged content

1 Introduction

One of the standard features of today's major Web search engines are query suggestions, which aid the user in the formulation of their search queries whilst typing. Those suggestions are commonly generated using the collective intelligence of the search engine users which is stored in the search engine's query logs. Learning the behaviour of the search engine users and applying the knowledge by generating query suggestions is not an easy task, as large-scale query logs are noisy, may contain errors and logging artefacts.

In this work, we present our efforts on implementing query suggestions for `startpagina`[1], a Dutch Web search portal similar in spirit to the Open Directory Project[2]. It is currently relying on query suggestions offered by a major

The work was conducted during the first author's TU Delft Master thesis project at Sanoma.

[1] http://startpagina.nl

[2] Open Directory Project (now DMOZ): http://www.dmoz.org

P. Cimiano et al. (Eds.): ICWE 2015, LNCS 9114, pp. 165–181, 2015.
DOI: 10.1007/978-3-319-19890-3_12

Commercial Search Engine (CSE) instead of generating its own. Since interacting with those externally generated suggestions leads to general Web search results (which often include results not indexed by `startpagina`) many users leave `startpagina` in the middle of a search session and continue with a general Web search. While search engine switching (initiated by the user) is a well-known phenomenon [25], we consider this switch to be a rather unconscious one, as the users are "switched" to a different engine without their explicit request. In order to increase user retention, we use `startpagina`'s query log and implement a four-step query suggestion pipeline based on state-of-the-art approaches in (1) search session splitting [16,17], (2) the classification of query reformulations [9,19], (3) the generation of query-flow graphs, and, (4) the extraction of suggestions from such graphs [7–10].

Our main research questions focus on the effects of applying provenly effective methods of generating query suggestions in regular Web search engines to a more constrained search environment, which is similar to search on a social tagging portal. In contrast to regular Web search, our experimental environment indexes its contents through tags created by human annotators. Our search engine is limited in its ability to return results for all queries, as a given query must match a tag before the associated content can be returned. It is not useful to suggest queries for which no matching tag exists and thus no content is available. In this work, we investigate whether query logs can be used to generate relevant query suggestions in this context.

We derive six different models from state-of-the-art query-flow and term-query graph models [7–10] and compare their effectiveness to the suggestions provided by the CSE (our baseline that is currently in use at `startpagina`). In this particular use case we are able to achieve much higher coverage, that is, the models trained on our log data can provide valid suggestions, i.e. suggestions for which `startpagina` has results, for a much larger number of queries.

In the remainder of the paper, we first cover related work (§ 2), provide more details about `startpagina` (§ 3) and describe our approach (§ 4), before presenting our experiments (§ 5) and a discussing of the lessons learnt (§ 6).

2 Background

2.1 Search Sessions

Deriving search sessions, i.e. chronologically ordered sets of queries by a single user with a common search goal (within a certain time interval), from query logs is one of the necessary pre-processing steps to generate query-log based query suggestions. Search session splitting has been tackled by various researchers in the past, including [15–17]. Most works rely heavily on lexicographical and temporal properties; it was shown that those low-level features achieve nearly the same effectiveness for search session splitting as more complex semantic or result-set based features [16].

2.2 Query Reformulations

Another important aspect of our pipeline is the classification of query reformulations, i.e. in what manner the next query is altered with respect to the previous one, as the reformulation type itself can significantly alter the shape and dynamics of a query-flow graph [8,9]. Early work on user query behavior in web search defined various reformulation type classes [12,20]. These form the basis for the four reformulation types introduced in [9], which are: *specialisation* (.e.g query "elephant" is reformulated to "elephant tusk"), *generalisation* (e.g. moving from "elephant tusk" to "elephant"), *parallel move/equivalent rephrase* (replacing some terms with similar terms or phrase the same query intent differently), *same query/error correction* (applying small changes, often spelling correction, to the next query). Both Boldi et al. [9] and Huang et al. [19] provide an extensive list and description of features that can be used to detect the reformulation type of two subsequent queries. These include both lexicographical and temporal features.

2.3 Query Suggestion

Suggestions for a given query can be generated from a multitude of sources: document content, taxonomies (e.g. WordNet), query logs or a combination of those. The use of query logs is particularly popular, but at the same time limited to use cases where large-scale query logs are available.

Huang et al. [18] extracted suggestions based on co-occurring query terms in users' search sessions. They found this approach to outperform a pure document content analysis-based approach (performed over the top-k retrieved documents). Baeza-Yates et al. [2] combined clicks and retrieved documents by only considering those top-k documents that were actually clicked by users; new query terms are suggested based on the analysis of the clicked documents.

The notion of click graphs started to appear in 2000 [6]. A click graph is a bipartite graph consisting of two groups of nodes, query nodes and document nodes (URLs). There is an undirected edge in between two nodes if the document appears in the result set of a query and was clicked as well. Generating such a graph from a query log enables the use of a range of graph theoretic algorithms. In particular random walks on click graphs are a popular strategy to generate query suggestions, e.g. [13,14,21]. The main drawback of click graphs is the large amount of data required to generate high-quality graphs; not every user query yields a click, and not all search portals are frequented by a sufficient number of users to make click graphs a viable option.

This drawback has led to the use of query-flow graphs for query suggestion generation. A query-flow graph contains nodes constructed from the unique set of queries in the query log. These nodes are connected by a directed edge if the queries succeeded one another in a single search session. The weights of the edges correspond to the likelihood of the two queries belonging to the same query chain. This modelling strategy was first proposed in [7]. Numerous extensions have been proposed, for instance, in [8,9], different graphs are constructed by considering only a subset of edges based on reformulation types; in [3,4] the random walk is biased towards the query intent. Altering the graph itself, by adding shortcuts for very likely paths in the graph has been proposed by Anagnostopoulos et al. [1]. More recently, works have also began to extend such graphs with nodes on the term level: instead of considering only a query as atomic unit (i.e. a node in a graph), each unique term within a query is considered to be a node as well. An advantage of such a term-query graph [10] is that the model can generate suggestions for queries that have not been "seen" before, which is not possible in query-flow graphs. The transition of individual query terms has been added to the query-flow graph in Szpektor et al. [24] and Song et al. [23]. Both of these models have a semantic component as well through named-entity recognition and click-based topic extraction respectively. Since users' querying behaviour and the search system's back-end are likely to change over time, [5] investigated the effects of time on the construction of query-flow graphs. They concluded that query-flow graph indeed age due to the change in user interest.

Query-flow graphs and term-query graphs have shown to be a popular and successful approach to query suggestion generation. We investigate two query-flow graph models (the original model [7] and variations of the reformulation type model [8,9]) and one term-query graph model [10] and examine their applicability to our particular use case `startpagina`. We do not consider click graphs, as the amount of click data required is not suitable for our use case.

3 Startpagina

`startpagina` focuses specifically on the Dutch market. The search portal employs human annotators that manually determine whether or not a Web site d (written in Dutch) should be included in its index. For indexing purposes, annotators provide a number of *tags* $\mathcal{T}_{d_i} = \{t_1^i, ..., t_m^i\}$ for each d_i. Users can only retrieve d_i if their complete query matches a tag in $\mathcal{T}_{d_i}$. The entire tag space over all n documents presented in the index is $\mathcal{T} = \bigcup_{k=1}^{n} \mathcal{T}_{d_k}$. `startpagina` currently employs both auto-completion (offered by the employed commercial search engine) and instant-result mechanisms. Each typing action by a user results in one of the following:

- If the user's current query is a tag found in $\mathcal{T}$, the correspondingly tagged results are shown (instant results provided by `startpagina`).
- If the user's current query is not in $\mathcal{T}$, query suggestions are retrieved from the CSE's suggestion API. The suggestions are agnostic to the tag space $\mathcal{T}$, i.e. they are not restricted to terms and phrases that appear in $\mathcal{T}$. A click on any of the suggestions that are not in $\mathcal{T}$ leads the user to a standard Web search result page (SERP) provided by the CSE.

Figure 1 presents an overview of `startpagina`'s user search flow. The outcome on the left (leading the user to a target Web site) is the desired case: the user remains on `startpagina` until the final click. The outcome on the right (showing a SERP) is the case we are tackling in our work: the external suggestions should be replaced whenever possible (i.e. when we can generate suggestions $t_i \in \mathcal{T}$) with **startpagina**'s own suggestions. In cases where this is not possible, **startpagina** continues to rely on the CSE's suggestions. Overall, generating **startpagina** internal suggestions will keep more users engaged with the site, which in turn will improve user retention and user satisfaction.

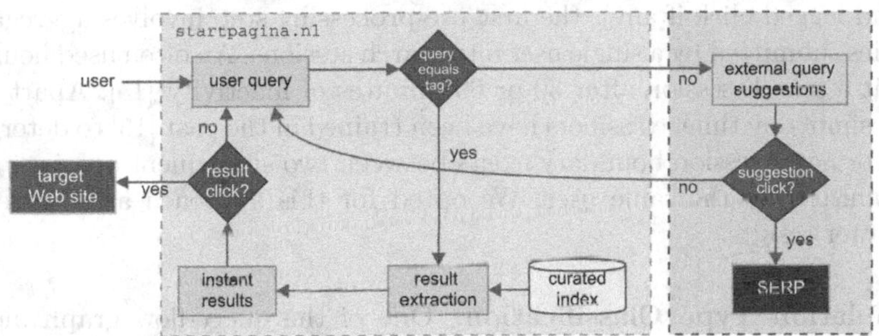

Fig. 1. High-level overview of **startpagina**'s current user search flow. Shown in red (suggestion component) is the part of the search flow we are tackling in this work.

On average, each month **startpagina** has more than 1.5 million unique visitors who conduct tens of millions of searches. A significant fraction[3] of searches result in the user leaving the site as their queries are not in $\mathcal{T}$ and thus no **startpagina** results are available.

The goal of our work is to provide for each user query which is not found in $\mathcal{T}$, a list of query suggestions that are found in $\mathcal{T}$. In this manner, when a user submits a search query for which no results are available, she instead receives a number of related query suggestions, all of which will lead to results within **startpagina**.

The content of **startpagina** is manually moderated and so are the tags that are used to describe and index it. This manual, human factor is similar to social tagging systems where the content and tags are generated by humans as well. The key difference is that **startpagina** has an editorial staff as opposed to having the system's users create and curate the content. Although this difference is important to note, our research does not focus on the content creation and curation but on using the collective intelligence of the search engine users to generate query suggestions. We therefore believe that our results extend to search engines that search through folksonomies as well.

4 Approach

Our query suggestions pipeline consists of four components: (1) search session splitting, (2) classification of query reformulation types, (3) generation of

[3] Due to the commercial nature of the portal, the exact numbers cannot be published here.

query-flow graphs, and, (4) deriving suggestions from them. The first two are necessary pre-processing steps to convert the query log into a suitable representation.

4.1 Pre-processing

Search Session Splitting. Given a typical query log (i.e. user-id, timestamp, query and logged click if any), the first pre-processing step involves aggregating the queries submitted by a single user into search sessions. An often used heuristic is to split a search session after 30 or 60 minutes of inactivity [15]. Apart from splitting simply by time, classifiers have been trained in the past [15] to determine whether or not a session boundary exists between two subsequent queries q_i and q_{i+1} submitted by the same user. We opted for this approach as it generally yields better results.

Reformulation Type Classification. One of the query-flow graph models we investigate is based on the intuition that different graphs should be build for different query reformulation types [9] as not all reformulations are equally useful for the generation of query suggestions. Thus, as a second component we implemented a classifier to determine the reformulation type of a pair of queries issued subsequently within a single search session. We distinguish between the following four types [9]: specialisation (**S**), generalisation (**G**), same query/error correction (**C**), and, parallel move/equivalent rephrase (**P**).

We treat both tasks (search session splitting and reformulation type classification) analogously, as they are similar in nature. We derive twenty-three features based on q_i and q_{i+1} individually as well as their temporal and syntactic relationship, in line with previous works [9,16,17,19]. An overview of these features is shown in Table 1. We employ a decision tree classifier (C5.0) as suggested in [9]. For search session splitting our classifier is binary, while for reformulation type classification we use n binary classifiers as well as the n-class classifier (where n is the number of reformulation types). The n binary classifiers are ordered according to their accuracy. If a query pair is classified with sufficient confidence by a classifier in the cascade, the remaining classifiers in the cascade are skipped for that pair [16].

To train the session splitting classifier, we manually annotated a set of randomly drawn *super-sessions* (a session of a single user split by the 60 minute inactivity heuristic is one super-session) from our query log and determined for each pair of subsequent queries whether or not they belong to the same session. Having trained the classifier, we then identified the sessions across the entire query log. In a second step we drew a sample of the search sessions identified in this manner and manually annotated the type of reformulation occurring. To compare our results directly with existing research, we also applied our implementation to a search session data set provided in [16] (we refer to it as `Hagen13`), which is based on the AOL query log.

We evaluate the effectiveness of the classifier through 5-fold cross-validation and report the following four metrics:

Table 1. Description of the 23 features used in both session splitting an query reformulation type classification. The following notation has been used in this table: $q^{pfx} \sqsubset q$ means that q^{pfx} is a prefix of q, q^{url} means that all URL elements like *http://* and *.com* have been stripped from q, and, $w(q)$ is the set of words in query q where the space character was used as a boundary between words.

#	Notation	Feature
$F1$	Δ_{ms}	time difference between q_i and q_{i+1} in milliseconds
$F2$	$\lvert q_i \rvert$	number of characters in q_i
$F3$	$\lvert q_{i+1} \rvert$	number of characters in q_{i+1}
$F4$	$F3 - F2$	difference in length between q_i and q_{i+1}
$F5$	$\texttt{Equals}(q_i,\ q_{i+1})$	boolean equality of q_i and q_{i+1}
$F6$	$\texttt{Equals}(q_i^{pfx},\ q_{i+1})$	boolean equality of q_i^{pfx} and q_{i+1}, with $\lvert q_i^{pfx} \rvert = \lvert q_{i+1} \rvert$
$F7$	$\texttt{Equals}(q_i,\ q_{i+1}^{pfx})$	boolean equality of q_i and q_{i+1}^{pfx}, with $\lvert q_i \rvert = \lvert q_{i+1}^{pfx} \rvert$
$F8$	$\texttt{Equals}(q_i^{url},\ q_{i+1}^{url})$	boolean equality of q_i^{url} and q_{i+1}^{url}
$F9$	$\lvert w(q_i) \rvert$	number of words in q_i
$F10$	$\lvert w(q_{i+1}) \rvert$	number of words in q_{i+1}
$F11$	$F10 - F9$	difference of number of words in q_i and q_{i+1}
$F12$	$\lvert w(q_i) \cup w(q_{i+1}) \rvert$	number of unique words combined
$F13$	$\lvert \{x \in w(q_i), y \in w(q_{i+1}) \mid x \sqsubset y\} \rvert$	number of words that were expanded
$F14$	$\lvert \{x \in w(q_i), y \in w(q_{i+1}) \mid y \sqsubset x\} \rvert$	number of words that were contracted
$F15$	$\lvert w(q_{i+1}) - w(q_i) \rvert - F10 - F11$	number of added words
$F16$	$\lvert w(q_i) - w(q_{i+1}) \rvert - F10 - F11$	number of deleted words
$F17$	$\texttt{Lev}(q_i, q_{i+1})$	Levenshtein distance between q_i and q_{i+1}
$F18$	$\frac{F17}{0.5 \cdot (F2+F3)}$	Levenshtein distance normalized by average length
$F19$	$\frac{F17}{F1}$	Levenshtein distance normalized by time difference
$F20$	$\texttt{CosSim}(\theta_{word,i},\ \theta_{word,i+1})$	cosine similarity of character 3-grams extracted from the individual words in a query
$F21$	$\frac{F20}{F1}$	cosine similarity ($F20$) normalized by time
$F22$	$\texttt{CosSim}(\theta_{query,i},\ \theta_{query,i+1})$	cosine similarity of the character 3-grams extracted from the query string as a whole
$F23$	$\frac{F22}{F1}$	cosine similarity ($F22$) normalized by time

- **Correctness**: the percentage of sessions that are completely correct, i.e. the start and end query are correctly identified and no split is introduced in-between;
- **Precision**: the percentage of boundaries that were correctly identified from all the boundaries that where classified as boundaries;
- **Recall**: the percentage of boundaries that were correctly identified of all the boundaries that should have been identified; and,
- **F-Measure**: with $\beta = 1.5$, as we consider false positives to be less harmful then false negatives (in the later case different search sessions are merged into one, leading to a degradation of the query-flow graph).

4.2 From Query-Flow Graphs to Query Suggestions

Query-Flow Graph. Boldi et al.'s query-flow graph [7–9] is a weighted, directed and annotated graph $G_{orig} = (V, E, W, T)$. The set of nodes V is defined as $V = V_{query} \cup \{t\}$ with V_{query} being the set of unique queries in a query log and t being a special node denoting the end of a search session. The set of edges $E \subseteq V \times V$ is a subset of all possible edges. An edge appears between nodes u and v if u was reformulated into v in at least one session in the query log. The edge (u,t) appears when u is the last query in a session. Edges are associated with weights, i.e. $w(u,v) = (0..1] \in W$. The weight is dependent on the frequency of the transition in the query log. Let $OUT(u)$ be the set of nodes that have an incoming edge from u. For every node it holds that: $\sum_{v \in OUT(u)} w(u,v) = 1$, which makes the graph essentially a Markov chain. Then, $w(u,v) = \frac{r(u,v)}{\sum_{i \in OUT(u)} r(u,i)}$; where $r(u,v)$ is the number of times that the transition from u to v occurred in the log. Finally, T is the set of annotations for each edge in E: each edge is annotated with the type of reformulation occurring between u and v. Edges directed to end node t are marked with special type X. Note that the original model did not have any annotations.

Slicing the Query-Flow Graph. As already mentioned, prior work [8,9] has investigated the use of a limited set of reformulation types to generate a more refined version of the query-flow graph. To create a slice of G_{orig}, we only retain those edges that are annotated with our chosen reformulation types; as an example, G_{SP} is the slice of G_{orig} which only contains reformulations of types specialisation and parallel moves. The edge weights are normalised so that $\sum_{v \in OUT(u)} w(u,v) = 1$. The special reformulation type X is assumed to be present in every slice.

Term-Query Graph. Another model that we consider is the term-query graph-based model [10], which again is an extension of G_{orig}. Typically, queries consist of a number of terms. In this model, we enlarge the graph to also add the set of unique terms of the query log as nodes, that is, $V = V_{query} \cup V_{term} \cup \{t\}$. The edge set E is also enlarged: there is an edge between a node $u \in V_{term}$ and $v \in V_{query}$ if v contains the term u. Note that no edges are directed towards term nodes and no direct edges exist between two term nodes. For a node $u \in V_{term}$ and $v \in V_{query}$, it holds that: $w(u,v) = \frac{1}{|OUT(u)|}$. Lastly we note that the reformulation type of an edge (u,v) with $u \in V_{term}$ and $v \in V_{query}$ is the special type X.

Generating Suggestions. Having discussed the different query-flow and term-query graphs, we now turn to the generation of query suggestions. We formulate this problem as follows: given a query q and a graph model G, generate a set of (usually no more than 5) suggestions that are relevant to q's intent.

It is important to note that if G is a query-flow graph model (either G_{orig} or $G_{reformulationTypes}$), we can only generate suggestions for "seen" queries, i.e. queries that are present in the query log from which G has been generated. If a query does not appear in the query log, we cannot generate suggestions for it. If q appears in G, we perform a random walk with restart from q's node, known as Personalized PageRank (PPR) [22]. The difference between PRP and standard PageRank [11] is that in PRP the random jump always jumps to our starting node, as opposed to jumping to a random node in the graph. The result of the random walk is a probability distribution (PPR scores), i.e. the probability of walking across a particular node in G when starting the walk in q. This is in effect the probability of users' submitting a particular query after the initial query q has been submitted. Since in this setup queries that occur very frequent in the query log have a large number of incoming edges with high weights, we normalise the PPR score by the standard PageRank score that each query (node) has. We then filter out all the suggestions that are not in tag space T, with the exception of special node t. The normalised PPR score is then used to rank the queries (nodes) and the highest scoring queries are selected as suggestions for our starting query q. The rank of node t in our generated ranking is also of importance: all queries (nodes) ranked below t have a lower likelihood of being submitted after q than the user stopping her search session. Thus, these queries are considered not to be useful and are stripped from the suggestion list (as well as t itself).

When G is the term-query graph, we first have to split the initial query q into $w_1, ..., w_m$ individual terms. We perform m random walks with restart, each one starting at one of the w_i (if they exist in the graph). The random walks are conducted in the same manner as described for the query-flow graphs. The result is m probability distributions, one for each of q's terms. We then calculate the Hadamard product [10] of these probability distributions, which assigns only to those suggestions that appear in all m distributions a score greater than zero. The suggestions are ranked by their Hadamard score and as before suggestions ranked below node t are removed from the final list of suggestions.

We experiment with eight models, five based on the query-flow graph and different reformulation types, one based on the term-query graph and two relying on the current system's suggestions that are generated by a commercial search engine.

Specifically, we investigate:

- $\mathbf{M_{orig}}$: basic query-flow graph including all reformulations types;
- $\mathbf{M_{GPC}}$: query-flow graph with generalis., parallel move and error correction;
- $\mathbf{M_{GPS}}$: query-flow graph with generalis, parallel move and specialis.;
- $\mathbf{M_{GCS}}$: query-flow graph with generalis, error correction and specialis.;
- $\mathbf{M_{PCS}}$: query-flow graph with parallel move, error correction and specialis.;
- $\mathbf{M_{TGM}}$): the term-query graph model including all reformulations types;

- **CSE suggestions overall**: we retrieve the top-5[4] suggestions for each test query from the system's currently employed CSE, independent of whether or not the suggestions are in $\mathcal{T}$ (i.e. leading to results in `startpagina`);
- **CSE suggestions** $\in \mathcal{T}$: we use the suggestions from the previous model (CSE suggestions overall) as a starting point and filter out all those that do not appear in tag space $\mathcal{T}$ (i.e. those that do not lead to results within `startpagina`).

Training and Evaluation. To train and evaluate our suggestions, we split our query log (ordered by time) into two sets, equivalent to "seen" and "unseen" queries. We generate the query-flow and term-query graphs on the seen set. We sample queries from the unseen set and derive query suggestions for them employing the eight models just described. For evaluation purposes, we ask human evaluators to judge the usefulness of the presented query suggestions to the initial query q as either *Useful*, *Somewhat Useful*, *Not Useful* or *Don't know*. The overall effectiveness of a model is the percentage of queries, for which the top-5 suggestions contain at least one *Somewhat Useful* suggestion (the so-called *u-score*) [8–10]. Additionally, we also evaluate the models according to their *coverage*, i.e. the number of queries for which suggestions are made at all. Since in our setup the tag space $\mathcal{T}$ is limited, the *u-score* alone is not sufficient to evaluate the effectiveness of our models.

5 Experiments

5.1 Data Set

We extract two data sets from `startpagina`'s query log: (1) data set `SP1` contains tens of millions of queries sampled from `startpagina`'s query log collected between April 14, 2014 and June 13, 2014; (2) data set `SP2` contains all queries issued in the seven days starting at June 14, 2014. We use `SP1` to train our classifiers and models. Data set `SP2` is employed to evaluate the query suggestions generated by our pipeline - this is a realistic setup, as we may be only able to (re-train) our models at particular moments in time.

5.2 Pre-processing

We randomly selected 974 super-sessions (i.e. a session split after 60 minutes of inactivity) from `SP1` and manually annotated the session boundaries within those super-sessions. Overall, we were able to unambiguously determine boundaries for 936 super-sessions, yielding 2,489 different search sessions with a total of 9,410 queries.

Our search session splitting classifier determines for each pair (q_i, q_{i+1}) of subsequent queries (submitted by a single user) whether they belong to the

[4] The API of the employed CSE imposes this limit.

same session or not. If not, q_i is considered to be the last query of session S_j while q_{i+1} is the first query of search session S_{j+1}. We use 5-fold cross-validation for training and testing.

The results are presented in Table 2. As baseline we report search session splitting based on minutes of inactivity (for each dataset, we empirically evaluated inactivity cutoffs between $[1, 2, .., 60]$ minutes and report the best performing one). While the inactivity based approach leads to 68% fully correctly identified sessions for SP1, our classifier-based approach makes correct decisions for 83% of the sessions. This result is verified on the public Hagen13 data set. When considering the learnt decision trees, the most significant features are the cosine similarity (both on the word and query level) as well as the Levenshtein distance normalised by the queries' time difference (i.e. $\frac{L(q_i,q_{i+1})}{\Delta_s}$). Overall, we conclude that we are able to split the Dutch startpagina sessions with sufficient accuracy for our purposes.

Table 2. Overview of search session splitting results achieved on two data sets

Splitting method	Data set	Correct	Precision	Recall	$F_{1.5}$-Measure
Inactivity (2 min)	SP1	68.46%	0.65	0.95	0.84
Classifier (C5.0)	SP1	82.64%	0.79	0.99	0.92
Inactivity (11 min)	Hagen13	67.35%	0.83	0.88	0.86
Classifier (C5.0)	Hagen13	84.51%	0.82	0.99	0.93

Having trained our search session splitter, we ran the classifier on the entire SP1 data set. We then randomly selected 1,806 query pairs from the identified sessions. For 1,738 pairs we were able to manually annotate them with their respective reformulation type (the remaining query pairs had unclear reformulations). We used those pairs to train and evaluate our reformulation type classifiers in a 5-fold cross-validation setup. The results show that query type reformulations can be classified effectively, yielding an accuracy of 85.9%.

Having determined the effectiveness of our classifier cascade, we classified all query pairs in SP1. We list the distribution of identified reformulation types in Table 3.

Interestingly, compared to previous works, in particular [9], which use Yahoo! query log data from 2008, we find considerable differences for the parallel move and specialisation types: parallel moves are found in less than 20% of all cases in SP1, while it is the most prevalent reformulation type in the Yahoo! logs (roughly 50% of all reformulations). In contrast, we find that in SP1 the S and C types occur with considerably higher frequency than found in the standard Web search setting. Despite the fact that for many queries startpagina does not return any results (because the query does not appear in T), more than 50% of the reformulations lead to more specific queries. This is contrary to our intuition, as we would expect users to back-off to more general queries in order to receive startpagina results. More research is needed to investigate this behaviour.

Table 3. Overview of the types of reformulations found in data set SP1 and in previously published works [9] (final two columns)

Reformulation type	SP1 $n = 4$	**Yahoo! UK, 2008**	**Yahoo! US, 2008**
G	13.01%	4.40%	9.50%
P	16.26%	47.70%	55.50%
C	18.16%	10.40%	5.00%
S	52.56%	37.50%	30.10%

5.3 From Query-Flow Graphs to Query Suggestions

We built the query-flow graphs from SP1 using our implemented pipeline: the query log was split into sessions, the reformulations were annotated, duplicate queries in succession were removed, and for each of the models a query-flow graph was generated. When computing (personalized) PageRank we set the random jump probability to $(1-\alpha) = 0.15$. Some basic graph statistics are shown in Table 4. While for most induced graphs the number of nodes and edges is comparable, $\mathbf{M_{GPC}}$ and $\mathbf{M_{TGM}}$ differ considerable with respect to the maximum out-degree and the number of edges. In slice $\mathbf{M_{GPC}}$, all edges that represent a specialization have been removed. We have shown in Table 3 that over half of the reformulation types in the graph are specializations so we expect the maximum outdegree to be lower for this slice. The border case nodes with a high outdegree have an even higher percentage of (outgoing) specialization edges, which explains the lower maximum outdegree in the overal graph. The higher number of nodes and edges in model $\mathbf{M_{TGM}}$ can be explained by the addition of the term nodes and the edges from the term nodes to the query nodes.

Table 4. Overview of the generated query-flow and term-query graphs based on data set SP1

	#nodes	**#edges**	**max. outdegree**
$\mathbf{M_{orig}}$	14,153,454	19,611,085	13,699
$\mathbf{M_{GPC}}$	14,153,454	12,638,766	775
$\mathbf{M_{GPS}}$	14,153,454	17,271,592	13,643
$\mathbf{M_{GCS}}$	14,153,454	16,697,988	13,650
$\mathbf{M_{PCS}}$	14,153,454	18,139,039	13,696
$\mathbf{M_{TGM}}$	17,686,843	59,658,990	552,735

We drew test queries from SP2 as follows: we partitioned SP2 into search sessions and randomly selected 282 of them. From each session, we then randomly drew a single query and generated the top 5 query suggestions based on each of our six models. We also captured the top 5 query suggestions from the system's currently used CSE. On average, each session contained 2.9 ($\sigma = 1.65$) queries.

Table 5 contains an example of query suggestions generated for the first query (underlined) of the following search session consisting of two queries: {<u>*egon*</u> $\rightarrow$ *aegon*}. Aegon is a multinational life insurance, pensions and asset management company. The user misspelled the name of the company in the first query. The final column lists the rating our human annotators assigned to the suggestion when taking the whole context of the search session into account.

We merged all suggestions generated for a query into a single list, removing duplications; due to the overlap in generated suggestions between the different models, the final list had far fewer than the possible $5 \times 7 = 35$ suggestions. On average 9.85 ($\sigma = 3.49$) unique suggestions were generated per query.

Table 5. Example of query suggestions generated for a query. From the short search session {*egon* $\rightarrow$ *aegon*} the first query (*egon*) was selected as the query to generate suggestions for. For each generated suggestion, all models generating it in the top 5 results are listed. Query suggestions that do not appear within $\mathcal{T}$ are marked with †. The final column contains the rating our human annotators: either U (*Useful*), US (*Somewhat useful*), or, NU (*Not useful*).

Query suggestions	**English translation**	**Model(s)** Orig	GCS	GPC	GPS	PCS	TGM	CSE	**Rating**
aegon	aegon	x	x	x		x	x		U
egon zehnder †	egon zehnder							x	NU
aegon hypotheek	aegon mortgage	x	x	x		x			U
aego	aego			x					NU
egon schiele †	egon schiele							x	NU
mijnaegon	myaegon			x					U
mijn aegon	my aegon				x		x		U
egon †	egon							x	NU
inloggen aegon	login aegon						x		U
aeg	aeg			x					SU
egon derksen †	egon derksen							x	NU
aegon verzekering	aegon insurance	x			x	x	x		U
aegon.nl	aegon.nl	x	x		x	x			U
aegon inloggen	aegon login	x	x			x	x		U
egon krenz †	egon krenz							x	NU

We recruited 31 native speakers of Dutch as human evaluators (11 human annotators employed at `startpagina` and 20 `startpagina` users). The evaluators were presented with a search session and the selected query (to derive suggestions for) from that session. To ensure that our evaluators made high-quality judgements, we asked them two initial questions for each session/query pair: (1) do all queries in the session have the same search goal (*yes/somewhat/no*), and, (2) do you understand the user's search intent (*yes/somewhat/no*). Each session/query pair was judged by a single evaluator. An evaluator could judge up to 20 session/query pairs. From the 282 session/query pairs, 40 sessions were judged by our evaluators as not having a single goal, while for an additional 53 sessions the evaluators were not able to clearly identify the intent of the session. For the remaining 189 session/query pairs with a total of 1886 suggestions, the evaluators were asked to rate the list of distinct suggestions with respect to their usefulness. The suggestions were presented in random order and the evaluators were unaware of the model(s) that generated the suggestion. In Table 6 we present the different models' effectiveness with respect to u-score and coverage.

Let's first discuss the influence of the reformulation types, when comparing the five reformulation type models (ignoring M_{TGM}) generated based on SP1. **S** & **G** are both important for coverage. This is not unexpected, as **S**-class reformulations account for more than 52% of all reformulations (Table 3). More interesting is the influence of the **G**-class edges. Although they account for only 13% of all reformulations (less than **P** or **C**), they are essential to achieve high coverage ($\mathbf{M_{orig}}$ achieves 88% coverage, $\mathbf{M_{PCS}}$ only 56%). We reason that startpagina's annotations play a role here: complex long queries rarely appear in $\mathcal{T}$, and thus simpler queries that generalise (i.e. are shorter and may appear in $\mathcal{T}$) are valuable. With respect to the u-score, i.e. the usefulness of the generated suggestions, we find that *including* the **P**-class (i.e. parallel moves) has the most negative effect (on average, models that include the P-class lose 10% in u-score). We speculate that parallel moves connect several distinct search paths together, thus adding noise to the reformulations.

The term-graph model ($\mathbf{M_{TGM}}$) exhibits the highest u-score across all our models, i.e. it generates the best suggestions for those queries, for which it is able to generate anything. At the same time though, the coverage is much lower than any of the other models (less than 36%), making it unusable in practice. This model was designed to have a higher coverage for queries that are not seen before. It is therefore notable that the model has the lowest coverage in our evaluation. The reason for this could be due to the limited tag space combined with the term-query model specific random walk method for generating suggestions. The individual lists of suggestions per random walk from a term are already sparse and the overlap between them is expected to be even more sparse (or non-existent). For future work it will be interesting to investigate models that combine reformulation type models with term-query graph models. Unfortunately, this is not feasible for the startpagina use case as the coverage for this combination would be very low and almost no suggestions could be made.

Overall, we conclude that when balancing the needs for usefulness and coverage, the basic model, i.e. $\mathbf{M_{orig}}$, which does not distinguish between reformulation types, is the best one to use.

When comparing our models' results to the CSE suggestions we first notice the low coverage CSE suggestions achieve - less than 26% of the individual generated suggestions are tags in startpagina's tag space $\mathcal{T}$. This is not surprising, as the CSE suggestions are agnostic to startpagina's content. With respect to u-score (which ignores whether or not the suggestions are in $\mathcal{T}$), CSE suggestions considerably outperform our models, indicating that there is a large potential for future improvements. Thus, we conclude that although the suggestions provided by the CSE are useful ones, they do not help in finding startpagina content most of the time.

Table 6. Overview of the query-flow graph models' effectiveness. All but the *CSE suggestions* are generated using `SP1` as training data.

	u-score	coverage
$\mathbf{M_{orig}}$	62.28%	88.36%
$\mathbf{M_{GPC}}$	63.78%	67.20%
$\mathbf{M_{GPS}}$	60.81%	78.31%
$\mathbf{M_{GCS}}$	70.07%	72.49%
$\mathbf{M_{PCS}}$	60.55%	55.67%
$\mathbf{M_{TGM}}$	72.05%	35.98%
CSE suggestions $\in \mathcal{T}$	83.67%	25.93%
CSE suggestions overall	87.36%	96.30%

When we consider the overal effectiveness of our models to generate *useful* suggestions, we find that more than half of all 1886 suggestions judged were deemed at least somewhat useful by our evaluators; more specifically: 28.2% of suggestions were deemed *useful*, 23.44% where *somewhat useful*, 44.11% were *not useful* and 4.24% suggestions were rated as *don't know*.

For 160 of the 189 queries, both $\mathbf{M_{orig}}$ and **CSE suggestions overall** could generate suggestions. In 75% of these cases, there was no overlap in the top-5 suggestions of both models. This indicates that our investigated approaches relying on query-flow and term-query graphs and `startpagina`'s query log are considerably different from the approaches and data employed by the CSE we compare our work against.

6 Conclusions

In this paper, we implemented and evaluated a pipeline that, based on a query log, generates query suggestions for unseen queries. We built on prior work, and investigated established approaches for search session splitting, reformulation type classification and the generation of query suggestions from query-flow and term-query graphs. We were able to successfully apply the results obtained in a regular Web search setting to the Dutch curated content search environment of `startpagina`. While search session splitting and reformulation classification yielded similar to existing work, the use of query-flow and term-query graphs showed a number of differences:

- We can improve the usefulness score (u-score) of the suggestions when only considering particular types of reformulations, as expected. In our case, leaving out class **P** (parallel move) increases the effectiveness. Contrary to prior work, **S** (specialisation) reformulation edges do not play a significant role.
- In contrast to the literature, which usually focuses on the u-score as effectiveness measure, we also need to take the coverage of a model into account.

Here, we observe a considerable degradation in coverage when only a subset of reformulations is considered; thus, there is a trade-off between accuracy and completeness. Depending on the optimisation goal, different models would have to be chosen.

- The term-query graph model produces the highest u-scores but, surprisingly, also has the lowest coverage by far. We reason that this is caused by the limited tag space $\mathcal{T}$ combined with the use of the term-query model specific random walk method.

Overall, we conclude that the state-of-the-art query suggestion models can successfully be applied to search environments where the content is described and indexed using tags. Not all user queries return results in such an environment but through harnessing the collective intelligence stored in the query logs we are still able to actively support individual users in their search missions. We found that a trade-off has to be made between the percentage of user queries for which we can generate suggestions and the usefulness of those suggestions. Although our use case is not a social tagging website and the tags on `startpagina` do not form a folksonomy, we believe that our results do apply to search engines in these types of environments. Our results certainly invite us to investigate combinations of the models described in this paper with collaborative filtering methodologies that are currently being used to suggest queries or tags on social tagging websites.

References

1. Anagnostopoulos, A., Becchetti, L., Castillo, C., Gionis, A.: An optimization framework for query recommendation. In: WSDM 2010, pp. 161–170 (2010)
2. Baeza-Yates, R., Hurtado, C.A., Mendoza, M.: Query recommendation using query logs in search engines. In: Lindner, W., Fischer, F., Türker, C., Tzitzikas, Y., Vakali, A.I. (eds.) EDBT 2004. LNCS, vol. 3268, pp. 588–596. Springer, Heidelberg (2004)
3. Bai, L., Guo, J., Cheng, X.: Query recommendation by modelling the query-flow graph. In: Salem, M.V.M., Shaalan, K., Oroumchian, F., Shakery, A., Khelalfa, H. (eds.) AIRS 2011. LNCS, vol. 7097, pp. 137–146. Springer, Heidelberg (2011)
4. Bai, L., Guo, J., Cheng, X., Geng, X., Du, P.: Exploring the query-flow graph with a mixture model for query recommendation. In: Proceedings of SIGIR Workshop on Query Representation and Understanding (2011)
5. Baraglia, R., Castillo, C., Donato, D., Nardini, F.M., Perego, R., Silvestri, F.: Aging effects on query flow graphs for query suggestion. In: CIKM 2009, pp. 1947–1950 (2009)
6. Beeferman, D., Berger, A.L.: Agglomerative clustering of a search engine query log. In: SIGKDD 2000, pp. 407–416 (2000)
7. Boldi, P., Bonchi, F., Castillo, C., Donato, D., Gionis, A., Vigna, S.: The query-flow graph: model and applications. In: CIKM 2008, pp. 609–618 (2008)
8. Boldi, P., Bonchi, F., Castillo, C., Donato, D., Gionis, A., Vigna, S.: Query suggestions using query-flow graphs. In: Proceedings of the 2009 Workshop on Web Search Click Data, pp. 56–63 (2009)

9. Boldi, P., Bonchi, F., Castillo, C., Vigna, S.: From "dango" to "japanese cakes": query reformulation models and patterns. In: WI 2009, pp.183–190 (2009)
10. Bonchi, F., Perego, R., Silvestri, F., Vahabi, H., Venturini, R.: Efficient query recommendations in the long tail via center-piece subgraphs. In: SIGIR 2012, pp. 345–354 (2012)
11. Brin, S., Page, L.: The anatomy of a large-scale hypertextual Web search engine. Computer networks and ISDN systems **30**(1), 107–117 (1998)
12. Bruza, P., Dennis, S.: Query reformulation on the internet: empirical data and the hyperindex search engine. In: RIAO 1997 (1997)
13. Cao, H., Jiang, D., Pei, J., He, Q., Liao, Z., Chen, E., Li, H.: Context-aware query suggestion by mining click-through and session data. In: SIGKDD 2008, pp. 875–883 (2008)
14. Craswell, N., Szummer, M.: Random walks on the click graph. In: SIGIR 2007, pp. 239–246 (2007)
15. Gayo-Avollo, D.: A survey on session detection methods in query logs and a proposal for future evaluation. Inf. Sci. **179**(12), 1822–1843 (2009)
16. Hagen, M., Gomoll, J., Beyer, A., Stein, B.: From search session detection to search mission detection. In: OAIR
17. Hagen, M., Stein, B., Rüb, T.: Query session detection as a cascade. In: CIKM 2011, pp. 147–152 (2011)
18. Huang, C.-K., Chien, L.-F., Oyang, Y.-J.: Relevant term suggestion in interactive web search based on contextual information in query session logs. JASIST **54**(7), 638–649 (2003)
19. Huang, J., Efthimiadis, E.N.: Analyzing and evaluating query reformulation strategies in web search logs. In: CIKM 2009 (2009)
20. Lau, T., Horvitz, E.: Patterns of search: analyzing and modeling web query refinement. In: UMAP 1999, pp. 119–128 (1999)
21. Mei, Q., Zhou, D., Church, K.W.: Query suggestion using hitting time. In: CIKM 2008, pp. 469–478 (2008)
22. Page, L., Brin, S., Motwani, R., Winograd, T.: The PageRank citation ranking: Bringing order to the web (1999)
23. Song, Y., Zhou, D., He, L.-w.: Query suggestion by constructing term-transition graphs. In: WSDM 2012, pp. 353–362 (2012)
24. Szpektor, I., Gionis, A., Maarek, Y.: Improving recommendation for long-tail queries via templates. In: WWW 2011, pp. 47–56 (2011)
25. White, R.W., Dumais, S.T.: Characterizing and predicting search engine switching behavior. In: CIKM 2009, pp. 87–96 (2009)

TV Goes Social: Characterizing User Interaction in an Online Social Network for TV Fans

Pedro Holanda, Bruno Guilherme, Ana Paula Couto da Silva(✉), and Olga Goussevskaia

Computer Science Department, Universidade Federal de Minas Gerais, Belo Horizonte, Brazil
{holanda,brunoguilherme,ana.coutosilva,olga}@dcc.ufmg.br

Abstract. The way people watch TV has been going through great changes in recent years. On the one hand, TV devices have turned into application development platforms with connectivity to the Internet. On the other hand, people are increasingly willing to share their TV watching habits with friends (and strangers) through online social networks. In this work we perform an analysis of tvtag, a social networking website for TV fans. We start by showing that tvtag, besides registering user preferences, captures real-time behavior, exhibiting increased user interaction on content air dates. Furthermore, we look into how different genres are distributed over content and characterize users according to how eclectic or narrow their interests are. In particular, we show that eclectic users tend to be less influential. Finally, we analyze how user activity can be used to predict content popularity.

Keywords: Online social networks · User behaviour characterization · Second-screen applications · Tvtag

1 Introduction

Understanding how people behave on Online Social Networks (OSNs) is a powerful tool for predicting if some of these networks will survive longer or not [18], impacting on the financial support to give them and the financial profit that can be gained from building and maintaining these networks. Furthermore, understanding how users interact with each other and with the available content provides precious insights for marketing strategies and for deciding if it is worth to maintain a specific product on the market.

It is not surprising that the television, a multi-billon dollar enterprise, also invests in advertising its contents over OSNs. TV channels encourage their audience to follow their profiles on different OSNs, such as Twitter and Facebook, where people are flooded with information related to their favorite TV shows.

Watching TV has always been a social experience. However, with an increasing number of personal gadgets, such as cell phones and tablets, acting as second screens in the living room, sharing our feelings about a TV episode or a

P. Cimiano et al. (Eds.): ICWE 2015, LNCS 9114, pp. 182–199, 2015.
DOI: 10.1007/978-3-319-19890-3_13

match now extends beyond our living room – it spans people connected to us via OSNs. This marriage between the "lean-back" TV environment and the more "lean-forward" Web surfing activity adds a new dimension to the entertainment business – the *Social TV*. In 2014, a study by Yahoo advertising [17] showed that 86% of users with access to mobile Internet used their smart phones while watching television, and 25% of them said they were browsing content related to the show they were watching. This suggests that the second-screen is no longer just a trend, but an integral aspect of media experiences. Social activity and participation on Twitter is now even ranking alongside traditional Nielsen ratings [1]. Nielsen social[1] releases a daily data set that collects the top 10 most-tweeted-about shows from the previous day and week.

Even though social TV and the second-screen have already become an important part of people's everyday lives, there is still little research characterizing these phenomena. In this work we focus our attention on analyzing how people share their TV and movie preferences with people beyond their homes. In particular, we analyze *tvtag*[2], an online social platform specifically designed for people to channel their social TV activities. We characterize tvtag user behavior, and use our analysis to shed light on how users interact in this OSN and how their preferences and activities may affect content popularity dynamics. We seek to answer several key questions:

- Is tvtag a predominantly real-time system, i.e., does user activity peak around air time of a show?
- How is user activity distributed among content, users, genres, and time?
- Are user evaluations mostly positive or negative?
- How are user interests distributed in the eclectic-to-homogeneous spectrum?
- Do eclectic users attract more followers and are therefore more influential?
- Is there a correlation between user activity before a release date and initial user engagement with a show?

Our analysis reveals interesting details about the operations of tvtag. In particular, we show that it can be viewed as a real-time, or second-screen, application; that users whose interests cross more than a handful of genres actually attract less followers; and we show that user activity before the release of a show is a good indicator of initial user engagement with the show. Therefore, it might be worthwhile to promote a new show on an OSN such as tvtag before actual release date in order to boost future audience.

The rest of the paper is structured as follows. In Sections 2 and 3 we describe the tvtag system, the dataset used and present initial analysis. In Sections 4 through 8 we present the characterization results and analysis. In Section 9 we discuss related work and in Section 10 we present our conclusions.

---

[1] www.nielsensocial.com

[2] During the course of this research project, tvtag actually shut down its services. Nevertheless, the data we were able to collect provides valuable insight into user behavior in this kind of OSN. In the future, we plan to make our dataset publically available and complement our analysis with data collected from other sources.

Table 1. Sampled dataset summary

Users	1,745,000
Users w/social connections	1,226,000
Movies	9,300
TV Shows	5,000
Genres (from TMDB)	26
TV shows w/ matched genre	3,050
Check-ins	92,077,000
Likes	52,776,000
Dislikes	3,033,000

2 Tvtag Overview

History: Originally named GetGlue, tvtag is a pioneer social network for entertainment, where users can check into TV shows and movies they are watching. The more users check in, the more the system learns about them and is able to make personalized recommendations. Launched back in 2010, tvtag user base rapidly grew from 30.000 to an estimated 4.5 million in late 2013, with a reported 500 million user activities, such as check-ins, likes and reviews, and partnerships with many entertainment content producers, such as HBO, ESPN, and Sony Pictures. In January 2015, to our surprise, tvtag shut down its services. Therefore, we performed our experiments on data collected up to that point and plan to complement the analysis with other data sources in the future.

Graph Structures: Tvtag is comprised by two main graph structures: the user-interest graph and the social graph. The user-interest graph arises from the interactions between users and content: users make check-ins to shows they watch, give likes and dislikes, leave comments and reviews. The social graph is generated by interactions among users: users connect through directed links by having followers and followees.

User Interface: Upon signing up, each tvtag user is invited to express some of her interests by marking what she likes and dislikes from a suggested list of shows. Once the profile is created, the user can follow other users and check into shows and movies she watches. The profile page exhibits a news stream with recent activities of her social connections and contents of interest. Every content in *tvtag*, such as a TV show, also has its own page, which includes all check-ins given by users, with corresponding timestamps, comments about the show posted in user pages, as well as those written directly on the show's page.

3 Datasets and Initial Analysis

Data Sources: In this work we aim to study the Social TV phenomenon. We used two data sources in our analysis: tvtag (introduced in Section 2) and TMDB (The Open Movie Database[3]). From tvtag we were able to collect information

[3] www.themoviedb.org

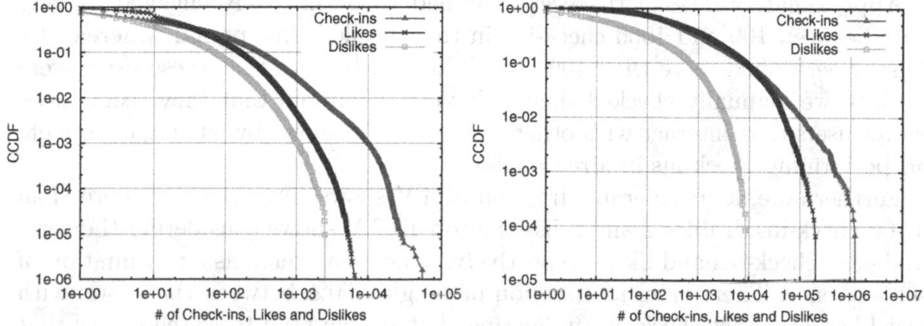

(a) Per user (excluding users with < check-ins(1M), likes(900K) and dislikes(1,6M))

(b) Per TV show (excluding shows with < check-ins(76), likes(6) and dislikes(910))

Fig. 1. CCDF of check-ins, likes and dislikes

about user preferences and activities related to TV contents, and from TMDB we obtained the corresponding metadata, comprised of information such as release and air dates, actors and directors, synopsis, and genre information about TV shows.

Data Collection: We implemented three Web crawlers to collect our data samples. The first crawler collects the user-interests graph of tvtag: it uses the web service provided by tvtag and downloads all check-ins, likes and dislikes of a user, having started with an initial random set of users and then augmented the graph coverage by following the user friendship network. The collected data sample, at the moment of writing, presents the best network coverage for the time period between 2011 and 2012, consisting of a total of approximately 29M check-ins, 21M likes and 1M dislikes in 2011 and 57M check-ins, 25M likes and 1M dislikes in 2012. The crawler continues to run at the time of writing, however, we have performed our analysis in the aforementioned time period due to a higher coverage ratio. The second crawler collects the social graph of tvtag, comprised by user's followers and followees. Our social graph analysis was performed on a graph with approximately 1.2M users and their followers. Our third crawler collected metadata from TMDB. We were collected 100% of movie and TV show information from TMDB. After matching the two datasets, we were able to obtain both user activity and metadata of approximately 3,000 TV shows. The total numbers of collected data can be seen in Table 1.

Initial Analysis: In Figures 1(a) and 1(b) we show the CCDF (complementary cumulative function distribution) of the number of check-ins, likes and dislikes performed per user and TV show, respectively. For the sake of clarity, we removed users and shows with zero check-ins, likes, and dislikes from the plots. Firstly, we observe that almost 52% of users (with at least one check-in) made at most 10 check-ins, revealing a low interactivity with the site content. On the other hand, approximately 50% of shows (with at least one check-in) received at most 350 check-ins.

Approximately 20% of the users revealed to be intensely engaged, having made between 100 and 1000 check-ins in the sampled time period, whereas 3% of users performed more than 1000 check-ins. To be sure that these users were not *bots*, we manually checked their behavior. We noted that they seem to be regular users that interact with other users and TV shows by writing comments and performing check-ins in a reasonable pattern.

Furthermore, a considerable fraction of TV shows (9%) received more than 10,000 check-ins. Tables 2 and 3 list the top 10 TV shows considering the total number of check-ins and likes, respectively, which may serve as an estimation of user audience. There is an intersection of roughly 50% between the shows with most likes and most check-ins, indicating that people tend to watch shows that they really enjoy.

Table 2. Top 10 TV shows in number of check-ins

TV show	Check-ins	Likes	Dislikes
Bing Bang Theory	1,972,968	206,769	4,935
True Blood	1,238,715	143,888	5,253
Walking Dead	1,159,322	159,704	2,444
Supernatural	1,117,981	109,901	5,089
Glee	949,049	153,192	8,403
Fringe	903,700	89,435	4,510
Once Upon a Time	875,683	82,481	1,630
Vampire Diaries	865,218	94,770	5,964
Game of Thrones	776,313	99,821	1,693
Dexter	749,978	139,011	3,598
Pretty Little Liars	666,265	77,870	4,806

Table 3. Top 10 TV shows in number of likes

TV show	Likes	Check-ins	Dislikes
Big Bang Theory	206,769	1,972,968	4,935
Family Guy	206,458	459,463	6,428
Simpsons	192,276	378,779	4,449
House	180,631	405,951	3,380
Walking Dead	159,704	159,322	2,444
Glee	153,192	949,049	8,403
HIMYM	143,998	537,257	4,095
True Blood	143,888	1,238,715	5,253
South Park	139,220	153,792	5,216
Dexter	139,011	749,978	3,598

Figures 1(a) and 1(b) also depict how people use like/dislike features. The result shows that users tend to be more positive than negative towards the TV shows. The dislike distribution has a stronger exponential decay when compared to the check-in and the like distribution decays. In our data sample, we have approximately 52M likes against 3M dislikes. More than 60% of users attributed more than 10 likes against 35% of users that performed the same amount of dislikes. Consequently, TV shows receive more likes than dislikes: 75% of them receive more than 10 likes, 32% of them receive more than 100 dislikes. The results may suggest that TV shows in tvtag meet users expectation.

Finally, in Table 4, we show the exponential fitting parameter α and the corresponding error for all distributions in Figures 1(a) and 1(b)[4]. All parameters are above 1, which means that the distributions mirror a non-exponential decay, in which a small portion of users is very engaged and a small portion of shows attracts intense user activity.

Table 4. Fitting parameters for distributions in Figures 1(a) and 1(b)

Users			Shows		
Check-in	Like	Dislike	Check-in	Like	Dislike
1.49 (0.007)	1.30 (0.008)	1.40 (0.01)	2.06 (0.016)	2.09 (0.016)	1.79 (0.021)

4 Genre Characterization

Genre Distribution: We start our analysis by examining what kind of content is available in tvtag. Thanks to the cross information we have from TMDB, we were able to categorize approximately 3,000 TV shows into 26 different genres. In our dataset, 63% of TV shows were labeled with one genre; 24% with 2 genres and 13% with 3 or more genres. Table 5 compares the top 10 genres (in terms of total number of available TV shows) in TMDB and tvtag. We can observe that 10 out of 10 genres in both lists are the same, even though the order and size of each genre differ between the two datasets. Comedy, Drama and Animation rank higher in tvtag. Drama, on the other hand, ranks higher in TMDB, followed by Comedy and Documentary. These discrepancies may be explained by differences in audience age groups. OSNs tend to attract younger audiences when compared to general TV public

Genre Popularity: A simple way of measuring a TV show's popularity is by counting the number of check-ins and likes it receives in an OSN. This measure has been widely used in literature for measuring content popularity [22]. In Figure 2 we look into how genre popularity changes during the sampled time period. We can observe that, for all genres, the number of check-ins peaks during the season release months (September/October) and after Christmas break (February). The numbers fall during Christmas break and summer vacations. Drama and comedy are the most popular genres in data we collected.

Genre Positivity: We looked into two measures of positivity. (1) User positivity, defined as the average number of likes given by a user to shows of a given

[4] Parameterization used the maximum likelihood estimation.

Table 5. Top 10 genres in number of TV shows in TMDB and tvtag datasets

TMDB		TVTag	
Genre	% of contents	Genre	% of contents
Drama	27.19	Comedy	39.11
Comedy	23.54	Drama	38.23
Documentary	14.65	Animation	18.20
Animation	14.02	Documentary	15.97
Action/Adventure	6.23	Action/Adventure	14.03
Sci-Fi/Fantasy	4.34	Sci-Fi/Fantasy	9.11
News	3.43	Mystery	4.92
Mystery	1.73	News	4.46
Family	0.91	Western	1.34
Western	0.82	Family	1.28

genre, and (2) Show positivity, defined as the ratio between the number of likes and dislikes given to shows of a given genre.

In Figure 3, we can se the average user positivity for all 26 genres in our dataset. It is not surprising to see that the most popular genres in terms of number of check-ins, such as Comedy, Drama and Animation, receive the highest number of likes from users, whereas less popular genres register less positivity from users.

We conjectured in Section 3 that people tend to be more positive than negative towards TV shows, regardless of the genre. Figure 4 corroborates this intuition, showing the ratio between *likes* and *dislikes* received by shows in each genre, over time. Interestingly, even though people are more engaged with Drama and Comedy genres, judging by the number of check-ins and likes per user (Figures 2 and 3), Mystery and Sci-Fi/Fantasy have the highest positivity ratios between August and October 2011. This result suggests that, although Drama and Comedy genres attract more likes, they also attract more dislikes.

5 Social Ties

Users in tvtag form a social network by following each other. We collected the followers and followees of approximately 1.2M users. In Figure 5(a) we plot the CCDF of the number of followers and followees per user. Both distributions follow the power-law distribution, with $\alpha = 1.41$ and error 0.02 and $\alpha = 1.36$ and error 0.01 exponential parameters, respectively. A small portion of users (1%) is followed by more than 100 users, whereas the vast majority (95%) has less than 10 followers. Similarly, only 1% of users follow ≥ 45 users, whereas 94% follow at most 10 other users.

In Figure 5(b), we plot the follower/followee ratio distribution per user. It can be seen that more than 80% of users have more followees than followers. A small portion (1%) have at least 10 times more followers than followees. This

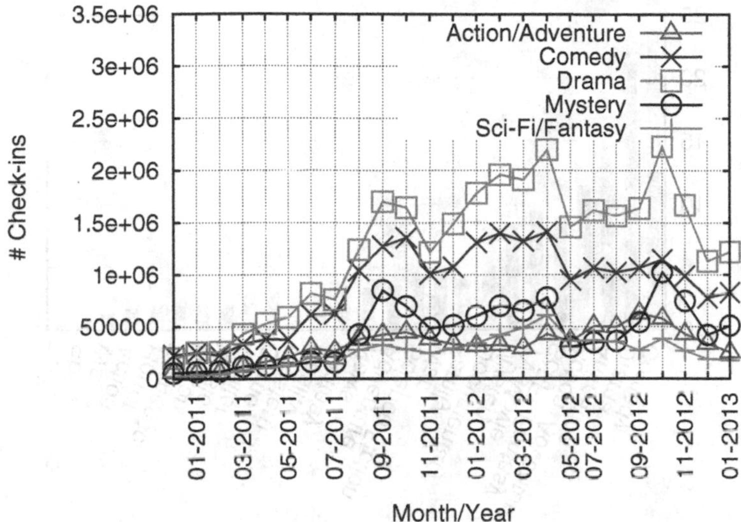

Fig. 2. Number of check-ins per genre over time

is an expected result, given the nature of this social relationship: some people attract a large amount of attention and it is up to them to return their attention to other users.

6 Second-Screen Behavior

In this section we analyze whether tvtag can be viewed as a real-time system, or if people tend to check into shows they like regardless of each show's air times. Tvtag provides us with a timestamp of every check-in, whereas TMDB gives us the information about the date and time of a show's release, as well as the date and time of the last aired episode. Tvtag provides GMT timestamps measured at the server and not locally at each user, so the time distribution of check-ins in our data sample, shown in Figure 6(a), has peak activity hours between 23:00 and 4:00, which roughly corresponds to the primetime span between Eastern and Pacific time zones.

Next, we analyze whether users increase their activity during the days when their favorite shows are broadcasted. In Figure 6(b), we consider 5% and 10% most popular TV shows[5], and plot the percentage of check-ins whose timestamps[6] fall

[5] The top 5% and 10% samples contain over 700 and 1400 shows, respectively, both covering a variety of genres

[6] For the purpose of our analysis, we subtracted 9 hours from the check-in timestamps, because tvtag uses GMT, which can be up to 9 hours ahead of primetime range. In this way, we were able to match the day of the week of the air times reported by TMBD and the corresponding check-in timestamps from tvtag.

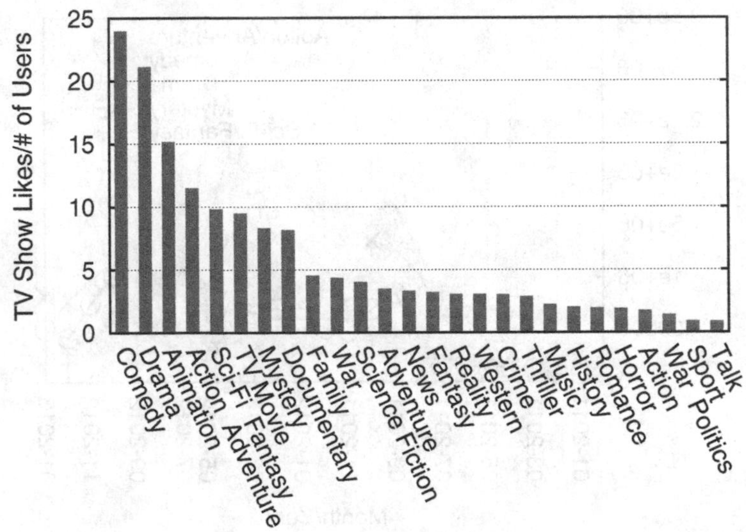

Fig. 3. User positivity per TV genre

on the same day of the week as the air date of the show's last aired episode. We count the check-ins in the month preceding the last aired episode, three preceding months and 6 preceding months, respectively. In Figure 6(b), the x-axis is 0 if the day of the week of the last air date coincides with the day of the week of the check-in; ± if the check-in was one day after or before the last air day, and so on. It can be observed that 65% of the check-ins to the 5% most popular shows that occur 1 month before the last air date fall on the same day of the week as the air date. For the 10% most popular shows, the number is over 60%. If we consider the preceding 3-month period, this ratio is over 55% for both groups, and if we consider the 6-month period, the number is close to 50% for both groups analyzed. The percentage of check-ins on day $\neq 0$ is $\leq 10\%$ for all sets analyzed. Overall, it can be clearly seen that user activity peaks during the days of the week when shows are broadcasted, indicating that tvtag behaves as a real-time, or second-screen, system, when TV programs of high popularity are considered.

7 Eclecticism and Popularity

In this section we analyze how user interests are distributed in the eclectic-to-homogeneous spectrum in terms of checked-in genres and how the level of eclecticism may affect user popularity.

In Figure 7, two measures of eclecticism are shown. The first measure counts the number of different genres of shows that users checked into during the entire sampled period[7]. The second measure counts the number of different genres

[7] Note that only the shows with matched genre information from TMDB were counted.

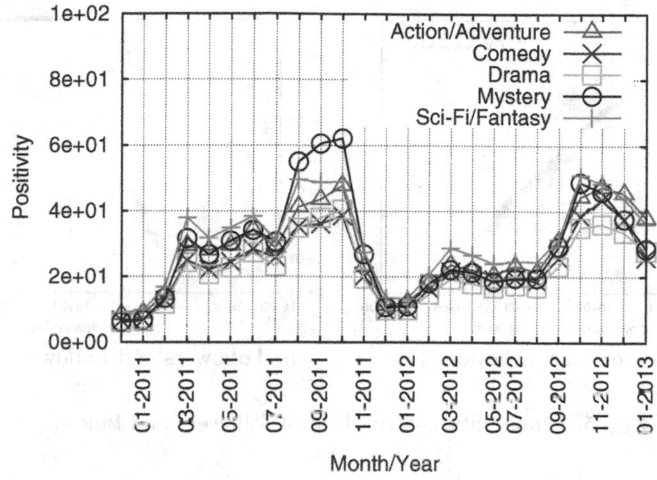

Fig. 4. Show positivity per TV genre over time (like-dislike ratio)

checked in by the user, with the restriction that at least 10% of her check-ins belong to each counted genre, i.e., occasional check-ins in different genres that did not sum up to a minimum of 10% were considered random and not counted. By the first measure, 13% of users are at one end of the spectrum, having checked into one single genre, and 10% of users are at the other end, having checked into more than 14 different genres. Approximately half of users checked into 5 genres or less. The second measure reveals that users are actually much less eclectic than that. More than a quarter of all users by the second measure checked into one single genre and more that 90% expressed interest in 4 genres or less.

In Figures 8 and 9 we analyze the relation between the eclecticism and popularity (number of respective followers) of users. Our hypothesis was that users whose interests are spread over a number of different genres tend to attract more followers. We grouped users according to the second measure of eclecticism, i.e., group 1 contains users who have checked into only one genre at least 10% of the time, group 2 those who checked into 2, and so on.

Figure 8 shows the mean number of followers for each group, as well as the number of users in each group. It can be seen that the group with the highest average number of followers is group 4 and the group with the highest number of users is group 3. Groups with eclecticism ≥ 5, on the other hand, have significantly less users although possess an average amount of followers close to other groups. The confidence intervals are tight, except for the groups with more than 6 genres, which means that users in these groups attracted either many or few followers, not having an homogeneous behavior.

Figure 9(a) shows the CDF of the number of followers for 9 eclecticism groups. It can be observed that users with less than 1000 followers are more or less evenly distributed among all groups, i.e., eclecticism does not seem to

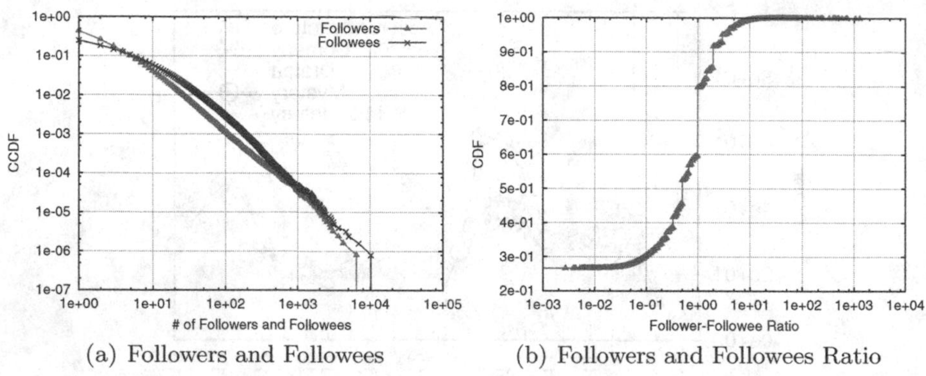

(a) Followers and Followees (b) Followers and Followees Ratio

Fig. 5. Probability Distribution of followers and follows

influence the distribution of followers among users. However, if we look into the most influential users, those with 1000 followers and more (see Figure 9(b)), we perceive that they belong exclusively to groups with eclecticism ≤ 4. Groups 3 and 4, in fact, contain the most influential users in tvtag, and groups with high eclecticism (with users who checked into ≥ 5 different genres) do not contain any of the most influential users.

These observations actually disprove our initial hypothesis that the more eclectic the more influential a user is. It turns out that moderately eclectic users are the ones who attract the most followers. One possible reason behind this is that people tend to follow "experts" is certain fields, and to become an expert one cannot excessively diversify one's interests.

8 Predicting Initial Audience Engagement

Popularity is the holy grail of TV shows. Producers, directors and actors expect to snatch the audience since the TV show's release, increasing its chance of surviving in the "TV jungle". It is crucial to grab people's attention since the TV show beginnings. The possibility of predicting audience engagement through simple models is a valuable tool for marketing strategies, since popularity attracts premium ad rates and boosts merchandise and content sales.

We propose a simple methodology that can be explored for predicting user engagement with a TV show, mainly in the earlier days after the release day. Our prediction strategy is motivated by a strong linear correlation observed between the number of likes before the release and the number of check-ins after the release date of a TV show. We analyzed a subset of 525 TV shows that were released in the years 2011 and 2012. We collected the likes before the show's release day and the check-ins performed one day and one month after the show's release. Figure 10 illustrate this correlation for a period of one day after the release day. We use a linear regression to observe the impact

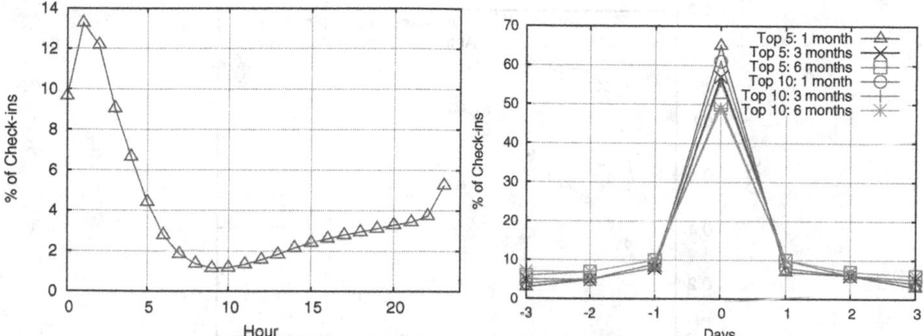

(a) Check-in hour-of-day (GMT) distribution at the server

(b) Second-screen behavior of 5% and 10% most popular TV shows: percentage of check-ins during the same day of the week of the last episode air date in the preceding 1, 3 and 6 months.

Fig. 6. Second-Screen Behavior

of the number of the pre-release likes on the initial show popularity, estimated by the number of check-ins after σ time units. We obtained the Pearson coefficients $\rho = 0.8750$ and $\rho = 0.9040$ for the regressions for time intervals 1-day and 1-month, respectively.[8]

In order to implement the prediction method, we divided our data sample into two subsets: the training set, Υ, to calculate the parameters, and the test set, Ω, to analyze the accuracy of the regression. We randomly selected the samples and computed the linear parameters for 1000 pairs of training and test sets. Tables 6 and 7 shows the a (curve slop), b (intercept point) and the determination R^2 (with 95% confidence intervals) coefficients of the linear regressions performed using 1000 random combinations of training and test sets. For all considered cases, R^2 value of the regression had mean values between 0.71 and 0.79. As expected, if we observe the behavior of more TV shows (increasing the training set size, Υ), we decrease the confidence interval.

As a further application example of the prediction method, we attempted to predict the initial user engagement of a show, which was released in 2014, i.e., one year after the release dates in our training set. We collected the likes (317) before the release of the Warner's Gotham and its check-ins 1-day (1,934) and 1-month (7,901) after the release day. With our simple model, by using 50% − 50% parameters, we obtained the values 1,591 for the number of check-ins one day after the release (18%) and 5,623 for the number of check-ins one month after

[8] Note that we discarded the shows with no popularity during the considered time period, i.e, shows with zero check-ins after the release, which was equal to 139 and 77 for 1-day and 1-month periods, respectively.

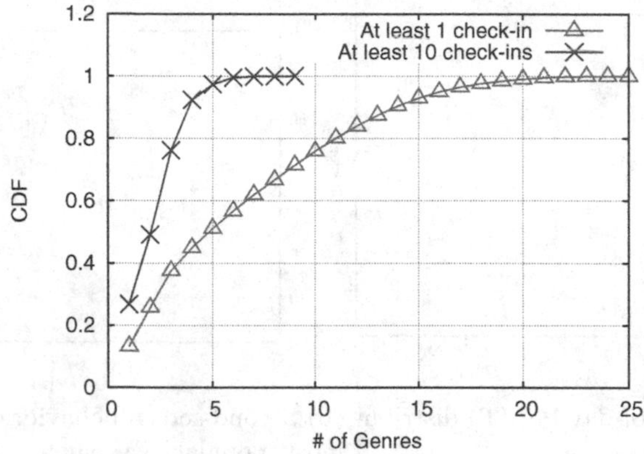

Fig. 7. User eclecticism: number of genres in user check-in history

Table 6. Predicting initial user engagement in the 1st *day* after the show's release day using the number of pre-release likes

Υ	Ω	1-Day		
		a	b	R^2
10%	90%	3.8500 ± 0.0435	368.2821 ± 10.085	0.7111 ± 0.0050
20%	80%	3.8801 ± 0.0148	352.7846 ± 3.5794	0.7342 ± 0.0018
30%	70%	3.9073 ± 0.0074	351.7603 ± 1.8233	0.7449 ± 0.0009
40%	60%	3.8999 ± 0.0042	351.9690 ± 1.0880	0.7480 ± 0.0006
50%	50%	3.9013 ± 0.0027	354.8540 ± 0.6946	0.7493 ± 0.0006
60%	40%	3.9083 ± 0.0018	352.7203 ± 0.4857	0.7469 ± 0.0005

the release (29%). Note that this underestimation error was amplified due to the growing size of tvtag overall network during the years 2013 and 2014.

We believe that our model is the first step to better understanding how an OSN for TV fans can be used to promote TV shows and increase future audiences. It demonstrates that it can be worthwhile for a TV network to invest in pre-release publicity on an OSN as a marketing strategy for increasing people's engagement with the first episodes and making them more likely to become fans of the show.

9 Related Work

Social TV and Second-screen Applications: Television has evolved from "lean-back" scheduled programming watching, constrained to our living rooms, into "lean-forward" entertainment, which includes sharing and discussing content, by individuals and groups, via various displays and media [8]. Authors in [15] study the viability of using social activity streams as a mechanism to detect and characterize television viewer behavior. However, the authors focused on

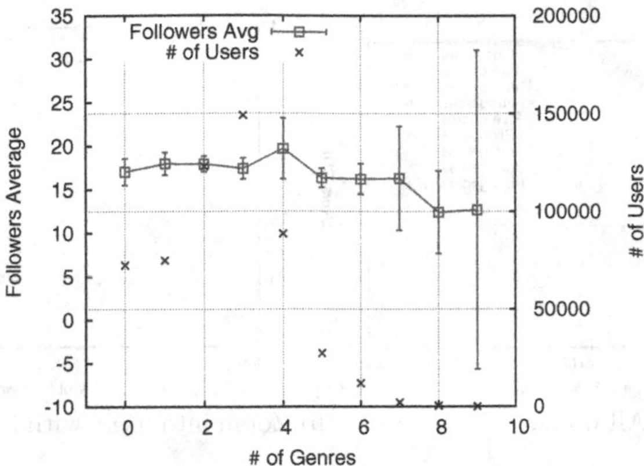

Fig. 8. Mean number of followers by user eclecticism (users grouped by number of checked-in genres)

Table 7. Predicting initial user engagement in the 1st *month* after the show's release day using the number of pre-release likes

Υ	Ω	1-Month		
		a	b	R^2
10%	90%	24.1259 ± 4.3691	805.1159 ± 172.169	0.7489 ± 0.0345
20%	80%	15.1780 ± 0.5046	767.7531 ± 91.551	0.7735 ± 0.0153
30%	70%	15.4168 ± 0.3132	721.7714 ± 59.980	0.7894 ± 0.0082
40%	60%	15.4826 ± 0.2199	706.7614 ± 41.831	0.7938 ± 0.0064
50%	50%	15.5068 ± 0.1647	707.9705 ± 31.509	0.7973 ± 0.0055
60%	40%	15.5516 ± 0.1261	698.3868 ± 23.946	0.7982 ± 0.0052

Twitter and Topsy[9], but do not characterize a specialized OSN for TV fans, which is probably more suitable for understanding how people relate to television content. Torrez-Riley [20] provide a historical perspective of television's role in engaging social interaction, and analyze how a new era of fragmented consumption and time-shifted viewing has altered this role. Furthermore, the author discusses the potential future of the ever-changing social TV industry and predicts what new adaptations will be implemented to engage and facilitate viewer relationships. However, no quantitative results are presented. Basapur *et al.* [6] describe the development and field trial of a second-screen TV experience, called FanFeeds, which allows authoring and consumption of time synchronized secondary content around TV shows. The participants of the experiment revealed that the prototype allowed them to better connect with their TV shows and have an enriched social life around live as well as time-shifted TV content. Geerts *et al.* [10] highlighted the importance of watching TV shows with

[9] www.topsy.com

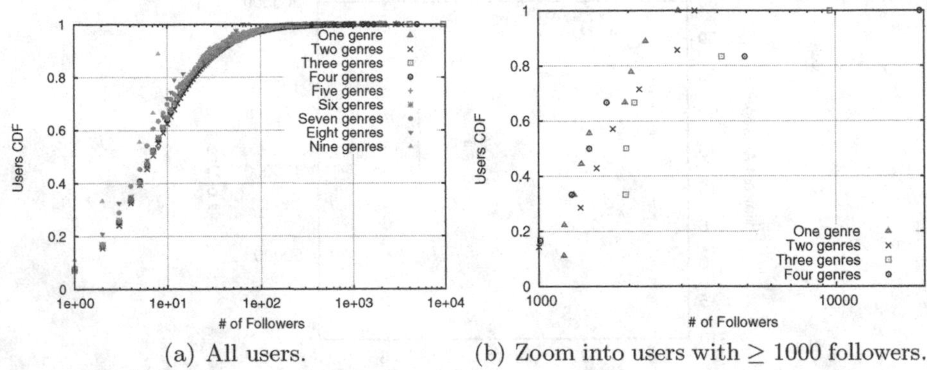

(a) All users.

(b) Zoom into users with ≥ 1000 followers.

Fig. 9. CDF of followers for each eclecticism group (users grouped by number of checked-in genres)

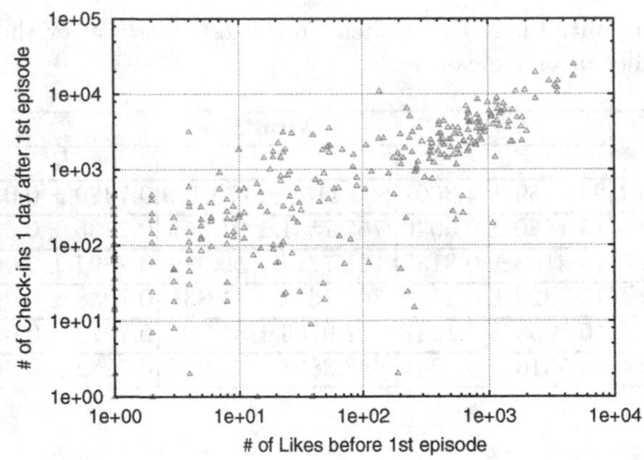

Fig. 10. Correlation between number of likes before and number of check-ins *one day* after the release day

friends via OSNs and how this action may influence their relationships. Finally, authors in [14] investigated user interactions with secondary screens during live and non-live transmission of TV programs. They also explored the role of hand-held devices in this second-screen interaction and performed statistical tests on more than 418,000 tweets from second screens for three popular TV shows.

OSN Characterization: The importance of OSNs has motivated researches to characterize different aspects of the most popular OSNs. The graph and social properties of Facebook [3,4,21], Twitter [9,12], Google+ [11], Last.fm[16] and Quora [23] have been carefully analyzed. Effects of user similarity in social media were explored in [2]. Authors in [5] analyzed the influence of people in promoting diffusion cascades in Twitter and found that the most influent are those with more followers. In [19], the authors proposed an univariate regression model to predict popularity of YouTube videos and Digg stories. There are other works that are interested in analyzing and predicting the content popularity in OSNs, e.g., [7,22]. However, there are few works that focus on capturing people's behavior towards television contents. Most of them use Twitter, a generic OSN to accomplish this task [13,15]. Even though there is a large pool of works devoted to studying the social and structural characteristics of OSNs, there is a lack of works looking into specialized OSNs for television fans.

10 Conclusions

In this work, we characterized tvtag, an OSN for television fans. Our analysis of tvtag revealed the following insights:

1. tvtag can be viewed as a real-time, or second-screen, application: user activity peaks during the days of the week when shows are broadcasted
2. Although groups of users that are interested in just a few (≤ 4) genres attract more users, the mean number of followers for all groups is almost the same. Then, we conclude that the level of eclecticism does not affect user popularity.
3. User activity before the release of a show is a good indicator of initial user engagement with the show: given a strong linear correlation between likes before show release and check-ins after its release, we proposed a linear regression model for predicting with reasonable error the user engagement in the first day and first month following the release day.

Even though in this work we analyzed one particular example of an OSN for TV fans, we believe that our work is a first step to better understanding people's engagement with television content through OSNs in general. As future work, we intend to enrich our analysis with data from other sources, possibly Twitter, IMDB, LastFm, or Reddit[10], for example by exploring user comments in these networks.

Acknowledgments. We would like to thank the anonymous reviewers for their valuable feedback. This work is supported in part by CNPq, FAPEMIG and LG Electronics in cooperation with Brazilian Federal Government through *Lei de Informatica*.

References

1. New nielsen research indicates two-way causal influence between twitter activity and tv viewership (2013). http://www.nielsen.com
2. Anderson, A., Huttenlocher, D., Kleinberg, J., Leskovec, J.: Effects of user similarity in social media. In: Proceedings of the Fifth ACM International Conference on Web Search and Data Mining, WSDM 2012, pp. 703–712. ACM, New York (2012)

[10] www.imdb.com,www.last.fm,www.reddit.com

3. Backstrom, L., Boldi, P., Rosa, M., Ugander, J., Vigna, S.: Four degrees of separation. In: Proceedings of the 4th Annual ACM Web Science Conference, WebSci 2012, pp. 33–42. ACM, New York (2012)
4. Backstrom, L., Kleinberg, J.: Romantic partnerships and the dispersion of social ties: a network analysis of relationship status on facebook. In: Proceedings of the 17th ACM Conference on Computer Supported Cooperative Work & #38; Social Computing, CSCW 2014, pp. 831–841. ACM, New York (2014)
5. Bakshy, E., Hofman, J.M., Mason, W.A., Watts, D.J.: Everyone's an influencer: quantifying influence on twitter. In: Proceedings of the Fourth ACM International Conference on Web Search and Data Mining, WSDM 2011, pp. 65–74. ACM, New York (2011)
6. Basapur, S., Mandalia, H., Chaysinh, S., Lee, Y., Venkitaraman, N., Metcalf, C.: Fanfeeds: evaluation of socially generated information feed on second screen as a tv show companion. In: Proceedings of the 10th European Conference on Interactive Tv and Video, EuroiTV 2012, pp. 87–96. ACM, New York (2012)
7. Benevenuto, F., Rodrigues, T., Almeida, V., Almeida, J., Ross, K.: Video interactions in online video social networks. ACM Trans. Multimedia Comput. Commun. Appl. **5**(5), 30:1–30:25 (2009)
8. Bondad-Brown, B.A., Ricea, R.E., Pearce, K.E.: Influences on tv viewing and online user-shared video use: Demographics, generations, contextual age, media use, motivations, and audience activity. Journal of Broadcasting & Electronic Media **56**, 471–493 (2012)
9. Cha, M., Haddadi, H., Benevenuto, F., Gummadi, K.P.: Measuring user influence in twitter: the million follower fallacy. In: ICWSM 2010: Proceedings of International AAAI Conference on Weblogs and Social (2010)
10. Geerts, D., Vaishnavi, I., Mekuria, R., van Deventer, O., Cesar, P.: Are we in sync?: synchronization requirements for watching online video together. In: Proceedings of the SIGCHI Conference on Human Factors in Computing Systems, CHI 2011, pp. 311–314. ACM, New York (2011)
11. Gonzalez, R., Cuevas, R., Motamedi, R., Rejaie, R., Cuevas, A.: Google+ or google-?: dissecting the evolution of the new osn in its first year. In: Proceedings of the 22nd International Conference on World Wide Web, WWW 2013, pp. 483–494. International World Wide Web Conferences Steering Committee, Republic and Canton of Geneva (2013)
12. Kwak, H., Lee, C., Park, H., Moon, S.: What is twitter, a social network or a news media? In: Proceedings of the 19th International Conference on World Wide Web, WWW 2010, pp. 591–600. ACM, New York (2010)
13. Lochrie, M., Coulton, P.: Sharing the viewing experience through second screens. In: Proceedings of the 10th European Conference on Interactive Tv and Video, EuroiTV 2012, pp. 199–202. ACM, New York (2012)
14. Mukherjee, P., Jansen, B.J.: Social tv and the social soundtrack: significance of second screen interaction during television viewing. In: Kennedy, W.G., Agarwal, N., Yang, S.J. (eds.) SBP 2014. LNCS, vol. 8393, pp. 317–324. Springer, Heidelberg (2014)
15. Narasimhan, N., Vasudevan, V.: Descrambling the social tv echo chamber. In: Proceedings of the 1st ACM Workshop on Mobile Systems for Computational Social Science - MCSS 2012, p. 33 (2012)
16. Pálovics, R., Benczúr, A.A.: Temporal influence over the last.fm social network. In: Proceedings of the 2013 IEEE/ACM International Conference on Advances in Social Networks Analysis and Mining, ASONAM 2013, pp. 486–493. ACM, New York (2013)

17. Raje, N.: Social tv and the "second screen" (2014). http://trivone.com/blog/social-tv-and-the-second-screen-2/
18. Ribeiro, B.: Modeling and predicting the growth and death of membership-based website. In: Proceedings of the 23rd International Conference on World Wide Web, pp. 653–664 (2014)
19. Szabo, G., Huberman, B.A.: Predicting the popularity of online content. Commun. ACM **53**(8), 80–88 (2010)
20. Torrez-Riley, J.: The social tv phenomenon: New technologies look to enhance televisions role as an enabler of social interaction
21. Ugander, J., Karrer, B., Backstrom, L., Marlow, C.: The anatomy of the facebook social graph (2011). CoRR, abs/1111.4503
22. Vasconcelos, M., Almeida, J., Gonçalves, M., Souza, D., Gomes, G.: Popularity dynamics of foursquare micro-reviews. In: Proceedings of the Second ACM Conference on Online Social Networks, COSN 2014, pp. 119–130. ACM, New York (2014)
23. Wang, G., Gill, K., Mohanlal, M., Zheng, H., Zhao, B.Y.: Wisdom in the social crowd: an analysis of quora. In: Proceedings of the 22nd International Conference on World Wide Web, WWW 2013, pp. 1341–1352. International World Wide Web Conferences Steering Committee, Republic and Canton of Geneva (2013)

Beomap: Ad Hoc Topic Maps for Enhanced Exploration of Social Media Data

Martin Leginus[1(✉)], ChengXiang Zhai[2], and Peter Dolog[1]

[1] Department of Computer Science, Aalborg University, Selma Lagerlofs Vej 300, 9220 Aalborg-East, Denmark
{mleginus,dolog}@cs.aau.dk

[2] Department of Computer Science, University of Illinois at Urbana-Champaign, 201 North Goodwin Avenue, Urbana, IL 61801, USA
czhai@cs.uiuc.edu

Abstract. Social media is ubiquitous. There is a need for intelligent retrieval interfaces that will enable a better understanding, exploration and browsing of social media data. A novel two dimensional ad hoc topic map is proposed (called Beomap). The main novelty of Beomap is that it allows a user to define an ad hoc semantic dimension with a keyword query when visualizing topics in text data. This not only helps to impose more meaningful spatial dimensions for visualization, but also allows users to steer browsing and exploration of the topic map through ad hoc defined queries. We developed a system to implement Beomap for exploring Twitter data, and evaluated the proposed Beomap in two ways, including an offline simulation and a user study. Results of both evaluation strategies show that the new Beomap interface is better than a standard interactive interface.

Keywords: Adaptive visualization · Adaptive browsing · Topic map · Social media

1 Introduction

To fully exploit the potential of social media data, there is a need for social analytics tools to enable more effective ways to understand, analyze and exploit social media information. An especially useful way to help users explore the information space is to visualize topics. Interfaces for visual exploration of topics proposed in [5,6] give users an understanding of underlying topic space and enable them to browse related topics. Further, these interfaces enable a user-centered exploration exploiting different machine learning techniques. These interfaces usually visualize relations between topics based on relevance scores but do not exploit other meta-data dimensions (e.g., popularity, sentiment or location) which might prevent the user from a more realistic understanding of underlying topic space. Moreover, it is not clear what a certain direction or position in the interface means e.g., what does it mean when a topic is presented

P. Cimiano et al. (Eds.): ICWE 2015, LNCS 9114, pp. 200–218, 2015.
DOI: 10.1007/978-3-319-19890-3_14

in the top right corner of the interface. Self-organizing maps [7] satisfy this partially, however the dimension cannot be flexibly modified by the user. Further, self-organizing maps are computationally expensive as well as difficult to clearly interpret horizontal and vertical axes. The last but perphaps the most crucial deficiency is the limited ability of a user to reach ad hoc relevant topics regions in a flexible way i.e., user-driven exploration. The user-driven exploration is different from machine-learning user centered exploration as it allows the user to completely control an exploration process.

In this paper, we propose a way to solve these limitations with a novel two dimensional ad hoc topic map (see Figure 1) which we refer to as Beomap (*beo* in latin means to make happy). The idea is to allow a user to define the meaning of a dimension using an arbitrary query to visualize an ad hoc topic map, which enables user-guided exploration and browsing of the underlying social media topics space. Such a Beomap has many desirable properties and advantages. First, Beomap would be especially useful to help users interact with search results when there is a missing aspect in the query (e.g., most top ranked results missed one query aspect), which often is the case when the search results are not satisfactory. We refer to a missing aspect as a need to view topics (from both inside as well as outside of search results) and underlying documents from a particular aspect/perspective. Beomap extends a standard ranking which is usually presented with an ordered list of topics into a two-dimensional ranking. The second dimension expresses how well a topic relevant to the main query also matches an additional aspect or a perspective which can be flexibly expressed with a second ad hoc query. The positive effect of this two-dimensional ranking enables easy understanding of topics orientation within the topic map i.e., a particular position of the depicted topic represents its closeness to the main query as well as to the second ad hoc query. Hence, users are better able to understand underlying topic structure between individual topics, which might lead to serendipitous discoveries. Further, Beomap enables a user to explore and navigate the topic space through user-chosen visualization metrics. The ad hoc topic map can also be generated and visualized according to a particular predefined visualization metric e.g., recency, relevance, popularity or location based dimension. Due to this, Beomap provides the means for enhanced browsing into related relevant topics from underlying social media data as well as the means for improved understanding of the topics structure.

The proposed topic map visualization is general enough and it can be applied to other domains where topic keywords are available or can be derived for a particular resource (other social media data e.g., Instagram, Facebook; folksonomy data e.g., Delicious, Bibsonomy and other forms e.g., research publications, news articles etc.).

To evaluate Beomap, we implemented BeomapApp a prototype system over social stream data from Twitter. The core component of the prototype system is a two-dimensional ad hoc topic map denoted as Beomap as well. To evaluate the proposed topic map, the offline browsing simulation of Beomap was performed which proved an enhanced retrieval of additional relevant tweets. We simulated various browsing strategies for Beomap and the baseline (see the detailed description of strategies in Section 4.1) assuming a user optimal behaviour i.e., an upper-bound scenario. The precision improvements of **BeomapBest**(the best strategy for Beomap) are significantly better than the **BLBest** (the best strategy for the baseline) (Wilcoxon signed rank test, $p < 0.00001$). The best precision versus user effort is attained with **BeomapMisAsp**, when a missing aspect of the query is used for Beomap generation. Moreover, the performed user study proves benefits of BeomapApp. Thirty one users consider the system as significantly more useful and are significantly more satisfied with the system than the baseline. Further, they perceive the system as a flexible tool for exploration, browsing and analysis of Twitter data as well as being easy to browse and interesting. Analyzed usage logs and acquired user comments about Beomap validate the benefits of two-dimensional ad hoc topic maps i.e., improved recall, more explored topics as well as positive comments about Beomap.

The structure of the paper is organized as follows. Section 2 positions our work with respect to existing information retrieval interfaces. Section 3 describes a novel two-dimensional topic map as well as several visualization metrics. Section 4 presents findings from the evaluation of Beomap (consisting of offline browsing simulation as well as user study). Section 5 discusses the benefits and limitations of Beomap. Section 6 summarizes the paper achievements and outlines future work.

2 Related Work

VizLinc [1] helps users to get an understanding of underlying data. It allows the user to find patterns and relations between mentioned entities and facilitates users to narrow down the existing documents to a fraction of only relevant ones. The system allows a text and entity search. The retrieved results can be also geo visualized in the map. Further, recognized entities matching a query are visualized in the graph. Entities are clustered and their neighbours can be exploited with the n-hop network functionality. The limitations of VizLinc are: (1) a graph exploration is limited only to n-hop neighbours - not possible adhoc browsing; (2) no meaningful explanation of direction within the visualized graph; (3) the system is not adapted for social media data where a meta-data annotation might be more challenging. Bron et at. [4] proposed a subjunctive exploratory search interface which supports exploration of multiple views on a topic as well as enables a discovery of patterns in the data. The proposed interface combines two side-by-side versions of an exploratory search interface that are extended with visualizations in which characteristics of the result sets can be depicted and compared. The performed user study indicates that the subjunctive interface enables users to define more diverse queries and to retrieve more diverse documents than with the standard exploratory search interface. Despite the benefits of the system, it is not possible to visualize user chosen metrics except of term frequencies and time.

Apolo, an interactive user interface [5], helps users to make sense of large graph data. The aim of the system is to support user-driven understanding of

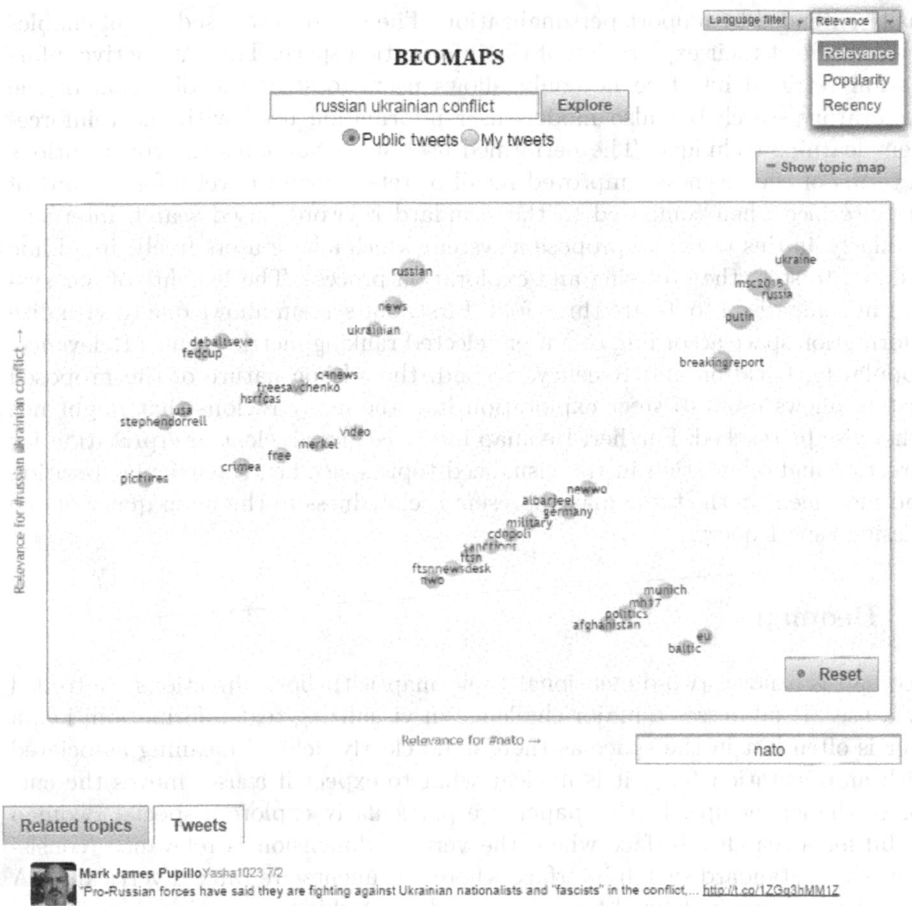

Fig. 1. Beomap is a two-dimensional topic map which supports ad hoc semantic dimensions that can be easily defined through a second query e.g. Nato. Further, it allows one to visualize a topic map with respect to the user defined meta-data metric e.g., Relevance. The topics in the top right corner are relevant for the main query as well as for the ad hoc dimension.

data. The underlying information landscape is adapted to user information need using Belief propagation algorithm. Users rated the system positively when used for sensemaking while browsing a scientific literature network. This work is in line with our motivation, to support user-driven exploration of the information landscape. The user-driven exploration in Beomap is achieved through a second ad hoc query dimension that allows users to regenerate freely a topic map according to user information need. The consequences of our design are a more realistic understanding of the underlying information landscape and the possibility of observing topic correlations between the main and second ad hoc query. Although, the adaptation is not the scope of this study, our system could be easily extended to support personalization. The system proposed by [6] enables users to direct their exploration of the information space. This interactive information retrieval interface not only allows users to steer the direction of the exploratory search but also models user information need with the reinforcement learning technique. The performed user study validates the contributions in terms of effectiveness (improved recall of relevant and novel information) of the interface when compared to the standard keyword based search interface. Similarly, in this work, we propose a system which allows users freely, in ad hoc fashion, to steer the browsing and exploration process. The benefits of our system in comparison to [6] are three-fold. First, our system allows one to visualize information space according to a user-selected ranking metric such as Relevance, Popularity, Location and Recency. Second, the ad hoc nature of the proposed system allows users to steer exploration into the many regions that might not otherwise be reached. Further, Beomap interface gives a clear interpretation for direction and orientation in the visualized topic space i.e., a particular position and movement in the topic map represents relatedness to the main query or the missing aspect query.

3 Beomap

Beomap is a novel two-dimensional topic map with both directions controlled by a user. It addresses a major challenge in visualizing text information, i.e., a user is often lost in the space as there is no clearly defined meaning associated with an orientation (e.g., it is unclear what to expect if a user moves the cursor to the left or up). In this paper, we particularly explore a special Beomap useful for a search interface where the vertical dimension is relevance (consistent with a standard search interface where documents are ranked vertically). A second dimension is defined by a user in ad hoc fashion by placing a query and choosing an appropriate visualization metric. The aim of Beomap is to "stretch" the standard linear relevance ordering to a two-dimensional ranking that would enable a user to examine visually the list based on how well topics match the second dimension, which can be defined flexibly by another query. Therefore, the second ad hoc dimension indicates whether a topic relevant to the main query is related to a missing aspect or a perspective. The second dimension can be visualized with a user-selected metric. Note that the second dimension is offered as an option, which the user can take as needed. Thus it is a very natural extension of the current search interface. A user can also easily go back to one dimension if needed. The possibility to change a visualization metric according to user needs provides new ways of user-driven exploration of underlying topic space and corresponding tweets. Hence, Beomap interface provides a new way of how to visualize user information need combined with arbitrary meta-data metric dimension (relevance, time, location, popularity or fuzzy metrics) which is different from the traditional way of visualizing with meta-data such as a time line, etc. The flexiblity to guide freely the exploration and browsing of topics within social media data through an ad hoc semantic dimension is different from established browsing interfaces like a faceted search or a word cloud. The existing interfaces provide only topics and aspects that are within the search results context; therefore, user ability to browse into remote topic regions is not supported.

To the best of our knowledge, no previous work has explored this kind of topic map, especially in the context of helping users interact with poor search results and for social media exploration. Beomap has many potential benefits. First, it would be particularly useful when a user would like to examine the missing aspect or would like to explore relevant tweets from a particular perspective or angle. Further, Beomap addresses the problem of orientation in text data visualization since it is not obvious what directions in the topic map mean (e.g., what does moving in a particular direction mean in the topic space?). Beomap provides a solution to this directions interpretation problem when visualizing text data. Beomap enables a better topic understanding by enabling one to view a topic from multiple aspects or perspectives which can be expressed flexibly through a second ad hoc dimension query. Further, allowing the user to select a visualization metric also improves a topic space understanding.

3.1 Various Metrics for Beomap ad Hoc Dimension

The visualization of a topic map is metric dependent. Hence, relatedness or closeness to the ad hoc query is calculated according to the user-selected metric. The calculation of the final score for a topic presented in the topic map is as follows: (1) Retrieve tweets matching a given query and calculate the metric score for each matching tweet; (2) Aggregate scores of mentioned keywords i.e., hashtags over the retrieved tweets; (3)Present keywords with the greatest levels of user-selected metric dimension in the topic map. In this work, we explored several metrics and analyzed in what situations these metrics might be useful for the end users. In the following, we present several metrics with a brief rationale: **Relevance** is a default metric in the Beomap system. The relevance score might be calculated with any retrieval ranking function. In this work, we utilize OKAPI BM25 retrieval function. Once relevance scores are calculated for the query matched tweets, the hashtags across tweets are aggregated such that final aggregated scores are obtained. The most relevant topics with respect to the main or second ad hoc query are visualized in the topic map. Obviously, the relevance based topic map allows users to explore and browse the topics that are relevant and related to the placed main or second ad hoc query. Further, it reveals how great the relevance relatedness is and what the relevance correlations are between individual topics. **Popularity** reflects a popularity of a topic keyword within the query matched tweets. **Time recency** calculates the recency score for topic keyword aggregating over tweets e.g., the more relevant tweets that are more recent attain a greater score. **Location** calculates a proximity with respect to the placed location-based queries. **Sentiment closeness** calculates for each tweet from the underlying collection a sentiment score. The sentiment scores are aggreagated according to a topic keyword and consequently visualized. This metric allows the user to explore positive or negative topics which can be either common or specific for both queries i.e., the main query as well as the ad hoc query. **Authority/Reputation** is a metric which would consider the tweet author's reputation within the social network for Beomap visualization. **Personalized** is a metric which adapts the visualization of the topic map with respect to user preferences as well as to the placed queries (when the system collects user preferences). In some scenarios, a **user customized metric** may be useful by combining some of the metrics described above.

3.2 Tasks Supported by Beomap Interface

The accurate definition of user supported tasks by Beomap interface enables one to define a basis for systematic comparison with other interfaces as well as for a further evaluation of the proposed interface. In this paper, we consider the following tasks as our targeted applications:

Missing aspect exploration: Find and browse relevant topics which are related to the main query as well as to the ad hoc missing aspect query. The second ad hoc query represents a missing aspect or a needed perspective when examining tweets that match the main query. For instance, users might be interested in this kind of task when the number of tweets matching the main query is large and users would like to examine only specific ones related to the missing aspect or requested perspective. Possible examples are: Which topics are relevant for the Russian Ukrainian conflict from the perspective of NATO, EU or Poland? Which topics are relevant to the placed query and are related as well to a particular geo-location?

Topics space understanding: Obtain topic space understanding and find relationships between interesting topics. Repeated examination of Beomap with respect to the main query and several second-dimension ad hoc queries combined with different meta-data metrics (repeating a missing aspect exploration task several times) will enable users to get an enhanced understanding of underlying topic space. Possible examples are: What topics are related and what are the relationships among them with respect to the main query e.g., Russian Ukrainian conflict?

The presented task types might be performed by users several times and combined in arbitrary order to accomplish the final goal i.e., finding relevant tweets that are not retrieved with the initial user standard keyword search.

3.3 Social Media Prototype System

We implement a prototype system for social media exploration and analytics. We refer to this system as BeomapApp. The BeomapApp consists of several components (see Figure 1). The main component is Beomap, a two-dimensional topic map that depicts a spatial distribution of topics according to a user selected visualization metric. Topics are presented according to two dimensions: (1) a relevance with respect to the main query (vertical dimension); (2) a metric-based closeness to the ad hoc second query. The topic map follows a two-dimensional cartesian coordinate system, presenting only the first quadrant. Hence, topics more related to the main query are presented in the top part of the map and topics related to the second ad hoc query are presented at the right side of the map. The topic map allows users to distinguish clearly which topics are related to the main or a second ad hoc query and the topics that are common for both queries. The common topics are presented in the top right corner of the map. The calculation of an exact position in Beomap is based on standard information retrieval ranking function OKAPI BM25 which can be defined as:

$$S(tw, Q) = \sum_{q_i \in Q \cap tw} TF(q_i, tw) \cdot IDF(q_i) \quad (1)$$

where

$$TF(q_i, tw) = \frac{f(q_i, tw) \cdot (k_1 + 1)}{f(q_i, tw) + k_1 \cdot (1 - b + b \cdot \frac{|tw|}{avgtwl})}$$

$$IDF(q_i) = \log \frac{N - n(q_i) + 0.5}{n(q_i) + 0.5}$$

and $f(q_i, tw)$ is a q_i term frequency within a tweet tw, $|tw|$ is the length of a given tweet tw, $avgtwl$ is average length of a tweet within the corpus, N is a total number of tweets in the corpus and $n(q_i)$ is the number of tweets that contain the term q_i. We set the following values for parameters $k_1 = 1.2$ and $b = 0.75$. When visualizing Beomap, we combine a main query Q_{main} and an ad hoc query Q_{adhoc} with logical OR into a query Q. Once a relevance score is computed for each tweet with respect to Q, we calculate an exact position for a particular hashtag h for a vertical dimension (y-axis) defined as:

$$pos_{vertical}(h) = \sum_{tw \in TW_{Q_{main} \cap h}} S(tw, Q)$$

where $TW_{Q_{main} \cap h} = \{tw | S(tw, Q) > 0, h \in tw, q_{main_i} \in tw\}$ is a set of all tweets which contain a particular hashtag h and at least one term q_{main_i} from the main query Q_{main} and the relevance score $S(tw, Q)$ with respect to the query Q is greater than 0. The calculation for the horizontal dimension (x-axis) is calculated in a similar way except that a set $TW_{Q_{main} \cap h}$ is replaced with $TW_{Q_{adhoc} \cap h}$

$$pos_{horizontal}(h) = \sum_{tw \in TW_{Q_{adhoc} \cap h}} S(tw, Q)$$

Due to long-tail distribution of hashtags in Twitter stream [10], there is a need to avoid depicting many hashtags with low levels of attained aggregated relevance scores in the same topic map region to provide an enhanced readability of the map. Hence, we order hashtags in an ascending order with respect to aggregated relevance score for each dimension and the rank position within the ordered set expresses a final position in the map for the given dimension. This solution is not optimal but we obtained the best topic map readability in comparison to standard scaling functions. Topics are represented in the bubble chart, each topic keyword is represented with a disk where the label is a topic keyword and the radius corresponds to a scaled topic popularity within the collection. We utilize log scaling to visualize a disk with the scaled topic popularity to make a topic map more readable. This is due to a long tail distribution of hashtags in the collection i.e., very few popular hashtags and many hashtags with low frequency occurrence. To obtain a full understanding of the topic map, the tooltip component was developed because topic keywords from social media data are not always easily understandable by the users e.g., *#tcot, #nomistrals4putin.* The tooltip is displayed when the user hovers over the particular topic in the map and presents a few relevant tweets for a given topic. The other components of the visual interface are two content panels displayed in tab view. In the first panel, a user can explore the most relevant topics to the placed queries with the corresponding summary tweets. The second content panel presents the most relevant tweets sorted according to the user selected metric. A user can place the main query in the input field located above the topic map and confirm it with the *Explore* button. Initially, the topic map is not visible to a user but can be diplayed by clicking on the button *Show topic map*. The user can define an ad hoc query through the input field which is located below the lower right corner of the topic map with the watermarked hint to enter the ad hoc dimension query. The ad hoc dimension metric can be chosen from the dropdown list which is presented in the top right corner of the interface.

3.4 Technical Implementation

The system has been developed with J2EE using Primefaces framework for the web interface and javascript JQPlot library for the topic map rendering. The backend application has been deployed to the Jboss application server 7 and the data were stored in Elasticsearch. The aggregation component of the Elasticsearch engine has been used for the calculations of metric dependent scores. The benefit of our implementation is easy deployment to the cloud infrastructure which might be needed for large data collections.

4 Evaluation

To validate contributions of Beomap as well as the social media exploration system BeomapApp, we perform an evaluation which consists of a simulated offline browsing evaluation of Beomap. Further, to validate the benefits of Beomap when integrated in a real application like BeomapApp, we perform a user study. We used the following hypotheses as guidelines when designing the evaluation of Beomap and BeomapApp. The hypotheses are presented below:

- $H1$: Beomap enables a more effective retrieval of additional relevant tweets (those that are relevant but not retrieved within the initial query top-k results) than in the baseline.
- $H2$: BeomapApp provides greater search and browsing satisfaction than the baseline.
- $H3$: BeomapApp is perceived by users as more useful and flexible than the baseline.
- $H4$: Using Beomap, participants will feel more familiar with the topics and contents of a collection than in the baseline.

4.1 Offline Simulation

To validate whether Beomap enables and facilitates navigation into relevant topics and consequent retrieval of relevant tweets which are difficult to retrieve with original query, we design the following offline evaluation. Similarly as in [11], we perform a simulated retrieval of additional relevant tweets where a user repeatably reformulates his/her queries. The aim is to validate whether Beomap facilitates more effective retrieval of additional relevant tweets. We retrieved available tweets with relevance judgments from TREC 2011 collection [9]. The relevance judgments sets were built using standard pooling technique. The tweets relevance was assessed with the three-points scale: (0: irrelevant, 1: relevant and 2: highly relevant). In this work, we consider both relevant and highly relevant tweets as equally relevant. The TREC2011 microblog corpus consists of fifty distinct queries and we denote each query as $Q_{original}$. We define a set of additional relevant tweets $R_{additional}$ as tweets that were rated relevant in TREC2011 but were not retrieved within the top k positions for the particular query $Q_{original}$. We aim to measure whether Beomap enhances retrieval of additional relevant tweets $R_{additional}$ in comparison to various baseline methods.

Baseline Methods. BL: This baseline method is based on the initial query $Q_{original}$. The precision at k is measured on top of tweets retrieved by $Q_{original}$ positioned from k to $2k$ rank with respect to the additional relevant tweets $R_{additional}$. This simulation can be perceived as if the user would like to retrieve more additional relevant tweets after already viewing some relevant tweets i.e., first top k tweets.

BLMR: This baseline method orders topic keywords e.g., hashtags by the aggregated relevance with respect to the $Q_{original}$. The most related relevant topic in combination with the $Q_{original}$ is used as a new query. The precision at k is measured on top of first top k tweets retrieved by the new query. This imitates user behaviour when the original query is automatically extended with the relevant related topic i.e., a query suggestion provided by a search engine.

BLBest: This method orders topics by aggregated relevance with respect to the $Q_{original}$. The best related relevant topic is combined with the $Q_{original}$ into a new query. The precision at k is measured on top of first top k tweets retrieved by the new query. This reflects user behaviour when the user carefully explores the provided list of query suggestions and picks the best with respect to his/her information needs.

Beomap Browsing Strategies. We compare baseline methods with the following browsing strategies of Beomap.

BeomapMisAsp: Thismethod corresponds to the missing aspect task definition (see Section 3.2). The aim is to support the exploration of topics and corresponding tweets related to the missing aspect as well as the matching original query. In this simulated evaluation, we define a missing aspect as a term from the multiple terms $Q_{original}$ which occurs the least within top k tweets returned by $Q_{original}$.

Consequently, the missing aspect is used as an input to the ad hoc dimension of Beomap. This browsing strategy assumes that a user examines topics presented in the topic map and picks the best topic. Finally, $Q_{original}$ is combined with the best node and precision at k is calculated with respect to $R_{additional}$ and the new query matching tweets. **BeomapMR:** This method retrieves the top most relevant topic keyword T with respect to the placed query $Q_{original}$. The relevant topic T is input for a second ad hoc dimension which leads to the generation of the topic map. A top relevant topic denoted as $T_{map}|T$ from the generated topic map is used for a query reformulation. The created query consists of $Q_{original}$, T and $T_{map}|T$. The precision at k is calculated with respect to $R_{additional}$ and the retrieved tweets. This replicates the similar user browsing strategy as **BLMR**; the only difference is further exploration of the topic map and selecting the most relevant topic with respect to the $Q_{original}$ as well as a second ad hoc query. The most relevant topic keyword from the topic map is the one with the highest average relevance score which incorporates relevance score with respect to the main query as well as to the ad hoc second query.

BeomapBest: This method is similar to **BLBest**. It assumes that the user examines all the related relevant topics and picks the best topic. The best topic is input for a second ad hoc dimension which leads to the generation of the topic map. Consequently, the best topic node is selected from the map i.e., a topic keyword which best suits user information need. The best topic node, the most related relevant topic (second ad hoc query) and $Q_{original}$ are combined into a new query. The precision at k is calculated with respect to $R_{additional}$ and the retrieved tweets for the new query. This browsing strategy is similar to **BLBest**. From the generated topic map, a user picks the best topic keyword.

Data Preprocessing. Topic maps generated from tweets' hashtags, when only a small twitter collection is considered, are sparse as only around 24% of tweets contain at least one hashtag. Thus, the generated topic map from hashtags, when an underlying tweets collection is small, prevent a complete retrieval of additional relevant tweets. To overcome this limitation, we have annotated tweets from TREC2011 corpus with recognized named entities using TextRazor tool. Each recognized entity has been converted into a hashtag i.e., Barack Obama transformed into #barackobama. In total, almost 77% of tweets contain at least one named entity which has been converted into a hashtag. Hence, 83% of tweets from TREC2011 corpus contains at least one hashtag or named entity. Almost, 90% of relevant tweets contain at least one hashtag or named entity.

Results. Obviously, the **BL** attains the lowest precision when retrieving additional relevant tweets. This supports a need for query reformulation and possible browsing of related relevant topics. The **BLMR** method attains higher precision than the **BL** as it extends the original query with the related relevant topic keyword which positively affects the retrieval of additional relevant tweets. The **BLBest** method examines a list of related relevant topics and assumes that the

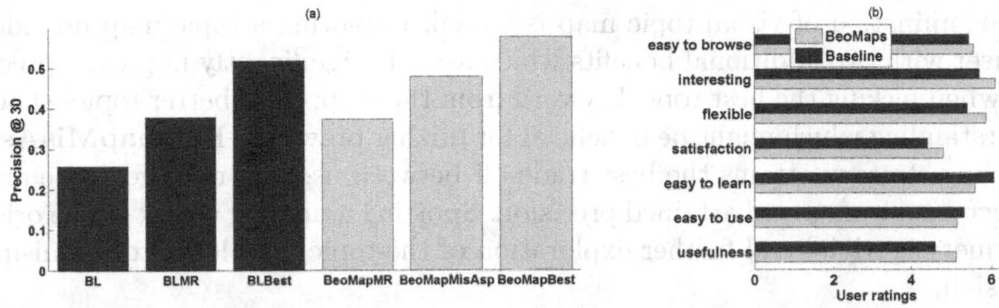

Fig. 2. Figure (a):Baseline methods are presented with black bars and yellow bars are corresponding to the browsing strategies of Beomap. We report means of measured precisions for individual queries from TREC2011 microblogging collection. Figure (b): Mean of user ratings for individual properties of both interfaces from the performed user study.

user would pick the best topic keyword and together with the original query form a new query. The browsing strategy **BeomapBest** attains higher precision as the best baseline method **BLBest**. Both methods **BeomapBest** and **BLBest** assume user optimal behaviour in selecting the best most relevant related topic which is used for the topic map creation in **BeomapBest**. Further, it assumes that the user picks the best topic keyword from the map. The evaluation reports the upper bound precision when (not) using topic maps. The precision improvements **BeomapBest** are significantly better than the **BLBest** (Wilcoxon signed rank test, $p < 0.00001$). Further, we report as well precision for missing aspect exploration method **BeomapMisAsp**, which achieves promising precision.

To illustrate the benefits of Beomap for the retrieval of additional relevant tweets, we examined the browsing logs of compared methods. For instance, the original query *White House spokesman replaced*, the **BLBest** method extended the original query with the *secretary* keyword. The Beomap methods attained better precision because of the topic keyword *carney* when the second ad hoc dimension query was *presssecretary* for the **BeomapBest** method. This indicates the benefits of Beomap, a discovery of important and relevant topics with respect to the original query. Similarly, for the original query *T*SA airport screening, the **BeomapBest** method included *Seattle* keyword into a new query and consequently attained higher precision than the baseline. At first sight, it is not obvious that Seattle is related to the original query but that is because of *Seattle man acquitted in TSA airport case.*

Normalization. Obviously, the defined browsing strategies should be compared carefully because each strategy requires different amounts of user effort to perform browsing and final retrieval. Comparing upper bound strategies of **BLBest** and **BeomapBest** is fair because in both cases a user has to choose the best node from topic keywords sorted by relevance which matches his/her given information need. Additional user effort is required when exploring a topic map in **BeomapBest** and consequent selection of the best node. However, the user examination of visual topic map is trivial. Exploring a topic map provides the user with two additional benefits which are: (1) significantly improved precision when picking the best topic keyword from the map; (2) a better topics space understanding which might be beneficial for further browsing. **BeomapMisAsp** browsing strategy attains the best trade-off between user effort to generate and inspect a topic map and attained precision. Spotting a missing aspect of the original query is trivial and further exploration of the topic map leads to promising precision.

Lessons. The simulated evaluation of Beomap validates the benefits of the ad hoc topic map for enhanced retrieval of additional relevant tweets i.e., tweets that are not retrieved with the original query (validates hypothesis $H1$). Also, the simulation proved that Beomap interface is suitable for exploration of topics related to the missing aspect of the original query when the best trade-off between user effort and precision is attained. Further, we found that when the second ad hoc dimension is generated with respect to the prominent aspect of the query, there are no improvements in comparison to the baseline. However, an advantage of Beomap generated with the prominent query is facilitated topics space understanding which might be beneficial for further exploration.

4.2 User Study

The purpose of the user study is three-fold: (1) to collect real users' feedback and opinions about Beomap; (2) to study the utility of the prototype system BeomapApp in comparison to a standard "Twitter like" list interface; (3) to understand what is the optimal intergration of Beomap into an application system. Participants in the study were asked to browse two different datasets; consequently we acquired their subjective assessments and opinions were acquired (similar to [2]). Further, we analyze log users' activities to explain the usage differences between two compared interfaces. We also measure standard information retrieval measures to compare both interfaces.

Participants. We recruited participants with Twitter accounts. The thirty-one study participants ranged in age from 18 to 38 years (average age 27.7). Fifteen were IT professionals, four were students (mathematics or economics background), and the other had careers in law, HR, design or the media. On average, they reported spending more than a half hour per week using Twitter. Further, they all reported using other social media services like Facebook (all participants), Linkedin (9 participants), Google+ (6 participants), Instagram (3 participants).

Compared Interfaces. The performed user study follows within-subjects design. Beomap system was compared with the standard Twitter-like list interface. To ensure that acquired subjective assessments of the systems were not biased because of the coloring or layout differences of the systems, we implemented the baseline system. The baseline system is visually similar to the tweets content panel in Beomap [1]. We implemented the baseline system instead of using an external one because of the following: First, we ensured that participants will perform their searching and browsing activities on top of the same tweets corpus when doing evaluation tasks using both systems. Second, we assured that usability of both systems will be comparable and with minimized if any visual nuances. To further ensure that our systems are at a similar level of usability, we consulted the HCI expert about both interfaces. The suggested changes were incorporated before the user study was conducted.

Procedure. Each test participant completed a pre-questionnaire before performing the evaluation. After each performed task, participants were asked to complete the questionnaire to obtain a subjective evaluation of Beomap and baseline. We used the standard USE questionnaire [8] and extended it with a few additional questions about the following system properties: *flexible tool for exploration, browsing and analysis of Twitter data,interesting, familiar with the collection, easy to browse.* Users rated each aspect of the interface on a 7-point Likert scale i.e., 1 for strongly disagree and 7 for strongly agree. We used a 7-point scale to be consistent with the [8]. To minimize carryover effects in our within-subjects design, participants performed two tasks with the following conditions. Each task was performed on top of a different tweets collection. Further, the interfaces and task order were alternated and counterbalanced among participants. Participants were asked to perform the following two tasks

Task 1: After your graduation you will be looking for a job in industry. You want information to help you focus on your future job seeking. You know it pays to know the market. You would like to find information about employment patterns in industry and what qualifications employers are looking for in future employees. Further, you would like to improve your knowledge about the job seeking process including how to prepare your resume, how to prepare yourself for the interview and other important hints. The task selection has been inspired by simulated work task situations [3]. The collection consists of $2.5M$ tweets retrieved during the second half of September 2014. The participant is asked to perform the following subtasks: (1) Provide a list of five relevant links to the articles related to the employment trends, required qualifications needed for your job and similar topics which are relevant to you; (2) Provide a list of five relevant links about job seeking tips and hints which are interesting and relevant for you.

Task 2: Imagine you are about to write a report about military conflict in Ukraine. Before starting the writing you should retrieve relevant tweets and articles related to the topic. The task selection has been inspired by the simulated work task situation from [6]. The collection consists of $130K$ tweets retrieved

[1] Screenshots as well as demo videos of both systems are available at https://sourceforge.net/projects/mleginus/files/beomaps/

during the second half of September 2014.Users are asked to perform the following subtasks: (1) In which Ukrainian cities are there fights and military conflicts between Ukraine and Russian oriented rebels? (2) Which Ukrainian and Russian politicians and their opinions with respect to the military conflict are mentioned on Twitter?

The following subsections describe a qualitative analysis of user study as well as quantitative analysis derived from the usage logs. In the end, we are presenting learned lessons.

4.3 Subjective Evaluation of Interfaces

To analyze acquired user ratings for individual properties of compared systems, we utilized Wilcoxon Signed Rank test for paired samples (ratings are non-continuous and non-normal). BeomapApp is considered significantly more useful than the baseline interface ($p < 0.0001$). Participants found BeomapApp a more flexible tool for exploration, browsing and analysis of Twitter data than the baseline. Hence, the improved usefulness and perception of flexibility for exploration, browsing and analysis validate the hypothesis $H3$. Further, users were significantly more satisfied with BeomapApp ($p < 0.04$). Additionally, users rated Beomap more interesting and easy to browse (results are not statistically significant). Because users were significantly more satisfied with BeomapApp as well as they perceived it as more easy to browse and more flexible for exploration, browsing and analysis partially validate the hypothesis $H2$. Users considered both systems similar when becominga familiarized with the collection. A limitation of the current BeomapApp implementation is lower ratings for the easy to use aspect in comparison to the baseline system ($p < 0.02$). Further, participants assigned BeomapApp lower ratings for the easy to learn aspect ($p < 0.01$) suggesting that BeomapApp is more difficult to learn in comparison to the standard keyword search to which users are exposed on a daily basis. Upon analyzing participants' negative comments about BeomapApp, however, we found that most of the opinions were related to the design of BeomapApp and not Beomap topic map. For instance, a user reported that BeomapApp is not that intuitive e.g., *Not intuitive at first; UI is a bit cluttered*. This indicates the importance of concerned and careful intergration of Beomap into a real world application so that a user will not become confused and Beomap could be fully exploited. The lessons related to the Beomap integration into a real application that were learned from this user study are: (1) ensure that the input field for a second ad hoc dimension query can be intuitively found by the user; (2) ensure that a user easily recognizes how to change and select the ad hoc metric for Beomap. These findings will be used for a further BeomapApp improvement which is part of our future work.

The order in which users accessed the systems influenced the user ratings. In particular, when users first used BeomapApp, the subsequent ratings for the baseline system (used in the second task) were lower (similar finding as in [12]).

4.4 Log Data

The analyzed user activities indicate that when using BeomapApp users are more active in placing more queries, higher numbers of clicked links and hashtags from the tweets and of course several clicks on the topic keywords in the topic map. The detailed statistics are presented in Table 1: The presented results indicate that users placed more queries, explored more hashtags and obtained an overview about other possibly relevant hashtags by seeing them in the topic map. Hence, these results support the hypothesis $H4$ that a user become more familiar with the topics and content of the collection. Further, a high average number of seen hashtags from the map validates the benefit of the Beomap for better topics structure understanding. We further analyzed placed queries to see whether the generated topic maps enhanced user ability to browse relevant related topics through query reformulations. For instance, when browsing tweets about conflict in Ukraine, Beomap helped users to discover keywords such as msf (*Doctors Without Borders/Médecins Sans Frontières*), russiainvadedukraine, natoforukraine,stoprussianaggression, savedonbasspeople, ukraineunderattack, ww3. Similarly, for the job search task where users discovered topic keywords such as tipshintsjob, employmenttrends, jobhints. Often, users used Beomap for exploration of cities (missing aspect) which were relevant to their job search queries. Whereas when using the baseline system, users mostly formulated standard queries as they are used to when utilizing a standard search engine.

Table 1. Average number of user activities for each considered interface

User activity	BeomapApp	Baseline
# queries	15.39	13.68
# clicked links	3.857	4.6
# clicked hashtags from tweets	1.35	1.12
# seen hashtags from map	37.17	X
# clicked hashtags from map	4.61	X

4.5 Participants' Feedback on Beomap

Users agreed that Beomap helped them to discover relevant topic keywords which enabled further browsing of other related relevant topic regions. The majority of users found Beomap useful *"It saves the time of a user by collecting the information in one place, it's also easy to use and interesting."*, *"Get a lot of info in a nutshell"* or *"fast data analysis"*. Users also appreciated the possibility to define a second ad hoc dimension e.g., *It aggregates tweets relevant to searched topic, and lets you sort the results by different criteria. The system also allows one to add a second topic to the search, and then creates a results map with tweet-to-topic relations. It simplifies the search for specific topics on twitter, and gives a graphic idea of the relation with other trending topics related to the search*. Several participants reported better topics structure understanding as well as an ability to explore relations between individual topics e.g., *"Quick overview of the topic within larger scope, correlation between topics and their relationship", "It simplifies the search for specific topics on twitter, and gives a graphic idea of the relation with other trending topics related to the search"*. Users also found Beomap easy to browse e.g., *Easy to browse interrelated data* and appreciated overall topic map visualization e.g., *The graphical way to present the relevance of the subjects is great.*.

Negative comments of participants were mostly related to the system itself and not to Beomap. A few users perceived the system as not very intuitive (analysis of possible reasons is discussed in Section Subjective evaluation of interfaces) e.g., *needs time to get used to it*. Another user reported a limited number of tweets in the system as a limitation e.g., *It's quite a nice system, perhaps you can update some more topics from twitter*. Several users as well reported that BeomapApp responded slower sometimes e.g., *a bit too slow*.

5 Discussions

Although we only explored the two-dimensional Beomap, the general idea of a topic map interface with ad hoc dimension and the possibility to visualize topics space with user-chosen metrics can be applied to many other systems. The generalization of this interface allows the user to exploit Beomap on top of different types of data e.g., social media data(Facebook, Flickr, Youtube, etc.), folksonomy data (Delicious, Bibsonomy, etc.), news articles or research publications. The current implementation of Beomap includes two dimensions for search interface but it is possible to extend the map into k-dimensions with k different ad hoc dimensions and user-defined metrics. Such a multi-dimensional topic map would enable users to examine their information need from multiple distinct missing aspects with different user-chosen metrics dimensions (e.g., putting sentiment polarity together with topical dimensions). It is also worth noting that the BeomapApp system has the potential to support many more applications than we explored. The performed evaluation of Beomap is based mostly on Relevance, Popularity or Recency metrics. However, the system can be easily extended with several different ad hoc metrics.

Further, suitable machine learning algorithms might be exploited to introduce new ad hoc metrics for an enhanced visualization of the topic map. For instance, one can train a classifier to detect a positive or negative sentiment of topics which can be further visualized with Beomap (a particular sentiment might be used as a missing aspect for an ad hoc dimension). To facilitate a selection of a missing aspect, simple analytics could be developed to test different alternatives of queries and to provide a user with the quantity of items matching each alternative.

Limitations: Our evaluation also reveals two limitations of Beomap. The first is when underlying items are not densely annotated with topic keywords e.g., a few hashtags on Twitter, a limited number of user tags in folksonomy data, etc. This might prevent users from finding and retrieving documents which are relevant but are not annotated with a topic keyword. To minimize this, underlying items might be annotated with named entity recognition or different machine learning based algorithms could be exploited for items annotation. The second limitation is that the controlled nature of the study prevents drawing more reliable conclusions when used by users over a longer period of time with real information needs.

6 Conclusions and Future Work

In this work, we proposed a novel interface (i.e., Beomap) for visualizing text information which allows a user to define ad hoc semantic dimensions with keyword queries. This feature not only makes the dimensions for visualizing topics in text more meaningful, but also naturally enables a user to explore the information space flexibly with arbitrary keyword queries. The topic map is two-dimensional with metric dependent visualization i.e., popularity, recency, proximity. The benefit of the topic map is the ability to steer browsing and exploration of underlying information space by the user through ad hoc queries into both topic map dimensions. Besides supporting ad hoc query-defined dimensions, the two-dimensional Beomap can also naturally support other metrics such as popularity,recency, proximity, etc., making it easy to do visual analytics. We evaluated the proposed Beomap in two ways. First, we used simulated user interaction with search results to compare the Beomap with multiple baselines representing state of the art interactive information exploration interfaces. The results show that Beomap improves the retrieval of additional tweets, the best trade-off between presicion versus user effort is attained when Beomap is generated with respect to the missing aspect of the query. Second, we conducted a user study to compare the BeomapApp system with a standard interface system for performing two information seeking tasks. The results show BeomapApp is perceived as more useful and that users were more satisfied with the system than the baseline. Further, they perceive the system as a flexible tool for exploration, browsing and analysis of Twitter data, and that is easy to browse, and interesting as well.

In the future, we plan to explore several directions. First, we will further evaluate the proposed Beomap with more users by deploying our prototype system on Amazon AWS (a grant is already approved for supporting this system) and making it available potentially for a large number of users Second, we will explore other social media such as Flickr, Instagram or folskonomy data, etc. Finally, the idea of allowing a user to define ad hoc semantic dimensions is not restricted to two dimensions.It would thus also be interesting to explore it with more than two dimensions, which can be particularly useful for visual text analytics.

References

1. Acevedo-Aviles, J.C., Campbell, W.M., Halbert, D.C., Greenfield, K.: Vizlinc: integrating information extraction, search, graph analysis, and geo-location for the visual exploration of large data sets
2. Bernstein, M.S., Suh, B., Hong, L., Chen, J., Kairam, S., Chi, E.H.: Eddi: interactive topic-based browsing of social status streams. In: Proceedings of the 23nd Annual ACM Symposium on User Interface Software and Technology, pp. 303–312. ACM (2010)
3. Borlund, P., Dreier, S.: An investigation of the search behaviour associated with ingwersen three types of information needs. Information Processing & Management **50**(4), 493–507 (2014)
4. Bron, M., Van Gorp, J., Nack, F., de Rijke, M., Vishneuski, A., de Leeuw, S.: A subjunctive exploratory search interface to support media studies researchers. In: Proceedings of the 35th International ACM SIGIR Conference on Research and Development in Information Retrieval, pp. 425–434. ACM (2012)
5. Chau, D.H., Kittur, A., Hong, J.I., Faloutsos, C.: Apolo: making sense of large network data by combining rich user interaction and machine learning. In: Proceedings of the SIGCHI Conference on Human Factors in Computing Systems, pp. 167–176. ACM (2011)
6. Glowacka, D., Ruotsalo, T., Konuyshkova, K., Kaski, S., Jacucci, G., et al.: Directing exploratory search: reinforcement learning from user interactions with keywords. In: Proceedings of the 2013 International Conference on Intelligent User Interfaces, pp. 117–128. ACM (2013)
7. Lagus, K., Honkela, T., Kaski, S., Kohonen, T.: Self-organizing maps of document collections: A new approach to interactive exploration. KDD **96**, 238–243 (1996)
8. Lund, A.M.: Measuring usability with the use questionnaire. Usability Interface **8**(2), 3–6 (2001)
9. Ounis, I., Macdonald, C., Lin, J., Soboroff, I.: Overview of the trec-2011 microblog track. In: Proceedings of the 20th Text Retrieval Conference, TREC 2011 (2011)
10. Tsur, O., Rappoport, A.: What's in a hashtag?: content based prediction of the spread of ideas in microblogging communities. In: Proceedings of the Fifth ACM International Conference on Web Search and Data Mining, pp. 643–652. ACM (2012)
11. Wang, X., Tan, B., Shakery, A., Zhai, C.: Beyond hyperlinks: organizing information footprints in search logs to support effective browsing. In: Proceedings of the 18th ACM Conference on Information and Knowledge Management, pp. 1237–1246. ACM (2009)
12. Yee, K.-P., Swearingen, K., Li, K., Hearst, M.: Faceted metadata for image search and browsing. In: Proceedings of the SIGCHI Conference on Human Factors in Computing Systems, pp. 401–408. ACM (2003)

CrowdSTAR: A Social Task Routing Framework for Online Communities

Besmira Nushi[1(✉)], Omar Alonso[2], Martin Hentschel[3], and Vasileios Kandylas[2]

[1] Department of Computer Science, ETH Zurich, Zurich, Switzerland
nushib@inf.ethz.ch

[2] Microsoft Corporation, Mountain View, CA, USA
{omalonso,vakandyl}@microsoft.com

[3] SnowFlake Computing, San Mateo, CA, USA
martin.hentschel@snowflakecomputing.com

Abstract. The online communities available on the Web have shown to be significantly interactive and capable of collectively solving difficult tasks. Nevertheless, it is still a challenge to decide how a task should be dispatched through the network due to the high diversity of the communities and the dynamically changing expertise and social availability of their members. We introduce CrowdSTAR, a framework designed to route tasks across and within online crowds. CrowdSTAR indexes the topic-specific expertise and social features of the crowd contributors and then uses a routing algorithm, which suggests the best sources to ask based on the knowledge vs. availability trade-offs. We experimented with the proposed framework for question and answering scenarios by using two popular social networks as crowd candidates: Twitter and Quora.

Keywords: Task routing · Social search · Question answering · Crowdsourcing · Expertise detection

1 Introduction

Social Task Routing is the problem of effectively routing tasks to the right crowds and the right users in online communities and social networks [4]. The need for solving tasks with the help of people is motivated by the fact that human intervention and skills can solve problems that are difficult to tackle by machines only. This motivation is even more crucial in *social search* (*i.e.* forwarding the question to a social network) where the semantic and context awareness of humans can help to increase the quality of Web search results as well as the users' satisfaction [12].

The challenge that we are addressing is how to find the best experts within the best matching crowd for a given task. This challenge is made more difficult because of the dynamically changing characteristics of networks and users. For example, the user base of a crowdsourcing platform or social network might significantly grow or shrink over time. Also, the activity of a single user may vary from being absolutely committed to only being marginally present or not present at all.

The main contribution of this work is a system for social task routing that combines expertise detection with social characteristics of users. We argue that

P. Cimiano et al. (Eds.): ICWE 2015, LNCS 9114, pp. 219–230, 2015.
DOI: 10.1007/978-3-319-19890-3_15

expertise detection is a crucial factor for the accuracy of a social task router, yet it is not sufficient. Equally important factors are the users' interactivity and availability characteristics. Therefore, the second main contribution of this paper is an exploration of the trade-offs between these dimensions. Our system, **CrowdSTAR** (**Crowd**sourced **S**ocial **T**ask **R**outing), investigates these aspects in the context of question-answering tasks using two popular social networks, Quora and Twitter.

2 Related Work

Social task routing stands at the boundary of major research fields like collaborative information seeking and crowdsourcing. Dustdar and Gaedke [4] were among the first to envision the general social routing principle supported by Web-scale workflows. Morris, Teevan, and Panovich [12] describe a thorough comparison between Web search and social search (*i.e.* forwarding questions to social networks). Further studies in the context of *community question answering* show that routing questions to Q&A communities increases the users' satisfaction [10,11].

The most relevant work to our problem definition is the one presented by Bozzon et al. [2]. The authors propose an generic resource-to-user graph model to represent any given crowd. Although the method does not take into account the social features of the experts, it provides a solid formal design for expertise matching and detection. Further analyses focus on the Q&A potential of crowds but yet do not make use of the social features [3,17]. Horowitz and Kamvar [6] explore the concept of social availability. Their work characterizes a social search engine (Aardvark) where people ask questions to other users via email and instant messaging. The availability of the members is not part of the user-topic model but works as a general pruning criterion. The expert search is isolated within a single network and within the circle of contacts of the person who is asking the question. Although this can be efficient for personal questions, it might not be as profitable for questions requiring a broader domain of competence. In the "IM-an-Expert" system proposed in [14], availability is not topical but it is defined as the the user status in an instant messaging system. Although the work does not use availability for task routing, it shows that it can impact the answer quality. Sung, Lee, and Lee [15] linearly combine (topical) availability with expertise into a single measure called *question affordance*.

Gathering expertise evidence in social networks is also an active field of research [1,2,5,13]. The generalized approach is to score candidate experts according to the likelihood of a person being an expert on query [1]. Pal and Counts define multiple features around the textual content a person generates [13] which are then also used as a scoring mechanism. The metrics explained in this study are built in the same spirit and elaborated for a better depiction of our vision.

An interesting line of work complementary to our study concerns task routing in networks with local knowledge [7,16]. This approach employs users in further routing tasks among each other to improve task assignment. Even though current

Table 1. Metric definitions of expertise

Metric	Definition
A	answer
CA	correct answer
P	post
OP	original non-conversational post
μ	average value among all users
N	total number of user data points

Table 2. Metric definitions of social availability

Metric	Definition
CP	conversational post
PQ	question presented to the user
AQ	question answered by the user
RT	average response time
LQ	last question presented
LA	last answer provided

results in this field are mainly theoretical and have not been studied in real-world applications, these ideas constitute a promising future work direction for CrowdSTAR and social task routing in general.

3 User Utility Model

CrowdSTAR adapts a multi dimensional user model to catalogue features of users from a utility perspective. The utility of a crowd member (*i.e.* her adequacy to solve a given task) is (1) topic-specific, (2) continuously changing, and (3) strongly affected by the user's social behavior in the network. In contrast to previous work [6], we decide to model more than one feature for each triple *<user, topic, crowd>* and use them altogether for routing purposes.

First, we identify two main dimensions for a given user part of a certain crowd on a particular topic: *Knowledge* and *Availability*. *Knowledge* is the dimension that captures the passive or active expertise on the topic while *Availability* shows the social involvement in answering questions or conversing on the same topic. Aiming for high knowledge is crucial but not sufficient. Accounts which seem to know a lot on a particular matter can be slow or not helpful in answering questions. In addition, the definition of these two dimensions is improved by decomposing them into two other sub-features. *Knowledge* is further divided into *Qualification* and *Interest* while *Availability* is broken down into *Responsiveness* and *Activity*. Semantically, the meaning of each of the features is as follows:

1. *Qualification*: How much original and qualitative content does the user generate? A user on Quora, for example, may be active on a subject by posting questions but this does not show that he is qualified. This feature also comprises the accuracy of the user since it includes the fraction of correct answers.

$$K_1(c,u,t) = \frac{\mathrm{CA}_{(c,u,t)} + \mu}{\mathrm{A}_{(c,u,t)} + N} + \frac{\mathrm{OP}_{(c,u,t)} + \mu}{\mathrm{P}_{(c,u,t)} + N} \tag{1}$$

2. *Interest*: How active and interested is the user? The aim is to compute the degree of interest on the topic with respect to the overall user content.

$$K_2(c,u,t) = \frac{\mathrm{P}_{(c,u,t)} + \mu}{\mathrm{P}_{(c,u)} + N} \tag{2}$$

3. *Responsiveness*: How responsive is the user to conversations and questions relevant to the topic? This feature can be exploited as a discriminative filter for distinguishing advertisement/company accounts from real human members. The average response time (RT) in the definition is useful to retrieve the answers faster.

$$A_1(c,u,t) = \frac{\mathrm{AQ}_{(c,u,t)} + \mu}{\mathrm{PQ}_{(c,u,t)} + N} + \frac{\mathrm{CP}_{(c,u,t)} + \mu}{\mathrm{P}_{(c,u,t)} + N} + \frac{1}{\mathrm{RT}_{(c,u,t)}} \tag{3}$$

4. *Activity*: How long has it been since the user's last contribution on the topic? Considering that human crowd members cannot be accessed continuously, this metric helps to increase user satisfaction by keeping them engaged without overloading.

$$A_2(c,u,t) = now - \max\{time(LQ_{(c,u,t)}), time(LA_{(c,u,t)})\} \tag{4}$$

The explanation of the acronyms used in the formal definition of features is given in Table 1 and 2. The variables μ and N are used to make the expertise detection less susceptible to low-frequency users (*i.e.* users that post only a few tweets) and spammers. This technique is similar to additive smoothing or Laplace smoothing.

Expertise Detection. There are two main challenges of expertise detection: *candidate selection* and gathering *expertise evidence* [1]. Candidate selection is the problem of finding candidate experts on a particular topic. Gathering expertise evidence is the problem of determining the strength of expertise of a candidate expert given the textual evidence. Candidate selection in our approach is achieved via two steps: (i) finding user-generated documents and (ii) selecting the authors of these documents as candidate experts. In the first step, we find user-generated documents (*e.g.*, tweets, questions, answers, posts) by matching all documents of a social network on a particular topic. Matching in Twitter is performed by checking whether the topic is contained in a tweet. In Quora, the content is tagged by users or editors with the topics it belongs to. In the second step, we choose as candidate experts the set of authors of the matched documents. Gathering expertise evidence is based on the two features of the Knowledge dimension: *Qualification* and *Interest*.

Social Availability. The social dimension of our user model is also topical as for the same level of expertise, people show different response rates on different arguments due to social trends or personal preferences. *Responsiveness* captures the responsiveness of the user to our tasks as well as to posts initiated by other users in the network. At the same time, it also includes the average response time on the topic. *Activity* then keeps track of the last Q&A event with the user on the topic. This means that a user that was recently asked on a topic will not be accessed on the same topic any time soon, yet he might still be a good candidate for other topics on which he is currently idle. The routing strategy described in the next section requires that the underlying features are up to date. From our observations it results that the social *Availability* features tend to change much faster than the *Knowledge* ones and they need to be updated more often.

4 Social Task Routing

According to Law and von Ahn [9] there exist two forms of assigning tasks to crowd members, referred to as push and pull approaches. Pull approaches let the users select the tasks, while the push approaches explicitly match the tasks to users. In our work, the social task routing belongs to the second form of task assignment but CrowdSTAR design is aware of the self-regulating events that happen in dynamic crowds where members can make free choices.

Routing Tasks within a Crowd. In order to consider all the features in the user utility model, the routing algorithm needs to explore the possible trade-offs between the features and access only those users which appear to dominate the rest of the crowd. For this purpose we select as a candidate user set the group of users which is not dominated by others in at least one of the dimensions. We refer to this candidate set as the *crowd skyline* for the topic associated to the task.

Figure 1 illustrates a sample output for two dimensions where the connected points represent the crowd skyline. Depending on the topic, the crowd expertise and how much redundancy one wants from the crowd, it can happen that the number of users in the skyline is not enough. For this purpose, we decide to continue running the skyline algorithm even beyond the first skyline. For example, in Figure 1 the data points connected by the dashed line represent the second skyline. The skyline computation uses the algorithm introduced by Kossmann et al. [8]. It applies a recursive nearest-neighbor search that continuously prunes from the search space regions that are dominated by the actual best data point not yet included in the skyline. The algorithm has a good pruning rate which is a necessary property for our routing algorithm to scale. Furthermore, a good property of the algorithm is the early output of skyline points, which is useful for very large data when it is not possible to wait until the whole computation finishes. We further prune the search space by disregarding users which have very low values in at least one of the axes (the dashed regions in Figure 1) because our experiments showed that these regions contain mostly spammy and non-responsive accounts.

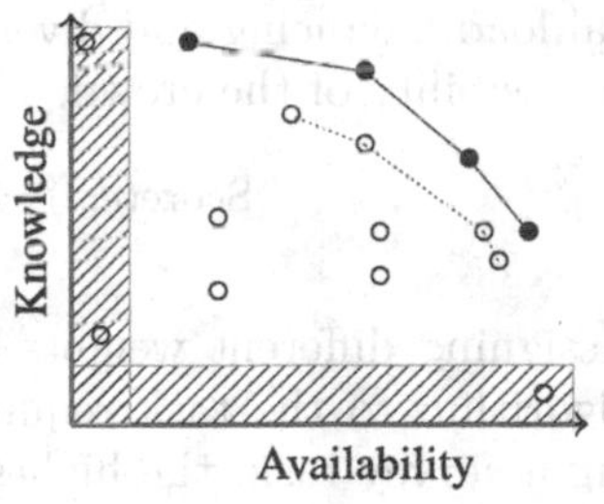

Fig. 1. Crowd skyline example

Whenever the user utility model is updated, the crowd skyline needs to be recomputed since different users may appear in the skyline. For instance, if a user has just answered a question, the respective *activity* is going to be updated with a very low value excluding this way the user from the candidate set to ask. Similarly, if someone gradually changes *interest* from photography to video and starts posting and answering more on the latter topic, the same switch will happen to his or her membership in the topic skyline. In our routing experiments we did not ask all the users in the skyline set since this would be too intrusive. Instead, we start in the middle of the skyline and then incrementally move towards the edges of the skyline in both directions. However, exploring different segments of the skyline is also effective as it gives a chance of participation and improvement to users that do not have the highest scores in all dimensions.

Routing Tasks across Multiple Crowds. The decision of crowd selection is based on an aggregate summary of each crowd. Although we index the features of all users, we do not use all of them to build the crowd summary. The summary includes only those members which will possibly be considered for question asking in the near future, *i.e.* the crowd skyline. The following formulation defines the summary of a crowd c on an arbitrary feature f for a topic t.

$$\text{Summary}(c,t,f) = \frac{\sum_{u \in \text{skyline}(c,t)} f(c,u,t)}{|\text{skyline}(c,t)|} \tag{5}$$

Having the summary on each dimension, the final crowd score of the crowd on the topic can be computed as a weighted linear combination of all the features. Note that *Activity* is excluded from the final score given that it is an individual load-balancing and diversification measure and should not affect the overall accessibility of the crowd.

$$\text{Score}(c,t) = \sum_{f \in \{K_1, K_2, A_1\}} (w_f \cdot \text{Summary}(c,t,f)) \tag{6}$$

Assigning different weights to the dimensions allows for adapting the routing algorithm to the task requirements. For example, if one is interested in solving a survey task, the highest weights should go to *interest* and *responsiveness* considering that the crowd members will only give their personal opinion and not actually solve a problem. For a fair comparison between crowds the number of users in the skyline of each crowd should be balanced which is very unlikely to happen given the different feature distributions. This problem is solved by choosing for both crowds an equal number of points as skyline representatives and moreover making use of the lower-level skylines.

5 CrowdSTAR System

CrowdSTAR is designed to help end users to solve challenging tasks with the help of human power available on the Web. One possible use case is to employ CrowdSTAR to propose to the user a set of candidate experts given the input query. Afterwards, the user can freely choose how many and which of the presented candidates to ask. In a second use case, the offered service not only finds the possible experts but also contacts them on behalf of the askers and then sends back the answers.

Components. Here we briefly describe each component of the CrowdSTAR system as depicted in Figure 2. All modules are implemented in C# and ran on a large computing cluster. The *Feature Collector* module gathers the textual evidence (*e.g.*, posts, native answers, questions, comments etc.) of users' expertise in Twitter and Quora regardless of their participation in CrowdSTAR.

Feature Monitor monitors in real time the activity of users in answering questions and sends this information to *Feature Index*. The latter uses the incoming data from the previous modules to recompute the changed dimensions of the user utility model. At the moment, the index keeps track of approximately the top 300,000 active users in Twitter and top 45,000 users in Quora. As soon as the *Feature Index* is updated on a certain topic, the *Skyline Builder* gets updated on the same topic by recomputing the skyline which is then used to refresh the crowd summary scores in the *Crowd Summarizer*. Finally, the *Task Router* routes the question according to the summarized crowd scores and the topical skylines. The posting process is done through the Twitter API while Quora does not provide an API yet and needs manual question posting. The budget here refers to the number of users to be asked as a degree of crowdsourcing redundancy that can be specified by the end user.

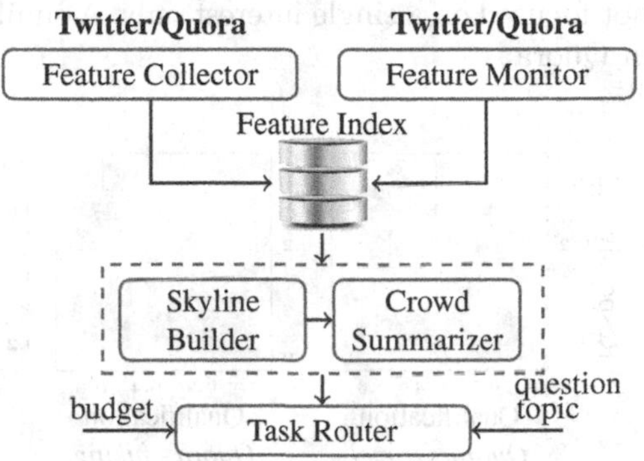

Fig. 2. CrowdSTAR architecture

6 Experimental Evaluation

In this section, we discuss how we collected the data for populating the user utility model and how we performed the routing experiments across and within Twitter and Quora. While we use proprietary data to run CrowdSTAR, we provide as much information as possible to make the experiments reproducible with similar systems.

Feature Collection. The features of each user were computed from the most recent one month interval. We focus on a broad range of topics (35 in total) from domains like technology, hobbies, news, and entertainment. In Quora we consider that a post falls within a topic if this is claimed from the author or Quora's maintenance staff since the mapping is highly accurate in this network. The posts in Twitter are not as structured. Thus, we categorize a tweet within a topic if the topic word explicitly appears in the tweet text. Involving topic-to-topic relationships would result into misleading outcomes (*e.g.*, a user who talks about *soccer* may not be an expert in *sport* and vice versa).

Table 3 shows an example of retrieving the top five users in Twitter with respect to *qualification* and *responsiveness* for topic *hiking*. Note that the most qualified users are famous accounts on the topic but not necessarily personal accounts, while the most responsive ones match to people who tend to answer and converse more on *hiking*. They are still knowledgeable but their attention is not focused on a single interest only. A similar phenomenon can also be observed in Quora.

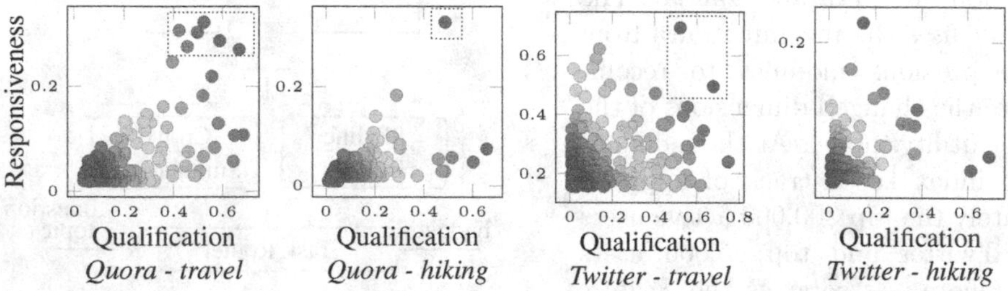

Fig. 3. Qualification and Interest for topics *travel* and *hiking* on Quora and Twitter.

In Figure 3 we show *qualification* and *responsiveness* for 200 most active users of both networks for topics *travel* and *hiking*. Users of the same color gradient would belong to the same skyline level as defined in our method. As expected, there is not necessarily a strong correlation between them (also the case for the other features) which supports once again the fact that using a linear combination or a generalization of all the features (*e.g.*, the total number of posts) is less informative and that the identified dimensions in the user utility model are present in real-world data. User data points of this nature, but of a larger scale, serve as an input for the social task routing algorithm. Ideally, we would like to choose only points that have very good scores on all the features such as those that fall within the dotted rectangles in the figure. In practice, this is not always feasible. For example, comparing the graphs for the two topics we can understand that the skyline region is more dense for popular and general topics like *travel*. For more specific ones like *hiking*, especially on Quora we can notice the existence of very few dominating experts.

Table 3. Example of top 5 Twitter users *w.r.t.* to qualification and responsiveness for topic *hiking*.

TOP 5 WHERE topic='hiking' ORDER BY			
QUALIFICATION		RESPONSIVENESS	
@hiking_camping	0.691	@thatoutdoorguy	0.223
@letsgoforahike	0.612	@nickandriani	0.169
@mightycrack	0.378	@astrogerly	0.141
@etravelhotels	0.367	@melissabravery	0.135
@outdoorgeardotd	0.367	@rsrigda	0.127

Question Posting. We created two different accounts on Twitter and Quora named respectively *@SocialQARouting* (`http://twitter.com/SocialQARouting`) and *Ada Floyd* (`http://www.quora.com/Ada-Floyd`), and used them for the purpose of conducting question routing experiments. Both accounts were first bootstrapped by gradually asking questions and posting other non-asking content. In Twitter we alternated two asking strategies: *introductory* and *simple greeting*. Also, we attached the #ask and #<topic> hashtags to the question text

Table 4. Comparison of Twitter and Quora task routing support.

	Quora	Twitter
Responsiveness	64%	44%
Questions answered	85%	44%
Average response time	~24 hours (1st response)	12.7 hours
Accuracy	80%-90% (manually evaluated)	
Asking tone	Formal	Informal
Question visibility	Many users	Mainly the assigned user
Human intervention	Thanking (built-in)	Introduction Greeting Thanking
Answer properties	Long and elaborated	140 char max and concise
Quality control	Upvotes and Editors	Candidates: #retweets, #favorites
Types of Q&A	Recommendation multiple items "How to" explanations Only interesting surveys	Recommendation single item Laconic explanations Survey and factual answers

to increase the interest of the user. We noticed that the most famous accounts prefer the introductory strategy while the others prefer a simple greeting. Quora members instead are used to a formal asking tone in contrast to Twitter where people tend to converse in a more relaxed and friendly way. The question promotion process was easier in Quora because it is intentionally designed for Q&A.

The main conclusion of this part of the work is that the networks that are primarily designed for task-solving need less human intervention for both the bootstrapping and the promotion phases because many necessary steps like introduction, thanking, rating, and rewarding are inherently present. Crowds of a more general purpose require additional human steps in the workflow, otherwise people tend to be reluctant to help. Indeed, in earlier stages of this project when we did not include any greeting, introductory or thanking messages the interaction was not satisfactory.

Task Routing. Table 4 shows the main results from routing 100 tasks to the targeted crowds. We received answers to 44% of the questions in Twitter and to 85% of the questions in Quora. Nevertheless, only 64% of the answers in Quora came from the users we pointed. The rest were given by other users interested in the same topic. The answers' accuracy was manually evaluated and varies between 80%–90% which confirms that when people feel confident to answer they are able to provide accurate insights.

Another major difference between the two crowds consists on the type of questions they can accommodate. Due to the message length restrictions in Twitter, it is possible to ask only short questions that can be answered with short replies. The answers in Quora are more elaborated and accordingly argued. We show some examples of questions routed to Quora and Twitter along with the respective retrieved answers in Table 5.

Table 5. Examples of questions routed to Twitter and Quora and the retrieved answers.

Question (Twitter)	Answer (Twitter)
@joshuariggins Do you know any good travel coffee mugs preferrably working for both cold and hot weather? #ask #travel	@SocialQARouting try @HydroFlask they are amazing. After 5 hrs with 170° coffee in it, left in 27° snow, it was still 115° hot
@NicoArts Why do you think magic realism is strongly related to the Latin American culture?	@SocialQARouting Sure! Seems to me it's almost entirely because of the works of author Gabriel García Márquez, link: http://en.wikipedia.org/wiki/Gabriel_Garc...
Hi @rickasaurus! Do you know whether there exists an active Machine Learning community within Twitter?	@SocialQARouting you may find this list helpful in your ongoing search https://twitter.com/rickasaurus/...
Question (Quora)	**Answer (Quora)**
What is the best way to rest during rock climbing?	When resting, remember to visualize the moves ahead, focus, breathe and try to release lactic acid from your arms. Read more: http://qr.ae/EsG00
How can a high-school history teacher make the class particularly interesting for the students?	Informative Wall Art. When in the eighth grade I had a history teacher whose room was an engaging learning aid because of the maps and posters on his wall. Read more: http://qr.ae/Estrp
How effective is orthodontics in grown ups?	Orthodontics for adults is very effective and given the recent advancements in orthodontic treatment, adult treatment is quicker and more convenient than ever. Read more: http://qr.ae/Esnpu

In both networks, members preferred to answer questions related to specific topics like *biking*, *hiking*, *poker* rather than general ones like *music*, *sport*, *travel*. A possible reason for this is that people tend to answer more on topics in which they have experience and are particularly enthusiastic of. This phenomenon constitutes an important implicit incentive for most of the Q&A applications and also for our study. According to our profile statistics in Quora, the most difficult questions to answer are those that either (i) belong to a narrow expertise domain (*e.g.*, "How much usability and cognition study is done before starting an architectural project?") or (ii) combine two domains together (*e.g.*, "What is an alternative backup solution for Mac OS X that is similar to Cobian?"). The most popular questions in terms of number of views, followers, and answer quality are queries that contain elements of entertainment, curiosity or professional interest (*e.g.*, "What is the most efficient starting strategy for Settlers of Catan?"). Another successful use-case for Q&A in CrowdSTAR is information gathering for building lists (*e.g.*, "Which are some well-known movie actors who also play on theater stages?'). In these cases, it is difficult to gather the whole answer by asking single individual. Many users instead are able to construct a complete and relevant answer.

7 Conclusions

In this paper, we proposed a general model for task routing in online crowds that combines expertise detection with social availability features. Furthermore, we presented the design and implementation of CrowdSTAR[1], a social task routing system. CrowdSTAR routes questions to responsive experts in an appropriate crowd. Yet, the system makes sure to not overload experts with requests by regulating the number of questions routed to individual users. CrowdSTAR currently supports two popular social networks, Twitter and Quora, but the architecture is extensible to other crowds. Our findings show that the proposed user utility model exists in real social networks and that experts are willing to answer questions which are more specific rather than general.

References

1. Balog, K., Fang, Y., de Rijke, M., Serdyukov, P., Si, L.: Expertise retrieval. Foundations and Trends in Information Retrieval **6**(2–3), 127–256 (2012)
2. Bozzon, A., Brambilla, M., Ceri, S., Silvestri, M., Vesci, G.: Choosing the right crowd: expert finding in social networks. In: Proc. of the 16th EDBT, pp. 637–648. ACM (2013)
3. Difallah, D.E., Demartini, G., Cudré, P.: Pick-a-crowd: tell me what you like, and i'll tell you what to do. In: Proc. of the 22nd WWW, pp. 367–374 (2013)
4. Dustdar, S., Gaedke, M.: The social routing principle. IEEE Internet Computing **15**(4), 80–83 (2011)
5. Ghosh, S., Sharma, N., Benevenuto, F., Ganguly, N., Gummadi, K.: Cognos: Crowdsourcing search for topic experts in microblogs. In: Proc. of the 35th SIGIR, pp. 575–590. ACM (2012)
6. Horowitz, D., Kamvar, S.D.: The anatomy of a large-scale social search engine. In: Proc. of the 19th WWW, pp. 431–440. ACM (2010)
7. Kleinberg, J.: The small-world phenomenon: An algorithmic perspective. In: Proc. of the 32nd Annual STOC, pp. 163–170. ACM (2000)
8. Kossmann, D., Ramsak, F., Rost, S.: Shooting stars in the sky: An online algorithm for skyline queries. In: Proc. of the 28th VLDB, pp. 275–286 (2002)
9. Law, E., von Ahn, L.: Human computation. In: Synthesis Lectures on Artificial Intelligence and Machine Learning, 13 (2011)
10. Li, B., King, I.: Routing questions to appropriate answerers in community question answering services. In: Proc. of the 19th CIKM, pp. 1585–1588. ACM (2010)
11. Liu, Y., Bian, J., Agichtein, E.: Predicting information seeker satisfaction in community question answering. In: Proc. of the 31st SIGIR, pp. 483–490. ACM (2008)
12. Morris, M.R., Teevan, J., Panovich, K.: A comparison of information seeking using search engines and social networks. In: Proc. of the 4th ICWSM, pp. 23–26. AAAI (2010)

[1] The technical report of the project was earlier released at http://arxiv.org/pdf/1407.6714v1.pdf.

13. Pal, A., Counts, S.: Identifying topical authorities in microblogs. In: Proc. of the 4th WSDM, pp. 45–54. ACM (2011)
14. Richardson, M., White, R.W.: Supporting synchronous social q&a throughout the question lifecycle. In: Proc. of the 20th WWW, pp. 755–764. ACM (2011)
15. Sung, J., Lee, J.G., Lee, U.: Booming up the long tails: discovering potentially contributive users in community-based question answering services. In: Proc. of the 7th ICWSM (2013)
16. Zhang, H., Horvitz, E., Chen, Y., Parkes, D.C.: Task routing for prediction tasks. In: Proc. of the 11th AAMAS, pp. 889–896. AAMAS (2012)
17. Zhou, Y., Cong, G., Cui, B., Jensen, C.S., Yao, J.: Routing questions to the right users in online communities. In: Proc. of the 25th ICDE, pp. 700–711. IEEE (2009)

Transforming Collaboration Structures into Deployable Informal Processes

C. Timurhan Sungur[1(✉)], Christoph Dorn[2], Schahram Dustdar[2], and Frank Leymann[1]

[1] Institute of Architecture of Application Systems, University of Stuttgart, Stuttgart, Germany
{sungur,leymann}@iaas.uni-stuttgart.de

[2] Distributed Systems Group, Vienna University of Technology, Vienna, Austria
{dorn,dustdar}@dsg.tuwien.ac.at

Abstract. Traditional workflow and activity-centric coordination offers limited process support to human collaborators when unanticipated situations predominate. Under such circumstances, informal processes focus on provisioning relevant resources for achieving collaboration goals. Resources include interaction mechanisms such as shared artifact, social networks, and publish/subscribe information dissemination as complex situations typically demand the close collaboration among multiple human process participants. Currently, however, there exists a gap between (i) selecting and configuring suitable interaction mechanisms (collaboration level) and (ii) deploying the respective collaboration platforms (IT level). In this paper, we present an approach and techniques for transforming collaboration structures into automatically deployable informal processes. We demonstrate how our tools support the specification of desirable collaboration capabilities subsequently deployed to multiple MediaWiki instances.

Keywords: Informal process essentials · Human architecture description language · Wiki · Collaboration configuration · Transformation

1 Introduction

Organizational processes range from ad-hoc activities to rigorously-defined workflows [19]. As flexibility and adaptation is required for unforseen situations, humans tend to execute most activities in those less well-defined processes—denoted in this paper as *informal processes.* With fewer a-priori specified flow conditions, however, comes the need for supporting coordination and collaboration among human process participants. Informal processes are hence inherently human-centric. Here, the traditional process modeling primitives (i.e., elements for tasks, control flow, data flow, etc) are often no longer suitable [15,30]. Other interaction dependency management patterns [17] such as *Shared Artifact*, *Social Network*, *Secretary/Principal*, *Master/Worker*, or *Publish/Subscribe* become increasingly relevant. Collaboration patterns allow modeling how multiple humans interact through messages, artifacts,

P. Cimiano et al. (Eds.): ICWE 2015, LNCS 9114, pp. 231–250, 2015.
DOI: 10.1007/978-3-319-19890-3_16

requests, etc, rather than having to express all work efforts by means of assigning a single task to a single process participant.

Multiple platforms implement the various collaboration patterns. Facebook and LinkedIn, for example, realize the Social Network pattern; MediaWiki [1], DokuWiki [2], and Google Documents realize the Shared Artifact pattern, Twitter the Publish/Subscribe pattern. Informal processes target unforeseen situations and thus require flexible coordination mechanisms. It is highly unlikely that, for example, a given wiki or social network platform in its initial, static configuration will remain suitable for all informal process purposes. We therefore argue that in human-intensive process environments, we need to treat coordination and collaboration mechanisms as resources that are specifically configured for each process instance. Statically provided collaboration mechanisms cause two types of problems: on the one hand, they may prove too flexible (e.g., pure email) and thus cannot properly support the process participants. Participants need then to execute all coordination actions manually without any monitoring, notification, protection, or other automation support. On the other hand, static configurations may lead to overly rigid coordination structures that quickly become inefficient to use or are abandoned altogether. An example are traditional workflow systems that exactly define who must do what in which order.

Providing collaboration mechanism as a configurable resource, however, entails a set of challenges. Typical resource management and provisioning mechanisms focus on fair, safe, or cheap access by individual clients [27]. Access privileges specify what a single client may or may not do with a particular resource. Collaboration mechanism resources, in contrast, are intrinsically subject to simultaneous, correlated use. Furthermore, collaborators enact process-centric roles that need finely-tuned, highly asymmetric usage capabilities (e.g., reading vs. writing, sending vs. receiving). While process participants are aware of these fine-grained collaboration-level requirements, IT personnel managing the actual resource have only insights into how to configure and deploy the corresponding software.

Our contribution in this paper are a set of models, transformations, and supporting framework for addressing these challenges. Our approach separates the specification of collaboration roles [16] from their provisioning details [30]. Along these lines, informal process participants utilize a collaboration-centric architecture description language for determining the required roles and collaboration actions for their particular informal process instance. This specification is tied to implementation artifacts via resource capabilities. Automatic deployment of implementation artifacts closes the gap between collaboration and IT level. We demonstrate the feasibility of specifying and deploying non-trivial collaboration structures based on a use case involving multiple wikis.

The remainder of this paper is structured as follows. Section 1.1 introduces an accompanying scenario. We subsequently provide background on applied models and techniques (Sec. 2) followed by an overview of our approach (Sec. 3).

[1] http://www.mediawiki.org/wiki/MediaWiki
[2] https://www.dokuwiki.org/dokuwiki

Section 4 describes the transformation and refinement process for mapping the collaboration specification to the providing software artifacts and their deployment. We demonstrate and discuss this procedure within the scope of a validating use case (Sec. 5). Section 6 compares related work to our approach before Section 7 completes this paper with an outlook on future work and conclusions.

1.1 Motivating Scenario

Suppose a research consortium envisions the knowledge collection and dissemination from project partners as well as the wider research community. Project members are, however, interesting in keeping preliminary articles on work in progress separated from stable, generally publishable results. The differences in the expected user base and work coordination call for significantly different user roles and access permission for each article type. The various ways people collaborate and engage in article authoring, quality management, commenting, and improving renders futile any attempt to adequately capture these in a traditional workflow-style model. Such a process model will exhibit rigid action sequences and inhibit ad-hoc collaboration. In most such environments, custom-made software is neither an option due to time and/or cost constraints. Resorting to pre-existing solutions such as a wiki is a step in the right direction. A standard wiki provides a suitable set of collaboration capabilities but rarely exhibits the right capability configuration by default. Given the permission model of a typical wiki software (e.g., MediaWiki), the scenario's article differences demand two wiki instances, each configured accordingly (see Fig. 1 left).

One potential configuration for an internal wiki instance may foresee user authentication even for merely reading articles. Editing and managing roles are kept simple and to a minimum. Each project participating organization allocates one quality manager who is also responsible for promoting regular users to editors. Editors obtain generous editing rights. For example, new articles are automatically approved; quality managers merely check changes to existing articles for sensitive data from time to time.

The external wiki, on the other hand, needs more sophisticated users groups. Specifically, the configuration needs to balance low entry barriers for consuming and contributing knowledge with measures targeting article spamming, vandalism, and edit wars. To this end, the wiki might allow anonymous read access, a basic set of editing rights for authenticated users, extensive editing rights for time-trusted experts, and separate roles for user management, article patrolling, and article protecting.

The project's members are only interested in determining the wiki configuration and understanding its implications at the collaboration level (in contrast to IT level configuration concerns such as security, persistence, and scalability). The following sections describe how to operationalize such separation of concerns.

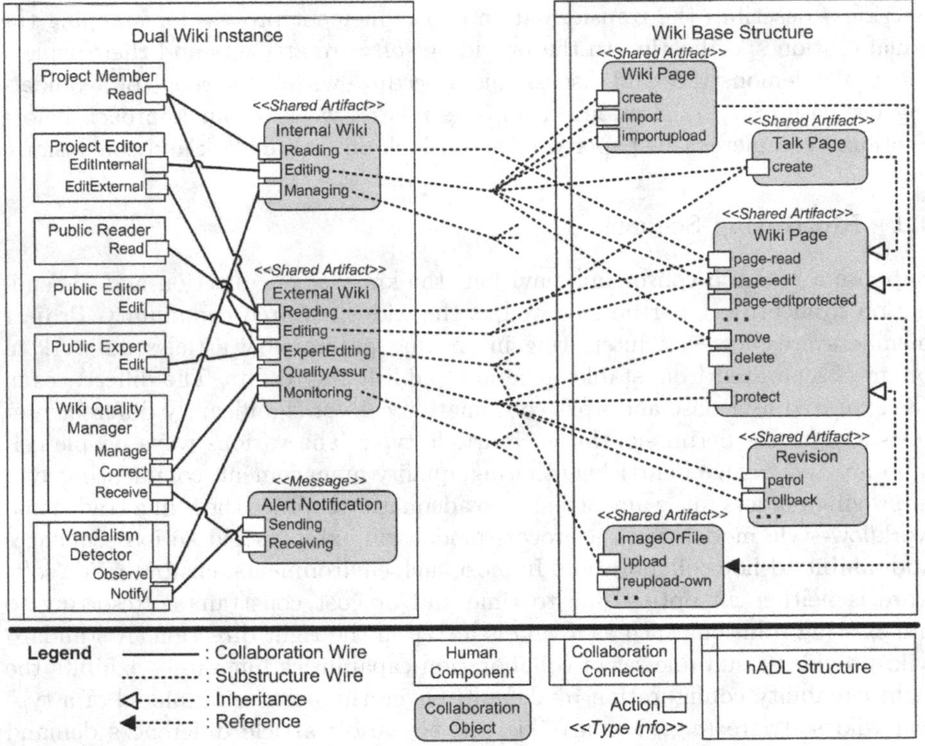

Fig. 1. Dual wiki scenario with substructure mapping in schematic hADL

2 Background

2.1 Human Architecture Description Language

The human Architecture Description Language (hADL) [16] provides a collaboration-centric component and connector view. A hADL model describes the collaboration structure in terms of the interacting user roles and their available interaction mechanisms. To this end, hADL distinguishes between *HumanComponents* and *CollaborationConnectors* to emphasize the difference between the primary collaborating users and non-essential, replaceable users that coordinate the collaboration. In our motivating scenario (Fig. 1 far left), project members, project editors, public read, public editor and public expert roles are the HumanComponents. The Wiki Quality Manager and Vandalism Detector roles represent CollaborationConnectors. They aren't strictly necessary, but greatly facilitate collaboration. A CollaborationConnector is thus responsible for the efficient and effective interaction among HumanComponents. It thereby may cover the full automation spectrum: from purely human, to software-assisted, to purely software implemented.

Users employ diverse means of interaction that range from emails, to chat rooms, shared wiki pages, and Q&A forums, to vote collection. These means implement vastly different interaction semantics: a message is sent and received, a shared artifact is edited, a vote can be cast. *CollaborationObjects* abstract from concrete interaction tools and capture the semantic differences in subtypes, e.g., *Message*, *Stream*, or *SharedArtifact*. In our example, the two *Wikis* (Fig. 1 mid left) provide collaboration in the form of a shared artifact, while the *Alert notification* provides messaging-centric capabilities. The actual notification mechanism may then be implemented through email, XMPP, SMS, or even a combination thereof.

Actions specify what capabilities a component or connector requires to fulfill his/her role, e.g., edit an article or receive an alert message. Complementary, *Actions* on CollaborationObject determine the offered capabilities. To this end, actions distinguish between *Create*, *Read*, *Update*, and *Delete* (CRUD) privileges. Action cardinalities further specify the upper and lower boundaries on the number of collaborators which may simultaneously have acquired the action's capabilities. The *Alert Notification Receiving* action, for example, thus demands at least one component or connector having receiving privileges when exhibiting an action cardinality of *(1..*)*.

Ultimately, *Collaboration Links* connect HumanComponent and CollaborationConnector actions to CollaborationObject actions, thus wiring up a particular collaboration structure. The *Structure* element provides a containment mechanism for complex, hierarchical CollaborationObjects and interaction patterns composed from the basic hADL elements. The scenario depicts the use of substructures for detailing the internal structure of each wiki collaboration object. The parent element references a pre-existing structure (here the Wiki Base Structure), and provides a mapping between parent action (e.g., Internal Wiki - Editing) and substructure action(s) (here Wiki Page - create, import ...) via substructure wires (Fig. 1 center, dashed lines). Multiple substructure wires between a single parent action and multiple sub actions imply *aggregation* semantics. Hence, the Internal Wiki editing action aggregates the Wiki Page create, import, import-upload, Page page-edit, etc capabilities. Likewise, two substructure wires from different parent actions to the same sub-action imply capability reuse, i.e., both parent actions make the sub-action's capability available. The substructure mechanism thus allows different configuration of the same base structures. Internal Wiki and External Wiki only need to exhibit the desired substructure wiring without having to duplicate the Wiki Base Structure.

2.2 Informal Process Essentials

Business process modeling languages, e.g., BPEL [26] and BPMN [2], enable capturing recurring activity patterns in various domains, e.g., manufacturing, health-care, IT, etc. Consequently, the activities, which frequently occur, can be documented, re-executed, and further improved. Typically, these activity-oriented process modeling approaches focus on the repeated activities and their structure. On the other hand, there are human-centric informal processes which cannot be well-defined using these activity-oriented approaches as their activities and sequences constantly change. Rather than using activity-oriented approaches, one captures the essential repeated information using resource-centric approaches such as Informal Process Essentials (IPE) [30]. The desired process result may be repeatedly obtained through selection of the same set of resources (and subsequently engaging them towards the collective goals of informal processes). IPE's resource-centric approach follows an agent-oriented style as an IPE model may specify resources that represent any type of active entities (humans, services, hardware, etc.) which then work autonomously towards the desired intentions of the respective informal process. Each IPE model contains the list of necessary resources to accomplish the target goal of the corresponding informal process. Each resource may exhibit various semantical relationships with other resources for specifying complex resource sets. These resources are typically provided by some services, i.e., resource organizers. Resource organizers are responsible for resource life-cycle operations of the resources within the corresponding process scope, i.e., they prepare the resources for the process execution and they release them upon process completion. Informal process actors are a special resource type. They work autonomously and make use of all other provided resources within the scope of their informal process instance. Resource organizers are added to the respective system on a plug-in basis. Each plug-in is responsible for the respective resource domain, e.g., a resource organizer plug-in for OpenTOSCA ecosystem. The combination of a domain specific resource organizer and its adapter results in a pluggable resource organizer. In the scope of this work, whenever we mention a specific resource organizer, we implicitly include its adapter.

An IPE model describes the the main intention that reflects the informal process' main goal. Each intention may be refined through sub-intentions that also may serve as constraints, e.g., "complete the process in one day". IPE model enactment depends on conditions in the surrounding execution environment. The IPE model's initial context specifies the triggers that signal when the model's corresponding resources should be initialized and subsequently work towards the informal process' main goal. Complementary to the initial context, the IPE model specifies the resulting context which specifies the conditions for determining the processes' main intention as successfully achieved. The expression of initial and final context is out of the scope of this work and will not be further discussed.

Fig. 2 illustrates the IPE Model for the motivating scenario. The IPE's collaborative resource specification is derived from the hADL architecture of the scenario. It details the various human performers who use the Wiki software in terms of their particular roles and permissions. The resources, that ultimately enact the collaboration roles, are organized by resource organizers, e.g., IT resources are organized by OpenTOSCA plug-in communicating with the OpenTOSCA ecosystem which is a cloud application management and deployment container. The main focus of this work is the transformation between the hADL model and

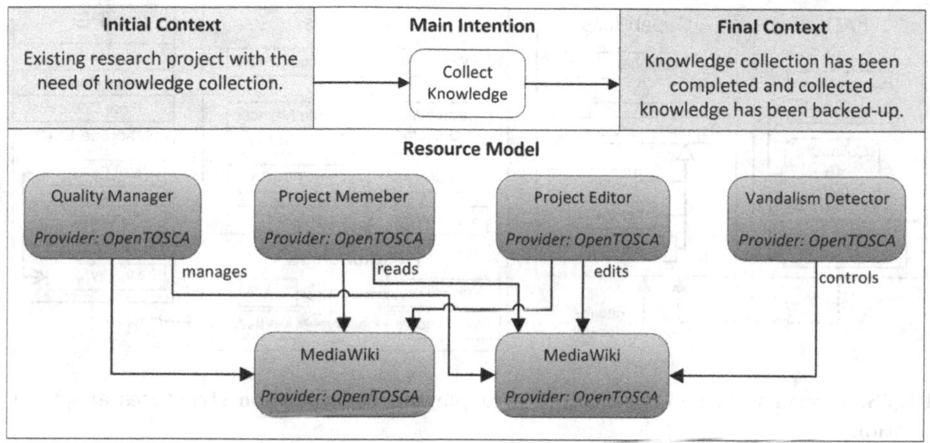

Fig. 2. Schematic IPE model of the dual wiki scenario

the resource model of an IPE model. In the following chapter, we will detail the interplay of hADL and IPE models and the relationships between them.

3 Approach

hADL models define high-level collaboration structures comprising human components, collaboration connectors, and collaboration objects without having to specify the underlying low-level deployment or implementation details. Instantiation of hADL models in an organizational context requires mapping hADL elements and their relations to specific, available resources of the respective organization. These resources abstract from provisioning details such as how a particular wiki is made available (e.g., in house on demand deployment via OpenTOSCA vs. external Software-as-a-Service provisioning) or how human participants become involved (e.g., via an organization internal OpenSocial-based platform vs. a LinkedIn external business social network). Resource relationships further specify which resources interact, but not how this interaction should be configured collaboration-wise. This concern, in turn, is best modeled in hADL.

Our approach (Fig. 3) aims at joining high-level hADL structures and low-level resources within the scope of an IPE model. Rather than directly mapping hADL and resource elements, our approach foresees their loose coupling via capabilities. hADL elements reference those capabilities which the ultimately selected resources needs to be able to fulfill. In contrast, resources specify both their complete capability set (e.g., for human-centric resources determined by their skill set), and their correspondingly required capabilities (to be provided by other resources). Our transformation logic takes a hADL model, capability definitions, and resources and produces an Informal Process Essentials (IPE) model. We outline the detailed transformation steps in the following section (Sec.4).

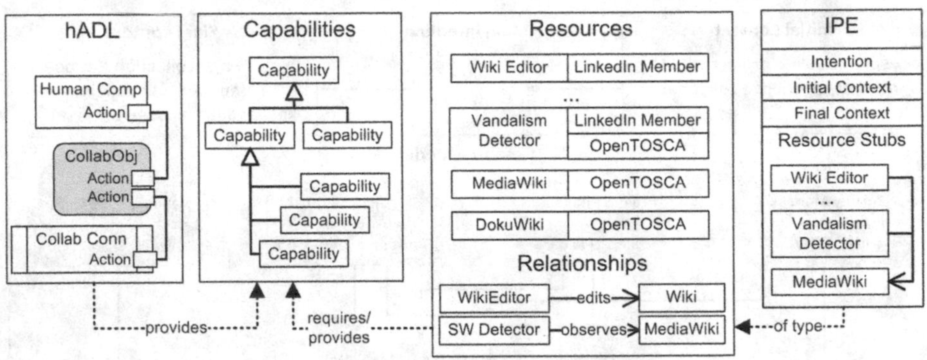

Fig. 3. Overview of models involved in deploying collaboration structures and their relations

Ultimately, the IPE model specifies a collaboration structure build from the participating resources, goals, and their initial/final contexts. It includes all details required for deploying and initializing resources upon informal process launch as well as their release at the end of the respective process. IPE models and corresponding tools (see Sec.5) thus constitute a realization environment for hADL models.

4 Transformation

The hADL-to-IPE transformation process relies on two complementary user roles. On the one hand, the *transformation principal* represents the informal process participant who drives the transformation for configuring the desired collaboration resources. In our scenario, one researcher from the lead project organization may assume this role. On the other hand, *resource principals* represent IT-level personnel who specify and maintain entries in the resource repository, capability repository, and hADL repository (see Fig. 5 center). Experts from an in-house IT department or at an external collaboration service provider typically assume this role.

4.1 Transformation Base Data

Our transformation assumes a bottom-up approach. Resource principals manage resource realizations. They utilize resource organizers such as OpenTOSCA for capturing the details required for instantiating and running resources (recall Section 2). Before a resource may become part of an IPE model, the resource principals first need to enhance resources with references to provided and required capabilities.

Resource principals also specify initial, basic hADL models; likewise with respective mappings to these capabilities. These basic hADL models primarily determine the structure of collaboration objects including their available actions but not their configuration in an actual informal process. For instance, in the motivating scenario (Section 1.1), the External and Internal Wiki (part of the hADL model under design) are built on top of a Base Wiki structure (from the hADL model repository). With increased use, the repository may eventually contain complete, specific hADL models depending on how useful the participants found the deployed configuration upon informal process completion. The management procedures involving resource principals, however, are outside the scope of this paper and thus not further discussed.

The transformation process relies on the concept of shared capabilities to bridge the different levels of abstraction, i.e., hADL and IPE, respectively, resource models. Typically, resources cannot operate on their own but require additional capabilities (i.e., requirements) that are provided by other resources. *Resource relationships* capture resource pairs with matching provided/required capabilities. A *Uses Wiki* relationship, for example, binds a Wiki Editor resource (requiring a Wiki capability) to a Wiki resource (providing a Wiki capability). Resource relationships are first class model elements at the same level of resources and managed within the resource repository.

Similar to resources, hADL human components, collaboration connectors, and collaboration objects reference capabilities. To this end, the capability model (visualized in Fig. 4) defines a core capability hierarchy for further extensions according to HumanComponent capability, CollaborationConnector capability, and CollaborationObject capability. Root-level BaseCapabilityProperties and customization thereof specify further details (based on hADL actions) needed for collaboration-centric configuration of domain-specific resources. Specifically, the *BaseCapabilityProperties* element contains basic hADL actions and/or composite actions. Example action specification refinements thereof include a simple *Wiki permission* in the former case and a *Wiki permission group* in the latter case, both defined within *WikiPermissionProperties*. The hADL model utilizes these refinement specifications whenever a human component, collaboration connector, or collaboration object exposes the corresponding capability. A hADL collaboration object exposing a *WikiCapability*, for example, may then exhibit simple Wiki permission actions and Wiki permission group actions. Likewise, the scenario's *External Expert Editor* exposes the *WikiEditorCapability* capability which in turn relies on the *WikiCapability* (via resource relationships), and thus calls for action types from the WikiPermissionProperties.

4.2 Transformation Procedure

The hADL-to-IPE transformation process is semi-automatic. The transformation principal needs only become involved for resolving ambiguities, select among multiple choices, and confirm the final IPE configuration. Fig. 5 displays the ideal sequence of the various transformation activities, i.e., error handling is omitted for sake of clarity.

The transformation principal engages in the hADL-to-IPE transformation process by creating a hADL model. The principal selects suitable collaboration

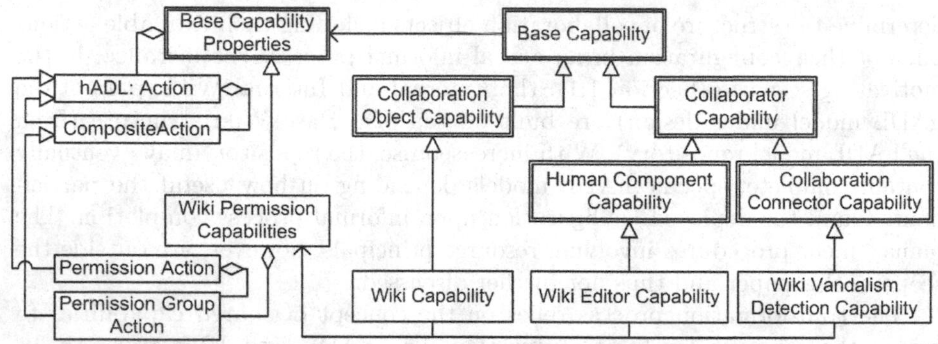

Fig. 4. Collaboration-centric capability model (double-edged elements are part of the base model, single-edged elements constitute extensions)

objects, human components, collaboration connectors, and structures thereof from the hADL repository. In our motivating scenario, the hADL repository contains the Wiki Base Structure and basic editor and manager components and connectors. These components and connectors typically exhibit only simple or even no actions but refer to capabilities. The transformation principals conducts three types of interleaving modeling activities.

- configuring the desired collaboration object configuration through selecting prepared hADL collaboration objects and (where applicable) rewiring their substructures.
- specifying the actual required component and connectors by copying, aggregating, creating or refining existing hADL collaborators from the hADL repository (e.g., merging a wiki reader with a notification dispatcher).
- linking collaborator actions and object actions, thereby completing the hADL model instance.

The resulting hADL model components, connectors, and objects exhibit a reference to their respective **provided** capabilities only. The required capabilities are automatically derived from the collaboration links during the *Generate IPE Stubs* step.

The IPE model determines a capability's configuration in terms of hADL actions. Whenever a collaboration object, component or connector contains a substructure, the specific wiring to subactions, therefore, needs pulling into the super structure. Otherwise, the information contained in the substructure mapping will be lost. The corresponding *Flatten hADL Model* step takes the initial hADL model and transforms it into a new hADL model where each action directly contains its related subactions.

The *Generate IPE Stubs* step creates a partial IPE model. The transformation logic generates an IPE *Resource* stub for each human component, collaboration connector, and collaboration object that references a (provided) capability. For instance, in the motivating scenario, the IPE model consists of stubs for

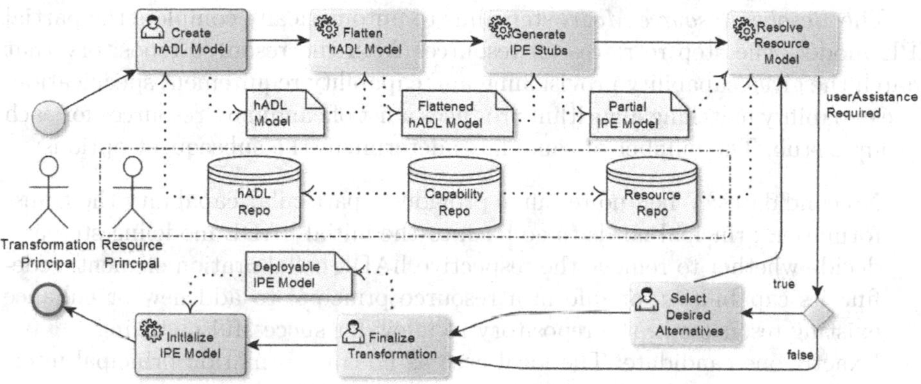

Fig. 5. hADL to IPE model transformation process (dotted lines represent dataflow, full lines depict control flow)

the External Editor, the Wiki Quality Manager, the External Wiki, the Internal Wiki, etc. A resource stub yet lacks a reference to an actual, existing resource enacting the respective hADL role in an informal process. Instead, the stub references the provided and required capabilities and provides their configuration in terms of the respective CapabilityProperties. The Project Editor resource stub, for example, features an IPE capability specification in the form of a WikiPermissionProperties element containing all hADL Project Editor actions (i.e., EditInternal, EditExternal) by copying them from the hADL model. A hADL link between a collaboration connector or a human component and a collaboration object implies that the former requires the capability of the latter. The links further define the precise subset of actions relevant to the requirement specification. Hence, the Project Editor stub features two IPE requirement specifications, both in the form of a WikiPermissionProperties element, each containing the linked hADL actions of the two hADL wiki objects (Internal Wiki - Editing composite action and External Wiki - Editing composite action).

The transformation logic additionally generates IPE *Resource Relationship* stubs based on the links in the flattened hADL input model. Resource relationship stubs describe which resource (stub) requires what other resource(s) (stubs) within the scope of the IPE model instance. The resource relationships ensure that ultimately the deployed Project Member resources, Project Editor resources, and Wiki Quality Manager resources have access to the same Internal Wiki resource, rather than each one having access to three separate wikis merely configured to each individual user resource. The exact relationship type, however, remains undecided as long as the IPE resource stubs remain without assigned resources from the repository. The concrete resource relationship type between Vandalism Detector and External Wiki depends on whether the ultimate resource will be software-based (and thus requires access to the Wiki via a machine API) or human-based (and thus requires access to the Wiki via a human consumable Web interface).

The *Resolve Resource Model* step aims to automatically complete the partial IPE model. The step retrieves all resources from the resource repository that match the given capability provisioning and capability requirement specification. The capability matching algorithm produces a list of candidate resources for each resource stub. The number of candidates determines the subsequent options:

- No candidates: When no resource provides a particular capability the transformation principal needs to go back to the initial hADL modeling step and decide whether to remove the respective hADL collaboration element, redefine its capabilities, or inform a resource principal to add new or enhance existing resources in the repository to allow for successful matching.
- Exactly one candidate: The ideal case as no transformation principal intervention is required.
- Multiple candidates: The transformation principal needs to *Select Desired Alternatives* upon which the control flow returns to the *Resolve Resource Model* step. For instance, a *VandalismDetectionCapability* can be provided by two different resources, e.g., a human resource or a software analyzer which detects violation patterns and notifies a users.

Having resolved the IPE resource stubs to concrete resources from the repository, the *Resolve Resource model* step commences with resolving the relationships stubs. During this process, the matching algorithm iterates through all relationship stubs and extracts compatible concrete relationship specifications candidates from the resource repository. To this end, the algorithm extracts the concrete resources references in the relationship stub and analyzes which relationship specification binds such a resource pair.

Similarly to before, having multiple relationship candidates requires the intervention of the transformation principal. Note that having no candidate for a particular resource relationship stub doesn't necessarily imply the need for restructuring the hADL model or resource relation specifications but rather having selected incompatible resources. For example, resource relationships in the repository may specify that a human Vandalism Detector is able to use both MediaWiki and DokuWiki resources while a software-based Detector is limited to MediaWiki. Hence, when selecting earlier the software-based Detector resource (for the VandalismDetection capability) and the DokuWiki resource (for the WikiCapability), the algorithm cannot find a concrete relationship. Consequently, the transformation process loops between *Resolve Resource Model* and *Select Desired Alternatives* until either all resource and resource relation stubs are resolved, or the resource principal aborts the process due to missing or mismatching resources and resource relationships, respectively.

4.3 Transformation Output Application

The hADL models lack information on the intentions and initial/final context of informal processes. The transformation principal completes the IPE model with these missing details in the *Finalize Transformation* step. This step also gives the resource principal a last opportunity for checking the generated resource model for completeness and correctness and adjusting it as needed. After these final manual configurations, the IPE model is ready for deployment whenever the execution environment matches the initial process context. For deployment, the various resource organizers obtain the IPE model, extract the hADL actions from each resource's capability requirements and capability provisioning specification for configuring and initializing the actual resource instances. For example, the WikiPermission actions and WikiPermissionGroup actions determine directly MediaWiki's permission configuration file.

5 Case Study Based on the OpenTOSCA Ecosystem

We have created a prototype for transformation procedure (all steps except for the first and last in Fig. 5) on top of our previous work [30] in order to test and validate our approach (see screenshots in Fig. 6). We realized the prototype as a REST-based web-service that reuses following specifications and tools: We apply the Topology Orchestration Specification for Cloud Applications (TOSCA) [6] for resource deployment. OpenTOSCA [5] is an open-source container (i.e., resource organizer) for cloud applications defined in TOSCA. Winery [24] is the corresponding modeling tool for specifying TOSCA-based applications. As TOSCA supports the concepts of capability and requirements, we use Winery as repository for capabilities, resources, and resource relationships. We defined domain-specific capabilities (in the *wikiCap* namespace) and corresponding capability property and action specification (in the *wtypes* namespace) for implementing the case study based on the motivating scenario. Due to page constraints we only provide some model excerpts in this section. A complete set of XML schemas, specifications, XSL transformations, input and output models as well as a proof-of-concept tool is available as supporting online material (SOM) at http://co-act.biz/downloads.

First, the transformation principal creates the hADL model using a hADL editor (outside of this paper's scope). The hADL editor loads the predefined, shared capabilities from Winery. The principal annotates the hADL modeling elements with the desired capability definitions (in our case those defined in the *wikiCap* namespace). The Listing 1.1 presents the hADL XML excerpt for the External Expert Editor from the motivating scenario Section 1.1. hADL's extension mechanism enables annotating each human component, collaboration connector, and collaboration object with the CapabilityRef elements containing the qualified name of a capability, e.g., *wikiCap:WikiEditorCapability* (see Listing 1.1 line 3).

```
<hADL:name>External Expert Editor</hADL:name>
  <hADL:extension>
    <depl:CapabilityRef>wikiCap:WikiEditorCapability</depl:CapabilityRef>
  </hADL:extension>
  <hADL:action id="external-expert-editExt">
    <hADL:name>edit</hADL:name>
    <hADL:primitive>CREATE</hADL:primitive>
    <hADL:primitive>READ</hADL:primitive>
    <hADL:primitive>UPDATE</hADL:primitive>
  </hADL:action>
</hADL:component>
```

Listing 1.1. hADL Human Component, XML excerpt

Running the set of XSL transformation and resource resolving steps (see upper right in screenshot Fig. 6) results in the IPE model (excerpt) in Listing 1.2 (full output available as SOM). The hADL component in Listing 1.1 becomes an IPE resource (line 1) consisting of a single provided capability (line 5 to 15), single requirement (line 17 to 37), and single relationship (line 39 to 45).

- the IPE capability segment simply refers to the provided capability (line 6) and a copy of the only Extern Expert's action defined in the hADL model.
- The IPE requirement segment references the required Wiki capability (line 17) as derived through navigating the hADL links. The requirement additionally exhibits a copy of the linked external wiki's expert editing action (lines 21 to 35) of type *WikiPermissionSetAction*. Note the action's domain specific element *groupName* (line 35) and subactions (line 28 to 33) used to configure the actual Wiki resource instance upon deployment.
- The IPE resource relationship segment indicates that the IPE resource External Editor ties to the IPE resource VWiki-Complex (line 43).

The IPE model content explained up to here represents the stub information and needs completion with actual resources from resource repository. In our case study, we search through human resources and IT resources in Winery. We converted also all available human resources to TOSCA NodeTypes and stored them in Winery. We subsequently iterate through all available human and IT resources. When checking a resource, we need to ensure that not only all hADL derived capability requirements are satisfied but also those referenced by the resources in Winery. At last, the relationships are selected based on the selected resources. In Listing 1.2, the stubs become complete by adding following resource, respectively relationship reference:

- External Editor specification maps to resource *wikiRes:Editor* (line 4).
- Relationship to VWiki-Complex maps to resource relationship *wikiResRel:edits* (line 40).

The resulting IPE Resource Model (see screenshot in Fig. 6 lower left) provides all necessary details to realize the desired resource model. In this case, it references certain TOSCA NodeTypes and RelationshipTypes. During initialization of the respective model, the resource organizer receives the resource information and executes the necessary domain specific operations. In case of TOSCA resources, first a topology is generated by converting TOSCA types (i.e., NodeTypes and RelationshipTypes) to TOSCA templates (i.e., NodeTemplates and RelationshipTemplates). Work of Hirmer et al. [22] supports the generation of a complete topology. Finally, we end up with a service template which contains the application topology. Such service templates can be deployed on declarative TOSCA containers [12].

```
<ipsm:Resource ipsm:id="MediaWiki.ExternalExpert" ipsm:name="External Expert Editor"
  ipsm:realizationDomain="http://www.uni-stuttgart.de/opentosca"
  xmlns:wikiCap="http://www.iaas.uni-stuttgart.de/ipsm/hadl/case-study/tosca/types"
  ipsm:type="wikiRes:Editor">
  <ipsm:CapabilityList>
    <ipsm:Capability ipsm:type="wikiCap:WikiEditorCapability">
      <ipsm:PropertyList>
        <hADL:action xmlns:hADL="http://at.ac.tuwien.dsg/hADL/hADLcore"
                     id="external-expert-editExt">
          <hADL:name>edit</hADL:name>
          <hADL:primitive>CREATE</hADL:primitive>
          <hADL:primitive>READ</hADL:primitive>
          <hADL:primitive>UPDATE</hADL:primitive>
        </hADL:action>
    ...
  <ipsm:RequirementList>
   <ipsm:Requirement  ipsm:requiredCapability="wikiCap:WikiCapability">
     <ipsm:PropertyList>
       <hADL:action
         xmlns:hADL="http://at.ac.tuwien.dsg/hADL/hADLcore"
         xmlns:wtypes="http://www.iaas.uni-stuttgart.de/ipsm/hadl/case-study/types"
         id="virtualwiki2-expert"
         xsi:type="wtypes:tMediaWikiPermissionSetAction">
        <hADL:name>Expert Editing</hADL:name>
        <hADL:primitive>READ</hADL:primitive>
        <hADL:primitive>UPDATE</hADL:primitive>
        <hADL:primitive>DELETE</hADL:primitive>
        <!-- subactions from references hADL substructure -->
        <btypes:SubAction
        xmlns:btypes="http://www.iaas.uni-stuttgart.de/ipsm/hadl/base/types"
            id="page-read" xsi:type="wiki:tMediaWikiPermissionAction">
          <hADL:name>read</hADL:name>
          <wiki:permission>read</wiki:permission>
        </btypes:SubAction>
        <!-- further subactions -->
        <wtypes:groupName>expert</wtypes:groupName>
      </hADL:action>
  ...
  <ipsm:RelationshipList>
    <ipsm:Relationship  ipsm:sourceDomain="http://www.uni-stuttgart.de/opentosca"
                        ipsm:type="wikiResRel:edits">
      <ipsm:TargetResourceList>
        <ipsm:TargetResource ipsm:targetDomain="http://www.uni-stuttgart.de/opentosca">
          VWiki-Complex</ipsm:TargetResource>
      </ipsm:TargetResourceList>
    </ipsm:Relationship>
  ...
```

Listing 1.2. Human Component as an IPE Resource, XML excerpt

Discussion. Our case study demonstrates the feasibility of separating collaboration-level resource configuration and system-level resource deployment of a real-world collaboration tool. Transformation principals need not know any technical details of the underlying technical infrastructure (here the configura-

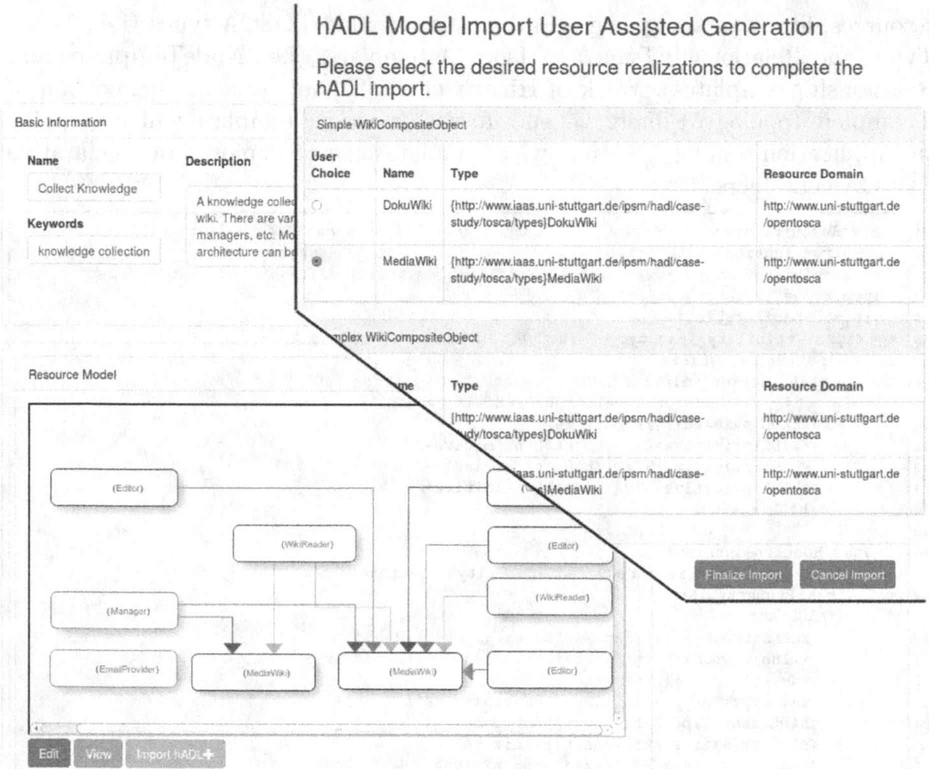

Fig. 6. hADL-to-IPE prototype screenshots

tion of MediaWiki software, web server, database, and hosting environment). The hADL model enables the principal to quickly perceive which permissions affect what collaboration mechanism (e.g., page, file, history) of a MediaWiki installation. Having multiple informal process participants access two wikis with different capabilities exemplifies our framework's ability to transform non-trivial, real-world hADL models to IPE models. We believe it's in the interest of the reader to keep subsequent deployment details out of this paper's scope as we build our case study on top of proven and mature tools and standards such as the OpenTOSCA container and Winery.

Our approach is applicable to collaboration platforms beyond wikis. The teaching support platform Moodle, for example, exhibits extensive configurability. Similar to MediaWiki, it supports the aggregation of collaboration capabilities into custom roles[3] and hence would be directly applicable to modeling in hADL and subsequent transformation to IPE.

[3] https://docs.moodle.org/24/en/Creating_custom_roles

6 Related Work

Web-based platforms, languages, and specifications such as CrowdSearcher [8], Jabberwocky [4], CrowdForge [23], or CrowdLang [25] aim at efficiently executing large-scale human-centric workflows. These approaches focus primarily on achieving sufficient quality at low costs when distributing, collecting, and filtering massive amounts of tasks. Interaction among task workers is not foreseen; all dependencies are modeled as task-centric workflow patterns [9]. Brambilla and Mauri integrate social network-centric actions into web applications via social primitives [11]. Their focus is on public social platforms (Facebook, Twitter, ...) and thus configuration and deployment of the collaboration structures remains out of scope.

Recently research efforts started explicitly targeting the integration of social media into business process management (BPM) technology. Brambilla et al. present design patterns for integrating of social network features in BPMN [10]. A social network user may engage in task-centric actions such as voting, commenting, reading a message, or joining a task. Böhringer utilizes tagging, activity streams, and micro-blogging for merging ad-hoc activities into case management [7]. Dengler et al. utilize collaborative software such as Wikis and social networks for coordinating process activities [14]. oBPM [20] is an approach for opportunistically modeling business processes in a bottom up manner. It thereby relies on task and artifact abstraction for coordination among participants. These approaches differ in two crucial aspects from our work: (i) they rely on a predefined process model, and (ii) they statically integrate social media resources.

The BPM community recognized the need for flexible processes early on [28], distinguishing among flexibility *by design*, *by deviation*, *by underspecification*, and *by change* [29]. Work on process flexibility, however, has the primary focus on the process specification and not on how to enable executable support for collaboration and coordination among process participants. Even traditional workflow description languages dedicated to modeling the human involvement such as Little-JIL [13], BPEL4People [1], or WS-HumanTask [3] foresee no explicit communication among process participants outside of tasks. Although BPEL4people supports four eyes, nomination, escalation, and chained execution scenarios; and WS-HumanTask allows attaching comments to tasks, all interaction is purely task-centric.

In our own recent work [15] we explored the integration of business process and collaboration patterns but didn't address ad-hoc collaboration resource deployment nor the context of informal processes. These informal processes are addressed by different approaches such as adaptive case management [21] or activity-centric computing [18]. However, these approaches focus primarily on activities and not resources. To this end, we have proposed a resource-oriented approach [30]. It enables the deployment of the resources in the context of an informal process context.

7 Conclusion and Outlook

Traditional workflow and activity-centric approaches are inadequate when organizations need to document and reuse best practices for solving problems of collaborative nature. Instead, tacit knowledge on suitable collaboration structures and their enactable informal process models constitute more fitting concepts. To this end, we presented a novel approach for transforming collaboration-level models (applying the human Architecture Description Language) into deployable technical informal processes (represented in IPE). We introduced the concept of shared capabilities as basis for transformation across different levels of abstraction. We subsequently detailed the various transformation steps and described their application in the scope of a validating case study and proof-of-concept tool involving real-world IT resources (i.e., MediaWiki) and human resources.

Having focused on the technical aspects (models, transformation, tools) in this paper, we are planning for more detailed, validating experiments involving more complex scenarios that we couldn't outline here due to page restrictions. These experiments will provide quantitative measures that serve as evidence on the benefits of our approach.

Acknowledgments. This work has been partially supported by Graduate School of Excellence advanced Manufacturing Engineering (GSaME)[4] and by the EU FP7 Smart-Society project, under Grant No. 600854.

References

1. BPEL4People. http://docs.oasis-open.org/bpel4people/bpel4people-1.1.pdf
2. BPMN 2.0. http://www.omg.org/spec/BPMN/2.0/PDF/
3. WS-HumanTask. http://docs.oasis-open.org/bpel4people/ws-humantask-1.1-spec-cs-01.pdf
4. Ahmad, S., Battle, A., Malkani, Z., Kamvar, S.: The jabberwocky programming environment for structured social computing. In: UIST 2011, New York, NY, USA, pp. 53–64 (2011)
5. Binz, T., Breitenbücher, U., Haupt, F., Kopp, O., Leymann, F., Nowak, A., Wagner, S.: OpenTOSCA – a runtime for TOSCA-based cloud applications. In: Basu, S., Pautasso, C., Zhang, L., Fu, X. (eds.) ICSOC 2013. LNCS, vol. 8274, pp. 692–695. Springer, Heidelberg (2013)
6. Binz, T., Breitenbücher, U., Kopp, O., Leymann, F.: TOSCA: Portable Automated Deployment and Management of Cloud Applications. In: Bouguettaya, A., Sheng, Q.Z., Daniel, F. (eds.) Advanced Web Services, pp. 527–549. Springer, New York (2014)
7. Böhringer, M.: Emergent case management for ad-hoc processes: a solution based on microblogging and activity streams. In: Muehlen, M., Su, J. (eds.) BPM 2010 Workshops. LNBIP, vol. 66, pp. 384–395. Springer, Heidelberg (2011)
8. Bozzon, A., Brambilla, M., Ceri, S., Mauri, A.: Reactive crowdsourcing. In: WWW 2013, pp. 153–164. International World Wide Web Conferences Steering Committee, Republic and Canton of Geneva, Switzerland (2013)

[4] http://www.gsame.uni-stuttgart.de/

9. Bozzon, A., Brambilla, M., Ceri, S., Mauri, A., Volonterio, R.: Pattern-based specification of crowdsourcing applications. In: Casteleyn, S., Rossi, G., Winckler, M. (eds.) ICWE 2014. LNCS, vol. 8541, pp. 218–235. Springer, Heidelberg (2014)
10. Brambilla, M., Fraternali, P., Vaca, C.: BPMN and design patterns for engineering social BPM solutions. In: Daniel, F., Barkaoui, K., Dustdar, S. (eds.) BPM Workshops 2011, Part I. LNBIP, vol. 99, pp. 219–230. Springer, Heidelberg (2012)
11. Brambilla, M., Mauri, A.: Model-driven development of social network enabled applications with WebML and social primitives. In: Grossniklaus, M., Wimmer, M. (eds.) ICWE Workshops 2012. LNCS, vol. 7703, pp. 41–55. Springer, Heidelberg (2012)
12. Breitenbücher, U., Binz, T., Képes, K., Kopp, O., Leymann, F., Wettinger, J.: Combining declarative and imperative cloud application provisioning based on TOSCA. In: Proceedings of the IEEE International Conference on Cloud Engineering, pp. 87–96 (2014)
13. Cass, A.G., Lerner, B.S., Sutton Jr. S.M., McCall, E.K., Wise, A.E., Osterweil, L.J.: Little-JIL/Juliette: a process definition language and interpreter. In: ICSE 2000, pp. 754–757. IEEE (2000)
14. Dengler, F., Koschmider, A., Oberweis, A., Zhang, H.: Social software for coordination of collaborative process activities. In: Muehlen, M., Su, J. (eds.) BPM 2010 Workshops. LNBIP, vol. 66, pp. 396–407. Springer, Heidelberg (2011)
15. Dorn, C., Dustdar, S., Osterweil, L.J.: Specifying flexible human behavior in interaction-intensive process environments. In: Sadiq, S., Soffer, P., Völzer, H. (eds.) BPM 2014. LNCS, vol. 8659, pp. 366–373. Springer, Heidelberg (2014)
16. Dorn, C., Taylor, R.N.: Architecture-driven modeling of adaptive collaboration structures in large-scale social web applications. In: Wang, X.S., Cruz, I., Delis, A., Huang, G. (eds.) WISE 2012. LNCS, vol. 7651, pp. 143–156. Springer, Heidelberg (2012)
17. Dorn, C., Taylor, R.N.: Analyzing runtime adaptability of collaboration patterns. Concurrency Computat.: Pract. Exper. (2014)
18. Dustdar, S.: Caramba Process-Aware Collaboration System Supporting Ad hoc and Collaborative Processes in Virtual Teams. Distributed Parallel Databases **15**, 45–66 (2004)
19. Ellis, C., Nutt, G.J.: Workflow: the process spectrum. In: Proceedings of the NSF Workshop on Workflow and Process Automation in Information Systems, pp. 140–145 (1996)
20. Grünert, D., Brucker-Kley, E., Keller, T.: oBPM – an opportunistic approach to business process modeling and execution. In: Fournier, F., Mendling, J. (eds.) BPM 2014 Workshops. LNBIP, vol. 202, pp. 463–474. Springer, Heidelberg (2015)
21. Herrmann, C., Kurz, M.: Adaptive case management: supporting knowledge intensive processes with IT systems. In: Schmidt, W. (ed.) S-BPM ONE 2011. CCIS, vol. 213, pp. 80–97. Springer, Heidelberg (2011)
22. Hirmer, P., Breitenbücher, U., Binz, T., Leymann, F.: Automatic topology completion of TOSCA-based cloud applications. In: Proceedings of CloudCycle14 Workshops, pp. 247–258. Bonn (2014)
23. Kittur, A., Smus, B., Khamkar, S., Kraut, R.E.: CrowdForge: crowdsourcing complex work. In: Proceedings of the 24th Annual ACM Symposium on User Interface Software and Technology, UIST 2011, pp. 43–52. ACM, New York (2011)
24. Kopp, O., Binz, T., Breitenbücher, U., Leymann, F.: Winery – a modeling tool for TOSCA-based cloud applications. In: Basu, S., Pautasso, C., Zhang, L., Fu, X. (eds.) ICSOC 2013. LNCS, vol. 8274, pp. 700–704. Springer, Heidelberg (2013)

25. Minder, P., Bernstein, A.: CrowdLang - first steps towards programmable human computers for general computation. In: AAAI Workshops (2011)
26. BPEL 2.0. http://docs.oasis-open.org/wsbpel/2.0/OS/wsbpel-v2.0-OS.pdf
27. Russell, N., van der Aalst, W.M.P., ter Hofstede, A.H.M., Edmond, D.: Workflow resource patterns: identification, representation and tool support. In: Pastor, Ó., Falcão e Cunha, J. (eds.) CAiSE 2005. LNCS, vol. 3520, pp. 216–232. Springer, Heidelberg (2005)
28. Sadiq, S.K., Sadiq, W., Orlowska, M.E.: Pockets of flexibility in workflow specification. In: Kunii, H.S., Jajodia, S., Sølvberg, A. (eds.) ER 2001. LNCS, vol. 2224, pp. 513–526. Springer, Heidelberg (2001)
29. Schonenberg, H., Mans, R., Russell, N., Mulyar, N., Aalst, W.: Process flexibility: a survey of contemporary approaches. In: Dietz, J.L.G., Albani, A., Barjis, J. (eds.) CAiSE 2008. LNBIP, vol. 10, pp. 16–30. Springer, Berlin Heidelberg (2008)
30. Sungur, C.T., Binz, T., Breitenbücher, U., Leymann, F.: Informal process essentials. In: EDOC 2014, pp. 200–209. IEEE (2014)

Raimond: Quantitative Data Extraction from Twitter to Describe Events

Thibault Sellam[1(✉)] and Omar Alonso[2]

[1] CWI, Amsterdam, The Netherlands
thibault.sellam@cwi.nl
[2] Microsoft Corporation, Mountain View, CA, USA
omalonso@microsoft.com

Abstract. Social media play a decisive role in communicating and spreading information during global events. In particular, real-time microblogging platforms such as Twitter have become prevalent. Researchers have used microblogging for a number of tasks, including past events analysis, predictions, and information retrieval. Nevertheless, little attention has been given to quantitative data extraction. In this paper, we address two questions: can we develop a mechanism to extract quantitative data from a collection of tweets, and can we use the salient findings to describe an event? To answer the first question, we introduce Raimond, a virtual text curator, specialized in quantitative data extraction from Twitter. To address the second question, we use our system on three events and evaluate its output using a crowdsourcing strategy. We demonstrate the effectiveness of our approach with a number of real world examples.

Keywords: Microblogs · Information extraction · Events analysis

1 Introduction

Microblogging platforms constitute an incredible source of data about events, especially during time-critical matters like disasters. Consider for instance the series of earthquakes which shook Japan in March 2011. In the days which followed the first shocks, millions of posts were written and shared on Twitter. These tweets came from a wide range of sources, including individuals, official organizations, and news agencies from various places around the world. Many of them were produced in real-time. The combination of volume, diversity, brevity and instantaneous reaction makes Twitter a powerful medium to understand how the world was responding.

In this paper, we investigate how to extract *quantitative information* from microblogs. For example, in the case of Japan, how many earthquakes actually stroked the country? How many casualties were reported? How much funds were unlocked to help? The event has a number of objective *quantitative properties*, such as cardinalities and measures. These properties are often associated with

P. Cimiano et al. (Eds.): ICWE 2015, LNCS 9114, pp. 251–268, 2015.
DOI: 10.1007/978-3-319-19890-3_17

numbers. Some of these properties change with time, e.g., the count of casualties. Others remain constant, like the funds offered by a particular organization. Our aim is to develop a systematic mechanism to extract this information.

Once extracted, quantitative data is a powerful resource to describe events. Charles Minard's carte figurative of Napoleon's campaign in Russia is a famous example of how to convey an event with numbers [23]. The second question we investigate in this paper is the following: to what extent can an automatic system build a narrative from quantities? We will introduce methods to clean and organize quantitative information. But as Tufte suggests, "graphical excellence begins with telling the truth about the data" [23]; we cannot completely discard humans assessment from the edition process.

Researchers have studied how to extract information automatically from web pages since the early days of the Web. Ultimately, the objective is to produce structured data, such as tables, from natural text. This task is a challenge simply because computers cannot understand languages as well as humans do. When we target well-defined classes of information (e.g., the date of a cultural event), we can look for characteristic keywords or expressions. But seeking quantitative data, in general, is much harder. We must deal with an immense range of vocabulary, expressions, interpretations and topics.

In this paper, we present Raimond, a virtual text curator. Raimond's goal is to collect, clean, organize and recommend fragments of text which contain quantitative information. Our system is organized as a pipeline, where each stage solves a different sub-problem. First, Raimond identifies relevant tweets which contain quantitative data. Then, it groups those tweets into sub-topics, removes the low quality content, and display the results. Given the complexity of the problem, we designed Raimond as a hybrid system. On one hand, we automated the data intensive parts of the extraction process. On the other hand, we let humans interpret the text through a crowdsourcing platform. To summarize, we make the following contributions:

- We analyze how quantitative data is conveyed on Twitter
- We describe Raimond, a system to extract, filter and organize quantitative information to describe events.
- We study three real-world examples
- We evaluate the effectiveness of our approach with crowdsourcing

This paper is organized as follows. In the next section, we present the notion quantfrag. In Section 3, we detail how Raimond extract quantitative data. Section 4 showcases Raimond with real-word examples. An evaluation is presented in Section 5. A survey of related work is presented in Section 6. Finally, we present our conclusions and outline future work.

Table 1. Illustration of our terminology

Tweet	`Japan update: five nuclear plants shut down in Japan, tsunami waves continue to hit`
Event	2011 Japan Earthquakes
Quantfrag	`five nuclear plants shut down in Japan`
Property	Nuclear plants shut down
Quantity	5
Is a Qweet?	Yes

2 Introducing the Quantfrag

Overview. The central concept behind Raimond is the **quantfrag**. A quantfrag is a snippet of text which contains a piece of quantitative information. Observe for instance the following tweets, recorded after the 2011 earthquakes in Japan[1]:

```
"Breaking News: A 8.8 earthquake just hit #Japan."
"At least 2,369 are missing after #quake. I have no words."
"This is insane. The Earth's rotation sped up by 1.6
microseconds. #japan #planet"
```

Each post contains some quantitative information, surrounded by comments or details about the context. We call quantfrags the fragments of text which contain the quantities. We highlight these fragments in bold in the example. Ideally, a quantfrag should contain enough information to understand the quantity, but no more. It should be self-contained, but short. This leads to our first definition:

Definition 1. *A quantfrag is a complete, minimal piece of text which describes a fact based on a quantity.*

Not all tweets contain quantfrags. We use the term **qweets** for those which do: a qweet is a Twitter post which contains a quantity. We illustrate our terminology in Table 1. Raimond's aim is to detect qweets, extract quantfrags, and present the collection in a browsable form.

Natural catastrophes are not the only events which yield quantitative data. The following quantfrags describe the 2014 World Cup Brazil-Germany game:

```
"BRA undefeated in 62 straight competitive home games since
1975"
"GER have now scored 221 goals in WorldCup history"
```

These quantfrags were produced during the 2014 Ukraine political crisis:

```
"EU to provide $15 billion help package to Ukraine"
"Crimea referendum: 97% voted to join Russia"
```

We will present these two topics in detail in Section 4.

[1] All the examples in this section are based on actual tweets. Nevertheless, we took the liberty to truncate the original posts to shorten the presentation.

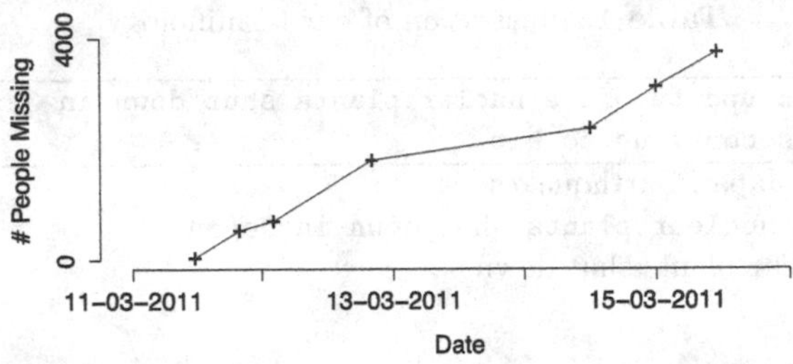

Fig. 1. Time series reconstituted from seven serial quantfrags

Detection. We now discuss how to detect qweets and quantfrags algorithmically. Most qweets contain numbers, written with letters or digits. However, Twitter data also contains a plethora of counter-examples. A post can describe a quantity without using any number:

```
"the country's strongest earthquake on record"
```

Also, it is not difficult to find numbers without quantities:

```
"Japan I pray 4 U"
"Please text the words Text Red Cross to 90999"
"Barack Obama will give a special address at 1130"
```

To complicate the matter further, many fragments form valid quantfrags, but they teach us little about the event:

```
"A fire has broken out at Cosmo Oil's 220,000 b/d Chiba
refinery after earthquake."
"I have a friend in japan. And he actually owes me ten bucks."
```

These examples show that reporting all tweets which contain numbers is a very naive solution. Raimond relies on the combination of several methods, which we will discuss thoroughly in the following section.

Single Quantfrags, Serial Quantfrags. During our experiments, we encountered two types of quantfrags. **Single quantfrags** state independent, self-contained facts. For instance, the following quantfrag is single:

```
"The Pacific Plate slid west by 79 feet"
```

Oppositely, **serial quantfrags** describe the same property of the event, but at different points in time. Therefore, they describe a time series. Here is an example of such fragments:

```
11 March 2011 - "530 people were reported missing after
#earthquake in Japan"
12 March 2011 - "about 1800 missing in #japan as a result of
#earthquake"
15 March 2011 - "at least 3,743 are missing #earthquake
#tsunami"
```

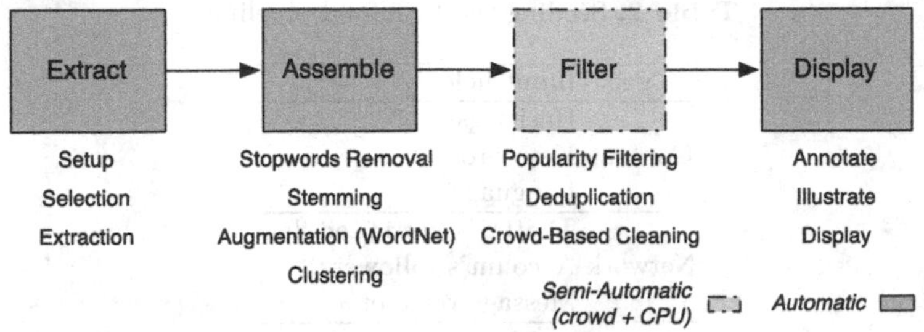

Fig. 2. Overview of the Raimond pipeline

These three quantfrags describe the number of people reported missing after the earthquakes, but at different points in time. They are particularly interesting because they let us reconstitute the original time series, as shown in Figure 1. One of Raimond's functions is to organize the quantfrags in subtopics, such that serial quantfrags are displayed together.

Validity. In general, qweets may contain approximations, omissions, exaggerations or time lags. Unfortunately, this noise is inherent to social data. For instance, thousands of tweets mentioned 88,000 missing people during the Japan earthquakes. We found no trace of the original report, and official sources hint that this number is largely overestimated[2]. Our aim is to depict microbloggers' views on events, regardless of their overlap with objective truth. Fact checking is, for now, beyond the scope of this study.

3 Methodology

Raimond's goal is to detect and organize quantfrags. To do so, it operates in four consecutive stages, pictured in Figure 2. First, Raimond detects the most promising tweets, and extracts the quantfrags. Then, it groups the fragments which cover the same topic. During the third phase, Raimond filters out the fragments which are irrelevant or not informative with a combination of coded rules and crowdsourcing. Finally, it labels and displays the clean groups.

3.1 Extracting Quantitative Data

During this first phase, Raimond detects the tweets associated to the event of interest, parses them and retrieves the quantfrags.

Setup. To seed the Raimond pipeline, we define an event configuration. The configuration specifies which authors to follow and which tweets to select. For our Japan example, we tracked the hashtag **#japan** during 5 days, and selected

[2] www.jst.go.jp/pr/pdf/great_east_japan_earthquake.pdf, page 13

Table 2. Seeding the Raimond pipeline

Type	Input field
Content	Hashtags
	Keywords
	Language
Network	Twitter's `verified` flag
	Account's followers
	Message retweets

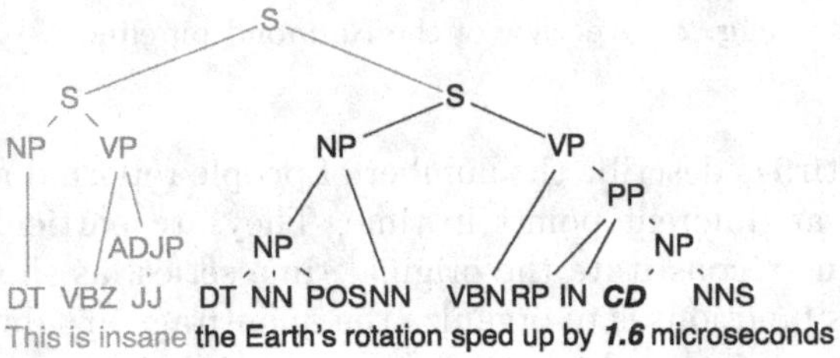

Fig. 3. Extracting quantfrags from the parse tree. The nodes of the tree represent constituent tags, as defined by the Penn Treebank. Our aim is to extract the subtree which contains the quantfrag. The quantfrag is highlighted in bold.

the posts with more than 25 retweets. Table 2 shows all the settings offered by Raimond. The aim of content-related parameters is to spot relevant tweets. Network-related parameters measure trust and influence.

Selection. Once the event configuration is defined, Raimond fetches the tweets from our archive, and it applies a filter to discard tweets with no quantities. At this point, we include every tweet which could potentially be interesting, regardless of it its quality - we value recall much more than precision. The filter relies on two tests, assembled in a disjunction. The first test uses a quantity classifier. The classifier is based on statistical learning, and it was trained internally for production purposes. For the second test, we wrote a set of regular expressions. These regular expressions detect cardinal and ordinal numbers, expressed with letters or numbers. At the end of this phase, we obtain a set of potential qweets, which typically contains lots of false positives.

Extraction. During this phase, Raimond extracts the quantfrags. Previously, we defined quantfrags as complete, minimal pieces of texts which convey a quantity. Unfortunately, evaluating whether a quantfrag is complete and minimal depends a lot on the user and the use case. Our definition is not practical. We propose to operationalize the notion as follows:

Definition 2 (operational). *A quantfrag is a grammatical clause which contains a quantity.*

To detect clauses with numbers, we use a grammatical parser. The parser takes a tweet as input, and returns a tree, as pictured in Figure 3. In this tree each node represents a grammatical constituent. We check if the tree contains a quantity, tagged `CD` (Cardinal number) in the example. If it does, we extract the smallest clause which contains this quantity (`S` in our example). If we detect several numbers, we extract one clause for each. We used an internal parser trained specifically for tweets, but several open source NLP suites can handle this type of task (e.g., Stanford NLP).

3.2 Assembling Quantfrags

In this phase, Raimond aggregates the quantfrags which describe the same topic, or, in some cases, the same variable (cf. serial quantfrags in Section 2). To achieve this, Raimond uses cluster analysis. As the quantfrags are short and noisy, preprocessing is crucial.

Preprocessing and Augmentation. To clean the quantfrags, we apply classic preprocessing operations: we replace smileys by keywords, we remove punctuation symbols and stop words, and we stem every term. Typically, the quantfrags we obtain are very short. This is problematic for clustering, because they are not likely to share terms. Consider for instance the following two quantfrags:

```
"Troops of 500+ to provide help"
"More than 500 militaries sent for assistance"
```

Both phrases have exactly the same meaning, yet they do not have any word in common. We use a lexical database, WordNet [13], to tackle this problem. For a given term, WordNet gives us hypernyms. Intuitively, a hypernym is a semantic superclass of a term. For instance, `army unit` is a hypernym of `troop`. Thanks to hypernyms, we can *augment* our quantfrags. We query the WordNet database for each noun and append the results to the fragment. This increases the chance that similar tweets share words. For instance, if we augment the first noun in each of our example tweets, we obtain:

"Troops *army unit military force* of 500+ to provide help"
"More than 500 militaries *military force organization* sent for assistance"

WordNet entries are organized in a hierarchy: hypernyms themselves have hypernyms. Therefore, we can expand our terms with several levels of generality. We used two levels of recursion in the example, we use three in our system.

In many cases, nouns have several competing WordNet entries. Each entry is represented by a set of synonyms, such as `assistance - aid - help`, or `assistance - financial aid - economic aid`. To resolve the ambiguity, we check how many of the synonyms are contained in the corpus, and keep the entry with the highest count. If the procedure finds no match, we take the most frequent sense. We refer the reader to the work of Hotho et al. for an empirical validation of this method [8].

Clustering. We represent the quantfrags with bags of words, and cluster them with agglomerative clustering [21]. We chose this approach because it is simple

Table 3. Parameters for the cluster analysis

Parameter	Range	Default
Distance	Cosine, Euclidean, p-Minkowski	Cosine
Linkage	Single, Complete, Average	Average
Maximum distance	0 - 1.0	0.9

enough to be tuned by non-technical users. Recall that agglomerative clustering operates bottom-up. To initialize the algorithm, we assign each quantfrag to its own cluster. Then, at each iteration, we detect which two clusters are the closest, and merge them. As the algorithm runs, the clusters get larger. We stop when we reached a threshold. The algorithm requires three parameters, summarized in Table 3. We must chose a distance function for quantfrags. For instance, the cosine distance is a well-established choice. We must also define how to compute the distance between clusters. Consider two clusters C_1 and C_2, and let d describe the distance measure we use for quantfrags. There are different ways to define how close these clusters are. We can use the the distance between their two closest points (single-link). In this case, we set $D(C_1, C_2) = \min\{d(x, y) : a \in C_1, y \in C_2\}$. We can use the distance between their two closes furthest points (complete-link). Then, $D(C_1, C_2) = \max\{d(x, y) : a \in C_1, y \in C_2\}$. This usually results in tighter clusters.

3.3 Filtering Irrelevant Quantfrags

During the two first phases, Raimond typically accumulates lots of false positives. Some quantfrags do not contain any quantity (`"Japan, I pray 4 u"`), are not related to the topic (`"Japan, thank you for Playstation 4!"`), are not informative (`"3 reasons why we must help Japan"`) or simply redundant. To make things worse, the clusters we detect are rarely perfect, as they may combine unrelated but lexically similar topics. To address this problem, we developed a cascade of filters, based on automatic rules and crowdsourcing. We summarize the filters in Table 4, and detail them below.

Table 4. Sequence of filters used to remove false positives

Precision Level	Filter	Computation
Cluster	Size	Machine
Quantfrag	Near-duplicates	Machine
Cluster	Relevance	Machine + Crowd
Quantfrag	Relevance	Machine + Crowd

Filtering on Popularity. Typically, the size of the clusters obey approximately a power-law distribution. We observe a few large clusters, and a long tail of micro-topics. Raimond gives the the option to select the large clusters (the head of the distribution) and discard the smaller groups. The rationale is that large clusters describe popular topics, while smaller clusters may contain noise, such as personal reaction or irrelevant facts.

Near-Duplicates Removal. So far, we have kept (near) duplicates to assess the popularity of the topics. We now eliminate the redundancy. In fact, this task is close to the clustering phase, described in 3.2. We detect near-duplicates with the exact same method, but we operate at a thinner granularity. We reuse the dendrogram structure produced at the end of the clustering phase, and we cut it at a low level of dissimilarity (by default, 0.1). We obtain lots of micro-clusters, we represent each of them by a representative quantfrag (by default, the most frequent one).

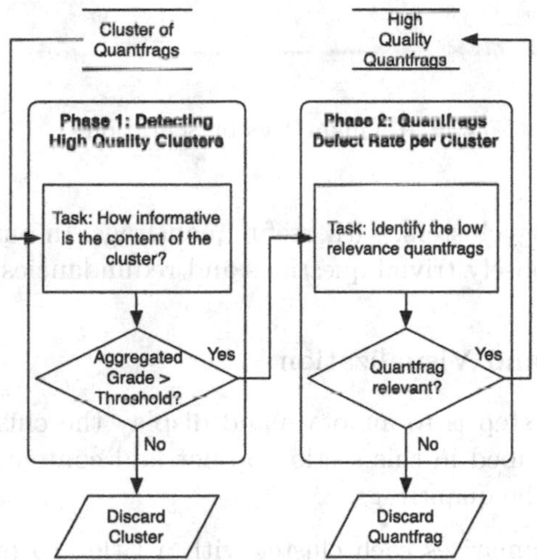

Fig. 4. Flow-Chart illustrating our crowdsourcing strategy to select high quality quantfrags

Crowd-Based Cleaning. At this stage, the collection of quantfrags still contains false positives, with numbers but no quantities. It also contains uninformative quantfrags, i.e., quantfrags which are technically valid but provide no useful information about the event. We discard those with human computation.

Our crowdsourcing strategy is based on two consecutive tasks. During the first task, workers evaluate the overall quality of the clusters. They assign a grade to each cluster, based on a relevance. We aggregate the scores, and check if the value is above a certain threshold. If not, we discard the cluster. We then run another task, in which the goal is to identify low quality quantfrags within the clusters. Figure 4 describes the overall process. We can think of this approach as a two-step quality control: the first phase checks if the cluster is relevant to the event. The second phase provides a defect rate per cluster. The final output

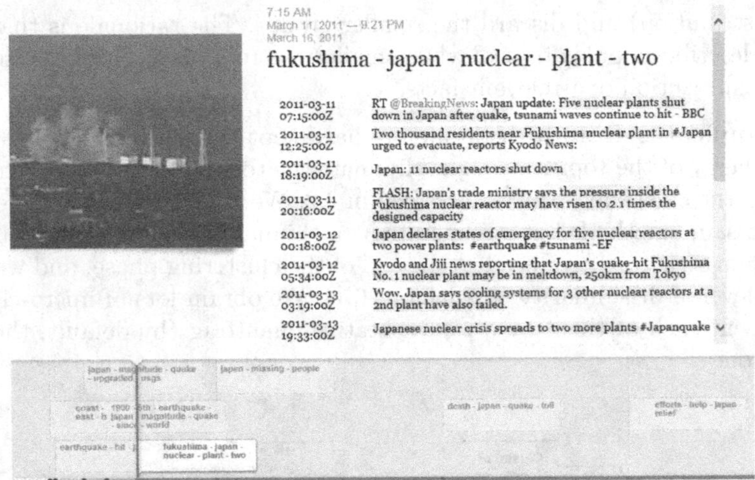

Fig. 5. Quantfrags presentation

is a set of high quality clusters, with useful quantfrags. In our surveys, we avoid spammers with purposely trivial questions and redundancies.

3.4 Annotation and Visualization

The aim of the last step is to annotate and display the clusters of quantfrags. The operations described in this section do not add content, but they enhance the presentation of the quantfrags.

Title. Raimond summarizes each cluster with a title. To produce the title, it creates documents by concatenating the quantfrags of each cluster. Then, it computes a tf-idf matrix, and reports the top k terms for each cluster/document (we set $k = 5$ for the rest of this paper).

Illustration. We observed that many qweets contain links to images. Our idea is to exploit these links to illustrate the clusters. Raimond parses the tweets for image URLs with a set of regular expressions. If it encounters such URLs, it tries to download the documents. It then presents the images side-by-side with the quantfrags in the interface. If a cluster links to several images, Raimond presents them sorted by decreasing order of popularity (using the number of retweets).

Display. Raimond's last task is to display the quantfrags. We provide a screenshot of the interface in Figure 5. The bottom part of the display presents the titles of the clusters on a timeline. To anchor the labels, we calculate *peak dates*. The peak date of a cluster is the timestamp at which it is the most popular. To calculate it, we retrieve the dates at which the quantfrags of the cluster are mentioned, estimate a density function with Gaussian density estimation and compute the mode of this distribution. We will present some examples in

Table 5. Data collection methodology and event configuration

	Ukraine	BRAvGER	Japan
Hashtags	`#ukraine`	`#bra #ger #bravger #brazil #germany`	`#japan`
Start date	1 Jan 2014	08 Jul 2014	10 Mar 2011
End date	15 May 2014	08 Jul 2014	15 Mar 2011
Author checks	Min. 200,000 followers Verified	Min. 200,000 followers Verified	Min. 25 retweets
#tweets	7,362,838	16,481,551	3,049,463

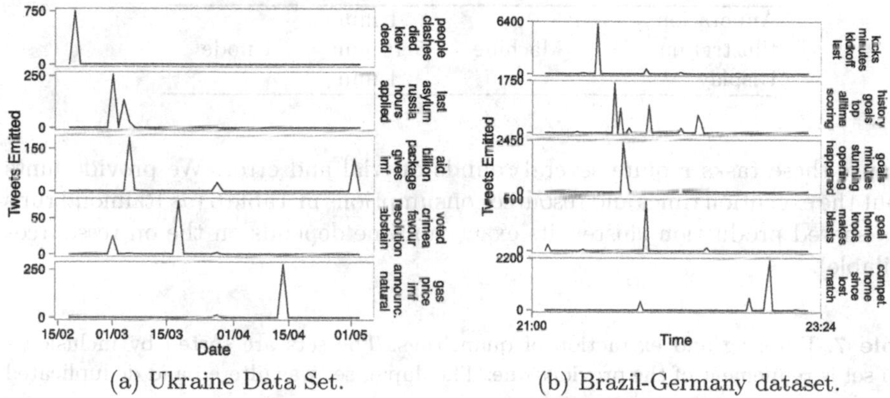

(a) Ukraine Data Set. (b) Brazil-Germany dataset.

Fig. 6. Popularity of the Clusters with Time

Section 4. Users can focus on a cluster by clicking on its title. Then, Raimond displays the quantfrags with their timestamps and the qweets from which they were extracted.

4 Use Cases

In this section, we present our experiments with three datasets. The first dataset is based the 2011 Japan earthquakes, discussed throughout the paper. The second dataset describes the political crisis in Ukraine, still ongoing at the time of writing. To obtain it, we tracked the hashtag `#ukraine` during 134 days. The third dataset contains tweets about the Brazil-Germany football game of the 2014 World Cup. Using five hashtags, we gathered approximately 16 millions of Tweets in less than 24 hours. We detail our data collection methodology and event configurations in Table 5.

In terms of implementation, Raimond runs partly on a cluster, and partly on a local machine. The cluster gives a huge throughput, but a low latency. The local machine operates the other around. Therefore, we implemented the operations which require no user intervention on the cluster (in particular the extraction). We run the Clustering step and parts of the Filtering step on the local machine,

Table 6. Hints about resource consumptions

Phase	Computation	Runtime	Resources
Extraction			
Selection	Machine	10-120 min	<500 nodes
Extractiom			
Preprocessing		30-90 min	
Augmentation	Machine		1 node
Clustering		1-5 min	
Popularity	Machine	<2 min	1 node
Deduplication			
Cleaning	Human	1-5 hours	>100 workers
Annotation		<1 min	
Illustration	Machine	5-10 min	1 node
Display		<1 min	

because these tasks require several rounds of trial and error. We provide hints about the execution times and resource consumptions in Table 6 (as Raimond runs on a shared production cluster, its exact runtime depends on the on ressources available).

Table 7. Filtering and extraction of quantfrags. The sets are sorted by inclusion - each set is refinement of the previous one. The Japan set was filtered and deduplicated before our experiments.

Dataset	Ukraine	BRAvGER	Japan
Tweets	7,326,838	16,481,551	3,049,463
. Trusted	441,151	992,980	NA
.. Unique	10,508	6,438	6,210
... Contain quantities	1,093	1,207	1,729
.... Quantfrags	718	762	1,354

Table 7 shows the size of the data as Raimond processes the tweets. We start with several million tweets. We tuned the pipeline to extract only those that come from official sources and news accounts (cf. Table 5). We obtain less than a million tweets (about 5% of the initial volume). This number includes the tweets written by official sources, but relayed by non-trusted individuals. After removing the retweets and the duplicates, we obtain less than 10,000 posts. This decrease is spectacular, but not surprising: by definition, popular accounts are massively retweeted. For instance, in the `BRAvGER` dataset, posts about spectacular actions and goals are retweeted by thousands of supporters. At the end of the pipeline, after filtering, cleaning and aggressive deduplication, we obtain a few hundred quantfrags.

Table 8 displays the labels of a few clusters generated by Raimond for the Japan dataset. As in our interface, we ordered the clusters by peak date. We observe that the topics are semantically intelligible. The first cluster describes

Table 8. Clusters from the Japan Dataset

Keywords	Peak	Size
quake, magnitude, upgraded, usgs, felt	11/03	4,029
nuclear, fukushima, plant, two, explosion	11/03	2,464
axis, moved, shifted, feet, earths	12/03	5,771
people, missing, tsunami, dead, quake	12/03	10,761
toll, death, quake, missing, tsunami	13/03	5,007
effort, help, donate, relief, redcross	13/03	7,414
plant, radiation, nuclear, fukushima, says	15/03	3,062

Table 9. Examples of clusters for the Ukraine dataset

Keywords	Peak Date	Size	Qweet
people, clashes, died, kiev, dead	18/02	1,128	"#Ukraine police say four officers have died in today's riots, 39 have sustained gunshot wounds and more than 100 others have been injured"
last, asylum, russia, hours, applied	01/03	451	"#UKRAINE: 143,000 Ukrainians have asked for asylum in #Russia for last two weeks"
aid, billion, package, gives, imf	05/03	330	"BREAKING: Top official says EU to provide #Ukraine $15 billion aid package in loans and grants"
voted, crimea, favour, resolution, abstained	14/03	765	"#Crimea parliament declares independence from #Ukraine after referendum. Final tally shows 97% voted to join #Russia"
gas, price, imf, announces, natural	13/04	406	"As the IMF announces aid package of $14-18bn for #Ukraine, the Ukrainian PM warns the price paid to Russia for gas will rise 79% from 1 Apr"
imposes, officials, sanctions, entry, russia	28/04	587	"BREAKING NEWS: #EU imposes sanctions on 21 officials from #Russia and #Ukraine over Crimea. More soon..."
donetsk, ballots, region, results, selfdefense	11/05	578	"Preliminary results show 89.7% support of self-rule in #Donetsk region, #referendum election commission says"

physical properties of the earthquake. The second one mentions the nuclear plant explosion which followed. Twitter users discuss the impact of the disaster on people and on the environment. Then, then they give more details about casualties, and encourage donations.

We show a few clusters created from the Ukraine dataset in Table 9. The quantfrags spread across a variety of small topics, such as casualties ("people, clashes, died"), international help ("aid, billion, package"), gas markets ("gas, price, imf") or sanctions ("imposes, officials, sanctions"). We describe the dynamics of the five first clusters in Figure 6a. To obtain these charts, we tracked the number of quantfrags produced for each cluster. We observe bursts, which

Table 10. Examples of clusters for the BRAvGER dataset

Keywords	Peak Time	Size	Qweet
reach, semifinals, first, country, consecutive	17:40:22	2,671	"GER is the first team ever to reach four straight #WorldCup semifinals."
kicks, minutes, every, kickoff, less	18:01:22	7,095	"Still more than two hours to go until kick-off... #Copacabana #Brazil "
history, goals, top, alltime, scoring	21:37:26	4,683	"#GER have now scored 221 goals in #WorldCup history, more than any other side and one ahead of #BRA."
goals, minutes, stun, opening, happened	21:47:02	3,535	" That. Just. Happened. Germany stun Brazil with 5 goals in the opening 29 minutes."
goal, home, kroos, makes, blasts	21:51:09	921	"#GER 5 goals in the first 29 minutes!" ''6-0... Germany got once and GOAL... #Amazing'' ''GOAL!!!! '79 Schurrle blasts home a pitch-perfect pass from Mueller to make it 7-0.''
klose, record, now, miroslav, goals	22:57:58	5,331	"#GER's Mirsolav Klose has a chance to break his record of 15 #WorldCup goals against Brazil."
competitive, home, since, lost, match	23:00:02	4,275	"Entering this match, Brazil had not lost a competitive game on home soil in 14,161 days. Until today.... #BRAvsGER"

last several hours, sometimes days. These bursts actually reflect real events. The first cluster describes the clashes which took place on February 18th and 20th. According to the quantfrags, this was the worse day of violence that Ukraine had known in 70 years. During the followed two weeks, several hundred thousands Ukrainians asked for asylum to Russia and a $15 billion Dollars help package was approved by the European Union. The fourth cluster describes the outcome of the Crimean status referendum, which happened on March 16th. Finally, the last cluster discusses a raise in consumer gas tariffs, requested by the IMF in exchange for a rescue loan.

Table 10 presents our Brazil-Germany dataset. As opposed to our previous example, the clusters are semantically close to each other - they are all somehow related to scoring goals. We highlight serial quantfrags in the fifth cluster ("goal, home, kroos"): the count of German goals is regulary incremented, finally reaching seven goals. We detail the dynamics of the clusters in Figure 6b. We see that they appear in short, intense bursts of several minutes. The game starts at 21.00, the first cluster discusses the kick-off. Within the first 30 minutes, the German team scores five goals. This triggers two consecutive clusters, explaining with quantities why the event is "historical" and "stunning". For instance, Germany is the first country to score 221 goals in a World Cup. With two goals

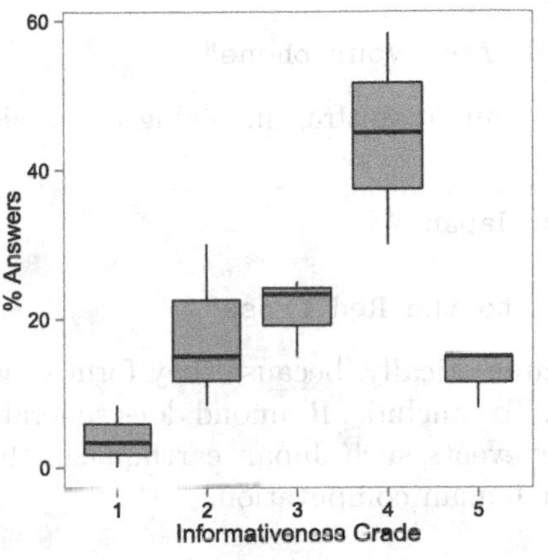

(a) Distribution of the grades for every datasets combined.

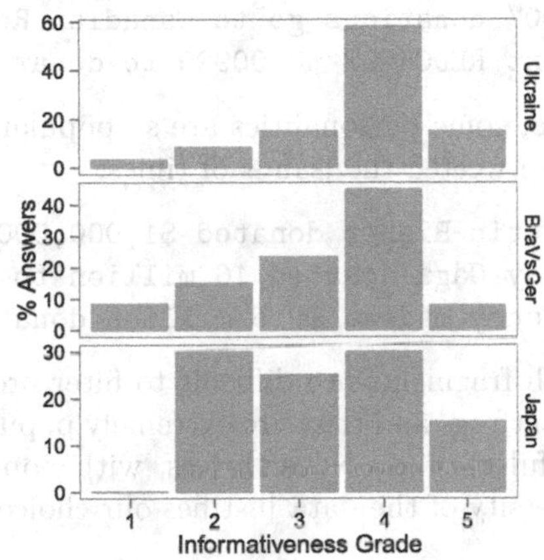

(b) Grades for each dataset.

Fig. 7. Crowdsourcing experiment results

in two minutes, the main attacker, Tony Kroos, has a cluster on his own. The last cluster shows that Brazil had not been defeated at home since 1975.

5 Crowdsourcing Experiments

In this Section, we evaluate the effectiveness of Raimond's output. We process the three datasets introduced in Section 4, and present the clusters to a set of crowdworkers. We ask them if the quantfrags contain quantitive information, and how *informative* this information is, with a grade between 1 (not informative) and 5 (very informative). As we only have a limited pool of workers, we decided to remove the crowd-based filtering step from the pipeline - to avoid having workers check their own work. Thus, our evaluation is conservative. We evaluated 70 clusters (20 for Ukraine and Brazil-Germany, 30 for Japan), containing between 2 and 75 quantfrags. Each cluster is reviewed by at least two workers.

Figure 7a represents the overall distribution of the grades. The neat dominance of the the value 4 indicates that most clusters are informative. Nevertheless, Raimond also returns some noise: about a fifth of the clusters have a grade lower than 2.

Figure 7b shows the grades for each dataset. The Ukraine and Brazil-Germany clusters have good scores. In the Ukraine case, more than 90% of the clusters have at least a grade of 3. Most of the noise comes from the Japan dataset. There are many informative clusters, but there are about as many irrelevant clusters. Further inspection revealed lots of calls for donations, such as:

```
"Txt ASIA to 30333 to donate $5."
"100% donations go to Canadian Red Cross"
"text REDCROSS to 90999 to donate $10 from your phone"
```

Also, some personalities are so popular that any quantfrag involving them will be retweeted thousands of times:

```
"Justin Bieber donated $1,000,000 to Japan."
"Lady Gaga donated 16 million to Japan"
"Disney made a $2.5 million donation to the Red Cross"
```

Such fragments are difficult to filter programmatically, because they form valid quantfrags and they are extremely popular. To conclude, Raimond does generate useful clusters. Nevertheless, with popular events such Japan earthquake, the diversity of the data justifies our choice for human computation.

6 Related Work

Studying events on social media has gained considerable interest in the last five years. In particular, catastrophes and emergency situations have attracted lots of attention [9]. The resulting works can be classified in four categories: event detection, event summarization, information extraction and visualization (note that these areas overlap). We describe these works below. There is to our knowledge no previous work on quantitative data extraction from Twitter.

Sayyadi et al. have published one the first study on event detection with social media, based on lexical community detection [20]. Sakaki et al. use microblogging to detect earthquakes and track their location [19]. Popescu and Pennachiotti focus on controversial events, which they recognize with supervised learning [16]. Petrović et al. focus on computational efficiency. They present a scalable algorithm based on Locality-Sensitive Hashing [14].

Authors have investigated how to extract key sentences to summarize a text for decades [11]. In 2001, Allan and Khandelwal proposed a method to summarize news coverage. They decompose a main event in sub-events with language models, and describe each sub-topic with a piece of news [2]. Several studies have extended this method to social data with more advanced statistical models. For instance, Chakrabarti et al. use a custom version of Hidden Markov Models to segment the events [6].

Extracting structured information about events from social media involves complex NLP methods. One of first the research effort on the topic was presented by Popsecu et al., who use entity extraction to recognize actors [17]. Benson et al. go one step further, as they infer structured records about entertainment events from Twitter [5]. Imran et al. combine several classifiers and a sequence labelling algorithm to extract structured information about disasters [10]. These approaches are generalized by Ritter et all, who introduce a method to analyze events in open domains. They present a pipeline, somehow similar to Raimond, which extracts names entities, event phrases, calendar dates and event type. Their pipeline combines cutom NLP tools and unsupervised learning [18].

Finally, several authors have studied how to create visual dashboards from Twitter to describe events. Diakopoulos et al. combine raw data, automatically-generated statistics (such as sentiment or relevance) and timelines to help journalists [7]. Marcus et al. propose a similar system, with geographical information and peak detection [12]. Alonso and Shiells introduce a display based on multiple timelines, and illustrate their method with sports events [4].

A number of studies resemble ours by their methods, but target other problems. Alonso et al. study to what extent crowdsourcing can be used to assess the interestingness of tweets [3]. For instance, NIFTY by Suen et al. is also an information extraction pipeline based on Twitter and unsupervised learning. However, it focuses meme-tracking [22]. More generally, news processing is an active related domain of research [1,15].

7 Conclusions and Future Work

Short posts on social networks provide lots of opportunities to communicate quantitative information. We described Raimond, a pipeline to extract this content from Twitter. We introduced quantfrags, and illustrated the concept with a number of examples. We presented how to extract quantfrags with the help of NLP techniques, how to organize them with clustering, and how to clean them with a hybrid automatic/crowdsourcing approach. Finally, we showcased quantfrags about a three real events. We described their semantics, their dynamics and evaluated their content.

We believe that many exciting developments can come from our work. We will generalize our pipeline to more general topics (not just events) and other data sources. We will also adapt it to real-time, incremental settings. Finally, we will investigate how to exploit our crowdsourced labels for machine learning.

More generally, the road for further automation lays wide open. Reconstituting time series from text without human intervention is still an open problem. This task implies many challenges: how can we normalize the quantfrags? How can we check the facts? How do we resolve inconsistencies? The technologies to be developed go far beyond the strict realm of social networks.

Acknowledgments. We thank Aitao Chen, from Microsoft Research for his NLP suite, his time and his insights. We thank Martin Kersten and Stefan Manegold for their support.

References

1. Ahmed, A., Ho, Q., Eisenstein, J., Xing, E., Smola, A.J., Teo, C.H.: Unified analysis of streaming news. In: Proc. WWW, pp. 267–276 (2011)
2. Allan, J., Gupta, R., Khandelwal, V.: Temporal summaries of new topics. In: Proc. SIGIR, pp. 10–18. ACM (2001)
3. Alonso, O., Marshall, C.C., Najork, M.: Are some tweets more interesting than others? #hardquestion. In: HCIR, p. 2. ACM (2013)

4. Alonso, O., Shiells, K.: Timelines as summaries of popular scheduled events. In: Proc. WWW, pp. 1037–1044 (2013)
5. Benson, E., Haghighi, A., Barzilay, R.: Event discovery in social media feeds. In: Proc. ACL, pp. 389–398. Association for Computational Linguistics (2011)
6. Chakrabarti, D., Punera, K.: Event summarization using tweets. In: Proc. ICWSM, pp. 66–73. AAAI Press (2011)
7. Diakopoulos, N.: Diamonds in the rough: Social media visual analytics for journalistic inquiry. In: Proc. VAST, pp. 115–122. IEEE (2010)
8. Hotho, A., Staab, S., Stumme, G.: Ontologies improve text document clustering. In: Proc. ICDM, pp. 541–544. IEEE (2003)
9. Imran, M., Castillo, C., Diaz, F., Vieweg, S.: Processing social media messages in mass emergency: A survey. In: CoRR. arXiv preprint: 1407.7071 (2014)
10. Imran, M., Elbassuoni, S., Castillo, C.: Practical extraction of disaster-relevant information from social media. In: Proc. WWW, pp. 1021–1024 (2013)
11. Luhn, H.: The automatic creation of literature abstracts. IBM Journal of Research and Development, 159–165 (1958)
12. Marcus, A., Bernstein, M., Badar, O.: Twitinfo: aggregating and visualizing microblogs for event exploration. In: Proc. CHI, pp. 227–236. ACM (2011)
13. Miller, G.A.: Wordnet: a lexical database for english. In: CACM, vol. 38, pp. 39–41. ACM (1995)
14. Petrović, S., Osborne, M., Lavrenko, V.: Streaming first story detection with application to twitter. In: NAACL, pp. 181–189. Association for Computational Linguistics (2010)
15. Phan, X.H., Nguyen, L.M., Horiguchi, S.: Learning to classify short and sparse text & web with hidden topics from large-scale data collections. In: Proc. WWW, pp. 91–100 (2008)
16. Popescu, A.M., Pennacchiotti, M.: Detecting controversial events from twitter. In: Proc. CIKM, p. 1873. ACM (2010)
17. Popescu, A.M., Pennacchiotti, M., Paranjpe, D.: Extracting events and event descriptions from Twitter. In: Proc. WWW, p. 105 (2011)
18. Ritter, A., Etzioni, O., Clark, S.: Open domain event extraction from twitter. In: KDD, p. 1104. ACM (2012)
19. Sakaki, T., Okazaki, M., Matsuo, Y.: Earthquake shakes Twitter users: real-time event detection by social sensors. In: Proc. WWW, pp. 851–860 (2010)
20. Sayyadi, H., Hurst, M., Maykov, A.: Event detection and tracking in social streams. In: Proc. ICWSM, pp. 311–314. AAAI Press (2009)
21. Sokal, R.R.: A statistical method for evaluating systematic relationships. U. Kansas Scientific Bulletin **38**, 1409–1438 (1958)
22. Suen, C., Huang, S., Eksombatchai, C., Sosic, R., Leskovec, J.: Nifty: a system for large scale information flow tracking and clustering. In: Proc. WWW, pp. 1237–1248 (2013)
23. Tufte, E.: The visual display of quantitative information. Graphics Press Cheshire, CT (1983)

A K-shell Decomposition Based Algorithm for Influence Maximization

Qian Zhao, Hongwei Lu, Zaobin Gan(✉), and Xiao Ma

School of Computer Science and Technology, Huazhong University of Science and Technology, Wuhan 430074, PR China
zqhuster@163.com, {luhw,zgan,cindyma}@mail.hust.edu.cn

Abstract. Influence maximization is an issue to find a K-node seed set of influential nodes that can maximize the number of influenced nodes in a social network, where K is a given parameter. A greedy algorithm can approximate the optimal result within a factor of $(1 - 1/e - \varepsilon)$, but it is computationally expensive. The degree-based heuristic algorithm is simple, but it is of unstable accuracy without considering propagation characteristics. To address these issues, a k-shell decomposition algorithm(KDA) for influence maximization is proposed under the linear threshold model in this paper. First, we present an improved greedy algorithm(IGA) by discarding some unnecessary calculations. Secondly, the network is decomposed using a k-shell decomposition method to calculate the potential influence of nodes. Finally the nodes with the largest potential influence and the nodes with the largest marginal influence degrees are selected at each step to compose a K-node seed set. The experimental results show that KDA can achieve both high efficiency and high accuracy, compared with the existing representative algorithms.

Keywords: Influence maximization · K-shell Decomposition · Information diffusion · Greedy selection strategy

1 Introduction

A social network is composed of nodes representing individuals and edges corresponding to relationship types between individuals such as friendship, collaboration, interaction, etc. This kind of complex network structure plays an important role for the spread of information in the form of "word-of-mouth". Motivated by the viral marketing and "word-of-mouth"marketing, Domingos and Richardson[1] proposed the problem of influence maximization in a social network. It aims to find a K-node seed set of influential nodes that can trigger the largest expected number of follow-ups for a parameter K, according to a chosen diffusion model.

One corresponding issue in marketing is product promotion. In order to market a new product with a limited budget, a company can select a small number of target customers in a social network by giving them some free samples of the new product, and expects that they can recommend the product to their

P. Cimiano et al. (Eds.): ICWE 2015, LNCS 9114, pp. 269–283, 2015.
DOI: 10.1007/978-3-319-19890-3_18

friends or influence their friends' behaviors, then their friends will influence their friends' friends, and so on. The cascade propagation will keep going. In this way, many individuals will eventually adopt the new product in the form of "word-of-mouth".

We call the small number of customers as influential individuals. So the problem here is how to choose a set of influential individuals who can trigger a massive cascade of influence. Analogously, for the spread of computer viruses on computer networks, the spread of infectious diseases in the crowd, and the spread of rumors in the society, and the like, the set of influential nodes needs to be targeted and removed to control the unhealthy diffusion. Hence, the problem of influence maximization can be also called as a target set selection problem and it has great practical significance in the marketing, the ad publishing, the virus spreading, and the public opinions pre-warning.

Kempe et al.[2] established that the optimization problem of influence maximization is NP-hard, and they proposed a GA(Greedy Algorithm) which is proved to provide a $(1-1/e-\varepsilon)$ approximation to the optimal result of influence maximization. It repeatedly picks the node with the maximal marginal influence degree and adds it to the seed set, until K is reached, so it is time-consuming and not the global optimal result. On the other hand, there exists some other heuristic algorithms, for example, the degree-based heuristic algorithm[2] is simple and has low computational cost, but it estimates influence spread using efficient heuristics, hence it is of unstable accuracy and has a unreliable performance.

In order to address these issues, we leverage the benefits of greedy algorithms and heuristic algorithms simultaneously, and propose a KDA algorithm for influence maximization.

The rest of this paper is as follows: In Section 2, the information diffusion models and the related work are presented. Section 3 discusses IGA and KDA in detail. Experimental results and analysis are given in Section 4, followed by conclusions and future work in Section 5.

2 Background

2.1 Information Diffusion Models

In the field of information diffusion, some diffusion models have been proposed. Generally, a network is abstracted as a graph $G(V, E)$, where V denotes the set of nodes, and E denotes the set of edges between two nodes. Each node has two states: active and inactive. Active nodes can influence other inactive nodes. The state of a node can be switched from being inactive to being active, but not vice versa. Most of the researches are based on two diffusion models, called the independent cascade model[3,4] and the linear threshold model[5].

The IC(Independent Cascade) model is a probabilistic information diffusion model. Each active node has its own independent cascade. At step t, an active node u has a single chance to influence its neighbor v with a probability b_{uv}. If u fails in activating v, then u will not attempt to activate v again. b_{uv} is a user-specified parameter, but Kemple et al.[2] think it will decrease over time and propose a decreasing cascade model. Kim et al.[6] proposed a new model CT-IC model, in which activation continues until a given time.

In the LT(Linear Threshold) model, an active node u has an influence weight b_{uv} on its neighbor v. $N(v)$ is defined as the neighborhood set of the node v. For every node v in the network, the total influence weights of its neighbors are subject to the constraint that $\sum_{u \in N(v)} b_{uv} \leq 1$. Each node v has a threshold θ_v ranging from $[0,1]$. At step t, an inactive node v becomes active if $\sum_{u \in A(v)} b_{uv} \geq \theta_v$, where $A(v)$ is the set of v's active neighbors. This model embodies a character of accumulation. At step t, if an active node u fails in activating its inactive neighbor v, then the influence will be accumulated and contribute to the latter activation. He et at.[7] proposed competitive LT model in which two competing opinions are spread in a LT model manner.

In both models, the process continues until no more activations are available. These two models reflects two aspects of social interaction. The IC model focuses on individual interaction and influence among friends in a social network, in which an individual is influenced independently by another one. While the LT model focuses on the accumulation influence, which is more suitable to reflect the social reality. For example, suppose some of our friends had bought a new product, we may be influenced by them to buy this product. So in this paper, we focus upon the LT model.

2.2 Related Work

Since Domingos and Richardson proposed the problem of influence maximization[1], it has drawn wide attention. GA in [2] is computationally expensive. Many efforts have been made to improve the efficiency of GA for influence maximization. Leskovec et al.[8] proposed an efficient approximation algorithm called CELF. It reduces the number of evaluations using the submodularity property of the influence maximization objective. But it cannot scale up to larger networks[11]. Chen et al.[12] proposed a NewGreedy algorithm to improve the greedy algorithm. Later CELF++[9] and UBLF[10] were proposed to improve CELF by exploiting submodularity. However, the number of activated nodes is not a submodular function of the targeted set for a fixed choice of thresholds[2].

Jiang et al.[13] proposed an algorithm based on simulated annealing to find the top-K influential nodes, but the initial temperature T_0 and the diminishing parameter ΔT are hard to choose. In [14], Borgs et al. presented a fast algorithm for influence maximization. Xu et al.[15] proposed an algorithm based on the influence transitivity, but its running time is 72% higher than that of GA in a graph with 15,437 nodes. Cheng et al.[16] proposed a novel framework IMRank with a remarkable efficiency and a high accuracy. Zhang et al.[17] proposed a novel method for identifying influential nodes in complex networks with community structure.

They are all designing using specific properties of the IC model, supposing the influence between individuals is independent, and do not apply to the LT model. To improve the efficiency of seed selection under the LT model, Chen et al.[18] proposed a scalable LDAG algorithm. Its idea is to construct a local DAG surrounding every node in the network and consider influence within it. Later Goyal et al.[19] proposed a SIMPATH algorithm by searching all the simple paths. It is based on the CELF optimization that iteratively selects seeds in a lazy forward manner. They adopted a parameter η to control the size of the neighborhood.

Ben-Zwi et at.[20] proposed an exact almost optimal algorithm for TARGET SET SELECTION. But the treewidth parameter determines the complexity to a large extent. Bhagat et al.[21] aimed to maximize the number of product adoptions based on the LT model. Goyal et al.[22] studied the problem of minimum target set selection. They added a threshold η, meaning that η nodes are eventually activated in the expected sense. In [23], Narayanam and Narahari proposed a SPIN algorithm based on the Shapley Value. But it relies on the evaluation of influence spreads of seed sets. Lu et al.[24] proposed a LMT algorithm for influence maximization. It computes the expected influence spread within a small number of hops. It solved the influence estimation problem by adding a hop constraint T.

Among existing algorithms for influence maximization, greedy algorithms give a guaranteed accuracy, but suffer from severe performance issues. The degree-based and some other heuristic algorithms have low computational cost, but they are of unstable accuracy. Therefore, a KDA algorithm is proposed in this paper.

3 The KDA Algorithm

In Section 3.1, the potential influence evaluation is introduced, and we improve the greedy algorithm in Section 3.2. Then a detailed description of the KDA algorithm is presented in Section 3.3.

3.1 Potential Influence Evaluation

The problem of influence maximization aims to find top-K nodes which can maximize the spread of influence. Since it is time-consuming to repeatedly pick K nodes with the maximal marginal influence degree, and the influence can be accumulated under the LT model, we can find some potential influential nodes by some heuristics. When the influence is accumulated enough, we can then use the greedy selection strategy to get the rest of the K seed nodes.

So far, there exists many evaluation approaches of individual influence. They are mainly based on the degree, closeness centrality[25], PageRank[26], and so on. But their time complexities are high. What's more, as shown in Fig. 1, though node 1's degree(4) is higher than node 15's(3), the degrees of node 1's neighbors are low. For node 15, though its degree is low, the degrees of its neighbors are high. So node 15 is more influential and will spread more widely than node 1. Therefore, the node with the largest degree may not be the most influential node in some cases, and the degree is actually not a good factor for individual influence evaluation.

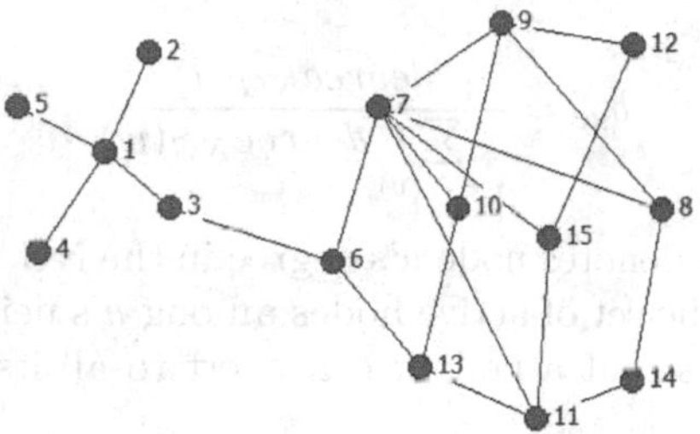

Fig. 1. A network with 15 nodes

Here, a k-shell decomposition method is used to evaluate the potential influence. It is proposed by Pittel et al. in [28]. Carmi et al.[27] used this method to find a model for the structure of the Internet. Although the k-shell decomposition method has limitations[17], Hu et al.[29] have showed that the most efficient spreaders are those located within the network core, as identified by k-shell decomposition. Using this method, a network is decomposed into its k-shells, and all nodes will get a k-shell value after the decomposition.

The k-shell method is described as follows. All nodes with degree 1 and their links are removed. After removing all the nodes with degree 1, some nodes may be left with one link, so we continue pruning the system iteratively until there is no node with degree 1 in the network. Those removed nodes are assigned to the 1-shell. In the same manner, the nodes with degree 2(or less) and their links are removed, creating 2-shell. The process continues, and let $k = 3, 4, ...$, until all the nodes in the network have been assigned to one of the shells.

Then as shown in Fig. 1, first, node 2, node 4 and node 5 with degree 1 are removed. After that, the remaining node 1 and node 3 are left with only one link, and both of them are removed. These removed nodes are assigned to the 1-shell. Then let $k = 2$, node 6, node 12, and node 14 with degre 2 are removed, after which, node 8 and node 13 are left with degree 2, so they are both removed. We continue removing nodes until all the nodes are removed. Finally all the remaining nodes in the network are assigned to the 2-shell. So node 1 is assigned to the 1-shell, and node 15 is assigned to the 2-shell. In this way, the larger the k-shell value of a node $v_i (i = 1, 2, ..., 15)$ is, the closer is v_i to the core of the network. So we can conclude that node v_i is more influential.

Because a node v is influenced by each neighbor u according to an influence weight b_{uv}, the influence weight is also another factor to determine nodes' potential influence. In the LT model, the influence weight b_{uv} is generally computed by $1/degree(v)$, considering the influence weights of v's every incoming edge are the same. But this evaluation neglects the difference between a node's neighbors. So Wang et al.[30] proposed a new estimate of b_{uv} by taking account of not only the number of v's neighbors but also how their neighbors connect to each other. First a NG(Neighbor Graph) of node v is constructed, made up of v, v's neighbors and the links between them. $N(v)$ is defined as the neighborhood set of v. Then b_{uv} is defined by formula 1.

$$b_{uv} = \frac{degree_{NG}(u)}{\sum\limits_{w \in N(v)} degree_{NG}(w)} \tag{1}$$

where $degree_{NG}(u)$ denotes node u's degree in the NG, rather than the whole network. Let $A(u)$ be the set of active nodes among u's neighbors. Then the sum of the influence weights that a node u can exert to all its inactive neighbors is defined by formula 2.

$$f(u) = \sum_{v \in N(u), v \notin A(u)} b_{uv} \tag{2}$$

b_{uv} ranges from 0 to 1, so $f(u)$ may be larger than 1, and can be mapped to the range of $[0, 1]$. Define $u_{k-shell}$ as the k-shell value of a node u. The larger the $u_{k-shell}$ is, the more likely u will be close to the core of the network. For the nodes in the same k-shell, if u's $f(u)$ is the largest, then u is obviously the most potential influential node. Hence, u's potential influence $p(u)$ can be defined by formula 3.

$$p(u) = u_{k-shell} \cdot (1 - e^{-f(u)}) \tag{3}$$

For the k-shell decomposition, many nodes may be assigned to the same shell. By formula 3, all the nodes' k-shell values are done some discount by the sum of the influence weights. So it's almost impossible for two nodes to have the same potential influence. The node u with the largest $p(u)$ is the most potential influential node.

3.2 Improved Greedy Algorithm

Given a network $G(V, E)$, V represents the set of nodes and E denotes the set of edges. S_{k-1} is the set of seed nodes at step k, $1 \leq k \leq K$, where K is the size of the seed set. If S_k is the set of initially active nodes(target set), then $R(S_k)$ is the set of active nodes at the end of the diffusion process. $\Delta R(v|S_{k-1}) = R(S_{k-1} \cup \{v\}) - R(S_{k-1})$ is the set of activated nodes with respect to the expected spread of the current seed set S_{k-1} at step k. Then $|\Delta R(v|S_{k-1})|$ is the marginal influence degree of node v. A_{k-1} is the set of active nodes at step k.

In general GA, we select the node u that provides the largest marginal influence degree at each step k, meaning the node $u = argmax_{v \in V \setminus A_{k-1}} |\Delta R(v|S_{k-1})|$. Then $S_k = S_{k-1} \cup \{u\}$ and A_k is updated. At each step, the seed is mined among all the inactive nodes. In fact, in the LT model for a fixed threshold, this greedy selection strategy is time-consuming.

Suppose that at step k, when computing node u's marginal influence degree, a node t is activated. In the LT model, the propagation continues until no more nodes can be activated, so obviously, $\Delta R(t|S_{k-1}) \subseteq \Delta R(u|S_{k-1})$, therefore, u's marginal influence degree is larger than t's. In this way, u is more likely to be selected as a seed instead of t. For a next inactive node v, whether v's marginal degree is larger or smaller than u's, t's marginal influence degree doesn't need to be computed later.

As argued above, it is unnecessary to compute the marginal influence degrees of all the inactive nodes at each step. For a node u, when u's marginal influence degree is computed, the nodes activated by u can be neglected and their marginal influence degrees don't need to be computed. Based on this idea, we can just compute part of the inactive nodes' marginal influence degrees at each step.

Because each step of IGA is the same operation, we just describe a step of IGA in Algorithm 1. n is the number of nodes in the network. Suppose that at step k, R_k is the total set of nodes activated by nodes whose marginal influence degrees are computed. At each loop, if a node u is subject to the constraint that $u \notin R_k$ && $u \notin A_{k-1}$, then it is selected to compute its marginal influence degree. Next the set R_k is updated. Finally, the node u_{max} with the maximal marginal influence degree can be acquired. Obviously, suppose that the number of the average diffusion steps is D for each node in the network, then the time complexity is $O(nD)$.

Algorithm 1. *FindMaxInfluence*

input: A_{k-1}, S_{k-1}, n

$effect = 0$ // meaning the marginal influence degree
$effect_{max} = 0$; $u_{max} = 0$
$R_k = \phi$ // initiate the R_k set
for $u = 1 : n$ **do**
  $\Delta R(u|S_{k-1}) = \phi$
  if $u \notin R_k$ && $u \notin A_{k-1}$ **then**
    $effect = |\Delta R(u|S_{k-1})|$
    $R_k = R_k \cup \Delta R(u|S_{k-1})$
   if $effect_{max} < effect$ **then**
     $effect_{max} = effect$
     $u_{max} = u$
   end if
  end if
end for

output: the node u_{max}

3.3 Algorithm Description

Using the characteristic of accumulation in the LT model, KDA has two phases: the heuristic selection and the greedy selection. The heuristic factor is c, $c \in [0, 1]$. The KDA algorithm is described in Algorithm 2. First we compute the k-shell values of all the nodes in the network. Then the influence weights are computed by formula 1. In phase 1, $p(u)$ is computed by formula 3, and the nodes with the largest $p(u)$ are selected heuristically as seeds in k_1 steps, where $k_1 = K - \lceil c \cdot K \rceil$. K is the size of the seed set. Then S_i and A_i are updated.

In phase 2, the number of steps is $k_2 = \lceil c \cdot K \rceil$. At each step, if a node has the largest marginal influence degree, then it is selected as a seed, where IGA is applied. Similarly, S_{i+k_1} and A_{i+k_1} are updated. After k_2 steps in phase 2, the set of seed nodes S_K can be acquired. It is obvious that when $c = 1$, the influence results of KDA are the same as that of GA.

Algorithm 2. KDA

input: $G(V, E)$, target set size K, factor c

1: $A_0 = A_1 = A_2 = ... = A_K = \phi$
2: $S_0 = S_1 = S_2 = ... = S_K = \phi$
3: $k_1 = K - \lceil cK \rceil$
4: $k_2 = \lceil cK \rceil$
5: **for** node $v \in V$ **do**
6: calculate $v_{k-shell}$
7: **end for**
8: **for** node $v \in V$ **do**
9: construct the NG(Neighbor Graph) for node v
10: **for** neighbor $u \in N(v)$ **do**
11: calculate b_{uv}
12: **end for**
13: **end for**
14: **for** i=1: k_1 **do**
15: $u = argmax_{v \notin A_{i-1}} p(v)$
16: $S_i = S_{i-1} \bigcup \{u\}$
17: let node u to influence other inactive nodes
18: update A_i
19: **end for**
20: **for** i=1: k_2 **do**
21: $u = findMaxInfluence(A_{i-1+k_1}, S_{i-1+k_1}, n)$
22: $S_{i+k_1} = S_{i-1+k_1} \bigcup \{u\}$
23: let node u to influence other inactive nodes
24: update A_{i+k_1}
25: **end for**

output: S_K

In Algorithm 2, the calculation of k-shell values in lines 5-7 needs $O(nd)$ time, where d is the average degree for every node. The lines 8-13 compute the influence by constructing NGs, so they take $O(nd)$ running time. The heuristic selection strategy in lines 14-19 need to calculate the potential influence degree, so the time complexity is $O(k_1(nd+D))$ in phase 1. The greedy selection strategy in lines 20-25 uses IGA described in Algorithm 1, then its time complexity is $O(k_2(nD+D))$

in phase 2. Therefore, the time complexity of KDA is determined by the greedy selection strategy in phase 2, and KDA's time complexity is $O(KnD)$.

4 Experimental Results and Analysis

In this section, KDA is tested on several network datasets ranging from small networks to large scale networks, to demonstrate the effectiveness and the efficiency of the KDA algorithm, compared with other well-known algorithms for influence maximization. The code is written in C language using the compiler VS2010. All the experiments are run on a 32-bit Windows 7 machine with 4GB memory.

4.1 Datasets

We select four datasets. These datasets vary in size and features thus we can test the performance of KDA in different cases. The four datasets include: a) **Email**, the Email network[31] is the network of e-mail interchanges between members of the Rovira i Virgili University(Tarragona)[1]. It has 1133 nodes and 5451 edges in total.

b) **Yeast-protein**, the Yeast Protein network[32] is the network of interactions between proteins[2], with 2361 nodes including 77 isolated nodes representing proteins and 6646 edges representing the interaction between proteins.

c) **PGP**, the PGP network[33] is a list of edges of the giant component of the network for secure information interchange[3]. It has 10680 nodes representing users and 24340 edges representing information interchange.

d) **NetHEPT**, the NetHEPT network is a collaboration network taken from the "High Energy Physics - Theory" section of the arXiv website[4]. It has 15233 nodes representing authors and 58891 edges representing co-authorship[5]. This dataset is widely used for influence maximization evaluation[11,18].

4.2 Algorithms Compared

In the experiments, θ_v is set as the classical threshold of 0.5 given by [2]. In the LT model, we use the b_{uv} described in formula 1 for the four graphs. Because so many algorithms are designed using specific properties of the IC model, much less work has been done for the LT model, we select some heuristics for the comparison and the LDAG algorithm[18] for the LT model. The compared algorithms include:

a) **Degree**, it's a heuristic algorithm based on the degree, considering high degree nodes as influential nodes[2].

---

1 http://deim.urv.cat/~alexandre.arenas/data/welcome.htm
2 http://vlado.fmf.uni-lj.si/pub/networks/data/bio/Yeast/Yeast.htm
3 http://deim.urv.cat/~alexandre.arenas/data/welcome.htm
4 http://arxiv.org/
5 http://research.microsoft.com/en-us/people/weic/graphdata.zip

b) **GA**, the GA algorithm picks K nodes with the maximal marginal influence gain[2].

c) **PageRank**, the PageRank algorithm is a link analysis algorithm to rank the importance of pages in the Web sites[26]. The damping factor is set as 0.85.

d) **LDAG**, it is proposed in [18], the parameter is set as $\theta = 1/320$ to control the size of the local LDAG for each node as recommended by the authors.

4.3 Experimental Results

The results of KDA with various K and c on Email and Yeast-protein are shown in Fig. 2. For a given K, when c varies, the results are different. When $c = 1$, the results of KDA are the same as that of GA. Fig. 2(a) shows the results on the Email dataset. When $K \leq 30$, KDA with $c = 0$ performs the worst, and when $K > 30$, GA performs worse than the others. The results with $c = 0.2$ and that with $c = 0.5$ are nearly the same. When $c = 0.8$ and $k = 50$, the influence degree decreases. KDA achieves the best performance when c is around 0.4.

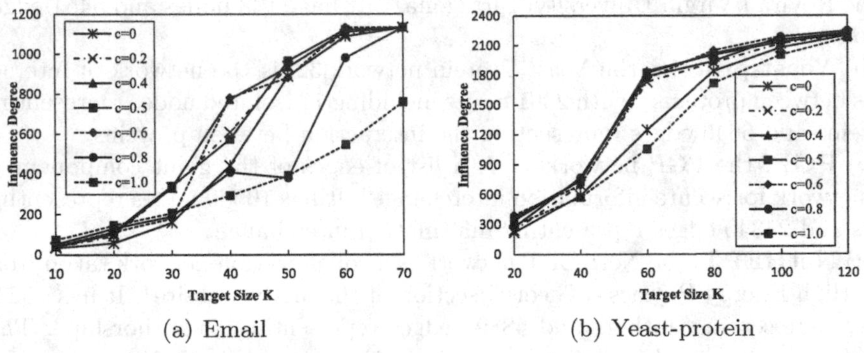

(a) Email (b) Yeast-protein

Fig. 2. Results of KDA with various K and c on networks

Fig. 2(b) demonstrates the results of KDA on Yeast-protein. The influence degree increases when K increases. There is not so much difference when c ranges from 0.4 to 0.6. It performs worse than others when $c = 1$ and $c = 0$.

Synthesize the experimental results on the above two datasets, it can be concluded that an appropriate c is important for a better diffusion of influence. The best performance of KDA is achieved when $c = 0.4$. It means that k_1 equals to $0.6 \cdot K$, and k_2 equals to $0.4 \cdot K$. KDA mines more seeds in phase 1 than in phase 2.

4.4 Comparison of the Seed Sets' Quality

The quality of the seed sets obtained from different algorithms is evaluated based on the influence spread. Higher the spread, better the quality. For better comparisons, we run five algorithms on four real datasets. The size of the seed is selected according to the size of the graph on different datasets. The comparison results are shown in Fig. 3.

In Fig. 3(a), when $K \leq 20$, GA performs a little better than KDA does. The reason is that when $K \leq 20$, k_1 is small, and the accumulated potential influence for KDA is not enough. We can see clearly that when $K \geq 30$, KDA performs consistently well comparing with the other four algorithms. LDAG performs better than the others when $K \geq 50$, but it is 25% lower than KDA. When $K = 70$, KDA can influence the whole network(1133 nodes) while the others can't. For Yeast-protein in Fig. 3(b), PageRank and Degree have similar performances and they both don't perform very well. LDAG just performs better than PageRank and Degree at some points. When $K = 120$, GA can reach KDA and they can both nearly influence the total nodes of the graph.

On the PGP dataset shown in Fig. 3(c), the curves of all the algorithms are nearly linear. GA is a litter lower than KDA. They can nearly influence the whole network when $K \geq 1300$. LDAG performs better than Degree and PageRank. The results on NetHEPT are shown in Fig. 3(d), GA performs a few percentage better than KDA when $K \geq 600$, but worse than KDA when $K < 600$.

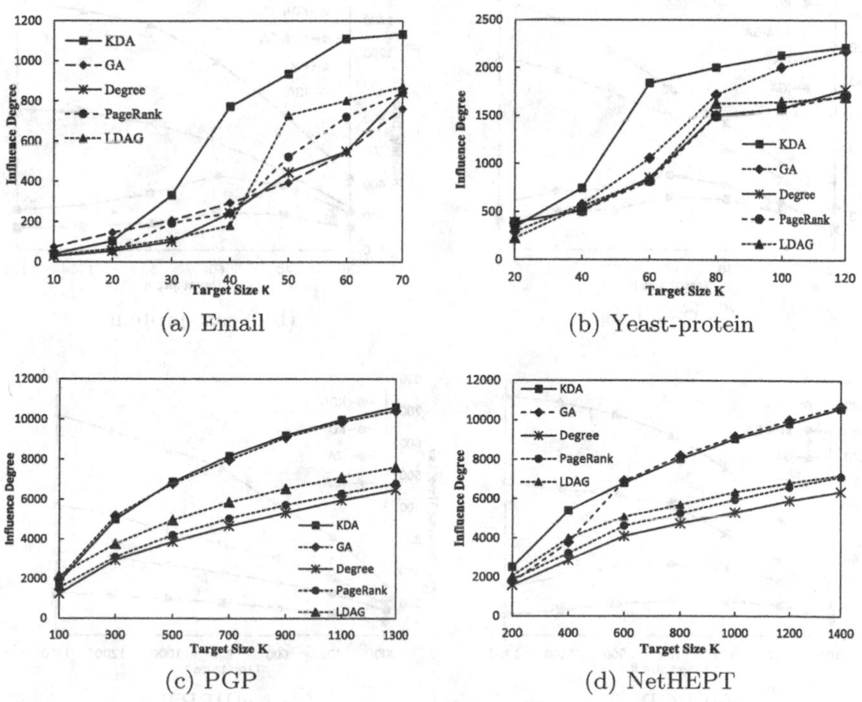

(a) Email (b) Yeast-protein

(c) PGP (d) NetHEPT

Fig. 3. Influence spread on four real datasets

From the four datasets, GA is the most unstable. It performs worse on Email as a whole, but better on NetHEPT. The unstable performance makes it unsuitable for the LT model to be applied in different types of networks. GA just picks up the node with the maximal marginal influence degree at each step, but KDA accumulates potential influence first, which will contribute to the later greedy selection. In this way, KDA can influence more nodes than GA. LDAG and KDA are both stable. Comparing with the heuristics PageRank and Degree without considering propagation characteristics, LDAG performs consistently well. But KDA performs better than LDAG. The seed nodes mined by KDA can influence more nodes than other algorithms for a given K under the LT model.

4.5 Analysis of the Time Complexity

Because the time complexity of KDA mainly depends on the greedy selection in phase 2, in this section, we compare KDA using IGA with that using GA to evaluate the efficiency of IGA on the running time. We refer to KDA with GA as KDA-GA. For better analysis, IGA is compared with GA at the same time.

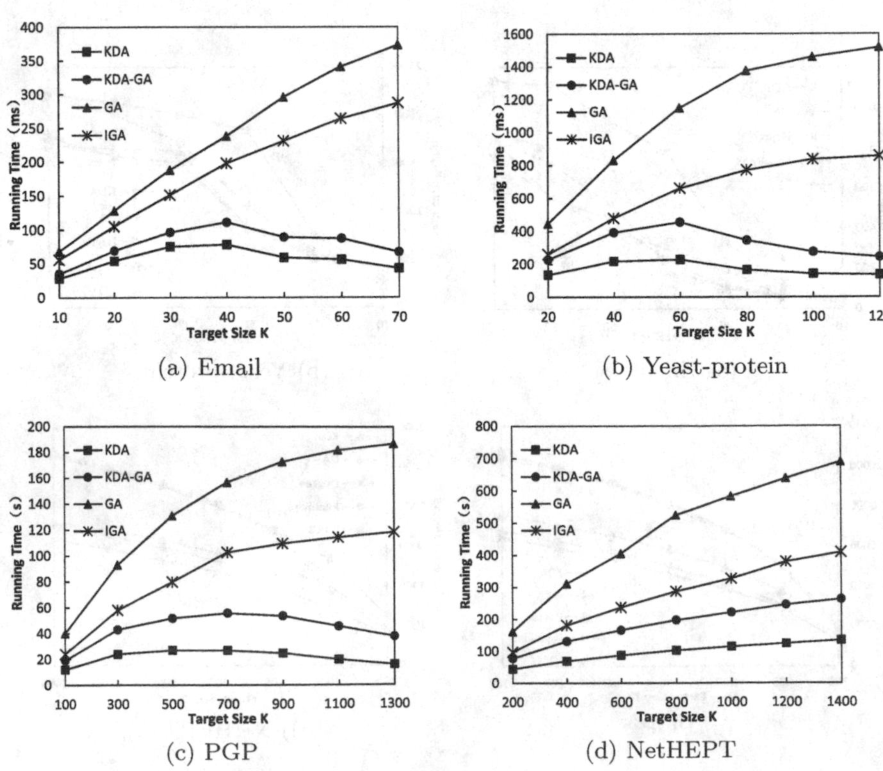

(a) Email (b) Yeast-protein

(c) PGP (d) NetHEPT

Fig. 4. Comparisons of running time on the real datasets

The results are shown in Fig. 4. It is clear that IGA reduces the running time significantly compared with GA, and IGA increases slower than GA. IGA is approximately twice as fast as GA on Yeast-protein and PGP. Using IGA in phase 2, KDA can reduce the running time by nearly one time compared with KDA-GA on the four datasets. So IGA is an efficient greedy selection strategy.

Note that for GA and IGA, when K increases, the running time increases on the four datasets. But for KDA and KDA-GA, the running time increases first and then decreases as K increases except on NetHEPT. In fact, on the first three datasets, it can influence the whole network with the maximal K from Fig. 4. What's more, the running time starts to decrease when K reaches nearly the half of the maximal K. On the Email dataset, the running time starts to decrease at $K = 40$. On Yeast-protein, it decreases at $K = 60$, and $K = 700$ on PGP. On NetHEPT, it cannot influence the whole network with $K = 1400$.

So we can conclude that if K is large enough according to different networks, then the potential influence degree can be accumulated to a certain degree, and the most potential nodes will be selected under the LT model. This will result in that the nodes will not diffuse too much in the greedy selection for KDA. In this way, it will take less time in phase 2, thus the total running time will decrease when K keeps increasing.

5 Conclusions and Future Work

In this paper, we investigate the problem of influence maximization under the LT model. To address the issues of high computational cost and unstable accuracy, a KDA algorithm for influence maximization is proposed. We present an improved greedy algorithm named IGA, which is applied in KDA to mine part of the seeds. KDA uses a k-shell decomposition to evaluate nodes' individual potential influence.

The KDA algorithm is tested on four real datasets along with some other algorithms. The experimental results show that KDA outperforms the others in terms of the influence spread. For the running time, IGA can reduce KDA's running time greatly when it is applied in KDA. Especially when K is large enough according to different networks, it will take less time for KDA. Therefore, KDA is an effective and efficient algorithm for influence maximization.

However, for the influence maximization evaluation, not only the maximization of influence spread should be considered, but also the time of diffusion for the mined top-K nodes should be investigated. In the future we will take the diffusion speed into account.

Acknowledgments. This research is funded by the National Nature Science Foundation of China (No. 61272406) and the Fundamental Research Funds for the Central Universities (HUST:2013TS101).

References

1. Domingos, P., Richardson, M.: Mining the network value of customers. In: Proceedings of the 7th ACM SIGKDD International Conference on Knowledge Discovery and Data Mining, pp. 57–66 (2001)
2. Kempe, D., Kleinberg, J., Tardos, E.: Maximizing the spread of influence through a social network. In: Proceedings of the 9th ACM SIGKDD International Conference on Knowledge Discovery and Data Mining, pp. 137–146 (2003)
3. Goldenberg, J., Libai, B., Muller, E.: Talk of the Network: A complex systems look at the underlying process of Word-of-Mouth. Marketing Letters **12**(3), 211–223 (2001)
4. Goldenberg, J., Libai, B., Muller, E.: Using complex systems analysis to advance marketing theory development. Academy of Marketing Science Review **9**(3), 1–18 (2001)
5. Granovetter, M.: Threshold models of collective behavior. American journal of sociology **83**(6), 1420–1443 (1978)
6. Kim, J., Lee, W., Hwanjo, Y.: CT-IC: Continuously activated and time-restricted independent cascade model for viral marketing. Knowledge-Based Systems **62**, 57–68 (2014)
7. He, X., Song, G., Chen, W., et al.: Influence blocking maxmization in social networks under the competive linear threshold model. In: SDM, pp. 463–474 (2012)
8. Leskovec, J., Krause, A., Guestrin, C., et al.: Cost-effective outbreak detection in networks. In: Proceedings of the 13th ACM SIGKDD International Conference on Knowledge Discovery and Data Mining, pp. 420–429 (2007)
9. Goyal, A., Lu, W., Lakshmanan, L.V.S.: CELF++: optimizing the greedy algorithm for influence maximization in social networks. In: Proceedings of the 20th International Conference Companion on World Wide Web, pp. 47–48. ACM (2011)
10. Zhou, C., Zhang, P., Guo, J., et al.: UBLF: an upper bound based approach to discover influential nodes in social networks. In: 13th International Conference on Data Mining, pp. 907–916. IEEE (2013)
11. Chen, W., Wang, C., Wang, Y.: Scalable influence maximization for prevalent viral marketing in large-scale social networks. In: Proceedings of the 16th ACM SIGKDD International Conference on Knowledge Discovery and Data Mining, pp. 1029–1038 (2010)
12. Chen, W., Wang, Y., Yang, S.: Efficient influence maximization in social networks. In: Proceedings of the 15th ACM SIGKDD International Conference on Knowledge Discovery and Data Mining, pp. 199–208 (2009)
13. Jiang, Q., Song, G., Cong, G., et al.: Simulated annealing based influence maximization in social networks. In: Proceedings of the 15th AAAI Conference on Artificial Intelligence, pp. 127–132 (2011)
14. Borgs, C., Brautbar, M., Chayes, J., et al.: Maximizing social influence in nearly optimal time. In: Proceedings of the ACM-SIAM Symposium on Discrete Algorithms, SODA, pp. 946–957 (2014)
15. Xu, W., Lu, Z., Wu, W., et al.: A novel approach to online social influence maximization. Social Network Analysis and Mining **4**(1), 1–13 (2014)
16. Cheng, S.Q., Shen, H.W., Huang, J.M., et al.: IMRank: influence maximization via finding self-consistent ranking (2014). arXiv preprint arXiv, 1402.3939
17. Zhang, X., Zhu, J., Wang, Q., et al.: Identifying influential nodes in complex networks with community structure. Knowledge-based Systems **42**, 74–84 (2013)

18. Chen, W., Yuan, Y., Zhang, L.: Scalable influence maximization in social networks under the linear threshold model. In: 10th International Conference on Data Mining, ICDM, pp. 88–97 (2010)
19. Goyal, A., Lu, W., Lakshmanan, L.V.S.: SIMPATH: an efficient algorithm for influence maximization under the linear threshold model. In: 11th International Conference on Data Mining, ICDM, pp. 211–220 (2011)
20. Ben-Zwi, O., Hermelin, D., Lokshtanov, D., et al.: An exact almost optimal algorithm for target set selection in social networks. In: Proceedings of the 10th ACM conference on Electronic commerce, pp. 355–362. ACM (2009)
21. Bhagat, S., Goyal, A., Lakshmanan, L.V.S.: Maximizing product adoption in social networks. In: Proceedings of the Fifth ACM International Conference on Web Search and Data Mining, pp. 603–612. ACM (2012)
22. Goyal, A., Bonchi, F., Lakshmanan, L.V.S., et al.: On minimizing budget and time in influence propagation over social networks. Social Network Analysis and Mining **3**(2), 179–192 (2013)
23. Narayanam, R., Narahari, Y.: A shapley value-based approach to discover influential nodes in social networks. IEEE Transactions on Automation Science and Engineering **8**(1), 1–18 (2011)
24. Lu, Z., Fan, L., Wu, W., et al.: Efficient influence spread estimation for influence maximization under the linear threshold model. Computational Social Networks **1**(1), 1–19 (2014)
25. Freeman, L.C.: Centrality in social networks conceptual clarification. Social networks **1**(3), 215–239 (1979)
26. Brin, S., Page, L.: The anatomy of a larege-scale hypertextual web search engine. Computer networks **30**(1), 107–117 (1998)
27. Carmi, S., Havlin, S., Kirkpatrick, S., et al.: A model of Internet topology using k-shell decomposition. Proceedings of the National Academy of Sciences **104**(27), 11150–11154 (2007)
28. Pittel, B., Spencer, J.H., Wormald, N.C.: Sudden emergence of a giant k-core in a random graph. Journal of Combinatorial Theory Series B **67**(1), 111–151 (1996)
29. Kitsak, M., Gallos, L.K., Havlin, S., et al.: Identification of influential spreaders in complex networks. Nat. Phys. **6**, 888–893 (2010)
30. Wang, Y., Feng, X.: A potential-based node selection strategy for influence maximization in a social network. In: Huang, R., Yang, Q., Pei, J., Gama, J., Meng, X., Li, X. (eds.) ADMA 2009. LNCS, vol. 5678, pp. 350–361. Springer, Heidelberg (2009)
31. Guimera, R., Danon, L., Diaz-Guilera, A., et al.: Self-similar community structure in a network of human interactions. Physical Review E **68**, 065103 (2003)
32. Sun, S., Ling, L., Zhang, N., et al.: Topological structure analysis of the protein-protein interaction network in budding yeast. Nucleic Acids Research **31**(9), 2443–2450 (2003)
33. Boguna, M., Pastor-Satorras, R., Diaz-Guilera, A., et al.: Models of social networks based on social distance attachment. Physical Review E **70**, 056122 (2004)

Semantic Web Applications

Keyword Pattern Graph Relaxation for Selective Result Space Expansion on Linked Data

Ananya Dass[1], Cem Aksoy[1], Aggeliki Dimitriou[2], and Dimitri Theodoratos[1(✉)]

[1] New Jersey Institute of Technology, Newark, USA
dth@njit.edu
[2] National Technical University of Athens, Athens, Greece

Abstract. Keyword search is a popular technique for querying the ever growing repositories of RDF graph data. In recent years different approaches leverage a structural summary of the graph data to address the typical keyword search related problems. These approaches compute queries (pattern graphs) corresponding to alternative interpretations of the keyword query and the user selects one that matches her intention to be evaluated against the data. Though promising, these approaches suffer from a drawback: because summaries are approximate representations of the data, they might return empty answers or miss results which are relevant to the user intent.

In this paper, we present a novel approach which combines the use of the structural summary and the user feedback with a relaxation technique for pattern graphs. We leverage pattern graph homomorphisms to define relaxed pattern graphs that are able to extract more results potentially of interest to the user. We introduce an operation on pattern graphs and we show that it can produce all relaxed pattern graphs. To guarantee that the result pattern graphs are as close to the initial pattern graph as possible, we devise different metrics to measure the degree of relaxation of a pattern graph. We design an algorithm that computes relaxed pattern graphs with non-empty answers in relaxation order. Finally, we run experiments to measure the effectiveness of our ranking of relaxed pattern graphs and the efficiency of our system.

1 Introduction

Keyword search is the most popular technique for querying data on the web because it allows the user to retrieve information without knowing any formal query language (e.g., SPARQL) and without being aware of the structure/schema of the data sources against which the keyword query is issued. The same keyword query can be used to extract data from multiple data sources with different structures and this is particularly useful in the web where the data sources that can provide the answers are not known in advance. Unfortunately, the convenience and the simplicity of keyword search comes along with a drawback. Keyword queries are imprecise and ambiguous. For this reason, keyword queries return a very large number of results. This is a typical problem

P. Cimiano et al. (Eds.): ICWE 2015, LNCS 9114, pp. 287–306, 2015.
DOI: 10.1007/978-3-319-19890-3_19

in IR. However, it is exacerbated in the context of tree and graph data where a result to a query is not a whole document but a substructure (e.g., a subtree, or a subgraph) which exponentially increases the number of results. As a consequence, the keyword search on graph data faces two major challenges: (a) effectively identifying relevant results and (b) coping with the performance scalability issue.

In order to identify relevant results, previous algorithms for keyword search over graph data compute candidate results in an approximate way by considering only those which maintain the keyword instances in close proximity [6,10,14,16,19,20,23,24]. The filtered results are ranked and top-k processed usually by employing IR-style metrics for flat documents (e.g., tf*idf or PageRank) adapted to the structural characteristics of the data [12,15,25,26]. Nevertheless, the statistics-based metrics alone cannot capture effectively the diversity of the results represented in a large graph dataset neither identify the intent of the user. As a consequence, the produced rankings are, in general, of low quality. Further, despite the size restriction of the candidate results, these algorithms are still of high complexity and they do not scale satisfactorily when the size of the data graph and the number of query keywords increases.

Leveraging the Structural Summary. In order to address these challenges recent approaches to keyword search on RDF data developed techniques which exploit a structural summary of the RDF graph [9,25,26]. This is a concept similar to the 1-index or data guide in tree databases. The structural summary summarizes the structure of an RDF graph and associates inverted lists of keyword instances (extensions) with nodes. A structural summary is typically much smaller than its RDF graph. These techniques use the structural summary to produce pattern graphs for a given keyword query. The pattern graphs are structured queries corresponding to interpretations of the imprecise keyword query. Evaluating the pattern graphs on the RDF graph, the candidate results for the keyword query can be produced. Interestingly, a pattern graph can be expressed as a SPARQL query, and all the machinery of query engines and optimization techniques developed for SPARQL can be leveraged to efficiently compute the results of the keyword query.

Benefits of the Structural Summary Approach. A structural summary approach can resolve the challenges mentioned above. Indeed, the pattern graphs can be ranked using a scoring function and the top-k of them be presented to the user. The user chooses one that best meets her intention, and only the corresponding structured query is evaluated against the data graph [25,26]. A more recent approach exploits semantic interpretations for the query keywords and a hierarchical clustering of the pattern graphs in order to select a relevant one [9]. Effectiveness studies show that the approaches based on the structural summary display good precision. Further, computing, ranking and identifying top-k subgraphs (query results) for a keyword query directly on the data graph is very expensive even when answers are computed in an approximate way [6,19]. In contrast, since the structural summaries are typically much smaller than the actual data, generating the relevant pattern graph can be done efficiently. Therefore, the structural summary-based approaches scale satisfactorily and compute answers of keyword queries efficiently even on large RDF graphs stored in external memory [8,9,25].

The Missing Relevant Result Problem. Despite its advantages, the structural summary-based approach for keyword search on RDF data has a drawback: since the structural summaries are approximate representations of the RDF graph data, the selected pattern graph might miss results which are relevant to the user intent. This might happen even if the user correctly selects the pattern graph which is relevant to her intent.

Our Approach. In this paper, we provide an approach for keyword search over RDF graph data which addresses the weakness of the structural summary based approach while maintaining its advantages. Our system enables gradual relaxation of a relevant pattern graph so that additional results of possible interest to the user are retrieved from the RDF graph, if needed (for example, if the original pattern graph returns no result or if the user wants to extract more semantically similar results).

Contribution. The main contributions of the paper are the following:

- We leverage pattern graph homomorphisms to define relaxed pattern graphs. Relaxed pattern graphs can expand the result space of an original pattern graph with semantically similar results (Section 3.1).
- We define an operation on pattern graphs (vertex split operation) in order to allow the construction of relaxed pattern graphs. A vertex split operation creates two split images of an entity variable vertex in a pattern graph and partitions its incident edges between the two vertices. We show that this operation is complete, that is, it can produce all the relaxed pattern graphs (Section 3.2).
- Since we want to relax a pattern graph so that the relaxed version is as close to the initial pattern graph as possible, we introduce three metrics to compare the degree of relaxation of relaxed pattern graphs and rank them. All three metrics take into account structural and semantic characteristics of the relaxed pattern graph and depend on the vertex split operations applied to the original pattern graph (Section 3.3).
- If an original pattern graph has an empty answer on an RDF graph, we would like to identify its vertices which contribute to this condition. We call these vertices empty vertices and we provide necessary and sufficient conditions for characterizing them in a pattern graph. Empty vertices are used to guide the relaxation process so that relaxed pattern graphs with non-empty answers are produced (Section 3.4).

- We design an algorithm which takes a pattern graph as input and gradually generates relaxed pattern graphs having non-empty answers. The algorithm returns the relaxed patterns graphs (and computes their answer in the RDF graph) in ascending order of relaxation (Section 3.5).
- We run experiments to measure the effectiveness of our ranking of relaxed pattern graphs and the efficiency of our system in computing relaxed pattern graphs and their answers. The results showed to be promising (Section 4).

2 Structural Summaries and Pattern Graphs

Data Model. Resource Description Framework (RDF) provides a framework for representing information about web resources in a graph form. The RDF vocabulary includes elements that can be broadly classified into Classes, Properties, Entities and Relationships. All the elements are resources. Our data model is an RDF graph defined as follows:

Definition 1 (RDF Graph). An *RDF graph* is a quadruple $G = (V, E, L, l)$ where:

V is a finite set of vertices, which is the union of three disjoint sets: V_E (representing entities), V_C (representing classes) and V_V (representing values).

E is a finite set of directed edges, which is the union of four disjoint sets: E_R (inter-entity edges called *Relationship* edges which represent entity relationships), E_P (entity to value edges called *Property* edges which represent property assignments), E_T (entity to class edges called *type* edges which represent entity to class membership) and E_S (class to class edges called *subclass* edges which represent class-subclass relationship).

L is a finite set of labels that includes the labels "type" and "subclass".

l is a function from $V_C \cup V_V \cup E_R \cup E_P$ to L. That is, l assigns labels to class and value vertices and to relationship and property edges.

Entity and class vertex and edge labels are Universal Resource Identifiers (URIs). Vertices are identified by IDs which in the case of entities and classes are URIs. Every entity belongs to a class. Fig. 1 shows an example RDF graph (inspired by the Jamendo dataset[1]). For simplicity, vertex and edge identifiers are not shown in this example graph.

Query Language Semantics. A *query* Q on an RDF graph G is a set of keywords. A *keyword instance* of a keyword k in Q is a vertex or edge label in G containing k. The *answer* of Q on G is a set of result graphs of Q on G. Each result graph is a minimal subgraph of G involving at least one instance of every keyword in Q and is formally defined below. In order to facilitate the interpretation of the semantics of the keyword instances, every instance of a keyword in Q is matched against a small subgraph of G which involves this

[1] http://dbtune.org/jamendo/

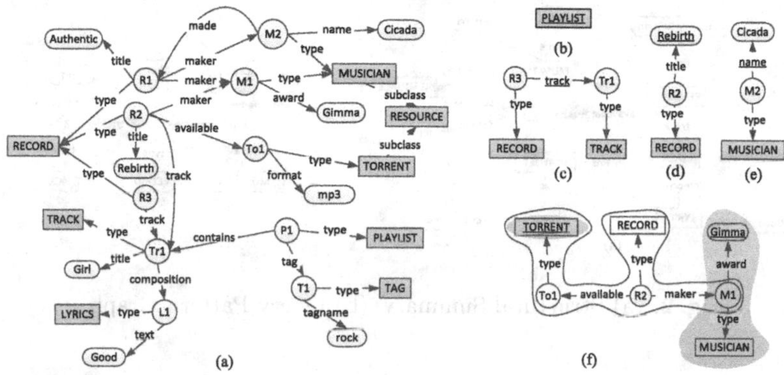

Fig. 1. (a) An RDF graph, (b), (c), (d) and (c) class, relationship, value and property matching constructs, respectively, (f) inter-construct connection and result graph

keyword instance and the corresponding class vertices. This subgraph is called *matching construct*. Figs. 1(b), (c), (d) and (e) show a class, relationship, value and property matching construct, respectively, for different keyword instances in the RDF graph of Fig. 1(a). Underlined labels in a matching construct denote the keyword instances. Each matching construct provides information about the semantic context of the keyword instance under consideration. For instance, the matching construct of Fig. 1(d) shows that `Rebirth` is the title of entity $R2$ of type Record.

A *signature* of Q is a function that matches every keyword k in Q to a matching construct of k in G. Given a query signature S, an *inter-construct connection* between two distinct matching constructs C_1 and C_2 in S is a simple path augmented with the class vertices of the intermediate entity vertices in the path (if not already in the path) such that: (a) one of the terminal vertices in the path belongs to C_1 and the other belongs to C_2, and (b) no vertex in the connection except the terminal vertices belong to a construct in S. Fig. 1(f) shows an inter-construct connection between the matching constructs for keywords `Torrent` and `Gimma` in the RDF graph of Fig. 1(a). The matching constructs are shaded and the inter-construct connection is circumscribed.

A subgraph of G is said to be *connection acyclic* if there is no cycle in the graph obtained by viewing its matching constructs as vertices and its inter-construct connections between them as edges. Given a signature S for Q on G, a *result graph* of S on G is a connected, connection acyclic subgraph of G which contains only the matching constructs in S and possibly inter-construct connections between them. A *result graph* for Q on G is a result graph for a signature of Q on G. Fig. 1(f) shows a result graph for the query {`Torrent`, `Cicada`} on the RDF graph of Fig. 1(a).

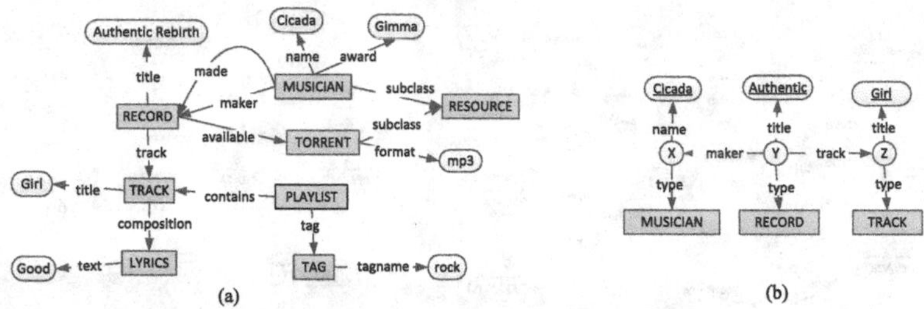

Fig. 2. (a) Structural Summary, (b) Query Pattern Graph

The Structural Summary and Pattern Graphs. In order to construct pattern graphs we use the structural summary of the RDF graph. Intuitively, the structural summary is a graph that summarizes the RDF graph.

Definition 2 (Structural Summary). The *structural summary* of an RDF graph G is a vertex and edge labeled graph constructed from G as follows:

1. Merge every class vertex and its entity vertices into one vertex labeled by the class vertex label and remove all the type edges from G.
2. Merge all the value vertices which are connected with a property edge labeled by the same label to the same class vertex into one vertex labeled by the union of the labels of these value vertices. Merge also the corresponding edges into one edge labeled by their label.
3. Merge all the relationship edges between the same class vertices which are labeled by the same label into one edge with that label.

Fig. 2(a) shows the structural summary for the RDF graph G of Fig. 1. Similarly to matching constructs on the data graph we define matching constructs on the structural summary. Since the structural summary does not have entity vertices, a matching construct on a structural summary possess one distinct entity variable vertex for every class vertex labeled by a distinct variable.

Pattern graphs are the subgraphs of the structural summary, strictly consisting of one matching construct for every keyword in the query Q and the connections between them without these connections forming a cycle.

Definition 3 (Pattern Graph). A *(result) pattern graph* for a keyword query Q is a graph similar to a result graph for Q, with the following two exceptions:

(a) The labels of the entity vertices in the result graph, if any, are replaced by distinct variables in the pattern graph. These variables are called *entity variables* and they range over entity labels.
(b) The labels of the value vertices are replaced by distinct variables whenever these labels are not the keyword instances in the result graph. These variables are called *value variables* and they range over value labels in the RDF graph.

Fig. 2(b) shows an example of a pattern graph, for the keyword query $Q = $ {`Cicada, Authentic, Girl`} on the RDF graph of Fig. 1.

Computing and Selecting Pattern Graphs. For computing the pattern graphs of a query on the structural summary, we use an algorithm which computes r-radius Steiner graphs [9]. The user selects a pattern graph by navigation through a two-level semantic hierarchical clustering system [9]. Nevertheless, the way the pattern graph is selected by the user is orthogonal to the relaxation method we present in this paper. Any other approach like those in [13,25–27] can be used for selecting the relevant pattern graph which will be relaxed.

3 Computing Relaxed Pattern Graphs

In order to expand the result set of the pattern graph chosen by the user and get additional results for the same query signature that involve the same classes, relationships, properties and values but additional entities, we relax this pattern graph. In this section, we first define relaxed pattern graphs. We then introduce an operation on pattern graphs, called vertex split operation, and we show that a pattern graph can be relaxed by applying vertex split operations. Relaxed pattern graphs which are semantically closer to the original pattern graph are preferable. Therefore, we introduced different metrics to compare the degree of relaxation of relaxed pattern graphs and characterize their closeness to the original pattern graph. Then, we elaborate on the reasons for a pattern graph having an empty answer. Finally, we design an algorithm which computes relaxed pattern graphs with non-empty answers ranked in ascending order of their degree of relaxation.

3.1 Relaxed Pattern Graphs

In order to define relaxed patterns, we need the concept of homomorphism between pattern graphs.

Definition 4 (Pattern Graph Homomorphism). Let P_1 and P_2 be two pattern graphs. A *homomorphism* from P_1 to P_2 is a function h from the variable vertices (entity variable and value variable vertices) of P_1 to the variable vertices of P_2 such that, if X is an entity variable vertex in P_1:

(a) for any type edge (X, c) in P_1, there is a type edge $(h(X), c)$ in P_2. That is, X in P_1 and $h(X)$ in P_2 are of the same type c.
(b) for every relationship edge (X, Y) in P_1 labeled by r, where Y is another entity variable in P_1, there is a relationship edge $(h(X), h(Y))$ in P_2 labeled by the same label r.
(c) for every property edge (X, Y) in P_1 labeled by p, where Y is a value variable vertex, there is a property edge $(h(X), h(Y))$ in P_2 labeled by the same label p.

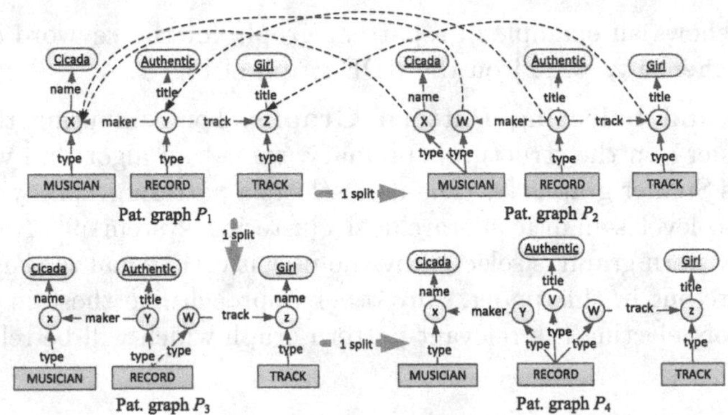

Fig. 3. An original pattern graph P_1 and relaxed pattern graphs P_2, P_3, P_4

(d) for every property edge (X, v) in P_1 labeled by p, where v is a value vertex labeled by the value (keyword) V, there is a property edge $(h(X), v')$ in P_2 labeled by the same label p, where v' is a value vertex also labeled by V.

Fig. 3 shows a homomorphism from the pattern graph P_2 to the pattern graph P_1. The vertex mapping is illustrated with dashed arrows. One can see, that there are also homomorphisms from P_3 and P_4 to P_1. However, there is no homomorphism from P_1 to any one of the other pattern graphs.

We use the concept of homomorphism to define a relation on pattern graphs.

Definition 5 (Relation $\prec$). Let P_1 and P_2 be two pattern graphs. We say that P_2 is a *relaxation* of P_1 or that P_2 is a *relaxed version* of P_1 if there is a homomorphism from P_2 to P_1 but there is no homomorphism from P_1 to P_2. In this case, we write $P_1 \prec P_2$.

In the example of Fig. 3, $P_1 \prec P_2$ and $P_1 \prec P_3 \prec P_4$. No other $\prec$ relationships hold between these patterns.

Clearly, relation $\prec$ is a strict partial order on the set of pattern graphs (it is irreflexive, asymmetric and transitive). We call its minimal elements *original* pattern graphs. The patterns initially presented to the user are original pattern graphs and one of them is selected and possibly relaxed. If an (original) pattern graph P has an embedding to an RDF graph, a relaxed version of P also has an embedding to the same RDF graph. The opposite is not necessarily true. Therefore, with relaxed pattern graphs we can expand the result set of an original pattern graph.

3.2 Vertex Splitting

A pattern graph is relaxed by applying the *vertex split* operation to one or more of its entity variable vertices. This operation “splits” an entity variable vertex in a pattern graph into two entity variable vertices of the same type and partitions the incident edges between the two new vertices as indicated by the operation.

Definition 6 (Vertex split operation). Let P be a pattern graph, v be an entity variable vertex in P connected with a type edge to a class vertex c, and $E = \{e_1, \ldots, e_k\}$, $k \geq 1$, be a proper subset of the set of non-type edges incident to v in P. Assume the edges $e_1, \ldots, e_k$, are connecting the pairs of vertices $(v, v_1), \ldots, (v, v_k)$, respectively. The *vertex split* operation $split(P, v, E)$ returns a pattern graph constructed from P as follows:
(a) Add to P a new entity variable vertex v' of type c.
(b) Remove all the non-type edges (incident to v) that occur in E.
(c) Add k edges $(v', v_1), \ldots, (v', v_k)$ having the same labels as the edges $e_1, \ldots, e_k$, respectively.

Splitting one or more of the vertices of an original pattern graph P results in a relaxed pattern graph (a relaxed version of P). Applying the split operation in sequence can create a pattern graph where the non-type edges incident to v are partitioned into more than two sets attached to different vertices, as desired.

Not all the entity variable vertices are interesting for splitting. This operation is defined only on candidate split vertices. An entity variable vertex is a *candidate split* vertex if it has at least two non-type edges.

As an example, consider the original pattern graph P_1 of Fig. 3. This is a pattern graph for the keyword query {`Cicada`, `Authentic`, `Girl`}. Applying $split(P_1, X, \{maker\})$ to P_1 results in the pattern graph P_2. Applying $split(P_1, Y, \{track\})$ to P_1 results in the pattern graph P_3. Applying in turn $split(P_3, Y, \{title\})$ produces the pattern graph P_4.

Any partitioning of the edges incident to a vertex in an original pattern graph can be obtained in a relaxed pattern graph by a successive application of vertex split operations. Therefore, one can see that if P_1 and P_2 are two pattern graphs, $P_1 \prec P_2$ iff P_2 can be produced from P_1 by applying a sequence of vertex split operations. In other words, the vertex split operation is sound and complete w.r.t. relaxed pattern graphs.

3.3 Measuring Pattern Graph Relaxation

Usually we want to relax a pattern graph so that it is as close to the initial pattern graph as possible. To this end, we introduce three metrics of decreasing importance to measure the degree of relaxation of a pattern graph. All these three metrics depend on the vertex split operations applied to the original pattern graph. The first one is called connectivity of the pattern graph. In order to define the connectivity of a pattern graph we use the concept of tightly connected pair of keyword instances. Two keyword instances in a pattern graph P are *tightly connected* if there exists a simple path between them which does not go through a class vertex. For instance, in the pattern graph of Fig. 4(b), the keyword instances `Rebirth` and `mp3` are tightly connected whereas the keyword instances `Cicada` and `Gimma` are not.

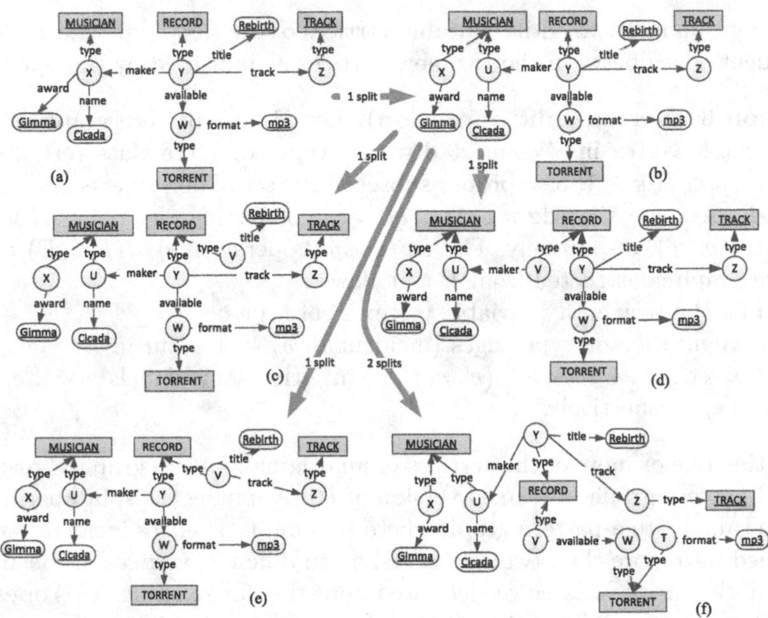

Fig. 4. (a) Original pattern graph (b), (c), (d), (e) and (f) relaxed pattern graphs

Definition 7 (Pattern graph connectivity). The *connectivity* of a pattern graph is the number of unordered keyword instance pairs that are strongly connected divided by the total number of unordered keyword instance pairs.

In an original pattern graph, all pairs of keyword instances are strongly connected. Therefore, its connectivity is 1. Relaxing such a pattern graph by applying the vertex split operation to any entity variable vertex produces a pattern graph of lower or same connectivity. For instance, the connectivity of the pattern graph in Fig. 4(a) is 1. The connectivity of the relaxed pattern graph of Figs. 4(b) is 0.73, the connectivity of that of Fig. 4(c) is 0.47 and the connectivity of those of Figs. 4(d), (e) and (f) is 0.33.

In order to distinguish between relaxed pattern graphs of the same pattern graph which have the same connectivity, we introduce another metric called *scatteredness* of a pattern graph. We first define the *distance* between two tightly connected keyword instances in a pattern graph as the number of vertices in a shortest path between them. For instance, in the pattern graph of Fig. 4(d) the distance between the tightly connected keyword instances of `Rebirth` and `mp3` is 2 while the distance between `Gimma` and `Musician` is 1.

A relaxed pattern graph partitions its keyword instances into sets of tightly connected keyword instances such that any two keyword instances which are tightly connected belong to the same set. The scatteredness of a pattern graph measures how sparsely are positioned the keyword instances within these sets.

Definition 8 (Scatteredness of a pattern graph). Let N be the sum of the distances between all the unordered keyword instance pairs that are tightly connected, and S be the total number of tightly connected unordered keyword pairs in a pattern graph P. The *scatteredness* of the tightly connected keyword instances of P (scatteredness of P for short) is N/S.

A relaxed pattern graph with smaller scatteredness is preferred over a pattern graph of the same connectivity but higher scatteredness since its keywords are assumed to be more closely related. In the example of Fig. 4, the patterns (d) and (e) have the same connectivity 0.33. However, the scatteredness of the pattern of Fig. 4(d) is 1 and that of the pattern of Fig. 4(e) is 2. We use the pattern graph scatteredness to rank the relaxed patterns of a pattern graph having the same connectivity. In our running example, the pattern of Fig. 4(d) is ranked before the pattern of Fig. 4(e).

Nevertheless, it is possible that multiple relaxed patterns of the same pattern graph have not only the same connectivity but also the same scatteredness. In order to differentiate between the degree of relaxation of such pattern graphs, we employ a third metric called *dispersion* of the keyword instances of a pattern graph. Roughly speaking this metric is used to capture how much the keywords are dispersed as a result of vertex split operations in the pattern graph. To formally define the keyword instance dispersion metric we introduce the concept of *split distance*. The *split distance* of two keyword instances in a pattern graph P is the minimum number of class vertices in the simple paths between these two keyword instances in P excluding the terminal vertices. For instance, in the pattern graph of Fig. 4(d), the split distance of the keyword instances of `Gimma` and `mp3` is 2 and that of `Gimma` and `Musician` is 0.

Definition 9 (Pattern graph keyword dispersion). The *keyword dispersion* of a pattern graph P is the sum of the split distances of all unordered pairs of keyword instances in P.

For example, the pattern graphs of Fig. 4(e) and (f) have the same connectivity (0.33) and the same scatteredness (2) whereas their keyword dispersion is 10 and 14, respectively. A pattern graph with a lower keyword dispersion is preferred over a pattern graph with a higher keyword dispersion. Hence, the pattern graph of Fig. 4(e) will be ranked higher than that of Fig. 4(f).

Given two pattern graphs P_1 and P_2, we say that, P_2 is equally or more relaxed than P_1, and we write $P_1 \leq_r P_2$, if: (a) $\text{conn}(P_1) \geq \text{conn}(P_2)$, or (b) $\text{conn}(P_1) = \text{conn}(P_2)$ and $\text{scatt}(P_1) \leq \text{scatt}(P_2)$, or (c) $\text{conn}(P_1) = \text{conn}(P_2)$ and $\text{scatt}(P_1) = \text{scatt}(P_2)$ and $\text{disp}(P_1) \leq \text{disp}(P_2)$. Any two pattern graphs are comparable w.r.t. $\leq_r$. If a set of pattern graphs is ranked with respect to $\leq_r$, with the less relaxed pattern graphs are ranked first, we say that it is ranked in *relaxation order*. Since split operations introduce additional type edges in the pattern graph it is not difficult to see that given two pattern graphs P_1 and P_2, if $P_1 \prec P_2$ then $P_1 \leq_r P_2$.

3.4 Identifying Empty Vertices for Relaxation

If an original pattern graph for a query has an empty answer on an RDF graph, we would like to identify vertices in the pattern graph which if not split, the relaxed pattern graph will keep producing an empty answer. Splitting these vertices does not guarantee that the relaxed query does have a non-empty answer. However, if we omit splitting any one of these vertices, the relaxed pattern graph will not return any results. We call these vertices *empty vertices.*

Definition 10 (Empty vertex). An entity variable vertex X in a pattern graph P on a data graph G is an *empty vertex* iff P or any relaxed version of P where X is not split has an empty answer on G.

We provide next conditions to characterize empty vertices in a pattern graph. Let X be an entity variable vertex of type c in a pattern graph P, $p'_1(X, Z'_1), \ldots, p'_m(X, Z'_m)$ be the property edges incident to X whose value vertices $Z'_1, \ldots, Z'_m$ are variables, $p_1(X, v_1), \ldots, p_n(X, v_n)$ be the property edges incident to X whose value vertices $v_1, \ldots, v_n$ are not variables (they are keyword instances), $r_1(X, Y_1), \ldots, r_k(X, Y_k)$ be the relationship edges from X to some other entity variable vertices $Y_1, \ldots, Y_k$ of type $c_1 \ldots c_k$, respectively, and $r'_1(X, Y'_1), \ldots, r'_l(X, Y'_l)$ be the relationship edges to X from some other entity variable vertices $Y'_1, \ldots, Y'_l$ of type $c'_1, \ldots, c'_l$, respectively (see Fig. 5). We call the graph of Fig. 5 the *star-join view* of the entity variable vertex X in P. One can see an entity variable vertex X is an empty vertex of pattern graph P on an RDF graph G iff the star-join view for X in P has an empty answer on G.

All empty vertices need to be split when relaxing a query in order to possibly get a nonempty answer for the query.

3.5 An Algorithm for Computing Relaxed Patterns

We provide now an algorithm which, given the pattern graph P chosen by the user, gradually generates relaxed pattern graphs of P having non-empty answers. The algorithm returns these pattern graphs and their answers in relaxation order. The number of relaxed pattern graphs returned is controlled by the user.

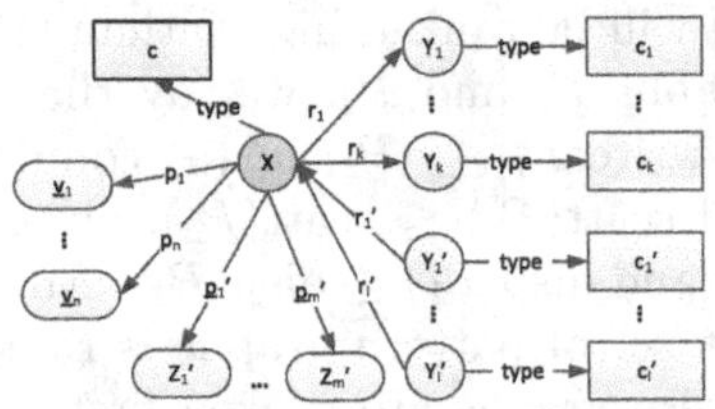

Fig. 5. Star-join view of entity variable vertex X

Algorithm 1.

Input: P: pattern graph.

Output: A list of relaxed pattern graphs of P with non-empty answers in ascending relaxation order. Every pattern is returned along with its answer.

1: $R = \{P\}$;
2: $MoreResults = True$;1
3: $Ans = \emptyset$;
4: **while** $R \neq \emptyset$ and $MoreResults$ **do**
5:     $P_{Top} \leftarrow$ the pattern in R with the highest rank;
6:     $R \leftarrow R - \{P_{Top}\}$;
7:     $EV \leftarrow ComputeEmptyVertices(P_{Top})$;
8:     Mark the new non-empty vertices in P_{Top};
9:     **if** $EV \neq \emptyset$ **then**
10:         $NewR \leftarrow GetRelaxedFromEmpty(P_{Top}, EV)$; ▷ all the relaxed patterns obtained by applying one vertex split operation to all empty vertices.
11:         Rank the patterns in $NewR$ in ascending relaxation order;
12:         $R \leftarrow$ merge R and $NewR$ into one list of patterns ranked in ascending relaxation order;
13:     **else**
14:         $Ans \leftarrow Evaluate(P_{Top})$;
15:         **if** $Ans \neq \emptyset$ **then**
16:             Output (P_{Top}, Ans);
17:             $MoreResults \leftarrow$ input from the user on whether more results are needed;
18:         **if** $Ans = \emptyset$ or $MoreResults$ **then**
19:             $MoreR \leftarrow GetRelaxed(P_{Top})$; ▷ all the new relaxed patterns obtained by applying one vertex split operation to a candidate split vertex.
20:             Rank the patterns in R in ascending relaxation order;
21:             $R \leftarrow$ merge R and $MoreR$ into one list of patterns ranked in ascending relaxation order;

The outline of our algorithm is shown in Algorithm 1. The input of this algorithm is an original pattern graph P. Data structure R is a list used to store pattern graphs (both original and relaxed). The variable $MoreResults$ reflects the user's choice of fetching more answers by further relaxing the pattern graphs in R. The algorithm first ranks the pattern graphs in R in ascending relaxation order (line 5). The pattern graph P_{Top} with the highest rank is chosen from R and its unmarked vertices are checked for emptiness (line 7). If P_{Top} has non-empty vertices, they are marked (line 8), and they (and their split images) remain marked in the relaxations of P_{Top}. If P_{Top} has empty vertices, it is further relaxed by applying one vertex split operation to all of its empty vertices in all possible ways. The resulting relaxed pattern graphs form a new list $NewR$ of relaxed pattern graphs (lines 9-10), which is then ranked in ascending relaxation order and is merged with the list R (lines 11-12). In contrast, if P_{Top} does not have any empty vertex, it is evaluated over the data graph and the set Ans of result graphs is non-empty, it is returned to the user along with the corresponding pattern graph P_{Top} (lines 14-16). In case the user wants more results, or the

Table 1. The keyword queries

Query #	Keywords	Chosen Pattern Graph Structure
1	teenage, text, fantasie, document	star-chain
2	signal, onTimeLine, 10002, recorded_as, sweet	chain
3	kouki, recorded_as, knees	star-chain
4	briareus, reflection, cool, girl	star
5	kouki, revolution, electro, good	star
6	nuts, spy4, chillout, track	star
7	biography, guitarist, track, lemonade	chain
8	divergence, track, obssession, format, mp32	star-chain
9	fantasie, performance, recorded_as, slipstream	chain
10	signal, recorded_as, fantasie, onTimeLine, 10001	chain

pattern graph P_{Top} produces an empty answer when evaluated over the data graph, P_{Top} is relaxed by applying one vertex split operation to all of its candidate split vertices in all possible ways and the generated relaxed pattern graphs are stored in a list $MoreR$ (lines 18-19). All the elements of $MoreR$ are then ranked and merged with the list R of pattern graphs (line 20-21). The whole process, as described in lines 5-21, continues until the user is satisfied with the results, or no more pattern graphs are left in R. The above discussion we can deduce that Algorithm 1 correctly computes its relaxed pattern graphs with non-empty answers in relaxation order.

4 Experimental Evaluation

We implemented our approach and run experiments to evaluate our system. The goal of our experiments is to assess (a) the effectiveness of the metrics introduced in ranking the relaxed pattern graphs, and (b) the feasibility of our system in producing and presenting to the user the relaxed pattern graphs and their answers in real time.

Dataset and Queries. We use Jamendo, a large repository of Creative Commons licensed music. Jamendo is a real dataset of 1.1M triples and of 85MB size containing information about musicians, music tracks, records, licenses and many other details related to them. Experiments are conducted on a standalone machine with an Intel i5-3210M @ 2.5GHz processors and 8GB memory.

Users were provided with different queries on the Jamendo dataset and selected the most relevant pattern graph among those provided by the system. We report on 10 queries. The queries cover a broad range of cases. They involve

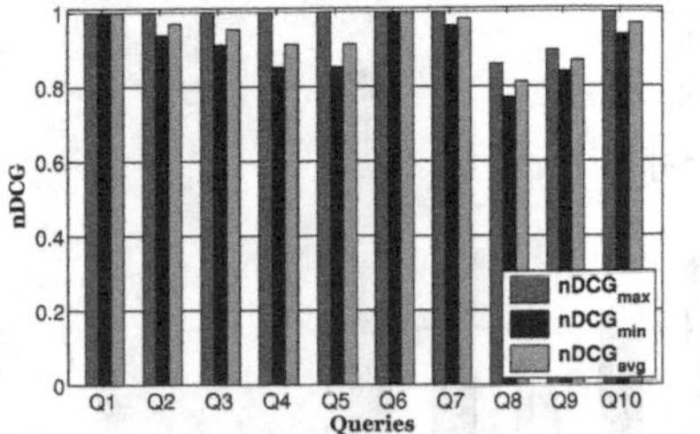

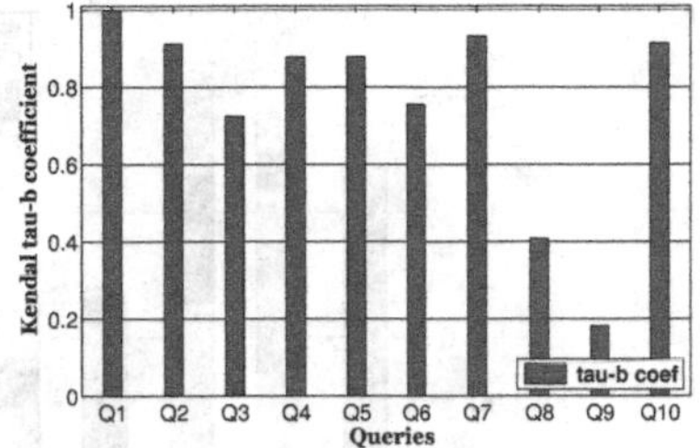

Fig. 6. (a) nDCG$_{max}$, nDCG$_{min}$ and nDCG$_{avg}$ (b) Kendall tau-b coefficient

from 3 to 5 keywords and their relevant pattern graph form a star or a chain or a combination of them. Table 4 shows the keyword queries and information about them.

Effectiveness in Ranking Relaxed Pattern Graphs. For our effectiveness experiments, we used expert users to determine the ground truth. For each query, a user selected, among those computed by the system, the pattern graph which is most relevant to the query. This is the original pattern graph. The user then is presented with all the relaxed pattern graphs that are generated by our algorithm (see Algorithm 1, Section 3.5) until the third relaxed pattern graph with a non-empty answer is produced and ranks them w.r.t to their semantic closeness to the original pattern graph. In order to measure the effectiveness of our technique in generating a ranked list of relaxed pattern graphs (ranked in relaxation order as described in Section 3.3), we are using two metrics: (a) *normalized discounted cumulative gain* (nDCG) [17], and (b) *Kendall tau-b rank correlation coefficient* [1]. Both of them allow comparing two ranked lists of items. Note that the list produced by the user (the correct ranked list) and one produced by our system might not form strict total orders. That is, there might be ties (relaxed pattern graphs with the same rank). We call the set of relaxed pattern graphs that have the same rank in a ranked list equivalence class. Equivalence classes need to be taken into account in measuring the similarity of the ranked lists.

The nDCG metric was first introduced in [17] based on two key arguments: (a) highly important items are more valuable than marginally relevant items, and (b) the lower the position of the relevant item in the ranked list, the less valuable it is for the user because the less likely it is that the user will ever examine the item. The *cumulative gain* (CG) for position n in the ranked list is the sum of the relevance scores of the items in the ranked positions 1 to n. A discounting function is used over cumulative gain to measure *discounted cumulative gain* (DCG) for position n, which is defined as the sum of the relevance scores of all the items at positions 1 to n, each divided by the logarithm of its respective position in the ranked list. The DCG value of a ranked list is the DCG value at

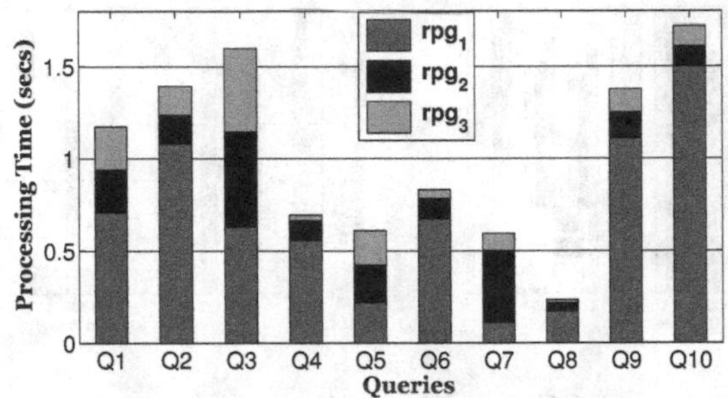

Fig. 7. Evaluation time for three consecutive relaxed pattern graphs

position n of the list where n is the size of the list. The *normalized discounted cumulative gain* (nDCG) is the result of normalizing DCG with the DCG of the correct list by dividing the DCG value of the system's ranked list by the DCG value of the correct ranked list. Thus, nDCG favors a ranked list which is similar to the correct ranked list.

In order to take into account equivalent classes of pattern graphs in the ranked lists, we have extended nDCG by introducing minimum, maximum and average values for it. The nDCG$_{max}$ value of a ranked list RL_e with equivalence classes corresponds to the nDCG value of a strictly ranked (that is, without equivalence classes) list obtained from RL_e by ranking the pattern graphs in the equivalence classes correctly (that is, in compliance with their ranking in the correct list). The nDCG$_{min}$ value of RL_e corresponds to the nDCG value of a strictly ranked list obtained from RL_e by ranking the pattern graphs in the equivalence classes in reverse correct order. The nDCG$_{avg}$ value of RL_e is the average nDCG value over all strictly ranked lists obtained from RL_e by ranking the pattern graphs in the equivalence classes in all possible ways. The nDCG values range between 0 and 1. Fig. 6(a) shows the nDCG$_{min}$, nDCG$_{max}$ and nDCG$_{avg}$ values for the queries of Table 1. As one can see, all the values are very close to 1.

The Kendall tau rank correlation coefficient [1] was proposed to address the problem of measuring the association between two different rankings of the same set of items. In our context, we want to see if the comparison of the ranked list produced by our system (the relaxation order) with the correct ranked list (defined by the expert user) suggests that the former possesses a reliable judgment of the closeness of the relaxed pattern graphs to the original pattern graph (which expresses the user's intention). However, the Kendall tau coefficient is useful when the ranked lists to be compared are strictly ranked. For this reason, we adopt here a variant called *Kendall tau-b coefficient* [1], which can deal with equivalent classes of items in the ranked lists. The value of the coefficient ranges from -1 to 1. If two items have the same (resp. different) relative rank order in the two lists, then the pair is said to be *concordant* (resp. *discordant*). If two items are in an equivalence class in at least one of the lists then the pair is neither concordant nor discordant. When the number of concordant pairs is much larger (resp. much less) than the number of discordant pairs, then the two lists are positively (resp. negatively) correlated, and the coefficient is close to 1 (resp. -1). When the number of discordant and concordant pairs are about the same, then the two lists are weakly correlated (the coefficient is close to 0). Fig. 6(b) shows the Kendall tau-b rank correlation coefficient for the queries of Table 1. As we can see, all the values are positive and in most cases very close to 1.

Efficiency of the System in Producing Relaxed Results. In order to asses the feasibility of our system, we ran our algorithm on the pattern graphs selected by the user for the queries of Table 4, and we measured the time needed to produce the first three consecutive nonempty relaxed pattern graphs and their answers. Many more relaxed pattern graphs are typically produced and ranked in the background, and a number of them are checked for empty answers. The queries were selected so that the original pattern graph for almost all of them has an empty answer. Fig. 7 shows the measured times. One can see that the displayed times for all the queries are interactive. The times needed to produce the second and third relaxed pattern graphs are usually shorter than for the previous relaxed pattern graphs since information about non-empty vertices is recorded and propagated down to the relaxations of the pattern graphs.

5 Related Work

In recent years, a number of papers address keyword search on graph data. Most of these approaches return answers which are trees [5,6,8,12,16,18,21]. Only few of them [20,23,24] return answers as graphs, subgraphs of the data graph. All the above approaches are proposed for generic graphs, and cannot be used directly for keyword search over RDF graph data. This is because the edges of an RDF graph represent predicates, which can also be matched by the keywords of a keyword query. The approaches proposed for keyword search on RDF data can be classified into two categories: (a) data-based approaches [11,12] and (b) schema-based approaches [9,13,22,25–27]. Data-based approaches rely on the data graph to produce answers. Although these approaches generate precise answers, they fail to scale well when the size of the data increases. In contrast, summary-based approaches rely also on a reduced size structural summary extracted from the data. In order to compute answers, these approaches focus on capturing the interpretations of a keyword query by mapping the keywords to elements of the structural summary and constructing pattern graphs. Given that keyword search is ambiguous, these approaches often exploit relevance feedback from the users in order to identify the users' intent [9,18,25]. A hierarchical clustering mechanism and user interaction at multiple levels of the hierarchy can be used to facilitate disambiguation of the keyword query and to support the computation of the relevant results. Such a mechanism is suggested in [2] in the context of tree data and in [9] in the context of RDF data. Although summary based approaches proved to have better performance scalability compared to data-based approaches, they provide an approximate solution and they might miss relevant results for a given keyword query. As RDF data graphs are practically schema free, a summary graph extracted from an RDF graph cannot capture completely all the information in the RDF graph. In this paper we provide a pattern graph relaxation technique to address this issue. Relaxation techniques are studied in [5,7,21]. These techniques are not directly related to our work since they are developed for XML and not RDF data and their goals and processes are different.

6 Conclusion

To address the drawback of structural summary-based approaches for keyword search on RDF graphs, while maintaining their advantages, we have presented a novel approach that permits the relaxation of the most relevant pattern graph selected by the user and expands its result space with similar results. We used pattern graph homomorphisms to introduce relaxed pattern graphs. We then defined an operation on pattern graphs and we show that it is sound and complete w.r.t. relaxed pattern graphs. In order to characterize the semantic closeness of relaxed pattern graphs to the original pattern graph, we introduced different syntax and semantic-based metrics that allow us to compare the degree of relaxation of relaxed pattern graphs. We studied properties of pattern graphs with empty answers and we use them to design an algorithm which computes relaxed pattern graphs with non-empty answers in ascending relaxation order. Our experimental results demonstrate the effectiveness of our approach in ranking the relaxed pattern graphs and the efficiency of our system in producing relaxed pattern graphs and their answers.

We are currently working on exploiting common subexpressions between relaxed pattern graphs and applying multiquery optimization techniques to further improve the performance of our system in computing keyword queries over large RDF repositories.

References

1. Agresti, A.: Analysis of ordinal categorical data. John Wiley & Sons (2010)
2. Aksoy, C., Dass, A., Theodoratos, D., Wu, X.: Clustering query results to support keyword search on tree data. In: Li, F., Li, G., Hwang, S., Yao, B., Zhang, Z. (eds.) WAIM 2014. LNCS, vol. 8485, pp. 213–224. Springer, Heidelberg (2014)
3. Aksoy, C., Dimitriou, A., Theodoratos, D.: Reasoning with patterns to effectively answer XML keyword queries. The VLDB journal 24(3): 441–465 (2015)

4. Aksoy, C., Dimitriou, A., Theodoratos, D., Wu, X.: *XReason*: a semantic approach that reasons with patterns to answer XML keyword queries. In: Meng, W., Feng, L., Bressan, S., Winiwarter, W., Song, W. (eds.) DASFAA 2013, Part I. LNCS, vol. 7825, pp. 299–314. Springer, Heidelberg (2013)
5. Amer-Yahia, S., Cho, S.R., Srivastava, D.: Tree pattern relaxation. In: Jensen, C.S., Jeffery, K., Pokorný, J., Šaltenis, S., Bertino, E., Böhm, K., Jarke, M. (eds.) EDBT 2002. LNCS, vol. 2287, pp. 496–513. Springer, Heidelberg (2002)
6. Bhalotia, G., Hulgeri, A., Nakhe, C., Chakrabarti, S., Sudarshan, S.: Keyword searching and browsing in databases using BANKS. In: ICDE, pp. 431–440 (2002)
7. Brodianskiy, T., Cohen, S.: Self-correcting queries for XML. In: CIKM (2007)
8. Dalvi, B.B., Kshirsagar, M., Sudarshan, S.: Keyword search on external memory data graphs. PVLDB **1**(1), 1189–1204 (2008)
9. Dass, A., Aksoy, C., Dimitriou, A., Theodoratos, D.: Exploiting semantic result clustering to support keyword search on linked data. In: Benatallah, B., Bestavros, A., Manolopoulos, Y., Vakali, A., Zhang, Y. (eds.) WISE 2014, Part I. LNCS, vol. 8786, pp. 448–463. Springer, Heidelberg (2014)
10. Ding, B., Yu, J.X., Wang, S., Qin, L., Zhang, X., Lin, X.: Finding top-k min-cost connected trees in databases. In: ICDE, pp. 836–845 (2007)
11. Elbassuoni, S., Blanco, R.: Keyword search over RDF graphs. In: CIKM (2011)
12. Elbassuoni, S., Ramanath, M., Schenkel, R., Weikum, G.: Searching RDF graphs with sparql and keywords. IEEE Data Eng. Bull., 16–24 (2010)
13. Fu, H., Gao, S., Anyanwu, K.: Disambiguating keyword queries on RDF databases using "Deep" segmentation. In: ICSC, pp. 236–243 (2010)
14. Golenberg, K., Kimelfeld, B., Sagiv, Y.: Keyword proximity search in complex data graphs. In: SIGMOD, pp. 927–940 (2008)
15. Guo, L., Shao, F., Botev, C., Shanmugasundaram, J.: XRANK: ranked keyword search over XML documents. In: SIGMOD, pp. 16–27 (2003)
16. He, H., Wang, H., Yang, J., Yu, P.S.: Blinks: ranked keyword searches on graphs. In: SIGMOD, pp. 305–316 (2007)
17. Järvelin, K., Kekäläinen, J.: Cumulated gain-based evaluation of IR techniques. ACM Trans. Inf. Syst. **20**(4), 422–446 (2002)
18. Jiang, M., Chen, Y., Chen, J., Du, X.: Interactive predicate suggestion for keyword search on RDF graphs. In: Tang, J., King, I., Chen, L., Wang, J. (eds.) ADMA 2011, Part II. LNCS, vol. 7121, pp. 96–109. Springer, Heidelberg (2011)
19. Kacholia, V., Pandit, S., Chakrabarti, S., Sudarshan, S., Desai, R., Karambelkar, H.: Bidirectional expansion for keyword search on graph databases. In: VLDB, pp. 505–516 (2005)
20. Kargar, M., An, A.: Keyword search in graphs: Finding r-cliques. VLDB (2011)
21. Kong, L., Gilleron, R., Mostrare, A.L.: Retrieving meaningful relaxed tightest fragments for XML keyword search. In: EDBT, pp. 815–826 (2009)
22. Le, W., Li, F., Kementsietsidis, A., Duan, S.: Scalable keyword search on large RDF data. IEEE Trans. Knowl. Data Eng. **26**(11), 2774–2788 (2014)
23. Li, G., Ooi, B.C., Feng, J., Wang, J., Zhou, L.: Ease: an effective 3-in-1 keyword search method for unstructured, semi-structured and structured data. In: SIGMOD, pp. 903–914 (2008)
24. Qin, L., Yu, J.X., Chang, L., Tao, Y.: Querying communities in relational databases. In: ICDE, pp. 724–735 (2009)

25. Tran, T., Wang, H., Rudolph, S., Cimiano, P.: Top-k exploration of query candidates for efficient keyword search on graph-shaped (RDF) data. In: ICDE (2009)
26. Wang, H., Zhang, K., Liu, Q., Tran, T., Yu, Y.: Q2Semantic: a lightweight keyword interface to semantic search. In: Bechhofer, S., Hauswirth, M., Hoffmann, J., Koubarakis, M. (eds.) ESWC 2008. LNCS, vol. 5021, pp. 584–598. Springer, Heidelberg (2008)
27. Xu, K., Chen, J., Wang, H., Yu, Y.: Hybrid graph based keyword query interpretation on RDF. In: ISWC (2010)

Approximate Continuous Query Answering over Streams and Dynamic Linked Data Sets

Soheila Dehghanzadeh[1(✉)], Daniele Dell'Aglio[2], Shen Gao[3], Emanuele Della Valle[2], Alessandra Mileo[1], and Abraham Bernstein[3]

[1] INSIGHT Research Center, NUI Galway, Galway, Ireland
soheila.dehghanzadeh@insight-centre.org
[2] DEIB, Politecnico of Milano, Milan, Italy
[3] Department of Informatics, University of Zurich, Zurich, Switzerland

Abstract. To perform complex tasks, RDF Stream Processing Web applications evaluate continuous queries over streams and quasi-static (background) data. While the former are pushed in the application, the latter are continuously retrieved from the sources. As soon as the background data increase the volume and become distributed over the Web, the cost to retrieve them increases and applications become unresponsive. In this paper, we address the problem of optimizing the evaluation of these queries by leveraging local views on background data. Local views enhance performance, but require maintenance processes, because changes in the background data sources are not automatically reflected in the application. We propose a two-step query-driven maintenance process to maintain the local view: it exploits information from the query (e.g., the sliding window definition and the current window content) to maintain the local view based on user-defined Quality of Service constraints. Experimental evaluation show the effectiveness of the approach.

1 Introduction

RDF Stream Processing (RSP) applications are becoming increasingly popular. For example, real-time city monitoring applications process public transportation and weather streams [13]; recommendation applications exploit micro-post streams and user profiles from social networks [7]; supply chain applications use commercial RFID data streams and product master data. RSP techniques, at the basis of those applications, proved to be valid solutions to cope with the high variety and velocity that characterize those data. However, more complex analyses can be performed by combining data streams with static or quasi-static background data. In a Semantic Web setting, background data is usually stored remotely and exposed through SPARQL endpoints [1].

Current RSP languages, like C-SPARQL [4], SPARQL$_{stream}$ [6], and CQELS-QL [12] support queries involving streaming and background data. Those languages are built as extensions of SPARQL 1.1 and consequently support the federated SPARQL extension [1] and the `SERVICE` clause that enables the remote evaluation of graph pattern expressions. However, to the best of our knowledge, implementations of those languages (RSP engines) invoke the remote

P. Cimiano et al. (Eds.): ICWE 2015, LNCS 9114, pp. 307–325, 2015.
DOI: 10.1007/978-3-319-19890-3_20

services for each query evaluation, without any optimization. For example, the C-SPARQL engine delegates the evaluation of the SPARQL operators to the ARQ engine[1]: `SERVICE` clauses are managed through sequences of invocations to the remote endpoints. This way, they generate high loads on remote services and have slow response times. Therefore, optimization techniques are highly needed to provide faster responses to this class of continuous queries.

Instead of pulling data from remote SPARQL endpoints at each evaluation, a possible solution is to store the intermediate results of SERVICE clauses in local views[2] inside the query processor. These types of solutions are widely adopted in databases to improve the performance, availability, and scalability of the query processor [9]. However, the freshness of the local view degrades over time due to the fact that background data in the remote service change and updates are not reflected in the local view. Consequently, the accuracy of the answer decreases. To overcome this issue, a *maintenance process* is introduced: it identifies the out-to-date (namely *stale*) data items in the local view and replaces them with the up-to-date (namely *fresh*) values retrieved from the remote services.

Consider a continuous query q over an RDF stream and quasi-static background data declared to be queryable in a SPARQL `SERVICE` clause. In this paper, we investigate the following problem: *given q, how can we adaptively refresh a local view of background data in order to satisfy Quality of Service constraints on accuracy and response time of the continuous answer?* The QoS constraints determine how much local view can be refreshed. In fact, the maintenance process should (1) limit the number of refresh requests according to responsiveness constraints and (2) maximize response accuracy w.r.t the limited refresh requests. In the following, we assume that the local view always contains all the elements needed to compute the current answer; that is, in this work we do not address the problem of view selection for local materialization [8].

In the first part of the paper, we analyze the problem. We present an example to show the drawbacks of the current solutions and to motivate the need of local views and maintenance processes in continuous queries with streaming and background data. Next, we formalize the problem and elicit the requirements to design maintenance processes in this setting.

In the second part of the paper, we present a solution for the class of queries where there is a unique equi-join between the `SERVICE` and the streaming graph pattern expressions. That is, the `SERVICE` has join variable as subject (object) of a triple pattern where the predicate is functional (inverse functional). In particular, this query class has a one-to-one mapping between the streaming and background data: thus, we do not cope with the join selectivity problem. It is worth noting that a relevant number of queries in the Stream Processing context are in this class [5,14]. Our solution is a query-driven maintenance process

---

[1] C-SPARQL Version 0.48; ARQ Version 2.11.1

[2] As in [9], with local view we broadly refer to any saved data derived from some underlying sources, regardless of where and how the data is stored. This covers traditional replicated data, data cached by various caching mechanisms and materialized views using any view selection methodology.

based on the following consideration: the accuracy of the current response is not affected by refreshing elements that are fresh or not involved in the current query. Thus, an efficient maintenance process should refresh local view entries that are both *stale* and *involved* in current query evaluation. We investigate the research question through two hypotheses.

The first hypothesis claims that *the accuracy of the answer can increase by maintaining part of the local view involved in the current query evaluation (HP1)*. Having materialized the intermediate results in a local view, the continuous queries join the local view with the stream. In fact, local view elements that are involved in current evaluation depend on the content of the stream in current evaluation which varies over different evaluations. We propose Window Service Join (WSJ), a join method to filter out local view elements that are not involved in current evaluation (i.e., their maintenance does not affect the response accuracy). In this way, the maintenance focuses on the elements that affect the accuracy of the current response.

The second hypothesis claims that *the accuracy of the answer increases by refreshing the (possibly) stale local view entries that would remain fresh in a higher number of evaluations (HP2)*. We propose Window Based Maintenance (WBM), a policy that assigns a score to the local view elements based on the estimated *best before time*, i.e., the time on which a fresh element estimated to become stale, and the number of next evaluations that the item is going to be involved. The former is possible by exploiting the change frequency of elements, while the second exploits the streaming part of the query and the window operator to (partially) foresee part of the future answers.

The paper is structured as follows. Section 2 introduces the main concepts at the basis of this work; Section 3 analyzes the problem, by providing a motivating example, the problem formalization and by identifying the requirements to design solutions. Section 4 presents the query-driven maintenance process, and an experimental evaluation is provided in Section 5. Finally, the paper closes with a brief review of relevant existing works in Section 6, and conclusions and future works in Section 7.

2 Background

An **RDF stream** S is a potentially unbounded sequence of time stamped informative units ordered by the temporal dimension:

$$S = ((d_1, t_1), (d_2, t_2), \ldots, (d_n, t_n), \ldots)$$

Where, given $(d_i, t_i) \in S$, t_i is the associated timestamp (as in [4,6,12], we consider the time as discrete), and d_i is an informative unit modelled in RDF, i.e., a set of one or more RDF statements. An RDF statement is a triple $(s, p, o) \in (I \cup B) \times I \times (I \cup B \cup L)$, where I, B, and L identify the sets of IRIs, blank nodes and literals respectively. An **RDF term** is an element of the set $(I \cup B \cup L)$.

An **RSP query language** allows to compose queries to be evaluated at different time instants in a continuous fashion: as the data in the streams change, different results are computed. Given a query q, the answer $Ans(q)$ is a stream where the results of the evaluations are appended. In general, RSP languages [4,6,12] extend the SPARQL query language [16] with operators to cope with streams.

SPARQL exploits **graph pattern expressions** to process RDF data; they are built by combining triple patterns and operators. A triple pattern is a triple $(ts, tp, to) \in (I \cup B \cup V) \times (I \cup V) \times (I \cup B \cup L \cup V)$, where V is the variable set. A graph pattern expression combines triple patterns using operators, e.g., unions, conjunctions, joins. The evaluation of graph pattern expressions produces a bag (i.e., un-ordered collections of elements that allow duplicates) of **solution mappings**; a solution mapping is a function that maps variables to RDF terms, i.e., $\mu : V \rightarrow (I \cup B \cup L)$. With $dom(\mu)$ we refer to the subset of V of variables mapped by μ. Given the focus of this paper, we present the `JOIN` and `SERVICE` operators. `JOIN` works on two bags of solution mappings Ω_1 and Ω_2:

$$join(\Omega_1, \Omega_2) = \{\mu_1 \cup \mu_2 \mid \mu_1 \in \Omega_1 \wedge \mu_2 \in \Omega_2 \wedge \mu_1 \text{ and } \mu_2 \text{ are compatible}\}$$

Two mappings are **compatible** if they assign the same values to the common variables[3], i.e., $\forall v \in dom(\mu_1) \cap dom(\mu_2), \mu_1(v) = \mu_2(v)$. We name **joining variables** the variables in $dom(\mu_1) \cap dom(\mu_2)$.

`SERVICE` is the clause at the basis of the federated extension [1], introduced in SPARQL 1.1. This clause indicates that a graph pattern expression has to be forwarded to and evaluated by a remote SPARQL endpoint. In this way, it is possible to retrieve only the relevant part of information to compute the query answer, instead of pulling the whole remote data and processing it locally.

Among operators in RSP languages, the **sliding window** is one of the most important ones. Due to the fact that streams are infinite, the query accesses the streaming data through **windows**, views over the stream that include subsets of the stream elements. The content of the window is a set of RDF statements and it can be processed through SPARQL expressions. In this work, we focus on time-based windows, that are defined through a time interval representing the portion of the stream they capture: a window $(o, c]$ contains all the elements $(d, t) \in S$ s.t. $o < t \leq c$. Time-based windows are generated by a time-based sliding window operator $\mathbb{W}$, defined through two parameters ω and β. The first, named **width**, defines the size of the windows (every window has an opening time o and a closing time c such that $c - o = \omega$); the second, named **slide**, defines the time step between windows (given two consecutive windows generated by $\mathbb{W}$ with opening time instants o_1 and o_2, $o_2 - o_1 = \beta$). When the width and the slide values are the same, the sliding window is named **tumbling window**: in this case, each element of the stream is in one and only one window, i.e., the stream is partitioned.

To close this section, we introduce the notion of accuracy and latency, that are used for the assessment of Quality of Service constraints. An RSP engine E is a system that evaluates continuous query over streams. Given a query q, $Ans(q)$ – the expected answer, and $Ans_E(q)$ – the answer provided by an engine E, the

[3] In this work, we do not treat the empty mappings.

accuracy $acc(E, q)$ is the ratio between the number of elements of $Ans_E(q)$ that are also in $Ans(q)$ and the total number of the elements in $Ans_E(q)$ (without repetitions) [15]. In a database system, the query latency is the time required to process the query answer. This definition has to be adapted for RSP engines, where queries are evaluated multiple times. In this case, the **query latency** is a set of values (one for each evaluation), and with $lat(E, q)$ we indicate the latency of the current evaluation of q in E.

3 Analysis of the Problem

In this section, we discuss the problem of maintaining local views in a Web stream processing. In Section 3.1, we discuss an example to highlight the critical aspects of the problem. In Section 3.2, we formalize the problem. Finally, in Section 3.3, we elicit the requirements of a solution for this problem. Those requirements take into account not only the aspects already studied in the database literature, but also new ones introduced by the Web setting and the presence of data streams.

3.1 Motivating Example

To motivate the problem introduced in Section 1, consider the following example[4]: the cloth brand ACME wants to persuade influential Social Network users to post commercial endorsements. To take precedence over the rival companies, the ACME Company wants to identify new influential users as soon as possible and persuade them. For this reason, ACME wants to develop an application on top of an RSP engine that runs a continuous query q (sketched in Listing 1.1) to identify the influential users.

Listing 1.1. Sketch of the query studied in the problem

```
1 REGISTER STREAM Ans(q) AS CONSTRUCT{ ?user a :InfluentialUser }
2 WHERE {
3   WINDOW W(200,20) ON S { ?user :isMentionedIn ?post [...] }
4   SERVICE BKG{ ?user :hasFollowers ?followerCount }
5   ... }
```

The identification process is based on two search criteria, associated to two main characteristics of influential users: first, users must be trend setters, i.e., there are more than 1000 posts mentioning them in the past 200 minutes. Second, the users must be famous, i.e., they have more than 10000 followers. ACME wants to have reports from the application every 20 minutes, and can accept approximate results with at least 75% accuracy. This identification process is encoded in the query q, that is evaluated over two input data: first, the micro-post stream is processed through a sliding `WINDOW` (in Line 3) to count the mentions; second, the number of follower (background data) is retrieved by invoking the

[4] Inspired by this SemTech 2011 talk: http://www.slideshare.net/testac/how-hollywood-learned-to-love-the-semantic-web.

BKG SPARQL endpoint (in Line 4) through the `SERVICE` clause. It is worth noting that the background data is quasi-static, which means the data changes very slowly, compared to the stream input.

An RSP engine can evaluate the joins involving `SERVICE` clauses with different strategies, as in SPARQL engines [2]. In the following, we analyze two of them. The first strategy, *Symmetrical Hash Join*, evaluates the *SERVICE* and the `WINDOW` graph pattern expressions, and then joins the results. The drawback of this strategy is the size of the `SERVICE` clause answer. In fact, its volume can be huge, and moving it from the remote endpoint to the local one is a time consuming task. Moreover, only a small subset of the `SERVICE` clause answer usually has compatible mappings in the `WINDOW` clause evaluation. So, most of the solutions retrieved from *BKG* are transferred and then discarded.

The second strategy, *Nested Loop Join* first evaluates the `WINDOW` graph pattern, and then submits a set of queries to the *BKG* service to retrieve the compatible mappings. This approach is the one currently implemented in query processors like ARQ (and consequently, in the C-SPARQL engine). In this case, only the relevant mappings for the current answer are retrieved (the triple pattern in Line 5 is bound with the values from the solution mappings of the `WINDOW` clause). However, this strategy also produces a high number of queries for the *BKG* SPARQL endpoint. In a continuous querying scenario, it can lead to a huge sequence of queries to be continuously sent to the remote service over time (and it could lead, in the worst case, to denial-of-service problem in *BKG*).

The *quasi-static* feature of the background data motivates the idea of materializing remote data in local views to limit the number of remote `SERVICE` invocations. In fact, local view eliminates the need of invoking `SERVICE` clauses. The local view is created by pulling the results of evaluating the `SERVICE` graph pattern at the system initialization (as in the first strategy). As alluded before, *BKG* data are changing. Thus, during the query evaluation, a *maintenance process* should refresh the data in local view to reflect those changes. The execution of the maintenance process is time consuming, due to the data exchange with the remote *BKG* service. In fact, the more frequent the maintenance process is applied, the more time is required to answer the current query. This leads to a loss of responsiveness but the response will be more accurate. Thus, the maintenance process should adjust the trade-off among accuracy and responsiveness of the evaluation. In database research, existing works on *adaptive maintenance* problem usually assume the existence of update streams [11] that push the changes in the local view; however, this assumption is rarely valid in a Web setting, where data are distributed and owned by different entities.

3.2 Problem Formalization

We can model the problem, in the context of an RSP engine E, as the execution of a continuous query q over an RDF stream S and a remote SPARQL endpoint BKG with some QoS constraints (α, ρ), i.e., the answer should have an accuracy equals or greater than α and should be provided at most in ρ time units. The output of the evaluation $Ans_E(q)$ is the sequence of answers produced by E

continuously evaluating q over time. The QoS constraints can be expressed in the following way:

$$(acc(E, q) > \alpha) \wedge (lat(E, q) < \rho) \text{ for each evaluation} \quad (1)$$

At each evaluation, the accuracy of the answer should be greater or equal to α, while the query latency should be lower or equal to ρ.

However, as the content of BKG changes over time, the evaluation of the SERVICE clause produces different solution mappings and consequently, the mappings in $\mathcal{R}$ become outdated and lead to wrong results. For this reason, each mapping $\mu^{\mathcal{R}} \in \mathcal{R}$ can be *fresh* or *stale*: $\mu^{\mathcal{R}}$ is fresh at time t if it is contained in the current evaluation of the SERVICE clause over BKG, it is stale otherwise, i.e., BKG changed and the evaluation of SERVICE produces a mapping μ^{S} different from $\mu^{\mathcal{R}}$.

A maintenance process selects a set of *elected* mappings $\mathcal{E} \subseteq \mathcal{R}$. The mappings in $\mathcal{E}$ will be refreshed through queries to the BKG SPARQL endpoint. The design of the maintenance process is key to the accuracy of the answer: if it correctly identifies the stale mappings and puts them in $\mathcal{E}$, the refresh action increases the number of fresh elements in $\mathcal{R}$ as well as in $Ans_E(q)$. If the number of update queries sent to BKG is high, the maintenance process is slow and influences the responsiveness of the query q. It is important to find stale mappings and put them in $\mathcal{E}$, to avoid unnecessary maintenance of still valid data.

To summarize, the problem is the design of a maintenance process to minimize both the number of stale elements involved in the computation of the current answer and the cost of the maintenance process w.r.t. the constraints on responsiveness and accuracy (α, ρ).

3.3 Elicitation of the Requirements

Requirements are critical to lead the design of the maintenance process. In fact, they specify the characteristics of the solution and ways to improve it.

Change Rate Distribution. Data in the background data set change with various rates. If the data elements change uniformly (i.e., all have similar change rates), oldest entries are highly likely to be stale entries. Thus, policies like Least Recently Updated (LRU) that updates the oldest entries, provides the best maintenance. However, in the Web it is possible to find many data sets where the uniform change rate assumption does not hold, e.g., DBPedia Live and social networks [17]. That is, the maintenance process should take into account various change rates of the data elements (requirement R1).

Furthermore, the change rate of a data element can vary overtime. For example, in Twitter, the follower number of a singer changes faster during concerts, and it changes slower when he is recording new albums. Thus, the maintenance process should be adaptive w.r.t the change rate variations at run-time (R2).

Query Features. Each query should satisfy the given constraints over responsiveness and accuracy (R3). The query processor should optimize the maintenance process to satisfy both of these constraints. However, there are cases where it is not possible to achieve the goal: when it happens, the maintenance process should raise an alert to the query processor (R4).

Moreover, it is possible to gather requirements while processing queries. First, the join between stream and quasi-static data exposes important information to improve the maintenance process: it may consider the join selectivity of mapping in the local view to identify those that have greater effect on accuracy (R5). Second, the streaming part of the query can be exploited by the maintenance process. In particular, the sliding window can enable the optimization the maintenance process: at each evaluation, the window slides, and part of the data is not removed from the window. Given the window definition, it is possible to compute how long a data item will remain in the system and use it in the maintenance process (R6), e.g., if two mappings have the same changing rate, we can update the one for which the compatible mapping from the stream has longer lifetime, as it has higher probability to save more future updates.

4 Solution

Our proposed solution is a query-driven maintenance process for the local view $\mathcal{R}$, in the context of the evaluation of continuous query q under QoS constraints on responsiveness and accuracy. The maintenance process is query-driven in the sense that it refreshes the mappings involved in the current query evaluation.

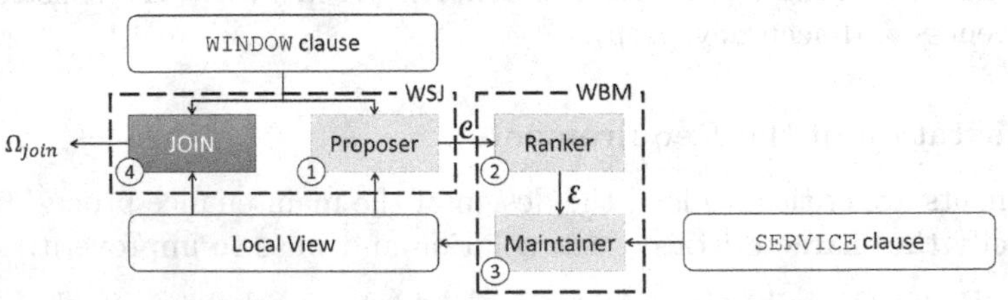

Fig. 1. The maintenance process components

The maintenance process identifies an elected set of mappings $\mathcal{E}$ and refresh them. The process, depicted in Figure 1, consists of the *proposer*, the *ranker* and the *maintainer* (the light gray boxes). The proposer (number 1 in the figure) selects the set $\mathcal{C}$ of candidate mappings for the maintenance from the local view $\mathcal{R}$. The idea behind the proposer is that the accuracy of the answer depends on the freshness of the mappings involved in the current query evaluation, so the maintenance should focus on them. The ranker (number 2 in the figure) computes the set $\mathcal{E} \subseteq \mathcal{C}$ of mappings to be refreshed; finally, the maintainer (number 3) refreshes the mappings in $\mathcal{E}$. After the maintenance process, the join (the dark gray box, number 4 in the figure) of the `WINDOW` and the

SERVICE expressions is computed by joining the results of the WINDOW clause evaluation with the local view (that contains the results of the SERVICE clause evaluation).

The solution is implemented in a system composed of two components, represented by the two dashed boxes in Figure 1. They are the Window Service Join method (WSJ) and the Window Based Maintenance policy (WBM). The former, presented in Section 4.1, performs the join and starts the maintenance process (as proposer); the latter, presented in Section 4.2, completes the maintenance process by ranking the candidate set and maintaining the local view. The intuition behind WBM is to prioritize the refresh of the mappings that are going to be used in the upcoming evaluations and that allows saving future refreshes.

As explained in Section 1, in the following we study the class of queries where there is a unique join between the WINDOW and the SERVICE graph pattern expressions. Moreover, to be compliant with SPARQL 1.0 endpoints, we assume that the queries sent to refresh the local view cannot make use of the VALUE clause. In other words, every query refreshes one replicated mapping.

4.1 The Window Service Join Method

WSJ performs the join and starts the maintenance process (as proposer). As explained above, the query answering process should take into account the QoS constraints (requirement R3) including latency and accuracy as defined in Equation 1. While the former can be tracked – the RSP engine can measure the query latency –, the latter can only be estimated, – the engine cannot determine if a mapping is fresh or stale, and consequently cannot compute the accuracy. This consideration leads the design of WSJ: it fixes the latency based on the responsiveness constraint ρ and maximize the accuracy of the answer accordingly.

To cope with the responsiveness requirement, we introduce the notion of *refresh budget* γ as the number of elements in $\mathcal{R}$ that can be maintained at each evaluation. As explained in Equation 1 the latency value should be lower or equal to the response time constraint ρ. Given the time r^q to evaluate the query [5], and the time to perform the maintenance process of γ elements ($\sum_{i=1}^{\gamma} r_i$), the latency of the engine E to execute the query q is:

$$\text{lat(E,q)} = r^q + \sum_{i=1}^{\gamma} r_i \leq \rho \tag{2}$$

Algorithm 1 shows WSJ. First invocation of the `next()` method retrieves the results of Ω_{join} (i.e., the block in Lines 1–12 is executed). That is, the WINDOW expression is evaluated and the bag of solution mappings Ω_{window} is retrieved from the WinOp operator (Lines 2–4). WSJ computes the candidate set $\mathcal{C}$ as the set of mappings in $\mathcal{R}$ compatible with the ones in Ω_{window} (Line 5). In fact, the mappings in $\mathcal{R}$ that are not compatible with the ones in Ω_{window} do not

[5] r^q includes the time to transform the query plan, optimize and evaluate it, and appending the output to the answer stream.

Algorithm 1. The WSJ next() method

```
1  if first iteration then
2      while WinOp has next do
3          append WinOp.next() to Ω_window
4      end
5      C = R.compatibleMappings(Ω_window);
6      M(C, γ);
7      it = Ω_window.iterator();
8  end
9  if it is not empty then
10     μ^W = it.next();
11     μ^R = R.compatibleMapping(μ^W);
12     return μ^W ∪ μ^R
13 end
```

affect the accuracy of the current query evaluation, so they are discarded. $\mathcal{C}$ and the refresh budget γ are the inputs of the maintenance policy M (Line 6), that refreshes the local view. Then, an iterator is initiated over Ω_{window} (Line 7). Finally, the join is performed (Lines 9–13) between each mapping in Ω_{window} and the compatible mapping from $\mathcal{R}$ and returned at each `next()` invocation.

Figure 2 shows the running example of this section. The join is performed at time 8. The local view $\mathcal{R}$ contains the result of the `SERVICE` clause evaluation(on the right): $\mu_a^{\mathcal{R}}$, $\mu_b^{\mathcal{R}}$, ..., $\mu_f^{\mathcal{R}}$. As described in Algorithm 1, WSJ first computes Ω_{window} (on the left): at time 8, it contains μ_a^W, μ_b^W, μ_c^W and μ_d^W. Next, WSJ starts the maintenance process. First, it filters $\mathcal{R}$ in order to build the candidate set $\mathcal{C}$ with the compatible mappings of the ones in Ω_{window}. $\mathcal{C}$ contains $\mu_a^{\mathcal{R}}$, $\mu_b^{\mathcal{R}}$, $\mu_c^{\mathcal{R}}$ and $\mu_d^{\mathcal{R}}$. The other two mappings in $\mathcal{R}$, $\mu_e^{\mathcal{R}}$ and $\mu_f^{\mathcal{R}}$, are not compatible with the mappings in Ω_{window}, so they are not considered for the refresh.

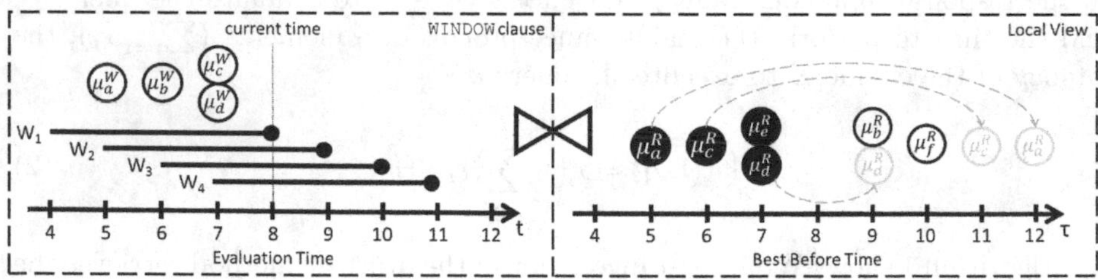

Fig. 2. An example of the maintenance process execution

4.2 The Window Based Maintenance Policy

The Window Based Maintenance (WBM) policy elects the mappings to be refreshed and maintains the local view accordingly. Its goal is to *maximize the accuracy of the query answer, given that it can refresh at most* γ *mappings at each evaluation.* WBM aims at identifying the stale mappings in the candidate set $\mathcal{C}$ and choose them for maintenance.

To determine if a mapping in $\mathcal{C}$ is fresh or stale, an access to the remote SPARQL endpoint BKG is required, and it is not possible (as explained above). To overcome this limitation, WBM computes the *best before time* of the mappings in $\mathcal{C}$: as the name suggests, it is an estimation of the time on which a fresh mapping becomes stale. Being only estimation, it is not certain that after the best before time the mapping becomes stale, but only *possibly stale.*

Algorithm 2. The M method

1 $\mathcal{PS}$ = possibly stale elements of $\mathcal{C}$;
2 **foreach** $\mu^{\mathcal{R}} \in \mathcal{PS}$ **do**
3   compute the remaining life time of $\mu^{\mathcal{R}}$;
4   compute the renewed best before time of $\mu^{\mathcal{R}}$;
5   compute the score of $\mu^{\mathcal{R}}$;
6 **end**
7 order $\mathcal{PS}$ w.r.t. the scores;
8 $\mathcal{E}$ = first γ mappings of $\mathcal{PS}$;
9 **foreach** $\mu^{\mathcal{R}} \in \mathcal{E}$ **do**
10     $\mu^{\mathcal{S}}$ = ServiceOp.next(JoinVars($\mu^{\mathcal{R}}$));
11   replace $\mu^{\mathcal{R}}$ with $\mu^{\mathcal{S}}$ in $\mathcal{R}$;
12   update the best before time τ of $\mu^{\mathcal{R}}$;
13 **end**

The maintenance policy operates as sketched in Algorithm 2. First, WBM identifies the possibly stale mappings. Next, WBM assigns a score to the possibly stale elements $\mathcal{PS}$ (Lines 2–6), in order to prioritize the mappings when the *refresh budget* is limited. The score is used to order the mappings. WBM builds the set of elected mappings $\mathcal{E} \subset \mathcal{PS}$ to be refreshed, by getting the top γ ones (Lines 7-8). Finally, the refresh is applied to maintain $\mathcal{R}$ (Lines 8–13): for each mapping of $\mathcal{E}$, WBM invokes the SERVICE operator to retrieve from the remote SPARQL endpoint the fresh mapping and replace it in $\mathcal{R}$. Additionally, in this block, the best before time values of the refreshed elements are updated. In the following, we go in depth in the algorithm using the example in Figure 2 to show how WBM works. We initialize the best before time of all local view elements with initial query evaluation time.

Identification of Possibly Stale Elements (Line 1). The core of WBM is the identification of possibly stale mappings. The local view $\mathcal{R}$ is modeled as:

$$\{(\mu_1^{\mathcal{R}}, \tau_1), (\mu_2^{\mathcal{R}}, \tau_2), \ldots, (\mu_n^{\mathcal{R}}, \tau_n)\}$$

Where $\mu_i^{\mathcal{R}}$ is the solution mapping in $\mathcal{R}$, and τ_i represents the current best before time. In Figure 2, the best before time values are shown on the right side of the picture (the black and white mappings in the local view), e.g., the best before time of $\mu_a^{\mathcal{R}}$ is 7, the one of $\mu_b^{\mathcal{R}}$ is 9 and the one of $\mu_c^{\mathcal{R}}$ is 6.

The set of possibly stale mappings $\mathcal{PS}$ is a subset of mappings in $\mathcal{C}$ such that their best before time is lower or equal to the current evaluation time. Continuing the example, given the candidate set $\mathcal{C} = \{\mu_a^{\mathcal{R}}, \mu_b^{\mathcal{R}}, \mu_c^{\mathcal{R}}, \mu_d^{\mathcal{R}}\}$, WBM selects the possibly stale mappings by comparing their best before time values with the the current time (8). The possibly stale mappings (the black mappings in the local view) are $PS = \{\mu_a^{\mathcal{R}}, \mu_c^{\mathcal{R}}, \mu_d^{\mathcal{R}}\}$. The best before time of $\mu_b^{\mathcal{R}}$ is 9, so this mapping does not need to be refreshed.

Computation of the Remaining Life Time (Line 3). The elements in $\mathcal{PS}$ have to be ordered to find the elected set $\mathcal{E}$. The ordering is based on two scoring values, presented in this and in the following step. The first is the number of next evaluations that involve the mapping. The continuous nature of the query and the presence of a sliding window allow to partially foreseeing which mappings are involved in the next evaluations. The **remaining life time** L is the number of future successive windows (i.e., evaluations) that involve the mappings in the local view $\mathcal{R}$. Given a sliding window $\mathbb{W}(\omega, \beta)$, we define L for the ith mapping $\mu_i^{\mathcal{R}}$ of $\mathcal{R}$ at time t as:

$$L_i(t) = \lceil \frac{t_i + \omega - t}{\beta} \rceil \tag{3}$$

Where t_i is the time that the compatible mapping μ_i^W enters the window.

Continuing the example in Figure 2, the remaining life time of $\mu_c^{\mathcal{R}}$ at the current time instant is $L_c(8) = 3$: the compatible mapping μ_c^W is in W_1, W_2 and W_3, so $\mu_c^{\mathcal{R}}$ is involved in three successive evaluations. Similarly, the values of $\mu_a^{\mathcal{R}}$ and $\mu_d^{\mathcal{R}}$ are 1 and 3 respectively.

Computation of the Renewed Best Before Time (Line 4). The second scoring value of WBM identifies the number of successive evaluations on which the element will remain (possibly) fresh, if refreshed now. In other words, first, WBS computes the *renewed best before time* τ_i^{next} of the mapping. The renewed best before time of the mapping $\mu_i^{\mathcal{R}}$ at time t is computed as:

$$\tau_i^{next} = \tau_i + I_i(t) \tag{4}$$

Where τ_i is the current best before time, and $I_i(t)$ is the **change interval**, and represents the time difference between the next and the current best before time. $I_i(t)$ is not known and has to be estimated. In fact, it is not possible to discover when the next change of a mapping is going to happen. In this paper, we estimate $I_i(t)$ using the change rate value of the element i.

In the running example, the renewed best before time of the elements in PS are shown by the arrows at the right of Figure 2 (the gray mappings): the one of $\mu_a^{\mathcal{R}}$ is 12, the one of $\mu_c^{\mathcal{R}}$ is 11 and the one of $\mu_d^{\mathcal{R}}$ is 9.

To have a scoring value comparable with the remaining life time value, it is necessary to normalize the renewed best before time with the window parameters

ω and β: this value, denoted with $V_i(t)$, is defined as:

$$V_i(t) = \lceil \frac{\tau_i^{next} - t}{\beta} \rceil$$

V measures in how many evaluation $\mu_i^{\mathcal{R}}$ will remain possibly fresh. The V values of $\mu_a^{\mathcal{R}}$, $\mu_c^{\mathcal{R}}$ and $\mu_d^{\mathcal{R}}$ at time 8 are respectively 4, 3 and 1.

Election of the Mappings to be Maintained (Lines 5–8). After the computation of $L_i(t)$ and $V_i(t)$, WBM assigns scores to the possibly stale elements to sort them for election. The score $score_i(t)$ of the ith mapping is defined as:

$$score_i(t) = \min(L_i(t), V_i(t)) \tag{5}$$

The idea behind this equation is to order the mappings based on number of refreshes that will be saved in the future. With regards to the example, $\mu_a^{\mathcal{R}}$ is the mapping with the highest renewed best before time, but the compatible mapping μ_a^W exits in the window W_2, so it is not going to be involved in the next evaluation unless μ_a^W enters the window again. In contrast, the compatible mappings of $\mu_c^{\mathcal{R}}$ and $\mu_d^{\mathcal{R}}$ exit respectively in W_3 and W_4, so the WBM prioritizes them. Between $\mu_c^{\mathcal{R}}$ and $\mu_d^{\mathcal{R}}$, the former has the priority on the latter. In fact, the renewed best before time of $\mu_c^{\mathcal{R}}$ is higher than the one of $\mu_d^{\mathcal{R}}$, and it does not need to be refreshed anymore in the (near) future. To summarize, the scores of the mappings in $\mathcal{PS}$ at time 8 are: $score_a(8) = 1$, $score_c(8) = 3$ and $score_d(8) = 1$.

Next, WBM ranks the $\mathcal{PS}$ entries by the score value (in decreasing order) and picks the top-γ to be refreshed. WBM picks randomly among mappings with same scores. It is worth noting that if the query q uses *a tumbling window*, the value of $L_i(t)$ is zero for all the elements and thus WBM sorts the possibly stale elements according to the $V_i(t)$ value. Given the refresh budget γ value 1, the elected mapping is $\mu_c^{\mathcal{R}}$, i.e., the one with the highest score (3).

Maintenance of the Local View (Lines 9–13). Finally, WBM refreshes the local view $\mathcal{R}$. WBM replaces each mapping in $\mathcal{E}$ with the respective fresh version retrieved from the remote service BKG. Additionally, WBM updates the best before time of the refreshed elements, by replacing the current best before time with the next one, as defined in Equation 4. Completing the example, the mapping $\mu_c^{\mathcal{R}}$ in $\mathcal{R}$ is replaced with the fresh value $\mu_c^{\mathcal{S}}$ retrieved by BKG, and the its best before time τ_c is updated to 11.

5 Experiments

In this section, we experimentally study the performance of WSJ and WBM to verify the validity of the hypotheses presented in Section 1. We set up two experiments: first (Section 5.1) investigates if WSJ improves the accuracy of the answer (HP1); second (Section 5.2) studies if WBM contributes to improve the accuracy of the answers (HP2). In the following, we describe the experimental setting to perform the experiments, inspired by the example in Section 3.1.

Data Set Preparation. An experimental data set is composed by streaming and background data. We built two data sets: one with real streaming data and synthetic background data; and one with real streaming and background data.

The *real streaming data* has been collected from Twitter. We identified four hundred Twitter verified users as a *user set*, and we collected three hours of tweets related to them. In the meanwhile, we also built the *real background data*, as the number of followers of the user set elements. We collected snapshots of the users' follower count every minute to keep track of the changes and to replay the evolution of the background data[6]. Additionally, we built the *synthetic background data* assigning a different change rate at each user (that is stable over time), and changing the follower count accordingly.

Query Preparation. The test query performs the join in Listing 1.1 between collected data. The query uses a window that slides every 60 seconds. Slides should be greater than or equal to intervals among consecutive snapshots to make sure that the current snapshot is different than the previous one.

5.1 Experiment 1

The first experiment aims at investigating the hypothesis HP1: *the accuracy of the answer can increase by maintaining part of the local view involved in the current query evaluation.* To verify this hypothesis, we follow a comparative approach: we evaluate the join using WSJ as join method, and we compare it with a set of baselines. As lower bound proposer, we consider the worst maintenance process (WST), that does no refresh local view throughout evaluations, i.e., it represents a proposer with an empty candidate set. As upper bound, we use BST (best): its candidate set consists of γ certainly stale elements (where γ is the refresh budget). This proposer cannot be applied in reality (as it is not possible to know if a local view element is stale or fresh), and we use it as upper bound. Finally, we use the proposer GNR: it uses the whole local view as candidate set, i.e., it maintains the local view without considering the query. To complete the maintenance process, a policy is required. We use two maintenance policies inspired by the random (RND) and Least-Recently Used (LRU) page replacement algorithms. RND picks γ mappings from the candidate set, while LRU chooses the γ least recently refreshed mappings in the candidate set.

Figure 3 shows the results of the experiment; the charts show the cumulative error over the multiple evaluations (the lower, the better). WST and BST are the lower and upper bounds so all the other results are between those two lines. It is possible to observe that GNR performs slightly better than the lower bound WST. Comparing GNR and WSJ, WSJ performs significantly better than GNR with both maintenance policies.

To study if the result generalizes, we repeated the experiment with different refresh budgets. To set the refresh budget, we first computed the average dimension of the candidate sets $|\bar{\mathcal{C}}| = 33$, and we set the refresh budget as 8%, 15% and

[6] It is worth to note that in this way we do not hit the Twitter API limits, see https://dev.twitter.com/rest/public/rate-limiting

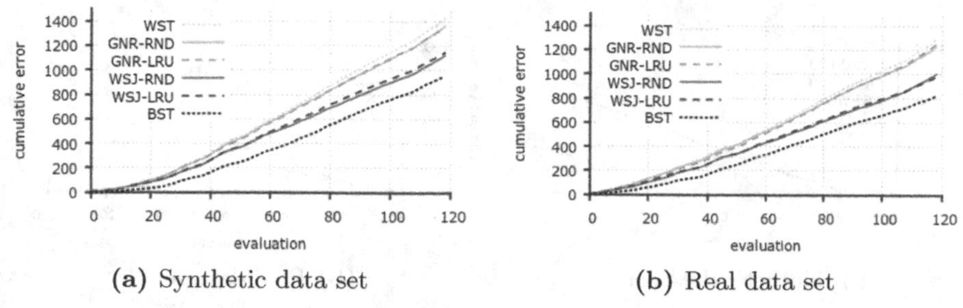

(a) Synthetic data set

(b) Real data set

Fig. 3. Evaluation of the WSJ proposer

Table 1. WSJ effect on maintenance accuracy in synthetic/real data sets

γ	Synthetic						Real					
	WST	GNR		WSJ		BST	WST	GNR		WSJ		BST
		RND	LRU	RND	LRU			RND	LRU	RND	LRU	
8%	0.23	0.26	0.27	**0.40**	0.38	0.49	0.30	0.34	0.33	0.46	**0.47**	0.56
15%	0.23	0.26	0.28	0.48	**0.51**	0.66	0.30	0.36	0.35	0.57	**0.58**	0.74
30%	0.23	0.32	0.33	0.64	**0.76**	0.94	0.30	0.41	0.41	0.68	**0.80**	0.98

30% of $|\bar{C}|$ (respectively 3, 5 and 10). Table 1 reports on the average accuracy for both the synthetic and the real data set. It is worth noting that WSJ shows better improvements than GNR when the refresh budget increases: moving γ from 8% to 30%, in the synthetic (real) data set GNR improves from 0.26 (0.27) to 0.32 (0.33), while WSJ improves the accuracy from 0.40 (0.38) to 0.64 (0.76). It happens because WSJ chooses the mappings from the ones currently involved in the evaluation, while GNR chooses from the whole local view. A similar trend is visible also when the real data set is considered.

5.2 Experiment 2

The second experiment aims at investigating the hypothesis HP2: *the accuracy of the answer increases by refreshing local view entries that estimated to be stale and would remain fresh in a higher number of evaluations.* This requires studying the performance of WBM. Like in the first experiment, we follow a comparative approach, and we compare WBM with other maintenance policies. As lower bound, we use WST (in this case represents a policy that does not refresh any mapping); as upper bound we use WBM*, i.e., the WBM policy that can access the real change time instants of the mappings from the remote service. Like BST, WBM* cannot be used in reality, due to the fact that change time instants are not available ahead of time. Finally, we use RND and LRU (presented in the previous section) as policies to make the comparison. Due to the good performance of WSJ, we used it as proposer for all policies.

Results of the experiments are shown in Figure 4. In both the synthetic and real data set cases, the WBM maintenance policy outperforms RND and LRU by having a lower cumulative error. This difference is more visible in the synthetic

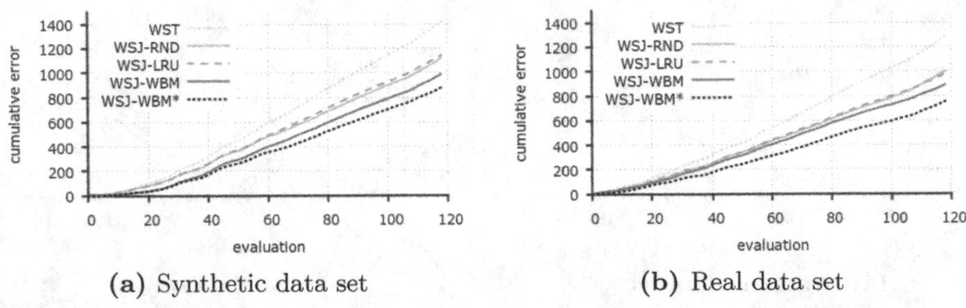

(a) Synthetic data set (b) Real data set

Fig. 4. Cumulative error of accuracy using WBM, LRU and RND as ranker

data set due to the fixed change rate assumption. Similarly, WST and WSJ-WBM* are lower and upper bounds respectively. Figure 4a and 4b shows that WSJ-WBM clearly outperforms baselines (WSJ-RND, WSJ-LRU).

We repeated the experiment with different time constraints (i.e., refresh budgets), in order to study the behavior of the policies under different situations. Results are shown in Table 2. In general WBM shows better performance than the two baseline policies we considered. However, WBM is more efficient on lower refresh budgets. Comparing WBM and WBM*, it is possible to notice that the accuracy difference increases as the refresh budget increases: WBM* accuracy move from 0.52 (0.59) for the synthetic (real) data set to 0.94 (0.98), while WBM moves from 0.46 (0.52) to 0.81 (0.80). In the experiment with the real data set, the estimation error is higher when the refresh budget is high; there WBM performance is equal to the LRU one.

Table 2. Accuracy comparison of LRU, RND & WBM in synthetic/real data sets

	Synthetic					Real				
γ	WST	WSJ RND	WSJ LRU	WSJ WBM	WSJ WBM*	WST	WSJ RND	WSJ LRU	WSJ WBM	WSJ WBM*
8%	0.23	0.39	0.38	**0.46**	0.52	0.30	0.45	0.47	**0.52**	0.59
15%	0.23	0.49	0.50	**0.60**	0.71	0.30	0.57	0.58	**0.61**	0.77
30%	0.23	0.64	0.76	**0.81**	0.94	0.30	0.68	**0.80**	**0.80**	0.98

6 Related Work

Local views, such as replicas and caches, materialize the content of remote sources in the query processor to improve availability, scalability and performance [9]. Any materialization methodology will lead to a trade-off among space/time. More materialization requires more space but will decrease the response time and vice versa. However, maintenance processes have to be introduced in order to update the view and reduce inconsistencies. View maintenance has been studied extensively in database community [3,9,11,19]. Any maintenance methodology will lead to a trade-off among response quality and time.

That is, the shorter maintenance intervals will lead to a higher response quality but will increase the response time due to the consumption of computational resources and vice versa. A common assumption among all maintenance methods is the existence of update streams, i.e, streams carrying the changes of the relations. An adaptive materialization strategy with an *eager view maintenance* (i.e., all the updates are processed on arrival) is proposed in [3]. It manages the trade-off among space and query response time and adaptively refines data for materialization by monitoring their cost/benefit ratio under different circumstances. In [11] a *lazy maintenance* (i.e., update processing can be postponed) solution is proposed. It works in cases where the cost of updating the views is high. In this work, authors propose a query-driven maintenance approach to apply a subset of update-stream so that user-defined constraints on the quality of the answer is not impaired. Providing approximate results according to the quality constraints is a well known problem [9]. In a similar attempt, [10] propose a technique to optimize the view maintenance process in order to target the trade-off between time and quality of the response. However, in a semantic web setting, update streams are not available because most of the SPARQL endpoints are not providing the update stream of their underlying data.

In [18] the time/quality trade-off has been addressed in a Semantic Web scenario: each query is split between the local query processor and a live query processor to achieve faster response than a live query processor and more fresh response than the local query processor. However, parameters to adjust the trade-off among freshness and fastness are fixed and therefore it is not possible to adjust them based on user-defined trade-off on a query basis.

7 Conclusions and Future Work

In this work, we studied the problem of evaluating continuous queries that access remote background data. Local views speed up the evaluation, but require maintenance processes to keep the replicated data updated. We elicited the requirements for designing a local view maintenance process, and we used them to build our solution. Considering the QoS constraints associated to the query (R3), the solution uses the available time to maximize the accuracy of the answer. It is done through two components, WSJ and WBM. WSJ identifies the candidate local view elements by keeping the compatible mappings from the WINDOW clause (R6). WBM identifies the set of possibly stale elements in WSJ output by considering the change rates (R1), and elects the ones to be maintained.

The maintenance process we propose can estimate the accuracy of the provided answer (R4): in fact, WBM identifies the set of possibly stale elements, and consequently the freshness of the response of the current evaluation. In future works, we plan to study the quality of this estimator.

A current limit of the solution is on how WBM estimates possibly stale elements. As explained, there is an error in the estimation of the best before time values, i.e., the time on which the elements in the local view may become stale. In future work, we aim at improving this estimation by exploring alternative methods to compute the time change interval $I_i(t)$, e.g., machine learning and event detection algorithms. More generally, we will extend WBM to take into account the requirements R2, i.e., the dynamic change rate of the elements.

A possible extension is related to the requirement R5. The current solution is designed for queries that have a one-to-one mapping between the results of `SERVICE` and `WINDOW` clauses. We aim at investigating the general case, where each mapping from the `SERVICE` clause evaluation join with a variable number of entries from the `WINDOW` clause evaluation. In those cases, various entries of local view affect the response accuracy differently. The maintenance policy should take this aspect into account when picking the local view entry to maintain.

Acknowledgments. This research has been partially funded by Science Foundation Ireland (SFI) grant No. SFI/12/RC/2289, EU FP7 CityPulse Project grant No.603095 and the IBM Ph.D. Fellowship Award 2014 granted to Dell'Aglio.

References

1. Aranda, C., Arenas, M., Corcho, Ó., Polleres, A.: Federating queries in SPARQL 1.1: Syntax, semantics and evaluation. J. Web Sem. **18**(1), 1–17 (2013)
2. Buil-Aranda, C., Polleres, A., Umbrich, J.: Strategies for executing federated queries in SPARQL1.1. In: Mika, P., et al. (eds.) ISWC 2014, Part II. LNCS, vol. 8797, pp. 390–405. Springer, Heidelberg (2014)
3. Babu, S., Munagala, K., Widom, J., Motwani, R.: Adaptive caching for continuous queries. In: ICDE 2005, pp. 118–129. IEEE (2005)
4. Barbieri, D.F., Braga, D., Ceri, S., Della Valle, E., Grossniklaus, M.: Querying RDF streams with C-SPARQL. SIGMOD Record **39**(1), 20–26 (2010)
5. Blanas, S., Patel, J.M., Ercegovac, V., Rao, J., Shekita, E.J., Tian, Y.: A comparison of join algorithms for log processing in mapreduce. In: SIGMOD 2010, pp. 975–986. ACM (2010)
6. Calbimonte, J., Jeung, H., Corcho, Ó., Aberer, K.: Enabling query technologies for the semantic sensor web. Int. J. Sem. Web Inf. Syst. **8**(1), 43–63 (2012)
7. Celino, I., Dell'Aglio, D., Della Valle, E., Huang, Y., Lee, T., Kim, S.-H., Tresp, V.: Towards BOTTARI: using stream reasoning to make sense of location-based micro-posts. In: García-Castro, R., Fensel, D., Antoniou, G. (eds.) ESWC 2011. LNCS, vol. 7117, pp. 80–87. Springer, Heidelberg (2012)
8. Goasdoué, F., Karanasos, K., Leblay, J., Manolescu, I.: View selection in semantic web databases. PVLDB **5**(2), 97–108 (2011)
9. Guo, H., Larson, P., Ramakrishnan, R.: Caching with good enough currency, consistency, and completeness. In: VLDB, pp. 457–468. VLDB Endowment (2005)
10. Guo, H., Larson, P., Ramakrishnan, R., Goldstein, J.: Relaxed currency and consistency: how to say good enough in SQL. In: SIGMOD, pp. 815–826. ACM (2004)
11. Labrinidis, A., Roussopoulos, N.: Exploring the tradeoff between performance and data freshness in database-driven web servers. PVLDB **13**(3), 240–255 (2004)
12. Le-Phuoc, D., Dao-Tran, M., Parreira, J.X., Hauswirth, M.: A native and adaptive approach for unified processing of linked streams and linked data. In: Aroyo, L., Welty, C., Alani, H., Taylor, J., Bernstein, A., Kagal, L., Noy, N., Blomqvist, E. (eds.) ISWC 2011, Part I. LNCS, vol. 7031, pp. 370–388. Springer, Heidelberg (2011)

13. Lécué, F., Tallevi-Diotallevi, S., Hayes, J., Tucker, R., Bicer, V., Sbodio, M.L., Tommasi, P.: Smart traffic analytics in the semantic web with STAR-CITY: Scenarios, system and lessons learned in Dublin City. J. Web Sem. **27**, 26–33 (2014)
14. Natsev, A., Chang, Y.-C., Smith, J.R., Li, C.-S., Vitter, J.S.: Supporting incremental join queries on ranked inputs. In: VLDB, pp. 281–290. Morgan Kaufmann (2001)
15. Parssian, A., Sarkar, S., Jacob, V.S.: Assessing information quality for the composite relational operation join. In: ICIQ, pp. 225–237. MIT (2002)
16. Schmidt, M., Meier, M., Lausen, G.: Foundations of sparql query optimization. In: ICDT, pp. 4–33. ACM (2010)
17. Sean, X., Xiaoquan, Z.: Impact of wikipedia on market information environment: Evidence on management disclosure and investor reaction. MIS Quarterly. Management Information Systems Research Center (2013)
18. Umbrich, J., Karnstedt, M., Hogan, A., Parreira, J.X.: Freshening up while staying fast: towards hybrid SPARQL queries. In: ten Teije, A., Völker, J., Handschuh, S., Stuckenschmidt, H., d'Acquin, M., Nikolov, A., Aussenac-Gilles, N., Hernandez, N. (eds.) EKAW 2012. LNCS, vol. 7603, pp. 164–174. Springer, Heidelberg (2012)
19. Viglas, S.D., Naughton, J.F., Burger, J.: Maximizing the output rate of multi-way join queries over streaming information sources. In: VLDB, pp. 285–296. VLDB Endowment (2003)

MIRROR: Automatic R2RML Mapping Generation from Relational Databases

Luciano Frontino de Medeiros[1], Freddy Priyatna[2(✉)], and Oscar Corcho[2]

[1] UNINTER, Curitiba, Brasil
luciano.me@uninter.com
[2] Ontology Engineering Group, Universidad Politécnica de Madrid, Madrid, Spain
ocorcho@fi.upm.es

Abstract. Two W3C recommendations exist for the transformation of RDB content into RDF: Direct Mapping (DM) and R2RML. The DM recommendation specifies the set of fixed transformation rules, whilst R2RML allows customising them. Here we describe the MIRROR system, which generates two sets of R2RML mappings. First, it creates a set of mappings that allow any R2RML engine to generate a set of RDF triples homomorphic to the ones that a DM engine would generate (they only differentiate in the URIs used). This allows R2RML engines to exhibit a similar behaviour to that of DM engines. Second, it produces an additional set of R2RML mappings that allow generating triples resulting from the implicit knowledge encoded in relational database schemas, such as subclass-of and M-N relationships. We demonstrate the behaviour of MIRROR using the W3C DM Test Case together with an extended version of one of its databases.

1 Introduction

The W3C RDB2RDF (Relational Database to Resource Description Framework) Working Group was created in 2009 with the mission to standardize languages for mapping relational data and relational database schemas into RDF and OWL. As a result of the work in the group, two recommendations were published in September 2012: Direct Mapping [1] and R2RML [2]. The former specifies the terms generation rules to be applied to generate automatically an RDF dataset that reflects the structure and content of the relational database. Since this may not be always adequate or optimal, especially in those cases when the relational database content needs to be transformed into RDF according to an existing ontology, R2RML allows customising the terms generation rules to be applied.

Hence R2RML provides more flexibility than its counterpart, the Direct Mapping specification. However, this comes at a cost for users interested in generating RDF from their relational databases: they need to learn how to create those R2RML mappings. Several tools have been made available to facilitate the task of mapping generation, as discussed in Section 2, but either they produce mappings in earlier RDB2RDF languages (e.g. the ODEMapster GUI, which produces R2O mappings) or are not usable enough (e.g. form-based tools that

P. Cimiano et al. (Eds.): ICWE 2015, LNCS 9114, pp. 326–343, 2015.
DOI: 10.1007/978-3-319-19890-3_21

only provide syntactic sugar to users, who still require a good knowledge of R2RML). An alternative approach to ease the burden of R2RML creation from users, making them more efficient, is to bootstrap the process with the creation of an initial R2RML mapping document that reflects the behaviour of the Direct Mapping specification, and then allow users to edit that document further, e.g. in a text editor. This has generally proven to be useful in our own work, since in many cases a large percentage of triple maps inside an R2RML mapping document are reused. This has also an additional positive side effect, which is the fact that any R2RML engine (e.g. morph-RDB) can be used to produce RDF following the Direct Mapping specification.

Furthermore, we have already pointed out that the Direct Mapping generates an RDF dataset that reflects the structure and content of the relational database. However, there are some well-known and widely-applied relational database patterns that usually encode some additional information that may be useful in this transformation process. For instance, some combinations of primary and foreign keys in relational tables are commonly used to represent parent-child, 1-N and M-N relationships between tables. This means that we may be able to push our approach further by generating as well some of that implicit information (such as subclass-of relationships, some specific object properties, etc.), in addition to the mappings generated following the Direct Mapping specification.

Motivational Example. Let us see an example, which will be used throughout the rest of the paper. Consider the database `D011`[1], from the W3C Direct Mapping Test Cases, with tables: `Student(ID, FirstName, LastName)` and `Sport(ID, Description)`, where `ID` is the primary key in both cases; and `Student_Sport( ID_Student, ID_Sport)`, where both columns form a composite primary key, and where `ID_Student` is a foreign key that refers to the column `ID` of the table `Student` and `ID_Sport` is a foreign key that refers to the column `ID` of the table `Sport`.

The constraints specified by the primary/foreign keys in the table `Student_Sport` represent an M-N relationship between table `Student` and table `Sport`. Thus, when transforming this database into RDF, one can expect that there will be an object property, for example `hasStudent`, with `Sport` as its domain and `Student` as its range, or viceversa with object property `hasSport`.

Now we will make the following modifications to that database, and will name the resulting database `D011B`. Figure 1 provides its graphical representation.

- Add another table `Person(ID, SSN)`, with `ID` as the primary key. We also add a foreign key constraint to the column `ID` of table `Student`, which refers to the column `ID` of the table `Person`. Then, we can see that there is a parent-child relationship, being the table `Person` the parent, and the table `Student` the child. This relationship implies that every property available in the parent is also inherited by the child, so that when we transform this database into RDF, the instances resulting from table `Student` will also have properties corresponding to the column `SSN` of the parent table `Person`.

[1] http://www.w3.org/2001/sw/rdb2rdf/test-cases/#D011-M2MRelations

Person	
ID (PK)	SSN
10	1234510
11	1234511
12	1234512

Contact		
CID (PK)	SID (FK)	Email
1	10	venus@hotmail.com
2	10	venus@gmail.com
3	11	fernando@yahoo.com
4	12	david@msn.com

Student		
ID (PFK)	FirstName	LastName
10	Venus	Williams
11	Fernando	Alonso
12	David	Villa

Student_Sport	
ID_Student (PFK)	ID_Sport (PFK)
10	110
11	111
11	112
12	111

Sport	
ID (PK)	Description
110	Tennis
111	Football
112	Formula1

Fig. 1. Graphical Representation of D011B Database

- Add another table `Contact(CID, SID, Email)` with `CID` as the primary key and `SID` as the foreign key that refers to the column `ID` in the table `Student`. The relationship between `Student` and `Contact` is a 1-N relationship, so we may expect to have an object property generated for this relationship, being `Student` the domain and `Contact` the range.

Contributions. The main contribution of this paper is the design and implementation of an algorithm that takes as an input a relational database and generates as an output an R2RML mapping document that includes two groups of mappings. The first group of mappings encodes the transformations that would be done by a Direct Mapping engine, with the only exception that the generated RDF will differ in the URIs that are generated for some RDF nodes. The second group of mappings encodes an additional set of transformations that exploit the implicit information that is normally contained in relational databases (e.g. subclass-of relationships, M-N relationships) and which are not exposed by directly following the Direct Mapping approach.

The rest of the paper is structured as follows. In Section 2 we discuss pre-R2RML and R2RML-compliant mapping generation systems. In Section 3 we present the core of our approach for the automatic generation of R2RML mappings from a relational database schema. In Section 4 we present some experiments applied to the set of test cases provided by the W3C RDB2RDF working group. In Section 5 we provide some conclusions on this paper and our planned future work.

2 Background and State of The Art

We start this section by providing some background on the two W3C recommendations that we have already referred to in the introduction: Direct Mapping and R2RML. Then we move into the description of some of the approaches that have been proposed so far for the generation of RDB2RDF mappings.

2.1 Background: W3C Direct Mapping and R2RML

As discussed in the introduction, the W3C **Direct Mapping** recommendation defines simple transformation rules to generate RDF from relational data, as follows:

- A rule to generate the subject URI that corresponds to each row of a database table. These subject URIs are the result of the concatenation of a base URI with the name of the primary key column, the symbol = and the value of the column, e.g., `<Student/ID=10>`. Blank nodes are generated in the case of tables that do not have any primary key defined.
- A rule to generate rdf:type triples from each row of a database table, e.g., `<Student/ID=10> rdf:type <Student>`.
- A rule to generate literal triples from each row of a database table. This rule generates the subject URI as the subject, the concatenation of the table name, the symbol # and the column name as the predicate, and the column value as the object. An example of a triple generated by this rule is the following: `<Student/ID=10> <Student#FirstName> "Venus"`.
- A rule to generate reference triples from each row of a datable table that contains a foreign key. This rule generates the subject URI as the subject, the concatenation of the table name, the string #ref- and the column name as the predicate, and the concatenation of the referenced table name, the primary key of the referenced table and the column value as the object. For example, this rule would generate the following triple: `<Contact/ID=1> <Contact#ref-SID> <Student/ID=10>`.

Unlike the Direct Mapping recommendation, **R2RML** allows users to specify the transformation rules to be applied. The most important R2RML elements are:

- `rr:TriplesMap`, used to transform database rows into RDF triples.
- `rr:LogicalTable`, used to specify the table (or view) whose rows are to be transformed.
- `rr:TermMap`, used to represent the term generation rules for components of the triples (subject, predicate, and object). There are three ways to specify them: constant (`rr:constant`), column `rr:column`, or template (`rr:template`).
- `rr:SubjectMap`, used to specify the transformation rules to generate the subjects of the triples.
- `rr:PredicateObjectMap`, used to specify the transformation rules to generate the pair of predicate and object of the triples, by means of `rr:PredicateMap` and `rr:ObjectMap`, respectively.

2.2 RDB2RDF Mapping Generation Approaches

Several works in the state of the art have dealt with the automatic or manual generation of RDB2RDF mappings.

The first group of systems that we can refer to is that of early RDB2RDF systems (e.g. ODEMapster [3], D2R Server [4], Triplify [5])[2], which used their own

[2] A longer list is available at http://d2rq.org/resources#projects

mapping languages to transform relational database content to RDF. They also had associated functionalities to ease the generation of such mappings, either manually or automatically. For example, the ODEMapster GUI was a NeOn Toolkit plugin that allowed specifying in a graphical manner the most common types of mappings that may be declared in the R2O language. D2R Server provides an automatic mapping generation functionality based on table and column names, as well as constraints such as primary and foreign keys, what is very similar to the one provided for the W3C Direct Mapping. This implementation was first available for the D2R language and later for R2RML. Triplify provides mapping templates for some well-known Web applications (e.g. WordPress, Joomla!, Drupal).

There are also other approaches that are independent from the mapping language and tool used to specify and run mappings. For instance, the authors in [6,10] analyse the different types of relationships that exist between relational tables, using primary and foreign keys, so as to determine the classes and properties of the expected results in RDF. However, no mappings are generated as a result of this analysis, what means that this work cannot be reused by other RDB2RDF engines. More recent work [7] has proposed a fixed set of rules for saturating mappings, once that the mappings between the relational database and an ontology have been defined by a domain expert. In fact, the motivation example that we have described in our example in section 1 is inspired by that work.

In [8] the authors proposed a semi-automatic mapping generation process, where R2RML mappings are generated based on a set of semantic correspondences (for classes and properties) defined by domain experts. And the authors in [9] present a GUI-based R2RML mapping editor to help non-expert users to create and modify their mappings.

However, none of the aforementioned approaches and systems deals with the automatic generation, from relational databases, of R2RML mappings that encode the implicit information that can be obtained from the relational database schema.

3 Automatic Generation of R2RML Mappings

Our process for automatically generating R2RML mappings from a relational database schema is depicted in Figure 2. The system receives as an input either the connection details to an existing database or a SQL file containing the database schema (represented by SQL DDL/DML statements). Then the process consists of two main steps:

1. **Identification of Relationships between Tables**. In this step, the relationships between tables are extracted, as well as their cardinality and the columns and constraints that are present in the database schema.
2. **Generation of R2RML Mappings**. In this step, the R2RML triples maps that correspond to the patterns identified in the previous step are generated.

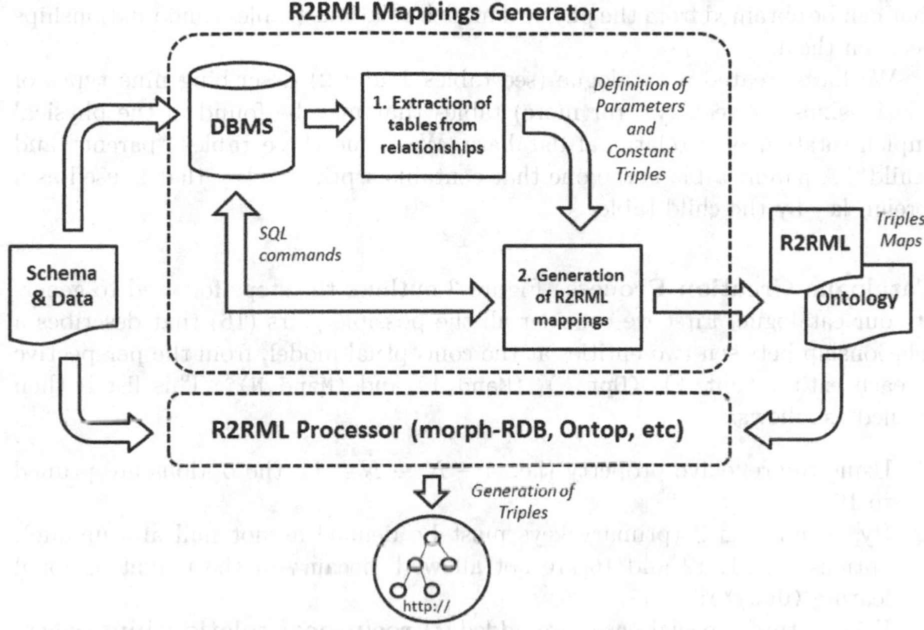

Fig. 2. A general overview of the R2RML mapping generation process in MIRROR

We consider two assumptions about the relational schema, so as to ensure completeness of the mapping process and preservation of information, as discussed in [10]:

1. The relational schema must be normalized, at least, in third normal form (3NF).
2. Primary keys must be defined as not null and unique.

Next we discuss about the typical patterns that can be found in a relational database schema and our approach to convert them into R2RML mappings.

3.1 A Catalogue of Typical Patterns in Relational Schemas

A typical database modeling process considers three types of models: **conceptual** (where the elements are described using an Entity-Relationship or an Extended Entity-Relationship diagram), **logical** (which uses the relational model and is independent of the target database management system) and **physical** (which depends on the underlying database management system, defines how data is stored and declares constraints and keys). While conceptual and logical models may in principle be the most adequate to understand the domain of a database, given their higher level of abstraction and technology independence, these models are not commonly available. Therefore, R2RML mapping generation algorithms need to be designed taking into account the information that can be obtained from the physical model: relations (tables) and relationships between them.

We have created a catalogue (see tables 1 and 2) describing nine types of relationships between two (or more) tables that may be found in the physical implementation of a relational database. We name these tables “parent“ and “child“. A parent table is the one that contains a primary key that is used as a foreign key by the child table.

Catalogue Creation Process. Figure 3 outlines the steps followed to generate our catalogue. First we consider all the possible pairs (16) that describes a relationship between two entities at the conceptual model, from the perspective of each entity: `(Opt,1)`, `(Opt,N)`, `(Mand,1)` and `(Mand,N)`[3]. This list is then pruned as follows:

1. Using the reflexive property (i.e., $1 - N \equiv N - 1$), the options are pruned to 10.
2. By assumption 2 (primary keys must be defined as not null and unique), options 10, 11, 12 and 16 are not allowed, because of the parent optional feature `(Opt,X)`:
3. Finally, three special cases are added: i) **reciprocal relationships**, where one parent may be (optionally) related to only one child, and one child may be related to only one parent, respectively; ii) **self (or recursive) relationships**, where one instance of the parent may be related to another instance of the same parent; and iii) **n-ary relationships**, which involve many relationships, having many child tables connected to one parent table.

As a result, the catalogue is reduced to nine patterns, which need to be detected in the physical model of the database.

Catalogue Description. These nine patterns are graphically depicted in tables 1 and 2, which shows how they are normally specified in the conceptual (already discussed), logical and physical models. In the **logical model** we specify the number of relations (tables) involved, as well as the type of relationship between them. In the **physical model** we describe whether null values are accepted in the key column (primary or foreign) of each relation.

Now we describe each of the rows of tables 1 and 2:

1. Rows 1 and 2a get transformed into a single table in the relational model (and hence also in the physical model).
2. Row 2b may be considered as a special case of row 5a. A special case of an IS-A relationship using two tables may be also considered here.
3. Row 3 indicates a reciprocal relationship case between two tables and it matches with twice 1:N case not mandatory, as row 5a also states.

[3] Opt and Mand refer to whether the relationship is optional or mandatory, and the second item refers to the maximum cardinality, which may be 1 or uningspecified.

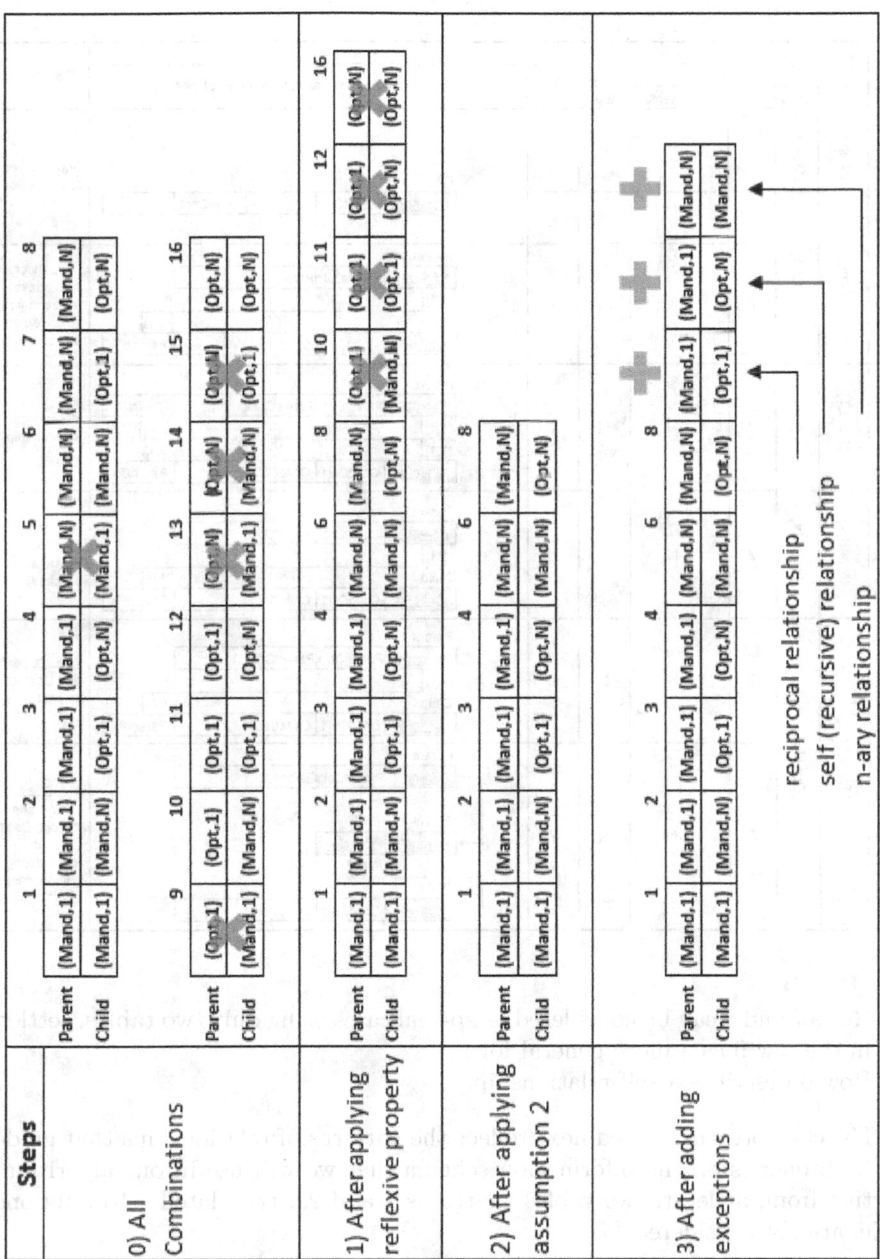

Fig. 3. Obtaining the Catalogue for Guiding the R2RML Mapping Generation

Table 1. Correspondences between conceptual, logical and physical models (rows 1 to 5)

		Conceptual		Logical		Physical			Comments
						Nullable		Graphical Representation for a Generic Model	
		Parent	Child	Tables	Relationships	Parent	Child		
1		(Mand,1)	(Mand,1)	1	-	N	-	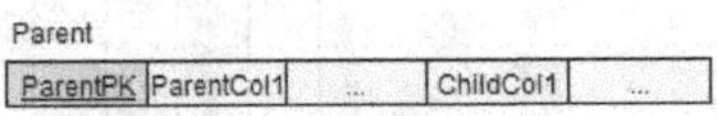 Parent ParentPK | ParentCol1 | ... | ChildCol1 | ...	One table, no relationships
2	a	(Mand,1)	(Opt,1)	1	-	N	-		
	b			2	1-N	N	Y	Parent ParentPK | ParentCol1 | ParentCol2 | ... (1,1) → (0,1) Child ChildPK | ChildCol1 | ChildCol2 | ... | ParentFK	Used for subclass relationships (e.g. *Person* and *Student*)
3		(Mand,1)	(Opt,1)	2	1-N	N	Y	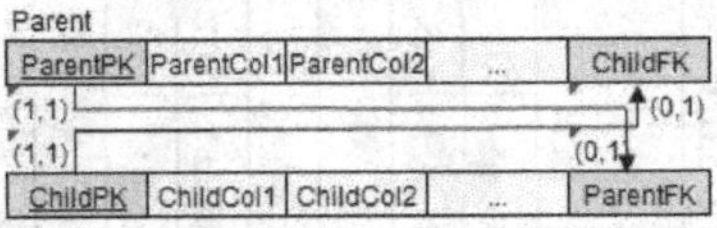 Parent ParentPK | ParentCol1 | ParentCol2 | ... | ChildFK (1,1) → (0,1) (1,1) → (0,1) ChildPK | ChildCol1 | ChildCol2 | ... | ParentFK	Reciprocal relationship
4		(Mand,1)	(Mand,N)	2	1-N	N	N	Parent ParentPK | ParentCol1 | ParentCol2 | ... (1,1) → (1,N) Child ChildPK | ChildCol1 | ChildCol2 | ... | ParentFK	(e.g. *Student* and *Contact*, mandatory case)
5	a	(Mand,1)	(Opt,N)	2	1-N	N	Y	Parent ParentPK | ParentCol1 | ParentCol2 | ... (1,1) → (0,N) Child ChildPK | ChildCol1 | ChildCol2 | ... | ParentFK	(e.g. *Student* and *Contact*, optional case)
	b			3	M-N	N	Y	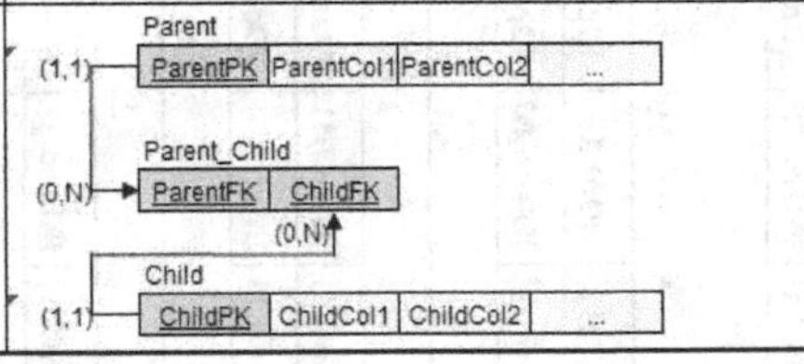 Parent (1,1) ParentPK | ParentCol1 | ParentCol2 | ... Parent_Child (0,N) ParentFK | ChildFK (0,N) Child (1,1) ChildPK | ChildCol1 | ChildCol2 | ...	(e.g. *Student*, *Sport* and *Student_Sport*, if considering optional case)

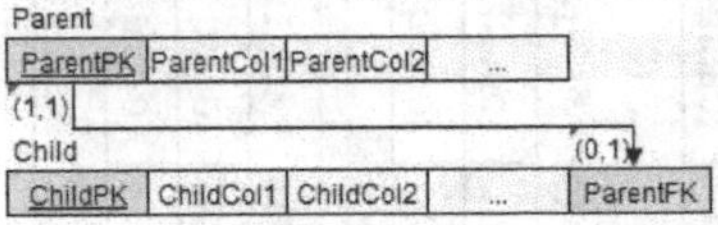

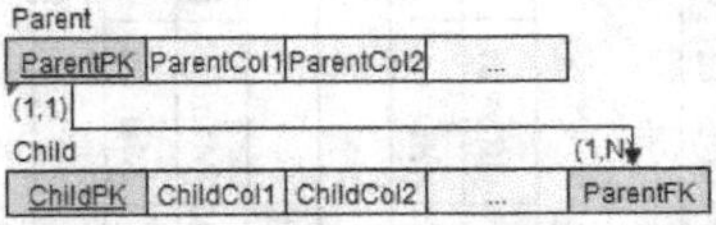

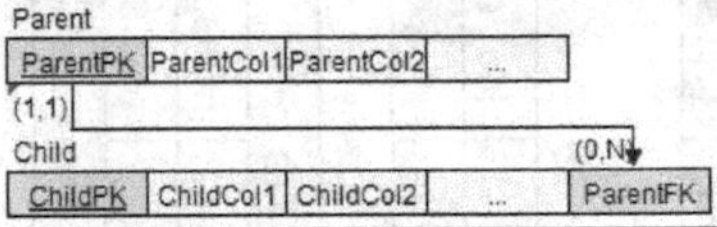

4. Rows 7 and 8 can be considered as special cases using only two tables, settled in the row 9 as a more general form.
5. Row 6 describes a self-relationship.

The categories described next reflect the patterns of relationships that guide the SQL queries on the information schema that we will use in our algorithm, starting from, at least, two tables (patterns 1 and 2a, translated into only one table, are not considered):

1. **1:N**, **optional** entity (rows 2b, 3, 5a, 6a and 6b).
2. **1:N**, **mandatory** entity (row 4)
3. **M:N** having **2 tables**, optional or mandatory (rows 5b, 7 and 8)
4. **M:N** having **more than 2 tables**, optional or mandatory (row 9)

Table 2. Correspondences between conceptual, logical and physical models (rows 6 to 9)

		Conceptual		Logical		Physical			Comments
						Nullable		Graphical Representation for a Generic Model	
		Parent	Child	Tables	Relationships	Parent	Child		
6	a	(Mand,1)	(Opt,N)	1	1-N	N	Y	Parent: ParentPK, ParentCol1, ParentCol2, ..., ParentFK; (1,1) → (0,N)	Self relationship (or recursive relationship)
	b			2	1-N	N	Y	Parent: ParentPK, ParentCol1, ParentCol2, ...; (1,1) → (0,N) Child: ChildPK, ParentFK, ChildCol1, ChildCol2, ...	
7		(Mand,N)	(Mand,N)	3	M-N	N	N	Parent: ParentPK, ParentCol1, ParentCol2, ... (1,1); Parent_Child: ParentFK, ChildFK (1,N), (1,N); Child: ChildPK, ChildCol1, ChildCol2 (1,1)	(e.g. tables *Student*, *Sport* and *Student_Sport*, mandatory case)
8		(Mand,N)	(Opt,N)	3	M-N	N	Y	Parent: ParentPK, ParentCol1, ParentCol2, ... (1,1); Parent_Child: ParentFK, ChildFK (0,N), (0,N); Child: ChildPK, ChildCol1, ChildCol2, ... (1,1)	Same as 5b
9		(Mand,N)	(Mand,N) or (Opt,N)	>=3	M-N	N	Y or N	Child: ChildPK, ChildCol1, ChildCol2, ... (1,1), (X,N); Parent_Child1: ParentFK, Child1FK (X,N); Parent: ParentPK, ParentCol1, ParentCol2, ... (1,1); Parent_ChildN: ParentFK, ChildNFK (X,N), (X,N); Child: ChildNPK, ChildNCol1, ChildNCol2, ... (1,1)	N-ary relationships (i.e. many different combinations involving rows 7 and 8)

3.2 Algorithms for the Generation of R2RML Mappings

Two different algorithms are proposed for R2RML mapping generation: one for 1:N relationships (Algorithm 1) and another one for M:N relationships (Algorithm 2).

In Algorithm 1 (Cardinality 1-N) the outer loop goes through all primary keys from the parent table, and executes three procedures that produce R2RML mapping components:

- *triplesMap(n)*: it stores an ordered, auto-incremented triples maps, indexed by n, according to the template `<#TriplesMap{n}>`.

- *logicalTable(RS)*: it stores the mapping component `rr:logicalTable` for the parent table RS.
- *subjectMap(RS, KS)*: it stores the mapping component `rr:subjectMap`, taking in account the template `rr:template "http://IRI/RS/{KS}"`, where `IRI` is a parameter defined by the user.

The inner loop stores the mapping component `rr:predicateObjectMap`. It loops through all the columns that belong to the parent table (represented by argument $attr(RS)$). When the index n is incremented, the graph for the child table is generated, considering now:

- *triplesMap(n)*: it has the same behaviour as for the parent table.
- *logicalTable(RT)*: it stores the mapping component `rr:logicalTable` for the child table RT.
- *subjectMap(RT, KT)*: it stores the mapping component `rr:subjectMap`, taking in account the template `rr:template "http://IRI/RT/{KT}"`.

After another inner loop with respect to the `rr:predicateObjectMap` for the child table, the algorithm registers the relationship, by means of the mapping component `rr:joinCondition`, linking the primary key KS from the parent table with the foreign key KT from the child table.

Algorithm 2 (Cardinality M-N) is different, since we use one more loop on all rows obtained from evaluation $[\![\phi]\!]_I$ (categories 3 and 4).

Algorithm 1 1-N Cardinality

```
Require: attr(φ) = {RS, KS, RT, KT}
if card([[φ]]_I) = 1 then
    n = 1
    for all KS do
        triplesMap(n)                         ▷ Generates triples map for RS (parent table)
        logicalTable(RS)
        subjectMap(RS, KS)
        for all attr(RS) do
            predicateObjectMap(attr(RS))
        end for
        n ← n + 1
        triplesMap(n)                         ▷ Generates triples map for RT (child table)
        logicalTable(RT)
        subjectMap(RT, KT)
        for all attr(RT) do
            predicateObjectMap(attr(RT))
        end for
        joinCondition(KS, KT)                 ▷ Generates join condition
        n ← n + 1
    end for
end if
```

Algorithm 2 M-N Cardinality

```
Require: attr(ϕ) = {RS, KS, RT, KT}
if card([[ϕ]]_I) > 1 then
    for all tuples in ϕ do
        n = 1
        for all KS do
            triplesMap(n)                    ▷ Generates triples map for RS (parent table)
            logicalTable(RS)
            subjectMap(RS, KS)
            for all attr(RS) do
                predicateObjectMap(attr(RS))
            end for
            n ← n + 1
            triplesMap(n)                    ▷ Generates triples map for RT (child table)
            logicalTable(RT)
            subjectMap(RT, KT)
            for all attr(RT) do
                predicateObjectMap(attr(RT))
            end for
            joinCondition(KS, KT)            ▷ Generates join condition
            n ← n + 1
        end for
    end for
end if
```

Subclass Identification. We use saturation to extend the set of R2RML mappings that has been initially created, exploiting subclass relationships that can be found in the database physical model. Unlike the work presented in [7], our work does not consider the use of an existing ontology to guide this saturation process. Our saturation approach considers two cases that can appear in the database physical model:

1. An IS-A relationship with cardinality 1-1 between a parent table and its child, having a common primary key table (row 2b from table 1).
2. An IS-A relationship with cardinality 1-N between a parent table and its child, becoming 1-1 after a data checking, testing whether any tuple in the parent table is related to only one tuple in the child table (it may happen with rows 4, 5a from 1, and 6a and 6b from table 2).

In these cases, the R2RML triple map for the child table is saturated with additional attributes from the parent table. An extra constant triple map is generated to feature explicitly the hierarchy, using `rdfs:subClassOf`.

Object Property Identification. Covering rows 5b from table 1; and 7, 8 and 9 from table 2, M-N relationships are represented by 3 tables. The binary table between parent and child tables, having the primary keys respectively as foreign keys, can be understood as an object property. Our R2RML mapping generator can create constant triples maps, templated as object property `ParentHasChild` and putting also its inverse, `ChildBelongsToParent`, using `owl:ObjectProperty`, `owl:inverseOf`, `rdfs:domain` and `rdfs:range`.

Datatype Property Identification. In the wake of the object properties handling, all columns of tables in the database schema are featured as datatype properties. The mapping generator creates constants triples maps (using `owl:DatatypeProperty`) considering the table to which the column belongs as the domain (using `rdfs:domain`), and the column data type as the range (using `rdfs:range`).

4 Implementation and Experimentation

The algorithms described in this paper have been implemented in MIRROR[4] (MappIng from Relational to Rdf generatOR) and have been integrated with morph-RDB[5] [11]. We have performed some experiments in order to show that our system can obtain R2RML mappings that encode the semantics in the W3C Direct Mapping specification, and furthermore that our system can generate R2RML mappings that also lift-up the implicit semantics encoded in the database.

We use two datasets in this experimentation: the set of databases provided in the Direct Mapping Test Cases, and we extend one of the databases (D011) to encode a parent-child relationship.

4.1 Experimentation Using the Direct Mapping Test Cases

The Direct Mapping Test Cases[6] is a test suite provided by the W3C RDB2RDF Working Group, which consists of a collection of test cases covering various database schemes such as databases without tables, databases with one table, with 1-N relationships, and with M-N relationships. In each of the test cases, the triples that can be expected as a result of applying Direct Mapping rules are provided. Thus, this test suite is a suitable source for us to evaluate our system, enabling us to see if our system produces the expected Direct Mapping results. In addition to that, we can also easily see the additional triples generated by the saturated mappings resulting from the identification of pattern relationships described in Section 3.

Here we discuss the database of Test Case `D011`, which consists of three tables `Student`, `Sport`, and `Student_Sport`. The table `Student_Sport` acts as a binary table that enables the M-N relationship between table `Student` and table `Sport`. The result of applying Direct Mapping rules over the database D011 can be seen in Listing 1.1.

[4] https://github.com/oeg-upm/MIRROR
[5] https://github.com/oeg-upm/morph-rdb
[6] http://www.w3.org/2001/sw/rdb2rdf/test-cases/

Listing 1.1. The Result of Applying Direct Mapping Rules Over D011 Test Case Database

```
<Student/ID=10> rdf:type <Student> .
<Student/ID=10> <Student#FirstName> "Venus".
<Student/ID=10> <Student#ID> 10 .
<Student/ID=10> <Student#LastName> "Williams" .
<Student/ID=11> rdf:type <Student> .
<Student/ID=11> <Student#FirstName> "Fernando".
<Student/ID=11> <Student#ID> 11 .
<Student/ID=11> <Student#LastName> "Alonso" .
<Student/ID=12> rdf:type <Student> .
<Student/ID=12> <Student#FirstName> "David".
<Student/ID=12> <Student#ID> 12 .
<Student/ID=12> <Student#LastName> "Villa" .
<Student_Sport/ID_Student=10;ID_Sport=110> rdf:type <Student_Sport> .
<Student_Sport/ID_Student=10;ID_Sport=110> <Student_Sport#ID_Student> 10 .
<Student_Sport/ID_Student=10;ID_Sport=110> <Student_Sport#ref-ID_Student> <Student/ID=10> .
<Student_Sport/ID_Student=10;ID_Sport=110> <Student_Sport#ID_Sport> 110 .
<Student_Sport/ID_Student=10;ID_Sport=110> <Student_Sport#ref-ID_Sport> <Sport/ID=110> .
<Student_Sport/ID_Student=11;ID_Sport=111> rdf:type <Student_Sport> .
<Student_Sport/ID_Student=11;ID_Sport=111> <Student_Sport#ID_Student> 11 .
<Student_Sport/ID_Student=11;ID_Sport=111> <Student_Sport#ref-ID_Student> <Student/ID=11> .
<Student_Sport/ID_Student=11;ID_Sport=111> <Student_Sport#ID_Sport> 111 .
<Student_Sport/ID_Student=11;ID_Sport=111> <Student_Sport#ref-ID_Sport> <Sport/ID=111> .
<Student_Sport/ID_Student=11;ID_Sport=112> rdf:type <Student_Sport> .
<Student_Sport/ID_Student=11;ID_Sport=112> <Student_Sport#ID_Student> 11 .
<Student_Sport/ID_Student=11;ID_Sport=112> <Student_Sport#ref-ID_Student> <Student/ID=11> .
<Student_Sport/ID_Student=11;ID_Sport=112> <Student_Sport#ID_Sport> 112 .
<Student_Sport/ID_Student=11;ID_Sport=112> <Student_Sport#ref-ID_Sport> <Sport/ID=112> .
<Student_Sport/ID_Student=12;ID_Sport=111> rdf:type <Student_Sport> .
<Student_Sport/ID_Student=12;ID_Sport=111> <Student_Sport#ID_Student> 12 .
<Student_Sport/ID_Student=12;ID_Sport=111> <Student_Sport#ref-ID_Student> <Student/ID=12> .
<Student_Sport/ID_Student=12;ID_Sport=111> <Student_Sport#ID_Sport> 111 .
<Student_Sport/ID_Student=12;ID_Sport=111> <Student_Sport#ref-ID_Sport> <Sport/ID=111> .
<Sport/ID=110> rdf:type <Sport> .
<Sport/ID=110> <Sport#ID> 110 .
<Sport/ID=110> <Sport#Description> "Tennis" .
<Sport/ID=111> rdf:type <Sport> .
<Sport/ID=111> <Sport#ID> 111 .
<Sport/ID=111> <Sport#Description> "Football" .
<Sport/ID=112> rdf:type <Sport> .
<Sport/ID=112> <Sport#ID> 112 .
<Sport/ID=112> <Sport#Description> "Formula1" .
```

Listing 1.2. The Generated R2RML Mappings Correspond to Direct Mapping Triples

```
<#TriplesMap5> a rr:TriplesMap;
    rr:logicalTable [ rr:tableName "student"; ];
    rr:subjectMap [ rr:class <Student>; rr:template "Student/{ID}"; rr:termType rr:IRI; ];
    rr:predicateObjectMap [ rr:predicate <Student#ID>; rr:objectMap [ rr:column "ID"; rr:datatype xsd:integer ; ];];
    rr:predicateObjectMap [ rr:predicate <Student#FirstName>;rr:objectMap [ rr:column "FirstName"; rr:datatype xsd:string ; ];];
    rr:predicateObjectMap [ rr:predicate <Student#LastName>; rr:objectMap [ rr:column "LastName"; rr:datatype xsd:string ; ]; ].

<#TriplesMap10> a rr:TriplesMap;
    rr:logicalTable [ rr:tableName "student_sport"; ];
    rr:subjectMap [ rr:class <Student_Sport>; rr:template "Student_Sport/{ID_Student}/{ID_Sport}"; rr:termType rr:IRI;];
    rr:predicateObjectMap[rr:predicate <Student_Sport#ID_Student>;rr:objectMap[rr:column "ID_Student";rr:datatype xsd:integer ;];];
    rr:predicateObjectMap[rr:predicate <Student_Sport#ID_Sport>;rr:objectMap[rr:column "ID_Sport";rr:datatype xsd:integer ;];];
    rr:predicateObjectMap [rr:predicate <Student_Sport#ref-ID_Student>;rr:objectMap [
        rr:parentTriplesMap <#TriplesMap5>;rr:joinCondition [ rr:child "ID_Student"; rr:parent "ID"; ];];];
    rr:predicateObjectMap [ rr:predicate <Student_Sport#ref-ID_Sport>;rr:objectMap [
        rr:parentTriplesMap <#TriplesMap1>; rr:joinCondition [ rr:child "ID_Sport"; rr:parent "ID"; ];];].

<#TriplesMap1> a rr:TriplesMap;
    rr:logicalTable [ rr:tableName "Sport"; ];
    rr:subjectMap [ rr:class <Sport>;rr:template "Sport/{ID}";rr:termType rr:IRI;];
    rr:predicateObjectMap [rr:predicate <Sport#ID>;rr:objectMap [ rr:column "ID"; rr:datatype xsd:integer ; ]; ];
    rr:predicateObjectMap [rr:predicate <Sport#Description>;rr:objectMap [ rr:column "Description"; rr:datatype xsd:string ; ];].
```

When the same database schema and instance are passed to MIRROR, it generates the R2RML mappings shown in Listing 1.2.

Listing 1.3. Direct Mapping triples of morph-RDB Result Over D011 Test Case Database

```
<Student/10> rdf:type <Student> .
<Student/10> <Student#FirstName> "Venus"^^xsd:string .
<Student/10> <Student#ID> "10"^^xsd:integer .
<Student/10> <Student#LastName> "Williams"^^xsd:string .
<Student/11> rdf:type <http :// example.com/Student .
<Student/11> <Student#FirstName> "Fernando"^^xsd:string .
<Student/11> <Student#ID> "11"^^xsd:integer .
<Student/11> <Student#LastName> "Alonso"^^xsd:string .
<Student/12> rdf:type <http :// example.com/Student> .
<Student/12> <Student#FirstName> "David"^^xsd:string .
<Student/12> <Student#ID> "12"^^xsd:integer .
<Student/12> <Student#LastName> "Villa"^^xsd:string .
<Student_Sport/10/110> rdf:type <Student_Sport> .
<Student_Sport/10/110> <Student_Sport#ID_Student> "10"^^xsd:integer> .
<Student_Sport/10/110> <Student_Sport#ref-ID_Student> <Student/10> .
<Student_Sport/10/110> <Student_Sport#ID_Sport> "110"^^xsd:integer> .
<Student_Sport/10/110> <Student_Sport#ref-ID_Sport> <Sport/110> .
<Student_Sport/11/111> rdf:type <Student_Sport> .
<Student_Sport/11/111> <Student_Sport#ID_Student> "11"^^xsd:integer> .
<Student_Sport/11/111> <Student_Sport#ref-ID_Student> <Student/11> .
<Student_Sport/11/111> <Student_Sport#ID_Sport> "111"^^xsd:integer> .
<Student_Sport/11/111> <Student_Sport#ref-ID_Sport> <Sport/111> .
<Student_Sport/11/112> rdf:type <Student_Sport> .
<Student_Sport/11/112> <Student_Sport#ID_Student> "11"^^xsd:integer> .
<Student_Sport/11/112> <Student_Sport#ref-ID_Student> <Student/11> .
<Student_Sport/11/112> <Student_Sport#ID_Sport> "112"^^xsd:integer> .
<Student_Sport/11/112> <Student_Sport#ref-ID_Sport> <Sport/112> .
<Student_Sport/12/111> rdf:type <Student_Sport> .
<Student_Sport/12/111> <Student_Sport#ID_Student> "12"^^xsd:integer> .
<Student_Sport/12/111> <Student_Sport#ref-ID_Student> <Student/12> .
<Student_Sport/12/111> <Student_Sport#ID_Sport> "111"^^xsd:integer> .
<Student_Sport/12/111> <Student_Sport#ref-ID_Sport> <Sport/111> .
<Sport/110> rdf:type <Sport> .
<Sport/110> <Sport#ID> "110"^^xsd:integer> .
<Sport/110> <Sport#Description> "Tennis"^^xsd:string> .
<Sport/111> rdf:type <Sport> .
<Sport/111> <Sport#ID> "111"^^xsd:integer> .
<Sport/111> <Sport#Description> "Football"^^xsd:string> .
<Sport/112> rdf:type <Sport> .
<Sport/112> <Sport#ID> "112"^^xsd:integer> .
<Sport/112> <Sport#Description> "Formula1"^^xsd:string> .
```

Upon receiving these mappings, morph-RDB (or any other R2RML processor) generates a set of triples (see Listing 1.3) that correspond to the ones generated by Direct Mapping, hence we call them Direct Mapping triples.

Listing 1.4. R2RML Mappings that Generate the Extra Triples

```
<#TriplesMap15> a rr:TriplesMap;
  rr:logicalTable [ rr:sqlQuery
    "SELECT DISTINCT t_39025.ID_Student AS ID_Student, t_39025.ID_Sport AS ID_Sport
      FROM (sport AS t_01724 JOIN student_sport AS t_39025 ON ((t_01724.ID=t_39025.ID_Sport)))
      JOIN student AS t_83317 ON ((t_83317.ID=t_39025.ID_Student))" ];
  rr:subjectMap [ rr:termType rr:IRI; rr:template "Sport/{ID_Sport}"; ];
  rr:predicateObjectMap [ rr:predicate <SportHasStudent>;
  rr:objectMap [ rr:template "Student/{ID_Student}" ]; ].
```

In addition to the mappings above, additional mappings are also generated, as shown in Listing 1.4. These mappings produce the triples that can be seen in Listing 1.5, which specify the relationship between Student and Sport, which are not generated by the Direct Mapping specification.

Listing 1.5. Extra triples of morph-RDB Result Over D011 Test Case Database

```
<Sport/110> <SportHasStudent> <Student/10> .
<Sport/111> <SportHasStudent> <Student/11> .
<Sport/111> <SportHasStudent> <Student/12> .
<Sport/112> <SportHasStudent> <Student/11> .
```

4.2 Experimentation Using `D011B`

For `D011B`, MIRROR generates the additional mappings shown in Listing 1.6:

- R2RML mappings that generate the triples that the instances of the class `Student` are also instances of the class `Person` (line 20-23) and that `SSN` is a property of `Student` because `Student` inherits properties of `Person` (line 24-27).
- R2RML mappings that generate relationships between `Student` and `Contact` (line 7-10).

Listing 1.6. R2RML Mappings Correspond to Subclass Generation and the Inherited `SSN` property in class `Student`

```
1  <#TriplesMap12> a rr:TriplesMap;
2     rr:logicalTable [ rr:sqlQuery
3          "SELECT DISTINCT t_37839.ID, t_11900.CID
4          FROM (student AS t_37839 JOIN contact AS t_11900 ON ((t_37839.ID=t_11900.SID)))" ];
5     rr:subjectMap [ rr:termType rr:IRI;
6          rr:template "http :// example.com/Student/{ID}"; ];
7     rr:predicateObjectMap [
8          rr:predicate ex:StudentHasContact;
9          rr:objectMap [ rr:template "http :// example.com/Contact/{CID}" ]; ];
10    ];
11 ].
12 <#TriplesMap18> a rr:TriplesMap;
13    rr:logicalTable [ rr:sqlQuery
14         "SELECT t_76159.ID, t_76159.FirstName, t_76159.LastName, t_40951.SSN
15         FROM person AS t_40951 JOIN student AS t_76159 ON (t_40951.ID=t_76159.ID)"
16    ];
17    rr:subjectMap [ rr:class ex:Student; rr:termType rr:IRI;
18         rr:template "http :// example.com/student/{ ID }";
19    ];
20    rr:predicateObjectMap[
21       rr:predicate rdf:type;
22       rr:objectMap [ rr:constant ex:Person ];
23    ];
24    rr:predicateObjectMap [
25         rr:predicate ex:Student#ssn;
26         rr:objectMap [ rr:datatype xsd: string ; rr:column "SSN";]
27    ];
28 ...
29 ].
```

5 Conclusion

We have presented a tool for the automatic generation of R2RML mappings from a relational database schema. These mappings can be used by any R2RML processor to generate a set of RDF triples that is similar to those resulting from Direct Mapping. Several types of relationships between tables in a physical model have been categorised. By means of a core query and two algorithms that extract and organize this information, mappings are generated.

MIRROR has been integrated with morph-RDB, what allows experimenting with the generated R2RML mappings. The process was tested using the DM test cases suite, with test D011 extended to D011B to cover more relationships. The additional mappings and extra triples resulting from subclasses, object properties and datatype properties have been also described.

In future works, we will cover other types of database systems, so as to make our work inline with xR2RML [12] and RML [13].

Acknowledgments. This research has been funded by Ministerio de Economía y Competitividad (Spain) under the project "4V: Volumen, Velocidad, Variedad y Validez en la Gestión Innovadora de Datos" (TIN2013-46238-C4-2-R). Luciano Frontino de Medeiros was supported by Fundación Carolina-Spain.

References

1. Arenas, M., Bertails, A., Prud, E., Sequeda, J., et al.: A direct mapping of relational data to RDF, W3C recommendation 27 september 2012 (2013)
2. Das, S., Sundara, S., Cyganiak, R.: R2RML: RDB to RDF mapping language. W3C recommendation, 27 september 2012 (2013)
3. Barrasa Rodríguez, J., Corcho, Ó., Gómez-Pérez, A.: R2O, an extensible and semantically based database-to-ontology mapping language (2004)
4. Bizer, C., Cyganiak, R.: D2R server-publishing relational databases on the semantic web. In: Poster at the 5th International Semantic Web Conference (2006)
5. Auer, S., Dietzold, S., Lehmann, J., Hellmann, S., Aumueller, D.: Triplify: lightweight linked data publication from relational databases. In: Proceedings of the 18th international conference on World wide web, pp. 621–630. ACM (2009)
6. Sequeda, J.F., Tirmizi, S.H., Corcho, O., Miranker, D.P.: Survey of directly mapping SQL databases to the semantic web. Knowledge Engineering Review **26**, 445–486 (2011)
7. Sequeda, J.F., Arenas, M., Miranker, D.P.: OBDA: query rewriting or materialization? in practice, both!. In: Mika, P., Tudorache, T., Bernstein, A., Welty, C., Knoblock, C., Vrandečić, D., Groth, P., Noy, N., Janowicz, K., Goble, C. (eds.) ISWC 2014, Part I. LNCS, vol. 8796, pp. 535–551. Springer, Heidelberg (2014)
8. Pequeno, V.M., Vidal, V.M., Casanova, M.A., Neto, L.E.T., Galhardas, H.: Specifying complex correspondences between relational schemas and RDF models for generating customized R2RML mappings. In: Proceedings of the 18th International Database Engineering & Applications Symposium, pp. 96–104. ACM (2014)

9. Sengupta, K., Haase, P., Schmidt, M., Hitzler, P.: Editing R2RML mappings made easy. In: International Semantic Web Conference (Posters & Demos), pp. 101–104 (2013)
10. Sequeda, J.F., Arenas, M., Miranker, D.P.: On directly mapping relational databases to RDF and OWL. In: Proceedings of the 21st international conference on World Wide Web, pp. 649–658. ACM (2012)
11. Priyatna, F., Corcho, O., Sequeda, J.: Formalisation and experiences of R2RML-based SPARQL to SQL query translation using morph. In: Proceedings of the 23rd international conference on World wide web, International World Wide Web Conferences Steering Committee, pp. 479–490 (2014)
12. Michel, F., Djimenou, L., Faron-Zucker, C., Montagnat, J.: xR2RML: Non-relational databases to RDF mapping. Technical report (2015)
13. Dimou, A., Vander Sande, M., Colpaert, P., Verborgh, R., Mannens, E., Van de Walle, R.: RML: a generic language for integrated RDF mappings of heterogeneous data. In: Proceedings of the 7th Workshop on Linked Data on the Web (LDOW2014), Seoul, Korea (2014)

Using Caching for Local Link Discovery on Large Data Sets

Mofeed M. Hassan(✉), René Speck, and Axel-Cyrille Ngonga Ngomo

AKSW, Department of Computer Science, University of Leipzig, Leipzig, Germany
{mounir,speck,ngonga}@informatik.uni-leipzig.de
http://aksw.org/

Abstract. Engineering the Data Web in the Big Data era demands the development of time- and space-efficient solutions for covering the lifecycle of Linked Data. As shown in previous works, using pure in-memory solutions is doomed to failure as the size of datasets grows continuously with time. We present a study of caching solutions for one of the central tasks on the Data Web, i.e., the discovery of links between resources. To this end, we evaluate 6 different caching approaches on real data using different settings. Our results show that while existing caching approaches already allow performing Link Discovery on large datasets from local resources, the achieved cache hits are still poor. Hence, we suggest the need for dedicated solutions to this problem for tackling the upcoming challenges pertaining to the edification of a semantic Web.

Keywords: Caching · Link discovery · Semantic web · Linked data

1 Introduction

The Web of Data is now an integral part of the Web which contains more than 60 billion facts pertaining to diverse domains including geo-spatial entities, bio-medicine and entertainment.[1] The architectural paradigm underlying the creation of data sources on the Data Web is very similar to that of the document Web and has led to creation of more than 300 knowledge bases, of which the largest pertain to geo-spatial data (LinkedGeoData) and medicine (LinkedTCGA). One of the most demanding steps while publishing data on the Data Web is the creation of links between knowledge bases. Here, the idea is to connect resources across knowledge bases to facilitate the development of applications based on distributed data, e.g., federated query processing and question answering.[2]

Formally, the link discovery problem can defined as follows [10]: Given two knowledge bases S and T as well as a relation R, find all the pairs (s, t) such that $R(s, t)$. For example, S could be the set of all cities in DBpedia while T could

[1] http://lod-cloud.net/state/
[2] http://www.w3.org/DesignIssues/LinkedData.html

P. Cimiano et al. (Eds.): ICWE 2015, LNCS 9114, pp. 344–354, 2015.
DOI: 10.1007/978-3-319-19890-3_22

be the set of all provinces in LinkedGeoData while R could be the `locatedIn` relation, which links two resources s and t when the polygon corresponding to s is completely contained in the polygon corresponding to t. Computing the set $M \subseteq S \times T$ of pairs that abide by R is quadratic in complexity when addressed in a naive manner. Hence, exisiting framework aim to approximate M by computing the set $M' = \{(s,t) : \delta(s,t) \leq \theta\}$, where θ is a threshold and δ is a distance function. Carrying out the computation of M' in a naive fashion is quadratic in time-complexity and linear in space complexity. Hence a large number of time-efficient algorithms for link discovery have been developed over the last years. To the best of our knowledge, all current implementations of such algorithms assume that the data to link (i.e., the sets S and T) can be held in memory. Novel works however show that this assumption is erroneous as large data sets such as LinkedGeoData and LinkedTCGA do not fit in the memory of machines used commonly for link discovery.

In this paper, we study how caching algorithms can be used to improve the space behavior of link discovery algorithms and how well the current approaches perform. To this end, we begin by presenting an architecture for combining caching and efficient link discovery approaches based on blocking and filtering. Thereafter, we present the set of caching algorithms. Then, we evaluate the performance of these algorithms on real data using the ORCHID algorithm as link discovery approach. We conclude the paper with a summary of our insights and a discussion of possible future work.

2 Caching

In this section, we present how caching can be used for Link Discovery. In particular, we begin by giving a general idea of the use of caching for Link Discovery. Thereafter, we present the caching approaches evaluated in this paper.

2.1 Caching for Link Discovery

Most time-efficient approaches for link discovery rely on reducing the number of comparisons of s and t by grouping elements of the source set to $S_i \subseteq S$ and elements of the target set to subsets $T_j \subseteq T$ and only comparing certain S_i with certain T_j. For example, two strings have a distance less or equal to 1 w.r.t. to the edit distance if they share at least one letter. If we assume that the resources in S and T are described by their labels and that δ is the edit distance on labels, then we can group the elements of S by the letters contained in their labels. In this case, S_i would be the subset of S such that the label of each of the resources in S_i contains the ith letter of the alphabet. If we define T_j similarly, then we would not need to compare S_i with T_j if $i \neq j$, leading to several comparisons not having to be carried out at all. The insight behind the use of caching for link discovery is that even when the sets S and T do not fit in memory, single elements of S and T do. Hence, given an element s of S, the data necessary to find all $t \in T$ such that $\delta(s,t) \leq \theta$ can be loaded in memory as required. Elements of t or even whole subsets T_i of T that are commonly used during computations should be cached so as to be read from memory during computations instead of being loaded from the hard drive, which is obviously more time-consuming.

We implemented these insights as follows (see Algorithm 1): Let A be a time-efficient algorithm and $A(s) \subseteq T$ be the set of all elements of T that are to be compared with s according the to algorithm A. We iterate over all $s \in S$ and call the function `load`$(A(s))$. This function encapsulates the cache and loads the portions of $A(s)$ that can be found in memory (i.e., in the cache) directly from the memory. The portions that cannot be found in the cache are loaded from external memory (e.g., the hard drive) sequentially and sent to the cache as well as to the `compare` method, which checks each of the loaded t for whether $\sigma(s,t) \geq \theta$ holds.

```
Data: Source S, target T, distance measure δ, distance threshold θ
Result: Set M ⊆ S × T
M = ∅;
for s ∈ S do
    A = load(s);
    for t ∈ A do
        if compare (s,t) == true then
            M = M ∪ {(s,t)}
        end
    end
    return M;
end
```

Algorithm 1. Basic caching-based approach to link discovery

2.2 Approaches

Caching strategies have several characteristics and can be classified by these [15]. These characteristics are the time since the last reference to an element in the cache (recency), the number of requests to an element in the cache (frequency), the size of an element in the cache (size), the cost to fetch an element (cost), the time since the last modification (modification), the time when an element gets stale and can be evicted from the cache (expiration) [15].

We choose as simple strategies First-In First-Out (FIFO) and First-In First-Out Second Chance (FIFO2ndChance), as a recency-based strategy Least Recently Used (LRU), as a frequency-based strategy Least Frequently Used (LFU), as a recency/frequency-based strategy Segmented Least Recently Used (SLRU) and as a function-based strategy Least Frequently Used with Dynamic Aging (LFUDA).

FIFO is a simple strategy. Once the cache is full, the cache element that has been longest in the cache is removed before the insertion of a new element. It is based on the idea of first-in-first-out (FIFO) lists [16].

FIFO2ndChance is a modified FIFO strategy in the way that a cache element that have been longest in the cache and was referenced in the past (i.e., used in a previous computation) in the past is removed but inserted again only once so that it gets a second chance. An unreferenced element that have been longest in the cache is removed.

LRU is based on the locality of reference and thus tries to predict future accesses to cache elements from previous accesses. The idea is to evict a cache element that led to the oldest hit in the cache. One of the main drawback of this approach is that the cache is not scan-resistant. Still, this is one of the most commonly used approaches [1].

LFU is based on a count of the number of accesses to entries in the cache is kept. The cache evicts the entries with the smallest frequency count when necessary. This approach is scan-resistant but does not make use of the locality of reference. The main drawbacks of this approach is that elements that were accessed often in the past and thus having a high count of the number of accesses can remain in the cache even when they are never requested in the future.

SLRU extends LRU by splitting the cache into an unprotected (US) and a protected segment (PS), while the former is used for new cache elements the later is reserved for popular elements. Both segments are LRU strategies but only elements in the US are evicted. New elements are inserted into the US and on an access to this element it is moved to the PS. Elements from the PS are moved back to the US as the most recently used element when the PS gets full.

LFUDA avoids the cache pollution drawback of LFU with a dynamic aging effect of the cached elements. It calculates a key value K for each element i in the cache with $K_i = F_i + L$ where F_i is the count of the number of accesses of i and L is the running age factor of the cache. L starts at 0 and is updated for each evicted element e to its key value (i.e., $L = K_e$). The strategy evicts the element with the smallest key value from the cache.

3 Experiments and Results

The goal behind our experiments was to determine whether current state-of-the art caching algorithms can be used for link discovery. Geographic domain provides large volume of data and require heavy computations. To this end, we assesses the performance of different caching approaches on real data w.r.t. to the runtime they required and the numbers of hits they were able to achieve. In the following, we begin by presenting the experimental setup used for our experiments. Thereafter, we present and discuss our results.

3.1 Experimental Setup

In the following, we present the setup used for our experiments.

Algorithm for Segmentation. We used the ORCHID [10] algorithm to compute the data segmentations. We used this algorithm for two reasons: First, it is reduction-ratio-optimal and does not tend to overgenerate data segmentations. Moreover, ORCHID can deal with geo-spatial data. This is important because the (to the best of our knowledge) currently largest data set on the Linked Open Data Cloud, i.e., LinkedGeoData, is a geo-spatial data set. Hence, the bias caused by unnecessary comparisons could be minimized while the size of the datasets used in our experiments could be maximized.

Data Set. LinkedGeoData dataset was selected because it is the largest data set on the Linked Open Data Cloud. It is a geospatial dataset generated by converting the data from the OpenStreetMap project[3] into RDF. Currently, LinkedGeoData includes approximately 30 billion triples which describe a.o. 3.8 million ways. Within our experiments, we used the differently sized fragments of the dump used in the original ORCHID paper, which contains all CBDs of ways in LinkedGeoData.

Caching Algorithms. We used the following approaches during our evaluation: FIFO, FIFO2ndChance, LRU, SLRU, LFU and LFUDA. For all approaches the evict size was set to be one. Variant cache sizes were used including 10, 100, 1K, 10K and 100K.

Setup. The evaluation was carried out in two phases. In the first phase, the size of data is 10^4 resources. Different distance thresholds of 0, 0.1, 0.3 and 0.5 km were used. Increasing the distance threshold results in the up rise of the number of compared polygons. This imposes more polygons to be cached and more computation time. The cache size was assigned to 10^3 for all caching approaches in the first phase. We selected the best three approaches for the second phase, which was a scalability evaluation. Here, we measured the number of hits and runtime of the approaches. The promoted approaches were opposed to different cache sizes measuring and comparing their run times and revealing the best performed approach. Cache sizes were 10^1, 10^2, 10^3, 10^4 and 10^5. In this phase the data size was increased to be 10^5 resources.

Hardware. The evaluation was carried out on a laptop running an Intel CoreTM i7 Quad Core 2.80GHz processor using 8G RAM.

[3] http://www.openstreetmap.org/

3.2 Results

In this section we present the results produced based on the aforementioned exponential setup. Figures 1 and 2 show the results of the first series on a sample of LinkedGeoData containing 10^4 resources, i.e., 10^4 polygons. The number of cache hits for each of the caching approaches w.r.t. different distance thresholds is presented in figure 1. It is noticeable that LFU achieves the lowest number of cache hits. SLRU also shows lower number of cache hits compared to the rest of the approaches that are almost close in the results. In figure 2, the runtimes of the different caching approach is depicted and it suggests that LRU, SLRU and FIFO have the lowest run times relative to different distance thresholds. It is clear that the lower number of hits the caching approach provides the longer time it takes for fetching or replacing the targeted data. In FIFO fetching and evicting data are performed in time complexity O(1). The simple iteration on polygons indexes implement by ORCHID the number of hits is high. For LRU and SLRU approaches, their implementations tend to avoid time-consuming updates for cache entries. Given that all approaches achieve similar numbers of cache hits the run time turns to be the effective factor in selecting the approaches for the next phase. Tables 1 and 2 give detailed insight on achieved results in this phase. The presented runtime values in Table 1 are in seconds for the sake of readability.

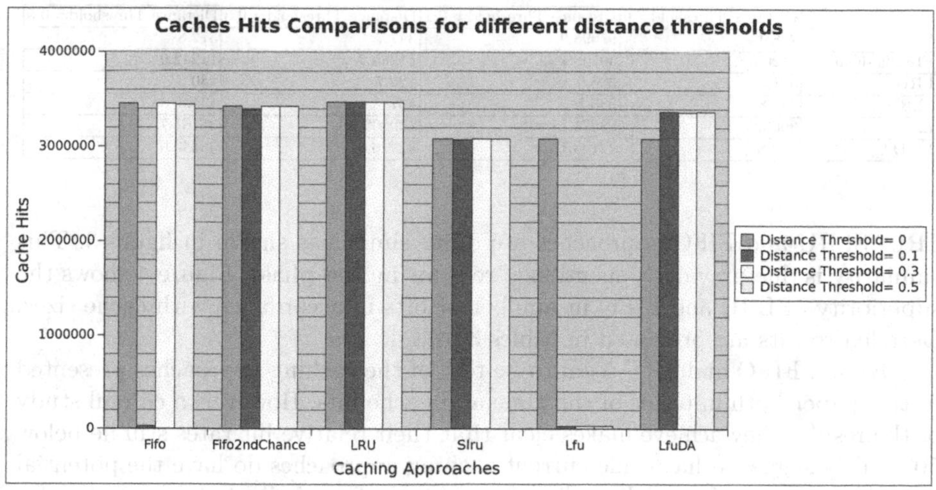

Fig. 1. Number of cache hits for different distance thresholds (dataset size = 10^4 resources)

The results of the second phase for different cache sizes are illustrated in figures 3 and 4. Note that we used a larger dataset of size 10^5 for this series of experiments. In contrast to the results of previous phase, the runtimes for

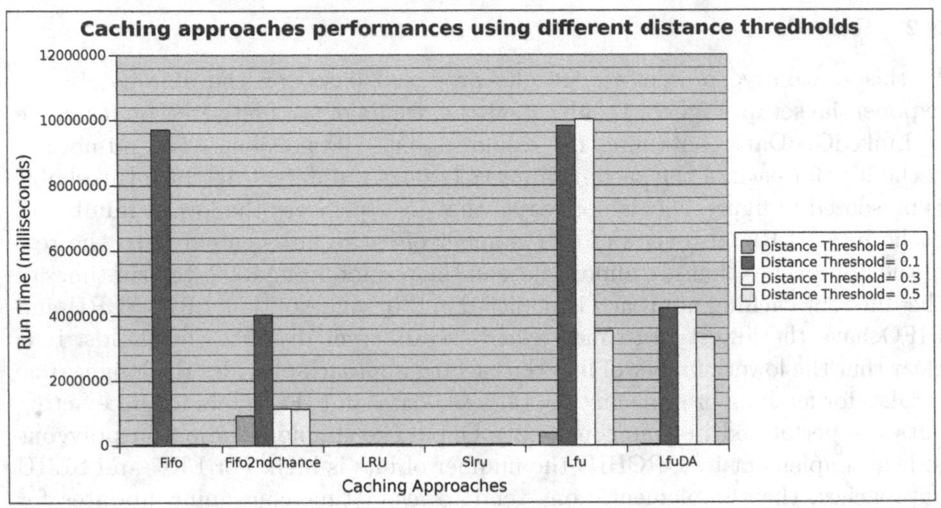

Fig. 2. Runtimes of the different caching approaches for different distance thresholds (dataset size = 10^4 resources)

Table 1. Runtimes of the different caching approachesand varying distance thresholds (dataset size = 10^4 resources)

CacheType	Distance Threshold= 0	Distance Threshold= 0.1	Distance Threshold= 0.3	Distance Threshold= 0.5
FIFO	278.4	97098.9	347.7	372.8
FIFO2ndChance	9120.6	40228.7	11285.2	11242.9
LRU	321.3	386.5	423.7	440.3
SLRU	343.8	388.1	437	435.8
Lfu	3903.2	98271.1	100202	35161.7
LfuDA	343.8	42185.1	42216.3	33240.6

LRU, SLRU and FIFO approaches are quite similar as shown in figure 3. This similarity is due previously mentioned reasons in first phase. Figure 4 shows the superiority of LRU and FIFO in number of hits in accordance with cache sizes. Detailed results are presented in tables 3 and 4.

Overall, FIFO and LRU seem to be test of the caching approaches presented in this paper both in terms of run time and cache hits. However, a careful study of the results they achieve makes clear that their relative hit rates still lie below 50%. This suggests that while current caching approaches do have the potential to reduce the runtime of link discovery approaches, dedicated approaches for link discovery could improve the quality of caching. The study thus suggests that dedicated approaches for link discovery should be investigated in future work to ensure the development of scalable link discovery approaches able to deal with Big Data.

Table 2. Number of hits for different caching approaches and varying distance thresholds (dataset size = 10^4 resources)

CacheType	Distance Threshold= 0	Distance Threshold= 0.1	Distance Threshold= 0.3	Distance Threshold= 0.5
FIFO	3456400	29052	3455933	3445072
FIFO2ndChance	3424230	3386093	3424230	3424270
LRU	3469912	3469912	3469404	3469871
SLRU	3082611	3073706	3082620	3082503
Lfu	3082611	29052	29059	29052
LfuDA	3082611	3369919	3363075	3369851

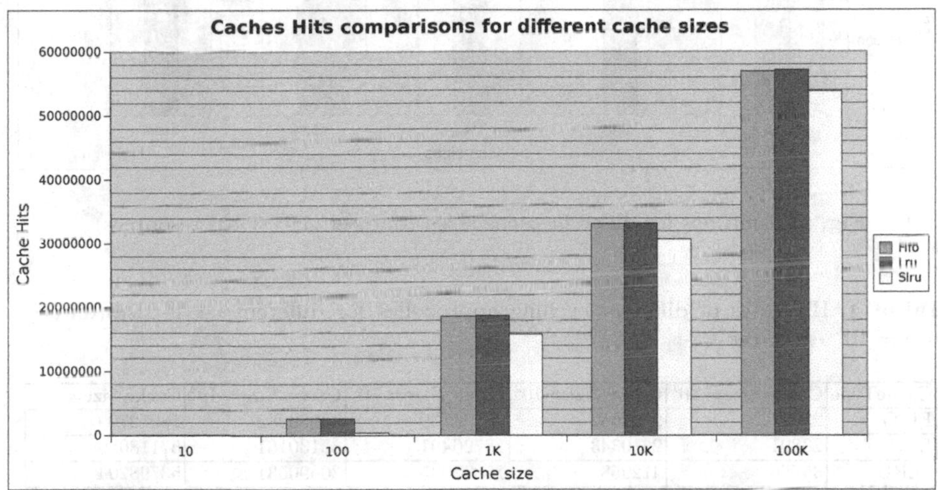

Fig. 3. Cache hits for different cache sizes (dataset size = 10^5 resources)

4 Related Work

A vast amount of literature has been produced to elucidate the problem of Link Discovery [7,9,11–13]. Still, with the growth of the size of the dataset at hand, improving the runtime of Link Discovery on large datasets becomes an increasingly urgent problem. Several approaches have been developed with the goal of improving the performance of Link Discovery approaches [8,11–13].

Caching follows the idea to store and reuse as much intermediary knowledge as possible to improve the runtime of the given algorithm. One of the most commonly used approaches is the Least Recently Used algorithm [14]. The idea

Table 3. Runtimes (seconds) for different cache sizes(dataset size = 10^5 resources)

CacheType	Cache Size= 10^1	Cache Size= 10^2	Cache Size= 10^3	Cache Size= 10^4	Cache Size= 10^5
FIFO	721.7	678.8	669.9	610.8	618.4
LRU	695.7	708.9	700.8	653.6	704.3
SLRU	714	907.4	658.7	694.2	700.6

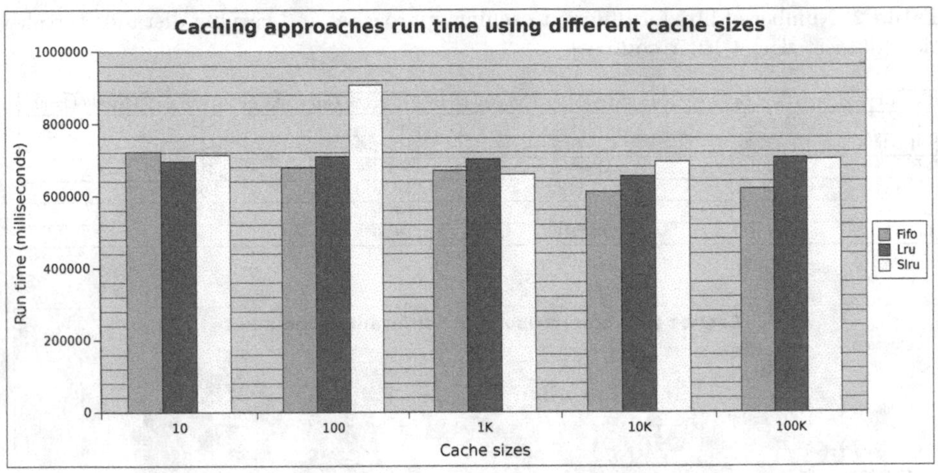

Fig. 4. Runtimes for different cache sizes (dataset size = 10^5 resources)

Table 4. Hit rates of different caching approaches for different cache sizes(dataset size = 10^5 resources)

CacheType	Cache Size= 10^1	Cache Size= 10^2	Cache Size= 10^3	Cache Size= 10^4	Cache Size= 10^5
FIFO	23927	2597652	18594739	33080982	56912799
LRU	23891	2610343	18726491	33130161	57118089
SLRU	34756	412958	15822935	30696531	53798204

behind this approach is simply to evict the entry that led to the oldest hit when the cache gets full. One of the main drawbacks of this approach is that the cache is not scan-resistant. Meanwhile, a large number of scan-resistant extensions of this approach have been created. For example, SLRU [6] extends LRU by splitting the cache into a protected and an unprotected area. The Least Frequently Used (LFU) [2] approach relies on a different intuition. Here, a count of the number of accesses to entries in the cache is kept. The cache evicts the entries with the smallest frequency count when necessary. This approach is scan-resistant but does not make use of the locality of reference. Consequently, it was extended by window-based LFU [5], sliding window-based approaches [3] and dynamic aging (LFUDA) [1] amongst others. Another commonly used caching strategy is based on the idea of first-in-first-out (FIFO) lists [16]. When the cache is full, this approach evicts the entry that have been longest in the cache. The main drawback of this approach is that it does not make use of locality. Thus, it was extended in several ways, for example by the "FIFO second chance" approach [16]. Other strategies such as Greedy Dual (GD*) [4] use a cost model to determine which entries to evict.

5 Conclusion and Future Work

In this paper, we presented an evaluation of different caching approaches integrated for link discovery. We used ORCHID as link discovery algorithm and measured the effect of cache sizes, dataset sizes and the distance thresholds on the performance of different caching strategies using real data. FIFO and LRU approaches were determine to be the best approaches for caching data when carrying out link discovery. Still, the relative hit rates of these approaches lie by less than 50%. Hence, our study suggests the need for dedicated caching approaches for link discovery. The development of such approaches will be carried out in future work.

References

1. Arlitt, M., Cherkasova, L., Dilley, J., Friedrich, R., Jin, T.: Evaluating content management techniques for web proxy caches. SIGMETRICS Performance Evaluation Review **27**(4), 3–11 (2000)
2. Breslau, L., Cao, P., Fan, L., Phillips, G., Shenker, S.: Web caching and zipf-like distributions: evidence and implications. In: INFOCOM, pp. 126–134 (1999)
3. Hou, W.-C., Wang, S.: Size-adjusted sliding window LFU - a new web caching scheme. In: Mayr, H.C., Lazanský, J., Quirchmayr, G., Vogel, P. (eds.) DEXA 2001. LNCS, vol. 2113, pp. 567–576. Springer, Heidelberg (2001)
4. Jin, S., Bestavros, A.: Greedydual* web caching algorithm - exploiting the two sources of temporal locality in web request streams. In: 5th International Web Caching and Content Delivery Workshop, pp. 174–183 (2000)
5. Karakostas, G., Serpanos, D.N.: Exploitation of different types of locality for web caches. In: Proceedings of the Seventh International Symposium on Computers and Communications, pp. 207–2012 (2002)
6. Karedla, R., Love, J.S., Wherry, B.G.: Caching strategies to improve disk system performance. Computer **27**, 38–46 (1994)
7. Lyko, K., Höffner, K., Speck, R., Ngomo, A.-C., Lehmann, J.: SAIM – one step closer to zero-configuration link discovery. In: Cimiano, P., Fernández, M., Lopez, V., Schlobach, S., Völker, J. (eds.) ESWC 2013. LNCS, vol. 7955, pp. 167–172. Springer, Heidelberg (2013)
8. Ngonga Ngomo, A.-C.: A time-efficient hybrid approach to link discovery. In: Proceedings of OM@ISWC (2011)
9. Ngonga Ngomo, A.-C.: Link discovery with guaranteed reduction ratio in affine spaces with Minkowski measures. In: Cudré-Mauroux, P., et al. (eds.) ISWC 2012, Part I. LNCS, vol. 7649, pp. 378–393. Springer, Heidelberg (2012)
10. Ngonga Ngomo, A.-C.: ORCHID – reduction-ratio-optimal computation of geo-spatial distances for link discovery. In: Alani, H., et al. (eds.) ISWC 2013, Part I. LNCS, vol. 8218, pp. 395–410. Springer, Heidelberg (2013)
11. Ngonga Ngomo, A.-C.: HELIOS – execution optimization for link discovery. In: Mika, P., et al. (eds.) ISWC 2014, Part I. LNCS, vol. 8796, pp. 17–32. Springer, Heidelberg (2014)
12. Ngonga Ngomo, A.-C., Auer, S.: Limes - a time-efficient approach for large-scale link discovery on the web of data. In: Proceedings of IJCAI (2011)

13. Ngomo, A.-C.N., Kolb, L., Heino, N., Hartung, M., Auer, S., Rahm, E.: When to reach for the cloud: using parallel hardware for link discovery. In: Cimiano, P., Corcho, O., Presutti, V., Hollink, L., Rudolph, S. (eds.) ESWC 2013. LNCS, vol. 7882, pp. 275–289. Springer, Heidelberg (2013)
14. O'Neil, E.J., O'Neil, P.E., Weikum, G.: The lru-k page replacement algorithm for database disk buffering. SIGMOD Rec. **22**, 297–306 (1993)
15. Podlipnig, S., Böszörmenyi, L.: A survey of web cache replacement strategies. ACM Comput. Surv. **35**(4), 374–398 (2003)
16. Tanenbaum, A.S., Woodhull, A.S.: Operating systems - design and implementation, 3rd edn. Pearson Education (2006)

YQL as a Platform for Linked-Data Wrapper Development

Jon Iturrioz, Iker Azpeitia(✉), and Oscar Díaz

University of the Basque Country (UPV/EHU), San Sebastián, Spain
{jon.iturrioz,iker.azpeitia,oscar.diaz}@ehu.eus

Abstract. Linked-Data Wrappers (LDWs) have been proposed to integrate Open APIs into the linked-data cloud. A main stumbling block is maintenance: LDWs need to be kept in sync with the APIs they wrap Hence, LDWs are not single-shot efforts, but sustained endeavors that developers might not always afford. As a result, it is not uncommon for third-party LDWs to stop working when their underlying APIs upgrade. Collaborative development might offer a way out. This requires a common platform and a community to tap into. This work investigates the suitability of the YQL platform for this job. Specifically, we look into two main properties for LDW success: effectiveness (i.e. the capability of YQL to enable users to develop LDWs) and scalability (i.e. graceful time degradation on URI dereferencing). The aim: moving LDW development from in-house development to collaborative development as promoted by YQL, on the hope of increasing LDWs' lifespan.

Keywords: Linked data wrappers · YQL · Open APIs

1 Introduction

The shortage of RDF end-points is hindering the development of the Web of Data. Turning existing data into RDF triplets might be conducted by data providers or data consumers. For example, the former is illustrated by R2RML [8] (for database sources) or OWL-S (for Web Service) [15]. Unfortunately, this approach has not caught on, suffering from the chicken-and-egg "cold-start" problem: providers (i.e. *eBay*, *Amazon*) lack a clear demand for RDF while consumers stick to JSON/XML because the learning curve and lifting effort to move to RDF. Alternatively, data consumers can construct themselves linked-data wrappers (LDWs) [4,5]. Third parties can develop LDWs at their own expense. In this case, maintenance becomes the main issue. Wrappers in general, and LDWs in particular, hold a tight coupling on the underlying platform (i.e. the Open API). If the API changes then, LDWs might need to be rewritten. The severity of this problem for LDWs stems from the frequency of change (APIs are reckoned to evolve regularly) and the developers' profile (in general research groups which might lack the resources in keeping LDWs on and running). The question is how to promote LDW development in a setting characterized by limited rewards and heavy maintenance. Collaborative development emerges as a possible answer.

P. Cimiano et al. (Eds.): ICWE 2015, LNCS 9114, pp. 355–373, 2015.
DOI: 10.1007/978-3-319-19890-3_23

Collaborative development rests on public availability and communication, usually via the Internet. This involves the existence of a platform. We look at Yahoo's YQL (*Yahoo Query Language*) platform [17] as an appropriate venue for LDW development. So far, this platform is being used for mashup developers to query, filter, and combine data across the Web through a single SQL-like interface. Turning YQL into a LDW platform, introduces two challenges:

- attracting producers. LDW development is programming intensive. Broadening the range of producers might be achieved by reducing the programming effort as well as embracing sibling communities. YQL facilitates both aims. First, YQL abstract the level at which API programming is conducted. Rather than facing API specifics, YQL hides this complexity through a table-like view. This speeds API programming in general, and LDW development in particular. Second, there already exists a YQL community. By adopting their own tools, we hope to tap into this community.
- attracting consumers. LDW continuous effort pays off if benefits go beyond breakout developers. So far, most LDWs are seldom used outside their research projects. If LDWs are to evolve beyond proof-of-concept, scalability issues should be considered. Graceful degradation of elapsed times promotes linkage with your LDW-supported linked data. YQL can help by providing load balancing that outperforms small-scale attempts to host LDW services.

Hence, this paper presents a case for YQL as an LDW platform by conducting two evaluations on effectiveness (i.e. the capability of YQL to enable users to develop LDWs with accuracy and completeness) (Section 4) and scalability (Section 5). So far, we focus on read-only API methods. We start by introducing a running example.

2 Running Example

The lack of services exposing linked-data is due to heterogeneous circumstances: technical (i.e. for complicated domains, mapping the underlying data representation to linked data formats is nontrivial), social (i.e. no demand on linked-data representation by the service community) or financial (i.e. no clear business model). Fortunately, in case the data is available under a liberal license[1], wrapping the data into a service separate from the original website, might be possible.

As an example, consider *Last.fm*. This is a music website that among other data, provides information about musical events. An Open API facilitates programmatic access to this data[2]. Output formats include XML and JSON but not linked data. As most current APIs, *Last.fm* behaves as a data silo with no interlinkage with other sources. Hence, moving *Last.fm* to the Linked Data (LD) cloud requires not only a change in the output format (e.g. JSON-LD [3]) but also

[1] See http://www.w3.org/TR/void/#license.

[2] http://www.last.fm/api

```
{
  "@context":{
    "rdfs":"http://www.w3.org/2000/01/rdf-schema#",
    "dc":"http://purl.org/dc/elements/1.1/",
    "mo":"http://purl.org/ontology/mo/",
    "event":"http://purl.org/NET/c4dm/event.owl#",
    "wth":"http://www.scs.ryerson.ca/~bgajdero/msc_thesis/code/ontologies/weather-ont-t2.owl",
    "dbpprop":"http://dbpedia.org/property/"
  },
  "@id":"http://rdf.onekin.org/lastfm/event/3986264",
  "@type":"mo:Performance",
  "dc:date":"Thu, 06 Nov 2014 20:00:00",
  "rdfs:label":"Guerrera",
  "event:place":"http://www.dbpedia.org/resource/Donostia",
  "mo:performer":"http://rdf.onekin.org/musicbrainz/artist/Guerrera",
  "dbpprop:hasPhotoCollection":"http://rdf.onekin.org/flickr/location/Donostia",
  "wth:hasWeather":"http://rdf.onekin.org/weather/location/Donostia"
}
```

Fig. 1. A *Last.fm* instance in JSON-LD format

setting links with other URI-addressable related sources. Figure 1 illustrates how an *event* instance might look like. Its URI is http://rdf.onekin.org/lastfm/event/3986264. Its description holds references to other resources such as the event's place (through the property *event:place*) or the event's performers (through the property *mo:performer*). This view is provided by a LDW which publicizes *Last.fm*'s event instances as URI-addressable resources by means of both lifting API-recovered data and interlinkaging it with other resources in the LD cloud. These issues are already covered in the literature [18][21,22].

Here, we rise a different concern. Our dismay is not so much about development but maintenance, i.e. how to increase the chances of our *Last.fm* LDW to be up and active in the medium run. The endeavor should not be underestimated. Open API upgrades are not uncommon, and development teams might need to change focus. No wonder distinct LDWs that properly worked at the time they were launched, they are no longer up at the time of this writing.

It is not odd for LDW efforts to stop working at some point: *Flickr wrappr* [4], *GoogleArt project to RDF*[3], *DBTune.org Artists*[4] (a wrapper on top of *Last.fm*), or *Twitter wrapper*[5]. Therefore, anecdotal evidence highlights the importance of maintenance for LDWs to be a sustainable foundation for the Web of Data. Collaborative code-development platforms come to the rescue.

[3] http://linkeddata.few.vu.nl/
[4] http://dbtune.org/
[5] http://km.aifb.kit.edu/services/twitterwrap/

3 Collaborative Code-Development Platforms and The YQL Web Service

A collaboration platform offers broad social networking capabilities to work processes. If this work is aimed at code development then, the platform provides repository hosting service, including distributed revision control and source code management. A main exponent of this kind of platforms is *GitHub*[6]. *GitHub* permits users to browse public repositories on the site. It provides social networking functions such as feeds, followers, wikis and a social network graph to display how developers work on their versions ("forks") of a repository. On top, services can be built that use *GitHub* as a repository. This is the case of YQL. YQL specializes on providing a framework for abstracting developers from the heterogeneity of API requests and its optimization. YQL is not thought for application development in general, but for abstracting from API heterogeneity. This specialization is what makes YQL attractive for LDW development. LDWs also aim at abstracting from Open APIs in terms of RDF end-points. The YQL Guide states "YQL Web Service enables applications to query, filter, and combine data from different sources across the Internet" [17]. LDWs pursuit similar goals. The difference stems from the abstraction at which these aims are conducted. YQL envisions the Web in term of tables (known as Open Data Tables (ODT)), and returns XML documents. By contrasts, LDWs support the linked-data view, and returns RDF triplets. This work is based on this likeness.

YQL statements have a SQL-like syntax, familiar to any developer with database experience. It aims at hiding APIs' specifics into a uniform table-like metaphor. The following YQL statement, for example, retrieves data about the event whose ID is *3986264:*

*select * from lastfm.event.getinfo where event="3986264"*

To access the YQL Web Service, a Web application can call HTTP GET, passing the YQL statement as a URL parameter, for example:

http://query.yahooapis.com/v1/public/yql?q=*select * from l*astfm.event.getinfo where event="3986264"

This setting is achieved through three mechanisms: *Open Data Tables* (ODT), the *Yahoo Query Language* (YQL), and the YQL console.

Open Data Tables. Broadly, ODTs are syntactic sugar for API parameters. Figure 2 shows the *lastfm.event.getInfo* ODT[7]. Main tags include *<meta>* and *<bindings>*. The former contains descriptive information about the ODT such as author, description or documentation link (3-7). The bindings (8-16) indicate how SQL operations are mapped into API calls. An entry exists for each operation (e.g. *<select>*, *<insert>*). The sample case illustrates the SELECT

[6] https://github.com/

[7] Full description at https://github.com/yql/yql-tables/blob/master/lastfm/lastfm.event.getinfo.xml.

```
1 <?xml version="1.0" encoding="UTF-8"?>
2 <table xmlns="http://query.yahooapis.com/v1/schema/table.xsd">
3  <meta>
4   <author>Jamie Matthews</author>
5   <description>YQL table for Last.fm Event.getInfo API method.</description>
6   <documentationURL>http://www.last.fm/api/show?service=292</documentationURL>
7  </meta>
8  <bindings>
9   <select itemPath="" produces="XML">
10    <urls><url>http://ws.audioscrobbler.com/2.0/?method=event.getinfo</url></urls>
11    <inputs>
12     <key id="event" type="xs:string" paramType="query" required="true" />
13     <key id="api_key" type="xs:string" paramType="query" required="true" />
14    </inputs>
15   </select>
16  </bindings>
17 </table>
```

Fig. 2. *lastfm.event.getinfo* ODT

case (9-15): *<url>* accounts for the URL pattern to invoke whereas *<input>* denotes the possible YQL statement input field. Each field (e.g. event) accounts for variables to be instantiated when SELECT is enacted.

The YQL Language. YQL includes *SELECT*, *INSERT* and *DELETE* statements that, behind the curtains, invoke the corresponding API methods by means of ODTs. ODTs hold all the intricacies of the underlying APIs. Specifically, benefits can be obtained from reusing of the authorization and authentication code from YQL, given the many access control mechanisms with APIs. In this way, YQL offloads processing that programmers would normally do on the client/server side to the *YQL* engine. Besides those provided by YQL itself (known as "built-in tables"), YQL permits the community to provide their own ODTs[8]. Once loaded in the YQL repository, an API's ODT makes this APIs YQL accessible.

The YQL Console[9] (see Figure 3). The YQL Console enables to run YQL statements interactively from your browser. Through this website, developers can check out their queries, look at the answers, and if satisfied, obtain the query's REST query counterpart. This URL can next be included in the user's programs.

The bottom line is that YQL provides ODTs as an alternative to direct API calls through optimization and abstraction. This is certainly of interest for LDW producers.

4 The LDW Community: The Producer Perspective

We believe a main challenge about LDW definition is not so much about "the how" but "the who". Good practices about LDW development already

[8] Community ODTs can be found at http://www.datatables.org/.

[9] http://developer.yahoo.com/yql/console/

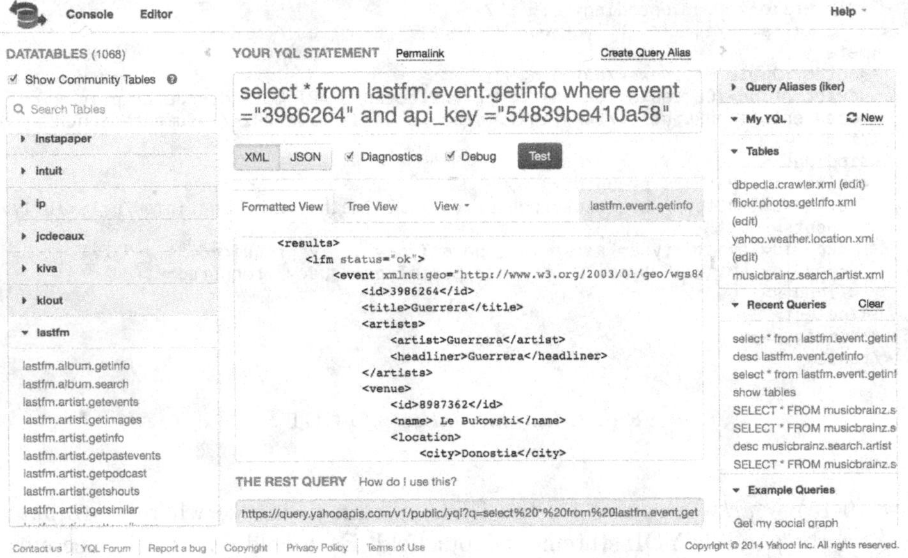

Fig. 3. The YQL console includes three main windows: the upper window contains the YQL statement; the middle window displays the statement's output (e.g. an XML document); the bottom window contains the URL counterpart of the YQL statement

exists [19]. The challenge is widen the programmer base. Two strategies: reducing LDW development effort & embracing other communities.

Reducing LDW Development Effort. So far, LDWs tend to start from scratch [18][21,22]. YQL promotes reuse through ODTs. ODTs encapsulate lowering and formatting concerns for a given API. If ODTs are shared, programs start development from ODTs (i.e. issuing SQL-like statements) rather than going down to the API services. As any other API programming, LDWs can also benefit from this approach. This entails a double wrapping: *YQL wraps APIs as tables while LDWs wrap tables as linked data.*

Benefits are twofold. First, LDWs are sheltered from changes in the underlying APIs. API upgrades are handled at the YQL-table level without impacting the LDWs built on top. Second, reuse. LDW developers can tap into existing YQL tables (1068 at the time of this writing).

Embracing Other Communities. At the time of this writing (March 2015), the page https://github.com/yql/yql-tables characterizes the YQL community along the following figures: 153 contributors, 3287 commits, 18 open issues, 14 closed, 14 open pull requests, 399 closed, 620 stars, and 425 forks. We believe LDW concerns are not so alien to API programmers. Broadly, wrapper definition pivots around two main issues: lowering (i.e. from URI dereferencing to API calls) and lifting (from API-call outputs to RDF resources). By moving to YQL, our hopes is to tap into this sibling community. However, evidences are needed that YQL is expressive enough to cater for LDW concerns.

```
1 <?xml version="1.0" encoding="UTF-8"?>
2 <table xmlns="http://query.yahooapis.com/v1/schema/table.xsd">
3 <meta>
4   <author>Iker Azpeitia</author>
5   <description> ODT for Last.fm event.getInfo API method. </description>
6   <documentationURL> http://www.last.fm/api/show?service=292 </documentationURL>
7   <sampleQuery>URIPattern: lastfm/event/{event}</sampleQuery>
8   <sampleQuery>URIexample: lastfm/event/3986264</sampleQuery>          LOWERING
9 </meta>
10 <bindings>
11   <select itemPath="" produces="XML">
12     <urls><url>http://ws.audioscrobbler.com/2.0/?method=event.getinfo</url></urls>
13     <inputs>
14       <key id="event" type="xs:string" paramType="query" required="true" />
15       <key id="api_key" type="xs:string" paramType="query" required="true" />
16     </inputs>
17   </select>
18   <function name="lifting">
19     <inputs>                                                            LIFTING
20       <pipe id="oneEventXML" paramType="variable" />
21       <key id="URI" paramType="variable" required="true"/>
22     </inputs>
23     <execute> <![CDATA[
24       var oneEventJSON= y.xmlToJson(oneEventXML);
25       var oneEventJSONLD={'@context':{rdfs:'http://www.w3.org/2000/01/rdf-schema#',
26       dc:'http://purl.org/dc/elements/1.1/', mo:'http://purl.org/ontology/mo/',
27       event:'http://purl.org/NET/c4dm/event.owl#', dbpprop:'http://dbpedia.org/property/',
28       wth:'http://www.scs.ryerson.ca/~bgajdero/msc_thesis/code/ontologies/weather-ont-t2.owl'}};
29       oneEventJSONLD['@id']= URI;
30       oneEventJSONLD['@type']='mo:Performance';
31       oneEventJSONLD['dc:date']=oneEventJSON.lfm.event.startDate;
32       oneEventJSONLD['rdfs:label']=oneEventJSON.lfm.event.title;
33       oneEventJSONLD['event:place']='http://dbpedia.org/resource/'
                                        +oneEventJSON.lfm.event.venue.location.city;
34       oneEventJSONLD['mo:performer']='http://rdf.onekin.org/musicbrainz/artist/'
                                        +oneEventJSON.lfm.event.artists.artist;
35       oneEventJSONLD['dbpprop:hasPhotoCollection']='http://rdf.onekin.org/flickr/location/'
                                        +oneEventJSON.lfm.event.venue.location.city;
36       oneEventJSONLD['wth:hasWeather']='http://rdf.onekin.org/weather/location/'
                                        +oneEventJSON.lfm.event.venue.location.city;
37       response.object = oneEventJSONLD;]]>
38     </execute>
39   </function>
40 </bindings>
41 </table>
```

Fig. 4. lastfm.event.getinfo LDW

The rest of this Section delves into these issues along three aspects: LDW development, LDW deployment and LDW adaptive maintenance.

4.1 LDW Development

This subsection builds upon YQL expressiveness to specify LDWs. As an example of reuse, we tap into the ODT in Figure 2, and turn it into a LDW (see Figure 4). The process includes two main steps.

First. YQL's *sampleQuery* tag is used to describe the URI pattern (line 7) and the URI grounding (line 8). When a linked wrapper server receives a URI (e.g. http://rdf.onekin.org/lastfm/event/3986264), it identifies the ODT at hand through pattern matching against the registered *URIPatterns* at deployment time. This pattern is attached to the linked wrapper server base URL (e.g. http://rdf.onekin.org/). The binding (lowering mapping) from URI pattern to

ODT input parameters is realized through pattern matching parameters (i.e. line 7 to line 14 {*event*} binding).

Second. YQL's *function* tag is recast for lifting: each YQL tuple (i.e. *oneEventXML*) is to be turned into an RDF individual (i.e. *oneEventJSONLD*). The lifting function holds *<inputs>* and *<execute>*. The former indicates the function's parameters which are set to *<pipe>* (i.e. holds "a tuple" of the ODT table described à la XML)(line 20) and *<key>* (i.e. to cast the ID for the returned RDF individual) (line 21). As for *<execute>*, it holds the JavaScript code that obtains JSON-LD out of the XML tuple (line 24-37). Interlinkage is also described here by constructing URIs out of existing parameters, e.g. *event:place* links to the *DBpedia* resource about the event's city (line 33)[10]. More interestingly, interlinkage can also be set with RDF individual counterparts of other API resources, e.g. *mo:performer* holds the URI for the event's artist kept at the *musicbrainz* API (line 34). Noteworthy, this interlinkage is realized through another LDW!

Let's check this out. Go to http://developer.yahoo.com/yql/console/ and paste the following snippet:

> *use 'https://raw.githubusercontent.com/onekin/ldw/master/events/ lastfm.event.getinfo.xml' as* ***lastfm****; select * from* ***lastfm*** *where event = '3986264' and api_key = '20b0801ddb96b112ce4db2dbae134e10'*
> *|* ***lastfm****.lifting ('http://rdf.onekin.org/lastfm/event/3986264');*

The sample LDW is held in *GitHub*. The snippet starts by keeping in *lastfm* the path to locate this LDW. Sentence *select* retrieves XML documents associated with event *"3986264"*. For each tuple, *lastfm.lifting* returns its JSON-LD counterpart. Once the LDW is checked out, it is time to deploy it. More examples of LDW's can be found at https://github.com/onekin/ldw.

4.2 LDW Deployment

A main goal of LDW Servers is to make LDWs dereferenceable datasets. A dataset is a set of RDF resources that are published, maintained or aggregated by a single provider. The term dataset has a social dimension: we think of a dataset as a meaningful collection of triples, that deal with a certain topic, originate from a certain source or process, are hosted on a certain server, or are aggregated by a certain custodian. This process comprises:

1. *Register*. LDWs need to be registered to be considered datasets. This process is realized in a LDW Server (e.g. http://rdf.onekin.org/ldw/). Once registered, the server starts listening URIs that conform to the LDW *URIPattern*.
2. *URI Dereference* (see Figure 5 steps 1..8). When one URI is invoked (e.g. http://rdf.onekin.org/lastfm/event/3986264) (step 1), the LDW server (i.e.

[10] The approach of linking to other datasets by appending something (e.g. the name of a city) to some other dataset's namespace URI works often, but in the most general case, it's a bit naive. In this case, the developer should resort to JavaScript to set the mapping.

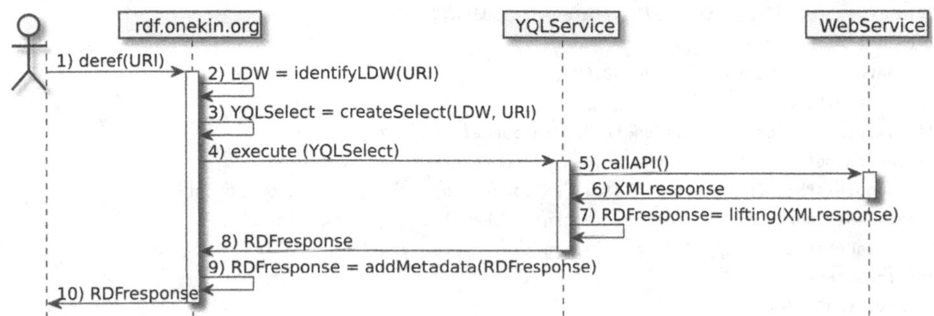

Fig. 5. Simplified sequence diagram

http://rdf.onekin.org) finds the LDW that matches the URI (step 2); lowers the URI to the corresponding YQL query (see the select in the previous section) (step 3); and sends the query to the YQL server (step 4). The YQL engine calls to the Web Service's API (steps 5 and 6) and applies the lifting function (step 7) resulting in a RDF resource description (step 8).

3. *Dataset Metadata Linkage.* Each resource pertains to a dataset. Each dataset contains metadata information that can be used in many situations, ranging from data discovery to cataloging and archiving. The Vocabulary of Interlinked Datasets (VoID) [2] is concerned with metadata about RDF datasets, and it is intended as a bridge between the publishers and users of RDF data. The server adds to the results a *void:inDataset* property that link to its VoID (Figure 5 step 9). This URI is also dereferenceable.
4. *Provenance Publication.* The ability to track the origin of data is a key component in building trustworthy, reliable applications [6]. A widely deployed vocabulary for representing such data is Provenance Ontology[11]. Provenance properties are automatically generated by the LDW server (Figure 5 step 9, resulting in the bottom part of the Figure 6[12]). The *prv:usedGuideline* indicates how the data has been created (i.e. points to the LDW URL), the *prv:performedBy* indicates who has performed the wrapping process (i.e. rdf.onekin.org), finally the source data is described in the *prv:usedData* property.

So far, we have addressed YQL's *modus operandi* for readers to judge its adjustment to LDW development practices. Next subsection conducts a quality-in-use evaluation on using YQL for LDW. We want to measure how effective are ODTs to define LDW along the lines of the previous description.

[11] Full description at http://purl.org/net/provenance/ns#.

[12] Data provided by the API does not conform to *xsd:date*. For simplification sake, we do not include here its cast.

```
"@id":"http://rdf.onekin.org/lastfm/event/3986264",
"@type":"mo:Performance",
"dc:date":"Thu, 06 Nov 2014 20:00:00",
"rdfs:label":"Guerrera",
"event:place":"http://www.dbpedia.org/resource/Donostia",
"mo:performer":"http://rdf.onekin.org/musicbrainz/artist/Guerrera",
"dbpprop:hasPhotoCollection":"http://rdf.onekin.org/flickr/location/Donostia",
"wth:hasWeather":"http://rdf.onekin.org/weather/location/Donostia",
"void:inDataset":"http://rdf.onekin.org/lastfm/event/event",
"prv:createdBy":{ ⊟
  "prv:usedGuideline":{ ⊟
    "@type":"prv:CreationGuideline",
    "foaf:homepage":"https://raw.githubusercontent.com/onekin/ldw/master/events/lastfm.eve
  },
  "prv:completedAt":"2015-03-04T15:53:03",
  "@type":"prv:DataCreation",
  "prv:usedData":{ ⊟
    "@type":"prv:DataItem",
    "foaf:homepage":"http://ws.audioscrobbler.com"
  },
  "prv:performedBy":"http://rdf.onekin.org"
}
```


Fig. 6. Resource dereference with provenance. Namespaces omitted.

4.3 LDW Adaptive Maintenance

Adaptive maintenance refers to the modification of a software product performed after delivery to keep it usable in a changed or changing environment. For LDWs, this changing environment include Open APIs and the Linked-Data cloud.

API Upgrades. This is not only a LDW problem. Applications using third-party APIs are well-aware of these problems. For example, Zibran et al. [23] found that among 1,513 bug reports related to various components of Eclipse, GNOME, MySQL, Python 3.1, and Android projects, 562 bug-reports were related to API usability issues. Likewise, mobile apps suffer also from similar problems [13]. Linares-Vásquez et al. provide empirical evidence about the relation between the success of apps (in terms of user ratings), and the change- and fault-proneness of the underlying APIs. Similar problems will likely emerge for LDWs.

Overcoming this problem requires mechanisms for change detection and change propagation. YQL can help. First, YQL provides a one-shot view of the health of ODTs (see Figure 7) so that willing-full members of the community can quickly spot where their work is required. Second, change propagation can be better localized by splitting LDW development in two stages: from API-to-table and from table-to-rdf. The former refers to traditional ODTs. In the best scenario, ODTs can be already available (i.e. not being part of the wrapping effort), and hence, its maintenance can be conducted by a different set of developers. As for the table-to-rdf stage, it involves leveraging the ODT to deliver

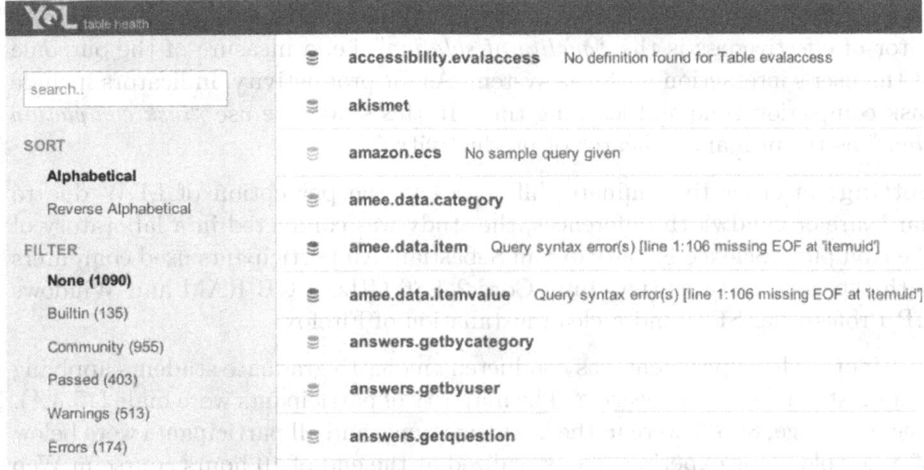

Fig. 7. YQL's health checker. ODTs are monitored for problems. A color code is used to indicate the outcome together with an automatically-generated symptom message.

JSON-LD. This part is less likely to be affected as long as the API upgrade does not involve parameter removals. The ODT-as-usual should shelter the second part from changes on the format, name and order of API parameters.

Linked Open Data (LOD) Cloud Expansion. New data sources are continuously being added to the LOD cloud. One could expect this growth resulted into a more bushy cloud with a higher degree on interlinkage. However, this does not come across in a study about the dynamics of LD [11]. Käfer et al. observe that, unlike the HTML world with an estimate of 25% in the number of new hyperlinks in a week period, LD seemed much more static. The authors indicate that "this seems counter-intuitive in that LD itself is fundamentally comprised of URIs and thus links". In the same vein, a recent study about the LD cloud concludes that only 56% of the 1014 datasets studied have external links [19]. This might be partially due to most linked-data sources be in-house wrappers. Here, adding links to brand-new LOD nodes is taken by the few wrapper's developers.

Here, distinct benefits can be hypothesized from collaborative LDW development. First, the larger the number of people, the greater the chances of spotting an interesting LOD node. Also, more people tend to imply more heterogeneous data needs, hence increasing the pressure for interlinkages. Finally, the burden of adding new links can be shared with people other than the initial developers.

4.4 Measuring Effectiveness

ISO-9126 provides a framework to evaluate quality in use which includes effectiveness (i.e. the capability of the software product to enable users to achieve specified goals with accuracy and completeness) and productivity (i.e.the relation between the capability of the software product to enable users to expend appropriate amounts of resources in relation to the effectiveness) [9]. A main indicator of effectiveness is the *"quality of solution"*, i.e. a measure of the outcome of the user's interaction with the system. As for productivity, indicators include task completion time and learning time. In this study, we use *"task completion time"* as the primary indicator of productivity.

Setting. In order to eliminate differences in the perception of LDW due to hardware or bandwidth differences, the study was conducted in a laboratory of the Computer Science Faculty of San Sebastián. All participants used computers with the same features (i.e., Intel Core 2 1.86 GHz, 3 GB RAM and Windows XP Professional SP3) and a clean installation of Firefox.

Subjects. The experiment was conducted among 15 graduate students applying in a Master in Web Engineering. The majority of participants were male (73.3%). Regarding age, 86.7% were in the 22-30 age range and all participants were below 35 years old. This experiment was realized at the end of 10 hours course in Web Programmable issues, where students familiarize with the YQL console, the YQL language and ODT specifications. As part of the Master degree, students followed a 30 hour Semantic Web course, where Linked Data concepts and RDF syntax were introduced. All of them were acquainted with JSON, but no JSON-LD. 5 students were expert JavaScript programmers, 5 had basic skills, and 5 knew the language but never code with it. All the students knew the existence of GitHub but only six had used it assiduously in previous projects.

Procedure. Before starting, a 45-minute talk was given, introducing the purpose, some practical examples of JSON-LD, one implemented LDW example[13] and the registration process on the LDW server. A user-guide sheet were distributed among participants with all this information. Next, subjects were faced with two scenarios, namely,

- from ODT to LDW. Here, students were given an existing ODT (i.e. *lastfm .events.getinfo*). The aim was to leverage this ODT to become a LDW. Tasks ahead include: URL pattern specification (i.e. lowering process) and lifting function definition. The latter involves ontologies identification, namespace handling, URI resource construction, URI class identification, properties XPath specification, multivalued attribute management and linkage pattern construction.
- from API to LDW. Here, students started from scratch, i.e. the API (in this case, the *authenticjobs.search* API[14]). This method returns the actual jobs that fulfill some input conditions. Besides the previously mentioned tasks, this scenario's demands include: API key obtention, API Endpoint localization, API parameter identification, and finally, ODT construction.

In order to measure productivity, participants had to annotate the start time and the finishing time. Finally, the subjects were directed to a *GoogleDocs* questionnaire to gather their opinion.

[13] https://github.com/onekin/ldw/blob/master/flickr/flickr.photos.getinfo.xml
[14] http://www.authenticjobs.com/api/documentation/

Table 1. Effectiveness. (a): from ODT to LDW. (b) from API to LDW

Task	#Students scenario (a)	#Students scenario (b)
API key obtention		12
API endpoint localization		15
API parameter localization		15
ODT construction		12
URL pattern specification	15	15
Ontologies identification	7	11
URI resource construction	13	12
Resource class identification	10	12
Properties XPath specification	15	11
Multivalue property management	2	5
Linkage pattern construction	11	12

Effectiveness Results. Table 1(a) shows the results for the first task: 13 out of 15 students completed the *LDW*. The criterium for success was the dereferenced of *Last.fm* events' URIs. During LDW development, none had problems to identify the *URL Pattern* that describes the lowering mapping. However, three had problems in specifying the *<function>* parameters that describe the lifting process. As expected, the *lifting* function caused most problems: all students lifted at least two attributes and created linked URI's to one resource; 13 correctly identified the URI of the resource (@id); 10 properly identified the type of the resource (@type: *mo:performance*); 7 provided appropriate namespaces (@context); finally, only 2 successfully processed multivalued attributes. The latter can be alleviated through a JavaScript library that helps managing multivalued attributes. Finally, interlinkage to other resources task was properly fulfilled by 11 students.

Table 1(b) depicts the outcome for the second endeavor: the development of the ODT plus the LDW. Compared with the first LDW, this task requires students to be familiarized with the *authenticjobs* API, identifying the required method and its input parameters. Additionally, students must register to *authenticjobs* to obtain the applications API Keys. Three students had problems to obtain this API keys. This API follows a standard REST query protocol similar to the *Last.fm* API, so students follow a clone-and-own approach by starting from the *flickr.photos.getinfo* ODT, and next, adapt it to the *authenticjobs'* specifics. This accounts for a new way of LDW development that collaborative development fosters. In the last step, that is, the ODT construction, 4 students had problems to identify the XPath where the result tuples were located. Once the ODT was created, moving to the LDW didn't involve any significant setback for most students (mainly due to the first lab being resolved some few hours before). Nevertheless, 3 students had problems to identify the ontology while 4 had difficulties to identify some complex XPaths from a service data (nested elements, attribute obtention, array position access). Once again, the main stumbling block stemmed from property multivalued attributes. Linkage to other services accounted for 0 links (3 students), 1 link (7 students), 2 link (4 students) and 3 links (1 student).

Productivity Results. We appreciate a considerable dispersion on the time involved in LDW development. The first LDW involved 20' on average while the second took 50' on average. Spend time was proportional to the student's JavaScript experience.

5 The LDW Community: The Consumer Perspective

LDW continuous effort pays off if beneficiaries go beyond breakout developers. So far, most LDWs are seldom used outside their research projects. If LDWs are to evolve beyond proof-of-concept, scalability issues should be considered. Graceful degradation of elapsed times should be obtained to ensure appropriate quality of service. YQL can help by providing load balancing that outperforms small-scale attempts to host LDW services. This section evaluates two scenarios:

- LDW overhead, i.e. additional latency introduced by the wrapping w.r.t direct API access, and
- LDW load balancing gains, i.e. difference between running a LDW in a server with and without load balancing.

Both studies were conducted over a AMD Turion 64 X2 2 GHz CPU with 4GB of memory, with a domestic 6Mbps WIFI LAN bandwidth. Measurements were realized through JMeter[15]. The experiment pivots around the *Flickr* website. The goal was to dereference a URI that contains a position (i.e. http://$flickrservice/location/52.453056/13.290556/) together with photos at this position. The wrapper was implemented in two ways:

- as an ad-hoc program (i.e. ***Flickrwrappr***). This accounts for the traditional scenario, and it is based on a wrapper service provided by the University of Mannheim[16]. The implementation accounts for 250 lines of PHP code.
- as an YQL's ODT (i. e. ***FlickrODT***). Here, the wrapper was developed and deployed using YQL infrastructure (available at https://github.com/onekin/ldw/blob/master/flickr/flickr.photos.getinfo.xml).

5.1 URI-Dereferencing Latency

We want to measure the latency introduced by wrapping w.r.t. directly invoking the *Flickr*'s API. To this end, dereferencing was conducted 1000 times with one call per second. The experiment was repeated three times at different hours of

[15] http://jmeter.apache.org/

[16] http://wifo5-03.informatik.uni-mannheim.de/flickrwrappr/. Interesting enough, this wrapper stopped working on June, 2014 as a result of a change in *Flickr*'s API (refer to http://code.flickr.net/2014/04/30/flickr-api-going-ssl-only-on-june-27th-2014/). We upgrade the code and install it in our server.

the day. Table 2 (lefthand side) shows the results. Outcomes indicate that wrapping involves a three-fold overhead compared with direct API calling. In addition, *Flickrwrappr* benefits from directly invoking API whereas *FlickrODT* only accesses *Flickr* indirectly through YQL services. This indirection costs 125ms in the median. We can tentatively conclude that for sparsely used wrappers, ODT indirection might improve maintenance but introduces a time penalty.

Table 2. Latencies. Lefthand side: latency average values (ms). Righthand side: median latency values based on a number of threads (ms).

	Flickr	Flickrwrappr	FlickrODT
Mean	212	646	851
Median	194	601	726
Min	188	515	615
Max	300	990	1223

#threads	Flickr	Flickrwrappr	FlickrODT
10	202	605	726
50	204	611	739
250	210	1251	802
2000	215	2371	957

5.2 URI-Dereferencing Scalability

This second experiment looks at wrapper behavior with different loads. Here, we subject the wrappers to different dereferencing petition loads: 10, 50, 250 and 2000 threads. The process is repeated 10 times every 5 seconds. Table 2 (righthand side) depicts the results. Here, *FlickrODT* outperforms *Flickrwrappr* as a result of the load balancing performed by the YQL platform. Whereas *FlickrODT* performance gracefully degrades, *Flickrwrappr* surpasses 611ms as the median latency when handling over 50 threads in parallel. This behavior is most important to ensure quality of service on the Web of Data. For wrappers supported by data owners (e.g. *DBpedia*) this might not be a problem, since they enjoy the resources to meet these figures. However, third-party collaboratively developed wrappers require YQL-like infrastructure to thrive. Otherwise, their poor quality of service might well discourage other end-points to set interlinkage with them.

6 Related Work

This section frames YQL into other attempts to facilitate LDW development: *D2RQ* [1], *DBpedia* [12], the *SA-REST* platform [20] *Karma* [22], *SWEET* [14], *LIDS/LOS* services [18][21], *Virtuoso Sponger* [10]. These platforms are compared along the following dimension (see Table 3): the data-source being wrapped, the wrapper language, and the existence of tools. Next paragraphs describe the specifics of each approach.

Data Sources. There are several initiatives to wrap heterogeneous data sources to the Linked Data. *D2RQ* platform wraps relational databases, *DBpedia* wraps Wikipedia HTML pages, and *SA-REST* focuses on Web Services. But it is the wrapping of REST API's where more initiatives showed up. This is inline with the tendency of publish data following this approach (a 75% of programmable web API offers this protocol). More encompassing approaches such as *Virtuoso Sponger*, offer a middleware for a variety data sources (relational, Web Service or REST). Unlike other approaches, data is not obtained on-the-fly but periodically uploaded. YQL permits wrappers upon REST services, and in general, any source that produces XML (e.g. XHTML).

Table 3. LDW Platforms

	Data sources	**Wrapper language**	**Tooling**
D2RQ	Relational DB	R2RML ontology	Code generator
Virtuoso Sponger	Relational DB and web resources	Virtuoso PL or C/C++ or Java	Clone
DBpedia	Wikipedia articles	WikiText template	Debug, clone
SA-REST platform	Web services	RDFa upon SAWSDL ontology	n/a
KARMA	REST	KARMA ontology	Programming by example
SWEET	REST	hREST upon MicroWSMO ontology	Annotation recommender
LIDS/LOS	REST	ontology + procedural	n/a
YQL	REST	YQL + JavaScript	Debug, clone cloud-deployment

Wrapper Language. Approaches attempt to find a compromise between expressiveness and learnability. This balance impacts the target audience. Domain-specific approaches focus on specific data sources (e.g. *Wikipedia* or relational databases) which permit lowering and lifting to be built-in. This accounts for more declarative wrapper specifications that easy user involvement. In the case of *DBpedia*, this specification is realized in terms of wiki templates, akin to the wiki origins of this initiative. In relational databases, wrapping is specified by R2RML ontology, where "TripleMaps" objects map tables and columns into RDF classes and properties, respectively. Departing from declarative specifications, other authors resort to general-purpose procedural languages (e.g. *YQL* and *Virtuoso Sponger*), wrapper ontologies (e.g. *Karma*), or a mixture (e.g. *SA-REST*, *SWEET* and *LIDS/LOS*), depending on the target audience (i.e. API programmers for *YQL* vs. Semantic Web community for *Karma*). Data services (e.g. *LIDS/LOS*) return data dynamically derived from supplied input parameters. The input can come in RDF format (Linked Open Services, *LOS*) or it can be a URI (Linked Data Services, LIDS). In both cases, the result is a RDF document. The wrapping is described using a RDF ontology together with some programming language (e.g. XSLT) for the lowering and the lifting. Finally, *Virtuoso Sponger* LDWs (known as Cartridges) resort to *Virtuoso PL*, a language that somehow blends SQL and C, or it can be defined in some procedural languages (e.g. C/C++ of Java).

Tooling. Promoting LDW goes through providing appropriate tools. This includes the existence of publicly available LDW repositories that permit clone&own, code generators, assistive editing, testing and debugging capabilities as well as cloud deployment. *RBA* [16] is a tool for semi-automatically generating customised *R2RML* Mappings from a database. Both *DBpedia* and YQL enjoy a LDW repository which is realized through wiki pages and *GitHub* repositories, respectively. *SWEET* offers a ontology assisted annotation recommender based on *Watson* [7]. *Karma* illustrates the most ground-breaking stance. Through a kind of "programming-by-example" approach, *Karma* permits end users to generate LDW automatically out of a set of examples of API calls.

7 Conclusions

Linked Data Wrappers (LDWs) permit Open APIs to become part of the LD cloud. This effort can be facilitated through LDW frameworks. This paper explores the potential of YQL to become such platform with a first focus on effectiveness and scalability. Results are promising in scalability, and, to some extent, also in effectiveness. We illustrate how common LDW matters can be built on top of YQL's ODT, and how students manage to develop LDWs on an average time frame of 20' to 50', depending on whether they can tap into an existing ODT or not.

We hypothesize that the *aging* of YQL's LDWs will improve w.r.t. traditional in-house LDWs. Rationales are twofold. First, LDWs are available through GitHub so open to public scrutiny and collaboration, while ODTs a more declarative than their Java counterparts. Second, by caring about performance, the chances of increasing trust that will eventual end up in interlinkage, would increase. This in turn might well result in more pressure to keep the LDW up. This has yet to be proven. However, the benefits are worthwhile: keeping in sync Open APIs, LDWs and the linked-data cloud.

Acknowledgment. This work is co-supported by the Spanish Ministry of Education, and the European Social Fund under contract TIN2011-23839 (Scripting).

References

1. D2RQ. Accessing Relational Databases as Virtual RDF Graphs. http://d2rq.org/
2. Describing Linked Datasets with the VoID Vocabulary (2011). http://www.w3.org/TR/void/
3. A JSON-based Serialization for Linked Data. W3C Recommendation (2014). http://www.w3.org/TR/json-ld/
4. Becker, C., Bizer, C.: Flickr wrappr: precise photo association. http://wifo5-03.informatik.uni-mannheim.de/flickrwrappr/

5. Bizer, C., Cyganiak, R., Gauß, T.: The RDF book mashup: from web APIs to a web of data. In: Proc. of Scripting for the Semantic Web Workshop at the ESWC. CEUR Workshop Proceedings (2007), ISSN 1613–0073. CEUR-WS.org/Vol-248/paper4.pdf
6. Buneman, P., Khanna, S., Wang-Chiew, T.: Why and where: a characterization of data provenance. In: Van den Bussche, J., Vianu, V. (eds.) ICDT 2001. LNCS, vol. 1973, pp. 316–330. Springer, Heidelberg (2000)
7. d'Aquin, M., Motta, E., Sabou, M., Angeletou, S., Gridinoc, L., Lopez, V., Guidi, D.: Toward a new generation of semantic web applications. IEEE Intelligent Systems **23**(3), 20–28 (2008)
8. Das, S., Sundara, S., Cyganiak, R.: R2RML: RDB to RDF Mapping Language. Tech. rep., W3C Recommendation (2012). http://www.w3.org/TR/r2rml/
9. Davis, I., Vitiello Jr, E.: ISO 9241–11. Ergonomic requirements for office work with visual displays terminals(VDTs) Part 11: Guidance on Usability (1998)
10. Erling, O., Mikhailov, I.: RDF support in the virtuoso DBMS. In: Pellegrini, T., Auer, S., Tochtermann, K., Schaffert, S. (eds.) Networked Knowledge - Networked Media. SCI, vol. 221, pp. 7–24. Springer, Heidelberg (2009)
11. Käfer, T., Abdelrahman, A., Umbrich, J., O'Byrne, P., Hogan, A.: Observing linked data dynamics. In: Cimiano, P., Corcho, O., Presutti, V., Hollink, L., Rudolph, S. (eds.) ESWC 2013. LNCS, vol. 7882, pp. 213–227. Springer, Heidelberg (2013)
12. Lehmann, J., Isele, R., Jakob, M., Jentzsch, A., Kontokostas, D., Mendes, P.N., Hellmann, S., Morsey, M., van Kleef, P., Auer, S., et al.: DBpedia-a large-scale, multilingual knowledge base extracted from Wikipedia. Semantic Web (2014)
13. Linares-Vásquez, M., Bavota, G., Bernal-Cárdenas, C., Penta, M.D., Oliveto, R., Poshyvanyk, D.: API change and fault proneness: a threat to the success of android apps. In: Proceedings of the 2013 9th Joint Meeting on Foundations of Software Engineering, pp. 477–487. ACM (2013)
14. Maleshkova, M., Pedrinaci, C., Domingue, J.: Semantic annotation of web APIs with SWEET. In: 6th Workshop on Scripting and Development for the Semantic Web, Colocated with ESWC (2010)
15. Martin, D., Burstein, M., Hobbs, J.: OWL-S: Semantic Markup for Web Services. Tech. rep., W3C Member Submission (2004). http://www.w3.org/Submission/OWL-S/
16. Neto, L.E.T., Vidal, V.M.P., Casanova, M.A., Monteiro, J.M.: *R2RML by assertion*: a semi-automatic tool for generating customised R2RML mappings. In: Cimiano, P., Fernández, M., Lopez, V., Schlobach, S., Völker, J. (eds.) ESWC 2013. LNCS, vol. 7955, pp. 248–252. Springer, Heidelberg (2013)
17. Network, Y.D.: Yahoo Query Language (YQL) guide. https://developer.yahoo.com/yql/guide/
18. Norton, B., Krummenacher, R., Marte, A., Fensel, D.: Dynamic linked data via linked open services. In: Proceedings of the Workshop on Linked Data in the Future Internet at the Future Internet Assembly (2010)
19. Schmachtenberg, M., Bizer, C., Paulheim, H.: Adoption of the linked data best practices in different topical domains. In: Mika, P., et al. (eds.) ISWC 2014, Part I. LNCS, vol. 8796, pp. 245–260. Springer, Heidelberg (2014)
20. Sheth, A.P., Gomadam, K., Lathem, J.: SA-REST: Semantically Interoperable and Easier-to-Use Services and Mashups. IEEE Internet Computing **11**(6), 91–94 (2007)

21. Speiser, S., Harth, A.: Integrating linked data and services with linked data services. In: Antoniou, G., Grobelnik, M., Simperl, E., Parsia, B., Plexousakis, D., De Leenheer, P., Pan, J. (eds.) ESWC 2011, Part I. LNCS, vol. 6643, pp. 170–184. Springer, Heidelberg (2011)
22. Taheriyan, M., Knoblock, C.A., Szekely, P., Ambite, J.L.: Rapidly integrating services into the linked data cloud. In: Cudré-Mauroux, P., et al. (eds.) ISWC 2012, Part I. LNCS, vol. 7649, pp. 559–574. Springer, Heidelberg (2012)
23. Zibran, M.F., Eishita, F.Z., Roy, C.K.: Useful, but usable? factors affecting the usability of APIs. In: 2011 18th Working Conference on Reverse Engineering (WCRE), pp. 151–155. IEEE (2011)

A Quantitative Comparison of Semantic Web Page Segmentation Approaches

Robert Kreuzer, Jurriaan Hage(✉), and Ad Feelders

Department of Information and Computing Sciences, Utrecht University, Utrecht, The Netherlands
robert.kreuzer@gmail.com, {J.Hage,A.J.Feelders}@uu.nl

Abstract. We compare three known semantic web page segmentation algorithms, each serving as an example of a particular approach to the problem, and one self-developed algorithm, WebTerrain, that combines two of the approaches. We compare the performance of the four algorithms for a large benchmark of modern websites we have constructed, examining each algorithm for a total of eight configurations. We found that all algorithms performed better on random pages on average than on popular pages, and results are better when running the algorithms on the HTML obtained from the DOM rather than on the plain HTML. Overall there is much room for improvement as we find the best average F-score to be 0.49, indicating that for modern websites currently available algorithms are not yet of practical use.

1 Introduction

Web page segmentation is the process of taking a web page, and partitioning it into so-called *semantic blocks* (or segments), that we define as

> A contiguous HTML fragment which renders as a graphically consistent block and whose content belongs together semantically.

Semantic blocks can in principle be deeply nested, although in practice people rarely consider nesting more than two or three levels. In this paper we do not consider the process of *labeling*, which takes a partitioning of a webpage into semantic blocks, and then assign labels to them taken from some ontology.

Human beings are very good at partitioning: even if a website is in a language we are not familiar with, it is clear to us what is an advertisement, what is a menu, and so on. Web page segmentation algorithms seek to automate this process: among the applications for automated segmentation we find mobile web, voice web, web page phishing detection, duplicate deletion, information retrieval, image retrieval, information extraction, user interest detection, visual quality evaluation, web page clustering, caching, archiving, semantic annotation and web accessibility [18].

In this paper we perform an empirical study of the usefulness of three web page segmentation *approaches*: the DOM-based approach, the visual approach

P. Cimiano et al. (Eds.): ICWE 2015, LNCS 9114, pp. 374–391, 2015.
DOI: 10.1007/978-3-319-19890-3_24

and the text-based approach. We also consider whether combining two of these approaches gives superior results. We compare the approaches by taking a representative algorithm for each, and evaluate their effectiveness in web page segmentation by comparing their outputs to a manually constructed ground truth. This should answer our first research question, which reads

RQ1: How well do different web page segmentation approaches perform on a large collection of modern websites? In particular, can we observe that the algorithms indeed fare worse on modern websites?

An additional, related research question we considered is the following:

RQ2: Can the results be improved by combining different approaches?

As we shall see in this paper, the answer to both these questions is affirmative. Although the algorithm that combines two of the approaches often outperforms the other algorithms, its effectiveness is still much below what we would like to see. A conclusion of this paper is then also that new, better algorithms should be sought to more effectively perform web page segmentation.

We have constructed two datasets: one with a number of popular websites, that we expected to be complex and therefore hard to deal with, and a second set with randomly selected websites to avoid having our results biased too much towards complicated websites. Our datasets are part of the contribution this paper offers, and are open for anyone to use[1].

The paper is structured as follows: in Section 2 we discuss the various approaches to web page segmentation, and our choice of algorithms for the comparison. We had to construct our own dataset of marked up web sites, and we discuss the process of doing so in Section 3. In Section 4 we provide the outcomes of our comparison, upon which we reflect in Section 5. Section 6 discusses related work, and Section 7 concludes.

2 Approaches and Algorithms

There are many algorithms for web page segmentation, and we cannot hope to consider them all. Instead, we opted to see which of the *approaches* to web page segmentation work well on modern websites. For each approach we chose a representative algorithm (typically the one that is generally most cited or compared against), obtained an implementation from others, or, in the absence of such an implementation, implemented the algorithm ourselves. The three approaches we consider are the DOM-based approach, the visual approach and the text-based approach.

2.1 The DOM-Based Approach (PageSegmenter)

In a DOM-based approach one simply looks at the DOM, the tree built by parsing the HTML, for cues on how to segment a page. (This tree does not include the

[1] https://github.com/rkrzr/dataset-random, https://github.com/rkrzr/dataset-popular, constructed by Kreuzer, El-Lari, Van Nuenen, and Hospes

properties added by external CSS files; these will only be present in the render tree.) The idea is that the HTML structure should reflect the semantics of the page. The quality of these approaches thus depends on how strongly this is the case. To do the segmentation they rely on detecting recurring patterns, such as lists and tables, and on heuristics, like headline tags working as separators, and links being part of the surrounding text. The approach is easy to implement and efficient to run, since one only needs to parse the HTML and not render the page. Complications are that there are many different ways to build an HTML document structure for the same content, styling and layout information is disregarded by design, and it will not work immediately in the presence of Javascript (unless you serialize the DOM first).

The PageSegmenter algorithm is an example of a DOM-based segmentation algorithm [16]. They tested their work experimentally against the TAP knowledge base [10] (which was not not available anymore for our study) and on a home-made dataset consisting of CS department websites. In [17], the authors also rate the individual blocks by learning a statistical predictor of segment content quality and use those ratings to improve search results.

The main idea of the PageSegmenter algorithm is that the root-to-leaf paths of leaf nodes can be analyzed for similarities to find nodes which likely belong to the same semantic block. An example of such a path is `/html/body/p/ul/li`. Now, if multiple adjacent siblings have the same such path it is a pretty safe assumption that they also semantically belong together, as they are structurally part of the same list.

In their paper the authors mention that they exclude text nodes from the tree where the text contains *modal verbs* (such as could, should, would...) in order to decrease noise. Our implementation does not do so, because this would make the algorithm language-specific, which is something we want to avoid. More details on how we implemented the algorithm precisely can be found in [15].

2.2 The Visual Approach (VIPS)

Visual approaches most resemble how a human segments a page, i.e. they operate on the rendered page itself as seen in a browser. They thus have the most information available, but are also computationally the most expensive because pages must be rendered. They often divide the page into separators, such as lines, white-space and images, and content and build a content-structure out of this information. They can take visual features such as background color, styling, layout, font size and type and location on the page into account. To render the page we need access to a browser engine, which complicates the implementation of an algorithm. Moreover, it clearly requires external resources such as CSS files and images in order to work correctly.

For this approach we elected the VIPS (Vision-based Page Segmentation) algorithm [5,6], which appears to be the most popular web page segmentation algorithm. As indicated by the name this algorithm is based on the rendered representation of a page. It analyzes the DOM after all the styling information from CSS rules have been applied and after Javascript files were executed (and potentially modified the tree). It is tightly integrated with a browser rendering engine since it needs to query for information such as the dimensions on screen of a given element. One thus has to decide on a fixed viewport size in advance on which the page should be rendered. Concretely, the algorithm builds a vision-based content structure, independent of the underlying HTML document, deciding during a top-down traversal whether something represents a visual block, or whether it should be subdivided further by using a number of heuristics, such as "if a sub-tree contains separators like the <hr> tag, subdivide". The authors tested their algorithm experimentally by sampling 140 pages from different categories of the Yahoo directory and running their algorithm on them and then manually assessing whether the segmentation was "Perfect", "Satisfactory" or "Failed". We used an existing implementation from Tomas Popela[2]; the original implementation was not available anymore.

2.3 The Text-Based Approach (BlockFusion)

The *text-based* approach differs from the other two in that it does not take the tree structure of the HTML into account at all. Algorithms only look at the (textual) content and analyze certain textual features like e.g. the text-density or the link-density of parts of a page. These techniques are grounded in results from quantitative linguistics which indicate that, statistically, text blocks with similar features are likely to belong together and can thus be merged in a single block. The optimal similarity threshold depends on the wanted granularity and needs to be determined experimentally. The algorithms tend to be fast and easy to implement since they work independently from the DOM, but like the DOM-based approach will not work with Javascript (unless you serialize the DOM first), do not not take structural and visual clues into account, and the extraction of sub-blocks requires local changes to the text-density threshold (since we can't employ document structure).

The representative chosen for the text-based approach is the BlockFusion algorithm [13]. The algorithm is based on the observation that the so-called *token density* can be a valuable heuristic to segment text documents. The token density of a text can simply be calculated by taking the number of words in the text and dividing it by the number of lines, where a line is capped to 80 characters. An HTML document is then first preprocessed into a list of atomic text blocks, by splitting on so-called separating gaps, which are HTML tags other than the <a> tag. For each atomic block the token density can then be computed. A merge strategy is then employed to merge blocks into progressively larger ones, if the difference between token densities of two adjacent blocks is below a certain threshold value. This is done repeatedly until no more blocks can be merged. Due to this design the algorithm does not support multiple levels of blocks by default, but by an extension in which we locally introduce a second smaller threshold value, and then call the BlockFusion algorithm on each (already merged) block, we can achieve a two-level hierarchy. BlockFusion was

[2] https://github.com/tpopela/vips_java

evaluated experimentally using a dataset consisting of 111 pages. We based our own implementation of this algorithm on an open source library from one of the BlockFusion authors [12], allowing us to stay close to the original implementation. We used a text density threshold value of $\vartheta_{max} = 0.38$, which was found to be the optimal value in the experimental evaluation [13].

2.4 A Combined Approach (WebTerrain)

The WebTerrain algorithm was developed as our own contribution to the segmentation problem. The main idea was to see if we can combine the different approaches from the other algorithms in order to improve upon the end result. The algorithm is based on a novel heuristic which inspired the name of the algorithm: Firefox has a little known feature which allows the user to see a 3D-rendered version of any website (choose Inspect Element after a right-click on any given page, and then click on the cube icon). The result looks similar to a geographic terrain map. This feature works by assigning an additional depth-value to each visible element on top of the common width- and height-values, which are already used in the normal 2D-representation of the page. The depth-value is simply the tree-level of the element. Experiments with this feature revealed that the elevation profile corresponds pretty well to what we would consider the semantic blocks of a web page. The heuristic that this observation leads to has the interesting property that it combines a plain structural approach with a rendering-based approach into one, since it not only takes the DOM tree into account but also the visibility and dimensions of each element. It is not possible to tell by simply looking at the original HTML document how it will ultimately be rendered. One does not know how much space each child of an element will take up on the screen, or if it will be visible at all. For this, one needs to actually render the page.

Further details about the various algorithms, implementations, complications, and how we extracted the necessary information from the outputs of the implementations are omitted for reasons of space, but can be found in [15].

3 The Datasets

Since web page segmentation is a fairly well-studied problem, many authors have done an empirical evaluation of their algorithms. The datasets and methods used for this evaluation vary widely. There appears to be no standard dataset for this problem, instead everyone seems to create their own dataset by first randomly sampling web pages (sometimes taken from a directory site such as http://dmoz.org) and then manually marking up the semantic blocks and often also labeling the blocks according to a predefined ontology. To further illustrate this, we consider how the three chosen known algorithms were validated by the authors that proposed them.

For the VIPS algorithm the authors did not first create a dataset with a ground truth. Instead they ran VIPS on their sample pages and then manually graded whether the segmentation of that page was "perfect", "satisfactory" or "failed". This approach is problematic on two levels: First, there is the obvious conflict of interest, since the authors themselves are grading the results of their own algorithm. Second, whether a segmentation is "perfect" or "satisfactory" is rather subjective and can thus not be repeated by others.

For the BlockFusion algorithm the authors did not use precision and recall, but instead they used two cluster correlation metrics, namely *Adjusted Rand Index* and *Normalized Mutual Information* to quantify the accuracy of the segmentation. They did first create a ground truth manually, but it is unclear whether this was done by the authors themselves or by volunteers.

For the PageSegmenter algorithm the authors did use precision, recall and F-Score in their evaluation. Differently from us they did not do this for all blocks in general on a page, but they divided the blocks into three classes first (which they call Concept, Attribute and Value) and applied the metrics to each of these classes. This again prevents a direct comparison as this division into three classes is specific to their algorithm and not applicable to other segmentation algorithms.

Before building our own dataset we investigated the datasets used by other authors to find out how they chose their sample pages, sample sizes and whether they downloaded only the HTML documents themselves, or the referenced external resources as well. Furthermore we wanted to see whether any of these datasets would be suitable for our study as well.

We found five datasets. The manually labeled ones vary in size from 105 to 515, with the exception of the TAP knowledge base [10] at a size of 9,068 which was a semantically labeled database that was used as a test-bed for the Semantic Web but is unfortunately not available anymore. The Web pages are sampled completely at random in [7], in [13] they are taken from the Webspam UK-2007 dataset[3,4,8] comprising over 100 million pages, which is focused on labeling hosts into spam/nonspam, in [14] they first downloaded 16,000 random pages from the directory site www.dmoz.org and randomly selected sample pages. Also, [16] distinguishes between template-driven and non-template-driven Web pages (i.e. pages generated by a web page authoring system and hand-coded ones).

The block assignment was sometimes done by the authors and sometimes by volunteers, the latter being preferable to avoid bias. It is not always mentioned what granularity of blocks was used (i.e. whether only top-level blocks were marked up or sub-blocks as well), but no one specifically mentioned marking up sub-blocks which leads us to the assumption that no sub-blocks were highlighted. Since none of these datasets are available online or from the authors directly we were unable to confirm this.

One other notable observation is that all datasets seem to consist only of HTML documents without any of the external resources referenced from the pages. While this is certainly partly due to the datasets being already up to 11 years old, when web pages on average were still a lot less complex than they are now, this is not realistic anymore for websites that are currently on-line. We discuss why later on in this section.

Neither of these potential benchmarks turned out to be suitable: either the authors of the papers never replied to our inquiries, and in the one case that we did find the dataset it was not suitable for our purposes since it was focused on news websites, and only included the original HTML sources and no external resources. The latter is a problem in our case, because all algorithms that depend on a rendered representation of the page will deliver very different results for a page with all external resources and one without. In conclusion, we decided to construct our own benchmark set, which we have made publicly available (see the footnote in Section 1).

External Resources in Web Pages. Modern web pages can and typically do reference a number of external resources that are necessary to render the page properly. These include images, videos, CSS files, Javascript files, and lesser known ones like font files, JSON or XML files, favicons, and vector graphic files.

Clearly, if you render only the HTML document itself then the result will usually be vastly different from the page including all resources. Mainly for this reason we decided to build a dataset consisting of HTML documents together with all their external resources (and all links rewritten accordingly so that they point to the right files). Javascript poses a real challenge for any kind of Web page analysis. Since a Javascript program can modify the DOM arbitrarily and furthermore load in more data or other Javascript programs from external sources, it is possible that the original HTML document and the rendered page have virtually nothing in common.

In effect, if we want to be able to validate algorithms that employ the visual approach, we must include in our dataset all the external resources that a given web page needs to be visualized. To retrieve, for a given web page, all such external resources is not a trivial exercise. For example, CSS files have the ability to refer to other CSS files, and these may again refer to ever more such files. Javascript is particularly hard to deal with since it is a Turing complete language (unlike HTML and CSS). In practice we solve the problem by simply running the Javascript programs, but whether we have in fact retrieved all resources that we shall ever need is undecidable in general. The best practical solution we could find is the `wget` utility, using finely tuned parameters[3]. It handles all of the difficulties mentioned above except references from within Javascript programs, and it also rewrites the links so that they all point to the right locations. We found that the downloaded pages rendered identical or nearly identical to the online version in most cases. The pages that used Javascript references to an extent that they could not be properly rendered offline were excluded from the dataset (18 out of 100 for the random dataset and 30 out of 100 for the popular dataset).

Having retrieved the web pages and the associated resources, they had to be marked up so that we would have a ground truth to compare the algorithms against. We implemented a small program, called Builder, in Javascript that,

[3] The magic incantation is: wget -U user_agent -E -H -k -K -p -x -P folder_name -e robots=off the_url

given the url of the web page, allows one of our volunteers to easily mark up the web page and store the results. It is run by clicking a bookmarklet which will load and run the Javascript program from our server. It then works by highlighting the DOM node the user is hovering over with the mouse, allowing her to select that block and showing her a menu where she can choose what type of block it is. The possible choices to classify a block were:

High-level-blocks Header, Footer, Content, Sidebar
Sub-level-blocks Logo, Menu, Title, Link-list, Table, Comments, Ad, Image, Video, Article, Searchbar

This block ontology was chosen with the goal of being comprehensive and it was divided into High-level blocks and Sub-level blocks (or level 1 and level 2 blocks) since Web pages can be segmented on different levels of granularity. E.g. a content-block can have a title, an image and an article as sub-blocks. While in principle there is no upper limit to how many levels of granularity you can have on a page, we found two levels to be sufficient in the majority of cases and have thus restricted ourselves to that.

For robustness we implemented the following solution to marking up the web pages in which the client (for marking up the web pages) and the server (serving the local version of the web pages) reside on the same machine: we first make the full page available offline using `wget`, then open that page in a browser, load the Builder, and add all the blocks and finally serialize the changed DOM to disk again. If one subsequently wants to get out all the blocks of a page one can do so using a simple Xpath query[4].

We built two different datasets, one containing only popular pages and one containing randomly selected pages. This was done to see if the algorithms performed differently on random and on popular pages on average. For the popular dataset we took the top 10 pages from the 10 top-level categories from the directory site http://dir.yahoo.com/. The chosen categories were Arts & Humanities, Business & Economy, Computer & Internet, Entertainment, Government, Health, News & Media, Science and Social Science. We believe this gives us a representative sample of popular websites, although not of websites in general. We manually checked all websites whether they still rendered properly after having been downloaded and removed the ones that were broken, which left us with a total of seventy popular pages in the dataset.

For the random websites we made use of the web service from
http://www.whatsmyip.org/random-website-machine/
to generate a hundred links, which we then downloaded. The service boasts over four million pages in its database and the only filtering done is for adult content, which makes it sufficiently representative for the Internet as a whole. After removing pages that did not render properly offline we ended up with a random dataset consisting of 82 pages.

The marking up of the semantic blocks on these pages was done by three volunteers. They were instructed to first mark up all the level-1 blocks they could

[4] Xpath query to get all blocks: '//*[@data-block]'

find and subsequently all the level-2 blocks within each level-1 block, according to the generic ontology we gave earlier in this section.

When establishing the ground truth with the help of outsiders, we must in some way be reasonably sure that this "truth" is objective enough. In other words, can we expect the intuitive understanding of what is a semantic block among our test persons to be aligned, and, moreover, in line with what the average person surfing the Web would say? The work of [16] reports an overlap of 87.5% between eight test subjects who they asked to mark up the same web pages. Although the sample is small, it corresponds to our own anecdotal experience. However, we did find that we had to be specific about the level of granularity (e.g. "the most high-level (i.e. biggest) blocks and their most high-level sub-blocks"), since there can be many levels.

4 Results

In this section we present the results of our evaluation of the four different segmentation algorithms. We tested all algorithms in a number of different configurations using a custom testing framework that abstracted the differences in implementations and normalized the results, which could subsequently be analyzed statistically [15].

First, we tested them on the two different datasets which we created for this purpose: the randomly selected dataset and the popular dataset. The first one consists of 82 random pages and the second one of 70 popular pages, all marked up by our assessors. We chose these two types of datasets to test whether the algorithms perform differently on random and on popular pages on average.

As a second variable we ran the algorithms on both the original HTML, i.e. the HTML document downloaded from the source URL via a single GET request, and the DOM HTML, i.e. the HTML document obtained by waiting for all external resources to load and then serializing the DOM. As there appears to be a trend to build pages dynamically on the client-side using Javascript, we were interested to see whether our results would reflect this. It is also of note that our tool to mark up blocks manually was browser-based and thus operated on the DOM, making the DOM HTML the true basis of our ground truth. We believe this is a more sensible basis than the original HTML, since it is what the user ultimately sees when viewing a page, and it also is what the creator of the page intended as the final result.

Finally we used two metrics to compare the generated results to the ground truth, the exact match metric and the fuzzy match metric. Both of them compare the string contents of the blocks to each other. Each block is serialized to only text with all HTML tags removed and white-space and newlines removed as well. For the exact match metric it then simply checks for string equality. This is of course a very strict criterion, as a minimally different string would be counted as false, while for most applications it would likely be perfectly sufficient. For this reason we also do a fuzzy string comparison to check for a similarity ratio of better than 0.8 between strings.

Table 1. Results for Random-HTML-Exact (left) and Random-HTML-Fuzzy (right). Note that the reported numbers are averages over 82 web pages. E.g., the reported F-score was computed by first computing the F-score for each web page, and then taking the average of these 82 F-scores. Therefore the reported values for Precision, Recall and F-score may not satisfy the formula for the F-score as given in the text.

Alg.	Prec.	Rec.	F-Sc.	Retr.	Hits
BF	0.03	0.06	0.04	25.99	0.77
PS	0.11	0.27	0.14	46.96	2.97
VIPS	0.07	0.06	0.06	7.42	0.91
WT	0.25	0.22	0.21	10.9	2.23

Alg.	Prec.	Rec.	F-Sc.	Retr.	Hits
BF	0.06	0.11	0.07	25.99	1.51
PS	0.19	0.45	0.24	46.96	5.24
VIPS	0.28	0.16	0.17	7.42	1.99
WT	0.48	0.43	0.42	10.9	4.5

So all together there are four testing variables: algorithms, datasets, HTML-type and metrics. This yielded 32 test runs in total, the results of which are presented in Table 1-4. For each algorithm we show the average Precision, Recall and F-Score values. Precision is a measure of quality that is defined as the fraction of relevant results out of all retrieved results. Recall is a measure of quantity that is defined as the fraction of retrieved results out of all relevant results. The F-Score is a combination of the two, defined as $F = 2 * \frac{P*R}{P+R}$. Additionally we also show the average number of retrieved blocks, valid hits (i.e. the number of relevant results returned by the algorithm) and the total number of relevant results (determined by the ground truth). The latter is interesting as it shows the difference in the average number of retrieved blocks and it also shows differences between the two datasets.

The Random Dataset

We first present the results of running the four different algorithms on the dataset consisting of 82 randomly selected pages. On average we have 12.24 relevant blocks on a random page. This number is the same for all the experiments with the random dataset. BlockFusion returns on average about twice as many blocks as there are relevant blocks. PageSegmenter returns about four times as many blocks as there are relevant blocks. VIPS returns too few blocks on average. Finally, WebTerrain is the closest in the number of retrieved results to relevant results. As we expected, results are considerably better for the fuzzy match metric as compared to the exact match.

The first two tables (see Table 1) show the results for the exact match metric (on the left), and the fuzzy match metric (on the right) for the random dataset with HTML input. Under the exact match metric, Precision and Recall are generally very low. BlockFusion (BF) and VIPS recognize hardly anything. Precision is highest for WebTerrain (WT)) and Recall is highest for PageSegmenter (PS). Precision and Recall are clearly better for the fuzzy match metric with the number of hits roughly doubling. Especially VIPS improves substantially, indicating that a number of its blocks were only slightly off from the ground truth. The best F-Score (0.42, WebTerrain) is still rather low.

Table 2. Results for Random-DOM-Exact (left) and Random-DOM-Fuzzy (right)

Alg.	Prec.	Rec.	F-Sc.	Retr.	Hits
BF	0.08	0.14	0.09	30.96	1.79
PS	0.11	0.39	0.16	65.04	4.47
VIPS	0.36	0.21	0.24	9.24	2.73
WT	0.34	0.29	0.29	10.58	3.04

Alg.	Prec.	Rec.	F-Sc.	Retr.	Hits
BF	0.1	0.17	0.12	30.96	2.35
PS	0.15	0.51	0.2	65.04	6.12
VIPS	0.51	0.26	0.3	9.24	3.33
WT	0.57	0.49	0.49	10.58	5.33

For the DOM HTML input (see Table 2), we again observe a notable improvement when comparing the exact to the fuzzy match metric, but not quite as dramatic as for the original HTML. The number of retrieved blocks is generally higher (slightly lower for WebTerrain), reflecting the observation that the DOM HTML is typically more complex (things are added, rather than removed).

BlockFusion is performing poorly under the exact match metric, but better than on the original HTML. PageSegmenter again exhibits low precision and high recall. VIPS has the best precision but lower recall, while WebTerrain does similarly on both, giving it the best F-Score. For the fuzzy match metric, we see about a 50% improvement compared to the exact match metric. WebTerrain and VIPS have the highest precision, and PageSegmenter and WebTerrain have the highest recall. Compared to the original HTML we see some improvements as well, especially for the VIPS algorithm. Overall we see the highest scores here out of all benchmarks.

The Popular Dataset

We now turn to the the dataset consisting of 70 popular pages. On average we have about 16.1 relevant blocks on a page: 16.15 for BlockFusion, 16.22 for PageSegmenter, 16.11 for VIPS, and 16.09 for WebTerrain. The slight variation in relevant blocks is because we had to exclude a few (no more than four) pages for some of the algorithms, as they would not be handled properly due to issues in their implementation (e.g. a GTK window would simply keep hanging).

Between the original HTML and the DOM HTML one can see that the number of retrieved blocks universally goes up, giving another sign that the DOM HTML generally contains more content. Overall the results are again better for the DOM HTML, questioning the use of the original HTML in web page segmentation algorithms.

Again, we start by looking at the variations that work on the original HTML input, see Table 3. The pattern seen in the random dataset repeats: results for the fuzzy match metric are about twice as good as for the exact match metric. Both BlockFusion and PageSegmenter return decidedly too many blocks on average, but only PageSegmenter can translate this into high recall scores. VIPS and WebTerrain are fairly close to the relevant number of blocks. For the exact match metric, the results are generally poor with WebTerrain having the best precision and PageSegmenter having the best recall. The results are better

Table 3. Results for Popular-HTML-Exact (left) and Popular-HTML-Fuzzy (right)

Alg.	Prec.	Rec.	F-Sc.	Retr.	Hits
BF	0.03	0.06	0.03	72.85	1.07
PS	0.05	0.24	0.08	124.43	4.05
VIPS	0.07	0.09	0.07	16.72	1.17
WT	0.18	0.17	0.16	13.86	2.19

Alg.	Prec.	Rec.	F-Sc.	Retr.	Hits
BF	0.05	0.12	0.06	72.85	2.07
PS	0.09	0.42	0.13	124.43	6.74
VIPS	0.13	0.15	0.12	16.72	2.23
WT	0.37	0.35	0.33	13.86	4.81

Table 4. Results for Popular-DOM-Exact (left) and Popular-DOM-Fuzzy (right)

Alg.	Prec.	Rec.	F-Sc.	Retr.	Hits
BF	0.03	0.08	0.04	81.75	1.34
PS	0.05	0.27	0.07	163.71	4.56
VIPS	0.13	0.14	0.12	19.51	2.25
WT	0.27	0.28	0.26	14.75	3.77

Alg.	Prec.	Rec.	F-Sc.	Retr.	Hits
BF	0.04	0.12	0.06	81.75	2.13
PS	0.07	0.41	0.11	164	6.68
VIPS	0.19	0.21	0.17	19.51	3.29
WT	0.47	0.46	0.42	14.74	6.43

for the fuzzy match metric, but overall still not convincing. Again WebTerrain and PageSegmenter are the best for precision and recall respectively.

Finally, we consider the two tables for DOM HTML input for the popular dataset (Table 4). Similar to what we saw in the random dataset the improvement from exact to fuzzy matches is smaller than it was for the original HTML, but still substantial.

For the exact match metric, the results are overall better than for original HTML with the biggest gains for VIPS and WebTerrain. WebTerrain has both the highest precision and the highest recall in this test. The results for the popular dataset are the best again, as in the random dataset, when running on the DOM HTML and using the fuzzy match metric. The results for BlockFusion are again the worst. PageSegmenter has again low precision and high recall. Noticeably different is VIPS, as it does not exhibit a high precision, as it did for the random dataset. Recall is similar, though slightly lower. WebTerrain exhibits the highest precision and recall, but precision is 0.1 points lower and recall 0.03 points lower than for the random dataset.

5 Reflection

In this section, we discuss the results of the previous section in some detail. We first consider what the observed effects were of the various testing variables.

Random vs. Popular Datasets. As can be seen from our results all algorithms perform virtually always better on the random pages than on the popular pages. We believe this is due to the increased complexity of popular pages, which can be seen from the fact that they on average had 32% more blocks than a random page. Furthermore we also found that a popular page on average consists of 196.2 files in total (this number includes all the external resources referenced from a page), while a random page only consists of 79.4 files on average. The number of retrieved blocks are also universally higher for all algorithms on the popular pages. But while the number of blocks in the ground truth was only 32% higher, the numbers for the algorithms increased by (much) more than that: BlockFusion 164.1%, PageSegmenter 152.1%, VIPS 111.1%, WebTerrain 39.3%. It thus seems that the algorithms do not scale well with increasing complexity. This could also partly explain why our results are generally less favorable than what has been found in earlier publications, as they are up to 10 years old, and the Web has become much more complex since then. It also shows the need for new techniques that deal well with this increased complexity.

Exact vs. Fuzzy Match Metric. We found that the number of recognized blocks improved significantly when using the fuzzy match metric as opposed to the exact match metric, as was to be expected. We believe that the results from the fuzzy match metric are generally more valuable since the quality of blocks will still be sufficient for most applications. Furthermore it can easily be adjusted to find more or less precise matches by adjusting the matching ratio.

Original HTML vs. DOM HTML. Comparing the original and the DOM HTML we found that the results of the segmentation for the DOM HTML are virtually always better, which is true for all algorithms on both datasets. This is due to the fact that the DOM HTML is what the user ultimately sees in the browser, it is thus the final result of the rendering process. While in the past it might have been sufficient to analyze only the original HTML, this is not true any more. As the Web becomes more dynamic and the use of Javascript to manipulate the page becomes more prevalent, there is not necessarily a link between original and DOM HTML any more. This also implies that one cited advantage of text-based segmentation algorithms, namely that they do not require the DOM to be built and are thus very fast, is not true any longer, as even for these algorithms it is necessary to obtain the final HTML for optimal results.

The Four Segmentation Algorithms. The four algorithms differ widely in their performance, and none of them performed well enough to be universally applicable, as the highest average F-Score was 0.49 (WebTerrain). Our comments here pertain to the test runs using the fuzzy match metric and the DOM HTML because we consider those the most relevant. But the general conclusions hold for the other testing combinations as well.

BlockFusion. This algorithm showed the worst performance on both datasets. Both precision and recall are very low (< 0.1 and < 0.2 respectively). It also returns too many blocks on average (2.5x too many for the random dataset and 5.1x too many for the popular dataset). We could thus not repeat the results from [13]. We conclude that a solely text-based metric is not sufficient for a good segmentation, but that it can be used to augment other approaches.

PageSegmenter. This algorithm exhibits low precision and (relatively) high recall (< 0.2 and > 0.4 respectively). This is due to the fact that it retrieves by far the most blocks of all algorithms (5.3x too many for the random dataset and 10.1x too many for the popular dataset). The number of false positives is

Table 5. ANOVA summary

	Df	Sum Sq	Mean Sq	F value	p-value
algorithm	3	3.55	1.18	333.41	¡ 2e-16
html	1	0.35	0.35	98.24	¡ 2e-16
dataset	1	0.37	0.37	104.55	¡ 2e-16
metric	1	0.66	0.66	185.48	¡ 2e-16
algorithm:html	3	0.22	0.07	20.97	2.10e-13
algorithm:dataset	3	0.07	0.02	6.59	0.000198
algorithm:metric	3	0.12	0.04	11.66	1.38e-07
html:dataset	1	0.05	0.05	14.61	0.000136
html:metric	1	0.02	0.02	5.60	0.018055
dataset:metric	1	0.00	0.00	0.55	0.456698
Residuals	2298	8.15	0.00		

thus very high. It would thus be interesting to see if this algorithm could be optimized to return fewer blocks while retaining the good recall rates.

VIPS. This algorithm showed the biggest difference between the random and the popular dataset. Precision was high and recall mediocre for the random dataset (0.51 and 0.26 respectively), while both were low for the popular dataset (0.19 and 0.21 respectively). It is not clear why there is such a substantial difference. The number of retrieved results is slightly too low for the random dataset, while it is slightly too high for the popular dataset (25% too low and 21% too high respectively). In terms of the F-Score the VIPS algorithm was second-best.

WebTerrain. This algorithm showed relatively high precision and recall for both datasets (both > 0.4). It retrieved slightly too few blocks for both datasets (14% too few for the random dataset and 8% too few for the popular dataset). We thus find that a combination of structural and rendering-based approaches enhances overall results. Furthermore the terrain heuristic seems promising. Future work could therefore likely improve upon these results by using more sophisticated combinations of different approaches and heuristics.

Analysis of Variance. We performed an analysis of variance (ANOVA) to test the impact of the four factors `algorithm` (with levels: `blockfusion`, `pagesegmenter`, `VIPS`, `WebTerrain`), `html` (levels: `dom`, `html`), `dataset` (levels: `popular`, `random`) and `metric` (levels: `exact`, `fuzzy`) on the F-score; see Table 5.

To reduce the non-normality of the dependent variable, we performed a Box-Cox transformation of the F score. The transformation is defined as:

$$Y^{(\lambda)} = \begin{cases} \frac{Y^{\lambda}-1}{\lambda} & \text{for } \lambda \neq 0 \\ \ln Y & \text{for } \lambda = 0 \end{cases}$$

where we defined $Y = Fscore + 1$ because Y is required to be strictly positive. We selected the value of λ that yielded the highest log-likelihood value, using a simple grid search [9]. This resulted in $\lambda = -3.45$.

We can read from the column labeled *p-value* that for all terms except `dataset:metric` the null hypothesis of 'no effect' will be rejected at the conventional significance level of $\alpha = 0.05$. To avoid confusion we note that the Analysis of Variance was performed on the (transformed) F *scores* obtained for different combinations of factor levels, which is an entirely different quantity then the F *statistic* (reported in the column *F value* in Table 5) which is used to test the significance of different (combinations of) factors in explaining the variation in observed F *scores*.

We see in Table 5 that the four factors `algorithm, html, dataset` and `metric` are all highly significant (p-value < 2e-16) in explaining observed variation in F-scores. The analysis thus confirms our intuition that these factors are relevant for an analysis of web page segmentation algorithms.

We also included *interaction terms* in the analysis (all the colon-separated variables, such as `algorithm:html`). An interaction term is the product of two variables that can in itself be a significant predictor of the outcome. A high significance for an interaction term $x : y$ means that x and y interact, i.e. the effect of x on the outcome (i.e., the F-score) is different for different values of y.

In Table 5 we see that all interaction terms are significant at $\alpha = 0.05$, except for the term dataset:metric. The term dataset:metric not being significant means that the influence of metric on the F-score is typically similar for both popular and randomly selected pages. This is consistent with the results reported in Section 4, where we found that the fuzzy metric always returns a higher F-score than the exact metric, for both randomly selected and popular web pages.

Threats to Validity. As in any empirical study there are various threats to validity. Unless noted otherwise, all discussed threats are to external validity.

A threat to construct validity concerns the implementations and our interpretations of the algorithms. Because we had to make these interpretations, and we did not obtain answers to our e-mails about these interpretations from the authors, we run the risk that we are not exactly measuring their algorithm, but a variation thereof. Detailed discussions of these issues can be found in [15].

In our study, we compare approaches to web page segmentation by looking at a particular instance of each approach. In our selection we have chosen well-known, often-cited representatives of each approach. To compensate, we have made our framework and datasets open for everyone to use, so that others can easily extend upon our work, by implementing other instances of the paradigms testing these against the ones that we have implemented.

When it comes to the experimental data, we used two datasets: one with popular web pages, mainly because doing well on pages that are often read by people is something an algorithm should be rewarded for, but also to serve as a "worst-case" since we expected these websites to be more complex than the average website. Since we also did not want to bias too much towards such pages, we also included a large sample of random pages, with the aim of increasing external validity. However, we did have to drop 48 out of 200 web pages, because when rendered locally they differed from the original web page. This means that our results may not generalize to websites that modify the DOM extensively. using Javascript.

The mark up was performed according to a particular ontology (Section 3), which may hurt external validity. We do believe our ontology to be generic enough to be applicable to most existing websites. A second issue at this point is construct validity: did the participants who marked up the websites for us understand the ontology, and what was expected of them? To make sure that that was the case, the first author first explained the ontology to them, and checked five segmentation results for each participant to see whether they had understood him well enough. It was also verified for a few sample pages that the volunteers agreed on the web page segmentation for those pages. We note that our test subjects all have an IT background, which may decrease external validity.

An issue in our study is that one of the algorithms we consider has been of our own devising. We note, however, that having confirmed that our implementation was correct, i.e., it behaved as we designed it to do on a few web pages, we did not make any modifications to it during or after we ran our experiments. This to avoid the danger of overfitting our algorithm to the chosen datasets.

6 Related Work

A comprehensive discussion of related work can be found in [15]. Here, we restrict ourselves to a selection that is most closely related to our work here.

The research on structuring information on web pages into semantic units goes back to at least [11]. Subsequent authors tried to automate the process of locating where the information of interest resided. The process can be broken into two distinct steps: segmentation (what belongs together in blocks) and labeling (what is the best description for the block, in terms of some chosen ontology).

In [14], the approach is based on heuristics that take visual information into account. They built their own basic browser engine to accomplish this, but do not take style sheets into account, and they avoid calculating rendering information for every node in the HTML tree. They then define a number of heuristics on the rendered tree assuming that the areas of interest on a page are header, footer, left menu, right menu and center of the page, and where they should be located, e.g. header on top. The authors test their algorithm experimentally for a dataset for which they manually label areas on 515 different pages. Their overall accuracy in recognizing targeted areas is 73%.

In [7], the authors turn the DOM tree into a complete graph, where every DOM node is a vertex in the graph. Each edge is then assigned a weight that denotes the cost of putting these two vertices into the same segment. The weights are learned from a dataset regarded as the ground truth by looking at predefined visual- and context-based features. Finally they group the nodes into segments by using either a correlation clustering algorithm, or an algorithm based on energy-minimizing cuts; the latter performs considerably better. Their evaluation is based on manually labeled data (1088 segments on 105 different web pages).

Baluja [2] focuses on the application of optimizing existing web pages for mobile phones by, first, dividing the web page into a 3x3-grid. The user can then interactively arrange for the website to be optimized for mobile phone screen. The page segmentation algorithm is based on clues from the DOM combined with a number of computer vision algorithms. Specifically, they use an entropy measurement to construct a decision tree that determines how to segment the page. They test their approach on a number of popular websites where they achieve good results in most cases (they rarely cut through coherent texts). One artificial limitation of their approach is that it divides the page into at most 9 segments, but it seems possible to adapt it to other grid sizes.

In [1], the authors improve upon the VIPS algorithm, by improving the first phase of visual block extraction. They divide HTML tags (including the ones introduced by HTML 5) not into three classes but into nine instead, and define new separation rules for these classes based on visual cues and tag properties of the nodes. No empirical evaluation of their algorithm is provided.

We found only one paper that, like us, is focused on comparing existing approaches to web page segmentation and labeling: [18]. The classification of about 80 papers is largely qualitative including bottom-up vs. top-down, DOM-based vs. visual, how the evaluation of the approaches is measured (precision and recall, success rate, or execution time), and whether specific heuristics are employed based on assumptions about the layout of web pages.

7 Conclusion and Future Work

We have compared the performance of four algorithms for web page segmentation. Our work shows that the three older algorithms BlockFusion, PageSegmenter and VIPS, performed worse than they did in their original publications, something which we believe is due to increasing complexity of websites and their ever more dynamic behavior due to the growing prevalence of DOM manipulations via Javascript. This belief is affirmed by our finding that the algorithms do better on randomly selected websites than on the more complicated popular ones. It does seem that combining two approaches to segmentation is a promising direction for further research, as shown by the consistently highest F-scores of the WebTerrain algorithm, although more research is needed to make (automatic) web page segmentation pratical. Promising-looking directions are more sophisticated combinations of different approaches and more directed segmentation algorithms that e.g. only focus on certain segments on a page or that target only specific domains of websites.

References

1. Akpinar, E., Yesilada, Y.: Vision based page segmentation: extended and improved algorithm. Technical report, Middle East Technical University Northern Cyprus Campus, January 2012

2. Baluja, S.: Browsing on small screens: recasting web-page segmentation into an efficient machine learning framework. In: Proceedings of the 15th International Conference on World Wide Web (WWW 2012), pp. 33–42. ACM Press (2006)
3. Boldi, P., Rosa, M., Santini, M., Vigna, S.: Layered label propagation: a multiresolution coordinate-free ordering for compressing social networks. In: Proceedings of the 20th International Conference on World Wide Web (WWW 2011). ACM Press (2011)
4. Boldi, P., Vigna, S.: The WebGraph framework I: compression techniques. In: Proceedings of the Thirteenth International World Wide Web Conference (WWW 2004), pp. 595–601. ACM Press, Manhattan (2004)
5. Cai, D., Yu, S., Wen, J.-R., Ma, W.-Y.: Extracting content structure for web pages based on visual representation. In: Zhou, X., Zhang, Y., Orlowska, M.E. (eds.) APWeb 2003. LNCS, vol. 2642, pp. 406–417. Springer, Heidelberg (2003)
6. Cai, D., Yu, S., Wen, J.R., Ma, W.Y.: VIPS: a visionbased page segmentation algorithm. Technical report, Microsoft Technical Report, MSR-TR-2003-79 (2003)
7. Chakrabarti, D., Kumar, R., Punera, K.: A graph-theoretic approach to webpage segmentation. In: Proceedings of the 17th International Conference on World Wide Web (WWW 2008), pp. 377–386. ACM Press (2008)
8. Crawled by the Laboratory of Web Algorithmics, University of Milan, http://law.di.unimi.it/. Yahoo! research: "Web spam collections". http://law.di.unimi.it/webdata/uk-2007-05/
9. Fox, J.: Applied Regression Analysis and Generalized Linear Models. Sage, 2nd edition (2008)
10. Guha, R., McCool, R.: TAP: a semantic web test-bed. Web Semantics: Science, Services and Agents on the World Wide Web **1**(1), 81–87 (2003)
11. Hammer, J., Garcia-Molina, H., Cho, J., Aranha, R., Crespo, A.: Extracting semistructured information from the web. In: Proceedings of the Workshop on Management of Semistructured Data, pp. 18–25 (1997)
12. Kohlschütter, C., Fankhauser, P., Nejdl, W.: Boilerplate detection using shallow text features. In: Proceedings of the Third ACM International Conference on Web Search and Data Mining, WSDM 2010, pp. 441–450. ACM, New York (2010)
13. Kohlschütter, C., Nejdl, W.: A densitometric approach to web page segmentation. In: Proceedings of the 17th ACM Conference on Information and Knowledge Management, pp. 1173–1182 (2008)
14. Kovacevic, M., Diligenti, M., Gori, M., Milutinovic, V.: Recognition of common areas in a web page using visual information: a possible application in a page classification. In: IEEE International Conference on Data Mining (ICDM 2002), pp. 250–257 (2002)
15. Kreuzer, R.: A quantitative comparison of semantic web page segmentation algorithms (MSc thesis) (2013). http://www.cs.uu.nl/wiki/Hage/SupervisedMScTheses
16. Vadrevu, S., Gelgi, F., Davulcu, H.: Semantic partitioning of web pages. In: Ngu, A.H.H., Kitsuregawa, M., Neuhold, E.J., Chung, J.-Y., Sheng, Q.Z. (eds.) WISE 2005. LNCS, vol. 3806, pp. 107–118. Springer, Heidelberg (2005)
17. Vadrevu, S., Velipasaoglu, E.: Identifying primary content from web pages and its application to web search ranking. In: Proceedings of the 20th International Conference on World Wide Web (WWW 2011), Hyderabad, India (Companion Volume), pp. 135–136. ACM Press (2011)
18. Yesilada, Y.: Web page segmentation: A review. Technical report, Middle East Technical University Northern Cyprus Campus, March 2011

A Semantic Framework for Sequential Decision Making

Patrick Philipp[1(✉)], Maria Maleshkova[1], Achim Rettinger[1], and Darko Katic[2]

[1] Institute AIFB, Karlsruhe Insitute of Technology, Karlsruhe, Germany
{patrick.philipp,maria.maleshkova,achim.rettinger}@kit.edu
[2] HIS, Karlsruhe Institute of Technology, Karlsruhe, Germany
darko.katic@kit.edu

Abstract. Current developments in the medical domain, not unlike many other sectors, are marked by the growing digitalisation of data, including patient records, study results, clinical guidelines or imagery. This trend creates the opportunity for the development of innovative decision support systems to assist physicians in making a diagnosis or preparing a treatment plan. To this end, complex tasks need to be solved, requiring one or more interpretation algorithms (e.g. image processors or classifiers) to be chosen and executed based on heterogeneous data. We, therefore, propose a semantic framework for sequential decision making and develop the foundations of a Linked agent who executes interpretation algorithms available as Linked APIs [9] on a data-driven, declarative basis [10] by integrating structured knowledge formalized in RDF and OWL, and having access to meta components for optimization. We evaluate our framework based on image processing of brain images and ad-hoc selection of surgical phase recognition algorithms.

Keywords: Sequential decision making · Linked APIs · Meta learning · Planning

1 Introduction

Inspired by the medical domain, we are interested in sequential decision making under uncertainty for complex tasks of arbitrary complexity. Consider a scenario in image processing which comprises several subtasks. An image, first, has to be filtered for distorting elements and normalized in terms of color. The image, then, has to be aligned with other images in the knowledge base to ease interpretation. Depending on the request of an enduser, one eventually has to segment the image and annotate it by using machine learning approaches. We are given access to a large set of interpretation algorithms eligible for each of these and other subtasks (e.g normalization, registration or segmentation). There is no trivial way to automate this process for a variety of user requests and scenarios. With no domain expert around, we might already fail to execute an interpretation algorithm with the correct data or to decide if the resulting segmentation is good or not. To make it even more complex, we might also be faced with multiple

P. Cimiano et al. (Eds.): ICWE 2015, LNCS 9114, pp. 392–409, 2015.
DOI: 10.1007/978-3-319-19890-3_25

eligible interpretation algorithms for a single subtask and need to decide which one to choose.

We summarize such an environment as highly heterogeneous in terms of tasks, interpretation algorithms and data. Endusers of such complex tasks often are no domain experts or only experts in a small subset of available interpretation algorithms. In addition, with a growing number of possibilities, it becomes intractable for domain experts to manually optimize complex tasks. Enabling automatic execution of complex tasks by sequential decision making, hence, is an important subject. The longterm goal is to develop a system (or agent) which knows how to optimally choose sequences of available interpretation algorithms for a given complex task as illustrated in fig. 1.

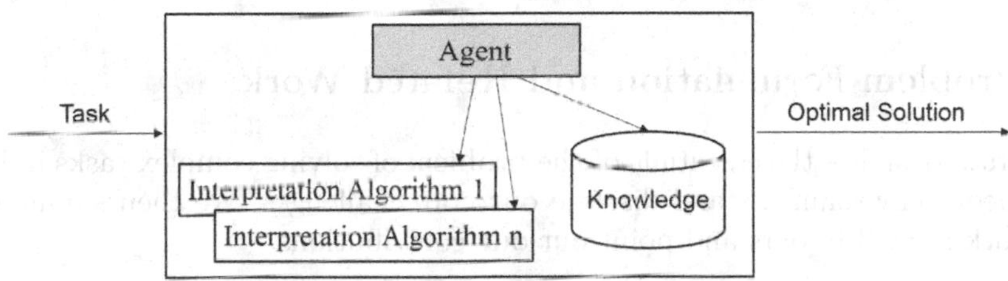

Fig. 1. An agent able to find optimal solutions for tasks

We build on prior work in the Semantic Web which centers around semantically enriched web services (so-called Linked APIs) [9], [2] and their data-driven, declarative execution (with Linked Data-Fu [10]). Equipped with these powerful technologies, we now concentrate on building a framework to enable decision making under uncertainty. Based on access to interpretation algorithms for a complex task, one can develop *meta components* and easily plug them into the current workflow. These meta *components* can comprise any strategy to choose interpretation algorithms for a task.

Although these strategies do not have to be sophisticated, we especially focus on enabling adequately complex methodologies to be flexibly and easily used. We argue that such complex approaches are necessary, if a vast amount of different kinds of information is available. Besides training samples, this might comprise manually modelled domain expert knowledge, statistical knowledge from studies or enduser feedback given in arbitrary situations. We will introduce two such *meta components* which make use of available structured knowledge to choose among interpretation algorithms.

Our contributions are threefold; we

(i) disclose different meta strategies for sequential decision making in heterogeneous domains and provide first results on their interplay with Linked Data,

(ii) enable flexible integration and testing of meta strategies within the semantic framework and
(iii) describe two meta components for (sequential-) decision making and their applications to medical scenarios.

The remainder of this paper is structured as follows. We formalize the problem in section 2 and show where our work has commonalities and differences to other approaches. The single components of our framework are, subsequently, being introduced in section 3. Section 4, then, integrates the components and shows how we solve complex tasks. In section 5, we show how our framework works in practise based on two medical scenarios and thereby dwell on a *meta learning* and an *abstract planning* component. We discuss current developments and possible improvements in section 6 and conclude the paper in section 7.

2 Problem Formulation and Related Work

We, first, formalize the essentials of the problem of solving complex tasks in heterogeneous environments and disclose our core challenges. We then summarize the work related to ours and point out our contributions.

2.1 Problem: Solving Complex Tasks with Access to Heterogeneous Interpretation Algorithms

Let X be the set of all tasks, Y the set of all abstract tasks and A the set of all available interpretation algorithms. Let further S be the set of *abstract states* defined by a subset of objects O, literals L and relations R. We denote, for simplicity, F_{s_k} as the set of features of a state s_k (i.e. a subset of $O \times R \times O$ and $O \times R \times L$). A grounded state $g(s_k)$ depicts an instance of s_k in nature. The set A_{s_k} defines the subset of applicable interpretation algorithms in s_k which is known to some degree. We, thus, assume that an interpretation algorithm $a_i \in A$ can be defined by a subset of features of F in a similar way as states $s_k \in S$. Knowing A_{s_k} depends on how we define features $f \in F$ for s_k and a_i. Let $T(s, a, s')$ be the transition function for some state s and interpretation algorithm a ending in s'. Our knowledge of $T(s, a, s')$, again, depends on the available features for s, a and s'. $T(g(s), a, g(s'))$ is not known and requires further knowledge to be approximated. A task $x(g(s_1), s_K)$ is a function defined on a grounded start state $g(s_1)$ and an abstract goal state s_K. Reaching an unknown grounded goal state $g(s_K)$ takes 1 to n state transitions $(g(s), a, g(s'))$. To solve $x(g(s_1), s_K)$, we need to find a sequence of interpretation algorithms a_i ending in the unknown grounded goal state $g(s_K)$ with high probability. An abstract task $y(g(s_1), s_K)$ is defined similarly but we need to find any sequence $a_1, \ldots, a_n$ to get from $g(s_1)$ to s_K. Our setting is much related to a Markov Decision Process (MDP) (S, A, T, R, γ) with R, in addition, being the reward function for state, interpretation algorithm pairs (s, a) and γ the discount factor. The latter regulates the influence of future interpretation algorithms a_i taken in future steps s_k on the value estimations of current states and actions. Defining $R(s,a)$ for $x(g(s_1), s_K)$ is not straightforward as $g(s_K)$ is unknown. An absorbing state with $R(s_k, a_i) = 0$ can be artificially modelled to denote the goal s_K.

We define **abstract planning** as trying to solve an *abstract task* $y(g(s_1), s_K)$. Here, we ignore that multiple interpretation algorithms a_i might be available for s_k. **Meta learning** considers $|A_{g(s_k)}| > 1$ and tries to solve a subtask $x_{A_{g(s_k)}}(g(s_k), s_K))$ to find optimal the a_i (or combination of multiple a_i) for $g(s_k)$. **Planning** deals with solving $x(g(s_1), s_K)$ with known T and R, and **planning-related learning** considers T, R unknown and tries to approximate them (as, for instance, is done in model-based reinforcement learning).

We will only deal with abstract planning and meta learning in this work, as they do suffice for our practical applications (see section 5), but stress that the planning task and the planning-related learning task are highly interesting and important. Based on the problem setting, we derived the following needs for our semantic sequential decision making framework:

Need for a Controlled & Semantic Vocabulary. If we want to have tasks automatically executed based on state-goal pairs; tasks, data and algorithms need to be using a common vocabulary.

Need for Accessibility & Scalability. The pool of algorithms needs to be accessible in real-time and available for many concurrent tasks. New interpretation algorithms should be readily available to be used and evaluated.

Need for Data-driven & Declarative Execution. With a large number of available interpretation algorithms for a state s_k, it will quickly become intractable to manually define and evaluate all possible permutations. By executing interpretation algorithms when they match s_k, we gain flexibility and can delegate the optimization problem. With growing experience, one could generalize the learnt optimal decisions to similar s_k.

Need for Meta Learning Components. As the optimization problem is neither trivial nor homogeneous, it might not be solvable by a single piece of software. One rather needs several meta components which are experts for different s_k.

2.2 Existing Frameworks

There is an ongoing research interest in so-called 'workflow systems' that enable describing and executing algorithms of different kinds. The work centered around semantic workflows [3] aims to enable the automatic composition of components in large-scale distributed environments. Generic semantic descriptions support combining algorithms and enable formalizing ensembles of learners. Therefore, conditions and constraints need to be specified. The framework also automatically matches components and data sources based on user requests.

Wood et al. [12] create abstract workflows as domain models which are formalized using the Web Ontology Language (OWL) and enable dynamic instantiation of real processes. These models can then be automatically converted into more specific workflows resulting in OWL individuals. The components can be reused in another context or process, and one can share abstract representations across the Web through OWL classes.

Automatic orchestration of analytical workflows is studied in [1]. The system essentially uses a planner, a leaner and a large (structured-) knowledge base to solve complex tasks. A large amount of potential workflows are taken into account to answer a user specified query with the optimal choice. The decision process comprises complex learning and planning approaches, and entails exploring large possible feature spaces. Lastly, atomic actions are lifted with semantic annotations to better adapt to user queries.

In contrast to previous approaches, our framework benefits from a combination of RDF and OWL, minimizing the efforts required for describing the algorithms and the used data. We use a data-driven approach to execute workflows and work towards completely automatic, declarative and optimal compositions of such. Our novel contribution essentially enables to develop powerful *Linked agents* capable of solving complex tasks in heterogeneous environments. Besides, only a small fraction of the above approaches employ a structured knowledge base. We are able to store structured performance-related information and try to reuse this evidence in order to optimize results. In addition, with the *Linked agent*, we can flexibly integrate new kinds of structured knowledge as well as so-called *meta components* to optimize decision making under uncertainty.

3 Components for Learning Optimal Web Service Pipelines

Our system infrastructure comprises four core component types:

1. Linked Interpretation Algorithms
2. A Structured Knowledge Base
3. Linked Meta Components
4. A Data-Driven Execution Engine (the Linked Agent)

Fig. 2 illustrates the framework components. We will now explain their respective functionality and put things together in section 4.

3.1 Structured Knowledge Base

A structured knowledge base stores both metadata and data, and provides a common and controlled vocabulary. Our framework uses the Resource Description framework (RDF) and the Web Ontology Language (OWL) for annotating raw data and modelling ontologies. As the Linked Data principles suggest, persistent URIs to resources have to be available and provide sufficient information

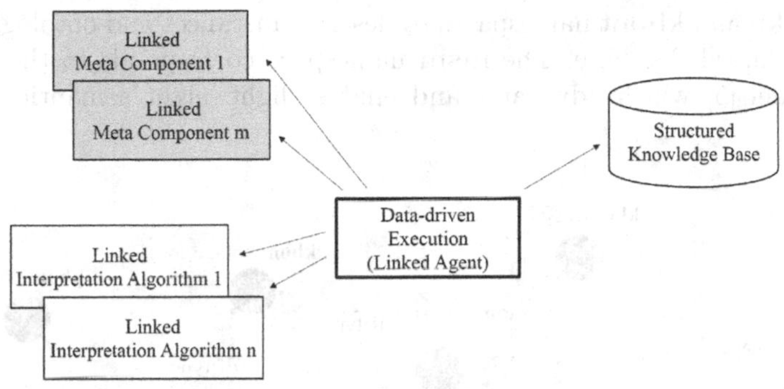

Fig. 2. Schematic Overview of the Framework

for lookups. Appropriate concepts for interpretation algorithms and data were modelled to enable the integration of new components. Fig. 5 depicts the components of the structured knowledge base used in our medical scenarios.

3.2 Linked Interpretation Algorithms

We deploy interpretation algorithms as web services to make them easily accessible in our infrastructure. We follow the idea of Linked Data web services (i.e. Linked APIs [9]) and applied them to medical interpretation algorithms in [2]. A *Linked interpretation algorithm* (an interpretation algorithm lifted to a Linked API) provides a standardized description of its functionality by reusing elements of the structured knowledge base. The description also defines how to communicate with the Linked interpretation algorithm and how to execute its methods. A minimal set of information of the description is summarized in table 1.

Table 1. Minimal description for Linked interpretation algorithms

Non-functional requirements	Functional requirements
Domain Experts	*Inputs*
Service Endpoint	*Preconditions*
Example request & response	*Outputs*
Algorithm class	*Postconditions*

An intuitive example of an arbitrary image processor is given in fig. 3. An image, defined in a data type ontology, is part of a pre- and postcondition of a Linked interpretation algorithm. Pre- and postconditions define strict rules about the states before- and after executing the Linked interpretation algorithm. The degree of detail of both pre- and postcondition is strongly dependent on the wrapping process of the respective interpretation algorithm. If semantics and interpretation algorithm are strongly intertwined, fine-grained semantics with rich information are available.

We use **kb** and **kbont** namespaces to describe instances and ontologies available in the knowledge base. The **msm** namespace corresponds to the minimal service model [5] which advocates and enables lightweight semantics for web services.

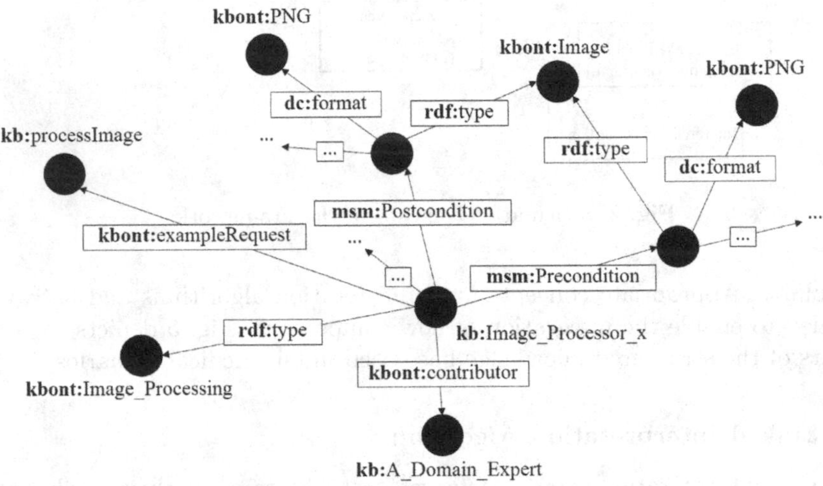

Fig. 3. An exemplary Linked image processor (namespaces omitted)

3.3 Linked Meta Components

There might be numerous approaches to choose, on a meta level, among Linked interpretation algorithms given $g(s_k)$. Such strategies generate policies which can be naive, sophisticated, biased on subjective criteria or otherwise. We enable flexible using, testing and exchanging of potentially powerful meta approaches in terms of so-called *Linked meta components*. Linked meta components are essentially Linked APIs and implement any decision making strategy of arbitrary complexity. To have access to all available interpretation algorithms, we assume a structured knowledge base linking to them.

A Linked meta component specifies the amount of information it needs by its precondition and is only called *iff* the agent can provide for all information. Besides a list of all available interpretation algorithms, a learner might, for instance, want to access a performance table which stores a history of validated results. We will discuss two cases of meta components, namely *abstract planning* and *meta learning*, in section 4 and show their practical application in section 5.

3.4 Data-Driven Execution (Linked Agent)

We integrate the prior components by using Linked Data-Fu [10]. The Linked Data-Fu rule-based execution engine describes and implements a formalism to virtually integrate data from different sources in real-time and have Linked APIs executed based on rules. In our framework, Linked Data-Fu searches eligible Linked meta components and Linked interpretation algorithms for (newly arrived) annotated data, and uses the structured knowledge base to execute them. Each Linked interpretation algorithm is represented as single rule which we automatically generate based on its description. Fig. 4 summarizes this process. When a state $g(s_k)$ fulfils the preconditions of a Linked interpretation algorithm, a HTTP POST request with grounded preconditions is issued to its service URI.

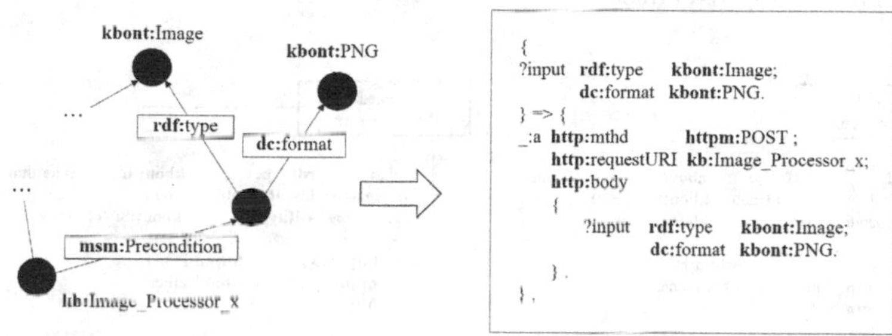

Fig. 4. A Linked Data-Fu rule for the Linked image converter

The automatic matching between Linked interpretation algorithms and structured data is highly advantageous. If interpretation algorithms have to be trained by samples, the agent can directly feed all annotated training data to the Linked interpretation algorithm. This is generally possible by merely defining rules for Linked Data-Fu. Even more important, with growing number of diverse Linked interpretation algorithms, we can automatically solve new complex tasks without additional manual effort.

We will refer to the Linked Data-Fu engine instantiated in our framework as *Linked agent.* The title is justified when combining the engine with appropriate Linked meta components, Linked interpretation algorithms and a structured knowledge base.

4 Solving Complex Tasks with Meta Learning and Abstract Planning

We will now explain the required interplay between the four components to enable sequential decision making for complex (abstract-) tasks $y(g(s_1), s_K)$ and $x(g(s_1), s_K)$. We, first, address the Linked abstract planning case where an abstract task $y(g(s_1), s_K)$ has to be solved by finding appropriate Linked interpretation algorithms a_i . Here, we do not try to distinguish between high- and low quality results (as this involves checking the instances), and trust the descriptions of Linked interpretation algorithms. Each Linked interpretation algorithm applicable in $g(s_k)$ *and* needed for reaching s_K will be chosen. The second case deals with Linked meta learning and builds on Linked interpretation algorithms selected by Linked abstract planning. An 'optimal' Linked interpretation algorithm is returned for $g(s_k)$ if $|A_{g(s_k)}| > 1$.

In fig. 5, we give a generic overview of interactions between the Linked agent and Linked meta components, Linked interpretation algorithms and the structured knowledge base. The Linked agent first queries the knowledge base to get all available Linked interpretation algorithms and then calls a Linked abstract planner. Based on the resulting set of candidate Linked interpretation algorithms for reaching goal s_K, it executes a Linked meta learner capable of dealing with the Linked interpretation algorithms. Finally, all 'optimal' Linked interpretation algorithms are being executed.

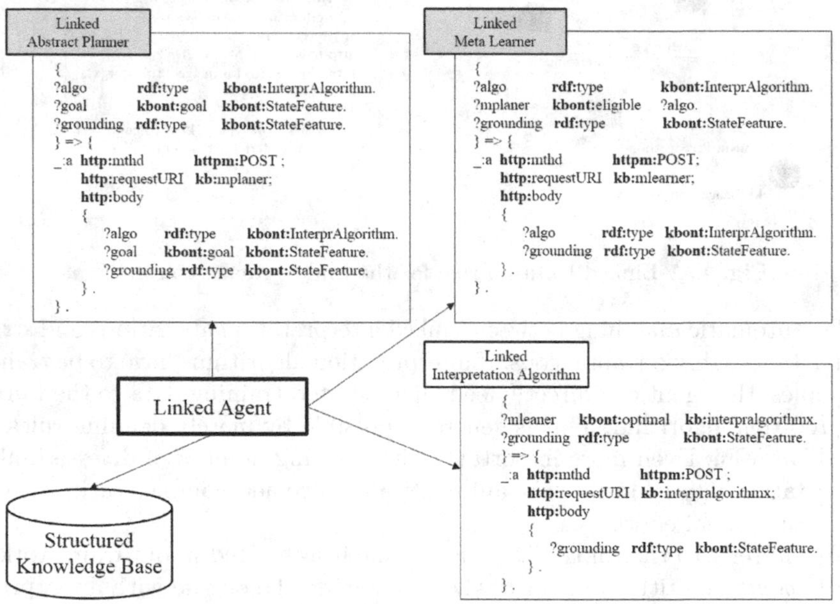

Fig. 5. Interactions within the framework to integrate Linked meta components

4.1 Linked Abstract Planning

Depending on a new task $y(g(s_1), s_K)$, the Linked agent evaluates the grounded state $g(s_k)$ in terms of rule checking. The Linked agent, therefore, keeps a set of automatically generated rules for each Linked interpretation algorithm. We cannot assume, however, that $g(s_k)$ only triggers interpretation algorithms which help reaching the goal s_K, as there might be a large amount of Linked interpretation algorithms. We, thus, need a Linked abstract planner to only return candidate Linked interpretation algorithms for reaching s_K.

A Linked abstract planner has to first query the structured knowledge base for all available Linked interpretation algorithms. It, then, decides which Linked interpretation algorithms are applicable to reach s_K based on an arbitrary mechanism and finally outputs a subset of A. Fig. 5 illustrates the agent rule to call the Linked abstract planner depending on its precondition. We describe one implementation of a Linked abstract planner in section 5.2.

4.2 Linked Meta Learning

In the meta learning setting, we want to find an optimal Linked interpretation algorithm a_i solving a subtask $x_{A_{g(s_k)}}(g(s_k), s_K))$. We assume to know candidates $A_{g(s_k)}$ of Linked interpretation algorithms to reach s_K (e.g. due to a Linked abstract planner), but are still faced with uncertainty about their performances given $g(s_k)$. Solving the learning setting can be approached with simple heuristics, but might require complex machine learning approaches to give good estimates. With our framework, we enable using any meta learning approach by wrapping it as Linked meta learner.

We reuse the Linked abstract planner and integrate a Linked meta learning component by creating a rule for the Linked agent. Fig. 5 describes the generic rule and section 5.3 introduces a Linked meta learner for one of our medical scenarios. The Linked meta learner outputs one Linked interpretation algorithm a_i for $A_{g(s_k)} > 1$ if the preconditions of Linked meta learner and a_i match. Otherwise, no decision is made on A_{s_k} and all candidates will be executed by the Linked agent. Note that multiple outputs of Linked interpretation algorithm could be combined (e.g. by a weighted majority voting) if a Linked meta learner was used after all eligible Linked interpretation algorithms have been executed, slightly changing the interactions found in fig. 5. The linked meta learner would, additionally, expect results of the Linked interpretation algorithms to compute their weights.

5 Medical Scenarios with Meta Components and Evaluations

We now introduce two scenarios set in the medical domain and illustrate possible Linked meta components. The first scenario deals with image processing. We developed a Linked abstract planner to derive eligible Linked interpretation algorithms for the so-called brain tumour progression mapping (TPM). In the second scenario, we optimized the choice among two Linked interpretation algorithms for phase recognition in minimal invasive surgeries with a Linked meta learner. Both scenarios use a common instantiation of our framework. We will start by explaining the shared components and subsequently focus on the individual scenarios.

5.1 A Semantic Framework for Medical Sequential Decision Making

The medical framework with its interpretation algorithms and data is being developed within the Cognition-Guided Surgery project [1]. Every interpretation

[1] http://www.cognitionguidedsurgery.de/

algorithm considered in the scenarios was wrapped as Linked interpretation algorithm. We modelled the descriptions with domain experts and developers of the interpretation algorithms, and integrated them in a central instance of a Semantic MediaWiki (SMW). We use an instance of XNAT [2] to store patient-relevant data and provide a RDF wrapper which lifts XNAT with semantic concepts. The knowledge base can be considered as union between the SMW and its links to other resources, such as XNAT.

Linked interpretation algorithms can automatically be executed with the Linked agent. We implemented a conversion mechanism from Linked interpretation algorithm descriptions to Linked agent rules (see fig. 4), and, thus, reduced the manual work for integrating new Linked interpretation algorithms. The Linked agent crawls the hierarchy imposed by XNAT according to simple rules and executes every Linked interpretation algorithm per patient if it is eligible. While this only covers offline scenarios, we can easily extend the setting to the online case. The complete framework with two Linked meta components is illustrated in fig. 6.

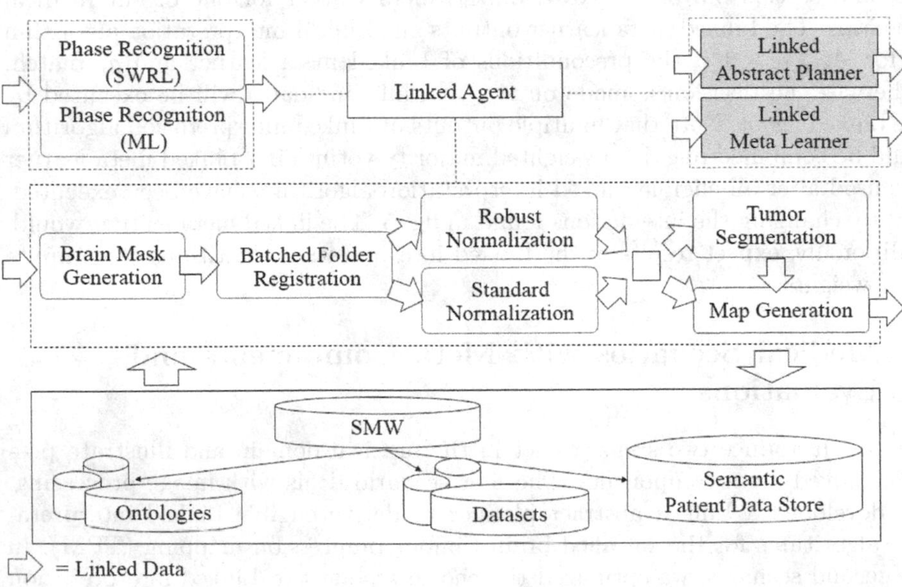

Fig. 6. The Semantic Framework for Medical Sequential Decision Making (extended based on [7])

5.2 Tumour Progression Mapping in the Semantic Framework

Tumour Progression Mapping (TPM) is an approach to visualize brain tumours in their progression over time. One, thereby, focusses on supporting radiologists

[2] http://www.xnat.org/

in their daily work. Radiologists, otherwise, would have to assess the irregular growth of brain tumours based on raw headscans which causes a lot of extra effort. When generating a TPM, different types of images are used and produced, and adequate interpretation algorithms need to be executed in correct order and with correct subsets of images.

The TPM generation process is illustrated in the framework overview (fig. 5). The images are stored in our knowledge base and converted into a common format. A mask for the brain region is created by the next interpretation algorithm, ensuring that subsequent tasks are not influenced by bones or other structures. A registration algorithm, then, spatially registers all brain images of a patient. The following normalization task adapts the intensities of MRI scans and generates similar values for similar tissue types. If additional annotations for a patient are available, the normalization becomes more robust by making use of a different normalization interpretation algorithm. The TPM can now be created by invoking the appropriate interpretation algorithm. An optional additional interpretation algorithm can automatically segment tumours and integrate the results into the map.

We studied how to wrap interpretation algorithms used in the TPM setting in [2] and initially applied Linked Data-Fu in [8], [7]. We now integrate these ideas into the semantic framework and introduce a Linked meta planner.

A Linked Abstract Planner for TPM. We developed Linked interpretation algorithms for every step in the TPM generation process. Listing 1.1 contains the preconditions of the brain stripping algorithm ('Brain Mask Generation') with headscan and initialization images as inputs.

```
?inputImage       rdf:type     kbont:Headscan;
                  dc:format    "image/nrrd".

?brainImage       rdf:type     kbont:BrainAtlasImage;
                  dc:format    "image/mha".

?brainAtlasMask   rdf:type     kbont:BrainAtlasMask;
                  dc:format    "image/mha".
```

Listing 1.1. Preconditions of the Linked brain mask generation algorithm

We created a finite MDP by using the pre- and postconditions of Linked interpretation algorithms to define abstract states s_k with local scopes, i.e. we only consider preconditions of s_k. The transition probabilities T are defined in equation 1 and make up an $S \times (A+1) \times S$ matrix by adding a dummy interpretation algorithm pointing to the goal state, when the latter was reached. The reward function R is a $S \times (A+1)$ matrix (see equation 2). By using any strategy to solve the MDP (e.g value iteration), we find eligible Linked interpretation algorithms to solve the task.

$$T(s,a,s') = \begin{cases} t_{sas'} = \frac{1}{|A_{s_k}|} & \exists(s,a,s') \text{ with respect to } F_s \text{ and } F_{s'} \\ t_{sas'} = 0 & \text{otherwise} \end{cases} \quad (1)$$

$$R(s,a) = \begin{cases} r_{sa} = 1 & \text{if } a \text{ equals dummy algorithm and } s \text{ equals goal} \\ r_{sa} = 0 & \text{otherwise} \end{cases} \quad (2)$$

The resulting Linked abstract planner takes as input Linked interpretation algorithms, patient information of type **kbont:**ImageFeature (i.e. $g(s_k)$), and goal state **kbont:**TumorProgressionMapping (i.e. s_K), and returns a set of eligible Linked interpretation algorithms. The abstract Linked Data-Fu rule for the Linked abstract planner is depicted in listing 1.2. The Preconditions for the brain mask generation algorithm (see listing 1.1) could, then, replace the abstract image features.

```
{
?algo          rdf:type        kbont:InterprAlgorithm.
?goal          kbont:goal      kbont:TumorProgressionMapping.
?grounding     rdf:type        kbont:ImageFeature.
} => {
_:a    http:mthd          httpm:POST ;
       http:requestURI    kb:mplanermdp;
       http:body
    {
        ?algo          rdf:type        kbont:InterprAlgorithm.
        ?goal          kbont:goal      kbont:TumorProgressionMapping.
        ?grounding     rdf:type        kbont:ImageFeature.
    } .
} .
```

Listing 1.2. Linked Data-Fu rule for executing the Linked abstract planner

Evaluation. A part of the evaluation of the Linked TPM scenario was conducted in [7] and [2]. The TPM generation process was shown to work based on the descriptions of the single Linked image processing algorithms and an initial implementation of Linked Data-Fu without a Linked meta planner. We showed that no substantial overhead is produced while executing the interpretation algorithms on the web and that the correct pipeline is built automatically.

Our Linked abstract planner, now, creates a finite MDP and automatically constructs T and R based on the available Linked interpretation algorithms A, the goal s_K and the current grounding $g(s_k)$. Consider a grounding $g(s_k)$ for the brain stripping algorithm (listing 1.1) and the goal **kbont:**TumorProgressionMapping with all paths to the TPM being possible. Besides the 6 Linked interpretation algorithms involved in the TPM process, the algorithm pool consists of 2 Linked phase recognizers of the subsequent scenario. We use a discount factor of 0.9, perform value iteration and derive $V =< 0.32805.0.3645, 0.405.0.405, 0.45, 0.45, 1.00, 0, 0 >$ after 6 iterations. States with values greater than zero depict preconditions of Linked interpretation algorithms which have to be executed to reach the goal (except for the absorbing goal state s_K).

5.3 Surgical Phase Recognition in the Semantic Framework

Surgical phase recognition is one step towards reducing the information overload for surgeons during surgery. Depending on the current phase, one could display an adequate subset of information, which benefits the surgeons in his or her decision making. To recognize the phase, one might leverage a variety of sensor outputs. In this scenario, only activity triples consisting of the currently used instrument, the performed action and the corresponding anatomical structure are used to determine the current phase (e.g. <Scalpel, cut, Gallbladder >).

The interpretation algorithms we considered for our learning scenario consisted of a rule-based interpretation algorithm using the Semantic Web Rule Language (SWRL) introduced in [4] and a machine learning (ML)-based phase recognition algorithm which takes in training samples (i.e. annotated surgeries). Both algorithms have varying degrees of performance and make mistakes in their predictions, as shown in table 2. If one could learn in which situations the respective interpretation algorithms excel, it would be highly beneficial. Our first approach to empirically learn the optimal phase recognition algorithm was mentioned in [7] and is now explained in terms of a generalizable Linked meta learner.

Table 2. Performance evaluation of phase recognition algorithms in 5 different surgeries

Algorithm	Surgery 1	Surgery 2	Surgery 3	Surgery 4	Surgery 5
ML-based	$0,9062$	$0,6635$	$0,9032$	$0,4484$	$0,6383$
SWRL	$0,9315$	$0,7753$	$0,89$	$0,8137$	$0,7241$

A Linked Meta Learner for Surgical Phase Recognition. We developed Linked interpretation algorithms for both phase recognition algorithms, and defined their inputs and outputs in terms of semantic pre- and postconditions [7]. See listing 1.3 for the preconditions of the Linked ML-based phase recognition algorithm. The postcondition simply states that the result has to be of type **kbont:**Phase which ensures, by inference, that only modelled phases can occur. The resulting Linked interpretation algorithms need to be initialized with a laparoscopic ontology with concepts for the surgical setting. The ML-based phase recognizer, in addition, has to be trained with samples.

```
?trainingSample  rdf:type           kbont:Surgery.

?ontology        rdf:type           kbont:Ontology.

?event           rdf:type           kbont:SurgicalEvent;
                 kbont:instrument   ?instrument;
                 kbont:action       ?action;
                 kbont:structure    ?structure.


?instrument      rdf:type           kbont:Instrument.
?action          rdf:type           kbont:InstrumentalProperty.
?structure       rdf:type           kbont:TreatedStructure.
```

Listing 1.3. Preconditions of the Linked ML-based algorithm

We developed a Linked meta learner for the setting of two competing Linked phase recognition algorithms. As it is quite specific and works only for Linked phase recognition algorithms, we define a less general description of the Linked meta learner. Listing 1.4 depicts the rule for executing the Linked meta learner. It assumes available candidate Linked interpretation algorithms to recognize surgical phases and outputs the highest weighted option. Please note that we can elegantly define the generality of the Linked meta learner based on the concept types we use. If it was able to optimally choose among two or more image processors as well, we could easily express that in the pre- and postconditions.

```
{
?algo        rdf:type        kbont:PhaseRecognitionAlgorithm.
?mplaner     kbont:eligible  ?algo.
?grounding   rdf:type        kbont:StateFeature.
} => {
_:a   http:mthd        httpm:POST;
      http:requestURI  kb:mlearnerheuristic;
      http:body
   {
      ?algo        rdf:type    kbont:PhaseRecognitionAlgorithm.
      ?grounding   rdf:type    kbont:StateFeature
   } .
} .
```

Listing 1.4. Linked Data-Fu rule for executing the Linked meta learner

The Linked meta learning component assesses the performance of a given Linked phase recognizer based on training samples close to the current state $g(s_k)$. It trains the ML-based phase recognizer on $n-1$ samples and predicts on the remaining surgery. The Linked meta learner repeats the process n times and derives the probability for a candidate with respect to $g(s_k)$ based on its performance on similar samples. The heuristic is summarized in algorithm 1.

Algorithm 1. Meta Learning Heuristic given Linked interpretation algorithms L, number of neighbours to consider k, state s_k, cut t

$N \leftarrow$ nearestNeighbours($g(s_k)$, k)
$T \leftarrow$ set of training samples cut into t subsets T_i
for all T_i **do**
    for all $l \in L$ **do**
        train(l, $T \setminus T_i$) //if possible
        updatePerformanceTable(l, T_i)
for all $l \in L$ **do**
    $w_l \leftarrow$ estimatePerformance(l, N)
$w_l^\star \leftarrow \arg\max_{l \in L} w_l$
return l

Evaluation. We determined the nearest neighbours based on the similarity between the current activity triple and the ones in the training set. The total success rate of the Linked meta learning component reached a better success rate than the best phase recognizer or was at least able to compete [7]. The results are summarized in table 3. In general, meta approaches learning a probability distribution over such algorithms often provide stabler results in the longterm, but often fail to choose the optimal algorithm for every single $g(s_k)$ in hindsight.

Table 3. Performance evaluation of the Linked meta learner [7]

Algorithm	Surgery 1	Surgery 2	Surgery 3	Surgery 4	Surgery 5
Linked meta learner	0,9332	0,7786	0,9180	0,7782	0,7238

6 Discussion

Our framework builds on the use RDF and OWL to describe the functionality of meta components, interpretation algorithms and data, and their conditions for execution. We use the pre- and postconditions of a Linked interpretation algorithm to decide if it is generally eligible for a (grounded-) state, and employ Linked meta components to find and choose among candidates for a specific goal. One could relax the impact of the pre- and postconditions and shift the decision to Linked meta components. This is useful for generalization or for dealing with situations where few semantics are available. In addition, solving a task is dependent on the available pool of Linked interpretation algorithms. If the goal cannot be reached, the Linked abstract planner does not return any Linked interpretation algorithm and if no competing candidate is available, the Linked meta learner only returns the single option. Besides, we do not limit our framework to the medical domain but want to stress the added value in heterogeneous use cases.

In case of abstract planning and MDPs, we only leveraged semantics to a small degree in terms of pre- and postcondition matchings. We want to investigate the potential advantages of richer classes such as relational MDPs [6]. In addition, linked meta components can make large use of an arbitrary amount of features besides their preconditions. Linked interpretation algorithm descriptions, although potentially modelled by domain experts, do not necessarily capture all relevant dependencies. Hence, learning the optimal feature subset of F_{s_k} to better estimate transition probabilities $T(s, a, s')$ or enriching F_{s_k} with more features seem interesting extensions to our framework. We also want to develop new Linked meta components for the pure planning and planning-related learning task as defined in section 2.

Since we enable to use multiple Linked meta components at once, one could have them compete as well. This is what Vilalta & Drissi [11] depict as curse of infinite bias. We want the system to be self-adaptive and improve with experience, which it already does to some extent by automatically considering training samples or further data sources. However, each of these Linked meta components has some kind of bias in terms of their methodology used. It is very interesting to have meta components compete with each other but the question how to deal with bias is important on its own.

7 Conclusion

We introduced our work on a semantic framework for sequential decision making in a heterogeneous environment. We reused established techniques of the Semantic Web to develop a data-driven, declarative framework for Linked interpretation algorithms and extended it with means to solve complex tasks. We, therefore, defined the problem of complex task solving in our setting and distinguished between (abstract-) planning- and (meta-) learning scenarios, with initial observations on the interplay with Linked Data (contribution (i)). By now, abstract planning and meta learning can be realized with appropriate Linked meta components, which can be naturally integrated with the Linked agent (contribution (ii)). We described two exemplary medical use cases which did benefit from our framework. The image processing and sensor interpretation algorithms were wrapped as Linked APIs and executed by the Linked agent. The two meta learning components for the use cases realized and optimized the pipeline construction for solving the complex tasks (contribution (iii)). We, finally, discussed current shortcomings of our framework, potential improvements we are investigating and the long-term goal of a self-adaptive framework.

Acknowledgments. This work was carried out with the support of the German Research Foundation (DFG) within projects I01, A01, R01, I04, SFB/TRR 125 "Cognition-Guided Surgery". We especially thank Stefanie Speidel, Christian Weber, Michael Götz, Anna-Laura Wekerle, Miriam Klauß, Hannes Kenngott and Beat Müller-Stich for support with the medical use cases.

References

1. Beygelzimer, A., Riabov, A., Sow, D., Turaga, D.S., Udrea, O.: Big data exploration via automated orchestration of analytic workflows. In: Proceedings of the 10th International Conference on Autonomic Computing (ICAC 13), pp. 153–158. USENIX, San Jose (2013)
2. Gemmeke, P., Maleshkova, M., Philipp, P., Götz, M., Weber, C., Kämpgen, B., Zelzer, S., Maier-Hein, K., Rettinger, A.: Using linked data and web apis for automating the pre-processing of medical images. COLD (ISWC) (2014)
3. Gil, Y., Gonzalez-Calero, P.A., Kim, J., Moody, J., Ratnakar, V.: A semantic framework for automatic generation of computational workflows using distributed data and component catalogues. Journal of Experimental & Theoretical Artificial Intelligence **23**(4), 389–467 (2011)
4. Katić, D., Wekerle, A.-L., Gärtner, F., Kenngott, H., Müller-Stich, B.P., Dillmann, R., Speidel, S.: Knowledge-driven formalization of laparoscopic surgeries for rule-based intraoperative context-aware assistance. In: Stoyanov, D., Collins, D.L., Sakuma, I., Abolmaesumi, P., Jannin, P. (eds.) IPCAI 2014. LNCS, vol. 8498, pp. 158–167. Springer, Heidelberg (2014)
5. Kopecky, J., Gomadam, K., Vitvar, T.: hrests: An html microformat for describing restful web services. In: IEEE/WIC/ACM International Conference on Web Intelligence and Intelligent Agent Technology, 2008. WI-IAT 2008, vol. 1, pp. 619–625. IEEE (2008)
6. van Otterlo, M.: The logic of adaptive behavior: knowledge representation and algorithms for adaptive sequential decision making under uncertainty in first-order and relational domains, vol. 192. Ios Press (2009)
7. Philipp, P., Katic, D., Maleshkova, M., Rettinger, A., Speidel, S., Wekerle, A.L., Kämpgen, B., Kenngott, H., Studer, R., Dillmann, R., Müller, B.: Towards cognitive pipelines of medical assistance algorithms. In: Proc. Computer Assisted Radiology and Surgery (CARS) (2015)
8. Philipp, P., Maleshkova, M., Götz, M., Weber, C., Kämpgen, B., Zelzer, S., Maier-Hein, K., Rettinger, A.: Automatisierte verarbeitung von bildverarbeitungsalgorithmen mit semantischen technologien. In: Bildverarbeitung fÃijr die Medizin (BVM), pp. 263–268 (2015)
9. Speiser, S., Harth, A.: Integrating linked data and services with linked data services. In: Antoniou, G., Grobelnik, M., Simperl, E., Parsia, B., Plexousakis, D., De Leenheer, P., Pan, J. (eds.) ESWC 2011, Part I. LNCS, vol. 6643, pp. 170–184. Springer, Heidelberg (2011)
10. Stadtmüller, S., Speiser, S., Harth, A., Studer, R.: Data-fu: A language and an interpreter for interaction with read/write linked data. In: Proceedings of the 22nd International Conference on World Wide Web, pp. 1225–1236 (2013)
11. Vilalta, R., Drissi, Y.: A perspective view and survey of meta-learning. Artificial Intelligence Review **18**(2), 77–95 (2002)
12. Wood, I., Vandervalk, B., McCarthy, L., Wilkinson, M.D.: OWL-DL domain-models as abstract workflows. In: Margaria, T., Steffen, B. (eds.) ISoLA 2012, Part II. LNCS, vol. 7610, pp. 56–66. Springer, Heidelberg (2012)

Generating Semantic Snapshots of Newscasts Using Entity Expansion

José Luis Redondo García[1(✉)], Giuseppe Rizzo[1], Lilia Perez Romero[2], Michiel Hildebrand[2], and Raphaël Troncy[1]

[1] EURECOM, Sophia Antipolis, France
{redondo,giuseppe.rizzo,raphael.troncy}@eurecom.fr
[2] CWI, Amsterdam, The Netherlands
{L.Perez,M.Hildebrand}@cwi.nl

Abstract. TV newscasts report about the latest event-related facts occurring in the world. Relying exclusively on them is, however, insufficient to fully grasp the context of the story being reported. In this paper, we propose an approach that retrieves and analyzes related documents from the Web to automatically generate semantic annotations that provide viewers and experts comprehensive information about the news. We detect named entities in the retrieved documents that further disclose relevant concepts that were not explicitly mentioned in the original newscast. A ranking algorithm based on entity frequency, popularity peak analysis, and domain experts' rules sorts those annotations to generate what we call Semantic Snapshot of a Newscast (NSS). We benchmark this method against a gold standard generated by domain experts and assessed via a user survey over five BBC newscasts. Results of the experiments show the robustness of our approach holding an Average Normalized Discounted Cumulative Gain of 66.6%.

Keywords: Semantic Video Annotation · Entity expansion · Newscasts

1 Introduction

With the emergence of both citizen-based and social media, traditional information TV channels have to re-think their production and distribution workflow processes. We live in a globalized world where events are the result of complex interactions between many diverse agents along time. The interpretation of those news stories is problematic because of two issues: *i)* the *need of background*, viewers often need to be aware of other facts that happened in a different temporal or geographic dimension and *ii)* the *need of completeness*, a single description of an event is often not enough to capture the complete story, because it is normally incomplete, biased or partially wrong. Some TV applications assist viewers in consuming news programs, but they still need to be fed with meaningful details concerning a news item. The most common strategy to get this information is to enrich the original content with additional data collected from external sources.

P. Cimiano et al. (Eds.): ICWE 2015, LNCS 9114, pp. 410–419, 2015.
DOI: 10.1007/978-3-319-19890-3_26

However, this results in large amounts of unreliable and repeated information, leaving to the user the burden of processing the large amounts of potentially related data to build an understanding of the event.

One strategy reported in the literature for having such a mechanism is to perform named entity extraction over the newscast transcript [6]. However, the set of named entities obtained from such an operation is generally insufficient and incomplete for expressing the context of a news event [4]. Sometimes, entities spotted within a document are not disambiguated because the textual clues surrounding the entity are not precise enough, while in other cases, some relevant entities are simply not mentioned in the transcripts. In this paper, we automatically retrieve and analyze additional documents from the Web where the same event is also described, in a process called Newscast Named Entity Expansion. By increasing the size of the set of documents to analyze, we improve the coverage of the context and the representativeness of the list of entities, reinforcing relevant entities and finding new ones that are potentially interesting. This approach is able to produce a ranked list of entities called Newscast Semantic Snapshot (NSS), which includes the initial set of detected entities in subtitles with other event-related entities captured from the surrounding documents.

The paper is organized as follows: Section 2 presents some related work. Section 3 describes our approach for generating NSS. Section 4 details the different ranking algorithms used for ordering the list of candidate entities. The experimental settings are described in Section 5. We summarize our main findings and outline some future work in Section 6.

2 Related Work

The need of a NSS for feeding second screen applications is a concept we have already investigated in some previous research work and prototypes [7], proving the benefit of browsing the "surrounding context" of a newscasts. The same idea[1] was presented in the Iberoamerican Biennial of Design (BID)[2] with great feedback from users and experts. In the domain of Social Networks, named entities are used for identifying and modeling events and detecting breaking news. In [10], the authors emphasize the importance of spotting entities contained in short user generated posts in order to better understand their topic. Entities have been used for video classification when the textual information attached to a video contains temporal references (e.g. subtitles) [5].

In the literature, there are some approaches relying in similar expansion techniques. Set expansion using the Web has been applied to the problem of unsupervised relation learning [1], deriving features for concept-learning [2], or computing similarity between attribute values in autonomous databases [15]. In [12], authors proposed a system called SEAL (Set Expander for Any Language). SEAL works by automatically finding semi-structured web pages that contain lists of items and aggregating these lists in a way that the most promising items are ranked higher.

[1] https://vimeo.com/119107849

[2] http://www.bid-dimad.org

The same authors published an improved version of the algorithm [13], increasing the performance by expanding a couple of randomly selected seeds and accumulating information along different iterations. Our approach focuses on maximizing the quality of a single search query for obtaining the most appropriate set of related documents to be analyzed. Another approach that works extending a set of entities is [11], which combines the power of semantic relations between language terms like synonymy and hyponymy and grammar rules in order to find additional entities in the Web sharing the same category that the ones provides as input. To the best of our knowledge, the only related work in the news domain that has been carried out grounding the power of enriching the set of initial entities by using an entity expansion algorithm is a previous paper of ours [8]. It includes a naive document collection strategy with no filtering of entities, it proposes an entity ranking algorithm based on the appearance of the entities in the collected documents, and it exploits the DBpedia knowledge base as a way to ensure the coherence of the final list of entities. The work presented in this paper builds over and extend this work in several directions: document retrieval mechanism, semantic annotation and creation of the NSS.

3 Newscast Entity Expansion Approach

Our approach for generating Newscast Semantic Snapshots is composed of five main steps: query formulation, document retrieval, semantic annotation, annotation filtering, and annotation ranking. Fig. 1 depicts the expansion process.

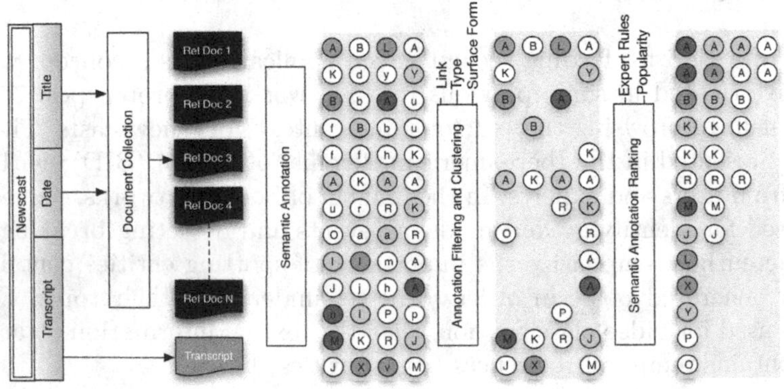

Fig. 1. Schema of Named Entity Expansion Algorithm

Query Formulation. Newscast broadcasters offer metadata about the items they publish, which is normally available together with the audiovisual content itself. In this work, we build the query $q = [\text{h}, \text{t}]$, where h is the video heading, and t is the publication date.

Document Retrieval. The retrieval stage has the intent to collect event-related documents from the open Web as result of the query q. It selects a set of the documents D over which the semantic annotation process is performed. The quality and adequacy of the collected documents sets a theoretical limit on how good the resulting news annotations are.

Semantic Annotation. In this stage, we perform a named entity recognition analysis with the objective of reducing the cardinality of the textual content from the set D of documents $\{d_1, ..., d_n, d_{n+1}\}$ where d_{n+1} refers to the original newscast transcript. HTML tags and other markup annotations are removed. The feature space is then reduced and each document d_i is represented by a bag of entities $E_{d_i} = e_{1_{d_i}}, ..., e_{n_{d_i}}$, where each entity is defined as a triplet $(surface\_form, type, link)$.

Annotation Filtering and Clustering. The Document Retrieval stage expands the content niche of the newscast. At this stage, we apply coarse grained filtering of the annotations E obtained from the previous stage, applying a $f(E_{d_i}) \rightarrow E'_{d_i}$ where $\left|E'_{d_i}\right| < \left|E_{d_i}\right|$. The particular strategies used will be further explained with the experimental settings in Section 5. Named entities are then clustered applying a centroid-based clustering operation based on strict string similarity over the $link$, and in case of mismatch, the Jaro-Winkler string distance [14] over the $surface\_form$. The output of this phase is a list of clusters containing different instances of the same entity.

Semantic Annotation Ranking. The bag of named entities E'_{d_i} is further processed to promote the named entities which are highly related to the underlined event. We propose a ranking strategy based on entity appearance in documents, popularity peak analysis and domain experts' rules in order to sort the annotations to generate the Semantic Snapshot of the considered Newscast (NSS).

4 Ranking Strategy

The unordered list of entities is ranked to promote those that are potentially interesting for the viewer. The strategies presented below rely on the assumption that entities appearing often in the retrieved documents are more important. We propose two different functions for scoring the frequency of the entities. We then consider two orthogonal functions which exploit the entity popularity in the event time window and the domain experts' knowledge.

4.1 Frequency-Based Function

We first rank the entities according to their absolute frequency within the set of retrieved documents D. Defining the absolute frequency of the entity e_i in a collection of documents D as $f_a(e_i, D)$, we consider the scoring function $S_F = \frac{f_a(e_i,D)}{|E|}$, where $|E|$ is the cardinality of all entities across all documents. In Fig. 2 (a) we can observe how entities with high S_F are on the right side of the plot and become part of the NSS.

4.2 Gaussian-Based Function

The S_F function privileges entities which appear the most. However, from a viewer's perspective, these frequent entities often represent concepts that have been so present in media that they have become too obvious to them. To approximate this scoring strategy, we rely on a Gaussian curve which penalizes both lowly and highly repeated entities. By characterizing the entities in terms of their Bernoulli appearance rate across all documents $f_{doc}(e_i)$ and applying the Gaussian distribution over those values, we promote entities distributed around the mean $\mu = \frac{|D|}{2}$ via the function $S_G = 1 - \left|\frac{f_{doc}(e_i)}{|D|} - 1\right|$ (Fig. 2 (b)).

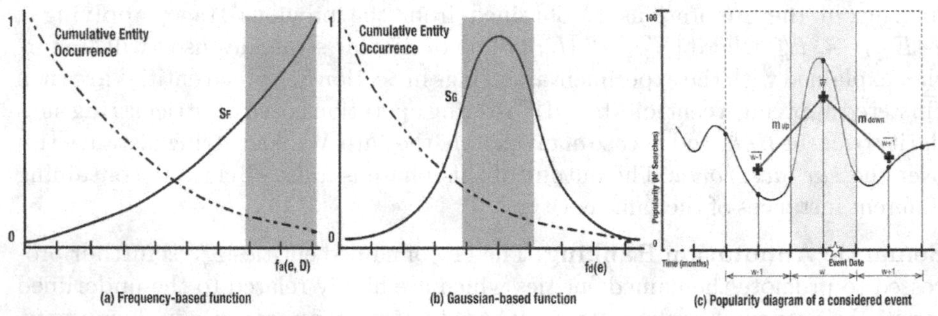

Fig. 2. (a) depicts the Decay function of the entity occurrences in the corpus and the S_F, (b) represents the Gaussian-based function S_G, with the entities highly important over the mean, and (c) the calculation of the popularity score for a considered event

4.3 Orthogonal Functions

Popularity Function. We propose a function that considers variations in entity popularity values (commonly named as popularity peaks) around the date of the studied event. Pure frequency-based approaches fail to promote certain entities which are barely mentioned in related documents but eventually become interesting for viewers. The only solution is to rely on external sources providing indications about the entity popularity, like Google Trends[3] or Twitter[4].

The procedure for getting $P_{peak}(e_i)$ is depicted in Fig. 2 (c). Using the label of an entity e_i, we obtain a list of pairs $[t, P]$ where P is the popularity score of an entity at the instant of time t. Afterward, we create three consecutive and equally long temporal windows around t: w_t containing the date itself, another one just immediately behind w_{t-1} and a last one after the previous two w_{t+1}. In a next step, we approximate the area inside the regions by calculating the average of the points contained in them, obtaining $\overline{w-1}$, $\overline{w}$ and $\overline{w+1}$.

[3] https://www.google.com/trends
[4] https://twitter.com

The variation in area between popularity under $\overline{w-1}$ and $\overline{w}$, and $\overline{w}$ and $\overline{w+1}$ give the values m_{up} and m_{down} respectively, which are normalized and combined into a single score for measuring how significant the increase in volume of searches was for that studied entity label. By empirically studying the distribution of the popularity scores of the entities belonging to a newscast, we have observed that it follows a Gaussian curve. This fact will help us to better filter out popularity scores that are not able to trigger valid conclusions.

Expert Rules Function. The knowledge of experts in the domain like journalists can be materialized in the form of rules that correct the scoring output produced by former ranking strategies. The preconditions for activating those rules involve entity features such as type, number of documents where they appear, or the nature of the sources where the documents are coming from. Actions triggered consist of adjustments in the relevance score according to a factor Op_{expert}, which intends to recreate expert's judgements for promoting or penalizing those candidate entities: $S_{expert}(e) = S_{F-1}(e) * Op_{expert}$.

5 Experimental Settings and Evaluation

In this section, we describe the experimental settings and we present the results of our evaluation against our golden standard. To the best of our knowledge, there was no evaluation dataset suited to this task, so we have built our own. With this objective in mind, we selected 5 news videos and manually extracted entities from the subtitles, video image, text contained in the video, articles related to the subject of the video and entities suggested by an expert. After building a candidate set of entities, we presented this set to 50 participants via an online survey and asked them to rate their level of interestingness. The methodology for building this dataset is described in details at https://github.com/jluisred/NewsEntities, together with the list of entities and scores per video which represent our golden standard.

Inspired by studies in Web search engines, we have based our evaluation procedure in a measure called Average Normalized Discounted Cumulative Gain ($MNDCG$ at N), which is based on the assumption that resulting documents can have different degrees of relevance for one particular task [3]. As the relevant documents in our gold standard are scored according to users' relevance, this measure can provide a more exhaustive judgment about the adequacy of the generated NSS. Concerning N, we have empirically studied the whole set of queries and main ranking functions observing that values of $MNDCG$ decreasingly improve until they reach a stable behavior from $N = 10$ on.

5.1 Experimental Settings

Document Retrieval. We rely on the Google Custom Search Engine (CSE) API service[5] by launching a query $q = [\text{h}, \text{t}]$. The maximum number of retrieved document is set to 50. The CSE engine also considers other parameters that need to be tuned up:

[5] https://www.google.com/cse/all

1. Web sites to be crawled. We have considered five possible values: search over the whole set of Web pages indexed by Google, search over a set of 10 internationals English speaking newspapers[6] (*L1*), search in the set of 3 international newspapers used in the gold standard creation (*L2*), prioritize results from in *L1* but still consider other sites, and prioritize content in *L2* but still consider other sites.
2. Temporal dimension. We consider the time window $T_{Window} = [\mathrm{t} - d, \mathrm{t} + d]$, with two possible values for d: 3 days and one week.
3. In addition, Google CSE can filter results according to the Schema.org types. In our experiments we tried with [NoFilter, Person&Organization Filtering]

Semantic Annotation. We use [9] which applies machine learning classification of the entity type given a rich feature vector composed of a set of linguistic features, the output of a properly trained Conditional Random Fields classifier and the output of a set of off-the-shelf NER extractors supported by the NERD Framework[7]. We used it as an off-the-shelf entity extractor, using the offered classification model trained over the newswire content.

Annotation Filtering and Clustering. In order to get rid of some non-pure named entities which are not well considered by viewers and experts, we have applied three different filtering approaches: filtering according to their NERD type[8] (*F1*), in our case, we keep only Person, Location, and Organization, removing entities with confidence score under first quarter of the distribution (*F2*), and keeping only entities with capitalized surface form (*F3*). A first pre-selection by setting to default the rest of steps of the approach led us to discover that 3 of the filters (*F1*, *F3*, and combination *F1_F3*) were producing the best MNDCG values.

Semantic Annotation Ranking. For the current experiment, we run both Frequency and Gaussian based functions, together with the orthogonal strategies based on popularity and expert rules. Regarding the *popularity* dimension, we rely on Google Trends, which estimates how many times a search-term has been used in a given time-window. Since Google Trends gives results with a monthly temporal granularity, we have fixed the duration of w to 2 months to keep the sample representative. With the aim of keeping only those findings backed by strong evidence, we have filtered the entities with peak popularity value higher than $\mu + 2 * \sigma$. Those entities will adjust their former scores with the popularity values via the following equation: $S_P(e) = R_{score}(e) + Pop_{peak}(e)^2$. Concerning the *Expert Rules* dimension, we have considered three rules to be applied over the three main entity types. The different Op_{expert} values have been deduced by relying on the average score per entity type computed in the survey. Organizations have gotten a higher weight (0.95), followed by Persons (0.74), and by Locations (0.48) that are badly considered and therefore lower ranked in general. A last rule applied over entities appearing in less than two sources $f_{doc}(e_i) < 2$ automatically discards the matched instances ($Op_{expert} = 0$).

[6] http://en.wikipedia.org/wiki/List_of_newspapers_in_the_world_by_circulation
[7] http://nerd.eurecom.fr
[8] http://nerd.eurecom.fr/ontology

5.2 Results

Given the different settings for each phase of the approach, we have a total of $20 * 4 * 4 = 320$ different runs that have ranked according to $MNDCG_{10}$. In addition, we have considered two baselines:

Baseline 1 (BS1): Former Entity Expansion Implementation. A previous version of the News Entity Expansion algorithm was already published in [8]. The settings are: Google as source of documents, temporal window of 2 Weeks, no Schema.org selected, no filter strategy applied, and only frequency-based ranked function with no orthogonal appliances.

Baseline 2 (BS2): TFIDF-based Function. To compare our functions with other traditional frequency based approaches, we selected the well-known TF-IDF. It measures the importance an entity in a document over a corpus of documents D, penalizing those entities appearing more frequently along the whole set of documents.

$$tf(e_i, d_j) = 0.5 + \frac{0.5 \times f_a(e_i, D)}{max\{f_a(e'_i, D) : e'_i \in d_j\}}, idf(e_i, d_j) = log \frac{|D|}{\{d_j \in D : e_i \in d_j\}} \quad (1)$$

We aggregated the different $tf(e_i, d_j) \times idf(e_i, d_j)$ into a single score via the function $S_{TFIDF}(e) = \frac{\sum_{j=1}^{n} tf(e, d_j) \times idf(e)}{|D|}$.

Table 1. Executed runs and their configuration settings, ranked by $MNDCG_{10}$

Run	Collection			Filtering	Functions			Result			
	Sources	T_{Window}	Schema.org		Freq	Pop	Exp	$MNDCG_{10}$	MAP_{10}	MP_{10}	MR_{10}
Ex0	Google	2W		F1+F3	Freq		✓	0.666	0.71	0.7	0.37
Ex1	Google	2W		F3	Freq		✓	0.661	0.72	0.68	0.36
Ex2	Google	2W		F3	Freq	✓	✓	0.658	0.64	0.6	0.32
Ex3	Google	2W		F3	Freq			0.641	0.72	0.74	0.39
Ex4	L1+Google	2W		F3	Freq		✓	0.636	0.71	0.72	0.37
Ex5	L2+Google	2W		F3	Freq		✓	0.636	0.72	0.7	0.36
Ex6	Google	2W		F1+F3	Freq			0.626	0.73	0.7	0.38
Ex7	L2+Google	2W		F3	Freq			0.626	0.72	0.72	0.37
Ex8	Google	2W		F1+F3	Freq	✓	✓	0.626	0.64	0.56	0.28
Ex9	L2+Google	2W		F1+F3	Freq		✓	0.624	0.71	0.7	0.37
Ex10	Google	2W		F1	Freq		✓	0.624	0.69	0.62	0.32
...	...	...	...	...	...	...	...	...	...	...	...
Ex78	Google	2W	✓	F1+F3	Gaussian		✓	0.552	0.66	0.66	0.34
Ex80	L2+Google	2W	✓	F1+F3	Gaussian		✓	0.55	0.69	0.7	0.36
Ex82	L1	2W	✓	F3	Gaussian		✓	0.549	0.68	0.64	0.33
...	...	...	...	...	...	...	...	...	...	...	...
BS2	Google	2W			Freq			0.473	0.53	0.42	0.22
...	...	...	...	...	...	...	...	...	...	...	...
BS1	Google	2W			TFIDF			0.063	0.08	0.06	0.03

In Table 1 we present the top 10 runs together with some lower configurations after position 78 and scores of the baseline strategies:

- Our best approach has obtained a $MNDCG_{10}$ score of 0.662 and a MAP_{10} of 0.71, which are reasonably good in the document retrieval domain.

- Our approach performs much better than *BS1* and by far better than *BS2*. The very low score of this last baseline reveals that traditional TF-IDF function is designed to measure the relevance of an item referred to the document that contains it and not the whole collection.
- Regarding the Document Retrieval step, using Google as source alone or together with other whitelists gives better results than restricting only to particular whitelists. The biggest T_{Window} of 2 weeks performs better in all cases, while the use of Schema.org does not bring significant improvement except when applied over the Gaussian function (see runs 78, 80, 82).
- The best Filter strategy is *F3*, followed by the combination *F1_F3*. In conclusion, capitalization is a very powerful clue for refining the candidate list.
- Absolute frequency function performs better than Gaussian in all top cases.
- Expert Rules improves NSS for almost every configuration possible.
- Popularity-based function does not seem to improve significantly the results. However, a further manual study of the promoted entities has revealed that the method is bringing up relevant entities like for example *David Ellsberg* for the query "Fugitive Edward Snowden applies for asylum in Russia". This entity is barely mentioned in the collected documents, but its role in the whole story is quite relevant[9], since he published an editorial with high media impact in The Guardian praising the actions of Snowden in revealing top-secret surveillance programs of the NSA.

6 Conclusion

In this paper, we have presented an approach for automatically generating Newscast Semantic Snapshots. By following an entity expansion process that retrieves additional event-related documents from the Web, we have been able to enlarge the niche of initial newscast content. The bag of retrieved documents, together with the newscast transcript, is analyzed with the objective of extracting named entities referring to persons, organizations, and locations. By increasing the size of the document set, we have increased the completeness of the context and the representativeness of the list of entities, reinforcing relevant entities and finding new ones that are potentially interesting inside the context of that news item. We assessed the entire workflow against a gold standard, which is also proposed and published in this paper. The evaluation has showed the strength of this approach, holding an $MNDCG_{10}$ score of 0.666, outperforming the two studied baselines.

Future research interests include tailoring the entity ranking functions to particular news categories: sport, politics, business, etc. via supervised techniques (Learning to Rank). We are investigating how relations between entities specified in knowledge bases or inside the collected documents can be used to better rank them and even generate a graph-based NSS. We also plan to use our approach as a means to suggest relevant entities in the process of the ground truth creation, in order to bring possible missing entities that were not identified because of human limitations in exhaustively covering the whole context of the news item.

[9] http://en.wikipedia.org/wiki/Daniel_Ellsberg

Acknowledgments. This work was partially supported by the European Union's 7th Framework Programme via the project LinkedTV (GA 287911).

References

1. Cafarella, M.J., Downey, D., Soderland, S., Etzioni, O.: Knowitnow: Fast, scalable information extraction from the web. In: Human Language Technology Conference(HLT-EMNLP-2005), pp. 563–570 (2005)
2. Cohen, W.W.: Automatically extracting features for concept learning from the web. In: Seventeenth International Conference on Machine Learning, ICML 2000, pp. 159–166. Morgan Kaufmann Publishers Inc., San Francisco (2000)
3. Croft, W.B., Metzler, D., Strohman, T.: Search engines: Information retrieval in practice. Addison-Wesley, Reading (2010)
4. Henzinger, M., Chang, B.-W., Milch, B., Brin, S.: Query-free news search. In: Proceedings of the 12th International Conference on World Wide Web, WWW 2003, pp. 1–10. ACM, New York (2003)
5. Li, Y., Rizzo, G., Redondo Garcia, J.L., Troncy, R.: Enriching media fragments with named entities for video classification. In: 1st Worldwide Web Workshop on Linked Media (LiME 2013), Rio de Janeiro, Brazil (2013)
6. Li, Y., Rizzo, G., Troncy, R., Wald, M., Wills, G.: Creating enriched youtube media fragments with nerd using timed-text. In: 11th International Semantic Web Conference (ISWC 2012), November 2012
7. Redondo-García, J.L., Hildebrand, M., Romero, L.P., Troncy, R.: Augmenting TV newscasts via entity expansion. In: Presutti, V., Blomqvist, E., Troncy, R., Sack, H., Papadakis, I., Tordai, A. (eds.) ESWC Satellite Events 2014. LNCS, vol. 8798, pp. 472–476. Springer, Heidelberg (2014)
8. Redondo Garcia, J.L., De Vocht, L., Troncy, R., Mannens, E., Van de Walle, R.: Describing and contextualizing events in tv news show. In: 23rd International Conference on World Wide Web Companion, pp. 759–764 (2014)
9. Rizzo, G., van Erp, M., Troncy, R.: Benchmarking the extraction and disambiguation of named entities on the semantic web. In: 9th International Conference on Language Resources and Evaluation (LREC 2014) (2014)
10. Steiner, T., Verborgh, R., Gabarro Vallés, J., Van de Walle, R.: Adding meaning to social network microposts via multiple named entity disambiguation apis and tracking their data provenance. International Journal of Computing Information Systems and Industrial Management **5**, 69–78 (2013)
11. Tran, M.-V., Nguyen, T.-T., Nguyen, T.-S., Le, H.-Q.: Automatic named entity set expansion using semantic rules and wrappers for unary relations. In: Asian Language Processing (IALP), pp. 170–173, December 2010
12. Wang, R.C., Cohen, W.W.: Language-independent set expansion of named entities using the web. In: Seventh IEEE International Conference on Data Mining, ICDM 2007, Washington, DC, USA, pp. 342–350 (2007)
13. Wang, R.C., Cohen, W.W.: Iterative set expansion of named entities using the web. In: Eighth IEEE International Conference on Data Mining, ICDM 2008, Washington, DC, USA, pp. 1091–1096 (2008)
14. Winkler, W.E.: Overview of record linkage and current research directions. In: Bureau of the Census (2006)
15. Wolf, G., Khatri, H., Chokshi, B., Fan, J., Chen, Y., Kambhampati, S.: Query processing over incomplete autonomous databases. In: 33rd International Conference on Very Large Data Bases, VLDB 2007, pp. 651–662 (2007)

Adaptive Faceted Search for Product Comparison on the Web of Data

Alex Stolz[(✉)] and Martin Hepp

Universitaet der Bundeswehr Munich, D-85579 Neubiberg, Germany
{alex.stolz,martin.hepp}@ebusiness-unibw.org

Abstract. In this paper, we study the appropriateness of adaptive faceted search as a search paradigm for e-commerce on the Web of Data. We provide preliminary evidence that the product space in a sample dataset narrows down logarithmically by the number of product features used in a query, and show that the usability of an adaptive, instance-driven faceted search interface is comparable to approaches with hard-wired product features, while improving the depth of product search and comparison.

Keywords: E-commerce · Product comparison · Faceted search · Usability · SUS · HCI · Linked data · Semantic Web · RDF · SPARQL

1 Introduction

In the recent years, companies have started to add structured e-commerce data published as RDFa and Microdata markup to HTML Web pages. Such product, store, and offer data, while mainly provided for major search engines like Google and primarily based on the GoodRelations and schema.org vocabularies, forms a promising data source for novel Web applications and services.

Unfortunately, the available means for exploring this giant RDF graph of e-commerce information are limited. The diversity of products and data sources, the inherent learning effects during search, the heterogeneity in terms of data semantics with the resulting need to align data schema elements on the go, and the sparsity of the graph of product information, create special requirements for product comparison solutions that are currently not met. On top of the technical challenges, products and services are typically characterized by a vast variety of product features that influence the overall utility of a certain product, trade-offs between such features, and a significant variation in item prices. Consequently, product comparison includes multi-dimensional, non-linear decisions.

Conventional search approaches fall short with structured product data at Web scale. Information retrieval, e.g. keyword search, essentially flattens multi-dimensional product descriptions to simple, one-dimensional term matches. On the other extreme, query formulation as with SPARQL is generally very complex and lacks mediation between the conceptual models of the data vs. the mental models of human users. Other methods suggested for browsing RDF data (e.g.

P. Cimiano et al. (Eds.): ICWE 2015, LNCS 9114, pp. 420–429, 2015.
DOI: 10.1007/978-3-319-19890-3_27

Tabulator [6]) are very low-level for serious product search. As a result of these shortcomings, consumers tend to narrow down the set of candidate offers very early in the search process, which bears the risk that potentially interesting product offers are eliminated prematurely. Also, results are highly biased towards a single product or offer dimension (e.g. low prices) [15].

In this paper, we show that *faceted search* ([19]; cf. [16]), a special form of exploratory search [11], is appropriate for product comparison on the Web of Data. Faceted search is well established both in practice (e.g. eBay[1] and Amazon[2]) and in academia as a way to guide users through option spaces (e.g. [8,13,23]). In a nutshell, it constitutes a multi-dimensional interaction paradigm based on facet-value pairs, e.g. product dimensions, that dynamically adapt with the actual data.

2 Requirements for Faceted Search

This section defines important requirements for product search that can to a large extent be readily met by faceted search interfaces over RDF data.

- *Regard multi-dimensionality of products:* The complexity and dynamics of products and services necessitate multi-parametric searches based on distinguishing properties and attributes of product entities, which, on the Web of Data, can be realized by considering the structure of the available data.
- *Support learning about the option space:* Search is an iterative, incremental learning process (e.g. [12, p.9]) rather than a static, one-shot query. For example, users grasp new information about the option space in every search turn [5], possibly leading to changes in price expectation. Thus, users need a way to relax or refine their constraints and preferences based on how those modify the size of the option space.
- *Facilitate incremental, user-driven schema alignment:* For product search with incremental learning, it is not only vital to assist in navigating and pruning the option space, but also to actively engage the user in the search process. Since users are likely to learn about correspondences in the underlying product features during the user interaction, the approximate alignment of conceptual elements should be integrated in the iterative search process, and be fed back to the graph. E.g., a user interface could ask the user for approval of a possible match between two product features. In an RDF environment, corresponding axioms can be easily added to the existing data as named RDF graphs – potentially managed on a per-user basis.
- *Take into account the popularity of conceptual elements in the instance data:* A user interface that is solely based on the schema elements defined in the underlying ontologies is inefficient, because the user lacks information about the availability of matching data (e.g. whether a property is used at all) and the relevance of a constraint on the option space (e.g. whether products differ

[1] http://www.ebay.com/

[2] http://www.amazon.com/

in that property). Due to a sparsely populated graph of product information on the Web, efficient user interfaces should thus adapt to the actual usage of schema elements in the data rather than be based on schema definitions.

- *Utilize metrics for the efficiency of the search process:* An efficient search interface presents choices to the user that help to quickly narrow down the option space, e.g. by proposing discerning features that partition the option space in the best possible way, or by suggesting properties that promise the highest utility to a given user need. The user dialog in faceted search is fundamentally a decision tree problem, where the user interaction steps are branches of the tree. Because the facets are orthogonal to each other, the decision tree can be constructed in any order [13]. However, if we want to optimize the search efficiency for the user, we have to create and, if necessary, update the resulting tree based on a "best split" strategy known from decision tree research in data mining [18, p.158]. Popular algorithms from literature, e.g. ID3 [14], iteratively choose attributes maximizing the information gain. In this context, [10] mention some popular facet-pair suggestion strategies, namely relying on frequency, probability, and the information gain. The authors in [22] further give an overview over different metrics appropriate for product search to help decide which facets to present to the user.

3 Experiments

This paper investigates the appropriateness of faceted search interfaces for the Web of Data. To test for two fundamental aspects of search interfaces, namely search efficiency and usability, we first measure the impact of specificity in product search on the size of the result set using a simulation of random walks. Then, we conduct a usability study where we contrast a data-driven, adaptive faceted search interface with a second alternative with hard-wired product features.

3.1 Impact of Search Specificity on the Size of the Result Set

We simulated a number of product searches to find out how dispersed the search space for products is and how well a faceted search approach on average performs regarding partitioning the option space.

Method. We took a random sample of 875 automobile offers[3] from the *mobile.de* car listing Web site. We extracted the product features from the respective Web pages and populated an RDF graph via mapping product features to properties from the VSO ontology[4]. For the sake of simplicity, we did not take into account quantitative values for our simulation, but only qualitative and datatype properties. The variety of qualitative and datatype properties over the whole dataset

[3] More precisely, we took random result page numbers between 1 and 100 for random price ranges between 1 and 100, 000 Euros.

[4] http://purl.org/vso/ns

Table 1. Variety of properties and values in automobile dataset

Property	Variety of Values
http://purl.org/vso/ns#bodyStyle	6
http://purl.org/vso/ns#color	24
http://purl.org/vso/ns#condition	5
http://purl.org/vso/ns#feature	60
http://purl.org/vso/ns#fuelType	10
http://purl.org/vso/ns#meetsEmissionStandard	5
http://purl.org/vso/ns#transmission	3

is shown in Table 1. These numbers give a total of 113 possible property-value pairs. From this range of possible property-value combinations, we drew one item at random and started from there 100 random walks with each simulating ten consecutive selection steps. After every selection step, we randomly picked a property-value pair from the reduced option space, which we obtained by issuing a proper SPARQL query.

Results. Figure 1 outlines the results of our simulation. At the beginning (step 0), the option space always entails the full range of 875 car offers. In search step 1, the median of the 100 iterations already goes down to circa 150 results, i.e. in 50% of the cases the first filtering step sorts out an average of more than 700 out of 875 automobiles. After having selected three product features, the median of the option space decreases to only three items.

As a possible constraint, our random walk does not include UNION clauses, i.e. the disjunctive selection of multiple facet values which would expand the option space (e.g. select a car that offers either manual or automatic transmission). However, we argue that this expansion operation does anyway occur rarely in practice when users seek interesting product offers.

Discussion. We can see clearly from the analysis that the space of possibly matching products decreases logarithmically with the number of features specified in a query. This confirms our assumption that learning about the option space, i.e. how relaxing and refining requirements and preferences based on the set of remaining choices, is a critical part of product search interaction. It also highlights that in specific branches of product search and thus sparsely populated decision trees, a search interface can benefit from being dynamically generated directly from the data about products and their characteristics.

Of course, the findings presented are currently based on a single sample data set of 875 cars, albeit those have been selected randomly from a very significant real dataset from a car sales portal. The effect of the number of features might be less significant if we took into account the correlation of features (e.g. that a stronger engine is likely to be found in combination with more seating capacity), which we deliberately abstracted from by selecting the features randomly. We would counter, however, that exactly these correlations between product features

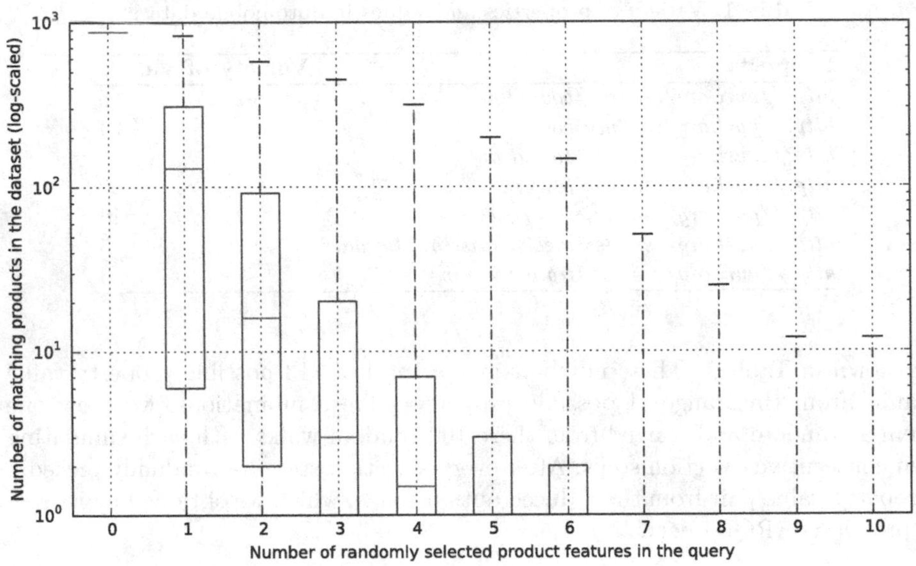

Fig. 1. Random walk simulation over a decision tree for 875 automobile offers

are unknown ex ante to a person exploring a product space and thus stress the importance of the learning effect of iterative product search.

3.2 Usability Studies of Faceted Search Interfaces for Products

Faceted search interfaces have recently attracted significant research interest. Various demonstrators, user studies, and evaluations repeatedly attest them superior usability in contrast with other search paradigms (e.g. [8,10,13,24]). In a survey in [23], the authors systematically compare faceted search with other popular search paradigms.

In here, we conduct a user study in order to find out whether an instance-driven search interface has a negative impact on usability, because hard-wired, consolidated user interfaces found in today's commercial faceted search applications have the advantage that the displayed facets can be based on popular mental models of human users. Instance-driven, adaptive faceted search interfaces bear the risk of being confusing to users, as the facets and facet names presented to users may change dynamically depending on the available data.

Method. In order to evaluate a potentially negative effect, we first developed an instance-driven, adaptive faceted search interface[5] for product comparison on the Web of Data, that addresses the requirements outlined in Sect. 2. Then, we prepared an identical search interface except for relying on hard-wired product

[5] http://www.ebusiness-unibw.org/tools/product-search/

Table 2. Results of SUS experiments

	Students		Crowdsourcing	
	A	B	A	B
No. participants	39	29	50	50
No. incorrect answers	5	3	13	9
No. answers considered	39	29	37	41
Avg. SUS score	66.54	72.59	65.00	68.75

features[6]. As the data to present in our two search interfaces, we used a random subset of 25 car offers out of the random sample of 875 car offers from *mobile.de*.

We set up a usability study according to the System Usability Scale (SUS) [7] score. The questionnaire encompasses ten brief questions where each response is represented by a five-point Likert scale ranging from *strongly agree* to *strongly disagree*. SUS questions are designed to alternate between positive and negative statements. In addition, we included a gold question to filter out unreliable candidates based on an incorrect response. We placed the gold question at the end of the questionnaire. Otherwise, we feared that participants would possibly give up too early, because it required a bit of effort to look at the information displayed in the search interface. Finally, we asked for optional feedback, which we used in a later analysis for interpreting the results. We put the questionnaire online so that users could test the search interface and answer to questions remotely.

We conducted two separate usability studies. The first one we ran with undergraduate students from our University, who specialize in business management or related fields. They were asked to assess the usability of the original, dynamic search interface *A* and, later, to repeat the same task with the amended search interface *B*. Our second experiment was harnessing crowd workforce from the CrowdFlower platform. As compared to the students experiment, we ran the usability test for both search interfaces *A* and *B* in parallel with two distinct groups of participants.

Results. In the following, we report on the empirical results obtained from the two usability studies, as summarized in Table 2.

Usability Experiment with Students. The task completion rate (cf. [17]) for students was 34/39 = 87% for search interface *A*, and 26/29 = 90% for search interface *B*. For students' ratings, we decided against eliminating incorrect answers to the gold question, because a closer investigation of individual responses revealed that students were not fooled by the alternating pattern of SUS questions rotating between positive and negative statements.

Search interface *A* achieved an average SUS score of 66.54, which is slightly below the average of 68[7], which was the mean SUS score among 500 system

[6] http://www.ebusiness-unibw.org/tools/product-search-static/

[7] http://www.measuringu.com/sus.php

usability studies. Taking on the qualitative, "adjective" rating introduced in [4], the search interface is considered *good* (SUS score close to 71.4). By comparison, search interface B obtained an average SUS score of 72.59. We stated the following null hypothesis to test the difference in the usability scores for significance:

Null Hypothesis. *There is no difference among SUS scores for search interfaces A and B obtained by two student samples from the same population.*

A Shapiro-Wilk test revealed that we cannot assume that both SUS score samples are normally distributed (p-values of 0.03 and 0.06), thus we compared the two samples using a non-parametric statistical test, the Wilcoxon rank-sum test.

The average usability scores assigned by our students to search interface A ($median = 70.00$) did not differ significantly from usability scores assigned to search interface B ($median = 75.00$), $W = -1.45$, $p = 0.15$, $r = -0.18$.

Usability Experiment with Crowdsourcing. Unlike in the previous experiment, we did only accept contributions by crowd workers who correctly answered the gold question. The task completion rate for crowd workers was $37/50 = 74\%$ for search interface A, and $41/50 = 82\%$ for search interface B.

Search interface A achieved an average SUS score of 65.00, which is below 68, but still *good* according to [4]. Search interface B obtained an average SUS score of 68.75. The null hypothesis below was used to test whether the usability scores significantly differ:

Null Hypothesis. *There is no difference among SUS scores for search interfaces A and B obtained through two different samples of crowd workers.*

A Shapiro-Wilk test revealed that we cannot assume that both SUS score samples are normally distributed (p-values of 0.13 and 0.01), thus we compared the two samples using a non-parametric statistical test, the Wilcoxon rank-sum test.

The average usability scores assigned by the first group of crowd workers to search interface A ($median = 65.00$) did not differ significantly from usability scores assigned to search interface B by the second group of crowd workers ($median = 73.75$), $W = -1.30$, $p = 0.19$, $r = -0.15$.

Discussion. This analysis shows that, in principle, a fully dynamic search interface directly based on product features found in the data, is not systematically less intuitive for users than one based on established, hard-wired product features used in existing car portals. However, we see a small negative effect in usability, which we expected, because the static, hard-wired set of search dimensions allows a higher degree of users' familiarity with the terminology and conceptual model of a search interface. We conclude from that small negative effect that a data-driven search interface for products comes at a cost, which must be compensated for by additional gains in precision, recall, and eventually the utility of the finally selected product.

We would also like to stress that a usability-based evaluation of novel search interfaces has a systematic weakness, because it only analyzes how well a user can handle the interface, but not the quality of the choices eventually made (e.g. how well the finally selected product meets the user's needs). As we have shown in the first part of this section, the sparsity and heterogeneity of the product space indicates that a more precise navigation in the option space can return much better product matches.

4 Related Work

Within the frame of this work, we deem mostly relevant three research directions, namely (1) adaptive faceted search interfaces, (2) faceted search over RDF data, and (3) faceted product search on the Semantic Web.

4.1 Adaptive Faceted Search

In adaptive faceted search interfaces, user controls dynamically adapt to the actual data restricted by the current selection. An adaptive faceted search interface was proposed in [1] to investigate content within Twitter streams. Facets and facet values are computed based on semantic enrichment of Twitter messages. The search interface adapts according to frequency, user profile, temporal context, and diversification. In [20], the author aims to facilitate information access on the Web via an adaptive, exploratory search relying on multiple search paradigms. Another work related to personalized faceted search over Web document metadata was proposed in [10], where facet views adapt according to user ratings.

4.2 Faceted Search over RDF Data

As an easy-to-use alternative for SPARQL querying, faceted search gained wide attraction as a search paradigm for RDF data. Faceted search as a means to navigate over arbitrary datasets with structured data was formalized in [13]. A similar approach develops a formal model for question answering based on faceted queries and regards also ontological reasoning [2]. The work in [8] combines the ease-of-use of faceted search with the expressive power of the SPARQL query language. In comparison to the two other works that operate on set operations over resources, this approach provides navigation through query transformations at the syntactic level. Some large-scale faceted search interfaces over real RDF datasets were suggested in [9] and [3]. In [9], the authors built a faceted search interface over structured Wikipedia infobox data (DBPedia). The work in [3] studies limitations of conventional faceted search systems, and presents a faceted search interface over Yago.

4.3 Faceted Search over Structured E-Commerce Data

The work in [21] presents a faceted product search interface over structured e-commerce data from the Web. The data store[8] presently contains a selection of

[8] http://xploreproducts.com/

product offers along with review data from selected online stores. In comparison to our research that proposes fully data-driven product search, this work only supports basic commercial properties of product offers, and categorizes products into a rigid category structure.

5 Conclusions

In this paper, we have studied the appropriateness of data-driven, adaptive faceted search interfaces for navigating the sparse graph of Linked Open Data for e-commerce on the Web with explicit support for user learning about the option space. We have provided preliminary evidence that the selection steps in faceted search interfaces drill down the option space logarithmically, and have shown that the usability loss of a dynamic, instance-driven faceted search interface in comparison to an approach with hard-wired product features is insignificant.

The small-scale usability study in this paper also indicates that users apparently have gotten used to search interfaces that expose rigid navigation structures optimized for individual application domains. While viable in smaller and controlled settings, it is not feasible for e-commerce over Linked Open Data, where diverse and dynamic product domains need to be consolidated. A large-scale evaluation with real e-commerce data from the Web is planned for future work.

Acknowledgments. The authors would like to thank Florian Ott for kindly supporting us in setting up and hosting the necessary infrastructure of our search systems, and all the undergraduate students at Universitaet der Bundeswehr Munich who participated in the usability study.

References

1. Abel, F., Celik, I., Houben, G.-J., Siehndel, P.: Leveraging the semantics of tweets for adaptive faceted search on twitter. In: Aroyo, L., Welty, C., Alani, H., Taylor, J., Bernstein, A., Kagal, L., Noy, N., Blomqvist, E. (eds.) ISWC 2011, Part I. LNCS, vol. 7031, pp. 1–17. Springer, Heidelberg (2011)
2. Arenas, M., Cuenca Grau, B., Kharlamov, E., Marciuška, S., Zheleznyakov, D.: Faceted search over ontology-enhanced RDF data. In: Proceedings of the 23rd ACM International Conference on Information and Knowledge Management (CIKM 2014), pp. 939–948. ACM, Shanghai (2014)
3. Arenas, M., Cuenca Grau, B., Kharlamov, E., Marciuška, S., Zheleznyakov, D.: Towards semantic faceted search. In: Poster Proceedings of the 23rd International World Wide Web Conference (WWW 2014 Companion), pp. 219–220. ACM, Seoul (2014)
4. Bangor, A., Kortum, P., Miller, J.: Determining What Individual SUS Scores Mean: Adding an Adjective Rating Scale. Journal of Usability Studies **4**(3), 114–123 (2009)
5. Bates, M.J.: The Design of Browsing and Berrypicking Techniques for the Online Search Interface. Online Information Review **13**(5), 407–424 (1989)

6. Berners-Lee, T., Chen, Y., Chilton, L., Connolly, D., Dhanaraj, R., Hollenbach, J., Lerer, A., Sheets, D.: Tabulator: exploring and analyzing linked data on the semantic web. In: Proceedings of the 3rd International Semantic Web User Interaction Workshop (SWUI 2006), Athens, GA, USA (2006)
7. Brooke, J.: SUS - A quick and dirty usability scale. In: Jordan, P., Thomas, B., Weerdmeester, B., McClelland, I. (eds.) Usability Evaluation in Industry, pp. 189–194. Taylor & Francis (1996)
8. Ferré, S., Hermann, A.: Semantic search: reconciling expressive querying and exploratory search. In: Aroyo, L., Welty, C., Alani, H., Taylor, J., Bernstein, A., Kagal, L., Noy, N., Blomqvist, E. (eds.) ISWC 2011, Part I. LNCS, vol. 7031, pp. 177–192. Springer, Heidelberg (2011)
9. Hahn, R., Bizer, C., Sahnwaldt, C., Herta, C., Robinson, S., Bürgle, M., Düwiger, H., Scheel, U.: Faceted wikipedia search. In: Abramowicz, W., Tolksdorf, R. (eds.) BIS 2010. LNBIP, vol. 47, pp. 1–11. Springer, Heidelberg (2010)
10. Koren, J., Zhang, Y., Liu, X.: Personalized interactive faceted search. In: Proceedings of the 17th International World Wide Web Conference (WWW 2008), pp. 477–485. ACM, Beijing (2008)
11. Marchionini, G.: Exploratory Search: From Finding to Understanding. Communications of the ACM **49**(4), 41–46 (2006)
12. Morville, P., Callender, J.: Search Patterns. O'Reilly Media (2010)
13. Oren, E., Delbru, R., Decker, S.: Extending faceted navigation for RDF data. In: Cruz, I., Decker, S., Allemang, D., Preist, C., Schwabe, D., Mika, P., Uschold, M., Aroyo, L.M. (eds.) ISWC 2006. LNCS, vol. 4273, pp. 559–572. Springer, Heidelberg (2006)
14. Quinlan, J.R.: Induction of Decision Trees. Machine Learning **1**(1), 81–106 (1986)
15. Sacco, G.M.: The intelligent E-store: easy interactive product selection and comparison. In: Proceedings of the Seventh IEEE International Conference on E-Commerce Technology (CEC 2005), pp. 240–248. IEEE, Munich (2005)
16. Sacco, G.M., Tzitzikas, Y.: Dynamic Taxonomies and Faceted Search: Theory, Practice, and Experience. Springer, Heidelberg (2009)
17. Sauro, J., Lewis, J.R.: Estimating Completion Rates from Small Samples Using Binomial Confidence Intervals: Comparisons and Recommendations. Proceedings of the Human Factors and Ergonomics Society 49th Annual Meeting (HFES 2005) **49**(24), 2100–2104 (2005)
18. Tan, P.N., Steinbach, M., Kumar, V.: Introduction to Data Mining, 1 edn. Addison-Wesley (2005)
19. Tunkelang, D.: Faceted Search. Morgan & Claypool (2009)
20. Tvarožek, M.: Exploratory Search in the Adaptive Social Semantic Web. Information Sciences and Technologies Bulletin of the ACM Slovakia **3**(1), 42–51 (2011)
21. Vandic, D., van Dam, J.W., Frasincar, F.: Faceted Product Search Powered by the Semantic Web. Decision Support Systems **53**(3), 425–437 (2012)
22. Vandic, D., Frasincar, F., Kaymak, U.: Facet selection algorithms for web product search. In: Proceedings of the 22nd ACM International Conference on Information and Knowledge Management (CIKM 2013), pp. 2327–2332. ACM, San Francisco (2013)
23. Wei, B., Liu, J., Zheng, Q., Zhang, W., Fu, X., Feng, B.: A Survey of Faceted Search. Journal of Web Engineering **12**(1), 41–64 (2013)
24. Yee, K.P., Searingen, K., Li, K., Hearst, M.A.: Faceted metadata for image search and browsing. In: Proceedings of the SIGCHI Conference on Human Factors in Computing Systems (CHI 2003), pp. 401–408. ACM, Fort Lauderdale (2003)

SUMMA: A Common API for Linked Data Entity Summaries

Andreas Thalhammer(✉) and Steffen Stadtmüller

Karlsruhe Institute of Technology, Karlsruhe, Germany
{andreas.thalhammer,steffen.stadtmueller}@kit.edu

Abstract. Linked Data knowledge sources such as DBpedia, Freebase, and Wikidata currently offer large amounts of factual data. As the amount of information that can be grasped by users is limited, data summaries are needed. If a summary relates to a specific entity we refer to it as entity summarization. Unfortunately, in many settings, the summaries of entities are tightly bound to user interfaces. This practice poses problems for efficient and objective comparison and evaluation.

In this paper we focus on the question of how to make summaries exchangeable between multiple interfaces and multiple summarization services in order to facilitate evaluation and testing. We introduce SUMMA, an API definition that enables to decouple generation and presentation of summaries. It enables multiple consumers to retrieve summaries from multiple providers in a unified and lightweight way.

Keywords: Web APIs · Entity summarization · Evaluation · Testing · User interfaces · Linked data

1 Introduction

With the growth of Open Data on the Web a plethora of information sources covering diverse topics and domains are readily available to information consumers. The abundance of information that can be found on single entities can even be increased with the integration of different data sources with semantic links (Linked Open Data). However, when it comes to the presentation of such information, there are often limits on the amount of data that can be rendered in interfaces and grasped by end users. These limits give rise to the requirement to only show the most important data in visualizations, i. e. a summary. The amount of commercial systems that offer entity summaries are on the rise [7,10,17]. Due to their proprietary nature, these systems tightly couple their user interface and backend in accordance to their specific requirements. Also the data sources from which these commercial summaries are derived are mostly not publicly available. As a consequence, it becomes hard to exchange, evaluate, and compare the output of summarization systems in an objective manner. In order to facilitate accessibility of entity summaries it is necessary to identify the principal properties of entity summarization systems, create a corresponding data model, and to adhere to the best practices of Web APIs.

P. Cimiano et al. (Eds.): ICWE 2015, LNCS 9114, pp. 430–446, 2015.
DOI: 10.1007/978-3-319-19890-3_28

To enable clients to easily consume the summaries of entities from different summarization services we propose SUMMA, a uniform lightweight interface design based on a request/response vocabulary and the Representational State Transfer (REST) interaction paradigm. The approach enables to combine a diverse selection of summarization approaches on a single Web site and to switch from one service to another even during user navigation. The proposed API aligns with the Linked Data interaction model. Our approach treats the summarization approach itself as a black box while preserving the possibility to define the required parameters of an entity summarization system in a uniform manner. Thus clients can easily substitute or combine the employed entity summarization system in a plug-and-play fashion. Existing summarization systems can easily offer summaries with the SUMMA API in addition to their deployed user interfaces. In order to facilitate evaluation, the API aims at supporting researchers and practitioners in the following settings:

- *Quantitative Evaluation*: SUMMA enables consumers to retrieve summaries of entities in their most pure form (a ranked list of RDF statements). As such, reverse engineering tasks such as disambiguating strings to URIs (e.g. mapping "`recompense`" to http://dbpedia.org/ontology/award) are not needed for automatic comparison of different approaches.
- *Qualitative Evaluation*: Commonly, multiple systems are placed next to each other in qualitative evaluation settings for entity summarization and subjects are asked to choose one or more. To support this, a SUMMA client can present summaries of multiple different summarization systems in a uniform way. In this way it can be ensured that style elements (such as pictures, borders, colors, etc.) do not play a significant role in the subjects' decision making process.
- *A/B Testing*: Evaluation with A/B testing is commonly applied in industry settings. SUMMA enables to change the technology that produces summaries while the user interface stays the same. By tracking the interaction with each variant it is possible to compare the effects of technology changes.

For our approach, we provide an open-source reference implementation and deployment as well as an empirical evaluation. The source code of the reference implementation as well as a deployment are available online. In the empirical evaluation, we measure the overlap of our established requirements with the features of real-world systems. This study includes interfaces of well known search engines like Bing, Google, and Yahoo as well as entity presentations of well-known news portals.

The remainder of this paper is organized as follows: In Section 2 we present a requirement analysis for a uniform entity summarization API as well as the API itself. In Section 3 we introduce the implementation as well as its deployment. The evaluation in Section 4 introduces an empirical study that assesses the applicability of our approach to real-world user interfaces. In Section 5 we analyze the most related approaches and outline how we differ from them. Section 6 concludes the paper and provides an outlook on our future work.

2 SUMMA API Definition

In its most basic form, a summary of an entity can be produced by two given parameters:

URI A URI that identifies the entity.
k A number k that defines an upper limit of how many facts about the entity should be presented.

While it is obvious that there is a need for an unambiguous reference to the entity, it could be argued that a summary could also be specified by a given compression level. For example, we could specify that 30 % of all facts about the given entity should be contained in the summary. In this respect, we would like to point out that concise presentations (for which we are aiming) are better declared with an upper limit rather than a given percentage. This is due to the fact that knowledge bases commonly cover well documented entities as well as a long tail of sparsely documented ones: in this respect, 30 % could mean 20,000 facts for some entities while only 3 for others.

When defining a uniform interface for entity summarization, various specifics that are inherent to the definition of RDF itself have to be considered as well. This ranges from the possibility to have multiple labels for vocabulary or data items to the more complex summaries that consider n-ary relations[1] or enable full property chains. Next to these features, other requirements include the grouping of statements and the restriction to a predefined set of properties. In the following we present an overview of all further requirements of the API:

Languages In many knowledge bases, labels in different languages for resources and properties are commonly available. In order to avoid multiple requests or queries to different knowledge sources we find it necessary to include labels of one or more languages in the output of the summary.
Multi-hop Search Space It might be necessary (think of n-ary relations or reification) or interesting to include statements in the summary that do not directly involve the targeted entity but are connected through one or more hops. For example, a max hop parameter of 1 (default) only considers statements where the entity is either in the subject or object role, while a max hop of 2 could cover facts that are still about the entity but are modeled via an n-ary relation. Further hops are possible.
Property Restriction A summary can be targeted to a predefined set of properties. An example would be to restrict the summary of a movie to {`dbpedia:starring`} or {`dbpedia:starring, dbpedia:director`}. This feature is very useful if the interface has reserved space for specific features such as a map presenting geolocations or pictures. These features can be retrieved in a separate request.

[1] "Defining N-ary Relations on the Semantic Web" – http://www.w3.org/TR/swbp-n-aryRelations

Statement Groups Rather than ranking statements only individually, the system could form groups or clusters of statements and, if applicable, provide names for these groups.

These features and their compositions enable very specific views on entities although they are still abstract enough to be applicable to any knowledge base, be it encyclopedic or proprietary. In general, also the following considerations have to be taken into account:

Resources/Literals Linking to other resources (i.e., URI identified entities) supports exploration aspects while textual information (represented as literals) satisfies more the information need about the specific entity. For visualization purposes any resource URI included in a summary has to be accompanied by a literal description which enables a user-friendly rendering of the resource. Clients consuming the summary can therefore ignore the resource URIs and only use literals for presentation.

Outgoing/Incoming Links For any unidirectional relation `:x :link :y` a second relation can be established in the way `:y :link_by :x`. In many cases displaying such a relation in a summary of `:y` makes sense as it covers information about it. Knowledge bases such as DBpedia, Freebase, and Wikidata enable to retrieve incoming links from other resources of the respective knowledge base with queries. For Linked Data in general, many incoming links can be retrieved with crawls as provided e.g. by the BTC [5].

Our approach consists of two main components with a strong interplay:

- The **SUMMA Vocabulary** can be used to frame summary requests, which can be submitted to a summarization engine. Servers can interpret the given parameters in the request and produce result sets with the vocabulary that are in accordance to the provided parameters.
- The description of the **RESTful Web Service** provides a clear guideline for the interplay between summary consumers and producers.

In the following, we first introduce the *SUMMA Vocabulary* and thereafter the *RESTful Web Service* interaction guideline.

2.1 SUMMA Vocabulary

The *SUMMA Vocabulary* offers various parameters that help to configure and represent a summary. During the design of the vocabulary we took the above considerations into account. An overview of the vocabulary is depicted in Figure 1. In the following we introduce all classes and properties:

Summary This class describes the abstract concept of a summary of an entity. The URIs of instances of this class are constructed with all query parameters.

SummaryGroup This class describes a group of statements. The entity summarization system does not necessarily have to produce groups. If groups are formed, it is completely up to the summarization system what is meant by them or if they come with a label in the desired language.

entity This predicate with domain Summary and range `rdfs:Resource` points to the entity that is summarized. As an example, the object of this property could be a DBpedia or Freebase entity. This property is mandatory for the API.

topK This property defines the maximum number of statements that are being returned. This property is mandatory for the API.

statement This property with domain Summary and range `rdf:Statement` attaches statements to a summary in the response context.

maxHops This property defines the maximum number of hops in the graph the interface is able to represent. The default value is set to 1, which means that all properties in the immediate vicinity of the focused entity are being considered.

path This property enables to include the full paths in the returned statements of the summary. For each statement that is included in the summary that does not directly involve the focused entity, a path that shows how the current statement relates to the entity needs to be provided. This situation can occur if the maximum of hops is greater than 1. For more than 2 hops, this relation is needed multiple times until the object statement of path includes a triple that contains the focused entity.

language This property defines the languages in which the output literals should be available. We recommend to use a fixed vocabulary like RFC 4646[2] for this.

group The group property enables summaries to form groups of statements. Attaching a group directly to a statement enables clients to ignore the property if present but not supported.

fixedProperty If there is already some background knowledge on the summarizer's side about the underlying data structure it can request properties that it wants to show in any case. Multiple different properties can be defined in this way and thereby restricting the output to the defined set of properties.

Next to this vocabulary, we make use of the vRank[3] vocabulary [9], XSD[4] and OWL[5]. The vRank vocabulary is necessary to include the computed scores of each statement by the summarization service. A summary typically includes more than one `rdf:Statement`. Although in some syntaxes constructs such as `summa:statement [ a rdf:Statement; ...], [ a rdf:Statement; ... ] .` could be mistaken for ordered lists, the group of statements is returned as a set. To determine an order between the statements additional information is required. In this respect, we choose to use vRank rather than `rdf:List` to enable summarization systems to publish the ranking scores. Listing 1.1 exemplifies the use of the vRank vocabulary in combination with a reified `rdf:Statement`.

[2] RFC 4646 – http://www.ietf.org/rfc/rfc4646.txt

[3] vRank – http://purl.org/voc/vrank#

[4] XSD – http://www.w3.org/2001/XMLSchema#

[5] OWL – http://www.w3.org/2002/07/owl#

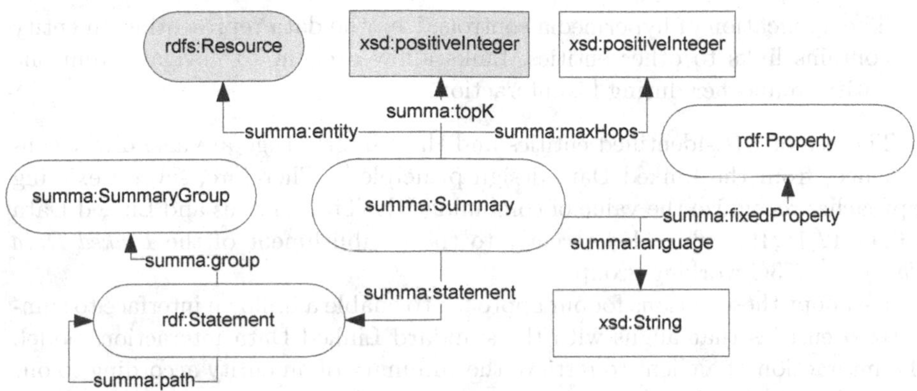

Fig. 1. The SUMMA Vocabulary. Mandatory parameters in grey

The *SUMMA Vocabulary* is published at http://purl.org/voc/summa/. Exemplary usages of the vocabulary are shown in Listing 1.2 for input and in Listing 1.3 for output (see Appendix A).

Listing 1.1. Example for using vRank for ranking a RDF Statement.

```


[ rdf:type rdf:Statement ;
  rdf:subject dbpedia:Barack_Obama ;
  rdf:predicate dbpedia-owl:birthDate ;
  rdf:object  "1961-08-04"^^xsd:date ;
  vrank:hasRank [ vrank:rankValue "33.11"^^xsd:float] ]
```

Listing 1.2. Example for a summary request that is sent via POST (namespaces omitted).

```
[ a :Summary;
:entity dbpedia:Barack_Obama ;
  :topK "2"^^xsd:positiveInteger ;
  :language "en" ;
  :maxHops "2"^^xsd:positiveInteger ;
  :fixedProperty dbpedia-owl:birthDate ;
  :fixedProperty dbpedia-owl:birthPlace . ]
```

2.2 RESTful Web Service

According to the Richardson maturity model [8] REST is identified as the interaction between a client and a server based on three principles:

- The use of URI-identified entities.
- The use of a constrained set of operations, i. e., the HTTP methods, to access and manipulate entity representations.

- The application of hypermedia controls, i. e., the data representing an entity contains links to other entities. Links allow a client to navigate from one entity to another during his interaction.

The use of URI-identified entities and their interlinkage are also direct consequences from the Linked Data design principles[6]. Therefore, several existing approaches recognize the value of combining RESTful services and Linked Data [2,6,11,12,18,19], which led recently to the establishment of the *Linked Data Platform*[7] W3C working group.

We adopt these notions for our approach to enable a uniform interface to summarized entities that aligns with the standard Linked Data interaction model. The interaction of a client to retrieve the summary of an entity according to our approach is depicted in Figure 2 and works as follows:

1. A client can send a summary request for an entity to a server offering a summarization service via an HTTP POST request.
2. The response to the request contains the summarized entity in its payload, as well as a URI in the location header field that identifies the created summary.
3. The client can use the URI of the summary for further lookups of the summary via HTTP GET.

Since summaries can be looked up via HTTP GET, we enable simple caching mechanisms for the clients. The URI of the summary also enables to include direct links in other web resources to the summary. To construct the URI that identifies a given summary, we adopt the approach from [11], where the URI contains key/value pairs that correspond to the properties in the original summary request. Note, that the server does not have to store the created summaries for allowing the direct lookup but can calculate the summary on-the-fly for GET requests as well as by interpreting the key/value pairs in the URI.

A client can also skip the first interaction via POST and anticipate how the URI of a summary would look like as the lookups are computed in the same way as the original POST request. However, we keep both interaction schemes in place in order to enable a clear formulation of a request as well as a clean cacheable lookup.

3 Implementation

The SUMMA API definition is based on Web standards such as the HTTP protocol and RDF. Summary producers as well as consumers can be implemented in a variety of programming languages. However, in order to demonstrate feasibility and to facilitate adoption, we provide a reference implementation based on Java Jersey[8] (server) and JavaScript (client).

---

[6] http://www.w3.org/DesignIssues/LinkedData.html

[7] http://www.w3.org/2012/ldp/charter

[8] Jersey – https://jersey.java.net/

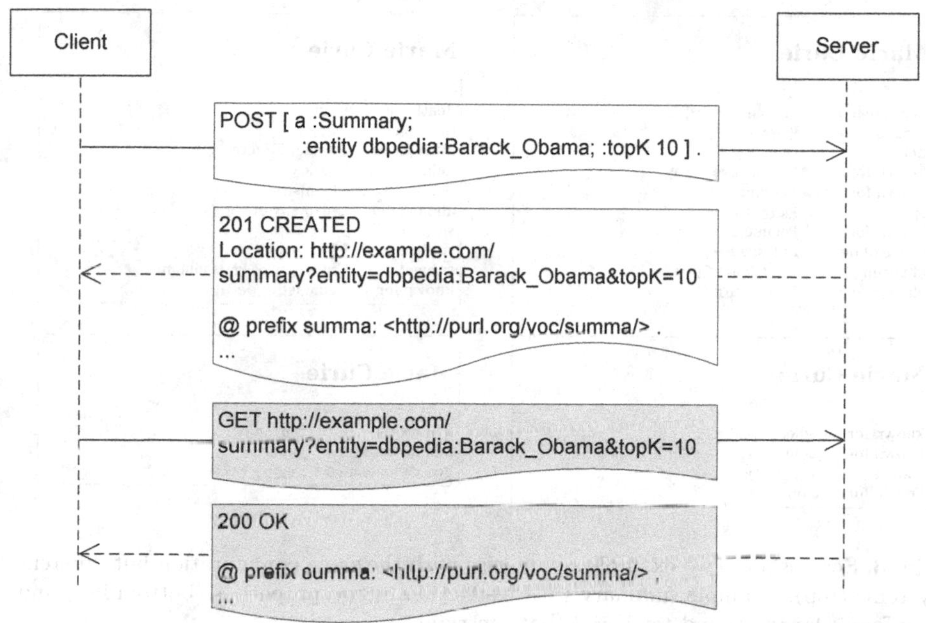

Fig. 2. Messages for first interaction: white. Messages for second interaction: grey

summaServer The summaServer application is an Apache Tomcat server application that fully implements the SUMMA API. It provides a naïve summarization method for DBpedia entities. This summarization method ranks objects (only outgoing links are considered) based on the number of their incoming links within Wikipedia. All necessary information (including the link counts) is available via the official DBpedia SPARQL endpoint.[9] The source code of summaServer application is published at https://github.com/athalhammer/summaServer and licensed with GPLv3.[10] Deployments of the summaServer application and another summarization method [15] can be found at the following addresses:

- http://km.aifb.kit.edu/summaServer
- http://km.aifb.kit.edu/summa

summaClient The summaClient library is a lightweight JavaScript application that interacts with servers that implement the SUMMA API. It enables visualization and interaction with the results of multiple summarization engines at a single Web page (see Figure 3). The source code of the summaClient library is published at https://github.com/athalhammer/summaClient and licensed with GPLv3. A deployment of the summaClient library can be found at http://people.aifb.kit.edu/ath/summaClient/.

[9] DBpedia SPARQL endpoint – http://dbpedia.org/sparql
[10] GPLv3 – http://www.gnu.org/copyleft/gpl.html

Marie Curie

death place	France
birth place	Warsaw
field	Chemistry
known for	Radioactive decay
known for	Radium
spouse	Pierre Curie
known for	Polonium
cause of death	Aplastic anemia
children	Irène Joliot-Curie
alma mater	ESPCI ParisTech

Marie Curie

death place	France
birth place	Warsaw
birth place	Russian Empire
field	Physics
field	Chemistry
alma mater	University of Paris
subject	1867 births
subject	1934 deaths
subject	University of Paris alumni
known for	Radioactive decay

Marie Curie

known for	Radioactive decay
known for	Radium
spouse	Pierre Curie
known for	Polonium

Marie Curie

lieu de décès	France
lieu de naissance	Varsovie
lieu de naissance	Empire russe

Fig. 3. Screenshot: Two example summaries with the same configuration but different systems (top). Example summary with restriction to two properties (bottom left) and a different language and $topK = 3$ (bottom right).

4 Evaluation

In our evaluation we inspect interfaces from well-known providers such as the Google Knowledge Graph (GKG) [10], Microsoft Bing Satori/Snapshots [7], or Yahoo Knowledge [17]. We assess whether the expressibility of these interfaces could be served via the SUMMA API. Thus, we provide empirical evidence about the general applicability of the API for any kind of RDF entity summary.

For our evaluation, we select the entity summarization systems of the three major search engines (mentioned above) as well as systems from the Alexa Top News sites[11] that offer factual knowledge about entities. We select two of the top 25 news portals offering infoboxes about entities. These are Forbes[12] and BBC news[13]. Our hypothesis is that the defined API could serve all of these interfaces, thus potentially enabling them to switch between different entity summarization services without changing their layout. For this, we focus on five entities from diverse domains: Spain, Dirk Nowitzki, Ramones, SAP, Inglourious Basterds. These entities are representatives for a country, a person (or athlete), a band, a company (or organization), and a movie. We have to note that, at the time of writing, BBC only supports summaries of countries, Forbes supports only summaries of persons and organizations, and Yahoo only supports persons and movies. For these systems our insights will be focused on the supported types. Some of the analyzed systems use also fixed schema patterns or a combination of

[11] http://www.alexa.com/topsites/category/Top/News
[12] Forbes, e. g. http://www.forbes.com/profile/dirk-nowitzki/
[13] BBC news, e. g. http://www.bbc.com/news/world-europe-17944958

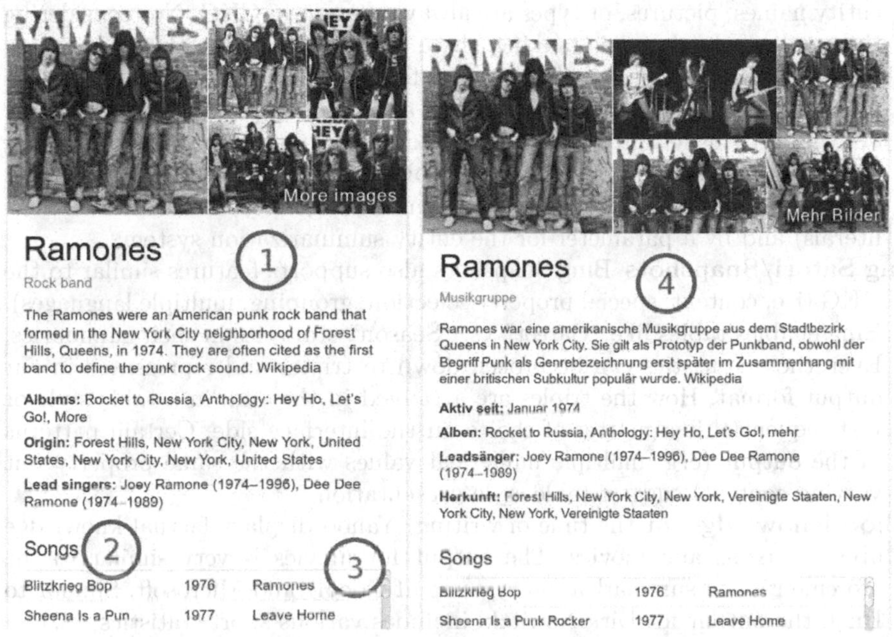

Fig. 4. Screenshot of the GKG representation of the "Ramones": 1) Specific properties such as the type and the Wikipedia description are always there (Property Restriction). 2) Several statements are gathered in a group named "Songs" (Statement Groups). 3) N-ary relations - in this case title, year, and album - are supported (Multi-hop Search Space). 4) The summary is offered in multiple languages (Languages).

entity-specific summaries and schema patterns. We assume that even with using only fixed schema patterns the content requirements at the interface remain the same. This still suits our evaluation scenario as our main goal is to decouple summary and presentation: the way in which the summaries were generated is not relevant (black box). We also tried to include research prototypes into our evaluation. However, although this research field is very active recently [1,13, 14,16,20], our system SUMMARUM [15] is currently the only research prototype that is available online.

In the following we will analyze for each of the above-mentioned interfaces on whether they would be able to consume data from the API without changing their layout. We assume both, the URI of the entity and the maximum number of facts (topK) as standard parameters. Figure 4 demonstrates the analysis of the interfaces.

Google Knowledge Graph For some facts, GKG uses contexts about the data items (e.g. Wikipedia abstracts, population numbers, dates of marriage, release year of album, role names, etc.). In RDF, these contexts are represented as n-ary relations. Our API supports summaries over such constructs with the multi-hop search space. Further, certain properties such as entity names, pictures, or types are always present in GKG. Not considering the result of the dynamic ranking, these properties can be addressed with a separate summary request that involves fixed properties. Further, GKG supports special groups of statements, such as a the group of albums of a band. We support this feature by enabling to add a group to each statement by the entity summarization system. GKG is able to adapt the interface to different languages. This is supported by RDF (multi-linguality of `rdfs:label`, i. e. literals) and by a parameter for the entity summarization system.

Bing Satori/Snapshots Bing Snapshots also supports features similar to the GKG (i. e. context, special property selection, grouping, multiple languages). Bing enables tables like "Career" vs. "Season" statistics in their summaries. Even these statistics can be broken down to triples and represented in our output format. How the triples are arranged in the end, in a table style or just sequential is a matter of choice on the interface side. Certain patterns in the output (e. g. multiple numerical values with the same property but varying context) suggest table-style presentation.

Yahoo Knowledge At the time of writing, Yahoo displays factual knowledge about persons and movies. The output for movies is very similar to the aforementioned summarization systems of Google and Microsoft. Similar to Bing, the output for Dirk Nowitzki includes various sport statistics. Like in Bing, this data can be covered by our output model. Entities representing other persons are very similar to the standard output of Google and Bing. Yahoo currently does not offer summaries in multiple languages.

Forbes The interface shows basic properties of persons and companies in a key-value style. Selected properties such as the label or a picture are present for any entity. Similar to GKG, for some properties the context is added, e. g. "As of June 2014". For companies, Forbes forms two groups. "At a Glace" and "Forbes Lists". All these features are supported by our defined data model. Like Yahoo, Forbes does not offer their summaries in different language versions.

BBC news The BBC news portal includes summaries of countries only. Like in Forbes, this data contains mainly key-value pairs and is easy to be represented with our output format. Also presenting multi-hop information is needed, as the presented images have a caption that is also shown. BBC does not define groups of facts and does not offer other languages than English.

The complete results of the evaluation are presented in Table 1. Overall we found that all the requirements that these interfaces need in order to offer all their functionality can be fulfilled by the proposed API.

5 Related Work

For the related work we distinguish between two kinds of approaches: systems that add an additional layer between a SPARQL endpoint and data consumers (as such serving as direct data providers) and approaches that introduce formalisms that enable ranked views on Linked Data.

Table 1. Requirements per interface. The checked features are supported by the specific interface, the crossed ones are not required.

Features	Google	Bing	Yahoo	Forbes	BBC
Languages	✓	✓	×	×	×
Multi-hop Search Space	✓	✓	✓	✓	✓
Property Restriction	✓	✓	✓	✓	✓
Statement Groups	✓	✓	✓	✓	×

Pubby[14] is used to add an intuitive interface to SPARQL endpoints. It enables to consume entities and ontologies on a per-concept basis directly in various formats. For entities, it considers attached literal values in all available languages as well as all incoming and outgoing relations. In general, Pubby implements the following pattern for resources described by their `URI`:

```
SELECT * WHERE {{<URI> ?p ?v . } UNION { ?v ?p <URI> . }}
```

This may result in a large set of facts that are directly related to the currently browsed entity. For machines as well as for human consumers all information about an entity is provided. In our approach we extend this mechanism by various configurable properties (e. g. maximum number of statements) that enable client interfaces to retrieve distilled versions of entities in a uniform way.

The Linked Data API[15] adds a RESTful layer on SPARQL endpoints. It enables developers who are not familiar with SPARQL or RDF in general to access SPARQL endpoints in a RESTful manner. As an example, it enables to represent selectors and filter options as request parameters in the following form: `http://example.com/university?country=UK&max-noStudents=10000`. Potential response formats include JSON, XML, RDF/XML, and Turtle. The Elda[16] system provides a reference implementation for the Linked Data API definition. The Linked Data API and SUMMA both add an additional RESTful layer on top of SPARQL endpoints. However, the rationales of both approaches are complementary: while the Linked Data API tries to make part of the SPARQL feature set more intuitively accessible using REST, we are focusing on defining a uniform RESTful interface that enables multiple services to provide concise views on the same entity in a uniform way.

Bizer et al. define Fresnel,[17] a vocabulary for selecting and formatting RDF data [3]. The vocabulary is supported by RDF browsers such as Longwell[18], Piggy Bank[19], or IsaViz[20]. It is devided into two main components, lenses and formats. While the lenses help on selecting which content should be presented the formats define the style in which the selected content should be presented.

[14] Pubby – http://wifo5-03.informatik.uni-mannheim.de/pubby/
[15] Linked Data API – https://code.google.com/p/linked-data-api/
[16] Elda – https://github.com/epimorphics/elda
[17] Fresnel – http://www.w3.org/2005/04/fresnel-info/manual/
[18] Longwell – http://simile.mit.edu/wiki/Longwell
[19] Piggy Bank – http://simile.mit.edu/wiki/Piggy_Bank
[20] IsaViz – http://www.w3.org/2001/r1/IsaViz/

Our work is mostly related to Fresnel Lenses: The predicates `fresnel:instance LenDomain` and `fresnel:classLensDomain` define the levels on which the lenses can be applied. The predicates `fresnel:showProperties` and `fresnel:hide Properties` define which properties of the instance or class are commonly shown and in which order. The order is defined with `rdf:List`. Moreover, the Fresnel Selector Language (FSL)[21] enables to define further restrictions, for example which properties of connected entities should be shown (e. g., `foaf:name`). The `fresnel:instanceLensDomain` in combination with the `fresnel:showProp erties` predicate and FSL enable quite particular decisions on which triples are included in the output and which are not. Eventually, however, covering specific triples for the output with Fresnel involves complex FSL patterns and, more importantly, still only provides a description of which information should be presented but not the information itself. Summarizing entities with respect to their individual particularities is possible but the lens descriptions would already cover much of the actual data. The remaining information such as the objects and all labels would have to be gathered at a different place. In other words, SUMMA provides access to entity-specific data while Fresnel, more abstractly, was designed to operate on the class level and to provide views. In fact, there are efforts to identify the most common properties per DBpedia class with surveys and crowd sourcing and to publish them as Fresnel lenses [1]. The SUMMA API could be used for interpreting such class-level lenses and for delivering the respective content accordingly. In addition, the SUMMA API explicitly enables entity-specific summaries that are beyond the scope of Fresnel.

Federated SPARQL queries[22] offer the possibility to query knowledge bases distributed over multiple endpoints with a single query. Summaries that are computed offline could be stored at one endpoint while the actual summarized knowledge base that contains further information (such as labels) is available at a different endpoint. A single federated query would retrieve triples specific to an entity while the SPARQL `LIMIT` clause would enable different summary sizes. As in our approach, the endpoint for the summary can be easily exchanged. Summaries that are computed online (e. g., depending on the user's geolocation, language, the time of the day, etc.) can get too complex in order to be retrieved with SPARQL queries of any kind. Intermediately storing the result in an endpoint in order to make it retrievable with SPARQL adds significant overhead to a process that needs to be performed in a range of few 100 milliseconds.

Roa-Valverde et al. introduce a vocabulary for sharing ranking computations over RDF data [9]. This enables to provide detailed information about ranking computations in RDF. Properties include ranking values and time stamps as well as algorithm descriptions and configurations. We use the vRank vocabulary in order to provide ranking values to the client interface.

Harth introduces VisiNav [4], a system that allows for new interaction principles within the Web of Data. The system is based on four key concepts that support search and navigation: *Keyword Search*, *Object Focus*, *Path Traversal*,

---

[21] Fresnel Selector Langauge (FSL) – http://www.w3.org/2005/04/fresnel-info/fsl/

[22] SPARQL 1.1 Federated Query – http://www.w3.org/TR/sparql11-federated-query/

and *Facet Selection*. Our API clearly supports *Object Focus* as it is specifically designed to deliver entity-specific summaries. We also support *Path Traversal* and *Facet Selection*. However, the two concepts become quite similar if you do not distinguish between incoming and outgoing connections. More specifically, we slightly reinterpret the *Facet Selection* concept as we form the union rather than the intersection ("... the user can reformulate the query and obtain increasingly specific result sets" [4]). Like our approach VisiNav also provides ranked views on data. VisiNav strongly couples the user interface and the back end. As such, the rankings and views on the data can only be displayed with the VisiNav system. In this paper, we provide a way to enable decoupling of the interfaces and their respective ranking back end.

In conclusion, we can state that the idea of browsing Linked Data with concise presentations is well established and real-world applications are taking up this idea [7,10,17]. To the best of our knowledge, all previous research approaches for presenting RDF data in a concise way are based on schema patterns and do not provide the data itself. In this paper we introduce a novel approach that supports the evaluation, exchange, and comparison of entity summaries in a lightweight way.

6 Conclusion and Future Work

We introduced an API that enables entity summarization systems to publish summaries in a uniform way. Further, it enables consumers to access summaries of Linked Data entities from a multitude of summarization services through a single lookup mechanism. Our empirical evaluation shows that the SUMMA API could be applied to already existing commercial systems while the reference implementations provide evidence for feasibility and facilitate adoption. The SUMMA API for comparison and evaluation is already deployed for use in industry and research.

We are currently in the process of implementing SUMMA adapters to other summarization systems. In addition, we plan to implement a portal where different entity summarization services are gathered and described also in accordance to their non-functional properties, e. g. response time and availability. Also, context-specific and personalized summaries that lead to the extensions of the SUMMA API are currently ongoing work.

Acknowledgments. The research leading to these results has received funding from the European Union Seventh Framework Programme (FP7/2007-2013) under grant agreement no. 611346 and by the German Federal Ministry of Education and Research (BMBF) within the Software Campus project "SumOn" (grant no. 01IS12051).

A Appendix

Listing 1.3. Example response in Turtle (common namespaces omitted).

```
@prefix : <http://purl.org/voc/summa/>.
@prefix vrank: <http://purl.org/voc/vrank#>.
@prefix dbpedia: <http://dbpedia.org/resource/>.
@prefix dbpedia-owl: <http://dbpedia.org/ontology/>.

<http://ex.com/summary?
entity=dbpedia:Barack_Obama&topK=2&language=en&maxHops=2&
fixedProperty=dbpedia:birthDate,dbpedia:birthPlace>
  a :Summary ;
:entity dbpedia:Barack_Obama ;
:topK "2"^^xsd:Integer ;
:language "en" ;
:maxHops "2"^^xsd:Integer ;
:fixedProperty dbpedia-owl:birthDate ;
:fixedProperty dbpedia-owl:birthPlace ;
:statement

[ rdf:type rdf:Statement ;
  rdf:subject dbpedia:Barack_Obama ;
  rdf:predicate dbpedia-owl:birthDate ;
  rdf:object "1961-08-04"^^xsd:date ;
  :group <http://ex.com/group/12> ;
  vrank:hasRank [ vrank:rankValue "3213.101"^^xsd:float ] ] ,

[ rdf:type rdf:Statement ;
  rdf:subject dbpedia:Honolulu ;
  rdf:predicate dbpedia-owl:areaCode ;
  rdf:object "808"@en ;
  vrank:hasRank [ vrank:rankValue "2323.433"^^xsd:float ] ;
  :path [ rdf:type rdf:Statement ;
    rdf:subject dbpedia:Barack_Obama ;
    rdf:predicate dbpedia-owl:birthPlace ;
    rdf:object dbpedia:Honolulu ] ] .

<http://ex.com/summary?
entity=dbpedia:Barack_Obama&topK=2&language=en&maxHops=2&
fixedProperty=dbpedia:birthDate,dbpedia:birthPlace#id>
  owl:sameAs dbpedia:Barack_Obama .

dbpedia:Barack_Obama rdfs:label "Barack Obama"@en .
dbpedia-owl:birthDate rdfs:label "birth date"@en .
dbpedia:Honolulu rdfs:label "Honolulu"@en .
dbpedia-owl:areaCode rdfs:label "area code"@en .
dbpedia-owl:birthPlace rdfs:label "birth place"@en .
<http://ex.com/group/12> rdfs:label "Important Dates"@en .
```

References

1. Assaf, A., Atemezing, G.A., Troncy, R., Cabrio, E.: What are the important properties of an entity? In: Presutti, V., Blomqvist, E., Troncy, R., Sack, H., Papadakis, I., Tordai, A. (eds.) ESWC Satellite Events 2014. LNCS, vol. 8798, pp. 190–194. Springer, Heidelberg (2014)
2. Berners-Lee, T.: Read-Write Linked Data, August 2009. http://www.w3.org/DesignIssues/ReadWriteLinkedData.html (accessed November 26, 2012)
3. Pietriga, E., Bizer, C., Karger, D.R., Lee, R.: Fresnel: a browser-independent presentation vocabulary for RDF. In: Cruz, I., Decker, S., Allemang, D., Preist, C., Schwabe, D., Mika, P., Uschold, M., Aroyo, L.M. (eds.) ISWC 2006. LNCS, vol. 4273, pp. 158–171. Springer, Heidelberg (2006)
4. Harth, A.: VisiNav: A system for visual search and navigation on web data. Web Semantics: Science, Services and Agents on the World Wide Web **8**(4) (2010)
5. Käfer, T., Harth, A.: Billion Triples Challenge data set (2014). http://km.aifb.kit.edu/projects/btc-2014/
6. Krummenacher, R., Norton, B., Marte, A.: Towards linked open services and processes. In: Berre, A.J., Gómez-Pérez, A., Tutschku, K., Fensel, D. (eds.) FIS 2010. LNCS, vol. 6369, pp. 68–77. Springer, Heidelberg (2010)
7. Qian, R.: Understand your world with bing (2013). http://blogs.bing.com/search/2013/03/21/understand-your-world-with-bing/
8. Richardson, L., Ruby, S.: RESTful Web Services. O'Reilly Media (2007)
9. Roa-Valverde, A., Thalhammer, A., Toma, I., Sicilia, M.-A.: Towards a formal model for sharing and reusing ranking computations. In: Proc. of the 6th Intl. Workshop on Ranking in Databases In conjunction with VLDB 2012 (2012)
10. Singhal, A.: Introducing the knowledge graph: things, not strings (2012). http://googleblog.blogspot.com/2012/05/introducing-knowledge-graph-things-not.html
11. Speiser, S., Harth, A.: Integrating Linked Data and services with Linked Data Services. In: Antoniou, G., Grobelnik, M., Simperl, E., Parsia, B., Plexousakis, D., De Leenheer, P., Pan, J. (eds.) ESWC 2011, Part I. LNCS, vol. 6643, pp. 170–184. Springer, Heidelberg (2011)
12. Stadtmüller, S., Speiser, S., Harth, A., Studer, R.: Data-fu: a language and an interpreter for interaction with read/write linked data. In: Conference on World Wide Web (2013)
13. Sydow, M., Pikua, M., Schenkel, R.: The notion of diversity in graphical entity summarisation on semantic knowledge graphs. Journal of Intelligent Information Systems, 1–41 (2013)
14. Thalhammer, A., Knuth, M., Sack, H.: Evaluating entity summarization using a game-based ground truth. In: Cudré-Mauroux, P., Heflin, J., Sirin, E., Tudorache, T., Euzenat, J., Hauswirth, M., Parreira, J.X., Hendler, J., Schreiber, G., Bernstein, A., Blomqvist, E. (eds.) ISWC 2012, Part II. LNCS, vol. 7650, pp. 350–361. Springer, Heidelberg (2012)
15. Thalhammer, A., Rettinger, A.: Browsing DBpedia entities with summaries. In: Presutti, V., Blomqvist, E., Troncy, R., Sack, H., Papadakis, I., Tordai, A. (eds.) ESWC Satellite Events 2014. LNCS, vol. 8798, pp. 511–515. Springer, Heidelberg (2014)
16. Thalhammer, A., Toma, I., Roa-Valverde, A.J., Fensel, D.: Leveraging usage data for linked data movie entity summarization. In: Proc. of the 2nd Int. Ws. on Usage Analysis and the Web of Data (USEWOD2012) Co-Located with WWW 2012, Lyon, France, 2012, vol. abs/1204.2718 (2012)

17. Torzec, N.: Yahoo's knowledge graph (2014). http://semtechbizsj2014.semanticweb.com/sessionPop.cfm?confid=82&proposalid=6452
18. Verborgh, R., Steiner, T., Van Deursen, D., Van de Walle, R., Valls, J.G.: Efficient runtime service discovery and consumption with hyperlinked RESTdesc. In: Proceedings of the 7th International Conference on Next Generation Web Services Practices (NWeSP 2011), Salamanca, Spain (2011)
19. Wilde, E.: REST and RDF granularity (2009). http://dret.typepad.com/dretblog/2009/05/rest-and-rdf-granularity.html
20. Danyun, X., Cheng, G., Yuzhong, Q.: Preferences in wikipedia abstracts: Empirical findings and implications for automatic entity summarization. Inf. Process. Manage. **50**(2), 284–296 (2014)

Quality and Accessibility Aspects of Web Applications

Two Factor Authentication Made Easy

Alex Q. Chen[1(✉)] and Weihan Goh[2]

[1] School of Computer Engineering, Nanyang Technological University, Singapore, Singapore
alexqchen@acm.org
[2] Singapore Institute of Technology, Singapore, Singapore
Weihan.Goh@SingaporeTech.edu.sg

Abstract. Authentication on the Web is a challenge that can have a negative effect on user experience if it becomes overly complicated and cumbersome. This experience is even more crucial for older and visually impaired users due to their functional abilities. Web applications typically authenticate users by requesting for information that only the user knows (e.g. password). To enhance security, two-factor authentication (2FA) are increasingly implemented, which require the user to manually transfer information between 2FA devices and the Web application. This process can impose usability barriers and stress on human's memory. This paper proposes a technique to mitigate such issues by using wearables as the 2FA device, and to allow authentication information to be transferred seamlessly and automatically from the device to the Web application. From our preliminary results, older users found our approach less stressful on the human's memory and easier to use.

1 Introduction

The presence of adversaries with capabilities to coerce users into surrendering their unique proofs of knowledge (e.g. passwords) strengthens the need for a two-factor authentication (2FA) model. However, providing 2FA on the Web imposes barriers to accessibility and usability. The 2FA model requires users to possess memory abilities and the capability to work between devices or applications to transfer the 2FA information. These requirements impose barriers for visual and motor impaired users; especially for the elderly due to deteriorating memory [18] and cognitive functioning capabilities. These issues suggest a gap to improve the implementation of 2FA in Web applications.

These days, older people are under higher social pressure from family members, such as their children and grandchildren, to use mobile devices [15]. A study on issues faced by old people when using mobile phones suggested that older people use technology only when no alternative method of communication is available [13]. More can be done to help these people adapt to technological advancements, especially when coping with important tasks like security. This paper proposes an approach that incorporates wearables to handle the second factor authentication in Web applications. Our approach is designed to reduce

P. Cimiano et al. (Eds.): ICWE 2015, LNCS 9114, pp. 449–458, 2015.
DOI: 10.1007/978-3-319-19890-3_29

interaction between devices and users, improving the usability but maintaining soundness and integrity of the security aspects. Our aim is to improve the usability of the 2FA model rather than reinventing it.

2 Accessing Secure Websites

Analysing online security techniques from the usability perspective exposes weaknesses of the system from the human factors element. Often, security processes use widgets as components to construct the user interface of a Web application. Web widgets are components of a Web page that affect how the content is presented and which content to present. Frequently, users are left unaware that changes in the content have taken place [7]. These findings make elderly users vulnerable, as they feel confused when dynamic content is orchestrated without the user's awareness. Highlighting the importance of keeping elderly users aware of the changes to content. Furthermore, introducing new functions to older adults can be intimidating [23]. Older adults are often not confident when using mobile phones. When met with problems, they prefer to recognise and solve them.

Elderly people are less receptive to technology and computer applications than those of younger age. Computer anxiety, fluid intelligence, and crystallised intelligence are important predictors of acceptance for older adults [9]. One of the main factors includes memory performance directly affected by social context [8]. The feeling of being stereotyped by ageing and memory has direct influence on the relationship between age and memory performance.

Service providers are adopting 2FA solutions because it can improve security at lower user effort [21], and improvements to existing security challenges, such as reinventing CAPTCHA to make it accessible to visually impaired users [12] has also been attempted. However, [12] only attempts to make CAPTCHA more accessible rather than improving the model so that it will integrate with existing systems and reduce the overall barriers imposed by the CAPTCHA model. Others attempted to address the accessibility barriers from another perspective. One study designed a generic tool to assist older users when interacting with dynamic Web content [14]. This technique provides help to the user when using a Web page, but it is not capable to deal with dynamic contents that span across multiple devices like what is required of the 2FA model.

Few studies have investigated alternative approaches to implement existing 2FA models on Web applications for the elderly, and the visually and motor impaired. A study covering mobile application trends for the ageing society reported that, commonly, only products and services to provide telemonitoring and alarm systems, user location, and tracking devices are developed [19]. More need to be done to make online security systems and models more intuitive for the ageing and disabled community.

3 Authentication Models

Authentication information can be classified as either (1) what the user knows, (2) what the user possesses, or (3) what the user inherently is [22]. The first is

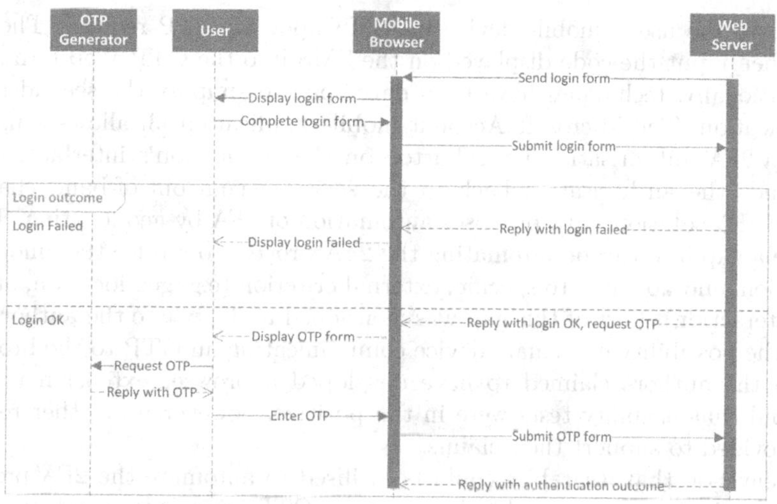

Fig. 1. A high-level overview of a Web 2FA sequence

ubiquitous - information like passwords falls into such category, and its effectiveness relies upon the non-disclosure of the proof of knowledge. However, with the advent of highly sophisticated coercion techniques and data breaches resulting in the leakage of such information [2,4], plus bad user practices (e.g. selecting weak passwords [1]), this is no longer the case.

Web service providers (e.g. Google, Dropbox, etc.) have increasingly adopted two-factor authentication (2FA) to mitigate weaknesses in the single-factor authentication model. This typically comes in the form of requesting for a one-time password (OTP) - a single-use code obtainable from the user's OTP device, upon successful completion of the first factor authentication. After receiving a correct OTP, the verifier is entitled to believe that the user has possession of the device capable of generating or receiving the OTP. While there can be many ways to generate OTPs [5,20], there are Informational and Internet Standard RFCs published detailing standard OTP algorithms [16,17].

Figure 1 gives a high-level overview of a generic Web 2FA authentication sequence. The difference between 2FA and single-factor authentication can be seen here. The first few transactions up to the submission of credentials via the login form remain the same for both. However, for 2FA, depending on the outcome of the first factor authentication, the Web application would either return a login failure, or request for an OTP. For the latter, the user would submit an OTP obtained from the OTP generator to the Web application.

One of the most common forms of an OTP generator is an OTP token device (see Figure 2a). Such device would require the user to generate an OTP, then input the digits displayed on the device's screen into the OTP Web form. Another option is to use SMS-based OTPs, where the OTP is generated by a third-party, and sent to the user's mobile device via SMS upon an OTP request. The user would then input the code displayed on the SMS into the OTP Web form.

Additionally, techniques have been developed to simplify the second factor authentication. The Microsoft Account mobile application [3] allows a user to trigger a 2FA authorisation via a button on the application's interface, which then sends the authorisation back to the server via an out-of-band channel. Another 2FA solution, [11], proposes automation of 2FA by geo-location. There is hence a gap in terms of automating the 2FA process to reduce the amount of interaction, and not tie it to specific, external criterion (e.g. geo-location, out-of-band interaction). Part of this gap was mentioned in [6], where the authors discussed the possibility of a smart device communicating an OTP to the browser. Though the authors claimed to have developed a browser extension to that effect and that usability tests were in the positive, however no further reports were provided to support their claims.

We envision that wearables could be utilised to automate the 2FA process. In such an instance, a wearable becomes an OTP generator, producing and returning an OTP when requested by a securely paired device. From there, the OTP is passed to the verifier over the network. This concept can be extended to mobile Web applications, and the entire process can thus be automated, without being tied to external criterion, but instead to the proximity and secure pairing between the wearable and mobile device accessing the Web application.

4 User Evaluation Setup

To better understand existing 2FA implementations and our proposed approach, a collection of phantom applications was developed to simulate how standard 2FA are implemented, and how our approach is perceived. We investigated how participants performed when accessing sensitive data on the Web using a smart mobile phone. The evaluation consists of three investigations: (1) the OTP is sent via a SMS; (2) the OTP is generated by a token device; and (3) using our approach to automate the 2FA process via a wearable device (smart watch). Seven Southeast Asian Chinese participants were recruited: 3 within the University and 4 from the neighbourhood residents' committees. Their age ranged between 51 and 72 years old, with a mean age of 59, of which 4 are males and 3 females. All participants are right-handed and have never used a smart watch prior to the investigations. All participants have experience with smart phones and proof of knowledge authentication (e.g. passwords), but only six have used proof of possession authentication (second factor authentication).

Three sets of phantom applications were developed to simulate the generation and processing of 2FA information. Each set of applications consists of two parts - an Android mobile Web browser application implementing a WebView instance, and a phantom Web application residing on a server within the University. The phantom mobile browser provides an interface between its code and the Web application, accessible via JavaScript, and statistics such as number of clicks and elapsed time for the evaluation were gathered. The phantom browser

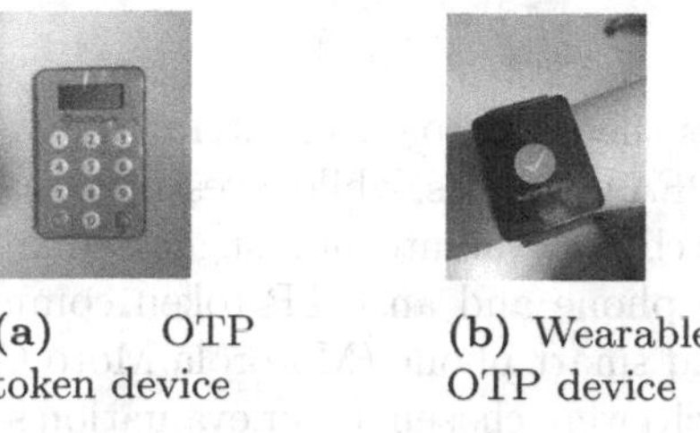

(a) OTP token device (b) Wearable OTP device

Fig. 2. OTP generators

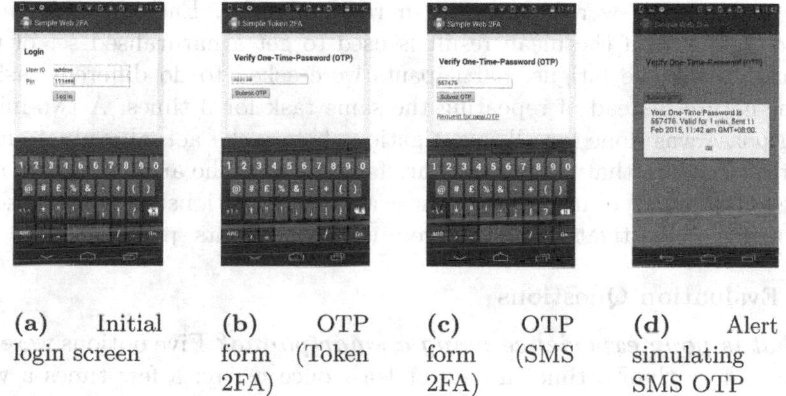

(a) Initial login screen (b) OTP form (Token 2FA) (c) OTP form (SMS 2FA) (d) Alert simulating SMS OTP

Fig. 3. Web application components for the Token and SMS investigations

for the SMS investigation is capable of generating alerts simulating SMS OTP messages (see Figure 3d) and synchronising of the OTP with the phantom Web application. The phantom applications for the Token investigation, on the other hand, do not verify the OTP submitted, though participants were not told of this and are asked to key in the digits exactly as shown on the OTP token (token used is shown in Figure 2a). For the Watch investigation, a listener was implemented on the wearable to trigger a short vibration and display a notification (see Figure 2b) once an OTP request message is received from the phantom browser. The entire second factor authentication does not require participants to transfer the OTP.

In all investigations, phantom mobile Web applications simulate a 2FA-capable online banking site. Each of them has similar login screens (see Figure 3a) to request for a user identification and PIN. Once the entire authentication process is completed successfully, the participant is shown a menu screen displaying common online banking transactions. Their difference, however, is in the second factor authentication - for the Token and SMS investigations, participants are required to enter the OTP as shown on the token and simulated SMS respectively into the OTP forms (see Figures 3b and 3c), while for the Watch investigation, no user intervention is required for the second factor authentication.

User Studies

Investigation (1) requires the participant to interact with a smart mobile phone when using mainstream 2FA processes, while investigation (3) uses a smart mobile phone and a smart watch to evaluate our suggested approach. Investigation (2) uses a smart mobile phone and an OTP token commonly issued by banks in Singapore. An Android smart phone (Motorola Moto G 2nd Generation) and smart watch (LG G Watch) were chosen in our evaluation setup due to their availability and compatibility. The smart phone has a 5-inch 720x1280 touch screen, and the smart watch a 1.65-inch touch screen. All evaluations assume that the smart phone and smart watch were set up and paired for the tests.

The user studies were conducted in random order. Each investigation is repeated 3 times and the mean result is used to get a naturalised set of measurements. To reduce fatigue, participants were asked to do different tasks of the same nature instead of repeating the same task for 3 times. A two-minute training phase was done for all investigations before the actual evaluation was conducted to ensure that participants are familiar with the authentication models. The following set of initial and post evaluation questions were also asked to understand the investigations better from the participants' perspective.

Initial Evaluation Questions

A1 ***What is your experience using a smartphone?*** Five options were provided: More than 3 times a day; at least once a day; a few times a week; rarely; no experience.

A2 ***What is your experience using a smart watch?*** Similarly, 5 options were provided: More than 3 times a day; at least once a day; a few times a week; rarely; no experience.

A3 ***Have you used the 2FA model before? If yes, discuss your experience with the 2FA model?***

Post-Evaluation Questions

C1 ***Of the 3 investigations conducted, which investigation do you prefer? Explain the reasons for your selection.***

C2 ***Using a 7-point Likert scale, rate how confident are you with the method used by the investigations. From the perspective whether the method is secure and sound.*** The participant will rate the 3 investigations individually; 1 is the worst and 7 very secure and sound.

C3 ***Of the 3 investigations conducted, you specified that investigation X method is the technique you feel most confident with. Explain the reasons for your selection.***

C4 ***Using a 7-point Likert scale, rate the ease of use for the 3 investigations.*** The participant will rate the 3 investigations individually; 1 is difficult to use and 7 very easy to use.

C5 ***During the evaluation, did you feel it was memory stressful in any part? If yes, could you name the investigation(s) from the 3 investigations conducted and describe why you felt that way.***

C6 ***Using a 7-point Likert scale, rate the level of stressfulness on your memory for the 3 investigations.*** The participant will rate the 3 investigations individually; 1 not stressful at all and 7 very stressful on the human's memory.

C7 ***Do you have any remarks or suggestions for the pilot study?***

5 Preliminary Results

This paper unveils our first steps to overcome the barriers in 2FA-enabled Web applications. In the evaluation, we examined two existing approaches for 2FA in Web applications, against our approach to address the 2FA-imposed barriers users faced. An improvement to accept 2FA when using our approach was noticed. During the evaluation, the performance and usability of all three investigations' approaches were measured. In Table 1, the median time taken to complete the authentication process for the three investigations show that our technique is the quickest. On seven occasions, users took > 1 attempts to pass through the first factor authentication, though most first factor challenge was successfully completed in one attempt. Table 1 also shows the median number of attempts to login and OTP generation for each investigation.

Older participants were noticed to tap more than once to select the textfields while entering their user identification and PIN. This behaviour is especially so when the participant attempts to switch between the user identification textfield and the PIN textfield. Often, most participants seem uncertain what to do with the OTP provided during their first attempt in each investigations (this observation is only noticed for the SMS and Token investigation).

In the post-evaluation questions, 5 participants chose the Watch investigation as their preferred choice (see Table 1) because the approach is simple and automatic. They commented that if the security aspects are dealt with properly, they would prefer to use it. Such responses were surprising, as none of them had used a smart watch before. Two participants mentioned that they do not know how the smart watch works. They were concerned about the process and security aspects, and they also raised concerns about the smart watch being hacked.

Table 1. Evaluation's measurements and participants choices

	SMS	Token	Watch
Evaluation Measurements			
Median time taken (seconds)	17.05	16.08	0.27
Median number of login attempts	1	1	1
Median number of OTP generated	1	1	1
Post-Evaluation Questions			
Preferred investigation (C1)	2	0	5
Confidence levels σ	1.13	1.53	1.83
Ease of Use levels σ	2.06	1.63	0.53
Stress on human's memory levels σ	2.23	1.99	0.76
Most stressful on human's memory (C5)	1	6	0

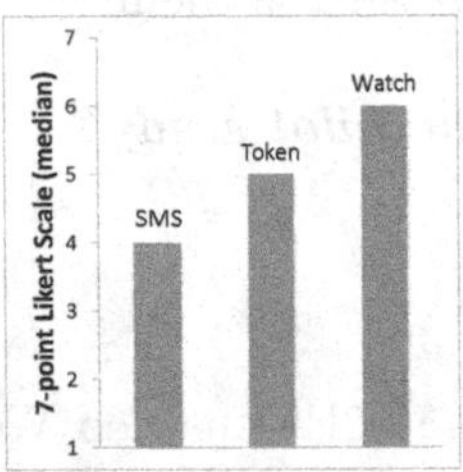

(a) Confidence level. The larger the value the more confident with the approach.

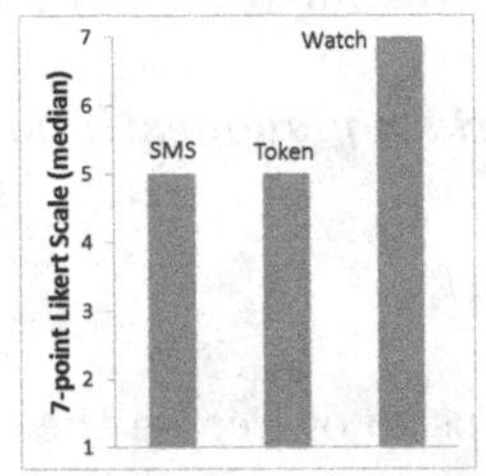

(b) Ease of use. The larger the value the easier the approach was to use.

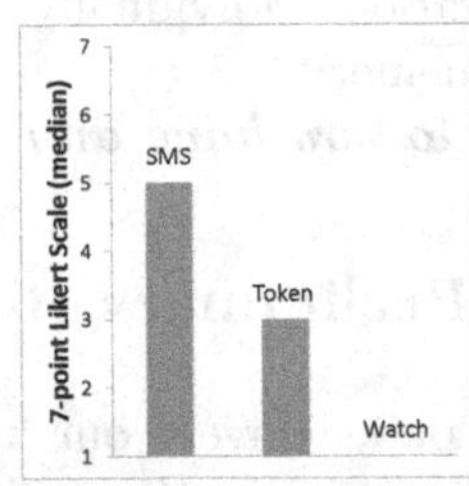

(c) Stress on human memory. The smaller the value the less stress on human memory.

Fig. 4. Post evaluation questions

The participants were asked in question C5 to choose which investigation that they feel was the most stressful on the human's memory. Six participants chose the SMS investigation, while one chose the Token investigation. The outlier participant (72 years old) was also the only participant that has never used 2FA prior to the evaluation. He raised issues with the small font size on the token's display and the contrast that makes it difficult to read. He also commented that the time provided to read the OTP is too short, thus, he has to request for a new OTP 3 times. The participants were asked to rate the three investigations based on their confidence of the technique (Post-evaluation question C2), the ease of using the technique (Post-evaluation question C4), and how stressful were the techniques on the human's memory (Post-evaluation question C6). The ratings were collected using a 7-point Likert scale and their median results are present in Figure 4 with the standard deviation listed in Table 1.

Users are more confident with the Watch approach than the token and SMS approaches (see Figure 4a). They also found it easier to use the Watch technique (see Figure 4b). Among the investigations, Figure 4c shows that the Watch technique was the least stressful on the human's memory. However, three participants commented that due to the lack of understanding of the security aspects of the Watch technique, they would fall back on the Token approach.

6 Discussion and Future Works

Participants were noted to be wary over the security aspects of the Watch approach, but strongly supported the concepts since it makes the process simpler and quicker, while maintaining the additional security. Further investigation discovered 4 participants describing the Token to be more trustworthy because the banks issued them. Interestingly, none of the participants realised that for the Token investigation, the phantom Web application could not verify whether an

OTP submitted is the same as the one generated by the token. This finding suggests that these participants placed their trust in authority over the technique applied, thus emphasising the need for a new approach, such as ours, to minimise the false sense of security. Finally, at least 3 participants raised their concerns that carrying around security tokens is troublesome and without it one cannot complete the authentication process. These concerns fall in line with the findings reported in [10], which strengthens our case for an alternative approach.

The investigations focus primarily on usability aspects of the Web applications using the three 2FA approaches. As such, security was not implemented in the applications and neither was the complete implementation of the 2FA techniques. Issues with equipment set up and connectivity are also not taken into account. Limitations by the devices and operating systems are also not considered. The small sample size of 7 participants only highlights the main issues of our proposed approach. However, this pilot study is meant only to be a feasibility investigation.

More can be done to improve our approach and minimise the barriers older people faced when challenged with security issues. A more thorough evaluation over a larger pool of participants is suggested for future work. User issues pertaining to Byzantine failures between the devices' communication are also encouraged to be examined. In addition to that, stronger 2FA authentication protocols can be investigated for use in conjunction with our proposed second factor authentication approach.

7 Conclusion

Our investigation revealed that users found existing 2FA-enabled Web applications are not without flaws. Older adults found 2FA tokens can be difficult to read and use, while the SMS technique is stressful on the human's memory. To overcome the usability barriers imposed by the 2FA model, we proposed an alternative approach to automate the 2FA process through the use of wearables, to remove the need for users to be the information conveyor. This reduction in user interaction to complete the 2FA process has proven to be less stressful on the human's memory and makes the experience easier.

Besides benefiting older adults, this pilot study could also assist visually and motor impaired users to adapt to security imposed on mobile devices. We envision that our approach can provide an alternative for second factor authentication; targeting older adults and those less functionally capable, to make 2FA-enabled Web applications more seamless by a broader group of users.

References

1. business password analysis - trustwave. https://gsr.trustwave.com/topics/business-password-analysis/2014-business-password-analysis/ (accessed February 13, 2015)
2. Is leaked? https://isleaked.com/ (accessed: February 13, 2015)
3. Microsoft account - android apps on google play. https://play.google.com/store/apps/details?id=com.microsoft.msa.authenticator&hl=en (accessed: February 13, 2015)

4. Security alerts from knowem: Gmail hack. https://securityalert.knowem.com/ (accessed: February 13, 2015)
5. Alghathbar, K., Mahmoud, H.: Noisy password scheme: A new one time password system. In: Canadian Conference on Electrical and Computer Engineering, CCECE 2009, pp. 841–846 (2009)
6. Ben-David, A., Berkman, O., Matias, Y., Patel, S., Paya, C., Yung, M.: Contextual OTP: Mitigating Emerging Man-in-the-Middle Attacks with Wireless Hardware Tokens. In: Bao, F., Samarati, P., Zhou, J. (eds.) ACNS 2012. LNCS, vol. 7341, pp. 30–47. Springer, Heidelberg (2012)
7. Brown, A., Jay, C., Chen, A.Q., Harper, S.: The Uptake of Web 2.0 Technologies, and Its Impact On Visually Disabled Users. Universal Access in the Information Society **11**, 185–199 (2012)
8. Chasteen, A.L., Bhattacharyya, S., Horhota, M., Tam, R., Hasher, L.: How feelings of stereotype threat influence older adults' memory performance. Experimental Aging Research **31**(3), 235–260 (2005)
9. Czaja, S.J., Charness, N., Fisk, A.D., Hertzog, C., Nair, S.N., Rogers, W.A., Sharit, J.: Factors predicting the use of technology: Findings from the center for research and education on aging and technology enhancement (create). Psychology and Aging **21**(2), 333–352 (2006)
10. De Cristofaro, E., Du, H., Freudiger, J., Norcie, G.: A comparative usability study of Two-Factor authentication (2014). http://arxiv.org/abs/1309.5344
11. Grim, E.: Two-factor authentication systems and methods (2013). https://www.google.com/patents/US8578454, US Patent 8,578 454
12. Holman, J., Lazar, J., Feng, J.H., D'Arcy, J.: Developing usable CAPTCHAs for blind users. In: Proceedings of the 9th International ACM SIGACCESS Conference on Computers and Accessibility, ASSETS 2007 pp. 245–246. ACM (2007)
13. Kurniawan, S.: Older people and mobile phones: A multi-method investigation. International Journal of Human-Computer Studies **66**(12), 889–901 (2008)
14. Lunn, D., Harper, S.: Providing assistance to older users of dynamic web content. Computers in Human Behavior **27**(6), 2098–2107 (2011)
15. Mallenius, S., Rossi, M., Tuunainen, V.K.: Factors affecting the adoption and use of mobile devices and services by elderly people-results from a pilot study. Paper presented at the 6th Annual Global Mobility Roundtable, Los Angeles, CA (2007)
16. M'Raihi, D., Bellare, M., Hoornaert, F., Naccache, D., Ranen, O.: RFC 4226-HOTP: An HMAC-Based One-Time Password Algorithm (2005)
17. M'Raihi, D., Machani, S., Pei, M., Rydell, J.: RFC 6238-TOTP: Time-Based One-Time Password Algorithm (2011)
18. Perlmutter, M., Mitchell, D.B.: The Appearance and Disappearance of Age Differences in Adult Memory, vol. 8, ch. 7, pp. 127–144. Springer, US (1982)
19. Plaza, I., Martín, L., Martin, S., Medrano, C.: Mobile applications in an aging society: Status and trends. Journal of Systems and Software **84**(11), 1977–1988 (2011)
20. Rubin, A.D.: Independent one-time passwords. In: Proceedings of the 5th Conference on USENIX UNIX Security Symposium, SSYM 1995, vol. 5, pp. 15–15. USENIX Association (1995)
21. Sasse, M.A., Palmer, C.C.: Protecting you. IEEE Security & Privacy **12**(1), 11–13 (2014)
22. Shirey, R.: Rfc 4949-internet security glossary (2007)
23. Zhou, J., Rau, P.L., Salvendy, G.: Age-Related Difference In The Use Of Mobile Phones. Universal Access in the Information Society **13**(4), 401–413 (2014)

Web Applications Composition and Mashups

REST Web Service Description for Graph-Based Service Discovery

Rosa Alarcon, Rodrigo Saffie, Nikolas Bravo(✉), and Javiera Cabello

Computer Science Department, Pontificia Universidad Catolica de Chile, Santiago, Chile
ralarcon@ing.puc.cl, {rasaffie,ngbravo,jacabell}@uc.cl

Abstract. Unlike WSDL/SOAP based services, REST services lack a widely accepted service description since it increases the coupling between clients and servers, hampering service evolution. In practice, REST services are described through informal, ad-hoc and semi-structured documents, often written in natural language, which worsens the level of coupling. Most of the few REST service descriptions currently proposed follow an operation-centric approach with unclear additional benefits for developers and consumers. We propose a service description model focused on hypermedia allowing the generation of a graph that captures state transitions in an *activity layer*; we also capture resource, transition, and response semantics in a *semantic layer*. Using graph queries we traverse the graph and facilitate service discovery and composition. The service model was implemented as Microdata-based annotations, and a JSON description. A prototype was developed using Neo4J, and a set of real Web APIs was chosen to illustrate our approach.

1 Introduction

The Web is an Internet-scale distributed *hypermedia* that provides a uniform way of accessing information through embedding *action* controls within the information retrieved from remote sites (i.e. *representations*). These features have made possible for the Web to evolve from a content-distribution platform to an application platform, and nowadays, to a distributed services platform, where functionality can be integrated into new services for massive consumption.

There are two main approaches to provide Web services. One is based on WSDL/SOAP standards and is pervasive in B2B scenarios; the other called REST services or Web APIs (Application Programmable Interfaces) is pervasive in the Web. Web APIs are a popular way of providing *service connectors* while avoiding the complexity of the stack of technologies and standards that SOAP-based Web services require. In practice, Web APIs present some drawbacks such as RPC calls tunneled over HTTP, and limited service evolvability since they introduce coupling between clients and servers by means of *service descriptions* written in natural language, typically provided as HTML pages. REST services, on the other hand, require additional constraints such as content-negotiation, the appropriate use of network protocol and hypermedia (to include links and

P. Cimiano et al. (Eds.): ICWE 2015, LNCS 9114, pp. 461–478, 2015.
DOI: 10.1007/978-3-319-19890-3_30

controls in the service response) so that clients know the actions available at any point in the interaction. In practice, most of the self-called REST services lack some constraints (mainly hypermedia).

REST Web services discovery and composition consider the provision of services destined to be consumed by other services (e.g. a machine-client). Like Web APIs, REST services are generally accompanied with informal documents (e.g. HTML pages), written in natural language, describing the resource types at the application domain level and the set of *entry points* (static URIs), URI patterns, authentication mechanisms, supported protocols, operations, media types and samples requests and responses. However, service discovery and composition still lack an extensible and universal strategy that facilitates machines to interact with services [1]. HTML documentation written in natural language not only introduces high coupling between clients and servers as well as unexpected complexity (e.g. the description fails to present clearly the assumptions, configurations, requirements, preconditions or secondary effects) but also makes impossible for machines to make sense on the usage of the service interface. Hence, a common practice is the provision of libraries that embed the service description rules and hide its complexity. Such approach typically becomes outdated, inaccurate or unclear forcing machine-client developers to engage in trial-error phases to allow client recovery. Under these conditions, automatic service discovery and composition are hard to support or plainly impossible to automate. The main difficulty is that current descriptions require human intelligence to understand the service's expectations about the client. Few attempts have been made to propose machine-readable REST service descriptions. Moreover, such descriptions fail to accommodate the REST architectural constraints, and focus extensively on the operations provided by the services instead of the flexibility that the REST uniform interface offers, such as the hypermedia constraint.

In this paper we present RAD (REST API Description), which is a service description that considers the REST uniform interface constraint, that is, identification of resources; manipulation of resources through representations, self-descriptive messages, and hypermedia as the engine of application state. We present two implementations of RAD: in JSON, allowing the generation of human-readable documentation; and in Microdata that can be embedded in the HTML service description. Both implementations are based on the RAD metamodel which considers an *activity* layer, capturing resource state transition mechanism, and a *semantic* layer, which captures the resource's and transition's semantics.

The result is a graph that captures both the underlying graph of state transitions modeled by a REST service and the semantic graph associated. Service discovery consists of discovering the nodes corresponding to entrypoints, and service composition corresponds to the discovery of paths in the graph that allows satisfying certain goal. We described three popular Web APIs using RAD, and we implemented a couple of use cases to demonstrate the feasibility of our approach.

2 Background

REST, the *Representational State Transfer* [2], is an architectural style that determines a set of constraints such as functional extensibility (i.e. code on demand) and stateless client-server interaction (i.e. the server shall not store context information about the client, which remains responsible for storing such information and providing it as-needed in the request messages). It also requires interaction visibility, metadata providing cache control information, and a uniform interface between *architectural* components. The uniform interface requires the identification of resources, manipulation of resources through representations, self-descriptive messages, and hypermedia as the engine of application state.

Data is the central element in REST, being the *resource* the basic information abstraction, which has associated a *resource identifier*, minted by the resource author. A resource is a conceptual mapping to a set of entities or *representations* whose format is negotiable. Resources are abstract and are realized by representations making unnecessary to classify resources according to a type or implementation (since the representation is served to the client, whereas the resource itself is hidden by the server). Representations comprise data and *metadata* (about the data, the *representation*, the *resource*, etc.) indicating the current or intended resource state, or the value of other resource.

Client's requests include *control data*, a resource identifier, and an optional representation. Servers perform actions on the resources according to the request and provide a response that may include control and resource metadata, and an optional representation. Control data determines the purpose of the message (requested action, response meaning) and the actions of intermediary components such as caches. Representation's data format is known as *media type*; representations convey the set of state transitions available for a resource at a determined state in the form of links and controls (from now on just links). User agents (e.g. Web browsers) behave as engines that move a Web application from one state to the next according to the end-user actions (i.e. by executing a link or control).

3 Related Work

3.1 REST Service Description

Some languages have been proposed to create REST services descriptions. For instance, WSDL [3] is a standardized language used to describe WSDL/SOAP services and REST services, it follows an RPC operation-oriented style and do not support hypermedia, content negotiation or metadata. The Web Application Description Language (WADL) [4] describes REST services in terms of *resources*, URI patterns, media types and schemas of the expected *request* and *response*. Representations support parameters with links to other resources. However WADL do not provide support for link discovery or URI generation for new resources, ignoring the dynamic nature of REST. The resulting model is operation-centric and introduces additional complexity with unclear benefits for both human and machine-clients. These descriptions are kept independently from the service so that maintainability issues may arise [5].

Semantic descriptions have been also proposed for REST services. For instance, RESTdesc [6] expresses REST service functionality in RDF, including a request's preconditions, postconditions, and quantifiers. Resources are typed and links semantics are also considered. The description itself is highly flexible and complex; it requires knowing the resources' URIs in advance in order to perform advanced queries. Less complex approaches are SA-REST [7] and hREST [8]; both propose a new resource (e.g. an HTML document) containing the input and output parameters, methods, and URIs, written as RDFa property value pairs (SA-REST) [9] or Microformat annotations [10] (hREST). Links and forms are supported but dynamic discovery of resources following such links is not considered. Microformats are not extensible and they require specific processing rules for each domain [1], [11]. RDFa solves Microformats limitations since they are generic and can be combined and extended, however, it is more complex [12].

RESTdoc [13] is a framework based on Microformats including adapters to transform the data to RDFS automatically, reducing the development complexity. RESTdoc also includes machine-learning techniques to infer the graph of interlinked resources from the user behavior; however, it ignores hypermedia. [14] and [15] go a step forward and infer the semantic model from request-response samples or from the HTML documentation pages. Like RESTdoc, they infer relationships between resources but ignore the hypermedia links. Hydra [16] is a vocabulary that allows providers to describe a Web API in terms of a main entry point, and a set of resources (classes), properties, and links, which are CRUD operations over HTTP. Resources and link semantics are handled as references to external entities following a JSON-based format (JSON-LD). Hydra moves a step forward in recognizing the relevance of hypermedia, but introduces non-REST concepts such as CRUD operations.

Industry approaches such as RAML, the RESTful API Modeling Language (http://raml.org/), proposes a YAML and JSON open specification for describing practical REST APIs that are human and machine readable, but leaving out the issues related to the REST hypermedia constraint. Similar approaches are proposed by Swagger (http://swagger.io/), Blueprint (https://apiblueprint.org/), and Mashape (https://www.mashape.com/), which provide either a resource-oriented description with various degrees of completeness or even a framework that generate mockup code. Again, neither of them includes hypermedia support nor a strategy for service discovery or composition.

3.2 REST Service Discovery

REST Service Discovery techniques follow either a directory-based (services are registered in either a centralized or a decentralized directory), directory less (a P2P overlay structure plays the directory role) or a hybrid infrastructure. The discovery, selection or matchmaking itself is performed by similarity algorithms that follow a logic-based (reasoning) or non-logic based (data mining, graph matching, schema matching, text similarity, among others) approach [17].

Nowadays the de facto service open central repository is *ProgrammableWeb* (www.programmableweb.com) with 12.889 Web APIs (retrieved by February 2015). It hosts self-declared REST APIs, but in practice many of them partially satisfy the REST constraints. The lack of a standardized service description for REST has a negative effect on global service discovery. For instance, in Programmable Web, services search is based on keyword match of service's description and metadata. Service discovery is a difficult task due to its large number, diversity of names and technical aspects.

In [18] a model for naming service interfaces from their objects, processes and business logic is proposed. An iterative search engine that filters the results based on the resources relationships enables service search. In [19], the goal is to discover similar service's operations. WADL described services are stored in a centralized repository; service's operation match is based on common parameters, using WordNet [20] to exploit similarity of synonyms. Another centralized repository, iServe, stores hREST described services as graphs interconnecting resources and parameters at the semantic level [21]. Service discovery consists of identifying resources and parameters using SPARQL queries on the graph.

A REST service is a collection of addressable and dereferenceable resources interconnected by links that determine the possible state transition for each resource. Hence, we focus on entrypoint discovery, that is, the links that make possible for a user to perform an action and achieve a goal.

3.3 REST Service Composition

Dynamic service composition is an important challenge, it requires generating a composition plan (control flow), selecting the required Web services, coordinating conversations between services (including data flow) and executing the composition at runtime. It is typically based on business constraints, on planning with user interaction, on context, on the data model, or on the service's signatures (inputs and outputs). REST service composition research focuses on orchestration, with JOpera [22] being the most complete framework. JOpera models control and data flow visually, and an engine executes the resulting composed service. In [23], control flow is specified in SPARQL and services could be WSDL/SOAP-based endpoints or REST resources. In [24] control and data flow is modeled and implemented using a Petri Net whereas interaction and communication with the resources themselves is mediated by a service description called ReLL [25]. ReLL is based on a hypermedia-oriented metamodel where links are considered first-class citizens. In [26] the BPEL composition language is extended through specialized activities that make possible resources invocation. Hypermedia constraint is implemented via inspection of responses. Data-Fu [27] is an RDF-based declarative language that allows developers to express service interaction as HTTP operations to change resource's state and retrieve response's data (which is an RDF graph). The hypermedia constraint is not considered and only links between resources (at the semantic level) can be discovered.

4 An Illustrative Example

In order to illustrate our approach we present the following scenario consisting of three Web APIs:

Spotify https://developer.spotify.com/web-api/,
Songkick https://www.songkick.com/developer/,
Uber https://developer.uber.com/.

The Spotify API provides access to its music streaming service's catalogue. The Songkick API provides access to a live music database with information about upcoming and past concerts as well as setlists. The Uber API allows the user to ask for transportation service types, price and an estimated time of arrival (ETA), as well as user's profile and activity. Let's consider the following use cases for service discovery and composition:

Discovery:
A user wants to find a given artist's playlists.
Such goal can be satisfied by GET operations (i.e. reflection) on resources provided by both Songkick, which provides the setlist for a given musical event, and Spotify, which provides an artists top tracks. The interfaces of both services are quite different from one another, so it is necessary to rely on its semantics rather than the syntactic description.

Composition:
A user wants to attend a concert but her favorite band is not in town. She decides to go to a similar artist's concert and needs to know the venues where they will play as well as information of taxis to reach the event.
Such goal can be satisfied by GET operations (i.e. retrieve artists and concerts data, consult on prices, etc.) on resources provided by Songkick or Spotify (similar artists, venues). The interaction with Uber requires to consult for fares and ETA (through GET) in order to request a taxi later. Again, interfaces are heterogeneous and service's semantics will make possible to discover the appropriate resource. In addition, it is necessary to follow various steps and support a failure path (e.g. there may be no similar band, the venue could be too far away in distance or time, or the cab price may be too high or too late). Also it is important to consider the semantics of the operations since a resource may include several links in their representation corresponding to various GETs, POSTs, etc., each with different semantics.

In the following sections we present RAD, a metamodel for REST service description, as well as the implementation of the described scenarios.

5 REST API Description (RAD)

The proposed metamodel is depicted in Figure 1. We separate modeling elements into two layers: a semantic layer that captures semantics of resources, parameters and actions; and an activity layer that is responsible for modeling REST service's interaction components. In our model, links are first-class citizens and represent an `Action` at a business level of abstraction.

`Actions` are key in our model, they are associated to operations, that is, a network protocol method (e.g. HTTP GET, HTTP POST, etc.) applied to a given `Resource`. Actions semantics or `Action Concept` denotes the intention of the operation at a business level (e.g. to buy, to rent, to search, etc.). Actions encapsulate state transition operational details and semantics. For instance, depending on the parameters, the resources https://api.spotify.com/v1/search will respond a GET operation with representations of *albums*, *artists*, *playlist* and *tracks*. At an operational level (i.e. HTTP), these invocations are the same, but at a business level they convey different semantics. Hence, we model each request as a separate link that is composed of one operation (e.g. an HTTP method) performed on a resource, requiring (or not) a set of parameters. An operation execution produces a response or representation that corresponds to a concept.

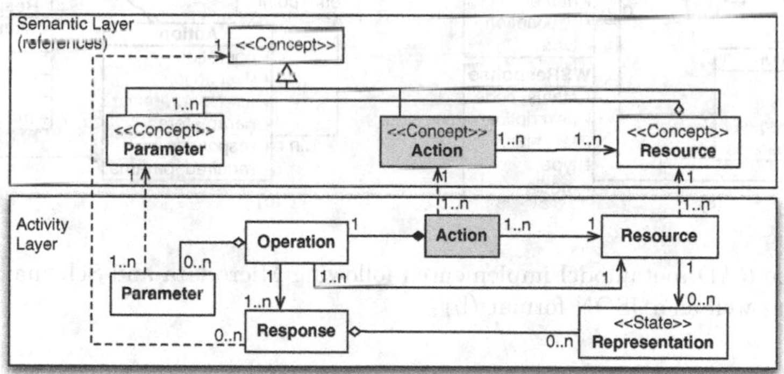

Fig. 1. The RAD metamodel includes a semantic and an activity layer

5.1 Semantic Annotations in RAD

Semantic descriptions have clear advantages; they can be integrated and used in combination with HTML hierarchy enriching its elements and attributes. Lightweight data formats such as Microformats and Microdata are easy to use by developers, they do not interfere with the information to be presented to the end user, and they can be understood by machines, while keeping all the information in one file. Semantic descriptions seem to be a good alternative to facilitate the automation of service discovery and invocation. In our model, Parameters, Resources and Links are associated with a corresponding Concept that models the semantics of each element in a Semantic Layer.

In our case, we extended Schema.org (http://schema.org/) data model with a set of concepts following the RAD metamodel as seen in Figure 2(a). We also implemented the RAD metamodel using JSON for creating a separate and complete description of a RESTful web service as seen in Figure 2(b). In this case, we do not determine the representation of such semantics but follow the SAWSDL/SAREST [28] approach in that the binding between elements in each layer is achieved through a model reference attribute that links and maps service elements to the semantic model.

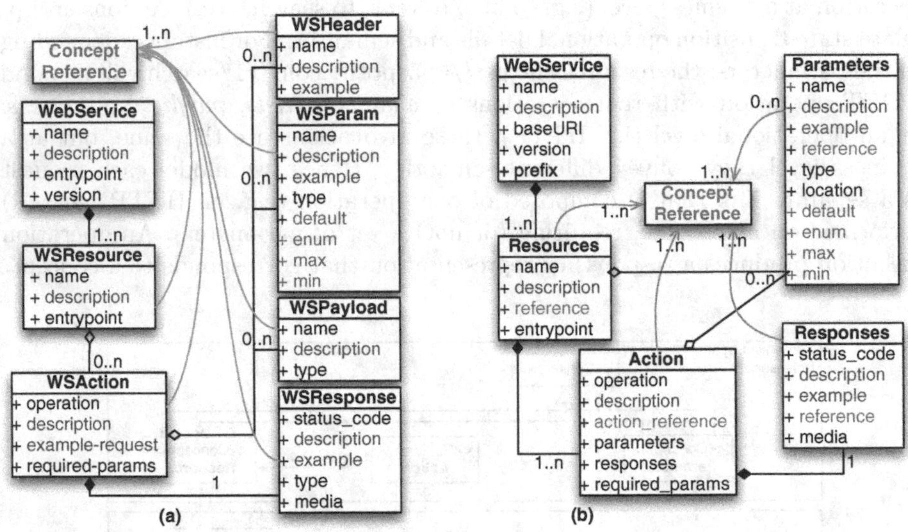

Fig. 2. The RAD metamodel implemented following Microdata and Schema.org principles (a) as well as a JSON format (b)

5.2 RAD Implementation in Microdata

We implemented the RAD metamodel using Microdata for the semantic annotation of RESTful web services (i.e. HTML description pages). Microdata is simple, flexible and more adaptable than other techniques for semantic description such as Microformats or RDFa [1]. Microdata syntax is simple and includes the *itemscope*, *itemtype* and *itemprop* HTML attributes. Each HTML content element is considered an item, each item consists of key-value pairs where *itemprop* is the key and the HTML content element is the value. Itemscope defines a new item that corresponds to the *subject* being described, while itemtype specifies its *type* (i.e. the associated concept). Both itemtype and itemprop can take any value, but in order to facilitate that concepts are understood properly, such values must correspond to a shared vocabulary between service providers and consumers.

The Schema.org data models and Microdata results in a simple structure that facilitates adding explicit semantics to HTML content without additional complexity. Schema.org vocabulary (derived from RDF Schema, as a semantic model) is a hierarchical vocabulary of markup schemas for primitive and specialized data types or `Things`, such as `Action`, `Events`, etc. It is promoted by Bing,

```
<div itemscope itemtype="http://schema.org/WebService">
  <h1 itemprop="name">Uber API<h1>
  <meta itemprop="entrypoint" content="http://developer.uber.com/">
  <div itemprop="resource" itemscope itemtype="http://schema.org/WSResource">
    <meta itemprop="entrypoint" content="/v1/estimates/time">
    <h2 itemprop="name">TIME ESTIMATES</h2>
    <p itemprop="description">The Time Estimates endpoint returns ETA's... </p>
    <h3>Resource</h3>
    <div itemprop="action" itemscope itemtype="http://schema.org/WSAction">
      <meta itemprop="reference" content="http://schema.org/Action/GetAction/GetTaxiTravelTimeCollectionAction">
      <meta itemprop="required_params" content="start_latitude AND start_longitude">
      <p><span itemprop="operation">GET</span> /v1/estimates/time<p>
      <h3>Query Parameters</h3>
      <ul>
        <li itemprop="param" itemscope itemtype="http://schema.org/WSParam">
          <p>Name: <span itemprop="name">start_latitude</span></p>
          <p>Type: <span itemprop="type">float</span></p>
          <p>Description:  <span itemprop="description">Latitude component of location.</span</p>
          <meta itemprop="reference"
           content="http://schema.org/Thing/Intangible/StructuredValue/GeoCoordinates/latitude">
        </li>
        <li itemprop="param" itemscope itemtype="http://schema.org/WSParam">
          <p>Name: <span itemprop="name">start_longitude</span></p>
          <p>Type: <span itemprop="type">float</span></p>
          <p>Description: <span itemprop="description">Longitude component of location.</span></p>
          <meta itemprop="reference"
           content="http://schema.org/Thing/Intangible/StructuredValue/GeoCoordinates/longitude">
        </li>
      </ul>
      <h3>Response</h3>
      <div itemprop="response" itemscope itemtype="http://schema.org/WSResponse">
         <meta itemprop="status_code" content="200">
         <meta itemprop="media" content="application/json">
...
```

Fig. 3. A snippet depicting the usage of Microdata and Schema.org principles for describing the *Time estimates* resource, for the arrival of a taxi in Uber

Google and Yahoo! as HTML markup that Web search engines use to improve the display of search results. The schemas extensibility mechanism is based on the "/" separator to specify "paths" that specializes a data type or a property. `Data Types` and `Enumerations` are written in camelcase starting with a capital letter, whereas `Properties`, also written in camelcase, start with a lowercase.

Schema.org does not consider descriptions for web services (neither WSDL/-SOAP nor REST). A `WebService` is the entity that encompasses the service elements; a service can contain one or more REST resources (`WSResource`). Certain actions may be performed on resources (`WSAction`) specifying the HTTP required operation (e.g. GET, POST, etc) and parameters (`WSParam`) to be sent in the request as well as their `type`, `default` values and `enumerated` values. Parameters may be included as headers (`WSHeader`) or in the payload (`WSPayload`). Attributes such as `name` and `example` and `description` are included only for documentary purposes. The expected `response` of the operation is also included. All attributes are optional; they may or may not be present in the description.

The model was applied to a Web API available on the Web: the Uber Products API https://developer.uber.com/v1/endpoints/. Figure 3 presents a simplified snippet of our Microdata approach for annotating the `Time Estimates` resource of the Uber Products API. For simplicity, we have removed style classes.

5.3 RAD Implementation in JSON

The JSON implementation satisfies two requirements, to generate human-readable documentation, and to allow machine clients to understand the rules under which they must interact with the service. An implementation overview can be seen in Figure 2(b). A REST Web Service is described by a human-readable `name` and `description` elements, a `base URI` (it may refer to the root service entrypoint), and a `version` identifier (a string). As observed in Figure 4, a *prefix* is a key-value namespace (starting with the '@' symbol) that shortens references to semantic elements (*Concept* in Figure 2(b)).

```
{
 "name": "Songkick",
 "baseURI": "http://api.songkick.com/api/3.0",
 "version": "3.0",
 "description": "The Songkick API gives you easy access to the biggest live music ....",
 "prefixes": {
   "@schema": "http://schema.org",
   "@Thing": "@schema/Thing",
   "@Action": "@schema/Action",
   "@apikey": "@Thing/CreativeWork/SoftwareApplication/WebApplication/apikey/songkickApiKey",
   "@identifier": "@Thing/identifier",
   "@artist_id": "@identifier$Organization/PerformingGroup/MusicGroup/songkickId",
   "@Collection": "@Thing/Collection",
   ...
 },
 "resources": {
    "/artists/{@artist_id}/similar_artists.json": {
       "name": "Collection of similar artists",
       "reference": "@Collection/MusicGroupCollection",
       "description": "A list of artists similar to a given artist, based on our tracking and ....",
       "actions": {
          "get": {
               "description": "Get a list of artists similar to a given artist.",
               "reference": "@Action/SearchAction/SearchMusicGroupAction",
               "additional_doc": "http://www.songkick.com/developer/similar-artists",
               "required_params": "apikey",
               "parameters": {
                 "apikey": {
                   "name": "API Key",
                   "description": "Your API Key",
                   "reference": "@apikey",
                   "type": "string",
                   "example": "ABC123DEFG"
                 }
               },
               "responses": {
                   "200": {
                     "description": "On success, the HTTP ...",
                     "media": [
                         "application/json"
                     ],
                     "reference": [
                         "@Collection/MusicGroupCollection"
                     ]
..
```

Fig. 4. A snippet depicting the usage of JSON for describing the *Similar Artists* resource

Unlike the Microdata model, the JSON model describes a set of resources; hence, Web services are composed of `Resources` described by a human-readable `name` and `description` elements, and a conceptual entity representing its semantics through a `reference` (a URI). `Resources` are the keystones of our description. Each `Resource` has an entrypoint, some entrypoints are absolute URLs whereas others refer to resource instances and hence the URL includes parameters whose values must be solved at runtime (`type="path"`); such parameters are also associated (reference) to a concept. `Resources` as a whole have also a reference to its corresponding resource `Concept`, as well as a human-friendly `name` and `description`.

`Actions` are associated to operations, that is, a network protocol method (e.g. HTTP GET, HTTP POST, etc.) applied to a given `Resource`. Each operation has a reference to an `Action Concept` as well as a human-friendly `description`. Operations have also `Parameters` and a logical expression that allow developers to specify the rules that determine which parameters are required. `Parameters` have a `name`, `type` (boolean, string, etc.), a location (path, url, header, or body), a `reference` to a concept, and optional specifications depending on each type such as `maximum`, `minimum`, `enumeration`, and `default` values. An `example` of possible values is also considered. Finally, a `Response` fully connects the graph by containing a reference to a `Concept`, which is expected to be returned together with an HTTP `status code`, `description` and `media type`. Naturally we are describing the characteristics of an expected response, however due to the dynamic nature of REST the actual response may vary.

5.4 Prototype Implementation

We implemented a prototype of our proposal storing Web services information (nodes and arcs) in the graph database Neo4j. This database was chosen because of its high flexibility, performance and scalability. There are two possible inputs for the current implementation: a Microdata annotated HTML description, and a JSON description. We implemented two Python parsers, the first one transforms Microdata annotated HTML descriptions into JSON; the second one processes JSON descriptions and generates the nodes and arcs to be stored in the database using the Py2neo library. JSON descriptions are validated by JSON Schema before being parsed.

6 Validation

Service descriptions, either in Microdata or JSON implementation, are parsed to generate a graph (Figure 5). Nodes and arcs are labeled with attributes: rounded rectangles for nodes, and square rectangles for arcs. Nodes and arcs have an internal identifier in the graph, GRI (Graph Resource Identifier).

`Resources`, `Operations`, `Parameters`, and `Responses` are nodes in the graph, whereas `Actions` become a semantic arc connecting resources and operations. `Resources`, `Actions`, `Responses`, and `Parameters` are associated to `Concepts` through a `reference` arc. `Concepts` themselves are nodes described by two attributes, a `URI` and a `label` indicating its type. `Concepts` can be part of a complex semantic model such as an ontology (e.g. see relationship "isA" from node 6 to 3) or not, depending on the providers choice. For the case of parameters, they are classified into 4 types (path, url, header, and body) and they refer to a `Concept Parameter`. Relationships between RAD activity layers are also included and annotated with the semantics of the relationship (e.g. uses and results) and a GRI identifier. Figure 6 presents the result obtained when parsing the JSON and Microdata descriptions corresponding to the three APIs described in the illustrative example.

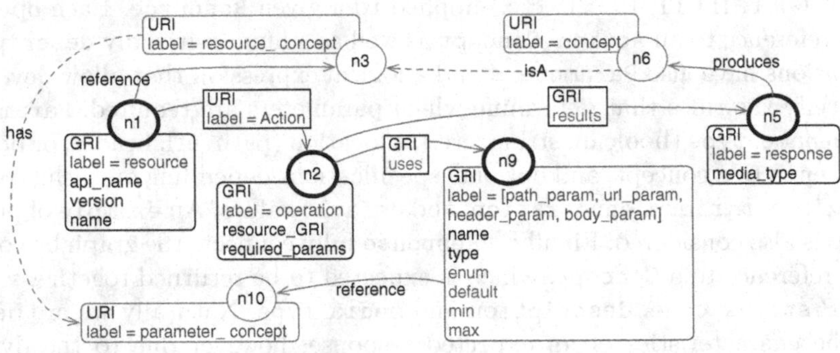

Fig. 5. The structure of the graph produced from JSON and Microdata implementation

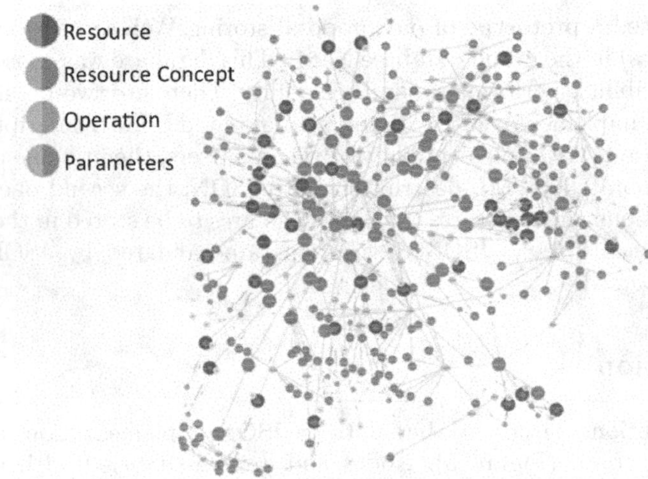

Fig. 6. The resulting graph, after parsing Spotify, Songkick and Uber APIs

```
(a) MATCH (concept)<-[:`is a`]-(resources)-[action]->(operations)-[:uses]->(parameters)
    WHERE concept.GRI=~ 'http://schema.org/Thing/CreativeWork/MusicPlaylist.*'
    AND action.GRI = 'http://schema.org/Action/GetAction/GetMusicRecordingCollectionAction'
    AND concept: `Resource Concept`  AND resources: Resource  AND operations: Operation
    AND parameters: Parameter
    RETURN concept, resources, operations, parameters

(b) MATCH (concept)<-[:`is a`]-(resources)-[action]->(operations)-[:uses]->(parameters), (operations)-[:results]-(responses)
    WHERE concept.GRI = 'http://schema.org/Thing/Collection/MusicGroupCollection'
    AND action.GRI = 'http://schema.org/Action/GetAction/GetMusicGroupCollectionAction/GetSimilarArtistsAction'
    AND concept: `Resource Concept`  AND resources: Resource  AND operations: Operation
    AND parameters: Parameter        AND responses: Response
    RETURN concept, resources, operations, responses, parameters

(c) MATCH (concept)<-[:`is a`]-(resources)-[action]->(operations)-[:uses]->(parameters), (operations)-[:results]-(responses)
    WHERE concept.GRI = 'http://schema.org/Thing/Collection/MusicEventCollection'
    AND action.GRI = 'http://schema.org/Action/SearchAction/MusicEventSearchAction'
    AND concept: `Resource Concept`  AND resources: Resource  AND operations: Operation
    AND parameters: Parameter        AND responses: Response
    RETURN concept, resources, operations, responses, parameters

(d) MATCH (concept)<-[:`is a`]-(resources)-[action]->(operations)-[:uses]->(parameters), (operations)-[:results]-(responses)
    WHERE concept.GRI = 'http://schema.org/Thing/Collection/TaxiCollection'
    AND action.GRI = 'http://schema.org/Action/GetAction/GetTaxiCollectionAction'
    AND concept: `Resource Concept`  AND resources: Resource  AND operations: Operation
    AND parameters: Parameter        AND responses: Response
    RETURN concept, resources, operations, responses, parameters

(e) MATCH (concept)<-[:`is a`]-(resources)-[action]->(operations)-[:uses]->(parameters), (operations)-[:results]-(responses)
    WHERE concept.GRI = 'http://schema.org/Thing/Collection/TaxiFareCollection'
    AND action.GRI = 'http://schema.org/Action/GetAction/GetTaxiFareCollectionAction'
    AND concept: `Resource Concept`  AND resources: Resource  AND operations: Operation
    AND parameters: Parameter        AND responses:Response
    RETURN concept, resources, operations, responses, parameters

(f) MATCH (concept)<-[:`is a`]-(resources)-[action]->(operations)-[:uses]->(parameters), (operations)-[:results]-(responses)
    WHERE concept.GRI = 'http://schema.org/Thing/Collection/TaxiTravelTimeCollection'
    AND action.GRI = 'http://schema.org/Action/GetAction/GetTaxiTravelTimeCollectionAction'
    AND concept: `Resource Concept`  AND resources: Resource  AND operations: Operation
    AND parameters: Parameter        AND responses:Response
    RETURN concept, resources, operations, responses, parameters
```

Fig. 7. Cypher queries to implement service discovery (a) and composition (b, to f) according to the example in section 4

6.1 Discovery

Let's consider again the Discovery example: *A user wants to find a given artist playlists.* Assuming that the user knows the Schema.org vocabulary, she must search for all `Resource Concepts` that are an instance of a `Musical Playlist` data type, as well as the parameters and operation required performing the HTTP request. Figure 7(a) shows such query, written in Cypher [29] which follows a syntax similar to SQL. As can be seen in Figure 7, Cypher queries are composed of three sections: the `MATCH` statement traverses the graph, through nodes (declared with parenthesis), relationships (if specified, declared with square brackets) and a direction (if specified, declared with arrows). When executed, the `MATCH` statement stores the nodes and relationships into variables. The `WHERE` statement imposes restrictions on such variables; and the RETURN statement determines the variables to be returned.

The query described in Figure 7(a) searches for graph fragments that hold the following form: *resource* nodes are linked through *action* arcs to *operation* nodes, which in turn are linked to *parameter* nodes through a uses arc (MATCH statement). In this case, the intended Action is to obtain a collection of music recordings (action.GRI="/GetMusicRecordingCollectionAction"); the Resource Concept is the set of music playlists (concept.GRI="/MusicPlaylist"). The result shown in Figure 8 reveals that there are two available operations for the given Action and Resource Concept, one provided by Songkick (a setlist for a given concert), and one by Spotify (the artists top tracks list).

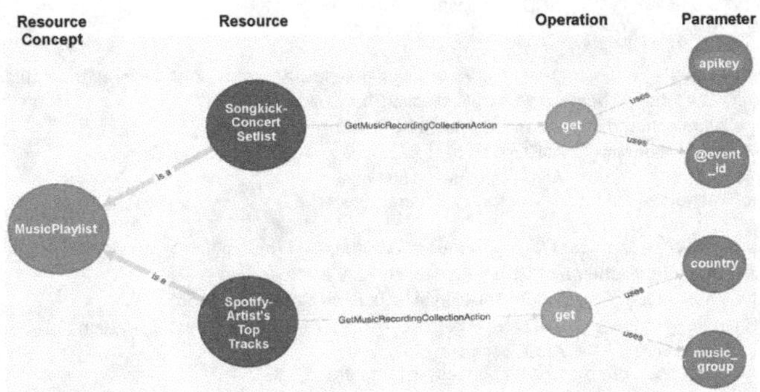

Fig. 8. Music playlists provided by Spotify and Songkick according to query (a) in Figure 7

6.2 Composition

Let's consider the Composition example: *A user wants to attend a concert but her favorite band is not in town. She decides to go to a similar artist concert and needs to know the venues where they will play as well as information of taxis to reach the event.* Again, assuming the user knows the Schema.org vocabulary, she needs to perform the following set of queries:

First, it is necessary to discover services allowing to search for similar artists (action.GRI="/GetSimilarArtistsAction"). Such services must provide resources of the MusicGroupCollection kind as a result. Figure 7(b) shows a Cypher query that follows the rules described in section 6.1. The query results are shown in Figure 9(a), we can observe that both Spotify and Songkick provide such feature although through different resources (*Related Artists* and *Similar Artist Collection*, respectively) and parameters. Semantically equivalent resources refer to the same concept in the extended Schema vocabulary. Equivalence between these resources is explicitly defined at a conceptual level in order to implement a prototype as a proof of concept.

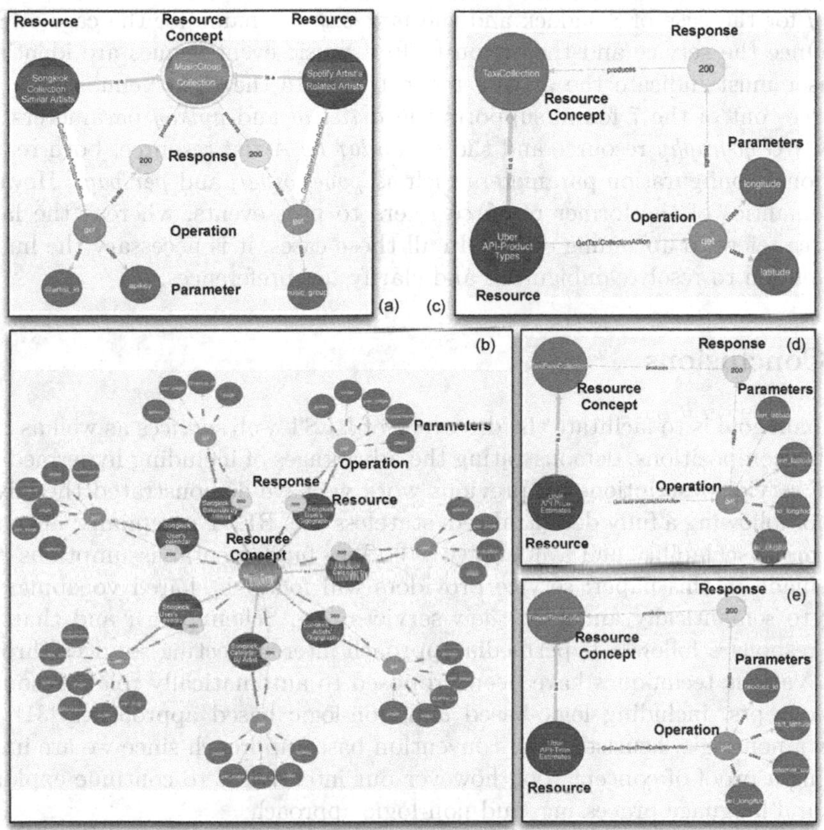

Fig. 9. Results for the various composition queries b to f in Figure 7

Afterwards, the user must search for information about the shows of the artists obtained in the previous query (Figure 7(c)). In this case, only Songkick can provide such functionality although through 7 resources (e.g. User's events, User's calendar, Calendar by Venue, etc.) as shown in Figure 9(b).

The next step is to find information about taxi availability to the found venues (Figure 7(d)). Now, only one service (Uber) provides an entrypoint to such request: `"/GetTaxiCollectionAction"` in Figure 9(c). Notice that in this case, the resource is more general than a *Taxi* concept, so it provides information of various product types, been one of them, the *TaxiCollection*. Queries (e) and (f) in Figure 7 presents the next steps: to find the estimated price and the estimated travel time and provide responses similar to the request for Taxi availability as shown in Figure 9(d) y (e).

Notice that, at this point, service composition cannot be performed automatically since it is necessary to support data flow. For instance, in order to find similar artists the user must provide information such as the *artists_id* and *apikey* for the case of Songkick and the *music_group* name for the case of Spotify. Once the service and the action to find music event venues are identified, the user must indicate the artist's name to locate the right venue. Only two resources out of the 7 found supports the *artist_id* and *apikey* parameters, the *Artist's Gigography* resource and the *Calendar by Artist* resource, both require additional configuration parameters such as *page*, *order*, and *per_page*. However the semantics of the former resource refers to past events, whereas the latter resource refers to upcoming events. In all these cases, it is necessary the human intervention to resolve ambiguities and clarify her preferences.

7 Conclusions

Our main goal is to facilitate the discovery of REST web services as well as their possible compositions, demonstrating the advantages of including hypermedia in REST service descriptions. In previous work we have demonstrated the advantages of following a fully decentralized, stateless (i.e. REST compliant) approach in terms of scalability and availability [30]. Two fundamental assumptions have been made in this paper: service providers will follow a shared vocabulary in order to semantically annotate their services (e.g. Schema.org); and that services responses follow a hypermedia approach interconnecting services through links. Various techniques have been proposed to automatically relate resources and concepts, including logic-based and non-logic based approaches [31]. We follow a non-logic, heuristic, and convention based approach since we are implementing a proof of concept tool, however our intention is to continue exploring a natural language processing, and non-logic approach.

Our proposal adds an extra layer to the REST architecture (i.e. business level supported by REST services) making maintenance a concern. A pending and no less important issue is data flow between operations, that is, how to transform response data into parameters to execute a new operation. The challenge not only relies on casting different data types (e.g. string, boolean, integer), but also on respecting and producing data that is semantically equivalent and which format could vary significantly (e.g. hash codes for different APIs that are produced following different protocols).

Natural language descriptions pose an additional challenge for machine-clients making it clear the need for introducing service semantics. Annotations seem to be a good alternative to achieve this goal, and Microdata is a good fit due to its simplicity, although other approaches such as Linked Data could be used. This proposal aims to provide a strategy for the discovery and composition of REST Web services, which foster service descriptions understandable by both developers and machines. As future work, we will focus on the discovery of relationships between resources at an activity and semantic level, as well as a more friendly way of expressing users needs.

References

1. Mayer, S., Guinard, D.: An extensible discovery service for smart things. In: Proceedings of the Second International Workshop on Web of Things, p. 7. ACM (2011)
2. Fielding, R.T.: Architectural styles and the design of network-based software architectures, Ph.D. dissertation, University of California, Irvine, Irvine, California (2000)
3. Chinnici, R., Gudgin, M., Moreau, J.-J., Schlimmer, J., Weerawarana, S.: Web services description language (wsdl) version 2.0 part 1: Core language, W3C working draft, vol. 26 (2004)
4. Hadley, M.: Web application description language, World Wide Web Consortium, Member Submission SUBM-wadl-20090831 (August 2009)
5. John, D., Rajasree, M.: Restdoc: Describe, discover and compose restful semantic web services using annotated documentations. International Journal of Web & Semantic Technology (IJWesT) 4(1) (2013)
6. Verborgh, R., Steiner, T., Van Deursen, D., De Roo, J., Van de Walle, R., Gabarró Vallés, J.: Description and interaction of restful services for automatic discovery and execution. In: Proceedings of the FTRA 2011 International Workshop on Advanced Future Multimedia Services (2011)
7. Lathem, J., Gomadam, K., Sheth, A.P.: Sa-rest and (s)mashups: Adding semantics to restful services. In: First IEEE International Conference on Semantic Computing (ICSC 2007), Irvine, California, pp. 469–476, September 2007
8. Kopecký, J., Gomadam, K., Vitvar, T.: Hrests: An html microformat for describing restful web services. In: 2008 IEEE/WIC/ACM International Conference on Web Intelligence, Sydney, Australia, pp. 619–625, December 2008
9. Adida, B., Birbeck, M., McCarron, S., Pemberton, S.: Rdfa in xhtml: Syntax and processing – a collection of attributes and processing rules for extending xhtml to support rdf, World Wide Web Consortium, Recommendation REC-rdfa-syntax-20081014, October 2008
10. Khare, R., Çelik, T.: Microformats: a pragmatic path to the semantic web. In: Proceedings of the 15th International Conference on World Wide Web, pp. 865–866. ACM (2006)
11. Adida, B.: hgrddl: Bridging microformats and rdfa. Web Semantics: Science, Services and Agents on the World Wide Web **6**(1), 54–60 (2008)
12. Bizer, C., Eckert, K., Meusel, R., Mühleisen, H., Schuhmacher, M., Völker, J.: Deployment of RDFa, Microdata, and Microformats on the Web – A Quantitative Analysis. In: Alani, H., Kagal, L., Fokoue, A., Groth, P., Biemann, C., Parreira, J.X., Aroyo, L., Noy, N., Welty, C., Janowicz, K. (eds.) ISWC 2013, Part II. LNCS, vol. 8219, pp. 17–32. Springer, Heidelberg (2013)
13. John, D., Rajasree, M.: Restdoc: Describe, discover and composerestful semantic web services using annotated documentations. International Journal of Web & Semantic Technology (IJWesT) 4(1) (2013)
14. Taheriyan, M., Knoblock, C.A., Szekely, P., Ambite, J.L.: Semi-automatically modeling web apis to create linked apis. In: Proceedings of the First Linked APIs workshop at the Ninth Extended Semantic Web Conference, May 2012. http://lapis2012.linkedservices.org/papers/2.pdf
15. Ly, P.A., Pedrinaci, C., Domingue, J.: Automated Information Extraction from Web APIs Documentation. In: Wang, X.S., Cruz, I., Delis, A., Huang, G. (eds.) WISE 2012. LNCS, vol. 7651, pp. 497–511. Springer, Heidelberg (2012)

16. Lanthaler, M., Gütl, C.: Hydra: A vocabulary for hypermedia-driven web apis. In: LDOW, Citeseer (2013)
17. Klusch, M.: Service discovery. In: Alhajj, R., Rokne, J. (eds.) Encyclopedia of Social Networks and Mining (ESNAM). Springer (2014)
18. Roy, M., Suleiman, B., Weber, I.: Facilitating Enterprise Service Discovery for Non-technical Business Users. In: Maximilien, E.M., Rossi, G., Yuan, S.-T., Ludwig, H., Fantinato, M. (eds.) ICSOC 2010. LNCS, vol. 6568, pp. 100–110. Springer, Heidelberg (2011)
19. Khorasgani, R.R., Stroulia, E., Zaïane, O.R.: Web service matching for restful web services. In: 13th IEEE International Symposium on Web Systems Evolution (WSE), 115–124. IEEE (2011)
20. Fellbaum, C.: WordNet. Wiley Online Library (1998)
21. Pedrinaci, C., Liu, D., Maleshkova, M., Lambert, D., Kopecky, J., Domingue, J.: Iserve: a linked services publishing platform. In: CEUR Workshop Proceedings, vol. 596 (2010)
22. Pautasso, C.: Composing RESTful Services with JOpera. In: Bergel, A., Fabry, J. (eds.) SC 2009. LNCS, vol. 5634, pp. 142–159. Springer, Heidelberg (2009)
23. Krummenacher, R., Norton, B., Marte, A.: Towards Linked Open Services and Processes. In: Berre, A.J., Gómez-Pérez, A., Tutschku, K., Fensel, D. (eds.) FIS 2010. LNCS, vol. 6369, pp. 68–77. Springer, Heidelberg (2010)
24. Alarcon, R., Wilde, E., Bellido, J.: Hypermedia-Driven RESTful Service Composition. In: Maximilien, E.M., Rossi, G., Yuan, S.-T., Ludwig, H., Fantinato, M. (eds.) ICSOC 2010. LNCS, vol. 6568, pp. 111–120. Springer, Heidelberg (2011)
25. Alarcón, R., Wilde, E.: Restler: Crawling restful services. In: Rappa, M., Jones, P., Freire, J., Chakrabarti, S. (eds.) 19th International World Wide Web Conference, pp. 1051–1052. ACM Press, Raleigh (2010)
26. Haupt, F., Fischer, M., Karastoyanova, D., Leymann, F., Vukojevic-Haupt, K.: Service composition for rest. In: IEEE 18th International Enterprise Distributed Object Computing Conference, EDOC 2014, pp. 110–119. IEEE (2014)
27. Stadtmüller, S., Speiser, S., Harth, A., Studer, R.: Data-fu: A language and an interpreter for interaction with read/write linked data. In: Proceedings of the 22nd International Conference on World Wide Web, pp. 1225–1236. International World Wide Web Conferences Steering Committee (2013)
28. Sheth, A.P., Gomadam, K., Lathem, J.: Sa-rest: Semantically interoperable and easier-to-use services and mashups. IEEE Internet Computing **11**(6), 91 (2007)
29. Holzschuher, F., Peinl, R.: Performance of graph query languages: comparison of cypher, gremlin and native access in neo4j. In: Proceedings of the Joint EDBT/ICDT 2013 Workshops, pp. 195–204. ACM (2013)
30. Bellido, J., Alarcón, R., Pautasso, C.: Control-flow patterns for decentralized restful service composition. ACM Transactions on the Web (TWEB) **8**(1), 5 (2013)
31. Lee, Y.-J.: Semantic-based data mashups using hierarchical clustering and pattern analysis methods. Journal of Information Science and Engineering **30**(5), 1601–1618 (2014)

Live, Personal Data Integration Through UI-Oriented Computing

Florian Daniel(✉)

University of Trento, Via Sommarive 9, I-38123 Povo, TN, Italy
daniel@disi.unitn.it

Abstract. This paper proposes a new perspective on the problem of data integration on the Web: the one of the Surface Web. It introduces the concept of UI-oriented computing as a computing paradigm whose core ingredient are the user interfaces that build up the Surface Web, and shows how a sensible mapping of data integration tasks to user interface elements and user interactions is able to cope with data integration scenarios that so far have only be conceived for the Deep Web with its APIs and Web services. The described approach provides a novel conceptual and technological framework for practices, such as the integration of data APIs/services and the extraction of content from Web pages, that are common practice but still not adequately supported. The approach targets both programmers and users alike and comes as an extensible, open-source browser extension.

Keywords: Data integration · UI-oriented computing · Mashups

1 Introduction

Data integration is the problem of "combining data residing at different sources, and providing the user with a unified view of these data" [12]. The traditional focus of data integration has been on databases, most notably relational databases, and on the problem of (re)writing queries over integrated views. With the advent of the World Wide Web, which as a matter of fact is a worldwide database, the focus has shifted toward the Web and data whose formats range from well structured (e.g., relational databases) to semi-structured (e.g., XML data) to unstructured (e.g., data inside Web pages) [3].

The most notable technologies today to publish and access these kinds of data over the Web are SOAP/WSDL Web services [1], RESTful Web services [10], RSS/Atom feeds, or static XML/JSON/CSV resources. Alternatively, data may be rendered in and scraped from HTML Web pages, for example, using tools like Dapper (http://open.dapper.net) or similar that publish extracted content again via any of the previous technologies.

All these technologies (except the Web pages) are oriented toward programmers, and understanding the underlying abstractions and usage conventions requires significant software development expertise. This makes data integration

P. Cimiano et al. (Eds.): ICWE 2015, LNCS 9114, pp. 479–497, 2015.
DOI: 10.1007/978-3-319-19890-3_31

a prerogative of skilled programmers, turns it into a complex and time-consuming task (even for small integration scenarios), and prevents less skilled users from getting the best value out of the data available on the Web.

Namoun et al. [13] studied the domain of end-user development (EUD) with a specific focus on the Web and Web services. Their findings clearly show that people without programming skills simply don't know what services or data formats are and that they lack the necessary understanding of how software is developed. What they know is how to operate user interfaces (UIs). These findings confirm our own experience with the development of mashups, mashup tools, and EUD, where we tried to simplify the use of services, data sources, UI widgets, and similar: insisting on abstracting APIs or services that were invented for programmers does not mitigate enough the identified conceptual gap.

However, these findings also inspire a new perspective on the problem of integration on the Web, that of the Surface Web, and a novel computing paradigm that we call *UI-oriented computing* (UIC). The underlying observation is that on the Web almost everything that can be done via APIs, Web services and similar (the Deep Web) can also be done via the UIs of the respective Web applications. For instance, we are all accustomed to book our trips to conferences, including train tickets, hotel reservations, flight tickets and car rentals, without having to issue Web service calls ourselves and, hence, abandon the Surface Web. All functionalities we need are available through the UIs of the applications.

The *research question* UIC poses is thus if and, if yes, which of the conventional Web engineering tasks can be achieved if we start from the UIs of applications, instead of from their APIs or services. In our prior work [7], we already investigated how to turn UIs into programmable artifacts and introduced the idea of *interactive APIs* (iAPIs), that is, APIs users can interact with via suitable UIs. In this paper, we focus on the case of data integration following the UIC paradigm and show that the benefits that can be achieved are not only for users but also for programmers. Concretely, this paper makes the following contributions to the state of the art:

- A *conceptual model* for UI-oriented data integration;
- A *microformat* for HTML able to turn UIs into interactive APIs;
- The implementation of a *runtime middleware* for UI-oriented computing applications;
- The implementation of design time support for UI-oriented computing for both programmers (a *UIC JavaScript library*) and common users (an *interactive, visual editor*); and
- A *case study* of UI-oriented data integration in practice, demonstrating the philosophy and viability of the approach.

Next, we describe the scenario we have in mind, we identify its requirements and outline how we approach the design of a UI-oriented computing paradigm for the specific instance of data integration. We introduce the microformat for iAPIs, their runtime and design time support, and apply the UI-oriented computing paradigm to the example scenario. Then we compare the proposed paradigm with the state of the art and discuss benefits, limitations and future work.

2 Scenario and Approach

Let's imagine we would like to integrate the publications by two different authors into one list of publications, for example, to assemble a research group's publications starting from the individual group members' personal websites. Both source lists of publications are published via regular HTML Web pages and rendered as tables, itemized or numbered lists, or paragraphs. In order to group publications into topics, we would also like to filter publications based on given keywords (e.g., "iAPI") and eliminate possible duplicates if the two authors published a paper together. Eventually, we would like to be able to embed the integrated list of publications into the group's website in a permanent, yet dynamically updated fashion. That is, we do not want to extract and statically store the list of publications, but we would like the integrated list to dynamically fetch and integrate data on the fly each time we access the group's website.

Implementing the described scenario by starting from the UIs of the source pages is not possible with the current state of the art: integrating data on the Web still means either writing code to extract content from Web pages (which we want to prevent) or writing code to interact with Web services or APIs (which we do not have). UIs are still only interfaces toward applications and do not provide users with fine-grained access to backend APIs or services.

2.1 Assumptions

The *assumptions* to approach the scenario from a UI perspective are that (i) all data we are interested in are rendered inside common Web pages (at least part thereof), (ii) pages are encoded in HTML and rendered inside a Web browser, (iii) the developers integrating data are either programmers or users, and (iv) we do not want to directly manipulate any API or Web service of the Deep Web.

2.2 Requirements

The core requirements for a data integration paradigm based on UIs and UI interactions only can thus be summarized as follows:

- *Infrastructure requirements*
  1. UI elements, such as tables, lists, paragraphs and similar, must be turned into artifacts that can be programmed to enable data reuse.
  2. A suitable runtime environment is needed to execute programs.
  3. A UI-oriented computing middleware is needed to manage network communications among UI elements distributed over different applications.
- *User requirements*
  4. UI constructs and usage conventions are needed to enable the user to express data integration operations, such as data access, formatting, unions and similar via UI elements.
  5. Since users are not able to modify the source of pages, a persistent storage of UI-oriented data integration logics for repeated execution is needed.

- *Programmer requirements*
  6. Programmers must be enabled to programmatically integrate data starting from the abstractions of requirement 1.
  7. Programmers that have full access to the source of their Web pages may want to embed their integration logic directly into their pages.

2.3 Approach

In line with the UI orientation pushed forward in this paper, the approach to satisfy these requirements proposes a new kind of "abstraction": no abstraction. The intuition is to turn UI elements into interactive artifacts that, besides their primary purpose in the page (e.g., rendering data), also serve to access a set of operations that can be performed on the artifacts (e.g., reusing data). Operations can be enacted either interactively, for example, by pointing and clicking elements, choosing options, dragging and dropping them, and similar – all interaction modalities that are native to UIs – or programmatically.

A first version of the necessary technology we have already introduced in [7], i.e., *interactive APIs* (requirement R1); we refine them in this paper and equip them with the necessary runtime support. iAPIs come as a binomial of a *microformat* for the annotation of HTML elements with data structures and operations and a *UIC engine* able to interpret the annotations and to run UI-oriented data integrations (R2). The engine is implemented as a browser extension. A dedicated *iAPI editor* injects into the page *graphical controls* that allow the user to specify data integration logics interactively (R4). The UIC engine maps them to a set of iAPI-specific *JavaScript functions* implementing the respective runtime support. The library of JavaScript functions can also be programmed directly by programmers (R6), without the need for interacting with UI elements. To users, the UI elements act as proxies toward the features of the library. A UI-oriented computing *middleware* (R3) complements the library; both are part of the browser plug-in. It takes care of setting up communications among integrated applications (e.g., to load data dynamically from third-party pages) and of storing interactively defined integration logics in the browser's *local storage* (R5). Programmers with access to the source code of a page can inject their JavaScript code directly into it (R7).

3 Publishing Data

In principle, each type of content accessible via the Surface Web can be extracted and reused as is for the development of new, composite applications. In practice, there are however several limitations to this approach, which makes content extraction not robust if not properly supported by the providers of the data. For instance, HTML has been invented to describe documents with content, layout and styles and less for the description of data. As a consequence, data structures are not always clearly identifiable from the HTML markup of a page, for example, because inconsistent markup elements are used for similar data structures.

That is, HTML markup may be ambiguous when it comes to understanding data structures. Next, the layout and style of applications typically evolve over time, e.g., to stick to changing tastes of their users. Some modifications do not affect the structure of the HTML markup and, hence, do not affect possible data extraction logics; other modifications however alter the HTML markup and extraction methods may fail to adapt. Finally, big datasets may be published either inside one page using the vertical extension of the page or they may be paginated, that is, split over multiple pages interlinked by data navigation controls. Data spread over multiple pages is again hard to extract.

A UI-oriented approach to publishing data must take these issues into account and devise a technique that allows the provider of the data to describe and advertise available data sources and the consumer to rely on a robust interface toward them, so as to be able to build dependable software on top of it. The solution we propose in this paper is equipping the HTML markup of pages with suitable *annotations* that (i) identify interactive APIs inside Web pages, (i) guide the access to data, and (ii) act as a contract between provider and consumer.

3.1 Identifying Data Sources

Data on the Web are structured into Web pages and rendered by the browser using a variety of different visualization elements in function of the data structures to be rendered: tables, itemized or enumerated lists, paragraphs, `div` elements, or similar can all be seen as proxies toward the data they render. Which exact elements inside a page in fact do provide access to reusable data can be identified by suitably annotating them. For instance, the following code fragment identifies a table as an iAPI (`h-iapi`) that provides access to data that can be *extracted* from the page, specifically a dataset of publications (`e-data:Publications`):

```
<table id="1" class="h-iapi e-data:Publications"> ... </table>
```

The annotation follows the conventions of the *microformats 2* proposal (http://microformats.org/wiki/microformats2). The convention is based on CSS class names and makes use of prefixes to facilitate the implementation of parsers. Specifically, the prefixes used in the proposed iAPI microformat are (Table 1 summarizes the instructions used in this paper and introduced in the following): `h-*` for the root classname that identifies the microformat, `e-*` for elements to be parsed as HTML, `p-*` for text properties, and `u-*` for URLs.

The previous annotation of the table did not provide any link to external resources. This means the data published through the iAPI can be extracted from the HTML markup. If the provider of the data in addition wants to link the table with an *external data source*, such as an RSS feed, a JSON file, or a RESTful or SOAP/WSDL Web service, this can be done by adding a `u-json`, `u-rss` or `u-xml` instruction as shown in the following code lines:

```
<table id="1" class="h-iapi e-data:Publications u-json:http://source">
   ... </table>
```

Table 1. Summary of the microformat instructions to annotate data source iAPIs

Instruction	Description
h-iapi	Qualifies the annotated HTML element as iAPI
e-data:label	Qualifies the iAPI as data source; label is a human-readable description
e-item:label	Identifies data items inside a feed of data; label names items
p-attr:label	Structures data items into attributes; label names attributes
h-card	Identifies the h-card microformat (http://microformats.org/wiki/h-card)
u-json:url	Identifies a JSON data source; url specifies the URL of the source
u-rss:url	Identifies an RSS data source; url specifies the URL of the source
u-xml:url	Identifies an XML data source; url specifies the URL of the source
e-item:label:key	Identifies data items inside an external data source; label gives a name to data items; key tells how to identify the item in the data source
p-attr:label:key	Structures data items into attributes; label gives names to data attributes; key tells how to identify the attribute in the data source

If no external link is provided, data is mandatorily extracted from the HTML markup. If an external link is provided, data can either be extracted from the markup or fetched from the linked resource. The external resource is particularly helpful when data are paginated, and it would not be possible to extract the complete dataset from one page. In this case, the external resource can provide direct access to the full dataset with one single query.

3.2 Describing Data Structures

The structure of rendered data is typically not evident on the Web. Some HTML elements are self-evident, such as tables, which have attributes (columns) and items (rows), while others are less able to express structural information, such as lists, paragraphs, `div` elements or plain text. Supporting the reuse of data therefore means equipping standard HTML elements with additional semantics that express the necessary structural information. Again, this can be achieved with sensible annotations of the HTML markup.

There are two ways to annotate iAPIs, in order to describe data structures: If data already comply with any of the microformats proposed by microformats.org, such as h-adr for addresses or h-card for business cards, the respective microformat can be used. If instead a custom data structure is needed, it is possible to annotate the iAPI with iAPI-specific instructions.

A data iAPI based on a *microformat* is annotated as shown in the following for the case of an h-card:

```
<div id="1" class="h-iapi e-data:Contact h-card">
  <span class="p-name">Florian Daniel</span>
  <span class="p-org">University of Trento</span>
</div>
```

The instruction `h-iapi` qualifies the `div` as iAPI, `e-data:Contact` tells that the data published by the iAPI is a contact, while the instruction `h-card` is the standard annotation of the h-card microformat, which proposes a set of pre-defined instructions, e.g., `p-name` and `p-org`, to identify the name and the organization of the contact, respectively.

A data iAPI that uses a *custom data format* can be described as follows:

```
<table id="1" class="h-iapi e-data:Publications">
  <tr class="e-item:Publication">
    <td class="p-attr:Authors">F. Daniel and A. Furlan</td>
    <td class="p-attr:Title">The Interactive API (iAPI)</td>
    <td class="p-attr:Event">ComposableWeb 2013</td>
  </tr>
  ... </table>
```

The annotation of the root node of the iAPI is as before. The instruction `e-item:label` marks up data items of type `label` (Publication), while `p-attr:label` structures items into attributes of type `label` (Author, Title, Event).

If the data iAPI provides access to an *external data source*, it is generally not possible to derive the structure of the external data from the structure of the HTML elements inside the iAPI. In fact, it is not only necessary to describe the structure of the data, but also to specify how to identify the structure inside the external data source. The following code provides an example of how to annotated a JSON resource:

```
<table id="1" class="h-iapi e-data:Publications u-json:http://source
  e-item:Publication:pubs
  p-attr:Author:auth
  p-attr:Tile:title
  p-attr:Event:event">
  ... </table>
```

The instructions `e-item:label:key` and `p-attr:label:key` define data items and their attributes (Publication and Author, Title, Event) and how to identify them inside the data source using a `key` that can be looked up (pubs, auth, title, event). If no keys are defined for the data items, per default a flat structure of the data source is assumed: an array of structured items. That is, each first-level entry of the data source (be it JSON, RSS or XML) is interpreted as a data item, and the second-level entries are interpreted as attributes.

It is important to note that the described approach to annotate data focuses on two aspects of the data: structure (the nesting of elements) and meaning (the human-readable labels). For simplicity, the proposed microformat does not yet feature *data types*, such as date, integer, string, or similar. This has as a consequence that all data fields are interpreted as strings. The micorformat does not provide for machine-readable semantics either, e.g., using Semantic Web standards like RDF (http://www.w3.org/RDF/) or RDFa (http://www.w3.org/TR/xhtml-rdfa-primer/). The current target are humans.

4 Integrating Data

Expressing a data integration logic is usually achieved by coding the logic in some programming language equipped with constructs that enable fetching data, storing them in variables, modifying data structures, and so on. Starting from UIs, the constructs we have are, however, *UI elements* like tables or lists (identified by the iAPI annotations), *user interactions* like clicking, selecting, dragging and dropping, and *input forms* that can be used to ask for user inputs needed to configure the integration logic. In this section, we show how we use these UI constructs to enable an interactive, visual data integration paradigm. Then, we explain the functions of the underlying code library that (i) enables programmers to code UI-oriented data integrations and (ii) serves as target language to map the UI-oriented data integration logic into an executable format.

4.1 Interactive, Visual Data Integration

Following a UI-oriented perspective, we do not want to deal with technical aspects (the *how*); instead, we want to concentrate our focus on *what* we want to achieve. For instance, given a source page with a dataset x that we want to reuse and a target page that contains an empty table y, the problem is rather how to specify interactively that we want to "reuse the data of table/list x in the source page inside table y of the target page." That is, we want to express the data integration logic declaratively, without having to specify how this logic is executed.

In this respect, it is important to note that there does not exist one single correct mapping of data integration operations to UI constructs. Specifying that one wants to reuse a given dataset found inside a Web page can be done by filling a form with the necessary details, drawing a table and linking it to the dataset, copying and pasting the table from the source page to the target page, etc. All of these modalities may be suitable metaphors. Which one is best (if any) is an HCI question that is out of the scope of this paper.

Accessing Data. The first step toward the integration of different data sources is accessing and loading data. Given the types of data iAPIs described earlier, accessing data means either extracting data from the markup of annotated Web pages or fetching data from a JSON, RSS or XML resource. Loading the data then means visualizing them somehow inside a new page (the target page) – note that in a UI-oriented paradigm the "memory" is the UI space, in that what is not visible is not available for interaction and manipulation.

The mapping of the data access operation we propose in this paper is illustrated in Figure 1(a): a *drag and drop* user interaction of the identified dataset from the source page to the target page, more specifically from a source iAPI to a target iAPI. Dragging and dropping is a commonly used technique in modern software systems to copy or move objects or content. The assumption is that iAPIs inside a page are made visible to users via the graphical controls that allow the users to interact with the iAPIs.

Selecting, Projecting, Ordering Data. Once data are loaded into the target page, these can be manipulated by the user. The basic operations in this respect are selection and projection, the former specifying which characteristics data items should satisfy in order for them to be included, the latter specifying which attributes of the items should be included.

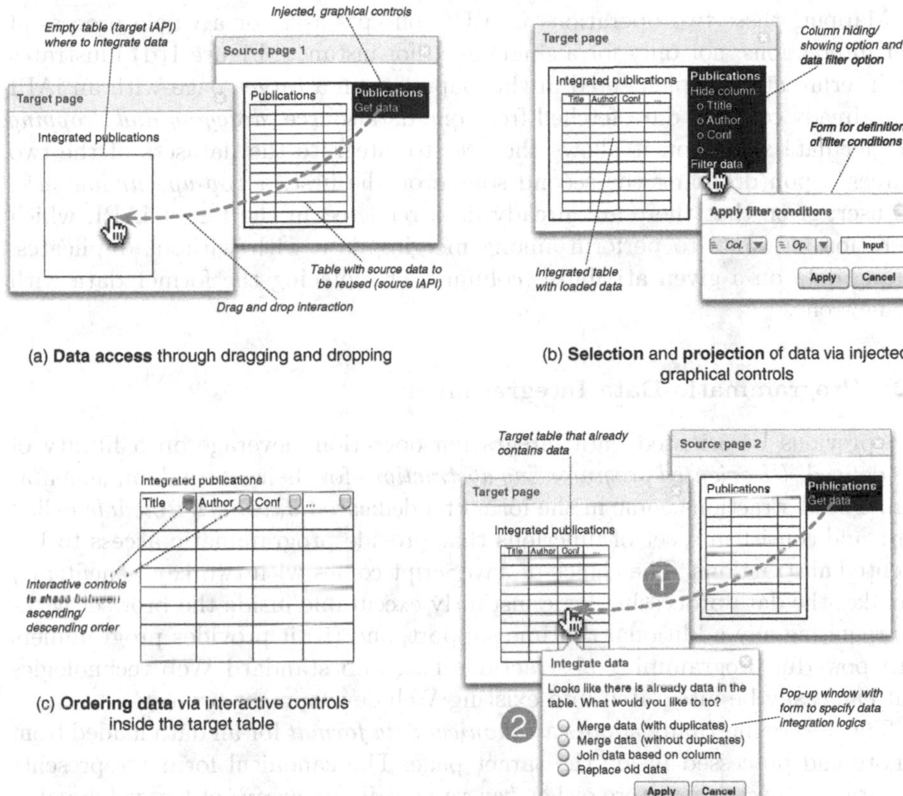

(a) **Data access** through dragging and dropping

(b) **Selection** and **projection** of data via injected graphical controls

(c) **Ordering data** via interactive controls inside the target table

(d) **Joining/merging data** by dropping new data on top of existing data and choosing a data integration operation

Fig. 1. Basic data integration operations mapped to UI elements and user interactions

One way of mapping these operations to UI constructs is illustrated in Figure 1(b): a *pop-up window* and an *input form* for the specification of filter conditions (selection) and *checkboxes* for hiding/showing attributes (projection). Both features are accessible via the graphical controls injected into the iAPI rendering the data fetched from the source page.

The order of data (typically ascending vs. descending vs. no order) can also be specified via suitable graphical controls. The typical solution to express the order of data in a table today is adding *order icons* to the heading of the table, such as illustrated in Figure 1(c). The order of data rendered using other visualizations, such as lists or simple paragraphs, can be specified by injecting similar icons when highlighted or via suitable entries in the respective iAPI's context menu.

Joining and Merging Data. Finally, the key to integration is bringing together different data sources. This means either joining or merging data (union), the latter with or without keeping possible duplicates in the integrated dataset.

Mapping these two operations into UI concepts asks for a whole process of user interactions, not only for a single one. For instance, Figure 1(d) illustrates the interpretation implemented in this paper: given a target page with an iAPI that already contains data fetched from one data source, *dragging and dropping* another data source on it allows the user to integrate the datasets of the two sources. Upon dropping the second source on the first, a *pop-up window* asks the user, given that there are already data rendered in the target iAPI, which operation he wants to perform among merging data with/without duplicates, joining data on a given attribute (column), or replacing the former data with the new one.

4.2 Programmatic Data Integration

The previous UI-oriented data integration operations leverage on a library of pre-defined, *UI-oriented programming abstractions* for their internal implementation. The abstractions come in the form of a dedicated *JavaScript module* called `iapi` and consist in a set of functions that provide programmatic access to UI-oriented abstractions. The choice of JavaScript comes with two key benefits: (i) it makes the data processing logic instantly executable inside the browser without requiring any additional runtime support, and (ii) it provides programmers with powerful programming abstractions based on standard Web technologies that can easily be integrated into existing Web development projects.

The library internally adopts a *canonical data format* for all data loaded from remote and processed inside the target page. The canonical format represents all data as objects that store either *key-value pairs* or *arrays* of key-value pairs. Each value can again be a key-value pair or an array of key-value pairs, and so on. The keys serve as identifiers of data items or attributes, the values are the actual data.

The functions of the library for UI-oriented data integration are (we discuss the details of how to visualize data in the next section):

- `iapi.fetchData(URL,id,callback(result))`: loads data from iAPI `id` in page `URL`; `callback(result)` names the callback function to be called once the fetched data (`result`) are available for use.
- `iapi.filter(data,filters,callback(result))`: filters items in `data` (data object in canonical format) according to the conditions expressed in `filters` in terms of common comparators, e.g., =, <, >, etc.
- `iapi.hide(data,options,callback(result))`: hides the attributes of `data` specified in `options`.
- `iapi.order(data,attribute,logic,callback(result))`: orders the items in `data` according to `logic` ("asc" or "desc") applied to `attribute`. If no order is specified, data are rendered in the order they are loaded.
- `iapi.unionAll(data1,data2,callback(result))`: computes the union of `data1` and `data2` and keeps possible duplicates in the result set.

- iapi.unionWithout(data1,data2,callback(result)): computes the union of data1 and data2 without keeping duplicates in the result set.
- iapi.join(data1,data2,attr1,attr2,condition,callback(result)): joins data1 and data2 based on the join condition condition (syntactically similar to filter conditions) applied to attributes attr1 and attr2.

All functions are asynchronous and make use of callback functions, so as not to block the regular processing of the host page while data are integrated.

5 Visualizing Data

Also for the formatting and rendering of data we distinguish the two paradigms illustrated before: interactive, visual vs. programmatic.

Interactive, Visual Data Visualization. From a UI perspective, the problem is the same as before for the data integration operations, that is, a mapping of data formatting operations to UI constructs is needed. Figure 2 illustrates the solution proposed in this paper: the user simply selects the preferred visualization format from a list of formats. For simplicity, the list of available formats is pre-defined in the visual editing mode, and new formats are added programmatically. The iAPI adapts its appearance on the fly.

Fig. 2. Formatting data interactively by choosing templates

Programmatic Data Visualization. The rendering of data visualizations can be achieved via dedicated HTML *templates* that, given a data object in canonical format, expand the template with the given data values. The design of templates is again based on the use of suitable annotations that specify the structural properties of the template as well as the iAPI annotations to be added to the data iAPI to be rendered. The following markup, for example, specifies a template for a table:

```
<table id="tbl" class="h-iapitemp h-iapi e-data:Publications">
  <tr> <td>Title</td> <td>Author</td> <td>Conf</td> </tr>
  <tr class="e-itemtemp e-item:Publication">
    <td class="e-attrtemp p-attr:Title"></td>
    <td class="e-attrtemp p-attr:Author"></td>
    <td class="e-attrtemp p-attr:Conf"></td>
  </tr>
</table>
```

The template fixes the header of the table (Title, Author and Conf) as well as the three td elements that will host the actual data values. The instruction h-iapitemp makes the table a template. The instructions e-itemtemp and `e-attrtemp` identify the markup to be repeated for data items and attributes. The attributes to be rendered are specified by the `p-attr:label` instruction that specifies the respective key inside the canonical data object to be rendered.

Given such a template, the programmatic visualization of a data object is achieved using the JavaScript instruction `$(selector).renderData(data, template)`. The function is a plug-in of jQuery (http://jquery.com), which is particularly powerful for the manipulation of DOM elements. The `selector` identifies the iAPI in which data are to be rendered; `data` and `template` (the HTML identifier) are the data object and template to be used. If no template is specified, a default visualization format is chosen, e.g., a table for bi-dimensional data or a list for uni-dimensional data (an array).

6 UI-Oriented Computing Infrastructure

In line with the UI orientation of the former sections, so far we did not concentrate on how to actually turn the described concepts into a running application. In fact, neglecting these aspects is the very idea of UI-oriented computing and the driver underlying the idea. However, enabling the introduced data integration paradigm requires the availability of a suitable UI-oriented computing infrastructure. The description of this infrastructure is the purpose of this section.

Figure 3 shows the internal architecture of the current prototype, which comes as a Google Chrome browser extension. The extension provides the browser with support for iAPIs and UI-oriented computing. The infrastructure comes with two core elements: a UIC engine for the execution of UI-oriented data integration logics and an iAPI editor for visual, interactive development. The *UIC engine* is split into two parts: The *background script* provides core middleware services, such as extension management (via its icon and pop-up menu), remote resource access, data parsing, and local storage management. The *content script* implements the `iapi` JavaScript library for programmatic UIC (the implementation is based on http://toddmotto.com/mastering-the-module-pattern), injects JavaScript code into the page under development, and provides for the rendering of data (using the jQuery plug-in). Content and background script communicate via Chrome system messages. The separation into the two scripts is imposed by Chrome's protection logic: only the background script has access to system features like local storage or extension management, while the content script is able to access and modify the DOM of the page shown in the browser. The *iAPI editor* comes as JavaScript code that is injected into the Web page under development. It parses the annotations of the iAPIs inside the page, augments them accordingly with graphical controls, and injects the event handlers necessary to intercept user interactions that can be turned into JavaScript data integration logics (in turn, injected into the page by the content script). Editor and content script communicate via standard HTML 5 messages.

One of the key features of the editor is the abilityto pre-render *templates* for data visualization. In fact, there are two types of templates, depending on their flexibility: *static* templates and *dynamic* templates. The former are templates

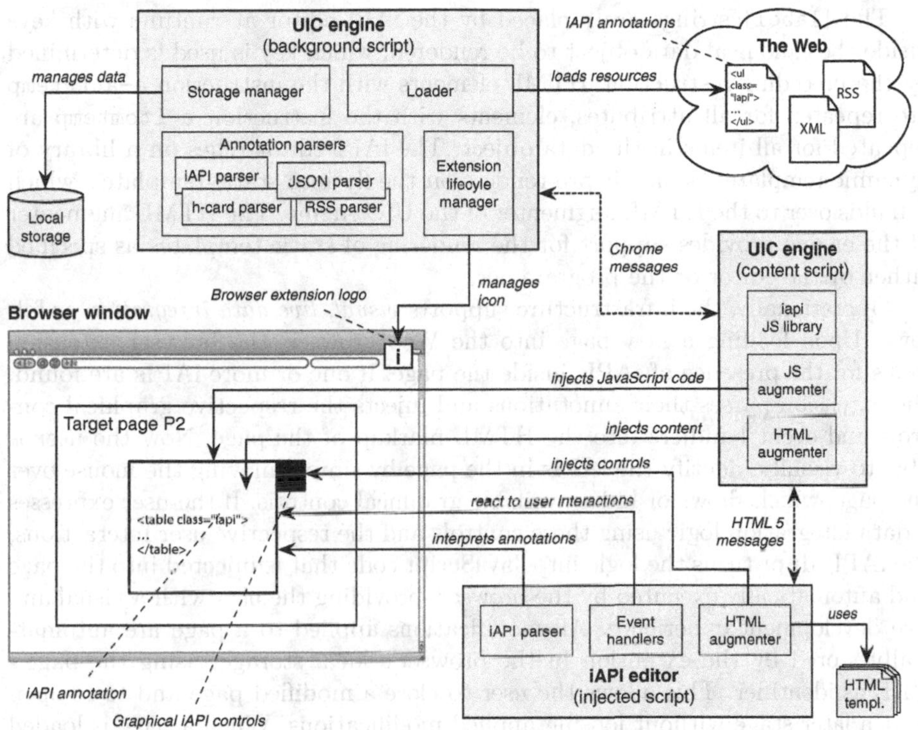

Fig. 3. Architecture of the UI-oriented computing environment as browser extension

whose structure is known at design time of the template, e.g., if the programmer wants to implement a data visualization for data whose structure is known (we discussed this case in the previous section). The latter are templates whose structure is only partially known at design time, since the structure of the data to be rendered is only known at rendering time of the data. This is the case of the visual, interactive development in which the structure of the data to be rendered is only known when actually interacting with a data iAPI. Static templates, instead, suit development scenarios in which the programmer embeds a purposefully tailored template in an own Web page.

The following markup implements, for example, the dynamic table template that could be used to generate the static template of the previous section:

```
<table id="tbl" class="h-iapitemp h-iapi e-data:[label]">
  <tr> <td class="e-attrtemp>[label]</td> </tr>
  <tr class="e-itemtemp e-item:[label]">
    <td class="e-attrtemp p-attr:[label]"></td>
  </tr>
</table>
```

The `[label]` strings are replaced by the iAPI editor at runtime with keys inside the canonical data object to be rendered; which key is used is determined by the preceding instruction. HTML elements with the instruction `e-attrtemp` are repeated for all attributes, elements with the instruction `e-itemtemp` are repeated for all items in the data object. The iAPI editor relies on a library of dynamic templates, which it pre-renders on the fly into static templates, which it hands over to the HTML augmenter of the UIC engine. The HTML augmenter of the engine provides support for the rendering of static templates as specified either by the editor or the programmer.

Operationally, the infrastructure supports *visual, live data integration* as follows: Upon loading a new page into the Web browser, the browser extension looks for the presence of iAPIs inside the page. If one or more iAPIs are found, the extension parses their annotations and injects the respective graphical controls and event handlers into the HTML markup of the page. Now the user is able to visually identify the iAPIs in the page by simply moving the mouse over the page, which shows or hides available graphical controls. If the user expresses a data integration logic using these controls and the respective user interactions, the iAPI editor turns the logic into JavaScript code that is injected into the page and automatically executed by the browser, providing the user with a visual and live development experience. All modifications applied to a page are automatically stored by the extension in the browser's local storage, using the page's URL as identifier. This allows the user to close a modified page and to re-open it at a later stage without loosing applied modifications. When a page is loaded into the browser, before enacting the iAPI editor the extension checks if the local storage already contains modifications to be applied. If yes, it loads them and injects them, restoring the state of the page as it was when the user abandoned the page the last time.

Programmatically developed data integrations are inserted by the programmer directly into the source markup of the page and contain both the JavaScript code of the integration logic and possible static HTML templates. This kind of integration is thus automatically executed by the Web browser when loading the page, thanks to the availability of the `iapi` JavaScript library, and does not require further interventions by the UIC runtime environment unless the user of the page decides to modify the page interactively.

Note that the clear separation of the visual, interactive development paradigm (the iAPIs with their graphical controls) from the programmatic development paradigm (JavaScript abstractions) also provides for a clear separation of the visual iAPI editor from the runtime environment. While the execution logic of data integrations always boils down to the operations discussed earlier in this paper, the interpretation of how these are best expressed via UI elements and user interactions is a matter of taste as well as of effective HCI. The implemented architecture makes it easy to develop different visual editors with different conventions than described on top of the current runtime environment.

The browser extension is available as open source on https://github.com/floriandanielit/interactive-apis. The code is currently being refactored.

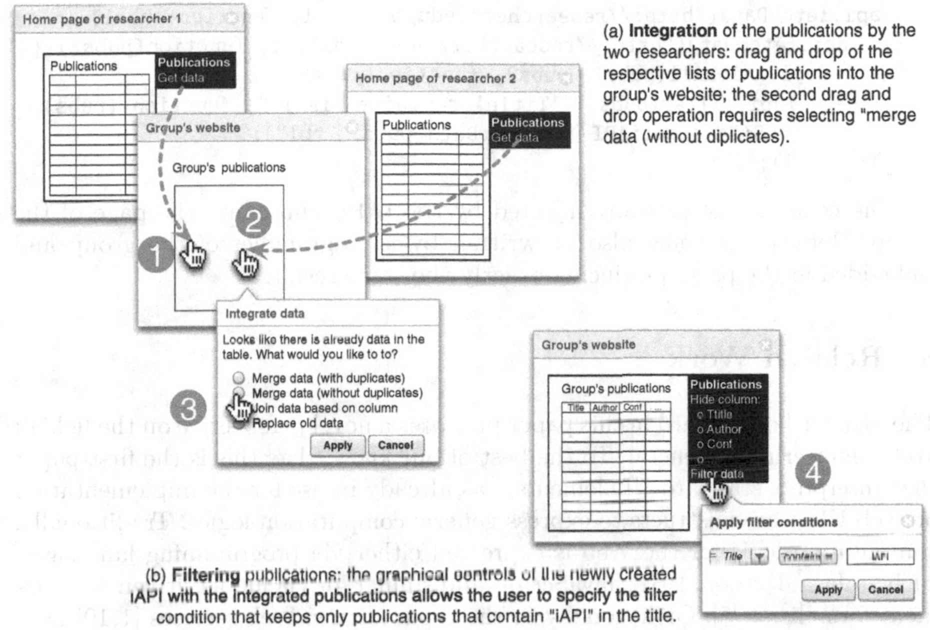

Fig. 4. UI-oriented computing solution to the initial data integration scenario

7 Case Study

We are now ready to come back to our initial data integration scenario and to show how it can be solved following the UIC approach. Figure 4 illustrates the steps that are necessary to develop the described data integration following the visual, interactive development paradigm. The whole process consists of four different steps: (1) dragging and dropping the list of papers of the first researcher into the group's website, (2) dragging and dropping the publications of the second researcher, (3) specifying that the two lists are to be merged without keeping duplicates. This produces an iAPI inside the group's website that contains all publications. In order to show only the publications on the specific topic "iAPIs," it is enough to configure a suitable filter through the iAPI's graphical controls (4). This ends the data integration process. Throughout all these steps, the user always experiences live the effect of his modifications, which allows him to easily understand whether the applied operations achieve the effect he expected or not.

The video available at http://www.floriandaniel.it/demo/uic.mp4 gives a more concrete feeling of the user experience of data integration as supported by the current prototype implementation of the iAPI editor and UIC engine. The showcased scenario is similar to the one of this paper, makes use of an auxiliary page for intermediate data formatting, and also uses the projection feature.

The JavaScript code that corresponds to the above scenario is as follows:

```
iapi.fetchData("http://researcher1.edu/pubs", 1, function(pubs1) {
  iapi.fetchData("http://researcher2.edu/pubs", 1, function(pubs2) {
    iapi.unionAll(pubs1, pubs2, function(pubs) {
      iapi.filter(pubs, "'Title' contains 'iAPI'", function (pubs) {
        $("#targetiAPI").renderData(pubs, "tbl");
}); }); }); });
```

The code is automatically injected by the iAPI editor into the page of the group. However, it could also be written by a programmer of the group and embedded in the page, producing exactly the same result.

8 Related Work

The idea pushed forward in this paper proposes a novel perspective on the field of Web engineering in general. To the best of our knowledge, this is the first paper that interprets standard UI elements – as already in use for the implementation of Web UIs – as constructs to express generic computation logics. Traditionally, computation logic for the Web is expressed either via programming languages, such as Java, Python, PHP, JavaScript, and similar, or via model-driven development formalisms [5]. Orthogonally to these paradigms, Web services [1,10] have emerged over the last decade as one of the most prominent Web technologies that influenced integration on the Web in general. Their focus, however, is on the application logic layer, not the presentation layer (the UIs) of applications.

Research on the reuse of UIs has mostly focused on the identification and definition of UI-centric component technologies, such as standard W3C widgets [14] and Java portlets [11] or proprietary formats [15], and the development of suitable integration environments [4,6]. The former essentially apply the traditional programmer perspective to UIs and still require integration at the application logic layer, e.g., via Java or JavaScript. The latter generally follow a black-box approach in the reuse of UIs: components are small, stand-alone applications and they are either included or excluded in a composition/workspace. The Web augmentation approach by Diaz et al. [9] is a partial exception: it allows for a fine-grained reuse of data among websites, starting from their UIs. The approach extracts data elements of limited size (individual labels or small fragments) without requiring additional annotations; on the downside, the approach still requires programming knowledge. None of these UI-centric approaches are however able to implement the data integration scenario approached in this paper.

Mashups [8] are the approach that comes closest to the described scenario; in fact, the discussed group website can be seen as a mashup, in particular, a data mashup. It could, for instance, be approached with the help of Yahoo! Pipes, JackBe Presto, or similar data mashup tools. Pipes (http://pipes.yahoo.com), for example, proposes a model-driven paradigm that starts from the assumption that the data to be integrated are available as RSS/Atom feeds or XML/JSON resources. This is not supported in our scenario, but can be achieved using content extraction tools like Dapper. The two lists of publications can then be merged, duplicates eliminated, and the final filter condition applied by selecting and configuring dedicated built-in constructs. The result is accessible as RSS feed via Yahoo! Pipes. Although the described logic is very similar to the one of our scenario, it still lacks the embedding of the result into the group's website, a task that requires manual development.

To aid both the extraction of content from HTML markup and the transparent invocation of backend Web services, this paper proposes the use of explicit annotations, similar to microformats (http://microformats.org). The approach does not yet focus on the annotation of data with semantics, as proposed by the Semantic Web initiative [2]. The goal of the annotations in this paper is to provide functional benefits to the consumers of data: annotations allow the injection of graphical controls that actually enable the UIC paradigm.

9 Discussion and Future Work

The goal of this paper is to propose a completely *new perspective* on a relevant problem in modern Web engineering, i.e., lightweight data integration. It does so from an original perspective, that of the UIs of applications, and in a holistic fashion. In fact, the proposed *UI-oriented computing* approach comes with all the ingredients that are necessary to turn it into practice: (i) a microformat for the annotation of data published inside Web pages or via common Web APIs/services, (ii) a UI-oriented development paradigm oriented toward users without programming skills (the interactive APIs), (iii) a UI-oriented development paradigm oriented toward programmers (the iAPI-specific JavaScript library), and (iv) a functioning runtime environment for UI-oriented data integrations (the browser extension).

On the one hand, UI-oriented computing *raises* the level of abstraction to programmers, who are provided with high-level, UI-specific constructs for data integration that allow them to neglect the technicalities of data access and manipulation. On the other hand, it *lowers* the level of abstraction to users, who are enabled to express data integrations by manipulating familiar UI constructs and do not have to learn programmer-oriented concepts that are abstract to them (e.g., Web services or database queries).

The approach further comes with a set of beneficial side effects: The *deployment* of iAPIs is contextual to the deployment of their host application, and they do not require separate deployment or maintenance. The *documentation* of iAPIs comes for free; the UI and the injected graphical controls already tell everything about them. The *retrieval* of iAPIs does not ask for new infrastructure or query paradigms; since iAPIs are an integral part of the Surface Web, it is enough to query for desired data via common Web search. All these make iAPIs and UI-oriented computing a natural integration paradigm for the Web with huge potential for fast prototyping, client-side customization, and EUD. The key difference of the proposed iAPI annotation from Semantic Web annotations is that they can immediately be turned into readily usable functionality, while generic semantic annotations lack clear target use cases and require clients to provide own implementations for their uses cases.

The *limitations* of UI-oriented computing as of today are the relatively low performance (UIs need to be instantiated locally), the missing support for more advanced uses cases beyond data integration, the lack of standardization, and, of course, the lack of annotated Web pages in general.

With our *future work*, we aim to address some of these limitations and to develop an iAPI annotation tool that allows one to "extract" iAPIs from third-party websites, to apply the UI-oriented computing approach also to forms (providing access to remote application logic) and sequences of user interactions (processes), and to propose an approach to clone complete iAPIs including their own UI. We aim to develop the respective iAPI microformat with the help of the community via the W3C Interactive APIs Community Group (http://www.w3.org/community/interative-apis).

Acknowledgments. My thanks go to A. Nouri and A. Zucchelli for their criticism and help with the implementation of the Google Chrome extension.

References

1. Alonso, G., Casati, F., Kuno, H., Machiraju, V.: Web Services: Concepts, Architectures, and Applications. Springer (2003)
2. Berners-Lee, T., Hendler, J., Lassila, O.: The semantic web. Scientific American, 34–43, May 2001
3. Cafarella, M.J., Halevy, A., Khoussainova, N.: Data Integration for the Relational Web. Proc. VLDB Endow. **2**(1), 1090–1101 (2009)
4. Cappiello, C., Matera, M., Picozzi, M., Sprega, G., Barbagallo, D., Francalanci, C.: DashMash: a mashup environment for end user development. In: Auer, S., Díaz, O., Papadopoulos, G.A. (eds.) ICWE 2011. LNCS, vol. 6757, pp. 152–166. Springer, Heidelberg (2011)
5. Ceri, S., Fraternali, P., Bongio, A., Brambilla, M., Comai, S., Matera, M.: Designing Data-Intensive Web Applications. Morgan Kauffmann (2002)
6. Chudnovskyy, O., Nestler, T., Gaedke, M., Daniel, F., Fernández-Villamor, J.I., Chepegin, V.I., Fornas, J.A., Wilson, S., Kögler, C., Chang, H.: End-user-oriented telco mashups: the OMELETTE approach. In: WWW 2012 (Companion Volume), pp. 235–238 (2012)
7. Daniel, F., Furlan, A.: The interactive API (iAPI). In: Sheng, Q.Z., Kjeldskov, J. (eds.) ICWE Workshops 2013. LNCS, vol. 8295, pp. 3–15. Springer, Heidelberg (2013)
8. Daniel, F., Matera, M.: Mashups: Concepts, Models and Architectures. Springer (2014)
9. Díaz, O., Arellano, C., Azanza, M.: A Language for End-user Web Augmentation: Caring for Producers and Consumers Alike. ACM Trans. Web **7**(2), 9:1–9:51 (2013)
10. Fielding, R.: Architectural Styles and the Design of Network-based Software Architectures. Ph.d. dissertation, University of California, Irvine (2007)
11. Hepper, S.: Java Portlet Specification, Version 2.0, Early Draft. Technical Report JSR 286, IBM Corp., July 2006. http://download.oracle.com/otndocs/jcp/portlet-2.0-edr-oth-JSpec/

12. Lenzerini, M.: Data integration: a theoretical perspective. In: PODS 2002, pp. 233–246 (2002)
13. Namoun, A., Nestler, T., Angeli, A.D.: Service composition for non-programmers: prospects, problems, and design recommendations. In: Brogi, A., Pautasso, C., Papadopoulos, G.A. (eds.) ECOWS, pp. 123–130. IEEE Computer Society (2010)
14. Web Application Working Group. Widgets Family of Specifications. Technical report, W3C, May 2012. http://www.w3.org/2008/webapps/wiki/WidgetSpecs
15. Yu, J., Benatallah, B., Saint-Paul, R., Casati, F., Daniel, F., Matera, M.: A framework for rapid integration of presentation components. In: WWW 2007, pp. 923–932 (2007)

Distributed Service Discovery in Mobile IoT Environments Using Hierarchical Bloom Filters

Hyeon-Jun Jo(✉), Jung-Hyun Kwon, and In-Young Ko

School of Computing, Korea Advanced Institute of Science and Technology, 291 Daehak-ro, Yuseong-gu, Daejeon 305-701, South Korea
{hyeonjun.jo,junghyun.kwon,iko}@kaist.ac.kr

Abstract. The Internet of Things (IoT) enables many devices to interact with each other in order to provide services to users. Especially, mobiles devices are becoming more powerful and common in everyday life, and it is essential to utilize their capabilities to provide services in IoT environments. In this paper, we propose a fast and flexible approach to discovering IoT-based services in mobile IoT environments. We applied Bloom filters to the configuration and management of distributed service registries to reduce the configuration cost, and to reduce the number of message exchanges between registries in updating information about available services. Especially, we extended the traditional Bloom filter to give it a hierarchical structure to more efficiently discover and manage information about the capabilities of IoT resources and the services that utilize them. We showed that performance increases and less message traffics in discovering available services by adding hierarchies to Bloom filters.

Keywords: Service discovery · Distributed service registries · Internet of things · Bloom filter

1 Introduction

In Internet of Things (IoT) environments, many real-world objects, from small sensors to vehicles, become smart objects that can be utilized to provide users with information and service capabilities [1] [2]. In addition, mobile devices such as smart phones, tablet PCs and wearable devices are becoming more powerful and common in everyday life, and they are regarded as important parts of IoT environments. We call the IoT environment, in which there are IoT devices that have mobility, a *mobile IoT environment*. Mobile Ad-hoc Network (MANET) [4] is being regarded as a promising technology to make connections among mobile IoT devices to make them interact with each other for user tasks. For example, the Thread group [7] is a mesh network, a type of MANET, which connects various household devices in a flexible and scalable manner.

In this mobile IoT environment, because of the mobility characteristic of IoT devices, connectivity among the devices is highly dynamic and spontaneous. Therefore, it is a challenging issue to discover and provide services that utilize the capabilities of mobile IoT devices in a reliable manner. In addition, since the status of services that

P. Cimiano et al. (Eds.): ICWE 2015, LNCS 9114, pp. 498–514, 2015.
DOI: 10.1007/978-3-319-19890-3_32

can be offered utilizing mobile IoT devices is volatile [3], it is necessary to effectively monitor and manage the availability and status of IoT-based services. The characteristics of the mobile IoT environment can be summarized as mobility, temporal connectivity, diversity, and large number of devices [4].

An IoT resource can be used by one or more services. In addition, services that utilize IoT resources work together to perform user tasks. A user task is a composition of services that provides capabilities that are necessary to accomplish a user's goal. Therefore, the challenging issue is to find appropriate services for a task out of the available services in the mobile IoT environment. Unlike service discovery in the traditional Web environment, in an IoT environment it is essential to effectively deal with dynamic changes in service availability and connectivity among resources. Therefore, *service discovery* in mobile IoT environments can be defined as follows: recognizing, configuring, and communicating of IoT resources and the services that utilize them [5]; finding available services in a dynamic manner; and managing status information [6].

In this paper, to meet these needs, we propose distributed service registries that enable fast and flexible service discovery in highly dynamic and spontaneous IoT-based service environments. A *service registry* stores information about the available services in an environment and provides clients with functions to find necessary services and to check the status of the services. To successfully build distributed service registries, it is essential to minimize the overhead of message exchanges between registries in order to find available services based on the IoT resources in a certain region. Especially, it is crucial to reduce the time overhead spent identifying resource capabilities of the available IoT devices, the services that can be provided by utilizing resource capabilities, and the tasks that can be performed by coordinating the available services.

In this work, we applied Bloom filters to the configuration and management of distributed service registries to reduce the configuration cost, and to reduce message exchanges in updating information about available services in dynamic mobile IoT environments. A *Bloom filter* converts a set of elements into an array by mapping each element of the set to a combination of index numbers. Each combination of index numbers is unique, and can later be used to identify an element of the set. For our distributed registry system, we convert each resource capability and service into a combination of integer numbers. Then, we project the combinations into coordinate points on a multi-dimensional coordinate system. Then, a registry can find necessary resource capabilities for a service on the coordinate system using the vector of the resource capabilities. On the coordinate system, each point means that the corresponding resource capability is available in the environment. In this way, availability of a service in a registry can be efficiently checked. Then, by sharing the converted points for available services with other neighboring registries, it is possible to maintain a global view of available services in the IoT environment.

Due to the false-positive problem of Bloom filters, we must control the range of unique index numbers and the number of hash functions to reduce the rate of generation of false-positive errors. The false-positive error rate depends on the total number of elements used. In other words, the higher the number of elements we use, the higher the number of hash functions will be needed. This causes a scalability problem. Therefore, we developed a *hierarchical Bloom filter* for the distributed service registries. We use multiple Bloom filters, each of which is used for a different level of the resource and the service hierarchies. The *resource-capability hierarchy* defines various types of resource capabilities in a hierarchical manner; *service hierarchy* defines a hierarchy of service capabilities. The two hierarchies are needed to help clients request services at various abstraction levels. With experiments using ns-3 simulator, we show that performance increases and less message traffics in discovering available services in an environment.

The remainder of the paper is organized as follows. In Section 2, we explain existing work on distributed service discovery. The characteristics of the mobile IoT-based service environment are described in Section 3; in Section 4, we explain the proposed approach of using Bloom filters to build an efficient distributed service registry system. Section 5 presents our experimental results and analyses. Finally, Section 6 concludes the paper with a brief discussion on our contribution and future work.

2 Related Work

Distributed service registries have been studied to overcome disadvantages such as bottleneck and single point of failure problems of centralized registry systems. First, a backbone network based approach was proposed [12] [13]. In this approach, a backbone network is formed using several nodes in an ad-hoc manner, and service registries are installed in the network nodes. This approach makes it possible to discover and manage services in distributed network nodes, but it may produce a lot of network traffic because a query to discover services is broadcasted to all registries in the network. Moreover, whenever there are any changes in the network nodes, the backbone network needs to be reformed to reflect the changes.

Service clustering methods have been developed to overcome the disadvantages of backbone network based approaches [14] [15]. The service clustering methods classify services in a network in different groups based on their types (e.g., node location) and choose a representative network resource to manage services in each group. This approach can reduce network traffic by sending a service-discovery query only to a specific cluster. However, it has the additional overhead of choosing a new representative for a cluster when the network changes. Although it is possible to use a static clustering method, one that does not consider network changes, such a method can still be problematic when the representative of a cluster is broken or not reachable.

There have also been studies on using distributed hash tables (DHT) for service discovery [16] [17]. In such an approach, each service has its unique key and the key and the location information of the service are stored in a hash table. Multiple registries distributed in a network environment are used to manage the table. The location information refers to a point in the entire area formed by all the service registries. Existing research assumes that each registry knows the correct location, which is hard to know because each registry knows location information for its local area, not for the global area.

There has been research on using a Bloom filter for service discovery. Sailhan et al. applied a Bloom filter to service description and reduced the size of service information stored in a registry [18]. This study, however, did not apply a Bloom filter to service-discovery queries exchanged among the service registries. Cheng et al. proposed a Counter Bloom filter to overcome the limitation of the traditional Bloom filter, in which stored hash values cannot be deleted after they are generated [19]. Using the Counter Bloom filter, service specifications that are stored in a registry can be deleted, and it is possible to reduce the size of the registry. However, this method cannot reduce the network traffic caused by the registries exchanging service information.

The aforementioned studies focused on fast information search within a service registry using a Bloom filter. Our study seeks not only to search service information fast inside a registry but also to reduce network traffic exchanged among registries by using a hierarchical Bloom filter, which is explained in Section 4.

3 Mobile IoT-Based Service Environment

The target environment that we consider in this work is an IoT-based service environment, in which various IoT resources and service gateways are deployed in a geographical region. The IoT resources and service gateways have mobility. The IoT resources are various types of IoT devices from tiny sensors to security cameras on streets, smartphones, and other IoT devices. Each IoT resource provides *resource capabilities*, which can be utilized to provide services. For the IoT resources that do not have enough computation and networking power to provide services, there are service gateways that proactively find IoT resources in the surrounding environment and make them accessible to provide services. A service needs to be bound to required resource capabilities in order to generate its service capability. The quality of a service is determined according to the capabilities of the IoT resources that are bound to the service. A *user task* is a composition of abstract services that define necessary capabilities to accomplish a user goal. A user task needs to be bound to service instances that provide service capabilities by utilizing IoT resources. There may be multiple service instances available for an abstract service of a task, and a service instance is chosen based on the quality requirements of a user.

Fig. 1 illustrates a mobile IoT-based service environment, including these core components. The *task layer* in Fig.1 is for selecting and running a user task. The *IoT resource layer* is composed of service gateways, service registries, and IoT resources. A *service gateway* discovers nearby IoT resources, and monitors changes in the surrounding environment to update the status information about the available IoT resources and service instances that utilize the IoT resources. The gateway has a connection range in which it can discover IoT resources. Gateways can be connected to each other and exchange information about available IoT resources and services that can be provided in a local environment. Smartphones and portable computing devices that have computing and networking capabilities can be used as gateways.

An IoT resource can be moved into an environment and can be dynamically discovered by nearby service gateways. An IoT resource can be utilized by one or more services. A service gateway usually has a limited *connection capacity* of maintaining connections to IoT resources. In addition, the number of gateways to which an IoT resource is connected and by which it can be monitored can be controlled by overall policy.

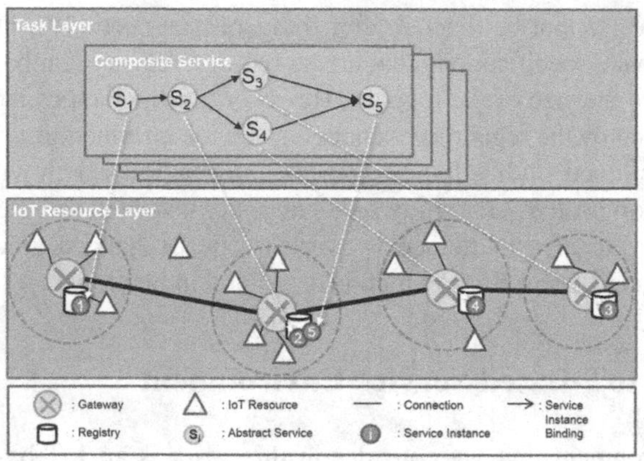

Fig. 1. Mobile IoT-based Service Environment

A service registry is deployed to a service gateway. A service registry stores the information about the IoT resources that are connected to the corresponding service gateway. It also identifies the services that can be provided by utilizing the IoT resources in a local environment, and maintains information about available services. Service registries also collaborate with each other by exchanging messages to monitor and share the status information about available services in the local environment. Therefore, it is possible to obtain information about available services by querying any of the service registries in the local environment.

4 A Hierarchical Bloom Filter for Distributed Service Registries

4.1 Hierarchies of Resource Capabilities and Services

We designed an ontology model to represent the relationship between the conceptual entities that are related to the resources and services in IoT-based service environments. Fig. 2 shows the model, which is composed of task, service, resource, and capabilities. The tasks, services, and resources provide their own capabilities, and the capabilities are compared against each other by the service discovery engine. A task is a composition of services and requires some service capabilities to provide its capabilities; a service requires certain resource capabilities to deliver its service capability.

To run a service instance, that instance needs to be bound to necessary resource capabilities. In our registry system, the required resource capabilities can be specified at different abstraction levels. The IoT resources that provide capabilities at a certain abstraction level that a service specifies, or more specialized capabilities than those of the abstraction level, are all considered as candidate IoT resources for the service. To support this, the resource capabilities are defined hierarchically by representing the subsumption relations (by using the 'subClassOf' relation) between the capabilities. Services are also defined similarly by representing the subsumption relations between service capabilities. The abstract services of a user task define their necessary service capabilities, which can be represented at various abstraction levels, and a query to find service instances for an abstract service can be made according to the abstraction levels specified.

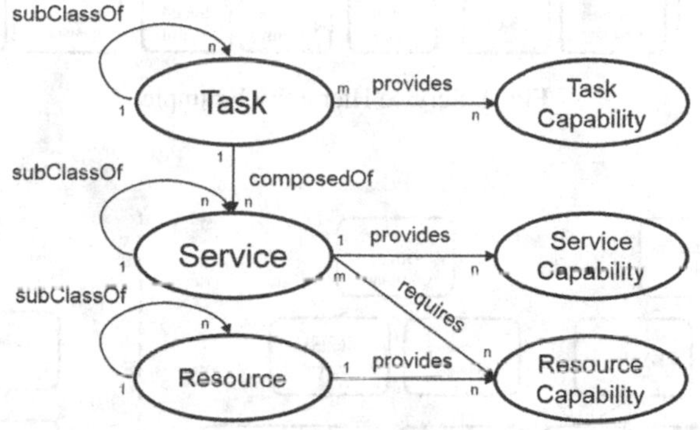

Fig. 2. Ontology Model for Mobile IoT Service Environment

By using the hierarchies of resource capabilities and services, it is also possible to identify services that can be run based on the available resource capabilities in a local environment. In addition, after recognizing the available services, user tasks that can be performed in the environment can be recommended to users.

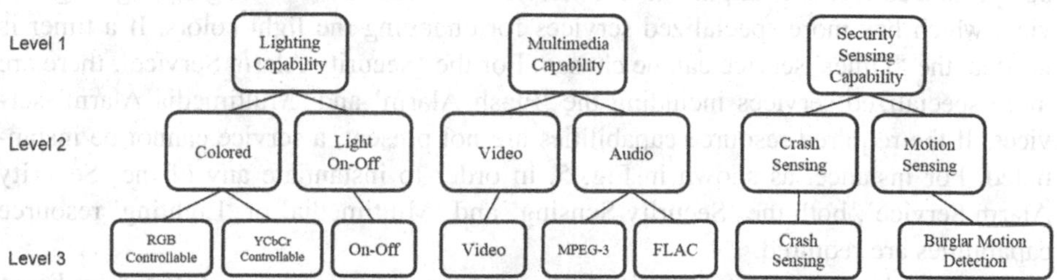

Fig. 3. Resource Capability Hierarchy Example

Fig. 3 shows a partial view of the resource capability hierarchy. The ‘Lighting’, ‘Multimedia’, and ‘Security Sensing’ capabilities are defined as the top-level capabilities, which can be divided into more specialized capabilities. For example, there are the ‘Colored’ lighting and simple ‘Light On-Off’ capabilities under the ‘Lighting’ capability, and the ‘Colored’ lighting capability can be further specialized into the ‘RGB Controllable’ and ‘YCbCr Controllable’ capabilities. If a service requires the ‘Colored’ lighting capability, any of the IoT resources that provide either of these specialized capabilities can be selected and bound to the service.

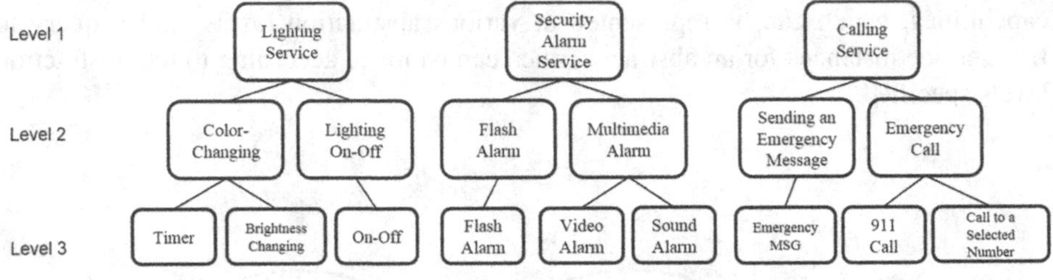

Fig. 4. Service Hierarchy Example

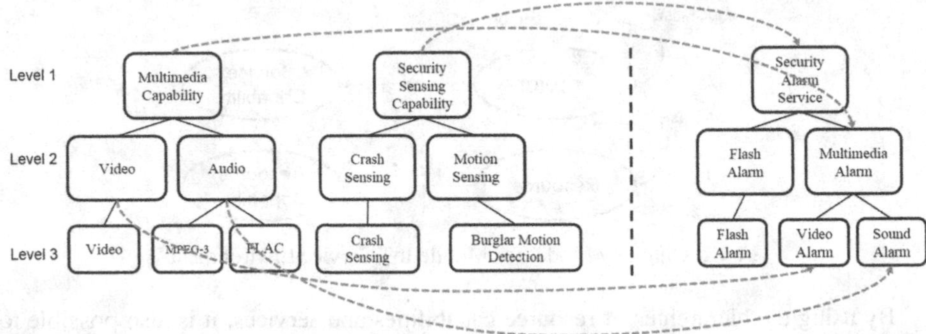

Fig. 5. An Example of Representing Relationship between Resource Capabilities and Services

Fig. 4 shows a part of the service capability hierarchy. The 'Lighting' service can be specialized into the 'Light On-Off' service, and the 'Color-changing' lighting service, which has more specialized services for changing the light colors. If a timer is needed, the 'Timer' service can be chosen. For the 'Security Alarm Service', there are more specialized services including the 'Flash Alarm' and 'Multimedia Alarm' services. If the required resource capabilities are not present, a service cannot be instantiated. For instance, as shown in Fig. 5, in order to instantiate any of the 'Security Alarm Service', both the 'Security Sensing' and 'Multimedia' or 'Lighting' resource capabilities are required.

A user task can be performed if all the abstract services are instantiated by being bound to required IoT resources. For example, the 'Secure a car' task requires two services, the 'Lighting' and 'Security Alarm' services, which can be instantiated by using the 'Lighting', 'Multimedia', and 'Security Sensing' capabilities.

4.2 Hierarchical Bloom Filters

A Bloom filter is a probabilistic data structure used to test if an element is a member of a set or not [8]. A Bloom filter is composed of a bit array and a set of hash functions. Once the bit array is made by performing the hash functions for a set of elements, it is possible to efficiently check if a specific element is in the set or not without searching all the elements. Some lookup mechanisms are necessary to implement a Bloom filter to avoid unnecessary search [9] [10]. The hash functions generate a series of integers for each element. These integers represent the positions (indices) in

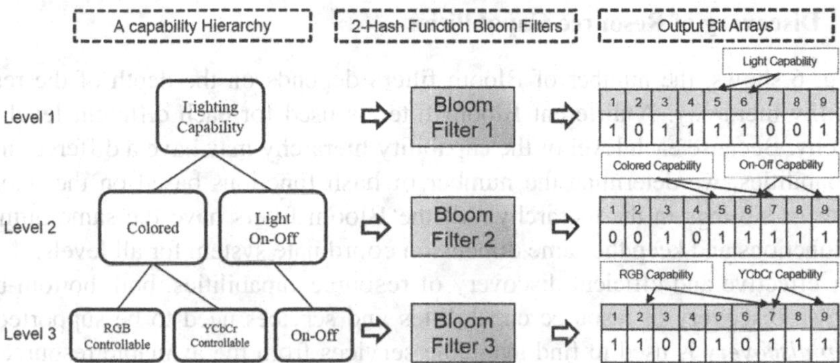

Fig. 6. Bloom Filters Applied to the Resource Capability Hierarchy

the bit array. The number of integers is determined based on the number of hash functions. In other words, every element is assigned a unique sequence of integers as a result of performing the hash functions. We can decide whether an element is in the set or not by checking specific positions of the bit array.

A *hierarchical Bloom filter* is a set of Bloom filters, each of which corresponds to one level of the resource capability hierarchy. Fig. 6 shows an example of the application of a hierarchical Bloom filter to the 'Lighting' capability hierarchy. In this example, since each Bloom filter has two hash functions, each capability is converted into two integers. In the figure, the 'Lighting' capability is represented by the integer numbers, 5 and 6, the 'Colored' lighting capability is converted to 5 and 7, and the 2 and 7 integer numbers are assigned to the 'RGB Controllable' lighting capability.

A Bloom filter has a 100% recall rate, which means that there are no false-negative errors but there may be false-positive errors. If there are false-positive errors, the resource capabilities and/or services that are not actually available may appear as if they are available during the service discovery process. Therefore, it is critical to manage the rate of false-positive errors so that it is very low. We can configure the rate of generating false-positive errors by resizing the number of hash functions and the length of the bit array. Equation (1) shows how to calculate the rate of false-positive errors [11]. In the equation, n is the number of elements managed by a Bloom filter, k is the number of hash functions, and m is the length of the bit array. Equation (1) means that the Bloom filter makes a tradeoff between the length of the bit array and the rate of false-positive errors. An increase of the number of hash functions causes an increase of the dimensions of the coordinate system, and generates more computational overhead in the discovering of services. Therefore, we determine the number of hash functions first, and then set the acceptable rate of false-positive errors by adjusting the length of the bit array.

$$(1-[1-\frac{1}{m}]^{kn})^k \approx (1-e^{-kn/m})^k \tag{1}$$

4.3 Discovery of Resource Capabilities

As Fig. 6 shows, the number of Bloom filters depends on the depth of the resource capability hierarchy. A different Bloom filter is used for each different level of the hierarchy. Because each level of the capability hierarchy may have a different number of capabilities, we determine the number of hash functions based on the maximum number of siblings in the hierarchy. All the Bloom filters have the same number of hash functions and keep the same dimension coordinate system for all levels.

For effective and efficient discovery of resource capabilities, both bottom-up and top-down discovery of resource capabilities and services need to be supported. *Bottom-up discovery* is used to find available services from the available resource capabilities found in a local environment. *Top-down discovery* is used to find necessary resource capabilities for instantiating an abstract service of a user task. There should be also a fast and simple method to reduce the overhead of exchanging messages to find available services based on the resource capabilities that exist in an environment. In addition, since the integer numbers that are generated by Bloom filters do not have any regularity but are rather almost random, we need a method to represent the hierarchical relations between levels of resource capabilities.

Algorithm 1 Convert Resource Capabilities to Vectors

```
Require: Capability C
Require: Capacity Hierarchy CH
Require: Number of Hash Functions in a Bloom Filter HF
Set capabilityVector to HF dimensional vector
Set all elements in capabilityVector to 0
Set Number of digits to shift per each hash function to digitsToShift
while C in CH do
    resourceDescription = getResourceDescription(C)
    hashValues = applyBloomfilter(resourceDescription)
    for axis = 0, axis < length(hashValues) do
        hashValues[axis]* = power(10, digitsToShift[axis])
        capabilityVector[axis]+ = hashValues[axis]
    C = getParentNode(C)
```

To meet these requirements, we have developed a method to map all the Bloom filter output values of resource capabilities in a coordinate space. Algorithm 1 shows the procedure of converting a resource capability into a coordinate point by using Equation (2). In the equation, L is the level of the resource capability hierarchy, BF_l is an integer number of a resource capability generated by a Bloom filter of level l, and D_l is the digit of the bit array of the Bloom filter of level l. Using this method, we can represent any resource capability as a numeric vector rather than as a string description. For instance, in Fig. 3, the 'Lighting' capability is represented as $\vec{V}_L(500, 600)$, the 'Light On-off' capability as $\vec{V}_B(560, 690)$, the 'Colored' lighting capability as $\vec{V}_C(550, 670)$, the 'RGB' lighting capability as $\vec{V}_R(552, 677)$, and the 'YCbCr' lighting capability as $\vec{V}_Y(557, 679)$.

$$\text{Resource Capability A}, \vec{V}_A = (\bar{p}_1, \bar{p}_2, \bar{p}_3, \dots, \bar{p}_k)$$

$$\text{Bloom Filter of Level } l, BF_l(A) = (i_{l,1}, i_{l,2}, i_{l,3}, \dots, i_{l,k})$$

$$D_l = \begin{cases} l = L, D_l = 0 \\ l < L, D_l = \sum_{j=l+1}^{L} d_j \end{cases}, d_j = Digit\ of\ BF_j(A)$$

$$\text{For } \vec{V}_A, \bar{p}_k = \sum_{l=0}^{L}\{i_{l,k} \times 10^{D_l}\} \quad (2)$$

Each service registry shares the vector points of its own resource capabilities with other registries in a certain geographical region. The messages that are exchanged between registries are composed of the vector point information, and the location and name of the service registries. The vector points of the resource capabilities and services that are stored in a service registry can be projected to a coordinate system. Each point represents the location of a resource capability. Since a service may require multiple resource capabilities, we represent the location of a service as the median point of the required resource capabilities. By specifying a resource capability at a certain abstraction level, all the specialized resource capabilities can be included in the area in the coordinate system. Resource capabilities that are siblings belong to different areas in the coordinate system.

Fig. 7 shows the vector convergence of the resource capabilities shown in Fig. 3, and the mappings of the resource capabilities to a coordinate system. Different shadow areas indicate different types of capabilities at different abstraction levels. More specialized resource capabilities are shown in smaller areas in the coordinate system. In addition, in Fig. 7, similar or alternative resource capabilities are shown as close to each other. Therefore, alternative resource capabilities can be found efficiently by searching a small area rather than searching the entire coordinate space. However, an alternative resource capability found in the space may belong to a totally different abstraction level if there is a higher-level boundary to the alternative. Therefore, we need to find alternative resource capabilities at the highest abstraction level.

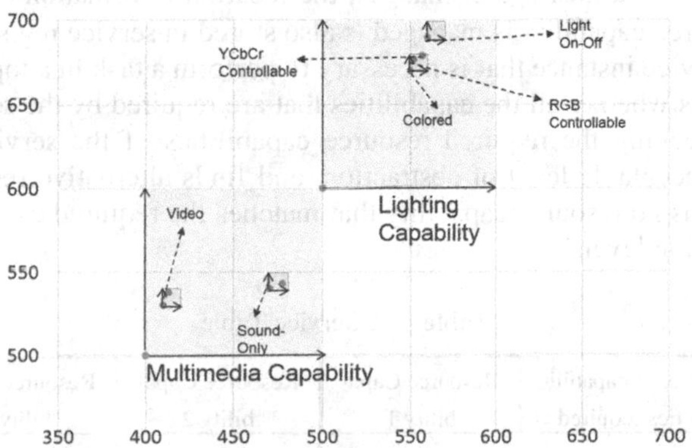

Fig. 7. Vector Conversion of Resource Capabilities

4.4 Discovery of Services

We have designed a *service table* that keeps the status information of the resource capabilities that are necessary to instantiate a service. This table enables both bottom-up and top-down discovery of service instances that are needed to perform a user task. Table 1 is an example of the service table; it includes the names of registered services, the number of resource capabilities required for each service, and the resource capabilities that are necessary for each service. Required resource capabilities of a service can be represented at various abstraction levels in the service table.

Algorithm 2 Discovery of Available Services

```
Require: Service Table ST
Require: Capability Hierarchy CH
availableService = []
for service in ST do
    requiredResourceCapabilities=ST[service]
    matchingResourceCapabilities=[]
    for rc in requiredResourceCapabilities do
        if rc in the terminals of CH then
            //There are exact services providing rc
            matchingResourceCapabilities.append(rc)
        else if rc in the non-terminals of CH then
            //There are alternative services providing rc
            matchingResourceCapabilities.append(rc)
    if requiredResourceCapabilities == matchingResourceCapabilities then
        availableService.append(service)
```

Once the coordinate system for resource capabilities is generated, as Algorithm 2 shows, the availability of a resource capability can be checked efficiently by looking up the vector point of the resource capability in the coordinate system. After comparing service tables with identified resource capability points, available services can be efficiently identified. In addition, when available resource capability points are shared between registries via message exchanges, the location information of the registry in which the resource capability is managed is also stored in service registries.

To find a service instance that is necessary to perform a task in a top-down manner, a registry checks whether all the capabilities that are required by the service are available. While checking the required resource capabilities of the service, the registry considers the acceptable level of abstraction, and finds alternative resource capabilities when there is no resource capability that matches the required capability specified for that abstraction level.

Table 1. A Service Table

Service	No. of capabilities required	Resource Capability 1	Resource Capability 2	Resource Capability 3	...
A	1	(x_1, y_1)	-	-	...
B	3	(x_6, y_6)	(x_2, y_2)	(x_3, y_3)	...
C	2	(x_4, y_4)	(x_5, y_5)	-	...

Another set of Bloom filters is used to discover user tasks by identifying available service instances. The discovery process is similar to the one that we explained in the previous sections. The available services are shared as a point; then, the available tasks are identified from all the shared service points by using a *task table*, which plays a role similar to that of the service table. The difference between a service table and a task table is that a task table includes information about the sequence of composing services.

5 Experiment and Analysis

Experiments are conducted to show how the pointed problems are solved. First, we expect that a Bloom filter itself will have a space advantage in representing each resource capability and service. In addition, by using a Bloom filter we expect that messages between distributed service registries will be generated with shorter lengths. We suggest hierarchical Bloom filters to overcome the problem of computing overhead when identifying available services. The Bloom filters generate a unique sequence of numbers for each resource capability and shares the integer numbers. After sharing, each service registry is able to quickly identify available services by comparing the integer numbers.

Furthermore, hierarchical Bloom filters are suggested for the identification of available services in a more flexible manner. This process reduces the searching space when seeking resource capabilities for each service; the final computing time is reduced more than it is when using non-hierarchical Bloom filters.

5.1 Experiment Settings

In comparison to the traditional service discovery approach, which exchanges service descriptions encoded as Simple Object Access Protocol (SOAP) messages, our approach generates much less network traffic because the Bloom filters convert the full service descriptions into simple integers. In addition, comparisons between bit arrays take much less computing time than does the comparing of SOAP XML messages. Therefore, in this experiment, rather than comparing the Bloom filter based approach and the traditional SOAP-based approach, we focus on evaluating the effectiveness of the two different approaches to applying Bloom filters: the non-hierarchical and the hierarchical Bloom filter approaches.

The dataset that we use for the experiment is generated by constructing hierarchies of resource capabilities and services, and by classifying the instances of IoT resources and services under the hierarchies in a randomized manner. For service instances, we use the Web service dataset,[1] which is composed of practical Web services data. We do not parse all information from the Web service data set; however, we use them as input for the Bloom filters. We generate various hierarchies of resource capabilities and services. The various hierarchies have different maximum numbers of siblings under a parent. When creating the relationships between resources and services, we

[1] http://www.wsdream.net/dataset.html

assign a maximum of five resource capabilities to a service and a maximum of five service capabilities to a user task.

During the experiment, we check the effectiveness of the approaches by changing the number of registries, the number of capabilities per service registry, the total number of resource capabilities and services, the depth of the resource capability and service hierarchies, and the number of hash functions for each Bloom filter. We measure the computing time for a service registry to identify available services based on IoT resources that are available in a local environment. In addition, we measure the amount of message traffic generated while identifying the available services. In the experiment, we check the computing time and message traffics while changing the number of resource capabilities and services from 30 to 400. In addition, we randomly allocate up to 30 resource capabilities for each service registry, and make a service to be associated with maximum 5 resource capabilities in a randomized manner. In addition, we test our approach with changing the depth of the hierarchies from 2 to 4.

In this experiment, we simulate the mobile IoT environment by using the ns-3[2] simulator, which is commonly used in network simulations. In this simulation environment, we created service gateways, and IoT resources that can be connected via Wi-Fi 802.11b. The simulation is performed by using a desktop computer running Ubuntu 12.04 (32-bit) with Intel Core i7-2600 (3.40GHz) with 16.00GB of RAM.

5.2 Experiment Result and Analysis

Fig. 8 compares the computing time and message traffics between the non-hierarchical Bloom filter and the hierarchical Bloom filters with different depths (with 2 to 4 levels). As shown in Fig. 8 (a), all the cases of using the hierarchical Bloom filter take much less computing time than the case of using the non-hierarchical Bloom filter. In addition, the gap between the non-hierarchical and hierarchical Bloom filter approaches gets wider as the number of resource capabilities and services increases. The difference between the non-hierarchical Bloom filter approach and the hierarchical Bloom filter approach with four levels is about 490µs when there are 40 resource capabilities and services, and the difference reaches up to 1,020µs when there are 400 resource capabilities and services. We expect that there will be more performance improvement of discovering services when there are more number of resource capabilities and services that need to be managed in a local IoT environment by the distributed service registries.

The computing time of the hierarchical Bloom filter approaches increase slightly as the depth of the hierarchies increases. This time overhead is due to the increase of the time to access multiple integers that correspond to the levels in the hierarchies. The simulation is performed by using a high-performance desktop computer. In practical IoT environments, service gateways are usually located in mobile devices that have much less computing power than the desktop computer. Therefore, we expect that the performance gain that we obtained by using the hierarchical Bloom filters will be significant in real IoT-based service environments. In addition, the performance of individual service registries is critical to improve the overall performance of discovering services in a

---

2 https://www.nsnam.org

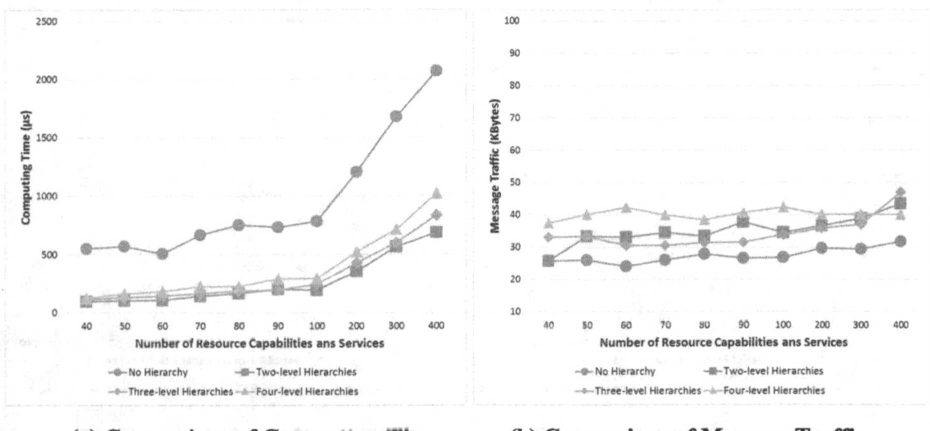

(a) Comparison of Computing Time **(b) Comparison of Message Traffic**

Fig. 8. Comparisons between Non-Hierarchical and Hierarchical Bloom Filters with Three Hash Functions

wide area where there are many resource capabilities and services to manage by a number of service registries.

As shown in Fig. 8 (b), the non-hierarchical Bloom filter generates the least amount of message traffic. Regarding to the hierarchical Bloom filter approaches, the message traffic increases slightly as the depth of the resource capability and service hierarchies increases. This is due to the fact that the hierarchical Bloom filters generate longer bit arrays as the depth of the hierarchies increases. However, the differences between the non-hierarchical and hierarchical Bloom filter approaches are not significant (maximum 18Kbyte difference) in mobile IoT environments where the network bandwidth is usually greater than 10Mbps (with Wi-Fi connections).

As the number of resource capabilities and services increase, it is necessary to increase either the number of hash functions or the depth of the resource capability and service hierarchies. In Fig. 8, we showed that having levels in the hierarchies causes a slight increase in computing time and message traffic. Fig. 9 compares the computing time and message traffics between the cases of using two hash functions and three hash functions for the Bloom filters with four levels in the hierarchies. As can be seen in the figure, having an additional hash function causes some overhead in computing time and message traffic. This is because it is necessary to manipulate and transmit more number of integers, as there is more number of hash functions.

In addition, the computing overhead caused by increasing the number of hash functions is relatively lager than the overhead generated by increasing the depth of the hierarchies. In other words, when there are 400 resource capabilities and services to manage, there is an increase of about 220µs in computing time as we add an additional hash function, whereas there is about 100µs increase in computing time when we increase the level of the hierarchies from 3 to 4. However, there is no significant difference in terms

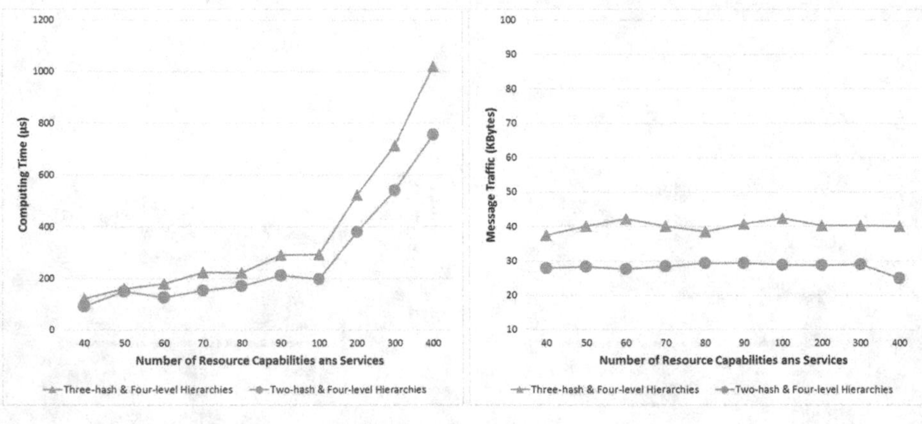

(a) Comparison of Computing Time **(b) Comparison of Message Traffic**

Fig. 9. Comparisons between Different-Hash Four Level Bloom Filters

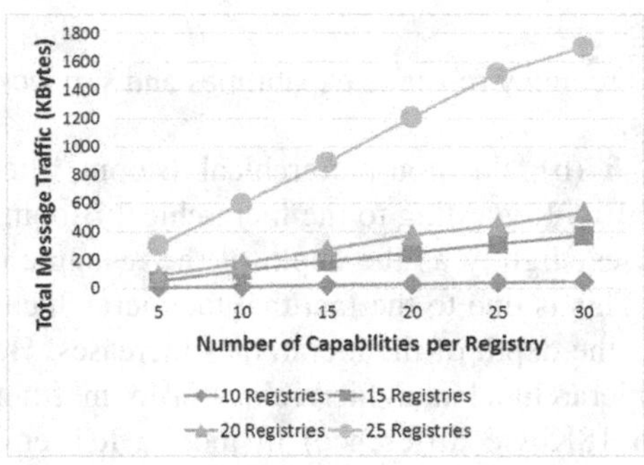

Fig. 10. Message Traffic Generated by Different Number of Registries

of the message traffic increased by having an additional hash function and adding a level in the hierarchies (about 15Kbyte increase vs. about 18Kbyte increase). Therefore, to handle more number of resource capabilities and services, it is more efficient to increase the depth of the hierarchies rather than adding more hash functions to the distributed service discovery system.

Fig. 10 compares the amount of message traffic generated by the service registries as we increase the number of service registries in an IoT environment. For each of the cases of having 10, 15, 20 and 25 service registries, we checked the trend of message traffic increase as we increase the number of resource capabilities that need to be managed by a service registry. All the cases show a linear increase in message traffic. However, as can be seen in the figure, the rate of message-traffic increase gets higher as there is more number of service registries. This is because there should be more interactions among the registries if their number increases in an environment. However, the amount of message-traffic increase is not significant when we increase the number of service registries up to 20 (maximum 500Kbyte increase when the number of service registries increases from 10 to 20). This result implies that the proposed approach is scalable to the number of service registries. However, to maintain the amount of message traffic in an IoT environment at a certain level, it is necessary to limit the number of service registries in the local area.

6 Conclusion

A mobile IoT environment is the service environment where diverse mobile IoT resources produce various capabilities that can be utilized to provide users with services that are necessary to accomplish their tasks. In this environment, it is essential to efficiently manage and find resource capabilities and services, of which availability and connection status are dynamically changed. In this paper, we have proposed an efficient approach to discovering IoT-based services in mobile IoT environments. We applied Bloom filters to the configuration and management of distributed service registries to reduce the configuration cost, and to reduce the number of message exchanges between registries in updating information about available services in dynamic mobile IoT environments. Especially, we extended the traditional Bloom filter to give it a hierarchical structure to discover more efficiently and manage information about the capabilities of IoT resources and the services that utilize them. We conducted a simulation of discovering services in a highly dynamic mobile IoT environment; our results proved that our approach is much more efficient than existing distributed service discovery approaches.

Our contribution is in that we have designed an ontology model for managing the information about user tasks, services and resource capabilities, and developed the hierarchical Bloom filtering approach that enables the significant reduction of the search space for discovering resource capabilities or services. In addition, we applied the hierarchical Bloom filtering approach to make distributed service registries to efficiently collaborate with each other to find resource capabilities and services that are spread in a mobile IoT environment.

As the future work, we firstly plan to extend the approach to handle more dynamic situations such as addition and/or removal of resource capabilities and services, and join and/or leave of service registries to and/or from an IoT environment. In addition, we will make the hierarchical Bloom filters more extensible and flexible to handle a large number of IoT resources and services, and to reflect the dynamic changes on the structures of the resource-capability and service hierarchies. We will also make the vectors of services and resource capabilities contain additional information such as quality of services so that users can select a service or resource capability by considering more specific quality requirements and/or constraints when there are the same or similar services and resource capabilities to choose from. We will also test our approach in a real test-bed environment that we are currently building in our campus.

Acknowledgement. This work was supported by the Dual Use Technology Program (UM13018RD1).

References

1. Broll, G., Rukzio, E., Paolucci, M., Wagner, M., Schmidt, A., Hussmann, H.: Perci: Pervasive service interaction with the internet of things. Internet Computing **13**(6), 74–81 (2009). IEEE
2. De, S., Barnaghi, P., Bauer, M., Meissner, S.: Service modelling for the Internet of Things. In: 2011 Federated Conference on Computer Science and Information Systems (FedCSIS), pp. 949–955. IEEE (2011)
3. Verma, R., Abhishek, S.: A novel web service directory framework for mobile environments. In: 2014 IEEE International Conference on Web Services (ICWS), pp. 614–621. IEEE (2014)
4. Kozat, U.C., Leandros, T.: Network layer support for service discovery in mobile ad hoc networks. In: INFOCOM 2003, Twenty-Second Annual Joint Conference of the IEEE Computer and Communications. IEEE Societies, vol. 3, pp. 1965–1975. IEEE (2003)
5. Zhu, F., Mutka, M.W., Ni, L.M.: Service discovery in pervasive computing environments. IEEE Pervasive computing **4**(4), 81–90 (2005)
6. Bettstetter, C., Renner, C.: A comparison of service discovery protocols and implementation of the service location protocol. In: Proceedings of the 6th EUNICE Open European Summer School. Innovative Internet Applications (2000)
7. Thread Group. http://threadgroup.org
8. Bloom, B.H.: Space/time trade-offs in hash coding with allowable errors. Communications of the ACM **13**(7), 422–426 (1970)
9. Dharmapurikar, S., Krishnamurthy, P., Sproull, T., Lockwood, J.: Deep packet inspection using parallel Bloom filters. In: IEEE Symposium on High Performance Interconnects (HotI), Stanford, CA, pp. 44–51 (2003)
10. Dharmapurikar, S., Krishnamurthy, P., Taylor, D.E.: Longest prefix matching using Bloom filters. In: Proceedings of the 2003 Conference on Applications, Technologies, Architectures, And Protocols For Computer Communications, ACM Sigcomm, pp. 201–212 (2003)
11. Mitzenmacher, M., Upfal, E.: Probability and computing: Randomized algorithms and probabilistic analysis, pp. 107–112. Cambridge University Press (2005)
12. Kozat, U.C., Tassiulas, L.: Service Discovery in Mobile Ad Hoc Networks: An Overall Perspective on Architectural Choices and Network Layer Support Issues. Ad Hoc Networks **2**(1), 23–44 (2004)
13. Sailhan, F., Issarny, V.: Scalable service discovery for MANET. In: Third IEEE International Conference Pervasive Computing and Communincations, pp. 8–12 (2005)
14. Klein, M., König-Ries, B., Obreiter, P.: service rings — a semantic overlay for service discovery in Ad Hoc networks. In: Network-Based Information Systems at Database and Expert Systems Applications, Prague, pp. 180–185 (2003)
15. Schiele, G., Becker, C., Rothermel, K.: Energy-efficient cluster-based service discovery for ubiquitous computing. In: 11th ACM SIGOPS European Workshop, Belgium (2004)
16. Sivavakeesar, S., Gonzalez, O.F., Pavlou, G.: Service discovery strategies in ubiquitous communication environments. Communications Magazine **44**(9), 106–113 (2006)
17. Tyan, J., Mahmoud, Q.H.: A comprehensive service discovery solution for mobile ad hoc networks. Mobile Networks and Applications **10**(4), 423–434 (2005)
18. Sailhan, F., Issarny, V.: Scalable service discovery for MANET. In: Third IEEE International Conference on Pervasive Computing and Communications, 2005, pp. 235–244 (2005)
19. Cheng, S., Chang, C.K., Zhang, L.J.: An efficient service discovery algorithm for counting bloom filter-based service registry. In: 2009 IEEE International Conference on Web Services, pp. 157–164 (2009)

A Methodology and Tool Support for Widget-Based Web Application Development

Petru Nicolaescu(✉) and Ralf Klamma

Advanced Community Information Systems (ACIS) Group,
RWTH Aachen University, Ahornstr. 55, 52056 Aachen, Germany
{nicolaescu,klamma}@dbis.rwth-aachen.de
http://dbis.rwth-aachen.de

Abstract. Due to the rapid evolution of Web technologies and standards like WebRTC for the real-time Web, there is a reengineering pressure on many existing Web applications for not getting outdated and for reducing costs and maintainance efforts. In this paper, we propose a methodology designed to support developers through an application reengineering process for achieving modular and scalable Web applications, by bridging the old and the new: a RESTful microservice architecture with a presentation layer composed from widgets. The methodology is based on empirical studies conducted with the help of the widget developer community and proposes an agile development cycle and guidelines for the redesign activities. Based on its principles, we developed a tool that has been used in the methodology evaluation for modeling the widget-based Web applications. The obtained results show that the approach and the proposed architecture are suitable for enabling the future generation of widget-based applications.

Keywords: Web widgets · Web development · Community information systems · Widgetizing methodology · Web application reengineering

1 Introduction

Rapid prototyping of Web applications and a well designed software architecture are active topics within the Web Engineering research community. With the rise of real-time Web technologies such as Web sockets, WebRTC, XMPP and the emergence of new Web architectures and engineering practices such as microservice architecture and continuous integration, existing applications need to be reengineered in order to take advantage of the new enabled opportunities and to avoid becoming obsolete. In this context, developers can benefit from a structured approach to redesign existing applications or develop new ones.

This paper presents a methodology for (re)engineering Web applications using Web widgets and microservices. Previous work has shown many benefits of modeling Web applications [1] for their model-based generation, mashing up widgets to form complex applications [2] and using Web widgets in distributing user interfaces [3] or in enabling near real-time collaboration [4]. Therefore, our methodology means to combine such approaches in order to obtain

P. Cimiano et al. (Eds.): ICWE 2015, LNCS 9114, pp. 515–532, 2015.
DOI: 10.1007/978-3-319-19890-3_33

a systematic way to develop powerful widget Web applications. It targets the multi-user/multi-device setting, where the applications need to be lightweight, scalable, collaborative and easily portable across devices.

The methodology proposes an agile development cycle for rapid prototyping and a model and architecture which can be used to redesign existing systems to multi-tier Web applications composed from RESTful microservices [5] [6] that partially or fully implement the logic for Web widgets as corresponding frontend elements.

Throughout this work, by *classic (single-user) Web applications* we refer to the applications that need to be reengineered. Usually, such applications have a tier architecture, with a logic tier (consisting of SOAP or RESTful Web services, Java enterprise technology), a shared data model (relational, XML, JSON, etc.) and a front-end with predefined page navigation. By reengineering we refer to the development cycle needed for transforming such a classic Web application in order to obtain a new, widget-based Web application. *Web widgets* have been initially used as interactive single purpose tools for displaying and/or updating information. Defined in the W3C Packaged Web Apps specification, they are full-fledged client-side applications with a clear-cut functionality. Their structure allows them to be shared, reused, mashed up, personalized in different contexts and on different types of devices. Due to their characteristics, our methodology considers them as perfect interface components for microservices, in the context of software modularization and feature minimization.

"Widgetizing" denotes the process of building a uniform, complex widget-based application, where the building components are widgets with clear-cut functionality which follow certain principles described in the rest of the paper, such as: function as front-ends to microservices, can be easily added to existing widgetized apps, can be modeled and generated, allow near real-time collaboration features (e.g. shared editing, message propagation, awareness of user actions). The widgets in such an application environment are assumed to communicate using interwidget communication (IWC). The microservice architectural style (described by Martin Fowler in his blog[1]) is an approach to building a compact application as a suite of small services, each running in its own process and communicating via lightweight mechanisms (e.g., HTTP, REST), where these services are independently deployable.

The methodology principles resulted from our experience in reengineering applications from various domains (cultural heritage, informal learning, modeling) and from an extensive literature survey. These were then validated and sorted using an empirical study with the help of the widget developer community. The study, together with the top requirements is presented in Sect. 2. Next, Sect. 3 describes the methodology with a focus on the design of widgetized applications. For designing and reengineering such widget applications, we have implemented a widgetizing editor prototype that follows the methodology principles and can showcase the core concepts that we propose, shortly described in Sect. 4. The prototype and the methodology specification have been evaluated

[1] http://martinfowler.com/articles/microservices.html

by widget developers with promising results and are presented in Sect. 5. Finally, the related work and conclusions and outlook are described in Sect. 6 and Sect. 7. The hereby presented methodology is a very important step towards achieving a platform for modeling and generating complex widget-based Web applications.

2 Widgetizing Methodology Requirements

Based on an extensive literature research (cf. Sect. 6) of existing Web engineering methods for mashups and Web widgets, we have extracted a set of most important common points and issues suitable for widgetizing scenarios. Based on these, we have performed a user study with widget developers with the goal to sort and detect the requirements for our methodology. The study was conducted using an online questionnaire which gathered feedback from 42 members of the widget developer community, ranging from middle to proficient expertise levels, from both academic and industry environments. In order to engage as many experts in the area as possible, the questionnaire was distributed via mailing lists, forums and email addresses. The targets were communities such as Apache Rave, Shindig, iGoogle as well as researchers that published works about Web widgets in Web engineering conferences.

Apart from user demographics questions, the questions were divided into

- Considerations, concepts and approaches for designing Web widgets and widget applications (DR)
- Pros and cons for widget-based Web applications (WR)
- Implementation, architecture and limitations of widget-based Web applications (IR)
- User/developer expectations from a widgetizing methodology (UR)

The questionnaire contained both structured and unstructured questions. The structured questions used a one to five likert scale, five representing the best and one the worst rating.

The majority of the participants have been involved in developing Web widgets from scratch (34), Web widget modification (36) and Web applications redesign to widget-based versions (28). More specific tasks include user interface design (38), testing (30), service development (29) and designing the persistence layer (17). The platforms where the participants worked on include Netvibes, iGoogle, Yahoo Pipes, Apache Rave, IBM Mashups and ROLE SDK.

Some of the most important results for the widgetizing design considerations are presented in Fig. 1.

The results show that the compatibility of the messages exchanged between widgets (in terms of inputs, outputs, storage, services, etc.) has a high priority for developers. Other important aspects of widgetizing are clearly performance, state preservation and enabling the application to migrate different functionalities to heterogeneous devices. In this case, the support of the widget platform for distribution is necessary, whereas identifying and separating the functionality appropriately for each widget is critical.

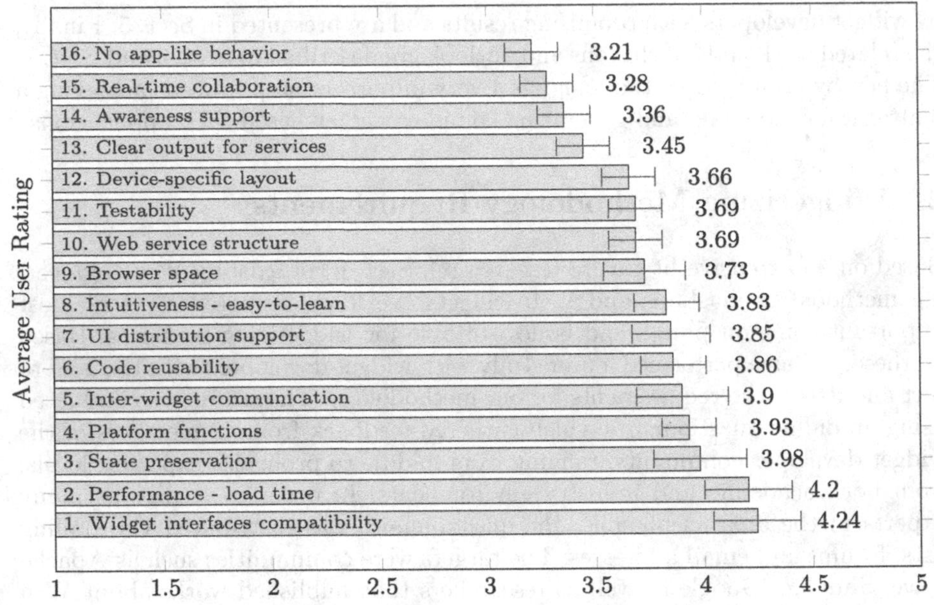

Fig. 1. Designing Widget Web Application Requirements (DR)

We also aimed to gather strengths and weaknesses of widget-based environments. Our findings show that developers want to use widgets because of features such as reusability (WR1. 88%), allowing personalization (WR2. 79%), supporting real-time collaborative tasks (WR3. 67%), instant updates and real-time operations (WR4. 62%).

However, there are also difficulties to create or reengineer widget applications with the above described features. Regarding the separated implementation of the client-side from the server-side in widget application development, 49% of the participants voted for implementing the server-side first, then design the client-side. 29% preferred a mixed approach and 17% have chosen to design the client-side first, then the server-side. Our results show that developers need support for taking such development decisions. Moreover, 64% of the participants stated that the widget-based applications require more interaction sequences to be tested (WR5.) and that it can be more difficult to use inter-widget communication than the classical Web applications' internal communication (WR6. 71%). These difficulties motivate the need of a methodology that provides assistance in implementing the widget-to-widget events to ease such development efforts and ensure consistency of the widgetized application (in terms of interactions and events).

Figure 2 depicts the survey results for the development approach of widget-based Web applications. As it can be observed, following the RESTful architectural style to improve the portability of the user interface was highly rated.

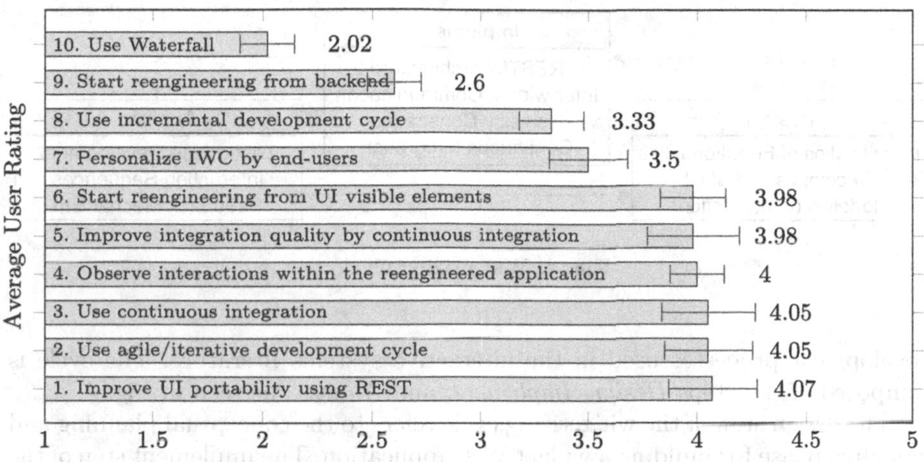

Fig. 2. Results for Implementation Approaches Requirements (IR)

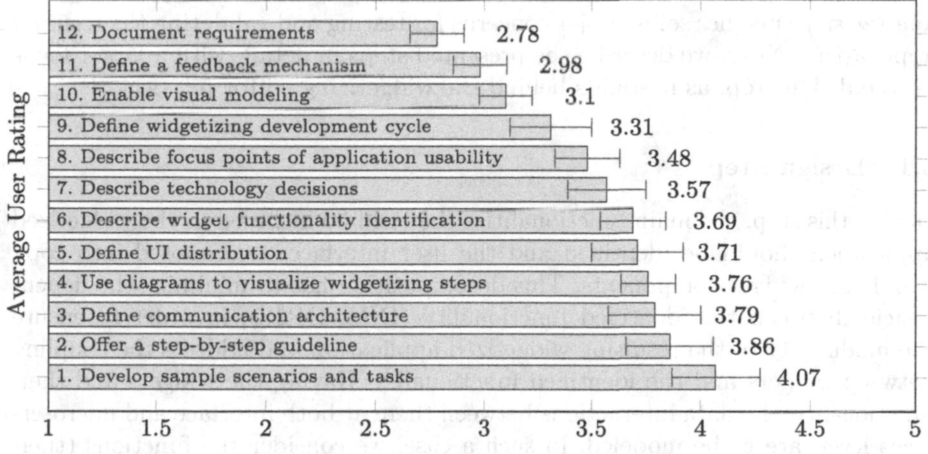

Fig. 3. Results for User/Developer Expectations (UR)

The last part of our survey, regarding developers' expectations from a widgetizing methodology can be visualized in Fig. 3.

3 Methodology

In the following, we present the major concepts of our proposed methodology and explain the rationale for considering them. We have defined a widgetizing cycle that adopts a simple iterative approach inspired by adaptive software

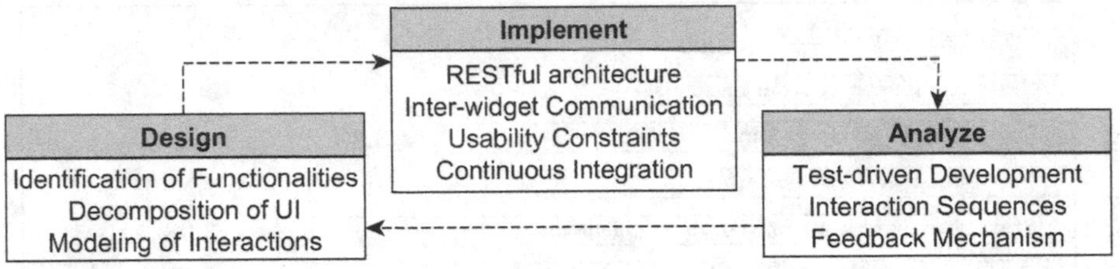

Fig. 4. Widgetizing Cycle

development processes used in the interactive systems literature. The cycle is composed of the steps *Design*, *Implement*, and *Analyze*, as seen in Fig. 4.

The design step of the widgetizing cycle refers to the conceptual planning and modeling phase for building a widget Web application. The implement step of the methodology specifies an architecture instance based on the concepts explained in the design step. In order to support developer concerns expressed during the initial studies, this step offers solutions for inter-widget communication and collaboration, to be considered during the process of widgetizing. Finally, the analyze step specifies some major concerns for testing and validating the resulted applications. Next, we describe the presented steps in detail, with a larger focus on the design step, as it stands behind the widgetizing editor (cf. Sect. 4).

3.1 Design Step

During this step, the main functionalities that will be included in the widgetized application should be identified and the user interface decomposed into core, standalone widget components. This decomposition has to minimize the dependencies between the identified functionality (DR1, DR13), in order to ensure the modularity of the resulting widgetized application and address the coupling between widgets and the identified functionality. Having the widgets and their functionality, the data interactions between them at both interface and microservices levels are to be modeled. In such a case, we consider the functions (their content being defined via inputs and outputs), events and their corresponding interface elements as being part of the lowest needed decomposition level.

As hinted in the overview given above, in a reengineering scenario (in the light of the initial study feedback), we consider the *identification of functionalities* and *decomposition of user interface* (DR1, DR6, DR10, IR1, IR4, IR6, UI5, UI6) to be the major first steps to widgetize an application. For classic Web applications this can be achieved by analyzing the data relationships and interactions from, to and within both the backend and frontend.

In order to structure the widgets and functions identification and develop the proper conceptual support for the methodology, we have constructed a model (cf. Fig. 5) that captures the different elements needed to be specified and related during the widgetizing process.

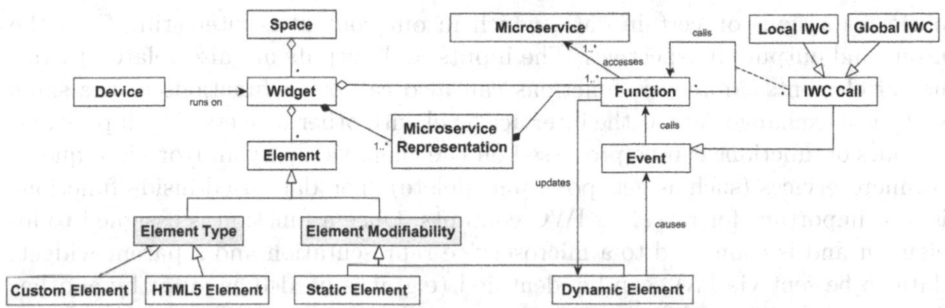

Fig. 5. A Conceptual Model of the Widgetized Platform

A space is the highest dimension of a widgetized platform that aggregates all the widgets selected for widgetizing a given application. The space encapsulates knowledge about the dependencies of its contained widgets and is also responsible for providing a platform for widget-related services (DR4). Among such services one can consider the widget rendering container(DR9), inter-widget communication and near real-time collaboration (DR5, DR15) and state preservation services(DR3), as well as the logic for managing users and devices (DR7). The IWC messages propagation can be achieved across widgets, devices and users and should be available at the space (widget container) level. The state preservation refers to maintaining the state of the various widgets composing a Web application, such that they can be reloaded, distributed across devices, etc. without losing their internal runtime data. As already mentioned in the introduction, the mapping recommendation is that widgets can be used as visualization components for one or more microservices but the number of associations should be kept to a minimum to ensure the resulting widgets follow their definition. Candidate widgets are most commonly visible via detecting separated panels, headings, navigation bars, embedded contents, and grids. In this case, our methodology specifies certain points to help developers detect main functionalities via examining user interface elements for detecting individual Web widgets. Technically however, for reengineering an application starting from the classic Web application's interface, it is not a trivial task to compute a fully-automatic conversion mechanism to identify and decompose the main functionalities of an application using the front-end code (IR6).

The microservice representation is a user interface Web component with a core functionality, corresponding to a backend microservice. In order to ensure scalability, rapid prototyping and a modular state-and-device independent architecture, the microservices are assumed to follow the REST principles (such as simplicity, stalesness and uniform interfaces) (IR1).

A function can serve more purposes. For example, it can realize the connection to microservices (within the scope of a widget) for a given microservice representation. Also, functions can fulfill utility operations (e.g. validating the user input on the client side). In this case, they are not attached to a microservice representation but run directly within the scope of a widget. A function performs actions on certain data, which in our context is interesting from the input and outputs perspectives. The inputs and outputs are also related to values of elements. Moreover, functions can also call other functions in the same widget or exchange data at the interface level with other widgets. The inputs and outputs of functions can be processed on the client side only and/or via requests to microservices (such as get, post, put, delete). The data used inside functions is also important for revealing IWC contents. Once a function is assigned to an element and is connected to a microservice representation and a parent widget, data to be sent via IWC can be identified (e.g. it is needed as input by another function linked to a different microservice representation). As an example, in our widgetizing editor, developers were given the possibility to create and assign certain data used by functions and indicate its collaborative or local usage (DR1, DR5).

In the widgetizing context, by elements we refer to user interface components used for rendering (e.g. HTML components). Our approach distinguishes using view inheritance between different elemens, considering their type and modifiability. Based on W3C HTML5 [7] definitions of elements and experience gained from several reengineering projects (e.g. widget-based Web application for collaborative modeling tasks and applications for semantic video annotation), we sorted out HTML5 elements that would often give developers guidelines for detecting main functionalities to be identified in decomposed widgets. Basically, these element types can also be mapped to entities from other known Web modeling metamodels from the literature, such as the UIElement from the UWE metamodel [8], "DisplayUnit" from WebML's hypertext package [9], etc.

Dynamic elements are any user interface elements with an event attribute and/or event listener that evokes an interaction to occur in a Web application. They can process information and/or invoke an activity at the user interface level. As an example, buttons are most common subjects to be identified as dynamic elements (triggers) in Web applications. In a widgetizing context, dynamic elements can also be information-related elements that do not fire an event in the Web application, but only receive data from certain functions. Elements may function with three different purposes, as they either handle inputs via the user interface (e.g., text fields, calenders, checkboxes), or they can be used to display backend info/results (table columns, list items, paragraphs) without evoking an interaction. Due to limited space, we have not included such specifications or any automatization considerations in the current work.

Events can be caused from dynamic elements upon fulfilling certain conditions (e.g., onclick, onchange, onsubmit) that fire an action in the browser. Therefore, a new event can only be assigned to an identified dynamic element in the widgetizing process. Furthermore, once an event is triggered by an element, a function can be called. For designing a new event, developers need to specify its parent trigger, event-handler attribute, and the event handler attribute's value. Thus, we can obtain the *modeling of the interactions* by specifying such structure of events and functions with their exchanged data.

By performing this modeling, developers will have a clear view of how the events (which can also be identified from the existing traditional single-user application) should be shaped and appropriately distributed in a widgetized application's architecture. In order to let developers manually construct a widget architecture for redesign, we implemented a widgetizing editor following the identification and event modeling principles of the design step.

Furthermore, to support developers in using the editor for performing the identifications, we have also developed a workflow diagram using PetriNets. This reflects the applicability of the design step and can point to what to follow next (UR1, UR2) based on the conditions and the progress of design. The workflow can be used as a guideline to be followed for modeling each interaction accordingly. In case of new requirements, needed improvements, or new identifications, the workflow can be iteratively applied over existing data, as well as in scenarios of developing a widget application from scratch.

3.2 Implement Step

RESTful architectural model for widget development ensures the portability of the microservices and user interface across multiple platforms and scalability of the various components [10].

As componentization of services has been studied for different purposes, there also exist equivalent architectures. In the microservice architecture, each service manages its own database. This type of approach for persistence layer suits better to widget-based applications as it can tackle larger volumes of traffic and can scale easily. Furthermore, there is no need for transactions as sharing data of independent Web services can be dealt with by a structured IWC mechanism.

We integrated the approach of componentization and the conceptual model of our widgetizing methodology to obtain an architecture template (cf Fig. 6). According to our proposed widgetizing framework, microservices for each widget run independent from each other. As one single widget can invoke more than one microservice, the services that are used by the same widget work also discrete from each other in terms of persistence.

In a collaborative widget environment, specification of *Inter-widget Communication* (DR5) messages and real-time collaboration data types are critical for widget orchestration (DR1), work productivity, real-time updates (DR14) and collaboration awareness (DR15). Collaboration between users is obtained via publishing global IWC messages, which allow browser-to-browser communication. Modeled interactions in the design step of the widgetizing methodology helps developers to specify the type of IWC messages for each event. Hence, contents assigned as collaborative/local for an event's function should be implemented and divided accordingly. Developers should consider the aspect of IWC messages in terms of functionality and collaboration awareness. Generally, for each IWC message to published, a description of IWC message based on functionality, IWC type (global or local), data to pass to other widgets and a widget and user identification can be specified [3]. In our widget development experience we used a JSON lightweight format for the IWC messages, with the above

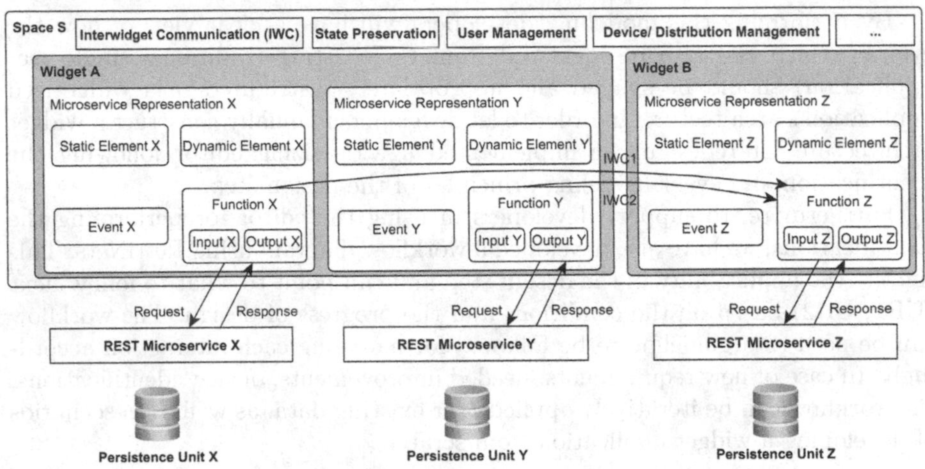

Fig. 6. An Instance of a Widgetized Architecture Template

mentioned structure. In general, simple conversions can ensure the data format transformation between various widgets, given that this has been agreed upon.

Separation of IWC messages is also a usability concern for specifying which information to pass to which widget, and what to make visible afterwards in the widget space for a better user experience. In terms of *usability constraints* (DR2, DR12), widgetizing is also an approach related to layout matters. The widget containers often allow users to resize the interface of Web widgets to provide flexibility for a personalized layout. Therefore, the user interface elements that Web widgets contain need to be designed with minimal tooling, in a responsive way. Depending on the tooling in a Web widget, the container is also subject to constraints in the size and layout. In modern development scenarios, this approach also handles the distribution of Web widgets into devices with smaller screens such as smartphones or tablets.

3.3 Analyze Step

The analyze step refers to testing and validating widgetized applications. Here, automated tests should be performed, the IWC message interoperability should be validated, the resulted application should be checked against the specified widgetizing model and architecture, etc. Furthermore, improvements and new features should be carefully analyzed and included in the widgetizing cycle. In case of the detection of inappropriate modeling of interactions, wrong widget/microservice representations identifications or other bugs in the specification, developers should follow the cycle by returning to the previous proposed steps.

Test-driven development deals with achieving an environment for automated testing and enabling the iterations of the widgetizing cycle for solving problems and integrating new features. Testing a collaborative widget-based Web application is a challenging task due to debugging complexity. Therefore, applicability of test-driven development is a well-suited approach for widgetizing scenarios, lowering the risk of errors and bugs while also improving the code quality.

Each *interaction sequence* should be tested after it has been implemented. In order to ensure compatibility of widgets, developers should build test units for all interactions corresponding to the sequence of widget-to-widget communication. Because our process is iterative, regression testing and continuous integration (IR3) should be used to ensure new bugs are not inserted with new iterations and to facilitate rapid prototyping.

How end-users perceive a system to improve their practice is critical to its success and therefore opinions from all users (experts/novices, supervisors/workers) are equally valid. Feedback may reveal faults, new identification and decomposition tasks, interaction models and new features to be implemented. Based on previous experience, we recommend the usage of feedback platforms for agile processes and social requirements engineering tools, that allow developers and end-users to interact, communicate and work collectively on development issues.

4 The Widgetizing Editor

Based on our methodology we have implemented a prototype in order to evaluate the feasibility of the design step, the completeness of the methodology and to assess to which extent the identifications and the reengineering approach in the design phase can be (semi) automatized. The editor consists of 8 different widgets with specific functionalities, namely *Widgets, Micro-services, Elements, Events, Functions, Contents, Interactions*, and *Architecture* and is presented in Fig. 7. Each widget models the concepts explained in Sect. 3. The aim was to provide developers a collaborative and widget-based platform that enables them to try and visualize the design step of the methodology by modeling a well-designed widget architecture. The prototype editor supports developers to model interactions and perform the decomposition of classic Web applications collaboratively, with an increased consistency via HTML5 catalog work and achieve and visualize the widgetized Web application architecture.

The prototype is built using the ROLE SDK[2] [11] which provides built-in community management system, collaborative designing and widget space management introduced. The widgets are developed using HTML5 and JavaScript and Bootstrap to provide responsiveness and easy-to-use user interface.

5 Evaluation

For the evaluation of the main concepts of widgetizing methodology and its tool support, we conducted a questionnaire-based user study with the participation of 19 developers and researchers and a face-to-face structured evaluation with 9 widget developers. The questionnaire participants already possessed widget development experience (74%), the rest being end-users of such applications.

[2] ROLE SDK. http://sourceforge.net/projects/role-project/files/role-m10-sdk

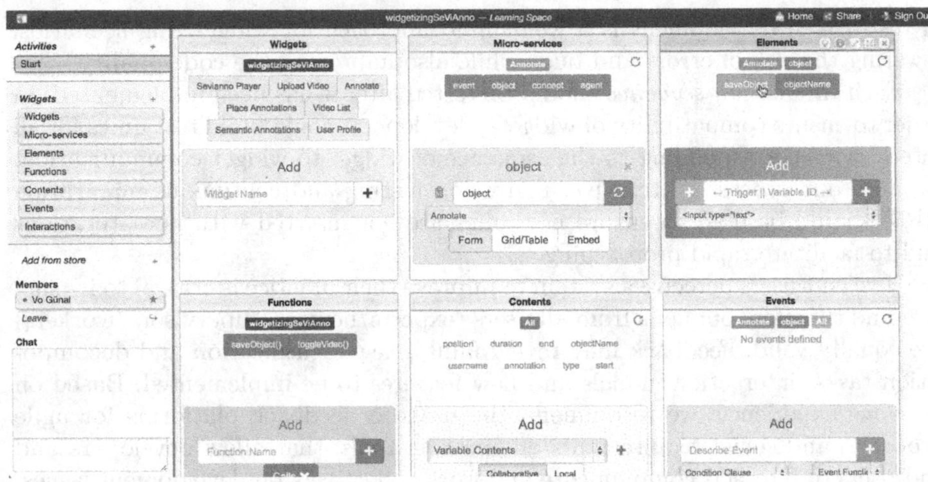

Fig. 7. User Interface of the Widgetizing Editor

Among the participants were also users that were included in the initial survey. Because we wanted to gather feedback from as many widget experts as possible, the widgetizing methodology and its main steps were described in a video, which also showcased the modeling prototype based on a real-world example. The goals were to help the participants to understand the methodology and its realization and assess the fulfillment of the main requirements. The video included the widgetizing cycle steps and an example of a widgetizing scenario – reengineer a semantic video annotation application with the use of the widgetizing editor prototype. The evaluation was performed using a questionnaire with structured questions (based on a one to five likert scale) and unstructured questions. The summary of the results are reflected in 8.

The experimental laboratory study included computer scientists well familiar with widget development. This second evaluation was performed in order to eliminate any confusion or misunderstandings that could have occurred in the first evaluation step and to be able to observe the participants and their actions during the evaluation. Another goal of this evaluation was to study if such a shared editor can help developers in modeling their reengineered applications and if the editor can be a starting point for automatizing the process. For this step, two widgetizing tasks were prepared for the design step to be performed by the participants - both without a time limit. We conducted individual sessions, where each participant was given a 5-minute tutorial about widgetizing, the concepts of our widgetizing model and the editor. After the short tutorial, we provided structured tasks of a widgetizing scenario to the participants. After performing them using the editor, all participants filled out a questionnaire meant to evaluate the methodology in practice. The questionnaire contained structured fields and additional unstructured fields for user comments. For the structured questions,

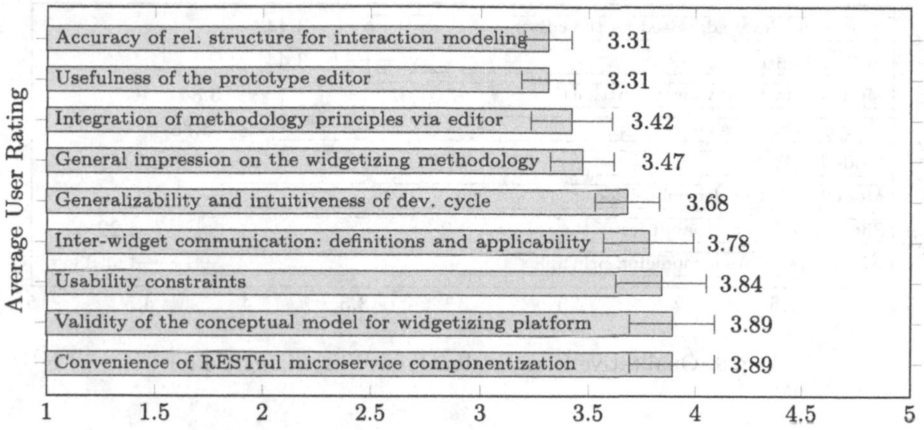

Fig. 8. Results from the Online Methodolody Evaluation

the questionnaire used a one to five likert scale, five representing the best and one the worst rating. The results are presented in Fig. 9.

During the online evaluation, the widgetizing methodology was rated with 3.47 from 5. The results show that the main requirements identified in the beginning of our study were considered satisfactory fulfilled by the participants in the evaluation. Based on the qualitative results collected, the iterative widgetizing development cycle proposed is well suited for modern development scenarios with constant changes of requirements and the needs for improvement, including transforming classic applications to widget-based collaborative Web suites. Despite the limited amount of time and disadvantage of distant presentation, we also got feedback from participants on the widgetizing prototype based on the sample scenario demonstrated in the video. The majority of participants stated that it would be useful to model an intuitive widget architecture in the design step via the presented widgetizing editor that was rated with 3.31 in average.

Moreover, based on the feedback gathered during the hands-on study, developers considered that modeling the widgetized applications in an editor together with an automatic approach for generating the basic structure of such an application would increase the implementation efficiency, lead to better organized, modular, structured and inter-compatible applications.

RESTful microservice componentization was considered to be very appropriate by the developers in the context of modular coding and increasing scalability for widgetizing scenarios. Hence, the recommended approaches for implementation of the widgetizing process specified by the methodology can be considered to function as a valid guidance during the designing, coding and testing phases of widget development/reengineering.

Based on the use of the editor on the given task, participants rated the intuitiveness with 3.44 in average. Based on their estimation, the required proficiency level for using the widgetizing editor was above average (3.44), but we consider that the difficulty can be lowered by creating precise and structured

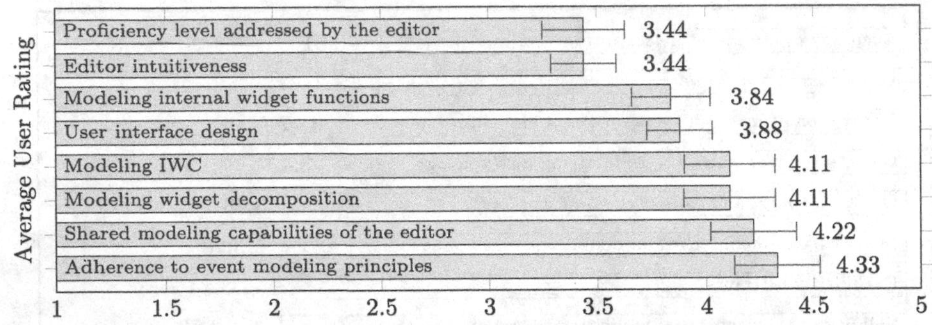

Fig. 9. Qualitative User Feedback on Widgetizing Editor

user instructions for the editor and by introducing (semi) automatic steps for connecting the elements, functions and events in the editor. Via comments some of the participants requested the increase of intuitiveness and user awareness by features that enable users with interactive recommendations, that can support them as they interact with the editor. We consider that such recommendations can be achieved from our model, during the modeling stage and involving more the different modeling actions of users.

The resulted model of the widgetizing step via the editor was rated 4.11 in average. Thus, 77% of the participants found the model they constructed very convenient to point to a feasible decomposed widget application design. Furthermore, the model for designing inter-widget communication via the editor was also rated 4.11. Participants found it easy to point to inter-widget communication messages to be implemented based on the hierarchical information of interacted data and interacting functions of events. The participants rated the event modeling concepts with 4.32 in average. These results support that the prototype provides developers very helpful information based on the decomposition and event modeling phases of the design step of our widgetizing methodology for enabling them to have a well-designed widget architecture model for the implementation step. Designing the architecture in a shared modeling space via widgetizing editor was considered to be a well-suited idea to have well-designed widget models by 88% of the participants, as it was rated with 4.22 in average. As such, the majority of widget developers believed that designing architecture models in a shared platform would increase the accessibility, designer/developer awareness and communication, and the quality of the widgetized model. We strongly believe that our approach for identifying main functionalities, decomposing the user interface and modeling of interactions will enable developers to have well-suited widget architecture models for more consistent and more productive widget implementations. The results show a positive influence of the widgetizing methodology upon widget application development and a high impact of the widgetizing editor upon performing the widgetizing steps.

5.1 Limitations

Due to time restrictions, we could not conduct studies with developers for modeling real applications using the widgetizing editor. Even though the editor itself was developed according to the methodology principles, we could not observe the reengineering process for third party applications at this stage or evaluate its real-time collaboration features. However, we would like to research how the learning curve of the widgetizing editor would progress for developers in a longer-term. Due to the same reasons, the analysis step of our widgetizing methodology was not properly evaluated and requires further study, especially in terms of automated testing. Finally, even though we consider the usage of secure protocols such as WebRTC, security is not part of the study, as we wished to concentrate on other non-functional requirements closer to the core of our research.

6 Related Work

The current section summarizes existing research related to different aspects covered in the widgetizing methodology, i.e. RESTful services, service composition, services and widget development, widget-based applications, widget distribution across devices and widget-based software systems. Together with the NRT collaboration and the widgets vs. services relationship, these were the most important comparison points that were considered for our methodological approach.

In a widgetizing scenario, using a lightweight infrastructure where services can be built with minimal tooling impacts the widget structure and the IWC design. Pautasso et. al [6] summarize the benefits of RESTful Web services, mentioning the easy development of clients for RESTful services, discovery of Web resources via URIs and hyperlinks and scalability due to the statelessness properties to a large number of clients and usage of lightweight messaging formats (e.g. JSON). *MashupAdvisor* [12] is a tool that follows a proposed framework aiming to increase the efficiency of mashup building process for non-programmer users. The tool estimates and recommends relevant outputs for the desired mashups using a repository. Its contribution is overcoming complex design processes for mashup inputs and outputs despite the increasing number of external services, sources, and operations by proving a design-time assistance. While it supports mashup communications using a semantic matcher for the interactions, there is no comprehensive focus on the overall widget application design or on collaborative tasks or cross-browser communication. *Omelette* [13] is a similar application that provides an assisted development environment helping end users compose existing Web services and build mashup applications. By integration of automated composition and pattern recognition methods, it provides a platform to aid users on availability, usage and configuration of desired components.

Building user interfaces and handling layouts for multiple heterogeneous user devices and different kinds of users is not scalable for human programmers and thus requires automated solutions [14]. In this case, Web widgets usually hold scalable limited display size, such that multiple widgets fit on one computer screen in a browser or single widgets fit on limited-size mobile device screens

[3]. Furthermore, having multiple widgets in the same application increases the possibility of performing more complex activities, and functionality of the application. The widget migration in such environments can be obtained by means of IWC mechanisms. An important point of applying IWC in a distributed environment is to support it both locally (e.g., via HTML5 Web Messaging [7]) and remotely (e.g., via XMPP). Concerning widget distribution systems, this concept is well reflected by the DireWolf framework [3]. Another approach is offered by *The Media Enrichment Project* [15], which focuses on real-time synchronization between a video on one display and the presentation of related information on the same or any other display within a Web browser. *MultiMasher* [16] is another tool for developing multi-device mashups that provides an easy selection for distributing and mashing up user interface (UI) elements, suited for an iterative design process as it implements first mechanisms for saving, loading, and merging multi-device mashups. Such approaches could be easily integrated during the widgetizing steps to enable distribution of widgets across devices.

Regarding development environments, *Mapping Web Personal Learning Environments* [17] covers the recent developments in mashup/widget environments, seen as Personal Learning Environments (PLEs). The aim of the study is to map the dimensions depending on several platforms, and guide developers for the decision of which environment to use comparing the identified features from the investigated platforms. The space concept of the widgetizing methodology design step has been specified using such PLE descriptions, using our previous experience from the ROLE FP7 European project.

With the emergence of service-oriented computing, empowering end-users to develop applications by composing individual services has further enhanced the prospects of supporting end-user development in mashup-based applications [18]. Several mashup editors have already been introduced by the industry, including *Yahoo Pipes*[3], *Intel Mash Maker*[4], and *IBM Mashup Center*[5], which allow their users to create mashups without any programming involved, by drag-and-drop services, operators, feeds and/or user inputs and visually connecting them [12]. These type of approaches are more appropriate for designing custom and collaborative applications. *ROLE SDK* spaces are also well-suited for widget-based collaborative application design as they possess lightweight features for the server-side, and high portability in the context of user interfaces, allowing interactions with complex IWC.

7 Conclusions

In this paper we present a widgetizing methodology meant to guide developers on how to redesign classical (single-user) Web applications as widget-based collaborative Web applications. The methodology eases the implementation efforts in widget developer communities, helping them to create relevant models of

[3] Yahoo Pipes. http://pipes.yahoo.com/pipes
[4] Intel Mash Maker. http://intel.ly/1a3qDsB
[5] IBM Mashup Center. http://ibm.co/1fBaSwB

widgetized applications. Furthermore, it guides to achieve interoperability and rapid prototyping. The first evaluation results showed that the methodology and a related widgetizing editor can be successfully used to design and specify such widget applications. As such, they pave the way to a new approach in designing and implementing applications for various communities that can effortless benefit from features such as real-time collaboration, state preservation, awareness using cutting edge protocols such as XMPP or WebRTC. Therefore, as future work we wish to implement a widgetizing editor with full support for communities of developers and end-users, where widgets and microservices can be modeled collaboratively, in order to generate collaborative Web applications that benefit of the principles already exposed in this work. For this purpose, we want to integrate the widgetizing editor with our existing SyncMeta [4] real-time modeling framework and enhance the resulted system with code generation capabilities.

Acknowledgments. This research was funded in part by the European Commission in the "Layers" (FP7-318209) project. We thank Volkan Günal for the prototype implementation and his contributions and all participants to our study for their time and valuable feedback.

References

1. Schwinger, W., Retschitzegger, W., Schauerhuber, A., Kappel, G., Wimmer, M., Pröll, B., Castro, C.C., Casteleyn, S., de Troyer, O., Fraternali, P., Garrigos, I., Garzotto, F., Ginige, A., Houben, G.J., Koch, N., Moreno, N., Pastor, O., Paolini, P., Ferragud, V.P., Rossi, G., Schwabe, D., Tisi, M., Vallecillo, A., van der Sluijs, K., Zhang, G.: A survey on web modeling approaches for ubiquitous web applications. International Journal of Web Information Systems **4**(3), 234–305 (2008)
2. Wilson, S., Daniel, F., Jugel, U., Soi, S.: Orchestrated User Interface Mashups Using W3C Widgets. In: Harth, A., Koch, N. (eds.) ICWE 2011. LNCS, vol. 7059, pp. 49–61. Springer, Heidelberg (2012)
3. Kovachev, D., Renzel, D., Nicolaescu, P., Koren, I., Klamma, R.: DireWolf: A Framework for Widget-based Distributed User Interfaces. Journal of Web Engineering **13**(3&4), 203–222 (2014)
4. Derntl, M., Erdtmann, S., Nicolaescu, P., Klamma, R., Jarke, M.: Echtzeitmetamodellierung im Web-Browser. Lecture Notes in Informatics **225**, 65–80 (2014)
5. Beyer, D., Chakrabarti, A., Henzinger, A.T.: Web service interfaces. In: Proceedings of the 14th International Conference on World Wide Web (WWW 2005), pp. 148–159 (2005)
6. Pautasso, C., Zimmermann, O., Leymann, F.: RESTful web services vs big web services. In: Proceedings of 17th International Conference on World Wide Web (WWW 2008), pp. 805–814 (2008)
7. Hickson, I., Berjon, R., Faulkner, S., Leithead, T., Navara, E.D., O'Connor, E., Pfeiffer, S.: HTML5. W3C Recommendation, W3C (2014). http://www.w3.org/TR/html5/
8. Koch, N., Pigerl, M., Zhang, G., Morozova, T.: Patterns for the model-based development of RIAs. In: Gaedke, M., Grossniklaus, M., Díaz, O. (eds.) ICWE 2009. LNCS, vol. 5648, pp. 283–291. Springer, Heidelberg (2009)

9. Schauerhuber, A., Wimmer, M., Kapsammer, E.: Bridging existing web modeling languages to model-driven engineering. In: Workshop Proceedings of the Sixth International Conference on Web Engineering (ICWE 2006) (2006)
10. Fielding, R.T.: Architectural Styles and the Design of Network-based Software Architectures. PhD thesis, University of California, Irvine (2000)
11. Govaerts, S., Verbert, K., Dahrendorf, D., Ullrich, C., Schmidt, M., Werkle, M., Chatterjee, A., Nussbaumer, A., Renzel, D., Scheffel, M., Friedrich, M., Santos, J.L., Duval, E., Law, E.L.-C.: Towards responsive open learning environments: the ROLE interoperability framework. In: Kloos, C.D., Gillet, D., Crespo García, R.M., Wild, F., Wolpers, M. (eds.) EC-TEL 2011. LNCS, vol. 6964, pp. 125–138. Springer, Heidelberg (2011)
12. Elmeleegy, H., Ivan, A., Akkiraju, R., Goodwin, R.: Mashup advisor: a recommendation tool for mashup development. In: Proceedings of IEEE 15th International Conference on Web Services (ICWS 2008), pp. 337–344 (2008)
13. Chudnovskyy, O., Nestler, T., Gaedke, M., Daniel, F., Fernández-Villamor, J.I., Chepegin, V., Fornas, J.A., Wilson, S., Kögler, C., Chang, H.: End-user-oriented telco mashups: the OMELETTE approach. In: Proceedings of the 21st International Conference Companion on World Wide Web (WWW 2012 Companion), pp. 235–238 (2012)
14. Duarte, C., Carriço, L., Jorge, J., Oviatt, S., Gonçalves, D., Leiva, L.: Interaction-based user interface redesign. In: Proceedings of ACM International Conference on Intelligent User Interfaces (IUI 2012), pp. 311–312 (2012)
15. Krug, M., Wiedemann, F., Gaedke, M.: Media enrichment on distributed displays by selective information presentation: a first prototype. In: Sheng, Q.Z., Kjeldskov, J. (eds.) ICWE Workshops 2013. LNCS, vol. 8295, pp. 51–53. Springer, Heidelberg (2013)
16. Husmann, M., Nebeling, M., Norrie, M.C.: MultiMasher: a visual tool for multi-device mashups. In: Sheng, Q.Z., Kjeldskov, J. (eds.) ICWE Workshops 2013. LNCS, vol. 8295, pp. 27–38. Springer, Heidelberg (2013)
17. Palmér, M., Sire, S., Bogdanov, E., Gillet, D., Wild, F.: Mapping web personal learning environments. In: Proceedings of the 2nd Workshop on Mash-Up Personal Learning Environments (MUPPLE 2009) (2009)
18. Minhas, S., Sampaio, P., Mehandjiev, N.: A framework for the evaluation of mashup tools. In: Proceedings of IEEE International Conference on Services Computing (SCC 2012), pp. 431–438 (2012)

Curtains Up! Lights, Camera, Action! Documenting the Creation of Theater and Opera Productions with Linked Data and Web Technologies

Thomas Steiner[1,2](✉), Rémi Ronfard[3], Pierre-Antoine Champin[1], Benoît Encelle[1], and Yannick Prié[4]

[1] CNRS, Université de Lyon, LIRIS – UMR 5205, Université Lyon 1, Lyon, France
{tsteiner,pierre-antoine.champin}@liris.cnrs.fr,
benoit.encelle@univ-lyon1.fr

[2] Google, Hamburg, Germany

[3] Inria Grenoble Rhône-Alpes / LJK Laboratoire J. Kuntzmann - IMAGINE, Saint-Ismier, France
remi.ronfard@inria.fr

[4] CNRS, Université de Nantes, LINA – UMR 6241, Nantes, France
yannick.prie@univ-nantes.fr

Abstract. For this paper, in the context of the French research project Spectacle en Ligne(s), we have recorded the entire set of rehearsals of one theater and opera production using state-of-the-art video equipment. The resulting raw video and audio tracks as well as manually generated annotation data were then preprocessed in order to localize actors and detect their dialogues. Based on these preprocessing steps, we have built a Web-based hypervideo application that allows for navigation through performance time, space, and time using modern HTML5 Web technologies like the emerging Web Components standard. We publish and consume the annotation data as Linked Data Fragments, a novel way to make triple-based structured data available in a scalable way. Researchers interested in the genetic analysis of live performances can, thanks to our application, better understand the different steps to a chef dœuvre. A demo of the application is available at http://spectacleenlignes.fr/hypervideo/.

Keywords: Hypervideo · Web components · Linked data fragments · Video analysis · Audio analysis · Theater · Opera · Rehearsal · live production

1 Introduction

1.1 Project Background

The objective of the *Spectacle en Ligne(s)*[1] project is to create a video corpus of live theater and opera rehearsals and to explore the uses of this archive

[1] Project website: http://spectacleenlignes.fr/

P. Cimiano et al. (Eds.): ICWE 2015, LNCS 9114, pp. 533–543, 2015.
DOI: 10.1007/978-3-319-19890-3_34

for pedagogic, research, and mediation purposes. The project is funded by the French National Agency of Research (ANR) as part of the project call *"Corpus, data and research tools in human and social sciences"*.[2] Adopting an interdisciplinary approach, the project is structured around three complementary areas of research: *(i)* sociological research for the study of public and existing performance archives, *(ii)* technological research for the chained capturing and publishing of challenges of Open Access, *(iii)* mediation research of audiences for the design of new usage scenarios of the archive. The project ended in December 2014.

1.2 Hypervideo Background

The term *hypervideo* is commonly used to refer to *"a displayed video stream that contains embedded user-clickable anchors"* [13,14] and annotations, allowing for navigation between the video and other hypermedia elements. In a 2006 article in *The Economist*, the authors write[3] *"[h]yperlinking video involves the use of 'object-tracking' software to make filmed objects, such as cars, clickable as they move around. Viewers can then click on items of interest in a video to watch a related clip; after it has played, the original video resumes where it left off. To inform viewers that a video is hyperlinked, editors can add highlights to moving images, use beeps as audible cues, or display still images from hyperlinked videos next to the clip that is currently playing."* In standard literature, hypervideo is considered a logical consequence of the related concept of *hypertext* [2]. In contrast to hypertext, hypervideo necessarily includes a time component, as content changes over time. In consequence, hypervideo has other technical and aesthetic requirements than hypertext, the most obvious one being appropriate segmentation in scenes or even objects. The opportunities for feature-rich semantic hypervideos are endless, only limited by feasibility and ease of their creation. In this paper, we share our approach to affordably and practically document the creation of theater and opera productions with video and Web technologies.

1.3 Paper Contributions

Our contributions with this paper are two-fold. First, we show how modern HTML5 Web technologies and the emerging Web Components [4] standard can be used for the documentation of theater and opera productions; the resulting hypervideo Web Components[4] [16] as well as the demo application[5] created for *Spectacle en Ligne(s)* based thereon are made available publicly as open source. Second, we make use of Semantic Web technologies, namely Linked Data Fragments [20], to publish *and* consume[6] the annotation data that was created

[2] *French: "Corpus, données et outils de la recherche en sciences humaines et sociales"*
[3] From hypertext to hypervideo: http://www.economist.com/node/7904166
[4] Polymer Hypervideo: https://github.com/tomayac/polymer-hypervideo
[5] *Spectacle en Ligne(s)* demo application: spectacleenlignes.fr/hypervideo/
[6] *Spectacle en Ligne(s)* data portal: http://spectacleenlignes.fr/query-ui/

during the recording phase. This approach allows us to make our structured data reusable by others as Linked Data [3] on the one hand, and shows its feasibility by "eating our own dog food" through using this data ourselves on the other.

2 Related Work

Related work can be regarded under the angles of online video annotation creation, large-scale Linked Data efforts for video, and video documentation of theatrical performances. Many have combined Linked Data and video, typical examples are [7] by Lambert *et al.* and [6] by Hausenblas *et al.* There are several text track enriching approaches based on named entity recognition, for example, [10] by Li *et al.* or [15] by us. The online video hosting platform YouTube lets publishers add video annotations in a closed proprietary format. From 2009 to 2010, YouTube had a feature called Collaborative Annotations [1] that allowed video consumers to collaboratively create video annotations. In [19], Van Deursen *et al.* present a system that combines Media Fragments URI [18] and the Ontology for Media Resources [9] in an HTML5 Web application to convert media fragment annotations into a WebVTT [12] file that can be used by HTML5-enabled players. Building on their work, in [17], we additionally allowed for writing annotations by letting annotators create WebVTT cues with an editor. Popcorn.js[7] is an HTML5 JavaScript media framework for the creation of interactive contextual media mixes by letting users link other media to moving images, optionally facilitated by PopcornMaker.[8] McAuley reports in [11] findings from ten years of experimentation with recording formats and analysis for the documentation of theatrical performances. In [8], Lan and Morgan investigate the effects of retroactive and focused self-monitoring through videotaping, on children's theater performance and found that retroactive self-monitoring enhanced theater performance. Giesekam examines in [5] the use of film and video in theaters and evaluates the impact and effectiveness of such developing multimedia technologies on practices in dramaturgy and performance.

3 Hypervideo Web Components

In this section, we first provide necessary background on the emerging Web Components standard and then describe the generic hypervideo Web Components that were created in the context of the *Spectacle en Ligne(s)* project.

3.1 Introduction to Web Components

Web Components is a set of specifications, which let Web developers leverage their HTML, CSS, and JavaScript knowledge to build widgets that can be reused

[7] Popcorn.js: http://popcornjs.org/
[8] PopcornMaker: https://popcorn.webmaker.org/

easily and reliably.[9] According to a (recently discontinued) W3C Working Draft introductory document,[10] the component model for the Web ("Web Components") consists of five different pieces that we will list in the following.

Imports which defines how templates, decorators and custom elements are packaged and loaded as a resource.

Shadow DOM which encapsulates a DOM subtree for more reliable composition of user interface elements.

Custom Elements which let authors define their own elements, with new tag names and new script interfaces.

Decorators which apply templates based on CSS selectors to affect rich visual and behavioral changes to documents.

Templates which define chunks of inert markup that can be activated for use.

At time of writing, partial native support for Web Components has landed in a number of Web browsers, however, for the majority of browsers, a so-called polyfill solution is still required. A polyfill is a piece of code that provides the technology that developers expect the browser to provide natively in the near future. We rely on the Polymer project[11] to provide Web Components support.

3.2 Implementation Details

We have developed a number of Web Components for the creation of hypervideos. These Web Components are behaviorally grouped together by a common naming convention. In Polymer, all element names have to start with the prefix `polymer` and contain a dash in order to add a namespace which avoids conflicts with existing elements. However, this requirement is seen as a bad practice by some, as it makes Web Components seem like being "owned" by the Polymer framework.

`<polymer-hypervideo>` is the parent element of all other elements. It accepts the attributes `src` for specifying a set of space-separated video sources (to support different encodings), and—analog to the native HTML5 video attributes—`width` and `height` for specifying the video's dimensions, then `poster` for specifying the video's poster frame, and finally `muted` to specify if the video should be initially muted.

`<polymer-data-*>` is a set of data annotation elements that includes the two shorthand annotation types `<polymer-data-actor>` for annotating video actors and `<polymer-data-overlay>` for annotating visual overlays, and the generic `<polymer-data-annotation>` for other annotations.

`<polymer-track-*>` are the two elements `<polymer-track-chapters>` and `<polymer-track-subtitles>`, which rely on WebVTT [12] text tracks of the types "chapters" and "subtitles" that they enrich with automatically generated chapter thumbnails and a full text subtitle view.

---

[9] Web Components: http://www.chromium.org/blink/web-components

[10] Discontinued W3C Working Draft document: http://www.w3.org/TR/2013/WD-components-intro-20130606/ [4]

[11] Polymer project: http://www.polymer-project.org/

<polymer-visualization-*> currently provides the following two visualization elements <polymer-visualization-timeline> on the one hand and <polymer-visualization-toc> on the other that create a timeline view and a table of contents that put all encountered <polymer-track-*> and <polymer-data-*> elements in a temporal context.

We have made an online demo application available at http://hypervideo.herokuapp.com/demo.html that showcases these Web Components and recall that we share their implementation as open source. These components communicate with each other through standard JavaScript events, so when a components needs to communicate its state to another, *e.g.*, <polymer-hypervideo> the current playtime to a <polymer-visualization-timeline>, it fires an event that components can subscribe to and react upon.

3.3 Evaluation of the Web Components Design Choice

The creation of new Web Components is a not too difficult task for an experienced Web developer. Especially Polymer's <seed-element>[12] makes getting started straight-forward. Support for Web Components has partially landed natively in Web browsers, which means the polyfill has to do less and less work emulating native support. Existing bugs are generally fixed in a timely manner in the frequent new releases of Polymer. Communication between Web Components can be subject to race conditions, as event listeners may not yet have been created at the time an event is being sent. Especially with dynamically created Web Components this can be an issue, also across browsers. We had to introduce short timeouts for certain Web Components before they propagate their properties up to their parent Web Component. Nevertheless, Web Components were the right design choice. The ease of use of the finished Web Components and the fact that Web Components can be created and interacted with using JavaScript like regular HTML elements outweigh the development effort.

4 Linked Data Publication and Consumption

4.1 Introduction to Linked Data

The portal LinkedData.org defines Linked Data [3] as being "about using the Web to connect related data that wasn't previously linked, or using the Web to lower the barriers to linking data currently linked using other methods." It uses Web technologies like the Hypertext Transfer Protocol and Unique Resource Identifiers (URIs) to create typed links between different sources. Tim Berners-Lee defined the four rules for Linked Data in a W3C Design Issue as follows.

[12] Polymer <seed-element>: https://www.polymer-project.org/docs/start/reusableelements.html

1. Use URIs as names for things.
2. Use HTTP URIs so that people can look up those names.
3. When someone looks up a URI, provide useful information, using the standards (RDF, SPARQL).
4. Include links to other URIs, so that they can discover more things.

4.2 Linked Data Fragments

Various access mechanisms to Linked Data exist on the Web, each of which comes with its own trade-offs regarding query performance, freshness of data, and server cost/availability. To retrieve information about a specific subject, one can dereference its URL. SPARQL endpoints allow to execute complex queries on RDF data, but they are not always available. While endpoints are more convenient for clients, individual requests are considerably more expensive for servers. Alternatively, a data dump allows interested parties to query locally. However, data dumps risk to get outdated quickly. Users then have to download the updated data dump again or work with data diffs. Linked Data Fragments [20] provide a uniform view on all such possible interfaces to Linked Data, by describing each specific type of interface by the kind of fragments through which it allows access to the dataset. Each fragment consists of three parts.

data: all triples of this dataset that match a specific selector;
metadata: triples that describe the dataset and/or the Linked Data Fragment;
controls: hypermedia links/forms that lead to other Linked Data Fragments.

This view allows to describe new interfaces with different trade-off combinations. One such interface is triple pattern fragments, which enables users to host Linked Data on low-cost servers with higher availability than public SPARQL endpoints. Such a light-weight mechanism is ideal to expose mid-size datasets.

4.3 Data Portal and Linked Data Fragments Web Component

We use the Linked Data Fragments server implementation Server.js[13] by Ruben Verborgh and also make a browser interface available that is based on Verborgh's Linked Data Fragments client implementation Browser.js.[14] We expose the data at the URL http://spectacleenlignes.fr/query-ui, which is host to a user interface that allows for SPARQL queries to be executed. Verborgh's original `ldf-client` library was written for a Node.js environment. We have compiled it using browserify,[15] a tool that allows modules designed for Node.js to be used from a Web browser context. This allows us to query our Linked Data portal from a browser context using a declarative Web Component called `<polymer-ldf-client>`[16] that we have also released as open source.

---

[13] Server.js: https://github.com/LinkedDataFragments/Server.js
[14] Browser.js: https://github.com/LinkedDataFragments/Browser.js
[15] Browserify: http://browserify.org/
[16] LDF Web Component: https://github.com/tomayac/polymer-ldf-client

4.4 Evaluation of the Linked Data Fragments Design Choice

Linked Data Fragments turned out to be a good design choice. Our mid-size dataset fits the use case perfectly well. Building upon Linked Data Fragments' promise to keep the server simple and enable smart clients, we can support complex queries on our dataset even on commodity hardware. While the processing speed may not in all cases compete with a performant native SPARQL query engine, the streaming nature of Linked Data Fragments results delivery allows the user to see and process partial results as they come, or simply to wait for the complete result. Our `<polymer-ldf-client>` Web Component supports both kinds of operation through a `responseFormat` attribute.

5 The *Spectacle en Ligne(s)* Demo Application

We recall the objective of the *Spectacle en Ligne(s)* project, which is to create a video corpus of live theater and opera rehearsals and to explore the uses of this archive for pedagogic, research, and mediation purposes. The demo application should facilitate the navigation through performance time, performance space, and rehearsal time of the recorded œuvres. It was built on top of the hypervideo Web Components that were introduced in Section 3 and uses the project's Linked Data portal described in Section 4 through a dedicated Web Component. From the recording phase, we have several video tracks for each rehearsal day as well as WebVTT text tracks and manual annotations from the preprocessing phase. Manual annotations mainly contain act and scene data, sparse mise en scène data, and in some cases information on the acting persons in a particular scene.

5.1 Data Flow

Starting with a list of all available videos (the demo application does not contain the full list of all recordings), we first obtain the relevant WebVTT text track for the selected video and via JavaScript create an empty `<polymer-hypervideo>` container. The text track is of type chapters (see [12] for available types) and is converted to a `<polymer-track-chapters` element that gets appended to the `<polymer-hypervideo>` container. We interpret chapters as text cues in the œuvres, which allows us to navigate directly into them. All chapters from the `<polymer-track-chapters` element are automatically displayed on a dynamically inserted `<polymer-visualization-timeline>` element. In continuation, we then query the Linked Data portal for all annotations available for this video using a dynamically inserted `<polymer-ldf-client>` Web Component. Incoming annotations are converted to `<polymer-data-annotation>` elements that are then placed on the `<polymer-visualization-timeline>` element. Finally, we obtain a WebVTT text track of type subtitles (again see [12]) that contains the spoken text of each text cue of the œuvre in the video in question. We dispose of HTML documents of the recorded œuvres that show the text and mise en scène instructions in a human-friendly way. Using common CSS selectors, we identify text cues in this document and align them with the text cue data from the WebVTT subtitles text track. This allows us to visually highlight text cues in the human-friendly documents upon cue change events that are sent by the `<polymer-hypervideo>` element. Figure 1 shows all Web Components and the human-readable documents in action for three different iterations.

5.2 Enabled Navigation Patterns

As outlined earlier, we have several videos for each rehearsal day. Actors rehearsed the acts of each œuvre on different days and not necessarily in chronologically correct order. In the simplest form, we allow for consuming the videos in sequential order to revive the rehearsal days and to see act by act, scene by scene, text cue by text cue how the actors and the metteur en scène worked on them. Each annotation, represented through yellow blocks in the timeline beneath the video in Figure 1, acts as a hyperlink that makes the video jump right to the annotation's time code. The same holds true for the chapter annotations that represent the text cues, displayed as green blocks in the timeline. Most interesting to the user probably is the navigation by text cue, where the user can see how a certain text cue evolved over time. Figure 1 shows act 1, cue 7.9 on three different days, starting with the first lecture of the text at a table on day 1, over to an early rehearsal on day 8 on a private stage, and ending with the technical mise en scène on day 40 on the public stage. Upon mouse-over on the main video, a hovering semi-transparent navigation control gets displayed that lets the user navigate to the next or previous rehearsal day, or the next or previous text cue. Additionally, three select boxes on top of the main video allow for focused by-text-cue, by-video, and by-rehearsal-day navigation.

5.3 Evaluation of the Demo Application

Through our groundwork with the hypervideo and Linked Data Fragments Web Components, building the final application was a rather straight-forward task. All that was missing was the application logic that orchestrates the different Web Components. The whole application required no more than 500 lines of JavaScript code.[17] As we make all source codes of the involved Web Components and the application itself available, future reuse of our work in other theater or opera performances is rendered possible. The opera and theater partners of the *Spectacle en Ligne(s)* project particularly appreciated the complete freedom of navigation in the whole recording archive. By dissolving the temporal order of the rehearsals in the application, they could analyze and study the progress of the different scenes, acts, and even text cues on a level of detail not seen before.

---

[17] *Spectacle en Ligne(s)* demo: https://github.com/tomayac/postdoc/tree/master/demos/polymer-hypervideo/spectacle-en-lignes

(a) Day 1, first complete lecture at the table, http://spectacleenlignes.fr/hypervideo/#lecture-a-la-table_4af0d0a10/7-9

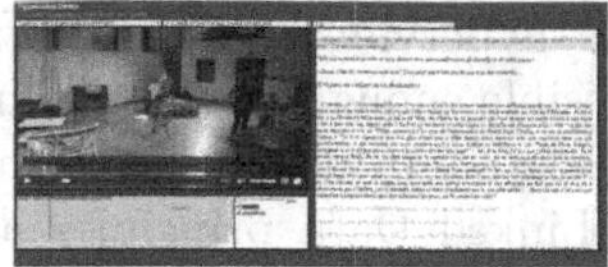

(b) Day 8, ongoing rehearsals of act 1, http://spectacleenlignes.fr/hypervideo/#travail-sur-lacte-3-et-lacte-1-jour-8_c0d547_a54/7-9

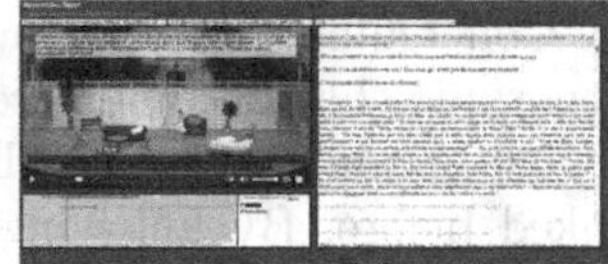

(c) Day 40, final technical mise en scène, http://spectacleenlignes.fr/hypervideo/#filage-technique-jour-40-deuxieme-partie_58b2a6_SON_GRESILLE_a1/7-9

Fig. 1. Evolution of act 1, cue 7.9 of T. Williams' *Chatte sur un toit brûlant*

6 Conclusions and Future Work

In this paper, we have first described the objectives of our project *Spectacle en Ligne(s)*. Second, we have introduced the concept of hypervideo, followed by a look at related works in the areas of online video annotation creation, large-scale Linked Data efforts for video, and video documentation of live theatrical and musical performances. In continuation, we provided necessary background on the emerging Web Components standard. As the first contribution of our paper, we have implemented and evaluated hypervideo Web Components that can be used to create hypervideos in a declarative way through nothing but custom HTML tags. Objects or temporal points of interest in the hypervideos can be annotated, such annotations then appear on an interactive timeline. We have then looked at Linked Data sharing principles and introduced Linked Data Fragments as an appropriate way to share our annotation data for others and ourselves to consume in a scalable manner. The second contribution is a Web Component that allows for interacting with Linked Data Fragments in a streaming or polling way again purely declaratively. Finally, we have combined all generated Web Components in a demo application that showcases the power and simplicity of our approach. The source codes of all involved Web Components and the application itself are available as open source to encourage broad reuse.

Future work will mainly concentrate on the hypervideo Web Components. We will evaluate their usefulness for further use cases like, for example, Web video courses and improve them accordingly if necessary. As we have repeatedly expressed, the Web Components standard is still in flux. As more and more Web browsers will gain native support for Web Components, existing timing challenges that we encountered occasionally will be resolved. Work on more hypervideo features has already started like camera selection or inter-hypervideo communication for synchronized hypervideo experiences. On the Linked Data side, we want to further improve the retrieval speed of Linked Data Fragments in our Web Component by allowing for parallel multiplexed query requests.

Concluding, through our hypervideo Web Components, creating a basic hypervideo has become accessible enough that standard Web developers can do it. The promise of Linked Data are synergies between data that was not interlinked before. By following Linked Data principles and thanks to our Linked Data Fragments Web Component, these synergies can be reached in the context of a Web application with very reasonable effort. We encourage others to reuse our Web Components in their own applications and to further extend and improve them.

References

1. Bar, S., et al.: YouTube's collaborative annotations. In: Webcentives 2009, 1st International Workshop on Motivation and Incentives, pp. 18–19 (2009)
2. Berners-Lee, T.: WorldWideWeb: Proposal for a HyperText Project. Proposal, W3C (1990). http://www.w3.org/Proposal.html
3. Berners-Lee, T.: Linked Data (2006). http://www.w3.org/DesignIssues/LinkedData.html
4. Cooney, D., Glazkov, D.: Introduction to Web Components. Working Draft, W3C, June 2013. http://www.w3.org/TR/components-intro/
5. Giesekam, G.: Staging the Screen: The Use of Film and Video in Theatre. Palgrave Macmillan (2007)
6. Hausenblas, M., Troncy, R., Raimond, Y., Bürger, T.: Interlinking multimedia: how to apply linked data principles to multimedia fragments. In: Linked Data on the Web Workshop (LDOW 2009) (2009)
7. Lambert, D., Yu, H.Q.: Linked data based video annotation and browsing for distance learning. In: SemHE 2010: The Second International Workshop on Semantic Web Applications in Higher Education (2010)
8. Lan, W.Y., Morgan, J.: Videotaping as a Means of Self-Monitoring to Improve Theater Students' Performance. The Journal of Experimental Education **71**(4), 371–381 (2003)
9. Lee, W., Bailer, W., Bürger, T., et al.: Ontology for Media Resources 1.0. Recommendation, W3C, February (2012). http://www.w3.org/TR/mediaont-10/
10. Li, Y., Wald, M., Omitola, N., Shadbolt, T., Wills, G.: Synote: weaving media fragments and linked data. In: Bizer, C., Heath, T., Berners-Lee, T., Hausenblas, M. eds. LDOW of CEUR Workshop Proceedings, vol. 937 (2012)
11. McAuley, G.: The Video Documentation of Theatrical Performance. New Theatre Quarterly **10**(5), 183–194 (1994)
12. Pfeiffer, S., Hickson, I.: WebVTT: The Web Video Text Tracks Format. Draft Community Group Specification, W3C, November 2013
13. Sawhney, N., Balcom, D., Smith, I.: HyperCafe: narrative and aesthetic properties of hypervideo. In: Proceedings of the the Seventh ACM Conference on Hypertext. HYPERTEXT 1996, pp. 1–10. ACM, New York (1996)
14. Smith, J., Stotts, D.: An Extensible Object Tracking Architecture for Hyperlinking In Real-time and Stored Video Streams. Carolina, Technical Report (2002)
15. Steiner, T.: SemWebVid - making video a first class semantic web citizen and a first class web bourgeois. In: Proceedings of the ISWC 2010 Posters & Demonstrations Track of CEUR, vol. 658, pp. 97–100, November (2010)

16. Steiner, T., Champin, P.-A., Encelle, B., Prié, Y.: Self-contained semantic hypervideos using web components. In: Verborgh, R., Mannens, E. eds. ISWC Developers Workshop 2014, CEUR-WS, pp. 96–101, October 2014
17. Steiner, T., Mühleisen, H., Verborgh, R., et al.: Weaving the web(VTT) of data. In: Proceedings of the 7th Workshop on Linked Data on the Web, April 2014
18. Troncy, R., Mannens, E., Pfeiffer, S., et al.: Media Fragments URI 1.0 (basic). Recommendation, W3C, September 2012. http://www.w3.org/TR/media-frags/
19. Van Deursen, D., Van Lancker, W., Mannens, E., et al.: Experiencing Standardized Media Fragment Annotations Within HTML5. Multimedia Tools and Applications, pp. 1–20 (2012)
20. Verborgh, R., et al.: Querying datasets on the web with high availability. In: Mika, P., et al. (eds.) ISWC 2014, Part I. LNCS, vol. 8796, pp. 180–196. Springer, Heidelberg (2014)

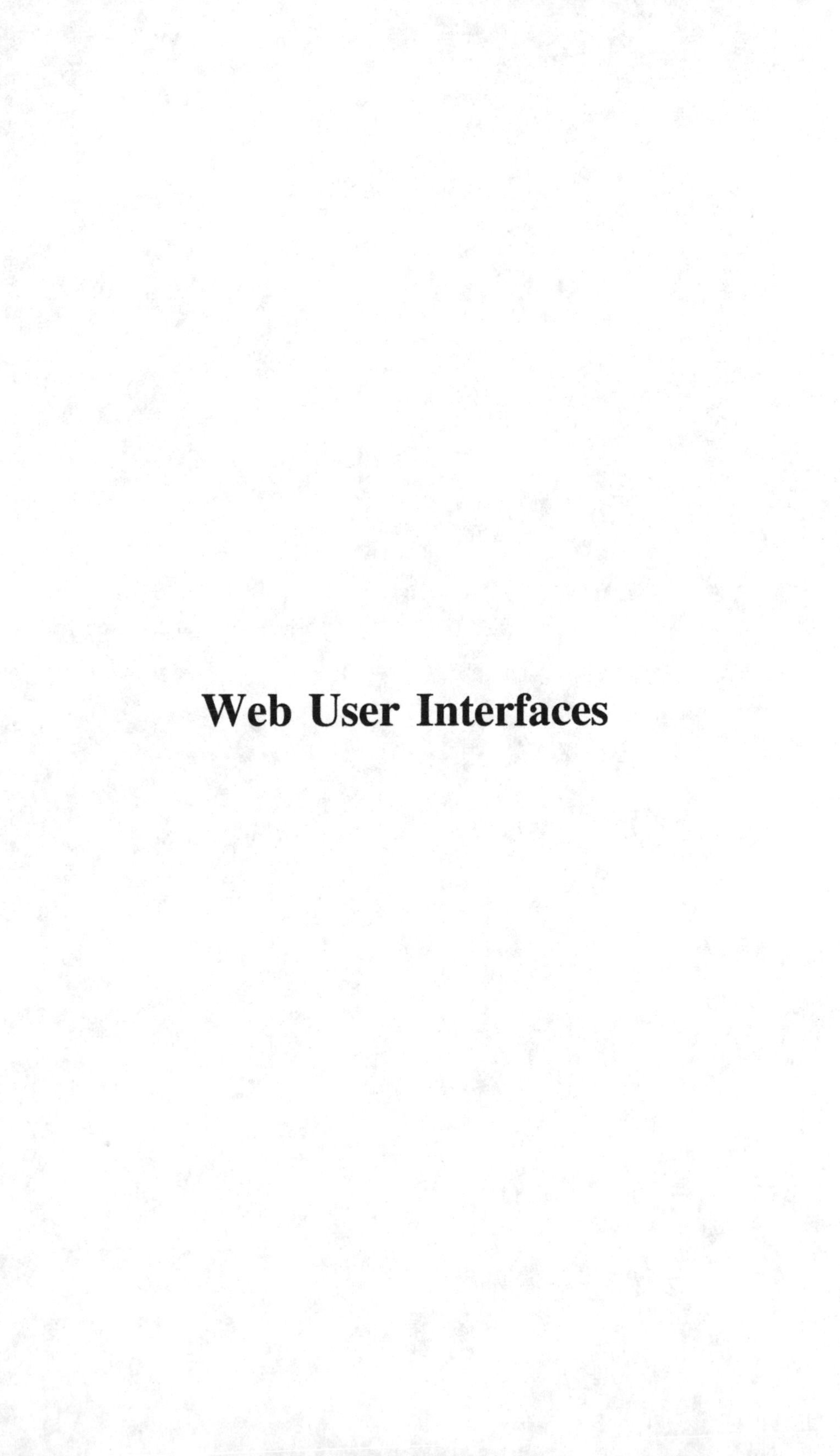

Web User Interfaces

Getting the Query Right: User Interface Design of Analysis Platforms for Crisis Research

Mario Barrenechea, Kenneth M. Anderson(✉), Ahmet Arif Aydin, Mazin Hakeem, and Sahar Jambi

Department of Computer Science, University of Colorado Boulder, Boulder, CO, USA
{mario.barrenechea,ken.anderson,ahmet.aydin,mazin.hakeem, sahar.jambi}@colorado.edu

Abstract. Web-based data analysis environments are powerful platforms for exploring large data sets. To ensure that these environments meet the needs of analysts, a human-centered perspective is needed. Interfaces to these platforms should provide flexible search, support user-generated content, and enable collaboration. We report on our efforts to design and develop a web interface for a custom analytics platform—EPIC Analyze—which provides interactive search over large Twitter data sets collected during crisis events. We performed seven think-aloud sessions with researchers who regularly analyze crisis data sets and compiled their feedback. They identified a need for a "big picture" view of an event, flexible exporting capabilities, and user-defined coding schemes. Adding these features allowed EPIC Analyze to meet the needs of these analysts and enable exploratory research on crisis data.

Keywords: User interfaces · Data-intensive systems · Crisis informatics

1 Introduction

We live in an era of big data. Our ability to generate and collect large amounts of data is having a transformative effect on the types of analysis we can perform. The term "big data" refers to a variety of techniques and technologies that enable this transformation and enable the creation of data-intensive software systems. These systems must collect, store, index, analyze, and annotate large sets of data and there are significant challenges in making these systems scalable, reliable, and efficient. Another class of challenges exist with respect to designing the user interface of these systems. These interfaces must provide users with a sense of scale, present details on demand, provide overviews, and provide a flexible set of operations that execute at interactive speeds.

We work in an area known as crisis informatics [15]; crisis informatics is a multidisciplinary research area that examines the socio-technical relationships among people, information, and technology during crisis events. It mainly examines the qualitative and quantitative aspects of social media data produced by members of the public during times of mass emergency. Our project—Project

P. Cimiano et al. (Eds.): ICWE 2015, LNCS 9114, pp. 547–564, 2015.
DOI: 10.1007/978-3-319-19890-3_35

EPIC—has been collecting crisis data sets from Twitter since Fall 2009; we have now amassed approximately 2.5B tweets across hundreds of events [2,3,18]. As a result, we have been designing and developing a data analysis environment—EPIC Analyze [1]—that provides a variety of services to help Project EPIC analysts explore and understand our large Twitter data sets.

As a result, we have been wrestling with a number of thorny design issues related to the design of data-intensive systems and their user interfaces [7]. In this paper, we report on the challenges we have encountered with designing user interfaces for services that enable the browsing, filtering, and annotation of large crisis data sets. For these services, our goals have been to a) provide interactive response times, to b) make it easy to query, filter, and explore a large data set, to c) ease the management and filtering of user-defined data, and to d) provide collaboration capabilities for our users. Drawing on techniques from human-centered computing, software engineering, and web engineering, our goal is to simplify the access to large crisis data sets and provide capabilities that allow EPIC Analyze to function as a vehicle for exploratory research on crisis data. To evaluate our efforts, we performed think-aloud sessions with seven researchers who regularly analyze crisis data sets and compiled their feedback. Their feedback drove the creation of the most recent version of EPIC Analyze.

This paper is organized as follows. In Section 2, we situate our work with respect to related research. In Section 3, we present the user interface and services of the current version of EPIC Analyze and then, in Section 4, we describe the evaluation we performed on a prior version of EPIC Analyze that led to the feedback that influenced the creation of the current version. In Section 5, we describe the data models and services in EPIC Analyze that make the user interface presented in Section 3 possible. Finally, we present avenues for future work and our conclusions in Section 6.

2 Related Work

We now present work related to our research on user interface design of data-intensive systems for crisis informatics. We start with a discussion on the challenges associated with interfaces for big data systems. We then present work in crisis informatics that provides insight into the needs of Project EPIC analysts. Finally, we discuss the importance of software architecture and design in producing data-intensive systems that are scalable, reliable, and efficient.

2.1 Interface Design for Big Data Systems

Software and web engineering researchers and practitioners face challenges with capturing, processing, integrating, analyzing, and archiving big data. To add to that burden, the goal for human-centered computing research in this domain is to put the power of big data systems into the hands of non-technical users [8]. Creating intuitive, flexible, and extensible user interfaces that allow users to pull from structured and unstructured data sources, query and analyze the data, and make more informed claims about the data, are the objectives of big data interfaces. Users of such interfaces do not need to become familiar with big data frameworks—e.g. MongoDB, Redis, Cassandra, Spark, etc.—but need to have confidence that the systems built on top of them are reliable and efficient; otherwise they may choose to stay away from working with big data or seek to use other technologies that do not have the same capacity for scale and thus be forced out of taking advantage of the benefits that big data analysis can provide.

Systems like Wrangler [11] and Google Refine (http://openrefine.org/) decrease the amount of work required to transform data; this allows those not proficient in programming to work in this space, converting large data sets into the format they need. For large time series data sets, there are several advances in diverse domains. The LifeFlow system [24] aggregates event data from hospital visits and room transitions and visualizes them to identify problems in triaging or resource allocation. Splunk (http://www.splunk.com) is a commercial data analysis platform for working with time series data, providing a pipe-based textual language to manipulate data. There are shortcomings to these tools, however. Wrangler, Refine, and LifeFlow do not provide support for user-generated annotations and do not enable collaboration among multiple users. Splunk's programming language is flexible but has a significant learning curve, especially for analysts not familiar with the pipe-and-filter architectural style.

One must also appreciate the infrastructure that is built behind such interfaces; often the design of the software infrastructure itself shapes the look and feel of the interface (as we will discuss in Section 5). With data analysis platforms, it is not good enough to just display a web page with filters for querying a database. Oussalah et. al [14] presents a web-based analysis environment that ties in semantic and spatial analyses of tweets in addition to straightforward search capabilities. This work inspired aspects of the design of EPIC Analyze, especially with respect to providing a suite of integrated services to the end user.

2.2 Crisis Informatics

Crisis informatics is an emerging field of study that examines the socio-technical relationships among people, information, and technology during mass emergency [15]. During disaster, lots of data is generated on social media. Crisis informatics has thus quantitatively and qualitatively examined social media during mass emergency events to understand socio-behavioral phenomena of self-organization [21,23], policy change [9], information sharing between unofficial and official sources [17,22], and crowdwork [16,23]. While much has been written on these topics, research methods for collecting, storing, and making sense of these vast amounts of social media data is unwieldy, time-consuming, and expensive. As software and web engineering researchers in crisis informatics, we seek to study how to design systems that support the methods employed by research analysts in crisis informatics and how such systems may change those methods over time. We view EPIC Analyze as a system that supports both of these goals.

2.3 Software Architecture

With respect to software architecture and the design of data-intensive systems, it is important to identify useful software architectural patterns as well as the right combinations of middleware and persistence software to efficiently, scalably, and reliably support social media data collection and analysis [1–3,6,14]. It is important that these systems be reliable to ensure 24/7 operation; it is almost impossible to go "back in time" to collect Twitter data after an event has occurred. As such, these systems need to be running continuously to be ready to spring into action when an event of interest occurs.

3 EPIC Analyze

EPIC Analyze [1] is a data analysis platform that builds on top of our previous work on EPIC Collect [2,18], a system designed for reliable and scalable social media collection. EPIC Analyze extends EPIC Collect with an architecture designed to support social media analytics (see Fig. 1). These systems support an analysis workflow that starts when an event of interest has been detected. Project EPIC analysts monitor Twitter for keywords of interest and use the EPIC Event Editor (a simple web application) to associate those keywords with a new event. EPIC Collect detects the presence of this new event and submits its keywords (along with the keywords of all other active events) to Twitter's Streaming API. It collects tweets containing those keywords and stores them in Cassandra. Our four-node Cassandra cluster can store terabytes of information and serves as the foundation for the work performed by EPIC Analyze.

3.1 The EPIC Architecture

The architecture for EPIC Analyze shown in Fig. 1 builds on top of EPIC Collect's storage mechanism (Cassandra) via the use of Datastax Enterprise

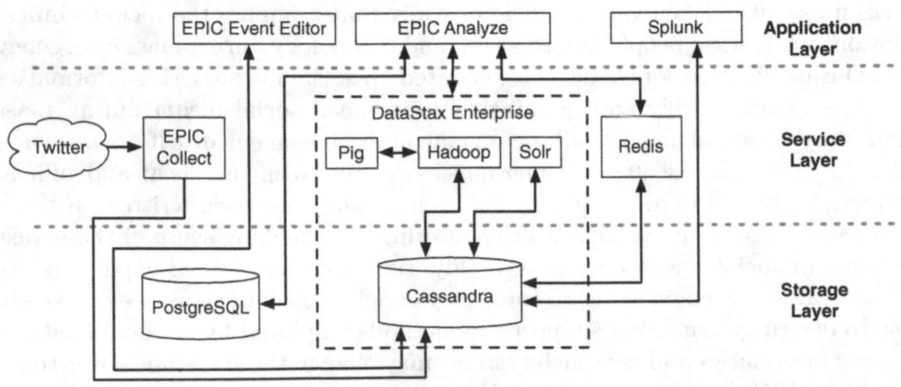

Fig. 1. EPIC Analyze Software Architecture

(http://www.datastax.com/) and its integrated versions of Solr, Pig, and Hadoop. Each of these components can be used to help index, search, or process our large Twitter data sets. We make use of PostgreSQL to store comments and annotations made by analysts while working with EPIC Analyze. EPIC Analyze is itself implemented as a Ruby on Rails web application that knows how to access all of the infrastructure provided by EPIC Collect and Datastax Enterprise. In addition, it makes use of Redis to cache the results of frequently accessed queries and data. Finally, a third-party data analysis tool—Splunk—is used as an alternative method for viewing and analyzing Twitter data, especially as it is streaming in during an active data collection and before it has been indexed by Solr and ready for use within EPIC Analyze.

3.2 The EPIC Analyze Application

EPIC Analyze is a web application that provides scalable and efficient filtering, analysis, and annotation capabilities on large Twitter data sets.

Browsing, Searching, and Visualizing. When an analyst logs in, she sees a list of data sets that have been indexed by EPIC Analyze (e.g. "2013 Boulder Flash Floods"). Once a data set has been selected, an analyst can view the tweets page-by-page in the EPIC Analyze browser (see Fig. 2.c). The browser provides an overview of the data set via a timeline that shows the volume of tweets over time at the top of the browser. On the right hand side, a detailed view of a single "page" of fifty tweets is displayed. On the left hand side, a form for querying the data set and its annotations is presented. If an analyst clicks a tweet, all of its relevant metadata is displayed in an in-line form for easy viewing; this form also contains links that take the analyst to see the original tweet on Twitter. On the timeline, analysts can click and drag (see Fig. 2.a) to specify a start and end date that will be used for all subsequent queries.

The filter form on the left allows analysts to search the data set by tweet or by annotation. The tab for tweet-based search presents a list of tweet attributes that can be used to filter an entire data set. The form supports standard boolean operations for advanced search; any number of tweet attributes can be used to specify a query. Backend services such as Solr and PostgreSQL are used to implement these queries and to provide facets. For instance, an analyst can click the Keyword filter field to see a dropdown list of all keywords associated with that data set (along with the number of times each keyword appears in the data set). This provides analysts with an idea of how popular (or unpopular) a certain keyword was and may guide or refine the questions they ask of the data set.

The tab for annotation search offers the analyst the ability to make queries against user-generated content. Annotations include both labels and comments and are visible to all analysts working on a data set to foster collaboration during the analysis process. These annotations can be queried using the same logical operations and faceting capabilities described above for tweet-based search. Submitted queries are processed quickly, often within a few seconds; we credit this performance to the design of EPIC Analyze's software infrastructure.

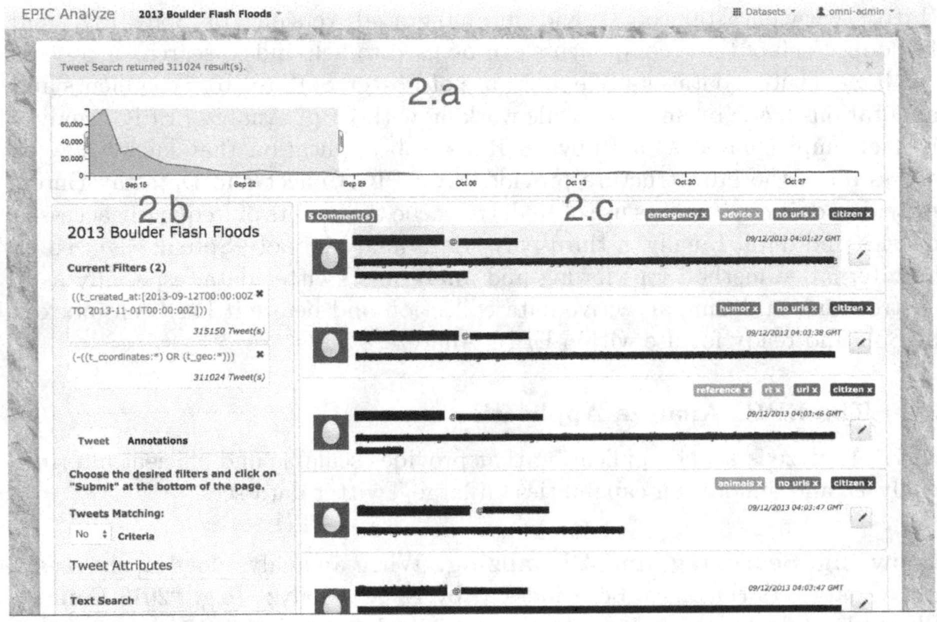

Fig. 2. The EPIC Analyze Browser. (Tweets are hidden for privacy reasons.)

After a query has been submitted and the result set has been filtered to match, the query appears in the "Current Filters" section of the user interface (see Fig. 2.b). This list provides a summary of the queries that were performed in the past and that are in effect as the analyst drills down further into a data set. Analysts can choose to delete a filter in this list or they can *jump to* a filter by clicking on its name. Such a click will render the result set for the filters up to that point. This first-class interface for queries provides a more tangible experience when analyzing data sets, and places the analyst in control over the analysis process.

Annotating Tweets. If an analyst wants to annotate a tweet, she can click on the pencil icon that appears on the right side of each tweet; this action causes an annotation form to appear next to the tweet. The analyst has the option to annotate the entire tweet or to annotate just portions of the text of the tweet. In this latter case, the browser updates the annotated text to appear in a color associated with the label making the annotation readily identifiable in future analysis sessions. Analysts can also comment on the tweet; multiple comments appear in a conversation thread (one per tweet) that appears in the annotation form. The browser indicates that comments exist for a particular tweet by displaying the number of comments for a tweet at the top of its display.

The annotation of tweets is a recognized and critical activity for crisis informatics research. Methods for doing so are documented in empirical studies

[9,17,22,23], but before our work with EPIC Analyze the process of annotating tweets in crisis data sets was laborious and error prone, tolerated only because it was the only way to conduct the research at the time. EPIC Analyze's support for annotations has been welcomed by Project EPIC analysts; they especially like its ability to allow search and filtering over the annotations.

However, future feature enhancements have been identified and include automating the tagging of tweets with labels—especially for large data sets—and allowing analysts to create and/or load their own labels (i.e. coding schemes) for a data set. In particular, the label becomes more than just a textual annotation but is instead a mapping scheme between values found in a tweet and a particular label. For example, analysts may want to tag all existing and future tweets that come from the user name "News6" as "local media." We intend to add this feature to EPIC Analyze in the near future.

Other Features. Research analysts can perform other useful functions with EPIC Analyze. For example, once they have applied a set of filters against a data set, and the resulting set of tweets is useful for future analysis, they can save the state of the result set as a new data set. With this feature, analysts can now engage in more localized analysis with other analysts without having to search a large data set from scratch each time. Secondly, as previously documented in [13], the ability to export these data sets in well-known formats is critical. For this reason, EPIC Analyze allows analysts to export result sets to CSV. Additionally, all annotation labels and comments that have been used to tag the tweets that appear in the result set also appear in the CSV. Finally, with the help of Redis and a job framework known as Resque, EPIC Analyze provides analysts and administrators with the ability to write Hadoop jobs or other scripts that process each tweet in the data set. This job framework is already used by EPIC Analyze to automatically sort large Twitter data sets by multiple sort dimensions, such as tweet id, screen name, and retweet count [4].

4 Evaluation of EPIC Analyze's User Interface

EPIC Analyze has been in constant design and development since Fall 2013. In that time, we have had multiple opportunities to respond to user feedback to make small improvements to the system here and there. However, we became interested in whether EPIC Analyze supports the analytical workflows that Project EPIC analysts employ to perform their research. We turned to task-oriented usability methods to evaluate whether these workflows can be performed with the EPIC Analyze user interface and whether it provides an enjoyable user experience [5]. In this section, we describe a user interface evaluation that we performed via think-aloud sessions on a previous version of the system interface (the one prior to the interface described in Section 3). Based on the results of these sessions, we developed the interface that EPIC Analyze now provides.

4.1 The Research Analysts

We interviewed seven crisis informatics researchers who self-identify as information scientists with specializations that draw from other disciplines, such as geography, journalism, and computational social science. These analysts all work for Project EPIC and work on events ranging from the 2014 Carlton Complex Wildfires in Washington (40,000 tweets), the 2013 Boulder Flash Floods (1 million tweets), the 2013 Japan Earthquake event (1.9 million tweets), and the 2012 Hurricane Sandy event (22 million tweets).

Previous work examined the work processes and tools used by research analysts in this domain [13]. In our study, we observed that they access data in diverse ways, from using commercial analytical tools such as Tableau and Splunk to more programmable interfaces like R and Python. Furthermore, their work processes are different based on their research: one analyst reports that she uses social network analysis methods in Python to model relationships of Twitterers within a data set, but she is often concerned about the representativeness of the data set. To address this concern, this particular analyst wrote her own scripts to filter the data sets such that she has a representative sample that can help answer her research questions.

Some analysts have stronger programming skills and are comfortable with programmatically retrieving data from EPIC Collect, storing it in their own databases, and scaffolding web pages of their analysis on top of that data. Still others use basic—yet powerful—tools, such as spreadsheets. Related work [10] shows that there is considerable overlap in functional power and usability with these tools since they are so well-known and understood; this poses challenges for adoption of other tools that can support these workflows, sometimes with greater analytical power. However, these productivity tools do fall short in some use cases, such as annotating tweets with labels and comments, which is necessary for qualitative and quantitative analysis. To understand how EPIC Analyze, therefore, may become useful to these analysts, we performed think-aloud sessions to see if EPIC Analyze could solve some of their current struggles and support their current and future analysis workflows.

4.2 Think Aloud Protocol Runs

We performed a series of think-aloud protocol runs to gather feedback on the progress we had made on the system interface, which included full search of most tweet-based metadata, support for creating and searching annotations on tweets, and creating new data sets out of previously-run filters (see Fig. 3). Think-aloud runs are well-known as a traditional usability method that captures feedback on a task that the user performs without any help or guidance from the interviewer [12]. We prepared several tasks that analysts should be able to perform without any prior experience with using EPIC Analyze. These tasks reflect the bulk of functionality that is available to use for any given data set in EPIC Analyze. In all seven interviews, we asked the research analyst to perform the following tasks or to answer the following questions:

1. Open an event that interests you
2. Investigate a tweet and look at all of its attributes.
3. How can you view the tweets from only the first or last day of this data set?
4. How can you get tweets written in Spanish? How about Spanish and French?
5. Can you find tweets that either have the word "bomb" in the text or are from a specific user? What about both?
6. How can you get back tweets with annotations?
7. How can you comment on a tweet that has already been commented on?

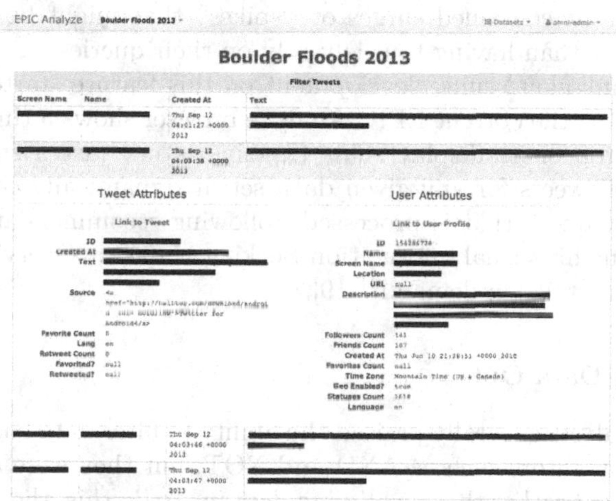

Fig. 3. Previous Version of EPIC Analyze

Each research analyst completed the tasks without any difficulty. All of them enjoyed using the interface and the general look-and-feel of the application. About half of them found it surprising that certain filters—such as issuing a query for both Spanish and French tweets—was supported. Almost all analysts complained that there was no "reset" button at the bottom of the query interface to clear text and other selections from the form. Some analysts complained that the filter result notification bar—which displays the results of the filtered result set when the query has finished—should stay on the screen rather than flashing away. This would create a reference point for the analyst in understanding how effective their query was. Also, they described the need for summative statistics, such as total dataset size, dataset date range, and keyword search terms (a feature already present but not very visible). One analyst suggested that all currently applied filters be displayed at the top of the search interface. As shown in Section 3, all of this feedback has been addressed.

After the tasks were performed, each interviewee was asked free-form questions about their experience with the interface. These semi-structured interviews at the end of the think-aloud session were critical to obtain a unique perspective on how and why these analysts would or would not use EPIC Analyze for future analysis. We now describe additional issues raised by the analysts.

4.3 The Big Picture

Analysts described the desire to see a "big picture view" of the event. The big picture refers to the extent to which analysts understand the context of their analysis through space, time, and control. They admitted that viewing thousands of pages was daunting and that they would prefer digging into the data after queries returned a more manageable set of data, on the order of hundreds of tweets. In order to achieve that, they suggested, it would be beneficial to have a way of displaying volume of tweets over time. That way, they could identify temporal areas that contained surges or "spikes" that might be interesting to investigate, rather than having to solely rely on their queries.

After the think-aloud runs, development on this feature started right away. As shown in Fig. 2, the current EPIC Analyze browser shows a timeline of tweet activity at the top of its display. This timeline is not just a static depiction of the volume of tweets for any given data set; it dynamically conveys volume of tweets for any query that is processed, following recommendations made by Schneiderman and his Visual Information-Seeking Mantra: "Overview first, zoom and filters, then details-on-demand" [19].

4.4 Filtering Data Out

The research analysts generally praised the ability to filter data based on conventional boolean operators such as AND and NOT, but they were also interested in *filtering data out* rather than *qualifying data in*. To do this, the unary operand NOT must be used to set up a query so that results that do not satisfy the filter values are returned. Analysts claim that this is useful because of the nature of their investigations into the data. Sometimes the most meaningful (and yet sparse) data comes from official sources, as in [9], and sometimes from "unofficial sources" who are tweeting about important local information, as in [22].

Of course, implementing this extra operand poses challenges for the interface. It is easy to imagine placing checkboxes at the beginning of each filter input option on the filter form, representing whether or not the analyst would like to filter this input in or out. But that leads to a lot more choices that, if improperly designed, may pose confusion and additional cognitive load on the analyst. In our most recent version of the EPIC Analyze interface, we have placed a drop-down list at the top of the filter form that includes three choices for filtering operators: AND, OR, and NOT. Analysts can choose exactly one option that will be applied to all filters in the interface at that time. Choosing the NOT operand will essentially group the filters with a locally implicit OR condition, and all filters are then prepended with a NOT clause in front of them. The reasoning behind this design decision is to abide by the observations we made during the think-aloud sessions and semi-structured interviews: analysts want to drill-down into data sets, not include as much data as possible. Specifically, when they are looking at a multi-million tweet data set, filtering out is a primary and important action that allows them to dig deeper into the data set for specific signals. Enabling the analyst with the NOT clause coupled with the OR condition over the AND condition achieves this: they are able to select more specifically what data will be filtered out. In future user studies, we plan to evaluate whether this mode of filtering out is preferable over using exclusive joins (AND clauses) between the filters.

The user interface task is not yet done after implementing the NOT operand, however. What if the analyst wants to make compound queries using these operators, such as "(X OR Y) AND Z"? How can the interface and the system support this? As we discuss in Section 5, we turned to data-modeling techniques to solve this problem.

4.5 VOST Deployment and Work Process Integration

Finally, there was interest expressed by one research analyst about integrating EPIC Analyze into established virtual community organizational settings. Specifically, this analyst performs research in collaboration with several virtual operations support teams, or VOSTs, in the emergency management community. Since 2011, VOSTs have been monitoring social media streams during disaster events to glean situational and actionable information coming from both official and unofficial sources [20]. This information, they argue, comes at a faster rate, is more verifiable, and discovers events in a time frame that traditional models of emergency management do not have the resources to handle. These VOSTs are now increasingly using social media as communication channels with the public to maintain situational awareness of the disaster as it is unfolding.

In discussing how EPIC Analyze can provide an information workspace for VOSTs, we discovered that the functionality previously described for automatically annotating tweets with labels is essential. As such, we have not yet deployed EPIC Analyze in this way; however this discovery provided further validation that such a feature is needed. We will return to studying the ability of EPIC Analyze to support these teams once this feature is implemented.

5 Data Modeling in EPIC Analyze

Data modeling in data-intensive systems is key to making them reliable, scalable, and efficient [1–3,18]. With respect to EPIC Analyze and its support for searching and filtering large data sets, we have observed that the data modeling decisions made in the lower layers of the software architecture impact how well EPIC Analyze is able to respond to query requests.

In this section, we describe the server-side facilities that respond to the queries made by an analyst. We illustrate this infrastructure by stepping through a typical search request-response cycle; we then discuss two data modeling challenges we faced in providing a good user experience and the techniques we employed to solve them. We connect these lessons with the impact that they had on improving EPIC Analyze's browsing interface.

5.1 A Day in the Life of a Query

The application architecture of EPIC Analyze (see Fig. 4) is composed of various components to properly serve HTTP requests coming from the user interface. Some of these components are tied to the application framework (Ruby on Rails), such as the Datasets Controller, QueryDispatcher, and Model interfaces, and some of them are acting as independent entities. For example, the EPIC Gem, which is a Ruby gem that helps query data sources like Cassandra, Solr, and Redis, is a separate library that is integrated for use within the EPIC Analyze application and serves other external use cases. We now present a typical request-response cycle to properly serve a query from the web interface and explain how each component serves an important function in this process.

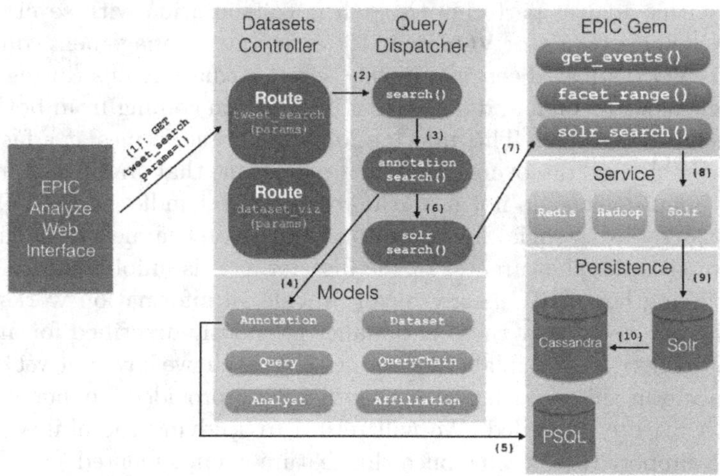

Fig. 4. EPIC Analyze Query Request Cycle

Important to this discussion are the objects that we have designed for this pipeline. The QueryChain object is a helper class designed for keeping track of Query objects, which are themselves encapsulations of query strings transformed from user input. More discussion of these two objects can be found in the next section. Additionally, it is important to highlight here that the data being computed and served are tweets, and so the common denominator between and among these data sources are the tweet id and its row key from Cassandra. Each secondary data source such as Solr and PostgreSQL may store additional information, such as enrichments to the data, but they are always bound to a tweet id and row key that are linked back to the primary data source, Cassandra. We refer to pairwise units of tweet id and row key as *tweet references*, because they represent the address for every tweet in the Cassandra cluster. More information on the data modeling decisions in our persistence layer with respect to these tweet references can be found in [1,18].

A typical search request for annotations or tweets in EPIC Analyze is made on the web interface and is illustrated by the following request-response cycle:

1. A request to issue a query through the web interface begins with a set of filter parameters that are sent via an HTTP GET request. The request is received by the datasets controller route named `tweet_search`; it is responsible for unpacking the request and invoking the QueryDispatcher to properly route the request's filter parameters to the appropriate data sources.
2. The QueryDispatcher receives the request payload and the current QueryChain object, which keeps track of Query objects in the order they were created in the user interface. The filter payload is sent through the Query constructor and—based on its parameters—is transformed into a Query subclass, either AnnotationQuery or SolrQuery. The main objective of QueryDispatcher is to send the QueryChain through to neighboring functions that process the query against our persistent data sources (PostgreSQL and Solr). In this case, an AnnotationQuery was created, and so QueryDispatcher passes the QueryChain instance to the `annotation_search` function.
3. The `annotation_search` function searches the QueryChain instance for AnnotationQuery instances, passes them to the Annotation model within the Rails framework, and returns search results of matching tweet references. This function is designed to aggregate the results from the AnnotationQuery instances found in the QueryChain and honor the logical operators that were expressed for each query. Since the system imposes a global AND operation between all Query instances, if an AnnotationQuery returns no results, we can short circuit the entire search operation and return no results back to QueryDispatcher which will, in turn, return no results back to the browser.
4. The Annotation model interface offers functionality for searching Annotation instances based on tweet ID, label name, label type, or comment. In this case, its search function is called with the current AnnotationQuery parameters and searches for Annotation instances that satisfy them.
5. Rails provides object-relational mapping facilities for linking model interfaces with various database systems, in this case PostgreSQL. Annotation instances are returned from calls to the Rails models and control flow is returned back to the QueryDispatcher.
6. At this point within the QueryDispatcher, either there are tweet references that have been returned from the Annotation model or not. If no results are returned, then logically-speaking, no further querying can satisfy the current request, so the QueryDispatcher will return nothing back to the datasets controller. In the normal case, however, control flow will continue with annotation-derived tweet references to the `solr_search` function.
7. The `solr_search` function collates SolrQuery instances from the QueryChain object and uses the EPIC gem to construct a Solr-based query. The function combines the query strings from these Solr Query instances

with any annotation-derived tweet references so that the impending Solr query is further constrained by the ids of those tweets.

8. The corresponding `custom_search` call is made within the EPIC gem; it accepts the query from the QueryDispatcher and makes the call to Solr.
9. Solr executes the query according to the parameters and returns paginated tweet references back to the QueryDispatcher.
10. With a paginated payload of tweet references, the QueryDispatcher must now resolve the tweet references to retrieve the full Tweet JSON object from the Cassandra cluster. It achieves this by calling the EPIC gem to make a batch call to fetch page-sized JSON objects from Cassandra. Once the resolved tweets are returned, the QueryDispatcher wraps them within Tweet object instances and returns them to the datasets controller, whereupon they are formatted into a response payload that is returned back to the analyst.

5.2 Query Visibility

While interfaces from tools like Google Refine, Wrangler, and Splunk have powerful ways to query against large amounts of data, some of them struggle with providing visibility in their effectiveness against the data. Google Refine will display updated counts on facets and the total, but that does not describe when or where the query affected the data most. Splunk does have a visual timeline that updates itself after each query but falls short of providing usable facilities to perform previous queries, or to string them together without having to learn a query language based on pipe commands. Not enough of these tools promote the *tangible* aspects of the queries that are issued: how to create, jump between, and destroy them, as well as to view their history. That is why we implemented the interface described in Section 3; it directly supports these features. To make this possible, we had to implement two new domain models: Query and QueryChain.

In previous versions of EPIC Analyze, querying was relatively straightforward. A simple filter form was designed to accommodate filtering most fields, including tweet text, retweet count, date created range, the presence of URLs, the presence of geo-coordinates, and more. After the user submitted the filter, the set of filter parameters was transformed into parameters that could be used to submit to Solr. This achieved basic querying against large data sets, but it did not provide any visibility into the queries after the result set was displayed. Recall that most of the research analysts we interviewed felt as though the interface was missing the "big picture" of the event. They did not want to be scouring through thousands of tweets page after page. They wanted to see how their queries were making a difference in filtering out the data.

These issues of visibility and tangibility were solved with the Query and QueryChain objects. As mentioned before, the Query object is an encapsulation of data attributes coming from the filter parameters on the web interface. The QueryChain object keeps track of the Query instances created and groups them by instance type to run queries against the appropriate data source. With these querying facilities established, it becomes straightforward to display them on the interface. A "Current Filters" section in the filter form displays a list of all of the queries that have previously been made.

Analysts now are able to create new queries, which will show up on the list after they have been processed. Analysts can also click on any one of these queries, and the datasets controller will identify an index that was linked to the clicked-on query. The QueryDispatcher is then able to re-arrange a subset of the queries with respect to the Query instance, whose name was clicked on, and execute them. The results reflect the query chosen, as well as the queries that came before it in the QueryChain. We refer to this user-action as *query-jumping* because the analyst is able to jump between previous queries to view the results that each one has made in drilling down into the data set. This provides visibility in the impact of each query, as well as control to the analyst in how to redirect analyst-made queries if (for example) the most recent query was not effective.

Additionally, analysts can delete any query along the chain, as shown in the filter form (see Fig. 2) with the X-mark next to each query name. Once deleted, the query will be removed from the QueryChain object, and the analyst will be able to continue making queries from the latest point while ignoring the effects of the deleted query. These query-based controls empower the analyst to make decisions without consequence: that is, the basic yet crucial operations that can be performed on queries is the basis for how analysts can drill down into the data set to identify the most important features for their research questions.

5.3 Query Expression

The ability to perform these operations on queries is critical for exploratory data analysis on large data sets, but not if the querying expression is not powerful enough. Based on our think-aloud sessions, we learned that the most basic querying operators—AND, OR, and NOT—reflected the kinds of queries that analysts wanted to make, such as: *Give me all of the tweets in the 2012 Hurricane Sandy data set that are geo-located, and then take away all the ones that have the screen name:"spammer123."* This kind of natural inquiry should be possible, assuming that the data fields are schematized under the data source and indexed for interactive response (in this case, Solr). However, what if the analysts want to make an additional query, such as, *Now, remove the tweets that have been previously tagged with:"social media" or "local/state government?"* How can a web interface provide the flexibility and expression for querying against multiple data sources? Current analytical tools either do not support this or struggle to provide timely responses for both dataset-specific and user-defined data.

Unbeknownst to the analyst, the nature of this problem requires insight into the complexity of algorithms needed to satisfy such heterogeneous queries. We observe here that there are naive ways to perform them, such as a brute force result set intersection: let the QueryDispatcher have the annotation search return tweet reference results based on the AnnotationQuery instances, and then let the Solr search return tweet references based on the SolrQuery instances. The resulting work now involves having to intersect these two result sets. However, the problem is that the result set coming from Solr is arbitrarily large—Solr indexes tweets for datasets that have millions of records. Performing the intersection between annotations and tweets would be burdensome and take too long to return back to the user responsively.

Again, data modeling helped us find a solution. Recall the search request-response cycle in Fig. 4. The Annotations database will return result sets that are sufficiently smaller on average than those returned by the Solr index. This is evident because while EPIC Analyze supports annotations on tweets during exploratory analysis, most analysts will not manually annotate on the order of more than thousands of tweets. Therefore, annotation-based tweet references can be processed independently before searching the Solr Index, regardless of the ordering of the Query instances in the QueryChain.

Indeed, the QueryDispatcher will send the QueryChain object to its `annotation_search` function to collate all of the AnnotationQuery instances and aggregate any tweet references that satisfy the annotation-based filters. For each query—issued with the AND, OR, or NOT operator by the analyst—the results are stored in a data structure we refer to as the *tweet reference groupings*; each group contains tweet references and the chosen operator for that query. Once complete, the annotation-based tweet reference groupings are fed into the Solr query as an extra argument, which strings together the tweet ids and joins them with the logical AND operator. That way, local filter operators and the implicit global AND between all queries in the QueryChain are represented, and Solr will process a result set that is constrainted by the tweet reference groupings generated by the annotation search.

This approach works solely because tweet references are the lowest common denominator among these data sources. If we were to include additional sources that provide further enrichments to the user experience, the data modeling would then easily extend to those technologies if they also persisted tweet references. For our application infrastructure, we have seen no observable latency in Solr calls given that annotation-based tweet reference groupings are passed into the Solr query. Indeed, since Solr is supported by computational resources in our infrastructure that support indexes of more than 4 million tweets, query results are usually completed in a few seconds.

6 Conclusions and Future Work

In this paper, we have presented our work on designing user interfaces for large-scale data analysis environments. We reported on challenges we faced designing a user interface for the browser of EPIC Analyze, our custom-designed analysis platform for crisis informatics research. Our work—influenced by our strong human-centered computing perspective—took advantage of feedback provided by seven Project EPIC analysts who work with crisis data sets on a daily basis. Their feedback led to a number of improvements that allowed EPIC Analyze to become a tool they use on a daily basis. We focused on a challenging user interface design puzzle—drilling down into a large data set—and showed how the solution required not just user interface elements but objects on the server side that allowed the problem to be cleanly modeled and implemented effeciently.

Future work on EPIC Analyze will support 1) automatic tagging of tweets with labels that match user-supplied rules; 2) geo-located tweets, including a map-based timeline that shows how tweets have appeared in a specific area over time; 3) social graphs that exist among Twitter users; and 4) streaming services that enable analysts to filter and monitor dynamic data through interactive real-time visualizations. For real-time data, the querying facilities will be decoupled from data sources like Cassandra and Solr and instead be designed to handle *any* data source. For each of these tasks, the user interfaces that we develop to support them will be the result of a highly-iterative participatory design process that is conducted in tandem with any modifications to the server side data model. We believe our approach can be applied to data analysis platforms in general and not just to platforms that support crisis informatics research.

Acknowledgments. This material is based upon work sponsored by the NSF under Grant IIS-0910586. We would like to thank the seven analysts who participated in our think-aloud sessions; their feedback helped us to improve EPIC Analyze.

References

1. Anderson, K.M., Aydin, A.A., Barrenechea, M., Cardenas, A., Hakeem, M., Jambi, S.: Design challenges/solutions for environments supporting the analysis of social media data in crisis informatics research. In: 48th Hawaii International Conference on System Sciences, pp. 163–172. IEEE, January 2015
2. Anderson, K.M., Schram, A.: Design and implementation of a data analytics infrastructure in support of crisis informatics research (nier track). In: 33rd International Conference on Software Engineering, pp. 844–847. ACM, May 2011
3. Anderson, K.M., Schram, A., Alzabarah, A., Palen, L.: Architectural implications of social media analytics in support of crisis informatics research. IEEE Bulletin of the Technical Committee on Data Engineering **36**(3), 13–20 (2013)
4. Aydin, A.A., Anderson, K.M.: Incremental sorting for large dynamic data sets. In: First IEEE International Conference on Big Data Computing Service and Applications. IEEE, March + April 2015
5. Bargas-Avila, J., Hornbæk, K.: Foci and blind spots in user experience research. Interactions **19**(6), 24 (2012)
6. Cameron, M.A., Power, R., Robinson, B., Yin, J.: Emergency situation awareness from twitter for crisis management. In: International Conference Companion on World Wide Web, pp. 695–698. ACM (2012)
7. Fisher, D., DeLine, R., Czerwinski, M., Drucker, S.: Interactions with big data analytics. Interactions **19**(3), 50–59 (2012)
8. Heer, J., Kandel, S.: Interactive analysis of big data. Crossroads **19**(1), 50–54 (2012)
9. Hughes, A.L., St. Denis, L.A.A., Palen, L., Anderson, K.M.: Online public communications by police & fire services during the 2012 hurricane sandy. In: Human Factors in Computing Systems, pp. 1505–1514. ACM (2014)
10. Jara Laconich, J.J., Casati, F., Marchese, M.: Social spreadsheet. In: Daniel, F., Dolog, P., Li, Q. (eds.) ICWE 2013. LNCS, vol. 7977, pp. 156–170. Springer, Heidelberg (2013)

11. Kandel, S., Paepcke, A., Hellerstein, J., Heer, J.: Wrangler: Interactive visual specification of data transformation scripts. In: Human Factors in Computing Systems, pp. 3363–3372. ACM (2011)
12. Lewis, C., Rieman, J.: Task-centered User Interface Design: A Practical Introduction. Department of Computer Science, University of Colorado, Boulder (1993)
13. McTaggart, C.: Analysis and Implementation of Software Tools to Support Research in Crisis Informatics. Master's thesis, University of Colorado (2012)
14. Oussalah, M., Bhat, F., Challis, K., Schnier, T.: A software architecture for Twitter collection, search and geolocation services. Knowledge-Based Systems **37**, 105–120 (2013)
15. Palen, L., Anderson, K.M., Mark, G., Martin, J., Sicker, D., Palmer, M., Grunwald, D.: A vision for technology-mediated support for public participation & assistance in mass emergencies & disasters. In: ACM-BCS Visions of Computer Science. British Computer Society (2010)
16. Palen, L., Soden, R., Anderson, T.J., Barrenechea, M.: Success and scale in a data-producing organization: The socio-technical evolution of openstreetmap in response to humanitarian events. In: Human Factors in Computing Systems. ACM (2015)
17. Sarcevic, A., Palen, L., White, J., Starbird, K., Bagdouri, M., Anderson, K.M.: "beacons of hope" in decentralized coordination: Learning from on-the-ground medical twitterers during the 2010 haiti earthquake. In: Computer Supported Cooperative Work, pp. 47–56. ACM (2012)
18. Schram, A., Anderson, K.M.: MySQL to NoSQL: Data modeling challenges in supporting scalability. In: Systems, Programming, Languages and Applications: Software for Humanity, pp. 191–202. ACM (2012)
19. Shneiderman, B.: The eyes have it: A task by data type taxonomy for information visualizations. In: IEEE Symposium on Visual Languages, pp. 336–343. IEEE (1996)
20. St. Denis, L., Hughes, A., Palen, L.: Trial by Fire: The Deployment of Trusted Digital Volunteers in the 2011 Shadow Lake Fire. In: Rothkrantz, L., Ristvej, J., Franco, Z. (eds.) International Conference on Information Systems for Crisis Response and Management, pp. 1–10 (2012)
21. Starbird, K., Palen, L.: "voluntweeters:" self-organizing by digital volunteers in times of crisis. In: Human Factors in Computing Systems, pp. 1071–1080. ACM (2011)
22. Starbird, K., Palen, L., Hughes, A., Vieweg, S.: Chatter on the red: What hazards threat reveals about the social life of microblogged information. In: Computer Supported Cooperative Work and Social Computing, pp. 241–250. ACM, February 2010
23. White, J., Palen, L., Anderson, K.M.: Digital mobilization in disaster response: The work & self-organization of on-line pet advocates in response to hurricane sandy. In: Computer Supported Cooperative Work and Social Computing, pp. 866–876. ACM (2014)
24. Wongsuphasawat, K., Guerra Gómez, J.A., Plaisant, C., Wang, T.D., Taieb-Maimon, M., Shneiderman, B.: Lifeflow: Visualizing an overview of event sequences. In: Human Factors in Computing Systems, pp. 1747–1756. ACM (2011)

Tilt-and-Tap: Framework to Support Motion-Based Web Interaction Techniques

Linda Di Geronimo(✉), Ersan Aras, and Moira C. Norrie

Department of Computer Science, ETH Zurich, CH-8092 Zurich, Switzerland
{lindad,norrie}@inf.ethz.ch, arase@student.ethz.ch

Abstract. Mobile devices in everyday use such as smartphones and tablets contain sensors capable of detecting the motion of the device in terms of the angle and speed of rotation. While these have been exploited in a range of mobile apps, little attention has been paid to how these could be used to support interaction on the web. To enable researchers and developers to explore new forms of interaction based on motion sensors, we introduce a framework that supports the rapid development of web applications featuring motion-based interaction. Our Tilt-and-Tap framework focuses on the combination of tilting and tapping as a means of interaction since this allows users to easily interact without changing their hand position. We present the features of the framework as well as details of its implementation, and then demonstrate its flexibility and ease of use through some examples. We also discuss issues of performance and portability.

Keywords: Web interaction framework · Mobile web · Motion sensors

1 Introduction

Mobile devices such as smartphones and tablets are now widely used for accessing digital media and services on the internet either through mobile apps or web browsers. For example, it has been reported that, between March 2013 and June 2014, the share of digital media time in the USA was 60% mobile and 40% desktop [1]. In the UK, it was estimated that, in August 2014, 76% of the digital population accessed the internet using a smartphone and 38% using a tablet[2].

Mobile apps are currently clear winners over the mobile web with estimates that 88% of access time on smartphones and 82% on tablets in the USA in June 2014 was via apps [1]. It has been suggested that the main reason for this is the fact that apps offer a better user experience as they have more control over how information is displayed and can be designed to take into account features of touch interaction such as sizing links in a finger-friendly way[3]. The adaptation of web sites to mobile devices has long been a topic of research and is now a part of standard web development practice known as responsive design [4]. However, the focus has very much been on adapting content and layout rather than modes of interaction. It is only relatively recently that researchers have

P. Cimiano et al. (Eds.): ICWE 2015, LNCS 9114, pp. 565–582, 2015.
DOI: 10.1007/978-3-319-19890-3_36

explored adaptation to touch and multi-touch [5], and frameworks have been developed to support forms of touch interaction beyond the standard pinch and pan gestures [6].

Modern smartphones and tablets incorporate cameras as well as proximity and motion sensors that offer the potential to support other forms of interaction worthy of exploration. While a variety of mobile apps have been developed that exploit such sensors, investigations of how these could be used to support web interactions and enhance the user experience are few and far between. We therefore decided to initiate research in this direction by exploring the potential use of motion sensors to enable users to interact with applications through combinations of tilting and tapping. Tilting gestures are defined based on the speed and orientation of the device as measured by accelerometer and gyroscope sensors. Our choice of interaction modes was to allow users to interact with a web application without requiring them to move the position of the hand(s) holding the device. In the case of smallscreens, it also allows users to interact with the device without occluding parts of the screen.

We developed the Tilt-and-Tap framework to support the rapid development of web applications that use tilting interactions in combination with other touch gestures and hence to support research on the potential use of motion-based web interaction. It is a jQuery[1]-based framework and builds on the HTML5 API which provides access to the sensor data as well as JavaScript. Development of Tilt-and-Tap not only allowed us to experiment with designing applications where tilt and tap are the primary forms of interaction, but also to investigate issues of performance and device-compatibility. In this paper, we discuss these issues in detail as well as presenting the framework and some example of its use.

Section 2 provides more background information on the use of motion sensors in mobile devices and related work. We then present the main features of the Tilt-and-Tap framework in Section 3 before going on to detail the two main forms of interaction—jerk tilting and continuous tilting—and how they are implemented in Section 4 and Section 5, respectively. By means of example, we show how the framework can be used and demonstrate its flexibility in Section 6. The performance and portability issues are discussed in Section 7. Concluding remarks are given in Section 8 along with an outline of future work.

2 Background

A number of research projects have investigated ways of exploiting the hardware sensors integrated in smartphones and tablets to go beyond simple touch-based interaction. One approach is to use the camera to capture in-air gestures [7–9], thereby enabling users to interact with an application without occluding any of the screen which is a major issue in small screen devices such as smartphones. However, this approach has the disadvantage that it requires the use of both hands—one to hold the device and one to perform the gestures. This also means

[1] http://jquery.com/

that it does not transfer naturally to tablets where both hands are often used to hold the device in order to reduce the strain.

Many researchers have therefore explored the use of the motion sensors, often in combination with touch, to achieve single-handed input in the case of smartphones. Generalising to tablets, the aim is to enable users to interact with applications using the hand or hands that hold the device without requiring them to move their holding position. This means, for example, that interactions could involve taps or gestures performed by a thumb.

Rekimoto [10] was one of the first to use motion sensors to perform tilting gestures. In his experiments, a user can select an item in a menu by pressing a physical button while rotating the device. Moreover, he also studied the use of the gyroscope as a means of inspecting a 3D object from different angles by simply moving the device.

Since this first study, tilt-based interactions have been explored in a number of projects with the main differences lying in the application settings studied and the implementations used. For example, Baglioni et al. [11] use different combinations of device roll and pitch to give eight gestures based on jerked tilt movements from the resting position to one of north, north-east, east, south-east, south, south-west, west or north-west to the opposing position and then back to the resting position. They illustrate the potential use of the interactions with three scenarios—switching between application windows, performing copy-paste between applications and controlling a music player. Other projects have used the acceleration data of the device to browse in a gallery [12], scroll a long document [13] or navigate a map [14,15].

In systems where the actions performed vary according to the extent of the tilting action, for example selecting an item within a menu or scrolling an amount proportional to the angle of the tilt, overshooting is a common issue. Cho et al. [12] try to avoid this issue by implementing a more complex algorithm for tilting gestures which involves the use of "attractors" around the desired target. They implemented this for the example of a photo browser and a study comparing it with a classic button-based interaction showed an improvement in usability.

Another major issue of motion-based interaction is the possibility of triggering tilting gestures accidentally. One proposed solution is to use motion-based gestures in combination with classic ones such as pressing a button or tapping the screen. Hinckley et al. [16] studied the combination of motion and touch using examples such as tapping the screen while tilting the device to zoom in on an image.

Finally, we note that tilting gestures have also been explored in cross-platform scenarios where mobile phones have been used to remotely control the interface of a large screen or tabletop [17,18].

Despite the wealth of research on tilt-based interaction, little consideration has been given to it in web contexts. Further, most of that research has focussed on specific categories of mobile devices, commonly smartphones. Since one of the main advantages of building on the web as opposed to developing mobile apps is the fact that it supports access from a wide range of devices, it is inherent in mobile web engineering to take a broader perspective and aim to cater for different categories of mobile devices. For this reason, we wanted to investigate the potential use of tilt-based interaction for a range of devices that included both smartphones and tablets, and develop a framework that would allow researchers and developers to quickly and easily experiment with interfaces using motion-based interaction techniques on any of these devices.

3 Tilt-and-Tap Framework

The main goal of the Tilt-and-Tap framework was to enable interaction designers and researchers to explore different styles and uses of motion-based interaction on the web with a view to establishing design guidelines that could enhance the mobile browsing experience in certain settings. A good starting point was to build on previous research on motion-based interaction and ensure that we could support the different forms of interaction that have been proposed.

Two basic styles of tilt-based interaction can be clearly distinguished. Some use a jerking action where there is a rapid movement from one position to another that corresponds to a discrete gesture. Often it is a small movement and in some cases may involve a movement forth and back so that the device returns to a resting position. We refer to this as *jerk tilting* and it is often used as some kind of toggle gesture such as for displaying/hiding menu items. Other applications use *continuous tilting* where the system performs an action continuously according to the speed of the device.

In addition to pure tilt-based interaction, it has also been proposed that tilt be combined with touch in various ways. Our Tilt-and-Tap framework therefore supports both jerk tilting and continuous tilting, and these can be used either in isolation or in combination with different kinds of touch actions such as tapping, double tapping and sustained touch. Any of these interactions can also be associated with some form of audio, visual or vibration feedback.

The framework is implemented as a jQuery plugin and to demonstrate its use we show simple examples of jerk and continuous tilting interactions alongside their implementations in Fig. 1.

In the top example, jerk tilting is used to open and close a black menu. To prevent accidental triggering of the operations, the tilting action is combined with a touch-hold on the red area in the lower right corner of the screen. To open the menu, the user touches the red area and tilts the device down. Later, tilting the device up while touching the red area will close the menu.

To implement this, a developer simply has to include script elements in their HTML file for jQuery and our framework, as well as the code shown to the right of the jerk tilting figure. The jQuery statement `$('#menu')` selects the element of the web page and binds it to the `tiltandtap` method of our framework. The developer only has to define and implement the callback function for the `tiltUp` and `tiltDown` events that, in this example, basically consists of using jQuery to change the CSS visibility property. The other parameters for `tiltUp` and `tiltDown` complete the definitions of the interactions by specifying the region

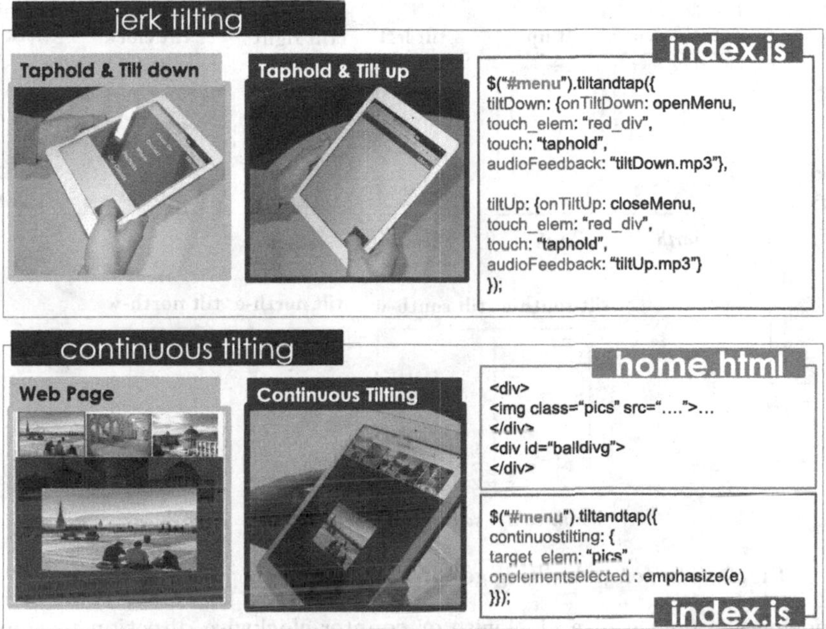

Fig. 1. Jerk and continuous tilting examples and their corresponding implementation

to be touched `touch_elem:"red_div"` and the touch action `touch: "taphold"` as well as the respective audio feedback files `tiltDown.mp3` and `tiltUp.mp3`.

In the bottom example shown in Fig. 1, continuous tilting is used to browse a gallery by continuously moving the device to the right or to the left. The scrolling speed depends on the speed of the device itself. Moreover, the picture currently selected is shown in full size in the lower part of the screen. This interaction is implemented using the `continuoustilting` event as shown in the code alongside the images of the web page. The set of target elements to be selected is defined by `target_elem: "pics"` which is all elements in the HMTL document with class `pics`. The other parameter specifies the callback function invoked when elements are selected which in this case will display a red border on the selected image in the gallery at the top and switch the image display in the main area accordingly.

4 Jerk Tilting

Tilt-and-Tap supports ten different jerk tilting interactions similar to the work presented by Baglioni et al. [11] but with the addition of the *tilt clock* and *tilt counter clock* gestures where the device is rotated clockwise or counter-clockwise as shown in Fig. 2. These two gestures were perhaps not studied by Baglioni et al. since they might not seem so natural with smartphones where the wrist positions required to perform them are quite awkward. However, they are much more natural with tablets where both hands are often used to hold the device

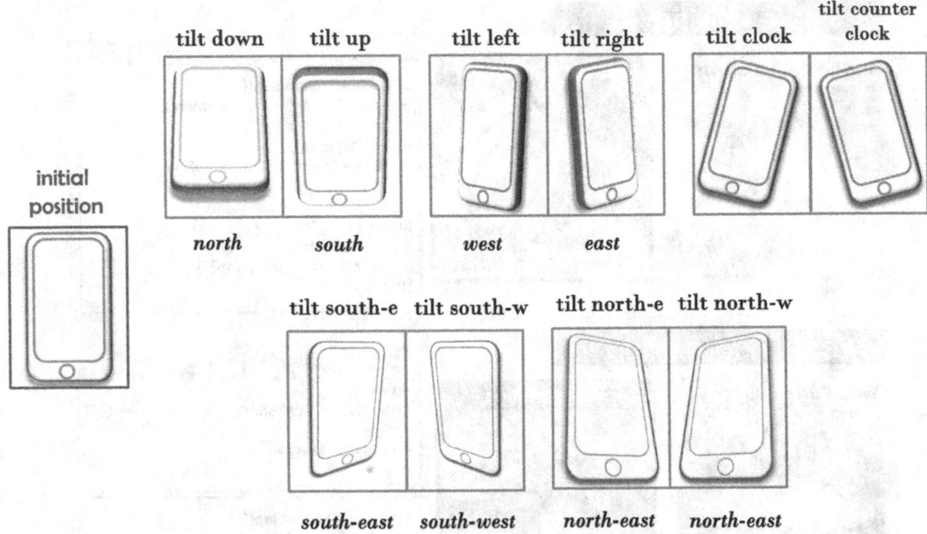

Fig. 2. The ten jerk tilting gestures relative to the initial position

and moving the device in a clockwise or counter-clockwise direction to change the orientation is common. As described in the previous section, each of these motions can also be combined with touch and feedback options.

Unlike previous projects on motion-based interaction, the goal of our project was to develop a general web framework based only on the standard web technologies HTML5 and JavaScript. Access to sensor data is via the HTML5 Device Orientation API events `DeviceOrientationChange` and `DeviceMotionChange`. `DeviceOrientationChange` returns information about the orientation of the device in the form of three values: `alpha`, `beta` and `gamma`. Those values represent the difference in position of the device with respect to three axes from a defined rest position flat on a surface as illustrated in Fig. 3.

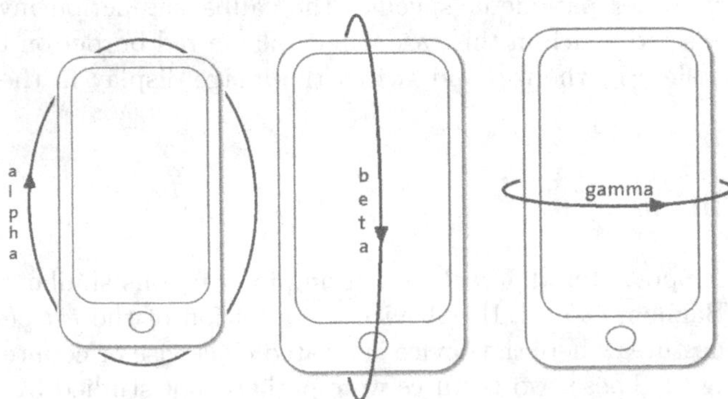

Fig. 3. Visual representations of values returned by the `DeviceOrientationChange` API: alpha, beta and gamma

`DeviceMotionChange` provides the acceleration of the device as a vector (x,y,z) of three coordinates in a 3D space. These coordinates describe the acceleration of the device to the right, forward and upwards directions, respectively, and they are calculated in m/s^2. Moreover, this function also returns a different version of the rotation data given by the `DeviceOrientationChange`, namely `rotationRate`, where the angles defined by `DeviceOrientationChange` are used to calculate the rate of change. Similar to `DeviceOrientationChange`, the `rotationRate` also gives three values `alpha`, `beta` and `gamma`, however, in this case, representing degrees per second.

These two events are called at regular intervals, which can change depending on the device and/or the browsers. However, in most of the browsers that we studied, this interval is 50ms. For both events, an `eventData` object is passed to the handler from which it can access the motion data described above. While the `DeviceOrientationChange` event only gives information about the orientation of the device, the `DeviceMotionChange` event gives information about `rotationRate` which we can determine not only the direction but also the acceleration used to move the device. For this reason, we use only `DeviceMotionChange` events to detect jerk tlting gestures.

Baglioni et al. [11] noticed that every time a jerk tilting gesture was performed, users automatically followed it with an opposite tilt interaction back towards the rest position. We refer to this as the recoil. In their work, the rest position refers to the device in a horizontal position as if flat on a table. Their implementation detects two different movements for each tilting interaction: the first in the direction of the tilting and the second towards the rest position. This solution assumes that the user is in a position where holding the device in their rest position is natural. This may not always be the case, for example, if they are lying on a sofa. Therefore, to avoid such assumptions and possible restrictions, we came up with the following alternative method for detecting a jerk tilting gesture that is both simple and efficient.

1. When the framework is initialised, it has an empty buffer of size three.
2. Every 50ms, the API returns an object containing the three values (`alpha`, `beta`, `gamma`) for the `rotationRate` of the device and we store it in the first free position in the buffer.
3. When the buffer is full, we check the last object stored:
   (a) If any of the sensor values in the object are bigger than the corresponding threshold, we save this information and go to step four.
   (b) If none of the values is larger than the threshold, we clear the buffer and start again from step one.
4. We call the function defined by the developer for the tilting gesture recognised.
5. We clear the buffer and discard the next three sensor readings to cater for recoil.

We show an example of this in Fig. 4 where the data corresponds to a tilt down gesture. When the tilt down gesture is performed, the beta value of the

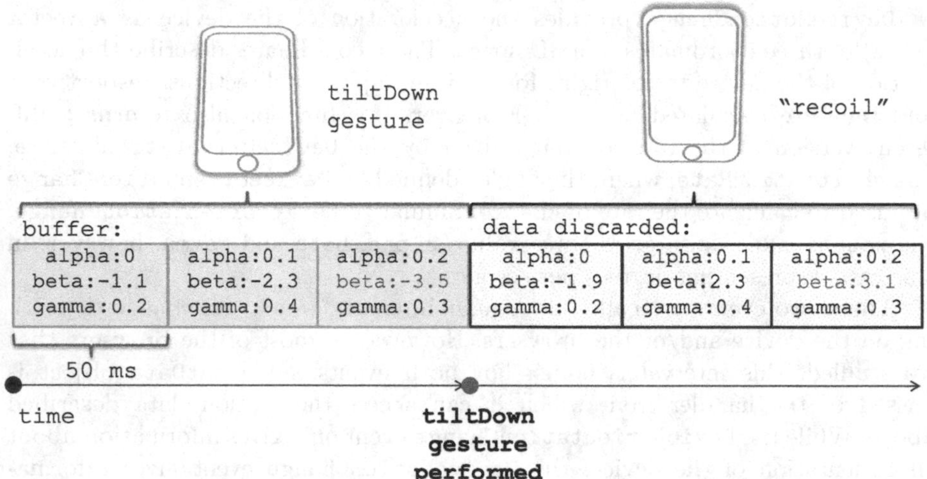

Fig. 4. Visual representation for the jerk tilting implementation

`rotationRate` object is affected and will return a negative value. If the absolute value is larger than the threshold (in this case 3) after 150ms, the tilt down gesture is recognised and the corresponding handler executed. As a result of recoil, it is likely that some of the beta values that follow are positive and could be falsely interpreted as tilt up if over the threshold as occurs in the last data object shown in the example. This is avoided since we discard the three data objects after the tilt down gesture is recognised.

Even though only the last object in the buffer is required to detect a gesture, we store the last three motion objects to be able to provide the developer with the motion history. This enables them to extend our implementation of jerk tilting recognition if desired by defining a different behaviour when the buffer is full (step 3 of the algorithm) without changing any other behaviour of the framework.

We note that the default size of the buffer as well as the thresholds were determined empirically based on our own experiments and they can differ depending on the browser used. We discuss this in more detail in Section 7. Moreover, all these values can be changed by the developer using the corresponding options available in the Tilt-and-Tap framework.

There are several other features offered by our framework for jerk tilting interactions. In Fig. 5, we show details of the main options for the `tiltUp` gesture. Note that the `thTiltUp` option allows us to distinguish between normal, medium or high jerk tilting interactions according to the tilt angle. The options are similar for all jerk tilting gestures (`tiltDown`, `tiltLeft`, `tiltRight`, `tiltClock`, `tiltCounterClock`).

5 Continuous Tilting

As already introduced in Section 3, we also support continuous tilting where the interactions continuously depend on the speed of the device. To design such

Option	Details		
	Description	Default Value	Possible Values
onTiltUp	Function to be called when a tilt up gesture is recognized	null	Name of an existing function
audioFeedback	Path of an audio file to be played when the tilt up gesture is recognized	null	A valid path of an audio file
vibrationFeedback	It indicates the intensity of the vibration when the tilting gesture is performed	0	Any number from 0 to 200
visualFeedback	It indicates the color of the border of the page when the tilting gesture is performed	null	Any CSS color (hex, string or RGB format)
touch	It indicates which other gesture is necessary to perform the tilting gesture	null	taphold, doubleTap, tap
touch_elem	If the pressing option is setted, it indicates the element of the DOM where the user has to perform the touch gesture	null	A valid selector
thTiltUp	Object that indicates the threshold for the tilt up gesture	{normal:3.1 medium:5.1 high: 6.9}	Any number for each of the intensity

Fig. 5. The main options for the `tiltUp` gesture

an interaction, we have taken inspiration from some previous works [12,14], but propose a different and more "visual" implementation. Our approach involves the use of a ball that, like a cursor, indicates the current position in the page. An example is shown in Fig. 6 where the ball will move back and forth along the horizontal bar below the images according to the direction, angle and speed of the horizontal tilting motion. It is important to note that while the ball can play an important role in suggesting that a horizontal tilting action is required and giving feedback to the user, a developer can choose if and how to display it. In the example, the viewport will be scrolled left or right depending on the position of the ball and the currently selected image element is indicated by displaying a thick border.

The `DeviceMotionChange` event returns the `accelerationIncludingGravity` object that provides values for the device acceleration and direction in 3D space. The implementation involves five steps described below and for which pseudocode is given in Fig. 7.

1. `listElementToSelect`. This first step creates a doubly linked list of all the elements in the page with class `class_name` as specified by the developer. The elements in the list are ordered depending on their current position in

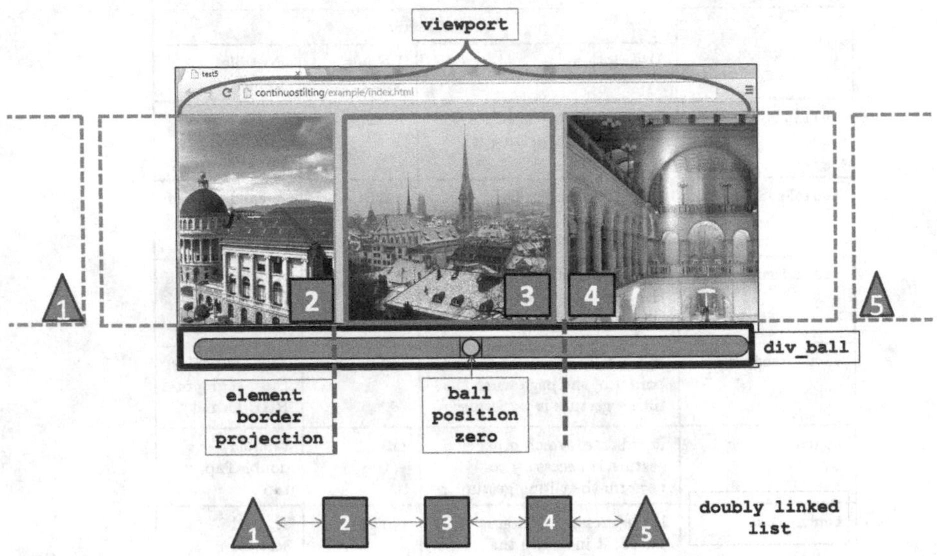

Fig. 6. Visual representation of the continuous tilting default implementation. The doubly linked list at the bottom represents the `target_element` in the page, where the rectangles correspond to elements that are visible in the viewport and the triangles to those that are currently not visible.

the page as determined by their coordinates and dimensions. Moreover, we store pointers to the first and last elements currently visible in the viewport as illustrated in Fig. 6. The list is created when the page is loaded and provides an easy means of checking which element is currently selected via the ball.

2. `moveViewPort`. Every 50ms, by default, we move the viewport depending on the tilt angle of the device.
3. `updateList`. Every 50ms, we check if the next or previous element in the list is now in the viewport depending on the tilt angle of the device. Moreover, we also check if any other elements are no longer in the viewport. Finally, we update the pointers.
4. `moveBall`. The ball is moved according to the direction and speed of the tilting. Again, thresholds are used to avoid reacting to minor movements that are probably accidental. The first time the function is called, the ball is located in the middle of the element specified by the developer. This means that the ball moves with respect to the starting position of the device rather than a pre-determined rest position, thereby accommodating different user positions such as lying on a sofa as opposed to sitting on a chair. The new position of the ball is calculated using its previous position and the current acceleration. Since the sign of the acceleration data can vary according to the browser, we set the variable `sign` as soon as a page is loaded according to the browser used. For the 1D case, the ball can only move to the left or right, while, in a 2D environment, it can move in all directions in the page.

```
onDocumentReady() {
listElementToSelect();
 onmotionchange (Acceleration data)
    {   updateList (data);
        moveViewport (data);
        moveBall (data);
        elemSelected ();
    }
}
```

```
listElementToSelect()
{
//foreach element in the page with class
//class_elem (specified by the developer)
foreach (element has class class_elem)
       {
      //element contains the ID of the element
      //its dimensions and coordinates
          list_elem [i]= element;
      //double linked list implementation
          list_elem [i] ->next =null;
          list_elem [i] ->prev =list_elem[i-1]
          list_elem[i-1] ->next =list_elm[i]

    //if element is the first one or the last
    //one visible in viewport maintain a
    //pointer to that element
          if(element first in viewport)
          {first_v = element;}
          if(element last in viewport)
          {last_v =element;}
       }
    //order elements in the doubly linked list
    //according on their position in the page
    orderList(list_elem);
}
```

```
moveBall (Acceleration data)
{//if the acceleration is bigger than a threshold
if(Δacc > th) {
 if (first call)
       {//set the ball in the centre of the div_ball
        setZeroPositionBall()
       }
 new_ball_position.top = ball.top + ((sign)·data.x·speed);
 new_ball_position.left = ball.left + ((sign)·data.y·speed);
//if the new position will put the ball outside the displayed
//page it does not move the ball
 if ( checkBallPosition (new_ball_position) ) {
       ball.top = new_ball_position.top;
       ball.left = new_ball_position.left;
     }
}
```

```
elemSelected()
{
  pointer = first_v;
  while (pointer != last_v; )
     {  //check if the ball is inside an element
        //(for a percentage defined by the developer) using its
        // dimension and coordinates
         if( isInside( ball.position, element, percentage))
         {
            cur = element;
            if( elemselected != cur)
             { elemselected = cur;
             //call the function defined by the user
             //when a new element is selected
               onElementSelected(elemselected);
             }
         return;
          }
     }
}
```

Fig. 7. Pseudocode of the default continuous tilting implementation with the first function called in the top left highlighted by a thicker border

5. `elemSelected`. We check which element is currently selected by simply checking the position of the ball. If the ball falls inside an element, we call the function `onElementSelected` defined by the developer. With the doubly linked list, this operation is done with a $O(s)$ complexity where s is the number of elements in the viewport. A possible optimisation would be to use an additional heap map with the position of the element as a key. However, since the number of elements is usually small, we opted for the simpler solution.

The default behaviour can easily be used by web developers with a basic knowledge of how to use a jQuery framework. For those with more programming skills, it is easy to extend these functions to give more control over the behaviour associated with each of these components.

As for jerk tilting, several options are available which we describe in Fig. 8. These allow a developer to specify whether the ball should be visible as well as its speed. Other options not shown in the Fig. 8 specify the size and the colour of the ball, the percentage overlap for a ball to be considered "inside" an element and its `dimensionality` which specifies whether it can move on only one axis or two.

For both jerk and continuous tilting, we also have an additional option that we call `activationGesture`. This option enables developers to decide how tilting interactions should be activated for their entire application. For example, a developer might specify a `tap`, `doubletap` or `taphold` on a specific area of the page.

Option	Details		
	Description	Default Value	Possible Values
targetClass	Class name of the elements that will be affected by the continuous tilting	null	A valid class name
elementPos	DOM element where to position the ball	Common DOM brother of the targetClass	A valid selector
visibility	It indicates if the ball will be visible or not	true	true, false
speed	A multiplier that increase or decrease the speed of the ball	null - speed decided only by the movement of the device	Any number. Positive numbers will increase the speed of the ball, while negative numbers will decrease the speed.
touch	It indicates which other gesture is necessary to perform the tilting gesture	null	taphold, doubleTap, tap
touch_elem	It indicates on which element the user has to perform the touch gesture	null	A valid selector
onElementSelected	The callback function called when the ball "selects" a targetElement	null	An existing function
onMoveViewport	The callback function to call anytime the device is moved	"Moves" the targetElement to the left if the ball falls to the left, and to the right if the ball falls to the right	An existing function

Fig. 8. List of the main options available for the `continuousTilting` interaction

6 Applications

In order to show the flexibility of the framework, we now present two web applications that we have implemented: YouTap and TiltZoo. As the names suggest, the first application is an extended version of one of the most famous websites on internet YouTube[2], while the second application refers to a zoo photo gallery.

In Fig. 9, we show the three main pages of YouTap. The home page simply shows a list of videos divided into different categories (music, sports, news etc.). If the user taps on a video, the page in the middle is displayed with the selected video shown in the lower portion and related videos placed on the top. In this page, the user can browse the related videos using a continuous tilting interaction to scroll to the left or right in the list. In this interaction, the user is helped by a green ball indicating the current position in the video gallery. If the user plays a video, the rest of the content becomes less visible to avoid confusion. At this point, the user can perform several tilting gestures to interact with the application. The user can skip to the next or previous video by jerk tilting the device to the left or to the right. Moreover, by hold tapping a red area at the bottom and tilting the device in some direction, the user can perform the following actions:

[2] https://www.youtube.com/

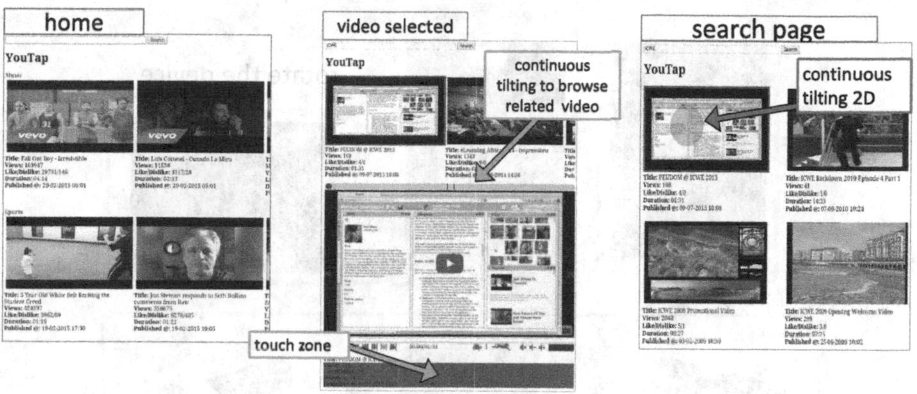

Fig. 9. Screenshots of the three main pages of YouTap

- **Soft tilt down/up**. It will turn the volume up or down by 20 units.
- **High tilt down/up**. It will mute or unmute the audio.
- **Soft tilt left/right**. It will skip to the next or previous 10 seconds of the video.
- **Medium tilt left/right**. It will skip the next or previous 30 seconds of the video.
- **High tilt left right**. It will skip the next or previous 120 seconds of the video.

As seen in the third page shown in Fig. 9, if the user searches for a video, the system will show a list of the results which can be browsed by tilting the device. In this case, a red ball is moved across the page corresponding to the tilt and when it is positioned over a particular thumbnail, a red border will be displayed. In the figure, it is positioned over the top left thumbnail. When a thumbnail is selected, a jerk tilt to the right will cause that video to be played.

With the second application, TiltZoo, our goal was to show how motion-based interactions can make the web more interactive and transform a simple picture gallery into a creative space. The scenario we envision is a one-page web site which can be browsed using two alternative modalities to show different pieces of information. The modalities are selected by changing the orientation of the device. When the device is used in portrait mode, as shown in Fig. 10, we allow the normal browsing experience that shows pictures and descriptions through common scrolling and tapping interactions (steps one and two). However, when the user rotates the device to landscape mode, a new view and different set of interactions becomes available (step three in Fig. 10). At this stage, the system waits for a double tap to activate the new motion-based modality. This can act as a switch to avoid unintended activation of tilting gestures. Once the tilting mode is activated, the user is free to explore a gallery of pictures, one at a time, as if they were displayed in a 3D space. When the user tilts the device to the right or to the left, the next or previous pictures are shown through a 3D animation that simulates the rotation of a cube. If the user wants to know more about

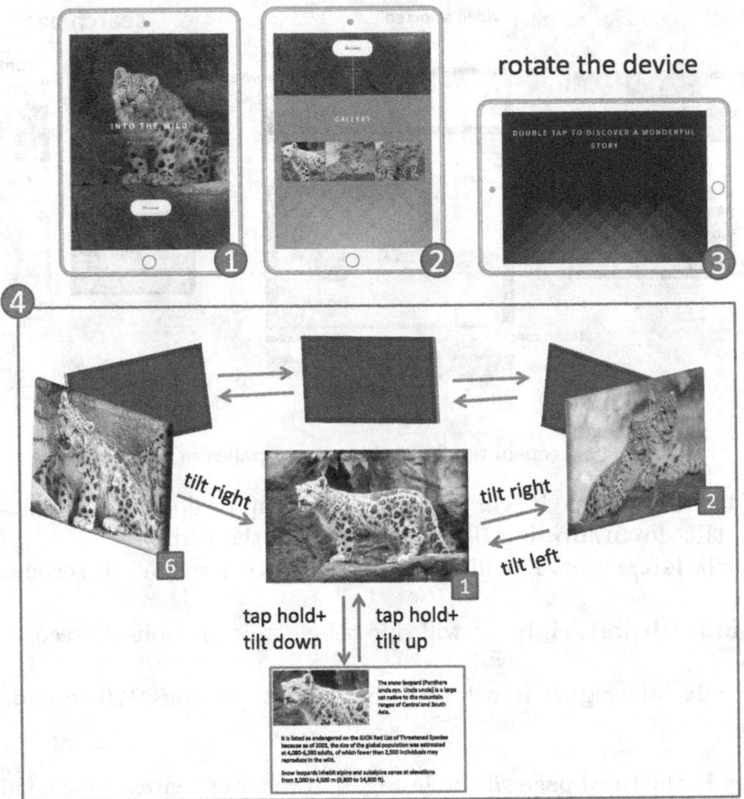

Fig. 10. TiltZoo application screenshots and its interaction flow

the picture they are currently viewing, they can hold tap on the picture and tilt down to access the bottom side of the cube where additional information is shown. To go back to the gallery, they have to simply hold tap on the page and tilt up. Finally, they can return to the normal browsing experience by rotating the device back to the portrait mode.

While YouTap has the goal of extending the current set of interactions available on YouTube, TiltZoo tries to make the browsing experience more creative and interactive. We have presented one possible way of enhancing such applications, but thanks to the flexibility of our framework many other approaches are possible. This flexibility derives directly from the amount of possible combinations of interactions available in Tilt-and-Tap. We believe that developers can take advantage of our framework to design and experiment with a wide range of innovative web applications that make use of motion-based gestures.

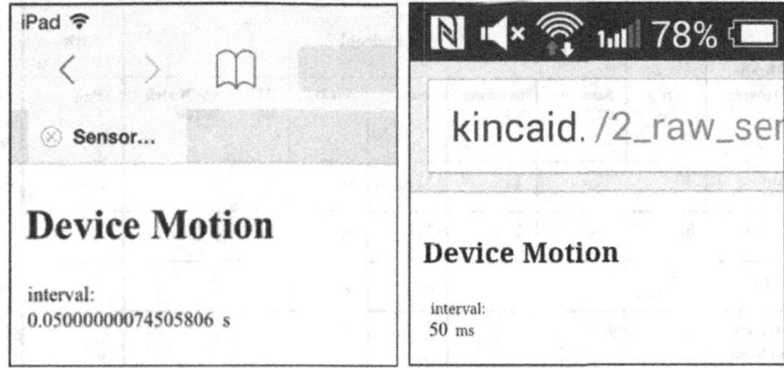

Fig. 11. Screenshots of a simple web page showing frequency of sensor data. The web page on the left is open in Safari on an iPad Air and the one on the right in Chrome on a Samsung tablet 8.4.

7 Discussion

A major challenge of our work was to build the framework using only generally available web APIs. Alternatively, we could have developed a more native solution using a platform such as Apache Cordova[3]. With this approach, it would have been possible to develop native Android applications using HTML, CSS and JavaScript without having to deal with the default behaviour of the browsers, thereby giving more freedom to developers. Despite these advantages, there are several problems with this approach. Even if native support would have been a simple way of demonstrating our ideas, access to information such as the motion data is not completely supported by these platforms, and it would have required a lot more effort to build the framework. Further, since one of the main goals of Tilt-and-Tap is to help developers use motion-based interactions, a jQuery plugin seemed the best way of providing widespread support. However, working with APIs that are still works in progress presented some challenges that we now discuss.

As described previously, the Tilt-and-Tap framework makes use of the HTML5 events `DeviceOrientationChange` and `DeviceMotionChange` to access sensor data. The Device Orientation API is not yet fully implemented by all browsers and not in the same way. The data returned by events is not the same in all browsers. For example, according to the specification, the frequency with which sensor data is made available should be given as a number specifying the number of milliseconds, but Safari and Chrome for the iPad and iPhone return a *long double* representing the frequency in seconds as shown in Fig. 11.

The specifics of the hardware sensors used in each mobile device also effects the data returned. We first analysed these problems by testing as many combinations of devices, platforms and browsers as possible to check if information found on the web at `cainuse.com` was reliable. We first used a simple application that just shows the data returned by the two events of interest to check support in different browsers

[3] http://cordova.apache.org/

API	Mobile Browser	Versio n	Android						iOS	Windows 8.1
			Samsung S2	Samsung 8.4	Nexus 5	Nexus 7	HTC M8	LG Watch W100	IPad	Nokia Lumnia 925
Device Orientation – Device Motion Change	Chrome	40	Yes	Yes	Yes	~	Yes	/	Yes	/
	Firefox	35	Yes	Yes	Yes	~	Yes	/	/	/
	Safari	9.1	/	/	/	/	/	/	Yes	/
	Internet Explorer	11	/	/	/	/	/	/	/	No
	WIB	1.0beta 19	/	/	/	/	/	Yes	/	/

Fig. 12. The compatibility table for `DeviceOrientationChange` and `DeviceMotionChange`. A / indicates that a device does not support a browser, while ~ indicates that the API is supported but suffers from various issues.

and platforms. The results are presented in Fig. 12[4]. According to `cainuse.com`, IE should support the two events, but in fact our application did not work. Moreover, we noticed that some devices have poor support for motion sensors returning a `beta` value of NaN (not a number) most of the time.

We then compared the data returned by `DeviceOrientationChange` and `DeviveMotionChange` for three different browsers and devices to determine the main differences between browsers and platforms. The main differences that we discovered are:

1. The range of the `beta` value for `DeviceOrientationChange` in Firefox and Chrome on Android devices is [-90,90], but [-180,180] on Safari and Chrome on iOS. However, the range of the `alpha` value for `DeviceOrientationChange` in Firefox and Chrome on Android devices is [-180,180], while it is [-90,90] in Safari and Chrome on iOS.
2. The `interval` data returned by Firefox is 100ms but 50ms in all other browsers tested.
3. The value `accelerationIncludingGravity.x` in Safari is positive if the device is tilted to the right and negative if tilted to the left. In all the other browsers, it is the opposite.
4. The sensing intervals are shown in seconds in Safari and Chrome on iOS, and in milliseconds on all other browser/device combinations.

Despite these issues, our framework works on all of the tested browser and device combinations listed in Fig. 12. We avoid the first three problems by using different thresholds and buffer sizes depending on the browser used. Our implementation is not affected by the fourth problem due to our use of a buffer.

Since such technologies are constantly evolving, it is not sure whether the HTML5 standard for the Device Orientation API will ever be completely followed

[4] As from evaluation on 25/03/2015.

by all of the main mobile browsers. One solution would be a more complex architecture involving a web server database that stores different settings (thresholds, interval unit measurements etc.) for each particular case. This database could be populated and updated by the crowd in order to cover as many combinations of browsers and devices as possible.

Another major issue concerning the use of motion sensor data in the web is performance related. Performance on small devices is already an issue for web developers since the processing power is not compatible with desktop computers. If functions have to be called every 50ms to check sensor data, this can seriously diminish the user experience due to the lags introduced. This was noticeable in our first efforts to implement continuous tilting which is why we opted for the simple solution based on doubly linked lists presented here that gives acceptable performance. We also implemented the tap, double tap and taphold recognition using only JavaScript to avoid the use of an external framework which could also have reduced performance. One possible future improvement would be to add a caching system to save time when pages are reloaded.

8 Conclusion

We have presented Tilt-and-Tap, a web-based framework that enlarges the set of possible interactions on the web and helps developers build web sites with motion-based interaction. We have built a number of application examples to demonstrate the flexibility of the framework and explore ways in which different tilting gestures combined with single, double and hold taps could be used to provide a set of rich interactions for web sites. In the future, we plan to carry out user studies with a view to establishing a set of design guidelines.

Other plans for future work include developing a visual tool that allows end-users to extend their web sites with motion-based interactions without the need for programming skills. This idea of bringing motion-based interactions into end-user development has already been discussed in the literature [19] but so far little has been done to support it in reality.

Another interesting direction of research is to investigate the use of tilting interaction in web-based cross device applications. For example, a user could interact with web applications on desktop computers or tablets by performing motion-based interactions using their smartwatch.

References

1. Perez, S.: Majority of Digital Media Consumption now takes place in Mobile Apps. TechCrunch (2014). http://techcrunch.com/2014/08/21/majority-of-digital-media-consumption-now-takes-place-in-mobile-apps/
2. Shaw, M.: Cross Channel Measurement - Understanding Consumer Behaviour Across Multiple Devices. Panel Presentation, AOP Conference (2014). http://www.comscore.com/Insights/Presentations-and-Whitepapers/2014/Cross-Channel-Measurement

3. Borley, R.: Why Smartphone Apps are killing the Mobile Web Browser. Dootrix (2014). http://dootrix.com/smartphone-apps-killing-mobile-web-browser/
4. Frain, B.: Responsive Web Design with HTML5 and CSS3. Packt Publishing (2012)
5. Nebeling, M., Norrie, M.C.: Beyond responsive design: adaptation to touch and multitouch. In: Casteleyn, S., Rossi, G., Winckler, M. (eds.) ICWE 2014. LNCS, vol. 8541, pp. 380–389. Springer, Heidelberg (2014)
6. Nebeling, M., Norrie, M.C.: jQMultiTouch: lightweight toolkit and development framework for multi-touch/multi-device web interfaces. In: Proc. 4th ACM SIGCHI Symposium on Engineering Interactive Computing Systems (EICS) (2012)
7. Yousefi, S., Kondori, F.A., Li, H.: Experiencing Real 3D Gestural Interaction with Mobile Devices. Pattern Recognition Letters **34**(8) (2013)
8. Song, J., Sörös, G., Pece, F., Fanello, S., Izadi, S., Keskin, C., Hilliges, O.: In-air gestures around unmodified mobile devices. In: Proc. 27th ACM User Interface Software and Technology Symposium (UIST) (2014)
9. Hürst, W., Wezel, C.V.: Gesture-Based Interaction via Finger Tracking for Mobile Augmented Reality. Multimedia Tools and Applications **62**(1) (2013)
10. Rekimoto, J.: Tilting operations for small screen interfaces. In: Proc. 9th ACM User Interface Software and Technology Symposium (UIST) (1996)
11. Baglioni, M., Lecolinet, E., Guiard, Y.: JerkTilts: using accelerometers for eight-choice selection on mobile devices. In: Proc. 13th Intl. Conf. on Multimodal Interfaces (ICMI) (2011)
12. Cho, S., Murray-Smith, R., Kim, Y.: Multi-context photo browsing on mobile devices based on tilt dynamics. In: Proc. 9th Intl. Conf. on Human Computer Interaction with Mobile Devices and Services (MobileHCI) (2007)
13. Eslambolchilar, P., Murray-Smith, R.: Tilt-based automatic zooming and scaling in mobile devices – a state-space implementation. In: Brewster, S., Dunlop, M.D. (eds.) Mobile HCI 2004. LNCS, vol. 3160, pp. 120–131. Springer, Heidelberg (2004)
14. Pahud, M., Hinckley, K., Iqbal, S., Sellen, A., Buxton, B.: Toward compound navigation tasks on mobiles via spatial manipulation. In: Proc. 15th Intl. Conf. on Human-Computer Interaction with Mobile Devices and Services (MobileHCI) (2013)
15. Tonder, B.V., Wesson, J.L.: Improving the Controllability of Tilt Interaction for Mobile Map-Based Applications. International Journal of Human-Computer Studies **70**(12) (2012)
16. Hinckley, K., Song, H.: Sensor synaesthesia: touch in motion, and motion in touch. In: Proc. SIGCHI Conf. on Human Factors in Computing Systems (CHI) (2011)
17. Boring, S., Jurmu, M., Butz, A.: Scroll, tilt or move it: using mobile phones to continuously control pointers on large public displays. In: Proc. 21st Annual Conf. of the Australian Computer-Human Interaction Special Interest Group (OZCHI) (2009)
18. Dachselt, R., Buchholz, R.: Natural throw and tilt interaction between mobile phones and distant displays. In: Proc. SIGCHI Conf. on Human Factors in Computing Systems, (CHI Extended Abstracts) (2009)
19. Paternò, F., Santoro, C., Spano, L.D.: Model-based design of multi-device interactive applications based on web services. In: Gross, T., Gulliksen, J., Kotzé, P., Oestreicher, L., Palanque, P., Prates, R.O., Winckler, M. (eds.) INTERACT 2009. LNCS, vol. 5726, pp. 892–905. Springer, Heidelberg (2009)

Harnessing WebGL and WebSockets for a Web-Based Collaborative Graph Exploration Tool

Björn Zimmer(✉) and Andreas Kerren

Department of Computer Science, ISOVIS Group, Linnaeus University, Vejdes Plats 7, SE-35195 Växjö, Sweden
{bjorn.zimmer,andreas.kerren}@lnu.se

Abstract. The advancements of web technologies in recent years made it possible to switch from traditional desktop software to online solutions. Today, people naturally use web applications to work together on documents, spreadsheets, or blogs in real time. Also interactive data visualizations are more and more shared in the web. They are thus easily accessible, and it is possible to collaboratively discuss and explore complex data sets. A still open problem in collaborative information visualization is the online exploration of node-link diagrams of graphs (or networks) in fields such as social sciences or systems biology. In this paper, we address challenges related to this research problem and present a client/server-based visualization system for the collaborative exploration of graphs. Our approach uses WebGL to render large graphs in a web application and provides tools to coordinate the analysis process of multiple users in synchronous as well as asynchronous sessions.

Keywords: Collaboration · Web user interfaces · WebGL · WebSockets · Network visualization · Graph drawing

1 Introduction

The advent of the Web 2.0 introduced a vast amount of interactive web applications such as text editors, online drawing tools or more advanced office suites (e.g., Google Docs). The online nature of these applications makes them feasible for collaboration, and an increasing amount of users spread across the globe work together to synchronously create and edit documents in web-based tools. These collaborative applications should assist users by providing insights about other users who are working on the same document to help everyone establishing a "common ground" (cf. Section 2 and [1,2]) in the shared workspace. Users should be able to notice if another user joins or leaves a session and be aware of the changes that other users are applying to a document. In addition, collaborative systems should also utilize concurrency control to solve arising conflicts when different users want to apply changes to the same part of a document simultaneously.

P. Cimiano et al. (Eds.): ICWE 2015, LNCS 9114, pp. 583–598, 2015.
DOI: 10.1007/978-3-319-19890-3_37

Information visualization researchers also use the web for making collaborative data visualizations available. The biggest advantage of these web-based applications is their convenient usage. Users do not have to download and install additional software packages or plug-ins to collaborate. It suffices to share a URL to start a collaborative session with other colleagues. This tackles a problem which was mentioned by Isenberg et al. [3] as one of the ongoing challenges in collaborative information visualization.

In this work, we focus on the cooperative analysis of complex node-link diagrams. These diagrams are usually explored by various domain experts, who would like to work together to improve the quality of the analysis process. This process can take place in a joint online session where everybody works *simultaneously* on one data set and discusses possible changes and insights in real-time with other users. In this case, an expert might want to see what the others are doing and if there are possibilities to coordinate the efforts and find a common ground. In another scenario, experts would like to work on the data set whenever time permits. In such an *asynchronous* setting, it would be interesting to quickly perceive changes that were performed by former analysts or to find out which parts of the data set were already explored by others.

We designed our visualization tool OnGraX to address special challenges for *synchronous* and *asynchronous* collaborative network analysis in a web-based environment. The graphs which are analyzed with the help of our system usually have a complex topology and various node attributes. But the available libraries for the visualization of graphs in web browsers are not sufficient enough, since their ability to render several thousand labeled nodes with different shapes and colors is quite limited. In this paper, we want to discuss the technical design decisions of our tool which enable us to provide an easy accessible web-based tool for the collaborative exploration of graphs. Note that all visualization details were published separately [4,5]. Here, we concentrate on the technical and engineering aspects of OnGraX. We will discuss the following points in detail:

- the utilization of WebGL to render graphs with several thousand labeled nodes of different shapes and color,
- the usage of WebSockets to provide real-time mouse and viewport positions of other users in synchronous sessions as well as fast response times for event synchronization, and
- efficiently storing the graph information and concurrency handling during collaborative sessions.

OnGraX is capable of visualizing graphs from various application domains, such as social networks (e.g., Facebook), networks in software engineering (UML-diagrams among other things), or biochemical networks. Currently, our tool is used for the collaborative analysis and data cleaning [6] of metabolic networks due to long lasting cooperations with biologists/bioinformaticians at several research institutions. This specific application serves as use case throughout this paper and focuses on the interactive exploration and analysis of biological networks based on the so-called Kyoto Encyclopedia of Genes and Genomes pathway database [7]. Building these biological networks is often based on complex experiments. In consequence, biologists of different domains and experience levels would like to explore the resulting networks together and check them for wrong entries or missing data and revise the networks wherever it is necessary.

The remainder of this paper discusses our solution for these challenges. The next section covers related work in graph visualization and web-based collaborative visualization. Our requirements are described in Section 3. An overview of our tool is given in Section 4, and the implementation as well as technical details are covered in Section 5. We discuss the benefits of our approach and future work in Section 6 and conclude in Section 7.

2 Related Work

Desktop applications for single users with the possibility to visualize graphs, such as Cytoscape [8], Gephi [9], Pajek [10], or Tulip [11], have been used before the advent of the Web 2.0. Available methods for graph visualizations are comprehensively overviewed in several surveys and books, for instance [12–14]. However, the idea of working collaboratively on complex data sets is becoming more and more attractive with the rapidly growing amount of data available. Thus, a good number of web-based visualizations were already introduced that support the public exploration of complex data sets [15]. Users are able to add comments on interesting visualizations and also discuss new insights with other users over the web. Several systems support those features, such as ManyEyes [16] or Sense.us [17]. In these web-based visualization systems, users are able to save bookmarks of specific views on a data set, and it is possible to add graphical annotations directly to the visualization. Dashiki [18] enables users to collaboratively build visualization dashboards with the help of a wiki-like syntax and interactive editors. However, the aforementioned systems are not suitable for our tasks, since they do not support the interactive visualization of node-link diagrams in a web browser. And, they do not provide any features for real-time interactions during synchronous collaboration settings.

Drawing graphs in a web browser is usually done with the help of already existing JavaScript libraries. Arbor.js [19] and Sigma.js [20] render the input graphs on a HTML5 canvas or via SVG-images, but they do not support OpenGL-enhanced rendering which limits the number of nodes and edges that can be rendered with a suitable frame rate. A faster solution is provided by VivaGraphJS [21]: this library uses a WebGL renderer to draw graphs and provides high performance during rendering, but gives only limited support for different and more complex node shapes. Additionally, these libraries are not able to efficiently render a lot of text, e.g., node labels for all nodes visible at the same time, which is one of the requirements for our tool as described in the next section.

A good overview of the field of collaborative visualization is given in the article of Isenberg et al. [3]. We follow their terminology and classify our approach as distributed, synchronous/asynchronous collaborative visualization method. In this work, we restrict ourselves on the collaborative visual analysis of networks.

For further readings on general aspects of visualization, human-computer interaction, computer-supported collaborated work, and collaborative visualization of other data types, we refer to the standard literature, for instance [2,15,22–25] (this list does not claim to be exhaustive).

The benefits of collaborative work are also discussed in an article on social navigation presented by Dieberger et al. [26]. Being able to see the usage history and annotations of former users might help analysts to filter and find relevant information more quickly. In order to be able to work together during a synchronous session, users have to know each other's interactions and views on the data set, usually referred to as "common ground" [1,2]. To find a common ground in node-link visualizations, we apply the techniques from the work of Gutwin and Greenberg [27] and show the viewports of other users as rectangles in the graph visualization.

There are also existing groupware frameworks and libraries to handle collaborative editing in the web with concurrency control, such as ShareJS [28] or Apache Wave [29]. They usually center on manipulating the DOM of collaborative websites and editing text in online documents without creating conflicts. Our approach concentrates on collaboration and awareness in a node-link based graph visualization which does not require to edit a lot of textual data, i.e., we focus on changing the structure and attributes of the graph instead. For this case, it suffices to use a traditional lock-based approach.

3 Requirements

Our goal was to design a system for analyzing complex graphs in distributed collaborative sessions. The initial process of beginning a collaboration should be as fast and easy as possible, thus the tool should also be available on the fly without requiring users to install specific software, plug-ins, or Java applets first. Additionally, users should be able to drop in and out of ongoing collaborative work without having to setup and plan each session individually—experts would like to work on a data set whenever they find the time and do not want to wait for others to join before they can start their analysis process. In this case, users who are joining an already ongoing session should be able to quickly catch up on what has been done before. Hence, the system should support logging all actions that are performed in a session and provide a way to quickly retrieve and analyze them to show important information to subsequent users. These actions include not only changes performed on a graph (such as deleting or changing the attributes of a node), but also the tracking and logging of every user's camera position. This assists subsequent analysts to identify regions of a graph that other users were already interested in if they work on the data set asynchronously. During a synchronous session however, changes applied to the graph should be distributed to all connected clients as fast as possible and users should be able to track each other's mouse and camera positions in real time to establish a common ground and be aware of everything that is going on in a session. The system also has to store the complete graph structure and additional graph attributes in an efficient way. And, it should handle conflicts that could arise during a collaborative session if two users want to change the same object in the graph at the same time.

In addition to the graph structure itself, nodes usually hold attributes (e.g., age, gender, or income for social networks). Rendering the nodes as simple dots is therefore not sufficient enough for our application areas since the shape, size, and color of nodes may have specific meanings; nodes may also have labels attached. Thus, our system should be able to render graphs with a considerable number of nodes and edges of different shapes and sizes with additional text labels on every node in an acceptable frame rate. Moreover, running computationally expensive tasks—such as calculating the layout of a graph, computing additional graph metrics, or aggregating the camera positions to show interesting regions—should not have a negative impact on the rendering performance on the clients. We summarize the technical requirements (TRs) of our tool as follows:

- TR 1. It should be possible to start a collaborative session on the fly without having to install software or plug-ins first.
- TR 2. The system should be able to render graphs with up to 6,000 nodes and edges with a good performance on standard computers.
- TR 3. It should be able to render nodes in various shapes and colors, with additional text labels on every node.
- TR 4. Changes to the graphs and mouse positions as well as viewports of other users should be distributed to all connected clients in (soft) real time.
- TR 5. The server should efficiently store the graph structure as well as the complete action history of a graph session in order to use this data for subsequent analysis processes.
- TR 6. The system should be able to manage concurrent graph changes during a collaborative session.
- TR 7. Computationally expensive processes, such as calculating the layout of a graph, should not interfere with the rendering performance of the graph visualization.
- TR 8. As the most graphs come with node and/or edge labels, the system should support fast and efficient text rendering.

4 General System Overview

OnGraX visualizes graphs as interactive node-link diagrams. Fig. 1 shows an overview of the tool right after joining an ongoing graph analysis session with two other users: Bob and Sue. Their viewports are represented as two dashed rectangles. Bob's position is shown in blue and Sue's position is shown in green (see Fig. 1(a) and (b)). The rectangles also contain their mouse cursors which are updated in real time. This makes it possible to point at interesting objects and coordinate collaborative work. Short animations (created with the tween.js [30] library) are used to facilitate user awareness about ongoing changes during a session. For instance, if nodes are deleted they will slowly grow in size and fade out instead of just disappearing. Recent actions which are performed during a session are tracked as small icons on the right-hand side of the screen (see Fig. 1(c)). These icons can be clicked to move the camera back and forth between the current camera position and the position where the event took place, enabling users to quickly check the ongoing work of other users. To not get overwhelmed with notifications, an additional dialog box allows users to configure which types of actions are tracked.

Apart from a simple chat window where users can discuss changes, it is also possible to pin textual annotations to nodes and edges. This gives analysts the possibility to pass information about performed changes in the graph to subsequent users, ask questions about specific objects, or delegate work to other users. In Fig. 1(d), an annotation that is pinned to a node is highlighted, along with the respective text in the annotations dialog in the bottom right corner. The text in the annotations dialog can also be clicked to move the camera to the respective annotated object in the graph if it is not in the current view. One problem with textual annotations is, that the original context in which an annotation was initially written could get lost if the respective graph region—where the annotation is pointing to—is changed during the course of a session or if the object with this annotation is deleted. We solve this problem by enabling analysts to temporarily revert the complete graph to an old state, giving them the possibility to view the graph in a state in which the annotation was originally written. This is done by clicking on any icon in the timeline at the bottom of the screen (see Fig. 1(e)). This action will undo all subsequent changes that were performed on the graph. While viewing an old state, icons to the right can be clicked to replay already performed changes and go forward in time, and icons on the left are used to undo additional changes to view even older states of the graph.

Analysts who join a session would like to be able to quickly find out which graph regions were already viewed or changed by other users, for instance to decide if they should work on another part of a graph or if they should double check on specific regions. In our case, we had to use a visualization method that does not interfere with the original graph visualization. Changing the colors or the size of nodes in the graph was not an option for us, because these properties are already mapped to other attributes. To still be able to show additional user data without affecting the original graph visualization, we use a heat map-based visualization approach. The heat map is drawn in the background of the graph visualization. It can be configured to only show data for specific users or to show data for all users together. Furthermore, it is possible to select a time frame (e.g., the last five minutes of the current analysis session) or a specific start and end date. This enables an analyst to review changes done in a collaborative session during a specific time frame or to check the work of a single user. The heat map can be configured to show two different data sources:

User viewports. Here, nodes are highlighted that were in the viewing area of all users during their analysis process. The server aggregates the logs of all node movements and user views to visualize the amount of seconds that nodes were in the viewports of all or specific users. This helps analysts to

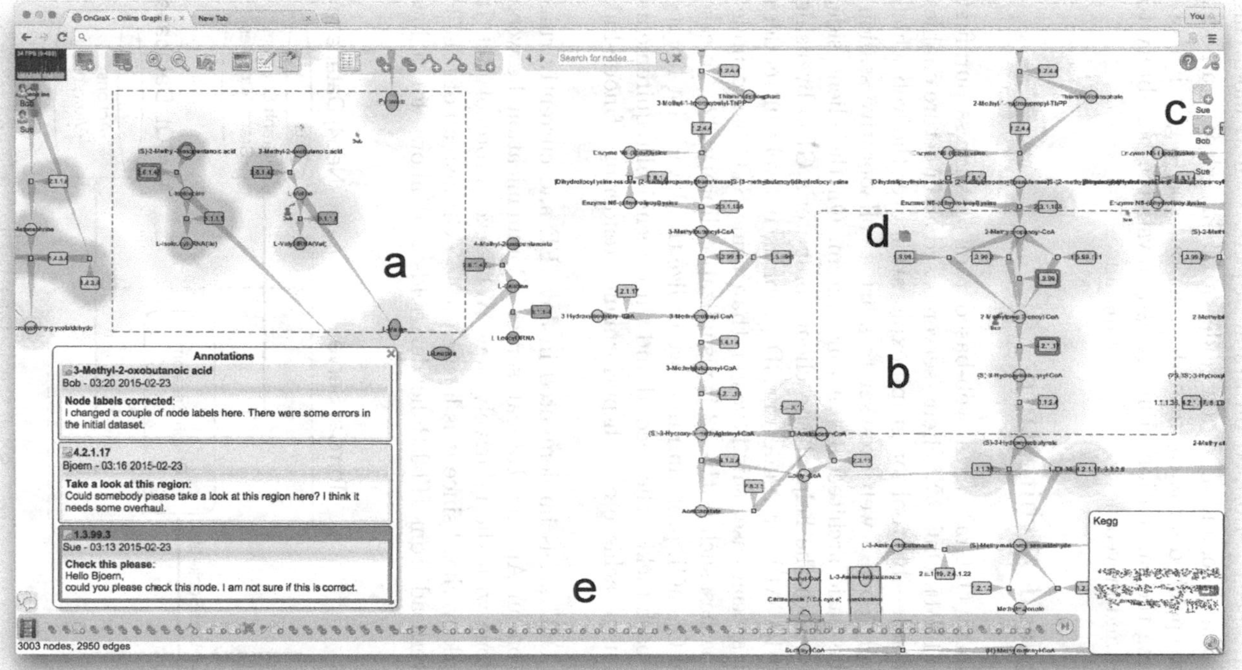

Fig. 1. Overview of our system. The image shows a part of a biochemical network with 3,003 nodes and 2,950 edges. The blue and green dashed rectangles (see (a) and (b)) are the viewing areas (viewports) of two other users who are exploring this graph simultaneously. The viewports and the mouse cursor of every user in a graph session are updated in (soft) real time. Here, the heat map in the background assists the analyst to identify regions of the graph that were of interest to the other users by highlighting all nodes based on their logged viewports. The symbols in the top-right corner of the screen (c) assist the analyst to keep track of recent actions performed by other users, such as adding or deleting nodes. Text annotations can be pinned to nodes and edges to discuss tasks, insights and questions with other users (d). The timeline (e) can be used to revert the graph to a previous state and replay applied changes.

quickly identify in which part of a graph another user was interested in and also to find out if there are any regions that were not viewed at all.

Graph changes. This option calculates a heat map based on the number of changes that have been performed on graph objects, such as modifying the shape or color of a node, adding a new node, or adding edges to a node. A multiplier can be specified for each individual action type to give it more or less weight during the calculation. This gives analysts the possibility to search for renamed and moved nodes only, for instance.

5 System Setup and Architecture

We decided to implement OnGraX as a web-based tool to address our first technical requirement (TR 1). OnGraX' client/server-based architecture enables us to provide an easily accessible tool for graph exploration over the web which allows analysts to simply open a web browser to start a collaborative session. Figure 2 illustrates the basic architecture of our system. On the client side, all graphs are rendered with the help of the client computer's GPU by using WebGL [31], a JavaScript API for rendering 3D graphics natively in modern web browsers. For our special case, this is faster than using SVG-based node-link visualization approaches, such as the d3.js visualization library [32]. To ease the process of low-level OpenGL programming, we utilize the JavaScript library three.js [33]. This approach tackles the second and third technical requirements (TR 2-3) and enables us to achieve a high-performance rendering of node-link diagrams.

The server side of OnGraX is implemented in Java EE and currently runs as a web application on an Apache Tomcat server. Communication between server and clients is done with the relatively new WebSocket protocol [34]. It suffers less from network overhead since it is layered over TCP instead of HTTP which removes the overhead from HTTP header fields and allows for a low

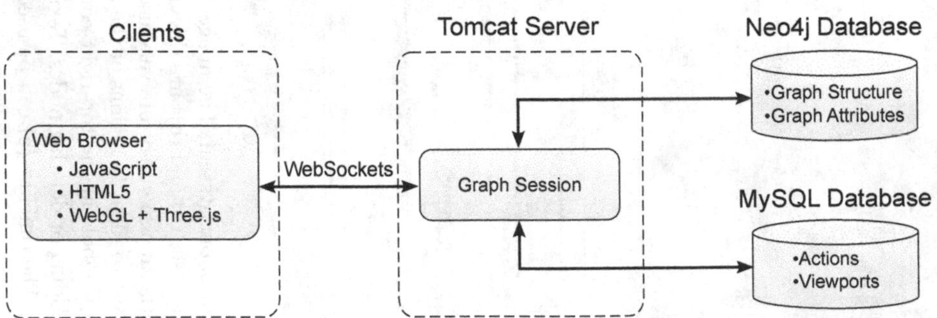

Fig. 2. General architecture of our system. Sessions are initialized on demand whenever a user joins a graph analysis session. The client-server communication is done via WebSockets. Every graph is stored in a separate Neo4j database, whereas all performed actions of a session are logged in a MySQL table.

latency two-way communication. Clients do not have to poll the server in regular intervals anymore to ask for updates. Instead, the server can send a message to all connected clients whenever an update on the client side is required. This allows our system to track the viewports and mouse positions of other users and distribute this information among all clients in real time and addresses our fourth technical requirement (TR 4).

Each graph is stored in a separate Neo4j [35] database. As soon as a user joins a graph session, the respective Neo4j database is initialized as an embedded database service on the server. As a graph-based database, Neo4j offers a convenient way to store our graphs together with all of their node/edge attributes and supports graph-like queries, such as shortest path calculations. It also simplifies other graph-related queries for community detection or applying clustering algorithms. For the remaining data, such as user data and login information, our system uses a MySQL database. Performed actions and all camera positions that are generated by the users while they are exploring a graph are also stored in a MySQL table. This data can be used later to visualize regions of a graph that were modified or viewed by other users. Using Neo4j to efficiently store the graph structure in conjunction with a MySQL database to log all events enables us to tackle our fifth technical requirement (TR 5).

Technical requirement number seven is addressed by using the server side part of our system for complex processes (TR 7). The Tomcat server currently runs on a Dell PowerEdge R720 with two Intel Xeon E5-2650 2.00GHz processors (eight cores each), 128GB RAM, and a Value MLC 3G SSD hard drive. This configuration provides more than enough computing power for our current purpose and future extensions like the calculation of complex graph layouts or running graph analysis algorithms on the server and distributing the results to all clients. Right now, all graphs analyzed with our tool already have precomputed layouts, but computing a layout for other graphs could easily be achieved by using a Java-based graph layout library, such as Jung [36].

5.1 Action and Conflict Handling

Since our system focuses on the collaborative exploration of graphs and not in the collaborative editing of text documents, we do not need sophisticated concurrency control systems which are usually used in such a case (e.g., operational transformation [37]). A pessimistic locking approach is sufficient enough for our scenario, since changes are usually performed directly on one or a couple of single nodes and node attributes. To address our sixth technical requirement (TR 6), we use a simple server-side queue to ensure that all clients visualize the same data structure. Whenever a user performs an action that would change the graph structure or any of the graph object's attribute—such as moving a node, changing the shape of a node, or adding a new edge between two nodes—an action request event is sent to the server. The server uses Neo4j's transaction system to open a new transaction and apply the changes to the stored graph. Only if the transaction is successful, the server reports this back to all connected clients, including the client who initiated the action. Figure 3 illustrates this approach.

All incoming actions are handled in a server-side queue, and an event is only applied if it is not in conflict with a previous event. This could happen if a user deletes a node, while a second user tries to add an edge to this node at exactly the same time. If the server processes the node delete action first, the second user's action will not be performed on the graph structure, and the user will receive a short notification instead, while his/her local graph visualization is updated to reflect the changes that where performed by the first user.

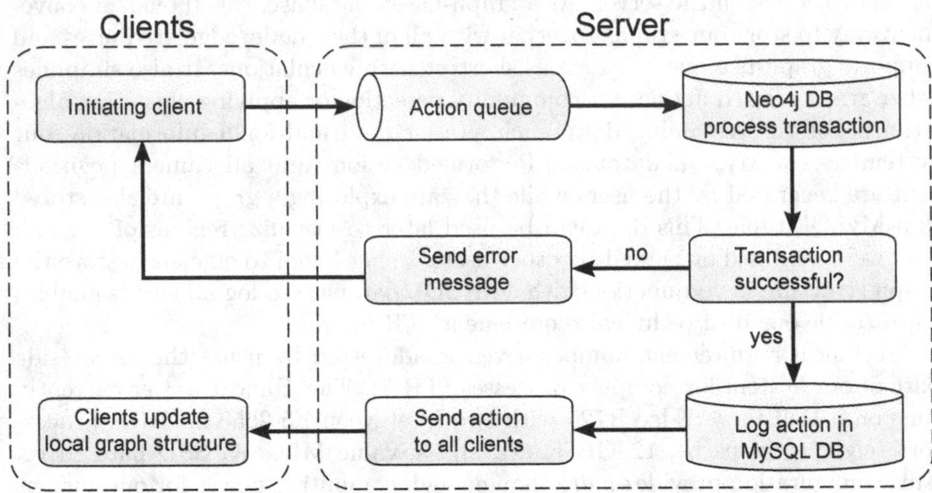

Fig. 3. Action handling between clients during a graph session. To avoid concurrent changes, actions that would affect the graph structure are sent as an action request event to a queue on the server. All clients only update their local graph visualization, if the transaction was applied successfully to the Neo4j database. In case of a conflict the action is not applied, and the initiating client receives an error message.

5.2 Calculation and Visualization of the Heat Map

As discussed in Section 4, we use a heat map-based visualization in the background of the node-link diagram (cf. Figure 1) to either show aggregated values of all logged user views to find regions of interest or applied node changes to get an overview of changes that were performed on a graph. If the heat map configuration is set to show the logged user views, the server calculates the heat map values by aggregating all logged user views with all node positions from all move actions that have been performed previously on the nodes. This process results in a heat map visualization that is robust against layout changes of the graph.

After the values are calculated and sent to the requesting client, they have to be visualized in the web browser without negative performance effects on the interactive graph visualization. To avoid having to render a lot of additional objects, we first draw the heat map values on an off-screen canvas element and create a single OpenGL texture from this canvas afterwards. The canvas represents the heat map values as an alpha map—for every node, a circular gradient is drawn which is based on the size and position of its related node. This creates an image with grayscale values ranging from 0 to 255. To create the actual colors for the heat map, each pixel value is used to lookup the color from a 1×256 pixel-wide color gradient. The gradient colors range from white, over green to red. Based on these color values, an OpenGL texture is created and put on a mesh in the background of the graph visualization. By using an alpha map as basis, we could also draw a heat map based on mouse positions or eye tracking data easily.

Getting the heat map values for all actions that were applied to all nodes of a graph only takes around 4 milliseconds on the server for a typical graph analysis session. Calculating the heat map based on user views and node positions takes considerably more time, because the server has to correlate all stored views with all logged node positions to get the number of seconds every node of the graph was viewed by a user while also considering layout changes. During our test sessions, the server calculated those values in about 60 milliseconds if the complete time frame was selected. The time also depends on the amount of stored user actions and node positions and will of course increase slightly if a graph analysis session is used for a longer time period and more actions are logged. However, since analysts are usually only interested in specific time frames which span over the course of a few days, this is not an important issue. Right now, the bottleneck during the heat map generation lies on the client side. The largest graph that is currently visualized with our system spans an area of 5,800×3,600 pixels. Drawing the alpha map on a canvas with the same size would take approximately 20 seconds, which is not adequate for generating a real-time heat map. Another problem occurs during the creation of the OpenGL texture, as the maximum texture size is limited by the client's graphic card. Current graphic cards support textures with up to 16,384×16,384 pixels, whereas older computers are limited to 2,048×2,048 pixels. We avoid this performance problem on the client side and achieve a real-time rendering for the heat map by drawing a scaled-down version of the alpha map if the graph area exceeds the size of 2,048×2,048 pixels. The resulting texture is then put on a mesh in the background of the visualization and stretched to the appropriate size of the graph.

An alternative and faster approach for generating the heat map would be to create the alpha map and the texture array directly on the server and send the array for the texture to the requesting client(s). But this would drastically increase the amount of traffic between server and clients. Therefore, we decided against this idea and settled for the slightly slower approach of drawing the heat map on the client side.

5.3 Rendering Text with WebGL

Drawing a large number of node labels was another challenge and requirement (TR 8) that we had to solve. The most convenient way—which can also be found in three.js forums—is to draw each node label on an offscreen canvas, render this canvas to an image and use this image as a sprite texture. This works well for a small amount of text strings. But for graphs with more than just a couple of hundred nodes, the JavaScript engine would have to create and render a large amount of textures, which is not fast enough and will eventually crash the JavaScript engine. To solve this, we adapted and modified the JavaScript-based solution from an online article of Heikkinen [38] for bitmap fonts, a common technique used in standard OpenGL rendering. Instead of creating a texture for each label, we just use one texture with all required letters on it. For each letter in a node label, two triangles are drawn and only the part of the texture with the position of the letter is mapped to this geometry. This is an extremely fast solution and the only drawback is, that the fonts do not scale nicely at very high zoom levels.

5.4 Performance

Upon joining a graph session, the complete graph structure is transferred to the client. This approach is fast enough for graphs with up to 6,000 nodes and edges. The download and initialization of all graphical objects on the client takes around three seconds. Unfortunately, this approach does not work for graphs with more than 6,000 nodes as it takes simply too long to transfer the whole data set to the client and generate all graphical objects in one single step. This may eventually lead to an error message in the client's browser stating that JavaScript is not responding anymore. Streaming the graph to the client by only sending an initial part and expanding the information as soon the user zooms out or further explores the graph would be a more convenient step and is planned for a future version of our tool. Picking up the idea of Gretarsson et al. [39], it would also be possible to render parts of the graph on the server and send them as images to the client where they are visualized until the complete data is loaded.

After the initialization phase, our tool renders a zoomed-out overview of our test graphs—which usually contain about 3,000 labeled nodes and edges—with 20 frames per second and 30-40 frames per second in a standard zoomed-in view on an early 2011 MacBook Pro (2,2GHz i7, 8GB memory, Radeon HD 6750M with 1,024MB video memory) with a screen resolution of 1,680×1,050 pixels. We also did a performance test with the same computer on a 4K monitor with a resolution of 3,840×2,160 pixels. Here, the overview is rendered with 10 frames per second and 20-28 frames per second for the zoomed-in view. The biggest graph visualized by with our system by now had 3,700 nodes and 7,500 edges. The initial data transfer while joining the session took about ten seconds. While rendering the complete overview of the graph was only possible with five frames per second, the standard zoom level of our users while working within the graph was rendered at around 10 to 15 frames per second with a 1,680×1,050 resolution. While this is not an optimal frame rate, the visualization still proved to be useable by our test users. Increasing the performance for bigger graphs is one of the next planned steps in our future work as discussed in the following section.

6 Discussion

We made our tool available to various experts in systems biology and bioinformatics at Monash University, Australia, and received mostly positive and also constructive feedback. They liked the idea of working together on their data sets by simply opening the visualization in a browser window. Seeing each others camera position in a synchronous session made it a lot easier for them to discuss and change specific parts of the graph, although one group of experts missed a voice chat directly in the tool. They would have preferred to be able to talk to each other directly without having to fall back to other programs, such as Skype or Google Hangouts. This could be addressed in a future version of our tool with the help of the new WebRTC standard [40] for real-time communications in browsers. Another group of biologists found the heat map visualization of user behavioral data quite useful. They would like to use OnGraX for the education of their students. A use case here would be to give students an already edited graph and ask them to revise the data set further as well as to verify the changes that have already been performed by previous users. Afterwards, the supervisors could review the steps that the students performed and also discuss and reflect the process online together with the students in a collaborative session.

There are still some technical issues that have to be addressed to improve the performance and usability of OnGraX. One task is to utilize Web Workers [41] to speed up the client-side part of the heat map generation. The user interface sometimes becomes unresponsive—depending on the client's hardware—for up to two seconds while the JavaScript engine generates the heat map texture. This caused a small inconvenience among some of our test users. Web Workers could be used to finish this calculation in a thread-like manner in the background of the web application, allowing the web page and user interface to remain responsive all the time.

In general, our tool is able to handle graphs with 10,000 nodes and edges on faster computers as we stated in [4], but some users with slower computers had performance issues during the exploration of graphs with more than 6,000 nodes. Using streaming techniques together with the idea of WiGis [39] to render parts of the graph on the server and only show them as images on the clients would be another possibility to improve the rendering performance and initialization times. Another technique would be to still send the whole data to the clients, but to render specified areas of a graph only once into a texture instead of rendering all graph objects in every frame. Users could then manually select areas to be rendered as a texture and only switch to full rendering on demand. If a subgraph that is rendered as a texture for one user is changed on another client, the changes only have to be rendered once again into the texture on the first user's client to update the information. Adapting this technique would enable us to visualize even bigger graphs with more than 10,000 nodes.

After implementing the aforementioned improvements, the next step will be to conduct a detailed user study to improve the user interface, find missing features and get detailed feedback about the usability of our system.

7 Conclusion

In this paper, we presented a collaborative system for visualizing graphs with several thousands of nodes and edges in a web-based environment. By using WebGL, the system is able to provide an interactive graph visualization with up to 6,000 labeled nodes and edges. With the help of our client/server-based system, analysts do not have to install any additional applications or browser plug-ins anymore. The start of a collaborative analysis session is simply done by opening a URL in a browser window. With this fundamental property of our visualization environment, we address one of the research challenges given in the article of Isenberg et al. [3]. Another challenge named by these authors is the need to develop so-called hybrid collaboration scenarios. Here, we provide users visualization and interaction techniques for analyzing data sets synchronously *and* asynchronously in a distributed environment. With the help of our tool, users can seamlessly drop in and out of ongoing sessions and do not have to wait for other users to start or finish their work. All actions performed during a session as well as the users' camera positions are tracked and can be visualized along with the graph data by using underlying heat map representations. This helps experts to analyze regions of a graph that were of interest or have been edited by former users, i.e., social navigation and guidance is maintained by the aggregated user activity in form of heat maps. Here, we address the "Collaboration & Awareness" challenge in web-based collaborative visualization that was raised by Heer et al. [15]. In the synchronous collaboration case, we provide another contribution (cf. "Pointing & Reference" challenge in [15]) namely that participants of an analysis session can follow the activities of the others (shared viewing areas) and point to specific nodes or edges by using brushing (shared node markers and mouse cursors). The use of WebSockets enables us to distribute this user data in real time among all connected clients.

Acknowledgments. The authors would like to thank Falk Schreiber and his colleagues at Monash University in Australia for constructive discussions and valuable feedback, as well as all students at Linnaeus University in Sweden who participated in our initial user studies.

References

1. Chuah, M., Roth, S.: Visualizing common ground. In: Proceedings of the International Conference on Information Visualization (IV 2003), pp. 365–372. IEEE (2003)
2. Heer, J., Agrawala, M.: Design Considerations for Collaborative Visual Analytics. Information Visualization **7**(1), 49–62 (2008)

3. Isenberg, P., Elmqvist, N., Cernea, D., Scholtz, J., Ma, K.-L., Hagen, H.: Collaborative Visualization: Definition, Challenges, and Research Agenda. Information Visualization **10**(4), 310–326 (2011)
4. Zimmer, B., Kerren, A.: Applying heat maps in a web-based collaborative graph visualization. In: Poster Abstracts, IEEE Information Visualization (InfoVis 2014), France, Paris (2014)
5. Zimmer, B., Kerren, A.: Sensemaking and provenance in distributed collaborative node-link visualizations. In: Abstract Papers, IEEE VIS 2014 Workshop: Provenance for Sensemaking, France, Paris (2014)
6. Kandel, S., Heer, J., Plaisant, C., Kennedy, J., van Ham, F., Riche, N.H., Weaver, C., Lee, B., Brodbeck, D., Buono, P.: Research directions in data wrangling: Visualizations and transformations for usable and credible data. Information Visualization **10**(4), 271–288 (2011)
7. KEGG: Kyoto Encyclopedia of Genes and Genomes. http://www.genome.jp/kegg/ (accessed July 10, 2014)
8. Shannon, P., Markiel, A., Ozier, O., Baliga, N.S., Wang, J.T., Ramage, D., Amin, N., Schwikowski, B., Ideker, T.: Cytoscape: a software environment for integrated models of biomolecular interaction networks. Genome Research **13**(11), 2498–2504 (2003)
9. Bastian, M., Heymann, S., Jacomy, M.: Gephi: an open source software for exploring and manipulating networks. In: International AAAI Conference on Weblogs and Social Media (2009)
10. Batagelj, V., Mrvar, A.: Pajek - analysis and visualization of large networks. In: Mutzel, P., Jünger, M., Leipert, S. (eds.) GD 2001. LNCS, vol. 2265, pp. 477–478. Springer, Heidelberg (2002). http://dx.doi.org/10.1007/3-540-45848-4_54
11. Auber, D.: Tulip: data visualization software. In: Graph Drawing, pp. 435–437 (2001)
12. von Landesberger, T., Kuijper, A., Schreck, T., Kohlhammer, J., van Wijk, J., Fekete, J.-D., Fellner, D.: Visual analysis of large graphs: State-of-the-art and future research challenges. Computer Graphics Forum **30**(6), 1719–1749 (2011). http://dx.doi.org/10.1111/j.1467-8659.2011.01898.x
13. Kerren, A., Purchase, H.C., Ward, M.O.: Multivariate Network Visualization, ser. Lecture Notes in Computer Science, vol. 8380. Springer (2014)
14. Kerren, A., Schreiber, F.: Network visualization for integrative bioinformatics. In: Chen, M., Hofestädt, R. (eds.) Approaches in Integrative Bioinformatics - Towards the Virtual Cell, pp. 173–202. Springer, Heidelberg (2014)
15. Heer, J., van Ham, F., Carpendale, S., Weaver, C., Isenberg, P.: Creation and collaboration: engaging new audiences for information visualization. In: Kerren, A., Stasko, J.T., Fekete, J.-D., North, C. (eds.) Information Visualization. LNCS, vol. 4950, pp. 92–133. Springer, Heidelberg (2008)
16. Viégas, A.B., Wattenberg, M., Ham, F.V., Kriss, J., Mckeon, M.: Many eyes: A site for visualization at internet scale. IEEE Transactions on Visualization and Computer Graphics **13**(6), 1121–1128 (2007)
17. Heer, J., Viégas, F., Wattenberg, M.: Voyagers and voyeurs: supporting asynchronous collaborative information visualization. In: ACM Human Factors in Computing Systems (CHI), pp. 1029–1038 (2007)
18. McKeon, M.: Harnessing the Information Ecosystem with Wiki-based Visualization Dashboards. IEEE Transactions on Visualization and Computer Graphics **15**(6), 1081–1088 (2009)
19. Samizdat Drafting Co. Arbor.js. http://arborjs.org (accessed January 2015)

20. Jacomy, A.: sigma.js. http://sigmajs.org (accessed January 2015)
21. Kashcha, A.: Vivagraphjs. https://github.com/anvaka/VivaGraphJS (accessed January 2015)
22. Kerren, A., Ebert, A., Meyer, J. (eds.): Human-Centered Visualization Environments, ser. LNCS Tutorial, vol. 4417. Springer, Heidelberg (2007)
23. Dix, A., Finlay, J.E., Abowd, G.D., Beale, R.: Human-Computer Interaction, 3rd edn. Prentice Hall, London (2003)
24. Baecker, R.M.: Readings in GroupWare and Computer-Supported Cooperative Work: Assisting Human-Human Collaboration, 1st edn. Morgan Kaufmann Publishers Inc., San Francisco (1994)
25. Kerren, A., Stasko, J.T., Fekete, J.-D., North, C. (eds.): Information Visualization, Human-Centered Issues and Perspectives, ser. Lecture Notes in Computer Science, vol. 4950. Springer (2008)
26. Dieberger, A., Dourish, P., Höök, K.: Social Navigation: Techniques for Building more Usable Systems. Interactions **7**(6), November 2000
27. Gutwin, C., Greenberg, S.: Design for individuals, design for groups: tradeoffs between power and workspace awareness. In: Proceedings of the 1998 ACM Conference on Computer Supported Cooperative Work, ser. CSCW 1998, pp. 207–216. ACM, New York (1998)
28. Gentle, J.: ShareJS - Live concurrent editing in your app. http://sharejs.org (accessed January 2014)
29. The Apache Software Foundation. Apache Wave. http://sharejs.org (accessed January 2014)
30. TweenJS. http://www.createjs.com/TweenJS (accessed January 2015)
31. Khronos Group. WebGL Specification. Editor's Draft 1, July 2014. http://www.khronos.org/registry/webgl/specs/latest (accessed January 2015)
32. Bostock, M.: D3 - data-driven documents. http://threejs.org (accessed January 2015)
33. Cabello, R.: Three.js. http://threejs.org (accessed January 2015)
34. World Wide Web Consortium. The WebSocket API. http://dev.w3.org/html5/websockets/ (accessed January 2015)
35. Neo Technology, Inc., Neo4j. http://neo4j.com (accessed January 2015)
36. O'Madadhain, J., Fisher, D., Nelson, T.: JUNG - Java Universal Network/Graph Framework. http://jung.sourceforge.net/ (accessed January 2015)
37. Ellis, C.A., Gibbs, S.J.: Concurrency control in groupware systems. SIGMOD Rec. **18**(2), 399–407 (1989)
38. Animating a Million Letters Using Three.js. http://www.html5rocks.com/en/tutorials/webgl/million_letters/ (accessed January 2015)
39. Gretarsson, B., Bostandjiev, S., O'Donovan, J., Höllerer, T.: WiGis: a framework for scalable web-based interactive graph visualizations. In: Eppstein, D., Gansner, E.R. (eds.) GD 2009. LNCS, vol. 5849, pp. 119–134. Springer, Heidelberg (2010)
40. World Wide Web Consortium. WebRTC. http://www.w3.org/TR/2015/WD-webrtc-20150210/ (accessed January 2015)
41. Web Workers. http://www.w3.org/TR/workers/ (accessed January 2015)

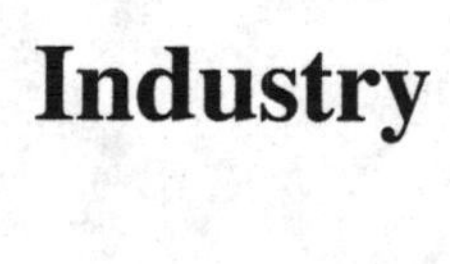
Industry

Challenges in Android Wear Application Development

Jukka Ahola(✉)

VTT Technical Research Centre of Finland LTD, Oulu, Finland
jukka.ahola@vtt.fi

Abstract. The research focus of this paper was to highlight current issues in wearable application development in Android Wear platform. The findings of the experimental research were discovered during the software development of a smart watch application, where the requirements and design were limited with the documented best practices. The results identify three issues, which should be addressed in the Android Wear platform roadmap, to better address the wearable application needs. The issues discussed are better wearable internet connectivity, virtual button support for watch faces, and software configurable language support for voice input. We propose those features to be added to the wearable platform roadmap to better support the global wearable business application ecosystems.

Keywords: Android · Google · Smart watch · Voice input · Wearable

1 Introduction

Recently, there has been wide interest in wearable technologies, where the leading global hardware manufacturers have announced their smart watch products in major technology events and conferences. The smart watch platforms are currently evolving in order to meet the usability and aesthetics expectations. [1,2].

However, recent experiments in our application development suggest that the Android Wear software platform [3] does not adequately address some of the usability features needed for smart wearable applications. Android Wear software platform and ecosystem is evolving and is backed by strong industrial partner support, but in its current form it is limiting the user scenarios the application developers are able to pursue.

The purpose of this paper is to highlight selected features needing improvement in the current Android Wear software platform. In this paper, we present three main issues in the wearable development experienced in our work and suggest solutions to overcome them. The rest of the paper is structured as follows: First, we describe what methods were used to identify the usability issues. Then we describe the findings and workarounds to the issues. We discuss the implications of the findings and propose a better way to handle the issues. Then we discuss the related work addressing similar topics and issues. Lastly we draw the conclusions and vision future work to this topic. The experimental results show that the current workarounds to the Android Wear platform address the issues, but require training and instructions for the designed user scenarios. The Android developer issues are discussed in specific developer forums [4,5].

P. Cimiano et al. (Eds.): ICWE 2015, LNCS 9114, pp. 601–604, 2015.
DOI: 10.1007/978-3-319-19890-3_38

2 Methods

The work was performed in 2014 in Finland. An Android watch face application was developed for the LG G Watch R smart watch paired with a Nexus 5 mobile. The development environment was Android Studio version 1.0 with Android SDK API version 24. LG G Watch R has a round display, which requires special attention when designing the graphical layouts.

3 Results

The Android Wear software platform does not support direct internet access from the watch [3]. The watch is connected to a smart phone through Bluetooth. The companion mobile application or service has to function as a proxy between the wearable application and the internet services. If the paired mobile application is not available for some reason, the user may not be aware of it and the wearable application is not getting the data from the web service. Wearable applications also rely on many services provided by the GoogleApiClient [3].

Android Wear compatible watches only have one physical button, and it is used to turn off the display or to return to the default watch face mode. Wear application can have buttons and other user interaction components in the application interface. However, the Android Wear application deactivates to the default power save mode after a short idle time. Watch face application is a long running application by default and is designed to display the time as shown in Figure 1. Android Wear takes over the touch events for watch face applications, preventing any action buttons to be triggered from the touch screen.

Android Wear supports receiving voice input from notifications. This requires the user to swipe the proper notification that triggers a separate activity to handle the voice input functionality. The speech recognition utilizes the the microphone on the wearable device, and translates it to text by using the Google cloud services. The voice input uses the language options configured and supported by the mobile phone. For instance, if the mobile phone default primary language is set to Italian, the wearable will attempt to recognize the speech in Italian. However, if you intend to override the language option programmatically from the Android Wear-application, the mobile phone will ignore it and use the default language options instead.

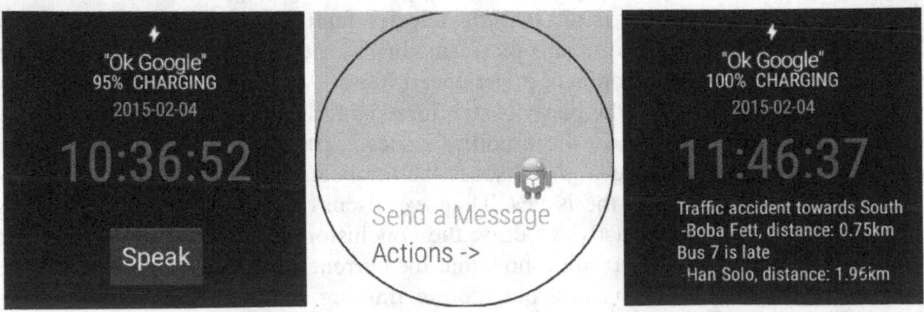

Fig. 1. Watch face application with a button and a voice input notification functionality

4 Discussion

The goal was to implement a wearable application, which is easily and quickly available, and able to send short spoken messages as text to the server. The application must be available with one touch. Watch face application was selected, because it activates itself with the push of a button and stays on until the user selects a different watch face application. Standard Android Wear applications can be configured to be long running applications by utilizing the wake lock feature. However, the application requires multiple swiping motions with accuracy to be activated, which can be troublesome in situations requiring attention elsewhere. The spoken language could not be changed in the watch face application due to the limitations in touch events and software configured language settings. The wearable application relies on the languages options configured on the mobile device. Currently the latest Android speech recognition supports two language options at the same time, where one language is selected as the primary language. This is a useful feature for localization, but cannot combine the two languages simultaneously, when you need to spell foreign street addresses in your speech. The wearable application currently has no understanding of the internet. It relies on the Bluetooth connection with the paired mobile companion application to delegate any web service requests and responses through mobile internet connectivity. The mobile application receives URL-addresses from the wearable application, and creates web requests with asynchronous responses back to the wearable application.

The following features would greatly benefit the future Android Wear platform:

- Wearable API that allows URL connections either directly or transparently through the connected mobile phone.
- Ability implement virtual software buttons to watch face applications for user interaction.
- Ability to programmatically control the language preference for voice input from the watch.

With the above features, the applications could be easily accessible in situations where the information needs to be accessed with limited eye-contact and touch interaction. The wearable application dependency from the companion mobile application would decrease with the support of internet networking library, making the development more straight forward and easier to maintain. Internationalization and localization would also be better supported, when the control is given to the wearable device on the wrist instead of the mobile device in the pocket. Watch Face applications for Android Wear could be more interactive with the support of virtual buttons, allowing users to trigger functionality directly from the watch face screen.

5 Conclusion and Future Work

Android Wear is a fascinating software platform capable of exchanging information in new ways. This paper identifies and discusses three important features currently missing in Android Wear platform that would greatly benefit wearable software developers. Direct internet connectivity, virtual button support for watch faces, and voice input localization should be considered to be included into the Android Wear platform to make meaningful wearable business applications. We will investigate alternative solutions and best practices to overcome the current limitations on the platform.

Acknowledgements. The described work discussed in this paper, is part of the Connecting Digital Cities activity of 2014, funded by EIT ICT Labs Knowledge and Innovation Community. The author wants to thank the colleagues participating the design and implementation of the system presented in this paper.

References

1. Morris, I.: Forbes (2014). http://www.forbes.com/sites/ianmorris/2014/12/30/google-needs-to-fix-android-wear-in-2015-to-fend-off-the-apple-watch/ (accessed February 4, 2015)
2. Fedewa, J.: Phandroid (2014). http://phandroid.com/2014/11/06/7-things-i-hate-about-android-wear/ (accessed February 4, 2015)
3. Android.com. https://developer.android.com/training/building-wearables.html (accessed February 4, 2015)
4. Stack Overflow. http://stackoverflow.com/questions/tagged/android-wear (accessed February 4, 2015)
5. Android Wear Developers. https://plus.google.com/communities/113381227473021565406 (accessed February 4, 2015)

Model-Driven Development Based on OMG's IFML with WebRatio Web and Mobile Platform

Roberto Acerbis[1], Aldo Bongio[1], Marco Brambilla[1,2(✉)], and Stefano Butti[1]

[1] WebRatio Srl., Como, Italy
{roberto.acerbis,aldo.bongio,stefano.butti}@webratio.com, marco.brambilla@polimi.it
[2] Politecnico di Milano. Dip. di Elettronica, Informazione e Bioingegneria, Milan, Italy

Abstract. The need for quick development of mobile applications, combined with the chronic shortage of IT personnel with skills in Web and mobile app development advocate for new approaches and tools. In this context, we propose a comprehensive tool suite called WebRatio Platform for model-driven development of web and mobile applications. The tool supports developers in the specification of the domain model and of the user interaction model for applications according to two extended versions of the OMG standard language called IFML (Interaction Flow Modeling Language). The extensions feature primitives tailored to web application development and to mobile systems. The tool features model-checking and full code generation that produces ready-to-publish Web and cross-platform mobile applications.

1 Introduction

Several researches have applied software engineering and Web engineering techniques to the specification of Web and multi-platform application interfaces and user interaction in broad sense. Among them, we can cite OO-HDM [8], WAE [2], WebDSL [4], OOH-Method [3], WebML [1], RUX-Model [6], HERA [9], and rapid UI development [7] and modeling languages like USIXML [5]. Commercial vendors are nowadays proposing tools for Web development, like Mendix (http://www.mendix.com) and Outsystems (http://www.outsystems.com) However, none of them has managed to become widely adopted in the software industry yet. For this reason, front-end development continues to be a costly and inefficient process, where manual coding is the predominant development approach, reuse is low, and cross-platform portability remains difficult.

In 2014, the Object Management Group has adopted a new standard called Interaction Flow Modeling Language (IFML), which supports the platform independent description of graphical user interfaces for applications accessed or deployed on such systems as desktop computers, laptop computers, PDAs, mobile phones, and tablets. IFML is inspired by WebML but adds several innovations: it increases separation of concerns, completely forbidding the integration of business logic into the user interaction specification; it defines a set of very generic concepts (the core of the language) which can be applied to any kind of

P. Cimiano et al. (Eds.): ICWE 2015, LNCS 9114, pp. 605–608, 2015.
DOI: 10.1007/978-3-319-19890-3_39

Table 1. Basic Core IFML concepts: description, notation, and platform-specific cases

Concept	Meaning	IFML Notation	PSM Example
View Container	An element of the interface that comprises elements displaying content and supporting interaction and/or other ViewContainers.	MailBox	Web page Window Pane.
View Component	An element of the interface that displays content or accepts input	Message List	An HTML list. A JavaScript image gallery. An input form.
Event	An occurrence that affects the state of the application	Name	
Action	A piece of business logic triggered by an event	Send	A database update. The sending of an email.
Navigation Flow	An input-output dependency. The source of the link has some output that is associated with the input of the target of the link		Sending and receiving of parameters in the HTTP request
Data Flow	Data passing between ViewComponents or Action as consequence of a previous user interaction.		
Parameter Binding Group	Set of ParameterBindings associated to an InteractionFlow (being it navigation or data flow)	<<ParamBindingGroup>> Title → AlbumTitle Year → AlbumYear	

user interface; it brings in the concept of event and asynchronous interactions; and it integrates seamlessly with UML and BPMN notations.

In this paper we describe our experience in implementing IFML for the Web and mobile domains [4] within the tool called WebRatio Platform, a model-driven, low-code development platform based on Eclipse that generates fully-functional Web applications and cross-platform mobile applications based on the Apache Cordova / PhoneGap framework.

2 The Interaction Flow Modeling Language (IFML)

The Interaction Flow Modeling Language (IFML) supports the platform independent description of graphical user interfaces for applications accessed or deployed on any systems and technological platform. The focus of the description is on the structure and behavior of the application front-end as perceived by the end user. With respect to the popular Model-View-Controller (MVC) model of an interactive application, the focus of IFML is mainly on the view part. IFML models support the following design perspectives (whose notation is summarized in Table 1): (1) The *view structure specification*, which consists of the definition of view containers; (2) The *view content specification*, which consists of the definition of view components, i.e., content publishing and data

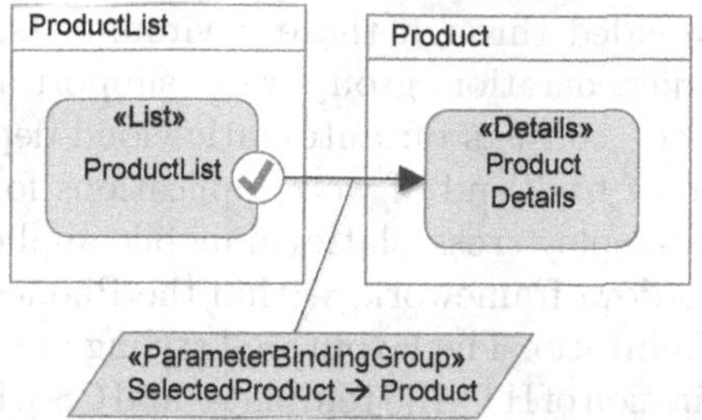

Fig. 1. Example of IFML model showing a list of products and the details view

entry elements contained within view containers; (3) The *events specification*, which consists of the definition of events (coming from users interaction, application logic, or external agents) that may affect the state of the UI; (4) The *event transition specification*, which consists of the definition of the effect of an event on the user interface; and (5) The *parameter binding specification*, which consists of the definition of the input-output dependencies between model elements. Furthermore, IFML can be complemented with external models for connecting to any kind of content model (representing databases, ontologies, file systems or other resources) and any kind of dynamic model (describing the business logic behind the application front end).

Figure 1 shows a simple example of IFML diagram, where a starting page displays a list of products and, upon selection by the user, a target page shows the details of the selected product.

3 WebRatio Platform

WebRatio Platform (www.webratio.com) is a model-driven low-code development tool based on IFML, which features two editions, respectively focusing on the design and development of Web and mobile applications. WebRatio Platform is implementing the Web-extended version of IFML and focusing specifically on Web applications. WebRatio Mobile Platform is implementing the mobile-extended version of IFML and focusing specifically on mobile applications. WebRatio provides three integrated environments:

- The modeling environment supporting the specification of IFML diagrams for the view description, UML class diagrams (or ER diagrams) for the information design, and optionally the integration with BPMN diagrams for the specification of business process aspects.
- The development environment for supporting the implementation of custom components, at the purpose of allowing personalized extensions of the modeling language based on vertical needs or native functionalities, as well as custom data and system integration requirements
- The layout template and style design environment, which allows the highest possible level of UI sophistication, thanks to full support of HTML 5, CSS and JavaScript based styling.

Based on the input provided through these environments, WebRatio provides model checking, full code generation, group–work support and lifecycle management. The generated code consists of: automatic cloud-deployed Java EE code covering both front-end of back-end of web applications for the Web version of WebRatio; and ready-to-deploy cross-platform mobile applications, based on the open-source Apache Cordova framework, within the PhoneGap distribution, for the Mobile version of WebRatio. The layout and styling of the target apps can be defined through the definition of HTML5 templates and CSS. By default, WebRatio Mobile builds apps that are fully functional even when not connected to the Internet (offline mode). It also provides a built-in solution for read/write data synchronization between the mobile device and the back end. The mobile app architecture is based on open and de facto standard libraries, such as Angular.js, JData, and Ionic.

In the deploy, integration and coherency between mobile and web application is granted by a common modeling approach. Web and mobile applications can be integrated with any existing back-end system with RESTful APIs; alternatively, one can build his own back-end using WebRatio Platform and a time-based cloud plans. The generated code base is human readable and maintainable, even outside WebRatio Platform. There are no proprietary or closed components in the generated code.

References

1. Ceri, S., Brambilla, M., Fraternali, P.: The history of WebML lessons learned from 10 years of model-driven development of web applications. In: Borgida, A.T., Chaudhri, V.K., Giorgini, P., Yu, E.S. (eds.) Conceptual Modeling: Foundations and Applications. LNCS, vol. 5600, pp. 273–292. Springer, Heidelberg (2009)
2. Conallen, J.: Building Web applications with UML. Addison Wesley (2002)
3. Gómez, J., Cachero, C., Pastor, O.: Conceptual modeling of device-independent web applications, pp. 26–39 (2001)
4. Groenewegen, D.M., Hemel, Z., Kats, L.C.L., Visser, E.: WebDSL: a domain-specific language for dynamic web applications. In: Harris, G.E. (ed.) OOPSLA Companion, pp. 779–780. ACM (2008)
5. Limbourg, Q., Vanderdonckt, J., Michotte, B., Bouillon, L., López-Jaquero, V.: USIXML: a language supporting multi-path development of user interfaces. In: Feige, U., Roth, J. (eds.) DSV-IS 2004 and EHCI 2004. LNCS, vol. 3425, pp. 200–220. Springer, Heidelberg (2005)
6. Linaje, M., Preciado, J.C., Sánchez-Figueroa, F.: A method for model based design of rich internet application interactive user interfaces. In: Baresi, L., Fraternali, P., Houben, G.-J. (eds.) ICWE 2007. LNCS, vol. 4607, pp. 226–241. Springer, Heidelberg (2007)
7. Schramm, A., Preußner, A., Heinrich, M., Vogel, L.: Rapid UI development for enterprise applications: combining manual and model-driven techniques. In: Petriu, D.C., Rouquette, N., Haugen, Ø. (eds.) MODELS 2010, Part I. LNCS, vol. 6394, pp. 271–285. Springer, Heidelberg (2010)
8. Schwabe, D., Rossi, G., Barbosa, S.D.J.: Systematic hypermedia application design with OOHDM. In: Proc. Hypertext 1996, pp. 116–128 (1996)
9. Vdovják, R., Frăsincar, F., Houben, G.-J., Barna, P.: Engineering Semantic Web Information Systems in Hera. Journal of Web Engineering **1**(1–2), 3–26 (2003)

Personal, Social and Event Organization Through Web and Mobile Apps: The Fluxedo Case

Max Bancora[1], Marco Brambilla[1,2(✉)], Davide Ripamonti[1], and Andrea Vaccarella[1]

[1] Fluxedo s.r.l., Como, Italy
{max.bancora,davide.ripamonti,andrea.vaccarella}@fluxedo.com
[2] Politecnico di Milano, Dip. Elettronica Informazione e Bioingegneria, Milano, Italy
marco.brambilla@polimi.it

Abstract. This paper presents Fluxedo, a platform that combines social network data, web interfaces, a mobile app, and information from events and venues, for allowing people to design their experience, plan their activities and engage with friends or colleagues in common tasks. The application is built through a set of Web engineering practices that include: model driven development, REST service design and invocation, interaction with public Web APIs (e.g., of social networks) and business process management (BPM).

1 Introduction

The main uses of web and mobile in the consumer market include social networking, content sharing and personal productivity. Some of these aspects sometimes converge, like in the case of social networking and personal productivity (including todo list and planning), which merge into socialization of task management, currently supported by a plethora of online services directed to the final user. However, all these tools share a common weakness: they don't provide any way for structuring the interactions, dependencies or constraints between tasks.

In this paper we discuss how the combination of model-driven development [3], social networking and business process management (BPM) can be fruitfully applied to personal and social task management in a consumer scenario. Our aim is to devise user-friendly mobile applications that hide the complexity of modeling behind extremely simple interfaces and interaction paradigms. The main challenge addressed is related to finding the appropriate level of complexity to be exposed to the user, because the expressive power should be complete enough for describing basic processes but also simple enough to let people understand, accept and use them in their everyday life, combined with social networking and content sharing capability.

We show the results of our studies at work in a commercial mobile application called Fluxedo (www.fluxedo.com). Fluxedo is a web and mobile app that allows users to create lists of items (i.e. activities), and assign those to other users via social networking means. Fluxedo can be seen as a to-do list app that integrates traditional features with new ones: users within a group of tasks (flow) receive notifications and can interact with the flow explicating whether they have already completed the task or not, as well as adding new tasks in the flow and change the tasks order.

P. Cimiano et al. (Eds.): ICWE 2015, LNCS 9114, pp. 609–612, 2015.
DOI: 10.1007/978-3-319-19890-3_40

2 Personal Organization on the Go

We identify the needs of users that want to combine personal organization, group and social activity planning, event participation and content sharing, under the name of *Personal Process Management (PPM)* [4, 5]. PPM focuses on:

- *Definition of the acceptable complexity of personal plans.*
- Definition of *social interactions, social sharing and gamification* aspects (i.e., the possibility of increasing engagement of users through mechanisms that are typical of games, such as points, badges and so on).
- Definition of monitoring and analytics dashboards for event organizers that want to have a bird's eye view on behavior of participants.

In their personal life organization, users have rather simple needs and usually aim at describing basic collaborative activities performed together with their acquaintances. In a field study performed with real perspective users, people declared the following requirements for this kind of applications:

- Easily specify task assignment to friends.
- Describe simple sequential constraints between tasks or the possibility of performing all actions altogether.
- Avoid dealing with complex decision points, involving definition of conditional expressions, complex event management, or process structures.
- Avoid graphical modeling of processes.
- Freely chat with other members and to exchange information and content.

Based on this, we studied a few variants of PPM and we tested them with end users [1]. The resulting execution model covers an extremely reduced expressive power with respect to classical BPM approaches, namely: atomic tasks, sequential task dependency, and task assignment to concrete actors (and not to roles), possibility of chatting and exchanging content freely with the group, and of attaching information to tasks (e.g., maps, photos, or documents). Therefore, the reuse of process models (in the sense of having several executions of them) is possible but not really frequent. One can instead think about neutral blueprints of processes to be instantiated several times (e.g., the specification of a typical "party planning" scenario). From the socialization perspective, the user needs are quite basic: they need the possibility of inviting users from social networks or mailing lists, they want them to see their tasks appear in the todo list in the right moment, and they want to award them somehow for the work done, e.g., through gamification mechanism. Notice that no graphical modeling notation, decision points, cycles, parallel executions, events or any other complex element is exposed to users.

3 Personal Organization on the Go

We implemented our findings by designing a mobile application with a model-driven approach based on the OMG's IFML standard [3]. Similarly, we designed the Web viewpoint of the application. Figure 1 shows some fragments of the model.

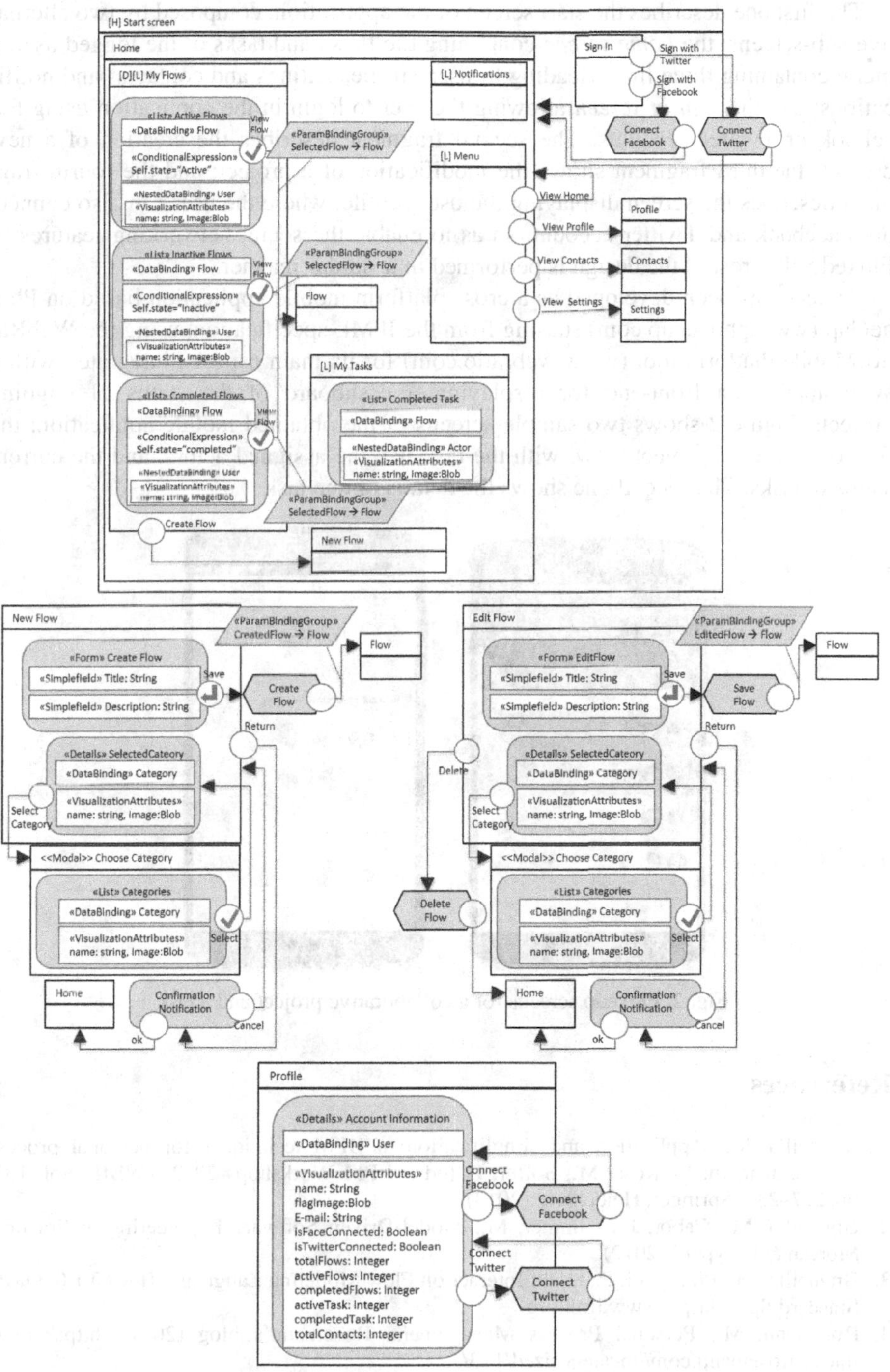

Fig. 1. IFML Model of the system (mobile ViewPoint)

The first one describes the start screen of the application, composed by two alternative sub-screens: the *home screen* containing the flows and tasks of the logged user, a menu containing three links (leading to user profile, settings and contacts) and notifications; and the *sign in screen* allowing the user to login in the application using Facebook or Twitter accounts. The second fragment describes the creation of a new project; the third fragment shows the modification of a project; and the fourth fragment describes the screen displaying the user profile, where the user can also connect his Facebook and Twitter account, so as to enable the social networking features of Fluxedo. The rest of the design is performed in a similar manner.

Fluxedo has been developed as a cross-platform mobile application based on PhoneGap (www.phonegap.com) starting from the IFML specification, using the WebRatio Mobile Platform tool (www.webratio.com) for its main aspects, integrated with a Web application front-end for displaying a dashboard of the status of ongoing projects. Figure 2 shows two sample screens of the obtained mobile application: the first one shows a project view, with the task list, the assigned actors, and the current status of tasks. The second one shows the details of one task.

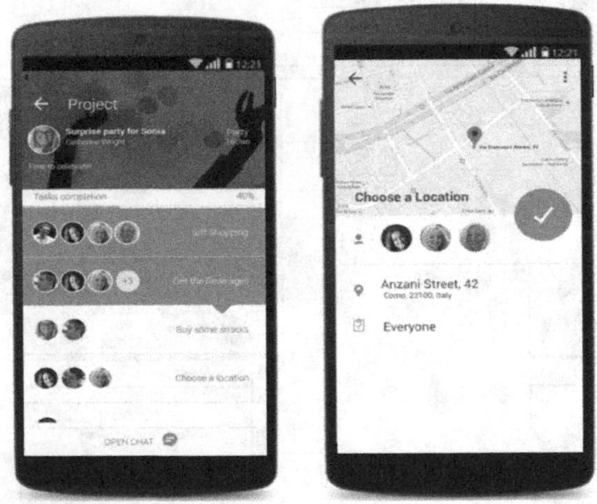

Fig. 2. Fluxedo screens for a collaborative project and a task

References

1. Brambilla, M.: Application and simplification of BPM techniques for personal process management. In: La Rosa, M., Soffer, P. (eds.) BPM Workshops 2012. LNBIP, vol. 132, pp. 227–233. Springer, Heidelberg (2013)
2. Brambilla, M., Cabot, J., Wimmer, M.: Model-Driven Software Engineering in Practice. Morgan & Claypool (2012)
3. Brambilla, M., Fraternali, P., et al.: Interaction Flow Modeling Language (IFML) 1.0. OMG Standard Spec. http://www.ifml.org
4. Rosemann, M.: Personal Process Management. Rosemann's blog (2011). http://www.michaelrosemann.com/uncategorized/113/
5. Weber, I., Paik, H.-Y., Benatallah, B., Vorwerk, C., Zheng, L., Kim, S.: Personal Process Management: Design and Execution for End-Users. UNSW-CSE-TR-1018, UNSW (2010)

Interactive Networks for Digital Cultural Heritage Collections - Scoping the Future of HistoGraph

Marten Düring[1], Lars Wieneke[1], and Vincenzo Croce[2(✉)]

[1] CVCE, Sanem, Luxembourg
{marten.duering,lars.wieneke}@cvce.eu
[2] Engineering Ingegneria Informatica spa, Rome, Italy
vincenzo.croce@eng.it

Abstract. Network visualizations are powerful albeit suggestive means to represent and explore complex relations between entities (people, places...) and have become increasingly popular in the humanities. In this article we briefly introduce the functionality of histoGraph, a technical demonstrator for the network-based analysis of photographs, survey current applications of network visualizations in the cultural heritage domain, and outline histoGraph's future development as an open source tool for the visualization of cultural heritage data.

1 Introduction

In the humanities the concept of truth is a fuzzy and relies on a more or less stable foundation of what is true. Network visualization are powerful albeit suggestive means to represent and explore complex relations between entities (people, words, places...) with great potential for the humanities and the cultural heritage sector. In this article we introduce the functionality of histoGraph, a demonstrator which exploits the surplus value of human touch for the identification of identities in historical image collections through a hybrid crowd-sourcing approach.

We distinguish two perspectives on network visualizations in the (Digital) Humanities: visualizations can be used to illustrate specific insights based on existing knowledge or to explore data and to discover something that is not yet known. Within this larger concept of visual analytics we also identify two perspectives: one that stipulates the idea of a holistic or "bigger" picture, so that we can gain insight by combining different information into one image (seeing the forest for the trees) and one that focuses on identifying the peculiar in a massive amount of information.

We propose to build a bridge between the two: an analytical tool to identify peculiarities and on the other hand an authoring tool for visual storytelling. This would offer us an interesting cross-connection with the idea of enhanced publication as it is understood by the Driver project [1]. Usually scientific publications contain read-only material that users can see but not act upon. What if we have a diagram that users can click on to manipulate the underlying dataset? histoGraph could offer a visualisation with an explanation but also let users select and then modify the analytical tool, to draw their own conclusions, to agree with the author or to challenge his findings.

P. Cimiano et al. (Eds.): ICWE 2015, LNCS 9114, pp. 613–616, 2015.
DOI: 10.1007/978-3-319-19890-3_41

2 The Tool in Digital Humanities

histoGraph was developed by the FP7-funded project CUbRIK [2] which focused on advanced multimedia search technologies. The current version creates a social network of people who appear in photos related to the history of European integration and automatically enriches the network with relevant sources based on keyword queries in full text. A demo is available online [3]. To create the network, faces in the historical photos need to be identified, a very challenging task for machines. Humans and machines therefore share this work and the input from one improves the performance of the other.

histoGraph introduces an effective interface to access collections of historical sources and to discover links among and entities within them. The integration of human expertise and machine computation opens up new possibilities to create a new type of applications. So far however, this potential remains largely untapped because of the significant requirements for such projects: The implementation and integration of advanced algorithms, for example for the identification of faces, requires specialized know-how and users from the humanities are challenged with defining unprecedented tasks for methods which haven't even emerged yet. histoGraph combines new approaches to engage the public to commit to humanities research, to facilitate exchange between users and to help us reach our audiences.

CUbRIK integrated research in computer science, the design of human-computation tasks, data visualization, social engineering and the humanities. Multimedia search is still a challenge and the CUbRIK project approached it from many different angles: Human-Machine-Interaction, face identification in photos and videos, copyright issues, gamification, content exploration and user communication. Alongside an app for exploring and searching fashion, histoGraph is one of two demos which implement the different modules developed by CUbRIK.

histoGraph is based on a collection of more than 3000 images which represent the main events and actors in the history of European integration hosted by the CVCE. To prepare the photos for the network, we use an image indexation pipeline which detects the location of individual faces in the photographs. A crowd of "click-workers" with no specific training double-checks whether the algorithms detected faces correctly or whether it missed some. In the next step, an automatic face recognition process is triggered that associates each of the now verified faces with a list of ten possible identities. This list of candidates is then disseminated for example through Twitter to a crowd of experts who vote for and comment on their preferred identity. The image metadata, for example the names of persons, the time or the place where an image was taken as well as contextual information about associated historical events can be reviewed by expert users and delegated to a crowd of specialists on the history of European Integration for review.

Based on the co-occurrence of persons in images, a social network is calculated which links individual persons with each other (**Fig. 1.** Screenshot of histoGraph's network visualization tool.). Connections gain in strength the more often persons appear together in an image. Users can interact with histoGraph in different ways, e.g. a click on a node leads to an ego-network of the selected person and a click on an edge displays documents, which mention both actors (**Fig. 2**). This feature is powerful since it guides users back to the primary sources on which a tie is based on and thereby makes it easier to understand what a tie and a node represent. Many of the documents stored in our collection come with a date of creation. This allows us to filter the network so it only displays connections of documents created within certain time spans.

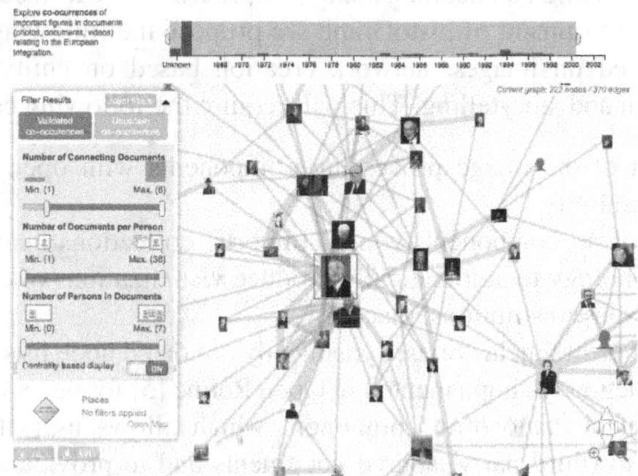

Fig. 1. Screenshot of histoGraph's network visualization tool

Fig. 2. Screenshot of histoGraph's tie contextualization

As introduced above a challenge for histoGraph and the Digital Humanities in general is the conception of truth. Scientists can rely on a more or less stable foundation of what is true, experiments can be replicated and measured precisely. In the humanities the concept of truth is far more complex: It is based on the insight, that there is no neutral or objective way to study human environments. The way in which questions are asked, when, by whom, how data is selected to answer them, by what means this data is analyzed and finally the way in which the results of such analyses are communicated and received all challenge the idea of "one truth". Persons may, for example, change careers, their home countries might be renamed or they choose to go by different names. This means that at different points in time there might be more than one "true" answer to the simple question "Who is this?". In order to represent the discursive nature of truth in the humanities we make use of a community-driven tool for question answering, similar to stackoverflow.com [4]. Users have the opportunity to answer questions and thus benefit from the knowledge within the expert crowd.

3 Conclusion

We envision that histoGraph fills this niche and becomes a general purpose context exploration and storytelling tool for research and teaching in cultural heritage, the humanities and journalism. Crucially, histoGraph will maintain its current ability to process photos and will also become capable of processing text documents and metadata. For future development of histoGraph we propose the following use cases: Network creation based on images, network creation based on entity co-occurrences, network annotation and storytelling. This will require the following components:

1. Redevelopment of the image processing components with open source solutions and enhanced usability
2. Development of a component which imports collections and uses language processing technology to automatically produce visualizations of co-occurring entities such as persons, institutions, places.
3. Development of browsing histories, dynamically up- dated node lists as well as logs of reversible user actions as implemented in Open Refine [5] for better orientation.
4. Development of an annotation component which allows users to manually link nodes and ties to (third party) source documents and to provide additional textual information
5. Redevelopment of the contextualization feature which visualizes such links to source documents for any node and tie
6. Development of map-based visualizations of data and hybrid map+network visualizations.

These are ambitious goals, which will require time, funding and a number of case studies for the development of prototypes. Network visualizations have unrivalled powers to make complex relations comprehensible – we hope that histoGraph will allow authors and audiences to make the most of this potential.

References

1. Driver project. http://www.driver-repository.eu/
2. CUbRIK project. http://www.cubrikproject.eu/
3. histoGraph demonstrator. http://histograph.eu/
4. Stack Overflow. http://stackoverflow.com/
5. Open Refine. http://openrefine.org/

A Framework for Business Mashup Applications

Vijay K. Naik

IBM T. J. Watson Research Center, Yorktown Heights, NY 10598, USA
vkn@us.ibm.com

Abstract. Mashup applications for business can lead to better business insights, marketing opportunities, and may provide opportunity to monetize the value locked in business data. To enable necessary experimentation with mashups by domain experts, we describe a development and runtime framework that exposes data level abstractions in the form of templates and automates the programming details associated with plumbing for mashups. The framework also provides runtime support to manage security, reliability, and other business application related enterprise IT concerns.

Keywords: Business mashup applications · Cloud service orchestration

1 Introduction

Mashups are web based applications that typically combine data, content, and application functions from multiple services on the internet and present those in a meaningful cohesive manner. Mashups may filter out subject specific types of information, blend different types of data to create new insights and even new information. By combining data from different sources, mashups help users uncover and understand hidden patterns, recognize correlations, gain competitive advantage, create business value, or simply create pure entertainment value. Data sources tend to be either static, or slowly changing, or dynamic and fast changing. GPS data, geographical data, national/state/city boundaries, webcam locations, language constructs, societal values etc. are examples of static or slowly changing data. Weather data, twitter trends, news headlines, stock prices, traffic patterns, webcam feeds, consumer spending patterns, public opinions, fashion trends, spread of deceases, demographics, census data are all examples of dynamically changing data. Combining data that change at different frequencies can often lead to interesting insights, bring out correlations, or help in making predictions in one dimension using information from another dimension. By juxtaposition of fast and slow changing and static forms of information and presenting in a contextually clear manner, mashups can attract more users, provide insights, and create value meaningful to the users.

Mashup applications provide an attractive opportunity for businesses to conduct market analysis, brand management, customer relations, forecasting, and for monetizing the value locked in enterprise data. However, to fully realize this potential value, domain experts need to experiment with many different combinations and patterns. In addition, the resulting application must also address security, reliability, and other

P. Cimiano et al. (Eds.): ICWE 2015, LNCS 9114, pp. 617–620, 2015.
DOI: 10.1007/978-3-319-19890-3_42

enterprise IT concerns. Today this requires domain expertise as well as low level programming skills to manage integration with web services and IT management services. This is often a high barrier for domain experts and for software engineers. Existing frameworks for mashup applications do not address many of the requirements inherent to business and enterprise environments.

In this paper, we describe a mashup development and run-time environment that (i) enables users to develop mashup applications without requiring deep software engineering or programming skills, (ii) provides composition mechanisms for encapsulating IT management functions with the mashup runtime and automates common integration patterns.

2 Mashup Business Applications

Mashup applications for business combine business sensitive data with external publically available and/or third party commercial data. These applications may be used internally for business analysis purposes or may be provided externally to customers, partners, and other interested parties. Like other business applications, mashup applications for business also need to satisfy certain non-functional requirements including security and privacy requirements adhering to compliance and regulatory concerns, availability and performance requirements, and failure handling according to predefined SLAs. To address these concerns, enterprise IT typically follow best practices for deploying and managing applications and associated supporting middleware and infrastructure services. The same practices need to be followed for mashup applications for businesses.

Enterprise IT mandate special handling of both business sensitive data and third party data: access to business sensitive data must be properly protected to remain compliant with various regulations while allowing access to the key aspects via the mashup applications; and externally obtained data needs to properly filtered and fenced off from the rest of the enterprise environment to meet security and compliance requirements. When external applications access enterprise data, proper care must be taken to address firewall issues to allow applications and services to access only the authorized data by authorized external parties without compromising the security of the rest of the enterprise.

Because mashups open up possibilities for combining data in numerous different ways and utility of a mashup application may be short lived and possibly of interest only to a small audience, mashup development processes need to be fast requiring low IT or development effort. Even end users who are not professional software engineers should be able to construct a mashup application with relatively minimum amount of effort and investment of time.

3 A Framework for Mashup Business Applications

A viable framework for developing and managing mashup business applications must provide: (i) low barrier to entry for domain experts and other users with low programming skills for developing mashup applications using only their domain knowledge; (ii) address for security, reliability, and other IT concerns; and (iii) provide enterprise grade support for mashup applications.

Our framework is based on the concept of using domain specific templates for capturing and providing the integration logic specific to each domain. Examples of domain specific templates are templates for Customer relations for brand management, Customer service for order tracking, Customer service for competitive positioning, Sales positioning for competitive pricing, Decision support for product placement, Transportation logistics for same day delivery, Risk modeling using real-time data, Emergency response for natural and man-made disasters, and so on. The templates are extensible and mechanisms are provided to import new templates. Templates incorporate domain specific data sources -- both public and private. From the template, script based composition tools are synthesized which then guide the end user to create their own mashup application within the context of that template. The composition tools provide access to functions for performing filtering, aggregation and other statistical operations, and analytics such as map-reduce on the data received from the data sources both pre- and post-data-mashup. Templates encapsulate the details of accessing data sources as well as manage the data flow to and from data operators. The mashup developer can focus on the data abstractions and on the content without having to worry about the underlying plumbing. In case of complex mashup applications, mashup developers may want to perform complex custom analysis during the mashup or post-mashup steps. This can be done by incorporating the mashup application within a server-side application developed using scripting languages such as Ruby or Node.js. Such an application would then provide the necessary logic for post-mashup analysis. Once a mashup application is developed using a template, it can then be previewed and published as a web application to be used by others.

Templates are extensible. However, extending the templates require some degree of programming experience and knowledge about the APIs supported by specific data provider web services. Similarly new domain specific templates can be added to the framework. Again this requires some degree of software engineering skills.

A library of data operators is provided to manipulate various types of structured and unstructured data streams, content feeds, and feeds from other mashup applications. This library is extensible and new operators can be added to the library. The operators can be in the form of URLs to services, self-contained applications, or modules to existing packages. Template developers may enable a subset of data operators that are suitable for a particular step in the flow which are then made available to mashup developer in the form of a catalog that they can use to select and apply for that stage. More experienced users can import their own data operators while developing a mashup application.

Once the mashup application is developed, internally it is represented as BPM workflow which orchestrates the steps of accessing and initializing data sources and executes the flow. Application developers submit their applications along with the specifications of their service requirements. These requirements are expressed in the form of attributes of services delivered by cloud-based infrastructure and platform service providers. The application may also be associated with explicit policies such as secure connections to data-sources, firewall rules, network authentication rules and keys, and the prescribed service levels. The underlying framework prepares the environment by acquiring instances of the necessary IT services from cloud service providers and then deploys and manages the application according to enterprise policies.

4 Related Work

In [1], authors characterize five popular mashup development tools and identify common and unique characteristics among these tools. They also identify desired characteristics that tools and frameworks need to provide for efficient mashup development. In [2], authors provide a survey of cloud service composition approaches and classify these approaches according eight categories they have identified. In [3], authors propose using domain specific mashup language developed using domain specific concepts. Using the language a domain-specific mashup tool and runtime platform is automatically generated. We share their goal of easing the burden of mashup development by using domain specific knowledge at the cost of reduced generality. However our approaches of using domain-specific knowledge differ. In [4], the author describes Microsoft SharePoint as a platform for enterprise mashups.

5 Conclusion

We have outlined a template based framework for developing mashup applications taking into enterprise IT considerations. Framework described here enables application developers to describe the data-sources and organize mashup operations within the context of a template. In case of complex mashup applications users also can specify the flow and operations during various stages of the flow. At run-time, the underlying integration logic and other plumbing needed to enable secure connectivity, enablement of IT management services for application lifecycle operations such scaling, failure handling, backup/recovery are automatically generated from the template. In a future publication we will describe details of template design and their implementation using specific example domains.

References

1. Yu, J., Benatallah, B., Casati, F., Daniel, F.: Understanding Mashup Development. IEEE Internet Computing **12**(5), 44–52 (2008)
2. Jula, A., Sundararajan, E., Othman, Z.: Cloud computing service composition: A systematic literature review. Expert Systems with Applications **41**, 3809–3824 (2014)
3. Soi, S., Daniel, F., Casati, F.: Conceptual development of custom, domain-specific mashup platforms. ACM Trans. Web **8**(3) (2014)
4. Arredondo, J.: SharePoint: A platform for enterprise mashups (2008). http://www.microsoft.com/mashups

The Inclusive Enterprise: Vision and Roadmap

Robert-Jan Sips[1], Alessandro Bozzon[2(✉)], Gerard Smit[1], and Geert-Jan Houben[2]

[1] Centre for Advanced Studies, IBM Benelux, Amsterdam, The Netherlands
{robert-jan.sips,gerard.smit}@ibm.nl.com
[2] Delft University of Technology, Delft, The Netherlands
{a.bozzon,g.j.p.m.houben}@tudelft.nl

Abstract. For companies across the globe, building and sustaining a talent pipeline has become top priority. *Job satisfaction* is a core reason for employee retention and has shown to be more dependent on the organisational climate, which includes aspects such as working conditions, leadership and *inclusion*, than on variables such as structure, size, and pay, which are easy to quantify and control. This paper presents a vision of an "Inclusive Enterprise", and elaborates on how a computer science approach can help to sense and foster inclusion and well-being in enterprise environments.

1 Introduction

For companies across the globe, building and sustaining a talent pipeline has become top priority An estimated 65% of executives report a lack of top talent in the ranks of their top 300 leaders and only 10% say that their companies retain most of their high performers [1]. Consequently, in the 21st century, a "war on talent" became a reality, with organisations competing with one another to hire and retain scarce human capital.

Job satisfaction (the "degree to which individuals like their jobs"), **inclusion** ("a sense of belonging: feeling respected, valued for who you are; feeling a level of supportive energy and commitment from others so than you can do your best work" [2]), and, in general, *well-being* have been shown to be a core reason for employee retention, leaving to *extrinsic factors*, such as salary and payment, a secondary role [3].

This paper presents a vision of an "Inclusive Enterprise", advocating **well-being** and **inclusion** as core properties of next generation enterprises.

To achieve this vision, we take a computer science angle, by asking ourselves the question: *how can computer systems help to foster inclusion and well-being in the enterprise?*. Indeed, variables such as organisation structure and size, and salary can be easily quantified and controlled; on the other hand, well-being and inclusion are difficult to capture and influence. The scientific challenge lies in the creation of methods and tools able to sense and affect the the organisational climate, to benefit its employees. In the remainder of this paper, we discuss our vision and report on the ongoing initiative within IBM Benelux, pursued with TU Delft.

P. Cimiano et al. (Eds.): ICWE 2015, LNCS 9114, pp. 621–624, 2015.
DOI: 10.1007/978-3-319-19890-3_43

2 The Vision

At the heart of our vision is an automated system that senses and influences the working environment of an employee.

We aim to address both the *physical* and the *personal* environment. The former concerns sensing of environmental properties like the level of noise and light intensity; but also work-related properties such as proximity of other people and the features of the current workstation. The personal environment includes less tangible factors, such as one's background, expertise, (cultural) bias, emotions, mood and satisfaction itself. All together, these properties can provide a snapshot of the current status of an employee, which can be in turn used to create a more inclusive and personalise work experience.

In order to be effective, we advocate for inclusive enterprise systems to comply with the "**Primum non nocere**" (first, do no harm) principle. While such a requirement is common to all personalised systems, the enterprise environment, and the fundamental role of work for human beings, puts major emphasis on the trust relationships that should be established between the employer, the system, and the employee. This leads to the following fundamental design properties:

Integration and Transparency: an inclusion system should seamlessly integrate with existing workflows and tools. To be effective, the system should not add cognitive burden to the user, while learning and adapting to short- and long-term changes in the user satisfaction and working conditions.
Engagement by Design: inclusion and well-being should be achieved without user intervention. When, however, interaction is required (e.g. for data provisioning or environmental sensing purposes), it should occur on a voluntary basis, and in an engaging context. The system may never rely on mandatory interactions and additional workload for employees.
Trustworthiness and Privacy by Design: the system deals with both work-related and personal information. Its functions and purposes should be transparent to the employee, and personal data should be managed with full supervision and consent of the user.
Reuse: the system should rely as much as possible on existing infrastructure, such as building management systems, enterprise collaborative work tools, and enterprise social media. This requirements is to safeguard existing investments in technological infrastructures, but also to support transparency.

The properties reflect our current understanding and experience in enterprise workforce engagement, and represent the pillars of our research efforts.

3 Building Blocks of Inclusive Enterprise Systems

Figure 1 summarises the main building blocks of an inclusive enterprise system. We envision a data-driven technical platform.

Data play a key role to fuel the sensing and interpretation activities required to understand and influence job satisfaction. The data will ideally be collected from existing infrastructure, such as Building Management Systems and (Enterprise) Social Media.

Online social media such as Facebook, Twitter and LinkedIn are used more and more by companies as a way to support business processes, marketing, and for competitive intelligence purposes. Web social data can provide precious information about the personal, working, and social dimensions of employees. For instance, in a previous work [4], we showed how online social media could be used as a vehicle for a better understanding of the internal and external corporate dynamics. Supported by the analytical capabilities of platforms such as IBM Bluemix and Watson, Web social data can give better insights about the background, expertise, skills, and values of employees, thus enabling personalised interaction and working experience.

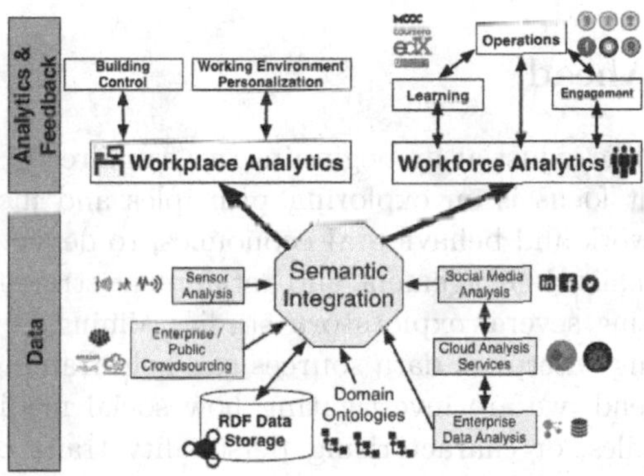

Fig. 1. High-level architecture of the data-driven inclusive workforce platform.

Physical enhancements provided by *smart devices* are helping to bridge the digital and physical worlds. Wearable technology is now collecting more data via sensors, communicating more information via displays, and truly augmenting a person's physical capabilities. Leveraging wearable devices allows companies to equip their employees with the technology they need to do better work, while improving operational efficiency and safety.

To cater for issues related to data sparseness, veracity, and sense-making, we envision a central role for *crowdsourcing* and *human computation*. Human can act as sensors for on-demand data creation, cleansing and linkage; we envision broad adoption of enterprise crowdsourcing techniques, including social sensing applications and pervasive human computation mechanisms.

The Role of Semantics. Thanks to state-of-the-art semantic technologies (best exemplified by cognitive computing initiatives like IBM Watson), we are working on creating a *semantic integration* layer for heterogenous environmental and social data. We plan to capitalise on existing standardisation efforts for semantic data representation, while integrating enterprise specific and domain-specific knowledge about the company, its organisation and structure. The semantic integration layer fuels the *workplace* and *workforce* analytics components, providing an unified and updated view on the current status of the company and its employees.

Elements of Inclusion. We stress the importance of *adaptation* and *engagement* as driving forces for inclusion, and as a main tool to influence satisfaction on the workplace. *Learning* is a fundamental right and duty of a modern workforce. Technological advances and quickly evolving societal (and work-related) challenges demand for continuous learning path, integrated (and driven) by both the duties, ambitions, and expectations of employees. To this end, *games with a purpose* and *gamification* techniques can be a main tool to drive engagement. In a recent work, we gathered strong evidence that a gamified experience can foster learning and social behaviour in employees.

4 The Path Ahead

While the research line is just at its beginning, we can already feature promising results. Our current focus is on exploring principles and methods from fields like psychology of work and behavioural economics, to devise worker modelling features, and personalised engagement and retainment strategies.

We are conducting several exploratory studies aiming at understanding to which extent existing enterprise data sources can help framing the status of an employee. To this end, we are investigating how social media can be used to elicit expertise profiles, or characterising personality traits of employees. The next step is to investigate how environmental and working conditions aspects can be inferred from data produced by employees. Whenever existing data are not sufficient, we will develop methods for (enterprise) social sensing aimed at data collection and enrichment.

Finally, we plan to experiment with ways to influence engagement and satisfaction. We are undergoing experiments aimed at providing better understanding of the fundamental principles of computer-mediated engagement mechanics in the enterprise.

References

1. Aguinis, H., Gottfredson, R.K., Joo, H.: Using performance management to win the talent war. Business Horizons **55**(6), 609–616 (2012)
2. Miller, F., Katz, J.: Inclusion Breakthrough: Unleashing the Real Power of Diversity. Berrett-Koehler Publishers (2002)
3. Hausknecht, J.P., Rodda, J., Howard, M.J.: Targeted employee retention: Performance-based and job-related differences in reported reasons for staying. Human Resource Management **48**(2), 269–288 (2009)
4. Bozzon, A., Efstathiades, H., Houben, G.-J., Sips, R.-J.: A study of the online profile of enterprise users in professional social networks. In: Proceedings of the Companion Publication of the 23rd International Conference on World Wide Web Companion, pp. 487–492. International World Wide Web Conferences Steering Committee (2014)

Fostering Innovation Through Coopetition: The *E015 Digital Ecosystem*

Maurilio Zuccalà(✉) and Irene Celino

CEFRIEL – Politecnico di Milano, Via Fucini 2, 20133 Milan, Italy
{maurilio.zuccala,irene.celino}@cefriel.com
http://www.cefriel.com

Abstract. Expo Milano 2015 is expecting to welcome millions of people from around the globe. They will visit the Universal Exposition and use local services provided by public and private organizations. Thus, this event is a major opportunity to introduce innovation in all aspects of urban life. The *E015 digital ecosystem* is a multi-stakeholder service-based environment enabling the realization and integration of advanced digital services made available before, during and also after the Expo by different stakeholders. E015 operates since 2013 and aims to become one of the legacies that the Expo will leave to Milan and to the European public and private system after the event.

1 Introduction

In 2015 the city of Milan is hosting the Universal Exposition [1]. This event represents a major opportunity to introduce digital innovation in all aspects of life and mobility: infrastructures, transport, cultural and social life, accommodation, services and facilities etc. Information Technology plays a key role in pursuing this goal, since it enables the creation of new functional and operational paradigms supporting the daily life of citizens and organizations. In fact, digital technologies can change the way the different stakeholders of a *smart territory* can effectively interact and cooperate.

The *E015 digital ecosystem* [2] was developed to support Expo Milano 2015 in tackling this challenge. E015 is a multi-stakeholder service environment enabling and fostering digital interoperability between organizations and companies, mainly in support of the realization of the smart territory concept. It aims to be neutral, multi-lateral, regulated, lightweight, extensible and scalable.

E015 enables new approaches to the design and implementation of advanced digital services. It provides members with lightweight participation guidelines and a set of shared and consolidated technical standards, processes and policies to develop their products – i.e., services, end-user applications and glossaries – and interoperate with other members. Membership is free, and it is open to everybody: organizations, companies and individuals.

E015 was promoted and founded in 2010 by major Italian associations of industries and companies – Confindustria, the Chamber of Commerce of Milan,

P. Cimiano et al. (Eds.): ICWE 2015, LNCS 9114, pp. 625–628, 2015.
DOI: 10.1007/978-3-319-19890-3_44

Confcommercio, Assolombarda and Unione del Commercio. In 2011, the public utility Expo 2015 S.p.A. became full partner of the initiative and operator of the ecosystem technical infrastructure, under the scientific coordination of CEFRIEL. As the result of the convergent efforts of various actors operating in the Milan Urban Area, pilot initiatives to test E015 were started by six large companies, i.e., the major national and regional transport players – SEA, ATM, Trenitalia, Trenord, Milano Serravalle - Milano Tangenziali, Infoblu - Autostrade per l'Italia. This led to the realization of a number of real-time services focused on the Milan Urban Area mobility domain: traffic information and camera views on ring roads; status and timetables of railway services, public transport and flights in Malpensa and Linate airports; status and availability of car parking and bike sharing stations. Such services were then leveraged by different end-user applications available as mobile apps, Web sites, info kiosks etc.

At the time of writing, E015 counts about 500 members and a steadily increasing number of services, end-user applications and shared glossaries covering several domains: mobility and travel, accommodation, cultural heritage, food and beverage, news and events etc. (the current full set of E015 assets can be browsed via the public Web site [2]).

The remainder of this paper briefly illustrates the E015 reference model, business perspective and achievements.

2 E015 Reference Model

E015 is an open API ecosystem [3]. It exploits the notion of API economy [6], which provides full, bidirectional and direct interoperability among autonomous distributed applications that access and exploit shared data-driven services. Ecosystem participants can publish their services (APIs), in terms of both functionalities and usage policies, to share their data assets through standard Web service interfaces. Other participants can then discover such services and leverage them, according to the respective usage policies, for building new value-added services or new integrated applications for end-users, thus contributing to the growth of the ecosystem. The interoperability model is based on open standards.

E015 participants can play one or more of these roles (see Fig. 1):

- **Service Providers** publish part of their own information assets in the ecosystem through APIs, so that other participants can use them for building value-added services as well as end-user applications.
- **End-User Application Providers** realize Web sites, mobile apps, information kiosks etc. providing end-users with value-added contents and functions by integrating the information provided in real-time through the ecosystem services and using shared glossaries.
- **Glossary Providers** propose standard ways to represent information in the ecosystem by means of taxonomies, ontologies etc. so that participants can rely on a set of shared and consolidated data models – i.e., the E015 "common language" – for developing their software products and for interoperating with other participants.

A number of **central infrastructural components** are in place to support the operations of the ecosystem, in particular: the main Web portal and interaction environment, the registry, a lightweight service monitoring component. The E015 architectural design is modular and extensible, so that existing components can be enhanced or new ones can be added in order to fulfill new business or technical needs and requirements. E.g., new evolution trends are currently being addressed, such as semantic interoperability and digital identity federation.

The ecosystem addresses governance both at the technical and the strategic level. In particular, it relies on the following internal roles:

- The **Technical Management Board** is in charge of managing the technical and procedural aspects of E015, e.g.: maintain, evolve and disseminate technical specifications and process guidelines; manage central infrastructural components; provide technical and procedural support to participants; monitor the availability of services.
- The **Governance Board** is in charge of long-term governance and strategic evolution of E015, e.g.: management of communication and relationship at national and international level; planning and management of long term ecosystem evolution.

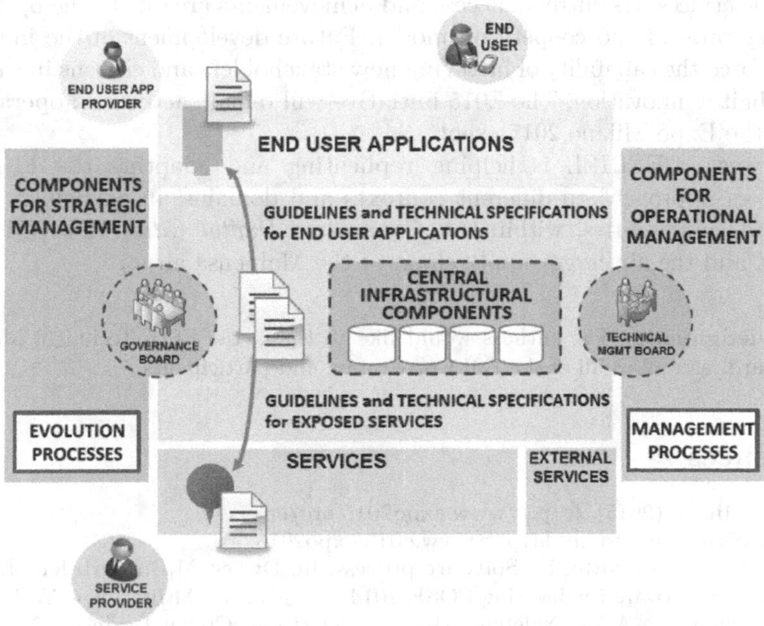

Fig. 1. High-level view of the E015 reference model

3 Coopetition in the Business Ecosystem

The "smartness" of a city or a territory derives from its ability of meeting, interacting, combining information, exploiting individual assets and pieces of knowledge in non-conventional ways, involving communities and stakeholders in an open participatory processes. This is why the founding principles of E015 are [3]: open standards, application mashup, and *coopetition*, i.e., cooperative competition – cooperation in the definition of the common architecture, standards, policies and governing processes; competition in the development of services and applications offered to the public [4].

Since the ecosystem opening in 2013, an exponentially increasing number of actors – among SMEs, large industrial companies, research institutions and public authorities – have joined E015 and are contributing services, end-user applications and glossaries. E015 thus represents an open innovation [5] process enabling new kinds of Public-Private Partnerships, and supporting new forms of institutional governance that better allow for service and information delivery.

4 Conclusion

The *E015 digital ecosystem* is enabling the creation of an innovative value chain involving private companies and public bodies by allowing rapid integration of data and services. Its current success and achievements are due to the open participatory process and coopetition model. Future development of the initiative will reinforce the capability of involving new stakeholders and citizens in the process of digital innovation. The E015 initiative will remain active and operational beyond the Expo Milano 2015 event.

Moreover, CEFRIEL is helping replicating and adapting the E015-like "ecosystem approach" to different contexts and domains, in particular: smart cities and communities, within the *Connecting Digital Cities* EIT ICT Labs Activity, and the air cargo supply chain of the Malpensa airport.

Acknowledgments. The authors would like to thank the E015 Technical Management Board, as well as all of the E015 promoters and participants.

References

1. Expo Milano (2015). http://www.expo2015.org/en
2. E015 digital ecosystem. http://www.e015.expo2015.org
3. Fuggetta, A., Di Nitto, E.: Software process. In: Dwyer, M.B., Herbsleb, J. (eds.) Future of Software Engineering FOSE 2014, pp. 1–12. ACM Inc., New York (2014)
4. Brandenburger, A.M., Nalebuff, B.J.: Co-opetition. Crown Business, New York (2011)
5. Chesbrough, H.W.: Open innovation: The New Imperative for Creating and Profiting from Technology. Harvard Business School Press, Boston (2003)
6. Gat, I., Succi, G.: A Survey of the API Economy. Agile Product & Project Management Executive Update **14**(6) (2013)

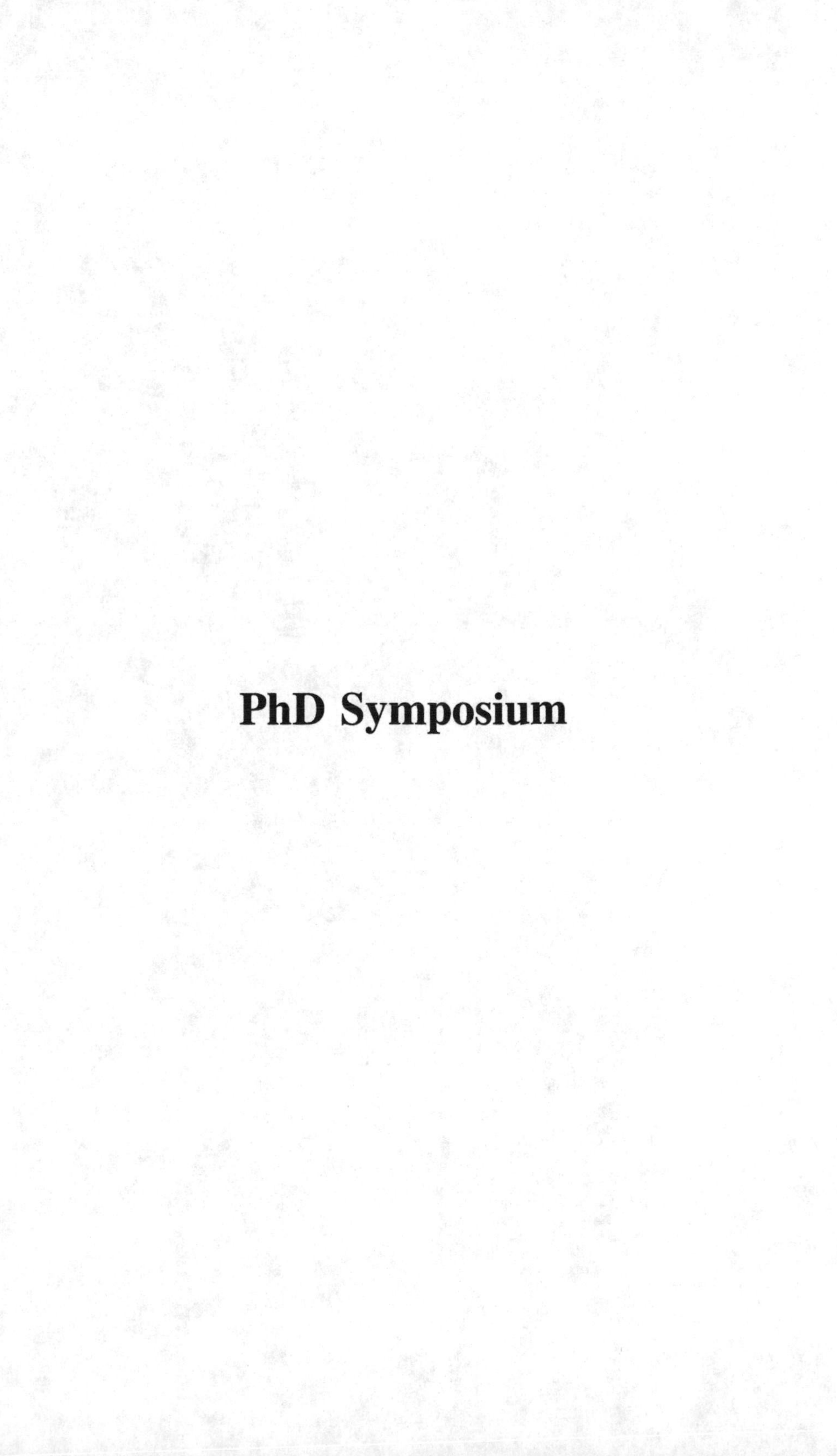

PhD Symposium

A Distributed Transaction Model for Read-Write Linked Data Applications

Nandana Mihindukulasooriya(✉), Raúl García-Castro, and Asunción Gómez-Pérez

Ontology Engineering Group, Escuela Técnica Superior de Ingenieros Informáticos, Universidad Politécnica de Madrid, Madrid, Spain
{nmihindu,rgarcia,asun}@fi.upm.es

Abstract. Read-write Linked Data applications provide a novel alternative to application integration that helps breaking data silos by combining the Semantic Web technologies with the REST design principles. One drawback that hinders the adoption of this approach in enterprise systems is the lack of transactions support. Transactions play a vital role in enterprise systems because inconsistent data can lead to problems, such as monetary losses or legal issues.

This paper presents a thesis that aims at defining a REST-compliant transaction model for distributed read-write Linked Data applications. The model extends the 'transactions as resources' approach using a set of hypermedia-controls defined by a transactions ontology and a multiversion concurrency mechanism. The author plans to formalize the transaction model which will then be evaluated to ensure the correctness and to perform a performance benchmark to evaluate the feasibility of using it in real world Linked Data applications.

Keywords: Transactions · Linked data · RESTful design

1 Introduction

Linked Data[1]-based application integration is getting traction as a novel approach for integrating data-intensive applications because of the benefits of Linked Data and Semantic Web technologies. Some advantages of this approach over existing approaches include: (a) global identifiers for data that can be accessed using the Web infrastructure and typed links between data from different applications; (b) the graph-based RDF data model that allows consuming and merging data from different sources without having to do complex structural transformations; and (c) explicit semantics of data expressed in RDF Schema or OWL ontologies which can be aligned and mapped to data models of other applications using techniques such as ontology matching [1]. In this context, *W3C Linked Data Platform*[2] (LDP) provides a standard RESTful protocol for read-write Linked Data ensuring interoperability.

[1] http://www.w3.org/DesignIssues/LinkedData.html
[2] http://www.w3.org/TR/ldp-primer/

P. Cimiano et al. (Eds.): ICWE 2015, LNCS 9114, pp. 631–634, 2015.
DOI: 10.1007/978-3-319-19890-3_45

Despite of these benefits, one of the main barriers for the wide adoption of this approach is the lack of transactions support. Traditionally, transactions ensure the atomicity, consistency, isolation, and durability (ACID) properties. However, the strong consistency properties of the ACID model may hinder other quality aspects of data-sharing systems as discussed by the *CAP* theorem [2] and the *PACELC* theorem [3]. To overcome these issues, new consistency models such as *BASE* [4] propose compromises between *consistency* and *availability/latency.*

The objective of this thesis is to develop a transaction model for read-write Linked Data applications that will provide strong consistency guarantees.

2 Related Work

Though a transaction model for Linked Data applications is a fairly new topic, several approaches for RESTful transactions have been proposed. One of the earliest approaches that is widely used in RESTful services is *batched transactions using the over-loaded POST method* [5]. *Atomic REST* follows an approach similar to batched transactions using mediators. The *transactions as resources* approach introduces a novel way of modeling transactions and the *RETRO model* further develops it using hypermedia controls to drive transaction state. An *optimistic technique for transactions using REST* and *a timestamp-based two phase commit protocol for RESTful services* use optimistic concurrency control mechanisms in contrast to pessimistic locking. The *Try-Cancel/Confirm (TCC)* pattern has been proposed to solve the specific business use case of reservation that only requires atomicity but not isolation.

The author has studied aforementioned models and the analysis of those models shows that they fail to provide consistency properties required by Linked Data applications due to several challenges [6]. For instance, the TCC model does not guarantee the isolation property and the other models that guarantee isolation do not support distributed transactions; the RETRO model needs a large number of HTTP round trips, which leads to a high overhead (refer to [6] for details).

3 Research Problems

The core research problem addressed in this thesis is how to design a transaction model that ensures strong consistency in distributed read-write Linked Data applications. The core problem is divided into three sub-problems:

RQ1. Which are the existing transaction models suitable for Linked Data applications? This question analyzes the state-of-the-art of REST-compliant transaction models and evaluates the current approaches based on the consistency model, applicability in the context of Linked data, challenges and limitations.

RQ2. How to design a REST-compliant transaction model for Linked Data applications? This question explores the possible compromises between REST constraints and strong consistency guarantees and investigates the possible ways of designing a transaction model that fits Linked Data applications.

RQ3. How to evaluate the proposed transaction model? This question evaluates the proposed model for both correctness and the practical usefulness in real world applications.

4 Methodology

First, a comprehensive analysis of the state of the art of RESTful transaction models was carried out with a Systematic Literature Review. The results were used to identify the existing RESTful transaction models, their applicability in the Linked Data application domain, and their gaps and challenges [6].

Second, a RESTful transaction model for Linked Data application has been defined that encloses the good features of the existing models whilst addressing their limitations. The proposed model is built on the *transactions as resources* model as the base and extends it with a well-defined transaction ontology to represent the transaction metadata as Linked Data. Using the ontology, transactions metadata will be represented as dereferenceable structured data serialized in machine readable RDF formats. The model explicitly defines the semantics of the media types used and allows clients to easily extract and process transaction metadata.

To achieve serializability, the transaction protocol adopts two version two-phase locking [7] that is used in the database domain to Linked Data applications. The proposed model provides solutions to the novel challenges of this approach when applied in the REST domain such as the management of provisional resource identifiers, identity conversions on commit and the management of relative URLs. Distributed transactions are handled by a transaction management service that is transparent to the client by communicating among a network of resource management services involved in the transaction. The model is currently implemented as an extension to the LDP4j framework [8], an open source Java-based framework for the development of interoperable read-write Linked Data applications.

Finally, the transaction model will be evaluated based on two main hypotheses. The first hypothesis is that the transaction model is correct, *i.e.*, it provides strong transaction guarantees. For this, the transaction model will be specified using a formal model that will define the restrictions of different states and the state transitions enforced by the model. We will follow a similar approach to what has been used by existing Web Service transaction protocols to prove the correctness by formalizing the proposed model using a method such as pi calculus or temporal logic (TLA+). The second hypothesis that will be evaluated is that the transaction model has a low-overhead and does not considerably affect the performance of the applications, *i.e.*, it will be feasible to use the model in real world Linked Data applications. A performance benchmark of the model implementation will be carried out to measure the performance of the transaction processing and the findings will be used to fine-tune the implementation and optimize the model.

5 Conclusions and Future Work

This paper presents a thesis on a novel REST-compliant transaction model for distributed read-write Linked Data applications. The model addresses the limitations of the previous approaches and provides strong consistency guarantees. The main contributions of this work include: (a) a thorough analysis of the impedance mismatches between the ACID transaction properties and the REST constraints, and (b) the definition, implementation, and evaluation of a transaction model for Linked Data applications that provides strong consistency guarantees.

As future work, we plan to expand the transaction protocol to cover different consistency levels and to define a high-level framework for transaction negotiation. The model is designed in a way that it provides a mechanism for the clients to express their preferences and expectations (e.g., similar to content negotiation on the Web). This enables the model to be extended to support other types of transactions (e.g., compensating transactions). Another aspect is the integration of the transaction model with the W3C LDP protocol in order to be proposed as a standardized W3C LDP extension.

Acknowledgments. The author is supported by the *4V: Volumen, Velocidad, Variedad y Validez en la gesti?n innovadora de datos* (TIN2013-46238-C4-2-R) project and he thanks Miguel Esteban-Gutiérrez for his valuable input related to this thesis.

References

1. Mihindukulasooriya, N., García-Castro, R., Esteban-Gutiérrez, M.: Linked data platform as a novel approach for enterprise application integration. In: Proceedings of the 4th International Workshop on Consuming Linked Data (COLD2013), Sydney, Australia (2013)
2. Brewer, E.A.: Towards robust distributed systems. In: Proceedings of the Nineteenth Annual ACM Symposium on Principles of Distributed Computing, PODC 2000, p. 7. ACM, New York (2000)
3. Abadi, D.J.: Consistency Tradeoffs in Modern Distributed Database System Design: CAP is Only Part of the Story. Computer **45**(2), 37–42 (2012)
4. Pritchett, D.: BASE: An Acid Alternative. Queue **6**(3), 48–55 (2008)
5. Kochman, S., Wojciechowski, P.T., Kmieciak, M.: Batched transactions for RESTful web services. In: Harth, A., Koch, N. (eds.) ICWE 2011 Workshops. LNCS, vol. 7059, pp. 86–98. Springer, Heidelberg (2012)
6. Mihindukulasooriya, N., Esteban-Gutiérrez, M., García-Castro, R.: Seven challenges for RESTful transaction models. In: Proceedings of the Companion Publication of the 23rd International Conference on World Wide Web, Seoul, South Korea, pp. 949–952 (2014)
7. Bernstein, P.A., Hadzilacos, V., Goodman, N.: Concurrency Control and Recovery in Database Systems, vol. 370. Addison-Wesley, New York (1987)
8. Esteban-Gutiérrez, M., Mihindukulasooriya, N., García-Castro, R.: LDP4j: a framework for the development of interoperable read-write linked data applications. In: Proceedings of the 1st ISWC Developers Workshop, Riva del Garda, Italy (2014)

Secure Storing of E-Health Records in the Cloud

Fabian Wiedemann(✉) and Martin Gaedke

Technische Universität Chemnitz, Chemnitz, Germany
{fabian.wiedemann,martin.gaedke}@informatik.tu-chemnitz.de

Abstract. Storing business sensitive data in the cloud is a huge challenge. Since disclosures of Edward Snowden, the trust in encryptions of the cloud provider decreased enormously. While this problem exists in many domains, like financial data, we identified a scenario in the e-Health sector. It is an important issue to preserve the patients' privacy when storing their e-Health records in the cloud. That is, encryption and decryption must be done by the client and it must be ensured that the cloud provider cannot access any e-Health record. Since a lot of e-Health records can be stored in such a system, it must be possible to search on the encrypted data without revealing any meta data or the records themselves. In this paper we present our planned research to securely store data in the cloud. We propose a first approach to deal with the identified requirements and describe our research methodology.

Keywords: Cloud · Security · Privacy · Encryption · Storage

1 Introduction

Over the last three years the usage of cloud computing by companies significantly increased [2]. Also, the revenue through cloud computing will grow within the next years by at least 15% annual [2]. On the one hand, important benefits why companies employ cloud computing are cost reduction in maintenance for software and infrastructure, higher scalability, and faster deployment of new software. On the other hand, a lot of companies in Germany hesitate to introduce cloud computing in their infrastructure. This is because they fear unauthorized access to sensitive business data [6].

One of the key issues companies need to deal with when using cloud computing is the privacy while storing personal data or business sensitive data in the cloud. Since the revelation of Edward Snowden, the trust in cloud providers regarding privacy issues decreased. While cloud providers encrypt the personal data or business sensitive data on the physical devices, they have the ability to decrypt the data and reveal them to others, like companies or official institutions, or process the data by their own. This is a huge obstacle for companies in using cloud computing, especially in sectors where privacy is important, like e-Health records or finance data.

P. Cimiano et al. (Eds.): ICWE 2015, LNCS 9114, pp. 635–638, 2015.
DOI: 10.1007/978-3-319-19890-3_46

We identified a scenario for storing e-Health records of patients in Germany in the cloud. The issue of privacy for the patient's e-Health records in Germany is regulated by a lot of laws and directives. To deal with these laws and directives special requirements need to be fulfilled by the software and cloud infrastructure.

2 Problem Analysis

Based on the described scenario of e-Health in Section 1, we analyze the following problem: Current cloud providers do not offer a secure and privacy-aware storage that fits legal requirements to store personal data, such as patient's e-Health records. In this context, we understand as secure and privacy-aware that the cloud provider will never have the ability to decrypt or reveal any information of the stored data.

The goal of our research is an approach that enables end users to securely store their personal data or business sensitive data in the cloud. For achieving the goal, we want to create a framework that supports web engineers to develop web applications that store their data in the cloud. The framework should consider privacy issues of the stored data and should never reveal any unencrypted data to third parties. To enable a wide usage of the framework, this needs to be applicable for any cloud provider.

3 Related Work

Literature to encryption partially deals with search-able encryption schemes. Bellare et al. in [1] and Song et al. in [4] focus on an encryption scheme which is secure against common attacks, while offering an efficient search on encrypted keywords. They propose an approach of a public-key encryption scheme that provides a deterministic encryption algorithm. That is, encrypting the same plain text, for example a keyword, two times with the same encryption key results in the same cipher text. Thus, searching on the encrypted keywords will provide the same results as searching on the plain keywords.

Besides the security topic in this research there is also related work in the context of software engineering. In [5] Vitali et al. describe an approach to build an e-Health infrastructure on the web. While our approach focuses on a client side encryption and storing only encrypted data, Vitali et al. developed a RESTful service to communicate e-Health records between medical practices, patients, and hospitals. Based on their recent work they evolved the framework SOLE to a REST architecture to reduce the overhead required by the previous one that uses SOAP for transmitting messages.

4 Approach

To deal with the problem described in Section 2, we propose a two-stage approach for secure storing documents in the cloud. One stage realizes the secure storing of the documents in the cloud (cf. Figure 1 (a)), while the other stage utilizes the requesting of the documents from the cloud (cf. Figure 1 (b)). Our approach works as follows.

First, the client extracts keywords from the documents that should be stored in the cloud (cf. ①). As keywords we understand anything that is related to the document, such as often used words as well as meta data. Afterwards, the client encrypts the documents and the keyword-file-table (cf. ②). The key used for encryption is only stored on the client and does not have to be revealed to the framework or the cloud. Both, the encrypted documents and the encrypted keyword-file-table are sent to the framework (cf. ③). The framework stores the encrypted keyword-file-table for an efficient lookup performed during a search request. The encrypted documents will be stored in the cloud (cf. ④).

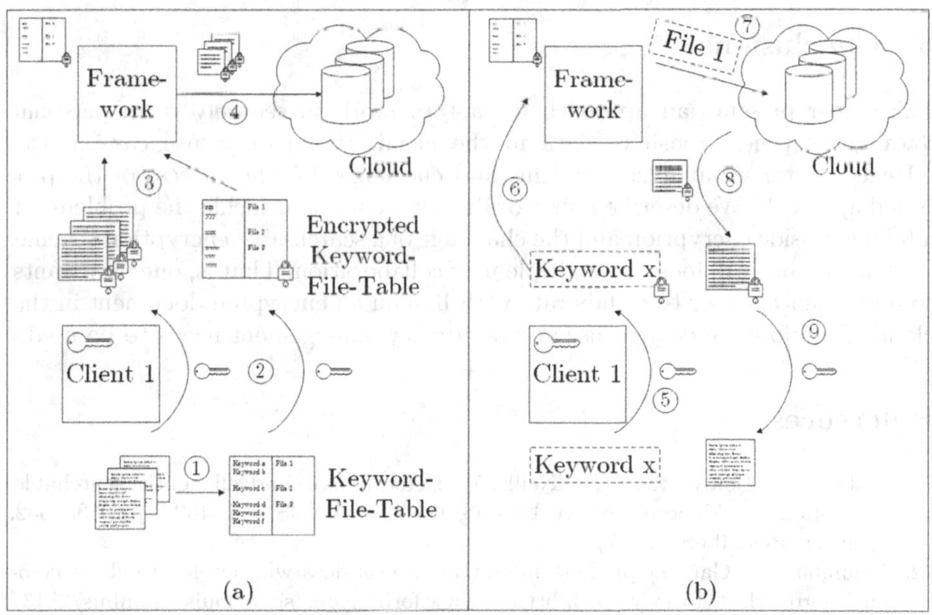

Fig. 1. Architecture of the approach

When the client wants to request a document to a specific keyword, the client encrypts the keyword using its stored key (cf. ⑤). The encrypted keyword is sent to the framework (cf. ⑥) and the framework can compute which document is requested based on the encrypted keyword-file-table. Afterwards, the framework requests the encrypted document from the cloud (cf. ⑦). The framework receives the encrypted document from the cloud and sends it to the client (cf. ⑧). In the last step, the client decrypts the encrypted document with its stored key and can process the document (cf. ⑨).

5 The Research Methodology

The research proposed in this paper will be structured following the Logical Framework Approach (LFA) [3]. LFA covers three stages of our research, i.e., identification, formulation, and evaluation. In the first stage, we identified the stakeholders of the proposed problem, i.e., doctors, nurses, patients, developers, and cloud providers. By interviewing and surveying these stakeholders we want to capture and analyze their problems. Based on the analyzed problems we derive objectives our approach needs to achieve. Within the formulation stage, we create measurable outcomes and define the scope of our research. Independently from LFA, we implement our approach between formulation and evaluation stage. In the last stage, we evaluate and measure how our objectives are fulfilled.

6 Conclusions

This paper presents an approach for a framework to securely store personal data and business sensitive data in the cloud. Based on a use case in the e-Health sector we analyze problems and challenges for the success of the proposed approach. We describe a first draft how we want to tackle the problems of a full client-side encryption and the challenge of a search-able encryption scheme.

Future work will focus on multiple user collaboration. That is, one user wants to invite another user to collaborate with him on an encrypted document in the cloud. Therefore, an easy to use and secure key management needs to be used.

References

1. Bellare, M., Boldyreva, A., O'Neill, A.: Deterministic and efficiently searchable encryption. In: Menezes, A. (ed.) CRYPTO 2007. LNCS, vol. 4622, pp. 535–552. Springer, Heidelberg (2007)
2. Columbus, L.: Gartner predicts infrastructure services will accelerate cloud computing growth, February 2013. http://www.forbes.com/sites/louiscolumbus/2013/02/19/gartner-predicts-infrastructure-services-will-accelerate-cloud-computing-growth/ (last accessed 2015–02-05)
3. European Commission: Project Cycle Management Guidelines, vol. 1 (2004). http://ec.europa.eu/europeaid/multimedia/publications/documents/tools/europeaid_adm_pcm_guidelines_2004_en.pdf
4. Song, D.X., Wagner, D., Perrig, A.: Practical techniques for searches on encrypted data. In: 2000 IEEE Symposium on Security and Privacy (S&P 2000), pp. 44–55. IEEE (2000)
5. Vitali, F., Amoroso, A., Roccetti, M., Marfia, G.: Restful services for an innovative e-health infrastructure: a real case study. In: 2014 IEEE 16th International Conference on e-Health Networking, Applications and Services (Healthcom), pp. 188–193. IEEE (2014)
6. Wallraf, B.: Cloud-monitor 2014. Tech. rep., KPMG AG (2014)

Knowledge Crowdsourcing Acceleration

Jie Yang([✉]), Alessandro Bozzon, and Geert-Jan Houben

Delft University of Technology, Mekelweg 4, 2628 CD Delft, The Netherlands
{j.yang-3,a.bozzon,g.j.p.m.houben}@tudelft.nl

Abstract. Crowdsourcing has recently become a powerful computational tool for data collection and augmentation. Although crowdsourcing has been extensively applied in diverse domains, most tasks are of low complexity such that workers are assumed to be endless, anonymous and disposable. By unlocking the value of human knowledge-related features, e.g., experience, expertise and opinion, we envision that crowdsourcing can reach its full potential to solve complex tasks. We aim at creating a comprehensive theory of crowdsourcing for knowledge creation, i.e., *knowledge crowdsourcing*, with a focus on developing methods and tools to control and accelerate knowledge creation process. Inspired by previous work, we describe a reference model of knowledge crowdsourcing acceleration, together with three case studies for model validation and extension. The results of our first case study on on-line knowledge creation demonstrate the potential contribution to web engineering.

Keywords: Crowdsourcing · Knowledge creation · Collaborative question answering · Enterprise expert finding · Urban computing

1 Introduction

Crowdsourcing is the process of sourcing tasks to large online crowds [1]. As a discipline, crowdsoucing recently emerged as a promising form of computation and knowledge generation [2], which provides effective methods for data collection and augmentation.

Motivation. Crowdsourcing has been usually studied as a computational tool, where tasks are assumed to be of low cognitive complexity, and workers to be endless, anonymous and disposable. Such crowdsourcing only takes little advantage of human capabilities, mostly only relying on the availability of workers. However, the rich, knowledge-related features of humans (i.e. expertise and skills), and their subjective perceptions are less considered. By fully unlocking the value of such inherent human abilities, crowdsourcing can reach its full potential, and enable the solution of more complex, cognitive intensive tasks.

Related Work. Although crowdsourcing has drawn much attention from researchers with diverse background, much less studies have been focusing on knowledge-related task crowdsourcing. The few studies addressing crowdsourcing

P. Cimiano et al. (Eds.): ICWE 2015, LNCS 9114, pp. 639–643, 2015.
DOI: 10.1007/978-3-319-19890-3_47

for knowledge creation present results that are difficult to compare, and of difficult generalization, as experiments are performed mostly on an ad-hoc basis. Typical tasks are solved as a bottom-up process. For instance, the processes of building wiki's or collaborative QA (CQA) systems, are not based on systematical crowdsourcing methods, but more on the spontaneus and autonomous contribution of volunteers. A comprehensive theory of *crowdsourcing* for *knowledge creation* is in demand [3].

Goal. Our work focuses on *knowledge crowdsourcing*, i.e. the process of designing, executing and coordinating crowdsourcing tasks that are knowledge intensive. Based on this definition, our goal is to develop the methods and tools required to control and accelerate the process of crowdsourced knowledge creation, by taking into account the rich set of knowledge-related features of humans, like experience, expertise, or opinion. We envision application in several domains, from the acceleration of the process of on-line knowledge creation, to the augmentation of subjective human perception data for better urban computing.

2 Methodology

Our path towards the creation of a more comprehensive theory of knowledge crowdsourcing builds upon a reference model, presented later in this section. Based on the initial model, we then follow an iterative improvement process based on its application to different real-world case studies, which, in turn, validate and extend the theory in each iteration. In this sense the case studies are important, as they serve as testbeds for validation, and basic resources for developing the knowledge crowdsourcing theory.

Initial Model. To control the process of knowledge crowdsourcing, we need to understand how it operates. Therefore a high-level reference model is to be proposed to capture its key steps. Our model follows the generic conceptual framework of human computation systems (HCS) [4]. It is applied in all case studies, such that their results, by conforming to a unified framework, could be better compared and, possibly, generalized.

Our model builds on the following key components: *1) Worker modeling* techniques to assess the worker skills and expertise; *2) Task modeling* techniques to represent the knowledge to be created; *3)* methods for *task assignment and recommendation*, and for *workflow control and optimization*, to enable quick and high-quality knowledge creation; and *4) tools* to support all the above. These components correspond to the key facets of conceptual framework of HCS: component 1 considers worker properties and engagement; component 2 defines the goal of a task; component 3 manages the problem-solving process.

Our work aim at showing how, by optimally combining the components described above, it will be possible to accelerate knowledge creation in a systematic and effective way. We envision that the accelerating methods and tools can be demonstrated in a new framework, built upon reference works in the field [5].

Case Studies. We identified 3 representative case studies where the knowledge creation task is complex, and crowdsourcing can be beneficial. Each case covers key components of our theory, while stressing different complexity dimensions.

On-line Knowledge Creation. This case study considers knowledge crowdsourcing in the open Web environment. Typical applications include CQA systems such as Stack Overflow and Yahoo! Answers, content curation systems like Reddit, and diverse on-line forums. Despite the high activeness of such systems, requests are not always satisfied due to the wide range of request difficulty and user expertise levels. In this use case, our research questions are: 1) how to model users with different levels of expertise; 2) how to model requests of different levels of difficulty; and 3) how to reduce time needed for obtaining good solutions/content. Section 3 presents initial results achieved with this case study.

Enterprise Knowledge Creation. This case study addresses the problem of knowledge creation in large companies. Tasks in this case are designed for enterprise interest, thus having narrow and focused knowledge needs. Requesters and workers are employees from the same company, thus offering crowds of a size smaller than that in the on-line case. Consequently, the challenges include: 1) modeling knowledge needs in task design; 2) modeling diverse facets of employees' expertise to match the task requirement; and 3) non-monetary incentive mechanisms (e.g. gamification) to engage workers, to cater for the presence of stronger monetary compensations (i.e. salary).

Urban Knowledge Creation. Crowdsourcing urban perception increases the availability of data to model urban conditions, for a better understanding of cities. In this case, crowds are engaged to source factual perception of urban environment (e.g., traffic congestion), but also subjective perception, such as travelers' emotional reaction to city spots. The later type of perception can be influenced by personalities or cultural backgrounds. Another important feature of this case study is that targeted workers are often very dynamic, yet geographically constrained. To summarize, this case study poses the following research questions: 1) properly embedding subjective element in task model; 2) modeling and eliciting general or subjective user features; and 3) instantly capturing and engaging the dynamic workers in the crowdsourcing workflow.

The three case studies have also important economical and societal value. Online knowledge creation platforms are important as it has been shown that they are reforming the ways people create and share knowledge on the Web. Enterprise knowledge creation, which is less studied, has the potential effect on boosting the performance of enterprise-level task execution. Urban knowledge creation addresses the challenge in optimizing the largest public living environment, i.e. cities, which already accommodate 72% of Europe population.

3 Results

This section presents our research results of the first case study, i.e. online knowledge creation. We focused on Stack Overflow, one of the most active CQA systems on the Web. Despite its success, a large portion of Stack Overflow questions do not receive good quality answers, and the average time for a question to obtain an answer is at a magnitude of days. Therefore, Stack Overflow is a perfect candidate to study techniques for accelerating knowledge creation.

Edit Suggestion. We first propose to better understand the impact of question quality on knowledge creation, by study methods to suggest the right edit to apply on poorly formulated questions. Based on a qualitative study that reveals the main functions of question edits, we presented a methodology to automatically detect whether a newly posted question needs an edit, and if so, what type of edit it needs. Experiments show that we can reach an F-measure of 0.7 for edit need prediction, and an F-measure of 0.76 for code type prediction. The detail of this research has been published in [6].

Expertise Identification. Identifying user expertise in CQA systems has been widely studied, while most of the research approximates user expertise with user activeness. We show in our recently published paper [7] that activeness does not necessarily strictly correlate with expertise. We proposed a novel expertise metric that is hardly influenced by activeness, based on which we define a group of users to approximate experts. By characterizing their behaviors, we show that they fit the image of experts better than experts defined by other metrics.

Question Routing. We are currently studying how better understanding the engagement of potential answerers can lead to better question routing, i.e. recommend questions to users to reduce answering time. We assume that questions of different topics require different combinations of user roles: questions relating to general skills may require active answerers engaged in discussion to ultimately generate a best answer, while questions relating to specific language or framework may only need one expert user to directly provide the right answer. Preliminary experiments show that optimizing the weights of user roles could improve the accuracy of question routing.

4 Future Works

We have instantiated knowledge crowdsourcing theory in on-line knowledge creation case, and demonstrated its potential benefits in several publications. With the promising results achieved so far, we plan to continue exploring knowledge crowdsourcing acceleration in enterprise (e.g. by collaborating with IBM Netherlands) and urban knowledge creation (e.g. in the context of the Amsterdam AMS initiative) cases, to further develop the theory with methods and tools.

References

1. Howe, J.: The Rise of Crowdsourcing. Wired Magazine **14**(6), 1–4 (2006)
2. Law, E., Ahn, L.V.: Human Computation. Synthesis Lectures on Artificial Intelligence and Machine Learning **5**(3), 1–121 (2011)

3. Kittur, A., Nickerson, J.V., Bernstein, M., Gerber, E., Shaw, A., Zimmerman, J., Lease, M., Horton, J.: The future of crowd work. In: CSCW 2013, pp. 1301–1318. ACM, New York (2013)
4. Malone, T.W., Laubacher, R., Dellarocas, C.: Harnessing Crowds: Mapping the Genome of Collective Intelligence. MIT Sloan Research Paper, No. 4732–09 (2009)
5. Bozzon, A., Brambilla, M., Ceri, S., Mauri, A.: Reactive crowdsourcing. In: WWW 2013, pp. 153–164. ACM, New York (2013)
6. Yang, J., Hauff, C., Bozzon, A., Houben, G.J.: Asking the right question in collaborative Q&A systems. In: Hypertext 2014, pp. 179–189. ACM, New York (2014)
7. Yang, J., Tao, K., Bozzon, A., Houben, G.-J.: Sparrows and owls: characterisation of expert behaviour in stackoverflow. In: Dimitrova, V., Kuflik, T., Chin, D., Ricci, F., Dolog, P., Houben, G.-J. (eds.) UMAP 2014. LNCS, vol. 8538, pp. 266–277. Springer, Heidelberg (2014)

Community-Driven Social Influence Analysis and Applications

Yang Zhang(✉) and Jun Pang

Faculty of Science, Technology and Communication, University of Luxembourg, Luxembourg, Luxembourg
{yang.zhang,jun.pang}@uni.lu

Abstract. Nowadays, people conduct a lot of activities with their online social networks. With the large amount of social data available, quantitative analysis of social influence becomes feasible. In this PhD project, we aim to study users' social influence at the community level, mainly because users in social networks are naturally organized in communities and communities play fundamental roles in understanding social behaviors and social phenomenons. Through experiments with a location-based social networks dataset, we start by demonstrating communities' influence on users' mobility, and then we focus on the influence of leaders in the communities. As a next step, we intend to detect users that act as structural hole spanners and analyze their social influence across different communities. Based on these studies, we plan to propose a unified approach to quantify users' social influence and investigate its applications, for example, in social interaction and behavior analysis.

1 Introduction

Online social networks (OSNs) have gained a lot of popularity and experienced fast growth during the past decade. Leading actors in OSNs including Facebook and Twitter have a huge amount of users. Nowadays, users share many information about themselves and conduct a lot of activities with their OSNs. With these large quantity of data regarding social behaviors, studies towards understanding human society become quantitatively achievable.

Social influence as a phenomena has been extensively studied [1]. In simple terms, it refers to the behavioral change of individuals affected by others. Common forms of social influence include conformity, peer pressure, leadership, etc. Understanding social influence is important and can result in many appealing applications, such as viral marketing, disease spread and urban planning.

Previous works have focused on computational models and algorithms on social influence in OSNs. Most of these works have considered social influence in the scope of the whole social graph. On the other hand, users of a social network are naturally organized in communities. Communities play a more important role

Y. Zhang—PhD student at the Computer Science and Communications research unit.

P. Cimiano et al. (Eds.): ICWE 2015, LNCS 9114, pp. 644–647, 2015.
DOI: 10.1007/978-3-319-19890-3_48

than friends on influencing a user's behavior, i.e., the influence is normally not from all his friends but certain communities. Therefore, community is the most useful resolution to study social influence. In this project, we aim to understand, model and quantify social influence at the community level.

2 Related Work and Our Approach

There are mainly two directions on modeling users' social influences. One is based on the social graph structure. Methods range from simple ones such as the number of friends to more sophisticated ones, such as the ones based on PageRank. The other direction to compute users' influence is through mining their behaviors in the past. For example, the authors of [2] quantify a Twitter user's influence through the number of users that retweet his tweets.

Besides quantifying users' influence, influence propagation has been studied as well. In [3], the authors have modeled a social network as a weighted graph where the weight on an edge reflects the influence between users. They propose two influence propagation models and solve the influence maximization as an optimization problem. Goyal et al. [4] have proposed three methods to compute influence on edges among users through the actions they have conducted.

One common drawback of the above methods is that the social network is considered as a whole. Instead, communities' influence play a more important role. For example, where a user goes for lunch is influenced by colleagues while his weekend plan depends on his family. In a broader view, communities' effectiveness have been demonstrated in other fields such as biology and physics. Therefore, we intend to study social influence at the community level.

To approach our project objectives, we first perform a case study on location-based social networks to demonstrate communities' influence. Sociological theories indicate that users' positions in social networks have a large impact on their influence. We then focus on users who are either the community leaders or structural hole spanners among communities. Having understood these users' behavior, we aim to propose a framework to quantify users' social influence.

3 Current Results

3.1 Community Detection

To study social influence at the community level, the first step would be discovering communities in a social network. Community detection algorithms have been well studied during the past decade and can be roughly classified into two kinds. Algorithms of the first kind detect communities based on certain metrics of the network structure such as clique and modularity. The second kind exploits attributes of the nodes in the social network. Depending on the dataset we are going to use, suitable schemes will be adopted to discover communities.

3.2 Community Influence

The first step of the project is to demonstrate that communities indeed play an important role on influencing users' behaviors. We have performed a case study on location-based social networks [5,6]. The dataset we use contains both users' location information and social relationships. We first propose a metric to quantify both a user's communities' and friends' influence. Through a comparison, we find that communities indeed have a stronger influence than friends on users' mobility. In addition, we show that different communities influence a user's mobility at different time or location. We further use a logistic model to predict a user's future location based on his communities' information, and the experimental results are promising.

3.3 Community Leader Influence

Leadership is a common social influence form. Leaders in a community are considered to have bigger influence than other members. To understand social influence, it is crucial to understand leaders' behaviors.

To find leaders in a community, we propose an algorithm that explores both the social graph structure and the behaviors users have conducted in the past. The leaders we find on a real-life social network dataset are distinguished from other members in the community in terms of the number of events they conduct and the number of friends they have. We further conduct several event prediction tasks on whether and when a community member will conduct a certain event given that leaders have already conducted the event before.

4 Future Work

4.1 Detecting Structural Hole Spanners

It has been proposed in sociology that users who act as intermediary between different communities have more control over the the social network in information diffusion. Users of this kind are termed as *structural hole spanners*. To discover structural hole spanners from the social network, Lou and Tang [7] have proposed two algorithms which are purely based on graph structure. However, besides social relationships, users also conduct a lot of actions in OSNs and these actions contain rich information about users' social behaviors. Therefore, we intend to consider not only the graph structure but also users' past behaviors to detect structural hole spanners. We plan to compare the accuracy of the structural hole spanners discovered by our algorithm with the algorithms proposed in [7]. To further demonstrate the effectiveness of our algorithm, we can explore structural hole spanners to study several interesting problems in social network analysis, such as community detection and event prediction.

4.2 Quantifying User Influence

Having demonstrated the communities' influence and how information are propagated in communities, we aim to quantify each user's influence in the social network by considering communities instead of the whole graph. The output of the quantification would be an influence score for each user in the network.

We start by assigning each user an *intra-community influence* based on his importance in his community. Intuitively, users such as leaders will receive a high score. The intra-community score can be computed based on both the social graph structure and events already conducted by the user. Then the second value we consider is how important a user is among different communities, namely *inter-community influence*. In this case, the previously mentioned structural hole spanners will get high scores. In the end, the social influence of a social network user is computed through his intra-community and inter-community scores. To show the effectiveness of our community-driven influence quantification method, experiments on various social network datasets will be conducted. The baseline models for comparison will include classical solutions such as PageRank.

4.3 Applications

Understanding social influence of users in OSNs is critical and will benefit many web applications (e.g., viral marketing) and real-life applications (e.g., urban planning). OSN operators who can exploit social influence to improve their quality of service. For example, our new social influence analysis can lead to the design of better event and venue recommender systems for OSNs to attract users. In a broader context, a suitable social influence model will also help to attack important problems, such as monitoring and controling disease spread.

References

1. Tang, J., Chang, Y., Liu, H.: Mining social media with social theories: a survey. SIGKDD Explorations Newsletter **15**(2), 20–29 (2014)
2. Bakshy, E., Hofman, J.M., Mason, W.A., Watts, D.J.: Everyone's an influencer: quantifying influence on twitter. In: Proc. 4th ACM International Conference on Web Search and Data Mining (WSDM), pp. 65–74. ACM Press, New York (2011)
3. Kempe, D., Kleinberg, J., Tardos, E.: Maximizing the spread of influence through a social network. In: Proc. 9th ACM Conference on Knowledge Discovery and Data Mining (KDD), pp. 137–146. ACM Press, New York (2003)
4. Goyal, A., Bonchi, F., Lakshmanan, L.V.: Learning influence probabilities in social networks. In: Proc. 3rd ACM International Conference on Web Search and Data Mining (WSDM), pp. 241–250. ACM Press, New York (2010)
5. Pang, J., Zhang, Y.: Location prediction: communities speak louder than friends. CoRR abs/1408.1228 (2014)
6. Pang, J., Zhang, Y.: Exploring communities for effective location prediction (poster paper). In: Proc. 24th World Wide Web Conference (Companion Volume) (WWW). ACM Press, New York (2015) (accepted)
7. Lou, T., Tang, J.: Mining structural hole spanners through information diffusion in social networks. In: Proc. 22nd International Conference on World Wide Web (WWW), pp. 825–836. ACM Press, New York (2013)

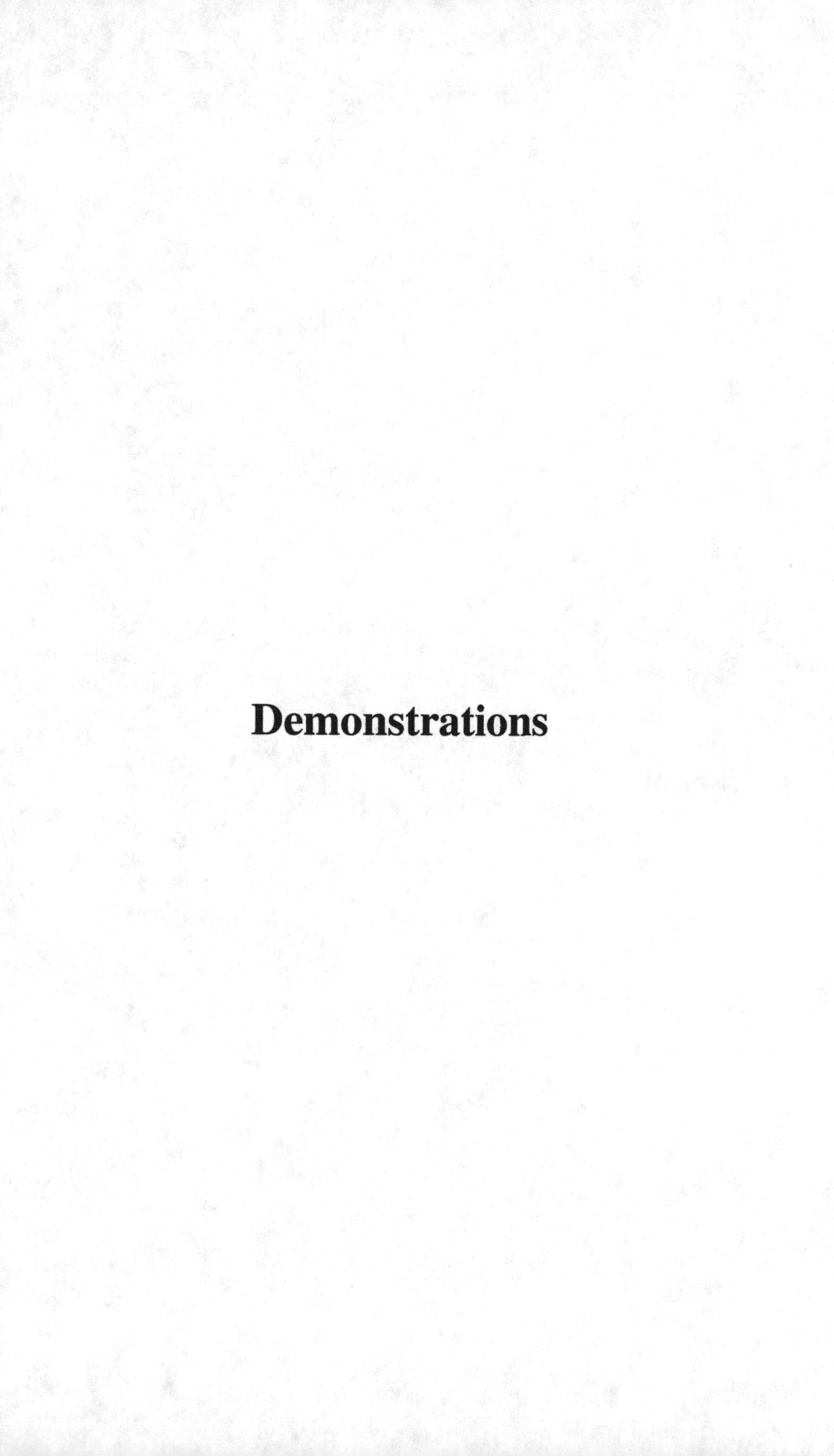

Demonstrations

Designing and Developing Context-Aware Mobile Mashups: The CAMUS Approach

Fabio Corvetta, Maristella Matera(✉), Riccardo Medana, Elisa Quintarelli, Vincenzo Rizzo, and Letizia Tanca

Dipartimento di Elettronica, Informazione e Bioingegneria,
Politecnico di Milano, Milan, Italy
{fabio.corvetta,vincenzo.rizzo}@mail.polimi.it,
{maristella.matera,elisa.quintarelli,letizia.tanca}@polimi.it,
r.medana@gmail.com

Abstract. CAMUS (Context-Aware Mobile mashUpS) is a framework for the design of mobile applications that dynamically collect and integrate heterogeneous resources (data sources and services) to offer integrated content and functions to mobile users in a context-aware fashion. CAMUS exploits a set of high-level abstractions for context and mashup modeling that hide the complexity resulting from service selection, invocation and integration. Generative techniques then enable the transformation of models into running code for mobile applications that flexibly respond to actual user needs as they vary in different situations of use.

Keywords: Mobile mashups · Context modeling · Context-aware mobile applications · End-user development

1 Introduction

Given the plethora of data and services today available online, it is often difficult to find on-the-fly the information or the applications that are appropriate to the current context of use [2]. This is even more true in the mobile scenario, where device resources (memory, computational power, transmission budget) are still limited. Given this evidence, our research focuses on the definition of methods and tools for the design and development of Context-Aware Mobile mashUpS (CAMUS). CAMUS apps dynamically collect and integrate data from documental, social and Web resources (accessed by means of Web APIs) and adapt the integrated content to the users' situational needs. They can offer multiple advantages thanks to their intrinsic capability of identifying pertinent data sources, selected on the basis of their adequateness with respect to the current users' needs, and pervasively presenting them to the final user in form of integrated visualizations deployed as mobile apps. This application paradigm overcomes the limits posed by pre-packaged apps and offers to users flexible and personalized applications whose structure and content may even emerge at runtime based on the actual user needs and situation of use.

P. Cimiano et al. (Eds.): ICWE 2015, LNCS 9114, pp. 651–654, 2015.
DOI: 10.1007/978-3-319-19890-3_49

The CAMUS framework does not only propose a new application paradigm; rather, as described in the following section, it paves the way to novel design methodologies and related tools for fast prototyping of mobile mashups, where context becomes a first-class modeling dimension improving *i)* the identification of the most adequate resources that can satisfy the users'information needs and *ii)* the consequent tailoring at runtime of the provided data and functions.

2 The CAMUS Framework

The CAMUS framework is characterized by design environments that, in line with recent approaches to visual programming of mashups, make intensive use of high-level visual abstractions [1]. Visual paradigms hide the complexity that is typical of service composition, data integration and mobile application programming, and assist CAMUS designers (even if non-experts in service composition) in the creation of personalized applications that can be run on multiple devices without the need of mastering different technologies. All the aspects that characterize the different contextual situations, i.e., the *dimensions* contributing to context, are modelled orthogonally with respect to the other instantaneous system inputs by means of the so-called *Context Dimension Model* [3,4], which provides the constructs to define at design-time the Universal Context Dimension Tree (*Universal CDT*), i.e., the set of possible contexts of use for a given domain of interest, expressed as a hierarchical structure consisting of *i)* context dimensions (black nodes), modeling the context variables, i.e., the different perspectives through which the user perceives the application domain (e.g., time, place, current company, interest topic), and *ii)* the allowed dimension values (white nodes), i.e., the variable values used to tailor the context-aware information (e.g., "evening", "New York", "with friends", "music"). Any subtree of the CDT with at most a value for each dimension represents a possible user context; variable values, detected at runtime through device sensors, then activate a given context. The adoption of a hierarchical structure allows us to employ different abstraction levels to specify and represent contexts.

Figure 1 represents the general organization of the CAMUS framework; it highlights its main architectural components and the flow of the different artifacts that enable the transition from high-level modeling notations to running code. The framework supports the activities of three main *personae*.

The *CAMUS administrator* is in charge of registering distributed resources (remote APIs or in-house services) into the platform, by creating descriptions of how the resources can be invoked and wrappers ensuring homogeneity of data formats. S/he also specifies the Universal CDT and the *mapping* between the identified context elements and some pertinent services among those previously registered. This mapping expresses the capability of services to return data and functions of interest with respect to the specified contexts. In other words, the Universal CDT expresses for each given context a virtual image of the relevant portion of the available resources.

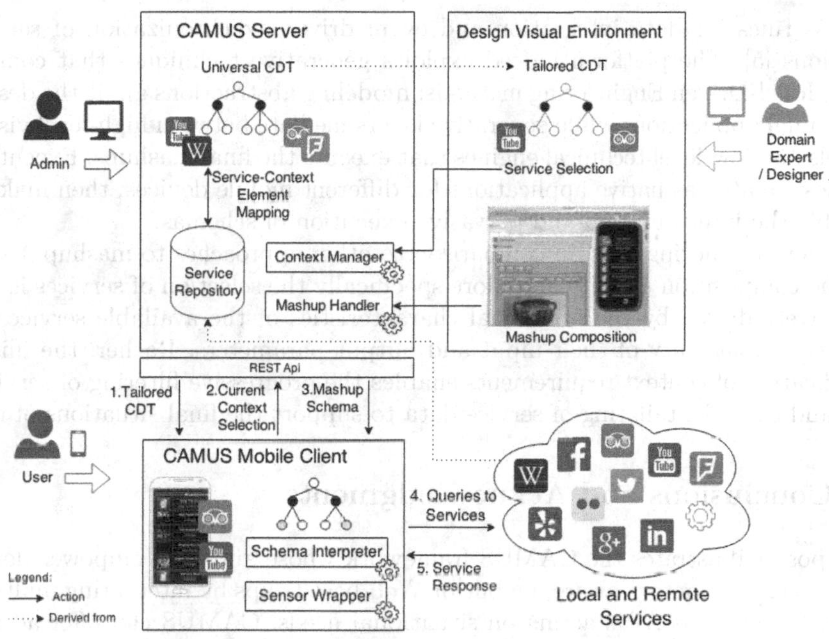

Fig. 1. Architecture of the CAMUS framework

The *CAMUS (MashUp) designer* starts from the image on the available resources represented by the universal CDT and, using a *Design Visual Environment*, defines the *Tailored CDT* by further refining the selection of possible contexts based on the needs and preferences of specific users or users' groups. The designer also defines how to mash up the identified services, i.e., how to integrate their result sets and synchronize their functions, and how to visualize the resulting information through unified views deployed as mobile apps. The result of this activity is an an XML-based *mashup schema*, automatically generated by the design environment based on a Domain Specific Language [5], which includes rules that at runtime guide the execution of the resulting app.

The *CAMUS (app) users* are the final recipients of the mobile app that offers a different bouquet of content and functions in each different situation of use. When the app is executed, the context parameter values that characterize the current situation, identified by means of a client-side *Sensor Wrapper*, are communicated to a server-side *Context Manager*. Based on the tailored CDT, this module computes the context-dependent parameters to instantiate queries to and invoke functions from the integrated services. The mashup schema created by the designer is interpreted locally (by means of a *schema interpreter*) to send parametric requests to the involved services and populate with the returned data the integrated views provided by the mobile app.

A dedicated module of the design environment, the *Mashup Handler*, translates the designers' visual composition actions into XML-based schemas that express rules for data integration and event-driven synchronization of service functions [5]. The platform indeed exploits generative techniques that comply with Model-Driven Engineering methods: modeling abstractions guide the design of the final applications while generative layers mediate between high-level visual models and low-level technical engines that execute the final mashups. Execution engines, created as native applications for different mobile devices, then make it possible the interpretation and pervasive execution of schemas.

It is worth noting that, in comparison to other approaches to mashup design [6], the composition activity and more specifically the selection of services is not exclusively driven by the functional characteristics of the available services or by the compatibility of their input and output parameters. Rather, the initial specification of context requirements enables the progressive filtering of services first and then the tailoring of service data to support the final situations of use.

3 Conclusions and Acknowledgments

This poster illustrates the CAMUS framework whose aim is to empower developers to create context-aware, mobile or Web-based apps by integrating multiple and heterogeneous APIs acting on situational needs. CAMUS can offer advantages in several application domains, as for instance tourism and enterprise, two domains for which our previous work already highlighted the need of methods and tools for the creation of flexible, situational applications [5]. Our current work is devoted to refining the implementation of the platform, and in particular to improve the integration of a visual mashup environment [5] with the CAMUS back-end. We thank the large group of students of Politecnico di Milano who enthusiastically contributed to the design and implementation of the first CAMUS prototype through which we assessed the feasibility of revising mashup composition practices through the introduction of context modeling concepts.

References

1. Ardito, C., Costabile, M.F., Desolda, G., Lanzilotti, R., Matera, M., Piccinno, A., Picozzi, M.: User-driven visual composition of service-based interactive spaces. J. Vis. Lang. Comput. **25**(4), 278–296 (2014)
2. Bianchini, D., Castano, S., De Antonellis, V., Ferrara, A., Quintarelli, E., Tanca, L.: RUBIK: Proactive, Entity-Centric and Personalized Situational Web Application Design. T. Large-Scale Data-and Knowledge-Cent. Syst. **13**, 123–157 (2014)
3. Bolchini, C., Curino, C., Orsi, G., Quintarelli, E., Rossato, R., Schreiber, F.A., Tanca, L.: And what can context do for data? CACM **52**(11), 136–140 (2009)
4. Bolchini, C., Orsi, G., Quintarelli, E., Schreiber, F.A., Tanca, L.: Context modeling and context awareness: steps forward in the context-addict project. IEEE Data Eng. Bull. **34**(2), 47–54 (2011)
5. Cappiello, C., Matera, M., Picozzi, M.: A UI-centric approach for the End-User Development of multi-device mashups. ACM Trans. on Web (to appear, 2015)
6. Daniel, F., Matera, M.: Mashups - Concepts, Models and Architectures. Data-Centric Systems and Applications. Springer (2014)

Release Adolescent Stress by Virtual Chatting

Jing Huang(✉), Qi Li, Yuanyuan Xue, Taoran Cheng, Shuangqing Xu, Jia Jia, and Ling Feng

Department of Computer Science and Technology, Tsinghua University, Beijing, China
{j-huang14,liqi13,xue-yy12,ctr10,xsq10}@mails.tsinghua.edu.cn
{jjia,fengling}@mails.tsinghua.edu.cn

Abstract. Many teenagers today live with stress. Due to their spiritual immaturity, teenagers cannot properly cope with stress, which probably brings such bad consequences as depression and even suicide. Hence, it is important to help teenagers timely resolve their stress. Many times, teenagers hesitate to express and reveal their negative emotion to the people nearby. In this paper, we present the design and implementation of a web-based virtual chatting tool, which can listen to, comfort, encourage the stressed teenagers and give useful solutions for their problems through chatting and thus releasing their stress. The tool also integrates social media micro-blog not only to support stress detection but also to provide useful resources for stress release.

Keywords: Adolescent · Virtual chatting · Stress · Release · Micro-blog

1 Introduction

Nowadays, people of various age groups are experiencing stress. Especially for the youth group, whose outlook on life and problem-solving ability are still immature, too much stress is easy to turn into severe consequences such as depression or even suicide. Parents, teachers and psychologists cannot offer help when teenagers refuse to express their stress to the people nearby, but rather turn to the virtual world for stress release. Hence, researchers try to help release teenagers' stress based on the virtual platform. Recently, the work in [3] proposed a chatting robot PAL, which could answer non-obstructive psychological domain-specific questions. It acts more like a Question&Answering (Q&A) system to match users' psychological questions from the numerous collected Q&A pairs and then selects suitable answers. However, only answering psychological questions offers limited help, for the stressed teenagers would pour forth their woes sentence by sentence instead of only asking questions and the comfort and encouragement for their experiences play a vital role in releasing their stress.

In this paper, we build a virtual chatting tool to communicate with teenagers like a virtual friend, comforting and encouraging teenagers to make them feel listened and understood, or a mentor, providing some useful solutions for their problems as well as guiding them to speak out what they can't say in real life

P. Cimiano et al. (Eds.): ICWE 2015, LNCS 9114, pp. 655–658, 2015.
DOI: 10.1007/978-3-319-19890-3_50

for cathartic stress relief. The tool extends our previous work [2] by integrating micro-blog for comprehensively learning the user's stress. Statistics show that 53% of 600 million registered micro-blog users are teenagers born after 1990, and every day produce over 200 million micro-blogs, of which main usage are self-expression [4]. Hence, by integrating users' micro-blog, the tool can be supplied much sentiment information to make some guesses and tentative inquiries about users' stress when the chatting sentences only offer incomplete information.

2 System Framework

Fig. 1 shows the tool framework. Its server consists of three components:

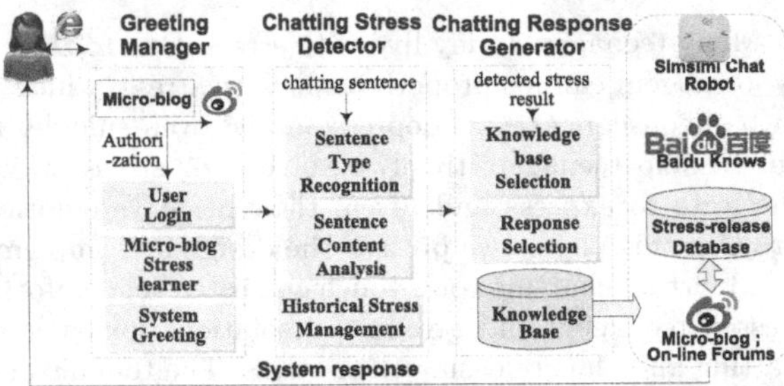

Fig. 1. Framework

- **Greeting Manager.** When a user logs into our tool, s/he can choose to use the micro-blog account to login or entry the chatting page directly. Fig. 2 shows the login interface of the tool. If the user authorizes us to access his/her micro-blog, *Micro-blog stress learner* module uses the method in [6] to learn his/her stress status based on the emoticons, punctuation marks, tweeting time, tweeting type as well as the text of recent tweets. Meanwhile, *System Greeting* module correspondingly adjusts the greeting sentence according to the detected result for better effect of stress release.
- **Chatting Stress Detector.** For a user's input sentence, *Sentence Type Recognition* module categorizes it into three different categories (interrogative question, rhetorical question or declarative sentence) for understanding user's expected answer. *Sentence Content Analysis* module detects user's stress status in the form of `(Stress, Category, SubCategory)` based on the established seven adolescent's stress-related lexicons. This module picks out the stress-related emotion and degree words to sense the user's stress level, namely denoting `Stress` ranged from 5 to 0. Then we use the LTP tool [1], a Chinese language processing tool for word segmentation and dependency analysis, to build a linguistic dependency tree of the sentence. The stress category/sub-category word, which has the the shortest path to the negative emotion word, is selected as the primary stress category/sub-category. Besides, the detected result is adjusted according to the historic detected results from the previous sentences or micro-blog, which is managed by the *Historical Stress Management* module.

Fig. 2. Login Interface

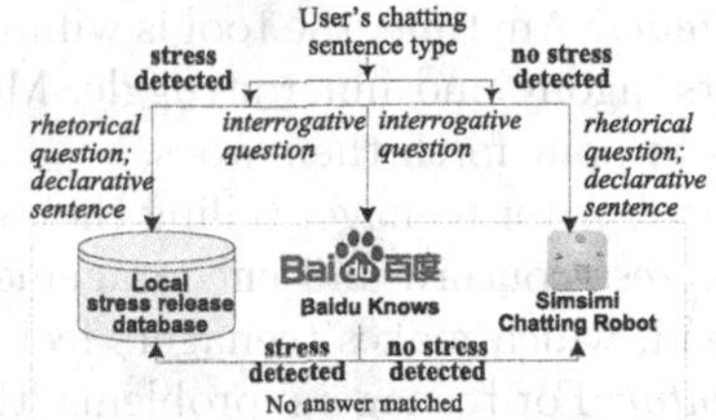

Fig. 3. Knowledge Base Selection Strategies

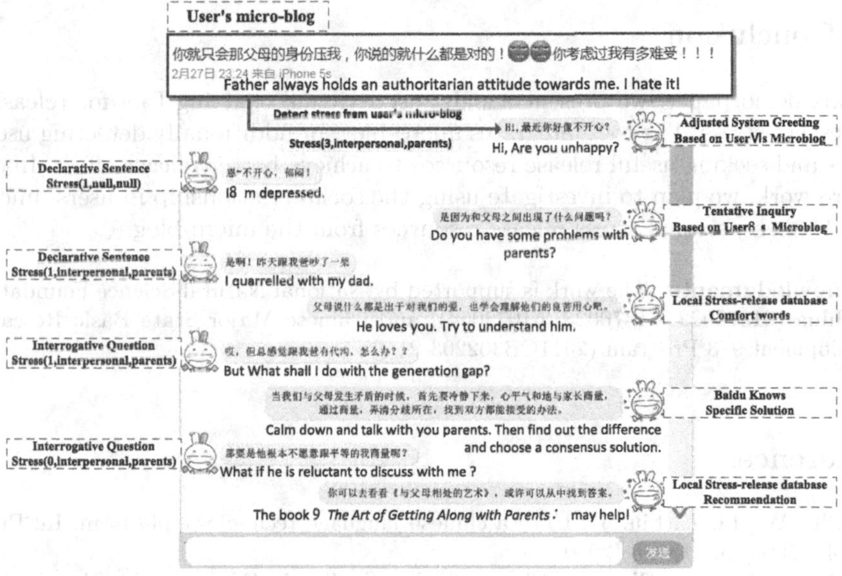

Fig. 4. A Chatting Example

– **Chatting Response Generator.** The knowledge base of the tool is comprised of three parts: local stress-release database, Chinese Q&A community Baidu Knows,which has six main topics about psychological questions and Simsimi [5],which provide public API for developers to establish their own chatting tool. According to different chatting sentence type and whether a user has stress, *Knowledge Base Selection* module chooses different knowledge base to get response. Fig. 3 shows the knowledge base selection strategies. According to the specific detected stress result, *Response Selection* module further chooses suitable responses from the corresponding knowledge base.

3 System Implementation

Fig. 4 shows a chatting example of our 10-participants user study. As it shows, the tool release teenagers' stress by acting the following roles:

A Listener: Anytime, the tool is willing and patient to listen to the teenagers' complaints, agony and inner struggle. Meanwhile, the tool can gradually guide teenagers to pour forth their woes.

A Friend: After teenager telling their stress, the tool says some words of comfort to express concern and encouragement to cheer up the depressed teenager like a friend, which makes teenagers feel understood and emboldened.

A Mentor: For teenagers' problems, the tool provides some specific solutions to help them get out of the trouble. Besides, the tool also recommends some helpful materials such as some related books and websites for their problems.

4 Conclusion

In this demo paper, we present a web-based virtual chatting tool for releasing adolescent stress. The tool integrates micro-blog for additionally detecting user's stress and seeking useful release resources to achieve better release effect. In our future work, we plan to investigate using the social relationship in users' micro-blog to seek personal stress release resources from the micro-blog.

Acknowledgments. The work is supported by National Natural Science Foundation of China (61373022, 61370023, 61073004), and Chinese Major State Basic Research Development 973 Program (2011CB302203-2).

References

1. Che, W., Li, Z., Liu, T.: LTP: a chinese language technology platform. In: Proc. of Coling, pp. 13–16 (2010)
2. Huang, J., Li, Q., Xue, Y., Cheng, T., Xu, S., Jia, J., Feng, L.: *Teenchat*: a chatterbot system for sensing and releasing adolescents' stress. In: Yin, X., Ho, K., Zeng, D., Aickelin, U., Zhou, R., Wang, H. (eds.) HIS 2015. LNCS, vol. 9085, pp. 133–145. Springer, Heidelberg (2015)
3. Liu, Y., Liu, M., Wang, X., Wang, L., Li, J.: Pal: a chatterbot system for answering domain-specific questions. In: Proc. of ACL, pp. 67–72. Citeseer (2013)
4. M. U. D. R. of Sina Microblog. http://data.weibo.com/report/reportdetail?id=76
5. SIMSIMI. Simsimi (2009). http://www.simsimi.com/
6. Xue, Y., Li, Q., Jin, L., Feng, L., Clifton, D.A., Clifford, G.D.: Detecting adolescent psychological pressures from micro-blog. In: Zhang, Y., Yao, G., He, J., Wang, L., Smalheiser, N.R., Yin, X. (eds.) HIS 2014. LNCS, vol. 8423, pp. 83–94. Springer, Heidelberg (2014)

Conflict Resolution in Collaborative User Interface Mashups

Michael Hertel, Alexey Tschudnowsky(✉), and Martin Gaedke

Technische Universität Chemnitz, Chemnitz, Germany
{Michael.Hertel,Alexey.Tschudnowsky,
Martin.Gaedke}@informatik.tu-chemnitz.de

Abstract. User Interface (UI) Mashups propose methods and techniques, which should enable non-programmers to develop their own widget-based solutions. At the moment the process of configuring UI mashups is mainly a single-user activity. Adding support for real-time collaboration to the composition tools could make the development process more "social" and, thus, further lower the entry barrier and make users more productive. The paper describes challenges and possible solutions to enable real-time collaboration in UI mashups with particular focus on resolution of conflicts, which can occur as a result of concurrent modifications. Implementation of the proposed mechanisms is demonstrated in the context of an open-source mashup platform Apache Rave.

Keywords: User interface mashups · Real-time collaboration · Operational transformation · Conflict resolution

1 Introduction

A UI mashup is a Web application, which is developed by the composition of components called widgets, which hide complexity of underlying technologies behind graphical user interfaces [8]. Interactions between widgets usually takes place over configurable connectors or emerge in a self-organized fashion based on capabilities of widgets. By developing UI mashups non-technical users should be enabled to solve situational problems faster and more efficiently [1].

Currently the majority of UI mashup composition tools are single-user applications. Enabling a collaborative use could yield added value to the platforms due to knowledge exchange, synergy effects and faster composition process [3]. However, building Web applications with real-time collaboration capabilities is a challenging task and requires a careful design of synchronization algorithms and conflict resolution mechanisms [2].

This paper describes an approach to integrate real-time collaboration capabilities to UI mashup development platforms. We demonstrate, how Operational Transformation (OT) algorithm [7] can be applied to maintain consistency of mashup models. The approach is implemented as an extension to Apache Rave[1], a publish-subscribe-based UI mashup platform.

[1] http://rave.apache.org/

P. Cimiano et al. (Eds.): ICWE 2015, LNCS 9114, pp. 659–662, 2015.
DOI: 10.1007/978-3-319-19890-3_51

2 Conflict Resolution Using OT

Conflicts emerge from concurrent actions that do not satisfy the consistency model as defined in [5]. OT as a concurrency control mechanism is well suited and increasingly applied for preserving consistency in real-time collaboration applications. OT consists of a generic control algorithm, a data model specific to a concrete application, operations and transformation functions. The fundamental concept of OT is the modification of conflicting operations by transforming them against all previously applied concurrent operations so that they eventually satisfy the consistency model.

2.1 Data Model

In the following we consider publish-subscribe-based UI mashups with user-defined communication restrictions as proposed in [6]. The following OT-specific data model is used. A mashup is a list of so called areas, which are lists of widgets. Widgets can not be placed freely on the workspace, but rather allocated to areas or re-ordered within them. Each widget has a set of properties, a view mode and a configuration of its inter-widget communication (IWC) behavior. Properties are unordered key-value pairs. Viewmode is a method of widget rendering: "normal", "minimized" or "maximized". IWC configuration is a set of restrictions, which describe, which receivers and which topics are forbidden to be used for message publications.

2.2 Operations

Each defined operation has to affect the OT data model for enabling consistency maintenance with OT. The concept of site identifiers is used for situations where a global unique decision is required, i.e., the same data was modified concurrently. Every operation transmits the unique identifier of its origin instance as the last parameter *sid*. It allows a global definite decision without a dedicated server. The following OT operations are defined for the synchronization of the mashup structure:

- *AddWidget*(*id*, *area*, *pos*, *width*, *height*, *viewmode*, *properties*, *iwcsettings*, *sid*) adds a new widget to the mashup into the *area* at the position *pos*.
- *MoveWidget*(*id*, *areaOld*, *posOld*, *areaNew*, *posNew*, *sid*) moves the widget to the given area *areaNew* at the position *posNew*.
- *RemoveWidget*(*id*, *area*, *pos*, *sid*) removes a component from the mashup.
- *ChangeViewmode*(*id*, *viewmode*, *sid*) sets the display mode of the widget with the identifier *id* to the given *viewmode*.
- *ReplaceWidgetProperty*(*id*, *key*, *value*, *sid*) replaces the current value of the property with the *key* for the component identified by the *id* with *value*.
- *ChangeConnectionSetting*(*publisherid*, *subscriberid*, *topic*, *state*, *sid*) specifies the rule provided by *state* that should be applied to the connection between the defined publisher and subscriber for the given *topic*.

2.3 Transformation Functions

The structural formula for each transformation T is $O'_a = T(O_a, O_b)$, which means that the operation O_a is transformed against the operation O_b and results in the transformed operation O'_a. To meet the convergence property with OT two transformation (or convergence) properties (TP) have been identified in [4]. Dedicated transformation functions have been developed for above operations, which satisfy TP1. It is assumed that the control algorithm can preserve TP2 because this embodies a common approach [7]. To validate the preservation of TP1 $Z_1 = Z_2$ must hold for all operations O_a and O_b and any initial state Z if $Z_1 = Z \circ O_a \circ T(O_b, O_a)$ and $Z_2 = Z \circ O_b \circ T(O_a, O_b)$. The composition operator $\circ$ represents the application of an operation O to the state Z resulting in the new state Z' including the impact of O in the context of $Z' = Z \circ O$. Due to the vast amount of possible constellations arising from the combination of all operations combined with every parameter proportion the verification of TP1 was automated with the help of VOTE[2].

3 Implementation

Apache Rave has been extended to support real-time collaboration and conflict resolution. We extended its mashup sharing functionality, which enabled to share configurations among platform users. However, further modifications to the shared mashup configuration were not synchronized in "real-time" and no conflict resolution was performed. We used the ShareJS[3] OT library for real-time mashup model synchronization and consistency preservation. Figure 1 shows

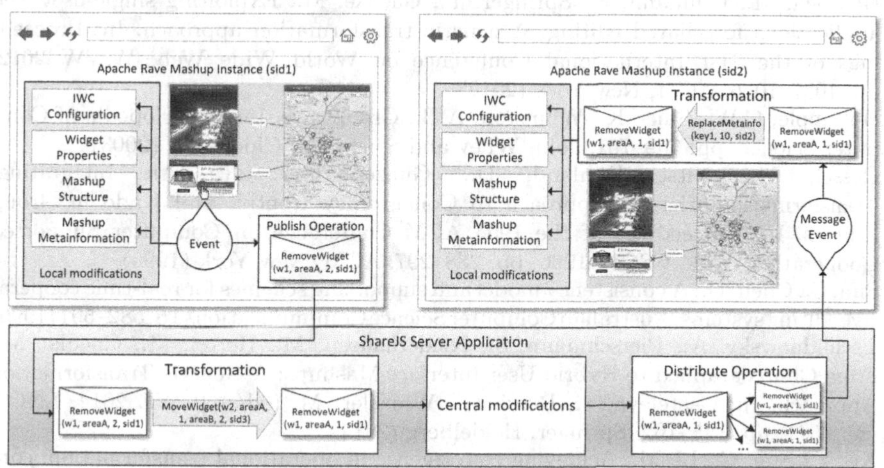

Fig. 1. Application of OT to collaborative UI mashups

[2] http://www-sop.inria.fr/coprin/urso/logiciels/
[3] http://sharejs.org/

the general process of the OT-based synchronization. Once an event initiates a local modification, a dedicated OT operation is issued to the ShareJS server. The server performs necessary transformations against all concurrent operations received previously. After that it applies the resulting operation to the global mashup configuration maintained by the server and propagates the operation to other collaborators. The receiving clients eventually transform this operation against not yet propagated local ones and apply the result.

Demonstration: An online demo of the approach can be found at https://vsr.informatik.tu-chemnitz.de/demos/conflict-resolution-ui-mashups.

4 Conclusions and Outlook

This paper demonstrated an approach to enable conflict resolution in collaborative UI mashups. Consistency preservation mechanisms based on OT were applied to publish-subscribe-based UI mashups.

Future research will focus on application of these mechanisms to other types of UI mashups. Another subject that is not yet considered are security concerns and rights management. Finally, support of OT undo functionality could further improve usability of mashups with real-time collaboration capabilities.

References

1. Cappiello, C., Daniel, F., Matera, M., Picozzi, M., Weiss, M.: Enabling End User Development through Mashups: Requirements, Abstractions and Innovation Toolkits. In: Piccinno, A. (ed.) IS-EUD 2011. LNCS, vol. 6654, pp. 9–24. Springer, Heidelberg (2011)
2. Heinrich, M., Lehmann, F., Springer, T., Gaedke, M.: Exploiting single-user web applications for shared editing: A generic transformation approach. In: Proceedings of the 21st International Conference on World Wide Web, WWW 2012, pp. 1057–1066. ACM, New York (2012)
3. Holsapple, C.W., Sims, K., Whinston, A.B.: Groupware. In: Encyclopedia of Computer Science, pp. 759–761. John Wiley and Sons Ltd., Chichester (2003)
4. Ressel, M., Nitsche-Ruhland, D., Gunzenhäuser, R.: An Integrating, Transformation-oriented Approach to Concurrency Control and Undo in Group Editors. In: Proceedings of the 1996 ACM Conference on Computer Supported Cooperative Work, CSCW 1996, pp. 288–297. ACM, New York (1996)
5. Sun, C., Chen, D.: A consistency model and supporting schemes for real-time cooperative editing systems. Australian Computer Science Communications **18**, 582–591 (1996)
6. Tschudnowsky, A., Pietschmann, S., Niederhausen, M., Hertel, M., Gaedke, M.: From Choreographed to Hybrid User Interface Mashups: A Generic Transformation Approach. In: Casteleyn, S., Rossi, G., Winckler, M. (eds.) ICWE 2014. LNCS, vol. 8541, pp. 145–162. Springer, Heidelberg (2014)
7. Xu, Y., Sun, C., Li, M.: Achieving convergence in operational transformation: conditions, mechanisms and systems. In: Proceedings of the 17th ACM Conference on Computer Supported Cooperative Work & Social Computing, CSCW 2014, pp. 505–518. ACM, New York (2014)
8. Yu, J., Benatallah, B., Casati, F., Daniel, F.: Understanding mashup development. IEEE Internet Computing **12**(5), 44–52 (2008)

Supporting the Development of Team-Climate-Aware Collaborative Web Applications

Sebastian Heil(✉), Marco Drechsel, and Martin Gaedke

Technische Universität Chemnitz, Chemnitz, Germany
{sebastian.heil,marco.drechsel,martin.gaedke}@informatik.tu-chemnitz.de

Abstract. Collaborative web applications are widely used in enterprises to support work in virtual teams. Here, monitoring mood is essential for team managers to intervene and restore optimal working conditions to ensure work success. To retrieve mood information from natural language communication, sentiment analysis techniques are necessary. This, however, requires expertise and is time-consuming if done individually for each web application. In this paper, we present TCAS which supports developers of collaborative web applications to leverage sentiment analysis for team climate assessment.

Keywords: Team climate assessment · Sentiment analysis · Collaboration

1 Introduction

Collaborative web applications for project, case or content management and enterprise social networks like Jive, Yammer and Salesforce Chatter are used in enterprises to support work in virtual teams. These teams are locally and temporally decoupled and formed to accomplish a common objective. Employees can work on a multiplicity of work items in different virtual teams. This leads to team managers having to oversee many different teams with distributed members.

Here, monitoring team climate is an important challenge as team climate, individual mood and job satisfaction are associated with each other. In this context, team climate is a combination of a team's level of activity and its sentiment state.

Team sentiment – the mood of the whole team, as expressed and perceived between team members – and the mood of the individual member are interlinked. [4] An employee's mood is an indicator of job satisfaction. [3] The team climate is an important factor for companies' productivity [4] and reputation and influences staff fluctuation. [8] In agile teams, happiness at work is even stated as essential for an organization's success and fostering creativity [7]. Monitoring team climate is therefore essential for team managers to intervene to avoid crises, restore optimal working conditions and ensure work success.

Manual observation of team climate is hardly feasible due to high team count, distributed members and high amount of text-based communication. To automatically retrieve mood information from natural language communication,

P. Cimiano et al. (Eds.): ICWE 2015, LNCS 9114, pp. 663–666, 2015.
DOI: 10.1007/978-3-319-19890-3_52

sentiment analysis techniques are necessary. Their application requires expertise applying suitable algorithms, determining parameters, combining results etc. Developing this functionality individually for each web application is time-consuming. Therefore, we propose a framework which supports developers of collaborative web applications to leverage sentiment analysis for team climate assessment. Section 2 introduces the Team Climate Assessment Service (TCAS), Section 3 discusses related work and Section 4 concludes the paper.

2 TCAS: Team Climate Assessment Service

Virtual teams are organized in different ways, e.g. in projects, cases, streams. They provide different types of information for team climate assessment, in particular communication and events. Communication is represented by messages between team members. Events, e.g. completion of a work task, occur at a certain point in time. Messages can be considered a specific event. We use JSON Activity Streams[1] as common format. Existing communication and events data can easily be mapped to this web standard format or is already available as activity streams.

For this demonstration, we describe TCAS applied to the project management domain as shown in Figure 1. 1) The project management system represents its projects as Activity Streams and invokes the TCAS. 2) Two components process the input: The activity analyzer utilizes event timestamps to determine the level of activity in the project. The mood analyzer applies sentiment analysis techniques to retrieve mood information from messages. 3) Results are mapped to the state model. It has two dimensions: activity (inactive, low, high) and mood (negative, neutral, positive). 4) A filtered list of relevant projects is returned to the project management system. By default, all states with negative mood indication or inactive activity are considered relevant. Figure 2 shows highlighting of theses critical instances in the VSRCM[2] case management system.

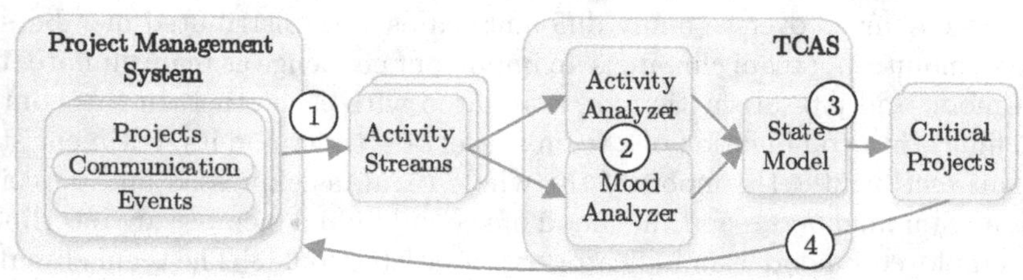

Fig. 1. Project Management Example of using TCAS

This allows team managers to intervene where either mood is poor or possible stagnation occurs. TCAS is customizable by developers. They can define

[1] http://tools.ietf.org/html/draft-snell-activitystreams
[2] https://vsr.informatik.tu-chemnitz.de/demos/vsrcm

Fig. 2. Critical cases highlighting using TCAS in VSRCM

thresholds for the state model dimensions and states considered relevant for filtering. The state model allows for easy extension: additional (e.g. domain-specific) analyzers can be added and incorporated as dimensions.

TCAS is implemented in C# as web service with REST API. Analyzers are run in parallel. The default mood analyzer filters activity streams for communication items using verbs post or create with object types note or message. The object's content value is the message text. Activity Streams allow arbitrary encoding of messages. Hence the filter is configurable, defaults as described above.

The analysis step is implemented as MapReduce algorithm. The map function applies sentiment analysis to each activity, the reduce function combines results taking into account the message age. More recent messages have a greater impact. To conduct sentiment analysis, different algorithms can be used as plugins. As a default, the Free Natural Language Processing Service[3] is used.

With TCAS focusing on reuse, developers of various types of collaborative web applications can leverage team climate assessment in their domain. Integration is addressed by employing JSON Activity Streams as common input format. For extensibility, parallel filters and the state model abstraction is provided.

Demonstration: For a screencast and further information, please visit https://vsr.informatik.tu-chemnitz.de/demos/vsrcm.

3 Related Work

Different services are available to extract sentiment information from natural language data like AlchemyAPI[4]. These services support development of sentiment-aware applications. In contrast, our approach allows to incorporate additional factors like team activity in order to evaluate the state of a virtual team: its team climate.

Sentiment analysis is also present in end user development. DashMash is a Web platform allowing end users to compose their analyses. [1] Our approach intends to support developers of arbitrary collaborative web applications.

Approaches like [6] use sentiment analysis to target market research by identifying the mood about products and brands expressed in the web. Others, like [5],

[3] http://www.mashape.com/loudelement/free-natural-language-processing-service
[4] http://www.alchemyapi.com/

enhance web search through sentiment information in order to improve users' access to the web. These approaches extract a crowd's sentiment about a given entity, while we evaluate general sentiment, i.e. mood, and level of activity of a given group.

Other approaches target communities or nations as a whole: [2] analyses tweets to obtain happiness values of the Twitter community. It constitutes the basis of a web service that correlates Twitter happiness with events.

Self-tracking systems provide measurement of team level happiness. They require employees to assess their happiness themselves. [7] So far an automated approach on team level is lacking, especially for team climate assessment.

4 Conclusion

In this paper we motivated team climate assessment for collaborative web applications. While specific applications of sentiment analysis exist in related work, we propose a development framework implemented as web service. To support developers, activity streams are used as common input format, a configurable set of analyzers is applied and the result is mapped into an extensible state model. We demonstrated the application of TCAS in a project management system.

In future work, feedback mechanisms need to be investigated. This way, the team climate assessment can be improved by learning and adaption to specific environments. In addition to activity levels, we plan to incorporate the dynamics of activity (e.g. increasing, decreasing, constant) in the state model. While this demonstration features a batch-processing model, continuous stream processing for reactive team climate detection requires further investigation.

References

1. Cappiello, C., Matera, M., Picozzi, M., Sprega, G., Barbagallo, D., Francalanci, C.: DashMash: A Mashup Environment for End User Development. In: Auer, S., Díaz, O., Papadopoulos, G.A. (eds.) ICWE 2011. LNCS, vol. 6757, pp. 152–166. Springer, Heidelberg (2011)
2. Dodds, P.S., et al.: Temporal patterns of happiness and information in a global social network: Hedonometrics and twitter. PLoS One 6(12) (12 2011)
3. Fisher, C.D.: Mood and emotions while working: missing pieces of job satisfaction? Journal of Organizational Behavior **21**(2), 185–202 (2000)
4. Kelly, J., Barsade, S.: Mood and Emotions in Small Groups and Work Teams. Organizational Behavior and Human Decision Processes **86**(1), 99–130 (2001)
5. Malinský, R., Jelínek, I.: Improvements of Webometrics by Using Sentiment Analysis for Better Accessibility of the Web. In: Daniel, F., Facca, F.M. (eds.) ICWE 2010. LNCS, vol. 6385, pp. 581–586. Springer, Heidelberg (2010)
6. Morinaga, S., et al.: Mining product reputations on the web. In: Proceedings of the Eighth ACM SIGKDD International Conference on Knowledge Discovery and Data Mining, KDD 2002, pp. 341–349. ACM, New York (2002)
7. Schiffer, B.: Agile Management Innovations: A Primer. Agile Product & Project Management 14(1) (2013)
8. Smith, F.J., Kerr, W.A.: Turnover factors as assessed by the exit interview. Journal of Applied Psychology **37**(5), 352–355 (1953)

Leveraging Social Data for Health Care Behavior Analytics

Xiang Ji[1], Paolo Cappellari[2(✉)], Soon Ae Chun[2], and James Geller[1]

[1] New Jersey Institute of Technology, Newark, NJ, USA
{xj25,james.geller}@njit.edu

[2] City University of New York, New York, NY, USA
{paolo.cappellari,soon.chun}@csi.cuny.edu

Abstract. User-generated social health data can provide valuable insights into the health care behavior and practices of patients for clinicians, policy makers and other patients. Social InfoButtons is a tool for integrating and analyzing social health data, using a semantic data integration framework that is flexible and extensible with respect to a variety of health data sources. The integration overlay provides a framework that semantically links data enabling cross dataset exploration and analysis. The unified data model for both scientific and social sources allows multi-dimensional analysis and the ability to explore and compare the expert knowledge with the actual health care practices of patients.

Keywords: Social health analytics · Data integration · Linked data

1 Introduction

We demonstrate Social InfoButtons a tool to semantically integrate and analyze health information from disparate data sources. Via a semantic overlay, the tool allows to correlate data from multiple, heterogeneous sources, thus enabling cross-dataset analytics. The goal is to enable end-users (i.e. patients, health practitioners, and organizations) to access and analyze social trends in health information in contrast to data provided by official and research sources.

The tool demonstrates the results illustrated in a recent paper [3]. Let us briefly provide background information and recall the main points. Nowadays, there are many different sources providing health data. The spectrum of information sources varies from the open data initiatives, to scientific resources, to social networks, including [4–6] to mention a few. With the number of health data sources growing, there is a need for unifying all health information into a unified health knowledge base, where the authoritative expert knowledge is complemented with the crowd wisdom from the social media. The main challenges are: (i) creating the knowledge base that has to integrate data in various formats, from highly structured to unstructured; and (ii) providing a simple way of accessing and analyzing the integrated information. The first challenge is addressed by semantically linking data from multiple sources via Semantic Web technology: core data required to run the analytics are extracted from all the

P. Cimiano et al. (Eds.): ICWE 2015, LNCS 9114, pp. 667–670, 2015.
DOI: 10.1007/978-3-319-19890-3_53

available sources and reconciled in a unified health data model stored in RDF format. To identify terms from different datasets that refer to the same concept, the Unified Medical Language System (UMLS) [1] is used. The UMLS provides a comprehensive vocabulary including multiple medical terms that refer to the same concepts. Together, the integration model and the UMLS-based reference ontology create a semantic overlay that enable cross-dataset exploration and analysis. The second challenge is addressed by providing analytics, presented in the demonstration, to answer health information questions, as highlighted in the study of Cimino et al. [2], however, in their case, for MDs.

In the demonstration we will show how users can: (i) easily access the unified knowledge base; (ii) explore and analyze health data via contextual analytics including keyword search, word clouds, trends, maps (and more) revolving around medical concepts such as condition, treatment, and symptoms; (iii) compare data from authoritative sources with social media data. In contrast to other research, Social InfoButtons can provide answers by relying on a comprehensive health knowledge base that includes both official and social data.

2 Demonstration

Social InfoButtons has a multi-tier architecture that reflects the overall approach described in Sec. 1. The main components are: data extraction and reconciliation, data storage, semantic linking and inference, analytics and UI. For the sake of space, we focus on the functionality of the analytics and the UI components, although the other components can be elucidated during the demo.

To illustrate the use of Social InfoButtons, let us refer to two scenarios (but more analytics will be shown in the demo): (i) a healthcare practitioner devising the best practice treatment for a patient; and (ii) an organization studying discrepancies between data from official reports and social trends. For the first scenario, consider a medical doctor, Christine, who has to prescribe a treatment for her patient Bob, who is a veteran suffering from Post-Traumatic Stress Disorder (PTSD). To best devise a treatment for Bob, in addition to consulting Bob's lab reports and electronic health record (EHR), Christine wants to see what treatments other patients with the same condition as Bob are following and what feedback they are providing in the social space. To do so, she would go to the Social InfoButtons home page[1] to perform a keyword search on the term "PTSD." The tool has an auto-complete as-you-type feature that suggest matching medical terms to the user. Submitting the request triggers a SPARQL query on our repository. Results are displayed in a page organized in four categories: 1) summary of social information (e.g. number of patients, patients' geographic distribution, topic cloud with most recent social posts, etc.), 2) list of treatments, each with associated side effects, 3) symptoms, and 4) contrast information (official vs. social data). It is important to emphasize that all results are supplied with a reference to the source they have been retrieved from. For instance, from each treatment in the list, the user can jump to the scientific

[1] http://cis.csi.cuny.edu:8080/SocialMedicalSearch

resources rather than to the social posts discussing the subject (either treatment or symptom). Thus, the user has the opportunity to explore additional information directly from the sources linked to topic of interest. Fig. 1a and Fig. 1b show parts (for the sake of space) of the result page. The first one shows the social summary for PTSD, including number of known patients and trending topics. The user can drill-down to access detailed information, including: the patients' profile data and location distribution, and the comments associated with each trending topic. From Fig. 1a, we can see that, for PSTD, "Veterans" is a trending topic in the social space: the user can click on the topic term and access associated social posts (e.g. tweets, see figure), if she wants to know more. Fig. 1b shows the list of treatments, each with a list of side effects as they are ranked by their popularity in the social space. Let us assume that Christine is considering prescribing a drug called Sertraline. By inspecting the result page, she discovers that a large percentage of Sertraline users have reported a side effect referred to as "emotional withdrawal" that is not listed in the drug documentation. At this point, if Christine wants to know more about the drug then she can follow the links, *PubMed* or *WebMD* (see the figure), that will lead her to the actual resources in the data source and their provenance. Alternatively, Christine may decide to inform Bob about this potential side effect and advise Bob to report to her whenever effect is observed. Conversely, she might discover further alternatives other patients with PTSD are adopting, thus she may decide to investigate whether any of such alternatives may suite Bob better.

Now, consider an organization, e.g., a government agency that wants to follow trends and understand whether discrepancies exist between official statistical data and social data. In this case, a knowledge worker from the organization may be asked to investigate what treatments patients are using but are not mentioned in scientific/official sources. Let's consider, for instance, Fibromyalgia, a common chronic pain condition for which, as with other medically unexplained syndromes, there is no universally accepted treatment. In such a case, exploring the unified knowledge base is even more valuable. The knowledge worker would start with a keyword search, as in the previous scenario. From the result page, by browsing the data contrast area, the user can trigger queries that display analytics contrasting data from official and social sources for Fibromyalgia. Fig. 1c displays a table listing the treatments for Fibromyalgia, along with the information whether each treatment occurs in official data or social data. Note, also, that results are ordered by popularity, in this case defined as the number of treatment occurrences in the social space. From the table, the user can discover that there is one treatment, *Cyclobenzaprine*, that occurs in social space only. At this point, further investigation can be initiated. As another example, if the organization wants to explore the distribution of the population afflicted by the condition *Asthma*, and how it compares with official data, the user has to submit a keyword search for the term "Asthma" and click on the map analytics option in the contrast area of the result page. The user would access an interactive map, supplemented with a heat layer, see Fig. 1d, where she can pinpoint the gender distribution by geographical area, and access contrast data via the given charts.

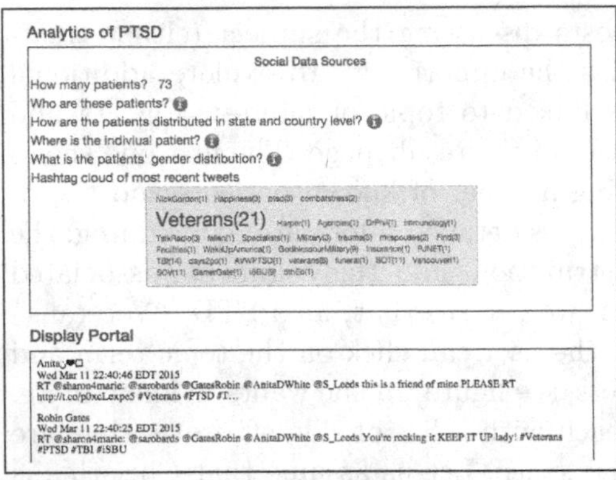

(a) Social Summary for PTSD

Treatments of the condition: PTSD (Post

Individual Therapy (Psychotherapy) pubmed webmed
Evaluated By **95** patients
Side Effects:

Sertraline (Prescription Drug) pubmed webmed
Evaluated By **25** patients
Side Effects:
(1) Weight gain 21%;
(2) Dry mouth (xerostomia) 20%;
(3) Loss of sex drive (libido) 18%;
(4) Fatigue 17%;
(5) Insomnia 11%;
(6) Emotional withdrawal 11%;

Citalopram (Prescription Drug) pubmed webmed
Evaluated By **22** patients
Side Effects:
(1) Fatigue 25%;
(2) Sex drive (libido) decreased 17%;
(3) Brain fog 15%;
(4) Anxious mood 14%;

(b) Conditions associated with PTSD

Treatment	Present in Social	Present in Authority
Duloxetine	Yes (1058)	Yes
Pregabalin	Yes (955)	Yes
Milnacipran	Yes (357)	Yes
Gabapentin	Yes (346)	Yes
Tramadol	Yes (201)	Yes
Cyclobenzaprine	Yes (188)	No

(c) Treatment Contrast for Fibromyaligia

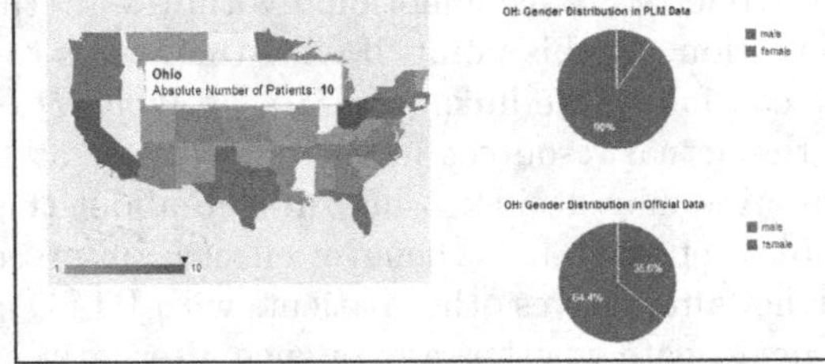

(d) Distribution Contrast for Asthma

Fig. 1. Snapshots of Analytics in Social InfoButtons

The main advantage of Social InfoButtons is the ability for users to explore and analyze both scientific and social media data in order to make better informed decisions, because of the larger, more inclusive knowledge available. Without Social InfoButtons, to achieve the same level of knowledge, a user would have to undergo a long and potentially expensive manual search process.

References

1. Bodenreider, O.: The unified medical language system (UMLS): integrating biomedical terminology. Nucleic Acids Research 32(Database-Issue), 267–270 (2004)
2. Cimino, J.J., Elhanan, G., Zeng, Q.: Supporting infobuttons with terminological knowledge. In: American Medical Informatics Association Annual Symposium, AMIA 1997, Nashville, TN, USA, October 25–29, 1997. AMIA (1997)
3. Ji, X., Chun, S.A., Geller, J.: Social infobuttons: Integrating open health data with social data using semantic technology. In: Proc. of the 5th International Workshop on Semantic Web Information Management, SWIM 2013, New York, NY, USA, June 23, 2013
4. Nyc open data. https://nycopendata.socrata.com (accessed: March 1, 2015)
5. Patientslikeme. https://www.patientslikeme.com (accessed: March 1, 2015)
6. Pubmed. http://www.ncbi.nlm.nih.gov/pubmed (accessed: March 1, 2015)

Collaborative Drawing Annotations on Web Videos

István Koren[(✉)], Petru Nicolaescu, and Ralf Klamma

Advanced Community Information Systems (ACIS) Group, RWTH Aachen University, Ahornstr. 55, 52056 Aachen, Germany
{koren,nicolaescu,klamma}@dbis.rwth-aachen.de
http://dbis.rwth-aachen.de

Abstract. Collaborative Drawing over a computer network, in particular on videos, usually requires some complex client-server architecture. In this paper, we want to demo an approach with the following distinctive features. On the client side we enable peer-to-peer collaborative video drawing in recent Web browsers supporting WebRTC. Developers can therefore embed it in arbitrary Web pages and users do not need to install any additional software. For persistence we use a microservice driven cloud approach which can be set up easily. All components are open source to facilitate wide use and further development. A use case evaluation showed promising results and will be presented in the demo.

1 Introduction

With the increasing mobility needed at the workplace, technologies for efficient collaboration come to the fore of various businesses. This shift is supported by mobile devices such as smartphones or tablets that make it possible to quickly turn to co-workers for ad-hoc help-seeking in remote locations or collecting useful bits and pieces of information for longer reflection. In many cases, capturing such information is realized using multimedia, such as images or videos. Yet, intuitive ways of collaboration for instructing colleagues, like highlighting certain parts on an architectural plan or marking hazardous spots in a video are not adequately attainable on today's information systems, even though technologies such as stylus pens for capacitive touchscreen devices like tablets exist. In particular, we are motivated by informal learning scenarios at construction sites, where new technical equipment and building materials are available frequently and companies struggle to cope with the growing speed of innovation while having decreasing resources for training.

To this end, we propose a Web-based toolkit for collaborative annotation of video data that is both reusable and extendable on the frontend and backend side. The demo consists of a video player that is overlaid by a drawing canvas onto which vector graphics can be collaboratively drawn on the frame level of the video. A master client, automatically designated by a calculated device profile, makes the annotations persistent using a backend service.

P. Cimiano et al. (Eds.): ICWE 2015, LNCS 9114, pp. 671–674, 2015.
DOI: 10.1007/978-3-319-19890-3_54

Our demo[1] is a seminal advancement of the DireWolf 2.0 framework [1] by using the underlying peer-to-peer communication technology with a standalone real-time collaboration framework, refining the user interface widgets as reusable components and adding a microservice-based backend for a scalable distribution.

We believe that other researchers may leverage our permissive open source work to further strengthen the Web as a device-independent platform for collaborative distributed applications.

2 Collaborative Video Drawing

We developed the video drawing prototype (cf. Figure 1) after evaluating our earlier SeViAnno system for semantic video annotation with construction companies [2]. Important requirements were the annotation of videos by drawing straight and free-hand lines, squares, circles and textual content. To support live inquiries, the drawings need to be synchronized in near real-time. As such, further requirements are consistency and automated conflict handling. To keep the mobile bandwidth low, we opted for vector-based instead of pixel graphics. Finally, we required a modular approach both on the front- and backend to be able to use the functionalities in other software projects as well.

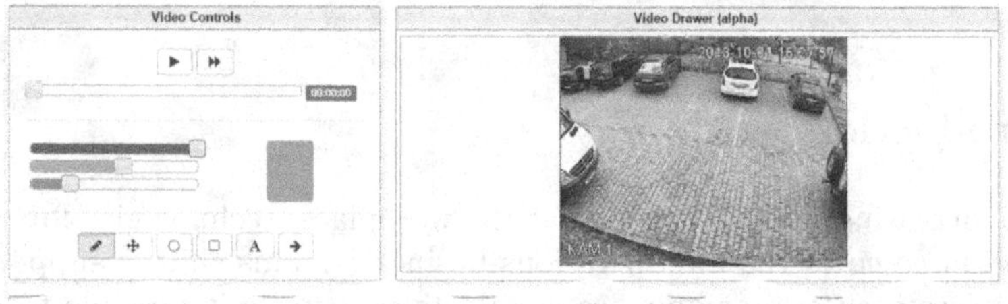

Fig. 1. Screenshot of the Video Drawing Tool Used in the Evaluation

The prototype allows the video selection from a list of videos uploaded by or shared with the user. The video may be started and stopped with a video controls toolbar that includes a player-like timeline. Existing drawings on certain frames are marked and clickable on the timeline for awareness reasons.

The specific drawing annotation types (free-hand, lines, squares, circles) can be selected in another toolbar. A video player displays the video and is overlaid by the drawing canvas. We chose to separate the controls from the video player to allow drawing over the borders of the video if desired so. Additionally, we leverage the widget distribution technologies introduced by DireWolf, i.e. the video canvas may be moved to a different device under the user's control, most usefully a touchscreen tablet.

[1] A demo video is available at http://goo.gl/iLy3gM

While a drawing is completed, it gets synchronized to other users looking at the specific video. I.e. users are seeing a live version of the current drawing. To ensure the persistence of the drawing, it is saved on a backend server.

Technically, the video widgets are implemented as Web Components [3], a recent Web standard that aims to provide reusable user interface components on the Web. Currently, Web Components are available as JavaScript library with so-called poly-fills, whereof there are some projects available. Although we currently use Polymer[2], the library should be easily exchangeable in the future, especially when the standard gets implemented natively in browsers.

The drawings are distributed as vector graphics to avoid having to send bandwidth-intensive pixel graphics on every change. Though remarkable work has been done in this respect, i.e. targeting the DOM layer as synchronized entity [4], we found available SVG based libraries to be too heavy for resource-constrained mobile devices. Therefore we employ the lightweight FabricJS[3] library that works with the JSON data, though it can also output SVG data.

The JSON data structure of the drawings gets automatically distributed to other users of the application watching the same video through our Yjs framework for shared editing of arbitrary data types [5]. Using an optimistic concurrency control algorithm, the framework is composed of a collaboration engine that maps certain data types, and connectors for message propagation. The video drawing prototype currently uses a JSON data type and the WebRTC connector of Yjs. For storing the shared state of the annotation on the server, a dedicated client is selected from the available collaborators. The selection is implemented using a score based on the device profile. Currently, mobile devices get lower scores due to their processing power, but the score can be adjusted to meet other requirements. If two or more devices have the same profile score, a decision is taken randomly.

On the backend, we employ a powerful REST-based microservice architecture with a security layer powered by OpenID Connect. OpenID Connect is a recent single sign-on standard that supports authentication and authorization of end users. The available videos are returned by a scalable cloud storage service based on OpenStack Swift. Another microservice accepts requests to save and retrieve the video annotation data in a MySQL database. Overall, our architecture is highly modular on both the HTML5 UI frontend with Web Components, as well as on the backend implemented as REST-based microservices.

3 Evaluation

We performed both a comparative technical evaluation as well as a user study to prove our concept. For the technical part, we measured which annotation type produced the biggest latency, which proved to be the creation of text objects with an average latency of 238.2 ms. The lowest latency were obtained for movements and rotations, with an average of 46 ms.

---

[2] see https://www.polymer-project.org/

[3] see http://fabricjs.com/

For the usability test, 15 people in groups of three people in a lab were asked to collaboratively draw certain annotations. Each user had to accomplish different tasks like highlighting certain objects in the video using rectangles and circles, pointing to objects using arrows, adding text annotations on screen, browsing through existing annotations using the video timeline and moving various annotations on the screen. During the test we encouraged users to talk to each other, to see how the speed of actions was perceived; in terms of this, the dragging feature was rated the highest. Furthermore, the tool was rated positive in terms of usability and performance.

4 Conclusion and Future Work

In this demo, we presented our prototype for drawing annotations on Web videos. The vector-based drawings are synchronized across devices using the infrastructural findings of our earlier DireWolf prototype and by employing Yjs, a newly developed Web-based collaborative editing framework.

Future work includes the generalization of the drawing canvas to be applicable to still images, live WebRTC video streams and other underlying content. Our evaluation study furthermore suggested adding more awareness features.

We are currently rolling out our prototype to real construction sites to further evaluate the applicability of our scenario and the technical approach. Finally, we want to use the prototype in a wide variety of Web applications ranging from the learning domain over requirements engineering for annotating screencasts.

Acknowledgements. The work has received funding from the European Commission's FP7 IP Learning Layers under grant agreement no 318209.

References

1. Koren, I., Bavendiek, J., Klamma, R.: DireWolf Goes Pack Hunting: A Peer-to-Peer Approach for Secure Low Latency Widget Distribution Using WebRTC. In: Casteleyn, S., Rossi, G., Winckler, M. (eds.) ICWE 2014. LNCS, vol. 8541, pp. 507–510. Springer, Heidelberg (2014)
2. Nicolaescu, P., Klamma, R.: SeViAnno 2.0: Web-Enabled Collaborative Semantic Video Annotation Beyond the Obvious. In: 12th International Workshop on Content-Based Multimedia Indexing 2014, pp. 1–6. IEEE (2014)
3. Glazkov, D., Ito, H.: Introduction to Web Components. Technical report. http://www.w3.org/TR/components-intro/ W3C (2014)
4. Heinrich, M., Lehmann, F., Springer, T., Gaedke, M.: Exploiting Single-User Web Applications for Shared Editing - A Generic Transformation Approach. In: Mille, A., Gandon, F.L., Misselis, J., Rabinovich, M., Staab, S. (eds.) 21st International Conference on World Wide Web 2012, WWW 2012, pp. 1057–1066. ACM, New York (2012)
5. Nicolaescu, P., Jahns, K., Derntl, M., Klamma, R.: Yjs: A Framework for Near Real-Time P2P Shared Editing on Arbitrary Data Types. In: Cimiano, P., Frasincar, F., Houben, G.J., Schwabe, D. (eds.) 15th International Conference on Web Engineering. LNCS, vol. 9114. Springer, Heidelberg (2015)

Yjs: A Framework for Near Real-Time P2P Shared Editing on Arbitrary Data Types

Petru Nicolaescu(✉), Kevin Jahns, Michael Derntl, and Ralf Klamma

RWTH Aachen University Advanced Community Information Systems (ACIS) Group, Ahornstr. 55, 52056 Aachen, Germany
{Nicolaescu,Jahns,Derntl,Klamma}@dbis.rwth-aachen.de
http://dbis.rwth-aachen.de

Abstract. Near real-time shared editing of documents in the Web browser has become popular for many applications like text writing, drawing, sketching and others. These applications require protocols for exchanging messages among user agents and for resolving editing conflicts. The available frameworks mostly rely on operational transformation approaches and often expose drawbacks like failing to scale, restriction to linear data structures and client-server architectures. In this paper we present Yjs, a lightweight open-source JavaScript framework that can be used for collaborative editing of arbitrary data types in peer-to-peer settings. The framework is based on a new operational transformation-like approach and supports communication protocols like XMPP and WebRTC. From an engineering perspective Yjs is easy to integrate into Web applications. Evaluations show that it has a favorable runtime complexity.

Keywords: Near real-time collaboration · Shared editing · Web framework

1 Introduction

Shared editing software enables multiple users to collaborate on shared data [3]. In a near real-time (NRT) setting, collaborators apply changes to their local copy, while concurrently sending and receiving notifications of those changes via some communication protocol. Google Docs is a good example of such an application. It uses Operational Transformation (OT) [1] and a client-server infrastructure for resolving conflicts occurring during NRT collaboration sessions. However, both existing literature [8] and practical experience show that current shared editing approaches do not scale well with the number of users in pure peer-to-peer settings. Moreover, they mostly enable collaboration on linear data structures but are not designed for non-linear ones (e.g., graphs, custom abstract data types). To overcome this gap we have developed Yjs[1], a framework that allows developers to conveniently add collaborative features to Web applications. It offers a

[1] Developer documentation and a demo can be found at http://y-js.org.

P. Cimiano et al. (Eds.): ICWE 2015, LNCS 9114, pp. 675–678, 2015.
DOI: 10.1007/978-3-319-19890-3_55

customizable approach for any required shared abstract data type. Based on a modular design Yjs contains a collaboration engine that resolves editing conflicts and ensures the shared data integrity across peers, and various connectors for propagating the collaboration-related updates across the network.

Our demo showcases the usage of Yjs on text, JSON and DOM elements (XML), using both WebRTC and XMPP connectors. As such, collaborative editing using text, HTML5 elements and HTML5 Web pages is part of the demo scenario. The focus is on the reliability and usability of the framework in ad hoc peer-to-peer settings. Presented recently in a lightning talk at the European open source conference in Brussels (FOSDEM'15), Yjs is already garnering interest from the open-source community. We target the adoption of NRT collaboration for existing and new Web applications by leveraging lightweight applications, where collaboration logic can be easily engineered on the client side.

2 Features of the Distributed Shared Editing Algorithm

Most OT frameworks support collaboration on text, JSON and/or XML [2,4,5]. However, due to the difficulty of implementation and dealing with known OT collaboration puzzles, they fail to scale with the number of users in peer-to-peer environments [8]. Namely, they do not always converge or they need a centralized mechanism for creating a total order for local operations. Moreover, in terms of applying operations on a local copy of a shared data, in a client-server approach there are n execution orders, where n is the number of users, whereas in a peer-to-peer approach, the clients have one connection to every collaborator and there are $n(n-1)!$ execution orders that need to be considered. Yjs proposes a new type of algorithm and a modular implementation that scales to peer-to-peer communication between the clients. The algorithm, similar to efficient existing OT approaches [7,8] has a favorable time complexity. Instead of defining an operation as a tuple of position and content, we define it as an insertion between two other operations (similar to the WOOT approach[2]). This has positive implications on preserving the user intention for the order of applied operations and enables a worst-case time complexity of $O(C^2)$, where C is the number of concurrent operations at the same position.

Important advantages of Yjs' algorithm are therefore that it reduces time to synchronize shared data among clients (e.g., after a late join), can handle more clients at the same time and minimizes the space needed for propagated messages. Compared to classic OT algorithms it does not require propagation of complex internal structures (i.e., state vectors). Due to space limitations, details about the algorithm and its formal proof will be published in the near future.

3 Yjs Framework

In contrast to similar implementations that support only a very limited number of document structures, the Yjs framework encourages developers to build custom data types. A custom type can use existing types (e.g., from third parties)

[2] https://hal.inria.fr/inria-00071240/document

in order to give meaning on the actions on the data and can fire custom events. Among existing implemented types are *String*, *Array* and *Object*. Internally, a linear data type is represented as a doubly linked list. Each composing element (e.g., a character of a word) represents an item of the linked list having a predecessor and a successor. When an element is deleted by an operation, it will not be removed from the linked list, but its content will be set to *empty*. Only a built-in garbage collector can remove elements completely from the linked list, when it can assure that no conflicts will occur. Yjs is currently available as a collection of open-source JavaScript libraries on GitHub[3].

In order to keep the modularity and to be able to employ Yjs in various Web engineering settings, the communication protocols and the shared data type formats support are implemented as dedicated interchangeable components. This greatly simplifies the process of integrating the framework into an existing project, since existing projects typically use diverse communication protocols (e.g., Web Sockets, IWC, XMPP), and collaborate on various data types (e.g., XML, JSON, graphs). Support of different communication protocols is implemented in connector components, and the support for data types in type components. While the text document component only supports simple insert, delete and replace operations, the interface for XML documents inherits all the features (events, and DOM traversal / manipulation) of the browser DOM element. This means that the XML document can also be easily queried and manipulated via jQuery using its XML manipulation features.

4 Evaluation

To evaluate the scalability and correctness of Yjs we performed multiple automatic tests simulating many users working on a single shared document. Every user was represented by an instance of the Yjs framework. For this, we used a test connector that simulated a peer-to-peer environment, configurable with respect to number of users and actions that can be created. We connected each test user directly with all other users by means of the test connector (resulting in a total connected network). Furthermore, we enabled the option to restrict the collaboration to a specific data type (e.g., text or JSON with primitive data types and XML attributes). Among the test cases we considered various network delays in the peer-to-peer communication, generation of random operations created in different contexts and varying order of received operations at every peer [7].

Using this setting we created and executed 10000 actions on text and JSON with various test agents, ranging from 1 to 10. The tests ran on one single CPU only (Intel i7, 3.4 GHz). We ran the test 15 times to obtain solid average timings. The results showed that in average 100 actions per millisecond can be performed, which we consider to meet well the NRT collaboration expectations.

In terms of real-world applications, Yjs was used for enabling free-hand collaborative video annotation at frame level in near real-time. The annotation tool

[3] https://github.com/y-js

evaluation also showed that the framework outputs reliable results and that it is easy to use from a developer's perspective.

5 Conclusion and Future Work

Our proposed example scenarios showcase NRT collaboration on text, JSON elements and XML in terms of DOM (collaboratively building a Web page). The scenarios use both XMPP and WebRTC in order to demonstrate the trade-off between federation and responsiveness. Our results show that XMPP provides a better scaling in number of users than WebRTC, which in turn provides more efficient response times. We are currently implementing the undo functionality. Furthermore, we are investigating ways to persist the internal Yjs data representations for improved performance.

Yjs is being integrated in several open-source projects. We plan to use Yjs with our DireWolf framework [6] for widget distribution in order to synchronize the state between the Web components. Further usage of Yjs—also in the domain of mashup applications—is to integrate it as NRT collaboration and state preservation solution in modeling and widgetizing Web applications.

Acknowledgements. This research was funded in part by the European Commission in the projects "Layers" (FP7-318209) and "METIS" (531262-LLP-2012-ES-KA3-KA3MP).

References

1. Ellis, C.A., Gibbs, S.J.: Concurrency Control in Groupware Systems. SIGMOD Record **18**(2), 399–407 (1989)
2. Gerlicher, A.R.S.: A Framework for Real-Time Collaborative Engineering in the Automotive Industries. In: Luo, Y. (ed.) CDVE 2006. LNCS, vol. 4101, pp. 164–173. Springer, Heidelberg (2006)
3. Grudin, J.: Computer-Supported Cooperative Work: History and Focus. Computer **27**(5), 19–26 (1994)
4. Heinrich, M., Grüneberger, F.J., Springer, T., Gaedke, M.: Enriching Web Applications with Collaboration Support Using Dependency Injection. In: Brambilla, M., Tokuda, T., Tolksdorf, R. (eds.) ICWE 2012. LNCS, vol. 7387, pp. 473–476. Springer, Heidelberg (2012)
5. Ignat, C.-L., Norrie, M.C.: Multi-level Editing of Hierarchical Documents. Computer Supported Cooperative Work (CSCW) **17**(5–6), 423–468 (2008)
6. Kovachev, D., Renzel, D., Nicolaescu, P., Koren, I., Klamma, R.: DireWolf: A Framework for Widget-based Distributed User Interfaces. Journal of Web Engineering **13**(3&4), 203–222 (2014)
7. Sun, D., Sun, C.: Operation context and context-based operational transformation. In: Proceedings of the 20th Anniversary Conference on Computer Supported Cooperative Work (CSCW 2006), pp. 279–288 (2006)
8. Weiss, S., Urso, P., Molli, P.: Logoot: a scalable optimistic replication algorithm for collaborative editing on P2P networks. In: Proceedings of the 29th IEEE Conference on Distributed Computing Systems (ICDCS 2009), pp. 404–412 (2009)

OSMoSys: A Web Interface for Graph-Based RDF Data Visualization and Ontology Browsing

Achilleas Psyllidis

Delft University of Technology (TU Delft), Julianalaan 134 2628 BL, Delft, The Netherlands
A.Psyllidis@tudelft.nl

Abstract. This demo presents *OSMoSys*, a novel web interface for visualizing, exploring, and navigating through linked data, in RDF or OWL format. Unlike most of the available RDF visualizers that are desktop-based, offer static representations, and solely cater to experienced users, *OSMoSys* aims to provide an easy-to-use framework to facilitate data sharing across multiple domains and stakeholders. It further offers a dynamic and interactive representation and exploration system for RDF data and ontologies, through force-directed graphs and multi-pane interfaces. In addition, it is mainly based on JavaScript and HTML5. *OSMoSys* is demonstrated through an experimental prototype that exemplifies its potential value in the field of smart cities.

Keywords: RDF visualization · Web ontology browser · Force-directed graph · Semantic web · Linked data

1 Introduction

Presently, a plethora of tools and platforms for visualizing Resource Description Framework (RDF) data, as well as for developing and exploring ontologies, is increasingly becoming available. However, the majority of these tools are solely accessible via desktop-based applications that, additionally, require certain skills in knowledge representation and semantic technologies. As a consequence, their benefits can only be exploited by a limited group of experienced users.

Motivated by this challenge, the paper demonstrates *OSMoSys*, a novel web interface for visualizing, exploring, and navigating through RDF models, OWL (Web Ontology Language) ontologies and linked data. *OSMoSys* comprises two mutually linked components: (a) a web-based interface that enables the representation of RDF data and OWL semantic models as force-directed graphs and, further, allows interactive concept discovery, and (b) a browser that provides online access to the complete hierarchy of ontologies via a multi-pane user interface (UI). Currently, most of the developed RDF and ontology graphs are presented in static layouts, such as node-link diagrams and table or tile charts [1,2,3]. On the contrary, *OSMoSys* utilizes a dynamic graph representation, which also allows users to interactively adjust the level of detail (LOD) displayed to them.

The aim of the presented web interface is to provide an easy-to-use framework, accessible to a wide range of users, either experienced or amateur ones, so they can benefit from the potential of combined information sources. By not requiring sophis-

P. Cimiano et al. (Eds.): ICWE 2015, LNCS 9114, pp. 679–682, 2015.
DOI: 10.1007/978-3-319-19890-3_56

ticated competences in ontology modeling or related fields, it aspires to promote data sharing and reuse across various application domains that make use of linked data. The contributions of this paper are mainly three:

1. A user-friendly web interface for interactively exploring RDF and OWL models, displayed as a dynamic graph with variable levels of detail;
2. A browser for exploring ontologies online;
3. An experimental prototype, employing HTML5 and JavaScript, deployed for urban computing and smart cities applications to exemplify the system's potential.

A running instance of the *OSMoSys* demonstrator is available for consideration at `http://www.hyperbody.nl/demo/osmosys`.

2 The OSMoSys Web Interface and Experimental Prototype

2.1 Interactive Graph-Based RDF and OWL Visualization

OSMoSys displays RDF and ontology concepts (classes) as nodes, and relations (object, data, and annotation properties) as edges (Fig. 1). It makes use of the Sigma.js JavaScript library[1], which is specifically dedicated to graph drawing, so as to visualize linked data in RDF format or OWL ontologies. JavaScript was particularly chosen for its compatibility with the majority of available web browsers. To further achieve the force-directed graph layout, the Yifan Hu multilevel algorithm was employed [4]. The latter dynamically distributes the graph nodes based on the conceptual proximity of the entities they represent. In addition, the front-end utilizes jQuery[2], along with CSS3 and HTML5. *OSMoSys* receives as input RDF data either already existing on the web or in the form of newly ingested local files. In both cases, the data sources are first converted into JSON (JavaScript Object Notation) format, so as to easily be integrated in the JavaScript library.

For the purposes of the experimental prototype, *OSMoSys* was used for visualizing a recently developed ontology for smart city planning and management. The latter formally describes data from disparate sectors within a city and, therefore, makes extensive reuse of relevant external ontologies and controlled vocabularies. As such, it constitutes an interesting example case for testing and displaying the platform's potential. The complete ontology hierarchy, along with several open municipal data that were mapped into the semantic model and stored as RDF triples, were then loaded into *OSMoSys*.

Node size variations in the developed graph indicate whether a concept refers to a top class or a subclass (Fig. 1). In full display mode, the user can easily recognize the eleven top classes, around which the semantic model is organized (besides the default *owl:Thing*). As a user zooms in, the graph displays different levels of detail, gradually making all subclass labels visible, in a process called semantic zooming. Hovering over a class node highlights its label along with its immediate relations to other classes, for visual clarity purposes. By further selecting a highlighted graph entity, an information pane pops up on the right, containing additional details about the class itself, as well as

---

[1] http://sigmajs.org, Accessed March 12, 2015.
[2] http://jquery.com, Accessed March 12, 2015.

an index of all related entities. Moreover, the main graph display shows an isolated view of the selected concept and its connections. The user can easily return to the full network view, by choosing the corresponding option provided by the UI. Navigation through the ontology graph is also possible via the information pane index.

One of the key features of the *OSMoSys* visualization UI is the search module. Thereby, the user is provided with the possibility to discover a concept (or RDF data entity), by performing keyword search, without necessarily knowing the exact entity name in advance. All relevant results will appear as a list below the search field, on the left floating menu. In this way, the user can navigate the various results and, correspondingly, highlight the selected concepts and their relations on the main display. Besides the search modules, users are also provided with a group selection tool. The latter is currently capable of grouping concepts of the semantic model, based on their function as top-level, principal, or sub-classes.

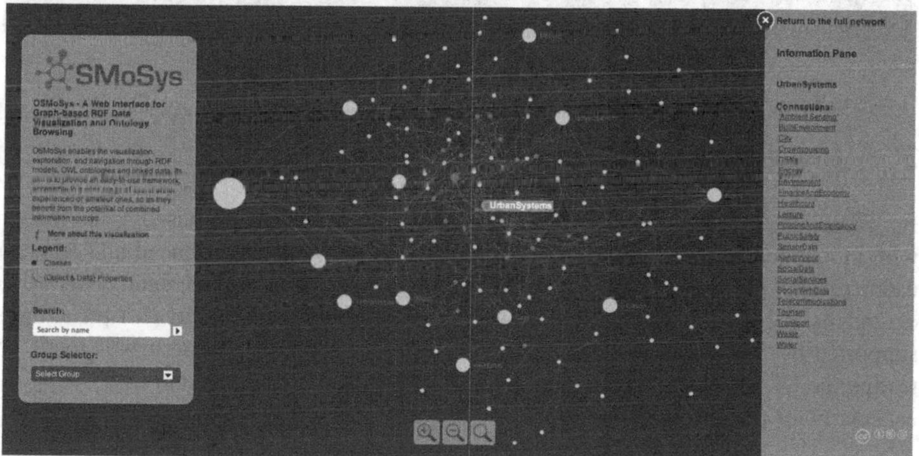

Fig. 1. Graph-based visualization of RDF data in the web-based *OSMoSys* user interface

2.2 Web Ontology Browser

In the case of OWL ontologies, besides the visualization interface, *OSMoSys* also offers an online browser that enables access to their complete hierarchy. The browser is directly accessible via a link on the information pane, described in the previous section.

The UI layout of the web ontology browser (WOB) is organized in three panes, providing different navigation possibilities and views of the ontology (Fig. 2). The upper-left pane lists the different ontology entities in groups of classes, object, data, and annotation properties, individuals, and data types. It also contains an option for returning back to the general overview. When any of the previous entity groups is selected, a complete index of the corresponding concepts in alphabetical order appears on the lower-left pane of the UI. Further, the main pane accommodates the full semantics, descriptions, and annotations of each selected entity, as well as its relations to other classes, and links to external vocabularies. The user can interactively browse the different entities and explore relations, either through the side-pane indexes or by directly clicking on any term included in the main pane. WOB is largely based on OWLDoc, as well as JavaScript and HTML5.

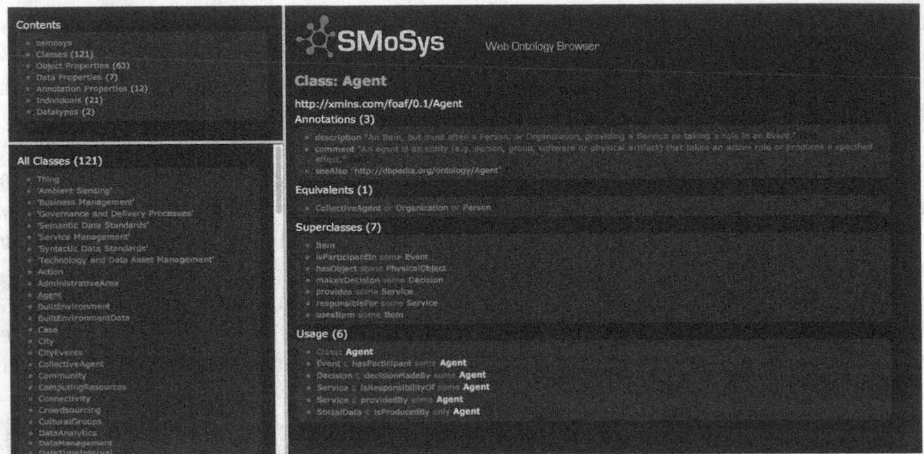

Fig. 2. Instance of the Web Ontology Browser

3 Conclusions and Future Work

By combining a user-friendly web interface for dynamic graph-based visualization with an online browser of RDF data, *OSMoSys* allows both experienced and amateur users to exploit the benefits of the increasingly available linked data. To further extend its accessibility potential, *OSMoSys* is largely based on JavaScript, as it is supported by the majority of contemporary browsers. Future research will focus on testing the UI with larger RDF datasets and also improving search and query support, especially for the ontology browser

Acknowledgments. This research is funded by the Greek State Scholarships Foundation (by the resources of the European Social Fund and the NSRF of 2007-2013) and the Alexander S. Onassis Foundation. It is also financially supported by the Foundation for Education and European Culture (IPEP) and the A. G. Leventis Foundation.

References

1. Schlegel, K., Weißgerber, T., Stegmaier, F., Seifert, C., Granitzer, M., Kosch, H.: Balloon synopsis: a modern node-centric RDF viewer and browser for the web. In: Presutti, V., Blomqvist, E., Troncy, R., Sack, H., Papadakis, I., Tordai, A. (eds.) ESWC Satellite Events 2014. LNCS, vol. 8798, pp. 249–253. Springer, Heidelberg (2014)
2. Stuhr, M., Roman, D., Norheim, D.: LODWheel: javascript-based visualization of RDF data. In: 2nd International Workshop on Consuming Linked Data (COLD 2011) (2011)
3. Berners-Lee, T., et al: Tabulator: exploring and analyzing linked data on the semantic web. In: 3rd International Semantic Web User-Interaction Workshop (2006)
4. Hu, Y.: Efficient and High Quality Force-Directed Graph Drawing. Mathematica **10**(1), 37–71 (2005)

Loop Discovery in Publish-Subscribe-Based User Interface Mashups

Alexey Tschudnowsky(✉) and Martin Gaedke

Technische Universität Chemnitz, Chemnitz, Germany
{alexey.tschudnowsky,martin.gaedke}@informatik.tu-chemnitz.de

Abstract. User interface (UI) mashups follow principles and architectures, which should enable even non-technical end users to develop their own widget-based applications. Recently, so-called choreographed solutions have been proposed, which lower the entry barrier even further: mashup designers are supposed to simply place widgets in a shared context and communication among them would emerge automatically. However, existing approaches for enabling self-organization among widgets do not take any measures to prevent undesired or faulty behavior like e.g., self-reinforcing loops or hunting. This paper demonstrates two developments to address this problem in the context of publish-subscribe-based UI mashups. The proposed algorithms are implemented as extensions to the open-source mashup platform Apache Rave.

Keywords: User interface mashups · Inter-widget communication · Loop discovery

1 Introduction

In the last years UI mashup platforms have been proposed, which have a goal to ease development of widget-based applications, and, thus, to involve non-programmers into the software development process. For example, OMELETTE [1] and ROLE [3] use publish-subscribe-based infrastructure to enable self-organization of widgets. In [2] widgets communicate without prior configuration by means of shared memory. These solutions (called choreographed UI mashups [6]) let end users focus on the selection and placement of required components only and unburden them from the task of configuration of communication behavior. Although the approach is promising, no measures have been proposed so far to prevent undesired and potentially dangerous communication such as self-reinforcing loops. The latter, however, can lead to a crash of the mashup, corruption of data or even cause financial losses as a result of calls to payed services.

Consider, for example, a publish-subscribe-based mashup, consisting of two widgets: the one, which shows locations of POIs around some given area on a map (W_{Map}), and the other, which displays details of some POIs in a table ($W_{Details}$). Once focus of W_{Map} is changed, details to items around are propagated to other widgets (POI description, location, contact data etc.). $W_{Details}$ receives the information and displays it to the user. A looping behavior in the mashup emerges, if

P. Cimiano et al. (Eds.): ICWE 2015, LNCS 9114, pp. 683–686, 2015.
DOI: 10.1007/978-3-319-19890-3_57

$W_{Details}$ immediately publishes coordinates of the POI, which is e.g., the closest to the current location of the user. This message would be delivered to W_{Map} and W_{Map} would move its focus to a new area. As a result a new message would be issued by W_{Map}, which would be delivered to $W_{Details}$ and the process would start for a new. Depending on the quality of widget implementation, the loop might either disappear after some iterations or become infinite leading to blocked UI or even crash of the browser.

This paper proposes mechanisms for early detection of looping behavior like the one above. Although, the mechanisms are demonstrated in the context of publish-subscribe-based UI mashups, they can be easily adapted to other choreography models such as shared memory as well.

2 Discovery of Looping Behavior

For description of the loop detection facilities we reuse the model and formal definitions of publish-subscribe-based UI mashups introduced in [5]. In the following, we make several additional definitions.

A published message $a =< w, t, data >$ (w – the publishing widget, t – the publication topic and $data$ – the content of the message) is called *user-triggered*, if it has been issued by w as a result of user interaction with w. It is called *subscription-triggered* by a', if it has been issued automatically after receipt of the publication message a' by w. Otherwise, a is called *internally-triggered*. Internally-triggered messages are e.g., timer events or push messages from remote services. According to this classification, we observe, that a continuous looping behavior as described in Section 1 can only be caused by widgets, which produce subscription-triggered messages. However, the triggering logic is not explicit and belongs to the black-box business logic of the widget (at least in the utilized model). As a result definite prediction of occurrence and of duration of "looping" communication can not be guaranteed. Therefore, we relax the original problem to detection of so-called *actual* and *potential* loops.

An *actual loop* L_a in a mashup M with threshold ε is a message sequence $L_a = (a_0, a_2, ..., a_n - 1)$ so that $\forall i \in \{0..n-1\} : a_i.t \in a_{i+1 mod n}.w.SUB \wedge time_{i+1 mod n} - time_i < \varepsilon$ with $time_i$ being occurrence time of a_i. The idea behind this definition is to provide as early loop prediction as possible - in this case, after the first iteration. A *potential* loop L_p in a mashup M is a sequence of widgets $L_p = (w_0, w_1, ...w_{n-1})$ so that $\forall w_i, w_{i+1 mod n} \in L_p : \exists t \in w_i.PUB : t \in w_{i+1 mod n}.SUB$. A potential loop represents sequence of senders, which can potentially (but not necessarily) yield an actual loop at mashup run-time.

2.1 Discovery Algorithms

For the discovery of *potential loops* we propose to analyze the mashup model and to identify possible communication paths among aggregated widgets. This can be efficiently done by pairwise comparison of their publication and subscription topics. The result of the analysis is a graph $G = (W, E)$, which has a directed edge $e \in E$ from widget $w_1 \in W$ to $w_2 \in W$ if and only if w_1 and w_2 can communicate over some topic $t \in w_1.PUB \cap w_2.SUB$. To identify potential loops (which correspond to strongly connected components in G by construction), we propose to apply Tarjan's algorithm [4]. Each widget in a strongly connected component can initiate or reinforce looping behavior (depending on internal logic and state) as there is a directed path between any pair of nodes (widgets).

Discovery of actual loops is based on traffic recorded on the publish-subscribe bus of a mashup execution environment. Issued messages are stored in the order and together with the time of their appearance in a buffer and the buffer is analyzed using the Algorithm 1 after each new incoming message.

Algorithm 1. Discovery of actual loops

Input : Mashup M, message sequence $A = (a_1, a_2, ..., a_n)$, threshold ε
Output: $L_a = \{a_{i1}, a_{i2}, ..., a_{ik}, a_n\}$ being an actual loop if the message a_n yields one, and $\emptyset$ otherwise

1. Construct a directed graph $G = (V, E)$ (so called *causality graph*):
   (a) Let $V = \{a_n\}, E = \emptyset$.
   (b) For each $a_i \in A \backslash \{a_n\} : a_n.t \in a_i.w.SUB$: add a_i to V and add (a_n, a_i) to E.
   (c) For each $i, j \in \{1..n-1\} : time_j - time_i < \varepsilon$:
   – Add a_i and a_j to V if they do not exist there yet
   – Add (a_j, a_i) to E.
2. Using a depth-first search with a_n as a start node, check if a_n belongs to a circle in G. If it is the case (meaning the message a_n causes an actual loop), return the circle vertexes. Return $\emptyset$ otherwise.

The above algorithm spans a directed graph on the sequence of recorded messages. Graph edges show 1) causal relationships between messages and 2) messages, whose senders will receive a_n after it has been emitted and, thus, can potentially trigger further communication. A circle in graph G containing a_n corresponds to the definition of an actual loop.

The complexity of the potential loop discovery algorithm is $O(|W|^2)$ with $|W|$ being the number of widgets in a mashup. The complexity of actual loop discovery is $O(n^2)$ with n being the number of buffered messages.

2.2 Implementation

The algorithms for discovery of potential and actual loops have been implemented in the context of Apache Rave[1]. The algorithm for potential loop discovery is implemented as a Javascript library, which is loaded during initialization of mashups. Currently, it should be triggered by mashup user each time a new widget is added. For discovery of actual loops, the message bus based on OpenAjaxHub [2] has been extended. Actual loop discovery takes place automatically

---

[1] http://rave.apache.org

[2] http://www.openajax.org/member/wiki/OpenAjax_Hub_2.0_Specification

as soon as a new message is published. The used buffer size is 100 (which significantly exceeds average number of widgets in a UI mashup). The threshold ε has been set to 10ms. It has been found empirically and should ensure, that user-widget interactions do not interfere with message publications caused by widgets themselves. The two extensions have direct access to mashup configuration and widget descriptors with corresponding publications and subscriptions. In case actual or potential loops are detected, mashup users are notified with suggestion to deactivate the message bus and, thus, to prevent any further communication.

Demonstration: A screencast and an online demo can be found at https://vsr.informatik.tu-chemnitz.de/demos/iwc-loops.

3 Conclusion

Looping behavior in choreographed UI mashups hasn't gained attention so far. However, its discovery and prevention are necessary requirements for reliability of resulting solutions. This paper presented facilities for discovery of so called potential and actual loops in publish-subscribed-based UI mashups. The algorithms proved to be effective and efficient for the utilized definitions and assumptions. However, they solve only relaxed problems. Current facilities do not detect "slow" loops, i.e., the ones, where time difference between published messages is larger than the chosen threshold ε. Second, they do not predict duration of loops - neither from the mashup configuration nor from the recorded traffic. Finally, loop warnings can be issued, if internally-triggered or user-triggered messages occur within the time ε from the last message publication. These deficiencies as well as application of the algorithms for other types of choreographed UI mashups are subjects of our future research.

References

1. Chudnovskyy, O., Nestler, T., et al.: End-user-oriented telco mashups: the omelette approach. In: WWW 2012 Companion Volume, pp. 235–238. ACM (2012)
2. Hoisl, B., Drachsler, H.: User-tailored inter-widget communication-extending the shared data interface for the apache wookie engine. In: ICL 2011, pp. 1123–1131. Kassel University Press (2010)
3. Isaksson, E., Palmer, M.: Usability and inter-widget communication in PLEs. In: MUPPLE-10. Sun SITE Central Europe, RWTH Aachen (2010)
4. Tarjan, R.E.: Data Structures and Network Algorithms. SIAM (1983)
5. Tschudnowsky, A., Pietschmann, S., Niederhausen, M., Hertel, M., Gaedke, M.: From choreographed to hybrid user interface mashups: a generic transformation approach. In: Casteleyn, S., Rossi, G., Winckler, M. (eds.) ICWE 2014. LNCS, vol. 8541, pp. 145–162. Springer, Heidelberg (2014)
6. Wilson, S., Daniel, F., Jugel, U., Soi, S.: Orchestrated user interface mashups using w3c widgets. In: Harth, A., Koch, N. (eds.) ICWE 2011. LNCS, vol. 7059, pp. 49–61. Springer, Heidelberg (2012)

NeLMeS: Finding the Best Based on the People Available Leveraging the Crowd

Fabian Wiedemann(✉), Ralph Sontag, and Martin Gaedke

Technische Universität Chemnitz, Chemnitz, Germany
{fabian.wiedemann,ralph.sontag,martin.gaedke}@informatik.tu-chemnitz.de

Abstract. An in-house crowd is composed of persons with different skills, where they can be assigned to different projects on demand. Persons forming an in-house crowd have to meet for different purposes, such as planning the project or distributing objectives. While scheduling meetings is an important task in a knowledge worker's daily business, the problem evolves by adding more specific constraints to the scheduling. It is difficult for a company that uses an in-house crowd to decide which project can be executed on which date. To deal with this problem we propose the NeLMeS approach. NeLMeS extends the principle of meeting scheduling by defining projects and their required skills as well as persons who have some skills. We present a first prototype that uses LinkedIn to extract person skills and schedules which project can be executed at each date.

Keywords: Crowdsourcing · Project management · Meeting scheduling · Web applications

1 Introduction

Crowdsourcing is an increasingly popular paradigm for accomplishing tasks for which persons or companies do not have the required manpower or specific skill [4]. While crowdsourcing in general involves external persons into sensitive internal processes of a company, the concept of an in-house crowd is more applicable. In an in-house crowd persons with different skills are employed who are not assigned to a specific department or division. That is, these persons can be assigned to several projects if their skills are required to accomplish diverse objectives within these projects. To organize the work of one project it is necessary to meet with persons involved in this project. For scheduling meetings efficiently, it would be beneficial to know which project can be executed on which date based on the available persons from the in-house crowd.

In [6] Sen and Durfee propose an approach for distributed meeting scheduling by defining a metric of the efficiency of scheduling the meeting. It takes into account the communication cost and total time taken to schedule the meeting. In [5] Lee and Pan describe an architecture which involves scheduling meetings utilizing a fuzzy agent. Neither approach, however, considers the skills a person

P. Cimiano et al. (Eds.): ICWE 2015, LNCS 9114, pp. 687–690, 2015.
DOI: 10.1007/978-3-319-19890-3_58

has and the skills that are required to execute a project. While expert finding in the crowd is not within the scope of this paper, there are several approaches which deal with expert finding, such as [1,3].

Scheduling a meeting can be formalized as follows: A date d_i is element of the set of all possible $Dates$. The subset of persons $Pers_i \subset Pers$ is defined by the persons which are available at a date d_i ($pers_g \in Pers_i : d_i \in pers_g.Dates$). The meetings where all persons can attend is $d_i : Pers_i = Pers \; \forall d_i \in Dates$.

This paper deals with the problem of planning which project $prj_j \in Prj$ can be executed at a certain date d_i. That is, persons $pers_k \in Pers$ has one or more skills $s_a \in S_k \subset S$ and a project prj_j requires different skills $s_b \in S_j \subset S$ to be executed.

The Next-Level-Meeting-Scheduler NeLMeS focuses on extending the classical scheduling meeting functionality by suggesting which projects can be executed at a scheduled date. Therefore, our approach is applicable in an in-house crowd scenario to suggest which project can be executed on which date.

This paper also presents a prototype illustrating the feasibility of our approach. It uses LinkedIn for extracting and incorporating person skills.

2 The Next-Level-Meeting-Scheduler NeLMeS

To deal with the scenario of an in-house crowd described in Section 1 NeLMeS implements the overall workflow depicted in Figure 1. When launching a new project one person has to be responsible for the organization, execution and success of this project. This person is the project's directly responsible individual (DRI). The DRI defines the objectives and derives a list of required skills based on these objectives. The list of required skills is used to find experts from the in-house crowd. Persons assigned to a project can vote for dates where they are available for a meeting. Based on the required skills of a project and the available persons the NeLMeS approach proposes which project meetings could be held on which date.

To schedule which project can be executed on which date, NeLMeS considers three inputs: on which date a person is available; which person owns which skill; which skill is required by which project to be executed. The output is a plan that proposes which project can be executed on which date.

For each date, NeLMeS checks whether a project can be executed. That is, the tool checks if the skills all available persons have will match the required skills of a project. This is defined as a maximum matching problem in bipartite graphs. Thus, one person can only provide one skill to a project even if the person has two or more required skills. In a bipartite graph, the vertices can be divided into two parts so that no two vertices in the same part are joined by an edge. A maximum bipartite matching is the cardinality maximal set of edges without common vertices in a bipartite graph.

We model a bipartite graph with all available persons at the selected date on the one side and the required skills for the selected project on the other side (cf. Algorithm 1 lines 4 and 5). Then, we insert edges between a person and a

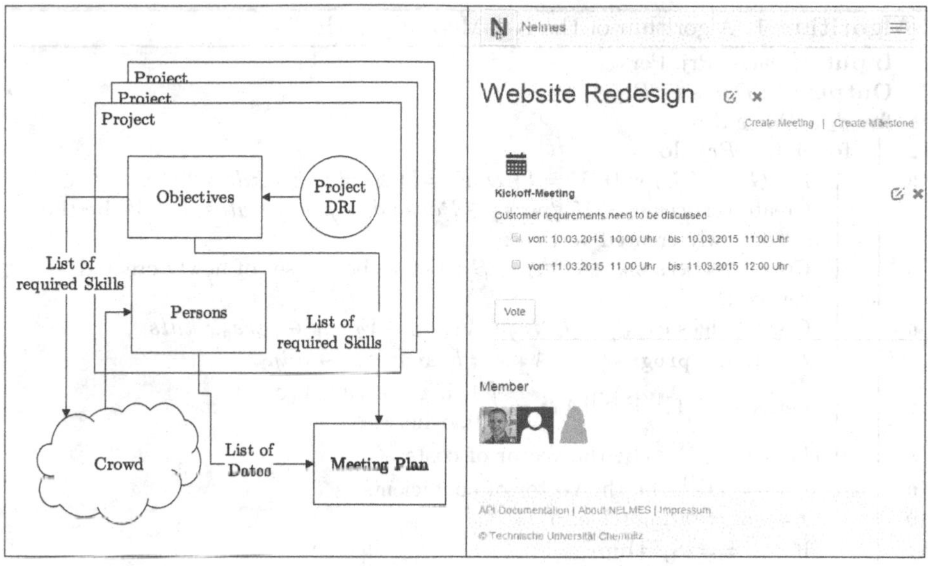

Fig. 1. Architecture of the NeLMeS approach

skill, if the person has that skill (cf. Algorithm 1 line 6). For this graph we have to solve a maximum bipartite matching. If the number of selected edges within a maximum bipartite matching is equal to the number of skills, the project can be executed at the selected date (cf. Algorithm 1 lines 11-13).

This maximum bipartite matching problem can be solved using linear programming. To solve this linear program NeLMeS employs the simplex algorithm [2]. While the Algorithm 1 results in a function (cf. line 12) which returns all possible projects prj_j for a given date d_i, our approach utilizes this function to generate the meeting plan for all given dates (cf. Figure 1).

For demonstrating NeLMeS we implemented a first prototype that uses LinkedIn as identity provider and for extracting person skills. Our prototype offers a RESTful API that is written in JavaScript and uses the runtime environment of node.js. To store data persistently we use the NoSQL database MongoDB. The front-end of our web application uses the frameworks Bootstrap for creating a responsive user interface that is easy to use on desktop computers as well as mobile devices.

Demonstration. The prototype presented in this paper is available for live testing at: http://vsr.informatik.tu-chemnitz.de/demo/nelmes/

3 Conclusion

NeLMeS eases scheduling meetings in an in-house crowd. After finding experts from the crowd it is possible to schedule which project can be executed at which

Algorithm 1. Algorithm of the NeLMeS approach

Input : Dates, Prj, Pers
Output: $f : Dates \rightarrow Prj$

for $d_i \in Dates$ **do**
  for $prj_j \in Prj$ **do**
    Let $G = (V, E)$ with $V = \{\}$ & $E = \{\}$ $S_j = prj_j.Skills$;
    Create vertices $v_g \in V$ $\forall pers_g \in Pers : d_i \in pers_g.Dates$; Let V_1 be the set of newly created vertices;
    Create vertices $w_h \in V$ $\forall s_h \in S_j$; Let V_2 be the set of newly created vertices;
    Create edges $e_{v_g,w_h} \in E$ $\forall v_g \in V_1, w_h \in V_2 : s_h \in pers_g.Skills$;
    `// Linear program as` $A * x = b$ `and` $c^T x \rightarrow min$
    Let $A \in \{0,1\}^{|V| \times |E|} | A_{v,e} = \begin{cases} 1, \text{ if } v \in e \ \forall v \in V, e \in E \\ 0, \text{ otherwise} \end{cases}$;
    Let $c = (-1)^{|E|}$ be the vector of costs;
    Let $b = (1)^{|V|}$ be the vector of coefficients;
    $x = simplexAlgo(A, b, c)$;
    if $1^T x == |S_j|$ **then**
      $f(d_i) = f(d_i) \cup d_i \mapsto prj_j$
    end
  end
end

date. We modeled the problem described in this paper as a maximum bipartite matching. This problem is solved by our approach utilizing the simplex algorithm. We present a first prototype that uses LinkedIn to extract person skill.

Future work will focus on extending our approach towards taking account of not only skills, but the different skill levels persons have. This transforms the problem into a more complex one by finding the best fitting assignment of persons and projects.

References

1. Bozzon, A., Brambilla, M., Ceri, S., Silvestri, M., Vesci, G.: Choosing the right crowd: expert finding in social networks categories and subject descriptors. In: Proc. of EDBT (2013)
2. Burkard, R.E., Cela, E.: Linear assignment problems and extensions. Springer (1999)
3. Heil, S., Wild, S., Gaedke, M.: CRAWL·E: distributed skill endorsements in expert finding. In: Casteleyn, S., Rossi, G., Winckler, M. (eds.) ICWE 2014. LNCS, vol. 8541, pp. 57–75. Springer, Heidelberg (2014)
4. Howe, J.: Crowdsourcing: A Definition. Crowdsourcing Weblog (2006)
5. Lee, C.S., Pan, C.Y.: An intelligent fuzzy agent for meeting scheduling decision support system. Fuzzy Sets and Systems **142**(3), 467–488 (2004)
6. Sen, S., Durfee, E.H.: A formal study of distributed meeting scheduling. Group Decision and Negotiation **7**(3), 265–289 (1998)

E-WISE: An Expertise-Driven Recommendation Platform for Web Question Answering Systems

Jie Yang(✉), Alessandro Bozzon, and Geert-Jan Houben

Delft University of Technology, Mekelweg 4, 2628 CD Delft, The Netherlands
{j.yang-3,a.bozzon,g.j.p.m.houben}@tudelft.nl

Abstract. This demo presents E-WISE, an expertise-driven recommendation platform built upon Web Question Answering (QA) systems to assist askers in question-answering process. Despite that crowdsourcing knowledge (e.g., on-line question-answering) is becoming increasingly important, it remains a big challenge to accelerate its process. E-WISE blends the recently developed methods for knowledge crowdsourcing acceleration, including *1)* an edit suggestion component to improve question quality; *2)* a question routing component that suggests a list of ranked answerers. Both components are automatic, and meanwhile enable a human controlling part: askers can make their decisions in selecting the right edits/answerers among the suggested ones, which guarantees the effectiveness of the suggesting components and provides feedback to the suggesting methods. E-WISE will be demonstrated through a case study on Stack Overflow – a popular QA systems, to exemplify its functions and potential in on-line knowledge creation.

Keywords: Crowdsourcing · Knowledge creation · Question answering · Edit suggestion · Question routing

1 Introduction

Crowdsourcing knowledge has recently been proposed as a promising topic, which solicits the rich set of knowledge-related features of humans (e.g. expertise, skills, experience and opinions), to solve complex and cognitive intensive tasks. The growing popularity of knowledge crowdsourcing systems, such as on-line QA platform (e.g. Stack Exchange[1] and Yahoo! Answers[2]), content curation systems (e.g. Reddit[3]), diverse on-line forums and wiki's, have demonstrated the great potential of knowledge crowdsourcing in on-line knowledge creation.

Although crowdsourcing has drawn much attention from diverse domains, knowledge crowdsourcing has been much less studied until the most recent [1]. In the case of on-line knowledge creation, typical tasks such as building wiki's or QA systems are performed on an ad-hoc basis. The non-existence of a comprehensive

[1] http://stackexchange.com/
[2] http://answers.yahoo.com/
[3] http://www.reddit.com

P. Cimiano et al. (Eds.): ICWE 2015, LNCS 9114, pp. 691–694, 2015.
DOI: 10.1007/978-3-319-19890-3_59

theory of knowledge crowdsourcing and a corresponding systematic engineering approach have induced big challenges: knowledge is usually created inefficiently. For instance in Stack Overflow[4], which is one of the most active QA systems on the web, there are more than 30% questions do not have any up-voted answer; furthermore, the average time for a question to receive an accepted answer is at a magnitude of days.

Recent advances in the research community have illuminated the possibility of developing methods and tools to support accelerating knowledge creation process. Question routing, for example, that actively routes the newly posted question to potential answerers, has been proposed as a promising method to accelerate QA process. Another direction in this research is to improve question quality. Poorly formulated questions (around 40% in Stack Overflow) needs to be edited after they were initially posted, as responses to comments or answers. Since the interactions between askers and other users lengthens the time for a question to obtain a good answer, it has been proposed to detect poorly formulated question and automatically suggest edit to improve question quality such that the QA process can be accelerated [2,3].

This demo introduces E-WISE, an expertise-driven recommendation platform that provides a continuous and complete line of assistance to askers in web QA systems. E-WISE supports related question retrieval, automatic edit suggestion, user modeling and question routing. The platform implements and integrates the state-of-the-art methods [3,4], thus contributing to the creation of a comprehensive theory of knowledge crowdsourcing acceleration. Another important feature of E-WISE is that askers are allowed to make their own decisions, with the assistance of the automatic recommending methods, i.e. edit and answerer suggestion. Therefore, E-WISE acts as a social machine [5] that fuses the complementary power of humans and computers for knowledge creation.

E-WISE will be demonstrated with an instantiation integrated with Stack Overflow. The attendees will be given the opportunity to interact lively with Stack Overflow through E-WISE, such as searching and posting questions on Stack Overflow, with the assistance of edit and answerer suggestion by E-WISE.

2 The E-WISE Architecture

Fig. 1 depicts the architecture of E-WISE. It comprises two phases, namely, off-line training and on-line searching and recommendation. Due to efficiency reason, the training phase trains recommenders off-line based on historical QA data imported from web QA systems; while on-line phase recommends edits and answerers to askers in real-time using the trained recommenders. Askers can interact lively with the QA systems through E-WISE, such that the actions taken by the askers can be written back to the QA sytems in real-time.

E-WISE consists of three components: related question searcher, edit suggester and question router. Standard information retrieving method is adopted for related question retrieval. While for edit suggestion and question routing, E-WISE implements our novel methods described in [3,4].

[4] http://stackoverflow.com/

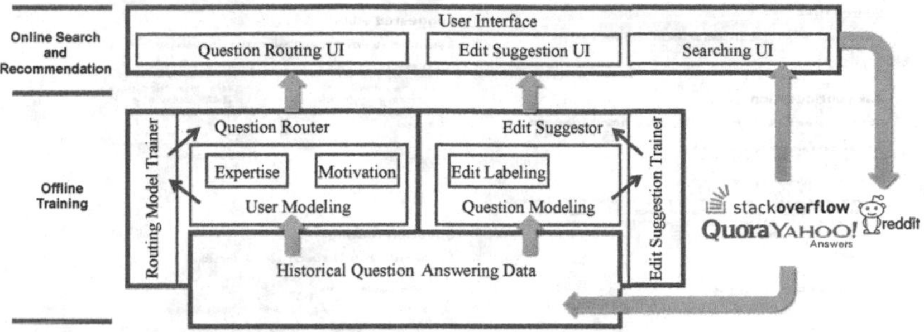

Fig. 1. System Architecture of E-WISE

Edit Suggester detects poorly formulated questions and suggests edits to improve question quality. Essentially, this component consists of two type of classifiers, one for edit/non-edit classification, the other one for edit type classification. The trainer takes (compressed) TFIDF representation of labeled questions as input, then trains the classifiers off-line for on-line edit suggestion.

After a question is classified as one that needs an edit, it will then be classified into some of pre-defined edit types. For instance the edit suggester of E-WISE for Stack Overflow defines the following edit types: *1)* Code, which indicates that the question needs to have a code snippet; *2)* SEC, indicating that the question needs clarification of either problem *S*tatement, *E*xample or *C*ontext; *3)* Attempt, which indicates that the asker needs to specify attempts that he has tried. The asker will receive a list of suggestions, and decide to reformulate their questions correspondingly. The asker is further provided the option to provide feedback to the system, by indicating whether or not the suggested edits are helpful.

Question Router. After the asker input a question, he can enable the question router to actively route his question to potential answerers. Question router contains a user modeling part that models the topic-wise expertise and motivation of answerers, which are considered as the most important answering properties in QA systems [4]. The basic assumption is that questions of different topics require different combinations of user roles: questions relating to general concepts may require motivated answerers engaged in discussion to ultimately generate a best answer, while some other questions relating to specific topic only need one expert user to directly provide the right answer.

Given a newly posted question, question router first matches the question to answerers according to the topics, then ranks the answerers according to expertise and motivation. Question router trains a learning-to-rank model off-line for on-line answerer ranking. It takes as input the user models (expertise, motivation) and historical QA data, and output the model for answerers suggestion. The asker will be shown a ranked list of answerers, together with their user profiles as the interpretation to help the asker in making decision of whom to route the question to. The asker is further provided with the option of removing or adding answerers.

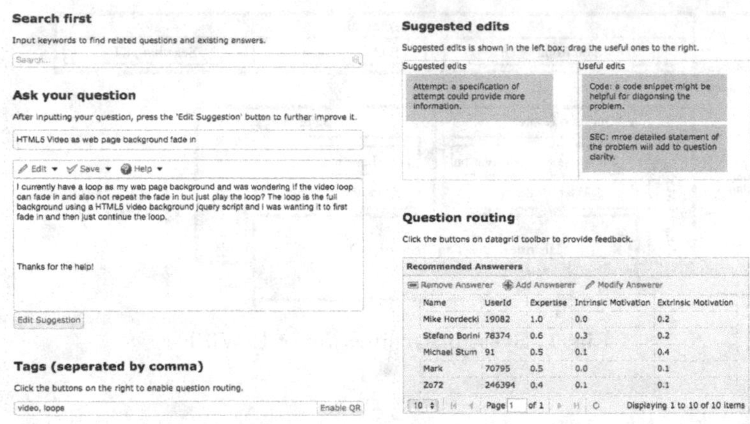

(a) User input interface. (b) Result and feedback interface.

Fig. 2. User interface

3 Demo Scenario: Stack Overflow

We demonstrate E-WISE with a case study on Stack Overflow. For performance reason, E-WISE takes the latest historical data for off-line training edit suggestor and question router; with the trained recommenders, E-WISE is seamlessly integrated with the live QA system, such that the askers are allowed to directly interact with Stack Overflow through E-WISE, e.g. searching related questions, post questions and inspect the profile of the suggested users.

Fig. 2a is the user interface in which askers can search, post questions, call edit suggester and question router. Fig. 2b is the user interface that displays suggested edits and answerers. Askers can interact with the results to provide feedback for both edit suggestion and question routing: suggested edits that are useful on the left box can be dragged to the right box to indicate the usefulness; answerers can be removed from or added to the routing list.

References

1. Kittur, A., Nickerson, J.V., Bernstein, M., Gerber, E., Shaw, A., Zimmerman, J., Lease, M., Horton, J.: The future of crowd work. In: CSCW 2013, pp. 1301–1318. ACM, New York (2013)
2. Ravi, S., Pang, B., Rastogi, V., Kumar, R.: Great question! question quality in community Q&A. In: ICWSM 2014, pp. 426–435. AAAI, Palo Alto (2014)
3. Yang, J., Hauff, C., Bozzon, A., Houben, G.J.: Asking the right question in collaborative Q&A systems. In: Hypertext 2014, pp. 179–189. ACM, New York (2014)
4. Yang, J., Tao, K., Bozzon, A., Houben, G.-J.: Sparrows and owls: characterisation of expert behaviour in stackoverflow. In: Dimitrova, V., Kuflik, T., Chin, D., Ricci, F., Dolog, P., Houben, G.-J. (eds.) UMAP 2014. LNCS, vol. 8538, pp. 266–277. Springer, Heidelberg (2014)
5. Hendler, J., Berners-Lee, T.: From the Semantic Web to Social Machines: a Research Challenge for AI on the World Wide Web. Artificial Intelligence **174**(2), 156–161 (2010)

Posters

Detaching Control from Data Models in Model-Based Generation of User Interfaces

Giorgio Brajnik[1,2(✉)] and Simon Harper[1]

[1] Computer Science School, University of Manchester, Manchester, UK
simon.harper@manchester.ac.uk
[2] Dipartimento di Matematica e Informatica, Università di Udine, Udine, Italy
brajnik@uniud.it

Abstract. A strength of IFML derives from its ability to support generation of a user interface by coupling data and control models. However, separation of concerns between different models (and in particular between models of control and of data) could be beneficial to better understand generation principles and expressivity limits, to support computation of design quality metrics, and to formulate intra-model transformation rules.

In the paper we show that such a separation is indeed possible using UML class and state diagrams. We present the generation rules that a compiler follows for producing user interfaces. Based on the adopted representation, we argue that certain expressive limits are due to the underlying foundation common of our approach and of IFML.

Keywords: Model-based user interface generation · Statecharts · UML · IFML · Low fidelity prototypes

1 Introduction

Model-based approaches for designing and developing user interfaces (UIs) often use platform independent meta-models that provide means to abstract data and control aspects. One of these approaches is Interaction Flow Modeling Language (IFML), an OMG standard aimed at modeling rich user interfaces [2] that is being used by industry to support automatic generation of web applications. The strength of IFML derives from its ability to support automatic generation of a web application and its user interface; this is made possible because it can express the abstract behavior of a UI through a very tight integration of data view components with a state transition representation.

In this paper we tackle the problem of detaching control from data specifications as they are used in IFML and see if, by providing a looser relationship between them, we can preserve the same expressive power and the ability to automatically generate UIs. This "separation of concerns" principle is often mentioned in the model-driven UI literature.

The are several reasons for doing so. A separate model of control helps understanding the conceptual framework upon which the generation principles can be

P. Cimiano et al. (Eds.): ICWE 2015, LNCS 9114, pp. 697–700, 2015.
DOI: 10.1007/978-3-319-19890-3_60

formulated; it can also help highlighting expressive limits, their reasons and possible solutions. A separate model of control can also be used in instrumenting the generation tool so that graph-theoretic metrics can be produced that bear upon usability (as suggested in [3,4]). These metrics would make interfaces and usability quantifiable (at least in part), and therefore would enable a data-driven approach to UI design that allows well founded comparisons of alternative designs. Finally, a separate model of control helps understanding if an algebra of models can be defined so that new models are automatically derived from existing ones. This could be extremely useful for deriving, for example, a mobile UI by applying certain operators on a model of a desktop UI.

However, at the moment, it is not clear if such a separation is possible without loosing the strong expressive power that IFML features. In the paper we show that such a separation is indeed possible, and that it can be achieved using UML class and state diagrams. Based on the adopted representation, we argue that certain expressive limits are due to the underlying foundation, that is common of our approach and of IFML. Limits deal with the inability to handle arbitrary undo/redo, to handle customizable toolbars, and to handle arbitrary instantiations of widgets.

2 Conceptual View of UICompiler

The following modeling elements are used by UICompiler, a tool that currently generates UIs starting from separate models of control and of data. (A) *State Machines*, expressed as UML state diagrams, which specify the behavior of each active UI component (such as a window of a browser). (B) *Events*, that represent user actions, events that are endogenous to the UI, or events pushed by an external agent. (C) *Data views*, which represent the conceptual model of the UI; *e.g.*, for a mail front end application the domain model comprises classes like `Message`, `Thread`, `Folder`, etc. They are defined as a system of classes with appropriate relationships. (D) *Annotations*, or XML fragments that are "attached" to model elements (to states, transitions or data views) and which are used to: (1) specify which data views should be used in a state to display information, and which specific variables of the state machine are used to populate them; (2) what is the domain, in terms of data views, of the parameters used in parametric events; (3) which widgets have to be embedded into states, and which transitions are embedded within widgets; (4) which custom templates (of custom widgets) to include within the prototype being built; (5) what is the effect on data of actions associated to transitions or states. State machines, events and data views are specified following UML 2.4.

The basic postulate underlying UICompiler is that the structure of the UI in terms of widgets and containers, and its changes over time, are determined by the state machine model. Said in other terms, available actions shape the structure of the UI. Two assumptions are important to support such a postulate: (1) A state should be identified by available user actions and non-user events. In other words, the set of transitions leaving a state should distinguish that state from other ones. (2) A state and its ancestors should be annotated in such a way that all the information needed by the user to decide which action to take next are rendered.

UICompiler embodies three general design principles: (A) The generated UI should include a representation of each active state, which should provide triggers for all the user actions that can be taken from that state. In this way each state represents an interaction context. (B) Nesting of states should reflect nesting of UI containers and widgets. In this way changes between interaction contexts depend on what actions are taken. (C) Concurrent regions should correspond to sibling components in the UI. This lets the user of the UI to work on any of the available interaction contexts, each corresponding to an active region

UICompiler does not attempt to produce visually appealing layouts and styles. Instead, the UI it generates can be easily styled with CSS (in the current desktop platform) thanks to classes and identifiers that are automatically injected into the DOM of the running UI. In this way, the designer can enhance at will aesthetics of the UI. Beyond providing flexibility to UI designers, in this way automated approaches to derive optimal layouts (*e.g.*, [5]) could be easily deployed.

UICompiler is a Java application that takes as input an XMI file that represents the state machine and class models; its content is parsed, several syntactic and semantic checks are applied (including checking that transitions leaving pseudo-states do not have event triggers, or that at most one event is specified for a compound transition), state machines are flattened, data views are transformed into JSON instances, and finally through a number of templates (for the top level state machine, for each state and transition) the final code is generated. At the moment only a desktop platform is supported, and code is generated in HTML, CSS and Javascript (jQuery).

3 Discussion

We are instrumenting UICompiler so that it can compute graph-theoretic metrics that bear upon usability (as done, for example, in [4]). In [1] we present preliminary results where the compiler uses the flattened version of the UML state machine model to compute the "betweenness" metric to identify states or transitions that are central in an interaction structure and that therefore should be free from usability defects.

So far we have applied UICompiler to a dozen of applications, and have found that all the UML state machine constructs were needed at one point or another. This suggests that the representation is minimal. We also discovered the following conceptual limitations.

Instances of Components. Right now it is not possible to specify, using a single UML state machine, that a model could include an arbitrary number of instances of a sub-state machine. For example, in catalog browser of an e-commerce website there could be n products, all sharing a particular interaction structure (such as expanding/collapsing, rotating, comparing). Right now one has to duplicate a composite state n times, and n has to be known at modeling time. We plan to overcome this limitation by allowing the designer to dynamically instantiate UML classes that represent UI components, each with its own interaction structure. When doing that, however, static analysis of the model with graph-theoretic metrics would suffer, because the graph changes whenever these components are instantiated.

Toolbar Customizations. Another limit of UML state machines used for UI specification lies in the fact that models cannot specify that a user can customize a UI by changing its toolbars. This requires that new states are dynamically created, with new transitions. In other words, that the state machine model changes dynamically. We plan to overcome this limit again by the ability to dynamically instantiate new state machines.

Undo and Redo. At the moment these capabilities can be included in prototypes generated by UICompiler only if they are programmed within the delivery platform (*e.g.*, explicitly programmed in Javascript). Because UML state machines are based on finite state machines, the stack-oriented management of history required by undos and redos cannot be expressed. However, it would be nice if they could be specified explicitly in the models so that graph-theoretic metrics could consider them.

These limitations are not specific to UICompiler, as they apply to all the approaches based on finite state representations, including IFML. Another fundamental limit of all these approaches is the inability to represent "natural UIs", namely those where the user interacts through a continuous stream of events, such as when using an eye tracker, a body movement tracker, or remote controllers whose position and orientation can be tracked.

References

1. Brajnik, G., Harper, S.: Model-based engineering of user interfaces to support cognitive load estimation in automotive applications. In: Kun, A., Froelich, P. (eds.) Cognitive Load and In-Vehicle Human-Machine Interaction Workshop; adjuct Proceedings of the 5th Int. Conference on Automotive User Interfaces and Interactive Vehicular Applications. ACM Press, Eindhoven (October 2013)
2. OMG: Interaction flow modeling language (IFML), ftf - beta 1. Tech. rep., OMG (March 2013). http://www.omg.org/spec/IFML/1.0
3. Thimbleby, H.: Press on: principles of interaction programming. The MIT Press (2007)
4. Thimbleby, H., Oladimeji, P.: Social network analysis and interactive device design analysis. In: Proc. of Engineering Interactive Computing Systems 2009, pp. 91–100. ACM Press (2009)
5. Zeidler, C., Lutteroth, C., Weber, G.: Constraint solving for beautiful user interfaces: how solving strategies support layout aesthetics. In: CHI New Zealand 2012. ACM Press, Dunedin (2012)

Graph-Based Methods for Clustering Topics of Interest in Twitter

Hugo Hromic(✉), Narumol Prangnawarat, Ioana Hulpuş, Marcel Karnstedt, and Conor Hayes

Insight Centre for Data Analytics, National University of Ireland Galway (NUIG), Galway, Ireland
{hugo.hromic,narumol.prangnawarat,ioana.hulpus,marcel.karnstedt, conor.hayes}@insight-centre.org
http://www.insight-centre.org

Abstract. Online Social Media provides real-time information about events and news in the physical world. A challenging problem is then to identify in a timely manner the few relevant bits of information in these massive and fast-paced streams. Most of the current topic clustering and event detection methods focus on user generated *content*, hence they are sensible to language, writing style and are usually expensive to compute. Instead, our approach focuses on mining the *structure* of the graph generated by the interactions between users. Our hypothesis is that bursts in user interest for particular topics and events are reflected by corresponding changes in the structure of the discussion dynamics. We show that our method is capable of effectively identifying event topics in Twitter ground truth data, while offering better overall performance than a purely content-based method based on LDA topic models.

1 Introduction

Twitter is possibly today the most widely used *microblogging* system in the world, allowing for real-time broadcasting of short messages (or *Tweets*) among friends and followers. This vast stream of content, despite containing a large amount of noisy data, also contains relevant and updated information [6,7]. Being able to timely identify these topical "gold nuggets" within busy social streams becomes essential to help users discover potentially interesting content.

The majority of existing approaches for topic finding in Twitter focus on [1]: (a) *textual features*, e.g. using topic models [9], keeping track of bursty words [3] or clustering trending Tweets [5], and (b) *activity dynamics*, e.g. monitoring keyword usage patterns [10] or analysing Tweet/Retweet interactions [2,12]. On the one hand, text-based approaches are inherently sensitive to the writing style and language (e.g. English, Chinese), where colloquial expressions dominate and are often expensive to process. On the other hand, activity-based approaches are faster but less effective in presence of noise and mostly dependant on the a priori chosen seed keywords or terms.

In this paper we propose to instead focus on a more efficient *structure-based* approach, which can be less expensive to process than text-based techniques,

P. Cimiano et al. (Eds.): ICWE 2015, LNCS 9114, pp. 701–704, 2015.
DOI: 10.1007/978-3-319-19890-3_61

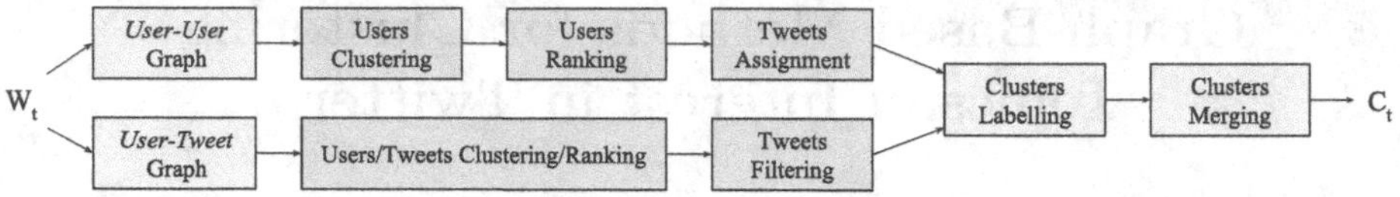

Fig. 1. Per-window processing pipeline for topics clustering. $W_t = \{tw_0, tw_1, \cdots, tw_n\}$ is a window of n Tweets at a time t and C_t is a resulting topics clustering configuration for the same time.

thanks to a simpler graph model; and less sensitive to noise compared to an activity-based approach that ignores the connection between user interactions.

It is well understood that events and topics generate bursts in Twitter activity [2]. Thus, we hypothesise that by modelling this activity as edges in a *Twitter interaction graph* we can capture bursty topics and events by using graph analysis methods. Therefore, we mine for groups of tightly connected users and Tweets under the assumption that these groups represent an emerged topic or event.

2 Graph-Based Pipeline for Topics Clustering

Our topic clustering approach is built around a processing pipeline (Figure 1) where an incoming stream of Tweets is received from Twitter and aggregated using a sliding window approach to generate two alternative graph representations of Twitter interactions (Figure 2(a)). The first is a **User-to-User (UU)** perspective (Figure 2(b)), where edges represent links between the author of a Tweet and all the mentioned, retweeted or replied users in it. The second is a bipartite **User-to-Tweet (UT)** view (Figure 2(c)), where edges link users to their posted Tweets, replies, Retweets, or posts in which they have been mentioned.

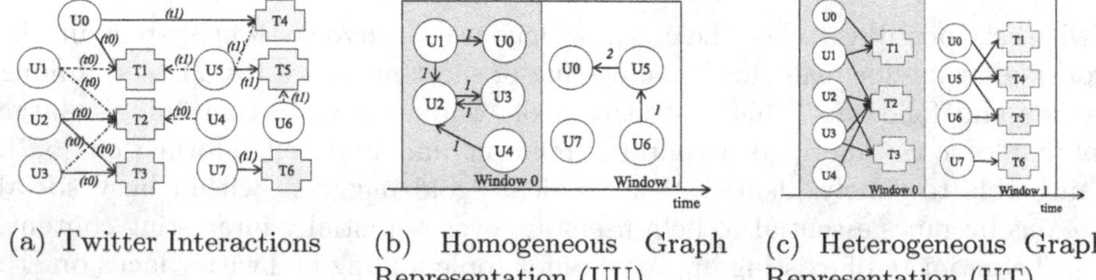

(a) Twitter Interactions (b) Homogeneous Graph Representation (UU) (c) Heterogeneous Graph Representation (UT)

Fig. 2. Graph models for Twitter interactions across processing windows. U-nodes denote users, T-nodes denote Tweets. Interaction types (edges): solid → *tweeted*, dashed → *mentionedIn*, dotted → *repliedIn* and dashed/dotted → *retweeted*.

Topic clusters are extracted from the above networks. For the UU Graph approach, we use the OSLOM community finding algorithm [8] to produce a set of user communities based on tightly interacting users. The users inside each community are ranked using the PageRank algorithm and their latest Tweets are selected to form clusters of Tweets. For the heterogeneous UT Graph, we use the RankClus algorithm [14] to build clusters of ranked Tweets. Tweets ranked lower than a given threshold are removed.

At this stage, the resulting clusters from both of our graph models do not have any topic information. For this we perform two post-processing steps for labelling and merging topically similar groups. First, we label each Tweet cluster by the top-k most frequent hashtags occurring in its Tweets. If no hashtag is found, then we extract the top-k most frequent named entities using the Python NLTK library[1]. Second, to minimise topic redundancy among clusters, i.e. those with similar labels, we combine the clusters that have the same first-n labels, ordered by their usage frequency.

3 Experiments and Results

To test our approach we use a third-party human annotated ground truth Twitter dataset containing a number of known public events, that we consider as *topics*, and their associated Tweets [11]. We constructed 28 day-long sliding windows and extracted labelled topic clusters for each. These were generated by our proposed pipeline, as well as a topic model approach using LDA [9] which serves as our text-based baseline. Our evaluation measured two aspects: clustering quality (using the F_1-Measure of Precision and Recall, see Figure 3) and runtime performance (Figure 4). In both experiments, our structure-based approach outperforms the baseline.

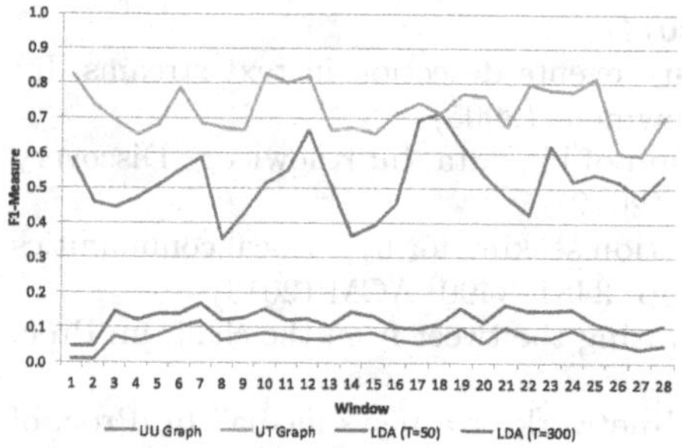

Fig. 3. Per-window F_1-Measure for both of our network types and the LDA topic models method (using two settings)

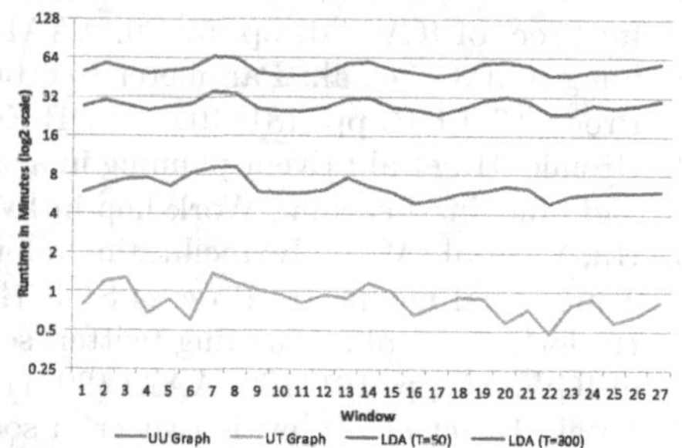

Fig. 4. Per-window runtime performances – in log scale – for all the studied methods (graph- and text-based)

4 Conclusions and Future Work

We proposed a graph-based processing pipeline for clustering topics of interest in Twitter. For this, we presented two different types of graphs for modelling interactions between users, one that only represents User-to-User actions, and another that captures the relations between users and Tweets. Based on the homogeneous

[1] Available in http://www.nltk.org

model, in 2012 we successfully developed *Whassappi* [4], a prototype mobile application for topic finding aimed at the visitors of the final leg of the Volvo Ocean Race 2012 in Ireland. We experimented with two state of the art network clustering algorithms, one for each type of graph. Our experiments and results support our hypothesis that analysis of user interactions through graph mining reveal discussions that ultimately correlate with human annotated events. Moreover, our approach outperformed a baseline text-based LDA topic model technique. Our study opened some interesting research questions that we plan to address in the future. For example, we noticed distinctive graph patterns for various types of events: the properties of the graph clusters and their nodes might potentially be used for classifying events. In this regard, one of our future objectives is to devise methods able to describe events, for instance to distinguish between local or personal topics, and events of world-wide interest [13].

Acknowledgements. This work was supported by Science Foundation Ireland (SFI) partly under Grant No. 08/SRC/I1407 (Clique) and partly under Grant No. 12/RC/2289 (Insight Centre for Data Analytics).

References

1. Atefeh, F., Khreich, W.: A survey of techniques for event detection in twitter. In: Computational Intelligence. Wiley Online Library (2013)
2. Chierichetti, F., et al.: Event detection via communication pattern analysis. In: Proc. of ICWSM, pp. 51–60. AAAI (2014)
3. Fung, G.P.C., et al.: Parameter free bursty events detection in text streams. In: Proc. of VLDB, pp. 181–192. VLDB Endowment (2005)
4. Hromic, H., et al.: Event panning in a stream of big data. In: Knowledge Discovery and Machine Learning Workshop in LWA (2012)
5. Hu, Y., et al.: Whoo.ly: facilitating information seeking for hyperlocal communities using social media. In: Proc. of SIGCHI, pp. 3481–3490. ACM (2013)
6. Hurlock, J., et al.: Searching twitter: separating the tweet from the chaff. In: Proc. of ICWSM, pp. 161–168. AAAI (2011)
7. Kwak, H., et al.: What is twitter, a social network or a news media? In: Proc. of WWW, pp. 591–600. ACM (2010)
8. Lancichinetti, A., et al.: Finding statistically significant communities in networks. In: PloS one, vol. 6, p. e18961. Public Library of Science (2011)
9. Lau, J.H., et al.: On-line trend analysis with topic models: #twitter trends detection topic model online. In: Proc. of COLING, pp. 1519–1534. Citeseer (2012)
10. Marcus, A., et al.: TwitInfo: aggregating and visualizing microblogs for event exploration. In: Proc. of SIGCHI, pp. 227–236. ACM (2011)
11. McMinn, A.J., et al.: Building a large-scale corpus for evaluating event detection on twitter. In: Proc. of CIKM, pp. 409–418. ACM (2013)
12. Popescu, A.M., et al.: Detecting controversial events from twitter. In: Proc. of CIKM, pp. 1873–1876. ACM (2010)
13. Prangnawarat, N., et al.: Event analysis in social media using clustering of heterogeneous information networks. In: Proc. of FLAIRS. AAAI (2015)
14. Sun, Y., et al.: RankClus: integrating clustering with ranking for heterogeneous information network analysis. In: Proc. of EDBT/ICDT, pp. 565–576. ACM (2009)

Towards Strategy Patterns for Evaluating Usability

Belen Rivera[1], Pablo Becker[1], Philip Lew[2], and Luis Olsina[1(✉)]

[1] GIDIS_Web, Engineering School at Universidad Nacional de La Pampa, La Pampa, Argentina
belenrs@yahoo.com, {beckerp,olsinal}@ing.unlpam.edu.ar
[2] School of Computer Science and Engineering, Beihang University, Beijing, China
philiplew@gmail.com

Abstract. In this paper, we propose a holistic quality evaluation approach for usability and user experience (UX), which relies on quality views and strategy patterns. A quality view relates accordingly an entity super-category, e.g., product, system, system in use, with a quality focus such as internal quality (IQ), external quality (EQ), and quality in use (QinU). Usability and UX are higher-level characteristics that should be linked to quality views appropriately. Also quality views support 'influences' and 'depends on' relationships. With a concrete evaluation or improvement project goal, our approach selects and instantiates a suitable strategy from a set of strategy patterns.

1 Introduction

It is well known that Usability and UX are significant quality characteristics of web and mobile applications and thus their evaluations are becoming increasingly important in the mobile gadgetry industry as well. However, looking at the state-of-the-art literature we found that Usability and UX are poorly linked to target entity categories (e.g., Product, System and System in use) with quality focuses such as IQ, EQ and QinU and their quality models. A *quality view* relates accordingly an entity super-category with a quality focus. Also quality views support *influences* and *depends on* relationships between views. Moreover, a *quality model* represents the quality focus by means of a set of characteristics, sub-characteristics and attributes. Thus, Usability and UX sub-characteristics and attributes, as non-functional requirements to be evaluated are often included in quality models [5].

On the other hand, quality views and their relationships are paramount for defining measurement, evaluation (ME) and change (MEC) strategies and *strategy patterns* to be used as resources in ME/MEC projects. We define the term strategy as; "*principles, patterns, and particular domain concepts and framework that may be specified by a set of concrete processes, in addition to a set of appropriate methods and tools as core resources for achieving a project goal* " [1]. In the last decade, we have earned experience in developing specific strategies. For instance, we have developed GOCAME (*Goal-Oriented Context-Aware Measurement and Evaluation*), and SIQinU (*Strategy for Improving Quality in Use*) strategies, which were applied in several concrete evaluation and improvement projects [4, 5, 6]. Regarding the above strategy definition, both strategies share the principle of three integrated capabilities, namely: the *ME domain conceptual base and framework*, the *process perspective specifications*, and the *method*

P. Cimiano et al. (Eds.): ICWE 2015, LNCS 9114, pp. 705–708, 2015.
DOI: 10.1007/978-3-319-19890-3_62

specifications. However, we recently have envisioned the idea of packaging the earned experience into strategy patterns.

It is recognized that patterns have had and still have significant impact in software and web engineering [3]. In a nutshell, the pattern's aim is to provide a general and reusable solution to a recurrent problem. In this sense, we have observed that strategy patterns can be applied to recurrent ME or MEC problems of any project. Therefore, the major contributions of this research are: (i) *Add a quality view component* to a ME conceptual framework, which allows instantiating quality views and quality models accordingly; (ii) *Specify strategy patterns for different quality views and project goals* such as evaluation and improvement for Usability and UX.

Following this introduction, Section 2 analyzes the quality view component and strategies. Section 3 discusses some strategy patterns and summarizes conclusions.

2 Quality Views and Strategy Patterns

In a given ME or MEC project one or more entity super-category can be chosen as, for example, System and System in use, which can be evaluated by means of the EQ and QinU focuses, respectively. The quality focus is the highest abstraction level concept of a quality model. Next, we represent the *quality view* component added to the previously developed C-INCAMI conceptual components [6].

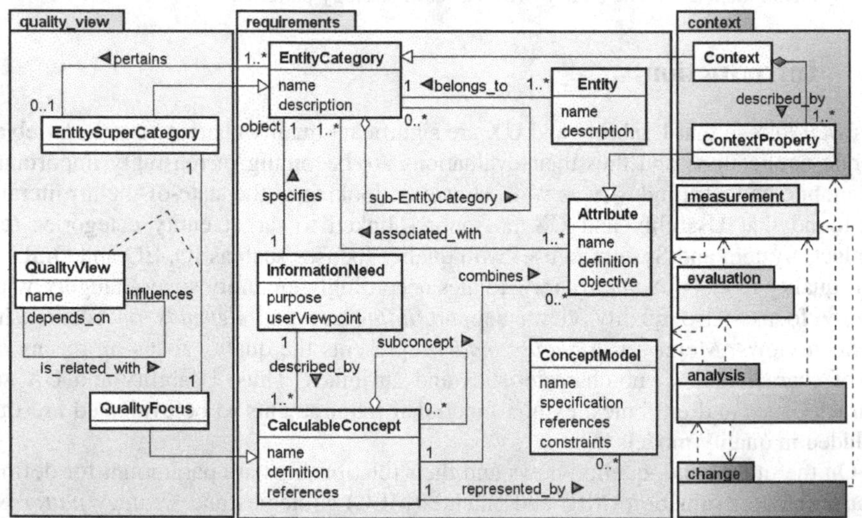

Fig. 1. C-INCAMI conceptual components enhanced with the new *quality_view* component

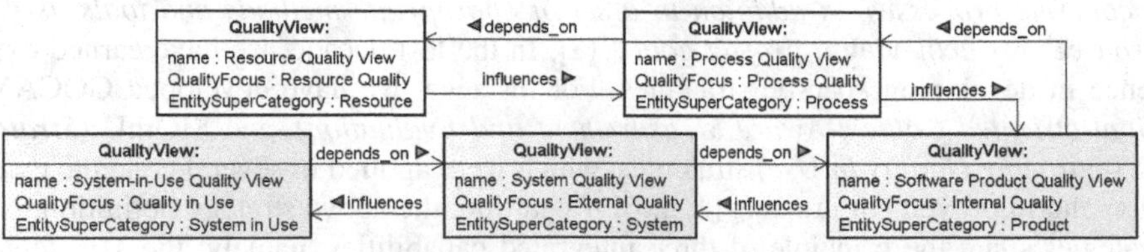

Fig. 2. An instantiation of typical quality views from the *quality_view* component

Fig. 1 shows the added *quality_view* component which allows the instantiation of quality views by means of the *QualityView* concept. Examples of concrete quality views are depicted in Fig. 2. A quality view is the association between an entity super-category (*EntitySuperCategory*) and a quality focus (*QualityFocus*). Moreover, the added component allows representing two relations between quality views. For instance, Fig. 2 shows that the System Quality view *influences* the System-in-Use Quality view and, in turn, the latter *depends on* or is determined by the former.

When evaluating Usability and UX for mobile and web entities, suitable quality views should be considered [5]. For this aim, potential views are the three yellow-colored quality views in Fig. 2, namely: Software Product, System and System-in-Use Quality views. For each quality view, and particularly for its quality focus, a quality model should be selected. A question that a reader might ask is: to which quality focus can Usability and UX characteristics be related? In short, Usability can be related to the IQ and EQ focuses, while UX to the QinU focus [2, 5].

On the other hand, the fact of modeling quality views and their relationships is crucial for the aim of selecting strategies, since they are chosen considering quality views to be evaluated according to the project goal. Each integrated strategy should support simultaneously the three principles as indicated in Section 1.

In the last decade, we developed specific strategies such as GOCAME and SIQinU, which have been employed in concrete evaluation and improvement projects. GOCAME embraces one quality view, and SIQinU two quality views. For instance, SIQinU supports the QinU/EQ/QinU evaluation and improvement cycles, starting evaluations from Task-based and/or Perception-based System-in-use entities, and their corresponding characteristics and attributes. Thus, we have employed SIQinU in the JIRA case study [4] for the most frequently used "Entering a new defect" task. SIQinU relates just the System-in-Use Quality view with the System Quality view exploring the abovementioned relationships between views.

To summarize, our *holistic quality evaluation approach* was used by means of quality views and specific strategies. However, we have recently observed that a ME or MEC strategy can be applied to recurrent problems of any ME/MEC project. Thus, we sought to develop a set of strategy patterns that offer reusable and instantiable solutions. Patterns are essentially 'experience in a can', for our case, ready to be opened and used by evaluators. We have specified a set of strategy patterns, following a specification template which includes: (1) *name*: A descriptive and unique name; (2) *alias*: Acronym or other names; (3) *intent*: Main objective for the pattern; (4) *motivation* (*problem*): Problem which solves the pattern; (5) *applicability*: Situations in which the pattern can be applied; (6) *structure* (*solution*): Generic structure and instantiable solution that the pattern offers; (7) *known uses*: References of real usage; (8) *scenario of use*: Concrete example and illustration for the instantiated pattern. For space reasons, the strategy patterns will be documented in a follow-up manuscript.

3 Final Remarks

Using our holistic approach, *ME/MEC strategies* are chosen for evaluation and improvement embracing one or more *quality views* to accomplish the project goal. To this end, we have also envisioned to design a set of strategy patterns as a way of packaging general and reusable solutions for common, recurrent problems/goals within measurement, evaluation and change/improvement situations for specific projects. Hence, a strategy pattern, according to the project goal and the amount of involved quality views can be selected from the set of strategy patterns. For example, if the project aims at assessing just one *quality view*, i.e., to understand the current situation of an entity category with regard to the corresponding quality focus, then the GOCAME_1V strategy pattern is the suitable. The pattern intention is to provide a solution in the instantiation of a ME strategy aimed at supporting an understanding project goal when one quality view is considered. The GOCAME_1V generic process consists of six activities. Note that this pattern can be used to evaluate either IQ, or EQ, or QinU focuses considering Usability concepts.

On the other hand, if the project involves MEC goals for one *quality view* then the GOCAMEC_1V strategy pattern should be selected. Furthermore, if the project involves MEC goals for two *quality views* then the GOCAMEC_2V strategy pattern should be chosen. Recall that in Fig. 2, between two quality views, the *depends on* and *influences* relationships can be used. If we consider for a while, the System Quality and the System-in-Use Quality views, these relations embrace the hypothesis that evaluating and improving the EQ of a system is one means of improving the QinU of a system in use. Similarly, evaluating the QinU can provide feedback to improve the EQ. Thus, the GOCAMEC_2V strategy pattern embeds this hypothesis. A concrete strategy derived from this pattern is the so-called SIQinU –used in an industrial case [4]-, which supports the QinU/EQ/QinU improvement cycles. Note that the GOCAMEC_2V strategy pattern can be instantiated to two another related quality views, such as Resource and Process Quality views, taking into account for instance that a resource quality (e.g. a new integrated tool) influences the process quality (e.g. a development process), and vice versa the process quality depends on the resource quality.

References

1. Becker, P., Papa, F., Olsina, L.: Process ontology specification for enhancing the process compliance of a measurement and evaluation strategy. CLEI Electronic Journal **18**(1), 1–26 (2015). Paper 2, ISSN 0717-5000
2. Bevan, N.: Extending quality in use to provide a framework for usability measurement. In: Kurosu, M. (ed.) HCD 2009. LNCS, vol. 5619, pp. 13–22. Springer, Heidelberg (2009)
3. Folmer, E., Bosch, J.: Experiences with software architecture analysis of usability. International Journal of Information Technology and Web Engineering **3**(4), 1–29 (2008)
4. Lew, P., Olsina, L., Becker, P., Zhang, L.: An Integrated Strategy to Systematically Understand and Manage Quality in Use for Web Applications. Requirements Engineering Journal, Springer, London **17**(4), 299–330 (2012)
5. Olsina, L., Santos, L., Lew, P.: Evaluating mobileapp usability: a holistic quality approach. In: Casteleyn, S., Rossi, G., Winckler, M. (eds.) ICWE 2014. LNCS, vol. 8541, pp. 111–129. Springer, Heidelberg (2014)
6. Olsina, L., Papa, F., Molina, H.: How to measure and evaluate web applications in a consistent way. In: Rossi, G., Pastor, O., Schwabe, D., Olsina, L. (eds.) Web Engineering: Modeling and Implementing Web Applications, pp. 385–420. HCIS Springer book (2008)

Scope-Aware Delegations in Distributed Social Networks

Anna Scholtz(✉), Stefan Wild, and Martin Gaedke

Technische Universität Chemnitz, Chemnitz, Germany
{anna.scholtz,stefan.wild,martin.gaedke}@informatik.tu-chemnitz.de

Abstract. Swiftly meeting challenges by distributing tasks to the most suitable knowledge workers is an important matter, especially for network-centric organizations. In such distributed work environments delegations help to solve tasks faster, but also require measures to prevent delegatees from exceeding assigned competencies. By providing universal identification, WebID by W3C can assist in establishing a basis for distributed collaboration. Yet, it does not allow users for delegating access rights to others in a controlled way to act on their behalves. This paper presents the DASC approach to enable scope-aware delegations in distributed social networks using WebID. We introduce a vocabulary to describe delegations including associated constraints and demonstrate a prototypical implementation of DASC within an existing WebID identity provider.

Keywords: Security · Delegation · Semantic web · Social web · WebID

1 Introduction

Network-centric organizations have been rapidly growing in number since the advent of the 21st century [1]. As things are going increasingly faster in our globalized world, it is vital to meet challenges in time by breaking complex activities down into smaller, more manageable tasks and swiftly distribute them to the knowledge workers who are best-suited for carrying them out. Enabling to organize loosely-coupled teams without implying further system dependencies, distributed social networks are well-suited for the knowledge work domain.

A distributed online social network can be implemented using W3C's WebID specification [2]. With WebID, users get a globally accessible and platform-independent identity they can use for authentication and building connections. Therefore, WebID employs three artifacts: A user, like Alice, authenticates herself using a *WebID certificate*. It contains her *WebID URI* and her public key. This *WebID URI* represents a specific identity of user Alice and refers to a *WebID profile* that stores her identity data in a machine-readable way as RDF triples.

Despite the benefits of delegation, it is not an intrinsic part of WebID yet. To prevent delegatees, like Bob, from improperly using profile data and access rights, such WebID extension would need to be aware of the delegation scope defined by a delegator, e.g., restricting the delegation to a specific service and time period.

P. Cimiano et al. (Eds.): ICWE 2015, LNCS 9114, pp. 709–712, 2015.
DOI: 10.1007/978-3-319-19890-3_63

Based on the conceptual foundation for preventing exploitation of personal user data established in [4], this paper discusses how to realize such security feature in practice. We provide three main contributions: First, a process model and semantic vocabulary that specify delegations with associated constraints to define the delegatee's scope, called DASC. Second, a proof-of-concept implementation of DASC and third, the integration into an existing WebID identity provider.

The paper is organized as follows: We discuss related work in Section 2, present and demonstrate DASC in Section 3 and conclude the paper in Section 4.

2 Related Work

While delegation in a closed context is not a new extension to existing identity systems, scope-aware on-behalf-of delegation for distributed social networks is.

OAuth (`http://tools.ietf.org/html/rfc6749`) is a widely used open standard to authorization. It enables users to grant third-party services access to their personal resources, with a *Resource Owner* delegating rights to a *Client* requesting access to a protected resource. While OAuth facilitates restricting the *Client*'s scope of action, it does not directly integrate with existing authentication routines.

XML-based languages such as SAML and XACML allow for detailed specification of authorization and delegation aspects, yet they lack semantic features including high expressiveness, self-descriptiveness and machine interpretability.

Tramp et al., discuss another approach for delegation based on WebID in [3], which distinguishes involved agents by their roles as *secretary* (delegatee) and *principal* (delegator). A WebID URI stored in the principal's WebID profile denotes the secretary, which in turn adds to each HTTP request issued on the principal's behalf the `X-On-Behalf-Of` HTTP header field containing the principal's WebID URI. Extending each HTTP request in such way does not only increase complexity, but also decrease interoperability and applicability.

3 Scope-Aware Delegations Through DASC

Devising DASC, an approach for Delegations Aware of SCope, we aimed at making as few changes as possible to the original WebID identification and authentication mechanism [2]. The conceptual model of DASC defines a delegation as a set consisting of the delegatee's WebID URI, a task to be fulfilled and constraints to determine the scope of action as a whitelist. A delegation-enabled WebID certificate is issued to delegatee Bob. It enables him to authenticate to services and act on Alice's behalf. To identify the real subject that is using the service, such certificate contains both of their WebID URIs. When delegatee Bob authenticates to a service using this certificate, the service can retrieve delegator Alice's WebID profile, which describes the delegation by referring to delegatee Bob by his WebID URI and by specifying other parameters, like constraints.

Transforming the conceptual into a physical model, the delegation-enabled WebID certificate is an X.509 client certificate that contains the *Subject Alternative Name* (SAN) denoting delegatee Bob and the *Issuer Alternative Name*

(IAN) denoting Alice as delegator. To define scope-aware delegations, we extend the delegator's WebID profile by specific RDF statements: The `delegatee` is represented by his WebID URI. The `task` is a URI pointing to the description of the work to be done. Delegators can define constraints, e.g., regarding `domain` or `validity`, from an extensible set. A thus specified delegation is shown below:

```
<WebID URI delegator> sociddea:delegate [
  sociddea:delegatee <WebID URI delegatee>;
  sociddea:task <URI to task description>;
  sociddea:delegationConstraints [
    sociddea:delegationValidity DEADLINE;
    sociddea:delegationDomain SERVICE;  ] ]
```

Listing 1.1. Structure of the delegation parameters

As we cannot prevent attackers from creating a delegation-enabled WebID certificate on their own, it is mandatory to include additional protective measures in the delegator's WebID profile and verify them whenever required. Assuming an attacker creates a WebID certificate containing his WebID URI as SAN and Alice's WebID URI as IAN, he would not be enabled to authenticate to a service as Alice's delegatee. This is because the delegation parameters of Alice's WebID profile, retrieved by the service, do not contain the attacker's WebID URI.

To illustrate our argumentation, Figure 2 depicts the delegation process as BPMN. Figure 1 shows DASC integrated into Sociddea - a WebID identity provider. On the left in Figure 1 Alice's view is featured when creating a delegation whereas the right part shows Bob's view on her WebID profile with delegations only concerning him. The numbers in Figure 2 correlate with those in Figure 1.

When Alice initiates the delegation, she has to describe the delegation parameters and optionally define constraints of domain and validity (cf. ①). After these parameters are added to her WebID profile (cf. ②), she can inform Bob. When Bob

Fig. 1. Delegation creation in Sociddea – Delegator: ① Defining delegation parameters and ② storing in WebID Profile. Delegatee: ③ Viewing delegations on the delegator's WebID profile and ④ creating a delegation-enabled WebID certificate.

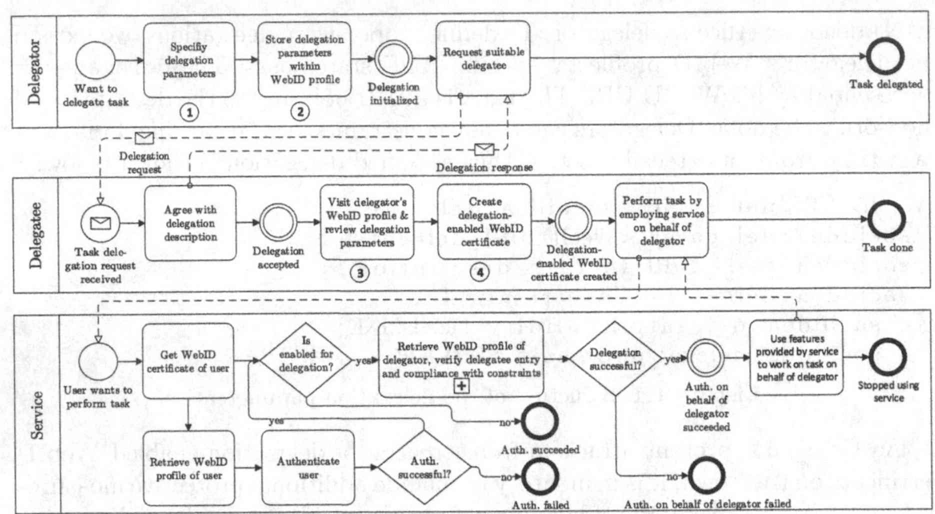

Fig. 2. Delegation process as business process model

visits Alice's WebID profile, he sees relevant delegations only concerning him (cf. ③). Once he decides to work on one task, he creates a delegation-enabled WebID certificate (cf. ④). He can then use this certificate to authenticate to a service that supports the delegation approach. The service requests Bob's and Alice's WebID profile to check the delegation constraints in Alice's WebID profile.

Further information about DASC and Sociddea, including screencasts and a demo, is available at: `https://vsr.informatik.tu-chemnitz.de/demos/sociddea`

4 Conclusion

This paper presented DASC, an approach for scope-aware delegations in distributed social networks using WebID. We introduced a vocabulary to specify delegations, modeled the DASC delegation process using BPMN, and showed a prototypical implementation of DASC integrated into a WebID identity provider.

Future work will focus on delegating a task to a group of subjects and to provide more precise restrictions, further analysis is needed on the constraints.

References

1. Abrams, R.S.: Uncovering the Network-Centric Organization (2009)
2. Story, H.: WebID Specifications (2014). `http://www.w3.org/2005/Incubator/webid/spec/`
3. Tramp, S., Story, H., et al.: Extending the WebID protocol with access delegation. In: COLD2012 (2012)
4. Wild, S., et al.: ProProtect3: An Approach for Protecting User Profile Data from Disclosure, Tampering, and Improper Use in the Context of WebID. TLDKS **19**, 87–127 (2015)

Balancing Isolation and Sharing of Data in Third-Party Extensible App Ecosystems

Florian Schröder[1], Raphael M. Reischuk[2](✉), and Johannes Gehrke[3]

[1] Saarland University, Saarbrücken, Germany
[2] ETH Zurich, Zürich, Switzerland
reischuk@inf.ethz.ch
[3] Cornell University, Ithaca, NY, USA

Abstract. In the landscape of application ecosystems, today's cloud users wish to personalize not only their browsers with various extensions or their smartphones with various applications, but also the various extensions and applications themselves. The resulting personalization significantly raises the attractiveness for typical Web 2.0 users, but gives rise to various security risks and privacy concerns, such as unforeseen access to certain critical components, undesired information flow of personal information to untrusted applications, or emerging attack surfaces that were not possible before a personalization has taken place. We propose a novel extensibility mechanism to implement personalization of existing cloud applications towards (possibly untrusted) components in a secure and privacy-friendly manner. More details of the results can be found in the long version [4] of this paper.

1 Introduction

Today's Web 2.0 users wish to personalize their devices and applications – from minorly invasive *customizations* (such as changing the visual appearance) to functionality-extending changes that constitute true forms of *extensibility*. Not only smartphones, tablets, and browsers are in focus of personalization, but also existing Rich Internet Applications (RIAs) should be customizable – and even extensible – in previously unforeseen directions [1–3].

Such user-driven personalizations (sometimes interchangeably referred to as customizations) inhabit extensible app ecosystems for web components and influence the *content*, the *style*, and the *functionality* of interactive web systems: the welcome page of Amazon.com shows different items for Alice as compared to Bob (content), an aged user might wish to have a larger font size for displaying text on his tablet or desktop computer (style), while a teenage user might long for advanced features to publish media data from any smartphone application to Facebook without waiting for her OS provider to support the desired features (functionality). Customization of content and style was traditionally referred to as personalization in the literature [2,5]. However, with the advent of Web 2.0, *extensibility* of functionality has become a novel and the most challenging component in the area of personalization.

One of the central difficulties of realizing extensibility is to faithfully address the various security and privacy aspects that naturally arise when functionality

P. Cimiano et al. (Eds.): ICWE 2015, LNCS 9114, pp. 713–716, 2015.
DOI: 10.1007/978-3-319-19890-3_64

is extended in a user-driven manner. While customization of content and style usually imposes no security vulnerabilities, extensibility of functionality (i.e., incorporating new program components in existing environments) faces – apart from the functional issues – also a number of security-related challenges [4,5].

2 Formal App Ecosystem Model

We consider the n-dimensional universe $\mathcal{P}^n$ of *principal classes* $\mathcal{P}^n := \langle \mathcal{P}_1, \ldots, \mathcal{P}_n \rangle$ that subsumes all instances of the particular class $\mathcal{P}_i$, e.g., users, components, locations, etc. Furthermore, we define the *data storage* as the set of all data items $\mathcal{D}$. Each such item is required to have a unique *owner* principal in each dimension, which would be affected by an operation on the particular data item. More precisely, for each data item $d \in \mathcal{D}$, we define $\mathit{aff}_{\mathcal{P}_i} : \mathcal{D} \to \mathcal{P}_i$ to represent the *affected principal* in dimension i. The affected principals may be determined with arbitrary semantics, according to the operation type, information flow, inference prevention, etc. For instance, items in `WHERE` clauses of SQL queries can be captured, or timing information in the analysis of side-channels.

In order to access data items, a principal can issue a request $r \in \mathcal{R}$. We define $\mathit{scope}_{\mathcal{D}} : \mathcal{R} \to \wp(\mathcal{D})$ to determine the scope of data items for such a request, i.e., the set of *affected data items* per request.

As motivated in [4], we want to enable *sharing* between principals of the same dimension, e.g., user Alice wants to share her favorite music files with user Bob. We thus require a function $\mathit{sh}_{\mathcal{P}_i} : \mathcal{P}_i \times \mathcal{P}_i \times \mathcal{D} \to \{0,1\}$ for each dimension $\mathcal{P}_i$ if sharing from one principal to another is defined for a specific data item.

Finally, the main access control policy $\mathit{req\_valid} : \mathcal{R} \times \mathcal{P}_1 \times \ldots \times \mathcal{P}_n \to \{0,1\}$ decides whether a given request is valid for all principals associated with this request (the *issuers*). More specifically, a request r is considered permissive if for each affected principal p_i, we have that either p_i itself is the issuer of r, or that p_i has explicitly shared the requested data with the actual issuer. Formally, $\mathit{req\_valid}(r, p_1, \ldots, p_n)$ iff

$$\forall d \in \mathit{scope}_{\mathcal{D}}(r) \colon \bigwedge_{i=1}^{n} \mathit{aff}_{\mathcal{P}_i}(d) = p_i \;\vee\; \mathit{sh}_{\mathcal{P}_i}(\mathit{aff}_{\mathcal{P}_i}(d), p_i, d).$$

We show how to instantiate the generic model into a concrete existing model [4]. This instantiation constitutes a general role model for extensible app ecosystems. We show how to incorporate common relational database models within our instantiated model. Furthermore, we show a *wiring methodology* to implement sharing between components by establishing links between the database tables owned by the particular components.

3 Example Application and Evaluation

We illustrate how to conveniently extend an existing application with new functionality, based on the techniques introduced in [4]. More specifically, we take a SAFE application of an interactive social network and add an incremental search functionality modeled as a set of independent f-units.

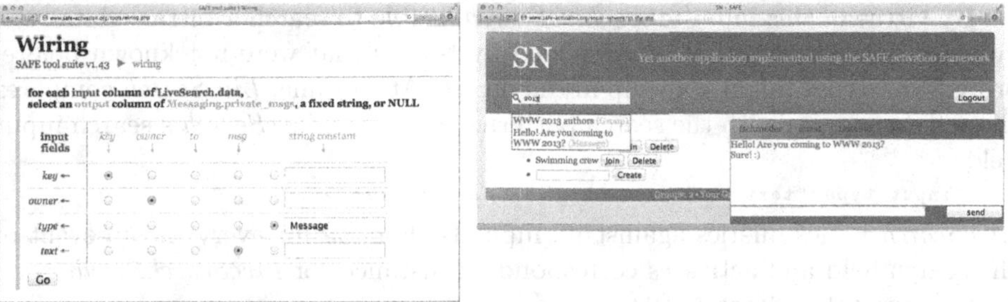

Fig. 1. Screenshots: Schema matching between *Messaging* and *LiveSearch* (left), and the extended application in which the external *LiveSearch* f-unit displays results obtained from customizable sources (right)

Initial Application. In addition to various other features, the initial social network application comprises the common functionality of *group membership* which is implemented by an f-unit *Groups*. Any authenticated user may create a group, which can be joined by other users. As f-units are required to state appropriate output tables for the sake of extensibility, *Groups* provides the public output table `all_groups` with a declaration of data and one invariant:

```
OUTPUT TABLE all_groups (
  SELECT name, gid AS key, owner FROM groups
  INVARIANT ALL )
```

The output table exposes the group names to the wiring process [4]: If wired to `all_groups`, other f-units can access the names of all available groups. The invariant `ALL` makes the group information public, i.e., readable for every user.

Furthermore, an f-unit *Messaging* implements an instant messaging functionality and defines an output table `private_msgs` as the set of all messages (local table `conversations`) that can be associated with the current user:

```
OUTPUT TABLE private_msgs (
  SELECT    msg_id AS key,  msg,  uid_from AS owner,  uid_recipient AS to
  FROM      conversations
  INVARIANT is(owner,@uid) OR is(to,@uid) )
```

Per default, every user may access output table rows with a matching owner column `is(owner,@uid)`. However, the specified invariant replaces this default behavior by potentially allowing foreign f-units to access both sent and received messages of the particular user they are currently connected to.

Adding Functionality. Given the initial application, we will now add a common *incremental search* functionality. By this means, the f-unit *LiveSearch* monitors a text input field for typing events, searches all its available datasets for the input pattern, and displays matching rows. We have equipped *LiveSearch* with an input table `data` that can be wired to output tables of other f-units.

```
INPUT TABLE data ( text TEXT, type VARCHAR(20), key KEY, owner OWNER )
```

The input table has two main data fields: `text` for arbitrary textual content (e.g., chat messages, group titles, poll descriptions), and `type` for an informal description of the search source type (e.g., messages, groups, polls).

By virtue of this input table, *LiveSearch* is able to search arbitrary data sets, even for data sources that are provided by f-units that were not known before, or by f-units that might come up in the future. At runtime, *LiveSearch* compares these data sources with the search patterns entered in *LiveSearch*'s search input field:

```
<input type="text" name="search" id="searchField">
```

LiveSearch issues queries against its input table `data` for every `keyup`-event of the search field and activates corresponding instances of *LiveSearchResults*:

```
<activate:LiveSearchResults
 query="SELECT text AS result, type AS info
       FROM data
       WHERE text LIKE CONCAT('%',REPLACE('$#search',' ','%'),'%')"
 refresh="searchField.keyup" />
```

Wiring. In the social network setting, the search engine shall include the groups of the social network in its search results. In order to provide *LiveSearch* with the actual group names, the wiring of *Groups*.`all_groups` into *LiveSearch*.`data` maps `key` $\mapsto$ `key`, `name` $\mapsto$ `text`, the constant `'Group'` $\mapsto$ `type`, and `owner` $\mapsto$ `owner`. Furthermore, upon integration of *Messaging*, the new feature of searching in both sent and received messages is stated by the wiring in Figur 1 (left): `key` $\mapsto$ `key`, `msg` $\mapsto$ `text`, the constant `'Message'` $\mapsto$ `type`, and `owner` $\mapsto$ `owner`.

Evaluation. The right-hand side of Figure 1 shows the resulting application: a wired input table allows *LiveSearch* to display search results generically for datasets of both *Groups* and *Messaging*. The wiring of *Groups*.`all_groups` and *Messaging*.`private_msgs` into *LiveSearch*.`data` results in a safe setting that reflects the modularity and extensibility paradigms, as depicted above. The implementation of *LiveSearch* benefits from various features and concepts that are offered by the described extensions of SAFE. For instance, the result set of *LiveSearch* can be arbitrarily augmented at run-time, and the wiring allows for easy integration of new functionality into an existing app ecosystem, without affecting already established apps. Privacy-aware collaboration across f-units thus only relies on a sufficiently generic interface of all involved f-units, formed by input and output tables.

References

1. Arellano, C., Díaz, O., Iturrioz, J.: Opening Personalization to Partners: An Architecture of Participation for Websites. In: Brambilla, M., Tokuda, T., Tolksdorf, R. (eds.) ICWE 2012. LNCS, vol. 7387, pp. 91–105. Springer, Heidelberg (2012)
2. Jørstad, I., Thanh, D.V., Dustdar, S.: Personalisation of next generation mobile services. In: Norrie, M.C., Dustdar, S., Gall, H.C. (eds.) UMICS 2006 (2007)
3. Reischuk, R.M., Backes, M., Gehrke, J.: SAFE extensibility for data-driven web applications. In: 21st Int. Conf. on World Wide Web, pp. 799–808. ACM (2012)
4. Schröder, F., Reischuk, R.M., Gehrke, J.: Balancing isolation and sharing of data for third-party extensible app ecosystems (2015). http://arxiv.org/abs/1412.7641
5. Toch, E., Wang, Y., Cranor, L.F.: Personalization and privacy: a survey of privacy risks and remedies in personalization-based systems. User Modeling and User-Adapted Interaction **22**(1–2), 203–220 (2012)

An Empirical Study of the Use of Multi-dimensional Contexts for Collaborative-Filtering-Based Service Recommendations in IoT Environments

Joo-Sik Son(✉), Han-Gyu Ko, and In-Young Ko

School of Computing, Korea Advanced Institute of Science and Technology, KAIST, Daejeon, Republic of Korea
{sonjoosik,kohangyu,iko}@kaist.ac.kr

Abstract. Collaborative filtering (CF) based recommendation techniques involve the use of feedback information such as users' ratings on items to predict their preferences on new items. To recommend services in Internet of Things (IoT) environments by utilizing CF based techniques, it is however essential to take into account multi-dimensional context information such as temporal, social, and spatial context to deal with the dynamism characteristic of IoT environments. In this paper, we propose a user-service matrix model to represent the contextual dependency between users and services and to analyze the feasibility of using multi-dimensional context information with regard to the accuracy of service recommendations. We conducted an experiment to demonstrate our approach using datasets collected from practical IoT testbed environments in which various smart devices are installed.

Keywords: Collaborative filtering · Context-aware service recommendation · Internet of things

1 Introduction

With the considerable advances in mobile networking and embedded computing technologies, everyday consumer electronics become smart objects. Smart objects are connected via standard protocols such that they are always accessible through the Internet. In these Internet of Things (IoT) environments, the advent of ubiquitous computing environments becomes a reality; hence, users will be served with their desired services according to their needs via the cooperation of smart objects in a spontaneous manner [1]. However, on the other hand, this extension requires high complexity when identifying and providing appropriate services on the fly, as there are increasingly more potential sets of composite services through various smart objects [2]. To resolve this complexity problem, researchers have closely examined recommender systems. In particular, recommender systems based on collaborative filtering (CF) are regarded as the state-of-the-art, as the effectiveness of these systems has been demonstrated in e-commerce domains. CF-based recommender systems utilize the feedback information such as users' ratings on items and purchase history to predict their preferences then, recommend new items based on the predicted preferences. However, unlike recommending content or products, understanding users' current situations is more

P. Cimiano et al. (Eds.): ICWE 2015, LNCS 9114, pp. 717–720, 2015.
DOI: 10.1007/978-3-319-19890-3_65

important than measuring preferences to effectively recommend users with services in Internet of Things (IoT) environments because, although a user may have frequently enjoyed a "Watching a Movie" service, for example, it is hardly appropriate if the system recommends the service when the user is at work during the daytime. Therefore, contextual data such as the time and place of the target user should be incorporated to develop a CF-based service recommender system.

Table 1. Testbed settings in two different places

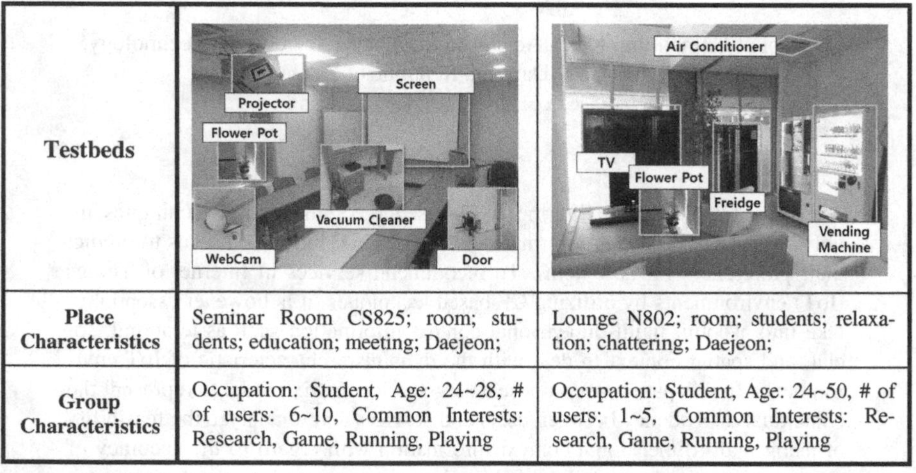

Testbeds		
Place Characteristics	Seminar Room CS825; room; students; education; meeting; Daejeon;	Lounge N802; room; students; relaxation; chattering; Daejeon;
Group Characteristics	Occupation: Student, Age: 24~28, # of users: 6~10, Common Interests: Research, Game, Running, Playing	Occupation: Student, Age: 24~50, # of users: 1~5, Common Interests: Research, Game, Running, Playing

In this paper, we propose a multi-aspect context model to capture a target user's situation. We then define dimensions of the proposed context model and instantiate sets of contextual factors for each dimension in testbeds after constructing the testbeds equipped with smart objects (please see Table 1). In addition, we describe the manner of generating the user-service matrix, which is the basic form of raw data used when applying the CF-based recommendation method. Finally, we empirically demonstrate whether the multi-dimensional context information can be used to improve the accuracy of the recommender system as well as which data have stronger effects on the recommendation accuracy. All experiments were performed using contextual data collected from the testbeds constructed as part of this study.

2 Multi-dimensional Context-Aware Service Recommendations

A smart space such as the testbeds that we described previously can have several meanings perceived by people over time based on their social interactions made in the space. As we presented in our earlier work [3], we call these different meanings assigned to a space as *placeness*, which is a diachronic representation of social and cultural activities. To discover and recommend services in a spontaneous manner without prior experiences in a given smart space, we exploit the experiences of people who have been at the place. Therefore, we need to determine what people have done by mining their experiences in the place. To do this, we identify 'what types and how many of users' have been at the place and identify 'what social activities' have been performed by the users in the place.

There are various types of model-based CF approaches. In this paper, we utilize Stochastic Gradient Descent (SGD) to apply the CF-based method to service recommendations. SGD is a gradient descent optimization method which can be used to minimize an objective function. In this work, we use the root mean square error (RMSE) as the objective function. RMSE is a metric which is used here to evaluate prediction accuracy levels. During the model learning process, the latent factors of users and items are mapped by a matrix-factorization process using singular value decomposition (SVD). Then, with the SGD technique, we can optimize the squared error. The model can include additional factors, such as the contextual information, because the increased dimension can be reduced by the SGD algorithm [4]. In this work, because it is necessary to consider the multi-dimensional contextual information of IoT environments, we use the SGD algorithm, which can deal with multi-dimensional input data effectively, to optimize the target function.

3 Experiments and Analysis

Table 2 shows the overall result of the experiment. This table shows the result when considering each contextual factor independently as well as the results of considering the aggregated contextual factors in each aspect, considering only the representative factors, and considering the aggregated contextual factors in all aspects. For the seminar room data, the case of considering the 'duration' contextual factor shows the best recommendation performance. This is because activities in the seminar room are usually pre-planned and changes on the activities are occasional. Contrary to the seminar room data, consideration of the 'noise' contextual factor results in the best recommendation accuracy in the lounge data. Compare to the seminar room, the lounge is a more dynamic place, where people come in and out frequently, and the activities performed by the people are much more flexible. This is the reason why the 'duration' contextual factor shows relatively low impact on the recommendations. However, the dynamic characteristic of the lounge tends to generate more noise and consideration of the 'noise' contextual factor contributes to improve the recommendation performance.

Table 2. The result of considering the contextual factors in multiple aspects

Contextual Information		Seminar Room		Lounge	
Aspect	**Factor**	**RMSE**	**Improvement**	**RMSE**	**Improvement**
Baseline		0.195278669	0 %	0.201059884	0
Temporal	Day	0.193245768	1.04 %	0.201372691	- 0.16
	Start Time	0.192672628	1.33 %	0.201302809	- 0.12
	Duration	**0.169284314**	**13.31 %**	0.199113007	0.97 %
	Aggregation	0.177093895	9.31 %	0.199858269	0.6 %
Spatial	Noise	0.190419091	2.49 %	**0.198706872**	**1.17 %**
	Brightness	0.179960872	7.84 %	-	-
	Aggregation	0.188342573	3.55 %	-	-
Social	The number of people	0.193881911	0.72 %	0.201274221	- 0.11 %
Aggregation	Representatives	0.179241705	8.21 %	0.199561041	0.75 %
	every factor	0.16996216	12.96 %	0.199457881	0.8 %

Although the results of analyzing the datasets from the seminar room and the lounge have some differences, there is a common characteristic that we can find. Both of the results show that it is essential to consider the aggregated contextual factors from different aspects. The accuracy of service recommendation increases as we consider more types of contextual factors in multiple aspects. This result strongly implies that consideration of various contextual factors during the CF-based service recommendation process is effective for the IoT-based service environments, which produce a rich set of contextual information.

4 Conclusion

In this paper, we described the empirical study that we conducted to evaluate the effectiveness of considering multi-dimensional contexts for service recommendations based on CF methods in IoT environments. First, we designed a placeness-based context model to capture users' situation in multiple aspects. We then collected data about the contextual factors in the temporal, spatial and social aspects from the testbeds that are equipped with smart objects. The experimental results showed that most of the contextual factors have positive impacts on service recommendations, and when multiple contextual factors are aggregated together, the performance improvement gets higher. Especially, we found that consideration of aggregated contextual factors from different aspects results in the best performance. These findings highly support that consideration of various contextual information in multiple aspects enables successful and accurate service recommendations in dynamic IoT environments.

Acknowledgement. This work was supported by ICT R&D program of MSIP/IITP. [B0101-14-0334, Development of IoT-based Trustworthy and Smart Home Community Framework].

References

1. Atzori, L., Iera, A., Morabito, G.: The Internet of Things: A survey. Computer Networks. **54**(15), 2787–2805 (2010). Elsevier
2. Vo, C.C., Torabi, T., Loke, S.W.: Task-oriented systems for interaction with ubiquitous computing environments. In: Sénac, P., Ott, M., Seneviratne, A. (eds.) MobiQuitous 2010. LNICST, vol. 73, pp. 332–339. Springer, Heidelberg (2012)
3. Ko, H.-G., Kim, T., Kim B., Lee, D., Ko, I.-Y., Hyun, S.J.: Place-aware opportunistic service recommendation scheme in a smart space with internet of things. In: IEEE 11th Consumer Communications and Networking Conference, pp. 477–482. Las Vegas (2014)
4. Koren, Y., Bell, R., Volinsky, C.: Matrix factorization techniques for recommender systems. Computer **8**, 30–37 (2009). IEEE

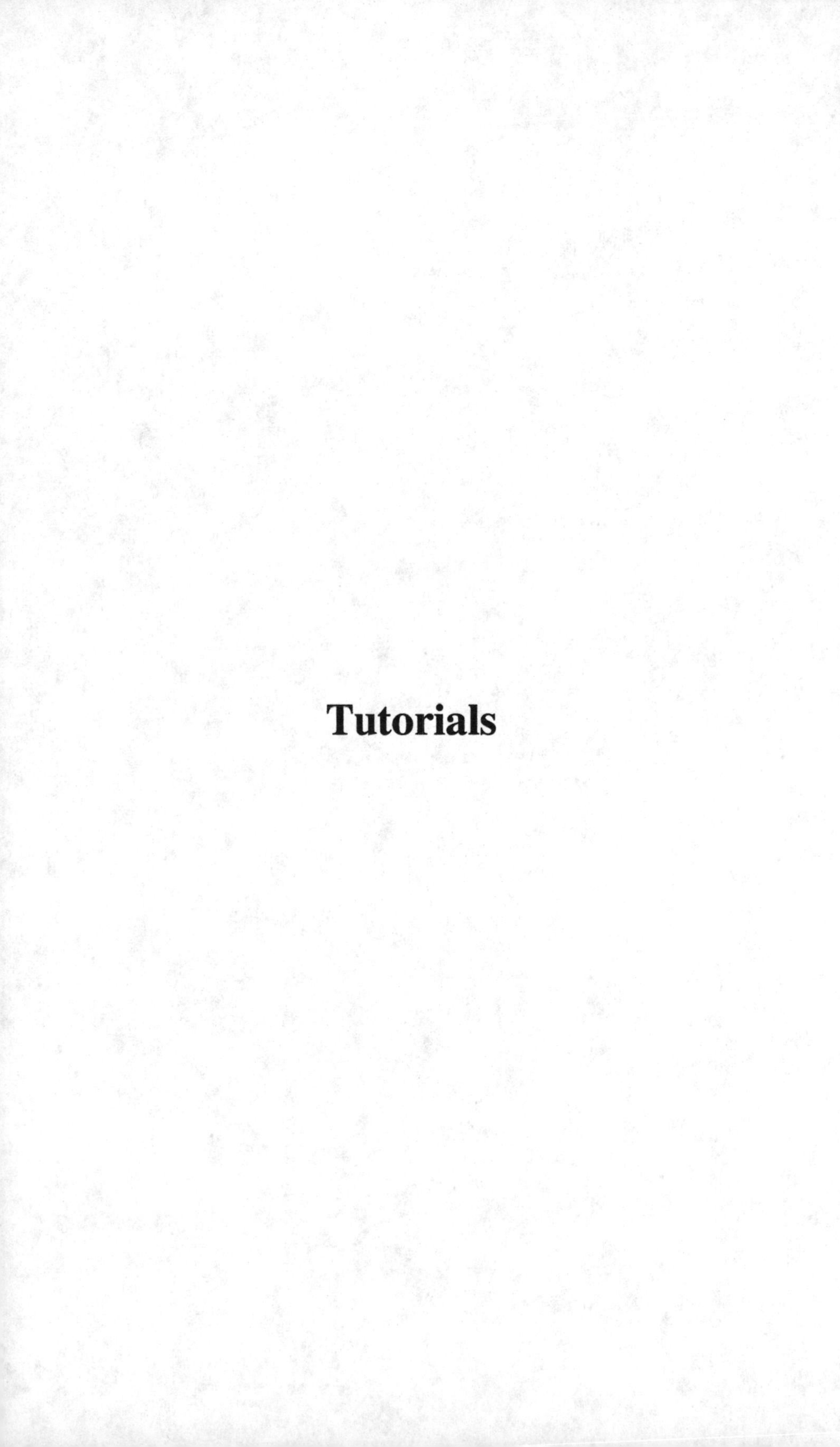

Tutorials

The Web of Data for E-Commerce: Schema.org and GoodRelations for Researchers and Practitioners

Martin Hepp(✉)

E-Business & Web Science Research Group, Universität der Bundeswehr München, Werner-Heisenberg-Weg 39, 85577, Neubiberg, Germany
mhepp@computer.org

Abstract. Schema.org is one of the main drivers for the adoption of Semantic Web principles by a broad number of organizations and individuals for real business needs. GoodRelations is a well-established conceptual model for representing e-commerce information, one of the few widely used OWL DL ontologies, and since 2012 the official e-commerce model of schema.org.

In this tutorial, we will (1) give a comprehensive overview and hands-on training on the advanced conceptual structures of schema.org for e-commerce, including patterns for ownership and demand, (2) present the full tool chain for producing and consuming respective data, (3) explain the long-term vision of Linked Open Commerce, and (4) discuss advanced topics, like access control, identity and authentication (e.g. with WebID); micropayment services, and data management issues from the publisher and consumer perspective. We will also cover research opportunities resulting from the growing adoption and the respective amount of data in RDFa, Microdata, and JSON-LD syntaxes.

Keywords: Schema.org · GoodRelations · Semantic Web · Ontologies · Microdata · OWL · RDFa · JSON-LD · Linked Open Data · E-Commerce · E-Business

1 Introduction

Schema.org [1] is one of the main drivers for the adoption of Semantic Web principles by a broad number of people for their real business needs. The resulting amount of real-world RDF[1] data exceeds a critical mass so that it becomes interesting as reference data for any kind of foundational Semantic Web research. At the same time, the schema.org ecosystem has become the source of, or catalyst for, many innovations in the field that reach out into core Semantic Web research, like the recent integration of transactions into schema.org [2], which is essentially a variant of the idea of Semantic Web Services (see e.g. [3]). In this tutorial, we want to cover the theoretical knowledge and practical skills for using schema.org for research and practical innovation.

[1] Including such that can be generated from Microdata, which is strictly speaking not an RDF syntax.

P. Cimiano et al. (Eds.): ICWE 2015, LNCS 9114, pp. 723–727, 2015.
DOI: 10.1007/978-3-319-19890-3_66

1.1 What Is GoodRelations?

GoodRelations[2] is a generic conceptual model that can be used to exchange information about products and services, pricing, payment options, other terms and conditions, store locations and their opening hours, and many other aspects of e-commerce, between networks of computer systems [4, 5]. The focus is on interoperability between Web sites and clients consuming the information given on those sites, but it can also be used for other purposes that require a common data model for information about technical and commercial aspects of products and business entities.

In essence, GoodRelations defines (1) a generic data structure and (2) unique identifiers for all elements of that data structure, i.e. its classes (entity types), properties (relationship types and attributes), and enumerated values (individuals). GoodRelations is available as an OWL DL Web ontology according to the W3C Web Ontology Language standard and can thus be used for exchanging data on the WWW, e.g. in Semantic Web and Linked Open Data projects.

GoodRelations is designed so that it fits any industry, any position in the value chain, and any country or legal environment. It is a truly generic model of information for offering any kind of goods (e.g. cameras, cars, consulting, medical treatment, etc.) to others and for specifying the expected compensation (e.g. money or other goods in barter trade) and conditions (e.g. indicating the time your offer expires or the payment methods accepted).

1.2 What Can I do with GoodRelations?

While it is impossible to enumerate all possible usages of GoodRelations, here is a list of prominent ones (taken from [5]):

1. **Search Engine Optimization** for Google, Yahoo, Bing, and Yandex with schema.org: Since November 2012, GoodRelations is the official e-commerce model of schema.org. schema.org is an initiative driven by several major search engines and allows site-owners to mark-up information in their Web content so that search engines can extract and process it better, i.e. more reliably and with less effort. In short, one can use the GoodRelations data model to add small data packets to Web pages in HTML that represent products and their features and prices, stores and opening hours, payment options and the like. Search engines will then be able to understand the content better and trigger many positive effects for the site in the search results, like Google Rich Snippets, or individualized relevance ranking.
2. **Product Information Management (PIM/PDM)** inside a single organization or a value chain: If you have to handle information about products and services from multiple sources, GoodRelations can serve as a global database schema for integrating the information, for it is typically easy to map existing data structures to GoodRelations. GoodRelations will then provide a common model to maintain, cleanse, consume, and share the data.

---

[2] http://purl.org/goodrelations/

3. **E-Commerce Data Quality Management:** One can also use GoodRelations to manage technical or commercial data from heterogeneous sources in graph databases (e.g. RDF triplestores) and implement data quality management projects on top of this model.

2 The Agent-Promise-Object-Compensation Model

As said, the goal of GoodRelations is to define a data structure for e-commerce that is

1. industry-neutral, i.e. suited for consumer electronics, cars, tickets, real estate, labor, services, or any other type of goods,
2. valid across the different stages of the value chain, i.e. from raw materials through retail to after-sales services, and
3. syntax-neutral, i.e. it should work in Microdata, RDFa, RDF/XML, Turtle, JSON, OData, GData, or any other popular syntax.

GoodRelations focuses on the early stages of business transactions, i.e. search and selection. Transactions were outside the initial scope, but have recently become relevant, as schema.org has started supporting transaction-related data.

At the very heart of GoodRelations is the assumption that most e-commerce information can be represented using just four entities [6]:

1. **An agent** (e.g. a person or an organization),
2. **A promise (offer) to transfer some rights** (ownership, temporary usage, a certain license, etc.) on some object or to provide some service,
3. **An object** (e.g. a camcorder, a house, a car, etc.) or service (e.g. a haircut), and
4. **An** expected **compensation** (e.g. an amount of money), to be provided by the accepting agent and related to the object or service.

A fifth entity that is often relevant is **a location from which that offer is available**(e.g. a store, a bus stop, a gas station, etc.).

This **Agent-Promise-Object-Compensation (APOC)** [6] principle can be found across most industries and is the source of the wide applicability of GoodRelations. It allows using the same vocabulary for offering a camcorder as for a manicure service or for the offer to dispose of used cars. The respective classes in GoodRelations are

- **gr:BusinessEntity** for the agent, i.e. the company or individual,
- **gr:Offering** for an offer to sell, repair, lease something, or to express interest in such an offer,
- **gr:ProductOrService** for the object or service,
- **gr:PriceSpecification** for the compensation, and
- **gr:Location** for a store or location from which the offer is available (in previous versions gr:LocationOfSalesOrServiceProvisioning).

Note that the object does not have to be a physical thing; it can also be a patent, a creative works, an action or happening, and the compensation does not have to be in money. GoodRelations makes minimal assumptions about what objects can be the subject of an offer, which bundles of rights can be offered, and about the nature of a compensation expected, if any.

3 GoodRelations in Schema.org

GoodRelations is a decade-long initiative and started as an independent Web vocabulary ("ontology") that was meant to be used in RDFa or other RDF-syntaxes (like RDF/XML, Turtle, etc.). In 2009, Yahoo started to honor GoodRelations in RDFa syntax, and in 2010 Google followed, creating significant incentives for real businesses to adopt this data model.

Initially, this all happened in the original GoodRelations namespace, i.e. with identifiers like

```
http://purl.org/goodrelations/v1#OpeningHoursSpecification
```

After the announcement of schema.org in 2011, we worked with Google, Bing, and Yahoo to integrate GoodRelations into schema.org. The result was released in 2012 and has since been an ongoing effort of evolving both projects in parallel. In essence, the integration into schema.org meant that (almost) any element from GoodRelations also became part of schema.org; for details, see [7]. Thanks to this, GoodRelations is now the official, extended e-commerce model of schema.org. Since schema.org is a single-namespace vocabulary (at least as of now), the result is that every GoodRelations element has now **two identifiers**, the original one, like

```
http://purl.org/goodrelations/v1#OpeningHoursSpecification
```

and the one in schema.org, like

```
http://schema.org/OpeningHoursSpecification
```

In some cases, the local part of the names differs between the original GoodRelations namespace and the derived version in the schema.org namespace, in order to be consistent with the existing naming conventions in schema.org, or because a similar element had existed before (for a full list of naming differences, see here[3]). For enumerations (individuals), the original namespace remains the official one, e.g. `http://purl.org/goodrelations/v1#Cash` for the payment method “cash”. This was decided because we wanted to reduce the number of new elements for schema.org.

[3] http://wiki.goodrelations-vocabulary.org/Cookbook/Schema.org#Naming_Differences

4 Contents of the Tutorial

In the ICWE 2015 tutorial, we (1) give a comprehensive overview and hands-on training on the advanced conceptual structures of schema.org for e-commerce, including patterns for ownership and demand, (2) present the full tool chain for producing and consuming respective data, (3) explain the long-term vision of Linked Open Commerce, (4) describe the main challenges for future research in the field, and (5) discuss advanced topics, like access control, identity and authentication (e.g. with WebID); micropayment services, and data management issues from the publisher and consumer perspective. We also cover research opportunities resulting from the growing adoption and the respective amount of data in RDFa, Microdata, and JSON-LD syntaxes.

Participants learn how to use the GoodRelations elements in schema.org to articulate information about business entities, products and services, prices, warranty, shop locations, terms and conditions, etc. This can improve the visibility of an offering in next generation Web search engines, allow more precise search, and support partners in the value chain to extract and reuse product model data easily. Attendees will also understand how such metadata can be used by search engines, browser extensions, and mobile applications, and how researchers can access and integrate respective data into their work.

Acknowledgments. This summary and the tutorial are heavily based on material that I wrote for the GoodRelations documentation at http://purl.org/goodrelations/.

References

1. http://schema.org
2. https://schema.org/docs/actions.html
3. Studer, R., Grimm, S., Abecker, A. (eds.): Semantic Web Services: Concepts, Technologies, and Applications. Springer, Heidelberg etc. (2007)
4. Hepp, M.: GoodrRlations: an ontology for describing products and services offers on the web. In: Gangemi, A., Euzenat, J. (eds.) EKAW 2008. LNCS (LNAI), vol. 5268, pp. 329–346. Springer, Heidelberg (2008)
5. http://wiki.goodrelations-vocabulary.org/Documentation/Intro
6. http://wiki.goodrelations-vocabulary.org/Documentation/Conceptual_model
7. http://wiki.goodrelations-vocabulary.org/Cookbook/Schema.org

Enabling the Web of (Linked Open) Data

Epaminondas Kapetanios[(✉)]

Faculty of Science and Technology, University of Westminster, London, UK
e.kapetanios@westminster.ac.uk

Abstract. In this tutorial, we will take a look at the Web of Data and the Linked Open Data (LOD) project, in particular, via the lenses of "emergent semantics", which is quintessential for a much sought after semantic interoperability in highly dynamic environments. We also review the Web of Data via the property of self-organisation, which is an essential property of emergent semantics systems. This approach is promising to tackle some of the challenges in relation with successful publishing, reusability and linking of open data on the Web, since data sets and their descriptions in such a dynamic environment are continuously evolving and, therefore, need to be explored and searched via approximate querying, pattern search and similarity functions.

Keywords: Web of data · Linked Open Data · Semantic interoperability · Semantic web · Pattern search · Information retrieval · Emergent semantics · Distributed semantics · Self-organisation

Synopsis

The World Wide Web changed dramatically the way we attempt to share knowledge by lowering the barrier to publishing and accessing documents as part of a global information space. This functionality has been primarily enabled by the generic, open and extensible nature of the Web, which is also a key feature in the Web's uncompromised growth. Recently, the Web also evolved from a global information space of linked documents to one where not only documents but data are linked too. Underpinning this evolution is a set of best practices for publishing and connecting structured data on the Web known as Linked Data. This, in turn, has led to viewing the Web as a global data space connecting data from diverse domains such as people, companies, books, scientific publications, films, music, television and radio programmes, genes, proteins, drugs and clinical trials, on-line communities, statistical and scientific data, and reviews.

The openness of the Web and the rise in numbers of linked datasets, however, created further issues with (re-)usability, as well as quality, performance, reliability of the infrastructure in the linked data ecosystem. To this extent, automating certain tasks, such as discovery, selection and optimisation, becomes more and more important as it is not enough anymore to argue that URIs and RDF are all one needs to explore the linked datasets. The possible links that can be followed from a starting URI raises both performance and trust issues. In addition, the dynamics of the data-sources

P. Cimiano et al. (Eds.): ICWE 2015, LNCS 9114, pp. 728–729, 2015.
DOI: 10.1007/978-3-319-19890-3_67

also has an impact on the discovery, selection and performance of crawling collections of datasets.

For instance, in order to find the right dataset and to make this dataset accessible for biologists, the developer has to go through the process of locating a dataset that contains information relevant to biologists' research interests, such as information about a specific organism, or more specifically, genomic information about a particular organism. Subsequently, find out how this dataset can be programmatically accessed, as an RDF dump, through SPARQL endpoint, or any other protocol. Mostly important though is to understand the content of the dataset in order to perform an alignment with other datasets. Moreover, a data consumer may have discovered several datasets as a result of an indexer query. The question then arises how to select appropriate datasets from this list of potential candidates, with the emphasis on how to define "appropriateness" along the dimensions of contents, interlinking with other data sets and vocabularies being used.

In this context, the tutorial will provide an overview of the current Linked Open Data (LOD) stack of technologies, with particular emphasis on search engines and technologies tailored to alleviate the task of discovery and selection of appropriate data sets for reusability and linking on the Web. The tutorial, however, will also take a look at the Web of Data (LOD project) via the lenses of "emergent semantics", which is quintessential for a much sought after semantic interoperability in dynamic environments, as well as self-organisation, which is an essential property of emergent semantics systems, and how this view has been embraced by search engines and technologies.

Alongside these considerations, the tutorial is built upon the principles of emergent semantics, e.g., semantic handshaking protocol, evolution from local interactions and agreements towards global ones, and semantic self-organisation, with emphasis on examples found in science and nature, e.g., magnetisation in Physics, or examples from biology and chemistry including the stripped patterns in Zebras, Fish and the ocular dominance columns of the brain. These patterns are produced due to the individual responses of the cells to local conditions and the response of the neighbouring cells. It will also build upon the principles of pattern search based information retrieval with the focus on how these apply to the highly dynamic environment of the Web of (Linked Open) Data for the sake of data reusability and interoperability. Particular emphasis will be given on patterns among high-level features in order to bridge the semantic gap in search.

Some Useful Links

1. http://www.semantic-web.at/LOD-TheEssentials.pdf
2. http://bit.ly/open-data-map
3. http://datacatalogs.org
4. http://okfn.org
5. http://www.opengovdata.org/home/8principles
6. http://opengovernmentdata.org

Author Index

Printed in the United States
By Bookmasters